Selected Chapters from

Core Concepts in Health

Tenth Edition Update

With Additional Readings

HPS 1040 Health Concepts and Strategies
Georgia Institute of Technology

Paul M. Insel
Stanford University

Walton T. Roth
Stanford University

Boston Burr Ridge, IL Dubuque, IA New York San Francisco St. Louis
Bangkok Bogotá Caracas Lisbon London Madrid
Mexico City Milan New Delhi Seoul Singapore Sydney Taipei Toronto

The McGraw-Hill Companies

Selected Chapters from
Core Concepts in Health, Tenth Edition Update
With Additional Readings

HPS 1040 Health Concepts and Strategies
Georgia Institute of Technology

This book is a McGraw-Hill Learning Solutions textbook and contains select material from *Core Concepts in Health*, Tenth Edition Update by Paul M. Insel and Walton T. Roth. Copyright © 2008 by The McGraw-Hill Companies, Inc. Reprinted with permission of the publisher. Many custom published texts are modified versions or adaptations of our best-selling textbooks. Some adaptations are printed in black and white to keep prices at a minimum, while others are in color.

1 2 3 4 5 6 7 8 9 0 MER MER 0 9 8 7

ISBN-13: 978-0-07-722575-9
ISBN-10: 0-07-722575-9

Custom Publishing Specialist: Katherine Kilburg
Production Editor: Carrie Braun
Printer/Binder: Mercury Print Productions

Brief Contents

Contents

PART TWO

Understanding Sexuality

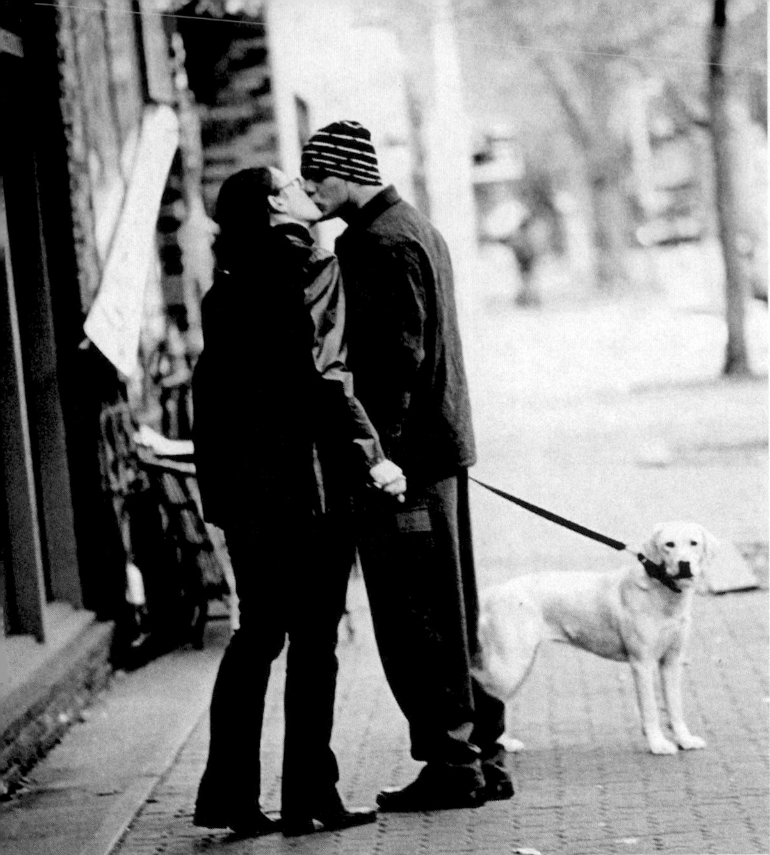

PART THREE

Making Responsible Decisions: Substance Use and Abuse

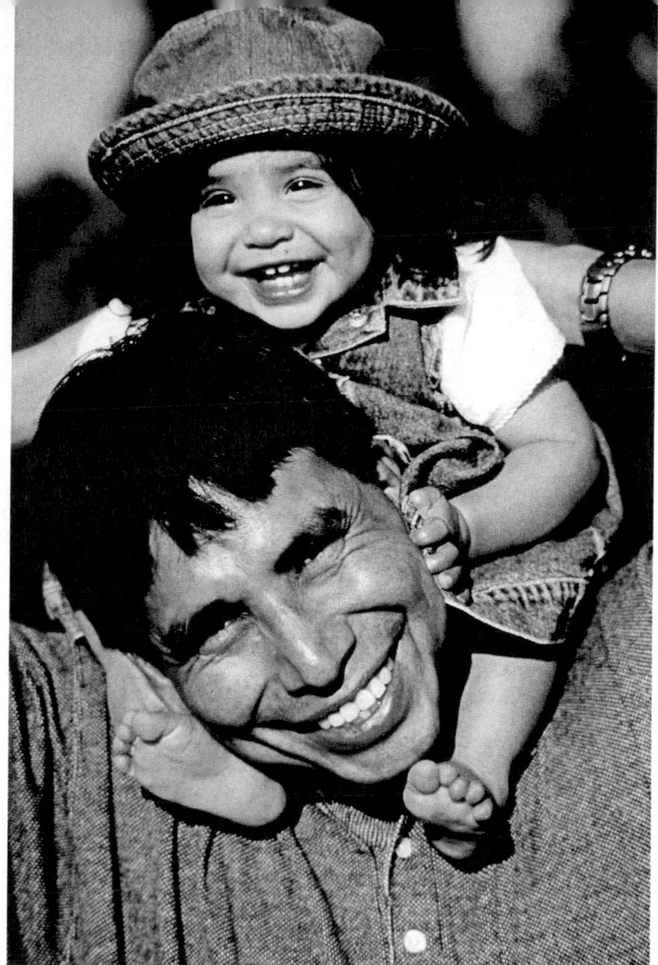

PART FOUR

Getting Fit

PART FIVE

Protecting Yourself from Disease

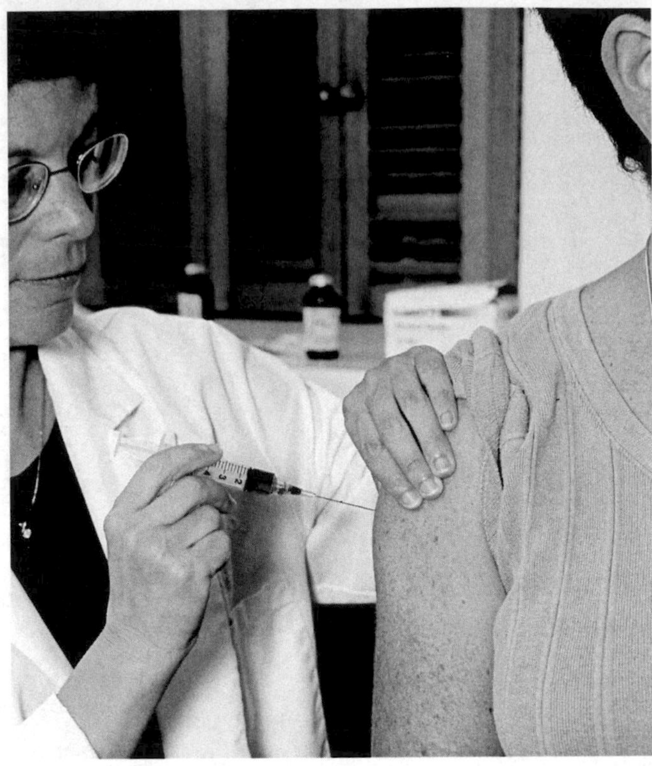

In the News

Mind/Body/Spirit

Take Charge

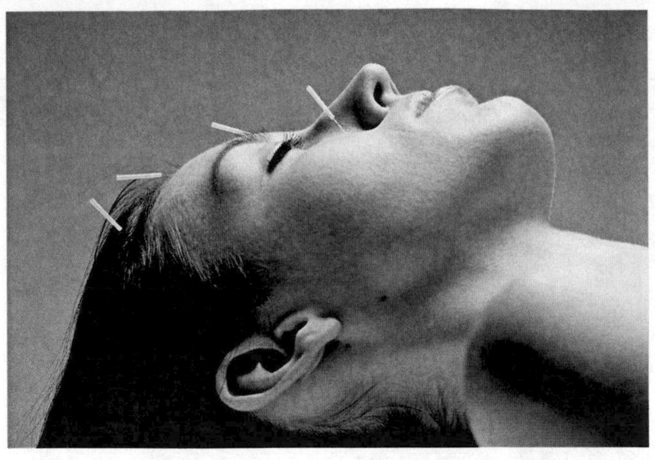

Critical Consumer

Dimensions of Diversity

Gender Matters

Assess Yourself

TOPICS OF SPECIAL CONCERN TO WOMEN

TOPICS OF SPECIAL CONCERN TO MEN

Note: The health issues and conditions listed here include those that disproportionately influence or affect women or men. For more information, see the Index under gender, women, men, and any of the special topics listed here.

DIVERSITY TOPICS RELATED TO ETHNICITY

Note: The health issues and conditions listed here include those that disproportionately influence or affect specific U.S. ethnic groups or for which patterns may appear along ethnic lines. For more information, see the Index under ethnicity, culture, names of specific population groups, and any of the topics listed here.

Preface

Core Concepts in Health has maintained its leadership in the field of health education for more than 30 years. Since we pioneered the concept of self-responsibility for personal health in 1976, hundreds of thousands of students have used our book to become active, informed participants in their own health care. Each edition of *Core Concepts* has brought improvements and refinements, but the principles underlying the book have remained the same. Our commitment to these principles has never been stronger than it is today.

OUR GOALS

Our goals in writing this book can be stated simply:

- To present scientifically based, accurate, up-to-date information in an accessible format
- To involve students in taking responsibility for their health and well-being
- To instill a sense of competence and personal power in students

The first of these goals means making expert knowledge about health and health care available to the individual. *Core Concepts* brings scientifically based, accurate, up-to-date information to students about topics and issues that concern them—exercise, stress, nutrition, weight management, contraception, intimate relationships, HIV infection, drugs, alcohol, and a multitude of others. Current, complete, and straightforward coverage is balanced with user-friendly features designed to make the text appealing. Written in an engaging, easy-to-read style and presented in a colorful, open format, *Core Concepts* invites the student to read, learn, and remember. Boxes, tables, artwork, photographs, and many other features highlight areas of special interest throughout the book.

Our second goal is to involve students in taking responsibility for their health. *Core Concepts* uses innovative pedagogy and unique interactive features to get students thinking about how the material they're reading relates to their lives. We invite them to examine their emotions about the issues under discussion, to consider their personal values and beliefs, and to analyze their health-related behaviors. Beyond this, for students who want to change behaviors that detract from a healthy lifestyle, we offer guidelines and tools, ranging from samples of health journals and personal contracts to detailed assessments and behavior change strategies.

Perhaps our third goal in writing *Core Concepts in Health* is the most important: to instill a sense of competence and personal power in the students who read the book. Everyone has the ability to monitor, understand, and affect his or her health. Although medical and health professionals possess impressive skills and have access to a huge body of knowledge that benefits everyone in our society, people can help to minimize the amount of professional care they actually require in their lifetime by taking care of themselves—taking charge of their health—from an early age. Our hope is that *Core Concepts* will continue to help young people make this exciting discovery—that they have the power to shape their futures.

ORGANIZATION AND CONTENT OF THE TENTH EDITION UPDATE

The organization of the book as a whole remains the same as in the tenth edition. The book is divided into seven parts: Part One, Establishing a Basis for Wellness, includes chapters on taking charge of your health (Chapter 1), stress (Chapter 2), and psychological health (Chapter 3). Part Two, Understanding Sexuality, opens with an exploration of communication and intimate relationships, including friendship, intimate partnerships, marriage, and family (Chapter 4) and then moves on to discuss physical sexuality (Chapter 5), contraception (Chapter 6), abortion (Chapter 7), and pregnancy and childbirth (Chapter 8). As in previous editions of *Core Concepts,* we devote a separate chapter to abortion to reflect both the importance of this issue and our belief that abortion is not a form of contraception and should not be included in the chapter on that topic.

Part Three, Making Responsible Decisions: Substance Use and Abuse, opens with a discussion of addictive behavior and the different classes of psychoactive drugs (Chapter 9), followed by chapters on alcohol (Chapter 10) and tobacco (Chapter 11). Part Four, Getting Fit, includes a detailed discussion of nutrition (Chapter 12), exercise (Chapter 13), and weight management (Chapter 14).

Part Five, Protecting Yourself from Disease, deals with the most serious health threats facing Americans today—cardiovascular disease (Chapter 15), cancer (Chapter 16), infectious diseases (Chapter 17), and sexually transmitted diseases (Chapter 18). Part Six, Accepting Physical Limits, explores aging (Chapter 19) and dying and death (Chapter 20). Part Seven, Living Well in the World, includes coverage of conventional and complementary medicine (Chapter 21), injury prevention (Chapter 22), and environmental health (Chapter 23).

Taken together, the chapters of the book provide students with a complete guide to promoting and protecting their health, now and through their entire lives, as individuals, as participants in a health care community and system, and as citizens of a planet that also needs to be protected if it is to continue providing human beings with the means to live healthy lives.

For the tenth edition update, all chapters were carefully reviewed, revised, and updated. The latest information from scientific and health-related research is incorporated in the text, and newly emerging topics and issues are discussed. The following list gives a sample of some of the current concerns addressed in the tenth edition update:

- Physical activity guidelines from the USDA, Surgeon General, American College of Sports Medicine, and American Cancer Society
- Nutrition guidelines, including the 2005 Dietary Guidelines for Americans, the USDA MyPyramid food guidance system, and the Mediterranean diet
- The increasing prevalence of overweight and obesity in the United States, along with associated health risks, contributing factors, and popular approaches to weight loss
- Trans fat and allergen food labeling requirements
- Emergency contraception (Plan B), contraceptive implants, the contraceptive ring, and other new contraceptive methods
- Tobacco addiction, tobacco advertising, and smoking cessation products
- Government rulings and warnings on ephedra, environmental tobacco smoke, the contraceptive patch, package inserts for prescription and OTC drugs, antidepressant use in children and adolescents, and more
- Pre-diabetes, diabetes, and insulin resistance
- Food safety issues, including mad cow disease, chemical contamination of fish, and outbreaks of illness from *E. coli* contamination
- Depression, suicide risk, and self-injury in young people
- Anorexia, bulimia, and disordered eating
- Use of performance-enhancing drugs by athletes
- HIV/AIDS prevention, testing, and treatment
- Avian flu, West Nile virus, drug-resistant tuberculosis, and other emerging infections
- Online social networking and dating Web sites
- Sources of stress and stress management strategies
- Risks of hormone replacement therapy for menopausal women
- The new human papillomavirus vaccine to prevent genital warts and cervical cancer
- Global climate change

The tenth edition update continues to emphasize the development of total wellness, with coverage of spiritual wellness and the close connections between mind and body. Key topics include paths to spiritual wellness; global religious views on tobacco use; the effects of stress on the brain, the immune system, and the course of pregnancy; the use of journal writing and spiritual practices to cope with stress; the benefits of volunteering; and the advantages of close connections with others. Chapter 4 includes information on the benefits of intimate relationships and strategies for building and maintaining healthy interpersonal relationships. Suggested journal writing activities on the Web site that accompanies the book help students to further explore their feelings and values.

Many other areas of special concern to students have also been expanded and updated in the tenth edition update. Chapters 2, 3, and 20 include expanded information on coping after terrorism or natural disasters and recognizing and dealing with post-traumatic stress disorder. Chapter 2 also includes information on the most common sources of stress for Americans as well as stressors common to nontraditional students. The coverage of drugs in Chapter 9 includes updated material on the nonmedical use of prescription pain relievers that contain oxycodone and hydorcodone, including Oxycontin and Vicodin, and the epidemic of methamphetamine use. The latest guidelines for healthy nutrient intakes and recommended patterns of physical activity are described in Chapters 12–14, along with expanded coverage of popular diets. Chapters 14 and 15 examine the health risks associated with diabetes, prediabetes, and insulin resistance, along with strategies for prevention and treatment. Chapter 17 includes a discussion of safety issues related to body art (tattoos and body piercing), and Chapter 18 provides an expanded look at the high rate of STDs among young adults. Prescription drug safety issues are highlighted in Chapter 21, including direct-to-consumer advertising and postapproval surveillance. Chapter 22 looks at terrorism and the magnitude and impact of interpersonal and collective violence worldwide. Chapter 23 includes the latest information on global warming, the hole in the ozone layer of the atmosphere, and the health effects of pollution.

Core Concepts takes care to address the health issues and concerns of an increasingly diverse student population. Although most health concerns are universal—we all need to eat well, exercise, and manage stress, for example—certain differences among people have important implications for health. These differences can be genetic or cultural, based on factors such as ethnicity, socioeconomic status, and age. Where such differences are important for health, they are discussed in the text or in highlight boxes called Dimensions of Diversity (described in greater detail below). Diversity topics in the tenth edition update include factors underlying health disparities, links between ethnicity and certain genetic diseases, the effects of culture on the expression of psychological disorders, high rates of HIV/AIDS among certain groups, and the relationships among ethnicity, poverty, educational attainment, and such risk factors as smoking, overweight, and exposure to pollutants.

Topics related to gender are also given special attention in the tenth edition update of *Core Concepts*. Key gender differences as well as issues of particular importance to women or men are discussed in the text and in highlight boxes called Gender Matters (described below). Gender-related topics include differences in such areas as responses to stress, risk of depression and suicide, communication styles, health effects from tobacco and alcohol use, heart attack symptoms, cancer rates and risk factors, muscular strength, life expectancy, dietary needs, body image, health care visits, grief, and risk of unintentional injuries and violence.

The health field is dynamic, with new discoveries, advances, trends, and theories reported every week. Ongoing research—on the role of diet in cancer prevention, for example, or on new treatments for HIV infection—continually changes our understanding of the human body and how it works in health and disease. For this reason, no health book can claim to have the final word on every topic. Yet within these limits, *Core Concepts* does present the latest available information and scientific thinking on innumerable topics.

To aid students in keeping up with rapidly advancing knowledge about health issues, *Core Concepts* also includes coverage of the Internet, a key source of up-to date information. Each chapter includes an annotated list of World Wide Web sites that students can use as a launching point for further exploration of important topics. Chapter 1 includes important information about evaluating health-related Web sites.

Ww Each chapter in the tenth edition update is also closely tied to the Web site developed as a companion to the text. Elements marked with the World Wide Web icon have corresponding links and activities on the *Core Concepts in Health* Online Learning Center (www.mhhe.com/insel10e). The Web site and other online supplements are described below in greater detail.

FEATURES OF THE TENTH EDITION UPDATE

This edition of *Core Concepts in Health* builds on the features that attracted and held our readers' interest in the previous editions. One of the most popular features has always been the **boxes,** which allow us to explore a wide range of current topics in greater detail than is possible in the text itself. The boxes are divided into eight categories, each in a different color and marked with a distinctive icon and label. Refer to the table of contents for a complete list of all the boxes in each category.

In the News boxes focus on current health issues that have recently been highlighted in the media. Topics include personalized medicine and other applications of the human genome project, same-sex marriage, antidepressant use and suicide risk in young people, innovations in contraception, factors contributing to the obesity epidemic in the United States, sports doping, the methamphetamine epidemic, avian flu, the impact of the baby boomers on society as they age, and global warming. Each In the News box is accompanied by the World Wide Web icon, indicating that the *Core Concepts* Online Learning Center has links to Internet resources students can use to learn more about the topic of the box.

Mind/Body/Spirit boxes focus on spiritual wellness and the close connections between people's feelings and states of mind and their physical health. Included in Mind/Body/Spirit boxes are topics such as paths to spiritual wellness, religious views of tobacco use, benefits of being a volunteer, sexual decision making and personal values, the placebo effect, how exercise fosters emotional wellness, and how stress can affect pregnancy and the immune system. Mind/Body/Spirit boxes emphasize that all the dimensions of wellness must be developed for an individual to achieve optimal health and well-being.

Take Charge boxes distill from each chapter the practical advice students need in order to apply information to their own lives. By referring to these boxes, students can easily find ways to foster friendships, for example; to become more physically active; to stay safe when using online social networking and dating Web sites; to reduce the amount of saturated and trans fats in their diets; to perform deep-breathing exercises for stress reduction; and to help a friend who has a problem with tobacco, drugs, or an eating disorder.

Critical Consumer boxes emphasize the key theme of critical thinking by helping students develop and apply critical thinking skills, thereby allowing them to make sound choices related to health and well-being. Critical Consumer boxes provide specific guidelines for evaluating health news and advertising, using food labels to make dietary choices, choosing a bicycle helmet, avoiding quackery, selecting exercise footwear, understanding health issues associated with tattooing and body piercing, getting an HIV test, using sunscreens and sunless tanning products, choosing smoking-cessation products, and making environmentally friendly shopping choices.

Dimensions of Diversity boxes are part of our commitment to reflect and respond to the diversity of the student population. These boxes give students the opportunity to identify any specific health risks that affect them because of who they are as individuals or as members of a group. Most Dimensions of Diversity boxes focus on issues related to U.S. ethnic groups, but some look at other dimensions, including socioeconomic status, age, and ability. Topics covered in these boxes include factors contributing to health disparities among ethnic minorities, diverse populations and stress, ethnic and cultural influences on psychological disorders, risk and protective factors for drug use related to ethnicity, rates of smoking and alcohol use among ethnic populations, ethnic foods, suicide among older men, exercise for people with special health concerns, and links between poverty and asthma.

In addition, some Dimensions of Diversity boxes highlight health issues and practices in other parts of the world, allowing students to see what Americans share with people in other societies and how they differ. Students have the opportunity to learn about laws and attitudes toward abortion in other countries, tobacco control around the world, the global pattern of HIV infection, and other topics of interest.

Gender Matters boxes highlight key gender differences related to wellness as well as areas of particular concern to men or women. An overview of key gender-related wellness concerns is provided in Chapter 1. Topics covered in later chapters include gender differences in rates of anxiety, depression, drug use, and cancer; in the symptoms and course of heart attack and STDs; and in responses to stress and grief. Other boxes look at the higher rates of autoimmune disorders in women and the higher rates of injuries in men.

Assess Yourself boxes give students the opportunity to examine their behavior and identify ways that they can change their habits and improve their health. By referring to these boxes, students can, for example, examine their eating habits, evaluate their fitness level, discover if they are at increased risk for cancer or cardiovascular disease, evaluate their driving habits, determine what triggers their eating, and examine their drinking and drug-taking behavior. These self-assessments are also included on the *Core Concepts in Health* Online Learning Center.

In Focus boxes highlight current wellness topics of particular interest. Topics include diabetes, Alzheimer's disease, headaches, carpal tunnel syndrome, cell phones and distracted driving, myths about organ donation, and shyness.

In addition to the boxes, many carefully refined features are included in the tenth edition update of *Core Concepts.* Each chapter opens with **Test Your Knowledge**—a series of 4 to 6 multiple choice and true-false questions, with answers. These self-quizzes facilitate learning by getting students involved in a variety of wellness-related issues. The questions emphasize important points, highlight common misconceptions, and spark debate.

Vital Statistics tables and figures highlight important facts and figures in a memorable format that often reveals surprising contrasts and connections. From tables and figures marked with the Vital Statistics label, students can learn about drinking and drug use among college students, alternative medicine use in the United States, world population growth, prevalence of psychological disorders, trends in public opinion about abortion, and a wealth of other information. For students who grasp a subject best when it is displayed graphically, numerically, or in a table, the Vital Statistics feature provides alternative ways of approaching and understanding the text. In addition, for each Vital Statistics table and figure, the *Core Concepts* Online Learning Center has links to sites where students can find the latest statistics and information.

Core Concepts features a wealth of attractive and helpful **illustrations.** The anatomical art, which has been prepared by medical illustrators, is both visually appealing and highly informative. These illustrations help students understand such important information as how blood flows through the heart, how the process of conception occurs, and how to use a condom. Other topics illustrated in the tenth edition update include diabetes, the effects of cocaine use on brain chemistry, the allergic response, the process of tumor development, osteoarthritis, MyPyramid, and trends in global temperature. These lively and abundant illustrations will particularly benefit those students who learn best from visual images.

Chapter-ending **Tips for Today** sections provide brief distillations of the major message of each chapter, followed by suggestions for a few simple things that students can try right away. Tips for Today are designed to encourage students and to build their confidence by giving them easy steps they can take immediately to improve their wellness.

Take Action, appearing at the end of every chapter, suggests hands-on exercises and projects that students can undertake to extend and deepen their grasp of the material. Suggested projects include interviews, investigations of campus or community resources, and experimentation with some of the behavior change techniques suggested in the text. Special care has been taken to ensure that the projects are both feasible and worthwhile.

The **Behavior Change Strategies** that conclude many chapters offer specific behavior management/modification plans relating to the chapter's topic. Based on the principles of behavior management that are carefully explained in Chapter 1, these strategies will help students change unhealthy or counterproductive behaviors. Included are strategies for dealing with test anxiety, quitting smoking, developing responsible drinking habits, planning a personal exercise program, phasing in a healthier diet, and many other practical plans for change.

Two quick-reference appendixes provide students with resources they can keep and use for years to come:

- **Appendix A,** "Nutritional Content of Popular Items from Fast-Food Restaurants," provides information on commonly ordered menu items.
- **Appendix B,** "Self-Care Guide for Common Medical Problems," provides information to help students assess and manage common symptoms, including fever, sore throat, indigestion, headache, and cuts and scrapes.

The latest emergency care guidelines for choking and cardiac arrest (the Heimlich maneuver and CPR) appear inside the back cover of the text, providing information that can save lives.

Several features from previous editions of *Core Concepts in Health* have been moved to the Online Learning Center. There, you'll find Communicate! exercises, which suggest strategies and activities for improving communication skills to enhance wellness; Journal Entry activities, which help students deepen their understanding of their wellness-related behaviors and become more skilled critical thinkers; and information about finding and evaluating Internet resources, formerly located in Appendix C.

LEARNING AIDS

Although all the features of *Core Concepts in Health* are designed to facilitate learning, several specific learning aids have been incorporated in the text. Learning objectives labeled **Looking Ahead** appear on the opening page of each chapter, identifying major concepts and helping guide students in their reading and review of the text. Important terms appear in boldface type in the text and are defined in a **running glossary,** helping students handle a large and complex new vocabulary.

Chapter summaries offer a concise review and a way to make sure students have grasped the most important concepts in the chapter. **For More Information** sections contain annotated lists of books, newsletters, hotlines, organizations, and Web sites that students can use to extend and broaden their knowledge or pursue subjects of interest to them. Also found at the end of every chapter are **Selected Bibliographies.** A complete **Index** at the end of the book includes references to glossary terms in boldface type.

TEACHING TOOLS

Available with the tenth edition update of *Core Concepts in Health* is a comprehensive package of supplementary materials designed to enhance teaching and learning.

Instructor's Media DVD

The **Instructor's Media DVD (ISBN 0-07-328238-3)** presents key teaching resources in an easy-to-use format. It is organized by chapter and works in both Windows and Macintosh environments. It includes the following teaching tools:

- The **Course Integrator Guide** includes learning objectives, extended chapter outlines, suggested activities, and lists of additional resources. It also describes all the print and electronic supplements available with the text and shows how to integrate them into lectures and assignments for each chapter. For the tenth edition update, the guide was prepared by Cathy Kennedy, Colorado State University.
- The **test bank** includes more than 3000 true-false, multiple choice, and short essay questions; it also includes two 100-question multiple choice tests that cover the content of the entire text. The answer key lists the page number in the text where each answer is found. Contributors to the tenth edition and tenth edition update test bank are Phil Kelly, Salem State University; Karen Vail-Smith, East Carolina University; and Kathy McGinnis, San Diego City College. Special thanks also go to our test bank reviewer panel: Phil Kelly; Betty Shepherd, Virginia Western Community College; Charla Blumell, East Carolina University; and Susan Moore, Western Illinois University.

  The test bank is available on the Instructor's Media DVD as Word files and with the EZ Test **computerized testing software.** EZ Test provides a powerful, easy-to-use test maker to create printed quizzes and exams. EZ Test runs on both Windows and Macintosh systems. For secure online testing, exams created in EZ Test can be exported to WebCT, Blackboard, PageOut, and EZ Test Online. EZ Test is packaged with a Quick Start Guide; once the program is installed, users have access to the complete User's Manual, including multiple Flash tutorials. Additional help is available at www.mhhe.com/eztest.
- The **PowerPoint slides** provide a lecture tool that you can alter or expand to meet the needs of your course. The slides include key lecture points and images from the text and other sources. For the tenth edition update, the PowerPoint presentations were created by Andrew Shim, Indiana University of Pennsylvania, and updated by Rob Hess, Community College of Baltimore County, Catonsville. As an aid for instructors who wish to create their own presentations, a complete **image bank,** including all the illustrations from the text, is also included on the Instructor's Media DVD.
- **Transparency masters and handouts**—more than 150 in all—are provided as additional lecture resources. The transparency masters feature tables showing key statistics and data, illustrations from the text and other sources, and key points from the text. Illustrations

of many body systems are also provided. The student handouts provide additional information and can be used to extend student knowledge on topics such as prediabetes, glycemic index, yoga for relaxation, and dealing with alcohol emergencies.

- A complete set of **Wellness Worksheets,** a student learning aid described below, is also included on the Instructor's Media DVD.
- Chapter-specific **video clips and images** are also available as additional lecture resources. They are designed to engage students and promote critical thinking and dialogue on relevant topics in personal health. The collection contains contemporary students interviews, news clips, and historical health videos on body images, depression, stress, genetics, spirituality, and many other topics.

Other Resources

- **Printed versions of key supplements**—the Course Integrator Guide, test bank, transparency masters, handouts, and Wellness Worksheets—are also available (ISBN 0-07-328243-X). The printed supplements are loose-leaf and three-hole-punched, ready to be placed in a binder.
- A set of 80 color **Transparency Acetates** (ISBN 0-07-328242-1) is available as a lecture resource. The acetates are not duplicates of the transparency masters on the Instructor's CD-ROM; many are from sources other than the text.
- Videos from **Films for Humanities** are also available.

Digital Solutions

The ***Core Concepts in Health*** **Online Learning Center** (www.mhhe.com/insel10e) provides many additional resources for both instructors and students. Instructor tools include downloadable versions of the Course Integrator Guide and all the PowerPoint slides, as well as links to professional resources. For students, there are learning objectives, self-quizzes and glossary flashcards for review, interactive Internet activities, and extensive links. The Online Learning Center also includes many tools for wellness behavior change, such as interactive versions of the Wellness Worksheets and a workbook for behavior change.

Classroom Performance System (CPS) brings interactivity into the classroom or lecture hall. CPS is a wireless response system that gives instructors and students immediate feedback from the entire class. Each student uses a wireless response pad similar to a television remote to respond instantly to polling or quiz questions. Contact your local sales representative for more information about using CPS with *Core Concepts in Health*.

PageOut (www.pageout.net) is a free, easy-to-use program that enables instructors to quickly develop Web sites for their courses. PageOut can be used to create a course home page, an instructor home page, an interactive syllabus that can be linked to elements in the Online Learning Center, Web links, online discussion areas, an online gradebook, and much more.

Instructors can combine Online Learning Center resources with popular course-management systems. The McGraw-Hill **Instructor Advantage program** offers access to a complete online teaching Web site called the Knowledge Gateway, toll-free phone support, and unlimited e-mail support directly from WebCT and Blackboard. Instructors who use 500 or more copies of a text can enroll in the Instructor Advantage Plus program, which provides on-campus, hands-on training from a certified platform specialist.

For more information about McGraw-Hill's digital resources, including how to obtain a password for PageOut, contact your local representative or visit McGraw-Hill on the Internet (www.mhhe.com/solutions).

Student Resources Available with *Core Concepts in Health*

In addition to resources available on the Online Learning Center, many other student resources are available. Contact your local representative to find out more about packaging any of the following with *Core Concepts in Health*.

- More than 100 **Wellness Worksheets** (ISBN 0-07-328253-7) are available to help students become more involved in their wellness and better prepared to implement successful behavior change. The worksheets include assessment tools, Internet activities, and knowledge-based reviews of key concepts. They are available shrink-wrapped with the text in an easy-to-use pad and on the Online Learning Center.
- **NutritionCalc Plus** (ISBN 0-07-321925-8) is a dietary analysis program with an easy-to-use interface that allows users to track their nutrient and food group intakes, energy expenditures, and weight control goals. It generates a variety of reports and graphs for analysis, including comparisons with the latest Dietary Reference Intakes (DRIs). The ESHA database includes thousands of ethnic foods, supplements, fast foods, and convenience foods, and users can add their own foods to the food list. NutritionCalc

Plus is available on CD-ROM (Windows only) or as an online version.

- **The Daily Fitness and Nutrition Journal** (ISBN 0-07-302988-2) is a handy booklet that guides students in planning and tracking a fitness program. It also helps students assess their current diet and make appropriate changes.
- The **Health and Fitness Pedometer** (ISBN 0-07-320933-3) can be packaged with copies of the text. It allows students to count their daily steps and track their level of physical activity.
- The interactive **HealthQuest CD-ROM** (ISBN 0-07-295117-6) helps students explore and change their wellness behavior. It includes tutorials, assessments, and behavior change guidelines in such key areas as stress, fitness, nutrition, cardiovascular disease, cancer, tobacco, and alcohol.

Additional supplements and many packaging options are available; check with your McGraw-Hill sales representative.

A NOTE OF THANKS

The efforts of innumerable people have gone into producing this tenth edition update of *Core Concepts in Health.* The book has benefited immensely from their thoughtful commentaries, expert knowledge and opinions, and many helpful suggestions. We are deeply grateful for their participation in the project.

Academic Contributors

Virginia Brooke, Ph.D., University of Texas Medical Branch at Galveston
Aging: A Vital Process

Theodore C. Dumas, Ph.D., Institute of Neuroscience, University of Oregon
Stress: The Constant Challenge

Thomas D. Fahey, Ed.D., California State University, Chico
Exercise for Health and Fitness

Michael R. Hoadley, Ph.D., Assistant Vice-President for Academic Affairs, Center for Academic Technology Support, Eastern Illinois University
Personal Safety: Protecting Yourself from Unintentional Injuries and Violence

Paul M. Insel, Ph.D., Stanford University
Taking Charge of Your Health

Nancy Kemp, M.D.
The Responsible Use of Alcohol; Sexually Transmitted Diseases

Charles Ksir, Ph.D., University of Wyoming
The Use and Abuse of Psychoactive Drugs

Howard Lee, M.D., M.P.H., Hematology and Oncology, Dominican Hospital, Santa Cruz, California
Cancer

Tova Marx, Ph.D.
Intimate Relationships and Communication

Nancy E. Mason, M.D., Department of Gynecology and Obstetrics, Stanford University School of Medicine
Abortion; Pregnancy and Childbirth

David Quadagno, Ph.D., Florida State University
Sex and Your Body

Jacob W. Roth, M.D., Dana Farber Cancer Institute, Harvard University
Dying and Death

Walton T. Roth, M.D., Stanford University
Psychological Health

James H. Rothenberger, M.P.H., University of Minnesota
Environmental Health

Judith Sharlin, Ph.D., R.D., Department of Nutrition, Simmons College
Weight Management

David S. Sobel, M.D., M.P.H., Director of Patient Education and Health Promotion, Kaiser Permanente Northern California
Conventional and Complementary Medicine: Skills for the Health Care Consumer

Mae V. Tinklenbeg, R.N., N.P., M.S.
Contraception

Jennifer A. Tremmel, M.D., S.M., Department of Cardiovascular Medicine, Stanford University Medical Center
Cardiovascular Health

R. Elaine Turner, Ph.D., R.D., University of Florida
Nutrition Basics

Patrick Zickler, Senior Science Writer, Masimax Resources, Inc.
Toward a Tobacco-free Society

Martha Zuniga, Ph.D., University of California, Santa Cruz
Immunity and Infection

Academic Advisers and Reviewers of the Tenth Edition and the Tenth Edition Update

Charlene Brown, Western Michigan University

Mary V. Brown, Utah Valley State College

Susan T. Burge, Cuyahoga Community College

Laura Burger, Grossmont College

Karen Camarata, Eastern Kentucky University
Jacquie Cottingham, Confederation College
Paula J. Dahl, Bakersfield College
Kathi Deresinski, Triton College
P. K. Doyle-Baker, University of Calgary
Maqsood M. Faquir, Palm Beach Community College
Kathi Fuller, Western Michigan University
Cathy Hammond, Morehead State University
Mary E. Iten, University of Nebraska at Kearney
Belinda L. Jones, North Carolina Central University
Roland J. Lamarine, California State University, Chico
Teresa A. Lyles, University of Florida
Susan A. Lyman, University of Louisiana at Lafayette
Lori S. Mallory, Johnson County Community College
Tom Pestolesi, Irvine Valley College
Roseann L. Poole, Tallahassee Community College
Donna Jeanne Pugh, Florida Metropolitan University
Bruce M. Ragon, Albany State University
Priscilla Rice, Bucks County Community College
Leah E. Robinson, Bucks County Community College
Stafford C. Rorke, Oakland University
Andrew Shim, Indiana University of Pennsylvania
Carol A. Smith, Elon University
Phillip B. Sparling, Georgia Institute of Technology
Debra Tavasso, East Carolina University
Jill M. Black, Cleveland State University
Ruth Dey, Johnson County Community College
Debra Engel, LaGuardia Community College
Ari Fisher, Louisiana State University
John Kowalczyk, University of Minnesota, Duluth
Priscilla MacDuff, Suffolk Community College
Marshall J. Meyer, Portland Community College
Richard E. Miller, George Mason University
Debby Singleton, Western Carolina University
Cynthia M. Smith, Central Piedmont Community College
Richard Stacy, University of Nebraska at Omaha
George Strickland, Lamar University
Jeremy Tiermini, Finger Lakes Community College
Deborah Vaughan, Contra Costa College
Lana Zinger, Queensborough Community College

Finally, we would like to thank the members of the *Core Concepts* book team at McGraw-Hill Higher Education. We are indebted to Kirstan Price, whose dedication and extraordinary creative energies have contributed so much to the success of this book; we are also indebted to Tim Huddleston for so ably taking on the role of developmental editor for the tenth edition update. Thanks also go to Chris Johnson, executive editor; Joe Diggins, sponsoring editor; Nick Agnew, executive marketing manager; Kate Engelberg, director of development; Julia D. Akpan, developmental editor for technology; Sarah B. Hill, editorial coordinator; Michele Perez, media producer; Ron Nelms, Jr.; media project manager; Chanda Feldman, production editor; Randy Hurst, production supervisor; Violeta Diaz, design manager; Robin Mouat, art manager; Nora Agbayani, photo researcher; and Marty Moga, permissions editor. To all we express our deep appreciation.

Paul M. Insel
Walton T. Roth

A Guided Tour of *Core Concepts in Health*

Are you looking for ways to improve your health behaviors and quality of life? Do you need help finding reliable wellness resources online? Would you like to boost your grade? *Core Concepts in Health* can help you do all this and much more!

ASSESS YOURSELF BOXES

Assess Yourself boxes give you the opportunity to evaluate your current level of wellness and pinpoint lifestyle behaviors that you can change. Assess Yourself boxes are marked with a World Wide Web icon to indicate that you can find them in an interactive format on the *Core Concepts in Health* Online Learning Center (www.mhhe.com/insel10e). Look for this icon throughout the text to identify elements that have corresponding activities and links on the Online Learning Center.

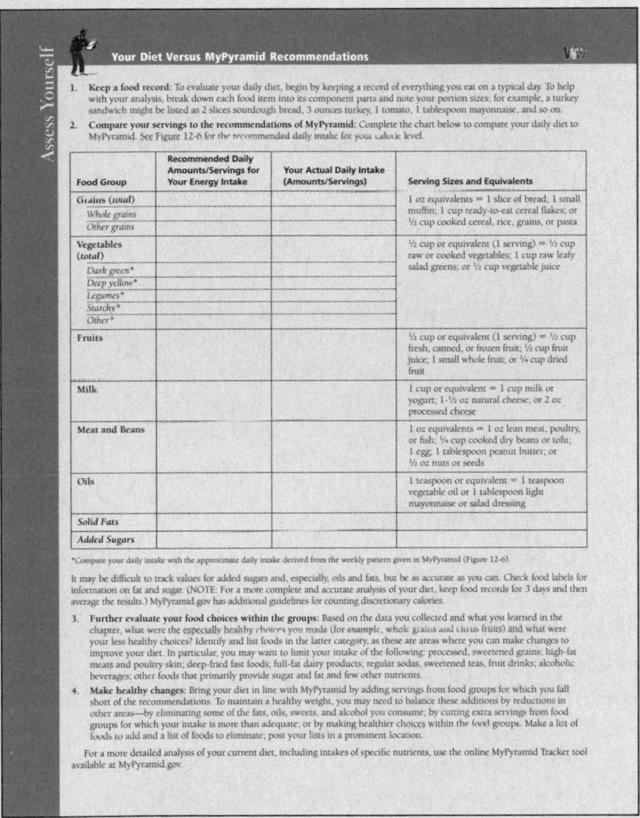

Assess Yourself

Your Diet Versus MyPyramid Recommendations

1. **Keep a food record:** To evaluate your daily diet, begin by keeping a record of everything you eat on a typical day. To help with your analysis, break down each food item into its component parts and note your portion sizes; for example, a turkey sandwich might be listed as 2 slices sourdough bread, 3 ounces turkey, 1 tomato, 1 tablespoon mayonnaise, and so on.
2. **Compare your servings to the recommendations of MyPyramid:** Complete the chart below to compare your daily diet to MyPyramid. See Figure 12-6 for the recommended daily intake for your calorie level.

Food Group	Recommended Daily Amounts/Servings for Your Energy Intake	Your Actual Daily Intake (Amounts/Servings)	Serving Sizes and Equivalents
Grains (*total*)			1 oz equivalents = 1 slice of bread; 1 small muffin; 1 cup ready-to-eat cereal flakes; or ½ cup cooked cereal, rice, grains, or pasta
Whole grains			
Other grains			
Vegetables (*total*)			½ cup or equivalent (1 serving) = ½ cup raw or cooked vegetables; 1 cup raw leafy salad greens; or ½ cup vegetable juice
*Dark green**			
*Deep yellow**			
*Legumes**			
*Starchy**			
*Other**			
Fruits			½ cup or equivalent (1 serving) = ½ cup fresh, canned, or frozen fruit; ½ cup fruit juice; 1 small whole fruit; or ¼ cup dried fruit
Milk			1 cup or equivalent = 1 cup milk or yogurt; 1-½ oz natural cheese; or 2 oz processed cheese
Meat and Beans			1 oz equivalents = 1 oz lean meat, poultry, or fish; ¼ cup cooked dry beans or tofu; 1 egg; 1 tablespoon peanut butter; or ½ oz nuts or seeds
Oils			1 teaspoon or equivalent = 1 teaspoon vegetable oil or 1 tablespoon light mayonnaise or salad dressing
Solid Fats			
Added Sugars			

*Compare your daily intake with the approximate daily intake derived from the weekly pattern given in MyPyramid (Figure 12-6).

It may be difficult to track values for added sugars and, especially, oils and fats, but be as accurate as you can. Check food labels for information on fat and sugar. (NOTE: For a more complete and accurate analysis of your diet, keep food records for 3 days and then average the results.) MyPyramid.gov has additional guidelines for counting discretionary calories.

3. **Further evaluate your food choices within the groups:** Based on the data you collected and what you learned in the chapter, what were the especially healthy choices you made (for example, whole grains and citrus fruits) and what were your less healthy choices? Identify and list foods in the latter category, as these are areas where you can make changes to improve your diet. In particular, you may want to limit your intake of the following: processed, sweetened grains; high-fat meats and poultry skin; deep-fried fast foods; full-fat dairy products; regular sodas, sweetened teas, fruit drinks; alcoholic beverages; other foods that primarily provide sugar and fat and few other nutrients.
4. **Make healthy changes:** Bring your diet in line with MyPyramid by adding servings from food groups for which you fall short of the recommendations. To maintain a healthy weight, you may need to balance these additions by reductions in other areas—by eliminating some of the fats, oils, sweets, and alcohol you consume; by cutting extra servings from food groups for which your intake is more than adequate; or by making healthier choices within the food groups. Make a list of foods to add and a list of foods to eliminate; post your lists in a prominent location.

For a more detailed analysis of your current diet, including intakes of specific nutrients, use the online MyPyramid Tracker tool available at MyPyramid.gov.

BEHAVIOR CHANGE STRATEGIES

Behavior Change Strategies provide specific behavior change plans for particular areas of wellness. Included are strategies for dealing with test anxiety, developing responsible drinking habits, quitting tobacco use, improving diet, planning a personal exercise program, and many other practical plans for change.

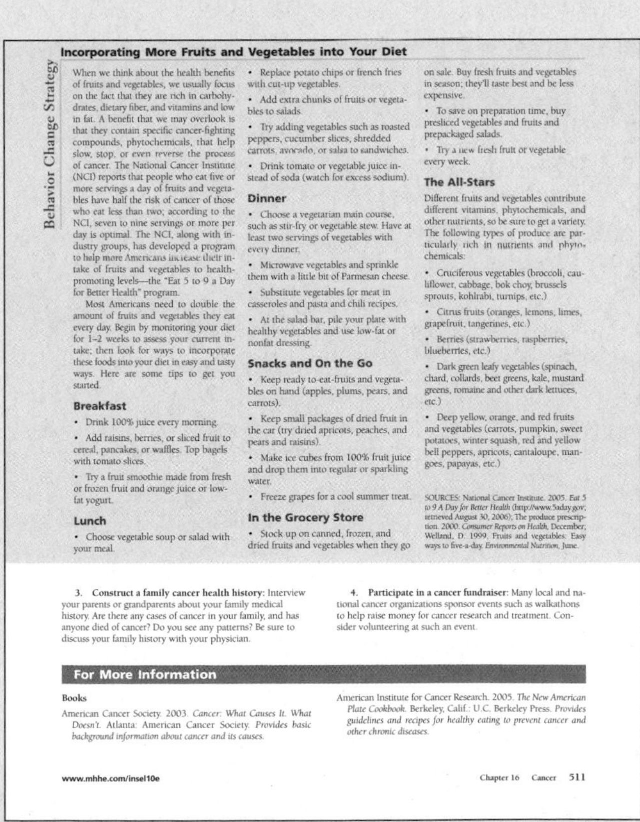

Behavior Change Strategy

Incorporating More Fruits and Vegetables into Your Diet

When we think about the health benefits of fruits and vegetables, we usually focus on the fact that they are rich in carbohydrates, dietary fiber, and vitamins and low in fat. A benefit that we may overlook is that they contain specific cancer-fighting compounds, phytochemicals, that help slow, stop, or even reverse the process of cancer. The National Cancer Institute (NCI) reports that people who eat five or more servings a day of fruits and vegetables have half the risk of cancer of those who eat less than two; according to the NCI, seven to nine servings or more per day is optimal. The NCI, along with industry groups, has developed a program to help more Americans increase their intake of fruits and vegetables to health-promoting levels—the "Eat 5 to 9 a Day for Better Health" program.

Most Americans need to double the amount of fruits and vegetables they eat every day. Begin by monitoring your diet for 1–2 weeks to assess your current intake; then look for ways to incorporate these foods into your diet in easy and tasty ways. Here are some tips to get you started.

Breakfast

- Drink 100% juice every morning.
- Add raisins, berries, or sliced fruit to cereal, pancakes, or waffles. Top bagels with tomato slices.
- Try a fruit smoothie made from fresh or frozen fruit and orange juice or low-fat yogurt.

Lunch

- Choose vegetable soup or salad with your meal.
- Replace potato chips or french fries with cut-up vegetables.
- Add extra chunks of fruits or vegetables to salads.
- Try adding vegetables such as roasted peppers, cucumber slices, shredded carrots, avocado, or salsa to sandwiches.
- Drink tomato or vegetable juice instead of soda (watch for excess sodium).

Dinner

- Choose a vegetarian main course, such as stir-fry or vegetable stew. Have at least two servings of vegetables with every dinner.
- Microwave vegetables and sprinkle them with a little bit of Parmesan cheese.
- Substitute vegetables for meat in casseroles and pasta and chili recipes.
- At the salad bar, pile your plate with healthy vegetables and use low-fat or nonfat dressing.

Snacks and On the Go

- Keep ready to-eat-fruits and vegetables on hand (apples, plums, pears, and carrots).
- Keep small packages of dried fruit in the car (try dried apricots, peaches, and pears and raisins).
- Make ice cubes from 100% fruit juice and drop them into regular or sparkling water.
- Freeze grapes for a cool summer treat.

In the Grocery Store

- Stock up on canned, frozen, and dried fruits and vegetables when they go on sale. Buy fresh fruits and vegetables in season; they'll taste best and be less expensive.
- To save on preparation time, buy presliced vegetables and fruits and prepackaged salads.
- Try a new fresh fruit or vegetable every week.

The All-Stars

Different fruits and vegetables contribute different vitamins, phytochemicals, and other nutrients, so be sure to get a variety. The following types of produce are particularly rich in nutrients and phytochemicals:

- Cruciferous vegetables (broccoli, cauliflower, cabbage, bok choy, brussels sprouts, kohlrabi, turnips, etc.)
- Citrus fruits (oranges, lemons, limes, grapefruit, tangerines, etc.)
- Berries (strawberries, raspberries, blueberries, etc.)
- Dark green leafy vegetables (spinach, chard, collards, beet greens, kale, mustard greens, romaine and other dark lettuces, etc.)
- Deep yellow, orange, and red fruits and vegetables (carrots, pumpkin, sweet potatoes, winter squash, red and yellow bell peppers, apricots, cantaloupe, mangoes, papayas, etc.)

SOURCES: National Cancer Institute. 2005. *Eat 5 to 9 A Day for Better Health* (http://www.5aday.gov; retrieved August 30, 2006); The produce prescription. 2000. *Consumer Reports on Health*, December; Welland, D. 1999. Fruits and vegetables: Easy ways to five-a-day. *Environmental Nutrition*, June.

3. **Construct a family cancer health history:** Interview your parents or grandparents about your family medical history. Are there any cases of cancer in your family, and has anyone died of cancer? Do you see any patterns? Be sure to discuss your family history with your physician.

4. **Participate in a cancer fundraiser:** Many local and national cancer organizations sponsor events such as walkathons to help raise money for cancer research and treatment. Consider volunteering at such an event.

For More Information

Books

American Cancer Society. 2003. *Cancer: What Causes It. What Doesn't.* Atlanta: American Cancer Society. *Provides basic background information about cancer and its causes.*

American Institute for Cancer Research. 2005. *The New American Plate Cookbook.* Berkeley, Calif.: U.C. Berkeley Press. *Provides guidelines and recipes for healthy eating to prevent cancer and other chronic diseases.*

www.mhhe.com/insel10e Chapter 16 Cancer 511

CRITICAL CONSUMER BOXES

Critical Consumer boxes are designed to help you develop and apply critical thinking skills so you can make sound choices related to wellness. Included are guidelines for evaluating health news and advertising, popular diets, and food and supplement labels; for choosing smoking cessation products, exercise footwear, and bicycle helments; for making environmentally friendly shopping choices; and much more.

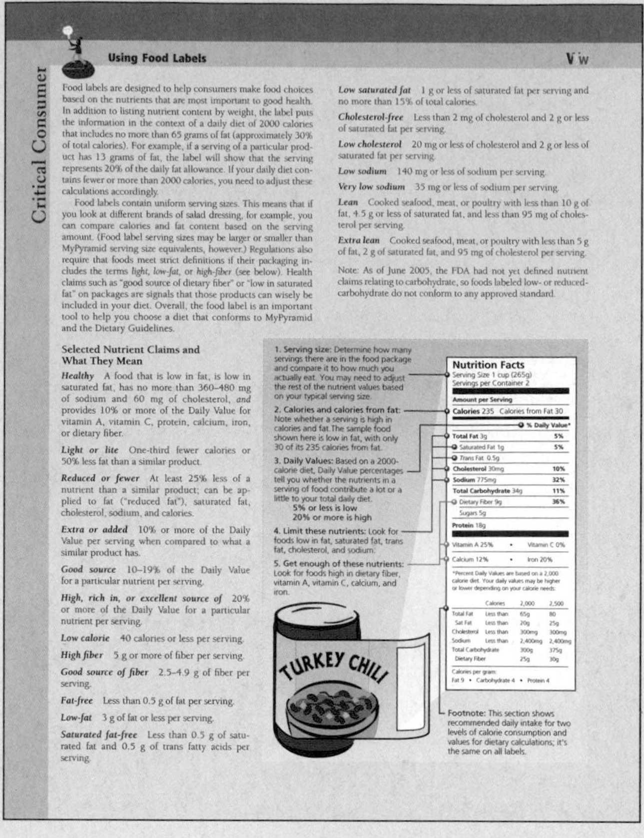

Critical Consumer

Using Food Labels

Food labels are designed to help consumers make food choices based on the nutrients that are most important to good health. In addition to listing nutrient content by weight, the label puts the information in the context of a daily diet of 2000 calories that includes no more than 65 grams of fat (approximately 30% of total calories). For example, if a serving of a particular product has 13 grams of fat, the label will show that the serving represents 20% of the daily fat allowance. If your daily diet contains fewer or more than 2000 calories, you need to adjust these calculations accordingly.

Food labels contain uniform serving sizes. This means that if you look at different brands of salad dressing, for example, you can compare calories and fat content based on the serving amount. (Food label serving sizes may be larger or smaller than MyPyramid serving size equivalents, however.) Regulations also require that foods meet strict definitions if their packaging includes the terms *light*, *low-fat*, or *high-fiber* (see below). Health claims such as "good source of dietary fiber" or "low in saturated fat" on packages are signals that those products can wisely be included in your diet. Overall, the food label is an important tool to help you choose a diet that conforms to MyPyramid and the Dietary Guidelines.

Selected Nutrient Claims and What They Mean

Healthy A food that is low in fat, is low in saturated fat, has no more than 360–480 mg of sodium and 60 mg of cholesterol, *and* provides 10% or more of the Daily Value for vitamin A, vitamin C, protein, calcium, iron, or dietary fiber.

Light or lite One-third fewer calories or 50% less fat than a similar product.

Reduced or fewer At least 25% less of a nutrient than a similar product; can be applied to fat ("reduced fat"), saturated fat, cholesterol, sodium, and calories.

Extra or added 10% or more of the Daily Value per serving when compared to what a similar product has.

Good source 10–19% of the Daily Value for a particular nutrient per serving.

High, rich in, or excellent source of 20% or more of the Daily Value for a particular nutrient per serving.

Low calorie 40 calories or less per serving.

High fiber 5 g or more of fiber per serving.

Good source of fiber 2.5–4.9 g of fiber per serving.

Fat-free Less than 0.5 g of fat per serving.

Low-fat 3 g of fat or less per serving.

Saturated fat-free Less than 0.5 g of saturated fat and 0.5 g of trans fatty acids per serving.

Low saturated fat 1 g or less of saturated fat per serving and no more than 15% of total calories.

Cholesterol-free Less than 2 mg of cholesterol and 2 g or less of saturated fat per serving.

Low cholesterol 20 mg or less of cholesterol and 2 g or less of saturated fat per serving.

Low sodium 140 mg or less of sodium per serving.

Very low sodium 35 mg or less of sodium per serving.

Lean Cooked seafood, meat, or poultry with less than 10 g of fat, 4.5 g or less of saturated fat, and less than 95 mg of cholesterol per serving.

Extra lean Cooked seafood, meat, or poultry with less than 5 g of fat, 2 g of saturated fat, and 95 mg of cholesterol per serving.

Note: As of June 2005, the FDA had not yet defined nutrient claims relating to carbohydrate, so foods labeled low- or reduced-carbohydrate do not conform to any approved standard.

1. Serving size: Determine how many servings there are in the food package and compare it to how much you actually eat. You may need to adjust the rest of the nutrient values based on your typical serving size.
2. Calories and calories from fat: Note whether a serving is high in calories and fat. The sample food shown here is low in fat, with only 30 of its 235 calories from fat.
3. Daily Values: Based on a 2000-calorie diet, Daily Value percentages tell you whether the nutrients in a serving of food contribute a lot or a little to your total daily diet.
5% or less is low
20% or more is high
4. Limit these nutrients: Look for foods low in fat, saturated fat, trans fat, cholesterol, and sodium.
5. Get enough of these nutrients: Look for foods high in dietary fiber, vitamin A, vitamin C, calcium, and iron.
TURKEY CHILI
Footnote: This section shows recommended daily intake for two levels of calorie consumption and values for dietary calculations; it's the same on all labels.
Nutrition Facts
Serving Size 1 cup (265g)
Servings per Container 2
Amount per Serving
Calories 235 Calories from Fat 30
% Daily Value*
Total Fat 3g 5%
Saturated Fat 1g 5%
Trans Fat 0.5g
Cholesterol 30mg 10%
Sodium 775mg 32%
Total Carbohydrate 34g 11%
Dietary Fiber 9g 36%
Sugars 5g
Protein 18g
Vitamin A 25% • Vitamin C 0%
Calcium 12% • Iron 20%
*Percent Daily Values are based on a 2,000 calorie diet. Your daily values may be higher or lower depending on your calorie needs:

	Calories	2,000	2,500
Total Fat	Less than	65g	80
Sat Fat	Less than	20g	25g
Cholesterol	Less than	300mg	300mg
Sodium	Less than	2,400mg	2,400mg
Total Carbohydrate		300g	375g
Dietary Fiber		25g	30g

Calories per gram:
Fat 9 • Carbohydrate 4 • Protein 4

TAKE CHARGE BOXES

Take Charge boxes present the practical advice you need to apply information from the text to your own life and to take charge of your health. Take Charge topics include breathing techniques for relaxation; guidelines for dealing with an alcohol emergency; and strategies for judging portion sizes, increasing physical activity, and improving communication.

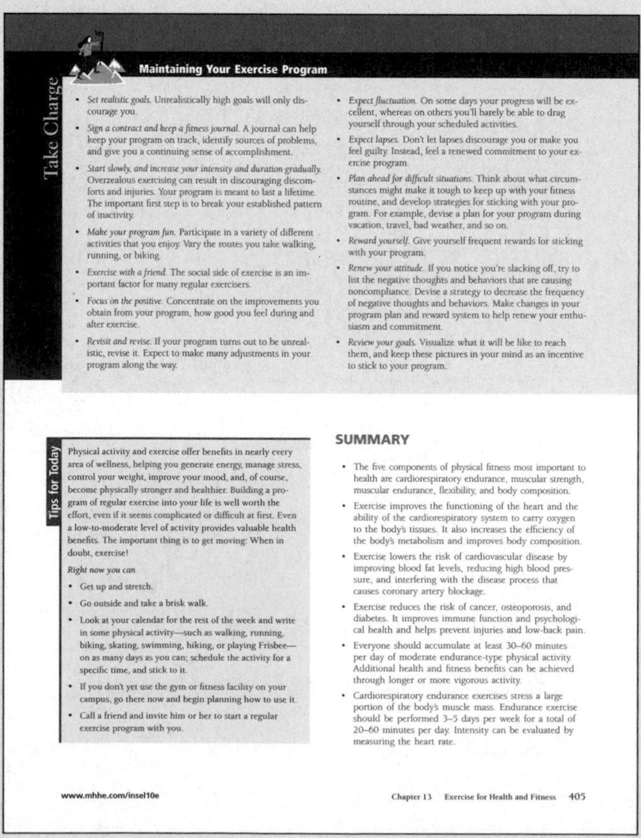

Take Charge

Maintaining Your Exercise Program

- *Set realistic goals.* Unrealistically high goals will only discourage you.
- *Sign a contract and keep a fitness journal.* A journal can help keep your program on track, identify sources of problems, and give you a continuing sense of accomplishment.
- *Start slowly, and increase your intensity and duration gradually.* Overzealous exercising can result in discouraging discomforts and injuries. Your program is meant to last a lifetime. The important first step is to break your established pattern of inactivity.
- *Make your program fun.* Participate in a variety of different activities that you enjoy. Vary the routes you take walking, running, or biking.
- *Exercise with a friend.* The social side of exercise is an important factor for many regular exercisers.
- *Focus on the positive.* Concentrate on the improvements you obtain from your program, how good you feel during and after exercise.
- *Revisit and revise.* If your program turns out to be unrealistic, revise it. Expect to make many adjustments in your program along the way.
- *Expect fluctuation.* On some days your progress will be excellent, whereas on others you'll barely be able to drag yourself through your scheduled activities.
- *Expect lapses.* Don't let lapses discourage you or make you feel guilty. Instead, feel a renewed commitment to your exercise program.
- *Plan ahead for difficult situations.* Think about what circumstances might make it tough to keep up with your fitness routine, and develop strategies for sticking with your program. For example, devise a plan for your program during vacation, travel, bad weather, and so on.
- *Reward yourself.* Give yourself frequent rewards for sticking with your program.
- *Renew your attitude.* If you notice you're slacking off, try to list the negative thoughts and behaviors that are causing noncompliance. Devise a strategy to decrease the frequency of negative thoughts and behaviors. Make changes in your program plan and reward system to help renew your enthusiasm and commitment.
- *Review your goals.* Visualize what it will be like to reach them, and keep these pictures in your mind as an incentive to stick to your program.

Tips for Today

Physical activity and exercise offer benefits in nearly every area of wellness, helping you generate energy, manage stress, control your weight, improve your mood, and, of course, become physically stronger and healthier. Building a program of regular exercise into your life is well worth the effort, even if it seems complicated or difficult at first. Even a low-to-moderate level of activity provides valuable health benefits. The important thing is to get moving: When in doubt, exercise!

Right now you can

- Get up and stretch.
- Go outside and take a brisk walk.
- Look at your calendar for the rest of the week and write in some physical activity—such as walking, running, biking, skating, swimming, hiking, or playing Frisbee—on as many days as you can; schedule the activity for a specific time, and stick to it.
- If you don't yet use the gym or fitness facility on your campus, go there now and begin planning how to use it.
- Call a friend and invite him or her to start a regular exercise program with you.

SUMMARY

- The five components of physical fitness most important to health are cardiorespiratory endurance, muscular strength, muscular endurance, flexibility, and body composition.
- Exercise improves the functioning of the heart and the ability of the cardiorespiratory system to carry oxygen to the body's tissues. It also increases the efficiency of the body's metabolism and improves body composition.
- Exercise lowers the risk of cardiovascular disease by improving blood fat levels, reducing high blood pressure, and interfering with the disease process that causes coronary artery blockage.
- Exercise reduces the risk of cancer, osteoporosis, and diabetes. It improves immune function and psychological health and helps prevent injuries and low-back pain.
- Everyone should accumulate at least 30–60 minutes per day of moderate endurance-type physical activity. Additional health and fitness benefits can be achieved through longer or more vigorous activity.
- Cardiorespiratory endurance exercises stress a large portion of the body's muscle mass. Endurance exercise should be performed 3–5 days per week for a total of 20–60 minutes per day. Intensity can be evaluated by measuring the heart rate.

www.mhhe.com/insel10e Chapter 13 Exercise for Health and Fitness 405

MIND/BODY/SPIRIT BOXES

Mind/Body/Spirit boxes focus on the close connections among people's feelings, states of mind, and physical health. Topics include religious views of tobacco use, effects of stress on the brain, sexual decision making and personal values, benefits of being a volunteer, expressive writing, and characteristics of a good death.

Mind/Body/Spirit

Help Yourself by Helping Others

Choosing to help others—whether as a volunteer for a community organization or through spontaneous acts of kindness—can enhance emotional, social, spiritual, and physical wellness. Surveys and studies indicate that the sense of purpose and service and the feelings of generosity and kindness that go with helping others may be as important a consideration for wellness as good nutrition and regular exercise. A 2006 study followed sedentary older people who joined a volunteer group called Experience Corps. The subjects' volunteer activities resulted in many of the same benefits as regular exercise, such as increased energy and vitality. Older adults who volunteer have higher levels of emotional and social wellness and lower rates of death.

In a national survey of volunteers from all fields, helpers reported the following benefits:

- Helper's high—physical and emotional sensations such as sudden warmth, a surge of energy, and a feeling of euphoria that occur immediately after helping
- Feelings of increased self-worth, calm, and relaxation
- A perception of greater physical health
- Fewer colds and headaches, improved eating and sleeping habits, and some relief from the pain of chronic diseases such as asthma and arthritis

Just how might helping benefit the health of the helper? By helping others, we may relieve our own distress and guilt over their problems. We focus on things other than our own problems, and we get a special kind of attention from the people we help. Helping others can be effective at banishing a bad mood or a case of the blues. Helping may block physical pain because we can pay attention to only a limited number of things at a given time. Helping others can also expand our perspective and enhance our appreciation for our own lives. Helping may benefit physical health by providing a temporary boost to the immune system and by combating stress and hostile feelings linked to the development of chronic diseases.

Helping others doesn't require a huge time commitment or a change of career. To get the most out of helping, keep the following guidelines in mind:

- *Make contact.* Choose an activity that involves personal contact.
- *Help as often as possible.* If your schedule allows, volunteer at least once a week. But, as with many parts of a wellness lifestyle, any amount of time helping is better than none.
- *Make helping voluntary.* Voluntary helping has positive results, whereas obligatory helping situations can actually increase stress.
- *Volunteer with others.* Working with a group enables you to form bonds with other helpers who can support your interests and efforts. Studies have found that the health benefits of volunteering are strongest for people who otherwise have low levels of social interaction.
- *Focus on the process, not the outcome.* We can't always measure or know the results of our actions.
- *Practice random acts of kindness.* Smile, let people go ahead of you in line, pick up litter, and so on.
- *Adopt a pet.* Several studies suggest that pet owners enjoy better health, perhaps by feeling needed or by having a source of unconditional love and affection.
- *Avoid burnout.* Recognize your own limits, pace yourself, and try not to feel guilty or discouraged. Take pride in being a volunteer or caregiver.

You can experience "helper's high" and the other personal rewards of volunteering as soon as you begin helping others. In addition to the benefits for you, volunteering has the added bonus of having a positive impact on the wellness of others. It fosters a sense of community and can provide some practical help for many of the problems facing our society today.

Financial planning for retirement is especially critical for women. American women are much less likely than men to be covered by pension plans, reflecting the fact that many women have lower-paying jobs or work part-time during their childbearing years. They tend to have less money vested in other types of retirement plans as well. Although the gap is narrowing, women currently outlive men by about 5–6 years, and they are more likely to develop chronic conditions that impair their daily activities later in life. The net result of these factors is that older women are almost twice as likely as older men to live in poverty. Women should investigate their retirement plans and take charge of their finances to be sure they will be provided for as they get older.

Adapting to Physical Changes

As described earlier in the chapter, there are many things a person can do to avoid or minimize the effects of the physical changes associated with aging. However, some changes in physical functioning are inevitable, and successful aging involves anticipating and accommodating these changes.

Decreased energy and changes in health mean that older people have to develop priorities for how to use their energy. Rather than curtailing activities to conserve energy, they need to learn how to generate energy. This usually involves saying yes to enjoyable activities and paying close attention to the need for rest and sleep.

www.mhhe.com/insel10e Chapter 19 Aging: A Vital Process 587

GENDER MATTERS

Gender Matters boxes highlight key gender differences related to wellness as well as areas of particular concern to men or women. Topics include gender differences in rates of anxiety, depression, drug use, and cancer; in the symptoms and course of heart attack and STDs; in styles of communication; and in responses to stress and grief.

Gender Matters

Women, Men, and Stress

Men and women alike experience stress, but they experience it differently.

Women and Stress

Women are more likely than men to find themselves balancing multiple roles, such as those of student, spouse, and parent. Women who work outside the home still do most of the housework—although today's husbands are helping in greater numbers than previous generations did—and housework isn't limited to cleaning or doing laundry. For example, more than 60% of women make all decisions about their family's health care, including decisions about elderly parents.

Women make up more than half the workforce but still face many workplace-related disparities that can be sources of stress. For example, women make less money than men in comparable jobs, are more likely to suffer sexual harassment or discrimination, and are less likely to be promoted into leadership positions.

The pressures of home, workplace, and school can create very high stress levels. This is especially true for women who see themselves in the traditional gender role as the family's primary caregiver.

Men and Stress

Men who fit a traditional male gender role may feel compelled to be in charge at all times. Their communication style may be competitive or aggressive, causing stress in interpersonal situations and limiting their ability to build a support network. Such men may keenly feel the responsibility to support a family, which can compound existing pressures at home and at work.

Key Stressors

A January 2006 survey conducted by the American Psychological Association, the National Women's Health Resource Center, and iVillage.com reported the percentages of men and women who feel stressed by the following issues:

	Women	Men
Money	28%	19%
Health of spouse/child	27%	20%
Health of parents	27%	20%
Children	24%	15%

In general, 51% of women reported that their stress affected them in some way, compared to 43% of men.

Physiological Differences and Stress

Because male testosterone levels rise from puberty onward, men tend to have higher blood pressure than women of the same age. This factor contributes to greater wear on the male circulatory system, sometimes increasing a man's risk for cardiovascular disease. A part of the brain that regulates emotions, the amygdala, is sensitive to testosterone. Thus, men may be predisposed to see social situations as more threatening than women do, resulting in more frequent stress responses.

Conversely, women have higher levels of oxytocin and are more likely to respond to stressors by seeking social support. This coping response may give women a longevity advantage over men by decreasing the risk of stress-related disorders. It does not, however, free women from stress-related ailments. Women are more likely than men to suffer stress-related hypertension, depression, and obesity. Recent research also shows that women who juggle multiple roles face an increased risk of heart disease, compared to women who do not need to balance different roles.

The General Adaptation Syndrome

Biologist Hans Selye, working in the 1930s and 1940s, was one of the first scientists to develop a comprehensive theory of stress and disease. Selye coined the term **general adaptation syndrome (GAS)** to describe what he believed was a universal and predictable response pattern to all stressors. He recognized that stressors could be pleasant, such as attending a party, or unpleasant, such as getting a flat tire or a bad grade. He called stress triggered by a pleasant stressor **eustress** and stress triggered by an unpleasant stressor **distress.** The sequence of physical responses associated with GAS is the same for both eustress and distress and occurs in three stages: alarm, resistance, and exhaustion (Figure 2-3).

Alarm This stage includes the complex sequence of events brought on by the activation of the sympathetic nervous system and the endocrine system—the fight-or-flight reaction. During this stage, the body is more susceptible to disease or injury because it is geared up to deal with a crisis. A person in this phase may experience headaches, indigestion, anxiety, and disrupted sleeping and eating patterns.

Resistance With continued stress, Selye theorized, the body develops a new level of homeostasis in which it is more resistant to disease and injury than it normally would be. During the resistance stage, a person can cope with normal life and added stress.

Exhaustion As you might imagine, both the mobilization of forces during the alarm reaction and the maintenance of homeostasis during the resistance stage require a considerable amount of energy. If a stressor persists or if several stressors occur in succession, general exhaustion results. This is not the sort of exhaustion people complain

Terms

gender role A culturally expected pattern of behavior and attitudes determined by whether a person is male or female.

general adaptation syndrome (GAS) A pattern of stress responses consisting of three stages: alarm, resistance, and exhaustion.

eustress Stress resulting from a pleasant stressor.

distress Stress resulting from an unpleasant stressor.

www.mhhe.com/insel10e Chapter 2 Stress: The Constant Challenge 39

IN THE NEWS BOXES

In the News boxes focus on current health issues that have recently been highlighted in the media, including such topics as same-sex marriage, stem cell research, avian flu, the methamphetamine epidemic, the growing prevalence of overweight and obesity, and global warming. In the News boxes are marked with the Web icon to indicate that the Online Learning Center has links to Web sites you can use to learn more about In the News topics.

In the News

The Next Influenza Pandemic—When, Not If?

Influenza Virus Basics

There are three main types of influenza viruses, designated A, B, and C. Influenza C usually causes only mild illness and has not been associated with widespread outbreaks. Types A and B, however, are responsible for **epidemics** of respiratory illness that occur almost every winter. Influenza A viruses are further divided into subtypes, based on differences in two surface antigens: hemagglutinin (H) and neuraminidase (N).

Influenza A viruses also differ from types B and C in that they can infect a variety of animals in addition to humans. Aquatic birds, such as ducks, are a natural reservoir for influenza A; they carry and can spread the virus but do not themselves become ill. Avian strains can infect and cause serious illness in domestic poultry and may also infect pigs, humans, and other mammals.

Antigenic Drift and Shift

Through replication errors and gene sharing, influenza viruses undergo constant change, enabling them to evade the immune system and thereby make people susceptible to influenza throughout life. A person infected with influenza does develop antibodies, but as the H and N antigens change, the antibodies no longer recognize the virus, and reinfection can occur.

Small changes in H and N antigens are referred to as *antigenic drift;* these changes are why the flu vaccine is reformulated each year. Fortunately, if the changes in H and N are small, the immune system may at least partially recognize the virus, giving many people some immune protection against the new strain.

Occasionally, an influenza A virus undergoes a sudden, dramatic change, called *antigenic shift*. If this occurs and the new virus spreads easily from person to person, a worldwide epidemic, called a **pandemic**, can occur because few people have any antibody protection against the virus. Antigenic shift occurs when an avian influenza virus mixes and exchanges genes with a human virus; this mixing may occur when a human or an animal such as a pig is simultaneously infected by both human and avian strains of influenza A.

Influenza pandemics usually occur about every 30 years or so. During the twentieth century, three major influenza pandemics occurred in humans:

- 1918–1919 ("Spanish flu"): About 20–40% of the world's population became ill, and as many as 40 million people died, including more than 500,000 Americans.
- 1957–1958 ("Asian flu")
- 1968–1969 ("Hong Kong flu")

The Next Pandemic

Many experts believe that an influenza pandemic is overdue, inevitable, and possibly imminent. Conditions that allow the mingling of flu viruses—including wild and domestic birds, humans, and other flu carriers living in crowded conditions and close proximity—exist in many parts of the world.

Scientists have been monitoring the progress of a strain of avian influenza A(H5N1) in Asia that has caused a small but deadly number of cases in humans. The initial outbreak in 1997–1998 killed 6 people in Hong Kong. Local authorities contained the outbreak quickly by tracing its source to infected chickens, ducks, and geese and then ordering the slaughter of all domestic poultry. Many experts believe that this quick action probably averted a pandemic.

The H5N1 strain doesn't pass easily to or between humans; the only case of human-to-human transmission involved a mother caring for a dying child. However, when it infects humans, it is deadly. Through mid-2006, outbreaks of H5N1 avian influenza were reported among migratory birds and poultry flocks in several countries in Asia, Africa, the Middle East, and Europe. Where those outbreaks occurred, people who came into close contact with infected birds became ill or died. As of mid-June 2006, 225 people worldwide were diagnosed with H5N1 infection and 128 of those victims died.

The more people who are infected, the greater the chance that avian and human strains will mix, producing an influenza virus that is easily transmitted between people. It is hoped that the resulting strain will be less lethal than the avian strain; human strains tend to be less deadly, and the quick death of avian hosts prevents the virus from being transmitted. However, one lesson from the 1918–1919 pandemic is that crowded human conditions—such as the army trenches, military hospitals, and troop transport ships associated with World War I—promote the development of lethal human flu strains.

Scientists are studying the virus to determine how many mutations it would take to allow H5N1 to pass easily between humans. In July 2006, drug manufacturer GlaxoSmithKline reported the development of a new vaccine that is more effective than current drugs against H5N1 influenza A. About 80% of persons immunized with the new drug developed antibodies after two low-dose injections. That compares to a 50% efficacy rate for previous drugs given at higher doses. The vaccine, which hasn't been shown to protect against mutated H5N1 viruses, is awaiting FDA approval.

pregnant woman, can be transmitted to a fetus, causing miscarriage, stillbirth, and severe birth defects, including deafness, eye and heart defects, and mental impairment. Mumps generally causes swelling of the parotid (salivary) glands, located just below and in front of the ears. This virus can also cause meningitis and, in males, inflammation of the testes.

Chicken Pox, Cold Sores, and Other Herpesvirus Infections The **herpesviruses** are a large group of viruses. Once infected, the host is never free of the virus. The virus lies latent within certain cells and becomes active periodically, producing symptoms. Herpesviruses are particularly dangerous for people with a depressed immune system, as in the case of

534 Part Five Protecting Yourself from Disease

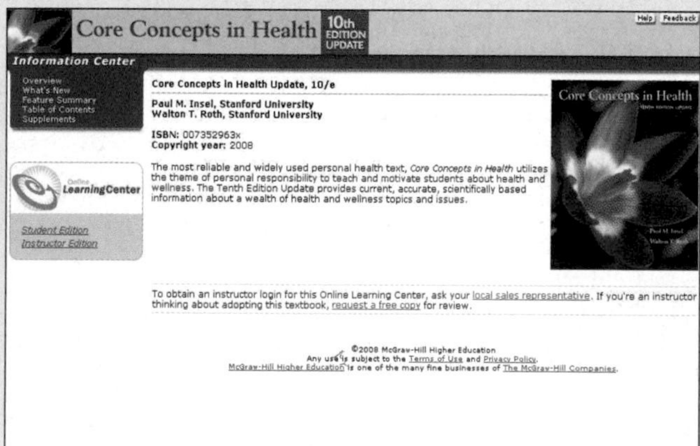

CORE CONCEPTS IN HEALTH ONLINE LEARNING CENTER

Visit the *Core Concepts in Health* Online Learning Center (www.mhhe.com/insel10e) for resources to help improve your grade and your level of wellness. You'll find chapter objectives and quizzes, flashcards, and many more study aids. You'll also find behavior change tools, interactive self-assessments, Internet activities, and links to reliable wellness-related sites.

Core Concepts in Health

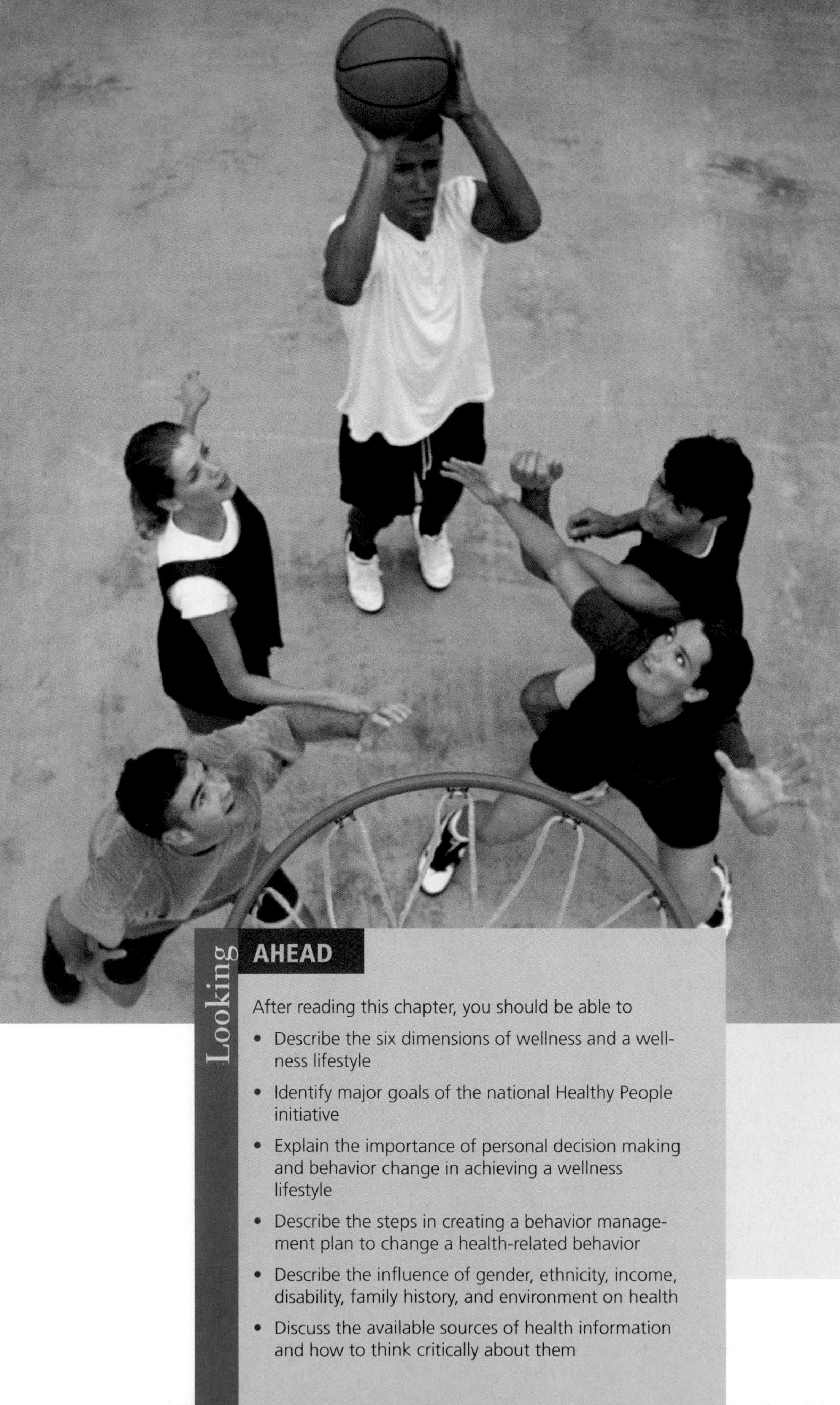

1

Looking AHEAD

After reading this chapter, you should be able to

- Describe the six dimensions of wellness and a wellness lifestyle
- Identify major goals of the national Healthy People initiative
- Explain the importance of personal decision making and behavior change in achieving a wellness lifestyle
- Describe the steps in creating a behavior management plan to change a health-related behavior
- Describe the influence of gender, ethnicity, income, disability, family history, and environment on health
- Discuss the available sources of health information and how to think critically about them

Taking Charge of Your Health

Test Your Knowledge

1. **In 1900, infectious diseases such as pneumonia and tuberculosis were responsible for more than one-third of all deaths in the United States.**
   True or false?
2. **The leading cause of death among Americans age 15–34 is unintentional injuries (accidents).**
   True or false?
3. **Which of the following lifestyle factors is the leading preventable cause of death for Americans?**
   a. alcohol abuse
   b. cigarette smoking
   c. poor dietary habits and lack of exercise
4. **Only 50% of health-related Web sites are nonpromotional and based on scientific information.**
   True or false?
5. **Which chronic condition is linked to the most deaths each year around the world?**
   a. obesity
   b. high blood pressure
   c. high cholesterol

ANSWERS

1. TRUE. A century later, infectious diseases cause only about 2% of all deaths; heart disease, cancer, and stroke are now responsible for more than 50% of all deaths among Americans.
2. TRUE. Homicide and suicide round out the top three leading causes of death for 15–34-year-olds; in this age group, the death rate for males is more than twice that of females.
3. B. Smoking causes about 435,000 deaths each year; poor diet and inactivity are responsible for about 365,000 deaths, and alcohol, more than 80,000.
4. FALSE. The number is closer to 35%. Most health-related Web sites sell products and/or are not based on scientific information.
5. B. According to the World Health Organization, high blood pressure is linked to 7.1 million deaths annually, worldwide. High cholesterol is associated with 4.4 million deaths per year, while 2.6 million people die as a result of obesity.

WW Visit the *Core Concepts in Health* Online Learning Center (www.mhhe.com/insel10e) for study aids and many additional resources.

A first-year college student resolves to meet the challenge of making new friends. A long-sedentary senior starts riding her bike to school every day instead of taking the bus. A busy part-time student organizes a group of coworkers to help plant trees in a blighted inner-city neighborhood. What do these people have in common? Each is striving for optimal health and well-being. Not satisfied to be merely free of major illness, these individuals want more. They want to live life actively, energetically, and fully, in a state of optimal personal, interpersonal, and environmental well-being. They have taken charge of their health and are on the path to wellness.

WELLNESS: THE NEW HEALTH GOAL

Wellness is an expanded idea of health. Many people think of health as being just the absence of physical disease. But wellness transcends this concept of health—for example, when individuals with serious illnesses or disabilities rise above their physical or mental limitations to live rich, meaningful, vital lives. Some aspects of health are determined by your genes, your age, and other factors that may be beyond your control. But true wellness is largely determined by the decisions you make about how to live your life. In this book, we will use the terms *health* and *wellness* interchangeably to mean the ability to live life fully—with vitality and meaning.

The Dimensions of Wellness

No matter what your age or health status, you can optimize your health in each of the following six interrelated dimensions. Wellness in any dimension is not a static goal but a dynamic process of change and growth (Figure 1-1).

Physical Wellness Optimal physical health requires eating well, exercising, avoiding harmful habits, making responsible decisions about sex, learning about and recognizing the symptoms of disease, getting regular medical and dental checkups, and taking steps to prevent injuries at home, on the road, and on the job. The habits you develop and the decisions you make today will largely determine not only how many years you will live, but also the quality of your life during those years.

Emotional Wellness Optimism, trust, self-esteem, self-acceptance, self-confidence, self-control, satisfying relationships, and an ability to share feelings are just some of the qualities and aspects of emotional wellness. Emotional health is a dynamic state that fluctuates with your physical, intellectual, spiritual, interpersonal and social, and environmental health. Maintaining emotional wellness requires monitoring and exploring your thoughts and feelings, identifying obstacles to emotional well-being, and finding solutions to emotional problems, with the help of a therapist if necessary.

Intellectual Wellness The hallmarks of intellectual health include an openness to new ideas, a capacity to question and think critically, and the motivation to master new skills, as well as a sense of humor, creativity, and curiosity. An active mind is essential to overall wellness, for learning about, evaluating, and storing health-related information. Your mind detects problems, finds solutions, and directs behavior. People who enjoy intellectual wellness never stop learning. They relish new experiences and challenges and actively seek them out.

Spiritual Wellness To enjoy spiritual health is to possess a set of guiding beliefs, principles, or values that give meaning and purpose to your life, especially during difficult times. Spiritual wellness involves the capacity for love, compassion, forgiveness, altruism, joy, and fulfillment. It is an antidote to cynicism, anger, fear, anxiety, self-absorption, and pessimism. Spirituality transcends the individual and can be a common bond among people. Organized religions help many people develop spiritual health. Many others find meaning and purpose in their lives on their own—through nature, art, meditation, political action, or good works.

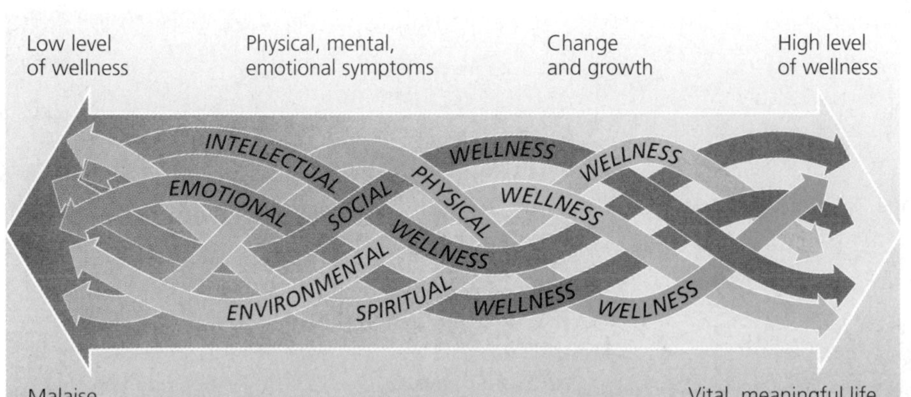

Figure 1-1 The wellness continuum. Wellness is composed of six interrelated dimensions, all of which must be developed in order to achieve overall wellness.

With wellness come health and vitality throughout the life span.

Interpersonal and Social Wellness Satisfying relationships are basic to both physical and emotional health. We need to have mutually loving, supportive people in our lives. Developing interpersonal wellness means learning good communication skills, developing the capacity for intimacy, and cultivating a support network of caring friends and/or family members. Social wellness requires participating in and contributing to your community, country, and world.

Environmental or Planetary Wellness Increasingly, personal health depends on the health of the planet—from the safety of the food supply to the degree of violence in a society. Other examples of environmental threats to health are ultraviolet radiation in sunlight, air and water pollution, lead in old house paint, and secondhand tobacco smoke in indoor air. Wellness requires learning about and protecting yourself against such hazards—and doing what you can to reduce or eliminate them, either on your own or with others.

The six dimensions of wellness interact continuously, influencing and being influenced by one another. Making a change in one dimension often affects some or all of the others. For example, regular exercise (developing the physical dimension of wellness) can increase feelings of well-being and self-esteem (emotional wellness), which in turn can increase feelings of confidence in social interactions and your achievements at work or school (interpersonal and social wellness). Maintaining good health is a dynamic process, and increasing your level of wellness in one area of life often influences many others (see the box "Ten Warning Signs of Wellness" on p. 4).

New Opportunities, New Responsibilities

Wellness is a relatively recent concept. A century ago, people considered themselves lucky just to survive to adulthood. A child born in 1900, for example, could expect to live only about 47 years. Many people died as a result of common **infectious diseases** and poor environmental conditions (unrefrigerated food, poor sanitation, air and water pollution). However, since 1900, the average life span has increased by more than 60%, thanks largely to the development of vaccines and antibiotics to prevent and fight infectious diseases and to public health campaigns to improve environmental conditions (Figure 1-2, p. 4).

But a different set of diseases has emerged as our major health threat, and heart disease, cancer, and stroke are now the top three causes of death in the United States (Table 1-1 on p. 5). Treating these and other **chronic diseases** has proved enormously expensive and extremely difficult. It has become clear that the best treatment for these diseases is prevention.

The good news is that people do have some control over whether they develop heart disease, cancer, and other chronic diseases. People make choices every day that either increase or decrease their risks for these diseases—lifestyle choices involving behaviors such as exercise, diet, smoking, and drinking. When researchers look at the lifestyle factors that contribute to death in the United States, it becomes clear that individuals can profoundly influence their own health risks (see Table 1-2 on p. 6 and the last column in Table 1-1). Smoking is the leading preventable cause of death among Americans, responsible for about 435,000 deaths each year; it is followed by obesity (about 112,000 deaths per year) and alcohol use (about 85,000 deaths per year). Preventable chronic diseases take a global toll, too. The World Health Organization (WHO) says 4.9 million people die annually from tobacco use, 2.6 million from

Terms

VW

wellness Optimal health and vitality, encompassing physical, emotional, intellectual, spiritual, interpersonal and social, and environmental well-being.

infectious disease A disease that is communicable from one person to another; caused by invading microorganisms such as bacteria and viruses.

chronic disease A disease that develops and continues over a long period of time; usually caused by a variety of factors, including lifestyle factors.

1. The persistent presence of a support network
2. Chronic positive expectations; the tendency to frame events in a constructive light
3. Episodic outbreaks of joyful, happy experiences
4. A sense of spiritual involvement
5. A tendency to adapt to changing conditions
6. Rapid response and recovery of stress response systems to repeated challenges
7. An increased appetite for physical activity
8. A tendency to identify and communicate feelings
9. Repeated episodes of gratitude and generosity
10. A persistent sense of humor

SOURCE: Ten warning signs of good health. 1996. *Mind/Body Health Newsletter* 5(1).

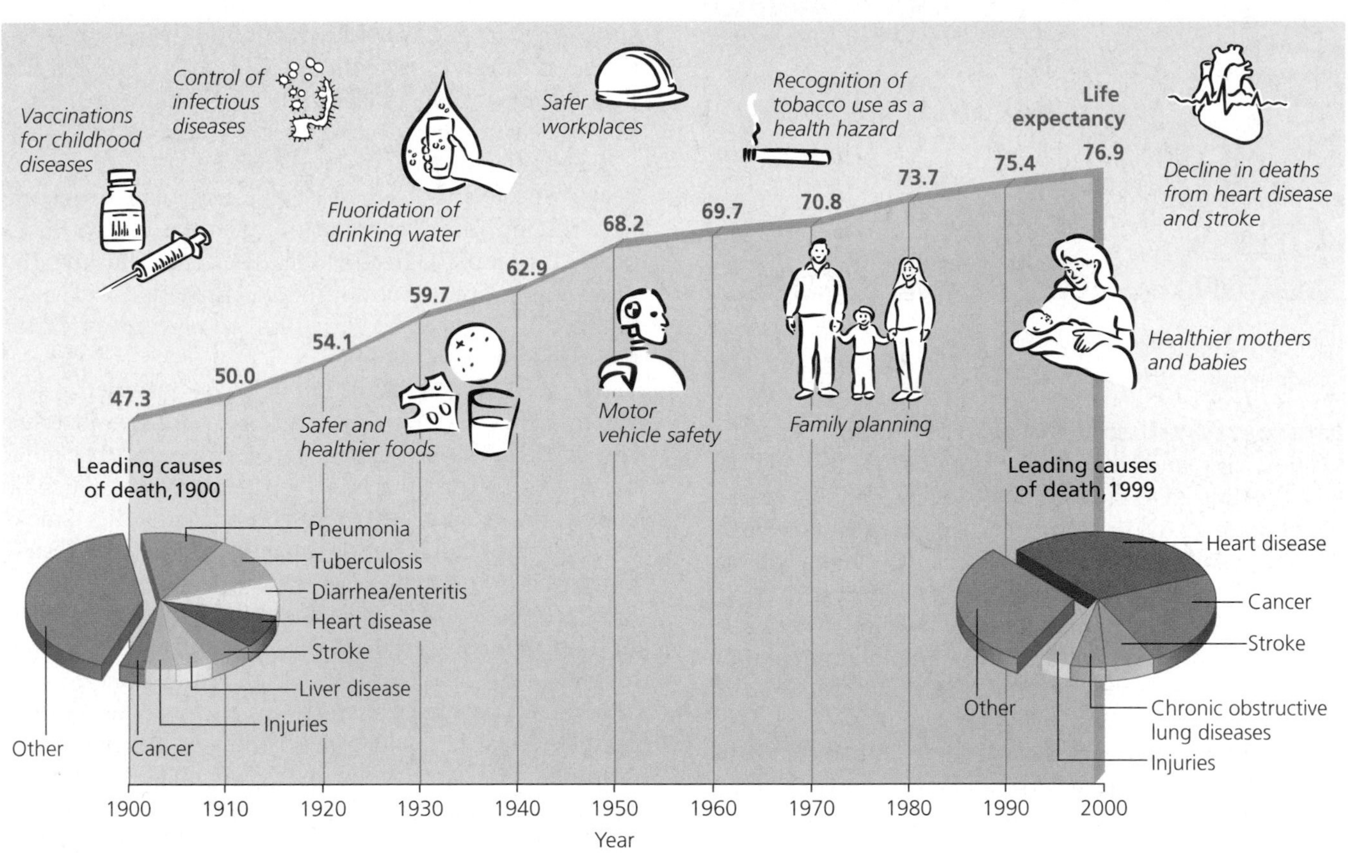

VITAL STATISTICS

Figure 1-2 Public health achievements of the twentieth century. During the twentieth century, public health achievements greatly improved the quality of life for Americans, and life expectancy rose from 47 to 77. A dramatic shift in the leading causes of death also occurred, with deaths from infectious diseases declining from over 33% of all deaths to just 2.2%. Heart disease, cancer, and stroke are now responsible for over 50% of all deaths among Americans.
SOURCES: National Center for Health Statistics. 2006. *Health, United States, 2006, with Chartbook on Trends in the Health of Americans.* Hyattsville, Md.: National Center for Health Statistics; Centers for Disease Control and Prevention. 1999. Ten great public health achievements—United States, 1900–1999. *Morbidity and Mortality Weekly Report* 48(12): 241–243.

VITAL STATISTICS

Table 1-1 Leading Causes of Death in the United States

Rank	Cause of Death	Number of Deaths	Percent of Total Deaths	Female/Male Ratio[a]	Lifestyle Factors
1	Heart disease	652,486	27.2	51/49	D I S A
2	Cancer[b]	553,888	23.1	48/52	D I S A
3	Stroke	150,074	6.3	61/39	D I S A
4	Chronic lower respiratory diseases	121,987	5.1	51/49	S
5	Unintentional injuries (accidents)	112,012	4.7	35/65	I S A
6	Diabetes mellitus	73,138	3.1	53/47	D I S
7	Alzheimer's disease	65,965	2.8	71/29	
8	Influenza and pneumonia	59,664	2.5	56/44	S
9	Kidney disease	42,480	1.8	52/48	D I S A
10	Septicemia (systemic blood infection)	33,373	1.4	56/44	A
11	Intentional self-harm (suicide)	32,439	1.4	20/80	A
12	Chronic liver disease and cirrhosis	27,013	1.1	36/64	A
13	Hypertension (high blood pressure)	23,076	1.0	62/38	D I S A
14	Parkinson's disease	17,989	0.8	43/57	
15	Assault (homicide)	17,357	0.7	50/50	
	All causes	2,397,615			

Key D Diet plays a part; I Inactive lifestyle plays a part; S Smoking plays a part; A Excessive alcohol consumption plays a part

[a]Ratio of females to males who died of each cause. For example, about the same number of women and men died of heart disease, but only about half as many women as men died of unintentional injuries and four times as many men as women committed suicide.

[b]Among people under age 85, cancer is the leading cause of death. Decreased rates of smoking have reduced deaths from both heart disease and cancer, but among ex-smokers, heart disease risk declines more quickly and to a greater degree than cancer risk.

Note: Although not among the overall top 15 causes of death, HIV/AIDS (12,995 deaths) is a major killer and is among the 10 leading causes of death among Americans age 15–44 years.

SOURCE: National Center for Health Statistics. 2006. Deaths: Final data for 2004. *Health E-stats.* Released November 24, 2006; Jemal, A., et al. 2005. Cancer statistics, 2005. *CA: A Cancer Journal for Clinicians* 55(1): 10–30.

obesity, 4.4 million from high cholesterol, and 7.1 million from high blood pressure.

One step in disease prevention is learning about wellness, illnesses, and treatments. A 2005 study by the Institute of Medicine, however, shows that 48% of adults are insufficiently literate in health-related issues, meaning they can't consistently find or assess information about their health. From these figures, it is clear that wellness cannot be prescribed; physicians and other health care professionals can provide information, advice, and encouragement—but the rest is up to each of us.

The Healthy People Initiative

Wellness is a personal concern, but the U.S. government has financial and humanitarian interests in it, too. A healthy population is the nation's source of vitality, creativity, and wealth. Poor health drains the nation's resources and raises health care costs for all.

The national Healthy People initiative aims to prevent disease and improve Americans' quality of life. Healthy People reports, published each decade since 1980, set national health goals based on 10-year agendas. The latest report, *Healthy People 2010,* proposes two broad national goals:

- *Increase quality and years of healthy life.* One way to measure quality of life is to count the number of "sick days" people endure—days they can't function normally due to illness. About 18% of Americans take 14 or more sick days each year, a number that continually rises. Along those same lines, Americans increasingly describe their health as fair or poor, rather than excellent or very good. Americans' life expectancy has increased significantly in the past century, but people can expect poor health to limit their activities and cause distress during the last 15% of their lives (Figure 1-3, p. 6). Health-related quality of life reflects a full range of functional capacity to work, play, and maintain satisfying relationships. This national goal stresses the importance of health status and quality of life, not just longevity.
- *Eliminate health disparities among Americans.* Many health problems today disproportionately affect certain American populations—for example, ethnic minorities, people of low socioeconomic status or educational attainment, and people with disabilities. *Healthy People 2010* calls for eliminating disparities in health status, health risks, and use of preventive services among all population groups within the next decade.

VITAL STATISTICS

Table 1-2 Actual Causes of Death Among Americans, 2000

	Number of Deaths Per Year	Percent of Total Deaths Per Year	Change in Number of Deaths Per Year Since 1990
Tobacco	435,000	18.1	+
Obesity*	112,000	4.6	+
Alcohol consumption	85,000	3.5	−
Microbial agents	75,000	3.1	−
Toxic agents	55,000	2.3	−
Motor vehicles	43,000	1.8	+
Firearms	29,000	1.2	−
Sexual behavior	20,000	0.8	−
Illicit drug use	17,000	0.7	−

Note: Actual causes of death are defined as lifestyle and environmental factors that contribute to the leading killers of Americans, including heart disease, cancer, and stroke. Microbial agents include bacterial and viral infections like influenza and pneumonia; toxic agents include environmental pollutants and chemical agents such as asbestos. Comparable calculations on actual causes of death were done for 1990 and 2000, and deaths from some causes increased (+) while for others, deaths declined (−).

*The number of deaths due to obesity is an area of ongoing controversy and debate. Recent estimates have ranged from 112,000 to 365,000.

SOURCES: Centers for Disease Control and Prevention. 2005. *Frequently Asked Questions About Calculating Obesity-Related Risk* http://www.cdc.gov/PDF/Frequently_Asked_Questions_About_Calculating_Obesity-Related_Risk.pdf; retrieved August 3, 2006. Mokdad, A. H., et al. 2005. Correction: Actual causes of death in the United States, 2000. *Journal of the American Medical Association* 293(3): 293–294. Mokdad, A. H., et al. 2004. Actual causes of death in the United States, 2000. *Journal of the American Medical Association* 291(10): 1238–1245.

Giving substance to these broad goals are hundreds of specific objectives—measurable targets for the year 2010—in many different focus areas that relate to wellness, including fitness, nutrition, safety, substance abuse, health care, and chronic and infectious diseases. Specific Healthy People targets serve as the basis for national monitoring and tracking of the health status and health risks of Americans and our use of health services. They encompass individual actions as well as larger-scale changes in environment and medical services. Examples of health promotion objectives from *Healthy People 2010,* as well as estimates of our progress toward these targets, appear in Table 1-3.

Healthy People 2010 reflects the changing attitude of Americans: an emerging sense of personal responsibility as the key to good health. The primary concerns of *Healthy People 2010* are the principal topics covered in this book. In many ways, personal wellness goals are no different from the national aspirations.

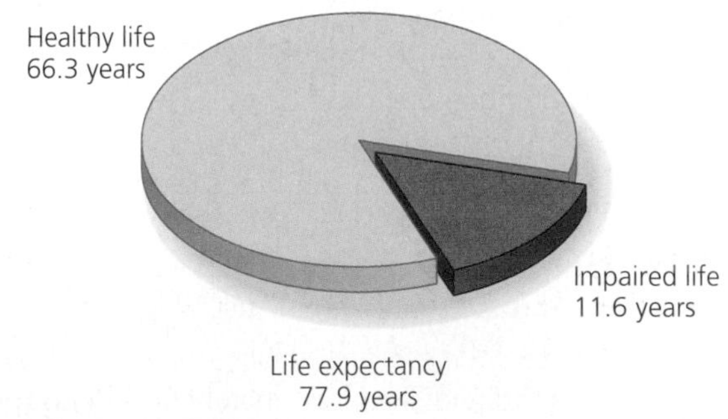

VITAL STATISTICS

Figure 1-3 Quantity of life versus quality of life. Years of healthy life as a proportion of life expectancy in the U.S. population.
SOURCES: National Center for Health Statistics. 2006. *Health, United States, 2006.* Hyattsville, Md.: National Center for Health Statistics. 2001. *Healthy People 2000 Final Review.* Hyattsville, Md.: Public Health Service.

Health Issues for Diverse Populations

Americans are a diverse people. Our ancestry is European, African, Asian, Pacific Islander, Latin American, and Native American. We live in cities, suburbs, and rural areas and work at every imaginable occupation. In no other country in the world do so many diverse people live and work together every day. And in no other country are the understanding and tolerance of differences so much a part of the political and cultural ideal. We are at heart a nation of diversity, and, though we often fall short of our goal, we strive for justice and equality among all.

When it comes to health, most differences among people are insignificant; most health issues concern us all equally. We all need to eat well, exercise, manage stress, and cultivate satisfying personal relationships. We need to know how to protect ourselves from heart disease, cancer, sexually transmitted diseases, and injuries. We need to know how to use the health care system.

But some of our differences, as individuals and as members of groups, do have important implications for health. Some of us, for example, have a genetic predisposition for developing certain health problems, such as high cholesterol. Some of us have grown up eating foods that raise our risk of heart disease or obesity. Some of us live in an environment that increases the chance that we will smoke

Table 1-3 Selected *Healthy People 2010* Objectives

Objective	Estimate of Current Status (%)	Goal (%)
Increase the proportion of people age 18 and older who engage regularly in moderate physical activity.	30	50
Increase the proportion of people age 2 and older who consume at least three daily servings of vegetables, with at least one-third being dark-green or orange vegetables.	3	50
Increase the prevalence of healthy weight among all people age 20 and older.	33	60
Reduce the proportion of adults 18 and older who use cigarettes.	21	12
Reduce the proportion of college students reporting binge drinking during the past 2 weeks.	39	20
Increase the proportion of pregnancies that are intended.	51	70
Increase the proportion of adults who take protective measures to reduce the risk of skin cancer (sunscreens, sun-protective clothing, and so on).	59	85
Increase the use of safety belts by motor vehicle occupants.	75	92
Increase the number of residences with a functioning smoke alarm on every floor.	87	100
Increase the proportion of people with health insurance.	84	100

SOURCE: National Center for Health Statistics. 2006. *DATA2010: The Healthy People 2010 Database: June 2006 Edition* (http://wonder.cdc.gov/data2010/obj.htm; retrieved July 17, 2006).

cigarettes or abuse alcohol. These health-related differences among individuals and groups can be biological—determined genetically—or cultural—acquired as patterns of behavior through daily interactions with our families, communities, and society. Many health conditions are a function of biology and culture combined. A person can have a genetic predisposition for a disease, for example, but won't actually develop the disease itself unless certain lifestyle factors are present, such as stress or a poor diet.

When we talk about health issues for diverse populations, we face two related dangers. The first is the danger of stereotyping, of talking about people as groups rather than as individuals. It's certainly true that every person is an individual with a unique genetic endowment and unique life experiences. But many of these influences are shared with others of similar genetic and cultural background. Statements about these group similarities can be useful; for example, they can alert people to areas that may be of special concern for them and their families.

The second danger is that of overgeneralizing, of ignoring the extensive biological and cultural diversity that exists among peoples who are grouped together. Groups labeled Latino or Hispanic, for example, include Mexican Americans, Puerto Ricans, people from South and Central America, and other Spanish-speaking peoples. Similarly, the population labeled American Indian includes hundreds of recognized tribal nations, each with its own genetic and cultural heritage. It's important to keep these considerations in mind whenever you read about culturally diverse populations.

Health-related differences among groups can be identified and described in the context of several different dimensions. Those highlighted in *Healthy People 2010* are gender, ethnicity, income and education, disability, geographic location, and sexual orientation.

Sex and Gender Sex and gender profoundly influence wellness. The World Health Organization (WHO) defines **sex** as the biological and physiological characteristics that define men and women; these characteristics are related to chromosomes and their effects on reproductive organs and the functioning of the body. Menstruation in women and the presence of testicles in men are examples of sex-related characteristics. **Gender** is defined as roles, behaviors, activities, and attributes that a given society considers appropriate for men and women. A person's gender is rooted in biology and physiology, but it is shaped by experience and environment—how society responds to individuals based on their sex. Examples of gender-related characteristics that affect wellness include higher rates of smoking and drinking among men and lower earnings among women (compared with men doing similar work).

Terms

sex The biological and physiological characteristics that define men and women.

gender The roles, behaviors, activities, and attributes that a given society considers appropriate for men and women.

Gender Matters

Women's Health/Men's Health

Men and women have different life expectancies, different reproductive concerns, and different incidences of many diseases. They have different patterns of health-related behaviors, and they respond differently to medications and other medical treatments. The lists below highlight just a few of the many gender differences that can affect wellness.

Women

- Women live longer than men (about 4 years, on average) but have higher rates of disabling health problems like arthritis, osteoporosis, and Alzheimer's disease.
- On average, women are shorter, have a lower proportion of muscle, and tend to have a "pear" body shape, with excess body fat stored in the hips. Obesity is more common in women than in men.
- Women score better on tests of verbal fluency, speech production, fine motor skills, and visual and working memory.
- Women experience heart attacks, on average, about 10 years later than men, but they have a poorer 1-year postattack survival rate. Women are more likely to experience atypical heart attack symptoms (such as fatigue and difficulty breathing) or "silent" heart attacks, which occur without chest pain.
- Women are more likely to have a stroke or to die from a stroke, but women are also more likely to recover language ability after a stroke affecting the left side of the brain.
- Women have lower rates of smoking but have a higher risk of lung cancer at a given level of exposure to cigarette smoke.
- Women become more intoxicated at a given level of alcohol intake.
- Women have stronger immune systems and are less susceptible to infection by certain bacteria and viruses, but they are more likely to develop autoimmune diseases like lupus.
- Women are more likely to react to stressors with a response called tend-or-befriend that involves social support; this response may give women a longevity advantage by reducing the risk of stress-related disorders.
- Women are more likely to suffer from depression and to attempt suicide.
- Women are more likely to suffer from migraine headaches and chronic tension headaches.
- Women are more likely to be infected with a sexually transmitted disease (STD) during a heterosexual encounter, and they are more likely to suffer severe and long-term effects from STDs, including chronic infection and infertility.

Men

- Men have a shorter life expectancy than women, but they have lower rates of disabling health problems.
- On average, men are taller, have a higher proportion of muscle, and tend to have an "apple" body shape, with excess body fat stored in the abdomen.
- Men score better in tests of visual-spatial ability—for example, the ability to imagine the relationships between shapes and objects when rotated in space.
- Men experience heart attacks, on average, about 10 years earlier than women, but they have a better 1-year postattack survival rate. Men are more likely to have classic heart attack symptoms like chest pain.
- Men are less likely to die from a stroke but are also more likely to have permanent loss of language ability following a stroke affecting the left side of the brain.
- Men have higher rates of smoking, spit tobacco use, and alcohol use and abuse.
- Men have higher rates of death from causes linked to intoxication, risk-taking behavior, firearms, unintentional injuries (car crashes, drowning), homicide, and suicide.
- Men are more likely to be exposed to toxic or cancer-causing chemicals on the job.
- Men have weaker immune systems and are more susceptible to infection by certain bacteria and viruses, but they are less likely to develop autoimmune diseases like lupus.
- Men are more likely to react to stressors with an aggressive or hostile response, a pattern that may increase the risk of stress-related disorders.
- Men have lower rates of depression and are less likely to attempt suicide; however, men are much more likely to succeed at suicide, and many more men than women die each year from suicide.
- Men are more likely to suffer from cluster headaches.
- Men are less likely to be infected with an STD during a heterosexual encounter.
- Men are more likely than women to suffer diseases such as alcoholism, ADHD, and Parkinson's disease.

The effects of sex and gender on wellness can be difficult to separate—but both are important. For example, rates of smoking among American women increased following changes in culturally defined ideas of appropriate behavior for women. This increase in smoking, combined with women's greater biological vulnerability to the cancer-causing agents in tobacco smoke, has led to a substantial increase in the number of deaths from lung cancer among women. See the box "Women's Health/Men's Health" for more on gender differences that impact wellness; throughout the text, boxes labeled Gender Matters focus on key wellness concerns for women and men.

Ethnicity Achieving the *Healthy People 2010* goal of eliminating all health disparities will require a national effort to identify and address the underlying causes of ethnic health disparities. Compared with the U.S. population as a whole, American ethnic minorities have higher rates of death and disability from many causes. These disparities result from a complex mix of genetic variations, environmental factors, and health behaviors.

Some genetic diseases are concentrated in certain gene pools, the result of each ethnic group's relatively distinct history. Sickle-cell disease is most common among people of African ancestry. Tay-Sachs disease afflicts people of Eastern European Jewish heritage and French Canadian heritage. Cystic fibrosis is more common among Northern Europeans. In addition to biological differences, many cultural differences occur along ethnic lines. Ethnic groups may vary in their traditional diets; their family and interpersonal relationships; their attitudes toward tobacco, alcohol, and other drugs; and their health beliefs and practices. All of these factors have implications for wellness. (See the box "Factors Contributing to Health Disparities Among Ethnic Minorities" on p. 10 for more information.")

The federal government collects population and health information on five broad ethnic minority groups in American society. (Figure 1-4 shows the current ethnic distribution of the United States.) Each group has some specific health concerns:

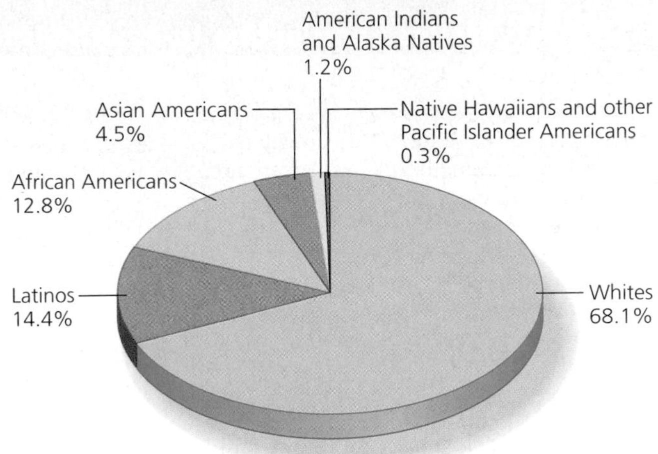

Note: Census respondents can choose more than one category, so percentages reflect both those who report one category and the approximately 2% of Americans who report two or more categories.

VITAL STATISTICS

Figure 1-4 Distribution of the U.S. population. SOURCE: U.S. Census Bureau. 2006. *Annual Estimates of Population by Race Alone or in Combination and Hispanic or Latino Origin for the United States.* Washington, D.C.: U.S. Census Bureau.

- *Latinos* are a diverse group, with roots in Mexico, Puerto Rico, Cuba, and South and Central America; many Latinos are of mixed Spanish and American Indian descent or of mixed Spanish, Indian, and African American descent. Latinos on average have lower rates of heart disease, cancer, and suicide than the general population, but higher rates of infant mortality and a higher overall birth rate; other areas of concern include gallbladder disease and obesity. At current rates, about one in two Latinas will develop diabetes in her lifetime.
- *African Americans* have the same leading causes of death as the general population, but they have a higher infant mortality rate and lower rates of suicide and osteoporosis. Areas of special concern for African Americans include high blood pressure, stroke, diabetes, asthma, and obesity. African American men are at significantly higher risk of prostate cancer than men in other groups, and early screening is recommended for them.
- *Asian Americans* include people who trace their ancestry to countries in the Far East, Southeast Asia, or the Indian subcontinent, including Japan, China, Vietnam, Laos, Cambodia, Korea, the Philippines, India, and Pakistan. Asian Americans have a lower death rate and a longer life expectancy than the general population. They have lower rates of coronary heart disease and obesity. However, health differences exist among these groups. For example, Southeast Asian men have higher rates of smoking and lung cancer, and Vietnamese American women have higher rates of cervical cancer.
- *American Indians and Alaska Natives* typically embrace a tribal identity, such as Sioux, Navaho, or Hopi. American Indians and Alaska Natives have lower death rates from heart disease, stroke, and cancer than the general population, but they have higher rates of early death from causes linked to smoking and alcohol use, including injuries and cirrhosis. Diabetes is a special concern for many groups; for example, the Pimas of Arizona have the highest known prevalence of diabetes of any population in the world.
- *Native Hawaiian and Other Pacific Islander Americans* trace their ancestry to the original peoples of Hawaii, Guam, Samoa, and other Pacific Islands. Pacific Islander Americans have a higher overall death rate than the general population and higher rates of diabetes and asthma. Smoking and obesity are special concerns for this group.

In some cases, however, medical disparities are starting to narrow. A 2005 survey of Medicare enrollees, for example, showed that the number of African Americans with diabetes who were taking steps to control their cholesterol rose by 46% between 1999 and 2003. The same survey showed that vastly more African Americans who suffer from heart disease were actively controlling their blood pressure.

Income and Education Inequalities in income and education underlie many of the health disparities among Americans. Income and education are closely related, and groups with the highest poverty rates and least education have the worst health status. These Americans have higher rates of infant mortality, traumatic injury and violent

To meet the *Healthy People 2010* goal of eliminating health disparities among ethnic minorities in the United States, the causes of these disparities must be identified and addressed. In studying the underlying causes of health disparities, it is often difficult to separate the many potential contributing factors.

Income and Education

Poverty and low educational attainment are the most important factors underlying health disparities. People with low incomes and less education have higher rates of death from all causes, especially chronic disease and injury, and they are less likely to have preventive health services such as vaccinations and Pap tests. They are more likely to live in an area with a high rate of violence and many other environmental stressors. They also have higher rates of unhealthy behaviors.

It is important to note that although ethnic disparities in health are significantly reduced when comparing groups with similar incomes and levels of education, they are not eliminated. For example, people living in poverty report worse health than people with higher incomes; but, within the latter group, African Americans and Latinos rate their health as worse than do whites (see figure). Infant mortality rates go down as the education level of mothers goes up; but among mothers who are college graduates, African Americans have significantly higher rates of infant mortality than whites, Latinos, and Asian Americans. These variations point to the complexity of health disparities.

Access to Appropriate Health Care

People with low incomes are less likely to have health insurance and more likely to have problems arranging for transportation to access care. They are also more likely to lack information about services and preventive care. But disparities persist even at higher income levels; for example, among nonpoor Americans, many more Latinos than whites or African Americans report having no insurance, no usual source of health care, and no health care visits within the past year. A 2006 study found that racial minorities have less access to better health care (such as complex surgery at high-volume hospitals) and receive lower quality care than whites. Factors affecting such disparities may include:

- *Local and regional differences in the availability of high-tech health care and specialists.* Minorities, regardless of income, may be more likely to live in medically underserved areas.
- *Problems with communication and trust.* People whose primary language is not English are more likely to be uninsured and to have trouble communicating with health care providers; they may also have problems interpreting health information from public health education campaigns. Language and cultural barriers may be exacerbated by an underrepresentation of minorities in the health professions.
- *Cultural preferences relating to health care.* Groups may vary in their assessment of when it is appropriate to seek medical care and what types of treatments are acceptable.
- *State and federal laws and programs.* Eligibility for Medicaid (a form of government insurance) varies by state and group. For example, Puerto Ricans are U.S. citizens and Cubans are classified as refugees, so people from these groups are immediately eligible for Medicaid; emigrants from other countries may not be able to access public insurance programs until 5 years after they enter the United States.

Culture and Lifestyle

As described in the chapter, ethnic groups may vary in health-related behaviors such as diet, tobacco and alcohol use, coping strategies, and health practices—and these behaviors can have important implications for wellness, both positive and negative. For example, African Americans are more likely to report consuming five or more servings of fruits and vegetables per day than people from other ethnic groups. American Indians report high rates of smoking and smoking-related health problems. Cultural background can be an important protective factor. For example, poverty is strongly associated with increased rates of depression; but some groups, including Americans born in Mexico or Puerto Rico, have lower rates of mental disorders at a given level of income and appear to have coping strategies that provide special resilience.

Discrimination

Racism and discrimination are stressful events that can cause psychological distress and increase the risk of physical and psychological problems. Discrimination can contribute to lower socioeconomic status and its associated risks. Bias in medical care can directly affect treatment and health outcomes.

Conversely, recent research shows that better health care results when doctors ask patients detailed questions about their ethnicity. (Most medical questionnaires ask patients to put themselves in a vague racial or ethnic category, such as Asian or Caucasian). Armed with more information on patients' backgrounds, medical professionals may find it easier to detect some genetic diseases or to overcome language or cultural barriers.

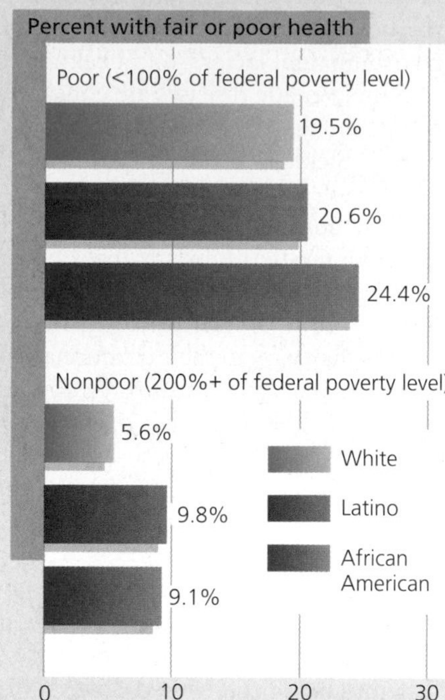

Self-rated health status. Respondents were asked to rate their health as excellent, very good, good, fair, or poor. Poverty is strongly associated with negative health status, but disparities persist even among nonpoor Americans.

SOURCES: National Center for Health Statistics. 2006. *Health, United States, 2006, with Chartbook on Trends in the Health of Americans.* Hyattsville, Md.: National Center for Health Statistics; Centers for Disease Control and Prevention. 2004. REACH 2010 surveillance for health status in minority communities. *MMWR Surveillance Summaries* 53(SS-6); Kaiser Family Foundation. 2003. *Key Facts: Race, Ethnicity, and Medical Care.* Menlo Park, Calif.: Kaiser Family Foundation; U.S. Department of Health and Human Services. 2001. *Mental Health: Culture, Race, and Ethnicity.* Rockville, Md.: U.S. Department of Health and Human Services.

death, and many diseases, including heart disease, diabetes, tuberculosis, HIV infection, and some cancers. They are more likely to eat poorly, be overweight, smoke, drink, and use drugs. They are exposed to more day-to-day stressors (such as the need to hold multiple jobs or deal with unreliable transportation) and have less access to health care services. A surprising finding from a 2006 study was that poor people living in wealthy neighborhoods had higher mortality rates than poor people living in moderate-income or low-income areas, perhaps because of the higher cost of living or psychosocial stressors. Many impoverished families are not only uninsured but rely on the local emergency room for their medical needs. Poverty and low educational attainment are far more important predictors of poor health than any ethnic factor.

Disability People with disabilities are those who have activity limitations, need assistance, or perceive themselves as having a disability. About one in five people in the United States has some level of disability, and the rate is rising, especially among younger segments of the population. People with disabilities are more likely to be inactive and overweight. They report more days of depression than people without disabilities. Many also lack access to health care services.

Geographic Location About one in four Americans currently lives in a rural area—a place with fewer than 2500 residents. People living in rural areas are less likely to be physically active, to use safety belts, or to obtain screening tests for preventive health care. They have less access to timely emergency services and much higher rates of injury-related death than people living in urban areas. They are also more likely to lack health insurance. Children living in dangerous neighborhoods—rural or urban—are four times more likely to be overweight than children living in safer areas.

Sexual Orientation The 1–5% of Americans who identify themselves as homosexual or bisexual make up a diverse community with varied health concerns. Their emotional wellness and personal safety are affected by factors relating to personal, family, and social acceptance of their sexual orientation. Gay, lesbian, and bisexual teens are more likely to engage in risky behaviors such as unsafe sex and drug use; they are also more likely to be depressed and to attempt suicide. HIV/AIDS is a major concern for gay men, and gay men and lesbians may have higher rates of substance abuse, depression, and suicide.

In this book, topics and issues in health that affect different American populations are given special consideration. Look for these discussions in the text and in boxes labeled Dimensions of Diversity. Also discussed in Dimensions of Diversity boxes are health issues and practices in other parts of the world. Explorations beyond the borders of the United States broaden our view, showing us both our common concerns and our divergent solutions.

CHOOSING WELLNESS

Wellness is something everyone can have. Achieving it requires knowledge, self-awareness, motivation, and effort—but the benefits last a lifetime. Optimal health comes mostly from a healthy lifestyle, patterns of behavior that promote and support your health now and as you get older. In the pages that follow, you'll find current information and suggestions you can use to build a better lifestyle. You'll also find tools for assessing yourself, for improving your communication skills, and for planning and carrying out specific behavior changes.

Factors That Influence Wellness

Our behavior, family health history, environment, and access to health care are all important influences on wellness. These factors, which vary for both individuals and groups, can interact in ways that produce either health or disease. For example, a sedentary lifestyle combined with a genetic predisposition for diabetes can greatly increase a person's risk of developing the disease. If this person also lacks adequate health care, he or she is much more likely to suffer dangerous complications from diabetes and have a lower quality of life.

Health Habits Scientific research is continuously revealing new connections between our habits and health. For example, heart disease is associated with smoking, stress, hostile and suspicious attitudes, a poor diet, and a sedentary way of life. Unfortunately, poor health habits take hold before many Americans reach adulthood. According to a 2005 study conducted by the Carolina Population Center and the University of North Carolina, 46% of white females age 19–26 reported they never exercised in an average week. About 67% of white males in the same age group reported that they engaged in binge drinking, and 31% were habitual smokers.

Other habits, however, are beneficial. Regular exercise can help prevent heart disease, high blood pressure, diabetes, osteoporosis, and depression and may reduce the risk of colon cancer, stroke, and back injury. A balanced and varied diet helps prevent many chronic diseases. As we learn more about how our actions affect our bodies and minds, we can make informed choices for a healthier life.

Heredity/Family History Your **genome** consists of the complete set of genetic material in your cells; it contains about 25,000 genes, half from each of your parents. **Genes**

Terms

genome The complete set of genetic material in an individual's cells.

gene The basic unit of heredity; a section of genetic material containing chemical instructions for making a particular protein.

control the production of proteins that serve both as the structural material for your body and as the regulators of all your body's chemical reactions and metabolic processes. The human genome varies only slightly from person to person, and many of these differences do not affect health. However, some differences do have important implications for health, and knowing your family health history can help you determine which conditions may be of special concern for you. Chapter 8 includes more information about how to put together and evaluate a family health tree.

Errors in our genes are responsible for about 3500 clearly hereditary conditions, including sickle-cell disease and cystic fibrosis. Altered genes also play a part in heart disease, cancer, stroke, diabetes, and many other common conditions; see the box "Personalized Medicine: Beyond the Human Genome Project." However, in these more common and complex disorders, genetic alterations serve only to increase an individual's risk, and the disease itself results from the interaction of many genes with other factors. For example, researchers have identified genes that clearly increase a woman's risk for breast cancer, but these genes explain only a small proportion of cases. In the small number of inherited cases, genetic alterations that increase the risk of cancer are present at birth in the genes of all the cells in the body. In the majority of cases, however, cancer results from genetic changes that occur after birth within particular cells—usually in response to behavioral and environmental factors. Another example of the power of behavior and environment can be seen in the more than 60% increase in the incidence of diabetes that has occurred among Americans since 1990. This huge increase is not due to any sudden change in our genes; it is the result of increasing rates of obesity caused by poor dietary choices and lack of physical activity (Figure 1-5).

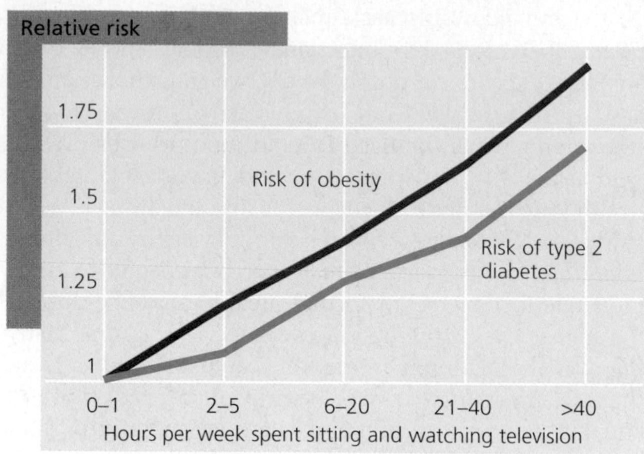

Figure 1-5 Sedentary lifestyle and risk of obesity and type 2 diabetes. Heredity and environment can play a role in the development of obesity and diabetes, but health habits are very important.
SOURCE: Hu, F. B., et al. 2003. Television watching and other sedentary behaviors in relation to risk of obesity and type 2 diabetes mellitus in women. *Journal of the American Medical Association* 289(14): 1785–1791. From T. D., Fahey, P. M. Insel, and W. T. Roth. 2007. *Fit and Well,* 7th ed., Fig. 1.4a, p. 8. New York: McGraw-Hill. Copyright © 2007 The McGraw-Hill Companies, Inc. Reprinted with permission.

Environment Your environment includes not only the air you breath and the water you drink but also substances and conditions in your home, workplace, and community. Are you frequently exposed to environmental tobacco smoke or the radiation in sunlight? Do you live in an area with poor air quality or high rates of crime and violence? Has alcohol or drug abuse been a problem in your family? These and other environmental factors all have an impact on wellness.

Access to Health Care Adequate health care helps improve both quality and quantity of life through preventive care and the treatment of disease. For example, vaccinations prevent many dangerous infections, and screening tests help identify key risk factors and diseases in their early, treatable stages. As described earlier in the chapter, inadequate access to health care is tied to factors such as low income and lack of health insurance. Cost is one of many issues surrounding the development of advanced health-related technologies.

Health Habits *Can* Make a Difference In many cases, behavior can tip the balance toward good health, even when heredity or environment is a negative factor. For example, breast cancer can run in families, but it also may be associated with being overweight and inactive. A woman with a family history of breast cancer is less likely to develop and die from the disease if she controls her weight, exercises regularly, performs breast self-exams, and has regular mammograms to help detect the disease in its early, most treatable stage.

Similarly, a young man with a family history of obesity can maintain a normal weight by being careful to balance calorie intake against activities that burn calories. If your life is highly stressful, you can lessen the chances of heart disease and stroke by learning ways to manage and cope with stress. If you live in an area with severe air pollution, you can reduce the risk of lung disease by not smoking. You can also take an active role in improving your environment. Behaviors like these enable you to make a difference in how great an impact heredity and environment will have on your health.

A Wellness Profile

What does it mean to be healthy today? A basic list of important behaviors and habits includes the following:

- Having a sense of responsibility for your own health and taking an active rather than a passive stance toward your life
- Learning to manage stress in effective ways
- Maintaining high self-esteem and mentally healthy ways of interacting with other people

Why do some people get cancer while others don't? Why is cancer more aggressive in one person than in another? Why does the same drug work for one person but not another? Why can one person benefit from the standard dose of a drug, while another requires half—or twice—the standard dose? The answers to such questions can sometimes be found in a person's genes. The goal of personalized medicine is to achieve the best medical outcome by choosing treatments that work with a person's genomic profile.

Genomics

Genomics is the study of genes and their function. Advances in genomics have started a revolution in our understanding of the complex interplay of genetic and environmental factors. That revolution, called "personalized medicine," is revealing thousands of new biological targets for the development of drugs. As a result, scientists are finding innovative ways to design new drugs and vaccines and to improve the diagnosis of disease.

Genetic information isn't usually used alone to make treatment decisions. Instead, it is used with factors such as family and medical histories, clinical exams, and other nongenomic diagnostic tests. Consider an example. BRCA1 is a breast cancer susceptibility gene first identified in 1994. Women who carry a mutation (abnormality) in this gene have a higher risk of breast or ovarian cancer than women who carry a normal version of the gene. The normal gene plays a role in repairing breaks in DNA. If the gene is mutated, this repair function may become disabled, leading to more DNA replication errors and cancerous growth. If a woman carries this genetic abnormality, her family history may indicate that she has a significant risk of breast or ovarian cancer and may be a candidate for targeted therapy. In this case, her physician may recommend a drug that turns off a particular enzyme that promotes the growth of cancer cells.

Proteomics

Proteomics is the study of proteins. Our genome provides the building blocks that describe who we are, but proteins make our bodies work. Your muscles are made of protein. If you want to pick up a glass, these proteins actually carry out your intentions. Proteins break down the food you eat so it can be absorbed in a form your body can use. Thoughts in your brain are stored by proteins.

The human genome contains about 25,000 genes. Those genes, however, contain the recipes for between 1 million and 5 million proteins. The continuous interaction of your genes, proteins, and other biochemical actions inside your body makes you who you are. In proteomics, proteins can be used to detect disease. Protein samples from blood or urine can reveal differences between a normal state and a diseased state, signaling an adverse event long before symptoms are apparent.

Pharmacogenetics

A person's environment, diet, and general health all influence how he or she responds to medicines—but genes are also important. *Pharmacogenetics* is the study of how individuals respond to medicines due to their genetic inheritance. The term has been pieced together from the words *pharmacology* (the study of how drugs work in the body) and *genetics* (the study of how traits are inherited).

Researchers in pharmacogenetics try to understand how a person's genes affect the way a medicine works in his or her body and what side effects are likely to occur. In the future, information harvested from this research will guide doctors in getting just enough of the right medicine to a person.

The Road to Personalized Medicine

Before doctors can dispense medications in such a personalized manner, researchers must pinpoint the proteins that medicines encounter in the body and determine how these proteins vary from person to person. Researchers must scrutinize the genes that form the basis for these protein differences. Scientists also must determine which genes contribute to diseases, such as cancer, heart disease, or asthma. Identifying such genes will provide scientists with an array of targets for future medicines.

Medical Innovations in the Twenty-First Century

Imagine a day when everyone's DNA has been processed onto computer chips to identify disease risks. Vaccines boost the immune system's ability to attack cancer cells. Natural hormones stimulate the growth of new blood vessels to bypass clogged arteries feeding the heart. Gene therapies encourage cancer cells to self-destruct or protect nerves from damage following a stroke. Cows are genetically engineered to produce beneficial drugs in their milk. These and other innovations—largely possible through pharmacogenetics—are now on the drawing board, being studied and tested.

- Understanding your sexuality and having satisfying intimate relationships
- Avoiding tobacco and other drugs; using alcohol responsibly, if at all
- Eating well, exercising, and maintaining healthy weight
- Knowing the facts about cardiovascular disease, cancer, infections, sexually transmitted diseases, and injuries and using your knowledge to protect yourself against them
- Understanding the health care system and using it intelligently
- Knowing when to treat your illnesses yourself and when to seek help
- Understanding the natural processes of aging and dying and accepting the limits of human existence
- Understanding how the environment affects your health and taking appropriate action to improve it

Incorporating these behaviors into your daily life may seem like a tall order, and in a sense it is the work of a lifetime. But the habits you establish now are crucial: They tend to set lifelong patterns. Some behaviors do more than set up patterns—they produce permanent changes in your health. If you become addicted to drugs or alcohol at age 20, for example, you may be able to kick the habit, but you will always face the struggle of a recovering addict. If you contract gonorrhea, you may discover later that your reproductive organs were damaged without your realizing it, making you infertile or sterile. If you ruin your knees doing the wrong exercises or hurt your back in an automobile crash, you won't have them to count on when you're older. Some things just can't be reversed or corrected.

HOW DO YOU REACH WELLNESS?

Your life may not resemble the one described by the wellness profile at all. You probably have a number of healthy habits and some others that place your health at risk. Maybe your life is more like this:

> It's Tuesday. Simon wakes up feeling blue, not really wanting to get out of bed. He wishes he knew what he wanted to do with his life. He wishes he'd meet someone new and fall in love. No time for breakfast, so he grabs a cup of coffee to drink during his first class. He hasn't done the reading and stares blankly at the teacher during the lecture. Later he goes to the student union and has a sugary doughnut and some more coffee; he lights up his first cigarette of the day. Lunch is a fast-food cheeseburger, french fries, and a shake. He spends the afternoon at the library desperately researching a paper that's due the next day, finally quitting at 6:00 and heading to the student union for a beer. He meets up with some buddies and joins them for pizza instead of having dinner at the dorm. By 11:00 he's tired, but he's written only one page of his paper, so he takes an upper to keep going. It makes his heart race and floods his head with so many ideas he has difficulty sorting them all out. He works feverishly and finally finishes at 4:00 the next morning. Exhausted, he falls asleep in his clothes. The next thing he knows, it's Wednesday morning, time to start a new day.

This is hardly an ideal lifestyle, but it's not unusual. Simon functions OK, meets his commitments, and shows some self-discipline. On the other hand, time gets away from him, and he doesn't get much exercise, doesn't eat as well as he could, and flirts with the dangers of taking drugs. Overall, he is low on energy and has little control over his life. He could be living a lot better.

Simon isn't alone in neglecting or abusing his health; many people fall into a lifestyle that puts their health at risk. Some aren't aware of the damage they're doing to themselves; others are aware but aren't motivated or don't know how to change; still others want to change but can't seem to get started. All of these are very real problems, but they're not insurmountable. If they were, there would be no ex-smokers, recovering alcoholics, or successful graduates of weight-loss programs. People can and do make difficult changes in their lives.

Taking big steps toward wellness may at first seem like too much work, but as you make progress, it gets easier. At first you'll be rewarded with a greater sense of control over your life, a feeling of empowerment, higher self-esteem, and more joy. These benefits will encourage you to make further improvements. Over time, you'll come to know what wellness feels like—more energy; greater vitality; deeper feelings of curiosity, interest, and enjoyment; and a higher quality of life.

Getting Serious About Your Health

Before you can start changing a health-related behavior, you have to know that the behavior is problematic and that you *can* change it. To make good decisions, you need information about relevant topics and issues, including what resources are available to help you change your behavior. You also need knowledge about yourself—how you relate to the wellness profile and what strengths you can draw on to change your behavior and improve your health.

Examining Your Current Health Habits Have you considered how your current lifestyle is affecting your health today and how it will affect your health in the future? Do you know which of your current habits enhance your health and which detract from it? Begin your journey toward wellness with self-assessment: Think about your own behavior and talk with friends and family members about what they've noticed about your lifestyle and your health.

Many people start to consider changing a behavior when they get help from others. An observation from a friend, family member, or physician can help you see yourself as others do and may get you thinking about your behavior in a new way. For example, Jason has been getting a lot of stomachaches lately. His girlfriend Anna notices other changes as well and suggests that the stress of classes plus a part-time job and serving as president of the school radio station might be causing some of Jason's problems. Jason never thought much about trying to control the stressors in his life, but with encouragement from Anna, he starts noticing what events trigger stress for him.

Landmark events can also get you thinking about behavior change. A birthday, the birth of a child, or the death of someone close to you can be powerful motivators for thinking seriously about behaviors that affect wellness. New information can also help you get started. As you read this text, you may find yourself reevaluating some of your health-related behaviors. This could be a great opportunity to make healthful changes that will stay with you for the rest of your life. To help determine whether your current health habits promote wellness, take the quiz in the box "Wellness: Evaluate Your Lifestyle" on page 16. Use the results to identify behaviors you could change to improve your health and well-being.

Choosing a Target Behavior A careful examination of your current lifestyle may reveal a number of habits that are candidates for change. To maximize your chances of success, don't try to change all your problem behaviors at once—to quit smoking, give up high-fat foods, start jogging, avoid drugs, get more sleep. Working on even one behavior change will make high demands on your energy. Concentrate on one behavior that you want to change, your **target behavior,** and work on it systematically. Start with something simple, like snacking on candy between afternoon classes or always driving to a particular class instead of walking or biking.

Obtaining Information About Your Target Behavior Once you've chosen a target behavior, you need to find out more about it. You need to know its risks and benefits for you—both now and in the future. How is your target behavior affecting your level of wellness today? For what diseases or conditions does this behavior place you at risk? What effect would changing your behavior have on your health?

You also need enough information to set an overall target for change. For some behaviors, this is simple. For example, if your target behavior is smoking, your goal will be to quit. But if your target behavior is something like a poor diet or an inactive lifestyle, you may need additional information to set an appropriate goal. Further investigation can help you determine that you should consume the equivalent of 4 cups of fruits and vegetables each day, for example, or that you should add 30–60 minutes of brisk walking to your daily routine.

To evaluate your target behavior and set an appropriate target for change, you'll need accurate information. As a starting point, use material from this text and from the resources listed in the For More Information section at the end of each chapter. See the box "Evaluating Sources of Health Information" on page 18 for tips on becoming a critical consumer of health information from a wide variety of sources.

Finding Outside Help Have you identified a particularly challenging target behavior, such as alcohol addiction, excessive overeating, or depression, that interferes with your ability to function or places you at a serious health risk? Outside help is often needed for changing behaviors or conditions that may be too deeply rooted or too serious for a self-management approach. If this is the case, don't be stopped by the seriousness of the problem—there are many resources available to help you solve it. On campus, the student health center or campus counseling center may be a source of assistance. Many communities offer a variety of services through adult education, health departments, and private agencies. Consult the yellow pages, your physician, your local health department, or the United Way; the last often sponsors local referral services.

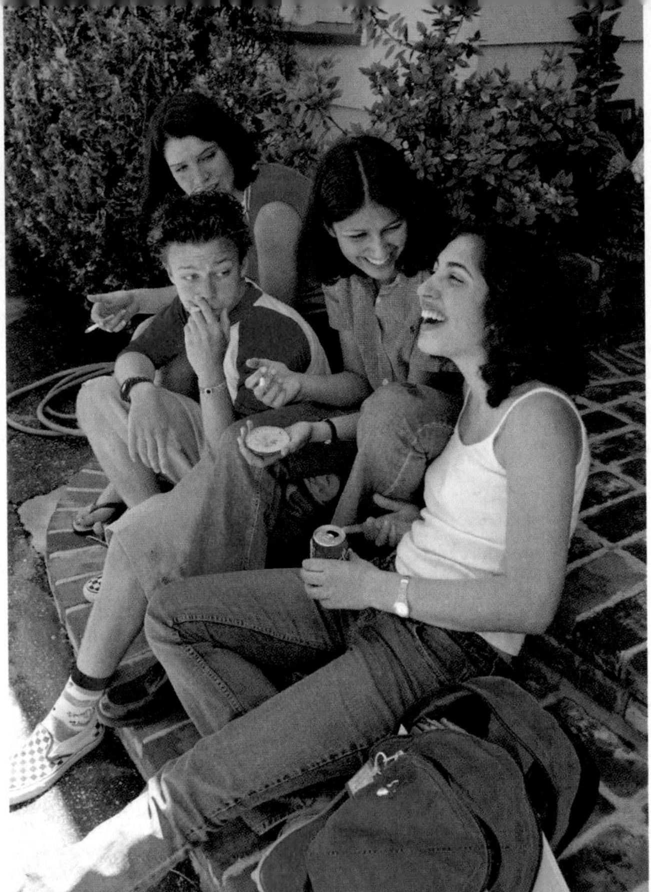

Changing powerful, long-standing habits requires motivation, commitment, and a belief that we are in control of our own behavior. To quit smoking, these young people must overcome a habit that is supported by their addiction to nicotine and by their social environment.

Building Motivation for Change

Knowledge is a necessary ingredient for behavior change, but it isn't usually enough to make people act. Millions of people smoke or have sedentary lifestyles, for example, even though they know it's bad for their health. To succeed at behavior change, you need strong motivation. Strategies for building motivation include examining the pros and cons of change, boosting self-efficacy, and overcoming key barriers to change.

Examining the Pros and Cons of Change Health behaviors have short-term and long-term benefits and costs associated with them. For example, in the short term, an inactive lifestyle allows for more time to watch TV and hang out with friends but leaves a person less able to participate in recreational activities. Over the long term, it increases the risk of heart disease, cancer, stroke, and

Term

target behavior An isolated behavior selected as the object of a behavior change plan.

All of us want optimal health. But many of us do not know how to achieve it. Taking this quiz, adapted from one created by the U.S. Public Health Service, is a good place to start. The behaviors covered in the quiz are recommended for most Americans. (Some of them may not apply to people with certain diseases or disabilities or to pregnant women, who may require special advice from their physician.) After you take the quiz, add up your score for each section.

Tobacco Use

If you never use tobacco, enter a score of 10 for this section and go to the next section.

		Almost Always	Sometimes	Never
1.	I avoid using tobacco.	2	1	0
2.	I smoke only low-tar/nicotine cigarettes *or* I smoke a pipe or cigars *or* I use smokeless tobacco.	2	1	0
	Tobacco Score:			

Alcohol and Other Drugs

		Almost Always	Sometimes	Never
1.	I avoid alcohol *or* I drink no more than 1 (women) or 2 (men) drinks a day.	4	1	0
2.	I avoid using alcohol or other drugs as a way of handling stressful situations or problems in my life.	2	1	0
3.	I am careful not to drink alcohol when taking medications, such as for colds or allergies, or when pregnant.	2	1	0
4.	I read and follow the label directions when using prescribed and over-the-counter drugs.	2	1	0
	Alcohol and Other Drugs Score:			

Nutrition

		Almost Always	Sometimes	Never
1.	I eat a variety of foods each day, including seven or more servings of fruits and vegetables.	3	1	0
2.	I limit the amount of total fat and saturated and trans fat in my diet.	3	1	0
3.	I avoid skipping meals.	2	1	0
4.	I limit the amount of salt and sugar I eat.	2	1	0
	Nutrition Score:			

Exercise/Fitness

		Almost Always	Sometimes	Never
1.	I engage in moderate exercise for 20–60 minutes, 3–5 times a week.	4	1	0
2.	I maintain a healthy weight, avoiding overweight and underweight.	2	1	0
3.	I do exercises to develop muscular strength and endurance at least twice a week.	2	1	0
4.	I spend some of my leisure time participating in physical activities such as gardening, bowling, golf, or baseball.	2	1	0
	Exercise/Fitness Score:			

Emotional Health

		Almost Always	Sometimes	Never
1.	I enjoy being a student, and I have a job or do other work that I like.	2	1	0
2.	I find it easy to relax and express my feelings freely.	2	1	0
3.	I manage stress well.	2	1	0

premature death. For successful behavior change, you must believe that the benefits of changing outweigh the costs.

Do a careful analysis of the short-term and long-term benefits and costs of continuing your current (target) behavior and of changing to a new, healthier behavior. Focus on the effects that are most meaningful to you, including those that are tied to your personal identity and values. For example, if you see yourself as an active person who is a good role model for others, then adopting behaviors such as regular physical activity and adequate sleep would support your personal identity. If you value independence and control over your life, then quitting smoking would be consistent with your values and goals. To complete your analysis, ask friends and family

	Almost Always	Sometimes	Never
4. I have close friends, relatives, or others I can talk to about personal matters and call on for help.	2	1	0
5. I participate in group activities (such as church and community organizations) or hobbies that I enjoy.	2	1	0

Emotional Health Score: ____________

Safety

1. I wear a safety belt while riding in a car.	2	1	0
2. I avoid driving while under the influence of alcohol or other drugs.	2	1	0
3. I obey traffic rules and the speed limit when driving.	2	1	0
4. I read and follow instructions on the labels of potentially harmful products or substances, such as household cleaners, poisons, and electrical appliances.	2	1	0
5. I avoid smoking in bed.	2	1	0

Safety Score: ____________

Disease Prevention

1. I know the warning signs of cancer, diabetes, heart attack, and stroke.	2	1	0
2. I avoid overexposure to the sun and use a sunscreen.	2	1	0
3. I get recommended medical screening tests (such as blood pressure checks and Pap tests), immunizations, and booster shots.	2	1	0
4. I practice monthly breast/testicle self-exams.	2	1	0
5. I am not sexually active *or* I have sex with only one mutually faithful, uninfected partner *or* I always engage in safer sex (using condoms) *and* I do not share needles to inject drugs.	2	1	0

Disease Prevention Score: ____________

What Your Scores Mean

Scores of 9 and 10 Excellent! Your answers show that you're aware of the importance of this area to wellness. More important, you are putting your knowledge to work for you by practicing good health habits. As long as you continue to do so, this area should not pose a serious health risk. It's likely that you are setting an example for your family and friends to follow. Since you scored high on this part of the quiz, you may want to focus on other areas where your scores indicate room for improvement.

Scores of 6–8 Your health practices in this area are good, but there is room for improvement. Look again at the items you answered with "Sometimes" or "Never." What changes can you make to improve your score? Even a small change can often help you achieve better health.

Scores of 3–5 Your health risks are showing! You may need more information about the risks you're facing and about why it's important for you to change these behaviors. Perhaps you need help in deciding how to successfully make the changes you want.

Scores of 0–2 Your answers show that you may be taking serious and unnecessary risks with your health. Perhaps you are not aware of the risks and what to do about them. You can easily get the information and help you need to improve, if you wish. The next step is up to you.

members about the effects of your behavior on them. For example, a roommate may tell you that he never ate candy in the evening until he started living with you, or a younger sister may tell you that your smoking habit influenced her decision to take up smoking.

Pay special attention to the short-term benefits of behavior change, as these can be an important motivating force. Although some people are motivated by long-term goals, such as avoiding a disease that may hit them in 30 years, most are more likely to be moved to action by shorter-term, more personal goals. Feeling better, doing better in school, improving at a sport, reducing stress, and increasing self-esteem are common short-term benefits of health behavior change. Many wellness behaviors are

Critical Consumer: Evaluating Sources of Health Information

General Strategies

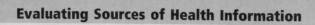

A key first step in sharpening your critical thinking skills is to look carefully at your sources of health information. Critical thinking involves knowing where and how to find relevant information, how to separate fact from opinion, how to recognize faulty reasoning, how to evaluate information, and how to assess the credibility of sources.

- *Go to the original source.* Media reports often simplify the results of medical research. Find out for yourself what a study really reported, and determine whether it was based on good science. What type of study was it? Was it published in a recognized medical journal? Was it an animal study, or did it involve people? Did the study include a large number of people? What did the authors of the study actually report in their findings? (You'll find additional strategies for evaluating research studies in Chapter 21.)
- *Watch for misleading language.* Reports that feature "breakthroughs" or "dramatic proof" are probably hype. Some studies will find that a behavior "contributes to" or is "associated with" an outcome; this does not imply a proven cause-and-effect relationship. Information may also be distorted by an author's point of view.
- *Distinguish between research reports and public health advice.* If a study finds a link between a particular vitamin and cancer, that should not necessarily lead you to change your behavior. But if the Surgeon General or the American Cancer Society advises you to eat less saturated fat or quit smoking, you can assume that many studies point in this direction and that this is advice you should follow.
- *Remember that anecdotes are not facts.* Sometimes we do get helpful health information from our friends and family. But just because your cousin Bertha lost 10 pounds on Dr. Amazing's new protein diet doesn't mean it's a safe, effective way for you to lose weight. Before you make a big change in your lifestyle, verify the information with your physician, this text, or other reliable sources.
- *Be skeptical, and use your common sense.* If a report seems too good to be true, it probably is. Be especially wary of information contained in advertisements. The goal of an ad is to sell you something, to create a feeling of need for a product where no real need exists. Evaluate "scientific" claims carefully, and beware of quackery (see Chapter 21).
- *Make choices that are right for you.* Your roommate swears by swimming; you prefer aerobics. Your sister takes a yoga class to help her manage stress; your brother unwinds by walking in the woods. Friends and family members can be a great source of ideas and inspiration, but each of us needs to find a wellness lifestyle that works for us.

Internet Resources

Evaluating health information from online sources poses special challenges; when reviewing a health-related Web site, ask the following questions:

- *What is the source of the information? Who is the author or sponsor of the Web page?* Web sites maintained by government agencies, professional associations, or established academic or medical institutions are likely to present trustworthy information. Many other groups and individuals post accurate information, but be sure to check their qualifications. (Check the home page or click on an "about us" or "who we are" link.) A 2006 national survey found that only one fourth of Americans check the source of the health information they find on the Internet.
- *How often is the site updated?* Look for sites that are updated frequently. Also check the "last modified" date of any specific Web page on a site.
- *What is the purpose of the page? Does the site promote particular products or procedures? Are there obvious reasons for bias?* Be wary of information from sites that sell specific products, use testimonials as evidence, appear to have a social or political agenda, or ask for money.
- *What do other sources say about a topic?* Be cautious of claims or information that appears at only one site or comes from a chat room or bulletin board.
- *Does the site conform to any set of guidelines or criteria for quality and accuracy?* Look for sites that identify themselves as conforming to some code or set of principles, such as those set forth by the Health on the Net Foundation or the American Medical Association. These codes include criteria such as use of information from respected sources and disclosure of the site's sponsors.

Additional strategies for locating and assessing health-related information from the Internet can be found on the *Core Concepts in Health* Web site (http://www.mhhe.com/insel10e).

associated with immediate improvements in quality of life. For example, surveys of Americans have found that nonsmokers feel healthy and full of energy more days each month than do smokers, and they report fewer days of sadness and troubled sleep; the same is true when physically active people are compared with sedentary people. Over time, these differences add up to a substantially greater quality of life for people who engage in healthy behaviors.

You can further strengthen your motivation by engaging your emotions and raising your consciousness about your problem behavior. This will enable you to focus on the current negatives of the behavior and to imagine the consequences if you don't make a change. Ask yourself: What do I want for myself, now and in the future?

For example, Ruby has never worried much about her smoking because the problems associated with it seem so far away. But lately she's noticed her performance on the volleyball team isn't as good as it used to be. Over the summer she visited her aunt, who has emphysema from smoking and can barely leave her bed. Ruby knows she wants to have children and a career as a teacher, and seeing her aunt makes her wonder if her smoking habit could make it difficult for her to reach these goals. She starts to wonder whether her smoking habit is worth the short- and long-term sacrifices.

Social pressures can also increase the motivation to make changes. In Ruby's case, anti-smoking ordinances keep her from smoking in her dorm and in many public places. The inconvenience of finding a place to smoke and the pressure from her roommate, who doesn't like the smoky smell of Ruby's clothes in their room, are among the short-term costs of Ruby's smoking habit that can add to her motivation to quit.

Boosting Self-Efficacy

When you start thinking about changing a health behavior, a big factor in your eventual success is whether you have confidence in yourself and in your ability to change. **Self-efficacy** refers to your belief in your ability to successfully take action and perform a specific task. Self-efficacy varies with each behavior and depends on many factors, including your level of self-esteem and your past experiences with your target behavior. Strategies for boosting self-efficacy include developing an internal locus of control, using visualization and self-talk, and obtaining encouragement from supportive people. Developing specific skills for change, discussed later in this chapter, is also critical for improving self-efficacy.

LOCUS OF CONTROL Who do you believe is controlling your life? Is it your parents, friends, or school? Is it "fate"? Or is it you? **Locus of control** refers to the figurative "place" a person designates as the source of responsibility for the events in his or her life. People who believe they are in control of their own lives are said to have an internal locus of control. Those who believe that factors beyond their control—heredity, friends and family, the environment, fate, luck, or other outside forces—are more important in determining the events of their lives are said to have an external locus of control. Most people are not purely "internalizers" or "externalizers"; their locus of control changes in response to the situation.

For lifestyle management, an internal locus of control is an advantage because it reinforces motivation and commitment. An external locus of control can actually sabotage efforts to change behavior. For example, if you believe you are destined to die of breast cancer because your mother died from the disease, you may view breast self-exams and regular checkups as a waste of time. In contrast, an internal locus of control is an advantage. If you believe you can take action to reduce your hereditary risk of breast cancer, you will be motivated to follow guidelines for early detection of the disease.

People who tend to have an external locus of control can learn to view the events in their lives differently and increase their feelings of self-efficacy. If you find yourself attributing too much influence to outside forces, gather more information about your target behavior. Make a list of all the ways that behavior change will improve your health. If you recognize and accept that you are in charge of your life, you're well on your way to wellness.

VISUALIZATION AND SELF-TALK One of the best ways to boost your confidence and self-efficacy is to visualize yourself successfully engaging in a new, healthier behavior. Imagine yourself turning down cigarettes, going for a regular after-dinner walk, or choosing healthier snacks. Also visualize yourself enjoying all the short-term and long-term benefits that behavior change will bring. Create a new self-image: What will you and your life be like when you become a nonsmoker, a regular exerciser, or a healthy eater?

You can also use self-talk, the internal dialogue you carry on with yourself, to increase your confidence in your ability to change. Counter any self-defeating patterns of thought with more positive or realistic thoughts: "Behavior change is difficult, but if I work at it, I will succeed," or "I am a strong, capable person, and I can maintain my commitment to change." Refer to Chapter 3 for more on self-talk.

ROLE MODELS AND OTHER SUPPORTIVE INDIVIDUALS Social support can also make a big difference in your level of motivation and your chances of success. Perhaps you know people who have reached the goal you are striving for; they could be role models or mentors for you, providing information and support for your efforts. Talk to them about how they did it. What were the most difficult parts of changing their behavior? What strategies worked for them? Gain strength from their experiences, and tell yourself, "If they can do it, so can I."

In addition, find a buddy who wants to make the same changes you do and who can take an active role in your behavior change program. For example, an exercise buddy can provide companionship and encouragement for times when you might be tempted to skip that morning jog. Or you and a friend can watch to be sure that you both have only one alcoholic beverage at a party. If necessary, look beyond your current social network at possible new sources of help, such as a support group. Later in this chapter, you'll learn some specific strategies for involving other people in your behavior change program.

Terms

self-efficacy The belief in one's ability to take action and perform a specific behavior.

locus of control The figurative "place" a person designates as the source of responsibility for the events in his or her life.

Identifying and Overcoming Key Barriers to Change Have you tried and failed to change your target behavior in the past? Don't let past failures discourage you; they can be a great source of information you can use to boost your chances of future success. Make a list of the problems and challenges you faced in your previous behavior change attempts; to this add the short-term costs of behavior change that you identified in your analysis of the pros and cons of change. Once you've listed these key barriers to change, develop a practical plan for overcoming each one. For example, if one of your key barriers for physical activity is that you believe you can't make time for a 40-minute workout, look for ways to incorporate shorter bouts of physical activity into your daily routine. If you always smoke when you're with certain friends, practice in advance how you will turn down the next cigarette you are offered. Developing strategies to cope with difficult situations is one of the most important factors in successful behavior change. You'll find additional advice and examples later in the chapter in the section "Developing Skills for Change."

Self-talk can also help overcome barriers. Make behavior change a priority in your life, and plan to commit the necessary time and effort. Ask yourself: How much time and energy will behavior change *really* require? Isn't the effort worth all the short- and long-term benefits?

Enhancing Your Readiness to Change

The transtheoretical, or "stages of change," model, developed by psychologists James Prochaska and Carlo DiClemente, has been shown to be an effective approach to lifestyle self-management. According to this model, you move through six well-defined stages as you work to change your target behavior. It is important to determine what stage you are in now so that you can choose appropriate strategies for progressing through the cycle of change (see the box "What Stage of Change Are You In?"). Using this approach can help you enhance your readiness and intention to change.

Precontemplation People at this stage have no intention of changing their behavior. They may be unaware of the risks associated with their behavior, or they may deny that their behavior will have any serious consequences for them. They may have tried unsuccessfully to change in the past and may now feel demoralized and think the situation is hopeless. They may also blame others for their problems.

If you are in the precontemplation stage, begin to move forward by raising your consciousness of your target behavior and its effects on you and those around you. Obtain accurate information about your behavior, and ask yourself what has prevented you from changing in the past. Enlist friends and family members to help you become more aware of your behavior and your reasons for continuing an unhealthy habit. Also find out more about the campus and community resources available to help you with behavior change.

Contemplation People at this stage are aware that they have a problem and have started to think and learn about it. They acknowledge the benefits that behavior change will have for them but are also very aware of the costs of changing. They wonder about possible courses of action but may feel stuck and unsure of how best to proceed.

At this stage, it's a good idea to begin keeping a written record of your target behavior—to help you learn more about it and to use when you begin to plan the specifics of your behavior change program. Work on your analysis of the pros and cons of change: Expand your list of the benefits, and problem-solve to overcome the key barriers on your list of the costs of changing. To be successful, you must believe that the benefits of change outweigh the costs. Engage your emotions and boost self-efficacy through visualization, self-talk, and the support of other people.

Preparation People at this stage plan to take action within a month and may already have begun to make small changes in their behavior. If you are in the preparation stage, your next step is to create a specific plan for change that includes a start date, realistic goals, rewards, and information on exactly how you will go about changing your behavior. You'll also want to prepare yourself emotionally and socially by practicing visualization and self-talk and by involving the people around you in your efforts at change. A step-by-step plan for developing a successful behavior change program is included in the next section of the chapter.

Action During the action stage, people outwardly modify their behavior and their environment. The action stage requires the greatest commitment of time and energy, and people in this stage are at risk for reverting to old, unhealthy patterns of behavior. If you are in the action stage, you'll need to use all the plans and strategies that you developed during earlier stages. In particular, be sure to plan ahead to overcome temptations and deal with problem situations.

Maintenance People at this stage have maintained their new, healthier lifestyle for at least 6 months. To guard against slips and relapses, they continue with all the positive strategies they used in earlier stages. Their confidence and self-efficacy increase. The maintenance stage typically lasts from 6 months to about 5 years.

Termination People at this stage have exited the cycle of change and are no longer tempted to lapse back into their old behavior. They have a new self-image and total self-efficacy with regard to their target behavior. This

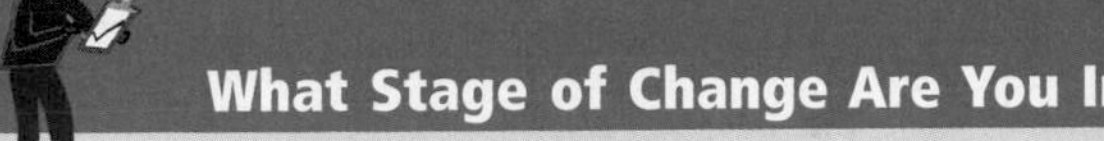

Assess Yourself

What Stage of Change Are You In?

To determine your stage, circle true or false for each of the following statements:

T F 1. I changed my target behavior more than 6 months ago.

T F 2. I changed my target behavior within the past 6 months.

T F 3. I intend to take action within the next month and have already made a few small changes in my behavior.

T F 4. I intend to take action on my target behavior within the next 6 months.

Find the stage that corresponds to your responses:

False for all four statements = Precontemplation

True for statement 4, false for statements 1–3 = Contemplation

True for statements 3 and 4, false for statements 1 and 2 = Preparation

True for statement 2, false for statement 1 = Action

True for statement 1 = Maintenance

SOURCE: Prochaska, J. O., C. A. Redding, and K. E. Evers. 2002. The transtheoretical model and stages of change. In K. Glanz, B. K. Rimer, and F. M. Lewis, eds., *Health Behavior and Health Education: Theory, Research, and Practice,* 3rd ed. San Francisco: Jossey-Bass.

stage applies to some behaviors, such as addictions, but may not be appropriate for others.

Lapses are a natural part of the process at all stages of change. Many people lapse and must recycle through earlier stages, although most don't go back to the first stage. If you lapse, use what you learn about yourself and the process of change to help you in your next attempt at behavior change.

Next, we'll take a closer look at the specific steps and skills involved in creating and implementing a plan for change.

Developing Skills for Change: Creating a Personalized Plan

Once you are committed to making a change, it's time to put together a detailed plan of action. Your key to success is a well-thought-out plan that sets goals, anticipates problems, and includes rewards.

1. Monitor Your Behavior and Gather Data

Begin by keeping careful records of the behavior you wish to change (your target behavior) and the circumstances surrounding it. Keep these records in a health journal, a notebook in which you write the details of your behavior along with observations and comments. Note exactly what the activity was, when and where it happened, what you were doing, and what your feelings were at the time. In a journal for a weight-loss or dietary-change plan, for example, you would typically record how much food you ate, the time of day, the situation, the location, your feelings, and how hungry you were (Figure 1-6). If your goal is to start an exercise program, use your journal to track your daily activities to determine how best to make time for your workouts. Keep your journal for a week or two to get some solid information about the behavior you want to change.

2. Analyze the Data and Identify Patterns

After you have collected data on the behavior, analyze the data to identify patterns. When are you hungriest? When are you most likely to overeat? What events seem to trigger your appetite? Perhaps you are especially hungry at midmorning or when you put off eating dinner until 9:00. Perhaps you overindulge in food and drink when you go to a particular restaurant or when you're with certain friends. Be sure to note the connections between your feelings and external cues such as time of day, location, situation, and the actions of people around you. Do you always think of having a cigarette when you read the newspaper? Do you always bite your fingernails when you're studying?

3. Set Realistic, Specific Goals Don't set an impossibly difficult overall goal for your program—going from a sedentary lifestyle to running a marathon within 2 months, for example. Working toward more realistic, achievable goals will greatly increase your chances of success. Your goal should also be specific and measurable, something you can easily track. Instead of a vague general goal such as improving eating habits or being more physically active, set a specific target—eating eight servings of fruits and vegetables each day or walking or biking for 30 minutes at least 5 days per week.

Date November 5		Day M [TU] W TH F SA SU								
Time of day	*M/S*	*Food eaten*	*Cals.*	*H*	*Where did you eat?*	*What else were you doing?*	*How did someone else influence you?*	*What made you want to eat what you did?*	*Emotions and feelings?*	*Thoughts and concerns?*
7:30	M	1 C Crispix cereal 1/2 C skim milk coffee, black 1 C orange juice	110 40 — 120	3	home	reading newspaper	alone	I always eat cereal in the morning	a little keyed up & worried	thinking about quiz in class today
10:30	S	1 apple	90	1	hall outside classroom	studying	alone	felt tired & wanted to wake up	tired	worried about next class
12:30	M	1 C chili 1 roll 1 pat butter 1 orange 2 oatmeal cookies 1 soda	290 120 35 60 120 150	2	campus food court	talking	eating w/ friends; we decided to eat at the food court	wanted to be part of group	excited and happy	interested in hearing everyone's plans for the weekend
	M/S = Meal or snack			H = Hunger rating (0–3)						

Figure 1-6 Sample health journal entries.

Whatever your ultimate goal, it's a good idea to break it down into a few small steps. Your plan will seem less overwhelming and more manageable, increasing the chances that you'll stick to it. You'll also build in more opportunities to reward yourself (discussed in step 4), as well as milestones you can use to measure your progress. If you plan to lose 15 pounds, for example, you'll find it easier to take off 5 pounds at a time. If you want to start an exercise program, begin by taking 10- to 15-minute walks a few times per week. Take the easier steps first and work up to the harder steps. With each small success, you'll build your confidence and self-efficacy.

4. Devise a Strategy or Plan of Action Next, you need to develop specific strategies and techniques that will support your day-to-day efforts at behavior change.

OBTAIN INFORMATION AND SUPPLIES Identify campus and community resources that can provide practical help—for example, a stop-smoking course or a walking club. Take any necessary preparatory steps, such as signing up for a stress-management workshop or purchasing walking shoes, nicotine replacement patches, or a special calendar to track your progress.

MODIFY YOUR ENVIRONMENT As you write in your health journal, you gather quite a lot of information about your target behavior—the times it typically occurs; the situations in which it usually happens; the ways sight, smell, mood, situation, and accessibility trigger it. You can probably trace the chain of events that leads to the behavior and perhaps also identify points along the way where making a different choice would mean changing the behavior.

You can be more effective in changing behavior if you control the environmental cues that provoke it. This might mean not having cigarettes or certain foods or drinks in the house, not going to parties where you're tempted to overindulge, or not spending time with particular people, at least for a while. If you always get a candy bar at a certain vending machine, change your route so you don't pass by it. If you always end up taking a coffee break and chatting with friends when you go to the library to study, choose a different place to study, such as your room.

It's also helpful to control other behaviors or habits that seem to be linked to the target behavior. You may give in to an urge to eat when you have a beer (alcohol increases the appetite) or when you watch TV. Try substituting some other activities for habits that seem to be linked with your target behavior, such as exercising to music instead of plopping down in front of the TV. Or, if possible, put an exercise bicycle in front of the set and burn calories while you watch your favorite show.

You can change the cues in your environment so they trigger the new, target behavior instead of the old one. Tape a picture of a cyclist speeding down a hill on your TV screen. Leave your exercise shoes in plain view. Put a chart of your progress in a special place at home to make your goals highly visible and inspire you to keep going. When you're trying to change an ingrained habit, small cues can play an important part in keeping you on track.

REWARD YOURSELF Another very powerful way to affect your target behavior is to set up a reward system that will reinforce your efforts. Most people find it difficult to

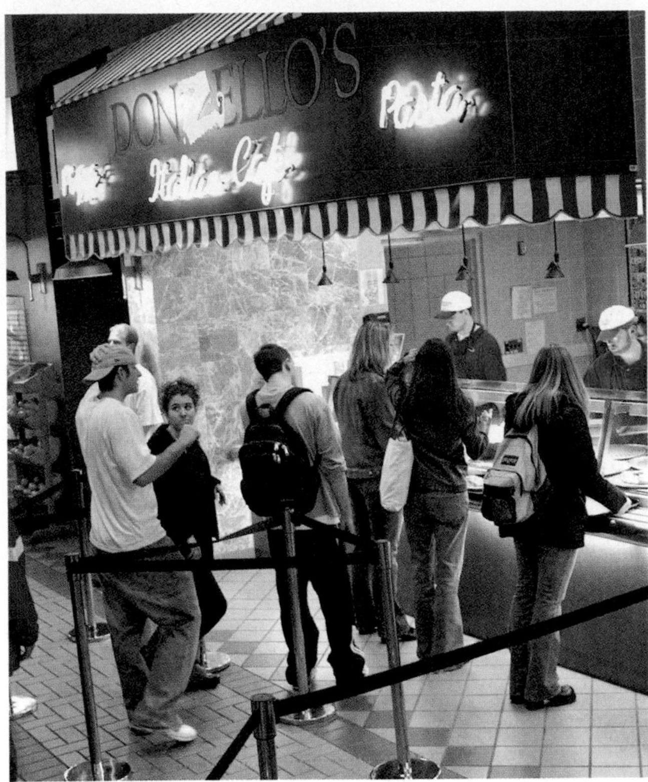

Your environment contains powerful cues for both positive and negative lifestyle choices. Identifying and using the healthier options available to you throughout the day is a key part of a successful behavior change program.

change long-standing habits for rewards they can't see right away. Giving yourself instant, real rewards for good behavior along the way will help you stick with a plan to change your behavior.

Carefully plan your reward payoffs and what they will be. In most cases, rewards should be collected when you reach specific objectives or subgoals in your plan. For example, you might treat yourself to a movie after a week of avoiding extra snacks. Don't forget to reward yourself for good behavior that is consistent and persistent—such as simply sticking with your program week after week. Decide on a reward after you reach a certain goal, or mark off the sixth week or month of a valiant effort. Write it down in your health journal and remember it as you follow your plan—especially when the going gets rough.

Make a list of your activities and favorite events to use as rewards. They should be special, inexpensive, and preferably unrelated to food or alcohol. Depending on what you like to do, you might treat yourself to a concert, a ball game, a new CD, a long-distance phone call to a friend, a day off from studying to take a long hike in the woods—whatever is rewarding to you.

INVOLVE THE PEOPLE AROUND YOU Rewards and support can also come from family and friends. Tell them about your plan, and ask for their help. Encourage them to be active, interested participants. Ask them to support you when you set aside time to go running or avoid second helpings at Thanksgiving dinner. You may have to remind them not to do things that make you "break training" and not to be hurt if you have to refuse something when they forget. To help friends and family members who will be involved in your program respond appropriately, you may want to create a specific list of dos and don'ts. Getting encouragement, support, and praise from important people in your life can powerfully reinforce the new behavior you're trying to adopt.

PLAN AHEAD FOR CHALLENGING SITUATIONS Take time out now to list situations and people that have the potential to derail your program and to develop possible coping mechanisms. For example, if you think that you'll have trouble exercising during finals week, schedule short bouts of physical activity as stress-reducing study breaks. If a visit to a friend who smokes is likely to tempt you to lapse, plan to bring nicotine patches, chewing gum, and a copy of your behavior change contract to strengthen your resolve.

5. Make a Commitment by Signing a Personal Contract

Once you have set your goals and developed a plan of action, make your plan into a personal contract. A serious personal contract—one that commits your word—can result in a higher chance of follow-through than will a casual, offhand promise. Your contract can help prevent procrastination by specifying the important dates and can also serve as a reminder of your personal commitment to change.

Your contract should include a statement of your goal and your commitment to reaching it. Include details of your plan: the date you'll begin, the steps you'll use to measure your progress, the concrete strategies you've developed for promoting change, and the date you expect to reach your final goal. Have someone—preferably someone who will be actively helping you with your program—sign your contract as a witness.

A Sample Behavior Change Plan

Let's take the example of Michael, who wants to improve his diet. By monitoring his eating habits in his health journal for several weeks, he gets a good sense of his typical diet—what he eats and where he eats it. Through self-assessment and investigation, he discovers that he currently consumes only about one serving of fruit per week, much less than the recommended three to five servings per day. He also finds out that fruit is a major source of fiber, vitamins, minerals, and other substances important for good health. He sets the target of eating three servings of fruit per day as the overall goal for his behavior change plan. Then Michael develops a specific plan for change that involves several changes in his behavior and his environment, which he describes in a contract that commits him to reaching his goal (Figure 1-7). Once Michael has signed his contract, he's ready to take action.

You can apply the general behavior change planning framework presented in this chapter to any target behavior. Additional examples of behavior change plans are presented in the Behavior Change Strategy sections that appear at the end of many chapters. In these, you'll find specific plans and advice for overcoming test anxiety (Chapter 2), reducing caffeine consumption (Chapter 9), quitting smoking (Chapter 11), beginning an exercise program (Chapter 13), eating more fruits and vegetables (Chapter 16), and many other positive lifestyle changes.

Putting Your Plan into Action

The starting date has arrived, and you are ready to put your plan into action. This stage requires commitment, the resolve to stick with the plan no matter what temptations you encounter. Remember all the good reasons you have for making the change—and remember that *you* are the boss.

Use all your strategies to make your plan work. Substituting behaviors is often very important—go for a walk after class instead of eating a bag of chips. Make sure your environment is change-friendly by keeping cues that trigger the problem behavior to a minimum. Also be sure to obtain as much support and encouragement from others as possible.

Use your health journal to keep track of how well you are doing in achieving your ultimate goal. Record your daily activities and any relevant details, such as how far you walked or how many calories you ate. Each week, chart your progress on a graph and see how it compares to the subgoals on your contract. You may want to track more than one behavior, such as the time you spend exercising each week and your weight.

If you don't seem to be making progress, analyze your plan to see what might be causing the problem. Possible barriers to success are listed in the section "Staying with It," along with suggestions for addressing them. Once you've identified the problem, revise your plan.

Be sure to reward yourself for your successes by treating yourself as specified in your contract. And don't forget to give yourself a pat on the back—congratulate yourself, notice how much better you look or feel, and feel good about how far you've come and how you've gained control of your behavior.

Staying with It

As you continue with your program, don't be surprised when you run up against obstacles; they're inevitable. In fact, it's a good idea to expect problems and give yourself time to step back, see how you're doing, and make some changes before going on again. If you find your program is grinding to a halt, try to identify what is blocking your progress. It may come from one of these sources.

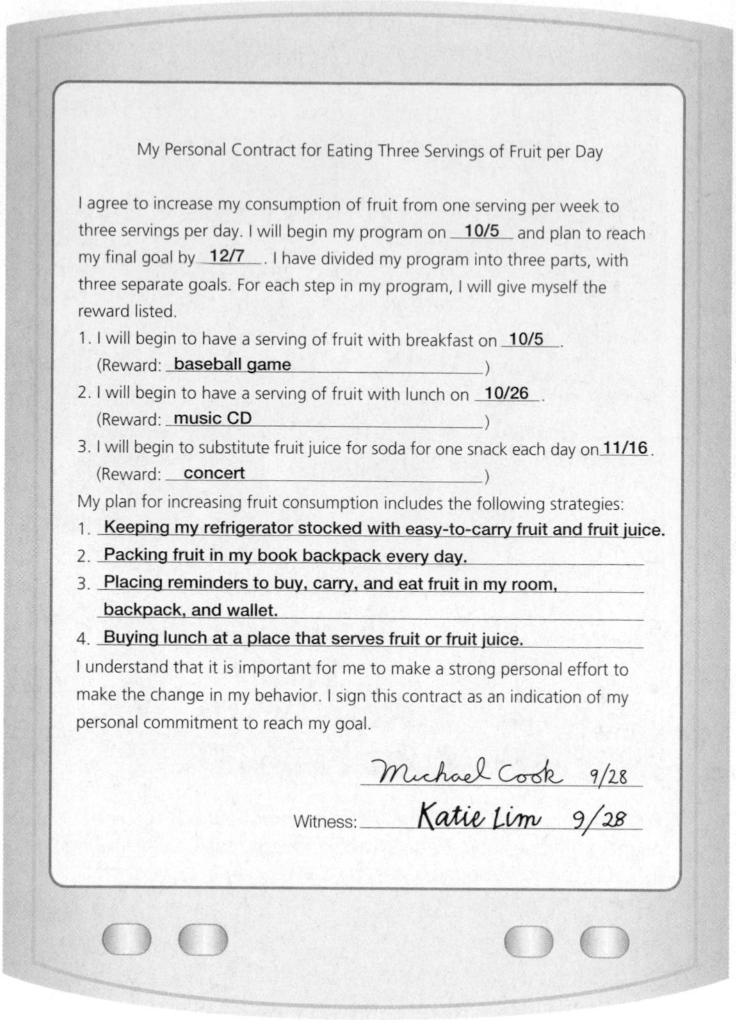

My Personal Contract for Eating Three Servings of Fruit per Day

I agree to increase my consumption of fruit from one serving per week to three servings per day. I will begin my program on **10/5** and plan to reach my final goal by **12/7**. I have divided my program into three parts, with three separate goals. For each step in my program, I will give myself the reward listed.

1. I will begin to have a serving of fruit with breakfast on **10/5**.
   (Reward: **baseball game**)
2. I will begin to have a serving of fruit with lunch on **10/26**.
   (Reward: **music CD**)
3. I will begin to substitute fruit juice for soda for one snack each day on **11/16**.
   (Reward: **concert**)

My plan for increasing fruit consumption includes the following strategies:

1. **Keeping my refrigerator stocked with easy-to-carry fruit and fruit juice.**
2. **Packing fruit in my book backpack every day.**
3. **Placing reminders to buy, carry, and eat fruit in my room, backpack, and wallet.**
4. **Buying lunch at a place that serves fruit or fruit juice.**

I understand that it is important for me to make a strong personal effort to make the change in my behavior. I sign this contract as an indication of my personal commitment to reach my goal.

Michael Cook 9/28

Witness: Katie Lim 9/28

Figure 1-7 A sample behavior change contract.

Social Influences Take a hard look at the reactions of the people you're counting on, and see if they're really supporting you. If they come up short, try connecting and networking with others who will be more supportive.

A related trap is trying to get your friends or family members to change *their* behaviors. The decision to make a major behavior change is something people come to only after intensive self-examination. You may be able to influence someone by tactfully providing facts or support, but that's all. Focus on yourself. If you succeed, you may become a role model for others.

Levels of Motivation and Commitment You won't make real progress until an inner drive leads you to the stage of change at which you are ready to make a personal commitment to the goal. If commitment is your problem, you may need to wait until the short-term costs of your target behavior make your life more unhappy or unhealthy; then your desire to change it will be stronger. Or you may find that changing your goal will inspire you to keep going. If you really want to change but your motivation comes and goes, look at your support system and at your own level of confidence. Building these up may be the key to pushing past a barrier. For more ideas, refer to the box "Motivation Boosters" on page 26.

Choice of Techniques and Level of Effort Your plan may not be working as well as you thought it would. Make changes where you're having the most trouble. If you've lagged on your running schedule, for example, maybe it's because you really don't like running. A group exercise class might suit you better. There are many ways to move toward your goal. Or you may not be trying hard enough. You do have to push toward your goal. If it were easy, you wouldn't need to have a plan.

Stress Barriers If you've hit a wall in your program, look at the sources of stress in your life. If the stress is temporary, such as catching a cold or having a term paper due, you may want to wait until it passes before strengthening your efforts. If the stress is ongoing, try to find healthy ways to manage it. For example, taking a half-hour walk after lunch may help. You may even want to make stress management your highest priority for behavior change (see Chapter 2).

Games People Play Procrastinating, rationalizing, and blaming—even when they want to change, people hold on fiercely to what they know and love (or know and hate). You may have very mixed feelings about the change you're trying to make, and your underlying motives may sabotage your conscious ones if you keep them hidden from yourself. Try to detect the games you might be playing with yourself so that you can stop them.

If you're procrastinating ("It's Friday already; I might as well wait until Monday to begin"), try breaking down your plan into still smaller steps that you can accomplish one day at a time. If you're rationalizing or making excuses ("I wanted to go swimming today, but I wouldn't have had time to wash my hair afterward"), remember that the only one you're fooling is yourself and that when you "win" by deceiving yourself it's not much of a victory. If you're wasting time blaming yourself or others ("Everyone in that class talks so much that I don't get a chance to speak"), recognize that blaming is a way of taking your focus off the real problem and denying responsibility for your actions. Try refocusing by taking a positive attitude and renewing your determination to succeed.

BEING HEALTHY FOR LIFE

Your first few behavior change projects may never go beyond the planning stage. Those that do may not all succeed. But as you taste success by beginning to see progress and changes, you'll start to experience new and surprising positive feelings about yourself. You'll probably find that you're less likely to buckle under stress. You may accomplish things you never thought possible—winning a race, climbing a mountain, quitting smoking. Being healthy takes extra effort, but the paybacks in energy and vitality are priceless.

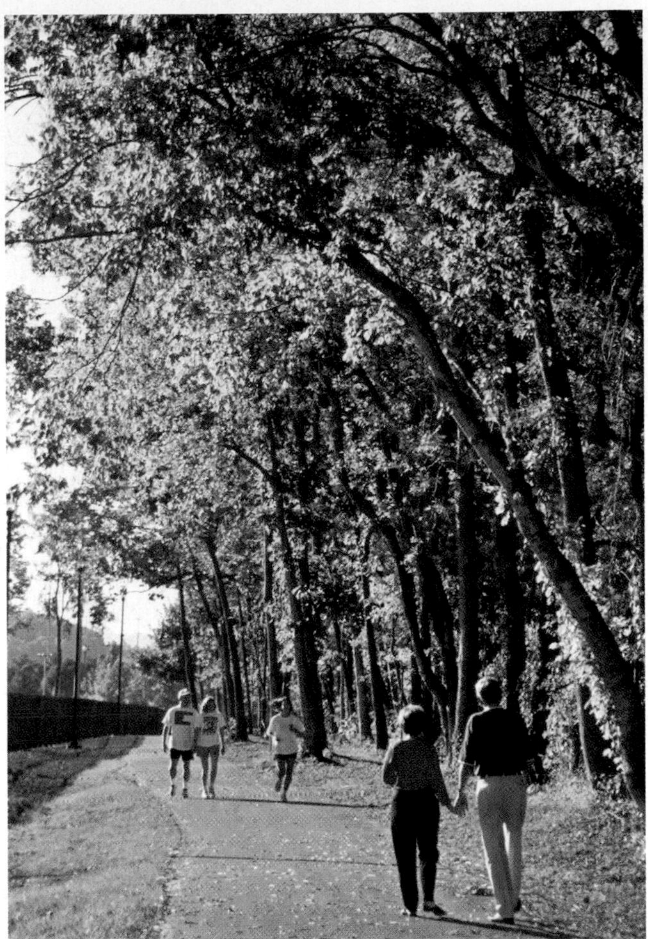

A beautiful day and a spectacular setting contribute to making exercise a satisfying and pleasurable experience. Choosing the right activity and doing it the right way are important elements in a successful health behavior change program.

Once you've started, don't stop. Remember that maintaining good health is an ongoing process. Tackle one area at a time, but make a careful inventory of your health strengths and weaknesses and lay out a long-range plan. Take on the easier problems first, and then use what you have learned to attack more difficult areas. Keep informed about the latest health news and trends; research is constantly providing new information that directly affects daily choices and habits.

Making Changes in Your World

You can't completely control every aspect of your health. At least three other factors—heredity, health care, and environment—play important roles in your well-being. After you quit smoking, for example, you may still be

Take Charge

Motivation Boosters

Changing behavior takes motivation. But how do you get motivated? The following strategies may help:

- Write down the potential benefits of the change. If you want to lose weight, your list might include increased ease of movement, energy, and self-confidence.
- Now write down the costs of not changing.
- Frequently visualize yourself achieving your goal and enjoying its benefits. If you want to manage time more effectively, picture yourself as a confident, organized person who systematically tackles important tasks and sets aside time each day for relaxation, exercise, and friends.
- Discount obstacles to change. Counter thoughts such as "I'll never have time to shop for and prepare healthy foods" with thoughts such as "Lots of other people have done it and so can I."
- Bombard yourself with propaganda. Subscribe to a self-improvement magazine. Take a class dealing with the change you want to make. Read books and watch talk shows on the subject. Post motivational phrases or pictures on your refrigerator or over your desk. Listen to motivational tapes in the car. Talk to people who have already made the change you want to make.
- Build up your confidence. Remind yourself of other goals you've achieved. At the end of each day, mentally review your good decisions and actions. See yourself as a capable person, in charge of your health.
- Create choices. You will be more likely to exercise every day if you have two or three types of exercise to choose from, and more likely to quit smoking if you've identified more than one way to distract yourself when you crave a cigarette. Get ideas from people who have been successful, and adapt some of their strategies to suit you.
- If you slip, keep trying. Research suggests that four out of five people will experience some degree of backsliding when they try to change a behavior. Only one in four succeeds the first time around. If you retain your commitment to change even when you lapse, you still are farther along the path to change than before you made the commitment. Try again. And again, if necessary.

inhaling smoke from other people's cigarettes. Your resolve to eat better foods may suffer a setback when you can't find any healthy choices in vending machines.

But you can make a difference—you can help create an environment around you that supports wellness for everyone. You can help support nonsmoking areas in public places. You can speak up in favor of more nutritious foods and better physical fitness facilities. You can include nonalcoholic drinks at your parties.

You can also work on larger environmental challenges: air and water pollution, traffic congestion, overcrowding and overpopulation, depletion of the atmosphere's ozone layer, toxic and nuclear waste, and many others. These difficult issues need the attention and energy of people who are informed and who care about good health. On every level, from personal to planetary, we can all take an active role in shaping our environment.

What Does the Future Hold?

Sweeping changes in lifestyle have resulted in healthier Americans in recent years and could have even greater effects in the years to come. In your lifetime, you can choose to take an active role in the movement toward increased awareness, greater individual responsibility and control, healthier lifestyles, and a healthier planet. Your choices and actions will have a tremendous impact on your present and future wellness. The door is open, and the time is now—you simply have to begin.

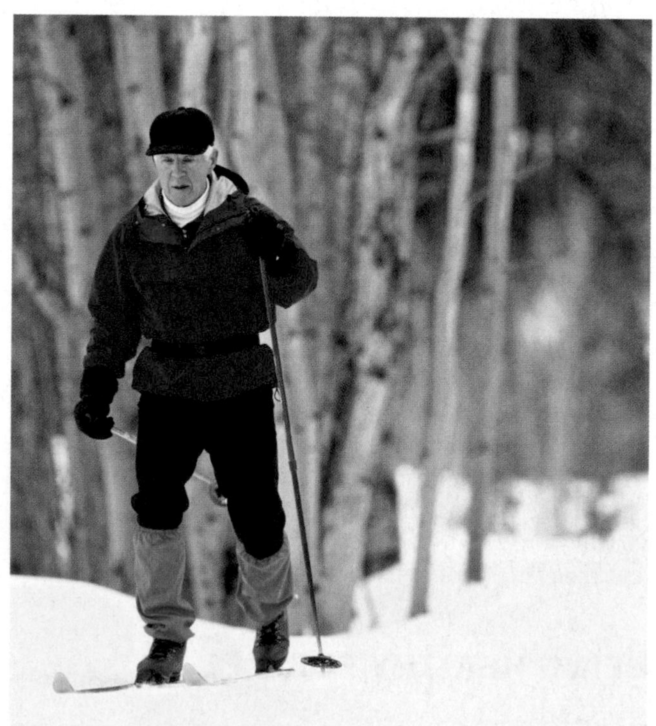

This retiree spends leisure time cross-country skiing. If you want to enjoy vigor and health in *your* middle and old age, begin now to make the choices that will give you lifelong vitality.

Tips for Today

You are in charge of your health! Many of the decisions you make every day have an impact on the quality of your life, both now and in the future. By making positive choices, large and small, you help ensure a lifetime of wellness.

Right now you can

- Go for a 15-minute walk.
- Have an orange, a nectarine, or a plum for a snack.
- Call a friend and arrange a time to catch up with each other.
- Start thinking about whether you have a health behavior you'd like to change. If you do, consider the elements of a behavior change strategy. For example,
    - Begin a mental list of the pros and cons of the behavior.
    - Think of one or two rewards that will be meaningful to you as you reach interim goals.
    - Think of someone who will support you in your attempts to make a behavior change—either someone who might want to make the same change you're contemplating or someone you can trust to provide you with encouragement. Talk to that person about your plan, get feedback, and ask for support.

SUMMARY

- Wellness is the ability to live life fully, with vitality and meaning. Wellness is dynamic and multidimensional; it incorporates physical, emotional, intellectual, spiritual, interpersonal and social, and environmental dimensions.
- As chronic diseases have become the leading cause of death in the United States, people have recognized that they have greater control over, and greater responsibility for, their health than ever before.
- The Healthy People initiative seeks to achieve a better quality of life for all Americans. The broad goals of the *Healthy People 2010* report are to increase quality and years of healthy life and to eliminate health disparities among Americans.
- Health-related differences among people that have implications for wellness can be described in the context of gender, ethnicity, income and education, disability, geographic location, and sexual orientation.
- Although heredity, environment, and health care all play roles in wellness and disease, behavior can mitigate their effects.
- Behaviors and habits that reinforce wellness include (1) taking an active, responsible role in your health; (2) managing stress; (3) maintaining self-esteem and good interpersonal relationships; (4) understanding sexuality and having satisfying intimate relationships; (5) avoiding tobacco and other drugs and restricting alcohol intake; (6) eating well, exercising, and maintaining healthy weight; (7) knowing about diseases and injuries and protecting yourself against them; (8) understanding and wisely using the health care system; (9) knowing when to seek treatment for an illness; (10) understanding and accepting the processes of aging and dying; and (11) understanding how the environment affects your health and working to improve the environment.
- To make lifestyle changes, you need information about yourself, your health habits, and resources available to help you change.
- You can increase your motivation for behavior change by examining the benefits and costs of change, boosting self-efficacy, and identifying and overcoming key barriers to change.
- The "stages of change" model describes six stages that people move through as they try to change their behavior: precontemplation, contemplation, preparation, action, maintenance, and termination.
- A specific plan for change can be developed by (1) monitoring behavior by keeping a journal; (2) analyzing the recorded data; (3) setting specific goals; (4) devising strategies for modifying the environment, rewarding yourself, and involving others; and (5) making a personal contract.
- To start and maintain a behavior change program you need commitment, a well-developed plan, social support, and a system of rewards.
- Although we cannot control every aspect of our health, we can make a difference in helping create an environment that supports wellness for everyone.

Take Action

1. **Start a health journal.** Use a daily planner or PDA as your health journal throughout the course; use it to track your behavior, your emotions, and other factors related to wellness. As a first journal activity, create lists of the positive lifestyle behaviors that enhance your well-being and the behaviors that detract from wellness. Use these lists as the basis for self-evaluation as you proceed through the book. The FamilyDoctor.org Web site offers suggestions for keeping a health journal, at http://familydoctor.org/838.xml. (Visit the Online Learning Center for health journal activities for each chapter.)

2. **Interview older family members.** Ask older members of your family (parents or grandparents) what they recall about patterns of health and disease when they were young. Did any of their friends or relatives die at an early age or of a disease that can now be treated? How have health concerns changed during their lifetime?

3. **Find a wellness role model.** Choose someone you consider to have embraced a wellness lifestyle. How is that person's overall health reflected in each of the dimensions of wellness? What can you borrow from her or his experiences and strategies for success in building a wellness lifestyle?

4. **Locate community resources.** Your school and community may present challenges to making healthy lifestyle choices, but they also have resources that can help you. Find out what local resources are "on your side" and can support your efforts at change; examples include free fitness facilities, stress-management workshops, and stop-smoking programs. As you become more aware of local resources and issues, you may also begin to identify ways that you could become involved to improve your community and its ability to promote wellness for all.

5. **Start building a family health history.** To help get started on your family health history, visit the site for the U.S. Surgeon General's Family History Initiative (www.hhs.gov/familyhistory). The instructions and forms from this site will help you organize your family tree and help you identify common diseases that may run in your family. Share the results with your health care provider. (For additional information on family health history, refer to Chapter 8.)

For More Information

Books

Komaroff, A. L., ed. 2005. *Harvard Medical School Family Health Guide*. New York: Free Press. *Provides consumer-oriented advice for the prevention and treatment of common health concerns.*

Prochaska, J. O., J. C. Norcross, and C. C. DiClemente. 1994. *Changing for Good: The Revolutionary Program That Explains the Six Stages of Change and Teaches You How to Free Yourself from Bad Habits*. New York: Morrow. *Outlines the authors' model of behavior change and offers suggestions and advice for each stage of change.*

Smith, P. B., M. MacFarlane, and E. Kalnitsky. 2002. *The Complete Idiot's Guide to Wellness*. Indianapolis, Ind.: Alpha Books. *A concise guide to healthy habits, including physical activity, nutrition, and stress management.*

Newsletters

Consumer Reports on Health (800-234-2188; http://www.ConsumerReportsonHealth.org)

Harvard Health Letter (800-829-9045; http://www.health.harvard.edu)

Harvard Men's Health Watch (877-649-9457)

Harvard Women's Health Watch (877-699-9457)

Mayo Clinic Health Letter (866-516-4974)

University of California at Berkeley Wellness Letter (800-829-9170; http://www.wellnessletter.com)

WW Organizations, Hotlines, and Web Sites

The Internet addresses (also called uniform resource locators, or URLs) listed here were accurate at the time of publication. Up-to-date links to these and many other wellness-oriented Web sites are provided on the links page of the *Core Concepts in Health* Web site (www.mhhe.com/insel10e).

Agency for Healthcare Research and Quality: Consumer Information. Provides materials on health plans and quality of care, prescription drugs, prevention and wellness, and consumer versions of evidence-based clinical practice guidelines for common conditions.
http://www.ahrq.gov/consumer

Centers for Disease Control and Prevention. Through phone, fax, and the Internet, the CDC provides a wide variety of health information.
800-311-3435
http://www.cdc.gov

Federal Trade Commission: Consumer Protection—Diet, Health, and Fitness. Includes online brochures about a variety of consumer health topics, including fitness equipment, generic drugs, and fraudulent health claims.
http://www.ftc.gov/bcp/menu-health.htm

FirstGov for Consumers: Health. Provides links to online brochures from a variety of government agencies.
http://www.consumer.gov/health.htm

Go Ask Alice. Sponsored by the Columbia University Health Service, this site provides answers to student questions about stress, sexuality, fitness, and many other wellness topics.
http://www.goaskalice.columbia.edu

Healthfinder. A gateway to online publications, Web sites, support and self-help groups, and agencies and organizations that produce reliable health information.
http://www.healthfinder.gov

Healthy People 2010. Provides information on Healthy People objectives and priority areas.
http://www.healthypeople.gov

MedlinePlus. Provides links to news and reliable information about health from government agencies and professional associations; also includes a health encyclopedia and information on prescription and over-the-counter drugs.
http://www.medlineplus.gov

MedlinePlus: Evaluating Health Information. Provides background information and links to sites with guidelines for finding and evaluating health information from the Web.
http://www.nlm.nih.gov/medlineplus/evaluatinghealthinformation.html

National Health Information Center (NHIC). Puts consumers in touch with the organizations that are best able to provide answers to health-related questions.
800-336-4797
http://www.health.gov/nhic

National Institutes of Health. Provides information about all NIH activities as well as consumer publications, hotline information, and an A to Z listing of health issues with links to the appropriate NIH institute.
http://www.nih.gov

National Women's Health Information Center. Provides information and answers to frequently asked questions.
800-994-WOMAN
http://www.4woman.gov

NOAH: New York Online Access to Health. Provides consumer health information in both English and Spanish.
http://www.noah-health.org

Office of Minority Health Resource Center. Promotes improved health among racial and ethnic minority populations.
http://www.omhrc.gov

Student Counseling Virtual Pamphlet Collection. Provides links to more than 400 pamphlets produced by different student counseling centers on a variety of wellness topics.
http://counseling.uchicago.edu/vpc

Surgeon General. Includes information on activities of the Surgeon General and the text of many key reports on such topics as tobacco use, physical activity, and mental health. You can also visit the site for the Surgeon General's Family History Initiative.
http://www.surgeongeneral.gov
http://www.hhs.gov/familyhistory

World Health Organization (WHO). Provides information about health topics and issues affecting people around the world.
http://www.who.int

The following are just a few of the many sites that provide consumer-oriented information on a variety of health issues:
FamilyDoctor.Org: http://www.familydoctor.org
InteliHealth: http://www.intelihealth.com
MayoClinic.com: http://mayoclinic.com
WebMD: http://webmd.com

The following sites provide daily health news updates:
CNN Health: http://www.cnn.com/health
MedlinePlus News: http://www.nlm.nih.gov/medlineplus/newsbydate.html
Yahoo Health News: http://dailynews.yahoo.com/h/hl

Selected Bibliography

American Cancer Society. 2006. *Cancer Facts and Figures—2006.* Atlanta: American Cancer Society.

American Heart Association. 2006. *2006 Heart and Stroke Statistical Update.* Dallas: American Heart Association.

Bren, L. 2005. Does sex make a difference? *FDA Consumer,* July–August.

Calle, E. E., et al. 2003. Overweight, obesity, and mortality from cancer in a prospectively studied cohort of U.S. adults. *New England Journal of Medicine* 348(17): 1625–1638.

Cauley, J. A., et al. 2005. Longitudinal study of changes in hip bone mineral density in Caucasian and African American women. *Journal of the American Geriatrics Society* 53(2): 183–189.

Casciano, D. A. 2005. Paving the way for safer, more effective drugs, food, and medical products. *FDA Consumer,* November–December.

Centers for Disease Control and Prevention. 1999. Achievements in public health, 1900–1999: Tobacco use, United States. *Morbidity and Mortality Weekly Report* 48(43): 986–993.

Centers for Disease Control and Prevention. 2004. REACH 2010 surveillance for health status in minority communities. *MMWR Surveillance Summaries* 53(SS-6).

Centers for Disease Control and Prevention. 2005. *Frequently Asked Questions About Calculating Obesity-Related Risk* (http://www.cdc.gov/PDF/Frequently_Asked_Questions_About_Calculating_Obesity-Related_Risk.pdf; retrieved July 10, 2006).

Centers for Disease Control and Prevention. 2005. Health-related quality of life surveillance—United States, 1993–2002. *MMWR Surveillance Summaries* 54(SS04).

Centers for Disease Control and Prevention. 2005. Racial/ethnic and socioeconomic disparities in multiple risk factors for heart disease and stroke, United States, 2003. *Morbidity and Mortality Weekly Report* 54(5): 113–117.

Centers for Disease Control and Prevention, Division of Nutrition and Physical Activity. 1999. *Promoting Physical Activity: A Guide for Community Action.* Champaign, Ill.: Human Kinetics.

Glanz, K., B. K. Rimer, and F. M. Lewis, eds. 2002. *Health Behavior and Health Education: Theory, Research, and Practice,* 3rd ed. San Francisco: Jossey-Bass.

How to keep those New Year's resolutions. 2006. *Harvard Health Letter,* January, 31.

Institute of Medicine. 2001. *Exploring the Biological Contributions to Human Health: Does Sex Matter?* Washington, D.C.: National Academy Press.

International Human Genome Sequencing Consortium. 2004. Finishing the euchromatic sequence of the human genome. *Nature* 431: 931–945.

Jemal, A., et al. 2005. Cancer statistics, 2005. *CA: A Cancer Journal for Clinicians* 55(1): 10–30.

Kaiser Family Foundation. 2003. *Key Facts: Race, Ethnicity, and Medical Care.* Menlo Park, Calif.: Kaiser Family Foundation.

Martin, G., and J. Pear. 2007. *Behaviour Modification: What It Is and How to Do It,* 8th ed. Upper Saddle River, N.J.: Prentice-Hall.

McClure, J. B. 2002. Are biomarkers useful treatment aids for promoting health behavior change? *American Journal of Preventive Medicine* 22(3): 200–207.

Mokdad, A. H., et al. 2004. Actual causes of death in the United States, 2000. *Journal of the American Medical Association* 291(10): 1238–1245.

Mokdad, A. H., et al. 2005. Correction: Actual causes of death in the United States, 2000. *Journal of the American Medical Association* 293(3): 293–294.

Muller, A. 2002. Education, income inequality, and mortality: A multiple regression analysis. *British Medical Journal* 324(7328): 23–25.

National Cancer Institute. 2004. *Cancer Facts: Cancer Clusters* (http://www.cancer.gov/cancertopics/factsheet/risk/clusters; retrieved July 10, 2006).

National Center for Health Statistics. 2004. Health behaviors of adults: United States, 1999–2001. *Vital and Health Statistics* 10(219).

National Center for Health Statistics. 2006. *Health, United States, 2006, with Chartbook on Trends in the Health of Americans.* Hyattsville, Md.: National Center for Health Statistics.

Office of Hawaiian Affairs. 2006. *Native Hawaiian Databook June 2006* (http://oha.org/pdf/databook/2006/Databook2006Health.pdf; retrieved July 10, 2006).

Ogden, C. L., et al. 2006. Prevalence of overweight and obesity in the United States, 1999–2004. *Journal of the American Medical Association* 295(13): 1549–1555.

Proteomics: Health at the cellular level. 2006. *Mayo Clinic Health Letter,* March.

Slater, M. D., and D. E. Zimmerman. 2002. Characteristics of health-related Web sites identified by common Internet portals. *Journal of the American Medical Association* 288(3): 316–317.

Steenland, K., et al. 2003. Deaths due to injuries among employed adults: The effects of socioeconomic class. *Epidemiology* 14(1): 74–79.

U.S. Census Bureau. 2005. *We the People: Women and Men in the United States.* Washington, D.C.: U.S. Census Bureau.

U.S. Department of Health and Human Services. 2000. *Healthy People 2010,* 2nd ed. Washington, D.C.: DHHS.

U.S. Department of Health and Human Services. 2001. *Mental Health: Culture, Race, and Ethnicity.* Rockville, Md.: U.S. Department of Health and Human Services.

Walsh, T., et al. 2006. Spectrum of mutations in BRCA1, BRCA2, CHEK2, and TP53 in families at high risk of breast cancer. *Journal of the American Medical Association* 295: 1379–1388.

Woodcock, J. 2005. Pharmacogenomics: On the road to "personalized medicine." *FDA Consumer,* November–December.

World Health Organization. 2006. Gender and HIV/AIDS (http://www.who.int/gender/hiv_aids/en; retrieved July 10, 2006).

World Health Organization. 2006. *Why Gender and Health?* (http://www.who.int/gender/genderandhealth/en; retrieved July 10, 2006).

2

Looking AHEAD

After reading this chapter, you should be able to

- Explain what stress is and how people react to it—physically, emotionally, and behaviorally
- Describe the relationship between stress and disease
- List common sources of stress
- Describe techniques for preventing and managing stress
- Put together a step-by-step plan for successfully managing the stress in your life

Stress: The Constant Challenge

Test Your Knowledge

1. **Which of the following events can cause stress?**
   a. taking out a loan
   b. failing a test
   c. graduating from college
   d. watching a hockey game
2. **Moderate exercise can stimulate which of the following?**
   a. analgesia (pain relief)
   b. birth of new brain cells
   c. relaxation
3. **High levels of stress can impair memory and cause physical changes in the brain.**
   True or false?
4. **For which of the following disorders is stress a risk factor?**
   a. diabetes
   b. arthritis
   c. premature menopause
   d. heart disease
5. **Which of the following can be a result of chronic stress?**
   a. violence
   b. heart attack
   c. stroke

ANSWERS

1. ALL FOUR. Stress-producing factors can be pleasant or unpleasant and can include physical challenges and the achievement of personal goals as well as what would commonly be perceived as negative events.
2. ALL THREE. Regular exercise is linked to improvements in many dimensions of wellness.
3. TRUE. Low levels of stress may improve memory, but high stress levels impair learning and memory and, over the long term, may shrink an area of the brain called the hippocampus.
4. ALL FOUR. Stress—interacting with heredity, personality, social environment, and behavior—increases vulnerability to many health problems.
5. ALL THREE. Chronic—or ongoing—stress can last for years. People who suffer from long-term stress may ultimately become violent toward themselves or others. They also run a greater than normal risk for certain ailments, especially cardiovascular disease.

Visit the *Core Concepts in Health* Online Learning Center (www.mhhe.com/insel10e) for study aids and many additional resources.

Everybody talks about stress. A 2006 survey by the American Psychological Association shows that 47% of American adults worry about the level of stress in their lives. People combat stress in many different ways. But what is stress? And why is it important to manage it wisely?

Most people associate stress with negative events: unpleasant life changes that create nervous tension. But stress isn't merely nervous tension. And it isn't something to be avoided at all costs (Figure 2-1). In fact, only death brings complete freedom from stress. Before we explore more fully what stress is, consider this list of common stressful situations or events:

- Interviewing for a job
- Running in a race
- Being accepted to college
- Going out on a date
- Watching a basketball game
- Getting a promotion

Obviously, stress doesn't arise just from unpleasant situations. Stress can also be associated with physical challenges and the achievement of personal goals. Stress-producing factors can be pleasant or unpleasant. More important than the type of stress you encounter, however, is the way you respond to stress—whether in positive, life-enhancing ways or in negative, counterproductive ways. The actions you take in response to stress are influenced by your biological predispositions, past experiences, and current circumstances. Although you cannot change who you are or what you've been through in the past, you *can* modify your behavior and seek out experiences that will improve your ability to deal with stress.

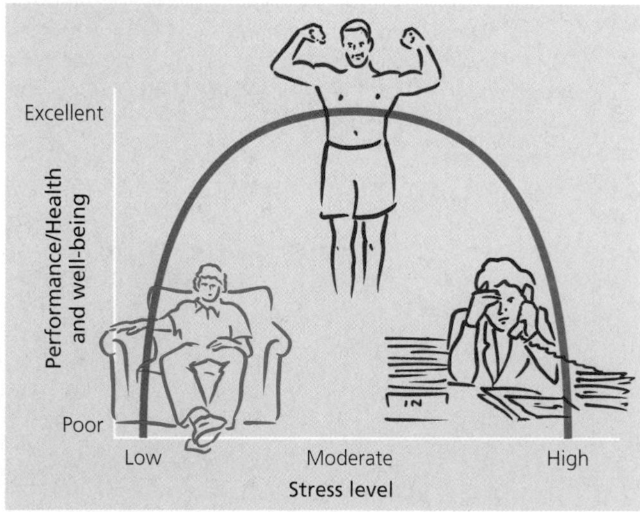

Figure 2-1 Stress level, performance, and well-being. A moderate level of stress challenges individuals in a way that promotes optimal performance and well-being. Too little stress, and people are not challenged enough to improve; too much stress, and the challenges become stressors that can impair physical and emotional health.

As a college student, you may be in one of the most stressful periods of your life (see the box "How High Is Your Stress Level?"). You may be on your own for the first time, or you may be juggling the demands of college with the responsibilities of a job, a family, or both. Financial pressures may be intense. Housing and transportation may be sources of additional hassles. You're also meeting new people, engaging in new activities, learning new information and skills, and setting a new course for your life. Good and bad, all these changes and challenges are likely to have a powerful effect on you, both physically and psychologically. Respond ineffectively to stress, and eventually it will take a toll on your sense of wellness. Learn effective responses, however, and you will enhance your health and gain a feeling of control over your life.

How do you know when your stress level is getting dangerously high? How can you develop techniques to cope positively with the stress that is part of your life? This chapter will help you discover answers to these questions.

WHAT IS STRESS?

Just what is stress, if such vastly different situations can cause it? In common usage, "stress" refers to two different things: situations that trigger physical and emotional reactions *and* the reactions themselves. In this text, we'll use the more precise term **stressor** for situations that trigger physical and emotional reactions and the term **stress response** for those reactions. A date and a final exam, then, are stressors; sweaty palms and a pounding heart are symptoms of the stress response. We'll use the term **stress** to describe the general physical and emotional state that accompanies the stress response. A person on a date or taking a final exam experiences stress.

Each individual's experience of stress depends on many factors, including the nature of the stressor and how the stressor is perceived. Responses to stressors include physical changes and emotional and behavioral responses.

Physical Responses to Stressors

Imagine that you are waiting to cross a street, perhaps daydreaming about a movie you saw last week. The light turns green and you step off the curb. Almost before you see it, you feel a car speeding toward you. With just a fraction of a second to spare, you leap safely out of harm's way. In that split second of danger and in the moments following it, you have experienced a predictable series of physical reactions. Your body has gone from a relaxed state to one prepared for physical action to cope with a threat to your life.

Two major control systems in your body are responsible for your physical response to stressors: the nervous system and the endocrine system. Through a variety of

Assess Yourself

How High Is Your Stress Level?

Ww

Many symptoms of excess stress are easy to self-diagnose. To help determine how much stress you experience on a daily basis, answer the following questions:

1. How many of the symptoms of excess stress listed in the table below do you experience frequently?
2. Are you easily startled or irritated?
3. Are you increasingly forgetful?
4. Do you have trouble falling or staying asleep?
5. Do you continually worry about events in your future?
6. Do you feel as if you are constantly under pressure to produce?
7. Do you often use tobacco, alcohol, or other drugs to help you relax?
8. Do you often feel as if you have less energy than you need to finish the day?
9. Do you have recurrent stomachaches or headaches?
10. Is it difficult for you to find satisfaction in simple life pleasures?
11. Are you often disappointed in yourself and others?
12. Are you overly concerned with being liked or accepted by others?
13. Have you lost interest in intimacy or sex?
14. Are you concerned that you do not have enough money?

Experiencing some of the stress-related symptoms or answering yes to a few questions is normal. However, if you experience a large number of stress symptoms or you answered yes to a majority of the questions, you are likely experiencing a high level of stress. Take time out to develop effective stress-management techniques. This chapter describes many coping strategies that can aid you in dealing with your college stressors. Additionally, your school's counseling center can provide valuable support.

Symptoms of Excess Stress

Physical Symptoms	Emotional Symptoms	Behavioral Symptoms
Dry mouth	Anger	Crying
Excessive perspiration	Anxiety or edginess	Disrupted eating habits
Frequent illnesses	Depression	Disrupted sleeping habits
Gastrointestinal problems	Fatigue	Harsh treatment of others
Grinding of teeth	Hypervigilance	Increased use of tobacco, alcohol, or other drugs
Headaches	Impulsiveness	Problems communicating
High blood pressure	Inability to concentrate	Sexual problems
Pounding heart	Irritability	Social isolation
Stiff neck or aching lower back	Trouble remembering things	

rapid chemical reactions affecting almost every part of your body, you are primed to act quickly and appropriately in time of danger.

Actions of the Nervous System The nervous system consists primarily of the brain, spinal cord, and nerves. Part of the nervous system is under voluntary control: commanding your arm to reach for a chocolate, for instance. The part that is not under conscious supervision, such as what controls the digestion of the chocolate, is known as the **autonomic nervous system.** In addition to digestion, it controls heart rate, breathing, blood pressure, and hundreds of other functions you normally take for granted.

The autonomic nervous system consists of two divisions. The **parasympathetic division** is in control when you are relaxed; it aids in digesting food, storing energy, and promoting growth. In contrast, the **sympathetic division** is activated during arousal or when there is an emergency, such as severe pain, anger, or fear. Sympathetic nerves use the neurotransmitter **norepinephrine** to exert their actions on nearly every organ, sweat gland, blood

Terms

Ww

stressor Any physical or psychological event or condition that produces stress.

stress response The physical and emotional changes associated with stress.

stress The collective physiological and emotional responses to any stimulus that disturbs an individual's homeostasis.

autonomic nervous system The branch of the nervous system that controls basic body processes; consists of the sympathetic and parasympathetic divisions.

parasympathetic division A division of the autonomic nervous system that moderates the excitatory effect of the sympathetic division, slowing metabolism and restoring energy supplies.

sympathetic division A division of the autonomic nervous system that reacts to danger or other challenges by almost instantly accelerating body processes.

norepinephrine A neurotransmitter released by the sympathetic nervous system onto target tissues to increase their function in the face of increased activity; when released in the brain, it causes arousal (increased attention, awareness, and alertness); also called *noradrenaline*.

vessel, and muscle to enable your body to handle an emergency. In general, it commands your body to stop storing energy and instead to mobilize all energy resources to respond to the crisis.

Actions of the Endocrine System One important target of the sympathetic nervous system is the **endocrine system.** This system of glands, tissues, and cells helps control body functions by releasing **hormones** and other chemical messengers into the bloodstream to influence metabolism and other body processes. Chemicals released into the blood are relatively free to travel throughout the body. The sites of action for circulating stress hormones are determined by specialized receptors in target tissues. Thus, stress hormones act only on those organs that have stress hormone receptors. Along with the nervous system, the endocrine system helps prepare the body to respond to a stressor.

The Two Systems Together How do both systems work together in an emergency? Let's go back to your close call with that car. Both reflexive and higher cognitive areas in your brain quickly make the decision that a large object traveling toward you at a high rate of speed is a threat and requires immediate action. A neurochemical message is promptly sent to the **hypothalamus,** a hormonal control center in the brain, that its services are needed, and it releases a chemical wake-up call to the nearby **pituitary gland.** In turn, the pituitary gland releases **adrenocorticotropic hormone (ACTH)** into the bloodstream. When ACTH reaches the **adrenal glands,** located just above the kidneys, it stimulates them to release **cortisol** and other key hormones into the bloodstream. Simultaneously, sympathetic nerves instruct your adrenal glands to release the hormone **epinephrine,** or adrenaline, which in turn triggers a series of profound changes throughout your body (Figure 2-2). Your hearing and vision become more acute. Bronchi dilate to allow more air into your lungs. Your heart rate accelerates and blood pressure increases to ensure that your blood—and the oxygen, nutrients, and hormones it carries—will be rapidly distributed where needed. Your liver releases extra sugar into your bloodstream to provide an energy boost for your muscles and brain. Your digestion halts. You perspire more to cool your skin. **Endorphins** are released to relieve pain in case of injury. Blood cell production increases.

It was Sir Walter Cannon who first called these almost-instantaneous physical changes, collectively, the **fight-or-flight reaction.** These changes give you the heightened reflexes and strength you need to dodge the car or deal with other stressors. Although these physical changes may vary in intensity, the same basic set of physical reactions occurs in response to any type of stressor, positive or negative.

The Return to Homeostasis Why doesn't your body remain in a hypervigilant state, perpetually ready for action? Why shouldn't your body always be prepared for a crisis? As you have probably guessed, it would be too exhausting. Your body actually resists dramatic changes. Whenever normal functioning is disrupted, such as during the fight-or-flight reaction, your body strives for **homeostasis,** a state in which blood pressure, heart rate, hormone levels, and other vital functions are maintained within a narrow range of normal.

Once a stressful situation ends, the parasympathetic division of your autonomic nervous system takes command and halts the reaction. It initiates the adjustments necessary to restore homeostasis. Your parasympathetic nervous system calms your body down, slowing a rapid heartbeat, drying sweaty palms, and returning breathing to normal. Gradually, your body resumes its normal "housekeeping" functions, such as digestion and temperature regulation. Damage that may have been sustained during the fight-or-flight reaction is repaired. The day after you narrowly dodge the car, you wake up feeling fine. In this way, your body can grow, repair itself, and acquire reserves of energy. When the next crisis comes, you'll be ready to respond—instantly—again.

The Fight-or-Flight Reaction in Modern Life The fight-or-flight reaction is a part of our biological

Terms

Ww

endocrine system The system of glands, tissues, and cells that secrete hormones into the bloodstream to influence metabolism and other body processes.

hormone A chemical messenger produced in the body and transported by the bloodstream to target cells or organs for specific regulation of their activities.

hypothalamus A part of the brain that activates, controls, and integrates the autonomic mechanisms, endocrine activities, and many body functions.

pituitary gland The "master gland," closely linked with the hypothalamus, that controls other endocrine glands and secretes hormones that regulate growth, maturation, and reproduction.

adrenocorticotropic hormone (ACTH) A hormone, formed in the pituitary gland, that stimulates the outer layer of the adrenal gland to secrete its hormones.

adrenal glands Two glands, one lying atop each kidney, whose outer layer (cortex) produces steroid hormones such as cortisol and whose inner core (medulla) produces the hormones epinephrine and norepinephrine.

cortisol A steroid hormone secreted by the cortex (outer layer) of the adrenal gland; also called *hydrocortisone.*

epinephrine A hormone secreted by the medulla (inner core) of the adrenal gland that affects the functioning of organs involved in responding to a stressor; also called *adrenaline.*

endorphins Brain secretions that have pain-inhibiting effects.

fight-or-flight reaction A defense reaction that prepares an individual for conflict or escape by triggering hormonal, cardiovascular, metabolic, and other changes.

homeostasis A state of stability and consistency in an individual's physiological functioning.

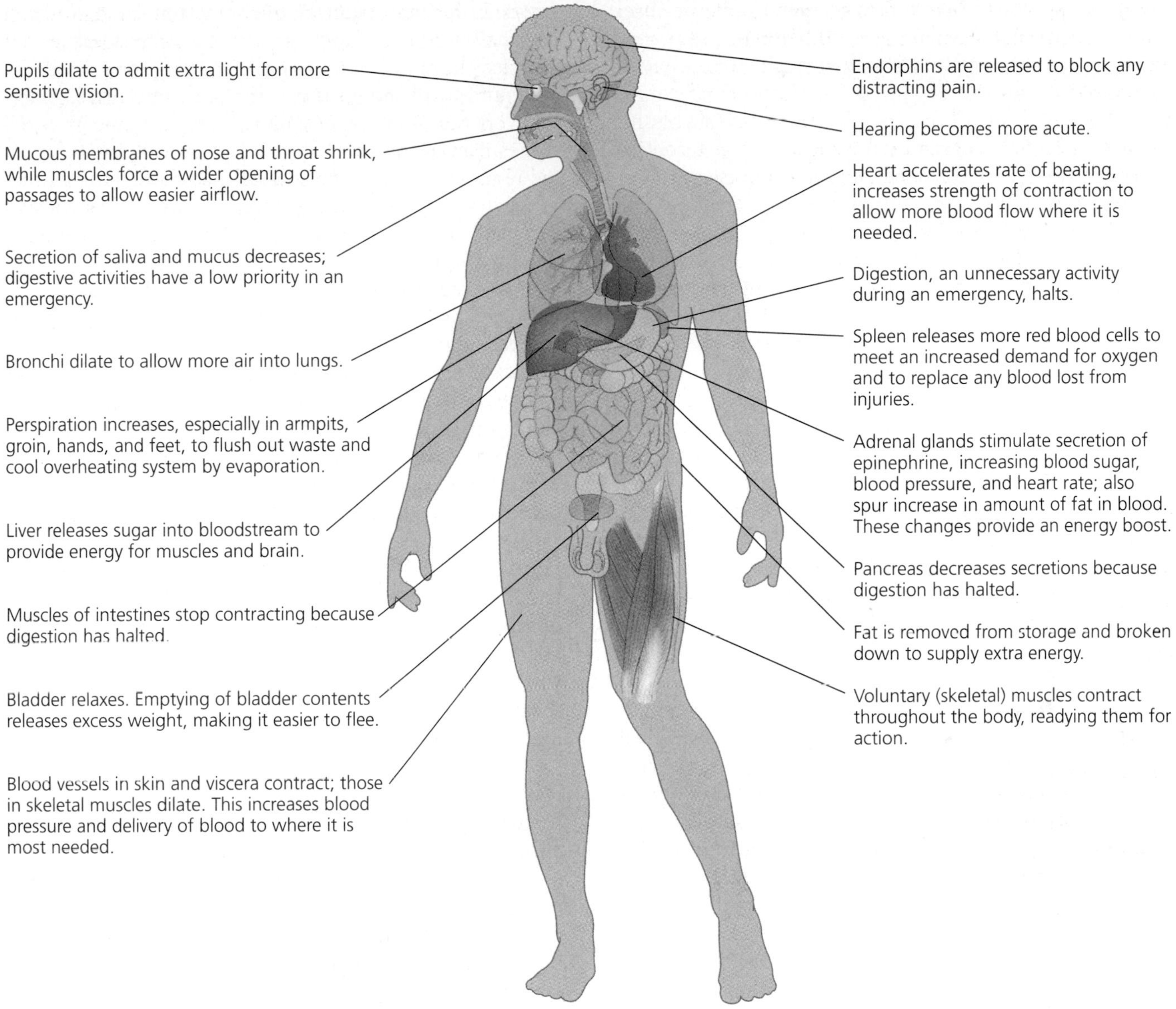

Pupils dilate to admit extra light for more sensitive vision.

Mucous membranes of nose and throat shrink, while muscles force a wider opening of passages to allow easier airflow.

Secretion of saliva and mucus decreases; digestive activities have a low priority in an emergency.

Bronchi dilate to allow more air into lungs.

Perspiration increases, especially in armpits, groin, hands, and feet, to flush out waste and cool overheating system by evaporation.

Liver releases sugar into bloodstream to provide energy for muscles and brain.

Muscles of intestines stop contracting because digestion has halted.

Bladder relaxes. Emptying of bladder contents releases excess weight, making it easier to flee.

Blood vessels in skin and viscera contract; those in skeletal muscles dilate. This increases blood pressure and delivery of blood to where it is most needed.

Endorphins are released to block any distracting pain.

Hearing becomes more acute.

Heart accelerates rate of beating, increases strength of contraction to allow more blood flow where it is needed.

Digestion, an unnecessary activity during an emergency, halts.

Spleen releases more red blood cells to meet an increased demand for oxygen and to replace any blood lost from injuries.

Adrenal glands stimulate secretion of epinephrine, increasing blood sugar, blood pressure, and heart rate; also spur increase in amount of fat in blood. These changes provide an energy boost.

Pancreas decreases secretions because digestion has halted.

Fat is removed from storage and broken down to supply extra energy.

Voluntary (skeletal) muscles contract throughout the body, readying them for action.

Figure 2-2 The fight-or-flight reaction. In response to a stressor, the autonomic nervous system and the endocrine system prepare the body to deal with an emergency.

heritage, a survival mechanism that has served humankind well. It enables our bodies to quickly prepare to escape from an injury or to engage in a physical battle. In modern life, however, the fight-or-flight reaction is often absurdly inappropriate. Many of the stressors we face in everyday life do not require a physical response—for example, an exam, a mess left by a roommate, or a red traffic light. Imagine that you are sitting quietly and then receive a letter saying that you have been denied a scholarship. You would probably quickly become more energized or alert, even irritated. You could feel a loss of appetite, and your respiration and heart rates would increase. Depending on the level of your response and state of physical fitness, you would feel other effects of sympathetic activation such as a slight throbbing in your upper extremities or temples, warmth in the face and neck region, and sweaty palms. The fight-or-flight reaction prepares the body for physical action regardless of whether such action is a necessary or appropriate response to a particular stressor.

Emotional and Behavioral Responses to Stressors

The physical response to a stressor may vary in intensity from person to person and situation to situation, but we all experience a similar set of physical changes—the fight-or-flight reaction. However, there is a great deal of variation in how people view potential stressors and in how people respond to them. For example, you may feel confident about taking exams but be nervous about talking to people you don't know, whereas your roommate may love challenging social situations but be very nervous about taking tests. Many factors, some external and some internal, help explain these differences. Your cognitive appraisal of a potential stressor will influence how that particular stressor is viewed. Two factors that can reduce the magnitude of the stress response are successful prediction and the perception of having some control over the stressor. For instance, obtaining course syllabi at the beginning of the term allows you to predict the timing of major deadlines and exams. Having this predictive knowledge also allows you to exert some control over your study and recreation plans and can thus help reduce the stress caused by exams.

Cognitive appraisal is highly individual and strongly related to emotions. The facts of a situation—Who? What? Where? When?—typically are evaluated fairly consistently from person to person. Evaluation with respect to personal outcome, however, varies: What does this mean for me? Can I do anything about it? Will it improve or worsen? If an individual perceives a situation as exceeding her or his ability to cope, the result can be negative emotions and an inappropriate stress response. If, on the other hand, a person perceives a situation as a challenge that is within her or his ability to manage, more positive and appropriate responses are likely.

Effective and Ineffective Responses Our emotional and behavioral responses to stressors are as critical to our overall experience of stress as are our physical responses. Common emotional responses to stressors include anxiety, depression, fear, or exhilaration. Although emotional responses are determined in part by inborn personality, we often can moderate or learn to control them. Coping techniques are discussed later in the chapter.

Our behavioral responses—controlled by the **somatic nervous system,** which manages our conscious actions—are under our control. Effective behavioral responses can promote wellness and enable us to function at our best. Ineffective behavioral responses can impair wellness and can even become stressors themselves. Depending on the stressor involved, effective behavioral responses may include talking, laughing, exercising, meditating, learning time-management skills, or finding a more compatible roommate. Inappropriate behavioral responses include overeating, substance abuse, or expressing hostility toward others.

Let's consider the different emotional and behavioral responses of students Amelia and David to a common stressor: the first exam of the semester. Both students feel anxious as the exam is passed out. Amelia relaxes her muscles and starts by writing the answers she knows. On a second pass through the exam, she concentrates carefully on the wording of each question. Some material comes back to her, and she makes educated guesses on the remaining items. She spends the whole hour writing as much as she can and checking her answers. She leaves the room feeling calm, relaxed, and confident that she has done well on the exam.

David responds to his initial anxiety with more anxiety. He finds that he doesn't know some of the answers, and he becomes more worried. The more upset he gets, the less he can remember; and the more he blanks out, the more anxious he gets. He begins to imagine the consequences of failing the course and berates himself for not having studied more. David turns in his paper before the hour is up, without checking his answers or going back to the questions he skipped. He leaves feeling depressed and angry.

As you can see, although both Amelia and David experienced the physical stress response as the exam was passed out, their emotional and behavioral responses were quite different—and led to very different outcomes. What determines these differences? Emotional and behavioral responses to stressors depend on a complex set of factors that include personality, cultural background, gender, and past experiences.

Personality and Stress In any stressful situation, some people seem nervous and irritable whereas others are calm and composed. Why do people respond so differently to stressors? Scientists remain unsure about the precise causes of these and other behavioral differences among individuals, but they are beginning to identify the brain mechanisms that interact to produce complex emotions and thought processes. **Personality,** the sum of behavioral, cognitive, and emotional tendencies, clearly affects how an individual perceives and reacts to stressors. To investigate the links among personality, stress, and overall wellness, researchers have looked at different constellations of characteristics, or "personality types."

TYPE A, B, AND C PERSONALITIES In the 1960s, researchers began separating people into two basic personality types, Type A and Type B. Type A individuals tended to be more controlling, schedule driven, competitive, and even hostile. Type B individuals were less hurried, more contemplative, and more tolerant of others.

These personality designations received much attention as a result of the findings of Meyer Friedman and Ray Rosenman, who showed that Type A individuals were more likely to have heart disease (they studied middle-age Caucasian males almost exclusively). However, later studies show that most Type A individuals are quite healthy and perhaps even more successful at surviving heart disease than Type B individuals of the same age and

Terms

somatic nervous system The branch of the nervous system that governs motor functions and sensory information; largely under our conscious control.

personality The sum of behavioral, cognitive, and emotional tendencies.

stage of disease; it may be that Type A people follow their medication and therapy schedules more exactly and tend to be more competitive against the disease. The only aspects of Type A personality that remain associated with a greater risk for heart disease in women and men of all ethnicities are anger, cynicism, and hostility (see Chapter 15 for more on the link between hostility and heart disease).

In terms of stress, Type A people may have a higher perceived stress level and greater coping difficulties, especially in social situations. They may react more explosively to stressors and become upset by events that others would consider only mild annoyances. Type B individuals, on the other hand, tend to be less frustrated by the flow of daily events and the actions of others.

Research into personality traits and cancer examined a Type C personality, characterized by difficulty expressing emotions, anger suppression, feelings of hopelessness and despair, and an exaggerated stress response to minor cognitive stressors. People who consistently show these traits have lower levels of immune cells important in fighting cancer as well as lower cancer survival rates. The heightened stress response associated with a Type C personality may be directly related to impaired immune function. Studies of Type A and C personalities suggest that it is beneficial to express your emotions but that consistent or exaggerated arousal or hostility toward others is unhealthy.

HARDINESS AND RESILIENCY Researchers have also looked at personality traits that seem to enable people to deal more successfully with stress. Psychologist Suzanne Kobasa examined "hardiness," a particular form of optimism. People with a hardy personality view potential stressors as challenges and opportunities for growth and learning, rather than as burdens. Hardy people tend to perceive fewer situations as stressful, and their reaction to stressors tends to be less intense. They are committed to their activities, have a sense of inner purpose, and feel at least partly in control of events in their lives.

Resiliency refers to personality traits associated with social and academic success in at-risk populations such as children from low-income families and people with mental or physical disabilities. Like hardy people, those with resiliency tend to set goals and face adversity through individual effort. The three basic types of resiliency center on how an individual responds to stress: nonreactive resiliency, in which a person does not react to stress; homeostatic resiliency, in which a person may react strongly but returns to baseline functioning fairly quickly; and positive growth resiliency, in which a person learns and grows. Resiliency is also associated with emotional intelligence and violence prevention.

People with a hardy or resilient personality typically have an internal locus of control. As described in Chapter 1, this means that they feel responsible for their own actions and in control of many of the events in their lives. This sense of control helps them cope with stress in a more positive way and put setbacks in proper perspective. Psychologist Martin Seligman coined the term "positive psychology," based on the idea that if young people are taught resiliency, hope, and optimism, they will be less susceptible to depression and will lead happier, more productive lives. People with an external locus of control—a belief that the events in their lives are controlled by outside factors—typically have more difficulties with stress. A person with an external locus of control may develop "learned helplessness"; in stressful situations, he or she believes it's pointless to even try to deal with stressors.

Can a Person Develop a Stress-Resistant Personality? Researchers have developed more complex and encompassing models that look at other factors that influence behavioral and emotional responses to stressors. Visit the Online Learning Center for self-assessments relating to personality types and traits such as assertiveness.

Researchers have also looked at the extent to which temperament and personality are inherited. Basic emotional response patterns such as the tendency to seek out new experiences appear to have a strong hereditary component; the underlying factor may be genes that influence the activities of neurotransmitters like serotonin and dopamine. On the other hand, character traits such as the degree to which a person is self-directed appear much more closely linked to sociocultural factors than to heredity. It is important to note that the relationship between genes and behavior is extremely complex, so that even traits with a strong genetic component are profoundly influenced by environment and experience.

Is there anything people can do to change their personality and become more stress-resistant? It is unlikely that you can change your basic personality. However, you can change your typical behaviors and patterns of thinking and develop positive techniques for coping with stressors. Strategies for successful stress management are described later in the chapter. For starters, though, try a few of the following:

- Build greater social support through meaningful relationships.
- Take advantage of opportunities to participate in and contribute to your family and community in productive ways.
- Set higher expectations for yourself with clear boundaries and fair, consistent expectations.
- Build life skills such as decision making, effective communication, and stress and conflict management.
- Do not try to control the outcome of every situation (for example, a team competition or a loved one's illness). Know your limitations and trust others.

Cultural Background Young adults from all over the world seek higher education at American colleges and universities. The vast majority of students come away from their undergraduate experience with a greater appreciation for other groups and cultures. However, when they are ignored, misunderstood, or disrespected, cultural differences in values, lifestyles, and what is considered to be acceptable behavior can be a source of stress and can lead to stereotyping, prejudice, discrimination, harassment, and even assault. The way you cope with stress and the way you interact with people of other cultures are influenced by the family and culture in which you were raised. Try to avoid the assumption that your way of life is the best or only way. If you take the time to learn about and from other cultures, you will become more aware of the potential strengths and weaknesses of your own culture. You will also reduce the likelihood of cultural differences becoming a source of stress for you.

Gender Like cultural background, our **gender role**—the activities, abilities, and behaviors our culture expects of us based on whether we're male or female—also affects our experience of stress. Some behavioral responses to stressors, such as crying or openly expressing anger, may be deemed more appropriate for one gender than the other. Strict adherence to gender roles can place limits on how a person responds to stress and can itself become a source of stress. Adherence to traditional gender roles can also affect the perception of a potential stressor. For example, if a man derives most of his sense of self-worth from his work, retirement may be a more stressful life change for him than for a woman whose self-image is based on several different roles.

Oxytocin, a hormone involved in social interaction and the regulation of mood, may underlie some of the gender differences in behavioral responses to stressors. Women produce more oxytocin than men do; and the hormone estrogen, which is more abundant in women, enhances its effects. Although both men and women experience the fight-or-flight physiological response to stress, women are more likely to respond behaviorally with a pattern of "tend-and-befriend"—nurturing friends and family and seeking social support and social contacts. Women are more likely to enhance their social networks in ways that reduce stress than to become aggressive or withdraw from difficult situations.

See the box "Women, Men, and Stress" for more on gender and stress.

Past Experiences Your past experiences significantly influence your response to stressors. For example, if you were unprepared for the first speech you gave in your speech class and performed poorly, you will probably experience greater anxiety in response to future assignments. If you had performed better, your confidence and sense of control would be greater, and you would probably experience less stress with future speeches. Effective behavioral responses, in this case careful preparation and visualizing yourself giving a successful speech, can help overcome the effects of negative past experiences.

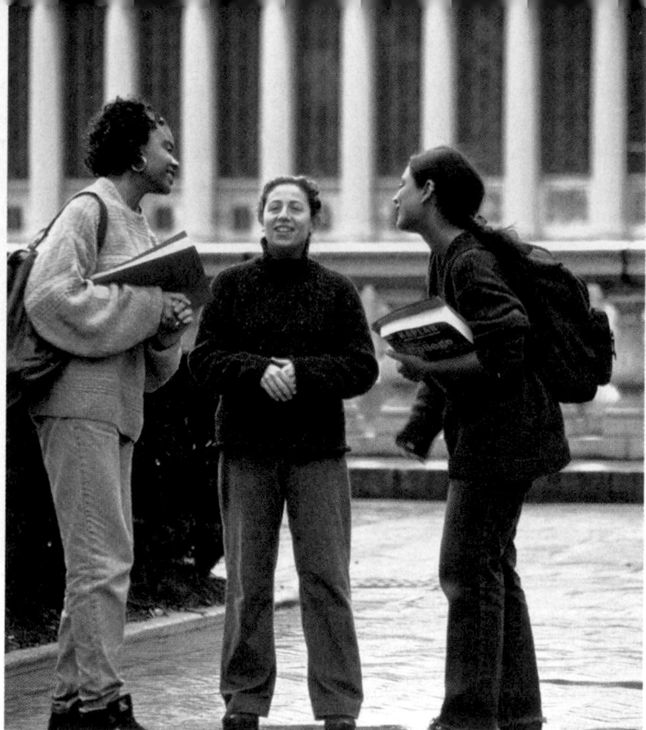

Research suggests that women are more likely than men to respond to stressors by seeking social support.

The Stress Experience as a Whole

Physical, emotional, and behavioral responses to stressors are intimately interrelated. The more intense the emotional response, the stronger the physical response. Effective behavioral responses can reduce stress; ineffective ones only worsen it. Sometimes people have such intense emotional responses and such ineffective or counterproductive behavioral responses to stressors that they need professional help with learning to cope. More often, however, people can learn to handle stressors on their own. Actions you can take to deal successfully with the stress in your life are described later in the chapter.

STRESS AND DISEASE

The role of stress in health and disease is complex, and much remains to be learned. However, evidence suggests that stress—interacting with a person's genetic predisposition, personality, social environment, and health-related behaviors—can increase vulnerability to numerous ailments. According to the American Psychological Association, 43% of adult Americans suffer health problems related to stress. Several related theories have been proposed to explain the relationship between stress and disease.

Gender Matters

Women, Men, and Stress

Men and women alike experience stress, but they experience it differently.

Women and Stress

Women are more likely than men to find themselves balancing multiple roles, such as those of student, spouse, and parent. Women who work outside the home still do most of the housework—although today's husbands are helping in greater numbers than previous generations did—and housework isn't limited to cleaning or doing laundry. For example, more than 60% of women make all decisions about their family's health care, including decisions about elderly parents.

Women make up more than half the workforce but still face many workplace-related disparities that can be sources of stress. For example, women make less money than men in comparable jobs, are more likely to suffer sexual harassment or discrimination, and are less likely to be promoted into leadership positions.

The pressures of home, workplace, and school can create very high stress levels. This is especially true for women who see themselves in the traditional gender role as the family's primary caregiver.

Men and Stress

Men who fit a traditional male gender role may feel compelled to be in charge at all times. Their communication style may be competitive or aggressive, causing stress in interpersonal situations and limiting their ability to build a support network. Such men may keenly feel the responsibility to support a family, which can compound existing pressures at home and at work.

Key Stressors

A January 2006 survey conducted by the American Psychological Association, the National Women's Health Resource Center, and iVillage.com reported the percentages of men and women who feel stressed by the following issues:

	Women	Men
Money	28%	19%
Health of spouse/child	27%	20%
Health of parents	27%	20%
Children	24%	15%

In general, 51% of women reported that their stress affected them in some way, compared to 43% of men.

Physiological Differences and Stress

Because male testosterone levels rise from puberty onward, men tend to have higher blood pressure than women of the same age. This factor contributes to greater wear on the male circulatory system, sometimes increasing a man's risk for cardiovascular disease. A part of the brain that regulates emotions, the amygdala, is sensitive to testosterone. Thus, men may be predisposed to see social situations as more threatening than women do, resulting in more frequent stress responses.

Conversely, women have higher levels of oxytocin and are more likely to respond to stressors by seeking social support. This coping response may give women a longevity advantage over men by decreasing the risk of stress-related disorders. It does not, however, free women from stress-related ailments. Women are more likely than men to suffer stress-related hypertension, depression, and obesity. Recent research also shows that women who juggle multiple roles face an increased risk of heart disease, compared to women who do not need to balance different roles.

The General Adaptation Syndrome

Biologist Hans Selye, working in the 1930s and 1940s, was one of the first scientists to develop a comprehensive theory of stress and disease. Selye coined the term **general adaptation syndrome (GAS)** to describe what he believed was a universal and predictable response pattern to all stressors. He recognized that stressors could be pleasant, such as attending a party, or unpleasant, such as getting a flat tire or a bad grade. He called stress triggered by a pleasant stressor **eustress** and stress triggered by an unpleasant stressor **distress.** The sequence of physical responses associated with GAS is the same for both eustress and distress and occurs in three stages: alarm, resistance, and exhaustion (Figure 2-3).

Alarm This stage includes the complex sequence of events brought on by the activation of the sympathetic nervous system and the endocrine system—the fight-or-flight reaction. During this stage, the body is more susceptible to disease or injury because it is geared up to deal with a crisis. A person in this phase may experience headaches, indigestion, anxiety, and disrupted sleeping and eating patterns.

Resistance With continued stress, Selye theorized, the body develops a new level of homeostasis in which it is more resistant to disease and injury than it normally would be. During the resistance stage, a person can cope with normal life and added stress.

Exhaustion As you might imagine, both the mobilization of forces during the alarm reaction and the maintenance of homeostasis during the resistance stage require a considerable amount of energy. If a stressor persists or if several stressors occur in succession, general exhaustion results. This is not the sort of exhaustion people complain

Terms

VW

gender role A culturally expected pattern of behavior and attitudes determined by whether a person is male or female.

general adaptation syndrome (GAS) A pattern of stress responses consisting of three stages: alarm, resistance, and exhaustion.

eustress Stress resulting from a pleasant stressor.

distress Stress resulting from an unpleasant stressor.

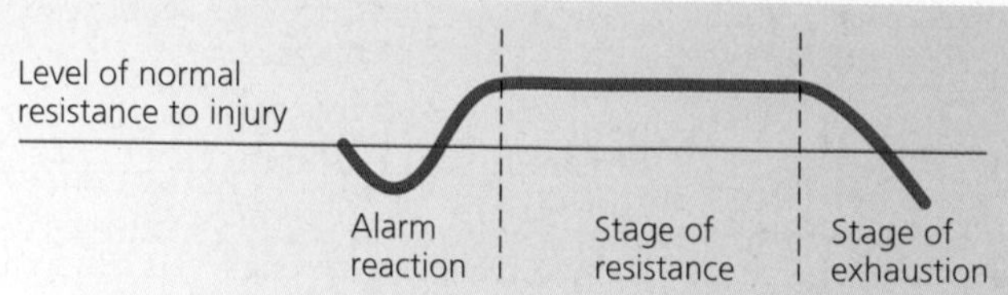

Figure 2-3 The general adaptation syndrome. Selye observed a predictable sequence of responses to stress. During the alarm phase, a lower resistance to injury is evident. With continued stress, resistance to injury is actually enhanced. With prolonged exposure to repeated stressors, exhaustion sets in, with a return of low resistance levels seen during acute stress.

of after a long, busy day. It's a life-threatening type of physiological exhaustion characterized by symptoms such as distorted perceptions and disorganized thinking.

Allostatic Load

While Selye's model of GAS is still viewed as a key contribution to modern stress theory, some aspects of it are now discounted. For example, increased susceptibility to disease after repeated or prolonged stress is now thought to be due to the effects of the stress response itself rather than to a depletion of resources (Selye's exhaustion state). In particular, long-term overexposure to stress hormones such as cortisol has been linked with health problems. (High cortisol levels are associated with metabolic syndrome, a condition linked to increased risk of heart disease, diabetes, depression, and osteoporosis; metabolic syndrome is discussed further in Chapter 15.)

The long-term wear and tear of the stress response is called the **allostatic load.** An individual's allostatic load is dependent on many factors, including genetics, life experiences, and emotional and behavioral responses to stressors. A high allostatic load may be due to frequent stressors, poor adaptation to common stressors, an inability to shut down the stress response, or imbalances in the stress response of different body systems. A high allostatic load is linked with heart disease, hypertension, obesity, and reduced brain and immune system functioning. In other words, when your allostatic load exceeds your ability to cope, you are more likely to get sick.

Psychoneuroimmunology

One of the most fruitful areas of current research into the relationship between stress and disease is **psychoneuroimmunology (PNI).** PNI is the study of the interactions among the nervous system, the endocrine system, and the immune system. The underlying premise of PNI is that stress, through the actions of the nervous and endocrine systems, impairs the immune system and thereby affects health. But although there is strong evidence that stress-related suppression of the immune system can increase vulnerability to disease in animals, the evidence in healthy humans is less clear. Even large stress-induced immune changes can have small clinical (medical) consequences because they are short-term or because the immune system has redundant components and compensates for changes. In short, the immune system is remarkably flexible and capable of substantial change without compromising health. On the other hand, chronic stress in individuals predisposed to or experiencing disease may have more substantial consequences.

Researchers have discovered a complex network of nerve and chemical connections between the nervous and endocrine systems and the immune system. In general, increased levels of cortisol are linked to a decreased number of immune system cells, or lymphocytes (see Chapter 17 for more on the immune system). Epinephrine and norepinephrine appear to promote the release of lymphocytes but at the same time reduce their efficiency. Interestingly, scientists have identified hormone-like substances called neuropeptides that appear to translate stressful emotions into biochemical events, some of which impact the immune system, providing a physical link between emotions and immune function.

It is important to note that different types of stress may affect immunity in different ways. For instance, during acute stress (typically lasting between 5 and 100 minutes), white blood cells are selectively redistributed into the skin, where they contribute to enhancement of the immune response. During a stressful event sequence, such as loss of a loved one or a personal trauma and the events that follow, there are typically no overall significant immune changes. Chronic stressors such as caregiving or unemployment have negative effects on almost all functional measures of immunity. Chronic stress may cause prolonged secretion of cortisol and may accelerate the course of diseases that involve inflammation, including multiple sclerosis, heart disease, and type 2 diabetes.

Mood, personality, behavior, and immune functioning are intertwined. For example, people who are generally pessimistic may neglect the basics of health care, become passive when ill, and fail to engage in health-promoting behaviors. People who are depressed may reduce physical activity and social interaction, which may in turn affect the immune system and the cognitive appraisal of a stressor. Optimism, successful coping, and positive problem solving, on the other hand, may positively influence immunity. The pattern of interaction between the stress and immune responses allows for regulation of energy mobilization and redirection that is necessary to fight attackers both within and without.

Links Between Stress and Specific Conditions

Although much remains to be learned, it is clear that people who have unresolved chronic stress in their lives or who handle stressors poorly are at risk for a wide range of health problems. In the short term, the problem might be just a cold, a stiff neck, or a stomachache. Over the long term, the problems can be more severe—cardiovascular disease (CVD), high blood pressure, impaired immune function, or accelerated aging.

Cardiovascular Disease During the stress response, heart rate increases and blood vessels constrict, causing blood pressure to rise. Chronic high blood pressure is a major cause of **atherosclerosis,** a disease in which blood vessels become damaged and caked with fatty deposits. These deposits can block arteries, causing heart attacks and strokes. The stress response can precipitate a heart attack in someone with underlying atherosclerosis. The stress response can also cause stress cardiomyopathy ("broken heart syndrome"), a condition that mimics a heart attack but doesn't actually damage the heart.

Certain types of emotional responses may increase a person's risk of CVD. So-called hot reactors, people who exhibit extreme increases in heart rate and blood pressure in response to emotional stressors, may face an increased risk of cardiovascular problems. As described earlier, people who tend to react to situations with anger and hostility are more likely to have heart attacks than are people with a less explosive, more trusting personality.

Stress has also been linked to some of the more recently identified risk factors for CVD, including elevated cholesterol. For example, inflammation is a key component of the damage to blood vessels that leads to heart attacks. Stress increases inflammation throughout the body. Stress-induced increases in inflammatory messenger molecules are also linked to elevated levels of homocysteine and c-reactive protein (CRP), two compounds that appear to be markers for CVD risk. Stress-related depression and anger are associated with elevated homocysteine levels, and job-related exhaustion is linked to high CRP levels in some people. Elevated CRP levels have also been implicated in insulin resistance and the development of diabetes, which is in turn a risk factor for CVD. Clearly, stress reduction can improve cardiovascular health. See Chapter 15 for more on CVD.

Altered Functioning of the Immune System

Sometimes you get sick when you can least afford it—during exam week, when you're going on vacation, or when you have a big job interview. As research in PNI suggests, this is more than mere coincidence. Some of the health problems linked to stress-related changes in immune function include the following:

- *Colds and other infections.* Stress can leave people more vulnerable to contracting a cold and less able to fight one off.
- *Asthma and allergies.* Stress is a trigger or aggravator of asthma, hives, eczema, and other allergies.
- *Cancer.* The immune system destroys abnormal cells; left unchecked, such cells can develop into cancerous tumors. Stress does not cause cancer, but by compromising the immune system, it may increase the risk of developing cancer and decrease the chance of surviving it.
- *Chronic disease flare-ups.* Symptoms of diseases such as genital herpes and HIV infection may flare up during episodes of stress. Stress may also distract people from their commitment to disease-management behaviors such as eating a healthy diet, exercising, and taking medications.

Psychological Problems The hormones and other chemicals released during the stress response cause emotional as well as physical changes (see the box "Stress and Your Brain"). Stress also activates the enzyme PKC, which influences the brain's prefrontal cortex. Excess PKC can negatively affect focus, judgment, and the ability to think clearly. Moreover, many stressors are inherently anxiety-producing, depressing, or both. Stress has been found to contribute to psychological problems such as depression, panic attacks, anxiety, eating disorders, and post-traumatic stress disorder (PTSD). PTSD, which afflicts war veterans, rape and child abuse survivors, and others who have suffered or witnessed severe trauma, is characterized by nightmares, flashbacks, and a diminished capacity to experience or express emotion. (For more information, see Chapter 3.)

Other Health Problems Many health problems may be related to uncontrolled stress. For example,

- *Digestive problems.* Stress is linked to stomachaches, diarrhea, and constipation. It may aggravate problems such as irritable bowel syndrome and ulcers.
- *Headaches.* Physiological changes associated with the stress response can cause tension headaches and trigger migraines (see the box "Headaches: A Common Symptom of Stress" on p. 43).

Terms

Vw

allostatic load The long-term negative impact of the stress response on the body.

psychoneuroimmunology (PNI) The study of the interactions among the nervous, endocrine, and immune systems.

atherosclerosis The buildup of fatty material in the lining of arteries that have become damaged from advancing age or high blood pressure; a leading cause of heart disease and stroke.

Mind/Body/Spirit

Stress and Your Brain

Like a computer that registers information in response to typing on a keyboard, your brain is able to respond to and store information about changes in your environment. Unlike a computer, your brain has the attribute of plasticity—it physically changes its structure and function in response to experience. Also unlike a computer, your brain is altered by psychological stress. Moderate stress enhances the ability to acquire information and remember daily events, while high levels of acute stress can impair learning. For example, people can often remember minute details following a fender bender but can't recall the events surrounding a major car crash. Thus, it is good to be a little bit nervous before an exam—but not highly anxious.

The effects of stress on brain form and function are apparent in a structure called the hippocampus, which is involved in learning and memory. High levels of chronic stress cause brain cells (neurons) in the hippocampus to shrink in size or die, thus impairing learning and memory. Exciting new research in neuroscience has revealed that the hippocampus actually grows new neurons during adulthood. However, stress acts to reduce new cell birth in the hippocampus, reducing the replacement of lost neurons. Together, these effects of stress result in fewer neurons and fewer connections between neurons in the hippocampus, thus decreasing the capacity for information processing. People who are depressed or who suffer from post-traumatic stress disorder have higher levels of stress hormones in their bloodstream and smaller hippocampi than others. Even in the absence of a serious disorder, it is thought that the accumulation of stress effects across the life span can contribute to brain aging. Thus, the way you cope with stress can affect the way your brain works both immediately and over the long term.

- *Insomnia and fatigue.* Chemical messengers produced during stress promote alertness and ward off sleep. Sleep disruption can produce fatigue and memory loss and lead to more serious health problems.
- *Injuries.* Stress may distract people, making them less vigilant about injury prevention behaviors such as wearing a safety belt. On-the-job injuries are also linked to job stress.
- *Endocrine effects and pregnancy complications.* Menstrual irregularities and impotence are both associated with periods of unusual stress. The stress response is an integral part of menstruation and pregnancy, but women who experience significant additional stress before or during pregnancy may have an increased risk of delivering a premature or low-birth-weight infant. Stress may also affect the timing and experience of menopause.
- *Type 2 diabetes.* In the most common form of diabetes, glucose builds up in the bloodstream because the body doesn't produce enough insulin and/or the body's cells are insulin resistant. Cortisol stimulates the release of glucose from the liver and muscle cells into the bloodstream; chronic stress may contribute to the development of diabetes and exacerbate symptoms in those who already have it. Stress also interacts with certain personality factors, including hostility and cynicism, to increase insulin resistance.
- *Premature aging.* Extended periods of stress may cause cellular damage, particularly to the DNA within cells. This damage may shorten cell life and hasten aging.

COMMON SOURCES OF STRESS

We are surrounded by stressors—at home, at school, on the job, and within ourselves. Being able to recognize potential sources of stress is an important step in successfully managing the stress in our lives.

Major Life Changes

Any major change in your life that requires adjustment and accommodation can be a source of stress. Early adulthood and the college years are associated with many significant changes, such as moving out of the family home. Even changes typically thought of as positive—graduation, job promotion, marriage—can be stressful. For older students, life changes may be different but just as powerful, such as the challenge of balancing school, work, and family responsibilities.

Clusters of major life changes may be linked to the development of health problems in some people. Research indicates that some life changes, particularly those that are perceived negatively, can affect health. However, personality and coping skills are important moderating influences. People with a strong support network and a stress-resistant personality are less likely to become ill in response to life changes than people with fewer resources.

Daily Hassles

Have you done any of the following in the past week?

- Misplaced your keys, wallet, or an assignment
- Had an argument with someone
- Waited in a long line, been stuck in traffic, or had another problem with transportation
- Worried about money
- Been upset about the weather

In Focus

Headaches: A Common Symptom of Stress

Are you among the more than 45 million Americans who have chronic, recurrent headaches? Headaches come in various types but are often grouped into three major categories: tension headaches, migraines, and cluster headaches. Other types of headaches have underlying organic causes, such as sinus congestion or infection.

Tension Headaches

Approximately 90% of all headaches are tension headaches, characterized by a dull, steady pain, usually on both sides of the head. It may feel as though a band of pressure is tightening around the head, and the pain may extend to the neck and shoulders. Acute tension headaches may last from hours to days, while chronic tension headaches may occur almost every day for months or even years. Psychological stress, poor posture, and immobility are the leading causes of tension headaches. There is no cure, but the pain can sometimes be relieved with over-the-counter painkillers and with therapies such as massage, acupuncture, relaxation, hot or cold showers, and rest.

If your headaches are frequent, keep a diary with details about the events surrounding each one. Are your headaches associated with late nights, academic deadlines, or long periods spent sitting at a computer? If you can identify the stressors that are consistently associated with your headaches, you can begin to gain more control over the situation. If you suffer persistent tension headaches, you should consult your physician.

Migraines

Migraines typically progress through a series of stages lasting from several minutes to several days. They may produce a variety of symptoms, including throbbing pain that starts on one side of the head and may spread; heightened sensitivity to light; visual disturbances such as flashing lights; nausea; and fatigue. About 70% of migraine sufferers are women, and migraine headaches may have a genetic component. Research suggests that people who get migraines may have abnormally excitable nerve cells in their brains. When triggered, these nerve cells send a wave of electrical activity throughout the brain, which in turn causes migraine symptoms. Potential triggers include menstruation, stress, fatigue, atmospheric changes, specific sounds or odors, and certain foods. The frequency of attacks varies from a few in a lifetime to several per week.

Keeping a headache journal can help a migraine sufferer identify headache triggers—the first step to avoiding them. In addition, many new treatments can help reduce the frequency, severity, and duration of migraines.

Cluster Headaches

Cluster headaches are extremely severe headaches that cause intense pain in and around one eye. They usually occur in clusters of one to three headaches each day over a period of weeks or months, alternating with periods of remission in which no headaches occur. About 90% of people with cluster headaches are male. There is no known cause or cure for cluster headaches, but a number of treatments are available. During cluster periods, it is important to refrain from smoking cigarettes and drinking alcohol, because these activities can trigger attacks.

For more on treating headaches, as well as warning signs for when a headache may signal a serious illness, refer to the self-care guide in Appendix B.

While major life changes are undoubtedly stressful, they seldom occur regularly. Psychologist Richard Lazarus has proposed that minor problems—life's daily hassles—can be an even greater source of stress because they occur much more often. People who perceive hassles negatively are likely to experience a moderate stress response every time they are faced with one. Over time, this can take a significant toll on health. Researchers have found that for some people daily hassles contribute to a general decrease in overall wellness. Remember, stress levels and coping abilities contribute to overall allostatic load.

College Stressors

College is a time of major life changes and abundant minor hassles. You will be learning new information and skills and making major decisions about your future. You may be away from home for the first time, or you may be adding extra responsibilities to a life already filled with job and family.

Academic Stressors Exams, grades, and choosing a major are among the many academic stressors faced by college students. In addition to an increased workload compared to that in high school, many students are unpleasantly surprised by the more rigorous evaluation of their work in college. Higher-quality efforts are expected of college students, so earning good grades takes more effort and dedication. Careful planning and preparation can help make academic stressors more predictable and manageable. Techniques for overcoming test anxiety, a common stress-related academic problem, are described in the Behavior Change Strategy at the end of the chapter.

Students close to graduation may find themselves faced with the need to plan for life after college—a potentially daunting task. Remember that you'll have many opportunities to change career paths in the future and that the training and life experience gained from one path can often be transferred to other endeavors.

In Focus

What Stresses Us Out?

In January 2006 the American Psychological Association, the National Women's Health Resource Center, and iVillage.com conducted a survey to determine Americans' leading sources of stress. Here are the results:

Money	59%
Work	59%
Health of parents or other family members	53%
Personal health concerns	50%
State of the world	50%
Health of spouse, partner, or children	48%
Children	41%

The same respondents reported the following physical or emotional problems related to their stress:

Nervousness/sadness	59%
Sleep problems	56%
Lack of interest, motivation, energy	55%
Fatigue	51%
Muscular tension	48%
Headaches	46%
Change in appetite	37%
Upset stomach/indigestion	32%
Tightness in chest	26%

Interpersonal Stressors The college years often involve potential stressors such as establishing new relationships and balancing multiple roles—student, employee, friend, spouse, parent, and so on. Social engagements may be exhilarating for some and painful for others. Viewed as an exciting challenge or an odious necessity, interacting with others involves attention, on-the-spot decision making, and energy expenditure—and it's stressful. Be yourself, go with the flow, and try not to be overly concerned with being liked by everyone you meet.

Time-Related Pressures Time pressures are a problem for most students, but they may be particularly acute for those who also have job and family responsibilities. Most people do have enough time to fulfill all of their responsibilities but fail to manage their time or their priorities effectively. For these people, it's important to make a plan and *stick to it*. Strategies for effective time management are described in the next section.

Financial Concerns As young adults leave home and become independent, financial responsibilities such as paying tuition, taking out loans, and managing living expenses are likely to arise. A financial budget is as important as effective time management for successfully dealing with college stress. Create a financial plan for each upcoming month or term so you can put your mind more at ease and concentrate on your studies.

Stressors Among Nontraditional Students Nontraditional students can be defined as individuals who, in addition to attending college, are married, a parent, a caretaker for an older family member, a full-time worker, and/or retraining for a new career. According to the National Center for Education Statistics, about 70% of undergraduates meet at least one of these criteria. Nontraditional students must often contend with the stress of increased responsibilities compared with traditional students, who are typically younger and have fewer demands on their time. Interestingly, nontraditional students have been shown to have higher class attendance, less worry about academic performance, and greater enjoyment of homework; they are more likely to report concern about family responsibilities. Traditional students report being more concerned with social and peer relationships.

Greater social support, especially from family and friends, is a stress buffer for married students and is related to better academic adjustment, personal and social adjustment, and commitment to college. However, married college students express greater marital distress than married couples not attending college. Married graduate students report more satisfaction with their educational programs but less satisfaction with their social and extracurricular activities, whereas commuting couples report less satisfaction with the time they are able to spend with their spouses compared with noncommuting couples. Time pressures may be especially severe for nontraditional students, so time-management strategies may be of particular importance.

Job-Related Stressors

Tight work schedules and overtime contribute to time-related pressures. Worries about job performance, salary, and job security are a source of stress for some people. Interactions with bosses, coworkers, and customers can also contribute to stress. High levels of job stress are also common for people who are left out of important decisions relating to their jobs. When workers are given the opportunity to shape how their jobs are performed, job satisfaction goes up and stress levels go down.

If job-related (or college-related) stress is severe or chronic, the result can be **burnout**, a state of physical, mental, and emotional exhaustion. Burnout occurs most often in highly motivated and driven individuals who feel that their work is not recognized or that they are not accomplishing their goals. People in the helping professions—teachers, social workers, caregivers, police officers, and so on—are also prone to burnout. For some who suffer from burnout, a vacation or leave of absence may be appropriate. For others, a reduced work schedule, better communication

Term

VW **burnout** A state of physical, mental, and emotional exhaustion.

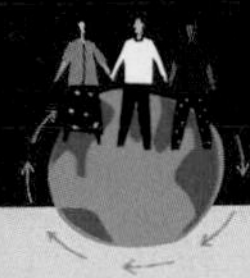

Dimensions of Diversity

Diverse Populations, Discrimination, and Stress

Stress is universal, but within the United States, a nation defined by its diversity, some groups face unique stressors and have higher-than-average rates of stress-related physical and emotional problems. These groups include ethnic minorities and people with low incomes, disabilities, or atypical gender identities or sexual orientations. Many of the unique stressors that affect special populations stem from prejudice—biased, negative attitudes toward a group of people.

Discrimination occurs when people act according to their prejudices; it can be blatant or subtle. Blatant examples of discrimination are not common, but they are major stressors akin to significant life changes. Examples include a swastika painted on a Jewish studies house, the defacement of a sculpture honoring the achievements of a gay artist, and bullying of poor children because they wear the same clothes to school each day. Subtler acts may occur much more frequently. For example, an African American student in a mostly white college town feels that shopkeepers are keeping an eye on him; a male-to-female transgendered individual believes she has been "clocked" (discovered) and treated with less respect by her professors and peers; a student using a wheelchair has difficulty with narrow aisles and high counters at local stores; and an obese executive is asked to purchase two seats on his business flights. Some of these social stressors are unique to certain groups, and it may be difficult for other people to understand how serious such stressors can be.

Recent immigrants to the United States must begin new lives in a new society; the stress associated with this process is called *acculturation stress*. Successful integration into a new society can occur in an open society where immigrants are free to retain any aspect of their cultural heritage and their native social customs and beliefs are valued. If there is great pressure to assimilate, minority immigrant groups may become disconnected from both their own culture and that of the host culture; marginalized groups can be targets of significant discrimination, even violence. Different immigrant groups experience variations in accultural stressors. For example, language barriers and limited formal education may make employment more difficult for some groups. In other groups, intense pressure is put on immigrant children to do well in school and enter high-paying professions to boost the honor and position of the family; these high expectations can be a source of stress, guilt, and alienation from the family.

Minorities often face additional job- and school-related stressors because of stereotypes and discrimination. They make less money than whites in comparable jobs and with comparable levels of education, and they may find it more difficult to achieve leadership positions. Many ethnic minorities must develop basic skills that natives of the host nation take for granted; for example, learning to speak English, balancing ancestral and American cultures, and finding employment sufficient to pay for basic necessities. All these types of stressors can contribute to higher levels of stress-related health problems among minorities.

On a positive note, many people who experience hardship, disability, or prejudice develop effective, goal-directed coping skills and are successful at overcoming obstacles and managing the increased stress they face. Resiliency, hopeful expectations for the future, and spiritual wellness all support successful coping.

with superiors, or a change in job goals may be necessary. Improving time-management skills can also help.

Problems at work are associated with health complaints. Some 32.9 million working days are lost annually from people taking time off because of illness. Mood and sleep disturbances, upset stomachs, headaches, and disturbed relationships with family and friends are examples of stress-related problems that are quick to develop, but the effects of job stress on chronic diseases are more difficult to see because chronic diseases take a long time to develop and can be influenced by many factors other than job stress. However, it is important to note that health care expenditures are nearly 50% greater for workers who report high levels of stress.

Employers are becoming more aware that unhealthy behaviors such as smoking and a sedentary lifestyle adversely affect the health and productivity of their employees and, ultimately, the bottom line. As a result, some employers are providing their employees with a variety of worksite-based health promotion and disease prevention programs, including stress-management programs. Worksite programs have been shown to improve employee health, increase productivity, and yield a significant return on investment for the employer.

Social Stressors

Social networks that affect stress may be real or virtual; each type can help boost your ability to deal with the stress in your life or can itself become a stressor.

Real Social Networks Although social support is a key buffer against stress, your interactions with others can themselves be a source of stress. As mentioned earlier, the college years are often a time of great change in interpersonal relationships. The community and society in which you live can also be major sources of stress. Social stressors include prejudice and discrimination. You may feel stress as you try to relate to people of other ethnic or socioeconomic groups. If you are a member of a minority ethnic group, you may feel pressure to assimilate into mainstream society. If English is not your first language, you face the added burden of conducting daily activities in a language with which you may not be completely comfortable. All of these pressures can become significant sources of stress. (See the box "Diverse Populations, Discrimination, and Stress" for more information.)

In the News

Coping After Terrorism or Natural Disasters

The United States has seen numerous disasters in recent years. Acts of terrorism—such as the Oklahoma City bombing in 1995 and the attacks of September 11, 2001—are seared into Americans' memory. Natural disasters such as Hurricanes Katrina and Rita, which hit the Gulf Coast in August 2005, caused devastation that will take years to clean up.

Nearly 3000 people died in the 9/11 attacks; hundreds were left homeless. Hurricane Katrina, the most devastating natural disaster in U.S. history, left 2.5 million residents without homes, transportation, or jobs. In a few hours, Katrina killed more than 1800 people and did an estimated $200 billion in damage to the U.S. economy. A year later, an estimated 500,000 residents in the area were said to still need mental health assistance.

Katrina also displaced as many as 100,000 college students. Several Southern colleges were heavily damaged and had to close their doors in order to recover, leaving students with nowhere to live or study.

People react to disasters in different ways. Even people not directly affected by a disaster may still suffer emotional reactions simply from watching endless coverage in the media. Responses can include disbelief, shock, fear, anger, resentment, anxiety, trouble concentrating or making decisions, mood swings, irritability, sadness, depression, panic, guilt, apathy, feelings of isolation or powerlessness, and many of the symptoms of excess stress (see the box on p. 33). While most people recover, some develop posttraumatic stress disorder (PTSD), a more serious condition. See Chapter 3 for information about PTSD.

If you are affected by a traumatic event, take these steps:

- Immediately after the event, pause and assess your situation.
- Allow yourself to mourn for others.
- Share your experiences and feelings with others. Be a supportive listener.
- Reassure children of their safety and remind them that they are not at fault.
- Take a break from media coverage, especially if you feel overwhelmed by it.
- Help others in any way you can, whether through financial contributions, participating in food or clothing drives, or volunteering to work with victims.
- Take care of yourself by eating a healthy diet, getting enough sleep, and using the stress-relief techniques discussed in this chapter.

If you still feel overwhelmed by emotion weeks later, consider getting professional help.

If you are displaced by a disaster—especially if you are a young adult living on your own for the first time—take the following steps as quickly as possible:

- Determine what you can control. Focus your efforts on those issues.
- Seek help immediately for important problems you cannot control. For example, local or national agencies may be on hand to provide basic necessities, transportation, or financial aid.
- Reach out to others affected by the event. Share, listen, and look for ways to offer support.
- Stay in touch with family. If possible, living with a relative or returning home may be a good short-term solution.
- Look for resources. For example, thousands of colleges welcomed students displaced by Katrina. Many offered free tuition, free housing, tutoring, and aid with other essentials. Schools reached out to displaced students online, in the media, and through teachers and counselors in the disaster area.

You can give yourself greater control in a disaster if you have an emergency plan. Create one that works for you; share it with people who are close to you. Organizations such as the Red Cross (http://www.redcross.org) offer resources that can help you prepare such a plan.

Virtual Social Networks New technologies can potentially be time-savers because we don't have to go home or to the office to check our e-mail or phone messages, and we can call on a cell phone rather than jot down notes to pass on at a later time. Telecommuting can ease the time pressures on people who find it necessary to work from home, such as parents with young children or people with disabilities. However, increased electronic interactivity can also impinge on our personal space, waste time, and cause stress. For example, count the number of times you check for e-mail or voice messages and find that you have none, or the times you are interrupted by messages that are relatively meaningless. If your instructor or supervisor knows that you are not tied to a land line, he or she may expect a greater degree of communication and the ability to meet unusual deadlines. If you are experiencing information overload, learn to use multimedia devices wisely. Give out your phone number only when it is absolutely necessary. Schedule times when you completely sever your electronic ties. Consider the financial savings that may arise from less frequent cell phone use.

Environmental Stressors

Claire loves the food at a certain restaurant, but she always feels "on edge" when eating there because of continuous loud background music. This is an example of an environmental stressor—some condition or event in the physical environment that causes stress. Environmental stressors include natural disasters, acts of violence, industrial accidents, and intrusive noises, smells, or sights. Like the loud music that bothers Claire, some environmental stressors are mere inconveniences that are easy to avoid. Others, such as pollen season for a hayfever sufferer or living next to a construction site, may be an unavoidable daily source of stress. For those who live in poor or violent neighborhoods or in a war-torn country, environmental stressors can be major life stressors (see the box "Coping After Terrorism or Natural Disasters").

Internal Stressors

Some stressors are found not in our environment but within ourselves. We pressure ourselves to reach goals and continuously evaluate our progress and performance. Setting goals and striving to reach them can enhance self-esteem if the goals are reasonable. However, unrealistic expectations can be a significant source of stress and can damage self-esteem. Other internal stressors are physical and emotional states such as illness and exhaustion; these can be both a cause and an effect of unmanaged stress.

Exercise is a particularly effective antidote to stress.

TECHNIQUES FOR MANAGING STRESS

What can you do about all this stress? A great deal. By shoring up your social support systems; improving your communication skills; developing and maintaining healthy exercise, eating, and sleeping habits; and learning to identify and moderate individual stressors, you can control the stress in your life. The effort is well worth the time: People who manage stress effectively not only are healthier but have more time to enjoy life and accomplish goals.

Social Support

Sharing fears, frustrations, and joys makes life richer and seems to contribute to the well-being of body and mind. Research supports this conclusion. One study of college students living in overcrowded apartments, for example, found that those with a strong social support system were less distressed by their cramped quarters than were the loners who navigated life's challenges on their own. Young adults who have strong relationships with their parents tend to cope with stress better than peers with poor parental relationships. Participation in a support group has been shown to improve the emotional health of cancer patients. Other studies have shown that married people live longer than single people and have lower death rates from a wide range of conditions. People in high-stress jobs fare better if they also have a supportive spouse. These workers tend to have lower blood pressure than workers with similar job-related stress but less supportive spouses. People with a strong social support system are also better able to withstand the stress of major life changes.

Allow yourself time to nourish and maintain a network of people you can count on for emotional support, feedback, and nurturance. Consider becoming a volunteer to help build your social support system and enhance your spiritual wellness. To evaluate your current social support system and to find strategies for strengthening your social ties, refer to the box "Healthy Connections" on page 48.

Communication

Do you often find yourself angry at others? Some people express their anger directly by yelling or being aggressive; others express anger indirectly by excessively criticizing others or making cynical comments. A person who is angry with others often has difficulty forming and maintaining successful social relationships. Better communication skills can help: Learn to listen to others and to express your needs and desires nonaggressively. Increase your communication skills in order to decrease stress in your relationships—at school, at work, and at home.

At the other extreme, you may suppress your feelings and needs entirely. You may have trouble saying no and allow people to take advantage of you. Many businesses encourage employees to take assertiveness training workshops to help them overcome shyness and resistance to communicating their needs. Such communication skills are also valuable in social relationships. (For a fuller discussion of how to enhance communication and resolve interpersonal conflicts, see Chapters 3 and 4.)

Exercise

Exercise helps maintain a healthy body and mind and even stimulates the birth of new brain cells. Regular physical activity can reduce various aspects of stress as well. One recent study found that taking a long walk can help decrease anxiety and blood pressure. Another study found that just a brisk 10-minute walk leaves people feeling more relaxed and energetic for up to 2 hours. People who exercise regularly react with milder physical stress responses before, during, and after exposure to stressors. People who took three brisk 45-minute walks a week

Mind/Body/Spirit

Healthy Connections

Meaningful connections with others can play a key role in stress management and overall wellness. A sense of isolation can lead to chronic stress, which in turn can increase your susceptibility to temporary illnesses like colds and to chronic illnesses like heart disease. Although the mechanism isn't clear, social isolation can be as significant to mortality rates as factors like smoking, high blood pressure, and obesity.

There is no single best pattern of social support that works for everyone. However, research suggests that having a variety of types of relationships may be important for wellness. To help determine whether your social network measures up, answer true or false for each of the following statements.

T/F 1. If I needed an emergency loan of $100, there is someone I could get it from.

T/F 2. There is someone who takes pride in my accomplishments.

T/F 3. I often meet or talk with family or friends.

T/F 4. Most people I know think highly of me.

T/F 5. If I needed an early morning ride to the airport, there's no one I would feel comfortable asking to take me.

T/F 6. I feel there is no one with whom I can share my most private worries and fears.

T/F 7. Most of my friends are more successful making changes in their life than I am.

T/F 8. I would have a hard time finding someone to go with me on a day trip to the beach or country.

To calculate your score, add the number of true answers to questions 1–4 and the number of false answers to questions 5–8. If your score is 4 or more, you should have enough support to protect your health. If your score is 3 or less, you may need to reach out. There are a variety of things you can do to strengthen your social ties:

- *Foster friendships.* Keep in regular contact with your friends. Offer respect, trust, and acceptance, and provide help and support in times of need. Express appreciation for your friends.
- *Keep your family ties strong.* Stay in touch with the family members you feel close to. Participate in family activities and celebrations. If your family doesn't function well as a support system for its members, create a second "family" of people with whom you have built meaningful ties.
- *Get involved with a group.* Do volunteer work, take a class, attend a lecture series, join a religious group. These types of activities can give you a sense of security, a place to talk about your feelings or concerns, and a way to build new friendships. Choose activities that are meaningful to you and that include direct involvement with other people.
- *Build your communication skills.* The more you share your feelings with others, the closer the bonds between you will become. When others are speaking, be a considerate and attentive listener. (Chapters 3 and 4 include more information on effective communication.)

Individual relationships change over the course of your life, but it's never too late to build friendships or become more involved in your community. Your investment of time and energy in your social network will pay off—in a brighter outlook now, and in better health and well-being for the future.

SOURCE: Friends can be good medicine. 1998. As found in the *Mind/Body Newsletter* 7(1): 3–6. Center for the Advancement of Health; Quiz from Japenga, A. 1995. A Family of Friends. *Health*, November/December, 1994. Adapted with permission. Copyright © 2001 *Health*® magazine. For subscriptions please call 800-274-2522.

for 3 months reported that they perceived fewer daily hassles. Their sense of wellness also increased.

These findings are not surprising since, as stated earlier, the stress response mobilizes energy resources and readies the body for physical emergencies. If you experience stress and do not physically exert yourself, you are not completing the energy cycle. You may not be able to exercise while your daily stressors occur—during class, for example, or while sitting in a traffic jam—but you can be active later in the day. Physical activity allows you to expend the nervous energy you have built up and trains your body to more readily achieve homeostasis following future disturbances in normal functioning.

It's not hard to incorporate light to moderate exercise into your day. Walk to class or bike to the store instead of driving. Use the stairs instead of the elevator. Take a walk with a friend instead of getting a cup of coffee. Go bowling, play tennis, or roller-skate instead of seeing a movie. Make a habit of taking a brisk after-dinner stroll. Plan hikes and easy bike outings for the weekends.

Consider taking a class in a kind of exercise you've always wanted to try, such as yoga, t'ai chi, square dancing, or fencing. The important thing is to find an activity that you enjoy, so it can become a habit and thereby an effective stress reducer. Chapter 13 presents guidelines for creating an exercise program to fit your individual needs and preferences.

Nutrition

A healthy diet will give you an energy bank to draw on whenever you experience stress. Eating wisely also will enhance your feelings of self-control and self-esteem. Learning the principles of sound nutrition is easy, and sensible eating habits rapidly become second nature when practiced regularly. (For more on sound nutrition, see Chapter 12.)

Avoiding or limiting caffeine is also important in stress management. Although one or two cups of coffee a day probably won't hurt you, caffeine is a mildly addictive stimulant that leaves some people jittery, irritable, and unable to sleep. Consuming caffeine during stressful situations can raise blood pressure and increase levels of cortisol. Tea, cola, some other soft drinks, chocolate, and more than a thousand over-the-counter drugs, including cold remedies, aspirin, and weight-loss preparations, also contain caffeine, sometimes in high doses.

Sleep

Lack of sleep can be both a cause and an effect of excess stress. Without sufficient sleep, our mental and physical processes steadily deteriorate. We get headaches, feel irritable, are unable to concentrate, forget things, and may be more susceptible to weight gain and illness. Levels of the stress hormones in the bloodstream vary throughout the day and are related to sleep patterns. Peak concentrations occur in the early morning, followed by a slow decline during the day and evening. Concentrations return to peak during the final stages of sleep and in the early morning hours. Acute sleep deprivation slows the daytime decline in stress hormones, so evening levels are higher than normal. A decrease in total sleep time also causes an increase in the release of stress hormones. Together, these changes may cause an increase in stress hormone levels throughout the day and may contribute to mental and physical deterioration. Fatigue and sleep deprivation are major factors in many fatal car, truck, and train crashes. Extreme sleep deprivation can lead to hallucinations and other psychotic symptoms as well as to a significant increase in heart attack risk.

According to the National Sleep Foundation's 2005 Sleep in America Poll, adults sleep an average of 6.8 hours on weeknights and slightly more on weekends. Most adults need 7–9 hours of sleep every night to stay healthy and perform their best. Adequate sleep improves mood, fosters feelings of competence and self-worth, and supports optimal mental and emotional functioning. If you are sleep-deprived, sleeping extra hours may significantly improve your daytime alertness and mental abilities.

Sleep occurs in two phases: rapid eye movement (REM) and non-REM. Non-REM sleep consists of four stages of successively deeper sleep, during which blood pressure, heart rate, temperature, and breathing rate drop, growth hormone is released, and brain wave patterns become slow and even. REM sleep, during which dreams occur, is characterized by the rapid back-and-forth movement of the eyes under closed eyelids. Heart rate, blood pressure, and breathing rate increase; brain activity increases to levels equal to or greater than those during waking hours. Muscles in the limbs relax completely, causing temporary paralysis and preventing the sleeper from acting out her or his dreams. A sleeper goes through several cycles of non-REM and REM sleep each night. Stress hormone levels are low during deep sleep and increase during REM sleep. The increase in REM sleep duration with each sleep cycle may underlie the progressive increase in circulating stress hormones during the final stages of sleep.

An April 2006 report by the Institute of Medicine said 50–70 million Americans suffer from chronic sleep disorders. More than 50% of adults have trouble falling asleep or staying asleep—a condition known as insomnia. The most common causes of insomnia are lifestyle factors, such as high caffeine or alcohol intake before bedtime; medical problems, such as a breathing disorder; and psychological stress. About 75% of people who suffer chronic insomnia report some stressful life event at the onset of their sleep problem. If you suffer from sleeping problems, try some of the strategies in the box "Overcoming Insomnia" on page 50.

Time Management

A surprising number of the stressors relate to time. Many people never seem to have enough time. Learning to manage your time is crucial to coping with the stressors you face every day. Three common factors that negatively impact time management for college students are perfectionism, overcommitment, and procrastination.

Perfectionism is the need to constantly improve a project, situation, or personal trait. It is frequently based on a self-deprecating fear of failure or harsh judgment by friends or family. Student perfectionists often spend an inordinate amount of time rewriting papers, reorganizing notes, and rearranging their work space to the point that they sacrifice social interaction and sleep. Perfectionists will torture themselves for getting an A-minus instead of an A on a test rather than congratulate themselves on a job well done. They will appraise the situation negatively using "should" statements: "I should have studied an hour more each night," "I shouldn't have taken so much time off last weekend," and so on. There is no such thing as perfection, so perfectionists are striving for unreachable goals. This unfulfilled effort increases stress and compromises time spent on other academic projects and social functions that are integral to a fulfilling college experience. If perfectionism is a problem for you, try not to put so much pressure on yourself. Focus on doing your best rather than trying to be the best. College is not a competition; it is a setting for personal growth. Accept your limits and try not to expect so much of yourself or others.

Overcommitters are less concerned with the quality of their efforts. Instead, they take on project after project and activity after activity because they find it difficult to say no or to accurately assess their current workload. Being well-rounded is admirable, but there is only so much one person can do. Overcommitters often feel they are missing

Take Charge

Overcoming Insomnia

Most people can overcome insomnia by discovering the cause of poor sleep and taking steps to remedy it. Insomnia that lasts for more than 6 months and interferes with daytime functioning requires consultation with a physician. Sleeping pills are not recommended for chronic insomnia because they can be habit-forming; they also lose their effectiveness over time.

If you're bothered by insomnia, try the following:

- Determine how much sleep you need to feel refreshed the next day, and don't sleep longer than that.
- Go to bed at the same time every night and, more important, get up at the same time every morning, 7 days a week, regardless of how much sleep you got. Don't nap during the day.
- Exercise every day, but not too close to bedtime. Your metabolism takes up to 6 hours to slow down after exercise.
- Avoid tobacco and caffeine late in the day, and alcohol before bedtime (it causes disturbed, fragmented sleep).
- If you take any medications (prescription or not), ask your doctor or pharmacist if they are known to interfere with sleep.
- Have a light snack before bedtime; you'll sleep better if you're not hungry.
- Use your bed only for sleep. Don't eat, read, study, or watch television in bed.
- Relax before bedtime with a warm bath (again, not too close to bedtime—allow about 2 hours for your metabolism to slow down afterward), a book, music, or relaxation exercises. Don't lie down in bed until you're sleepy.
- If you don't fall asleep in 15–20 minutes, or if you wake up and can't fall asleep again, get out of bed, leave the room if possible, and do something monotonous until you feel sleepy. Try distracting yourself with imagery instead of counting sheep; imagine yourself on a pleasant vacation or enjoying some beautiful scenery.
- If sleep problems persist, ask your physician for a referral to a sleep specialist in your area. You may be a candidate for a sleep study—an overnight evaluation of your sleep pattern that can uncover many sleep-related disorders.

out when they say no to something, and they often don't fully experience many college activities because they don't take the time to immerse themselves in any one thing.

Procrastination—putting something off until later—is a problem for many people. People who put off key tasks and decisions may sabotage personal relationships, college life, careers, and health. Although reasons for procrastination vary, it often camouflages self-doubt, an unreasonable desire for perfection, or a reluctance to make changes. People who set impossibly high standards for themselves may actually protect their self-esteem by procrastinating; if they fail to complete a project, for example, their work will never be evaluated.

If procrastination or another time-related stressor is a problem for you, try some or all of the following strategies for managing your time more productively and creatively:

- *Set priorities.* Divide your tasks into three groups: essential, important, and trivial. Focus on the first two. Ignore the third.
- *Schedule tasks for peak efficiency.* You've undoubtedly noticed you're most productive at certain times of the day (or night). Schedule as many of your tasks for those hours as you can, and stick to your schedule.
- *Set realistic goals, and write them down.* Attainable goals spur you on. Impossible goals, by definition, cause frustration and failure. Fully commit yourself to achieving your goals by putting them in writing.
- *Budget enough time.* For each project you undertake, calculate how long it will take to complete. Then tack on another 10–15%, or even 25%, as a buffer against mistakes, interruptions, or unanticipated problems.
- *Break down long-term goals into short-term ones.* Instead of waiting for or relying on large blocks of time, use short amounts of time to start a project or keep it moving. Say you have a 50-page report due and are about to panic. Divide the assignment into three tasks: research, outlining, and writing. Then budget enough time slots (of half an hour or an hour) to complete each task. Your steady progress will make you feel so much better that you'll be encouraged to continue.
- *Visualize the achievement of your goals.* By mentally rehearsing your performance of a task, you will be able to reach your goal more smoothly.
- *Keep track of the tasks you put off.* Analyze the reasons why you procrastinate. If the task is difficult or unpleasant, look for ways to make it easier or more fun. If you hate cleaning up your room, break the work into 10-minute tasks and do a little at a time. If you find the readings for one of your classes particularly difficult, choose an especially nice setting for your reading and then reward yourself each time you complete a section or chapter.
- *Consider doing your least favorite tasks first.* Once you have the most unpleasant tasks out of the way, you can have fun with the projects you enjoy more.
- *Consolidate tasks when possible.* For example, try walking to the store so that you run your errands and exercise in the same block of time.

- *Identify quick transitional tasks.* Keep a list of 5-minute tasks you can do while waiting or between other tasks, such as watering your plants, doing the dishes, or checking a homework assignment.
- *Delegate responsibility.* Asking for help when you have too much to do is no cop-out; it's good time management. Just don't delegate to others the jobs you know you should do yourself, such as researching a paper.
- *Say no when necessary.* If the demands made on you don't seem reasonable, say no—tactfully, but without guilt or apology.
- *Give yourself a break.* Allow time for play—free, unstructured time when you ignore the clock. Don't consider this a waste of time. Play renews you and enables you to work more efficiently.
- *Stop thinking or talking about what you're going to do, and just do it!* Sometimes the best solution for procrastination is to stop waiting for the right moment and just get started. You will probably find that things are not as bad as you feared, and your momentum will keep you going.

Strive for Greater Spirituality

Spirituality involves a high level of faith and commitment with respect to a well-defined worldview or belief system that gives a sense of meaning and purpose to existence. Spirituality also provides an ethical path to personal fulfillment that includes connectedness with self, others, and a higher power or larger reality. Overall, there appears to be a positive relationship between spirituality and adaptive coping, suggesting that aspects of spirituality and spiritual practices can play a significant role as a personal resource for coping. Spirituality can be enhanced through many activities, including participation in organized religion, spending time in nature or working on environmental issues, helping others, and engaging in personal spiritual practices such as prayer or meditation.

Despite the benefits of developing spiritual wellness, an ongoing survey of first-year college students found that the goal of succeeding financially has reached its highest point in over a decade, but the desire to "develop a meaningful philosophy of life" has dropped to its lowest point in the history of the survey. On a more positive note, the same survey found high levels of volunteerism among college students. Through volunteering and engaging in personal spiritual practices, we may gain meaning, direction, purpose in life, and a greater sense of connectedness.

Confide in Yourself Through Writing

Confiding in others can help maintain physical and psychological health following a major life trauma. Keeping a diary is analogous to confiding in others, except that you are confiding in yourself. This form of coping with severe stress may be especially helpful for those who are shy or introverted and find it difficult to open up to others. Although writing about traumatic and stressful events may have a short-term negative effect on mood, over the long term, stress may be reduced and positive changes in health occur. A key to promoting beneficial results with respect to health and well-being through journaling is to write about one's emotional responses to a stressful event. Set aside a special time each day or week to journal your feelings about stressful events in your life.

Cognitive Techniques

Some stressors arise in our own minds. Ideas, beliefs, perceptions, and patterns of thinking can add to our stress level. Each of the following techniques can help you change unhealthy thought patterns to ones that will help you cope with stress. As with any skill, mastering these techniques takes practice and patience.

Think and Act Constructively Worrying, someone once said, is like shoveling smoke. Think back to the worries you had last week. How many of them were needless? Think about things you *can* control. Try to stand aside from the problem, consider the positive steps you can take to solve it, and then carry them out. Remember, successful prediction of a stressful event is a major factor determining the magnitude of the stress response. In the evening, try to predict stressful events you might encounter the following day. Will you see someone who makes you feel uncomfortable? If so, decide now how you will interact with that person. Will you attend a class that doesn't hold your attention? Develop a strategy now that will help you maintain focus. Will you have to wait in line to register or buy tickets? If so, plan to pass the time by listening to music to relax or by catching up on some reading.

Take Control A situation often feels more stressful if you feel you're not in control of it. Time may seem to be slipping away before a big exam, for example. Unexpected obstacles may appear in your path, throwing you off course. When you feel your environment is controlling you instead of the other way around, take charge! Concentrate on what is possible to control, and set realistic goals. Be confident of your ability to succeed.

Problem-Solve Students with greater problem-solving abilities report greater adjustment to university life, higher motivation levels, lower stress levels while studying, and, on average, higher grades. When you find yourself stewing over a problem, take a moment to sit down with a piece of paper and go through a formal process of problem solving. Within a few minutes you can generate a plan. Try this approach:

1. Define the problem in one or two sentences.
2. Identify the causes of the problem.

Managing the many commitments of adult life—including work, school, and parenthood—can sometimes feel overwhelming and produce a great deal of stress. Time-management and problem-solving skills, including careful scheduling with a date book or handheld computer, can help people cope with busy days.

3. Consider alternative solutions; don't just stop with the most obvious one.
4. Weigh positive and negative consequences for each alternative.
5. Make a decision—choose a solution.
6. Make a list of what you will need to do to act on your decision.
7. Begin to carry out your list; if you're unable to do that, temporarily turn to other things.
8. Evaluate the outcome and revise your approach if necessary.

Modify Your Expectations Expectations are exhausting and restricting. The fewer expectations you have, the more you can live spontaneously and joyfully. The more you expect from others, the more often you will feel let down. And trying to meet the expectations others have of you is often futile.

Maintain Positivity If you catch your mind beating up on you—"Late for class again! You can't even cope with college! How do you expect to ever hold down a professional job?"—change your inner dialogue. Talk to yourself as you would to a child you love: "You're a smart, capable person. You've solved other problems; you'll handle this one. Tomorrow you'll simply schedule things so you get to class with a few minutes to spare." (Chapter 3 has more information on self-talk.)

Cultivate Your Sense of Humor When it comes to stress, laughter may be the best medicine. Even a fleeting smile produces changes in your autonomic nervous system that can lift your spirits. And a few minutes of belly laughing can be as invigorating as brisk exercise. Hearty laughter elevates your heart rate, aids digestion, eases pain, and triggers the release of endorphins and other pleasurable and stimulating chemicals in the brain. After a good laugh, your muscles go slack; your pulse and blood pressure dip below normal. You are relaxed. Cultivate the ability to laugh at yourself, and you'll have a handy and instantly effective stress reliever.

- Keep a humor journal. Write down funny things that you and others say, including unintentional slips of the tongue. Collect clever sayings that make you smile.
- Look at newspaper and magazine cartoons. Cut out those you find particularly funny and add them to your humor journal.
- Collect some funny props—clown noses, "arrow" headbands, Groucho glasses—that you can put on the next time you feel stressed or anxious. Or simply try making funny faces in front of a mirror.
- Watch funny films and television programs. In a study of college students, those who watched an episode of *Seinfeld* prior to giving an impromptu speech were less anxious and had a lower heart rate than those who didn't watch the program.

Weed Out Trivia A major source of stress is trying to store too much data. Forget unimportant details (they will usually be self-evident) and organize important information. One technique you can try is to "chunk" the important material into categories. If your next exam covers three chapters from your textbook, consider each chapter a chunk of information. Then break down each chunk into its three or four most important features. Create a mental outline that allows you to trace your way from the most general category down to the most specific details. This technique can be applied to managing daily responsibilities as well. Break down your daily tasks into three or four categories, such as academics, family and friends, fitness, and daily living. For each, list the three most important items for the day. Items on the family and friends list might include caring for a child, calling home, and helping a classmate; your daily living items might be going to the dentist, buying gas, and shopping for dinner. Cross items off your mental outline as you complete them to free up memory and attention for the unexpected.

Live in the Present Do you clog your mind by reliving past events? Clinging to experiences and emotions, particularly unpleasant ones, can be a deadly business. Clear your mind of the old debris; let it go. Free yourself to enjoy life today.

Go with the Flow Remember that the branch that bends in the storm doesn't break. Try to flow with your life, accepting the things you can't change. Be forgiving of faults, your own and those of others. Instead of anticipating happiness at some indefinite point in the future, realize that pleasure is integral to being alive. You can create it every day of your life. View challenges as an opportunity to learn and grow. Be flexible. In this way, you can make stress work for you rather than against you, enhancing your overall wellness.

Relaxation Techniques

First identified and described by Herbert Benson of the Harvard Medical School, the **relaxation response** is a physiological state characterized by a feeling of warmth and quiet mental alertness. This is the opposite of the fight-or-flight reaction. When the relaxation response is triggered by a relaxation technique, heart rate, breathing, and metabolism slow down. Blood pressure and oxygen consumption decrease. At the same time, blood flow to the brain and skin increases, and brain waves shift from an alert beta rhythm to a relaxed alpha rhythm. Practiced regularly, relaxation techniques can counteract the debilitating effects of stress.

If you decide to try a relaxation technique, practice it daily until it becomes natural to you, and then use it whenever you feel the need. You may feel calmer and more refreshed after each session. If one technique doesn't seem to work well enough for you after you've given it a good try, try another one. You'll know you've mastered a deep relaxation technique when you start to see subtle changes in other areas of your life: You may notice you've been encountering fewer hassles, working more efficiently, or enjoying more free time. None of the techniques takes long to do—for instance, just a few minutes away from the TV should do the trick.

Progressive Relaxation Unlike most of the others, this simple method requires no imagination, willpower, or self-suggestion. You simply tense, and then relax, the muscles in your body, group by group. The technique, also known as deep muscle relaxation, helps you become aware of the muscle tension that occurs when you're under stress. When you consciously relax those muscles, other systems of the body get the message and ease up on the stress response.

Start, for example, with your right fist. Inhale as you tense it. Exhale as you relax it. Repeat. Next, contract and relax your right upper arm. Repeat. Do the same with your left arm. Then, beginning at your forehead and ending at your feet, contract and relax your other muscle groups. Repeat each contraction at least once, breathing in as you tense, breathing out as you relax. To speed up the process, tense and relax more muscles at one time—both arms simultaneously, for instance. With practice, you'll be able to relax very quickly and effectively by clenching and releasing only your fists.

Visualization Also known as using imagery, **visualization** lets you daydream without guilt. Athletes find that the technique enhances sports performance, and visualization is even part of the curriculum at U.S. Olympic training camps. You can use visualization to help you relax, change your habits, or perform well—whether on an exam, a stage, or a playing field.

Next time you feel stressed, close your eyes. Imagine yourself floating on a cloud, sitting on a mountaintop, or lying in a meadow. What do you see and hear? Is it cold out? Or damp? What do you smell? What do you taste? Involve all your senses. Your body will respond as if your imagery were real. An alternative: Close your eyes and imagine a deep purple light filling your body. Now change the color into a soothing gold. As the color lightens, so should your distress.

Visualization can also be used to rehearse for an upcoming event and enhance performance. By experiencing an event ahead of time in your mind, you can practice coping with any difficulties that may arise. Think positively, and you can "psych yourself up" for a successful experience.

Meditation The need to periodically stop our incessant mental chatter is so great that, from ancient times, hundreds of forms of **meditation** have developed in cultures all over the world. Meditation is a way of telling the mind to be quiet for a while. Because meditation has been at the core of many Eastern religions and philosophies, it has acquired an "Eastern" mystique that has caused some people to shy away from it. Yet meditation requires no special knowledge or background. Whatever philosophical, religious, or emotional reasons may be given for

Terms

VW

relaxation response A physiological state characterized by a feeling of warmth and quiet mental alertness.

visualization A technique for promoting relaxation or improving performance that involves creating or re-creating vivid mental pictures of a place or an experience; also called *imagery*.

meditation A technique for quieting the mind by focusing on a particular word, object (such as a candle flame), or process (such as breathing).

Take Charge

Meditation and the Relaxation Response

Dr. Herbert Benson developed a simple, practical technique for eliciting the relaxation response.

The Basic Technique

1. Pick a word, phrase, or object to focus on. If you like, you can choose a word or phrase that has a deep meaning for you, but any word or phrase will work. Some meditators prefer to focus on their breathing.
2. Take a comfortable position in a quiet environment, and close your eyes if you're not focusing on an object.
3. Relax your muscles.
4. Breathe slowly and naturally. If you're using a focus word or phrase, silently repeat it each time you exhale. If you're using an object, focus on it as you breathe.
5. Keep a passive attitude. Disregard thoughts that drift in.
6. Continue for 10–20 minutes, once or twice a day.
7. After you've finished, sit quietly for a few minutes with your eyes first closed and then open. Then stand up.

Suggestions

- Allow relaxation to occur at its own pace; don't try to force it. Don't be surprised if you can't tune out your mind for more than a few seconds at a time; it's not a reason for anger or frustration. The more you ignore the intrusions, the easier doing so will become.
- If you want to time your session, peek at a watch or clock occasionally, but don't set a jarring alarm.
- The technique works best on an empty stomach, before a meal or about 2 hours after eating. Avoid times of day when you're tired—unless you want to fall asleep.
- Although you'll feel refreshed even after the first session, it may take a month or more to get noticeable results. Be patient. Eventually the relaxation response will become so natural that it will occur spontaneously, or on demand, when you sit quietly for a few moments.

meditation, its power derives from its ability to elicit the relaxation response.

Meditation helps you tune out the world temporarily, removing you from both internal and external sources of stress. It allows you to transcend past conditioning, fixed expectations, and the trivial pursuits of the psyche; it clears out the mental smog. The "thinker" takes time out to become the "observer"—calmly attentive, without analyzing, judging, comparing, or rationalizing. Regular practice of this quiet awareness will subtly carry over into your daily life, encouraging physical and emotional balance no matter what confronts you. For a step-by-step description of a basic meditation technique, see the box "Meditation and the Relaxation Response."

Another form of meditation, known as *mindfulness meditation,* involves paying attention to physical sensations, perceptions, thoughts, and imagery. Instead of focusing on a word or object to quiet the mind, you observe thoughts that do occur without evaluating or judging them. Development of this ability requires regular practice but may eventually result in a more objective view of one's perceptions. It is believed that a greater understanding of one's moment-to-moment thought processes (mindful awareness) provides a richer and more vital sense of life and improves coping. Studies also suggest that people who rate high in mindfulness are less anxious and better able to deal with stress; among people with specific health problems, mindfulness can provide substantial benefits.

Deep Breathing Your breathing pattern is closely tied to your stress level. Deep, slow breathing is associated with relaxation. Rapid, shallow, often irregular breathing occurs during the stress response. With practice, you can learn to slow and quiet your breathing pattern, thereby also quieting your mind and relaxing your body. Breathing techniques can be used for on-the-spot tension relief as well as for long-term stress reduction.

The primary goal of many breathing exercises is to change your breathing pattern from chest breathing to diaphragmatic ("belly") breathing. During the day, most adults breathe by expanding their chest and raising their shoulders rather than by expanding their abdomen. This pattern of chest breathing is associated with stress, a sedentary lifestyle, restrictive clothing, and cultural preferences for a large chest and a small waist. Diaphragmatic breathing, which involves free expansion of the diaphragm and lower abdomen, is the pattern of breathing characteristic of children and sleeping adults. (The diaphragm is a sheet of muscle and connective tissue that divides the chest and abdominal cavities.) Diaphragmatic breathing is slower and deeper than chest breathing. For instructions on how to perform diaphragmatic breathing, refer to the box "Breathing for Relaxation."

Hatha Yoga *Yoga* is an ancient Sanskrit word referring to the union of mind, body, and soul. The development and practice of yoga are rooted in the Hindu philosophy of spiritual enlightenment. The founders of yoga developed a system of physical postures, called *asanas,* designed to cleanse the body of toxins, calm and clear the mind, bring energy into the body, and raise the level of consciousness.

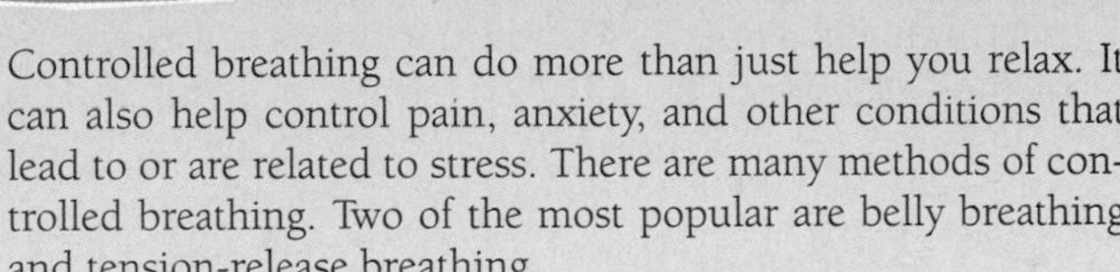

Breathing for Relaxation

Controlled breathing can do more than just help you relax. It can also help control pain, anxiety, and other conditions that lead to or are related to stress. There are many methods of controlled breathing. Two of the most popular are belly breathing and tension-release breathing.

Belly Breathing

1. Lie on your back and relax.
2. Place one hand on your chest and the other on your abdomen. Your hands will help you gauge your breathing.
3. Take in a slow, deep breath through your nose and into your belly. Your abdomen should rise significantly (check with your hand); your chest should rise only slightly. Focus on filling your abdomen with air.
4. Exhale through your mouth, gently pushing out the air from your abdomen.

Tension-Release Breathing

1. Lie down or sit in a chair and get comfortable.
2. Take a slow, deep breath into your abdomen. Inhale through your nose. Try to visualize the air moving to every part of your body. As you breathe in, say to yourself, "Breathe in relaxation."
3. Exhale through your mouth. Visualize tension leaving your body. Say to yourself, "Breathe out tension."

There are many variations on these techniques. For example, sit in a chair and raise your arms, shoulders, and chin as you inhale; lower them as you exhale. Or slowly count to 4 as you inhale, then again as you exhale.

Many yoga experts suggest breathing rhythmically, in time with your own heartbeat. Relax and listen closely for the sensation of your heart beating, or monitor your pulse while you breathe. As you inhale, count to 4 or 8 in time with your heartbeat, then repeat the count as you exhale. Breathing in time with soothing music can work well, too.

Experts suggest inhaling through the nose and exhaling through the mouth. Breathe slowly, deeply, and gently. To focus on breathing gently, imagine a candle burning a few inches in front of you. Try to exhale softly enough to make the candle's flame flicker, not hard enough to blow it out.

Practice is important, too. Perform your chosen breathing exercise 2 or more times daily, for 5–10 minutes per session.

SOURCES: Duke University. 2005. *Breathing for relaxation* (http://www.hr.duke.edu/sos/breathing.html; retrieved May 25, 2006); LIFE Center, Rehabilitation Institute of Chicago. *Pain: Breathing for relaxation* (http://lifecenter.ric.org/content/2996/; retrieved May 25, 2006).

Hatha yoga, the most common yoga style practiced in the United States, emphasizes physical balance and breathing control. It integrates components of flexibility, muscular strength and endurance, and muscle relaxation; it also sometimes serves as a preliminary to meditation.

A session of hatha yoga typically involves a series of *asanas,* held for a few seconds to several minutes, that stretch and relax different parts of the body. The emphasis is on breathing, stretching, and balance. There are hundreds of *asanas,* and they must be performed correctly in order to be beneficial. For this reason, qualified instruction is recommended, particularly for beginners. Regardless of whether you accept the philosophy and symbolism of different *asanas,* the practice of yoga can induce the relaxation response as well as develop body awareness, flexibility, and muscular strength and endurance.

Taijiquan A martial art that developed in China, taijiquan (or "tai chi") is a system of self-defense that incorporates philosophical concepts from Taoism and Confucianism. An important part of this philosophy is *chi,* an energy force that surrounds and permeates all things. In addition to serving as a means of self-defense, taijiquan aims to bring the body into balance and harmony with this universal energy in order to promote health and spiritual growth. It teaches practitioners to remain calm and centered, to conserve and concentrate energy, and to harmonize with fear. Taijiquan seeks to manipulate force by becoming part of it—"going with the flow," so to speak.

Taijiquan is considered the gentlest of the martial arts. Instead of using quick and powerful movements, taijiquan consists of a series of slow, fluid, elegant movements, which reinforce the idea of moving *with* rather than *against* the stressors of everyday life. The practice of taijiquan promotes relaxation and concentration as well as the development of body awareness, balance, muscular strength, and flexibility. It usually takes some time and practice to reap the stress-management benefits of taijiquan, and, as with yoga, it's best to begin with some qualified instruction.

Listening to Music Listening to music is another method of inducing relaxation. It has been shown to influence pulse, blood pressure, and the electrical activity of muscles. Studies of newborns and hospitalized stroke patients have shown that listening to soothing, lyrical music can lessen depression, anxiety, and stress levels. Exposure to rhythmic music has been shown to help people with

Taijiquan is among the many techniques for inducing the relaxation response. In addition to helping these men manage stress, regular practice of taijiquan will also improve their balance and increase their muscular strength and flexibility.

Parkinson's disease and other physical disabilities walk more steadily. Music therapy, which can involve both listening to music and creating music, has also been shown to be helpful in pain management, including lessening the need for anesthesia during labor. Although the effects of music are just beginning to be investigated, researchers have found that exposure to soothing music leads to reduced levels of the stress hormone cortisol and causes changes in the electrical activity in the brain.

To experience the stress-management benefits of music yourself, set aside a time to listen. Choose music that you enjoy and that makes you feel relaxed. To learn more about formal music therapy, contact the American Music Therapy Association (www.amta.org).

Biofeedback Using **biofeedback** helps people reduce the stress response by enabling them to become more aware of their level of physiological arousal. It involves mechanical monitoring of some measure of the physiological stress response, such as perspiration, heart rate, skin temperature, or muscle tension. A person receives feedback about his or her condition through the use of sound (a tone or music), light, or a meter or dial. For example, as heart rate increases, the tone becomes louder; as it decreases, the tone softens. Through trial and error, people can learn to reduce their physiological stress response through conscious control.

Term

Ww

biofeedback A technique in which monitoring devices are used to help a person become conscious of unconscious body processes, such as body temperature or blood pressure, in order to exert some control over them.

The point of biofeedback training is to teach how relaxation feels, how to induce relaxation, and how to transfer this skill to daily life (without the use of electronic equipment). In addition to monitoring equipment, biofeedback usually also requires the initial help of a therapist, stress counselor, or technician.

Other relaxation techniques include massage, hypnosis and self-hypnosis, and autogenic training. To learn more about these and other techniques for inducing the relaxation response, refer to For More Information at the end of the chapter.

Counterproductive Coping Strategies

College is a time when you'll learn to adapt to new and challenging situations and gain skills that will last a lifetime. It is also a time when many people develop habits, in response to stress, that are counterproductive and unhealthy and that may also last well beyond graduation.

Tobacco Use Many young adults who never smoked in high school—and who rebuked their parents for tobacco use—smoke their first cigarette in college, usually at a party or bar or in a dorm with friends. Cigarettes and other tobacco products contain nicotine, a chemical that enhances the actions of neurotransmitters. Many smokers report that smoking helps them to cope with stress by providing a feeling of relaxation, giving them something to do with their hands in social situations, or breaking up monotony and routine. Nicotine can make you feel relaxed and even increase your ability to concentrate, but it is highly addictive and nicotine dependence itself is considered a psychological disorder. Cigarette smoke also contains many other substances that are harmful to your lungs and circulatory system and that cause heart disease, stroke, lung cancer, and emphysema. These negative consequences far outweigh any beneficial effects, and tobacco use should be avoided. The easiest thing to do is to not start. See Chapter 11 for more on the health effects of tobacco use and for tips on how to quit.

Use of Alcohol and Other Drugs No college experience is complete without a party or two. Letting loose, dancing, laughing, and interacting with others—all are part of college parties and all can be very effective short-term coping strategies. However, partying in college is usually associated with drinking alcohol. Keg parties and drinking games can be fun, but they contribute to binge drinking and other forms of alcohol abuse. Like nicotine, alcohol is addictive, and many alcoholics find it hard to relax without a drink. Having a few drinks might make you feel temporarily at ease, and drinking until you're intoxicated may help you forget your current stressors. However, using alcohol to deal with stress places you at risk for all the short-term and long-term problems associated with alcohol abuse. It also does nothing to address the actual causes of stress in your life. Although moderate alcohol consumption may have potential health benefits for some people, many college students have patterns of drinking that detract from wellness. For more on the responsible use of alcohol, refer to Chapter 10.

Using other psychoactive drugs to cope with stress is also usually counterproductive:

- Caffeine raises cortisol levels and blood pressure and can make you feel more stressed; caffeine also disrupts sleep. Other stimulants, such as amphetamine, are used by some people in an attempt to cope with stress or sleepiness, making stress a risk factor for stimulant use. Stimulant drugs can activate the stress response, and they affect the same areas of the brain that are involved in regulating the stress response.
- Marijuana use is relatively common among college students, who report that they smoke marijuana in an effort to induce relaxation and for "mind expansion." Use of marijuana causes a brief period of euphoria and decreased short-term memory and attentional abilities. Physiological effects clearly show that marijuana use doesn't cause relaxation; in fact, some neurochemicals in marijuana act to enhance the stress response, and getting high on a regular basis can elicit panic attacks. To compound this, withdrawal from marijuana may also be associated with an increase in circulating stress hormones.
- Opioids such as morphine and heroin can mimic the effects of your body's natural painkillers and act to reduce anxiety. However, tolerance to opioids develops quickly, and many users become dependent.

In general, it's not a good idea to alter your body chemistry with drugs in order to cope with stress. In moderation, substances such as caffeine and alcohol appear to have some positive attributes—but their use has many pitfalls and does not directly address the causes of stress.

Unhealthy Eating Habits The nutrients in the food you eat provide energy and the substances needed to maintain your body. However, eating is also psychologically rewarding. We use food to end long days, to celebrate special events, and to enjoy the company of friends. The feelings of satiation and sedation that follow eating produce a relaxed state. However, regular use of eating as a means of coping with stress may lead to unhealthy eating habits. In fact, a 2006 survey by the American Psychological Association revealed that about 25% of Americans use food as a means of coping with stress or anxiety. These "comfort eaters" are twice as likely to be obese as average Americans.

Certain foods and supplements are sometimes thought to fight stress. Carbohydrates may reduce the stress response by promoting activity of the parasympathetic nervous system; however, a high-carbohydrate diet can lead to excessive weight gain in sedentary people and is not recommended as a strategy for coping with stressors. In addition, some evidence suggests that greater ingestion of carbohydrates, simple sugars, and fatty foods may actually be a predisposing factor for psychological distress. Many dietary supplements are marketed for stress reduction, but supplements are not required to meet the same standards as medications in terms of safety, effectiveness, and manufacturing (see Chapters 12 and 21).

Binge eating is defined as eating a large quantity of food in a discrete period of time, accompanied by a sense of lack of control over eating. Binge eating may serve as an avoidance coping strategy and a temporary escape. However, the loss of control over eating is associated with negative emotional states, and binge eating is a risky behavior associated with weight gain and serious eating disorders. A good strategy to avoid unhealthy binge-eating habits is to make sure you eat breakfast and lunch in the first half of your day—rather than waiting until the evening to consume a real meal. Eating early in the day increases your metabolism and gives you the energy to engage in all your activities. In addition, early meals will decrease feelings of hunger later in the day. See Chapters 12 and 14 for more on a healthy diet and on eating disorders.

CREATING A PERSONAL PLAN FOR MANAGING STRESS

What are the most important sources of stress in your life? Are you coping successfully with these stressors? No single strategy or program for managing stress will work for everyone, but you can use the principles of behavior management described in Chapter 1 to tailor a plan specifically to your needs. The most important starting point for a successful stress-management plan is to learn to listen to your body. When you learn to recognize the stress response and the emotions and thoughts that accompany it, you'll be in a position to take charge of that crucial moment and handle it in a healthy way.

Identifying Stressors

Before you can learn to manage the stressors in your life, you have to identify them. A strategy many experts recommend is keeping a stress journal for a week or two. Keep a log of your daily activities, and assign a rating to your stress level for every hour. Each time you feel or express a stress response, record the time and the circumstances in your journal. Note what you were doing at the time, what you were thinking or feeling, and the outcome of your response.

After keeping your journal for a few weeks, you should be able to identify your key stressors and spot patterns in how you respond to them. Take note of the people, places, events, and patterns of thought and behavior that cause you the most stress. You may notice, for example, that mornings are usually the most stressful part of your day. Or you may discover that when you're angry at your roommate, you're apt to respond with behaviors that only make matters worse. Once you've outlined the general pattern of stress in your life, you may want to focus on a particularly problematic stressor or on an inappropriate behavioral response you've identified. Keep a stress log for another week or two that focuses just on the early morning hours, for example, or just on your arguments with your roommate. The more information you gather, the easier it will be to develop effective strategies for coping with the stressors in your life. Use the situations in which your stress level has dissipated as positive reinforcement that you have the ability to adapt to your stressors. Rise to the challenge of those events that continue to cause you stress. Keeping a journal allows you to be a bit more analytical about what produces the most stress in your life and fills in where your conscious memory fails you.

Designing Your Plan

Earlier in this chapter, you learned about many different techniques for combating stress. Now that you've identified the key stressors in your life, it's time to choose the techniques that will work best for you and create an action plan for change. Finding a buddy to work with you can make the process more fun and increase your chances of success. Some experts recommend drawing up a formal contract with yourself.

Whether or not you complete a contract, it's important to design rewards into your plan. You might treat yourself to a special breakfast in a favorite restaurant on the weekend (as long as you eat a nutritious breakfast every weekday morning). If you practice your relaxation techniques faithfully, you might reward yourself with a long bath or an hour of pleasure reading at the end of the day. It's also important to evaluate your plan regularly and redesign it as your needs change. Under times of increased stress, for example, you might want to focus on good eating, exercise, and relaxation habits. Over time, your new stress-management skills will become almost automatic. You'll feel better, accomplish more, and reduce your risk of disease.

Getting Help

If the techniques discussed so far don't provide you with enough relief from the stress in your life, you might want to read more about specific areas you wish to work on, consult a peer counselor, join a support group, or participate in a few psychotherapy sessions. Excellent self-help guides can be found in bookstores or the library. Additional resources are listed in the For More Information section at the end of the chapter.

Your student health center or student affairs office can tell you whether your campus has a peer counseling program. Such programs are usually staffed by volunteer students with special training that emphasizes maintaining confidentiality. Peer counselors can guide you to other campus or community resources or can simply provide understanding.

Support groups are typically organized around a particular issue or problem. In your area, you might find a support group for first-year students; for reentering students; for single parents; for students of your ethnicity, religion, or national origin; for people with eating disorders; or for rape survivors. The number of such groups has increased in recent years as more and more people discover how therapeutic it can be to talk with others who share the same situation.

Short-term psychotherapy can also be tremendously helpful in dealing with stress-related problems. Your student health center may offer psychotherapy on a sliding-fee scale; the county mental health center in your area may do the same. If you belong to any type of religious organization, check to see whether pastoral counseling is available. Your physician can refer you to psychotherapists in your community. Not all therapists are right for all people, so be prepared to have initial sessions with several. Choose the one you feel most comfortable with.

Tips for Today

Some stress is unavoidable in life. How you respond to it is what determines whether you become stressed out or maintain your serenity. For the stress you can't avoid, develop a range of stress-management techniques and strategies.

Right now you can

- Sit in a comfortable chair and practice deep breathing for 5–10 minutes.
- Visualize a relaxing, peaceful place and imagine yourself experiencing it as vividly as possible; you might "feel" a gentle breeze on your skin or "hear" the soothing sound of a waterfall. Stay there as long as you can.
- Stand up and do some stretching exercises, such as gently rolling your head from side to side, stretching your arms out in front of your body and over your head, and slowly bending over and letting your arms hang toward the floor.
- Get out your date book and schedule what you'll be doing the rest of today and tomorrow. Pencil in a short walk and a conversation with a friend. Plan to go to bed 15 minutes earlier than usual.

SUMMARY

- When confronted with a stressor, the body undergoes a set of physical changes known as the fight-or-flight reaction. The sympathetic nervous system and endocrine system act on many targets in the body to prepare it for action.
- Emotional and behavioral responses to stressors vary among individuals. Ineffective responses increase stress but can be moderated or changed.

- Factors that influence emotional and behavioral responses to stressors include personality, cultural background, gender, and past experiences.
- The general adaptation syndrome (GAS) has three stages: alarm, resistance, and exhaustion.
- A high allostatic load characterized by prolonged or repeated exposure to stress hormones can increase a person's risk of health problems.
- Psychoneuroimmunology (PNI) looks at how the physiological changes of the stress response affect the immune system and thereby increase the risk of illness.
- Health problems linked to stress include CVD, colds and other infections, asthma and allergies, cancer, flare-ups of chronic diseases, psychological problems, digestive problems, headaches, insomnia, and injuries.
- A cluster of major life events that require adjustment and accommodation can lead to increased stress and an increased risk of health problems. Minor daily hassles increase stress if they are perceived negatively.
- Sources of stress associated with college may be academic, interpersonal, time-related, or financial pressures.
- Job-related stress is common, particularly for employees who have little control over decisions relating to their jobs. If stress is severe or prolonged, burnout may occur.
- New and changing relationships, prejudice, and discrimination are examples of interpersonal and social stressors.
- Social support systems help buffer people against the effects of stress and make illness less likely. Good communication skills foster healthy relationships.
- Exercise, nutrition, sleep, and time management are wellness behaviors that reduce stress and increase energy.
- Cognitive techniques for managing stress involve developing new and healthy patterns of thinking, such as practicing problem solving, monitoring self-talk, and cultivating a sense of humor.
- The relaxation response is the opposite of the fight-or-flight reaction. Techniques that trigger it, including progressive relaxation, imagery, meditation, and deep breathing, counteract the effects of chronic stress. Counterproductive coping strategies include smoking, drinking, and unhealthy eating.
- A successful individualized plan for coping with stress begins with the use of a stress journal or log to identify and study stressors and inappropriate behavioral responses. Completing a contract and recruiting a buddy can help your stress-management plan succeed.
- Additional help in dealing with stress is available from self-help books, peer counseling, support groups, and psychotherapy.

Take Action

1. **Interview friends or family members.** Choose someone who seems to deal particularly well with stress. Interview that person about his or her methods for managing stress. What strategies does he or she use? What can you learn from that person that can be applied to your own life?

2. **Check out local services.** Investigate the services available in your community—such as peer counseling, support groups, and time-management classes—to help people deal with stress. If possible, visit or gather information on one or more of them. Write a description and evaluation of their services, including your personal reactions.

3. **Try a stress-management technique.** Reread the techniques described in this chapter, and choose one to try for a week. After a trial period, evaluate the effectiveness of the strategy you chose. Did your stress level decrease during the week? Were you better able to deal with daily hassles and any more severe stressors that you encountered?

4. **Reach out to others by becoming a volunteer.** Whether or not you realize it, you likely have more physical, emotional, and intellectual resources than you need. Transfer some of these resources to people who would benefit greatly from just a few hours of your time and effort. In doing so, you may find that you also benefit in terms of greater self-esteem and appreciation for your own support system and the opportunities you have for a positive future. Look for an opportunity to volunteer to help others in your community.

For More Information

Books

Blonna, R. 2007. *Coping with Stress in a Changing World.* 4th ed. New York: McGraw-Hill. *A comprehensive guide to stress management that includes separate chapters on college stressors and spirituality.*

Greenberg, J. 2008. *Comprehensive Stress Management.* 10th ed. New York: McGraw-Hill. *Provides a clear explanation of the physical, psychological, sociological, and spiritual aspects of stress and offers numerous stress-management techniques.*

Kabat-Zinn, J. 2005. *Coming to Our Senses: Healing Ourselves and the World Through Mindfulness.* New York: Hyperion. *Explores the connections among mindfulness, health, and our physical and spiritual well-being.*

Pennebaker, J. W. 2004. *Writing to Heal: A Guided Journal for Recovering from Trauma and Emotional Upheaval.* Oakland, Calif.: New Harbinger Press. *Provides information about using journaling to cope with stress.*

WW Organizations and Web Sites

American Psychological Association. Provides information on stress management and psychological disorders.
http://www.apa.org; http://helping.apa.org

Dealing with Test Anxiety

Are you a person who doesn't perform as well as you should on tests? Do you find that anxiety interferes with your ability to study effectively before the test and to think clearly in the test situation? If so, you may be experiencing test anxiety. Two methods that have proven effective in helping people deal with test anxiety are systematic desensitization and success rehearsal.

Systematic Desensitization

Systematic desensitization is based on the premise that you can't feel anxiety and be relaxed at the same time.

Phase I: Constructing an Anxiety Hierarchy Begin the first phase by thinking of ten or more situations related to your fear, such as hearing the announcement of the test date in class, studying for the test, sitting in the classroom waiting for the test to begin, reading the test questions, and so on. Write each situation on an index card, using a brief phrase to describe it on one side of the card. On the other side, list several realistic details or prompts that will help you vividly imagine yourself actually experiencing the situation. For example, if the situation is "hearing that 50% of the final grade will be based on the two exams," the prompts might include details such as "sitting in the big lecture auditorium in Baily Hall," "taking notes in my blue notebook," and "listening to Professor Smith's voice."

Next, arrange your cards in order, from least-tense to most-tense situation. Rate each situation to reflect the amount of anxiety you feel when you encounter it in real life, to confirm your anxiety hierarchy. Assign ratings on a scale of 0–100, and make sure the distances between items are fairly small and about equal. When you're sure your anxiety hierarchy is a true reflection of your feelings, number the cards.

Phase II: Learning and Practicing Muscle Relaxation The second phase of the program involves learning to relax your muscles and to recognize when they are relaxed (see the description of progressive relaxation in this chapter). As you become proficient at this technique, you'll be able to go to a deeply relaxed state within just a few minutes. When you can do this, go on to the next phase of the program.

Phase III: Implementing the Desensitization Program Use the quiet place where you practiced your relaxation exercises. Sit comfortably and place your stack of numbered cards within reach. Take several minutes to relax completely, and then look at the first card, reading both the brief phrase and the descriptive prompts. Close your eyes and imagine yourself in that situation for about 10 seconds. Then put the card down and relax completely for about 30 seconds. Look at the card again, imagine the situation for 10 seconds, and relax again for 30 seconds.

At this point, evaluate your current level of anxiety about the situation on the card in terms of the rating scale you devised earlier. If your anxiety level is 10 or below, relax for 2 minutes and go on to the second card. If it's higher than 10, repeat the routine with the same card until the anxiety decreases. If you have difficulty with a particular item, go back to the previous item; then try it again. If you still can't visualize it without anxiety, try to construct three new items with smaller steps between them and insert them before the troublesome item. You should be able to move through one to four items per session. Sessions can be conducted from twice a day to twice a week and should last no longer than 20 minutes. It's helpful to graph your progress in a way that has meaning for you.

After you have successfully completed your program, you should be desensitized to the real-life situations that previously caused anxiety. If you find that you do experience some anxiety in the real situations, take 30 seconds or a minute to relax completely, just as you did when you were practicing.

Success Rehearsal

To practice this variation on systematic desensitization, take your hierarchy of anxiety-producing situations and vividly imagine yourself successfully dealing with each one. Create a detailed scenario for each situation, and use your imagination to experience genuine feelings of confidence. Recognize your negative thoughts ("I'll be so nervous I won't be able to think straight") and replace them with positive ones ("Anxiety will keep me alert so I can do a good job"). Proceed one step at a time, thinking as you go of strategies for success that you can later implement. These might include the following:

- Before the test, find out everything you can about it—its format, the material to be covered, the grading criteria. Ask the instructor for practice materials. Study in advance; don't just cram the night before. Avoid all-nighters.
- Devise a study plan. This might include forming a study group with one or more classmates or outlining what you will study, when, where, and for how long. Generate your own questions and answer them.
- In the actual test situation, sit away from possible distractions, listen carefully to instructions, and ask for clarification if you don't understand a direction.
- During the test, answer the easiest questions first. If you don't know an answer and there is no penalty for incorrect answers, guess. If there are several questions you have difficulty answering, review the ones you have already handled. Figure out approximately how much time you have to cover each question.
- For math problems, try to estimate the answer before doing the precise calculations.
- For true-false questions, look for qualifiers such as *always* and *never.* Such questions are likely to be false.
- For essay questions, look for key words in the question that indicate what the instructor is looking for in the answer. Develop a brief outline of your answer, sketching out what you will cover. Stick to your outline, and keep track of the time you're spending on your answer. Don't get caught with unanswered questions when time is up.
- Remain calm and focused throughout the test. Don't let negative thoughts rattle you. Avoid worrying about past performance, how others are doing, or the negative consequences of a poor test grade. If you start to become nervous, take some deep breaths and relax your muscles completely for a minute or so.

The best way to counter test anxiety is with successful test-taking experiences. The more times you succeed, the more your test anxiety will recede. If you find that these methods aren't sufficient to get your anxiety under control, you may want to seek professional help.

Association for Applied Psychophysiology and Biofeedback. Provides information about biofeedback and referrals to certified biofeedback practitioners.

http://www.aapb.org

Harvard Mind-Body Medical Institute. Provides information about stress-management and relaxation techniques.

http://www.mbmi.org

Medical Basis for Stress. Includes information on recognizing stress and on the physiological basis of stress, self-assessments for stress levels, and techniques for managing stress.

http://www.teachhealth.com

National Institute for Occupational Safety and Health (NIOSH). Provides information and links on job stress.

http://www.cdc.gov/niosh/topics/stress

National Institute of Mental Health (NIMH). Publishes informative brochures about stress and stress management as well as other aspects of mental health.

http://www.nimh.nih.gov

National Sleep Foundation. Provides information about sleep and how to overcome sleep problems such as insomnia and jet lag.

http://www.sleepfoundation.org

Student Counseling Virtual Pamphlet Collection. Links to online pamphlets from student counseling centers; topics include stress, sleep, and time management.

http://counseling.uchicago.edu/resources/virtualpamphlets/

Selected Bibliography

American Psychological Association. 2005. *The different kinds of stress* (http://www.apahelpcenter.org/articles/article.php?id=21; retrieved July 18, 2006).

American Psychological Association. 2005. *Learning to Deal with Stress* (http://helping.apa.org/articles/article.php?id=71; retrieved July 18, 2006).

American Psychological Association. 2006. *Stress and mind/body health* (http://apahelpcenter.mediaroom.com/file.php/87/Exec+Summary+Survey.doc; retrieved July 18, 2006).

Bouchard, T. J. Jr., and M. McGue. 2003. Genetic and environmental influences on human psychological differences. *Journal of Neurobiology* 54(1): 4–45.

Centers for Disease Control. 2005. *Coping with a Traumatic Event: Information for the Public* (http://www.bt.cdc.gov/masstrauma/copingpub.asp; retrieved July 18, 2006).

Cohen, S., W. J. Doyle, and A. Baum. 2006. Socioeconomic status is associated with stress hormones. *Psychosomatic Medicine* 68(3): 414–420.

Constantine, M. G., S. Okazaki, and S. O. Utsey. 2004. Self-concealment, social self-efficacy, acculturative stress, and depression in African, Asian, and Latin American international college students. *American Journal of Orthopsychiatry* 74(3): 230–241.

Frequent headaches, hidden dangers. 2006. *Consumer Reports on Health,* June.

Grossman, P., et al. 2004. Mindfulness-based stress reduction and health benefits: A meta analysis. *Journal of Psychosomatic Research* 57(1): 35–43.

Headaches. 2006. *Journal of the American Medical Association* 295(19): 2320.

How stress can make you forgetful, age faster. 2005. *Tufts University Health & Nutrition Letter,* February, 1.

Institute of Medicine Committee on Sleep Medicine and Research. 2006. *Sleep Disorders and Sleep Deprivation: An Unmet Public Health Problem,* ed. H. R. Colton and B. M. Altevogt. Washington, D.C. National Academies Press.

Lane, J. D., et al. 2002. Caffeine affects cardiovascular and neuroendocrine activation at work and home. *Psychosomatic Medicine* 64(4): 595–603.

Lauderdale, D. S., et al. 2006. Objectively measured sleep characteristics among early-middle-aged adults: The CARDIA study. *American Journal of Epidemiology* 164(1): 17–18.

MacGeorge, Erina L., et al. 2004. Stress, social support, and health among college students after September 11, 2001. *Journal of College Student Development* 45(6): 655–670.

Mayo Foundation for Medical Education and Research. 2005. *Stress: Why you have it and how it hurts your health.* (http://www.mayoclinic.com/health/stress/SR00001; retrieved July 18, 2006).

Meier-Ewert, H. K., et al. 2004. Effect of sleep loss on C-reactive protein, an inflammatory marker of cardiovascular risk. *Journal of the American College of Cardiology* 43: 678–683.

Melamed, S., et al. 2004. Association of fear of terror with low-grade inflammation among apparently healthy employed adults. *Psychosomatic Medicine* 66(4): 484–491.

National Mental Health Association. 2006. *Coping with disaster: Tips for college students on coping with war and terrorism.* (http://www.nmha.org/reassurance/collegeWarCoping.cfm; retrieved July 18, 2006).

Pickering, T. G. 2003. Effects of stress and behavioral interventions in hypertension—Men are from Mars, women are from Venus: Stress, pets, and oxytocin. *Journal of Clinical Hypertension* 5(1): 86–88.

Ridley, M. 2003. *Nature Via Nurture: Genes, Experience, and What Makes Us Human.* New York: HarperCollins.

Sax, L. J., et al. 2006. *The American Freshman: National Norms for Fall 2005.* Los Angeles: UCLA Higher Education Research Institute.

Schwarze, N. J., J. M. Oliver, and P. J. Handal. 2003. Binge eating as related to negative self-awareness, depression, and avoidance coping in undergraduates. *Journal of College Student Development* 44(5): 644–652.

Segerstrom, S. C., and G. E. Miller. 2004. Psychological stress and the human immune system: A meta-analytic study of 30 years of inquiry. *Psychological Bulletin* 130(4): 601–630.

Smyth, J., and R. Helm. 2003. Focused expressive writing as self-help for stress and trauma. *Journal of Clinical Psychology* 59(2): 227–235.

Stambor, Z. 2006. Stressed out nation. *Monitor on Psychology* 37(4) (http://www.apa.org/monitor/apr06/nation.html; retrieved August 8, 2006).

Steptoe, A., et al. 2004. Loneliness and neuroendocrine, cardiovascular, and inflammatory stress responses in middle-aged men and women. *Psychoneuroendocrinology* 29(5): 593–611.

Wetter, D. W., et al. 2004. Prevalence and predictors of transitions in smoking behavior among college students. *Health Psychology* 23(2): 168–177.

Wittstein, I. S., et al. 2005. Neurohumoral features of myocardial stunning due to sudden emotional stress. *New England Journal of Medicine* 352(6): 539–548.

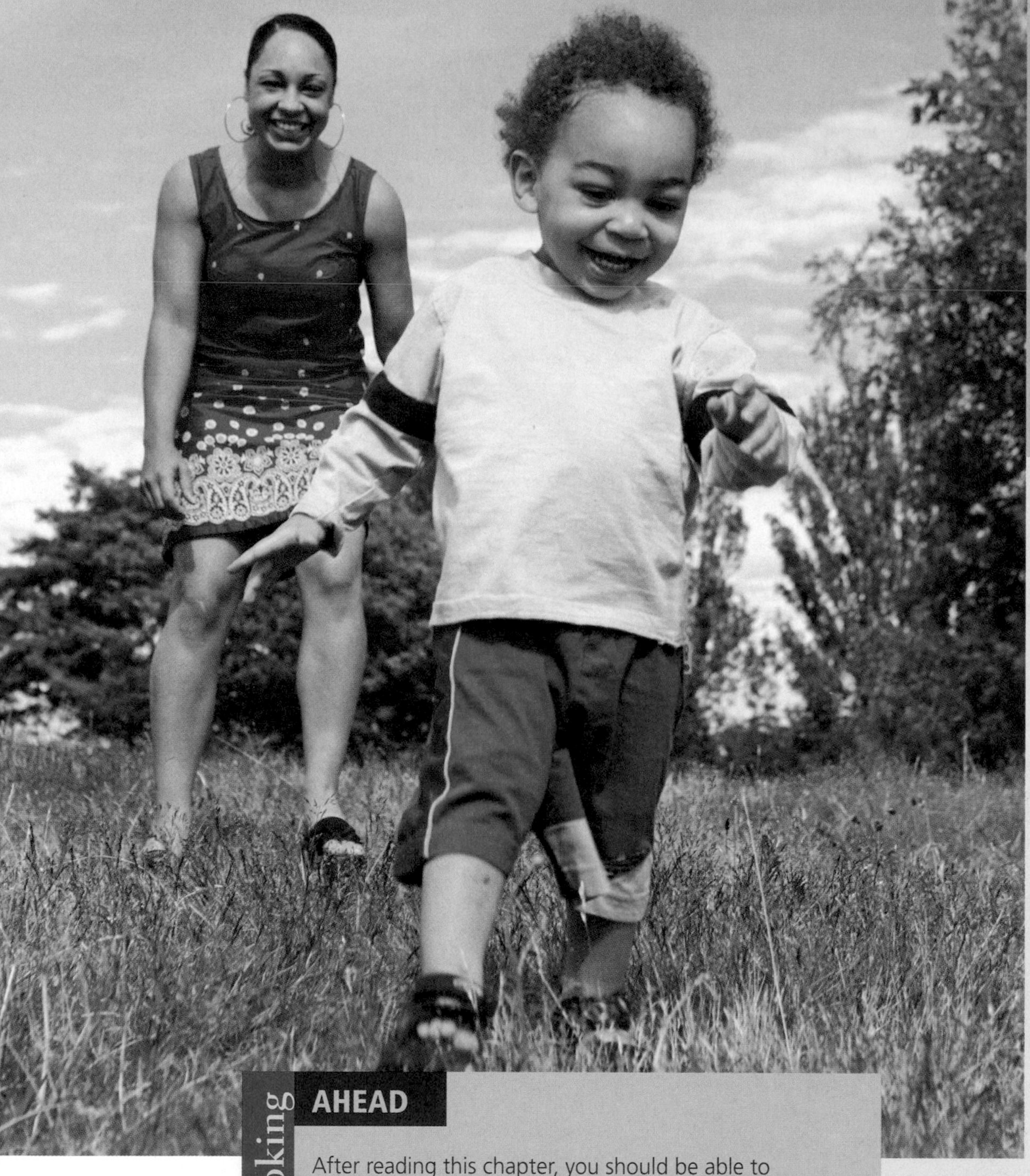

3

Looking AHEAD

After reading this chapter, you should be able to

- Describe what it means to be psychologically healthy
- Explain how to develop and maintain a positive self-concept and healthy self-esteem
- Discuss the importance to psychological health of an optimistic outlook, good communication skills, and constructive approaches to dealing with loneliness and anger
- Describe common psychological disorders and list the warning signs of suicide
- Explain the different approaches and types of help available for psychological problems

Psychological Health

Test Your Knowledge

1. **Normality is a key component of psychological health.**
True or false?
2. **Trying to think rationally about what bothers you won't get you very far, because psychological problems usually are due to emotions, not thinking.**
True or false?
3. **About how many Americans have a diagnosable psychological disorder during the course of a year?**
a. 5%
b. 10%
c. 20%
4. **People with enough willpower can force themselves to snap out of their depression.**
True or false?
5. **A person who attempts suicide but survives did not really intend to die.**
True or false?

ANSWERS

1. FALSE. Normality simply means being close to average, and having unusual ideas or attitudes doesn't mean that a person is mentally ill. The fact that people's ideas are varied makes life interesting and helps people respond in creative ways to life's challenges.
2. FALSE. Research has shown that getting people to adopt more realistic attitudes and beliefs about themselves and others can alleviate depression.
3. C. Other than substance-abuse problems, the most common types of disorders are simple phobias and depression. The majority of people with psychological disorders do not receive appropriate treatment.
4. FALSE. Depression, a disorder strongly linked to brain chemistry, can overcome whatever willpower a person has and make it impossible for her or him to make rational decisions—or any decisions at all.
5. FALSE. A person may intend to die but miscalculate the type or amount of drug needed or how to successfully carry out some other method of suicide.

Visit the *Core Concepts in Health* Online Learning Center (www.mhhe.com/insel10e) for study aids and many additional resources.

What exactly is psychological health? Many people over the centuries have expressed opinions about the nature of psychological (or mental) health. Some even claim that there is no such thing, that psychological health is just a myth. We disagree. We think there is such a thing as psychological health just as there is physical health—and the two are closely interrelated. Just as your body can work well or poorly, giving you pleasure or pain, your mind can also work well or poorly, resulting in happiness or unhappiness. Psychological health is a crucial component of overall wellness. (We are using "mental health" and "psychological health" interchangeably; the latter is the more current term, but it hasn't replaced "mental health" yet.)

If you feel pain and unhappiness rather than pleasure and happiness or if you sense that you could be functioning at a higher level, there may be ways you can help yourself—either on your own or with the aid of a professional. This chapter will explain how.

WHAT PSYCHOLOGICAL HEALTH IS NOT

Psychological health is not the same as psychological **normality.** Being mentally normal simply means being close to average. You can define normal body temperature because a few degrees above or below this temperature means physical sickness. But your ideas and attitudes can vary tremendously without your losing efficiency or feeling emotional distress. And psychological diversity is valuable; living in a society of people with varied ideas and lifestyles makes life interesting and challenging.

Conforming to social demands is not necessarily a mark of psychological health. If you don't question what's going on around you, you're not fulfilling your potential as a thinking, questioning human being. For example, our society admires the framers of the U.S. Constitution and the abolitionists who rebelled against injustices. If conformity signified mental health, then political dissent would indicate mental illness by definition (and we have seen that definition used by dictators). If such a definition were valid, Galileo would have been mad for insisting that the earth revolved around the sun.

Never seeking help for personal problems does not prove you are psychologically healthy, any more than seeking help proves you are mentally ill. Unhappy people may not want to seek professional help because they don't want to reveal their problems to others, may fear what their friends might think, or may not know whom to ask for help. People who are severely disturbed psychologically or emotionally may not even realize they need help, or they may become so suspicious of other people that they can be treated only without their consent.

We cannot say people are "mentally ill" or "mentally healthy" on the basis of symptoms alone. Life constantly presents problems. Time and life inevitably alter the environment as well as our minds and bodies, and changes present problems. The symptom of anxiety, for example, can help us face a problem and solve it before it gets too big. Someone who shows no anxiety may be refusing to recognize problems or do anything about them. A person who is anxious for good reason is likely to be judged more psychologically healthy in the long run than someone who is inappropriately calm.

Finally, we cannot judge psychological health from the way people look. All too often, a person who seems to be OK and even happy suddenly takes his or her own life. Usually such people lack close friends who might have known of their desperation. At an early age, we learn to conceal and lie. We may believe that our complaints put unfair demands on others. While suffering in silence can sometimes be a virtue, it can also impede getting help.

DEFINING PSYCHOLOGICAL HEALTH

It is even harder to say what psychological health *is* than what it is *not.* Psychological health can be defined either negatively as the absence of sickness or positively as the presence of wellness. The narrower, negative definition has several advantages: It concentrates attention on the worst problems and on the people most in need, and it tends to avoid value judgments about the best way to lead our lives. However, if we consider everyone to be mentally healthy who is not severely mentally disturbed, we end up ignoring common problems that can be addressed.

A positive definition—psychological health as the presence of wellness—is a more ambitious outlook, one that encourages us to fulfill our own potential. Freedom from disorders is only one factor in psychological wellness. During the 1960s, Abraham Maslow eloquently described an ideal of mental health in his book *Toward a Psychology of Being.* He was convinced that psychologists were too preoccupied with people who had failed in some way. He also disliked the way psychologists tried to reduce human striving to physiological needs or drives.

According to Maslow, there is a *hierarchy of needs,* listed here in order of decreasing urgency: physiological needs, safety, being loved, maintaining self-esteem, and self-actualization (Figure 3-1). When urgent needs like the need for food, water, shelter, sleep, and safety are satisfied, less urgent needs take priority. Most of us are well fed and feel reasonably safe, so we are driven by higher motives. Maslow's conclusions were based on his study of a group of visibly successful people who seemed to have lived, or be living, at their fullest, including Abraham Lincoln, Henry David Thoreau, Ludwig van Beethoven, Eleanor Roosevelt, and Albert Einstein, as well as some of his own friends and acquaintances. He stated that these people had achieved **self-actualization;**

Figure 3-1 Maslow's hierarchy of needs. People focus first on the needs at the bottom of the hierarchy because unless basic physiological needs are fulfilled, other needs have little meaning. Once urgent needs are satisfied, people can focus on higher motives. Those who make it to the top of the needs hierarchy achieve self-actualization—they have grown to fulfill much of their human potential and are able to act and make choices unfettered by unfulfilled needs at lower levels. SOURCE: Maslow, A. 1970. *Motivation and Personality,* 2nd ed. New York: Harper & Row.

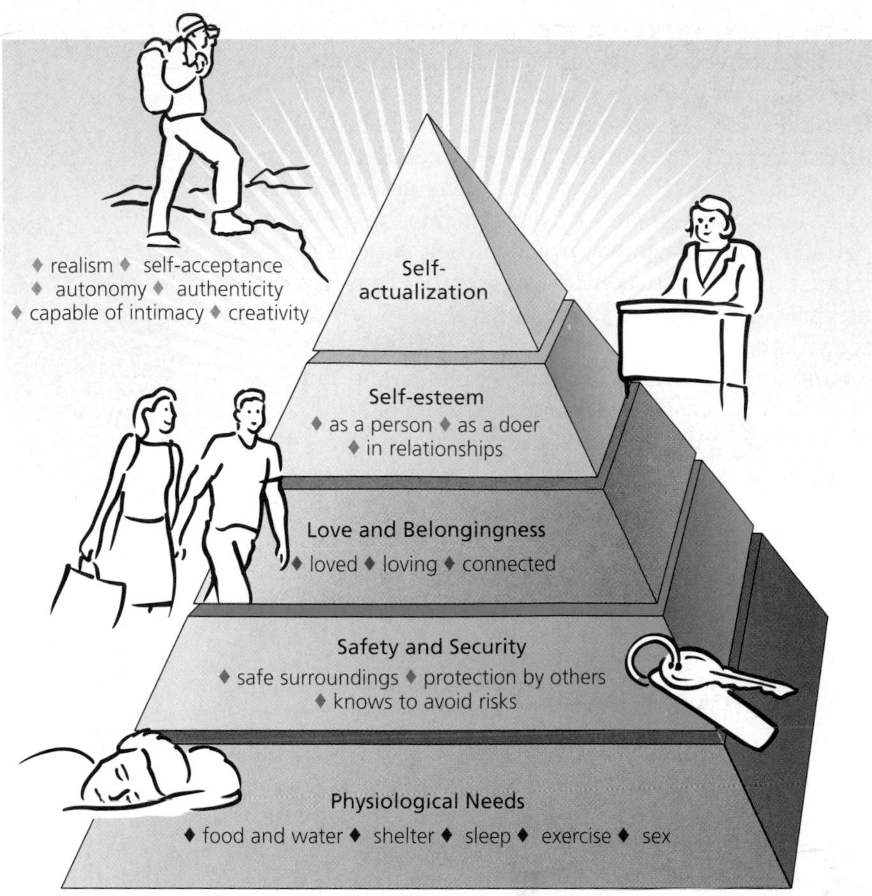

he thought they had fulfilled a good measure of their human potential and suggested that self-actualized people all share certain qualities.

Realism

Self-actualized people are able to deal with the world as it is and not demand that it be otherwise. If you are realistic, you know the difference between what is and what you want. You also know what you can change and what you cannot. Unrealistic people often spend a great deal of time and energy trying to force the world and other people into their ideal picture. Realistic people accept evidence that contradicts what they want to believe, and if it is important evidence they modify their beliefs.

Acceptance

Psychologically healthy people can largely accept themselves and others. Self-acceptance means having a positive **self-concept**, or *self-image,* or appropriately high **self-esteem.** Such people have a positive but realistic mental image of themselves and positive feelings about who they are, what they are capable of, and what roles they play. People who feel good about themselves are likely to live up to their positive self-image and enjoy successes that in turn reinforce these good feelings. A good self-concept is based on a realistic view of personal worth—it does not mean being egocentric or "stuck on yourself."

Being able to tolerate our own imperfections and still feel positive about ourselves helps us tolerate the imperfections of others. Psychologically healthy people tend to be optimistic about what they can expect from other people until experience proves their optimism to be unrealistic. Acceptance means being willing to interact with people who are imperfect and unlikely to change.

Autonomy

Psychologically healthy people are able to direct themselves, acting independently of their social environment. **Autonomy** is more than freedom from physical control

Terms

VW

normality The psychological characteristics attributed to the majority of people in a population at a given time.

self-actualization The highest level of growth in Maslow's hierarchy.

self-concept The ideas, feelings, and perceptions one has about oneself; also called *self-image.*

self-esteem Satisfaction and confidence in oneself; the valuing of oneself as a person.

autonomy Independence; the sense of being self-directed.

by something outside the self. Many people, for example, shrink from expressing their feelings because they fear disapproval and rejection. They respond only to what they feel as outside pressure. Such behavior is **other-directed.** In contrast, **inner-directed** people find guidance from within, from their own values and feelings. They are not afraid to be themselves. Psychologically free people act because they choose to, not because they are driven or pressured. They have an internal locus of control and a high level of self-efficacy (see Chapter 1).

Autonomy can give healthy people certain childlike qualities. Very small children have a quality of being "real." They respond in a genuine, spontaneous way to whatever happens, without pretenses. Being genuine means not having to plan words or actions to get approval or make an impression. It means being aware of feelings and being willing to express them—being unself-consciously oneself. This quality is sometimes called **authenticity**; such people are *authentic,* the "real thing."

A Capacity for Intimacy

Healthy people are capable of physical and emotional intimacy. They can expose their feelings and thoughts to other people. They are open to the pleasure of intimate physical contact and to the risks and satisfactions of being close to others in a caring, sensitive way. Intimate physical contact may mean "good sex," but it also means something more—intense awareness of both your partner and yourself in which contact becomes communication. Chapters 4 and 5 discuss intimacy in more detail.

Creativity

Psychologically healthy people are creative and have a continuing fresh appreciation for what goes on around them. They are not necessarily great poets, artists, or musicians, but they do live their everyday lives in creative ways: "A first-rate soup is more creative than a second-rate painting." Creative people seem to see more and to be open to new experiences; they don't fear the unknown or need to minimize or avoid uncertainty.

How did Maslow's group achieve their exemplary psychological health, and (more important) how can *we* attain it? Maslow himself did not answer that question, but it undoubtedly helps to have been treated with respect, love, and understanding as a child, to have experienced stability, and to have achieved a sense of mastery. As adults, since we cannot redo the past, we must concentrate on meeting current challenges in ways that will lead to long-term mental wellness. We must not consider ourselves failures if we do not become self-actualized in every way or at every moment. Self-actualization is an ideal to strive for, even if we never or only occasionally attain it to the fullest degree.

Self-actualized people respond in a genuine, spontaneous way to what happens around them. They are capable of maintaining close interpersonal relationships.

MEETING LIFE'S CHALLENGES

Life is full of challenges—large and small. Everyone, regardless of heredity and family influences, must learn to cope successfully with new situations and new people. For emotional and mental wellness, each of us must continue to grow psychologically, developing new and more sophisticated coping mechanisms to suit our current lives. We must develop an adult identity that enhances our self-esteem and autonomy. We must also learn to communicate honestly, handle anger and loneliness appropriately, and avoid being defensive.

Growing Up Psychologically

Our responses to life's challenges influence the development of our personality and identity. Psychologist Erik Erikson proposed that development proceeds through a

Terms

VW

other-directed Guided in behavior by the values and expectations of others.

inner-directed Guided in behavior by an inner set of rules and values.

authenticity Genuineness.

Table 3-1 Erikson's Stages of Development

Age	Conflict	Important People	Task
Birth–1 year	Trust vs. mistrust	Mother or other primary caregiver	In being fed and comforted, developing the trust that others will respond to your needs
1–3 years	Autonomy vs. shame and self-doubt	Parents	In toilet training, locomotion, and exploration, learning self-control without losing the capacity for assertiveness
3–6 years	Initiative vs. guilt	Family	In playful talking and locomotion, developing a conscience based on parental prohibitions that is not too inhibiting
6–12 years	Industry vs. inferiority	Neighborhood and school	In school and playing with peers, learning the value of accomplishment and perseverance without feeling inadequate
Adolescence	Identity vs. identity confusion	Peers	Developing a stable sense of who you are—your needs, abilities, interpersonal style, and values
Young adulthood	Intimacy vs. isolation	Close friends, sex partners	Learning to live and share intimately with others, often in sexual relationships
Middle adulthood	Generativity vs. self-absorption	Work associates, children, community	Doing things for others, including parenting and civic activities
Older adulthood	Integrity vs. despair	Humankind	Affirming the value of life and its ideals

SOURCE: Erikson, E. 1963. *Childhood and Society.* New York: Norton.

series of eight stages, extending throughout the life span. Each stage is characterized by a major crisis or turning point—a time of increased vulnerability as well as increased potential for psychological growth (Table 3-1).

The successful mastery of one stage is a basis for mastering the next, so early failures can have repercussions in later life. Fortunately, life provides ongoing opportunities for mastering these tasks. For example, although the development of trust begins in infancy, it is refined as we grow older. We learn to trust people outside our immediate family and to limit our trust by identifying people who are untrustworthy.

Developing an Adult Identity A primary task beginning in adolescence is the development of an adult identity: a unified sense of self, characterized by attitudes, beliefs, and ways of acting that are genuinely one's own. People with adult identities know who they are, what they are capable of, what roles they play, and their place among their peers. They have a sense of their own uniqueness but also appreciate what they have in common with others. They view themselves realistically and can assess their strengths and weaknesses without relying on the opinions of others. Achieving an identity also means that one can form intimate relationships with others while maintaining a strong sense of self.

Our identities evolve as we interact with the world and make choices about what we'd like to do and whom we'd like to model ourselves after. Developing an adult identity is particularly challenging in a heterogeneous, secular, and relatively affluent society like ours, in which many roles are possible, many choices are tolerated, and ample time is allowed for experimenting and making up one's mind.

Early identities are often modeled after parents—or the opposite of parents, in rebellion against what they represent. Later, peers, rock stars, sports heroes, and religious figures are added to the list of possible models. In high school and college, people often join cliques that assert a certain identity—the "jocks," the "brains," the "slackers." Although much of an identity is internal—a way of viewing oneself and the world—it can include things such as styles of talking and dressing, ornaments like earrings, and particular hairstyles.

Early identities are rarely permanent. A student who works for good grades and approval from parents and teachers one year can turn into a dropout devoted to hard rock and wild parties a year later. At some point, however, most of us adopt a more stable, individual identity that ties together the experiences of childhood and the expectations and aspirations of adulthood. Erikson's theory does not suggest that suddenly one day we assume our final identity and never change after that. Life is more interesting for people who continue to evolve into more distinct individuals, rather than being rigidly controlled by their pasts. Identity reflects a lifelong process, and it changes as a person develops new relationships and roles.

Developing an adult identity is an important part of psychological wellness. Without a personal identity, we begin to feel confused about who we are; Erikson called this situation an *identity crisis.* Until we have "found ourselves," we cannot have much self-esteem, because a self is not firmly in place.

How far have you gotten in developing your adult identity? Write down a list of characteristics you think a friend who knows you well would use to describe you. Rank them from the most to the least important. Your list might include elements such as gender, socioeconomic status, ethnic and/or religious identification, choice of college or major, parents' occupations, interests and talents, attitudes toward drugs and alcohol, style of dress, the kinds of people with whom you typically associate, your expected role in society, and aspects of your personality. Which elements of your identity do you feel are permanent, and which do you think may change over time? Are there any characteristics missing from your list that you'd like to add?

Another aid to developing an adult identity is to identify possible role models. Whom do you admire and want to be like? Which characteristics of that person do you want to emulate? How did that person acquire those characteristics, and how could you follow in her or his footsteps? Some role models might be willing to be mentors to you, spending time with you and sharing their wisdom.

Developing Intimacy Erikson's developmental stages don't end with establishing an adult identity. Learning to live intimately with others and finding a productive role for yourself in society are other tasks of adulthood—to be able to love and work.

People with established identities can form intimate relationships and sexual unions characterized by sharing, open communication, long-term commitment, and love. Those who lack a firm sense of self may have difficulty establishing relationships because they feel overwhelmed by closeness and the needs of another person. As a result, they experience only short-term, superficial relationships with others and may remain isolated. As described in Chapter 2, a lack of social support can affect getting both physical and psychological help. (Chapter 4 has more information about intimate relationships.)

Developing Values and Purpose in Your Life Erikson assigned his last two stages, generativity versus self-absorption and integrity versus despair, to middle adulthood and older adulthood. But these stages are concerned with values and purpose in life, issues that need to be addressed by young people and reexamined throughout life. Values are criteria for judging what is good and bad; they underlie our moral decisions and behavior. The first morality of the young child is to consider "good" to mean what brings immediate and tangible rewards, and "bad," whatever results in punishment. An older child will explain right and wrong in terms of authority figures and rules. But the final stage of moral development, one that not everyone attains, is being able to conceive of right and wrong in more abstract terms such as justice and virtue.

As adults we need to assess how far we have evolved morally and what values we actually have adopted, either explicitly or implicitly. Without an awareness of our personal values, our lives may be hurriedly driven forward by immediate desires and the passing demands of others. But are we doing things according to our principles? What are we striving for with our actions? Living according to values means considering your options carefully before making a choice, choosing between options without succumbing to outside pressures that oppose your values, and making a choice and acting on it rather than doing nothing. Your actions and how you justify them proclaim to others what you stand for.

A practical exercise for clarifying your values and goals is to write a draft of your obituary for a local newspaper. How would you like to be remembered? What would you like to have achieved? What will you have done to meet those goals? This obituary should not be a glorification, but an honest, realistic appraisal. End it by summarizing in a few sentences what was most important about your life. In reading what you have written, ask yourself, "How will I have to change to be the person I want to be?"

For more on developing meaning and purpose in your life, see the box "Paths to Spiritual Wellness." Visit the Online Learning Center for self-assessments that can help you identify your goals and values and suggest ways to boost your spiritual wellness.

Achieving Healthy Self-Esteem

Having a healthy level of self-esteem means regarding your self, which includes all aspects of your identity, as good, competent, and worthy of love. It is a critical component of wellness.

Developing a Positive Self-Concept Ideally, a positive self-concept begins in childhood, based on experiences both within the family and outside it. Children need to develop a sense of being loved and being able to give love and to accomplish their goals. If they feel rejected or neglected by their parents, they may fail to develop feelings of self-worth. They may grow to have a negative concept of themselves.

Another component of self-concept is integration. An integrated self-concept is one that you have made for yourself—not someone else's image of you or a mask that doesn't quite fit. Important building blocks of self-concept are the personality characteristics and mannerisms of parents, which children may adopt without realizing it. Later, they may be surprised to find themselves acting like one of their parents. Eventually, such building blocks should be reshaped and integrated into a new, individual personality.

A further aspect of self-concept is stability. Stability depends on the integration of the self and its freedom

Mind/Body/Spirit

Paths to Spiritual Wellness

Spiritual wellness means different things to different people. For many, it involves developing a set of guiding beliefs, principles, or values that give meaning and purpose to life. It helps people achieve a sense of wholeness within themselves and in their relationships with others. Spiritual wellness influences people on an individual level, as well as on a community level, where it can bond people together through compassion, love, forgiveness, and self-sacrifice. For some, spirituality includes a belief in a higher power. Regardless of how it is defined, the development of spiritual wellness is critical for overall health and well-being. Its development is closely tied to the other components of wellness, particularly psychological health.

There are many paths to spiritual wellness. One of the most common in our society is organized religion. Some people object to the notion that organized religion can contribute to psychological health and overall wellness, asserting that it reinforces people's tendency to deny real difficulties and to accept what can and should be changed. Freud criticized religion as wishful thinking; Marx called it an opiate to make the poor accept social injustice. However, many elements of religious belief and practice can promote psychological health.

Organized religion usually involves its members in a community where social and material support is available. Religious organizations offer a social network to those who might otherwise be isolated. The major religions provide paths for transforming the self in ways that can lead to greater happiness and serenity and reduce feelings of anxiety and hopelessness. In Christianity, salvation follows turning away from the selfish ego to God's sovereignty and grace, where a joy is found that frees the believer from anxious self-concern and despair. Islam is the word for a kind of self-surrender leading to peace with God. Buddhism teaches how to detach oneself from selfish desire, leading to compassion for the suffering of others and freedom from fear-engendering illusions. Judaism emphasizes the social and ethical redemption the Jewish community can experience if it follows the laws of God. Religions teach specific techniques for achieving these transformations of the self: prayer, both in groups and in private; meditation; the performance of rituals and ceremonies symbolizing religious truths; and good works and service to others. Christianity's faith and works are perhaps analogous to the cognitive and behavioral components of a program of behavior change.

Spiritual wellness does not require participation in organized religion. Many people find meaning and purpose in other ways. By spending time in nature or working on environmental issues, people can experience continuity with the natural world. Spiritual wellness can come through helping others in one's community or by promoting human rights, peace and harmony among people, and opportunities for human development on a global level. (The spiritual, psychological, and physical wellness benefits of helping others are discussed further in Chapter 19.) Other people develop spiritual wellness through art or through their personal relationships.

The search for meaning and purpose in life is reflected in Erikson's later stages of development. Particularly in the second half of life, people seem to have an urge to view their activities and consciousness from a transcendent perspective. Perhaps it is the approach of death that makes older people tend to take less interest in material possessions and to devote more time to interpersonal and altruistic pursuits. At every age, however, people seem to feel better if they have beliefs about the ultimate purpose of life and their own place in the universe.

from contradictions. People who have gotten mixed messages about themselves from parents and friends may have contradictory self-images, which defy integration and make them vulnerable to shifting levels of self-esteem. At times they regard themselves as entirely good, capable, and lovable—an ideal self—and at other times they see themselves as entirely bad, incompetent, and unworthy of love. While at the first pole, they may develop such an inflated ego that they totally ignore other people's needs and see others only as instruments for fulfilling their own desires. At the other pole, they may feel so small and weak that they run for protection to someone who seems powerful and caring. At neither extreme do such people see themselves or others realistically, and their relationships with other people are filled with misunderstandings and ultimately with conflict.

The concepts we have about ourselves and others are an important part of our personalities. And all the components of our self-concept profoundly influence our interpersonal relationships.

Meeting Challenges to Self-Esteem As an adult, you sometimes run into situations that challenge your self-concept: People you care about may tell you they don't love you or feel loved by you, or your attempts to accomplish a goal may end in failure. You can react to such challenges in several ways. The best approach is to acknowledge that something has gone wrong and try again, adjusting your goals to your abilities without radically revising your self-concept. Less productive responses are denying that anything went wrong and blaming someone else. These attitudes may preserve your self-concept temporarily, but in the long run they keep you from meeting the challenge. The worst reaction is to develop a lasting negative self-concept in which you feel bad, unloved, and ineffective—in other words, to become demoralized. Instead of coping, the

A positive self-concept begins in infancy. Knowing that he's loved and valued by his parents gives this baby a solid basis for lifelong psychological health.

demoralized person gives up, reinforcing the negative self-concept and setting in motion a cycle of bad self-concept and failure. In people who are genetically predisposed to depression, demoralization can progress to additional symptoms, discussed later in the chapter.

NOTICE YOUR PATTERNS OF THINKING One method for fighting demoralization is to recognize and test your negative thoughts and assumptions about yourself and others. The first step is to note exactly when an unpleasant emotion—feeling worthless, wanting to give up, feeling depressed—occurs or gets worse, to identify the events or daydreams that trigger that emotion, and to observe whatever thoughts come into your head just before or during the emotional experience. It is helpful to keep a daily journal about such events.

Consider the example of Jennifer, a student who went to the college counseling center because she'd been feeling "down" lately. Her social life had not been going well, and she had begun to think she was a boring, uninteresting person. Asked to keep a daily journal, she wrote that she felt let down and discouraged when a date who promised to meet her at 7:30 P.M. was 15 minutes late. She had these thoughts: "He's not going to come. It's my fault. He has more important things to do. Maybe he's with someone else. He doesn't like me. Nobody likes me because I don't have anything interesting to say. What if he had a car accident?"

People who are demoralized tend to use all-or-nothing thinking. They overgeneralize from negative events. They overlook the positive and jump to negative conclusions, minimizing their own successes and magnifying the successes of others. They take responsibility for unfortunate situations that are not their fault. The minute Jennifer's date was late, she jumped to the conclusion that he was not coming and blamed herself for it. From that point she jumped to more negative conclusions and more unfounded overgeneralizations. Patterns of thinking that make events seem worse than they are in reality are called **cognitive distortions.**

DEVELOP REALISTIC SELF-TALK Jennifer needs to develop more rational responses. For Jennifer, more rational thinking could be "He's a little late so I'll reread the study questions." If he still hasn't come after 30 minutes, she might call him to see if something is holding him up, without jumping to any conclusions about the meaning of his lateness.

In your own fight against demoralization, it may be hard to figure out a rational response until hours or days after the event that upset you. But once you get used to noticing the way your mind works, you may be able to catch yourself thinking negatively and change the thought process before it goes too far.

This approach is not the same as positive thinking—substituting a positive thought for a negative one. Instead, you simply try to make your thoughts as logical and accurate as possible. If Jennifer continues to think she's boring, she should try to collect evidence to prove or disprove that. If she has exaggerated her dullness, as do many demoralized people, her investigations may prove her wrong. For example, she might ask her friends their candid opinions about her personality, and she can observe whether people seem interested in continuing a conversation with her.

Demoralized people can be so tenacious about their negative beliefs that they make them come true in a self-fulfilling prophecy. Jennifer might conclude that she is so boring no one will like her anyway, so she may as well not bother to be involved in what's going on around her. This behavior could help her negative belief become a reality. For additional tips on how to change distorted, negative ways of thinking, see the box "Realistic Self-Talk."

Being Less Defensive

Sometimes our wishes come into conflict with people around us or with our conscience, and we become frustrated and anxious. If we cannot resolve the conflict by changing the external situation, we try to resolve the

Terms

VW

cognitive distortion A pattern of thinking that makes events seem worse than they are.

defense mechanism A mental mechanism for coping with conflict or anxiety.

Take Charge

Realistic Self-Talk

Do your patterns of thinking make events seem worse than they truly are? Do negative beliefs about yourself become self-fulfilling prophecies? Substituting realistic self-talk for negative self-talk can help you build and maintain self-esteem and cope better with the challenges in your life. Here are some examples of common types of distorted, negative self-talk, along with suggestions for more accurate and rational responses.

Cognitive Distortion	Negative Self-Talk	Realistic Self-Talk
Focusing on negatives	School is so discouraging—nothing but one hassle after another.	School is pretty challenging and has its difficulties, but there certainly are rewards. It's really a mixture of good and bad.
Expecting the worst	Why would my boss want to meet with me this afternoon if not to fire me?	I wonder why my boss wants to meet with me. I guess I'll just have to wait and see.
Overgeneralizing	(After getting a poor grade on a paper) Just as I thought—I'm incompetent at everything.	I'll start working on the next paper earlier. That way, if I run into problems, I'll have time to consult with the TA.
Minimizing	I won the speech contest, but none of the other speakers was very good. I wouldn't have done as well against stiffer competition.	It may not have been the best speech I'll ever give, but it was good enough to win the contest. I'm really improving as a speaker.
Blaming others	I wouldn't have eaten so much last night if my friends hadn't insisted on going to that restaurant.	I overdid it last night. Next time I'll make different choices.
Expecting perfection	I should have scored 100% on this test. I can't believe I missed that one problem through a careless mistake.	Too bad I missed one problem through carelessness, but overall I did very well on this test. Next time I'll be more careful.
Believing you're the cause of everything	Sarah seems so depressed today. I wish I hadn't had that argument with her yesterday; it must have really upset her.	I wish I had handled the argument better, and in the future I'll try to. But I don't know if Sarah's behavior is related to what I said or even if she's depressed. In any case, I'm not responsible for how Sarah feels or acts; only she can take responsibility for that.
Thinking in black and white	I've got to score 10 points in the game today. Otherwise, I don't belong on the team.	I'm a good player or else I wouldn't be on the team. I'll play my best—that's all I can do.
Magnifying events	They went to a movie without me. I thought we were friends, but I guess I was wrong.	I'm disappointed they didn't ask me to the movie, but it doesn't mean our friendship is over. It's not that big a deal.

SOURCE: Adapted from Schafer, W. 1999. *Stress Management for Wellness,* 4th ed. Copyright © 2000. Reprinted with permission of Wadsworth, a division of Thomson Learning: www.thomsonrights.com.

conflict internally by rearranging our thoughts and feelings. Some standard **defense mechanisms** are listed in Table 3-2 on page 72. The drawback of many of these coping mechanisms is that although they succeed temporarily, they are dead-ends that make finding ultimate solutions much harder. Some mechanisms, such as substitution and humor, can be very useful for coping, as long as they don't keep us from being who we want to be.

Recognizing your own defense mechanisms can be difficult, because they've probably become habits, occurring unconsciously. But we each have some inkling about how our mind operates. By remembering the details of conflict situations you have been in, you may be able to figure out which defense mechanisms you used in successful or unsuccessful attempts to cope. Try to look at yourself as an objective, outside observer would and analyze your thoughts and behavior in a psychologically stressful situation from the past. Having insight into what strategies you typically use can lead to new, less defensive and more effective ways of coping in the future.

Being Optimistic

Optimism and pessimism are abstract concepts that might seem to have more to do with philosophy than with psychological health. However, many psychologists believe that pessimism is not just a symptom of everyday depression but an important root cause as well. Pessimists not only expect repeated failure and rejection but also perversely accept it as deserved. Pessimists do not see themselves as capable of

Table 3-2 Defense and Coping Mechanisms

Mechanism	Description	Example
Projection	Reacting to unacceptable inner impulses as if they were from outside the self	A student who dislikes his roommate feels that the roommate dislikes him.
Repression	Expelling from awareness an unpleasant feeling, idea, or memory	The child of an alcoholic, neglectful father remembers him as a giving, loving person.
Denial	Refusing to acknowledge to yourself what you really know to be true	A person believes that smoking cigarettes won't harm her because she's young and healthy.
Passive-aggressive behavior	Expressing hostility toward someone by being covertly uncooperative or passive	A person tells a coworker, with whom she competes for project assignments, that she'll help him with a report but then never follows through.
Displacement	Shifting one's feelings about a person to another person	A student who is angry with one of his professors returns home and yells at one of his housemates.
Rationalization	Giving a false, acceptable reason when the real reason is unacceptable	A shy young man decides not to attend a dorm party, telling himself he'd be bored.
Substitution	Deliberately replacing a frustrating goal with one that is more attainable	A student having a difficult time passing courses in chemistry decides to change his major from biology to economics.
Humor	Finding something funny in unpleasant situations	A student whose bicycle has been stolen thinks how surprised the thief will be when he or she starts downhill and discovers the brakes don't work.

success, and they irrationally dismiss any evidence of their own accomplishments. This negative point of view is learned, typically at a young age from parents and other authority figures. But as an optimist would tell you, that means it also has the potential to be unlearned.

Psychologist Martin Seligman points out that we are more used to refuting negative statements, such as "The problem is going to last forever and ruin everything, and it's all my fault," when they come from a jealous rival rather than from our own mind. But refuting such negative self-statements is exactly what a pessimist must learn to do in order to avoid chronic unhappiness. Pessimists must first recognize and then dispute the false, negative predictions they generate about themselves. Seligman points out that learning to be optimistic is easier and more lasting than, for example, learning to eat less. Unlike refusing foods you love, disputing your own negative thoughts is fun—because doing so makes you feel better immediately.

Maintaining Honest Communication

Another important area of psychological functioning is communicating honestly with others. It can be very frustrating for us and for people around us if we cannot express what we want and feel. Others can hardly respond to our needs if they don't know what those needs are. We must recognize what we want to communicate and then express it clearly. For example, how do you feel about going to the party instead of to the movie? Do you care if your roommate talks on the phone late into the night? Some people know what they want others to do but don't state it clearly because they fear denial of the request, which they interpret as personal rejection. Such people might benefit from **assertiveness** training: learning to insist on their rights and to bargain for what they want. Assertiveness includes being able to say no or yes depending on the situation.

Because expressing feelings has become so central to popular psychology, many misconceptions have arisen. Neither "sharing" feelings with everyone on every occasion nor making important decisions based on feelings alone is a legitimate psychological health goal. But communicating your feelings appropriately and clearly is important. For example, if you tell people you feel sad, they may have various reactions. If they feel closer to you, they may express an intimate thought of their own. Or they may feel guilty because they think you're implying they have caused your sadness. They may even be angry because they feel obligated to help cheer you up.

Depending on your intention and your prediction of how a statement will be taken, you may or may not wish to make it. For example, if you say you feel like staying home tonight, you may also be implying something different. You could really be saying "Don't bother me" or opening a negotiation about what you would be willing to do that evening, given the right event or incentive.

Term

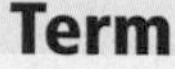

assertiveness Expression that is forceful but not hostile.

Good communication means expressing yourself clearly. You don't need any special psychological jargon to communicate effectively. (For tips, see the box "Guidelines for Effective Communication" in Chapter 4, p. 104.)

Dealing with Loneliness

The right balance between being alone and being with others is often hard to achieve. Some people are motivated to socialize by a fear of being alone—not the best reason to spend time with others. If you discover how to be happy by yourself, you'll be better able to cope with periods when you're forced to be alone—for example, when you've just broken off a romantic relationship, when you've moved to a new town, or when your usual friends are away on vacation.

Unhappiness with being alone may come from interpreting it as a sign of rejection—that others are not interested in spending time with you. Before you conclude that, be sure that you give others a real chance to get to know you. Examine your patterns of thinking: You may harbor unrealistic expectations about other people—for example, that everyone you meet must like you and, if they don't, you must be terribly flawed. You might also consider the possibility that you expect too much from new acquaintances and, sensing this, they start to draw back, triggering your feelings of rejection. Not everyone you meet is a suitable and willing person for a close or intimate relationship. Feeling pressure to have such a relationship may lead you to take up with someone whose interests and needs are remote from yours or whose need to be cared for leaves you with little time of your own. You will have traded loneliness for potentially worse problems.

Loneliness is a passive feeling state. If you decide that you're not spending enough time with people, take action to change the situation. College life provides many opportunities to meet people. In addition to classes and dorms, there are organizations of all kinds—hiking clubs, religious groups, advocacy groups, and so on—that offer a chance to meet others who share your interests. If you're shy, you may have to push yourself to join such groups. Look for something you've enjoyed in the past or in which you have a genuine interest. If your loneliness is the result of missing absent friends, remember that communication at a distance is cheaper and easier than ever before. For many people, e-mail and cell phones offer more immediate and satisfying contact than letters for keeping up with people in their lives.

Dealing with Anger

Common wisdom holds that expressing anger is beneficial for psychological and physical health. However, recent studies have questioned this idea by showing that overtly hostile people seem to be at higher risk for heart attacks. Angry words or actions don't contribute to psychological wellness if they damage relationships or produce feelings of guilt or loss of control. Perhaps the best way to resolve this contradiction is to distinguish between a gratuitous expression of anger and a reasonable level of self-assertiveness.

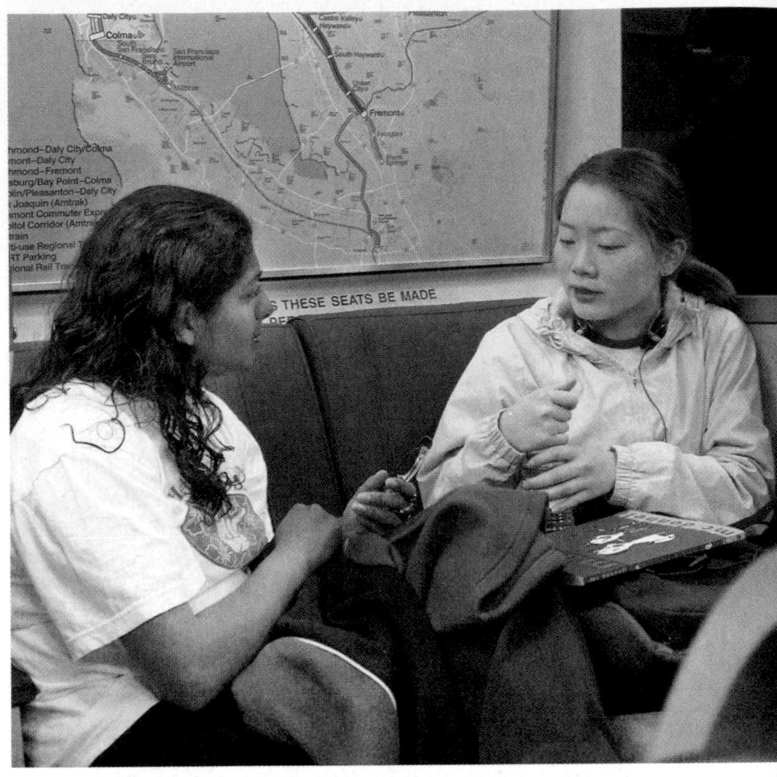

As these women express their thoughts and feelings to each other and listen attentively in response, they enhance their relationship, which in turn supports their psychological well-being.

At one extreme are people who never express anger or any opinion that might offend others, even when their own rights and needs are being jeopardized. They may be trapped in unhealthy relationships or chronically deprived of satisfaction at work and at home. If you have trouble expressing your anger, consider training in assertiveness and appropriate expressions of anger to help you learn to express yourself constructively.

At the other extreme are people whose anger is explosive or misdirected. The National Institute of Mental Health (NIMH) estimates that 7.3% of Americans suffer from intermittent explosive disorder (IED). IED is often accompanied by depression or another disorder. Explosive anger, or rage, like a child's tantrum, renders individuals temporarily unable to think straight or to act in their own best interest. During an IED episode, a person may lash out uncontrollably, hurting someone else or destroying property. Anyone who expresses anger this way should seek professional help.

Managing Your Own Anger If you feel explosive anger coming on, consider the following two strategies to head it off. First, try to *reframe* what you're thinking at that moment. You'll be less angry at another person if there is a possibility that his or her behavior was not intentionally directed against you. Did the man who cut into your lane on the freeway do it deliberately to spite you, or did he simply fail to see you? Look for possible mitigating factors that would make you less likely to blame him: Maybe he's late for a job interview and preoccupied with worries. If you're angry because you've just been criticized, avoid mentally replaying scenes from the past when you received similar unjust criticisms. Think about what is happening now, and try to act differently than in the past—less defensively and more analytically. What is it about me that makes it easy for this person to get my goat? Why am I taking it personally? Why am I acting like a jerk just because she did?

Second, until you're able to change your thinking, try to *distract* yourself. Use the old trick of counting to 10 before you respond, or start concentrating on your breathing. If needed, take a longer cooling-off period by leaving the situation until your anger has subsided. This does not mean that you should permanently avoid the issues and people who make you angry. When you've had a chance to think more clearly about the matter, return to it.

Dealing with Anger in Other People Anger can be infectious and disruptive to cooperation and communication. If someone you're with becomes very angry, respond "asymmetrically" by reacting not with anger but with calm. Try to validate the other person by acknowledging that he or she has some reason to be angry. This does not mean apologizing, if you don't think you're to blame, or accepting verbal abuse, which is always inappropriate. Try to focus on solving the problem by allowing the individual to explain why he or she is so angry and what can be done to alleviate the situation. Finally, if the person cannot be calmed, it may be best to disengage, at least temporarily. After a time-out, a rational problem-solving approach may become more successful.

PSYCHOLOGICAL DISORDERS

All of us have felt anxious at times, and in dealing with the anxiety we may have avoided doing something that we wanted to do or should have done. Most of us have had periods of feeling down when we became pessimistic, less energetic, and less able to enjoy life. Many of us have been bothered at times by irrational thoughts or odd feelings. Such feelings and thoughts can be normal responses to the ordinary challenges of life, but when emotions or irrational thoughts start to interfere with daily activities and rob us of our peace of mind, they can be considered symptoms of a psychological disorder.

Psychological disorders are generally the result of many factors. Genetic differences, which underlie differences in how the brain processes information and experience, are known to play an important role, especially in bipolar disorder and schizophrenia. However, exactly which genes are involved, and how they alter the structure and chemistry of the brain, is still under study. Learning and life events are important, too: Identical twins often don't have the same psychological disorders in spite of having identical genes. Some people have been exposed to more traumatic events than others, leading either to greater vulnerability to future traumas or, conversely, the development of better coping skills. Furthermore, what your parents, peers, and others have taught you strongly influences your level of self-esteem and how you deal with frightening or depressing life events (see the box "Ethnicity, Culture, and Psychological Disorders").

In this section, we'll take a closer look at some of the more common psychological disorders, including anxiety disorders, mood disorders, and schizophrenia. (Table 3-3 on p. 76 shows the likelihood of these disorders occurring during your lifetime and during the past year.) Elsewhere in this book you can learn about other disorders: sexual disorders in Chapter 5, disorders associated with drug and alcohol abuse in Chapters 9 and 10, eating disorders in Chapter 14, and Alzheimer's disease in Chapter 19.

Anxiety Disorders

Fear is a basic and useful emotion. Its value for our ancestors' survival cannot be overestimated; for modern humans, it provides motivation for self-protection and for learning to cope with new or potentially dangerous environmental or social situations. Only when fear is out of proportion to real danger can it be considered a problem. **Anxiety** is another word for fear, especially a feeling of fear that is not in response to any definite threat. Only when anxiety is experienced almost daily or in life situations that recur and cannot be avoided can anxiety be called a disorder. This section provides brief descriptions of the major types of anxiety disorders.

Simple Phobia The most common and most understandable anxiety disorder, **simple,** or **specific, phobia** is a fear of something definite like lightning or a particular animal or location. Examples of commonly feared animals are snakes, spiders, and dogs; frightening locations are often high places or enclosed spaces. Sometimes, but

Terms

Vw

anxiety A feeling of fear that is not directed toward any definite threat.

simple (specific) phobia A persistent and excessive fear of a specific object, activity, or situation.

social phobia An excessive fear of performing in public; speaking in public is the most common example.

panic disorder A syndrome of severe anxiety attacks accompanied by physical symptoms.

Dimensions of Diversity

Ethnicity, Culture, and Psychological Disorders

Psychological disorders differ in incidence and symptoms across cultures and ethnic groups around the world. This variability is usually attributable to cultural differences—factors such as how symptoms are interpreted and communicated, whether treatment is sought, and whether a social stigma is attached to a particular symptom or disorder. Cultural differences relating to acculturation, ethnic identity, coping styles, social support, racism, and spirituality can increase the risk for, or provide protection from, psychological disorders.

Expression of Symptoms

People from different cultures or groups may manifest or describe symptoms differently. Consider the following examples:

- In Japan, where showing respect and consideration for others is highly valued, people with social phobia may be more distressed about the imagined harm to others by their social clumsiness than at their own embarrassment.
- Older African Americans may express depression in atypical ways—for example, denying depression by taking on a multitude of extra tasks.
- Somatization, the indirect reporting of psychological distress through nonspecific physical symptoms, occurs across ethnic groups but is more prevalent among some, including African Americans, Puerto Ricans, and Chinese Americans.
- Schizophrenia may manifest with different delusions depending on the local culture.

Attitudes Toward Symptoms, Diseases, and Treatment

An important cultural factor is whether a group regards symptoms as a social, moral, or health problem. It is relatively easy for Americans of northern European descent to regard an emotional problem as psychological in nature and to there fore accept a psychological treatment. For other groups, symptoms of psychological distress may be viewed as a spiritual problem, best dealt with by religious figures.

Attitudes about disease influence whether patients will comply with professional treatment. For example, researchers looking at multiethnic clinics found that Southeast Asians were more likely than other groups to have no detectable blood levels of their prescribed antidepressant medication. The patients' respect for the authority of the physician made them reluctant to admit that they did not agree with the doctor's recommendations and had not followed them.

People from some groups may have little hesitation about communicating intimate, personal problems to professional care providers. However, for others, particularly men and members of certain ethnic groups, loss of emotional control may be seen as a weakness. In addition, the use of mental health services is viewed negatively in many cultures; this stigma may partly account for the fact that African Americans and Asian American/Pacific Islanders are only about half as likely as whites to use any type of mental health service. For all groups, culturally competent care is important to avoid misdiagnosis and inappropriate or ineffective treatment.

Genetic/Biological Risk Factors

Biology can also play a role in the differences seen among patients of different ethnic groups. There is accumulating evidence that genetic differences between ethnic groups can explain some differences in drug metabolism. For example, psychotropic drugs are broken down in the body by a specific enzyme known as CYP2C19. Reduction of the activity of this enzyme is caused by two mutations, one of which appears to be found only in Asian populations. People in whom the action of this enzyme is reduced are called poor metabolizers, who as a result are very sensitive to medications that are broken down by it. The percentage of poor metabolizers among Asians is about 20%; among Latinos, about 5%; and among whites, 3%. Asian patients thus tend to have more adverse reactions to the doses of drugs standardized principally on white patients in the United States.

SOURCES: Kleinman, A. 2004. Culture and depression. *New England Journal of Medicine* 351(10): 951–953; Kirmayer, L. J. 2001. Cultural variations in the clinical presentation of depression and anxiety: Implications for diagnosis and treatment. *Journal of Clinical Psychiatry* 62 (Suppl. 13): 22–28; Lin, K. M. 2001. Biological differences in depression and anxiety across races and ethnic groups. *Journal of Clinical Psychiatry* 62 (Suppl. 13): 13–19; Baker, F. M. 2001. Diagnosing depression in African Americans. *Community Mental Health Journal* 37(1): 31–38; U.S. Department of Health and Human Services. 2001. *Mental Health: Culture, Race, and Ethnicity—A Supplement to Mental Health: A Report of the Surgeon General*. Rockville, Md.: U.S. Department of Health and Human Services.

not always, these fears originate in bad experiences, such as being bitten by a snake. A special kind of simple phobia is fear of blood, injections, or seeing injured people. These fears usually come from a tendency to faint or become nauseated in such situations.

Social Phobia People with **social phobia** fear humiliation or embarrassment while being observed by others. Fear of speaking in public is perhaps the most common phobia of this kind. Extremely shy people can have social fears that extend to almost all social situations (see the box "Shyness" on p. 77). People with these kinds of fears may not continue in school as far as they could and may restrict themselves to lower-paying jobs where they do not have to come into contact with new people.

Panic Disorder People with **panic disorder** experience sudden unexpected surges in anxiety, accompanied by symptoms such as rapid and strong heartbeat, shortness of breath, loss of physical equilibrium, and a feeling of losing mental control. Such attacks usually begin in one's early twenties and can lead to a fear of being in crowds or closed places or of driving or flying. Sufferers fear that a panic attack will occur in a situation from which

VITAL STATISTICS

Table 3-3 **Prevalence of Selected Psychological Disorders Among Americans**

Disorder	Men: Lifetime Prevalence (%)	Men: Past Year Prevalence (%)	Women: Lifetime Prevalence (%)	Women: Past Year Prevalence (%)
Anxiety disorders				
Simple phobia	6.7	4.4	15.7	13.2
Social phobia	11.1	6.6	15.5	9.1
Panic disorder	2.0	1.3	5.0	3.2
Generalized anxiety disorder	3.6	2.0	6.6	4.3
Obsessive-compulsive disorder	1.7	0.5	2.8	0.8
Post-traumatic stress disorder	5.0	1.5	10.4	3.5
Mood disorders				
Major depressive episode	12.0	5.5	20.4	7.7
Manic episode	1.6	1.4	1.7	1.3
Schizophrenia and related disorders	1.0	0.8	0.5	0.4
Dementia	Depends on life expectancy	6.4 (age >=65)	Depends on life expectancy	5.7 (age >=65)

SOURCES: Kessler, R. C., et al. 2003. The epidemiology of major depressive disorder: Results from the National Comorbidity Survey Replication (NCS-R). *Journal of the American Medical Association* 289(23): 3095–3105; U.S. Department of Health and Human Services. 1999. *Mental Health: A Report of the Surgeon General.* Rockville, Md.: DHHS; Kessler, R. C., et al. 1995. Posttraumatic stress disorder in the National Comorbidity Survey. *Archives of General Psychiatry* 52(12): 1048–1060; Kessler, R. C., et al. 1994. Lifetime and 12-month prevalence of DSM-III-R psychiatric disorders in the United States. *Archives of General Psychiatry* 51(1): 8–19; Ferri, C. P., et al. 2005. Global prevalence of dementia: A Delphi consensus. *Lancet* 366: 2112–2117; Kukull, W. A., et al. 2002. Dementia and Alzheimer disease incidence. *Archives of Neurology* 59(Nov.): 1737–1776. (Note: Rates of the prevalence of dementia are highly dependent on how much impairment is considered dementia and on the age range of the population.)

escape is difficult (such as while in an elevator), where the attack could be incapacitating and result in a dangerous or embarrassing loss of control (such as while driving a car or shopping), or where no medical help would be available if needed (such as when a person is alone away from home). Fears such as these lead to avoidance of situations that might cause trouble. The fears and avoidance may spread to a large variety of situations until a person is virtually housebound, a condition called **agoraphobia.** People with panic disorder can often function normally in feared situations if someone they trust accompanies them.

Generalized Anxiety Disorder A basic reaction to future threats is to worry about them. **Generalized anxiety disorder (GAD)** is a diagnosis given to people whose worries have taken on a life of their own, pushing out other thoughts and refusing banishment by any effort of will. The topics of the worrying are ordinary concerns: Will I be able to pass the exam next Friday? Where will I get money to get my car fixed? Furthermore, the worrying is not completely unjustified—after all, thinking about problems can result in solving them. But this kind of thinking seems to just go around in circles, and the more you try to stop it, the more you feel at its mercy. The end result is a persistent feeling of nervousness, often accompanied by depression.

Obsessive-Compulsive Disorder The diagnosis of **obsessive-compulsive disorder (OCD)** is given to people with obsessions or compulsions or both. **Obsessions** are recurrent, unwanted thoughts or impulses. Unlike the worries of GAD, they are not ordinary concerns but improbable fears such as of suddenly committing an antisocial act or of having been contaminated by germs. For example, a parent may have an impulse to kill a beloved child, or a person may brood over whether he or she got HIV from a handshake. **Compulsions** are repetitive, difficult-to-resist actions usually associated with

Terms

agoraphobia An anxiety disorder characterized by fear of being alone away from help and avoidance of many different places and situations; in extreme cases, a fear of leaving home. From the Greek for "fear of the public market."

generalized anxiety disorder (GAD) An anxiety disorder characterized by excessive, uncontrollable worry about all kinds of things and anxiety in many situations.

obsessive-compulsive disorder (OCD) An anxiety disorder characterized by uncontrollable, recurring thoughts and the performing of senseless rituals.

obsession A recurrent, irrational, unwanted thought or impulse.

compulsion An irrational, repetitive, forced action, usually associated with an obsession.

post-traumatic stress disorder (PTSD) An anxiety disorder characterized by reliving traumatic events through dreams, flashbacks, and hallucinations.

In Focus: Shyness

Shyness is a form of social anxiety, a fear of what others will think of one's behavior or appearance. Physical signs include a rapid heartbeat, a nervous stomach, sweating, cold and clammy hands, blushing, dry mouth, a lump in the throat, and trembling muscles. Shy people are often excessively self-critical, and they engage in very negative self-talk. The accompanying feelings of self-consciousness, embarrassment, and unworthiness can be overwhelming.

To avoid situations that make them anxious, shy people may refrain from making eye contact or speaking up in public. They may shun social gatherings. They may avoid college courses or job promotions that demand more interpersonal interaction or public speaking. Shyness is not the same thing as being introverted. Introverts prefer solitude to society. Shy people often long to be more outgoing, but their own negative thoughts prevent them from enjoying the social interaction they desire. The consequences of severe shyness can include social isolation, loneliness, and lost personal and professional opportunities. Very shy people also have higher than average rates of other anxiety and mood disorders and of substance abuse.

Shyness is very common, with 40–50% of Americans describing themselves as shy. However, only about 7–13% of adults are so shy that their condition interferes seriously with work, school, daily life, or interpersonal relationships. Shyness is often hidden, and most shy people manage to appear reasonably outgoing, even though they suffer the physical and emotional symptoms of their anxiety. Many shy people do better in structured rather than spontaneous settings.

What causes people to be shy? Research indicates that for some the trait may be partly inherited. But for shyness, as for many health concerns, biology is not destiny. Many shy children outgrow their shyness, just as others acquire it later in life. Clearly, other factors are involved. The type of attachment between a child and his or her caregiver is important, as are parenting styles. Shyness is more common in cultures where children's failures are attributed to their own actions but successes are attributed to other people or events. People's experiences during critical developmental transitions, such as starting school and entering adolescence, have also been linked to shyness. For adults, the precipitating factor may be an event such as divorce or the loss of a job.

Recent surveys indicate that shyness rates may be rising in the United States. With the advent of technologies such as ATM machines, video games, voice mail, faxes, and e-mail, the opportunities for face-to-face interaction are diminishing. Electronic media can be a wonderful way for shy people to communicate, but they can also allow them to hide from all social interaction. In fact, one study found that greater use of the Internet was associated with a decline in participants' communication with family members, a reduction in the size of their social circles, and an increase in levels of depression and loneliness. It remains to be seen whether the first generation to have cradle-to-grave access to home computers, faxes, and the Internet will experience higher rates of shyness.

Shyness is often undiagnosed, but help is available. Shyness classes, assertiveness training groups, and public speaking clinics are available (see the Behavior Change Strategy at the end of the chapter). For the seriously shy, effective treatments include cognitive-behavioral therapy and antidepressant drugs.

If you're shy, try to remember that shyness is widespread and that there are worse fates. Some degree of shyness has an upside. Shy people tend to be gentle, supportive, kind, and sensitive; they are often exceptional listeners. People who think carefully before they speak or act are less likely to hurt the feelings of others. Shyness may also facilitate cooperation. For any group or society to function well, a variety of roles is required, and there is a place for quieter, more reflective individuals.

SOURCES: Furmark, T. 2002. Social phobia. *Acta Psychiatrica Scandinavica* 105(2): 84–93; Carducci, B. J. 1999. *Shyness: A Bold New Approach.* New York: Perennial; Kraut, R., et al. 1998. Internet paradox: A social technology that reduces social involvement and psychological well-being? *American Psychologist* 53(9): 1017–1031.

obsessions. A common compulsion is hand washing, associated with an obsessive fear of contamination by dirt. Other compulsions are counting and repeatedly checking whether something has been done—for example, whether a door has been locked or a stove turned off. People with OCD feel anxious, out of control, and embarrassed. Their rituals can occupy much of their time and make them inefficient at work and difficult to live with.

Post-Traumatic Stress Disorder People who suffer from **post-traumatic stress disorder (PTSD)** are reacting to severely traumatic events (events that produce a sense of terror and helplessness) such as physical violence to oneself or loved ones. Trauma occurs in personal assaults (rape, military combat), natural disasters (floods, hurricanes), and tragedies like fires and airplane or car crashes. Symptoms include reexperiencing the trauma in dreams and in intrusive memories, trying to avoid anything associated with the trauma, and numbing of feelings. Hyperarousal, sleep disturbances, and other symptoms of anxiety and depression also commonly occur. Such symptoms can last months or even years. PTSD symptoms often decrease substantially within 3 months, but in up to one-third of PTSD cases, the individual does not fully recover. Recovery may be slower in those who have previously experienced trauma or who suffer from ongoing psychological problems.

The terrorist attacks on September 11, 2001, brought PTSD into the spotlight. Among those affected were

Assess Yourself

Are You Suffering from a Mood Disorder?

Ww

You should get evaluated by a professional if you've had five or more of the following symptoms for more than 2 weeks or if any of these symptoms causes such a big change that you can't keep up your usual routine.

When You're Depressed

_____ You feel sad or cry a lot, and it doesn't go away.

_____ You feel guilty for no reason; you feel you're no good; you've lost your confidence.

_____ Life seems meaningless, or you think nothing good is ever going to happen again.

_____ You have a negative attitude a lot of the time, or it seems as if you have no feelings.

_____ You don't feel like doing a lot of the things you used to like—music, sports, being with friends, going out, and so on—and you want to be left alone most of the time.

_____ It's hard to make up your mind. You forget lots of things, and it's hard to concentrate.

_____ You get irritated often. Little things make you lose your temper; you overreact.

_____ Your sleep pattern changes: You start sleeping a lot more or you have trouble falling asleep at night; or you wake up really early most mornings and can't get back to sleep.

_____ Your eating pattern changes: You've lost your appetite or you eat a lot more.

_____ You feel restless and tired most of the time.

_____ You think about death or feel as if you're dying or have thoughts about committing suicide.

When You're Manic

_____ You feel high as a kite, like you're "on top of the world."

_____ You get unrealistic ideas about the great things you can do—things that you really can't do.

_____ Thoughts go racing through your head, you jump from one subject to another, and you talk a lot.

_____ You're a nonstop party, constantly running around.

_____ You do too many wild or risky things—with driving, with spending money, with sex, and so on.

_____ You're so "up" that you don't need much sleep.

_____ You're rebellious or irritable and can't get along at home or school or with your friends.

If you are concerned about depression in yourself or a friend, or if you are thinking about hurting or killing yourself, talk to someone about it and get help immediately. There are many sources of help: a good friend; an academic or resident adviser; the staff at the student health or counseling center; a professor, coach, or adviser; a local suicide or emergency hotline (get the phone number from the operator or directory) or the 911 operator; or a hospital emergency room.

SOURCE: National Institute of Mental Health. 2001. *Let's Talk About Depression* (http://www.nimh.nih.gov/publicat/letstalk.cfm; retrieved July 13, 2006).

survivors, rescue workers, passersby, residents of Manhattan in general, and, to some extent, television viewers around the world who saw countless repeated images of the devastation. An estimated 150,000 New Yorkers suffered PTSD following the attacks; some were still experiencing symptoms 5 years later. Hurricane Katrina had a similarly devastating effect; in one survey, 19% of police officers and 22% of firefighters in the Gulf Coast states reported symptoms of PTSD. Soldiers wounded in combat are also at risk for PTSD; among soldiers wounded in Iraq or Afghanistan, rates of PTSD increased during the first year after the injury, suggesting that the emotional impact deepens with time. When symptoms persist, and when daily functioning is disrupted, then professional help is needed.

Treating Anxiety Disorders Therapies for anxiety disorders range from medication to psychological interventions concentrating on a person's thoughts and behavior. Both drug treatments and cognitive-behavioral therapies are effective in panic disorder, OCD, and GAD. Simple phobias are best treated without drugs.

Mood Disorders

Daily, temporary mood changes typically don't affect our overall emotional state or level of wellness. A person with a mood disorder, however, experiences emotional disturbances that are intense and persistent enough to affect normal functioning. The two most common mood disorders are depression and bipolar disorder.

Depression The National Institutes of Health estimates that **depression** strikes nearly 10% of Americans annually, making it the most common mood disorder. Depression affects the young as well as adults; about 9% of adolescents aged 12–17 suffer a major depressive episode each year, and nearly 50% of college students report depression severe enough to hinder their daily functioning. Depression takes different forms but usually involves demoralization and can include

- A feeling of sadness and hopelessness
- Loss of pleasure in doing usual activities

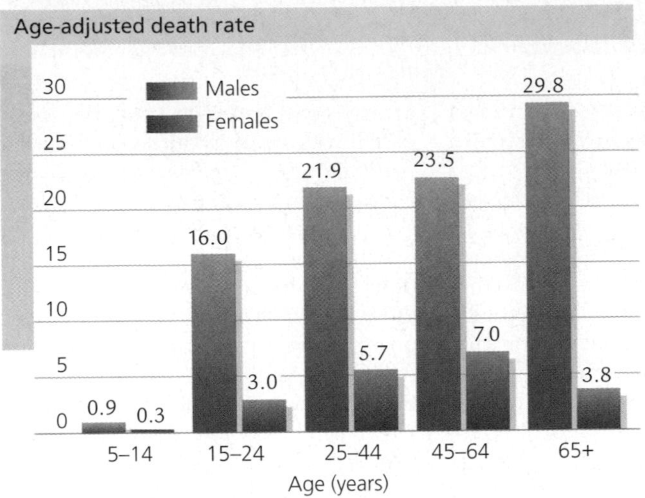

(a) Suicide rate by age and gender

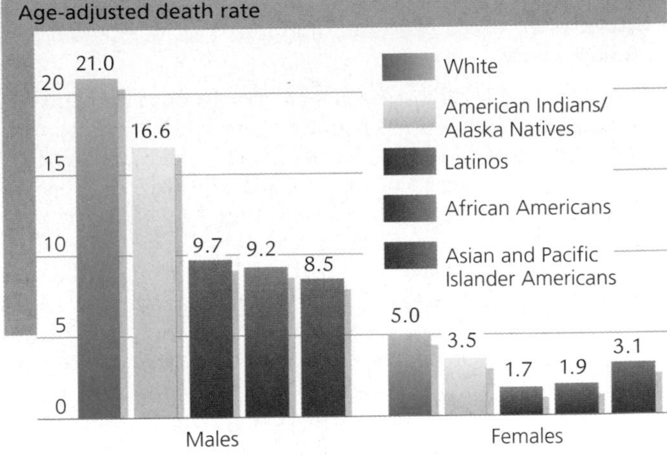

(b) Suicide rate by ethnicity and gender (all ages)

VITAL STATISTICS

Figure 3-2 Rates of suicide per 100,000 people in the United States. The rate of suicide varies by gender, age, and ethnicity. Rates are higher among men than women at all ages and are higher among whites compared to other groups. White men over age 65 have the highest rates of suicide. The national suicide rate is 10.8 per 100,000 people. These statistics are complete through 2003.

SOURCE: National Center for Health Statistics. 2006. *Health, United States, 2006.* Hyattsville, Md.: National Center for Health Statistics.

- Poor appetite and weight loss
- Insomnia or disturbed sleep
- Restlessness or, alternatively, fatigue
- Thoughts of worthlessness and guilt
- Trouble concentrating or making decisions
- Thoughts of death or suicide

A person experiencing depression may not have all of these symptoms. Sometimes instead of poor appetite and insomnia, the opposite occurs—eating too much and sleeping too long. (New research shows that depression may contribute to weight gains in young women.) People can have most of the symptoms of depression without feeling depressed, although they usually experience a loss of interest or pleasure in things (see the box "Are You Suffering from a Mood Disorder?").

In major depression, symptoms are often severe; a diagnosis of *dysthymic disorder* may be applied to people who experience persistent symptoms of mild or moderate depression for 2 years or longer. In some cases, depression is a clear-cut reaction to specific events, such as the loss of a loved one or failing in school or work, whereas in other cases no trigger event is obvious. When there is an obvious external trigger, depression may be termed "exogenous." If the trigger is internal, depression is characterized as "endogenous."

RECOGNIZING THE WARNING SIGNS OF SUICIDE One of the principal dangers of severe depression is suicide. Although a suicide attempt can occur unpredictably and unaccompanied by depression, the chances are greater if symptoms are numerous and severe. Additional warning signs of suicide include the following:

- Expressing the wish to be dead or revealing contemplated methods
- Increasing social withdrawal and isolation
- A sudden, inexplicable lightening of mood (which can mean the person has finally decided to commit suicide)

Certain risk factors increase the likelihood of suicide:

- A history of previous attempts
- A suicide by a family member or friend
- Readily available means, such as guns or pills
- A history of substance abuse or eating disorders
- Serious medical problems

In the United States, men have much higher suicide rates than women; white men over age 65 have the highest suicide rate (Figure 3-2). Whites and Native Americans have higher rates than most other groups, but rates among blacks have been rising and are now comparable to rates among whites. Women attempt three times as

Term

depression A mood disorder characterized by loss of interest, sadness, hopelessness, loss of appetite, disturbed sleep, and other physical symptoms.

Gender Matters

Depression, Anxiety, and Gender

The common belief that females are more emotional than males has both a positive and a negative side. On the one hand, women are thought to express positive emotions more clearly than men, especially those related to sympathy and caring. On the other hand, they are thought to be more prone to negative emotions such as depression and worry—an association supported in epidemiological studies of anxiety and mood disorders. One of the defining characteristics of a psychiatric disorder is that it interferes with daily activities and the ability to live a happy life. Thus, the higher incidence of anxiety and mood disorders in women is convincing evidence that they are more likely to suffer from emotional distress than are men.

Anxiety Disorders

Panic disorder is more than twice as common in women as in men, whereas obsessive-compulsive disorder occurs in men and women at about the same rate. In population surveys, social anxiety disorder is more common in women than in men, but men are more likely to seek treatment for it—perhaps because men are more likely to find it a barrier to success in white-collar jobs. In some surveys, PTSD is more common in women, but the incidence of PTSD depends on the incidence of traumatic events, which varies in different environments. Men are more often exposed to military combat, and women to rape. Trauma from motor vehicle crashes is a fairly common cause of PTSD in both sexes.

Depression and Suicide

Over their lifetimes, about 20% of women and 12% of men have serious depression. When women are depressed, they are more likely than men to experience guilt, anxiety, increased appetite and weight gain, and increased sleep. When women take antidepressants, they may need a lower dose than men; at the same dosage, blood levels of medication tend to be higher in women. An issue for women who may become pregnant is whether antidepressants can harm a fetus or newborn. The best evidence indicates that the most frequently prescribed types of antidepressants do not cause birth defects, although some studies have reported withdrawal symptoms in some newborns whose mothers used certain antidepressants.

Although suicidal behavior is strongly associated with depression, and depression is more prevalent in women, in the United States, many more men than women commit suicide. Until age 9, boys and girls have the same suicide rates; from 10 to 14 the boys' rate is twice as high; from 15 to 19, four times as high; and from 20 to 24, six times as high. Overall, about three times as many women as men attempt suicide, but women's attempts are less likely to be lethal. In the United States, 60% of male suicides involve firearms.

Factors Underlying Gender Differences

Why women have more problems with anxiety and depression than men is a matter of debate. Some experts think much of the difference is due to reporting bias: Women are more willing to admit to experiencing negative emotions, being stressed, or having difficulty coping. Women may also be more likely to seek treatment at a given level of symptoms.

Other experts point to biologically based sex differences, particularly in the level and action of hormones. Greater anxiety and depression in women compared with men is most pronounced between puberty and menopause, when female hormones are most active. However, this period of life is also the time in which women's social roles and expectations may be the most different from those of men. Women may put more emphasis on relationships in determining self-esteem, so the deterioration of a relationship is a cause of depression that can hit women harder than men. In addition, culturally determined gender roles are more likely to place women in situations where they have less control over key life decisions, and lack of autonomy is associated with depression.

The higher suicide rate among young men may relate to gender norms and expectations that men assert independence and physical prowess—sometimes expressed in risky, dangerous, and potentially self-destructive behavior. Such behavior, often involving drugs and alcohol and resulting in motor vehicle crashes, occurs more often in young people who later commit suicide. Even when suicidal intention is never expressed, suicidal impulses are often suspected of contributing to sudden deaths in this age group.

SOURCES: Sanz, E. J., et al. 2005. Selective serotonin reuptake inhibitors in pregnant women and neonatal withdrawal syndrome. *Lancet* 365(9458): 482–487; Kessler, R. C. 2003. Epidemiology of women and depression. *Journal of Affective Disorders* 74: 5–13; World Health Organization. 2002. *Gender and Mental Health.* Geneva: World Health Organization; Pigott, T. A. 1999. Gender differences in the epidemiology and treatment of anxiety disorders. *Journal of Clinical Psychiatry* 60 (Suppl. 18): 4–15; Langhinrichsen-Rohling, J., et al. 1998. Gender differences in the suicide-related behaviors of adolescents and young adults. *Sex Roles: A Journal of Research* 39(11–12): 839–854.

many suicides as men, yet men succeed at more than three times the rate of women (see the box "Depression, Anxiety, and Gender"). Suicide rates among adolescents and young adults and among adults over 65 have been falling for the last two decades.

Sometimes mistaken for suicide attempts are acts of self-injury, including cutting, burning, hitting, and other forms of self-inflicted harm. The prevalence of self-injury is estimated at 3–4% in the general population but is higher in adolescents, especially females. In a 2006 study, 17 percent of college students surveyed said they had injured themselves intentionally. A maladaptive coping strategy, self-injury is believed to provide relief from unbearable psychological distress or pain, perhaps through the release of endorphins. A variety of psychotherapeutic interventions can help people who injure themselves.

HELPING YOURSELF OR A FRIEND If you are severely depressed or know someone who is, expert help from a mental health professional is essential. Don't be afraid to

In Focus

Myths About Suicide

Myth People who really intend to kill themselves do not let anyone know about it.
Fact This belief can be an excuse for doing nothing when someone says he or she might commit suicide. In fact, most people who eventually commit suicide *have* talked about doing it.

Myth People who made a suicide attempt but survived did not really intend to die.
Fact This may be true for certain people, but people who seriously want to end their life may fail because they misjudge what it takes. Even a pharmacist may misjudge the lethal dose of a drug.

Myth People who succeed in suicide really wanted to die.
Fact We cannot be sure of that either. Some people are only trying to make a dramatic gesture or plea for help but miscalculate.

Myth People who really want to kill themselves will do it regardless of any attempts to prevent them.
Fact Few people are single-minded about suicide even at the moment of attempting it. People who are quite determined to take their life today may change their mind completely tomorrow.

Myth Suicide is proof of mental illness.
Fact Many suicides are committed by people who do not meet ordinary criteria for mental illness, although people with depression, schizophrenia, and other psychological disorders have a much higher than average suicide rate.

Myth People inherit suicidal tendencies.
Fact Certain kinds of depression that lead to suicide do have a genetic component. But many examples of suicide running in a family can be explained by factors such as psychologically identifying with a family member who committed suicide, often a parent.

Myth All suicides are irrational.
Fact By some standards all suicides may seem "irrational." But many people find it at least understandable that someone might want to commit suicide, for example, when approaching the end of a terminal illness or when facing a long prison term.

discuss the possibility of suicide with someone you fear is suicidal. You won't give them an idea they haven't already thought of (see the box "Myths About Suicide"). Asking direct questions is the best way to determine whether someone seriously intends to commit suicide. Encourage your friend to talk and to take positive steps to improve his or her situation. Most communities have emergency help available, often in the form of a hotline telephone counseling service run by a suicide prevention agency (check the yellow pages). If you feel there is an immediate danger of suicide, do not leave the person alone. Call for help or take him or her to an emergency room.

TREATING DEPRESSION Although treatments are highly effective, only about 35% of people who suffer from depression currently seek treatment. Treatment for depression depends on its severity and on whether the depressed person is suicidal. The best initial treatment for moderate to severe depression is probably a combination of drug therapy and psychotherapy. Stimulants such as amphetamines are not good antidepressants; much better are newer prescription antidepressants, although they may take several weeks to begin working, and patients may need to try multiple medications before finding one that works well. Therefore, when suicidal impulses are strong, hospitalization may be necessary.

Antidepressants work by affecting the activity of key neurotransmitters in the brain, including serotonin (Figure 3-3). The herbal supplement St. John's wort may also affect serotonin levels, but it is not subject to the same testing and regulation as prescription medications (see the box "Alternative Remedies for Depression" on p. 83). Anyone who may be suffering from depression should seek a medical evaluation rather than self-treating with supplements.

Electroconvulsive therapy (ECT) is effective for severe depression when other approaches have failed. In ECT, an epileptic-like seizure is induced by an electrical impulse transmitted through electrodes placed on the head. Patients are given an anesthetic and a muscle relaxant to reduce anxiety and prevent injuries associated with seizures. A typical course of ECT includes three treatments per week for 2 to 4 weeks.

One type of depression is treated by having sufferers sit with eyes open in front of a bright light source every morning. These patients have **seasonal affective disorder (SAD)**; their depression worsens during winter months as the number of hours of daylight diminishes, then improves with the spring and summer. The American Psychiatric Association estimates that 10–20% of Americans suffer symptoms that may be linked to SAD. SAD is more common among people who live at higher latitudes, where there are fewer hours of light in winter. Light therapy may work by extending the perceived length of the day

Terms

VW

electroconvulsive therapy (ECT) The use of electric shock to induce brief, generalized seizures; used in the treatment of selected psychological disorders.

seasonal affective disorder (SAD) A mood disorder characterized by seasonal depression, usually occurring in winter, when there is less daylight.

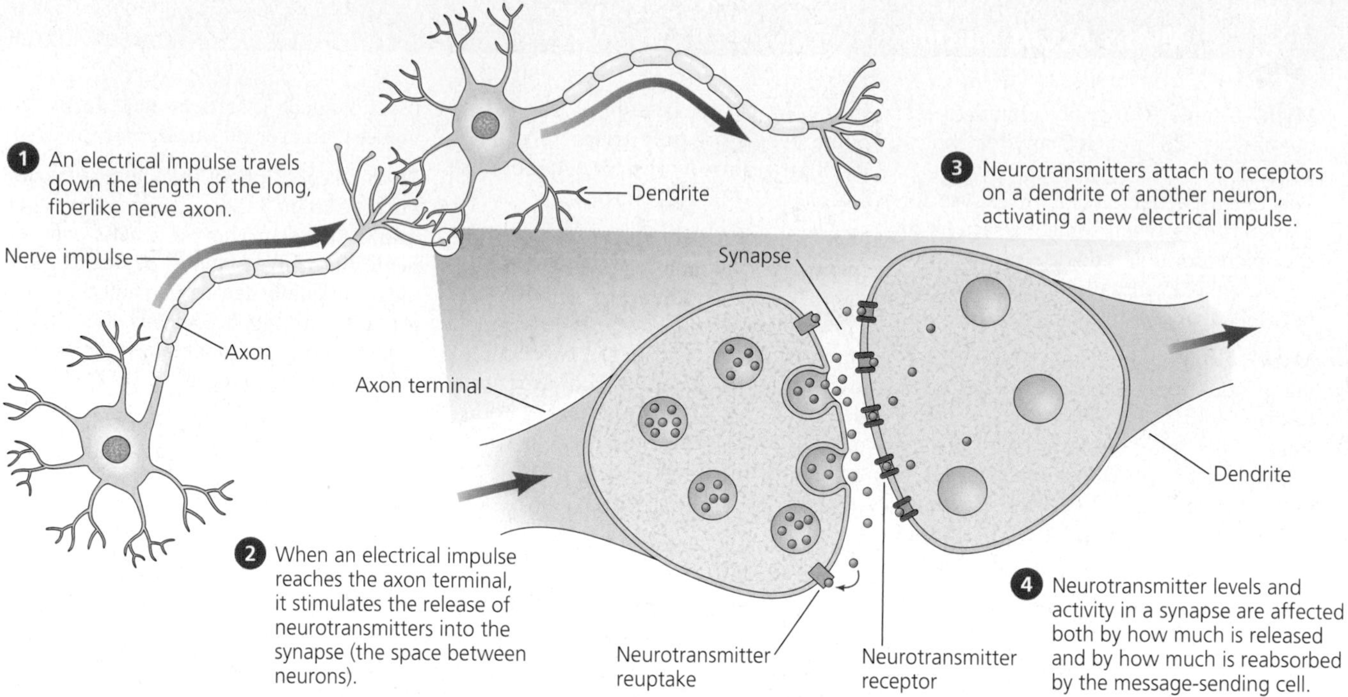

1 An electrical impulse travels down the length of the long, fiberlike nerve axon.
Nerve impulse
Axon
Dendrite
Axon terminal
Synapse
2 When an electrical impulse reaches the axon terminal, it stimulates the release of neurotransmitters into the synapse (the space between neurons).
3 Neurotransmitters attach to receptors on a dendrite of another neuron, activating a new electrical impulse.
Dendrite
Neurotransmitter reuptake
Neurotransmitter receptor
4 Neurotransmitter levels and activity in a synapse are affected both by how much is released and by how much is reabsorbed by the message-sending cell.

Figure 3-3 Nerve cell communication. Nerve cells (neurons) communicate through a combination of electrical impulses and chemical messages. Neurotransmitters such as serotonin and norepinephrine alter the overall responsiveness of the brain and are responsible for mood, level of attentiveness, and other psychological states. Many psychological disorders are related to problems with neurotransmitters and their receptors, and drug treatments frequently target them. For example, the antidepressant drug Prozac increases levels of serotonin by slowing the resorption (re-uptake) of serotonin.

and thus convincing the brain that it is summertime even during the winter months.

Mania and Bipolar Disorder People who experience **mania**, a less common feature of mood disorders, are restless, have a lot of energy, need little sleep, and often talk nonstop. They may devote themselves to fantastic projects and spend more money than they can afford. Many manic people swing between manic and depressive states, a syndrome called **bipolar disorder** because of the two opposite poles of mood. Tranquilizers are used to treat individual manic episodes, while special drugs such as the salt lithium carbonate taken daily can prevent future mood swings. Anticonvulsants (used to prevent epileptic seizures) are also prescribed to stabilize moods; examples are Tegretol (carbamazepine) and Lamictal (lamotrigene).

Gender Differences Although equal numbers of men and women suffer from bipolar disorder, women are nearly twice as likely as men to be clinically depressed. The Gender Matters box in this chapter discusses these differences further.

Schizophrenia

Schizophrenia can be severe and debilitating or quite mild and hardly noticeable. Although people are capable of diagnosing their own depression, they usually don't diagnose their own schizophrenia, because they often can't see that anything is wrong. This disorder is not rare; in fact, 1 in every 100 people has a schizophrenic episode sometime in his or her lifetime, most commonly starting in adolescence. However, because people who are directly or indirectly affected do not like to talk about schizophrenia, its frequency is not generally appreciated. In addition, schizophrenic people tend to withdraw from society when they are ill, another factor making it seem rarer than it is.

Scientists are uncertain about the exact causes of schizophrenia. Researchers have identified possible chemical and structural differences in the brains of people with the disorder as well as several genes that appear to increase risk. Schizophrenia is likely caused by a combination of genes and environmental factors that occur during pregnancy and development. For example, children born to older fathers have higher rates of schizophrenia, as do children with prenatal exposure to certain infections or medications.

Some general characteristics of schizophrenia include

- *Disorganized thoughts.* Thoughts may be expressed in a vague or confusing way.
- *Inappropriate emotions.* Emotions may be either absent or strong but inappropriate.
- *Delusions.* People with delusions—firmly held false beliefs—may think that their minds are controlled by outside forces, that people can read their minds,

Critical Consumer: Alternative Remedies for Depression

VW

Mainstream therapies for depression include medications accepted as safe and effective by government regulatory agencies, certain psychotherapies, and light therapy in the case of seasonal affective disorder. Yet, in surveys, 20% of people in the United States who suffer from depression report using unconventional therapies such as acupuncture, body movement therapy, homeopathy, qigong, faith healing, or herbs or other "natural" substances. With the exception of one herb, St. John's wort (*Hypericum perforatum*), these therapies have not been shown to be effective in double-blind placebo-controlled trials. Such trials are the only scientific way to show that a treatment has healing power beyond that of a **placebo.** (See Chapter 21 for more on different types of medical research studies.)

St. John's wort, a flowering plant that grows as a weed in the United States, has been reputed to have curative properties since the time of Hippocrates in ancient Greece. Modern pharmacological studies confirm that its active ingredients produce a number of biochemical and physiological changes in animals, although it's still unclear exactly how these changes might affect depression. Data from a number of studies suggest that St. John's wort could benefit people with mild to moderate depression, but concerns have been raised about the adequacy of those trials. Recently, two carefully designed trials were conducted on St. John's wort. In one, 375 mild to moderately depressed patients were randomly assigned to receive either a placebo or an extract of St. John's wort; the extract was statistically more effective than the placebo and did not have more side effects. In the other trial, 340 depressed patients were given either St. John's wort, a placebo, or sertraline, a prescription antidepressant. In that study, St. John's wort was no more effective than the placebo—but neither was sertraline. Because many other studies have shown sertraline to have better results than a placebo, this result casts doubt as to whether the study methods were sensitive enough to detect an antidepressant effect. In any case, consumers are left without a definitive answer on the effectiveness of St. John's wort.

An advantage of St. John's wort is that it causes fewer adverse effects than conventional antidepressants. In data from three studies including about 600 depressed patients, the herb produced no more adverse effects than did the placebo. There was no evidence of sedation, gastrointestinal disturbances, or other side effects associated with other antidepressants. However, the safety of St. John's wort in pregnancy has not been established, and it may interact with, and reduce the effectiveness of, certain medications, including oral contraceptives and some medications for treating heart disease, depression, HIV infections, and seizures.

One reason for the popularity of an herb for depression is that it doesn't require a prescription or any kind of contact with a physician or a therapist; for those who are not members of a generous health care plan, an herbal remedy may also be less expensive than a prescription antidepressant. On the other hand, people suffering from depression *should* seek professional advice and not try to get along entirely with self-diagnosis and self-help. If you are depressed enough to contemplate taking St. John's wort, you need to make an appointment to talk to a professional about your depression.

Bear in mind that St. John's wort does not work for everyone, and no expert advocates it for severe depression. Also, because herbal products are classified as dietary supplements, they are not scrutinized by the regulatory agencies that oversee prescription drugs. Thus, consumers have no guarantee that the product contains the herbs and dosages listed on the label (see Chapters 12 and 21 for more on dietary supplements).

SOURCES: Trautmann-Sponsel, R. D., and A. Dienel. 2004. Safety of Hypericum extract in mildly to moderately depressed outpatients: A review based on data from three randomized, placebo-controlled trials. *Journal of Affective Disorders* 82(2): 303–307; Lecrubier, Y., et al. 2002. Efficacy of St. John's wort extract WS 5570 in major depression: A double-blind, placebo-controlled trial. *American Journal of Psychiatry* 159(8): 1361–1366; Hypericum Depression Trial Study Group. 2002. Effect of *Hypericum perforatum* (St. John's wort) in major depressive disorder: A randomized controlled trial. *Journal of the American Medical Association* 287(14): 1807–1814; Shelton, R. C., et al. 2001. Effectiveness of St. John's wort in major depression. *Journal of the American Medical Association* 285 (15): 1978–1986.

that they are great personages like Jesus Christ or the president of the United States, or that they are being persecuted by a group such as the CIA.

- *Auditory hallucinations.* Schizophrenic people may hear voices when no one is present.
- *Deteriorating social and work functioning.* Social withdrawal and increasingly poor performance at school or work may be so gradual that they are hardly noticed at first.

None of these characteristics is invariably present. Some schizophrenic people are quite logical except on the subject of their delusions. Others show disorganized thoughts but no delusions or hallucinations.

Terms

VW

mania A mood disorder characterized by excessive elation, irritability, talkativeness, inflated self-esteem, and expansiveness.

bipolar disorder A mental illness characterized by alternating periods of depression and mania.

schizophrenia A psychological disorder that involves a disturbance in thinking and in perceiving reality.

placebo A chemically inactive substance that a patient believes is an effective medical therapy for his or her condition. To help evaluate a therapy, medical researchers compare the effects of a particular therapy with the effects of a placebo. The "placebo effect" occurs when a patient responds to a placebo as if it were an active drug.

A schizophrenic person needs help from a mental health professional. Suicide is a risk in schizophrenia, and expert treatment can reduce that risk and minimize the social consequences of the illness by shortening the period when symptoms are active. The key element in treatment is regular medication. At times medication is like insulin for diabetes—it makes the difference between being able to function or not. Sometimes hospitalization is temporarily required to relieve family and friends.

MODELS OF HUMAN NATURE AND THERAPEUTIC CHANGE

It is not surprising that beings as complicated as we humans cannot be satisfactorily encompassed by a single perspective. In fact, at least four different perspectives—biological, behavioral, cognitive, and psychodynamic—can be applied to human problems such as the psychological disorders discussed in this chapter. Each perspective has a distinct view of human nature, and from those views of human nature come distinct therapeutic approaches.

The Biological Model

The biological model emphasizes that the mind's activity depends entirely on an organic structure, the brain, whose composition is genetically determined. The activity of neurons, mediated by complex chemical reactions, gives rise to our most complex thoughts, our most ardent desires, and our most pathological behavior. Of course, no one can assert that environment and learning have no influence. Even if the brain is nothing but a supercomputer, it still has to be programmed by experience.

Biological researchers have investigated all of the psychological disorders we have discussed and have found genetic influences on anxiety and depression that cannot be accounted for by environment and learning. The fact that drugs can make anxiety and depression worse or better is evidence that chemicals in the brain influence our moods. Magnetic resonance imaging of the brain shows that the structure of the brain is slightly different in people with schizophrenia.

Pharmacological Therapy The most important kind of therapy inspired by the biological model is pharmacological therapy. A list of some of the popular medications currently used for treating psychological disorders follows. All require a prescription from a psychiatrist or other medical doctor. All have received approval from the U.S. Food and Drug Administration (FDA) as being safe and more effective than a placebo. However, as with all pharmacological therapies, these drugs may cause side effects. For example, the side effects of widely used antidepressants range from diminished appetite to loss of sexual pleasure. In addition, an individual may have to try several drugs before finding one that is effective and has acceptable side effects.

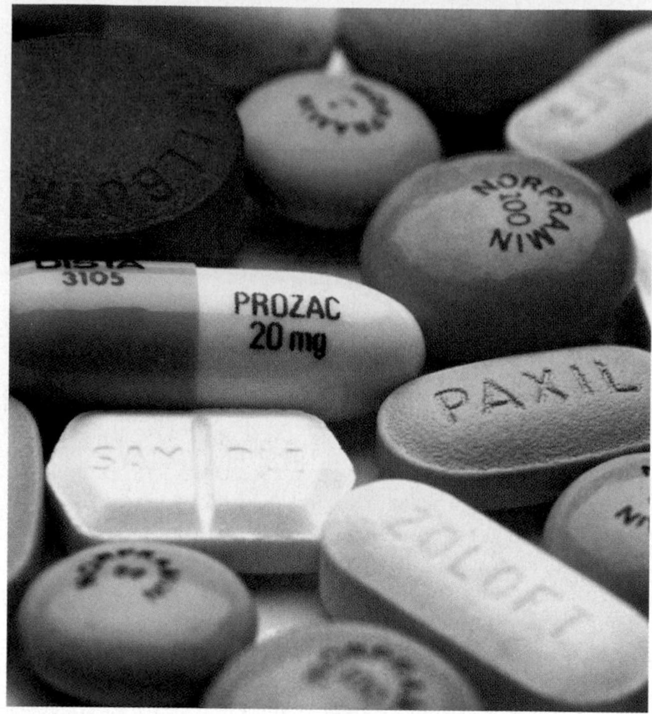

Pharmacological therapy (medication) is a common form of treatment for many psychological disorders. Medications can be very effective, but they do have risks and side effects, and they do not work for all patients.

1. *Antidepressants:* One group is called the selective serotonin re-uptake inhibitors (SSRIs) because of one of their mechanisms of action; this group includes Prozac (fluoxetine), Paxil (paroxetine), Zoloft (sertraline), Luvox (fluvoxamine), Celexa (citalopram), and Lexapro (escitalopram). Another group is called the tricyclics after their chemical structure; it includes Aventyl (nortriptyline) and Elavil (amitriptyline). Nardil (phenelzine) is a monoamine oxidase inhibitor. Antidepressants that do not fit into these groups include Effexor (venlafaxine), Welbutrin (buproprion), Serzone (nefazodone), and Remeron (mirtazapine). Surprisingly, these antidepressants are as effective in treating panic disorder and certain kinds of chronic anxiety as they are in treating depression. They may also alleviate the symptoms of OCD. In 2006, the FDA approved a form of buproprion for the treatment of SAD.
2. *Mood stabilizers:* Lithium carbonate and Depakote (valproic acid) are the most important mood stabilizers. They are taken to prevent mood swings that occur in bipolar disorder and certain kinds of schizophrenia.
3. *Antipsychotics:* Older antipsychotics include Haldol (haloperidol) and Prolixin (fluphenazine); newer

antipsychotics (sometimes called "atypical") are Clozaril (clozapine), Zyprexa (olanzapine), Risperdal (risperidone), Seroquel (quetiapine), Geodon (ziprasidone), and Abilify (aripiprazole). The drugs reduce hallucinations and disordered thinking in people with schizophrenia, bipolar disorder, and delirium, and they have a calming effect on agitated patients.

4. *Anxiolytics (antianxiety agents) and hypnotics (sleeping pills):* One of the largest and most prescribed classes of anxiolytics is the benzodiazepines, a group of drugs that includes Valium (diazepam), Librium (chlordiazepoxide), Xanax (alprazolam), and Ativan (lorazepam); Dalmane (flurazepam), Restoril (temazepam), and Halcion (triazolam) are benzodiazepines marketed as sleeping aids. Newer hypnotics are Sonata (zaleplon), Ambien (zolpidem), Lunesta (eszopiclone), and Rozerem (ramelteon).
5. *Stimulants:* Ritalin (methylphenidate) and Dexedrine (dextroamphetamine) are most commonly used for **attention-deficit/hyperactivity disorder (ADHD)** in children and less often in adults. Drugs of this type are also marketed under the names Adderall, Strattera, and Concerta. They are also used for daytime sleepiness in adults, as are purified caffeine (for example, No-Doz) and Provigil (modafinil).
6. *Anti-dementia drugs:* Dementia is an impairment in memory and thinking that occurs almost exclusively in the elderly. The most common type is Alzheimer's disease (see Chapter 19). Many people with this problem are now prescribed Aricept (donepezil) or Namenda (memantine). Other anti-dementia drugs are Exelon (rivastigmine) and Razadyne (galantamine).

Issues in the Use of Pharmacological Therapy

The discovery that many psychological disorders have a biological basis in disordered brain chemistry has led to a revolution in the treatment of many disorders, particularly depression. The new view of depression as based in brain chemistry has also lessened the stigma attached to the condition, leading more people to seek treatment, and antidepressants are now among the most widely prescribed drugs in the United States. The development of effective drugs has provided relief for many people, but the wide use of antidepressants has also raised many questions (see the box "Antidepressant Use in Young People" on p. 86).

Research indicates that for mild cases of depression, psychotherapy and antidepressants are about equally effective. For major depression, combined therapy is significantly more effective than either type of treatment alone. Psychotherapy may be particularly important for people whose condition has a strong psychosocial component. Therapy can help provide insight into factors that precipitated the depression, such as high levels of stress or a history of abuse. A therapist can also provide guidance in changing patterns of thinking and behavior that contribute to the problem.

What about the use of antidepressants to treat unwanted personality traits in psychologically healthy people? Anecdotal evidence suggests that Prozac and related drugs may help shy or pessimistic people become more outgoing and optimistic, for example. The potential use of antidepressants in this way has sparked ethical debate. By masking mental pain, will they interfere with people's connection to reality and to their own emotional experience and expression? This ethical debate extends to other pharmacological treatments for psychological disorders.

The Behavioral Model

The behavioral model focuses on what people do—their overt behavior—rather than on brain structures and chemistry or on thoughts and consciousness. This model regards psychological problems as "maladaptive behavior" or bad habits. When and how a person learned bad behavior is less important than what makes it continue in the present. Behaviorists analyze behavior in terms of **stimulus, response,** and **reinforcement.** The essence of behavior therapy is to discover what reinforcements keep an undesirable behavior going and then to try to alter those reinforcements. For example, if people who fear speaking in class (the stimulus) remove themselves from that situation (the response), they experience immediate relief, which acts as reinforcement for future avoidance and escape.

To change their behavior, fearful people are taught to practice **exposure**—to deliberately and repeatedly enter the feared situation and remain in it until their fear begins to abate. Clients are often asked to keep a daily behavior journal to monitor the target behavior and the events that precede and follow it. A student who is afraid to speak in class might begin his behavioral therapy program by keeping a diary listing each time he makes a contribution to a classroom discussion, how long he speaks, and his anxiety levels before, during, and after speaking. He would then develop

Terms

VW

attention-deficit/hyperactivity disorder (ADHD) A disorder characterized by persistent, pervasive problems with inattention and/or hyperactivity to a degree that is not considered appropriate for a child's developmental stage and that causes significant difficulties in school, work, or relationships.

stimulus Anything that causes a response.

response A reaction to a stimulus.

reinforcement Increasing the future probability of a response by following it with a reward.

exposure A therapeutic technique for treating fear in which the subject learns to come into direct contact with a feared situation.

In the News

Antidepressant Use in Young People

On September 14, 2004, an FDA advisory committee voted in favor of recommending a warning label for antidepressant drugs on the basis of evidence that their use increases the risk of suicidal thinking and behavior in children and adolescents. The committee based its conclusions on data from trials sponsored by pharmaceutical companies. Controversy immediately followed: Parents wondered why it had taken so long to come to this conclusion, because most of the data had been around for years.

Effectiveness

Drug treatment for depression is considered part of a success story in which people take seriously symptoms of depression and hints of suicidal thinking in children and teens. Over the past decade, the suicide rate among adolescents has fallen. Many factors have likely contributed to the decline, including stricter gun laws that make it harder for young people to gain access to guns. Drug treatment has also been considered a key factor in the decline in suicide rates.

A 2005 review of reported childhood depression cases showed that between 1995 and 2002 the number of pediatric psychotherapy sessions declined significantly while prescriptions for antidepressants rose. Most of those prescriptions were for drugs that had not been approved for use in children. To date, only one drug—fluoxetine (Prozac)—has been approved for use specifically in children and teens. Studies have found that fluoxetine causes a greater improvement than a placebo, but the combination of drug therapy and cognitive-behavioral therapy is more beneficial than either treatment alone. The placebo effect, in which people improve while taking pills containing inactive compounds, is significant in studies of depression and can exceed 30%—meaning almost a third of people receiving a placebo experience an improvement in their symptoms.

Many antidepressants other than fluoxetine, especially other SSRIs, are also prescribed to young people, but these other drugs haven't been shown to be effective for that age group. Unpublished research data indicates that some SSRIs are *not* effective in children and teens or are only slightly more effective than a placebo.

Safety

All medications have potential risks and side effects. The problem associated with SSRIs that caused the FDA to act is the possibility that they increase the risk of suicide in some young people, particularly in the period immediately following the start of medication use. When study results were pooled, researchers found that in the short term, about 2–3% of users have an increased risk of suicidal thoughts and actions beyond the risk inherent from depression itself.

Researchers aren't exactly sure what causes this effect. One theory is that SSRIs reverse the lethargy associated with depression more quickly than they relieve the depression itself, giving users the energy to contemplate suicide in the interim. Antidepressants may work differently on the brains of young people than on the brains of adults, so there may be as yet unidentified effects.

In October 2004, the FDA published a public health advisory about using antidepressants in children and teens. It emphasizes that young people who take antidepressants should be monitored closely, especially when starting a new medication or changing the dosage of a drug. The FDA told manufacturers to revise the labeling of their products to include a boxed warning and expanded warning statements. Depression is a serious illness that can increase the risk of suicide, and mental health professionals and patients must balance the risks of doing nothing against the potential risks and benefits of different types of treatments. These points were emphasized by the American Academy of Child and Adolescent Psychiatry in response to the FDA advisory.

In July 2005, the FDA issued a new advisory warning that antidepressants may increase the risk of suicide in adults and that adults who take antidepressants—like children who take antidepressants—should be monitored closely. The agency's investigation into this concern continues.

SOURCES: Food and Drug Administration. 2004. *FDA Proposed Medication Guide: About Using Antidepressants in Children or Teenagers* (http://www.fda.gov/cder/drug/antidepressants/SSRIMedicationGuide.htm; retrieved July 14, 2006); Newman, T. B. 2004. Treating depression in children: A black-box warning for antidepressants in children? *New England Journal of Medicine* 351(16): 1595–1598; Brent, D. A. 2004. Treating depression in children: Antidepressants and pediatric depression—the risk of doing nothing. *New England Journal of Medicine* 351(16): 1598–1601; Treatment for Adolescents with Depression Study (TADS) Team. 2004. Fluoxetine, cognitive-behavioral therapy, and their combination for adolescents with depression. *Journal of the American Medical Association* 292(7): 807–820; Stafford, R. S., et al. 2005. Depression treatment during outpatient visits by U.S. children and adolescents. *Journal of Adolescent Health* 37(6): 434–442.

concrete but realistic goals for increasing his speaking frequency and contract with himself to reward his successes by spending more time in activities he finds enjoyable.

Although exposure to the real situation works best, exposure in one's imagination or through the virtual reality of computer simulation can also be effective. For example, in the case of someone afraid of flying, an imagined scenario would likely be vivid enough to elicit the fear necessary to practice exposure techniques. The Behavior Change Strategy at the end of Chapter 2 provides a model program for reducing test anxiety; refer to Chapter 1 for general strategies for behavior change.

The Cognitive Model

The cognitive model emphasizes the effect of ideas on behavior and feeling. According to this model, behavior results from complicated attitudes, expectations, and motives rather than from simple, immediate reinforcements. When behavioral therapies such as exposure work, it is because they change the way a person thinks about the feared situation and his or her ability to cope with it.

According to one cognitive theory, recurring false ideas produce feelings such as anxiety and depression. Identifying and exposing these ideas as false should relieve the painful emotion. For example, people who are anxious are thinking, "Something bad is going to happen and I won't be able to handle it." The therapist challenges such ideas in three ways: showing that there isn't enough evidence for the idea, suggesting different ways of looking at the situation, and showing that no disaster is going to occur. The therapist does not just state his or her position but encourages clients to examine the logic of their own ideas and then to test their truth.

For example, a student afraid of speaking in class may harbor thoughts such as "If I begin to speak, I'll say something stupid; if I say something stupid, the teacher and my classmates will lose respect for me; then I'll get a low grade, my classmates will avoid me, and life will be hell." In cognitive therapy, these ideas will be examined critically. If the student prepares, will he or she really sound stupid? Does every sentence said have to be exactly correct and beautifully delivered, or is that an unrealistic expectation? Will classmates' opinions be completely transformed by one presentation? Do classmates even care that much? And why does the student care so much about what *they* think? People in cognitive therapy are taught to notice their unrealistic thoughts and to substitute more realistic ones, and they are advised to repeatedly test their assumptions.

The Psychodynamic Model

The psychodynamic model also emphasizes thoughts, but it asserts that false ideas cannot be fought directly because they are fed by other, unconscious, ideas and impulses. Symptoms are not isolated pieces of behavior but results of a complex system of secret wishes, emotions, and fantasies hidden by active defenses that keep them unconscious (see Table 3-2). The role of the past in shaping the present is often emphasized in psychodynamic therapy. By having the client speak as freely as possible in front of the therapist, the therapist can help the client achieve some insight into the reasons for his or her apparently irrational and self-defeating thoughts and actions. In essence, a trustworthy therapist helps clients become more honest with themselves. One contemporary version of this approach, interpersonal therapy, focuses on the relationship between the person and others. The therapist takes an active role in helping the client to understand and overcome self-isolation and to develop interpersonal skills.

Newer therapies referred to variously as humanistic, existential, or experiential are like psychodynamic therapies in encouraging self-awareness, but they focus more on the present and future than the past. Clients are encouraged to get in touch with their subjective experience (the here and now). The therapist acts as a guide to self-exploration and as a facilitator for expanding the client's inherent human potential.

Gradually exposing a person to a feared object or situation can help overcome phobias. Use of virtual reality goggles allows this individual to simulate a realistic public speaking situation without having to worry about the presence of an actual audience.

Evaluating the Models

Ignoring theoretical conflicts among psychological models, therapists have recently developed pragmatic *cognitive-behavioral therapies* that combine effective elements of both models in a single package. For example, the package for treating social anxiety emphasizes exposure as well as changing problematic patterns of thinking. Combined therapies have also been developed for panic disorder, obsessive-compulsive disorder, generalized anxiety disorder, and depression. These packages, involving ten or more individual or group sessions with a therapist and homework between sessions, have been shown to produce significant improvement.

Drug therapy and cognitive-behavioral therapies are also sometimes combined, especially in the case of depression. For anxiety disorders, both kinds of therapy are equally effective, but the effects of drug therapy last only as long as the drug is being taken, while cognitive-behavioral therapies produce longer-term improvement. For schizophrenia, drug therapy is a must, but a continuing relationship with therapists who give support and advice is also indispensable.

Psychodynamic therapies have been attacked as ineffective and endless. Of course, effectiveness is hard to demonstrate for therapies that do not focus on specific symptoms. But common sense tells us that being able to open yourself up and discuss your problems with a supportive but objective person who focuses on you and lets you speak freely can enhance your sense of self and reduce feelings of confusion and despair.

GETTING HELP

Knowing when self-help or professional help is required for mental health problems is usually not as difficult as knowing how to start or which professional to choose.

Self-Help

If you have a personal problem to solve, a smart way to begin is by finding out what you can do on your own. Some problems are specifically addressed in this book. Behavioral and some cognitive approaches are especially useful for helping yourself. They all involve becoming more aware of self-defeating actions and ideas and combating them in some way: by being more assertive; by communicating honestly; by raising your self-esteem by counteracting thoughts, people, and actions that undermine it; and by confronting, rather than avoiding, the things you fear. Get more information by seeing what books are available in the psychology or self-help sections of libraries and bookstores, but be selective. Watch out for self-help books making fantastic claims that deviate from mainstream approaches.

Some people find it helpful to express their feelings in a journal. Grappling with a painful experience in this way provides an emotional release and can help you develop more constructive ways of dealing with similar situations in the future. Research indicates that using a journal this way can improve physical as well as emotional wellness.

For some people, religious belief and practice may promote psychological health. Religious organizations provide a social network and a supportive community, and religious practices, such as prayer and meditation, offer a path for personal change and transformation.

Peer Counseling and Support Groups

Sharing your concerns with others is another helpful way of dealing with psychological health challenges. Just being able to share what's troubling you with an accepting, empathetic person can bring relief. Comparing notes with people who have problems similar to yours can give you new ideas about coping.

Many colleges offer peer counseling through a health center or through the psychology or education department. Peer counseling is usually done by volunteer students who have received special training that emphasizes confidentiality. Peer counselors may steer you toward an appropriate campus or community resource or simply offer a sympathetic ear.

Many self-help groups work on the principle of bringing together people with similar problems to share their experiences and support one another. Support groups are typically organized around a specific problem, such as eating disorders or substance abuse. Self-help groups may be listed in the phone book or the campus newspaper.

Professional Help

Sometimes self-help or talking to nonprofessionals is not enough. More objective, more expert, or more discreet help is needed. Many people have trouble accepting the need for professional help, and often those who most need help are the most unwilling to get it. You may someday find yourself having to overcome your own reluctance, or that of a friend, about seeking help.

Determining the Need for Professional Help

In some cases, professional help is optional. Some people are interested in improving their psychological health in a general way by going into individual or

Group therapy is just one of many different approaches to psychological counseling. If you have concerns you would like to discuss with a mental health professional, shop around to find the approach that works for you.

Critical Consumer

Choosing and Evaluating Mental Health Professionals

VW

College students are usually in a good position to find convenient, affordable mental health care. Larger schools typically have both health services that employ psychiatrists and psychologists and counseling centers staffed by professionals and student peer counselors. Resources in the community may include a school of medicine, a hospital, and a variety of professionals who work independently. Although independent practitioners are listed in the telephone book, it's a good idea to get recommendations from physicians, clergy, friends who have been in therapy, or community agencies rather than pick a name at random.

Financial considerations are also important. Find out how much different services will cost and what your health insurance will cover. If you're not adequately covered by a health plan, don't let that stop you from getting help; investigate low-cost alternatives. City, county, and state governments often support mental health clinics for those who can afford to pay little or nothing for treatment. Some on-campus services may be free or offered at very little cost.

The cost of treatment is linked to how many therapy sessions will be needed, which in turn depends on the type of therapy and the nature of the problem. Psychological therapies focusing on specific problems may require eight or ten sessions at weekly intervals. Therapies aiming for psychological awareness and personality change can last months or years.

Deciding whether a therapist is right for you will require meeting the therapist in person. Before or during your first meeting, find out about the therapist's background and training:

- Does she or he have a degree from an appropriate professional school and a state license to practice?
- Has she or he had experience treating people with problems similar to yours?
- How much will therapy cost?

You have a right to know the answers to these questions and should not hesitate to ask them. After your initial meeting, evaluate your impressions:

- Does the therapist seem like a warm, intelligent person who would be able to help you and interested in doing so?
- Are you comfortable with the personality, values, and beliefs of the therapist?
- Is he or she willing to talk about the techniques in use? Do these techniques make sense to you?

If you answer yes to these questions, this therapist may be satisfactory for you. If you feel uncomfortable—and you're not in need of emergency care—it's worthwhile to set up one-time consultations with one or two others before you make up your mind. Take the time to find someone who feels right for you.

Later in your treatment, evaluate your progress:

- Are you being helped by the treatment?
- If you are displeased, is it because you aren't making progress, or because therapy is raising difficult, painful issues you don't want to deal with?
- Can you express dissatisfaction to your therapist? Such feedback can improve your treatment.

If you're convinced your therapy isn't working or is harmful, thank your therapist for her or his efforts, and find another.

group therapy to learn more about themselves and how to interact with others. Clearly, seeking professional help for these reasons is a matter of individual choice. Interpersonal friction among family members or between partners often falls in the middle between necessary and optional. Successful help with such problems can mean the difference between a painful divorce and a satisfying relationship.

It's sometimes difficult to determine whether someone needs professional help, but it is important to be aware of behaviors that may indicate a serious problem. Following are some strong indications that you or someone you know needs professional help:

- If depression, anxiety, or other emotional problems begin to interfere seriously with school or work performance or in getting along with others
- If suicide is attempted or is seriously considered (refer to the warning signs earlier in the chapter)
- If symptoms such as hallucinations, delusions, incoherent speech, or loss of memory occur
- If alcohol or drugs are used to the extent that they impair normal functioning during much of the week, if finding or taking drugs occupies much of the week, or if reducing their dosage leads to psychological or physiological withdrawal symptoms

Choosing a Mental Health Professional

Mental health workers belong to several different professions and have different roles. Psychiatrists are medical doctors. They are experts in deciding whether a medical disease lies behind psychological symptoms, and they are usually involved in treatment if medication or hospitalization is required. Clinical psychologists typically hold a Ph.D. degree; they are often experts in behavioral and cognitive therapies. Other mental health workers include social workers, licensed counselors, and clergy with special training in pastoral counseling. In hospitals and clinics, various mental health professionals may join together in treatment teams. For more on finding appropriate help, see the box "Choosing and Evaluating Mental Health Professionals."

Tips for Today

Life inevitably brings change and challenge—they are a part of growth and development. Most of life's psychological challenges can be met with self-help and everyday skills—introspection and insight, honest communication, support from family and friends. Sometimes a psychological problem poses a greater challenge than we can handle on our own; for these situations, professional help is available.

Right now you can

- Consider the areas in your life where you can be creative (one of the qualities associated with self-actualization), whether in music, art, Web page design, party planning, or whatever you truly enjoy. With the knowledge that allowing your creative side to flourish is a valuable use of your time, plan a way to spend an hour or more on this activity this week.
- Sit down and write 100 positive adjectives that describe you (friendly, loyal, athletic, smart, musical, sensitive, and so on). If you can't think of 100 right now, write as many as you can and keep thinking about it over the next day or two until you reach 100.
- Take a serious look at how you've been feeling the past few weeks. If you have any feelings that are especially difficult to deal with, begin to think about how you can get help with them. Consider consulting the self-help section at the bookstore, talking to a trustworthy friend or peer counselor, or making an appointment with a staff person at the campus counseling center.
- Look at the list of defense mechanisms in Table 3-2. Do you recognize one you've used recently? Review the situation in your mind to see if there's a way you could have coped with it differently.

SUMMARY

- Psychological health encompasses more than a single particular state of normality. Psychological diversity is valuable among groups of people.
- Defining psychological health as the presence of wellness means that to be healthy you must strive to fulfill your potential.
- Maslow's definition of psychological health centered on self-actualization, the highest level in his hierarchy of needs. Self-actualized people have high self-esteem and are realistic, inner-directed, authentic, capable of emotional intimacy, and creative.
- Crucial parts of psychological wellness include developing an adult identity, establishing intimate relationships, and developing values and purpose in life.
- A sense of self-esteem develops during childhood as a result of giving and receiving love and learning to accomplish goals. Self-concept is challenged every day; healthy people adjust their goals to their abilities.
- Using defense mechanisms to cope with problems can make finding solutions harder. Analyzing thoughts and behavior can help people develop less defensive and more effective ways of coping.
- A pessimistic outlook can be damaging; it can be overcome by developing more realistic self-talk.
- Honest communication requires recognizing what needs to be said and saying it clearly. Assertiveness enables people to insist on their rights and to participate in the give-and-take of good communication.
- People may be lonely if they haven't developed ways to be happy on their own or if they interpret being alone as a sign of rejection. Lonely people can take action to expand their social contacts.
- Dealing successfully with anger involves distinguishing between a reasonable level of assertiveness and gratuitous expressions of anger, heading off rage by reframing thoughts and distracting oneself, and responding to the anger of others with an asymmetrical, problem-solving orientation.
- People with psychological disorders have symptoms severe enough to interfere with daily living.
- Anxiety is a fear that is not directed toward any definite threat. Anxiety disorders include simple phobias, social phobias, panic disorder, generalized anxiety disorder, obsessive-compulsive disorder, and post-traumatic stress disorder.
- Depression is a common mood disorder; loss of interest or pleasure in things seems to be its most universal symptom. Severe depression carries a high risk of suicide, and suicidally depressed people need professional help.
- Symptoms of mania include exalted moods with unrealistically high self-esteem, little need for sleep, and rapid speech. Mood swings between mania and depression characterize bipolar disorder.
- Schizophrenia is characterized by disorganized thoughts, inappropriate emotions, delusions, auditory hallucinations, and deteriorating social and work performance.
- The biological model emphasizes that the mind's activity depends on the brain, whose composition is genetically determined. Therapy based on the biological model is primarily pharmacological.
- The behavioral model focuses on overt behavior and treats psychological problems as bad habits. Behavior change is the focus of therapy.
- The cognitive model considers how ideas affect behavior and feelings; behavior results from complicated attitudes, expectations, and motives, not just from simple reinforcements. Cognitive therapy focuses on changing a person's thinking.
- The psychodynamic model asserts that false ideas are fed by unconscious ideas and cannot be addressed directly. Treatment is based on psychotherapy.
- Help is available in a variety of forms, including self-help, peer counseling, support groups, and therapy with a mental health professional. For serious problems, professional help may be the most appropriate.

Behavior Change Strategy

Dealing with Social Anxiety

Shyness is often the result of both high anxiety levels and lack of key social skills. To help overcome shyness, you need to learn to manage your fear of social situations and to develop social skills such as appropriate eye contact, initiating topics in conversations, and maintaining the flow of conversations by asking questions and making appropriate responses. As described in the chapter, repeated *exposure* to the source of one's fear—in this case, social situations—is the best method for reducing anxiety. When you practice new behaviors, they gradually become easier and you experience less anxiety. A counterproductive strategy is avoiding situations that make you anxious. Although this approach works in the short term—you eliminate your anxiety because you escape the situation—it keeps you from meeting new people and having new experiences. Another counterproductive strategy is self-medicating with alcohol or drugs. Being under their influence actually prevents you from learning new social skills and new ways to handle your anxiety.

To reduce your anxiety in social situations, try some of the following strategies:

- Remember that physical stress reactions are short-term responses to fear. Don't dwell on them—remind yourself that they will pass, and they will.
- Refocus your attention away from the stress reaction you're experiencing and toward the social task at hand. Your nervousness is much less visible than you think.
- Allow a warm-up period for new situations. Realize that you will feel more nervous at first, and take steps to relax and become more comfortable. Refer to the suggestions for deep breathing and other relaxation techniques in Chapter 2.
- If possible, take breaks during anxiety-producing situations. For example, if you're at a party, take a moment to visit the restroom or step outside. Alternate between speaking with good friends and striking up conversations with new acquaintances.
- Watch your interpretations; having a stress reaction doesn't mean that you don't belong in the group, that you're unattractive or unworthy, or that the situation is too much for you. Try thinking of yourself as excited or highly alert instead of anxious.
- Avoid cognitive distortions and practice realistic self-talk. Replace your self-critical thoughts with more supportive ones: "No one else is perfect, and I don't have to be either." "It would have been good if I had a funny story to tell, but the conversation was interesting anyway."
- Give yourself a reality check: Ask if you're really in a life-threatening situation (or just at a party), if the outcome you're imagining is really likely (or the worst thing that could possibly happen), or if you're the only one who feels nervous (or if many other people might feel the same way).
- Don't think of conversations as evaluations; remind yourself that you don't have to prove yourself with every social interaction. And remember that most people are thinking more about themselves than they are about you.

Starting and maintaining conversations can be difficult for shy people, who may feel overwhelmed by their physical stress reaction. If small talk is a problem for you, try the following strategies:

- Introduce yourself early in the conversation. If you tend to forget names, repeat your new acquaintance's name to help fix it in your mind ("Nice to meet you, Amelia").
- Ask questions, and look for shared topics of interest. Simple, open-ended questions like "How's your presentation coming along?" or "How do you know our host?" encourage others to carry the conversation for a while and help bring forth a variety of subjects.
- Take turns talking, and elaborate on your answers. Simple yes and no answers don't move the conversation along. Try to relate something in your life—a course you're taking or a hobby you have—to something in the other person's life. Match self-disclosure with self-disclosure.
- Have something to say. Expand your mind and become knowledgeable about current events and local or campus news. If you have specialized knowledge about a topic, practice discussing it in ways that both beginners and experts can understand and appreciate.
- If you get stuck for something to say, try giving a compliment ("Great presentation!" or "I love your earrings.") or performing a social grace (pass the chips or get someone a drink).
- Be an active listener. Reward the other person with your full attention and with regular responses. Make frequent eye contact and maintain a relaxed but alert posture. (See Chapter 4 for more on being an active listener.)

At first, your new behaviors will likely make you anxious. Don't give up—things *will* get easier. Create lots of opportunities to practice your new behaviors; your goal is to make them routine activities. For example, striking up a conversation with someone in a registration or movie line can help you practice your small-talk skills in a nonthreatening setting. Once you are comfortable doing that, you might try initiating brief conversations with classmates about academic topics—the upcoming midterm, for example, or an assignment. Following that, you might try something more challenging, such as discussing a more personal topic or meeting new people in a social setting.

Regular practice and stress-management skills are critical. Using these techniques, you can increase your social skills and confidence level at the same time that you decrease your anxiety. Eventually, you'll be able to sustain social interactions with comfort and enjoyment. If you find that social anxiety is a major problem for you and self-help techniques don't seem to work, consider looking into a shyness clinic or treatment program on your campus.

SOURCES: University of Texas at Dallas, Student Counseling Center. 2005. *Self-Help: Overcoming Social Anxiety* (http://www.utdallas.edu/counseling/selfhelp/social-anxiety.html; retrieved July 14, 2006); Carducci, B. J. 1999. *Shyness: A Bold New Approach.* New York: Perennial.

Take Action

1. **Become a peer counselor.** Many colleges and communities have peer counseling programs, hotline services (for both general problems and specific issues such as rape, suicide, and drug abuse), and other kinds of emergency counseling services. Some programs are staffed by trained volunteers. Investigate such programs in your school (through the health clinic or student services) or community (look in the yellow pages), and consider volunteering for one of them. The training and experience can help you understand both yourself and others.

2. **Consider assertiveness training.** Being assertive rather than passive or aggressive is a valuable skill that everyone can learn. To improve your ability to assert yourself appropriately, sign up for a workshop or class in assertiveness training on your campus or in your community.

3. **Support your spiritual side.** Turn off your phone, remove your watch, and spend some quiet time alone with your thoughts and feelings. Engage in an activity that contributes to your sense of spiritual well-being. Examples might include spending time in nature; experiencing art, architecture, or music; expressing your creativity; or engaging in a personal spiritual practice such as prayer, meditation, or yoga.

For More Information

Books

Antony, M. M. 2004. *10 Simple Solutions to Shyness: How to Overcome Shyness, Social Anxiety & Fear of Public Speaking*. Oakland, Calif.: New Harbinger. *Practical suggestions for fears of interacting with people you don't know.*

Clark, C. C. 2006. *Living Well with Anxiety: What Your Doctor Doesn't Tell You … That You Need to Know*. New York: Collins. *A practical guide to both medical and self-care treatments for anxiety disorders, with a focus on holistic approaches that include nutrition, herbal supplements, exercise, time management, and more.*

Flach, F. 2003. *Resilience: The Power to Bounce Back When the Going Gets Tough*. Rev. ed. Long Island City, N.Y.: Hatherleigh Press. *Provides practical suggestions for personal growth in the face of stress and change.*

Frances, A., and M. B. First. 1999. *Your Mental Health: A Layman's Guide to the Psychiatrist's Bible*. New York: Scribner. *A resource-packed reference with information on dozens of mental disorders; based on the APA's DSM-IV.*

Jenkins, J., D. Keltner, and K. Oatley. 2006. *Understanding Emotions*. 2nd ed. Oxford: Blackwell. *A comprehensive guide to emotions, including current research on the neuroscience of emotions, evolutionary and cultural approaches to emotion, and the expression and communication of emotions.*

Miklowitz, D. J. 2002. *The Bipolar Disorder Survival Guide: What You and Your Family Need to Know*. New York: Guilford Press. *Covers the origins, symptoms, and treatments for bipolar (or manic-depressive) disorder.*

Rubin-Deutsch, J. 2003. *Why Can't I Ever Be Good Enough? Escaping the Limits of Your Childhood Roles*. Oakland, Calif.: New Harbinger. *Presents strategies for transforming unhealthy patterns of thought and interaction from childhood into more healthy adult roles.*

Seligman, M. E. 2006. *Learned Optimism: How to Change Your Mind and Your Life* (Vintage Reprint Edition). New York: Vintage. *Introduces methods for overcoming feelings of helplessness and building a positive self-image that can contribute to emotional well-being.*

Thase, M. E., and S. S. Lang. 2006. *Beating the Blues: New Approaches to Overcoming Dysthymia and Chronic Mild Depression*. New York: Oxford University Press. *Describes strategies for changing negative thinking patterns that lead to discouragement and pessimism; also discusses newer medications and alternative therapies.*

WW Organizations, Hotlines, and Web Sites

American Association of Suicidology. Provides information about suicide and resources for people in crisis.
http://www.suicidology.org

American Psychiatric Association (APA). Provides facts on topics such as depression, anxiety, eating disorders, and medications.
888-357-7924; 703-907-7300
http://www.psych.org

American Psychological Association Consumer HelpCenter. Provides information about common challenges to psychological health and about how to obtain professional help.
800-964-2000
http://helping.apa.org

Anxiety Disorders Association of America (ADAA). Provides information and resources related to anxiety disorders.
http://www.adaa.org

Depression and Bipolar Support Alliance (DBSA). Provides educational materials and information about support groups.
800-826-3632
http://www.dbsalliance.org

Internet Mental Health. An encyclopedia of mental health information, including medical diagnostic criteria.
http://www.mentalhealth.com

MindZone. Offers information on mental health issues specifically for teens.
http://www.copecaredeal.org

NAMI (National Alliance on Mental Illness). Provides information and support for people affected by mental illness.
800-950-NAMI (Help Line)
http://www.nami.org

National Hopeline Network. 24-hour hotline for people who are thinking about suicide or know someone who is; calls are routed to local crisis centers.
800-SUICIDE
http://www.hopeline.com

National Institute of Mental Health (NIMH). Provides helpful information about anxiety, depression, eating disorders, and other challenges to psychological health.
866-615-6464; 301-443-4513
http://www.nimh.nih.gov

National Mental Health Association. Provides consumer information on a variety of issues, including how to find help.
800-969-NMHA
http://www.nmha.org

National Mental Health Information Center. A one-stop source for information and resources relating to mental health.
800-789-2647
http://www.mentalhealth.org

Psych Central: Dr. John Grohol's Mental Health Page. A guide to mental health resources on the Internet.
http://psychcentral.com

Surgeon General: Reports. Reports from the U.S. Surgeon General, including the 1999 report on mental health and the 2001 supplement on culture and ethnicity.
http://www.surgeongeneral.gov/library/reports.htm

World Health Organization: 2001 World Health Report. Focuses on mental health as a major cause of disability.
http://www.who.int/whr/2001/en

The following sites include interactive online assessments for various psychological problems:

Depression-screening.org: http://www.depression-screening.org
Freedom from Fear: http://www.freedomfromfear.com

Selected Bibliography

Adams, R. E., and J. A. Boscarino. 2006. Predictors of PTSD and delayed PTSD after disaster: The impact of exposure and psychosocial resources. *The Journal of Nervous and Mental Disease* 194(7): 485–493.

American Psychiatric Association. 2000. *Diagnostic and Statistical Manual of Mental Disorders,* 4th ed., Text Revision *(DSM-IV-TR).* Washington, D.C.: American Psychiatric Association Press.

American Psychiatric Association. 2005. *College Mental Health Statistics* (http://www.healthyminds.org/collegestats.cfm; retrieved July 14, 2006).

Antidepressants for children and adolescents: An update. 2006. *Harvard Mental Health Letter* 22(12): 4–5.

Benton, S. A., et al. 2003. Changes in counseling center client problems across 13 years. *Professional Psychology: Research and Practice* 34(1): 66–72.

Boscarino, J. A., R. E. Adams, and C. R. Figley. 2004. Mental health service use 1-year after the World Trade Center disaster: Implications for mental health care. *Annals of General Hospital Psychiatry* 5: 346–358.

Brenes, G. A., 2006. Age differences in the presentation of anxiety. *Aging and Mental Health* 10(3): 298–302.

Brenes, G. A., et al. 2002. Do optimism and pessimism predict physical functioning? *Journal of Behavioral Medicine* 25(3): 219–231.

Coryell, W. H. 2006. Clinical assessment of suicide risk in depressive disorder. *CNS Spectrums* 11(6): 455–461.

Cutler, J. L., et al. 2004. Comparing cognitive behavior therapy, interpersonal psychotherapy, and psychodynamic psychotherapy. *American Journal of Psychiatry* 161(9): 1567–1573.

Dervic, K., et al. 2004. Religious affiliation and suicide attempt. *American Journal of Psychiatry* 161(12): 2303–2308.

Fazel, S., and M. Grann. 2006. The population impact of severe mental illness on violent crime. *American Journal of Psychiatry* 163(8): 1397–1403.

Food and Drug Administration. 2005. Safeguards for children taking antidepressants strengthened. *FDA Consumer,* January/February.

Gunnell, D., P. K. Magnusson, and F. Rasmussen. 2005. Low intelligence test scores in 18-year-old men and risk of suicide: Cohort study. *British Medical Journal* 330(7484): 167.

Healy, D. 2006. Did regulators fail over selective serotonin reuptake inhibitors? *British Medical Journal* 333: 92–95.

Hershel, J., J. A. Kaye, and S. S. Jick. 2004. Antidepressants and the risk of suicidal behaviors. *Journal of the American Medical Association* 292(3): 338–343.

Hettema, J. M., et al. 2006. A population-based twin study of the relationship between neuroticism and internalizing disorders. *American Journal of Psychiatry* 163(5): 857–864.

Kasper, S., et al. 2006. Superior efficacy of St. John's wort extract WS(R) 5570 compared to placebo in patients with major depression: A randomized, double-blind, placebo-controlled, multi-center trial. *BMC Medicine* 4(1): 14.

Kendler, K. S., J. Myers, and C. A. Prescott. 2005. Sex differences in the relationship between social support and risk for major depression: A longitudinal study of opposite-sex twin pairs. *American Journal of Psychiatry* 162(2): 250–256.

Lewis, C. 2003. The lowdown on depression. *FDA Consumer,* January/February.

Licinio, J., and M. L. Wong. 2005. Opinion: Depression, antidepressants and suicidality: A critical appraisal. *Nature Reviews: Drug Discovery* 4(2): 165–171.

McGirr, A., et al. 2006. An examination of DSM-IV depressive symptoms and risk for suicide completion in major depressive disorder: A psychological autopsy study. *Journal of Affective Disorders* July 17, 2006.

Miller, M., D. Azrael, and D. Hemenway. 2002. Household firearm ownership and suicide rates in the United States. *Epidemiology* 13(5): 517–524.

Mufson, L., et al. 2004. A randomized effectiveness trial of interpersonal psychotherapy for depressed adolescents. *Archives of General Psychiatry* 61(6): 577–584.

Nathan, P. E., and J. M. Gorman, eds. 2002. *A Guide to Treatments That Work,* 2nd ed. Oxford: Oxford University Press.

National Institute of Mental Health. 2000. *Depression* (http://www.nimh.nih.gov/publicat/depression.cfm; retrieved July 13, 2006).

Nemeroff, C. B. 2006. The burden of severe depression: A review of diagnostic challenges and treatment alternatives. *Journal of Psychiatric Research* July 25 (Epub ahead of print).

Ozer, D. J., and V. Benet-Martinez. 2006. Personality and prediction of consequential outcomes. *Annual Review of Psychology* 57: 401–421.

Pampallona, S., et al. 2004. Combined pharmacotherapy and psychological treatment for depression: A systematic review. *Archives of General Psychiatry* 61(7): 714–719.

Rothwell, J. D. 2004. *In the Company of Others: An Introduction to Communication,* 2nd ed. New York: McGraw-Hill.

Schatzberg, A. F., J. O. Cole, and C. DeBattista. 2005. *Manual of Clinical Psychopharmacology,* 5th ed. Washington, D.C.: American Psychiatric Publishing.

Shedd, O. L., et al. 2004. The World Trade Center attack: Increased frequency of defibrillator shocks for ventricular arrhythmias in patients living remotely from New York City. *Journal of the American College of Cardiology* 44(6): 1265–1267.

Simeon, D., et al. 2003. Peritraumatic reactions associated with the World Trade Center disaster. *American Journal of Psychiatry* 160(9): 1702–1705.

Simon, O. R., et al. 2002. Characteristics of impulsive suicide attempts and attempters. *Suicide and Life-Threatening Behavior* 32(1 Suppl): 49–59.

Snow, V., S. Lascher, and C. Mottur-Pilson. 2000. Pharmacological treatment of acute major depression and dysthymia. *Annals of Internal Medicine* 132(9): 738–742.

Stahl, S. M. 2002. *Essential Psychopharmacology of Antipsychotics and Mood Stabilizers.* Cambridge: Cambridge University Press.

Substance Abuse and Mental Health Services Administration. 2005. *Depression among adolescents* (http://oas.samhsa.gov/2k5/youthDepression/youthDepression.htm; retrieved July 13, 2006).

Tsai, S. Y., et al. 2002. Risk factors for completed suicide in bipolar disorder. *Journal of Clinical Psychiatry* 63(6): 469–476.

Walsh, B. T., et al. 2002. Placebo response in studies of major depression. *Journal of the American Medical Association* 287(14): 1840–1847.

Zarit, S. H., and J. M. Zarit. 2006. *Mental Disorders in Older Adults: Fundamentals of Assessment and Treatment,* 2nd ed. New York: Guilford Press.

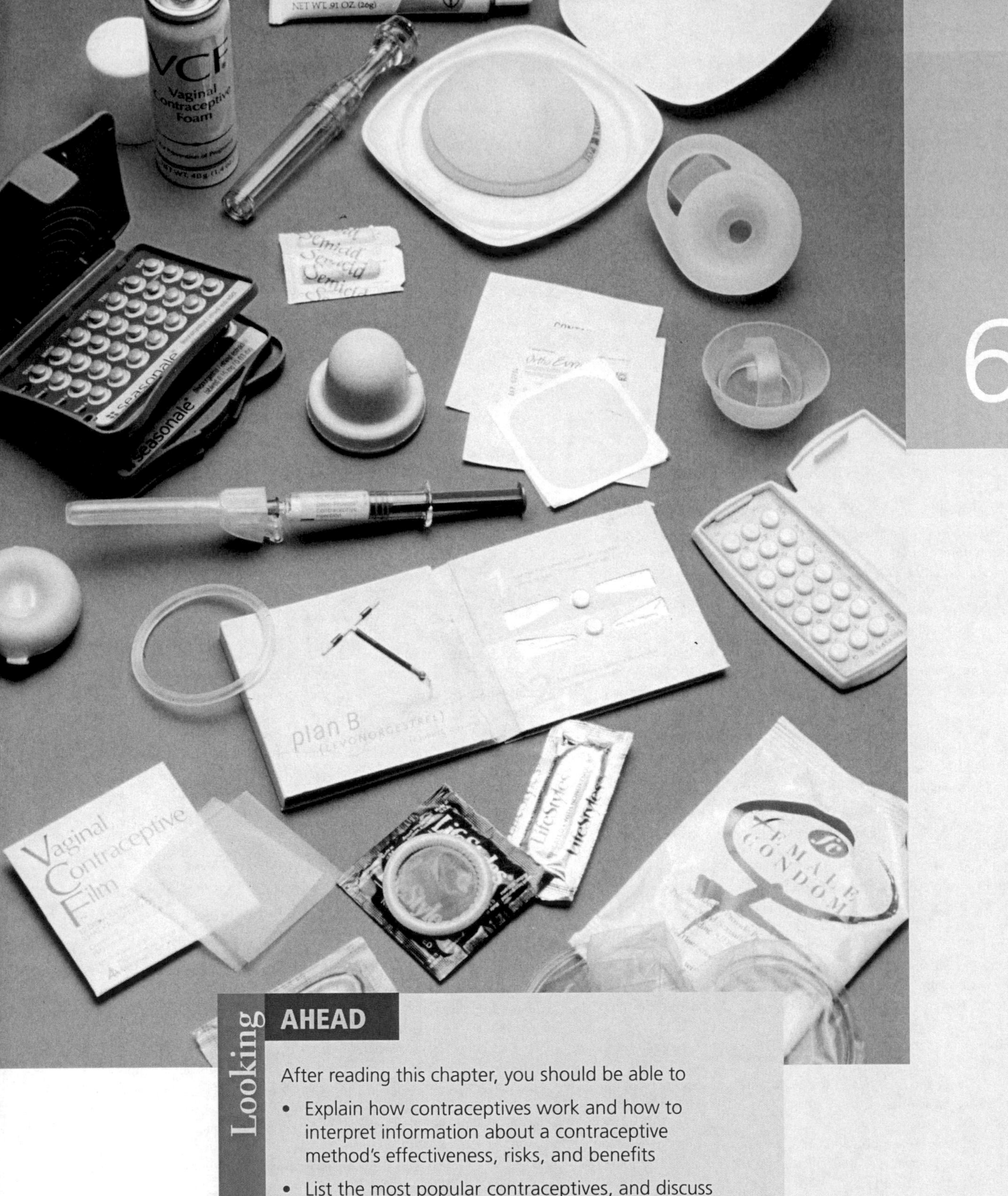

6

Looking AHEAD

After reading this chapter, you should be able to

- Explain how contraceptives work and how to interpret information about a contraceptive method's effectiveness, risks, and benefits
- List the most popular contraceptives, and discuss their advantages, disadvantages, and effectiveness
- Discuss issues related to contraception, including nonmarital sexual relationships, gender differences, sex education for teenagers, and communication between partners
- Choose a method of contraception based on the needs of the user and the safety and effectiveness of the method

Contraception

Test Your Knowledge

1. **Which of the following contraceptive methods offers the best protection against pregnancy? Which offers the best protection against sexually transmitted diseases?**
   a. oral contraceptives
   b. injectable contraceptives
   c. male condoms
   d. diaphragm with spermicidal foam
2. **Oral contraceptive users typically gain a significant amount of weight.**
   True or false?
3. **Hand lotion, Vaseline (petroleum jelly), and baby oil are good choices for condom lubricants.**
   True or false?
4. **About one in ten young people (age 15–24) reports having had unprotected sex because of the use of alcohol or other drugs.**
   True or false?
5. **Emergency contraception is now available without a prescription to women 18 and older.**
   True or false?

ANSWERS

1. B AND C. Injectable contraceptives are the most effective at preventing pregnancy; male condoms are the most effective against sexually transmitted diseases.
2. FALSE. Oral contraceptive use is not associated with significant, if any, weight gain; if there is an effect, it is small and may be due to short-term fluid retention.
3. FALSE. Only water-based lubricants such as K-Y Jelly should be used as condom lubricants. Any product that contains mineral oil can cause latex condoms to disintegrate, beginning within 60 seconds of its being applied.
4. FALSE. The figure is about one in four. Mixing alcohol, drugs, and sex substantially increases the risk of unprotected sexual activity, unintended pregnancy, and STDs.
5. TRUE. In August 2006, the Food and Drug Administration approved the use of Plan B, an emergency contraception product, as an over-the-counter drug for women 18 and older. It is stocked behind the counter in pharmacies because proof of age is required to purchase it.

Visit the *Core Concepts in Health* Online Learning Center (www.mhhe.com/insel10e) for study aids and many additional resources.

In her lifetime, an average woman's ovaries release over 400 eggs, 1 a month for about 35 years. Each egg is capable of developing into a human embryo if fertilized by one of the millions of sperm a man produces in every ejaculate. Furthermore, unlike most other mammals, humans are capable of sexual activity at any time of the month or year. These facts help explain why people have always had a compelling interest in controlling fertility and in preventing unwanted pregnancies. Historical writings dating back to the fourth century B.C. mention the use of douches, sponges, and crude methods of abortion. Other materials mentioned as potential contraceptives include lemon juice, parsley, seaweed, olive oil, camphor, and opium. Although not fully understood at the time, the underlying principle of these trial-and-error methods was the same as that of today's **contraceptives:** preventing **conception** by blocking the female's egg from uniting with the male's sperm, thereby preventing pregnancy.

Modern contraceptive methods are much more predictable and effective than in the past, and people in developed countries now have many options when it comes to making decisions about their sexual and contraceptive behavior. Worldwide, however, the situation is quite different. People in many countries have little access to contraceptive information and supplies. The World Health Organization estimates that 80 million women worldwide have unintended or unwanted pregnancies every year and half a million women die as a result of complications of pregnancy and chilbirth. Table 6-1 shows the numbers of intended and unintended pregnancies in the United States in 2001 (the most recent year for which complete data are available). About 44% of unintended pregnancies were carried to term that year; another 42% ended in abortion. The remainder ended in loss of the fetus for some other reason.

In addition to the primary purpose of preventing pregnancy, many types of contraception play an important role in protecting against **sexually transmitted diseases (STDs).** Being informed about the realities and risks and making responsible decisions about sexual and contraceptive behavior are crucial components of lifelong wellness. But because such decisions are emotional, complex, and difficult, people tend to avoid them or to deal with them ineffectively.

Although biological, social, and media pressures often encourage sexual activity at ever-younger ages, few forces in the United States support a factual, realistic discussion of the importance of either postponing sexual intercourse or using contraception when intercourse is chosen. Our present superficial approaches to education are clearly ineffective: The United States has one of the highest teen pregnancy rates of all developed nations. Because many of the changing roles of women are severely compromised by unplanned child rearing and because the option of abortion is becoming more restricted, the problem is even worse than the numbers show.

VITAL STATISTICS

Table 6-1 Intended versus Unintended Pregnancies in the United States: 2001

Total pregnancies	6,404,000
Intended	51%
Unintended	49%
Unintended pregnancies ending in abortion	42%
Pregnancy rate*	104
Abortion rate*	21
Unintended birth rate*	22

*Per 1000 women

SOURCE: Finer, L. B., and S. K. Henshaw. 2006. Disparities in rates of unintended pregnancy in the United States, 1994 and 2001. *Perspectives on Sexual and Reproductive Health* 38(2): 90–96.

This chapter provides basic information on the various contraceptive methods, including their advantages and disadvantages; STDs are discussed in Chapter 18. The issues raised should encourage you to think about your own beliefs and attitudes about sexual behavior and contraception and to discuss them with others. Among the most important choices of your life will be deciding what type of sexual involvement is best for you and when you are ready for a sexual relationship; equally critical is the commitment to always protect yourself against unwanted pregnancy and STDs.

PRINCIPLES OF CONTRACEPTION

A variety of effective approaches in preventing conception are based on different principles of birth control. **Barrier methods** work by physically blocking the sperm from reaching the egg. Diaphragms, condoms, and several other methods are based on this principle. *Hormonal methods,* such as oral contraceptives (birth control pills), alter the biochemistry of the woman's body, preventing **ovulation** (the release of the egg) and producing changes that make it more difficult for the sperm to reach the egg if ovulation does occur. So-called *natural methods* of contraception are based on the fact that egg and sperm have to be present at the same time if fertilization is to occur. Finally, *surgical methods*—female and male sterilization—more or less permanently prevent transport of the sperm or eggs to the site of conception.

All contraceptive methods have advantages and disadvantages that make them appropriate for some people but not for others or the best choice at one period of life but not at another. Factors that affect the choice of method include effectiveness, convenience, cost, reversibility, side effects and risks, and protection against STDs. Later in this chapter, we help you sort through these factors to decide

In Focus

Myths About Contraception

Myth Taking borrowed birth control pills for a few days before having sexual relations gives reliable protection against pregnancy.
Fact Instructions for taking birth control pills must be followed carefully to provide effective contraception. With most pills, this means starting them with a menstrual period and then taking one every day.

Myth Pregnancy never occurs when unprotected intercourse takes place just before or just after a menstrual period.
Fact Menstrual cycles may be irregular, and ovulation may occur at unpredictable times.

Myth During sexual relations, sperm enter the vagina only during ejaculation and never before.
Fact The small amounts of fluid secreted before ejaculation may contain sperm. This is why withdrawing the penis from the vagina just prior to ejaculation is not an effective method of contraception.

Myth If semen is deposited just outside the vaginal entrance, pregnancy cannot occur.
Fact Although sperm usually live about 72 hours within the woman's body, they can live up to 6 or 7 days and are capable of traveling through the vagina and up into the uterus and oviducts.

Myth Douching immediately after sexual relations can prevent sperm from reaching and fertilizing an egg.
Fact During ejaculation (within the vagina), some sperm begin to enter the cervix and uterus. Because these sperm are no longer in the vagina, it is impossible to remove them by douching after sexual relations. Douching may actually push the sperm up farther.

Myth A woman who is breastfeeding does not have to use any contraceptive method to prevent pregnancy.
Fact Frequent and regular breastfeeding may at times prevent ovulation, but not consistently and reliably. Ovulation and pregnancy may occur before the first period after delivering a baby.

Myth Women can't become pregnant the first time they have intercourse.
Fact *Any time* intercourse without protection takes place, sperm may unite with an egg to begin a pregnancy. There is nothing unique about first intercourse that prevents this.

Myth Taking a "rest" from the pill periodically is necessary for safety.
Fact There are no known medical benefits from taking a prolonged break from oral contraceptive use; the risks and benefits of ongoing pill use should be evaluated for each individual. Pregnancy commonly occurs when one method of contraception is stopped and not immediately replaced by another method.

Myth Pregnancy is impossible if partners have sex while standing up.
Fact Sperm can travel and reach the egg regardless of body position.

on the method that's best for you. (See the box "Myths About Contraception" to make sure you're not basing your current choices on common misinformation.)

Effectiveness, one of the factors listed earlier, requires further explanation. Contraceptive effectiveness is partly determined by the reliability of the method itself—the failure rate if it were always used exactly as directed ("perfect use"). Effectiveness is also determined by characteristics of the user, including fertility of the individual, frequency of intercourse, and, more important, how consistently and correctly the method is used. This "typical use" **contraceptive failure rate** is based on studies that directly measure the percentage of women experiencing an unintended pregnancy in the first year of contraceptive use. For example, the 8% failure rate of oral contraceptives means 8 out of 100 typical users will become pregnant in the first year. This failure rate is likely to be lower for women who are consistently careful in following instructions and higher for those who are frequently careless; the "perfect use" failure rate is 0.3%. Similarly, the 16% failure rate of typical diaphragm use can be decreased or increased significantly by how correct and consistent the woman is in using the device.

Another measure of effectiveness is the **continuation rate**—the percentage of people who continue to use the method after a specified period of time. This measure is important because many unintended pregnancies occur when a method is stopped and not immediately replaced with another. Thus, a contraceptive with a high continuation rate would be more effective at preventing pregnancy than one with a low continuation rate.

We turn now to a description of the various contraceptive methods, discussing first those that are reversible and then those that are permanent.

Terms

Vw

contraceptive Any agent that can prevent conception; condoms, diaphragms, intrauterine devices, and oral contraceptives are examples.

conception The fusion of ovum and sperm, resulting in a fertilized egg, or zygote.

sexually transmitted disease (STD) Any of several contagious diseases contracted through intimate sexual contact.

barrier method A contraceptive that acts as a physical barrier, blocking the sperm from uniting with the egg.

ovulation The release of the egg (ovum) from the ovaries.

contraceptive failure rate The percentage of women using a particular contraceptive method who experience an unintended pregnancy in the first year of use.

continuation rate The percentage of women who continue to use a particular contraceptive after a specified period of time.

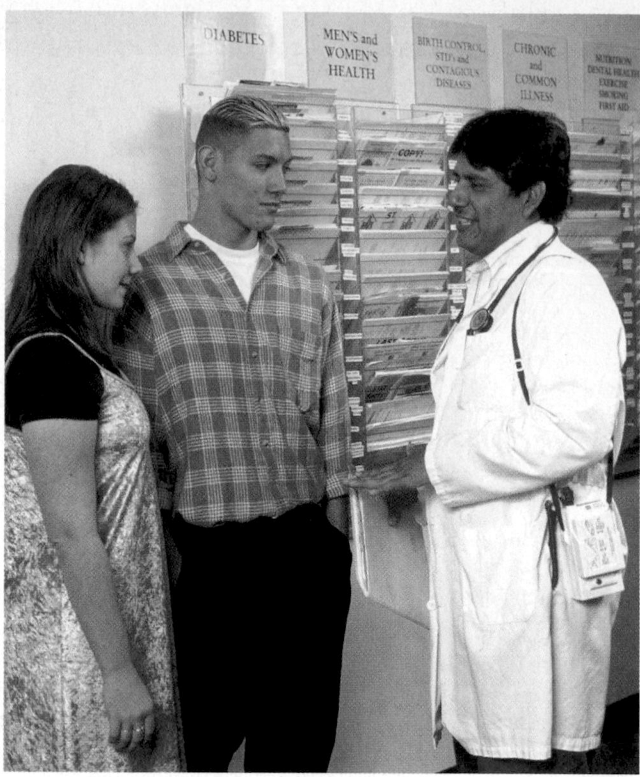

To be effective, contraceptives should be chosen thoughtfully and used correctly. A careful explanation by a health care professional will help this couple choose a method that is right for them.

REVERSIBLE CONTRACEPTION

Reversibility is an extremely important consideration for young adults when they choose a contraceptive method, because most people either plan to have children or at least want to keep their options open until they're older. In this section we discuss the reversible contraceptives, beginning with the hormonal methods, then moving to the barrier methods, and finally covering the natural methods.

Oral Contraceptives: The Pill

A century ago or more, a researcher made a key observation: Ovulation does not occur during pregnancy. Further research brought to light the hormonal mechanism: During pregnancy, the corpus luteum secretes progesterone and estrogen in amounts high enough to suppress ovulation. (Refer to Chapter 5 for a complete discussion of the hormonal control of the menstrual cycle.) **Oral contraceptives (OCs),** or birth control pills, prevent ovulation by mimicking the hormonal activity of the corpus luteum. The active ingredients in OCs are estrogen and progestins, laboratory-made compounds that are closely related to progesterone.

In addition to preventing ovulation, the birth control pill has other backup contraceptive effects. It inhibits the movement of sperm by thickening the cervical mucus, alters the rate of ovum transport by means of its hormonal effects on the oviducts, and may prevent implantation by changing the lining of the uterus, in the unlikely event that a fertilized ovum reaches that area.

The most common type of OC is the combination pill. Each 1-month packet contains 3 weeks of pills that combine varying types and amounts of estrogen and progestin. Most packets also include a 1-week supply of inactive pills to be taken following the hormone pills; others simply instruct the woman to take no pills at all for 1 week before starting the next cycle. During the week in which no hormones are taken, a light menstrual period occurs. Many different types of combination pills are available today, and if minor problems occur with one brand, a woman can switch to another.

A newer use schedule is the extended-cycle regimen, in which a woman takes active pills for 84 consecutive days, followed by inactive pills for a week; this pattern reduces the number of menstrual periods from 13 per year to just 4 per year. Seasonale and other new OCs are specifically packaged for extended use. Other OCs with hormones similar to Seasonale's may be used in the same way.

Another, much less common, type of OC is the minipill, a small dose of a synthetic progesterone taken every day of the month. Because the minipill contains no estrogen, it has fewer side effects and health risks, but it is associated with more irregular bleeding patterns.

A woman is usually advised to start the first cycle of pills with a menstrual period to increase effectiveness and eliminate the possibility of unsuspected pregnancy. She must take each month's pills completely and according to instructions. Taking a few pills just prior to having sexual intercourse will not provide effective contraception.

Hormonal adjustments that occur during the first cycle or two may cause slight bleeding between periods. This spotting is considered normal. Full effectiveness cannot be guaranteed during the first week because maximal levels of hormones haven't yet been reached. A backup method is recommended during the first week and any subsequent cycle in which the woman forgets to take any pills.

Since its approval by the FDA in 1960, the pill has remained a popular contraceptive in the United States. OC use declined temporarily in the late 1970s following publicity regarding possible increased risks of heart attack and stroke. However, these risks have been substantially reduced by the use of lower-dosage pills (those with 50 micrograms or less of estrogen) and the identification of women at higher risk for complications. Today, OCs are the most widely used form of contraception among unmarried women and are second only to sterilization among married women.

Advantages The main advantage of the oral contraceptive is its high degree of effectiveness in preventing pregnancy. Nearly all unplanned pregnancies result because the pills were not taken as directed. The pill is relatively simple to use and does not require any interruptions that could hinder sexual spontaneity. Most women also enjoy the predictable regularity of periods, as well as the decrease in cramps and blood loss. For young women, the reversibility of the pill is especially important; **fertility**—the ability to reproduce—returns after the pill is discontinued (although not always immediately).

Medical advantages include a decreased incidence of benign breast disease, iron-deficiency anemia, pelvic inflammatory disease (PID), ectopic pregnancy, colon and rectal cancer, endometrial cancer (of the lining of the uterus), and ovarian cancer. Women who have never used the pill are twice as likely to develop endometrial or ovarian cancer as those who have taken it for at least 5 years.

Disadvantages Although oral contraceptives do lower the risk of PID, they do not protect against HIV infection or other STDs in the lower reproductive tract. OCs have been associated with increased cervical chlamydia. Regular condom use is recommended for an OC user, unless she is in a long-term, mutually monogamous relationship with an uninfected partner.

The hormones in birth control pills influence all tissues of the body, and they can lead to a variety of minor disturbances. Symptoms of early pregnancy—morning nausea and swollen breasts, for example—may appear during the first few months of OC use. They usually disappear by the fourth cycle. Other side effects include depression, nervousness, changes in sex drive, dizziness, generalized headaches, migraine, bleeding between periods, and changes in the lining of the walls of the vagina, with an increase in clear or white vaginal discharge. Chloasma, or "mask of pregnancy," sometimes occurs, causing brown "giant freckles" to appear on the face. Acne may develop or worsen, but, in most women, using the pill causes acne to clear up, and it is sometimes prescribed for that purpose.

Serious side effects have been reported in a small number of women. These include blood clots, stroke, and heart attack, concentrated mostly in older women who smoke or have a history of circulatory disease. Recent studies have shown no increased risk of stroke or heart attack for healthy, young, nonsmoking women on lower-dosage pills. OC users may be slightly more prone to high blood pressure, blood clots in the legs and arms, and benign liver tumors that may rupture and bleed. OC use is associated with little, if any, increase in breast cancer and a slight increase in cervical cancer; however, earlier detection and other variables such as number of sexual partners may account for much of this increase. The link between OC use and cervical cancer appears to pertain primarily to women infected with human papillomavirus, an STD.

Birth control pills are not recommended for women with a history of blood clots (or a close family member with unexplained blood clots at an early age), heart disease or stroke, any form of cancer or liver tumor, or impaired liver function. Women with certain other health conditions or behaviors, including migraines, high blood pressure, cigarette smoking, and sickle-cell disease, require close monitoring.

When deciding whether to use OCs, each woman needs to weigh the benefits against the risks. To make an informed decision, she should seek the help of a health care professional (see the box "Obtaining a Contraceptive from a Health Clinic or Physician" on p. 156). A woman can take several steps to decrease her risk from OC use:

1. Request a low-dosage pill. (OCs recommended for most new users contain 30–35 micrograms of estrogen.)
2. Stop smoking.
3. Follow the dosage carefully and consistently.
4. Be alert to preliminary danger signals, which can be remembered with the word ACHES:

   Abdominal pain (severe)

   Chest pain (severe), cough, shortness of breath or sharp pain on breathing in

   Headaches (severe), dizziness, weakness, or numbness, especially if one-sided

   Eye problems (vision loss or blurring) and/or speech problems

   Severe leg pain (calf or thigh)
5. Have regular checkups to monitor blood pressure, weight, and urine, and have an annual examination of the thyroid, breasts, abdomen, and pelvis.
6. Have regular **Pap tests** to check for early cervical changes. Because OC use may temporarily increase some women's susceptibility to the STDs chlamydia and gonorrhea, regular screening for those diseases is also recommended, especially when condoms aren't being used.

For most women, the known, directly associated risk of death from taking birth control pills is much lower than the risk of death from pregnancy (Table 6-2, p. 157).

Effectiveness Oral contraceptive effectiveness varies substantially because it depends so much on individual factors. If taken exactly as directed, the failure rate is extremely low (0.3%). However, among average users, lapses

Terms

Vw

oral contraceptive (OC) Any of various hormone compounds (estrogen and progestins) in pill form that prevent conception by preventing ovulation.

fertility The ability to reproduce.

Pap test A scraping of cells from the cervix for examination under a microscope to detect cancer.

Critical Consumer

Obtaining a Contraceptive from a Health Clinic or Physician

VW

If you are a woman who is considering a method of contraception that requires a prescription or professional fitting or insertion, you'll need to go to a health clinic or a physician to get it. Many of the female methods—including the hormonal methods, IUDs, and the diaphragm and cervical cap—require at least an initial professional visit. The thought of visiting a physician's office or health clinic to discuss and obtain contraception makes many people nervous. Keep in mind that the people in the office are health care professionals who will not pass moral judgment on you. They are dedicated to meeting your health care needs. Knowing what to expect can help you get more from your visit.

Before Your Visit

You can prepare for a more successful visit by doing the following:

1. Pull together your personal and family medical history. Make sure it's accurate and up-to-date.
2. Review the section in this chapter titled "Which Contraceptive Method Is Right for You?" Carefully consider each topic, and discuss it with your partner if that would be helpful.
3. Write down any questions you have. Clarify in your own mind what you need to find out about your contraceptive options.
4. If you have questions about sexually transmitted diseases or other aspects of sexuality, write those down, too.
5. If you like, plan to have your partner, a friend, or a family member accompany you to your appointment.

During Your Visit

When you arrive, you'll probably be asked to fill out forms covering your background and medical history. A physician or staff member will then review the various contraceptive methods with you and answer your questions. She or he can help you evaluate the key factors affecting your choice of method, including health risks, lifestyle factors, cost, and protection against STDs. You may have blood and urine samples taken for lab tests.

The Physical Exam

Your physical exam will probably include a check of your breasts, external genitals, and abdomen, plus a Pap test and possible screening for certain STDs. The exam will help ensure that you can safely use the method you have chosen, as well as protect your overall health. If this is your first pelvic exam and/or you feel nervous or uncomfortable, tell the clinician, and ask her or him to explain each step of the examination.

For the pelvic exam, you will be asked to lie on your back on an examination table, with your feet in metal stirrups and your knees bent. The exam doesn't usually hurt. An instrument called a speculum will be inserted into the vagina to hold it open so the clinician can look at the cervix and vaginal walls. For the Pap test, the clinician will scrape some cells from the cervix and place them on a glass slide. These cells will be analyzed for any signs of cancer. You may feel a slight pressure while the cells are collected. The clinician will also check your internal organs by placing two gloved fingers into the vagina and the other hand on the lower abdomen. He or she will palpate (examine by touching) the uterus and ovaries to check for any abnormalities.

If you're getting a diaphragm or a cervical cap, you will be fitted for it at this time. The clinician will probably try different sizes to find the best fit and then will show you how to insert and remove it.

Following Your Exam

After your exam, a health care worker will either provide you with your contraceptive, arrange for a further appointment (if necessary), or give you a prescription. Make sure you know exactly how to use the method you've chosen. Written instructions and information may be available. Be sure you have a phone number you can call if you have questions later.

such as forgetting to take a pill do occur, and a typical first-year failure rate is 8%. The continuation rate for OCs also varies; the average rate is 68% after 1 year.

Contraceptive Skin Patch

The contraceptive skin patch, Ortho Evra, is a thin, 1¾-inch square patch that slowly releases an estrogen and a progestin into the bloodstream. The contraceptive patch prevents pregnancy in the same way as combination OCs, following a similar schedule. Each patch is worn continuously for 1 week and is replaced on the same day of the week for 3 consecutive weeks. The fourth week is patch-free, allowing a woman to have her menstrual period.

The patch can be worn on the upper outer arm, abdomen, buttocks, or upper torso (excluding the breasts); it is designed to stick to skin even during bathing or swimming. If a patch should fall off for more than a day, the FDA advises starting a new 4-week cycle of patches and using a backup method of contraception for the first week.

Advantages With both perfect and typical use, the patch is as effective as OCs in preventing pregnancy. Compliance seems to be higher with the patch than with OCs, probably because the patch requires weekly instead of daily action. Medical benefits are likely to be comparable to those of OCs.

Table 6-2 Contraceptive Risks

Contraceptive Method	Risk of Death in Any Given Year
Oral contraceptives	
Nonsmoker	1 in 66,700
Age less than 35	1 in 200,000
Age 35–44	1 in 28,600
Heavy smoker (25 or more cigarettes/day)	1 in 1,700
Age less than 35	1 in 5,300
Age 35–44	1 in 700
IUDs	1 in 10,000,000
Barrier methods, spermicides	none
Fertility awareness methods, withdrawal	none
Sterilization	
Laparoscopic tubal ligation	1 in 38,500
Hysterectomy	1 in 1,600
Vasectomy	1 in 1,000,000
Pregnancy and childbirth	1 in 10,000

SOURCE: Hatcher, R. A., et al. 2004. *Contraceptive Technology*, 18th rev. ed. New York: Ardent Media. Reprinted by permission of Ardent Media, Inc.

Disadvantages With patch use, additional measures must be taken for protection against STDs. Minor side effects are similar to those of OCs, although breast discomfort may be more common in patch users. Some women also experience skin irritation around the patch. More serious complications are thought to be similar to those of OCs, including an increased risk of side effects among women who smoke. However, because Ortho Evra exposes users to higher doses of estrogen than most OCs, patch use may further increase the risk of blood clots and other adverse effects. In 2006 the FDA approved an updated, bold-faced warning on the label of Ortho Evra, informing women of this possible increased risk.

Effectiveness With perfect use, the failure rate is very low (0.3%) in the first year of use. The typical failure rate is 8%. The product appears to be less effective when used by women weighing more than 198 pounds.

Vaginal Contraceptive Ring

The NuvaRing is a vaginal ring that resembles the rim of a diaphragm and is molded with a mixture of progestin and estrogen. The 2-inch ring slowly releases hormones and maintains blood hormone levels comparable to those found with OC use; it prevents pregnancy in the same way as OCs. A woman inserts the ring anytime during the first 5 days of her menstrual period and leaves it in place for 3 weeks. During the fourth week, which is ring-free, her next menstrual period occurs. A new ring is then inserted.

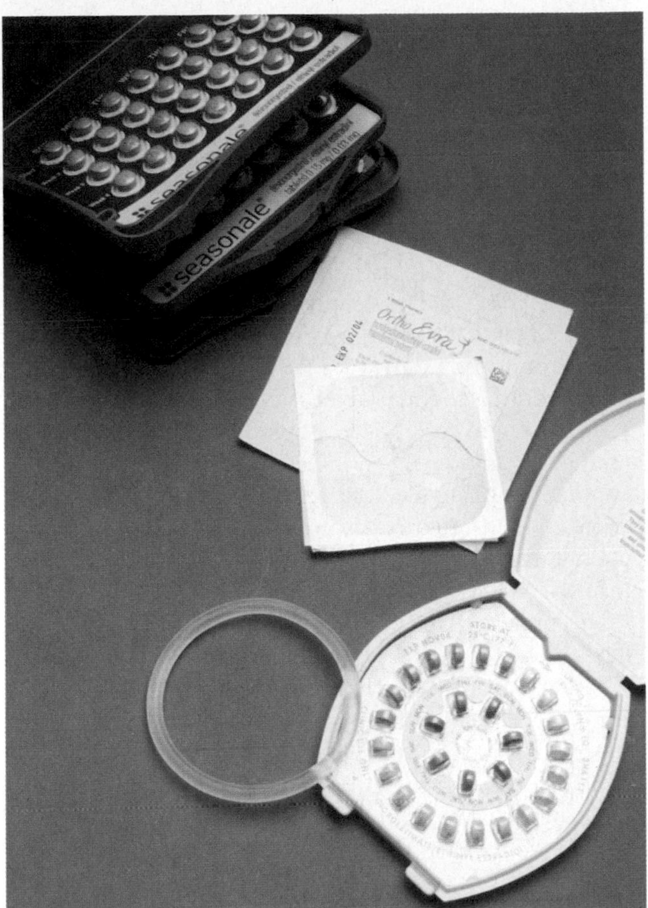

Reversible hormonal contraceptives are available in several forms. Shown here are the patch, the ring, and birth control pills.

Backup contraception must be used for the first 7 days of the first ring use or if the ring has been removed for more than 3 hours during use. A diaphragm is not recommended as a backup contraceptive with the NuvaRing because the ring may interfere with the placement of a diaphragm.

Advantages The NuvaRing offers 1 month of protection with no daily or weekly action required. It does not require a fitting by a clinician, and exact placement in the vagina is not critical as it is with a diaphragm. Medical benefits are probably similar to those of OCs.

Disadvantages The NuvaRing gives no protection against STDs. Side effects are roughly comparable to those seen with OC use, except for a lower incidence of nausea and vomiting. Other side effects may include vaginal discharge, vaginitis, and vaginal irritation. Medical risks also are similar to those found with OC use.

Effectiveness As with the pill and patch, the perfect use failure rate is 0.3% and the typical use failure rate is 8%.

Contraceptive Implants

Contraceptive implants are placed under the skin of the upper arm and deliver a small but steady dose of progestin (a synthetic progesterone) over a period of years. One such implant, called Norplant, consists of six flexible, matchstick-size capsules and provides protection for 5 years. Norplant was available in the United States in the 1990s. Because of lawsuits and related complaints, however, this implant is no longer distributed in the United States. A newer version of the product, called Jadelle (or Norplant II), is very similar to Norplant but consists of two slightly larger capsules. The new implant has been approved for 5-year use in the United States but is not yet available.

Implanon is a single, longer implant that was approved for use in the United States in 2006. This device, which is generally easier to insert and remove than the original Norplant, is effective for 3 years.

The progestins in implants have several contraceptive effects. They cause hormonal shifts that may inhibit ovulation and affect development of the uterine lining. The hormones also thicken the cervical mucus, inhibiting the movement of sperm. Finally, they may slow the transport of the egg through the fallopian tubes. Contraceptive implants are best suited for women who wish to have continuous and long-term protection against pregnancy.

Advantages Contraceptive implants are highly effective. After insertion of the implants, no further action is required; at the same time, contraceptive effects are quickly reversed upon removal. Because implants, unlike the combination pill, contain no estrogen, they carry a lower risk of certain side effects, such as blood clots and other cardiovascular complications. In addition, the progestin is released at a steady rate, in smaller quantities than are found in oral contraceptives. The thickened cervical mucus resulting from implant use has a protective effect against PID.

Disadvantages Like the pill, an implant provides no protection against HIV infection and STDs in the lower reproductive tract. Although the implants are barely visible, their appearance may bother some women. Only specially trained practitioners can insert or remove the implants, and removal is sometimes difficult.

The most common side effects of contraceptive implants are menstrual irregularities, including longer menstrual periods, spotting between periods, or having no bleeding at all. The menstrual cycle usually becomes more regular after 1 year of use. Less common side effects include headaches, weight gain, breast tenderness, nausea, acne, and mood swings. Cautions and more serious health concerns are similar to those associated with oral contraceptives but are less common.

Effectiveness Typical failure rates for Norplant are very low (0.05%) in the first year, increasing slowly with each additional year of use. The cumulative failure rate of Norplant at the end of 5 years is about 1.9%. The overall failure rate for Implanon is estimated at about 0.1%.

Injectable Contraceptives

Hormonal contraceptive injections were developed in the 1960s and are currently being used in at least 80 countries throughout the world. The first injectable contraceptive approved for use in the United States was Depo-Provera, which uses long-acting progestins. Injected into the arm or buttocks, Depo-Provera is usually given every 12 weeks, although it actually provides effective contraception for a few weeks beyond that. As another progestin-only contraceptive, it prevents pregnancy in the same ways as Norplant.

Lunelle, an injectable containing both estrogen and progestin, was approved for use in the United States in 2000. Lunelle injections are given every month rather than every 3 months as with Depo-Provera. Lunelle prevents pregnancy in the same way as OCs. (Lunelle became unavailable in 2002 following a voluntary recall and manufacturing hold; for its current status, check with your health care provider.)

Advantages Injectable contraceptives are highly effective and require little action on the part of the user. Because the injections leave no trace and involve no ongoing supplies, injectables allow women almost total privacy in their decision to use contraception. Like Norplant, Depo-Provera has no estrogen-related side effects; it requires only periodic injections rather than the minor surgical procedures of implant insertion and removal. Lunelle, which does contain estrogen, has many of the same benefits as oral contraceptives and may be preferred by women who do not want to take a pill every day.

Disadvantages Injectable contraceptives provide no protection against HIV infection and STDs in the lower reproductive tract. A woman must visit a health care facility every month (Lunelle) or every 3 months (Depo-Provera) to receive the injections. The side effects of Depo-Provera are similar to those of Norplant; menstrual irregularities are the most common, and after 1 year of using Depo-Provera many women have no menstrual bleeding at all. Lunelle causes less menstrual irregularity than Depo-Provera. Weight gain is a common side effect of both Depo-Provera and Lunelle. After discontinuing the use of Depo-Provera, women may experience temporary infertility for up to 12 months; with Lunelle, fertility usually returns within 2 to 3 months of the last injection.

Reasons for not using Depo-Provera are similar to those for not using Norplant; contraindications for Lunelle are similar to those for OCs. Although early animal studies indicated that Depo-Provera increases the risk of breast and other cancers, the FDA has concluded that worldwide studies and years of human use have shown the risk of cancer in humans to be minimal or nonexistent. Extended use of Depo-Provera is associated with decreased bone density, a risk factor for osteoporosis (see Chapter 12); women are advised to use Depo-Provera as a long-term contraceptive (longer than 2 years, for example) only if other methods are inadequate. Studies have found that bone density rebounds when use of Depo-Provera stops.

Effectiveness Perfect use failure rates are 0.3% for Depo-Provera and 0.5% for Lunelle. With typical use, failure rates increase to 3% for both types of injectables in the first year of use. The 1-year continuation rate for both Depo-Provera and Lunelle is about 56%.

Emergency Contraception

Emergency contraception refers to postcoital methods—those used after unprotected sexual intercourse. An emergency contraceptive may be appropriate if a regularly used method has failed (for example, if a condom breaks) or if unprotected sex has occurred. Sometimes called the "morning-after pill," emergency contraceptives are designed only for emergency use and should not be relied on as a regular method.

Until recently the most frequently used emergency contraceptive was a two-dose regimen of certain oral contraceptives. Researchers are still uncertain precisely how OCs work as emergency contraceptives. Opponents of their use argue that if they act by preventing implantation of a fertilized egg, they may actually be **abortifacients;** however, recent evidence indicates that prevention of implantation is not their primary mode of action. Postcoital pills appear to work primarily by inhibiting or delaying ovulation and by altering the transport of sperm and/or eggs; they do not affect a fertilized egg already implanted in the uterus.

Plan B is a newer product specifically designed for emergency contraception. It contains two progestin-only pills. The first pill should be taken as soon as possible (no more than 72 hours) after inadequately protected sex. The second pill should be taken 12 hours after the first. If taken within 24 hours after intercourse, Plan B may prevent as many as 95% of expected pregnancies. Overall, Plan B reduces pregnancy risk by about 89%. It is most effective if initiated in the first 12 hours. Possible side effects are similar to those associated with the OC regimen and can include nausea, stomach pain, headache, dizziness, and breast tenderness.

In August 2006, the FDA approved the use of Plan B as an over-the-counter (OTC) drug for women aged 18 and older. Prior to that time, it was available to all women by

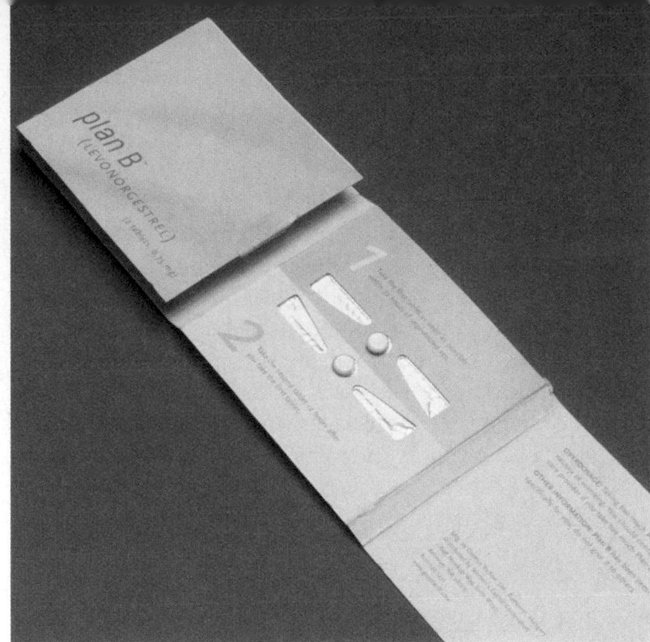

Emergency hormonal contraceptives can reduce the risk of pregnancy by nearly 90% if taken within 72 hours of unprotected intercourse. The most commonly used regimens for emergency contraception involve taking two doses of hormones about 12 hours apart.

prescription and in some states directly from pharmacists. It remains a prescription drug for those under age 18. Plan B is stocked behind the counter because proof of age or a prescription is required to purchase it.

Because of concerns about the drug's use by young teens, the manufacturer of Plan B, Duramed, agreed to a rigorous program of labeling, packaging, education, distribution, and monitoring called Convenient Access, Responsible Education (CARE). Among other things, Duramed has committed not to distribute Plan B through convenience stores or other retail outlets where younger women might have access to it without a prescription.

An FDA expert advisory panel had originally voted to approve Plan B as an OTC medication in 2004, but, in an unusual move, the FDA rejected the panel's recommendation, citing concern that young teens could not take the drug safely without a physician's guidance. The American College of Obstetricians and Gynecologists and other organizations responded that all scientific questions about the safety and use of Plan B had been resolved and that political considerations had influenced the FDA's decision. Only with strong Congressional pressure was OTC use of the drug finally approved.

Easy access to emergency contraception is important because the sooner the drug is taken, the more effective it is. Some clinicians advise women to keep a package of emergency contraception on hand in case their regular

Term

abortifacient An agent or substance that induces abortion.

contraception method fails. Research has found that ready access to emergency contraception does *not* lead to an increase in unprotected intercourse, unintended pregnancies, or STDs.

Despite FDA approval, not all physicians, hospitals, or pharmacists make emergency contraception available, even in cases of sexual assault. So-called refusal or conscience clauses, originally designed to allow physicians to refuse to perform abortions because of personal moral or religions objections, are being applied to a wider range of health care activities and participants. Increasingly, however, states are requiring pharmacies to carry Plan B. Call the Emergency Contraception Hotline (888-NOT-2-LATE) for more information about access.

Intrauterine devices, discussed in the next section, can also be used for emergency contraception: If inserted within 5 days of unprotected intercourse, they are even more effective than OCs. However, because their use is more complicated, they are not used nearly as frequently. In addition, the drug mifepristone is being studied as another possible option (see Chapter 7).

The Intrauterine Device (IUD)

The **intrauterine device (IUD)** is a small plastic device placed in the uterus as a contraceptive. Two IUDs are now available in the United States: the Copper T-380A (also known as the ParaGard), which gives protection for up to 10 years, and the Levonorgestral IUD (Mirena), approved in 2000, which releases small amounts of progestin and is effective for up to 5 years.

Researchers do not know exactly how IUDs prevent pregnancy. Current evidence suggests that they work primarily by preventing fertilization. IUDs may cause biochemical changes in the uterus and affect the movement of sperm and eggs; although less likely, they may also interfere with implantation of fertilized eggs. Mirena slowly releases very small amounts of hormones, which impedes fertilization or implantation.

An IUD must be inserted and removed by a trained professional. It can be inserted at any time during the menstrual cycle, as long as the woman is not pregnant. The device is threaded into a sterile inserter, which is introduced through the cervix; a plunger pushes the IUD into the uterus. The threads protruding from the cervix are trimmed so that only 1–1½ inches remain in the upper vagina (Figure 6-1).

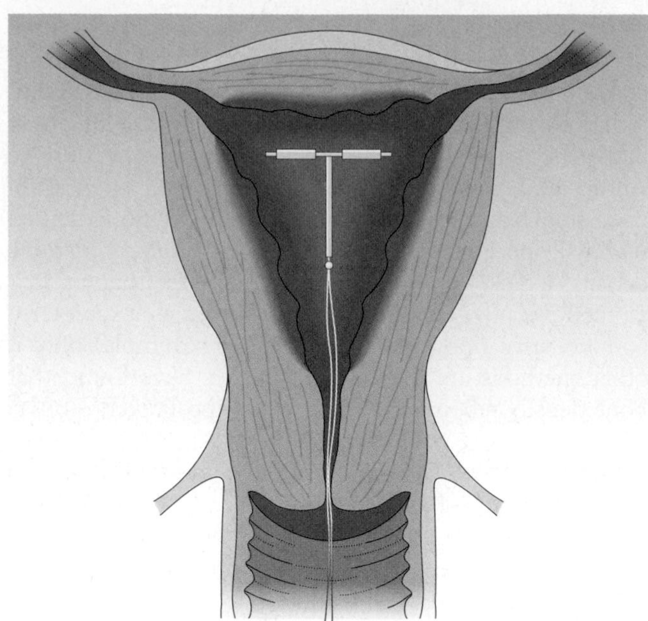

Figure 6-1 An IUD (Copper T-380A) properly positioned in the uterus. The attached threads that protrude from the cervix into the upper vagina allow the woman to check to make sure that the IUD is in place.

Advantages

Intrauterine devices are highly reliable and are simple and convenient to use, requiring no attention except for a periodic check of the string position. They do not require the woman to anticipate or interrupt sexual activity. Usually IUDs have only localized side effects, and in the absence of complications they are considered a fully reversible contraceptive. In most cases, fertility is restored as soon as the IUD is removed. The long-term expense of using an IUD is low.

Disadvantages

Most side effects of IUD use are limited to the genital tract. Heavy menstrual flow and bleeding and spotting between periods may occur, although with Mirena menstrual periods tend to become shorter and lighter over time. Another side effect is pain, particularly uterine cramps and backache, which seem to occur most often in women who have never been pregnant. Spontaneous expulsion of the IUD happens to 5–6% of women within the first year, most commonly during the first months after insertion. The older the woman is and the more children she has had, the less likely she is to expel the device. In about 1 of 1000 insertions, the IUD punctures the wall of the uterus and may migrate into the abdominal cavity.

A serious but rare complication of IUD use is pelvic inflammatory disease (PID). Most pelvic infections among IUD users occur shortly after insertion, are relatively mild, and can be treated successfully with antibiotics. However, early and adequate treatment is critical—a lingering infection can lead to tubal scarring and subsequent infertility.

Some physicians advise against the use of IUDs by young women who have never been pregnant because of the increased incidence of side effects in this group and the risk of infection with the possibility of subsequent infertility. IUDs are not recommended for women of any age who are at high risk for STDs. They are also unsuitable for women with suspected pregnancy, large tumors of the uterus or other anatomical abnormalities, irregular or unexplained bleeding, a history of ectopic pregnancy, or rheumatic heart disease. No evidence has been found linking IUD use to cancer. IUDs offer no protection against STDs.

Early IUD danger signals are abdominal pain, fever, chills, foul-smelling vaginal discharge, irregular menstrual periods, and other unusual vaginal bleeding. A change in string length should also be noted. An annual checkup is important and should include a Pap test and a blood check for anemia if menstrual flow has increased.

Effectiveness The typical failure rate of IUDs during the first year of use is 0.8% for the ParaGard and 0.1% for Mirena. Effectiveness can be increased by periodically checking to see that the device is in place and by using a backup method for the first few months after IUD insertion. If pregnancy occurs, the IUD should be removed to safeguard the health of the woman and to maintain the pregnancy. The continuation rate of IUDs is about 80% after 1 year of use.

Male Condoms

The **male condom** is a thin sheath designed to cover the penis during sexual intercourse. Most brands available in the United States are made of latex, although condoms made of polyurethane are also now available. Condoms prevent sperm from entering the vagina and provide protection against disease. Condoms are the most widely used barrier method and the third most popular of all contraceptive methods used in the United States, after the pill and female sterilization.

Condom sales have increased dramatically in recent years, primarily because they are the only method that provides substantial protection against HIV infection as well as some protection against other STDs. At least one-third of all male condoms are bought by women. This figure will probably increase as more women become aware of the serious risks associated with STDs and assume the right to insist on condom use. Women are more likely to contract an STD from an infected partner than men are. Women also face additional health risks from STDs, including cervical cancer, PID, ectopic pregnancy (which is potentially life-threatening), and infertility.

The man or his partner must put the condom on the penis before it is inserted into the vagina, because the small amounts of fluid that may be secreted unnoticed prior to **ejaculation** often contain sperm capable of causing pregnancy. The rolled-up condom is placed over the head of the erect penis and unrolled down to the base of the penis, leaving a half-inch space (without air) at the tip to collect semen (Figure 6-2, p. 162). Some brands of condoms have a reservoir tip designed for this purpose. Uncircumcised men must first pull back the foreskin of the penis. Partners must be careful not to damage the condom with fingernails, rings, or other rough objects.

Prelubricated condoms are available containing the **spermicide** nonoxynol-9, the same agent found in many of the contraceptive creams that women use. However, there is no evidence that spermicidal condoms are more effective than condoms without spermicide, even though they cost more. Furthermore, these condoms have been associated with urinary tract infections in women and, if they cause tissue irritation, an increased risk of HIV transmission.

If desired, users can lubricate their own condoms with contraceptive foam, creams, or jelly. If vaginal irritation occurs with these products, water-based preparations such as K-Y Jelly can be used. Any products that contain mineral or vegetable oil—including baby oil, many lotions, regular Vaseline petroleum jelly, cooking oils (corn oil, Crisco, butter, and so on), and some vaginal lubricants and anti-fungal or anti-itch creams—should never be used with latex condoms; they can cause latex to begin to disintegrate within 60 seconds, thus greatly increasing the chance of condom breakage. (Polyurethane is not affected by oil-based products.)

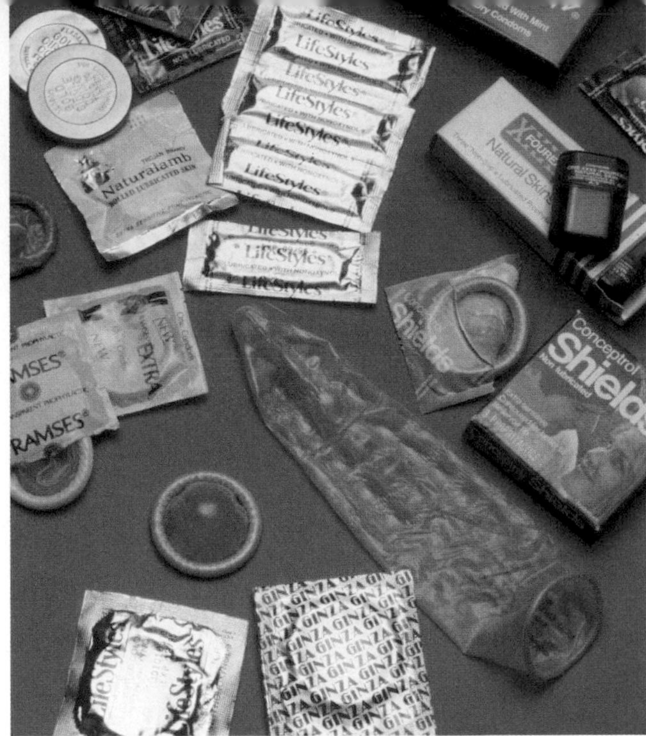

Condoms come in a variety of sizes, textures, and colors; some brands have a reservoir tip designed to collect semen. Used consistently and correctly, condoms provide the most reliable protection available against HIV infection for sexually active people.

Terms

intrauterine device (IUD) A plastic device inserted into the uterus as a contraceptive.

male condom A sheath, usually made of thin latex (synthetic rubber), that covers the penis during sexual intercourse; used for contraception and to prevent STDs.

ejaculation An abrupt discharge of semen from the penis after sexual stimulation.

spermicide A chemical agent that kills sperm.

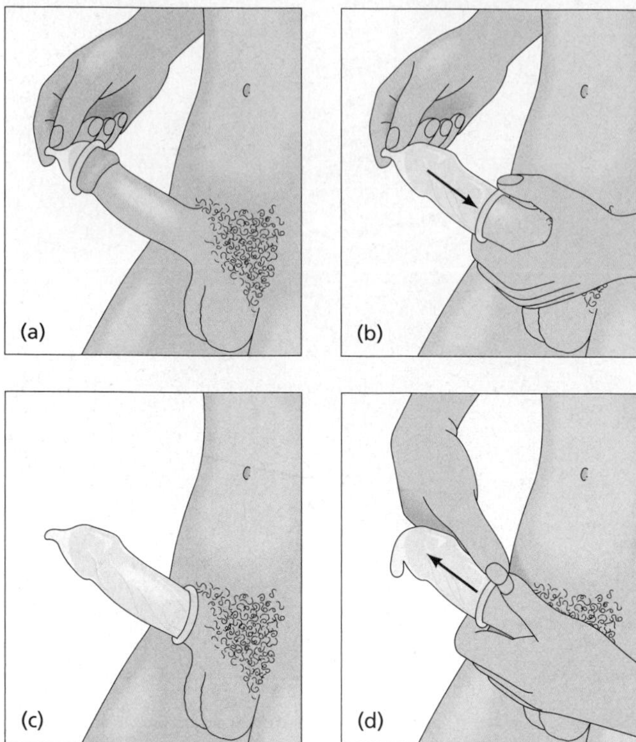

Figure 6-2 Use of the male condom. (a) Place the rolled-up condom over the head of the erect penis. Hold the top half-inch of the condom (with air squeezed out) to leave room for semen. (b) While holding the tip, unroll the condom onto the penis. Gently smooth out any air bubbles. (c) Unroll the condom down to the base of the penis. (d) To avoid spilling semen after ejaculation, hold the condom around the base of the penis as the penis is withdrawn. Remove the condom away from your partner, taking care not to spill any semen.

When the man loses his erection after ejaculating, the condom loses its tight fit. To avoid spilling semen, the condom must be held around the base of the penis as the penis is withdrawn. If any semen is spilled on the vulva, sperm may find their way to the uterus.

Advantages Condoms are easy to purchase and are available without prescription or medical supervision (see the box "Buying and Using Over-the-Counter Contraceptives"). In addition to being free of medical side effects (other than occasional allergic reactions), latex condoms help protect against STDs. A recent study determined that condoms may also protect women from human papilloma virus (HPV), which causes cervical cancer. Condoms made of polyurethane are appropriate for people who are allergic to latex. However, they are more likely to slip or break than latex condoms, and therefore may give less protection against STDs and pregnancy. (Lambskin condoms permit the passage of HIV and other disease-causing organisms, so they can be used only for pregnancy prevention, not the prevention of STDs.) Except for abstinence, correct and consistent use of latex male condoms offers the most reliable available protection against the transmission of HIV.

Disadvantages The two most common complaints about condoms are that they diminish sensation and interfere with spontaneity. Although some people find these drawbacks serious, others consider them only minor disadvantages. Many couples learn to creatively integrate condom use into their sexual practices. Indeed, it can be a way to improve communication and share responsibility in a relationship.

Effectiveness In actual use, the failure rate of condoms varies considerably. First-year rates among typical users average about 15%. At least some pregnancies happen because the condom is carelessly removed after ejaculation. Some may also occur because of breakage or slippage, which may happen 1–2 times in every 100 instances of use for latex condoms and up to 10 times in every 100 instances for polyurethane condoms. Breakage is more common among inexperienced users. Other contributing factors include poorly fitting condoms, insufficient lubrication, excessively vigorous sex, and improper storage (because heat destroys rubber, latex condoms should not be stored for long periods in a wallet or a car's glove compartment). To help ensure quality, condoms should not be used past their expiration date or more than 5 years past their date of manufacture (2 years for those with spermicide). It is important to note, however, that most condom failures are due to inconsistent or improper use, not problems with condom quality.

If a condom breaks or is carelessly removed, the risk of pregnancy can be reduced somewhat by the immediate use of a vaginal spermicide. Some clinicians recommend keeping emergency contraceptive pills on hand. If the emergency contraceptive Plan B is taken within 1 hour of inadequately protected sex, the failure rate is only about 0.14%. The most common cause of pregnancy with condom users is "taking a chance"—that is, occasionally not using a condom at all—or waiting to use it until after preejaculate fluid (which may contain some sperm) has already entered the vagina.

Female Condoms

A female condom is a latex or polyurethane pouch that a woman or her partner inserts into her vagina. Although the female condom is preferred in certain situations because it requires less participation on the part of the male partner, its overall popularity remains far below that of the male condom.

The female condom currently available is a disposable device that comes in one size and consists of a soft, loose-fitting polyurethane sheath with two flexible rings (Figure 6-3 on p. 164). The ring at the closed end is inserted into the vagina and placed at the cervix much like a diaphragm. The ring at the open end remains outside the vagina. The walls of the condom protect the inside of the vagina.

Buying and Using Over-the-Counter Contraceptives

You can buy several types of contraceptives without a prescription. These have several advantages—they are readily accessible and relatively inexpensive, they are moderately effective at preventing pregnancy, and some offer some protection against HIV infection and other STDs. But like all methods, over-the-counter contraceptives work only if they are used correctly. The following guidelines can help you maximize the effectiveness of your method of choice.

Male Condoms

- *Buy latex condoms.* If you're allergic to latex, use a polyurethane condom or wear a lambskin condom under a latex one. Lambskin condoms provide no STD protection; polyurethane condoms may provide less protection against pregnancy and STDs than latex condoms do, but more studies are needed.
- *Buy and use condoms while they are fresh.* Packages have an expiration date or a manufacturing date. Don't use a condom after the expiration date or more than 5 years after the manufacturing date (2 years if it contains spermicide).
- *Try different styles and sizes.* Male condoms come in a variety of textures, colors, shapes, lubricants, and sizes. Shop around until you find a brand that's right for you. Condom widths and lengths vary by about 10–20%. A condom that is too tight may be uncomfortable and more likely to break; one that is too loose may slip off.
- *Use "thinner" condoms with caution.* Condoms advertised as "thinner" are often no thinner than others, and those that really are the thinnest tend to break more easily.
- *Don't remove the condom from an individual sealed wrapper until you're ready to use it.* Open the packet carefully. Don't use a condom if it's gummy, dried out, or discolored. Keep extra condoms on hand.
- *Store condoms correctly.* Don't leave condoms in extreme heat or cold, and don't carry them in a pocket wallet.
- *Use only water-based lubricants.* Never use oil-based lubricants like Vaseline or hand lotion, as they may cause a latex condom to break. Avoid oil-based vaginal products.
- *Use male condoms correctly* (see Figure 6-2). Use a new condom every time you have intercourse. Misuse is by far the leading reason that condoms fail.
- *Use emergency contraceptive pills if a condom slips or breaks.*

Female Condoms

- *Make sure your condom comes with the necessary supplies and information.* The FC female condom comes individually wrapped. With your condom, you should receive a leaflet containing instructions and a small bottle of additional lubricant.
- *Buy and use female condoms while they are fresh.* Check the expiration dates on the condom packet and the lubricant bottle.
- *Buy several condoms.* Buy one or more for practice before using one during sex. Have a backup in case you have a problem with insertion or use.
- *Read the leaflet instructions carefully.* Practice inserting the condom and checking that it's in the proper position.
- *Use the female condom correctly.* Make sure the penis is inserted into the pouch and that the outer ring is not pushed into the vagina. Add lubricant around the outer ring if needed.
- *Use emergency contraception pills if a condom slips or breaks.*

Contraceptive Sponges

- *Buy and use contraceptive sponges when they are fresh.* Check the expiration date on each package.
- *Read and follow the package instructions carefully.* Moisten the sponge with water and place high in the vagina.
- *Use each sponge only once.* The sponge may be left in place for up to 24 hours without the addition of spermicide for repeated intercourse.

Spermicides

- *Try different types of spermicides.* You may find one type easier or more convenient to use. Foams come in aerosol cans and are similar to shaving cream in consistency. Foams are thicker than creams, which are thicker than jellies. Foams, creams, and jellies usually require applicators; spermicidal suppositories and films do not.
- *Read and follow the package directions carefully.* Cans of foam must be shaken before use. Jellies and creams are often inserted with an applicator just outside the entrance to the cervix. Suppositories and film must be placed with a finger.
- *Pay close attention to the timing of use.* Follow the package instructions for inserting the spermicide at the appropriate time before intercourse actually occurs. Spermicides have a fairly narrow window of effectiveness. Be sure to also allow the recommended amount of time for suppositories and films to dissolve.
- *Use an additional full dose for each additional act of intercourse.*
- *Leave the spermicide in place for 8 hours after the last act of intercourse.*
- *Consider using spermicides with another form of birth control.* These include a condom, diaphragm, or cervical cap. Combined use provides greater protection against pregnancy.

Emergency Contraceptive Pills

Plan B pills are highly effective when taken soon after unprotected intercourse. If you are 18 or older, you can purchase Plan B over the counter. It is stocked behind the counter, so you will have to request it from the pharmacist and show proof of age. It is not available at convenience stores or other retail outlets where younger women might have access to it without a prescription. To maximize effectiveness, follow the instructions on the package carefully.

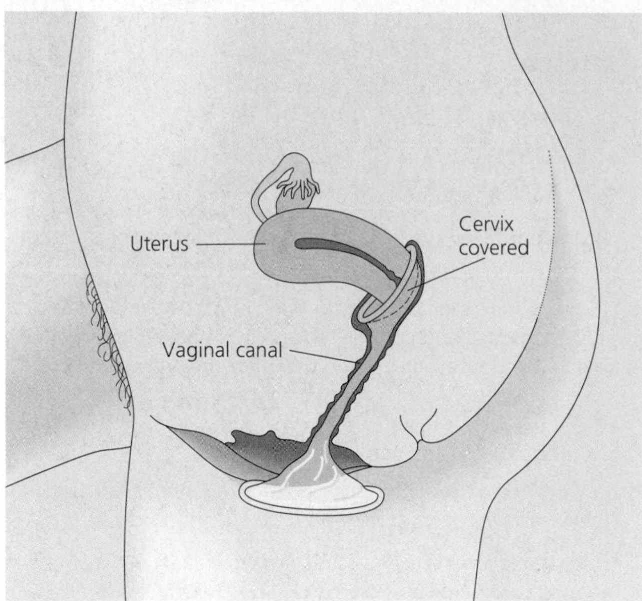

Figure 6-3 The female condom properly positioned.

The directions that accompany the condom should be followed closely. It can be inserted up to 8 hours before intercourse and should be used with the supplied lubricant or a spermicide to prevent penile irritation. As with male condoms, users need to take care not to tear the condom during insertion or removal. Following intercourse, the woman should remove the condom immediately, before standing up. By twisting and squeezing the outer ring, she can prevent the spilling of semen. A new condom should be used for each act of sexual intercourse. A female condom should not be used with a male condom because when the two are used together slippage is more likely to occur.

Advantages For many women, the greatest advantage of the female condom is the control it gives them over contraception and STD prevention. (Partner cooperation is still important, however.) Female condoms can be inserted before sexual activity and are thus less disruptive than male condoms. Because the outer part of the condom covers the area around the vaginal opening as well as the base of the penis during intercourse, it offers potentially better protection against genital warts or herpes. The polyurethane pouch can be used by people who are allergic to latex. And because polyurethane is thin and pliable, there is little loss of sensation. When used correctly, the female condom should theoretically provide protection against HIV transmission and STDs comparable to that of the latex male condom. However, in research involving typical users, the female condom was less effective in preventing both pregnancy and STDs. With careful instruction and practice, effectiveness can be improved.

Disadvantages As with the traditional condom, interference with spontaneity is likely to be a common complaint. The outer ring, which hangs visibly outside the vagina, may be bothersome during foreplay; if so, couples may choose to put the device in just before intercourse. During coitus, both partners must take care that the penis is inserted into the pouch, not outside it, and that the device does not slip inside the vagina. Female condoms, like male condoms, are made for one-time use. A single female condom costs about four times as much as a single male condom.

Effectiveness The typical first-year failure rate of the female condom is 21%. For women who follow instructions carefully and consistently, the failure rate is considerably lower. Although the female condom rarely breaks during use, slippage occurs in nearly one in ten users. The risk of being exposed to semen is higher if the relationship is new or short-term, if intercourse is very active, and if there is a large disparity between vagina and penis sizes. Having Plan B available as a backup contraceptive is recommended.

The Diaphragm with Spermicide

Before oral contraceptives were introduced, about 25% of all American couples who used any form of contraception relied on the **diaphragm.** Many diaphragm users switched to the pill or IUDs, but the diaphragm offers advantages that are important to some couples.

The diaphragm is a dome-shaped cup of thin rubber stretched over a collapsible metal ring. When correctly used with spermicidal cream or jelly, the diaphragm covers the cervix, blocking sperm from entering the uterus.

Diaphragms are available only by prescription. Because of individual anatomical differences among women, a diaphragm must be carefully fitted by a trained clinician to ensure both comfort and effectiveness. The fitting should be checked with each routine annual medical examination, as well as after childbirth, abortion, or a weight change of more than 10 pounds.

The woman spreads spermicidal jelly or cream on the diaphragm before inserting it and checking its placement (Figure 6-4). If more than 6 hours elapse between the time of insertion and the time of intercourse, additional spermicide must be applied. The diaphragm must be left in place for at least 6 hours after the last act of coitus to give the spermicide enough time to kill all the sperm.

To remove the diaphragm, the woman simply hooks the front rim down from the pubic bone with one finger and pulls it out. She should wash it with mild soap and water, rinse it, pat it dry, and then examine it for holes or cracks. Defects would most likely develop near the rim and can be spotted by looking at the diaphragm in front of a bright light. After inspecting the diaphragm, she should dust it with cornstarch (*not* talcum powder, which may damage it and irritate the vagina) and store it in its case.

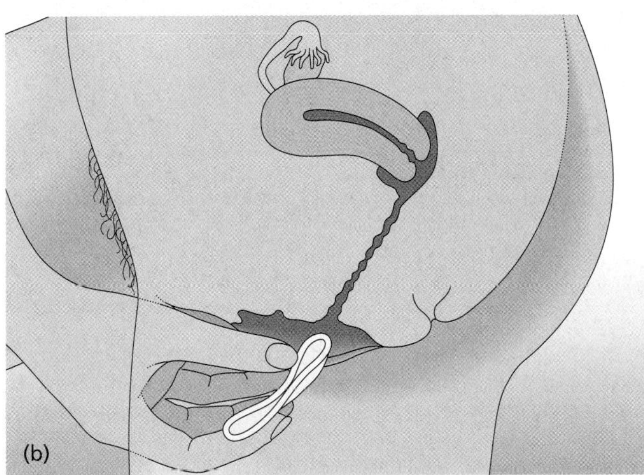

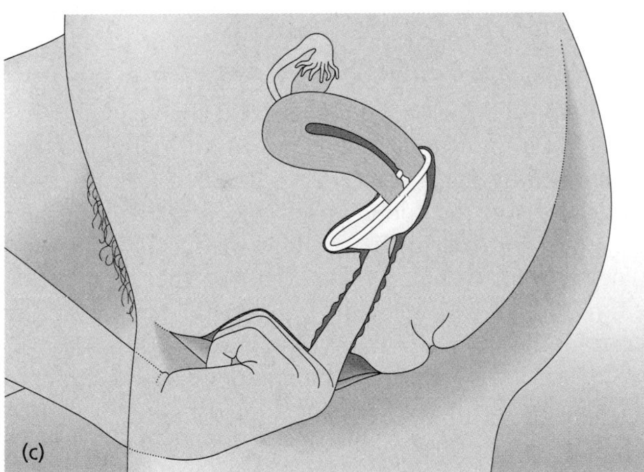

Figure 6-4 Use of the diaphragm. Wash your hands with soap and water before inserting the diaphragm. It can be inserted while squatting, lying down, or standing with one foot raised. (a) Place about a tablespoon of spermicidal jelly or cream in the concave side of the diaphragm, and spread it around the inside of the diaphragm and around the rim. (b) Squeeze the diaphragm into a long, narrow shape between the thumb and forefinger. Insert it into the vagina, and push it up along the back wall of the vagina as far as it will go. (c) Check its position to make sure the cervix is completely covered and that the front rim of the diaphragm is tucked behind the pubic bone.

Advantages Diaphragm use is less intrusive than male condom use because a diaphragm can be inserted up to 6 hours before intercourse. Its use can be limited to times of sexual activity only, and it allows for immediate and total reversibility. The diaphragm is free of medical side effects (other than rare allergic reactions). When used along with spermicidal jelly or cream, it offers significant protection against gonorrhea and possibly chlamydia, STDs that are transmitted only by semen and for which the cervix is the sole site of entry. Diaphragm use can also protect the cervix from semen infected with the human papillomavirus, which causes cervical cancer. However, the diaphragm is unlikely to protect against STDs that can be transmitted through vaginal or vulvar surfaces (in addition to the cervix), including HIV infection, genital herpes, and syphilis.

Disadvantages Diaphragms must always be used with a spermicide, so a woman must keep both of these somewhat bulky supplies with her whenever she anticipates sexual activity. Diaphragms require extra attention, since they must be cleaned and stored with care to preserve their effectiveness. Some women cannot wear a diaphragm because of their vaginal or uterine anatomy. In other women, diaphragm use can cause an increase in bladder infections and may need to be discontinued if repeated infections occur. It has also been associated with a slightly increased risk of **toxic shock syndrome (TSS),** an occasionally fatal bacterial infection. To diminish the risk of TSS, a woman should wash her hands carefully with soap and water before inserting or removing the diaphragm, should not use the diaphragm during menstruation or in the presence of an abnormal vaginal discharge, and should never leave the device in place for more than 24 hours.

Effectiveness The effectiveness of the diaphragm mainly depends on whether it is used properly. In actual practice, women rarely use it correctly every time they have intercourse. Typical failure rates are 16% during the first year of use. The main causes of failure are incorrect insertion, inconsistent use, and inaccurate fitting. Sometimes, too, the vaginal walls expand during sexual stimulation, causing the diaphragm to be dislodged. If a diaphragm slips during intercourse, a woman may choose to use emergency contraception.

Terms

VW

diaphragm A contraceptive device consisting of a flexible, dome-shaped cup that covers the cervix and prevents sperm from entering the uterus.

toxic shock syndrome (TSS) A bacterial disease usually associated with tampon use; can also occur in men; symptoms include weakness, cold and clammy hands, fever, nausea, and headache. TSS can progress to life-threatening complications, including very low blood pressure (shock) and kidney and liver failure.

Lea's Shield

Lea's Shield, a one-size-fits-all diaphragm-like device, was approved by the FDA in 2002 and is now available by prescription. Made of silicone rubber, it can be used by people allergic to latex, and it is not damaged by petroleum-based products. The shield has a valve allowing the flow of air and fluids from the cervix as well as a loop that aids in insertion and removal. The device may be inserted at any time prior to intercourse, but should be left in place for 8 hours after last intercourse; it can be worn for up to 48 hours. Like the diaphragm, it must be used with spermicide. Studies completed thus far have reported advantages, disadvantages, and failure rates similar to those of the diaphragm.

The Cervical Cap

The **cervical cap**, another barrier device, is a small flexible cup that fits snugly over the cervix and is held in place by suction. The Prentif cervical cap, a thimble-shaped latex cup, is no longer being produced by he manufacturer, but many are still in use. The FemCap cervical cap is a clear silicone cup with a brim around the dome to hold spermicide and trap sperm and a removal strap over the dome. It comes in three sizes and must be fitted by a trained clinician. It is used like a diaphragm, with a small amount of spermicide placed in the cup and on the brim before insertion.

Advantages Advantages of the cervical cap are similar to those associated with diaphragm use and include partial STD protection. It is an alternative for women who cannot use a diaphragm because of anatomical reasons or recurrent urinary tract infections. Because the cap fits tightly, it does not require a fresh dose of spermicide with repeated intercourse. It may be left in place for up to 48 hours.

Disadvantages Along with most of the disadvantages associated with the diaphragm, difficulty with insertion and removal is more common for cervical cap users. In addition, some studies have indicated that women who use the cap rather than the diaphragm initially have a higher rate of abnormal Pap test results. In most cases, these are due to inflammation or infections of the cervix, conditions that are easily treatable. As a safety precaution, the FDA requires that the cap be prescribed only for women with normal Pap tests and that a repeat Pap test be done after 3 months of use to confirm that no changes have occurred. Because there may be a slightly increased risk of TSS with prolonged use, the cap should not be left in place for more than 48 hours.

Effectiveness Studies indicate that the average failure rate for FemCap is 23%. For women who have never been pregnant or given birth vaginally, the failure rate is 14%, and for women who have given birth vaginally, the failure rate is 29%.

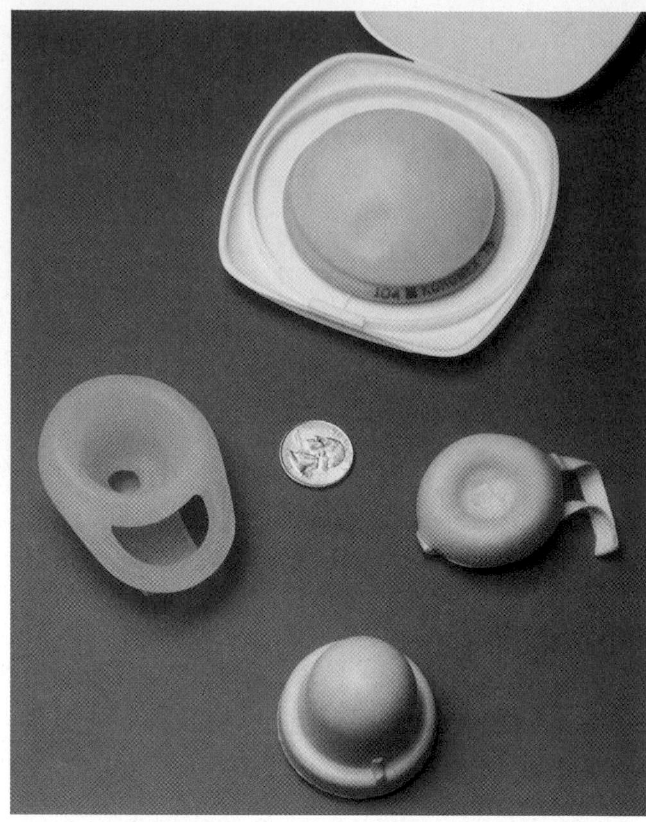

The diaphragm (top), Lea's Shield (left), and the Prentif cervical cap (bottom) work by covering the mouth of the cervix, blocking sperm from entering the cervix; all require a prescription. The sponge (right), which is available without a prescription or fitting, acts as a barrier, a spermicide, and a seminal fluid absorbent.

The Contraceptive Sponge

The **sponge** was sold in the United States between 1983 and 1995, at which time the original manufacturer decided to withdraw the contraceptive rather than bring its manufacturing plant up to FDA standards. The safety or effectiveness of the sponge itself was never in question, and FDA approval of the product was never rescinded. A new company bought the rights to the sponge and reintroduced it in Canada in 2003; the FDA approved the return of the sponge to the U.S. market in 2005.

The sponge is a round, absorbent device about 2 inches in diameter with a polyester loop on one side (for removal) and a concave dimple on the other side, which helps it fit snugly over the cervix. The sponge is made of polyurethane and is presaturated with the same spermicide that is used in contraceptive creams and foams. The spermicide is activated when moistened with a small amount of water just before insertion. The sponge, which can be used only once, acts as a barrier, as a spermicide, and as a seminal fluid absorbent.

Advantages The sponge offers advantages similar to those of the diaphragm and cervical cap, including partial protection against some STDs. In addition, sponges can be obtained without a prescription or professional fitting, and they may be safely left in place for 24 hours without the addition of spermicide for repeated intercourse.

Disadvantages Reported disadvantages include difficulty with removal and an unpleasant odor if left in place for more than 18 hours. Allergic reactions, such as irritation of the vagina, are more common with the sponge than with other spermicide products, probably because the overall dose contained in each sponge is significantly higher than that used with other methods. (It contains 1 gram of spermicide compared with the 60–100 mg present in one application of other spermicidal products.) If irritation of the vaginal lining does occur, the risk of yeast infections and STDs (including HIV) may increase. Because the sponge has also been associated with toxic shock syndrome, the same precautions must be taken as described for diaphragm use. A sponge user should be especially alert for symptoms of TSS when the sponge has been difficult to remove or was not removed intact. It is not known how much spermicide is absorbed through the vaginal walls with this device or what the possible effects are of recurring, extended exposure.

Effectiveness The typical effectiveness of the sponge is slightly lower than that of the diaphragm (20% failure rate during the first year of use) for women who have never experienced childbirth. For women who have had a child, however, sponge effectiveness is significantly lower than diaphragm effectiveness. One possible explanation is that its size may be insufficient to adequately cover the cervix after childbirth. To ensure effectiveness, the user should carefully check the expiration date on each sponge, as shelf life is limited.

Vaginal Spermicides

Spermicidal compounds developed for use with a diaphragm have been adapted for use without a diaphragm by combining them with a bulky base. Foams, creams, jellies, suppositories, and films are all available. Foam is sold in an aerosol bottle or a metal container with an applicator that fits on the nozzle. Creams and jellies are sold in tubes with an applicator that can be screwed onto the opening of the tube (Figure 6-5).

Foams, creams, and jellies must be placed deep in the vagina near the cervical entrance and must be inserted no more than 60 minutes before intercourse. After an hour, their effectiveness is drastically reduced, and a new dose must be inserted. Another application is also required before each repeated act of coitus. If the woman wants to **douche,** she should wait for at least 6 hours after the last intercourse to make sure that there has been time for the spermicide to kill all the sperm; douching is not recommended, however, because it can irritate vaginal tissue and increase the risk of various infections.

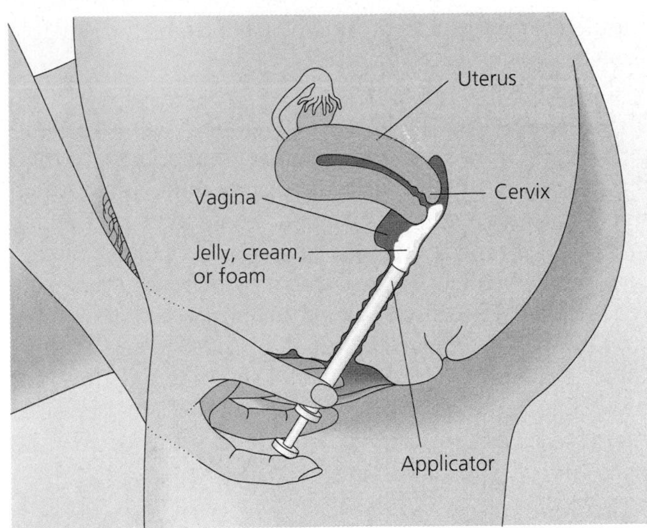

Figure 6-5 The application of spermicide.

The spermicidal suppository is small and easily inserted like a tampon. Because body heat is needed to dissolve and activate the suppository, it is important to wait at least 15 minutes after insertion before having intercourse. The suppository's spermicidal effects are limited in time, and coitus should take place within 1 hour of insertion. A new suppository is required for every act of intercourse.

The Vaginal Contraceptive Film (VCF)® is a paper-thin 2-inch square of film that contains spermicide. It is folded over one or two fingers and placed high in the vagina, as close to the cervix as possible. In about 15 minutes the film dissolves into a spermicidal gel that is effective for up to 1 hour. A new film must be inserted for each act of intercourse.

Advantages The use of vaginal spermicides is relatively simple and can be limited to times of sexual activity. They are readily available in most drugstores and do not require a prescription or a pelvic examination. Spermicides allow for complete and immediate reversibility, and the only medical side effects are occasional allergic reactions. Vaginal spermicides may provide limited protection against some STDs but

Terms

VW

cervical cap A small flexible cup that fits over the cervix, to be used with spermicide.

sponge A contraceptive device about 2 inches in diameter that fits over the cervix and acts as a barrier, spermicide, and seminal fluid absorbent.

douche To apply a stream of water or other solutions to a body part or cavity such as the vagina; not a contraceptive technique.

should never be used instead of condoms for reliable protection.

Disadvantages When used alone, vaginal spermicides must be inserted shortly before intercourse, so their use may be seen as an annoying disruption. Some women find the slight increase in vaginal fluids after spermicide use unpleasant. Spermicides can alter the balance of bacteria in the vagina. Because this may increase the occurrence of yeast infections and urinary tract infections, women who are especially prone to these infections may want to avoid spermicides. Also, this method does not protect against gonorrhea, chlamydia, or HIV. Overuse of spermicides can irritate vaginal tissues; if this occurs, the risk of HIV transmission may actually increase.

Effectiveness The effectiveness rates of vaginal spermicides vary widely, depending partly on how consistently and carefully instructions are followed. The typical failure rate is about 29% during the first year of use. Foam is probably the most effective, because its effervescent mass forms a denser and more evenly distributed barrier to the cervical opening. Creams and jellies provide only minimal protection unless used with a diaphragm or cervical cap. Spermicide is generally recommended only in combination with other barrier methods or as a backup to other contraceptives. Plan B provides a better backup than spermicides, however.

Abstinence, Fertility Awareness, and Withdrawal

Millions of people throughout the world do not use any of the contraceptive methods we have described, either because of religious conviction or cultural prohibitions or because of poverty or lack of information and supplies. If they use any method at all, they are likely to use one of the following relatively "natural" methods of attempting to prevent conception.

Abstinence The decision not to engage in sexual intercourse for a chosen period of time, or **abstinence,** has been practiced throughout history for a variety of reasons. Until relatively recently, many people abstained because they had no other contraceptive measures. Today, few American women rely on periodic abstinence as a contraceptive method. For those who do, other methods may simply seem unsuitable. Concern about possible side effects, STDs, and unwanted pregnancy may be factors. For others, the most important reason for choosing abstinence is a moral one, based on cultural or religious beliefs or strongly held personal values (see the box "Sexual Decision Making" on p. 139). Individuals may feel that sexual intercourse is appropriate only for married couples or for people in serious, committed relationships. Abstinence may also be considered the wisest choice in terms of an individual's emotional needs. A period of abstinence may be useful as a time to focus energies on other aspects of interpersonal or personal growth.

Anyone can practice abstinence at any time, including people who are not yet sexually active, those who are beginning a relationship with a new partner, and those who are not currently in a relationship. Couples may choose abstinence to allow time for their relationship to grow. A period of abstinence allows partners to get to know each other better and to develop trust and respect for each other. Many couples who do choose to abstain from sexual intercourse in the traditional sense turn to other mutually satisfying alternatives. When open communication between partners exists, many new avenues may be explored. These may include dancing, massage, hugging, kissing, petting, mutual masturbation, and oral-genital sex. A recent government study reported that more than one-half of American teens age 15–19 have engaged in oral sex. The number increases for those age 18–19.

The Fertility Awareness Method The basis for the **fertility awareness method (FAM)** is abstinence from coitus during the fertile phase of a woman's menstrual cycle. Ordinarily only one egg is released by the ovaries each month, and it lives about 24 hours unless it is fertilized. Sperm deposited in the vagina may be capable of fertilizing an egg for up to 6–7 days, so conception can theoretically occur only during 8 days of any cycle. Predicting which 8 days is difficult. It is done by either the calendar method or the temperature method. Information on cyclical changes of the cervical mucus can also help determine the time of ovulation.

The *calendar method* is based on the knowledge that the average woman releases an egg 14–16 days before her next period begins. Few women menstruate with complete regularity, so a record of the menstrual cycle must be kept for 12 months, during which time some other method of contraception must be used. The first day of each period is counted as day 1. To determine the first fertile, or "unsafe," day of the cycle, subtract 18 from the number of days in the shortest cycle (Figure 6-6). To determine the last unsafe day of the cycle, subtract 11 from the number of days in the longest cycle.

Terms

VW

abstinence Avoidance of sexual intercourse; a method of contraception.

fertility awareness method (FAM) A method of preventing conception based on avoiding intercourse during the fertile phase of a woman's cycle.

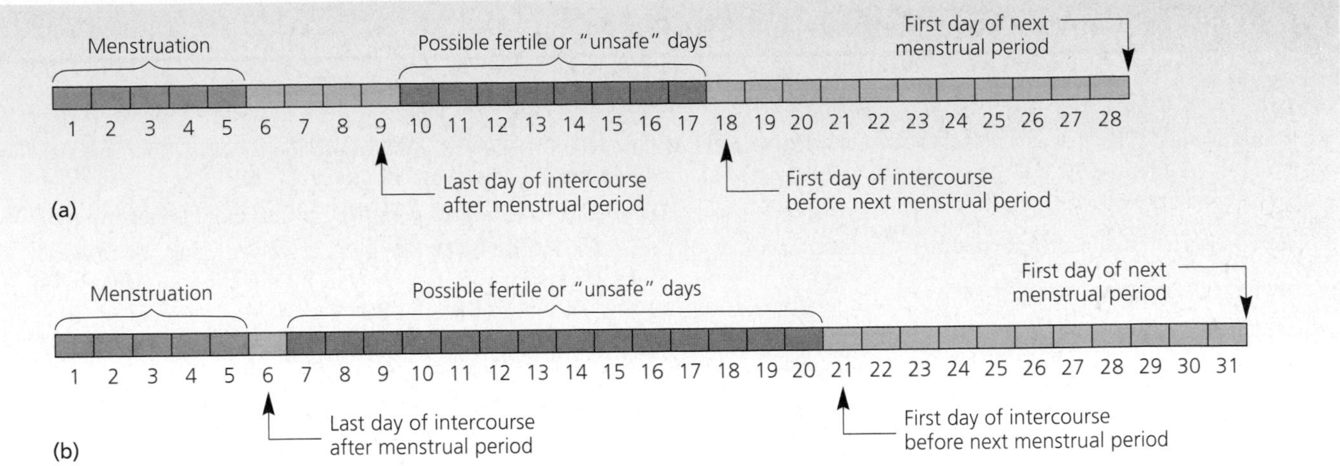

Figure 6-6 The fertility awareness method of contraception. This chart shows the safe and unsafe days for (a) a woman with a regular 28-day cycle and (b) a woman with an irregular cycle ranging from 25 to 31 days.

A variation of the calendar method known as the Standard Days Method (SDM) can be used by women with regular menstrual cycles between 26 and 32 days long. Couples must avoid unprotected intercourse on days 8 through 19 of the woman's cycle. Some women who use SDM use a string of color-coded beads known as CycleBeads™ to track their fertile days.

The *temperature method* is based on the knowledge that a woman's body temperature drops slightly just before ovulation and rises slightly after ovulation. A woman using the temperature method records her basal (resting) body temperature (BBT) every morning before getting out of bed and before eating or drinking anything. Once the temperature pattern is apparent (usually after about 3 months), the unsafe period for intercourse can be calculated as the interval from day 5 (day 1 is the first day of the period) until 3 days after the rise in BBT. To arrive at a shorter unsafe period, some women combine the calendar and temperature methods, calculating the first unsafe day from the shortest cycle of the calendar chart and the last unsafe day as the third day after a rise in BBT.

The *mucus method* (or Billings method) is based on changes in the cervical secretions throughout the menstrual cycle. During the estrogenic phase, cervical mucus increases and is clear and slippery. At the time of ovulation, some women can detect a slight change in the texture of the mucus and find that it is more likely to form an elastic thread when stretched between thumb and finger. After ovulation, these secretions become cloudy and sticky and decrease in quantity. Infertile, safe days are likely to occur during the relatively dry days just before and after menstruation. These additional clues have been found to be helpful by some couples who rely on the fertility awareness method. One problem that may interfere with this method is that vaginal infections or vaginal products or medication can also alter the cervical mucus.

FAM is not recommended for women who have very irregular cycles—about 15% of all menstruating women. Any woman for whom pregnancy would be a serious problem should not rely on FAM alone, because the failure rate is high—approximately 25% during the first year of use. FAM offers no protection against STDs.

Withdrawal In withdrawal, or coitus interruptus, the male removes his penis from the vagina just before he ejaculates. Withdrawal has a relatively high failure rate because the male has to overcome a powerful biological urge. In addition, because preejaculatory fluid may contain viable sperm, pregnancy can occur even if the man withdraws prior to ejaculation. Sexual pleasure is often affected because the man must remain in control and the sexual experience of both partners is interrupted.

Failure rates for typical use are about 27% in the first year. Men who are less experienced with sexual intercourse and withdrawal or who have difficulty in foretelling when ejaculation will occur have higher failure rates. Withdrawal does not protect against STDs.

Combining Methods

Couples can choose to combine the preceding methods in a variety of ways, both to add STD protection and/or to increase contraceptive effectiveness. For example, condoms are strongly recommended along with OCs whenever there is a risk of STDs (Table 6-3, p. 170). Foam may be added to condom use to increase protection against

Table 6-3 Contraceptive Methods and STD Protection

Method	Level of Protection
Hormonal methods	Do not protect against HIV or STDs in lower reproductive tract; increase risk of cervical chlamydia; provide some protection against PID.
IUD	Does not protect against STDs; associated with PID in first month after insertion.
Latex or polyurethane male condom	Best method for protection against STDs (if used correctly); does not protect against infections from lesions that are not covered by the condom. (Lambskin condoms do not protect against STDs.)
Female condom	Theoretically should reduce the risk of STDs, but research results are not yet available.
Diaphragm, sponge, or cervical cap	Protects against cervical infections and PID. Diaphragms, sponges, and cervical caps should not be relied on for protection against HIV.
Spermicide	Modestly reduces the risk of some vaginal and cervical STDs; does not reduce the risk of HIV, chlamydia, or gonorrhea. If vaginal irritation occurs, infection risk may increase.
FAM	Does not protect against STDs.
Sterilization	Does not protect against STDs.
Abstinence	Complete protection against STDs (as long as all activities that involve the exchange of body fluids are avoided).

Abstinence or sex with a mutually monogamous, uninfected partner is the surest way to protect yourself against HIV and other STDs. Barring this, correct and consistent use of latex male condoms provides the best protection against STDs.

both STDs and pregnancy. For many couples, and especially for women, the added benefits far outweigh the extra effort and expense.

Table 6-4 summarizes the effectiveness of available contraceptive methods.

PERMANENT CONTRACEPTION: STERILIZATION

Sterilization is permanent, and it is highly effective at preventing pregnancy. For these reasons, it is becoming an increasingly popular method of contraception. At present it is the most commonly used method both in the United States and in the world. It is especially popular among couples who have been married 10 or more years, as well as couples who have had all the children they intend to have. Sterilization provides no protection against STDs.

An important consideration in choosing sterilization is that, in most cases, it cannot be reversed and should be considered permanent. Although the chances of restoring fertility are being increased by modern surgical techniques, such operations are costly, and pregnancy can never be guaranteed. Some couples choosing male sterilization store sperm as a way of extending the option of childbearing.

Some studies indicate that male sterilization is preferable to female sterilization for a variety of reasons. The overall cost of a female procedure is about four times that of a male procedure, and women are much more likely than men to experience both minor and major complications following the operation. Furthermore, feelings of regret seem to be somewhat more prevalent in women than in men after sterilization. Men seeking vasectomies are typically white, married, relatively affluent and well educated, and privately insured.

Although some physicians will perform surgery for sterilization on request, most require a thorough discussion with both partners before the operation. Most physicians also recommend that people who have religious conflicts, psychological problems related to sex, or unstable marriages not be sterilized. Young couples who might later change their minds are also frequently advised not to undergo sterilization.

Terms

Vw

sterilization Surgically altering the reproductive system to prevent pregnancy. Vasectomy is the procedure in males; tubal sterilization or hysterectomy is the procedure in females.

vasectomy The surgical severing of the ducts that carry sperm to the ejaculatory duct.

vasa deferentia The two ducts that carry sperm to the ejaculatory duct; singular, vas deferens.

Table 6-4 Contraceptive Effectiveness

Method	Percentage of Women Experiencing an Unintended Pregnancy in the First Year of Use	
	Typical Use	Perfect Use
Mirena IUD	0.1	0.1
Male sterilization (vasectomy)	0.15	0.1
Female sterilization	0.5	0.5
ParaGard (Copper T-380A)	0.8	0.6
Lunelle injections	3	0.05
Depo-Provera injections	3	0.3
Oral contraceptives	8	0.3
Evra patch	8	0.3
NuvaRing	8	0.3
Male condom (latex or polyurethane)	15	2
Diaphragm with spermicide	16	6
Cervical cap with spermicide*	16	9
Sponge*	16	9
Female condom	21	5
Fertility awareness method	25	
Calendar alone		9
Combination of FAM methods		2
Withdrawal	27	4
Spermicides (alone)	29	18
Chance (no method)	85	85

*For women who have given birth, the rates of unintended pregnancy increase to 32% for typical use and 26% for perfect use for the cervical cap and to 32% for typical use and 20% for perfect use for the sponge.

SOURCE: Hatcher, R. A., et al. 2004. *Contraceptive Technology,* 18th ed. New York: Ardent Media. Reprinted by permission of Ardent Media, Inc.

Male Sterilization: Vasectomy

The procedure for male sterilization, **vasectomy,** involves severing the **vasa deferentia,** two tiny ducts that transport sperm from the testes to the seminal vesicles (see Figure 5-2). The testes continue to produce sperm, but the sperm are absorbed into the body. Because the testes contribute only about 10% of the total seminal fluid, the actual quantity of ejaculate is only slightly reduced. Hormone production from the testes continues with very little change, and secondary sex characteristics are not altered.

Vasectomy is ordinarily performed in a physician's office and takes about 30 minutes. A local anesthetic is injected into the skin of the scrotum near the vasa. Small incisions are made at the upper end of the scrotum where it joins the body, and the vas deferens on each side is exposed, severed, and tied off or sealed by electrocautery. A plastic clamp (Vasclip) the size of a grain of rice was approved by the FDA in 2003 and may become more popular as more physicians become trained and experienced in its use; although also permanent, the use of the clip may cause less tissue damage and pain following surgery. The incisions are then closed with sutures, and a small dressing is applied (Figure 6-7). Pain and swelling are usually slight and can be relieved with ice compresses, aspirin, and the use of a scrotal support. Bleeding and infection occasionally develop but are usually easily treated. Fewer complications occur with an alternative procedure involving a midline puncture rather than incisions; many physicians in the United States now perform this "no-scalpel" vasectomy. After either procedure, most men are ready to return to work in 2 days.

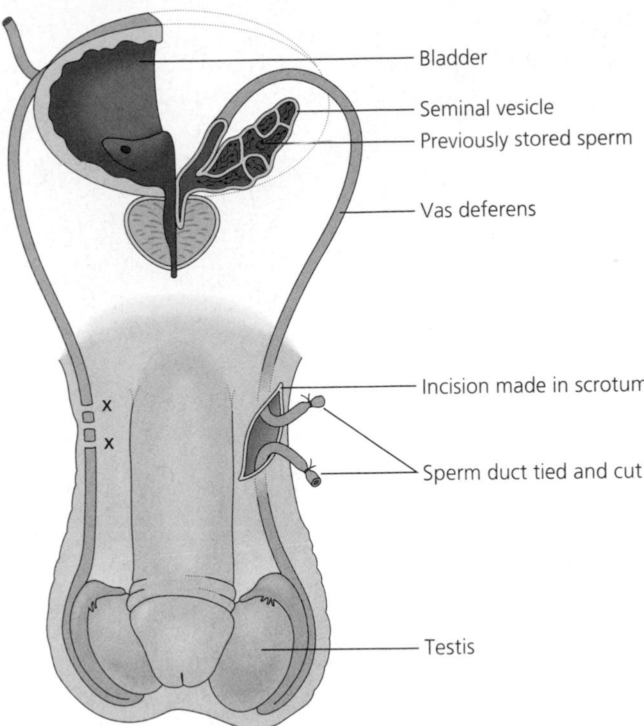

Figure 6-7 Vasectomy. This surgical procedure involves severing the vasa deferentia, thereby preventing sperm from being transported and ejaculated.

Men can have sex again as soon as they feel no further discomfort, usually after about a week. Another method of contraception must be used for at least 3 months after vasectomy, however, because sperm produced before the operation may still be present in the semen. Microscopic examination of a semen sample can confirm that sperm are no longer present in the ejaculate.

Vasectomy is highly effective. In a small number of cases, a severed vas rejoins itself, so some physicians advise yearly examination of a semen sample. The overall

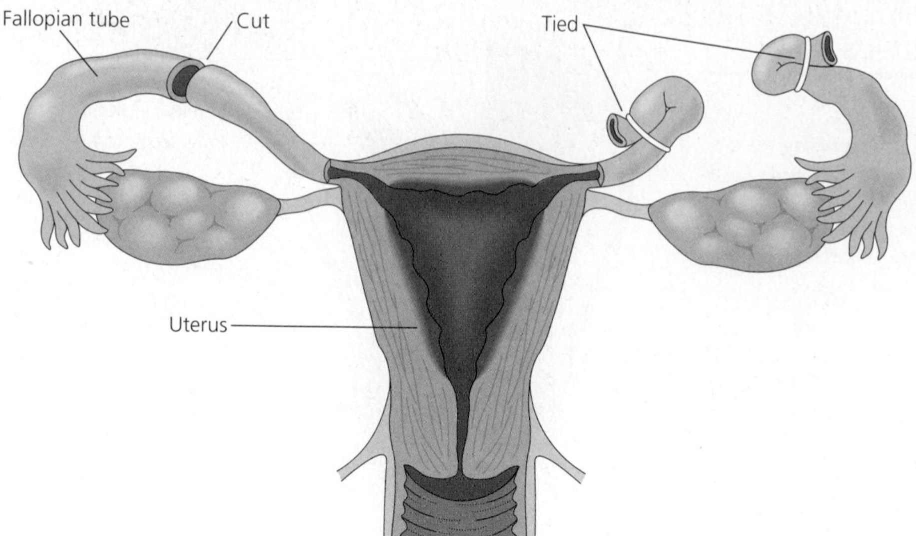

Figure 6-8 Tubal sterilization. This procedure involves severing or blocking the fallopian tubes, thereby preventing eggs from traveling from the ovaries to the uterus. It is a more complex procedure than vasectomy.

failure rate for vasectomy is 0.15%. No strong links have been found between vasectomy and chronic diseases, and the bulk of the evidence now indicates that men with vasectomies are not at increased risk for heart disease, prostate cancer, or testicular cancer.

Although some surgeons report pregnancy rates of about 80% for partners of men who have their vasectomies reversed within 10 years of the original procedure, most studies report figures in the 50% range. In at least half of all men who have had vasectomies, the process of absorbing sperm (instead of ejaculating it) results in antisperm antibodies that may interfere with later fertility. Other factors, such as length of time between the vasectomy and the reversal surgery, may also be important predictors of reversal success.

Female Sterilization

The most common method of female sterilization involves severing, or in some manner blocking, the oviducts, thereby preventing the egg from reaching the uterus and the sperm from entering the fallopian tubes (see Figure 5-1). Ovulation and menstruation continue, but the unfertilized eggs are released into the abdominal cavity and absorbed. Although progesterone levels in the blood may decline slightly, hormone production by the ovaries and secondary sex characteristics are generally not affected.

Tubal sterilization is most commonly performed by a method called **laparoscopy.** A laparoscope, a tube containing a small light, is inserted through a small abdominal incision, and the surgeon looks through it to locate the fallopian tubes. Instruments are passed either through the laparoscope or through a second small incision, and the two fallopian tubes are sealed off with ties or staples or by electrocautery (Figure 6-8). General anesthesia is usually used. The operation takes about 15 minutes, and women can usually leave the hospital 2–4 hours after surgery. Tubal sterilization can also be performed shortly after a vaginal delivery, or in the case of cesarean section immediately after the uterine incision is repaired.

Although tubal sterilization is somewhat riskier than vasectomy, with a rate of minor complications of about 6–11%, it is the more common procedure (see the box "Contraceptive Use Among American Women"). Potential problems include bowel injury, wound infection, and bleeding. Serious complications are rare, and the death rate is low.

The failure rate for tubal sterilization is about 0.5%. When pregnancies do occur, an increased percentage of them are ectopic. Some complaints of long-term abdominal discomfort and menstrual irregularity following tubal sterilization have been reported, but recent studies have not found any association between them. Because reversibility rates are low and the procedure is costly, female sterilization should be considered permanent.

A new female sterilization device was approved by the FDA in 2002. The Essure System consists of tiny spring-like metallic implants that are inserted through the vagina, into the fallopian tubes, using a special catheter. Within several months, scar tissue forms over the implants, blocking the tubes. A backup method may be used until a test shows that the tubes are occluded. Placement of the device doesn't require an incision or general anesthesia, and recovery time is quicker than that following tubal sterilization. Only clinicians with specialized training and equipment can perform this procedure, and in some cases a second procedure is required.

Terms

VW

tubal sterilization Severing or in some manner blocking the oviducts, preventing eggs from reaching the uterus.

laparoscopy Examining the internal organs by inserting a tube containing a small light through an abdominal incision.

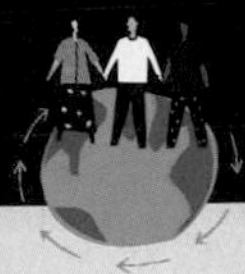

Contraceptive Use Among American Women

About 62 million women in the United States are in their childbearing years (15–44) and thus face decisions about contraception. Overall, about 62% of American women use some form of contraception, and most of the remaining 38% are either sterile, pregnant or trying to become pregnant, or not sexually active. Only 7% of American women are fertile, sexually active, and not seeking pregnancy *and* not using contraceptives; this small group accounts for almost half of the 3 million unintended pregnancies that occur each year. The unintended pregnancies that occur among contraceptive users are usually the result of inconsistent or incorrect use of methods. For example, one-third of barrier method users report not using their method every time they have intercourse.

Oral contraceptives and female sterilization are the two most popular methods among American women (see figure). However, choice of contraceptive method and consistency of use vary with age, marital status, and other factors:

- *Age:* Sterilization is much more common among older women, particularly those who are over 35 years of age and/or who have had children. Older women are also much more likely to use reversible methods consistently—they are least likely to miss pills and most likely to use barrier methods during every act of intercourse. Young women between ages 15 and 17 who use OCs are more likely by far to miss pills than women in any other age group.
- *Marital status:* Women who are or were married have much higher rates of sterilization than women who have never been married. Those who have never been married have high rates of OC and condom usage.
- *Ethnicity:* Overall rates of contraceptive use and use of OCs are highest among white women. Female sterilization, implants, and injectables are more often used by African American women and Latinas, and IUD use is highest among Latinas. Condom use is highest among Asian American women and similar across other ethnic groups. Male sterilization is much more common among white men than among men of other ethnic groups.
- *Socioeconomic status and educational attainment:* Low socioeconomic status and low educational attainment are associated with high rates of female sterilization and low rates of pill and condom use. However, women who are poor or have low educational attainment and who do use OCs have higher rates of consistent use than women who are wealthier or have more education. About 20% of women age 15–44 lack adequate health insurance, increasing the cost and difficulty of obtaining contraceptives.

Some trends in contraceptive use may also reflect the differing priorities and experiences of women and men. For example, female sterilization is more expensive and carries greater health risks than male sterilization—yet it is more than twice as common. (Worldwide, female sterilization is more than four times as common as male sterilization.) This pattern may reflect culturally defined gender roles and the fact that women are more directly affected by unintended pregnancy. In surveys, women rate pregnancy prevention as the single most important factor when choosing a contraceptive method; in contrast, men rate STD prevention as equally important.

SOURCES: Guttmacher Institute. 2005. *Facts in Brief: Contraceptive Use.* New York: Guttmacher Institute; Guttmacher Institute. 2005. *Issues in Brief: Preventing Unintended Pregnancy in the U.S.* (http://www.agi-usa.org/pubs/ ib2004no3.html; retrieved July 27, 2006); National Center for Health Statistics. 2004. Use of contraception and use of family planning services in the United States: 1982–2002. *Advance Data from Vital and Health Statistics,* No. 350; Grady, W. R., D. H. Klepinger, and A. Nelson-Wally. 1999. Contraceptive characteristics: The perceptions and priorities of men and women. *Family Planning Perspectives* 31(4): 168–175.

Contraceptive use among American women age 15–44 years.

Take Charge

Talking with a Partner About Contraception

Many people have a difficult time talking about contraception with a potential sex partner. How should you bring it up? And whose responsibility is it, anyway? Talking about the subject may be embarrassing at first, but imagine the possible consequences of *not* talking about it. An unintended pregnancy or a sexually transmitted disease could profoundly affect you for the rest of your life. Talking about contraception is one way of showing that you care about yourself, your partner, and your future.

Before you talk with your partner, explore your own thoughts and feelings. Find out the facts about different methods of contraception, and decide which one you think would be most appropriate for you. If you're nervous about having this discussion with your partner, it may help to practice with a friend.

Pick a good time to bring up the subject. Don't wait until you've started to have sex. A time when you're both feeling comfortable and relaxed will maximize your chances of having a good discussion. Tell your partner what you know about contraception and how you feel about using it, and talk about what steps you both need to take to get and use a method you can live with. Listen to what your partner has to say, and try to understand his or her point of view. You may need to have more than one discussion, and it may take some time for both of you to feel comfortable with the subject. *But don't have sex until this issue is resolved.*

If you want your partner to be involved but he or she isn't interested in talking about contraception, or if he or she leaves all the responsibility for it up to you, consider whether this is really a person you want to be sexually involved with. If you decide to go ahead with the involvement, you may want to enlist the support of a friend, family member, or health care worker to help you make and implement decisions about the essential issue of contraception.

Hysterectomy, removal of the uterus, is the preferred method of sterilization for only a small number of women, usually those with preexisting menstrual problems. Because of the risks involved, hysterectomy is not recommended unless the woman has disease or damage of the uterus and future surgery appears inevitable.

ISSUES IN CONTRACEPTION

The subject of contraception is closely tied to several issues that are currently receiving much attention in the United States, such as premarital sexual relations, gender differences, and sexuality education for teens.

When Is It OK to Begin Having Sexual Relations?

Answers to that question strongly affect a society's approach to contraception. Opinions on the appropriate age or time to begin having sex often determine one's views on sexuality education and contraception accessibility. Americans have a wide range of opinions on this issue: only after marriage; when 18 years or older; when in a loving, stable relationship; when the partners have completed their education and/or could support a child; whenever both partners feel ready and are using protection against pregnancy and STDs.

Opinions about appropriate sexual behavior shift from one decade to another. Although attitudes became more liberal during the 1960s and 1970s, people started having more restrictive views in the 1980s and 1990s. Today, the most common reasons for disapproving of sex are the risk of exposure to STDs, the risk of pregnancy, and moral or religious beliefs. According to recent data, most of today's young Americans are somewhat permissive regarding premarital sex. Although many approve of sexual relations for couples who are seriously dating or engaged to be married, they are less accepting of sexual intercourse on a first date or at the casual dating stage.

Closely related to the issue of beginning sexual relations is a more personal question: What would you consider the ideal amount of previous sexual experience for you and your partner? Again, opinions vary, especially in terms of what is desirable for men and for women. Limited experience is still more commonly deemed desirable for women, whereas being "sexually experienced" is often valued more highly for men.

As more women consider careers for themselves and therefore often delay childbearing and even marriage, the likelihood of sexual activity and the critical need for pregnancy and STD prevention only increase. As a result, making decisions about sexual activity and contraception becomes even more important to those starting college or a career. Unfortunately, however, many individuals in this age group—even those who protect their health in all other areas of their life—end up taking high risks in their sexual behavior. Ambivalence and a lack of communication about who will "take charge" are common and are partly due to the denial of, and hypocrisy about, sexual behavior that exists in our society. (For guidelines on improving your own communication, see the box "Talking with a Partner About Contraception.") Alcohol and drug use are also strongly linked to risky sexual behavior.

Term

VW **hysterectomy** Total or partial surgical removal of the uterus.

Future Methods of Contraception

Even the best of the present methods of contraception have drawbacks, and the search continues for the ideal method—more effective, safer, cheaper, easier to use, more readily available, easily reversible, and acceptable to more people. Many new methods are widely used in other countries long before they become available in the United States. This delay is partly due to higher costs of safety testing in the United States, greater liability risks for manufacturers, and lower levels of government funding for contraceptive research.

Despite delays, the past decade has seen several new methods approved and marketed in the United States, a trend that is likely to continue. The options expected to become available in the near future are variations of current methods: new combinations of hormones, new designs for IUDs and condoms, and new spermicides and microbicides that kill viruses and bacteria as well as sperm. Some of the other methods being studied are described below.

Lower-dose OCs

Several OCs with only 15 micrograms of estrogen are now available in Europe. These pills are likely to be marketed in the United States in the near future.

New Hormone Delivery Methods

New types of implants are being developed, and a kit for an *at-home version of the Lunelle injectable contraceptive* is also under development. This kit would allow women to self-administer the injections, eliminating the need for monthly clinic visits.

Similar to Norplant, *biodegradable implants* are placed under the skin and deliver small doses of hormones over a long period of time. Unlike Norplant, the capsules dissolve over time, eliminating the need for surgical removal. *Injectable microspheres,* tiny clusters of molecules filled with hormones, also dissolve as they deliver a steady dose of hormones over many months.

Hormonal Contraceptives for Men

Male and female hormones can interfere with sperm development in the male, just as they suppress ovulation in the female. One promising contraceptive under study combines a daily pill or implant containing a progestin with a testosterone pellet implanted under the skin and replaced every 12 weeks. This combination has been shown to reduce sperm production to zero in 80–90% of users. Some men report side effects similar to those women may experience when taking OCs: headaches, acne, and increased appetite.

Contraceptive Immunization

Immunity to fertility has occasionally (though rarely) occurred as a result of a man's being unintentionally sensitized to his own sperm cells. He then produces antibodies that inactivate sperm as if they were disease organisms. In theory, a woman could be purposely sensitized against her own egg cells or against her partner's sperm cells. Another immunocontraceptive under study targets just the zona pellucida (ZP), the protein covering of the egg cell. Immunization against ZP would temporarily block sperm from penetrating the egg without affecting normal egg development. Concerns that the antibodies may cross-react with untargeted hormones in the body have slowed research in this area.

Reversible Sterilization

Present methods of sterilization in both men and women are reversible 50–70% of the time. Several new techniques are being studied in the hope that restoring fertility can be made easier and more predictable. These techniques include injecting liquid silicone into the fallopian tubes, where it solidifies and forms a plug, and placing various types of clips and plugs on the vasa to totally block sperm flow. These plugs or clips could then be removed if an individual wanted to restore fertility.

Contraception and Gender Differences

A second issue, one all couples must confront, is the differing significance of contraception to women and men. The consequences of not using contraception are markedly different for men and women. In past years, women have accepted the primary responsibility of contraception, along with related side effects and health risks, partly because of the wider spectrum of methods available to them and partly because women have greater personal investment in preventing pregnancy and childbearing. Men still have very few contraceptive options, with condoms being the only reversible method currently available (see the box "Future Methods of Contraception"). Recently, however, men's participation has become critical, since condom use is central to safer sex even when OCs or other methods are being used by women.

Although dependent primarily on the cooperation of the man, condom use and the prevention of STDs have potentially greater consequences for the woman. Whereas men may suffer only local and short-term effects from the most common diseases (not including HIV infection), women face an increased risk of serious long-term effects, such as cervical cancer and/or pelvic infection with associated infertility, from these same prevalent STDs. In addition, women are more likely than men to contract HIV from an infected partner. In other words, although dependent on the male, condom use is clearly a more important issue for women. The female condom may offer a helpful alternative, but the cooperation of the male partner is still needed to ensure correct use.

Worldwide, condom use is increasing, but it remains low in developing countries, where it is often difficult for women to negotiate safe sex and condom use. The World Health Organization reports that the main factor in poor sexual health around the world is gender inequality.

The experience of an unintended pregnancy is also very different for men and women. Although men do suffer

Gender Matters

Men's Involvement in Contraception

What can be done to increase men's involvement in contraception? Health care professionals are taking the following approaches:

- Develop programs and campaigns that stress the importance of information, counseling, and medical care relating to sexual and reproductive matters from adolescence on. Men are less likely than women to seek regular checkups, but regular care for men would benefit men in their own right and both men and women as individuals, couples, and families.
- Recruit and train male health workers, who can be important advocates and role models for healthful behaviors. Expand educational material and clinical programs that focus on male contraception and reproductive health.
- Focus on men as obstacles to women's contraceptive use and as an untapped group of potential users. Educate men about the ways in which stereotypical views of male or female sexuality can inhibit good reproductive health for both men and women. Stress the importance of shared responsibility.
- Develop educational and clinical programs specifically targeted at young men. Men in their early 20s are most likely to engage in risky sexual behaviors and to have adverse reproductive health outcomes. Surveys indicate that most men use a condom the first time they have intercourse, but condom use subsequently declines—and there is much greater reliance on female contraceptive methods.

What can individuals do? Men can increase their participation in contraception in the following ways:

- Initiate and support communication regarding contraception and STD protection.
- Buy and use condoms whenever appropriate.
- Help pay contraceptive costs.
- Be available for shared responsibility in the resolution of an unintended pregnancy, should one occur.

SOURCES: United Nations Population Fund. 2004. *The State of World Population Report 2004*. New York: UNFPA; Alan Guttmacher Institute. 2004. *In Their Own Right: Addressing the Sexual and Reproductive Health of American Men*. New York: Alan Guttmacher Institute; Armstrong, B. 2003. The young men's clinic: Addressing men's reproductive health and responsibilities. *Perspectives on Sexual and Reproductive Health* 35(5): 220–225.

emotional stress from such an unexpected occurrence (and sometimes share financial and/or custodial responsibilities), women are much more intimately affected, obviously by the biological process of pregnancy itself as well as the outcome: abortion, adoption, or parenting. In addition, our societal attitudes are more severely punitive toward the woman and place much greater responsibility and blame on her when an unintended pregnancy occurs. Fortunately, there is growing interest in the roles and responsibilities of men in family planning (see the box "Men's Involvement in Contraception").

Sexuality and Contraception Education for Teenagers

A third controversial issue is sexuality education and pregnancy prevention programs for teenagers. Again, opinion in the United States is sharply divided. Certain groups are concerned that more sexuality education and especially the availability of contraceptives will lead to more sexual activity and promiscuity. They maintain that greater access to improved contraception was a key factor contributing to the sexual revolution in the 1960s and that the ensuing liberal sexual attitudes have been generally more destructive than helpful. They point to an increase in divorce, a rise in STDs, and a general relaxing of standards of morality as related negative effects.

Many in this group urge that sexuality education be handled in the home, where parents can instill moral values, including premarital abstinence. According to some in this group, young people should primarily be taught to "just say no." They see most public education about contraception, especially facilities that make supplies available, as only increasing the problem.

Other groups argue that encouraging the public availability of contraceptive information and supplies does not necessarily result in an increase in promiscuous sexual behavior, pointing to the fact that many young teenagers are already pregnant when they first visit a health care facility. These groups assert that parents are not effectively dealing with the issues and that a broader, coordinated approach involving public institutions, including schools, is needed, along with parental input. Many current programs focus on postponing sexual involvement but also emphasize contraceptive use for individuals who are sexually active. Increased availability of contraceptive information and methods is considered a necessary and realistic part of this approach.

The birth rate among U.S. teenagers 15 to 17 years of age fell to the lowest level ever recorded in 2004, but teen pregnancy and birth rates remain significantly higher than rates in other developed countries. The teen pregnancy rate in the United States is nearly twice that in Canada and Great Britain, for example, and approximately 4 times that in France, 5 times that in Germany, and 9 times that in the Netherlands. The teen abortion rate in the United States is nearly 8 times higher than in Germany, 7 times higher than in the Netherlands, and 3 times higher than in

How old should people be when they become sexually active? The answer depends on the personal values, beliefs, and experiences of the individuals involved.

France. The rate of gonorrhea among U.S. teens is more than 50 times higher than the rate in the Netherlands or France; rates of HIV infection, syphilis, and chlamydia among teens are also much higher in the United States. Levels of sexual activity and age at first intercourse do not differ significantly in these countries, but sexually active U.S. teens are less likely to use any contraceptive method and particularly less likely to use one of the more effective hormonal methods.

Reports by the Guttmacher Institute and Advocates for Youth have noted some attitudes and programs in other developed countries that may help explain their lower teen pregnancy rates:

- Childbearing is strongly regarded as adult behavior, to be considered when young people have completed their education, are in stable relationships, and are financially independent from their parents. This attitude is weaker and varies across regions and groups in the United States.
- Young people who are sexually active are expected to protect themselves and their partners from pregnancy and STDs, and state or public schools typically provide comprehensive information about prevention. More than one-third of U.S. school districts currently provide abstinence-only sexuality education.
- In many European countries, governments support large, long-term public education campaigns promoting responsible sexual behavior. These campaigns are direct and humorous, focus on safety and pleasure, and utilize many outlets, including the Internet, television, films, radio, and billboards.
- Young people in other developed countries typically have easier access to contraceptives and reproductive health services than do young people in the United States. Contraceptives are typically free or are inexpensive through national health insurance. U.S. teens may encounter logistical, financial, or legal barriers to contraceptive access. Some states have or are considering parental notification laws that would apply to minors seeking prescription contraceptives at family planning clinics. Surveys indicate that such laws are likely to increase the number of teens using no contraception or less effective over-the-counter contraceptives.

Sexuality and contraceptive education remains a volatile issue. Studies show that sexually active students who receive comprehensive sexuality education are more likely to use contraceptives and that those who are not sexually active are not encouraged to initiate having sex. Abstinence-only school programs, on the other hand, do not appear to reduce the number of teens who are having sex. Although a great deal of focus has been placed on HIV and STDs prevention, the nearly 1 million U.S. teenage pregnancies that occur each year are a serious public health problem and warrant much greater national attention.

WHICH CONTRACEPTIVE METHOD IS RIGHT FOR YOU?

The process of choosing and using a contraceptive method can be complex and varies from one couple to another. Each person must consider many variables in deciding which method is most acceptable and appropriate for her or him. Key considerations include those listed here:

1. *Health risks.* Is there anything in your personal or family medical history that would affect your choice of method? For each method you consider, what are the potential health risks that apply to you? For example, IUDs are not recommended for young women without children because of an increased risk of pelvic infection and subsequent infertility. Hormonal methods should be used only after a clinical evaluation of your medical history. Other methods have only minor and local side effects. Talk with your physician about the potential health effects of different methods for you.
2. *The implications of an unplanned pregnancy.* How would an unplanned pregnancy affect you and your future? If effectiveness is of critical importance to you, carefully consider the ways the effectiveness of each method can be improved. Abstinence is 100% effective, if maintained. If used correctly, hormonal methods offer very good protection against pregnancy. Barrier methods can be combined with spermicides (or with emergency contraception, when indicated) to improve their effectiveness.
3. *STD risk.* How likely are you to be exposed to any sexually transmitted diseases? Have you and your

Assess Yourself

Which Contraceptive Method Is Right for You and Your Partner?

If you are sexually active, you need to use the contraceptive method that will work best for you. A number of factors may be involved in your decision. The following questions will help you sort out these factors and choose an appropriate method. Answer yes (Y) or no (N) for each statement as it applies to you and, if appropriate, your partner.

_____ 1. I like sexual spontaneity and don't want to be bothered with contraception at the time of sexual intercourse.
_____ 2. I need a contraceptive immediately.
_____ 3. It is very important that I do not become pregnant now.
_____ 4. I want a contraceptive method that will protect me and my partner against sexually transmitted diseases.
_____ 5. I prefer a contraceptive method that requires the cooperation and involvement of both partners.
_____ 6. I have sexual intercourse frequently.
_____ 7. I have sexual intercourse infrequently.
_____ 8. I am forgetful or have a variable daily routine.
_____ 9. I have more than one sex partner.
_____ 10. I have heavy periods with cramps.
_____ 11. I prefer a method that requires little or no action or bother on my part.
_____ 12. I am a nursing mother.
_____ 13. I want the option of conceiving immediately after discontinuing contraception.
_____ 14. I want a contraceptive method with few or no side effects.

If you answered yes to the statements whose numbers are listed in the left-hand columns below, the method in the right-hand columns might be a good choice for you.

1, 3, 6, 10, 11, 12*	Oral contraceptives	2, 5, 7, 8, 12, 13, 14	Vaginal spermicides and sponge
1, 3, 6, 8, 10, 11	Contraceptive patch, vaginal ring	5, 7, 12, 13, 14	Diaphragm and spermicide, cervical cap
1, 3, 6, 8, 10, 11, 12*	Contraceptive injectables	5, 7, 13, 14	FAM and withdrawal
1, 3, 6, 8, 11, 12, 13	IUD		
2, 4, 5, 7, 8, 9, 12, 13, 14	Condoms (male and female)		

12*Progestin-only hormonal contraceptives (the minipill and Depo-Provera injections) are safe for use by nursing mothers; contraceptives that include estrogen are not usually recommended.

Your answers may indicate that more than one method would be appropriate for you. To help narrow your choices, circle the numbers of the statements that are *most* important for you. Before you make a final choice, talk with your partner(s) and your physician. Consider your own lifestyle and preferences, as well as the features of each method (effectiveness, side effects, costs, and so on). For maximum protection against pregnancy and STDs, you might want to consider combining two methods. It's also a good idea to be prepared for change; the method that seems right for you now may be inappropriate if your circumstances become different.

partner been screened for STDs recently? Have you openly and honestly discussed your past sexual behavior? Condom use is of critical importance whenever any risk of STDs is present. This is especially true when you are not in an exclusive, long-term relationship or when you are taking the pill, because cervical changes that occur during hormone use may increase vulnerability to certain diseases. Abstinence or activities that don't involve intercourse or any other exchange of body fluids can be a satisfactory alternative for some people.

4. *Convenience and comfort level.* How do your partner and you view each of the methods? Which would you most likely use consistently? The hormonal methods are generally ranked high in this category, unless there are negative side effects and health risks or forgetting to take pills is a problem for you. Some people think condom use disrupts spontaneity and lowers penile sensitivity. (Creative approaches to condom use and improved quality can decrease these concerns.) The diaphragm, cervical cap, contraceptive sponge, female condom, and spermicides can be inserted before intercourse begins but are still considered a significant inconvenience by some.

5. *Type of relationship.* How easy is it for you to talk with your partner about contraception? How willing is

he or she to be involved? Barrier methods require more motivation and sense of responsibility from *each* partner than hormonal methods do. When the method depends on the cooperation of one's partner, assertiveness is necessary, no matter how difficult. This is especially true in new relationships, when condom use is most important. When sexual activity is infrequent, a barrier method may make more sense than an IUD or one of the hormonal methods.

6. *Ease and cost of obtaining and maintaining each method.* If a physical exam and clinic follow-up are required, how readily accessible is this to you? Can you and your partner afford the associated expenses of the method? Investigate the costs of different methods. If you have insurance, find out if it covers any of the costs.

7. *Religious or philosophical beliefs.* Are any of the methods unacceptable to you because of your personal beliefs? For some, abstinence and/or FAM may be the only permissible contraceptive methods.

Whatever your needs, circumstances, or beliefs, *do* make a choice about contraception. Not choosing anything is the one method known *not* to work. (To help make a choice that's right for you, take the quiz in the box "Which Contraceptive Method Is Right for You and Your Partner?") This is an area in which taking charge of your health has immediate and profound implications for your future. The method you choose today won't necessarily be the one you'll want to use your whole life or even next year. But it should be one that works for you right now.

Tips for Today

Your decisions about contraception are among the most important you will make in your life. They affect your physical and emotional health, your relationship and family choices, and your career and life plans. Decisions about contraception are far too important to leave to chance.

Right now you can

- Close your eyes and visualize the life you hope to have in 5 years, 10 years, and 15 years. Does it include a relationship, a family, children? Are you doing anything right now—such as taking a chance on an unintended pregnancy—that could prevent you from realizing your dreams?
- If you are sexually active or considering becoming so, make an appointment with a physician or health care practitioner to discuss which contraceptive method is right for you.
- If you are sexually active, consider whether your sexual health or the nature of your relationship with your partner has changed since you made your current contraceptive choices. If you want to make changes, think about how to do so and how to discuss any changes with your partner.

SUMMARY

- Barrier methods of contraception physically prevent sperm from reaching the egg; hormonal methods are designed to prevent ovulation, fertilization, and/or implantation; and surgical methods permanently block the movement of sperm or eggs to the site of conception.
- The choice of contraceptive method depends on effectiveness, convenience, cost, reversibility, side effects and risk factors, and protection against STDs. The concept of effectiveness includes failure rate and continuation rate.
- Hormonal methods may include a combination of estrogen and progestins or progesterone alone. Hormones may be delivered via pills, patch, vaginal ring, implants, or injections.
- Hormonal methods prevent ovulation, inhibit the movement of sperm, and affect the uterine lining so that implantation is prevented.
- The most commonly used emergency contraceptives are two-dose regimens of OCs and Plan B, which is now available without a prescription to women 18 and older.
- How IUDs work is not clearly understood; they may cause biochemical changes in the uterus, affect movement of sperm and eggs, or interfere with the implantation of the egg in the uterus.
- Male condoms are simple to use, immediately reversible, and provide STD protection; female condoms are available but are more difficult to use.
- The diaphragm, Lea's Shield, cervical cap, and contraceptive sponge cover the cervix and block sperm from entering; all are used with or contain spermicide.
- Vaginal spermicides come in the form of foams, creams, jellies, suppositories, and film.
- So-called natural methods include abstinence, withdrawal, and fertility awareness method (FAM); the latter is based on avoiding intercourse during the fertile phase of a woman's menstrual cycle.
- Combining methods can increase contraceptive effectiveness and help protect against STDs.
- Vasectomy—male sterilization—involves severing the vasa deferentia. Female sterilization involves severing or blocking the oviducts so that the egg cannot reach the uterus.
- Key issues in contraception include decisions about when it is OK to have sex, gender differences in the significance of contraception, and sexuality education and contraception accessibility for teens.
- Issues to be considered in choosing a contraceptive include the individual health risks of each method, the implications of an unplanned pregnancy, STD risk, convenience and comfort level, type of relationship, the cost and ease of obtaining and maintaining each method, and religious or philosophical beliefs.

Take Action

1. **Visit a health care provider:** Make an appointment with a physician or other health care provider to review the health risks of different contraceptive methods as they apply to you. For each method, determine whether any risk factors associated with its use apply to you or your partner.

2. **Visit a drugstore:** Visit a local drugstore and make a list of the contraceptives sold there, along with their prices. Next, investigate the costs of prescription contraceptive methods by contacting your physician, medical clinic, and/or pharmacy. Estimate the annual cost of regular use for each method, and rank the methods from most to least expensive.

3. **Develop a public service campaign:** Devise a public service campaign that will encourage men to become more involved in contraception. Your campaign might use techniques such as TV and print advertisements, radio announcements, and posters. Look at other public service campaigns and advertisements for ideas. What sorts of images do you think would be motivational? What sort of tone and message do you think would be most effective?

For More Information

Books

Boston Women's Health Book Collective. 2005. *Our Bodies, Ourselves—A New Edition for a New Era.* New York: Simon & Schuster. *Broad coverage of many women's health concerns, with extensive coverage of contraception.*

Glasier, A., and B. Winikoff. 2005. *Fast Facts: Contraception,* 2nd ed. Oxford: Health Press. *Basic facts and figures related to contraceptive methods. Succinct and easy to read.*

Hatcher, R. A., et al. 2004. *Contraceptive Technology,* 18th ed. New York: Ardent Media. *A reliable source of up-to-date information on contraception.*

Hatcher, R. A., et al. 2005. *A Pocket Guide to Managing Contraception,* 2005–2007 ed. Tiger, Ga.: Bridging the Gap Foundation. *An easy-to-use, reliable source of contraceptive information.*

Hatcher, R. A., et al. 2005. *Safely Sexual,* 2nd ed. New York: Ardent Media. *Realistic recommendations on the prevention of unplanned pregnancy, as well as HIV infection and other STDs.*

Tone, A. 2001. *Devices and Desires: Men, Women, and the Commercialization of Contraception in the United States.* New York: Hill & Wang. *An engaging history of contraception in America.*

Organizations, Hotlines, and Web Sites

The Guttmacher Institute. A nonprofit institute for reproductive health research, policy analysis, and public education.
800-355-0244
http://www.agi-usa.org

Ann Rose's Ultimate Birth Control Links Page. A Web site with information on methods of birth control and decision-making strategies.
http://www.ultimatebirthcontrol.com

Association of Reproductive Health Professionals. Offers educational materials about family planning, contraception, and other reproductive health issues; the Web site includes an interactive questionnaire to help people choose contraceptive methods.
202-466-3825
http://www.arhp.org

Emergency Contraception Hotline. Provides information and referrals.
888-NOT-2-LATE

Emergency Contraception Web Site. Provides extensive information about emergency contraception; sponsored by the Office of Population Research at Princeton University.
http://www.not-2-late.com

It's Your Sex Life. Provides information about sexuality, relationships, contraceptives, and STDs; geared toward teenagers and young adults.
http://www.itsyoursexlife.com

Kaiser Family Foundation: Women's Health Policy: Contraception. Provides information and reports focused on how policies impact reproductive health care and access to contraceptives.
http://www.kff.org/womenshealth/contraception.cfm

Managing Contraception. Provides brief descriptions and tips for using many forms of contraception.
http://www.managingcontraception.com

Planned Parenthood Federation of America. Provides information on family planning, contraception, and abortion and provides counseling services.
800-230-PLAN
http://www.plannedparenthood.org

Reproductive Health Online (Reproline). Presents information on contraceptive methods currently available and those under study for future use.
http://www.reproline.jhu.edu

The following are some of the many organizations focusing on family planning and reproductive health issues worldwide:

Family Health International
http://www.fhi.org

Global Reproductive Health Forum at Harvard
http://www.hsph.harvard.edu/Organizations/healthnet

International Planned Parenthood Federation
http://www.ippf.org

Safe Motherhood
http://www.safemotherhood.org

United Nations Population Fund
http://www.unfpa.org

WHO World Health Day 2005: Make Every Mother and Child Count
http://www.who.int/world-health-day/2005/en

See also the listings for Chapters 5, 7, 8, and 18.

Selected Bibliography

Aegidius, K., et al. 2006. Oral contraceptives and increased headache prevalence: the Head-HUNT Study. *Neurology* 66(3): 349–353.

Amory, J. K. 2005. Male hormonal contraceptives: Current status and future prospects. *Treatments in Endocrinology* 4(6): 333–341.

Artz, L., et al. 2005. A randomized trial of clinician-delivered interventions promoting barrier contraception for sexually transmitted disease prevention. *Sexually Transmitted Diseases* 32(11): 672–679.

Awsare, N. S., et al. 2005. Complications of vasectomy. *Annals of the Royal College of Surgeons of England* 87(6): 406–410.

Bahamondes, L., et al. 2006. A prospective study of the forearm bone density of users of etonorgestrel- and levonorgestrel-releasing contraceptive implants. *Human Reproduction* 21(2): 466–470.

Chapman, L., and A. Magos. 2005. Currently available devices for female sterilization. *Expert Review of Medical Devices* 2(5): 623–634.

Crosby, R., et al. 2005. Condom discomfort and associated problems with their use among university students. *Journal of American College Health* 54(3): 143–147.

Dailard C. 2006. Contraception counts: Ranking state efforts. *Issues Brief* (Guttmacher Institute) (1): 1–7.

Dede, F. S., et al. 2006. Changes in menstrual pattern and ovarian function following bipolar electrocauterization of the fallopian tubes for voluntary surgical contraception. *Contraception* 73(1): 88–91.

Eisenberg, M. E., et al. 2005. Weight-related issues and high-risk sexual behaviors among college students. *Journal of American College Health* 54(2): 95–101.

Flores, J. B., et al. 2005. Clinical experience and acceptability of the etonorgestrel subdermal contraceptive implant. *International Journal of Gynaecology and Obstetrics* 90(3): 228–233.

Food and Drug Administration. 2005. *Patient Information Sheet: Norlegstromin/ethinyl estradiol (marketed as Ortho Evra).* 13 December (http://www.fda.gov/cder/drug/InfoSheets/patient/norlegstrominPIS.htm; retrieved August 7, 2006).

Forum on Child and Family Statistics. 2006. *America's Children in Brief: Key National Indicators of Well-Being, 2006* (http://childstats.gov; retrieved November 10, 2006).

Foulkes, R., et al. 2005. Opportunities for action: Addressing Latina sexual and reproductive health. *Perspectives on Sexual and Reproductive Health* 37(1): 39–41.

Frye, C. A. 2006. An overview of oral contraceptives: Mechanism of action and clinical use. *Neurology* 66(Suppl. 3): S29–36.

Funk, S., et al. 2005. Safety and efficacy of Implanon, a single-rod implantable contraceptive containing etonogestrel. *Contraception* 71(5): 319–326.

Glasier, A., and W. C. Shields. 2006. Can we improve contraceptive use? *Contraception* 73(1): 1–3.

Greer, J. B., et al. 2005. Short-term oral contraceptive use and the risk of epithelial ovarian cancer. *American Journal of Epidemiology* 162(1): 66–72.

Hahm, H. C., et al. 2006. Asian American adolescents' first sexual intercourse: Gender and acculturation differences. *Perspectives on Sexual and Reproductive Health* 38(1): 28–36.

Jensen, J. T. 2005. Contraceptive and therapeutic effects of the levonorgestrel intrauterine system: An overview. *Obstetrical and Gynecological Survey* 60(9): 604–612.

Johnson, L. A. 2005. Today Sponge to be available in U.S.—again. *San Francisco Chronicle,* 23 April, A2.

Kaufman, M. 2006. Plan B battles embroil states. *Washington Post,* 27 February, A01.

Kaunitz, A. M. 2005. Beyond the pill: New data and options in hormonal and intrauterine contraception. *American Journal of Obstetrics and Gynecology* 192(4): 998–1004.

Klein, J. D. 2005. Adolescent pregnancy: Current trends and issues. *Pediatrics* 116(1): 281–286.

Kripke, C. 2006. Cyclic vs. continuous or extended-cycle combined contraceptives. *American Family Physician* 73(5): 804.

Lesnewski, R., et al. 2005. Safety of and contraindications for use of intrauterine devices. *American Family Physician* 71(1): 95–102.

Matteson, K. A., et al. 2006. Unplanned pregnancy: Does past experience influence the use of a contraceptive method? *Obstetrics and Gynecology* 107(1): 121–127.

Mauck, C. K., et al. 2006. FemCap with removal strap: Ease of removal safety and acceptability. *Contraception* 73(1): 59–64.

Maugh, T. H. 2005. 70% of older teens have had oral sex. *San Francisco Chronicle,* 16 September, A3.

Monastersky, N., and S. C. Landau. 2006. Future of emergency contraception lies in pharmacists' hands. *Journal of the American Pharmacists Association* 46(1): 84–88.

Naz, R. K. 2005. Antisperm vaccine for contraception. *American Journal of Reproductive Immunology* 54(6): 378–383.

Niccolai, L. M., et al. 2005. Condom effectiveness for prevention of *Chlamydia trachomatis* infection. *Sexually Transmitted Infections* 81(4): 323–325.

Non-latex versus latex male condoms for contraception. 2006. *Cochrane Database of Systematic Reviews* (1): CD003550.

Peterson, H. B., and K. M. Curtis. 2005. Clinical practice. Long-acting methods of contraception. *New England Journal of Medicine* 353(20): 2169–2175.

Raine, T. R., et al. 2005. Direct access to emergency contraception through pharmacies and effect on unintended pregnancy and STIs: A randomized controlled trial. *Journal of the American Medical Association* 293(1): 54–62.

Sarkar, N. N. 2005. The combined contraceptive vaginal device (NuvaRing): A comprehensive review. *European Journal of Contraception and Reproductive Health Care* 10(2): 73–78.

Schreiber, C. A., et al. 2006. Effects of long-term use of nonoxynol-9 on vaginal flora. *Obstetrics and Gynecology* 107(1): 136–143.

Silvera, S. A., et al. 2005. Oral contraceptive use and risk of breast cancer among women with a family history of breast cancer: A prospective cohort study. *Cancer Causes Control* 16(9): 1059–1063.

Spermicide used alone for contraception. 2005. *Cochrane Database of Systematic Reviews* (4): CD005218.

Stanwood, N. L., et al. 2006. Self-injection of monthly combined hormonal contraceptive. *Contraception* 73(1): 53–55.

Stewart, F. H., et al. 2005. Extended use of transdermal norelgestromin/ethinyl estradiol: A randomized trial. *Obstetrics and Gynecology* 105(6): 1389–1396.

Tanne, J. H. 2006. FDA rejected contraception for political reason. *British Medical Journal* 332(7542): 624.

The ESHRE Capri Workshop Group. 2005. Noncontraceptive health benefits of combined oral contraception. *Human Reproduction Update* 11(5): 513–525.

Thottam, J. 2006. A big win for Plan B: Wal-Mart's about-face expands access to the "morning after" pill. *Time,* 13 March, 41.

Urdl, W., et al. 2005. Contraceptive efficacy, compliance and beyond: Factors related to satisfaction with once-weekly transdermal compared with oral contraception. *European Journal of Obstetrics, Gynecology, and Reproductive Biology* 121(2): 202–210.

Valappil, T., et al. 2005. Female condom and male condom failure among women at high risk of sexually transmitted disease. *Sexually Transmitted Diseases* 32(1): 35–43.

Wald, A., et al. 2005. The relationship between condom use and herpes simplex virus acquisition. *Annals of Internal Medicine* 143(10): 707–713.

Wooltorton, E. 2006. The Evra (ethinyl estradiol/norelgestromin) contraceptive patch: Estrogen exposure concerns. *Canadian Medical Association Journal* 174(2): 164.

World Health Organization. 2006. *Future of Sexual and Reproductive Health at Tipping Point, According to Global Study* (http://www.who.int/mediacentre/news/releases/2006/pr63/en/index.html; retrieved November 1, 2006).

9

Looking AHEAD

After reading this chapter, you should be able to

- Define and discuss the concepts of addictive behavior, substance abuse, and substance dependence
- Explain factors contributing to drug use and dependence
- List the major categories of psychoactive drugs and describe their effects, methods of use, and potential for abuse and dependence
- Discuss social issues related to psychoactive drug use and its prevention and treatment
- Evaluate the role of drugs and other addictive behaviors in your life and identify your risk factors for abuse or dependence

The Use and Abuse of Psychoactive Drugs

Test Your Knowledge

1. Addictions always involve drugs that cause physical withdrawal symptoms when the person stops taking them.
True or false?

2. Which of the following is the most widely used illegal drug among college students?
a. cocaine
b. hallucinogens
c. marijuana
d. heroin

3. Caffeine use can produce physical dependence.
True or false?

4. Which of the following drugs is most addictive?
a. marijuana
b. nicotine
c. Valium
d. LSD

5. About what percentage of street drugs contain the promised primary ingredient?
a. 50%
b. 66%
c. 75%

ANSWERS

1. FALSE. Both assertions in this statement are wrong. Addiction does not always involve a drug, but even when it does, withdrawing from that drug may not result in physical symptoms.
2. C. Marijuana ranks first, followed (in order) by cocaine, hallucinogens, and heroin. Alcohol remains by far the most popular drug among college students. However, the vast majority of college students (80%) report no drug use in the previous month.
3. TRUE. Regular users of caffeine develop physical tolerance, needing more caffeine to produce the same level of alertness. Many also experience withdrawal symptoms, such as headaches and irritability, when they decrease their intake.
4. B. Valium is also addictive, LSD and marijuana less so. Nicotine is believed to be the most highly addictive psychoactive drug.
5. A. This figure is even lower for drugs that are difficult to obtain or manufacture. Street drugs may be sold in unsafe dosages and are typically mixed ("cut") with cheaper and often more hazardous substances.

WW Visit the *Core Concepts in Health* Online Learning Center (www.mhhe.com/insel10e) for study aids and many additional resources.

The use of **drugs** for both medical and social purposes is widespread in America (Table 9-1). Many people believe that every problem, no matter how large or small, has or should have a chemical solution. For fatigue, many turn to caffeine; for insomnia, sleeping pills; for anxiety or boredom, alcohol or other recreational drugs. Advertisements, social pressures, and the human desire for quick solutions to life's difficult problems all contribute to the prevailing attitude that drugs can ease all pain. Unfortunately, using drugs can—and often does—have serious consequences.

The most serious consequences are abuse and addiction. The drugs most often associated with abuse are **psychoactive drugs**—those that alter a person's experiences or consciousness. In the short term, psychoactive drugs can cause **intoxication,** a state in which sometimes unpredictable physical and emotional changes occur. A person who is intoxicated may experience potentially serious changes in physical functioning, and his or her emotions and judgment may be affected in ways that lead to uncharacteristic and unsafe behavior. In the long term, recurrent drug use can have profound physical, emotional, and social effects.

This chapter introduces the general concept of addictive behavior and then focuses on the major classes of psychoactive drugs: their short- and long-term effects, their potential for abuse and addiction, and other issues related to their use. Alcohol and nicotine—two of the most widely used psychoactive drugs and those that have the greatest negative impact on wellness in terms of disease, injury, and death—are treated in detail in Chapters 10 and 11.

VITAL STATISTICS

Table 9-1 Nonmedical Drug Use Among Americans

	Percentage Using Substance in the Past 30 Days	
	College Students (age 18–22)	All Americans (age 12 and older)
Any illicit drug	21.2	8.1
Tobacco (all forms)	36.8	29.4
Cigarettes	30.6	24.9
Smokeless tobacco	5.3	3.2
Cigars	11.9	5.6
Pipe tobacco	1.2	0.9
Alcohol	62.4	51.8
Binge alcohol use	43.4	22.7
Marijuana/hashish	17.3	6.0
Cocaine	1.9	1.0
Crack	0.1	0.3
Heroin	0.1	0.1
Hallucinogens	1.5	0.4
LSD	0.2	0.0
Ecstasy	0.5	0.2
Inhalants	0.6	0.3
Psychotherapeutics*	5.7	2.6
Pain relievers	4.1	1.9
Tranquilizers	1.4	0.7
Stimulants	1.8	0.4
Methamphetamine	0.5	0.2
Sedatives	0.2	0.1

*Nonmedical use of prescription-type pain relievers, tranquilizers, stimulants, or sedatives.

SOURCE: Office of Applied Studies, Substance Abuse and Mental Health Services Administration. 2006. *Results from the 2005 National Survey on Drug Use and Health: National Findings,* September 2006 Update (http://oas.samhsa.gov/nhsda.htm; retrieved November 17, 2006).

ADDICTIVE BEHAVIOR

Although addiction is most often associated with drug use, many experts now extend the concept of addiction to other behaviors. **Addictive behaviors** are habits that have gotten out of control, with resulting negative effects on a person's health. Looking at the nature of addiction and a range of addictive behaviors can help us understand similar behaviors when they involve drugs.

Terms

drug Any chemical other than food intended to affect the structure or function of the body.

psychoactive drug A drug that can alter a person's consciousness or experience.

intoxication The state of being mentally affected by a chemical (literally, a state of being poisoned).

addictive behavior Any habit that has gotten out of control, resulting in a negative effect on one's health.

What Is Addiction?

The word *addiction* tends to be a highly charged one for most people. We may jokingly say we're addicted to fudge swirl ice cream or our morning jog, but most of us think of true addiction as a habitual and uncontrollable behavior, usually involving the use of a drug. Some people think of addiction as a moral flaw or a personal weakness. Others think addictions arise from certain personality traits, genetic factors, or socioeconomic influences. Views on the causes of addictions have an impact on our attitudes toward people with addictive disorders, as well as on the approaches to treatment.

Historically, the term *addiction* was applied only when the habitual use of a drug produced chemical changes in the user's body. One such change is physical tolerance, in which the body adapts to a drug so that the initial dose no longer produces the original emotional or psychological effects. This process, caused by chemical changes, means the user has to take larger and larger doses of the drug to achieve the same high. (Tolerance will be discussed in greater detail later in the chapter.) The concept of addiction as a disease process, one based in brain chemistry, rather than a moral failing, has led to many advances in the understanding and treatment of drug addiction.

Some scientists think that other behaviors may share some of the chemistry of drug addiction. They suggest that activities like gambling, eating, exercising, and sex trigger the release of brain chemicals that cause a pleasurable rush in much the same way that psychoactive drugs do. The brain's own chemicals thus become the "drug" that can cause addiction. These theorists suggest that drug addiction and addiction to other pleasurable behaviors have a common mechanism in the brain. In this view, addiction is partly the result of our own natural wiring.

However, and very important, the view that addiction is based in our brain chemistry does *not* imply that an individual bears no responsibility for his or her addictive behavior. Many experts believe that it is inaccurate and counterproductive to think of all bad habits and excessive behaviors as diseases. They point to other factors, especially lifestyle and personality traits, that play key roles in the development of addictive behaviors. Before we consider what those factors are, let's first look in more detail at what constitutes addictive behavior.

Characteristics of Addictive Behavior

It is often difficult to distinguish between a healthy habit and one that has become an addiction. Experts have identified some general characteristics typically associated with addictive behaviors:

- *Reinforcement.* Addictive behaviors are physically and/or psychologically reinforcing. Some aspect of the behavior produces pleasurable physical and/or emotional states or relieves negative ones.
- *Compulsion or craving.* The individual feels a strong compulsion—a compelling need—to engage in the behavior, often accompanied by obsessive planning for the next opportunity to perform it.
- *Loss of control.* The individual loses control over the behavior and cannot block the impulse to engage in it. He or she may deny that the behavior is problematic or may have tried but failed to control it.
- *Escalation.* Addiction often involves a pattern of escalation, in which more and more of a particular substance or activity is required to produce its desired effects. This escalation typically means that a person must give an increasing amount of his or her time, attention, and resources to the behavior.
- *Negative consequences.* The behavior continues despite serious negative consequences, such as problems with academic or job performance, personal relationships, and health; legal or financial troubles are also typical.

The Development of Addiction

There is no single cause of addiction. Instead, characteristics of an individual person, of the environment in which the person lives, and of the substance or behavior he or she abuses combine in an addictive behavior. Although addictive behaviors share many common characteristics, the importance of these different factors varies from one case to another, even when the addiction is to the same substance or behavior.

We all engage in activities that are potentially addictive. Some of these activities can be part of a wellness lifestyle if they are done appropriately and in moderation, but if a behavior starts to be excessive, it may become an addiction. An addiction often starts when a person does something he or she thinks will bring pleasure or help avoid pain. The activity may be drinking a beer, going on the Internet, playing the lottery, or going shopping. If it works, and the behavior does bring pleasure or alleviates pain, the person is likely to repeat it. He or she becomes increasingly dependent on the behavior, and tolerance may develop—that is, the person needs more of the behavior to feel the same effect. Eventually, the behavior becomes a central focus of the person's life, and there is a deterioration in other areas, such as school performance or relationships. The behavior no longer brings pleasure, but it is necessary to avoid the pain of going without it. What started as a seemingly innocent way of feeling good can become a prison.

Many common behaviors are potentially addictive, but most people who engage in them do not develop problems. The reason, again, lies in the combination of factors that are involved in the development of addiction, including personality, lifestyle, heredity, the social and physical environment, and the nature of the substance or behavior in question. For a behavior to become an addiction, these diverse factors must come together in a certain way. For example, nicotine, the psychoactive drug in tobacco, has a very high potential for physical addiction; but a person who doesn't choose to try cigarettes, perhaps because of family influence or a tendency to develop asthma, will never develop nicotine addiction.

Characteristics of People with Addictions

The causes and course of an addiction are extremely varied, but people with addictions do seem to share some characteristics. Many use the substance or activity as a substitute for other, healthier, coping strategies. People vary in their ability to manage their lives, and those who have the most trouble dealing with stress and painful emotions may be more susceptible to addiction.

Some studies have found that genetic factors play a role in risk for drug abuse. In addition, some people may have a genetic predisposition to addiction to a particular substance; such predispositions may involve variations in brain chemistry. People with addictive disorders usually have a distinct preference for a particular addictive behavior. They also often have problems with impulse control and self-regulation and tend to be risk takers.

Examples of Addictive Behaviors

The use and abuse of psychoactive drugs is explored in detail later in the chapter. In this section, we examine some behaviors that are not related to drugs and that can become addictive for some people.

The availability of gambling on the Internet makes it even more difficult for pathological gamblers to control their compulsion.

Compulsive or Pathological Gambling Many people gamble casually by putting a dollar in the office football pool, buying a lottery ticket, or going to the races. But some become compulsive gamblers, unable to control the urge to gamble, even in the face of financial and personal ruin. Most compulsive gamblers seek excitement even more than money. Increasingly larger bets are necessary to produce the desired level of excitement. A loss can lead to a perceived need to keep placing bets to win back the money. When financial resources become strained, the person may lie or steal to pay off debts. The consequences of compulsive gambling are not just financial; the suicide rate of compulsive gamblers is 20 times higher than that of the general population.

Compulsive gamblers may gamble to relieve negative feelings and become restless and irritable when they are unable to gamble. As with many addictive behaviors, compulsive gambling may begin or flare up in times of stress. The earlier a person starts to gamble, the higher the risk of compulsive gambling. Gambling is often linked to other risky behaviors, and many compulsive gamblers also have drug and alcohol abuse problems.

The American Psychiatric Association (APA) recognizes pathological gambling as a mental disorder and lists ten characteristic behaviors, including preoccupation with gambling, unsuccessful efforts to cut back or quit, using gambling to escape problems, and lying to family members to conceal the extent of involvement with gambling. In the United States, it is estimated that 1% of adults are compulsive (pathological) gamblers, and another 2% are "problem gamblers." As many as 4% of adults who live within 50 miles of a casino may be compulsive gamblers. These numbers may increase due to the spread of legalized gambling, both on the Internet and on American Indian tribal reservations.

In a recent survey of more than 10,000 students from more than 100 colleges, 42% of students reported having gambled at least once in the past year, and about 3% reported gambling at least once a week. Other characteristics associated with gambling among college students included more time watching TV, more time using a computer nonacademically, less time studying, lower grades, participation in intercollegiate athletics, and alcohol use and binge drinking.

Cognitive behavioral therapy has long been viewed as the most effective way to overcome pathological gambling. In a recent study, the drug nalmefene helped compulsive gamblers curb their addiction. The drug has not yet gained FDA approval for such use.

Sex and Love Addiction More controversial is the notion of addiction to sex or love. Some researchers believe that the initial rush of arousal and erotic or romantic chemistry produces an effect in the brain comparable to that of taking amphetamines or morphine. After a time, the brain becomes desensitized, and the addict must then seek his or her next rush by pursuing a new partner. According to this view, cheating on a partner, having many partners, and sexually victimizing others are behaviors parallel to drug-seeking behavior. Behaviors associated with sex addiction include an extreme preoccupation with sex, a compulsion to have sex repeatedly within a short period of time, spending a great deal of time and energy looking for partners or engaging in sex, using sex as a means of relieving painful feelings, and suffering negative emotional, personal, and professional consequences as a result of sexual activities.

Some experts are reluctant to call compulsive sexual activity a true addiction. However, even therapists who challenge the concept of sex addiction recognize that some people become overly preoccupied with sex, cannot seem to control their sex drive, and act in potentially harmful ways in order to obtain satisfaction. This pattern of sexual behavior does seem to meet the criteria for addictive behaviors discussed earlier.

Compulsive Spending or Shopping Compulsive spenders repeatedly give in to the impulse to buy much more than they need or can afford. For the compulsive shopper, spending may serve to relieve painful feelings such as depression or anxiety, or it may produce positive emotions such as excitement or happiness. Compulsive spenders usually buy luxury items rather than daily necessities. Men tend to buy cars, exercise equipment, and sporting gear; women tend to buy clothes, jewelry, and perfume. Some experts link compulsive shopping with neglect or abuse during childhood; it also seems to be associated with eating disorders, depression, and bipolar disorder. Some compulsive shoppers are helped by antidepressants.

Compulsive shoppers are usually significantly distressed by their behavior and its social, personal, and financial consequences. Characteristics of out-of-control spending include shopping in order to "feel better," using money or time that had been set aside for other purposes, hiding spending from others, and spending so much that the shopper goes into debt or engages in illegal activities such as shoplifting or writing bad checks. Like other addictive behaviors, compulsive shopping is characterized by a loss of control over the behavior and significant negative consequences.

Internet Addiction Some recent research has indicated that surfing the World Wide Web can also be addictive. In order to spend more time online, Internet addicts skip important social, school, or recreational activities, thereby damaging personal relationships and jeopardizing academic and job performance. Despite the negative consequences they are experiencing, they don't feel able to stop. The Internet addicts identified in one study averaged 38 online hours per week. Internet addicts may feel uncomfortable or be moody when they are not online. They may be preoccupied with getting back online and may stay there longer than they intend. A national survey published in 2006 found that more than 13% of respondents found it hard to stay off line for several days at a time. The study estimated that 5–10% of the U.S. population may experience Internet addiction. As with other addictive behaviors addicts may be using their behavior to alleviate stress or avoid painful emotions.

Activities by Internet addicts may take many forms, some of which, such as e-mail and chat rooms, are specific to the online format. However, widespread access to the Internet may expose many more people to other potentially addictive behaviors, including gambling, shopping, and sex. The Internet is convenient, easily accessible, and affordable; it is also anonymous, so people who might have hesitated to gamble or make expensive purchases in public may feel less inhibited when these activities can take place privately. There are thousands of online gambling sites and millions of online stores that allow people to gamble or shop from their homes at all times of the day or night; in addition, sites featuring online auctions or stock trading offer activities that are very similar to gambling. As described in Chapter 5, easy access to sexually oriented Web sites can lead to cybersex addiction for some people. It remains to be seen whether increasing access to the Internet among Americans will lead to more problems with addictive behaviors.

Other behaviors that can become addictive include eating, watching TV, working, and playing video games. Any substance or activity that becomes the focus of a person's life at the expense of other needs and interests can be damaging to health.

DRUG USE, ABUSE, AND DEPENDENCE

The substances most commonly associated with addiction are psychoactive drugs. Drugs are chemicals other than food that are intended to affect the structure or function of the body. They include prescription medicines such as antibiotics and antidepressants; nonprescription, or over-the-counter (OTC), substances such as alcohol, tobacco, and caffeine products; and illegal substances such as LSD and heroin. The use of drugs is not a new phenomenon in society; in fact, drug use has a long history.

The Drug Tradition

Using drugs to alter consciousness is an ancient and universal pursuit. People have used alcohol for celebration and intoxication for thousands of years. People in all parts of the world have discovered and exploited the psychoactive properties of various local plants, such as the coca plant in South America and the opium poppy in the Middle East and Far East.

Beginning in the nineteenth century, chemists were successful in extracting the active chemicals from medicinal plants, such as morphine from the opium poppy and cocaine from the coca leaf. This was the beginning of modern *pharmacy,* the art of compounding drugs, and of *pharmacology,* the science and study of drugs. From this point on, a variety of drugs began to be produced, including codeine, LSD, methamphetamine, and heroin (Figure 9-1).

Initially, the manufacture and sale of these new drugs were not regulated. Pure morphine or cocaine could be purchased by mail order, and the makers of patent medicines and tonics included potentially addictive drugs in their products without informing the consumer of either the ingredients or the dangers. The earliest version of the soft drink Coca-Cola contained cocaine, which accounted for the lift it provided.

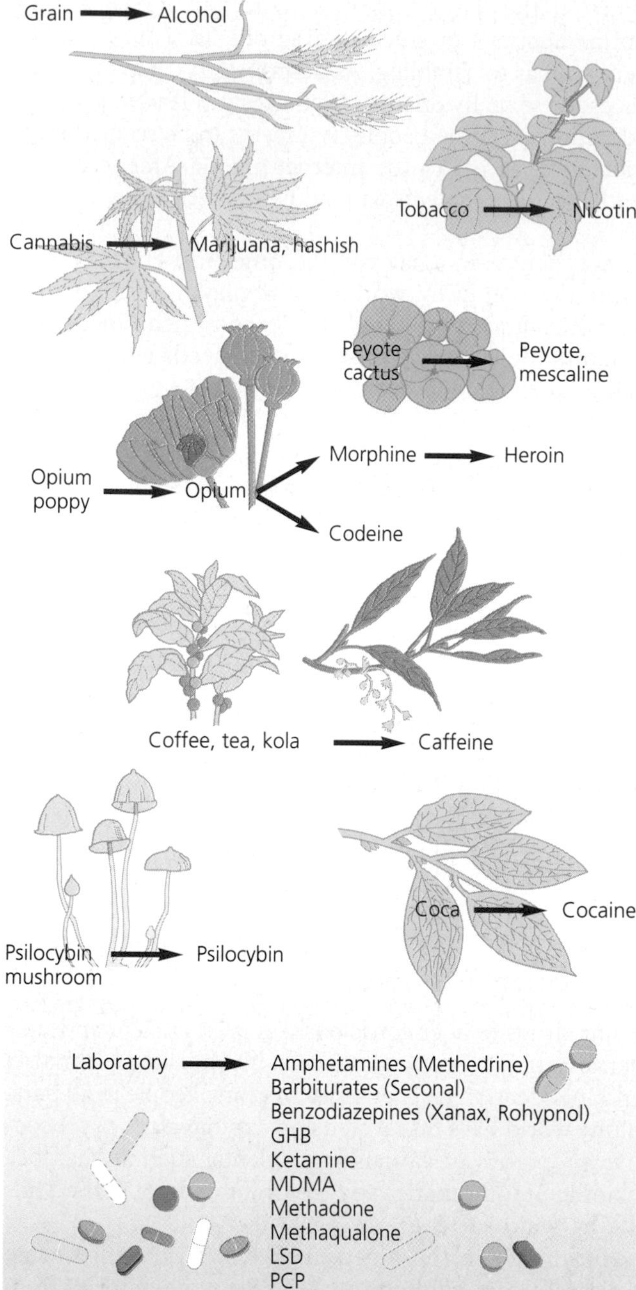

Figure 9-1 Sources of selected psychoactive drugs.

Drug addiction among middle-class Europeans and North Americans was more common by 1900 than at any time before or since. Concerns about drug addiction and the need to regulate drug sales and manufacture led in the early 1900s to the passage of U.S. federal drug laws. Middle-class use of the regulated drugs dropped, and drug use became restricted to, and increasingly identified with, criminal subcultures.

Nonmedical (recreational) drug use expanded in the general U.S. population during the 1960s and 1970s, reaching a peak in 1979. Drug use rates then declined until the early to mid-1990s, when drug use rates began to rise in certain age groups. Between 2002 and 2005, however, use of illicit drugs, including marijuana and methamphetamine, declined among youths aged 12–17, as did use of alcohol and tobacco. In young adults aged 18–25, overall drug use remained stable in 2005, although there was an increase in nonmedical use of narcotic pain relievers.

Drug Abuse and Dependence

The APA's *Diagnostic and Statistical Manual of Mental Disorders* is the authoritative reference for defining all sorts of behavioral disorders, including those related to drugs. The APA has chosen not to use the term *addiction,* in part because it is so broad and has so many connotations. Instead, the APA refers to two forms of substance (drug) disorders: substance abuse and substance dependence. Both are maladaptive patterns of substance use that lead to significant impairment or distress. Although the APA's definitions are more precise and more directly related to drug use, they clearly encompass the general characteristics of addictive behavior described in the last section.

Drug Abuse As defined by the APA, **substance abuse** involves one or more of the following:

- Recurrent drug use, resulting in a failure to fulfill major responsibilities at work, school, or home
- Recurrent drug use in situations in which it is physically hazardous, such as before or while driving a car
- Recurrent drug-related legal problems
- Continued drug use despite persistent social or interpersonal problems caused or exacerbated by the effects of the drug

The pattern of use may be constant or intermittent, and **physical dependence** may or may not be present. For example, a person who smokes marijuana once a week and cuts classes because he or she is high is abusing marijuana, even though he or she is not physically dependent.

Drug Dependence **Substance dependence** is a more complex disorder and is what many people associate with the idea of addiction. The seven specific criteria the APA uses to diagnose substance dependence are listed below. The first two are associated with physical dependence; the final five are associated with compulsive use. To be considered dependent, an individual must experience a cluster of three or more of these seven symptoms during a 12-month period.

1. *Developing tolerance to the substance.* When a person requires increased amounts of a substance to achieve the desired effect or notices a markedly diminished effect with continued use of the same amount, he or she has developed **tolerance.** For example, heavy heroin users may need to take ten times the amount they took at the beginning in order to achieve the desired effect; such a large dose would be lethal to a

nonuser. The degree to which tolerance develops varies widely depending on the drug.

2. *Experiencing withdrawal.* In an individual who has maintained prolonged, heavy use of a substance, a drop in its concentration within the body can result in unpleasant physical and cognitive **withdrawal** symptoms. The person is likely to take the substance to relieve or avoid those symptoms. Withdrawal symptoms are different for different drugs. For example, nausea, vomiting, and tremors are common for alcohol, opioids, and sedatives; for stimulants like amphetamines, cocaine, and caffeine, fatigue and irritability may occur. Other drugs have no significant withdrawal symptoms.
3. *Taking the substance in larger amounts or over a longer period than was originally intended.*
4. *Expressing a persistent desire to cut down or regulate substance use.* This desire is often accompanied by many unsuccessful efforts to reduce or discontinue use of the substance.
5. *Spending a great deal of time obtaining the substance, using the substance, or recovering from its effects.*
6. *Giving up or reducing important social, school, work, or recreational activities because of substance use.* A dependent person may withdraw from family activities and hobbies in order to use the substance in private or to spend more time with substance-using friends.
7. *Continuing to use the substance in spite of recognizing that it is contributing to a psychological or physical problem.* For example, a person might continue to use cocaine despite recognizing that she is suffering from cocaine-induced depression.

If a drug-dependent person experiences either tolerance or withdrawal, he or she is considered physically dependent. However, not everyone who experiences tolerance or withdrawal is drug dependent. For example, a hospital patient who is prescribed therapeutic doses of morphine to relieve pain may develop a tolerance to the drug and experience withdrawal symptoms when the prescription is discontinued. But without showing any signs of compulsive use, this individual would not be considered dependent. Dependence can occur without a physical component, based solely on compulsive use. For example, people with at least three symptoms of compulsive use of marijuana who show no signs of tolerance or withdrawal are suffering from substance dependence. In general, dependence problems that involve physical dependence carry a greater risk of immediate general medical problems and higher relapse rates.

Who Uses Drugs?

The use and abuse of drugs occur at all income and education levels, among all ethnic groups, and at all ages. Society is concerned with the casual or recreational use of illegal drugs because it is not really possible to know when drug use will lead to abuse or dependence. Some casual users develop substance-related problems; others do not. Some psychoactive drugs are more likely than others to lead to dependence (Table 9-2), but some users of even heroin or cocaine do not meet the APA's criteria for substance dependence. However, people who begin to use drugs at very young ages have a greater risk for dependence and serious health consequences.

Although we can't accurately predict which drug users will become drug abusers, researchers have identified some characteristics that place young people at higher-than-average risk for *trying* illicit drugs. Being male is one risk factor: Although gender differences in drug use are gradually narrowing, males are still about twice as likely as females to abuse illicit drugs (see the box "Gender Differences in Drug Use and Abuse" on p. 243). An adolescent who has a poor self-image; lacks self-control; uses tobacco; has an eating disorder; is aggressive, impulsive, or moody; or suffers from attention-deficit/hyperactivity disorder (ADHD) may be at increased risk for trying drugs. A thrill-seeking or risk-taking personality is another factor. People who drive too fast or who don't wear safety belts may have this personality type, which is characterized by a sense of invincibility. Such people find it easy to dismiss warnings of danger, whether about drugs or safety belts—"That only happens to other people; it could never happen to me."

Belonging to a peer group or family that accepts or rewards drug use is a significant risk factor for trying illicit drugs. One survey of people in drug treatment found that 20% had used drugs with their parents, usually before age 18. Chaotic home environments, dysfunctional families, and parental abuse also increase risk. Children with no parental monitoring after school

Terms

VW

substance abuse A maladaptive pattern of use of any substance that persists despite adverse social, psychological, or medical consequences. The pattern may be intermittent, with or without tolerance and physical dependence.

physical dependence The result of physiological adaptation that occurs in response to the frequent presence of a drug; typically associated with tolerance and withdrawal.

substance dependence A cluster of cognitive, behavioral, and physiological symptoms that occur in an individual who continues to use a substance despite suffering significant substance-related problems, leading to significant impairment or distress; also known as *addiction.*

tolerance Lower sensitivity to a drug so that a given dose no longer exerts the usual effect and larger doses are needed.

withdrawal Physical and psychological symptoms that follow the interrupted use of a drug on which a user is physically dependent; symptoms may be mild or life-threatening.

Table 9-2 Psychoactive Drugs and Their Potential for Producing Dependence

	Potential for Dependence	
Drug	Physical	Psychological
Nicotine	High	High
Heroin	High	High
Methamphetamine (smoked "ice")	High	High
Opium	High	High
Crack cocaine	Possible	High
Alcohol	Possible	Possible
Methaqualone	High	High
Barbiturates	High	Moderate
Amphetamine	Possible	High
Cocaine	Possible	High
Diazepam (Valium)	Low	High
PCP	Unknown	High
Chloral hydrate ("mickey")	Moderate	Moderate
Codeine	Moderate	Moderate
Marijuana	Unknown	Unknown
Hashish	Unknown	Unknown
Inhalants	Unknown	Moderate
Steroids	Possible	Possible
LSD	None	Unknown
Psilocybin	None	Unknown
MDMA (ecstasy)	Unknown	Unknown

SOURCES: National Clearinghouse for Alcohol and Drug Information. 2006. *Drugs of Abuse* (http://www.health.org/govpubs/rpo926; retrieved August 7, 2006); Beers, M. H., et al. 2006. *The Merck Manual of Diagnosis and Therapy,* 18th ed. New York: John Wiley & Sons.

are more likely to try illicit drugs than those with regular adult supervision. Adolescent girls who date boys 2 or more years older than themselves are more likely to use drugs. Young people who live in disadvantaged areas are more likely to be offered drugs at a young age, increasing their risk of drug use. Especially at younger ages, the risk of using drugs is higher for people who come from a single-parent family, for those whose parents failed to complete high school, and for those who are uninterested in school and earn poor grades. However, drug use rates among middle-class youths with college-educated parents tend to catch up with, and in some cases outstrip, those of other groups by the time students reach the twelfth grade.

What about people who *don't* use drugs? As a group, nonusers also share some characteristics. Not surprisingly, people who perceive drug use as risky and who disapprove of it are less likely to use drugs than those who believe otherwise. Drug use is also less common among people who have positive self-esteem and self-concept and who are assertive, independent thinkers who are not controlled by peer pressure. Self-control, social competence, optimism, academic achievement, and regular church attendance are also linked to lower rates of drug use (see the box "Spirituality and Drug Abuse" on p. 244).

Home environments are also influential: Coming from a strong family, one that has a clear policy on drug use, is another characteristic of people who don't use drugs. Young people who communicate openly with their parents and feel supported by them are also less likely to use drugs. Although parents may feel they have little effect on their children's drug-related attitudes and behaviors, evidence suggests that they can be a major influence. Some parents may wait too long to express a clear drug policy. Recent surveys indicate that attitudes about drugs and access and exposure to drugs change most dramatically between the ages of 12 and 13. Compared to a 12-year-old, a 13-year-old is about three times more likely to know teens who use and sell drugs and to know where and how to buy drugs. Yet nearly half of 13-year-olds report that their parents have never seriously discussed the dangers of illegal drugs with them.

Why Do People Use Drugs?

The answer to this question depends on both the user and the drug. Young people, especially those from middle-class backgrounds, are frequently drawn to drugs by the allure of the exciting and illegal. They may be curious, rebellious, or vulnerable to peer pressure. They may want to appear to be daring and to be part of the group. Young people may want to imitate adult models in their lives or in the movies. Most people who have taken illicit drugs have done so on an experimental basis, typically trying the drug one or more times but not continuing. The main factors in the initial choice of a drug are whether it is available and whether other people around are already using it.

Although some people use drugs because they have a desire to alter their mood or are seeking a spiritual experience, others are motivated primarily by a desire to escape boredom, anxiety, depression, feelings of worthlessness, or other distressing symptoms of psychological problems. They use drugs as a way to cope with the difficulties they are experiencing in life. The common practice in our society of seeking a drug solution to every problem is a factor in the widespread reliance on both illicit and prescription drugs.

For people living in poverty in the inner cities, many of these reasons for using drugs are magnified. The problems are more devastating, the need for escape more compelling. Furthermore, the buying and selling of drugs provide access to an unofficial, alternative economy that may seem like an opportunity for success.

Gender Matters

Gender Differences in Drug Use and Abuse

Men are more likely than women to use, abuse, and be dependent on illicit drugs. Rates of use are similar in males and females age 12–17, but among those 18 and older, more men than women use drugs and have problems associated with drug use (see table). Men account for about 80% of arrests for drug abuse violations, 70% of admissions for treatment, and 65% of drug-related deaths.

There are also gender differences in why and how young people use drugs. Young males tend to use alcohol or drugs for sensation seeking or to enhance their social status, factors tied to culturally based gender roles. Young women tend to use drugs to improve mood, increase confidence, and reduce inhibitions. Boys are likelier to receive offers to use drugs in public settings, whereas girls are likelier to receive offers in a private place such as a friend's residence.

Despite overall lower rates of drug use, females may have unique biological vulnerabilities to certain drugs, and they may move more quickly from use to abuse. Major life transitions, including the physical and emotional changes associated with puberty, increase the risk of drug use and abuse for girls more so than for boys. Certain other drug abuse risk factors are also more common in female adolescents, including depression, low self-esteem, eating disorders, and a history of physical or sexual abuse.

Adolescent boys and girls share some protective factors relating to drug abuse, including positive family relationships and extracurricular activities; religious involvement is protective for both boys and girls but may be more protective for girls. Among older men and women, marriage, children, and employment are associated with lower rates of drug abuse and dependence. Rates of drug abuse and dependence among married adults are less than half of those among unmarried adults; similar patterns are seen when comparing adults who live with children versus those who do not live with children and adults who are employed versus those who are unemployed.

	National Survey Results: Percent Reporting in Past Year	
	Males	**Females**
Illicit drug use*	16.9	12.2
Age 12–17	20.6	21.5
Age 18–25	37.9	29.9
Age 26 and older	12.5	8.1
Drove under influence of illicit drug	6.5	2.7
Illicit drug or alcohol abuse or dependence	12.7	6.2
Treatment for drug dependence	1.2	0.6

*Illicit drugs include marijuana/hashish, cocaine, heroin, hallucinogens, inhalants, and prescription-type psychotherapeutics used nonmedically.

SOURCES: Office of Applied Studies, Substance Abuse and Mental Health Services Administration. 2006. *Results from the 2005 National Survey on Drug Use and Health: National Findings*, September 2006 (http://oas.samhsa.gov/; retrieved November 17, 2006); Office of National Drug Control Policy. 2006. *Women and Drugs* (http://whitehousedrugpolicy.gov/drugfact/women/index.html; retrieved August 7, 2006); Office of Applied Studies, Substance Abuse and Mental Health Services Administration. 2006. *Treatment Episode Data Set (TEDS). Highlights—2004. National Admissions to Substance Abuse Treatment Services* (http:// wwwdasis.samhsa.gov/teds04/ tedshigh2k4.pdf; retrieved August 7, 2006).

Risk Factors for Dependence

Why do some people use psychoactive drugs without becoming dependent, whereas others aren't as lucky? The answer seems to be a combination of physical, psychological, and social factors. Research indicates that some people may be born with certain characteristics of brain chemistry or metabolism that make them more vulnerable to drug dependence. Other research suggests that people who were exposed to drugs while still in the womb may have an increased risk of abusing drugs themselves later in life.

Psychological risk factors for drug dependence include difficulty in controlling impulses and a strong need for excitement, stimulation, and immediate gratification. Feelings of rejection, hostility, aggression, anxiety, or depression are also associated with drug dependence. People may turn to drugs to blot out their emotional pain.

People with mental illnesses have a very high risk of substance dependence. Research shows that about one-third of people with psychological disorders also have a substance-dependence problem and about one-third of those have another mental disorder. People with two or more coexisting mental disorders are referred to as having **dual (co-occurring) disorders.** Diagnosis of psychological problems among people with substance dependence can be very difficult because drug intoxication and withdrawal can mimic the symptoms of a mental illness.

Term

dual (co-occurring) disorder The presence of two or more mental disorders simultaneously in the same person; for example, drug dependence and depression.

Vw

Mind/Body/Spirit

Spirituality and Drug Abuse

The use of alcohol and other drugs is intertwined with spirituality and religion. Some religions use drugs in the quest for spiritual transcendence: American Indian, Polynesian, African, and other indigenous religions have used psychoactive drugs such as peyote, khat, alcohol, and hashish for expanding consciousness and developing personal spirituality. For other religions, the use of psychoactive drugs is seen as a threat to spirituality. In Islam, for example, the consumption of alcohol and certain other drugs is strictly forbidden. Although there are diverse religious viewpoints on drug use, many religions infer some link between psychoactive drugs and spirituality.

In studies of American teens and adults, spiritual or religious involvement is generally associated with a lower risk of trying psychoactive drugs and, for those who do use drugs, a lower risk of heavy use and dependence. The mechanism for this protective effect is unclear; possibilities include the adoption of a strict code of behavior or set of principles that forbids drug use, the presence of a social support system for abstinence or moderation, and the promotion of a large, complex set of values that includes avoidance of drug use. The relationship between religious faith and avoidance of drug use appears to be even stronger in teens than in adults. One study found that teens who felt they had a personal relationship with the divine and/or who belonged to a more fundamentalist religious denomination were less likely to engage in substance use and abuse than other teens. Teens who attend 25 or more religious services per year are about half as likely to use illicit drugs compared with teens who attend services less frequently. Overall, people who spend time regularly engaging in spiritual practices such as prayer and transcendental meditation have lower rates of drug abuse.

People with current substance-abuse problems tend to have lower rates of religious affiliation and involvement and lower levels of spiritual wellness, characterized by a lack of a sense of meaning in life. One of the hallmarks of drug dependence is spending increasing amounts of time and energy obtaining and using drugs; such a pattern of behavior inevitably reduces the resources an individual puts toward developing physical, emotional, and spiritual wellness.

What about those seeking to break their dependence on drugs? Among people in treatment for substance abuse, higher levels of religious faith and spirituality may contribute to the recovery process. A study of people recovering from alcohol or other drug abuse found that spirituality and religiosity were associated with increased coping skills, greater optimism about life, greater resilience to stress, and greater perceived social support. If, for a particular individual, there is a spiritual aspect to his or her substance-abuse problem, then it is likely that spirituality may also play a role in recovery.

More research is needed to clarify the relationships among spirituality, religion, drug use, and recovery. One of the difficulties in conducting research in this area is the difficulty in defining and measuring spirituality and religious involvement. Spirituality is a complex part of human nature, involving behavior, belief, and experience. And although behaviors such as the spiritual practices of prayer or meditation can be measured, it is more difficult to determine what such practices mean to an individual and her or his overall sense of self.

SOURCES: Brown, A. E., et al. 2006. Alcohol recovery and spirituality: Strangers, friends, or partners? *Southern Medical Journal* 99(6): 654–657; Substance Abuse and Mental Health Network. 2004. Religious beliefs and substance use among youths. *NSDUH Report,* January; Plante, T. G., and D. A. Pardini. 2000. Religious denomination affiliation and psychological health: Results from a substance abuse population. Presented at the American Psychological Association Annual Convention, August 7; Miller, L., M. Davies, and S. Greenwald. 2000. Religiosity and substance use and abuse among adolescents in the national comorbidity survey. *Journal of the American Academy of Child and Adolescent Psychiatry* 39(9): 1190–1197.

Social factors that may influence drug dependence include growing up in a family in which a parent or sibling abused drugs, belonging to a peer group that emphasizes and encourages drug abuse, and living in poverty. Because they have easy access to drugs, health care professionals are also at a higher risk. To determine whether you are at risk, take the quiz in the box "Do You Have a Problem with Drugs?"

Other Risks of Drug Use

Dependence is not the only serious potential consequence of drug use. Each year, nearly 1.3 million emergency room visits are related to drug misuse or abuse.

Intoxication People who are under the influence of drugs—intoxicated—may act in uncharacteristic and unsafe ways because both their physical and mental functioning are impaired. They are more likely to be injured from a variety of causes, including falls, drowning, and automobile crashes; to engage in unsafe sex, increasing their risk for sexually transmitted diseases and unintended pregnancy; and to be involved in incidents of aggression and violence, including sexual assault.

Unintended Side Effects Psychoactive drugs have many physical and psychological effects beyond the alteration of consciousness. These effects range from nausea and constipation to paranoia, depression, and heart failure. Some drugs also carry the risk of fatal overdose.

Unknown Drug Constituents There is no quality control in the illegal drug market, so the composition, dosage, and toxicity of street drugs is highly variable.

Assess Yourself

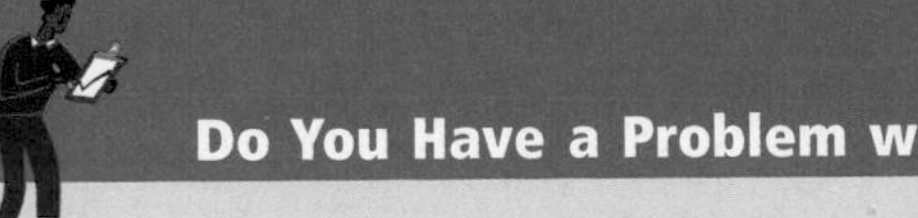

Do You Have a Problem with Drugs?

Answer yes (Y) or no (N) to the following questions:

_____ 1. Do you take the drug regularly?

_____ 2. Have you been taking the drug for a long time?

_____ 3. Do you always take the drug in certain situations or when you're with certain people?

_____ 4. Do you find it difficult to stop using the drug? Do you feel powerless to quit?

_____ 5. Have you tried repeatedly to cut down or control your use of the drug?

_____ 6. Do you need to take a larger dose of the drug in order to get the same high you're used to?

_____ 7. Do you feel specific symptoms if you cut back or stop using the drug?

_____ 8. Do you frequently take another psychoactive substance to relieve withdrawal symptoms?

_____ 9. Do you take the drug to feel "normal"?

_____ 10. Do you go to extreme lengths or put yourself in dangerous situations to get the drug?

_____ 11. Do you hide your drug use from others? Have you ever lied about what you're using or how much you use?

_____ 12. Do people close to you ask you about your drug use?

_____ 13. Are you spending more and more time with people who use the same drug as you?

_____ 14. Do you think about the drug when you're not high, figuring out ways to get it?

_____ 15. If you stop taking the drug, do you feel bad until you can take it again?

_____ 16. Does the drug interfere with your ability to study, work, or socialize?

_____ 17. Do you skip important school, work, social, or recreational activities in order to obtain or use the drug?

_____ 18. Do you continue to use the drug despite a physical or mental disorder or despite a significant problem that you know is made worse by drug use?

_____ 19. Have you developed a mental or physical condition or disorder because of prolonged drug use?

_____ 20. Have you done something dangerous or that you regret while under the influence of the drug?

The more times you answer yes, the more likely it is that you are developing a dependence on the drug. If your answers suggest dependence, talk to someone at your school health clinic or to your physician about taking care of the problem before it gets worse.

Studies of samples indicate that many street drugs don't contain their promised primary ingredient; in some cases, a drug may be present in unsafe dosages or mixed with other drugs to boost the effects. Careless manufacturing practices can result in the presence of toxic contaminants.

Risks Associated with Injection Drug Use

Heroin and related drugs are those most often injected, but cocaine, amphetamines, and other drugs, including steroids, may also be injected. Many injection drug users (IDUs) share or reuse needles, syringes, and other injection equipment, which can easily become contaminated with the user's blood. Small amounts of blood can carry enough human immunodeficiency virus (HIV) and hepatitis C virus (HCV) to be infectious. Through 2004, injection drug use accounted for about 25% of all HIV/AIDS cases; many more were attributed to sexual contact with IDUs. Injection drug use also accounts for 60% of HCV infections. About 15% of IDUs are infected with HIV; as many as 95% may carry HCV, according to the CDC. Unsterile injection practices can cause skin and soft tissue infections, which can progress to gangrene and be fatal if untreated. Other risks include endocarditis (infection of the heart valves), tuberculosis, and tetanus.

The surest way to prevent diseases related to injection drug use is never to inject drugs. Those who do inject drugs should use a new needle and syringe with each injection and should use sterile water and other equipment to prepare drugs. Bleach or boiling water may kill some viruses and bacteria, but they are not foolproof sterilization methods. Many viruses can survive in a syringe for a month or more.

Syringe exchange programs (SEPs)—in which IDUs can turn in a used syringe and get back a new one free—have been advocated to help slow the spread of HIV and reduce the rates and cost of other health problems associated with injection drug use. Opponents of SEPs argue that supplying addicts with syringes gives them the message that illegal drug use is acceptable and could thus exacerbate the nation's drug problem. However, studies have shown that well-implemented SEPs do not increase the use of drugs, and most offer AIDS counseling and provide referrals to drug treatment programs. Getting people off drugs is clearly the best solution, but there are far more IDUs (an estimated 1.5 million in the United States) than treatment facilities can currently handle.

Legal Consequences Many psychoactive drugs are illegal, so using them can result in large fines and/or imprisonment. The FBI reports nearly 1.7 million drug-related arrests each year. Possession of marijuana, heroin, or cocaine are the most commonly reported violations.

In the following sections of the chapter, you'll learn more about how drugs affect the body and how drug use and abuse affect individuals, families, and society as a whole.

HOW DRUGS AFFECT THE BODY

The psychoactive drugs discussed in this chapter have complex and variable effects, many of which can be traced to changes in brain chemistry. However, the same drug may affect different people differently or the same person in different ways under different circumstances. Beyond a fairly predictable general change in brain chemistry, the effects of a drug may vary depending on three general categories of factors: drug factors, user factors, and social factors.

Changes in Brain Chemistry

How can different drugs produce such different effects—making a person alert and wired or dull and sleepy? Psychoactive drugs produce most of their key effects by acting on brain chemistry in a characteristic fashion. Before any changes in brain chemistry can occur, however, molecules of the drug have to be carried to the brain through the bloodstream via a particular route of administration. A drug that is taken by mouth has to dissolve in the stomach, be absorbed into the bloodstream through the lining of the small intestine, and then pass through the liver, heart, and lungs before returning to the heart to be carried via arteries to the brain. A drug that is already dissolved and is injected directly into the bloodstream will reach the brain in much less time, and drugs that are inhaled and absorbed by the lungs travel to the brain even more rapidly. The more quickly a drug reaches the brain, the more likely the user is to become dependent.

Terms

pharmacological properties The overall effects of a drug on a person's behavior, psychology, and chemistry.

dose-response function The relationship between the amount of a drug taken and the intensity or type of the resulting effect.

time-action function The relationship between the time elapsed since a drug was taken and the intensity of its effect.

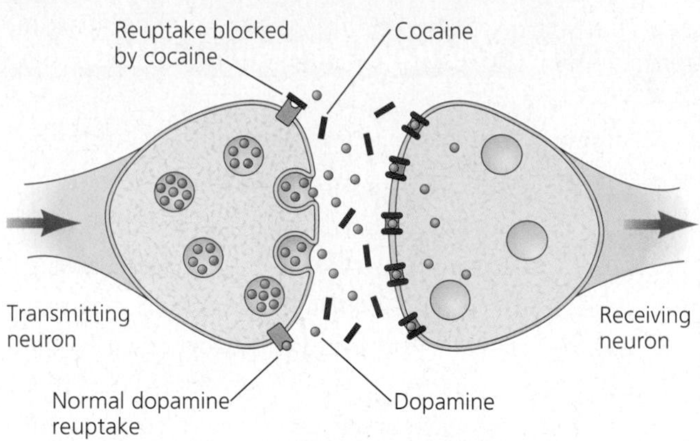

Figure 9-2 Effect of cocaine on brain chemistry. Under normal circumstances, the amount of dopamine at a synapse is controlled in part by the reuptake of dopamine by the transmitting neuron. Cocaine blocks the removal of dopamine from a synapse; the resulting buildup of dopamine causes continuous stimulation of the receiving neurons.

Once a psychoactive drug reaches the brain, it acts on one or more neurotransmitters, either increasing or decreasing their concentration and actions. Cocaine, for example, affects dopamine, a neurotransmitter thought to play a key role in the process of reinforcement—the brain's way of telling itself "That's good; do the same thing again." As described in Chapter 3, when a neurotransmitter is released by one neuron to signal another neuron, its level or concentration is controlled in part by the reuptake or resorption of the neurotransmitter by the releasing neuron. Cocaine inhibits the resorption of dopamine, thereby increasing the concentration of dopamine in the synapse and lengthening the time of its action (Figure 9-2). The euphoria produced by cocaine is thought to be a result of its effect on dopamine. Heroin, nicotine, alcohol, and amphetamines also affect dopamine levels through their effects on the brain.

The duration of a drug's effect depends on many factors and may range from 5 minutes (crack cocaine) to 12 or more hours (LSD). As drugs circulate through the body, they are metabolized by the liver and eventually excreted by the kidneys in urine. Small amounts may also be eliminated in other ways, including in sweat, in breast milk, and via the lungs.

Drug Factors

When different drugs or dosages produce different effects, the differences are usually caused by one or more of five different drug factors:

1. The **pharmacological properties** of a drug are its overall effects on a person's body chemistry, behavior, and psychology. The pharmacological properties also include the amount of a drug required to exert various effects, the time course of these effects, and other characteristics, such as a drug's chemical composition.

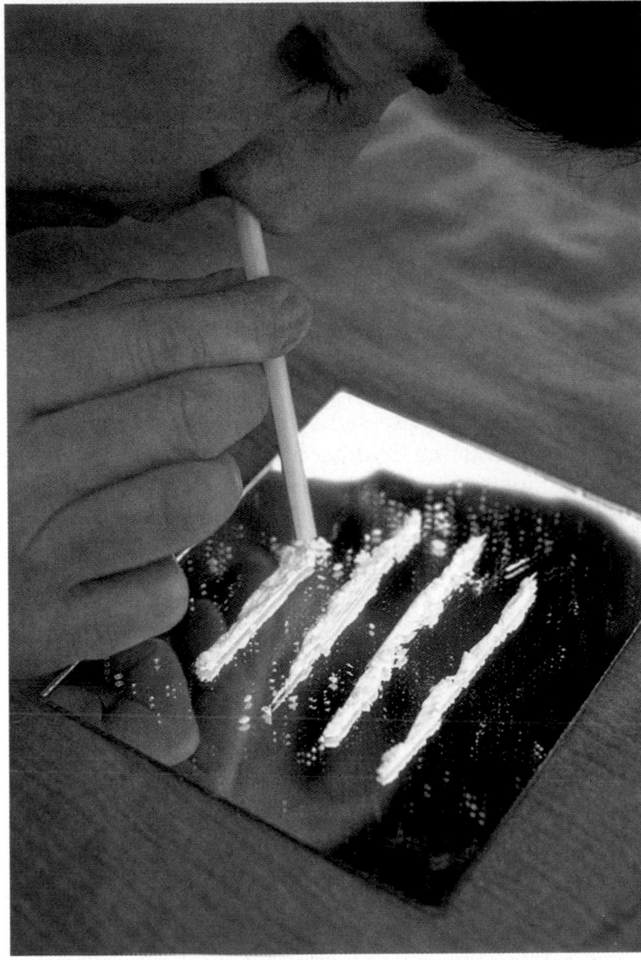

Method of use is one variable in the overall effect of a drug on the body. Sniffing, or snorting, cocaine produces effects in 2–3 minutes. With other methods, such as injecting it intravenously, inhaling vapors, or smoking crack, the effects of cocaine are felt within seconds.

2. The **dose-response function** is the relationship between the amount of drug taken and the type and intensity of the resulting effect. Many psychological effects of drugs reach a plateau in the dose-response function, so that increasing the dose does not increase the effect any further. With LSD, for example, the maximum changes in perception occur at a certain dose, and no further changes in perception take place if higher doses are taken. However, all drugs have more than one effect, and the dose-response functions usually are different for different effects. This means that increasing the dose of any drug may begin to result in additional effects, which are likely to be increasingly unpleasant or dangerous at high doses.

3. The **time-action function** is the relationship between the time elapsed since a drug was taken and the intensity of its effect. The effects of a drug are greatest when concentrations of the drug in body tissues are changing fastest, especially if they are increasing.

4. The person's *drug use history* may influence the effects of a drug. A given amount of alcohol, for example, will generally affect a habitual drinker less than an occasional drinker. Tolerance to some drugs, such as LSD, builds rapidly. To experience the same effect, a user has to abstain from the drug for a period of time before that dosage will again exert its original effects.

5. The *method of use (or route of administration)* has a direct effect on how strong a response a drug produces. Methods of use include ingestion, inhalation, injection, and absorption through the skin or tissue linings. Drugs are usually injected in one of three ways: intravenously (IV, or mainlining), intramuscularly (IM), or subcutaneously (SC, or skin popping). If a drug is taken by a method that allows the drug to enter the bloodstream and reach the brain rapidly, the effects are usually stronger and the potential for dependence greater than when the method involves slower absorption. For example, injecting a drug intravenously produces stronger effects than swallowing the same drug. Inhaling a drug, such as when tobacco or crack cocaine is smoked, produces very rapid effects on the brain.

User Factors

The second category of factors that determine how a person will respond to a particular drug involves certain physical and psychological characteristics. Body mass is one variable. The effects of a certain dose of a drug on a 100-pound person will be twice as great as on a 200-pound person. Other variables include general health and genetic factors. For example, some people have an inherited ability to rapidly metabolize a cough suppressant called dextromethorphan, which also has psychoactive properties. These people must take a higher-than-normal dose to get a given cough-suppressant effect.

If a person's biochemical state is already altered by another drug, this too can make a difference. Some drugs intensify the effects of other drugs, as is the case with alcohol and sedatives. Some drugs block the effects of other drugs, such as when a tranquilizer is used to relieve anxiety caused by cocaine. Interactions between drugs, including many prescription and OTC medications, can be unpredictable and dangerous.

One physical condition that requires special precautions is pregnancy. It can be risky for a woman to use any drugs at all during pregnancy, including alcohol and common OTC preparations like cough medicine. The risks are greatest during the first trimester, when the fetus's body is rapidly forming and even small biochemical alterations in the mother can have a devastating effect on fetal development. Even later, the fetus is more susceptible than the mother to the adverse effects of any drugs she takes. The fetus may even become physically dependent on a drug being taken by the mother and suffer withdrawal symptoms after birth.

Sometimes a person's response to a drug is strongly influenced by the user's expectations about how he or she will react (the psychological *set*). With large doses, the drug's chemical properties do seem to have the strongest effect on the user's response. But with small doses, psychological (and social) factors are often more important. When people strongly believe that a given drug will affect them a certain way, they are likely to experience those effects regardless of the drug's pharmacological properties. In one study, regular users of marijuana reported a moderate level of intoxication **(high)** after using a cigarette that smelled and tasted like marijuana but contained no THC, the active ingredient in marijuana. This is an example of the **placebo effect**—when a person receives an inert substance yet responds as if it were an active drug. (The placebo effect is discussed in more detail in Chapter 21.) In other studies, subjects who smoked low doses of real marijuana that they believed to be a placebo experienced no effects from the drug. Clearly, the user's expectations had a greater effect on the smokers than the drug itself.

Social Factors

The *setting* is the physical and social environment surrounding the drug use. If a person uses marijuana at home with trusted friends and pleasant music, the effects are likely to be different from the effects if the same dose is taken in an austere experimental laboratory with an impassive research technician. Similarly, the dose of alcohol that produces mild euphoria and stimulation at a noisy, active cocktail party might induce sleepiness and slight depression when taken at home while alone.

REPRESENTATIVE PSYCHOACTIVE DRUGS

What are the major psychoactive drugs, and how do they produce their effects? We discuss six different representative groups in this chapter: (1) opioids, (2) central nervous system depressants, (3) central nervous system stimulants, (4) marijuana and other cannabis products, (5) hallucinogens, and (6) inhalants (Figure 9-3). Some of these drugs are classified according to how they affect the body; others—the opioids and the cannabis products—are classified according to their chemical makeup. (For the sources of selected psychoactive drugs, see Figure 9-1.)

Opioids

Also called *narcotics,* **opioids** are natural or synthetic (laboratory-made) drugs that relieve pain, cause drowsiness, and induce **euphoria.** Especially in small doses, opioids have beneficial medical uses, including pain relief and cough suppression. Opium, morphine, heroin, methadone, codeine, hydrocodone, oxycodone, meperidine, and fentanyl are examples of drugs in this category. Opioids tend to reduce anxiety and produce lethargy, apathy, and an inability to concentrate. Opioid users become less active and less responsive to frustration, hunger, and sexual stimulation. These effects are more pronounced in novice users; with repeated use, many effects diminish.

Opioids are typically injected or absorbed into the body from the stomach, intestines, nasal membranes (from snorting or sniffing), or lungs (from smoking). Effects depend on the method of administration. If brain levels of the drug change rapidly, more immediate effects will result. Although the euphoria associated with opioids is an important factor in their abuse, many people experience a feeling of uneasiness when they first use these drugs. Users also often feel nauseated and vomit, and they may have other unpleasant sensations. Even so, the abuse of opioids often results in dependence. Tolerance can develop rapidly and be pronounced. Withdrawal symptoms include cramps, chills, sweating, nausea, tremors, irritability, and feelings of panic.

Rates of heroin use have always been low, but there are periodic episodes of increased use among some groups. Use among college students remains below 1%, but between 1991 and 2000 heroin use among high school seniors more than doubled, mostly due to increased rates of sniffing or smoking the drug. Although these users avoid the special disease risks of injection drug use, including HIV infection, dependence can readily result from sniffing and smoking heroin. In addition, the potentially high but variable purity of street heroin poses a risk of unintentional overdose. Symptoms of overdose include respiratory depression, coma, and constriction of the pupils; death can result.

Nonmedical use of prescription pain relievers that contain oxycodone and hydorcodone, including Oxycontin and Vicodin, has increased in recent years. When taken as prescribed in tablet form, these drugs treat moderate to severe chronic pain and do not typically lead to abuse. However, like other opioids, use of prescription painkillers can lead to abuse and dependence. Oxycodone and hydrocodone can

Terms

VW

high The subjectively pleasing effects of a drug, usually felt quite soon after the drug is taken.

placebo effect A response to an inert or innocuous medication given in place of an active drug.

opioid Any of several natural or synthetic drugs that relieve pain and cause drowsiness and/or euphoria; examples are opium, morphine, and heroin; also called *narcotic.*

euphoria An exaggerated feeling of well-being.

Category	Representative drugs	Street names	Appearance	Methods of use	Short-term effects
Opioids	Heroin	Dope, H, junk, brown sugar, smack	White/dark brown powder; dark tar or coal-like substance	Injected, smoked, snorted	Relief of anxiety and pain; euphoria; lethargy, apathy, drowsiness, confusion, inability to concentrate; nausea, constipation, respiratory depression
	Opium	Big O, black stuff, hop	Dark brown or black chunks	Swallowed, smoked	
	Morphine	M, Miss Emma, monkey, white stuff	White crystals, liquid solution	Injected, swallowed, smoked	
	Oxycodone, codeine, hydrocodone	Oxy, O.C., killer, Captain Cody, schoolboy, vike	Tablets, powder made from crushing tablets	Swallowed, injected, snorted	
Central nervous system depressants	Barbiturates	Barbs, reds, red birds, yellows, yellow jackets	Colored capsules	Swallowed, injected	Reduced anxiety, mood changes, lowered inhibitions, impaired muscle coordination, reduced pulse rate, drowsiness, loss of consciousness, respiratory depression
	Benzodiazepines (e.g., Valium, Xanax, Rohypnol)	Candy, downers, tranks, roofies, forget-me pill	Tablets	Swallowed, injected	
	Methaqualone	Ludes, quad, quay	Tablets	Injected, swallowed	
	Gamma hydroxy butyrate (GHB)	G, Georgia home boy, grievous bodily harm	Clear liquid, white powder	Swallowed	
Central nervous system stimulants	Amphetamine, methamphet-amine	Bennies, speed, black beauties, uppers, chalk, crank, crystal, ice, meth	Tablets, capsules, white powder, white crystals	Injected, swallowed, smoked, snorted	Increased heart rate, blood pressure, metabolism; increased mental alertness and energy; nervousness, insomnia, impulsive behavior; reduced appetite
	Cocaine, crack cocaine	Blow, C, candy, coke, flake, rock, toot	White powder, beige pellets or rocks	Injected, smoked, snorted	
	Ritalin	JIF, MPH, R-ball, Skippy	Tablets	Injected, swallowed, snorted	
Marijuana and other cannabis products	Marijuana	Dope, grass, joints, Mary Jane, reefer, skunk, weed	Dried leaves and stems	Smoked, swallowed	Euphoria, slowed thinking and reaction time, confusion, anxiety, impaired balance and coordination, increased heart rate
	Hashish	Hash, hemp, boom, gangster	Dark, resin-like compound formed into rocks or blocks	Smoked, swallowed	
Hallucinogens	LSD	Acid, boomers, blotter, yellow sunshines	Blotter paper, liquid, gelatin tabs, pills	Swallowed, absorbed through mouth tissues	Altered states of perception and feeling; nausea; increased heart rate, blood pressure; delirium; impaired motor function; numbness, weakness
	Mescaline (peyote)	Buttons, cactus, mesc	Brown buttons, liquid	Swallowed, smoked	
	Psilocybin	Shrooms, magic mushrooms	Dried mushrooms	Swallowed	
	Ketamine	K, special K, cat valium, vitamin K	Clear liquid, white or beige powder	Injected, snorted, smoked	
	PCP	Angel dust, hog, love boat, peace pill	White to brown powder, tablets	Injected, swallowed, smoked, snorted	
	MDMA (ecstasy)	X, peace, clarity, Adam	Tablets	Swallowed	
Inhalants	Solvents, aerosols, nitrites, anesthetics	Laughing gas, poppers, snappers, whippets	Household products, sprays, glues, paint thinner, petroleum products	Inhaled through nose or mouth	Stimulation, loss of inhibition, slurred speech, loss of motor coordination, loss of consciousness

Figure 9-3 Commonly abused drugs and their effects SOURCES: The Partnership for a Drug-Free America. 2006. *Drug Guide by Name* (http://www.drugfree.org/portal/drug_guide; retrieved August 7, 2006); U.S. Drug Enforcement Agency. 2006. *Photo Library* (http://www.usdoj.gov/dea/photo_library.html; retrieved August 7, 2006); U.S. Drug Enforcement Agency. 2005. *Drug Information* (http://www.usdoj.gov/dea/concern.concern.htm; retrieved August 7, 2006); National Institute on Drug Abuse. 2004. *Commonly Abused Drugs* (http://www.drugabuse.gov/DrugPages/DrugsofAbuse.html; retrieved August 7, 2006).

be abused orally; the long-acting form of oxycodone is also sometimes crushed and snorted or dissolved and injected, providing a powerful heroin-like high. When taken in large doses or combined with other drugs, oxycodone and hydrocodone can cause fatal respiratory depression. A 2006 study reported that overdoses from opioid painkillers kill more people than overdoses from either cocaine or heroin.

Central Nervous System Depressants

Central nervous system **depressants,** also known as **sedative-hypnotics,** slow down the overall activity of the **central nervous system (CNS).** The result can range from mild **sedation** to death, depending on the various factors involved—which drug is used, how it's taken, how tolerant the user is, and so on. CNS depressants include alcohol (discussed in Chapter 10), barbiturates, and other sedatives.

Types The various types of barbiturates are similar in chemical composition and action, but they differ in how quickly and how long they act. Drug users call barbiturates downers or downs and refer to specific brands by names that describe the color and design of the capsules: "reds" or "red devils" for Seconal, "yellows" or "yellow jackets" for Nembutal. People usually take barbiturates in capsules, but they may also inject them.

Antianxiety agents, also called sedatives or **tranquilizers,** include the benzodiazepines such as Xanax, Valium, Librium, clonazepam (Klonopin), and flunitrazepam (Rohypnol, also called roofies). Other CNS depressants include methaqualone (Quaalude), ethchlorvynol (Placidyl), chloral hydrate ("mickey"), and gamma hydroxy butyrate (GHB, or "liquid ecstasy").

Effects CNS depressants reduce anxiety and cause mood changes, impaired muscular coordination, slurring of speech, and drowsiness or sleep. Mental functioning is also affected, but the degree varies from person to person and also depends on the kind of task the person is trying to do. Most people become drowsy with small doses, although a few become more active.

Medical Uses Barbiturates, antianxiety agents, and other sedative-hypnotics are widely used to treat insomnia and anxiety disorders and to control seizures. Some CNS depressants are used for their calming properties in combination with **anesthetics** before operations and other medical or dental procedures.

From Use to Abuse People are usually introduced to CNS depressants either through a medical prescription or through drug-using peers. The use of Rohypnol and GHB is often associated with dance clubs and raves (see the box "Club Drugs"). The abuse of CNS depressants by a medical patient may begin with repeated use for insomnia and progress to dependence through increasingly larger doses at night, coupled with a few capsules at stressful times during the day.

Most CNS depressants, including alcohol, can lead to classical physical dependence. Tolerance, sometimes for up to 15 times the usual dose, can develop with repeated use. Tranquilizers have been shown to produce physical dependence even at ordinary prescribed doses. Withdrawal symptoms can be more severe than those accompanying opioid dependence and are similar to the DTs of alcoholism (see Chapter 10). They may begin as anxiety, shaking, and weakness but may turn into convulsions and possibly cardiovascular collapse and death.

While intoxicated, people on depressants cannot function very well. They are mentally confused and are frequently obstinate, irritable, and abusive. Even prescription use of benzodiazepines has been associated with an increased risk of automobile crashes. After long-term use, depressants like alcohol can lead to generally poor health and brain damage, with impaired ability to reason and make judgments.

Overdosing with CNS Depressants Too much depression of the central nervous system slows respiration and may stop it entirely. CNS depressants are particularly dangerous in combination with another depressant, such as alcohol. People who combine depressants with alcohol account for thousands of emergency room visits and hundreds of overdose deaths each year. Rohypnol is ten times more potent than Valium and can be fatal if combined with alcohol. GHB is often produced clandestinely, resulting in widely varying degrees of purity; it has been responsible for many poisonings and a number of deaths.

In recent surveys, about 3% of college students report having used a CNS depressant (other than alcohol) within the past month.

Central Nervous System Stimulants

CNS **stimulants** speed up the activity of the nervous or muscular system. Under their influence, the heart rate accelerates, blood pressure rises, blood vessels constrict, the pupils of the eyes and the bronchial tubes dilate, and gastric and adrenal secretions increase. There is greater muscular tension and sometimes an increase in motor activity.

Terms

VW

depressant, or sedative-hypnotic A drug that decreases nervous or muscular activity, causing drowsiness or sleep.

central nervous system (CNS) The brain and spinal cord.

sedation The induction of a calm, relaxed, often sleepy state.

tranquilizer A CNS depressant that reduces tension and anxiety.

anesthetic A drug that produces a loss of sensation with or without a loss of consciousness.

stimulant A drug that increases nervous or muscular activity.

In Focus

Club Drugs

Club drugs include a variety of very different drugs that are part of the popular dance culture of clubs and raves—all-night dance parties held in fields or abandoned buildings. Some people refer to club drugs as soft drugs because they see them as recreational—more for the casual, weekend user—rather than as addictive. But club drugs have many potential negative effects and are particularly potent and unpredictable when mixed with alcohol. Substitute drugs are often sold in place of club drugs, putting users at risk for taking dangerous combinations of unknown drugs.

MDMA *(ecstasy, E, X, XTC, Adam, hug drug, lover's speed):* Taken in pill form, MDMA (methylenedioxymethamphetamine) is a stimulant with mildly hallucinogenic and amphetamine-like effects. Users may experience euphoria, increased energy, and a heightened sense of belonging. In club settings, using MDMA can produce dangerously high body temperature and potentially fatal dehydration; some users experience confusion, depression, anxiety, paranoia, muscle tension, involuntary teeth clenching, blurred vision, nausea, and seizures. Even low doses can affect concentration, judgment, and driving ability. Tolerance can develop, leading users to take the drug more frequently (on a daily basis), to use higher doses, or to combine MDMA with other drugs, including Prozac, to enhance the drug's effects. A recent study demonstrated that loud music may prolong ecstasy's effects. This may explain, in part, ecstasy's popularity as a club drug. In addition to MDMA, many ecstasy tablets include other drugs such as methamphetamine, ephedrine, or cocaine. At high doses or mixed with other drugs, MDMA is extremely dangerous; most deaths linked to MDMA have occurred as a result of multidrug toxicity or traumatic injuries.

MDMA increases the activity of three neurotransmitters: serotonin, dopamine, and norepinephrine. Increases in serotonin are likely the cause of the drug's mood-elevating effects, but use of MDMA can deplete the brain of serotonin and may cause an emotional let-down (sadness, irritability, etc.) in the days following use. Animal studies have found that moderate to high doses of MDMA are toxic to nerve cells producing serotonin and may cause long-lasting damage; human studies are ongoing. MDMA users perform worse than nonusers on complex cognitive tasks of memory, attention, and general intelligence. Long-term effects may include physical symptoms and psychological problems such as confusion or paranoia. Research suggests that pregnant women who use MDMA are at increased risk for having a baby with congenital malformations and long-term impairment in memory and other cognitive functions.

LSD *(acid, boomers, yellow sunshines, red dragon):* A popular and potent hallucinogen, LSD (lysergic acid diethylamide) is sold in tablets or capsules, in liquid form, or on small squares of paper called blotters. LSD increases heart rate and body temperature and may cause nausea, tremors, sweating, numbness, and weakness. (See p. 256 for more on LSD.)

Ketamine *(special K, vitamin K, K, cat valium, jet):* A veterinary anesthetic that can be taken in powdered or liquid form, ketamine may cause hallucinations and impaired attention and memory. At higher doses, ketamine can cause delirium, amnesia, high blood pressure, and potentially fatal respiratory problems. Tolerance to ketamine develops rapidly.

GHB *(Georgia home boy, G, grievous bodily harm, liquid ecstasy):* GHB (gamma hydroxybutyrate) can be produced in clear liquid, white powder, tablet, and capsule form; it is often made in basement chemistry labs, where toxic substances may unintentionally be added or produced. GHB is a CNS depressant that in large doses or when taken in combination with alcohol or other depressants can cause sedation, loss of consciousness, respiratory arrest, and death. GHB may cause prolonged and potentially life-threatening withdrawal symptoms. Some products sold as dietary supplements for bodybuilding, weight loss, or insomnia contain the chemically similar compounds GBL (gamma butyrolactone) or BD (butanediol). It is illegal to sell products containing GHB, GBL, or BD for human consumption. The FDA has issued several warnings to prevent such items from being sold to the public.

Rohypnol *(roofies, roche, forget-me pill):* Taken in tablet form, Rohypnol (flunitrazepam) is a sedative that is ten times more potent than Valium. Its effects, which are magnified by alcohol, include reduced blood pressure, dizziness, confusion, gastrointestinal disturbances, and loss of consciousness. Users of Rohypnol may develop physical and psychological dependence on the drug.

An additional problem associated with GHB, Rohypnol, and several other club drugs is their potential use as "date rape drugs." Because they can be added to beverages surreptitiously, these drugs may be unknowingly consumed by intended rape victims. In addition to depressant effects, some drugs also cause *anterograde amnesia,* the loss of memory of things occurring while under the influence of the drug. Because of concern about GHB, Rohypnol, and other similarly abused drugs, Congress passed the "Drug-Induced Rape Prevention and Punishment Act," which increased federal penalties for use of any controlled substance to aid in sexual assault (see Chapter 23).

Small doses usually make people feel more awake and alert, less fatigued and bored. The most common CNS stimulants are cocaine, amphetamines, nicotine (discussed in Chapter 11), ephedrine, and caffeine.

Cocaine Usually derived from the leaves of coca shrubs that grow high in the Andes in South America, cocaine is a potent CNS stimulant. For centuries, natives of the Andes have chewed coca leaves both for pleasure and to increase their endurance. For a short time during the nineteenth century, some physicians were enthusiastic about the use of cocaine to cure alcoholism and addiction to the painkiller morphine. Enthusiasm waned after the adverse side effects became apparent.

Cocaine—also known as coke or snow—quickly produces a feeling of euphoria, which makes it a popular recreational drug. Cocaine use surged in popularity during the early 1980s, when the drug's high price made it a status drug. The introduction of crack cocaine during the 1980s made the drug available in smaller quantities and at lower prices to more people. The typical recreational user shifted rapidly from wealthy professionals snorting powdered cocaine to poor inner-city smokers of crack cocaine. In the general population, cocaine use peaked in 1985 with an estimated 3% of adult Americans reporting use. In recent surveys, about 1% of all adults and 2% of college students surveyed reported using cocaine in the previous month.

METHODS OF USE Cocaine is usually snorted and absorbed through the nasal mucosa or injected intravenously, providing rapid increases of the drug's concentration in the blood and therefore fast, intense effects. Another method of use involves processing cocaine with baking soda and water, yielding the ready-to-smoke form of cocaine known as crack. Crack is typically available as small beads or pellets smokable in glass pipes. The tiny but potent beads can be handled more easily than cocaine powder and marketed in smaller, less expensive doses.

EFFECTS The effects of cocaine are usually intense but short-lived. The euphoria lasts from 5 to 20 minutes and ends abruptly, to be replaced by irritability, anxiety, or slight depression. When cocaine is absorbed via the lungs, by either smoking or inhalation, it reaches the brain in about 10 seconds, and the effects are particularly intense. This is part of the appeal of smoking crack. The effects from IV injections occur almost as quickly—in about 20 seconds. Since the mucous membranes in the nose briefly slow absorption, the onset of effects from snorting takes 2–3 minutes. Heavy users may inject cocaine intravenously every 10–20 minutes to maintain the effects.

The larger the cocaine dose and the more rapidly it is absorbed into the bloodstream, the greater the immediate—and sometimes lethal—effects. Sudden death from cocaine is most commonly the result of excessive CNS stimulation that causes convulsions and respiratory collapse, irregular heartbeat, extremely high blood pressure, blood clots, and possibly heart attack or stroke. Although rare, fatalities can occur in healthy young people; among people age 18–59, cocaine users are seven times more likely than nonusers to have a heart attack. Chronic cocaine use produces inflammation of the nasal mucosa, which can lead to persistent bleeding and ulceration of the septum between the nostrils. The use of cocaine may also cause paranoia and/or aggressiveness.

Although the use of cocaine decreased in the general U.S. population after 1985, cocaine is responsible for more deaths and emergency room visits than any other illicit drug. This presumably reflects the fact that smoking crack is more toxic than snorting powdered cocaine. Most deaths result from people using cocaine in combination with another substance, such as alcohol or heroin.

ABUSE AND DEPENDENCE When steady cocaine users stop taking the drug, they experience a sudden "crash" characterized by depression, agitation, and fatigue, followed by a period of withdrawal. Their depression can be temporarily relieved by taking more cocaine, so its continued use is reinforced. A binge cocaine user may go for weeks or months without using any cocaine and then take large amounts repeatedly. Although not physically dependent, a binge cocaine user who misses work or school and risks serious health consequences is clearly abusing the drug.

COCAINE USE DURING PREGNANCY Cocaine rapidly passes from the mother's bloodstream into the placenta and can have serious effects on the fetus. A woman who uses cocaine during pregnancy is at higher risk for miscarriage, premature labor, and stillbirth. She is more likely to deliver a low-birth-weight baby who has a small head circumference. Her infant may be at increased risk for defects of the genitourinary tract, cardiovascular system, central nervous system, and extremities. It is difficult to pinpoint the effects of cocaine because many women who use cocaine also use tobacco and/or alcohol.

Infants whose mothers use cocaine may also be born intoxicated. They are typically irritable and jittery and do not eat or sleep normally. These characteristics may affect their early social and emotional development because it may be more difficult for adults to interact with them. Cocaine also passes into breast milk and can intoxicate a breastfeeding infant.

Research on the long-term effects of prenatal exposure to cocaine has been inconclusive. Initial findings of devastating effects have not been borne out. Recent studies suggest that prenatal cocaine exposure may cause subtle changes in the brain that affect specific cognitive and motor skills; behavioral problems—disorganization, poor social skills, and hyperactivity—have also been reported. Although fetal cocaine exposure is an important issue, the type and magnitude of effects produced by nicotine are similar, and there are nearly 20 times more infants exposed to cigarettes than to cocaine.

Amphetamines Amphetamines (uppers) are a group of synthetic chemicals that are potent CNS stimulants. Some common drugs in this family are amphetamine (Benzedrine), dextroamphetamine (Dexedrine), and methamphetamine (Methedrine). Popular names for these drugs include "speed," crank, chalk, crystal, and "meth." Crystal methamphetamine (ice), a smokable, high-potency form of methamphetamine, is popular in some cities. Easy to manufacture, ice is cheaper than crack and produces a similar but longer-lasting euphoria. The use of ice can quickly lead to dependence. In a recent survey of high school students, about 2% reported having used ice in the past year (see the box "The Meth Epidemic" on p. 256).

EFFECTS Small doses of amphetamines usually make people feel more alert. Amphetamines generally increase motor activity but do not measurably alter a normal, rested person's ability to perform tasks calling for challenging motor skills or complex thinking. When amphetamines do improve performance, it is primarily by counteracting fatigue and boredom. Amphetamines in small doses also increase heart rate and blood pressure and change sleep patterns.

Amphetamines are sometimes used to curb appetite, but after a few weeks the user develops tolerance and higher doses are necessary. When people stop taking the drug, their appetite usually returns, and they gain back the weight they lost unless they have made permanent changes in eating behavior.

FROM USE TO ABUSE Much amphetamine abuse begins as an attempt to cope with a temporary situation. A student cramming for an exam or an exhausted long-haul truck driver can go a little longer by taking amphetamines, but the results can be disastrous. The likelihood of making bad judgments significantly increases. The stimulating effects may also wear off suddenly, and the user may precipitously feel exhausted or fall asleep ("crash").

Another problem is **state dependence,** the phenomenon whereby information learned in a certain drug-induced state is difficult to recall when the person is not in that same physiological state. Test performance may deteriorate when students use drugs to study and then take tests in their normal, nondrug state. (Users of antihistamines may also experience state dependence.)

Methamphetamine intoxication leads to unsafe and uncharacteristic behavior. It has been linked to high-risk sexual activity and increased rates of STDs, including HIV infection (see Chapter 18 for more information).

DEPENDENCE Repeated use of amphetamines, even in moderate doses, often leads to tolerance and the need for increasingly larger doses. The result can be severe disturbances in behavior, including a temporary state of paranoid **psychosis,** with delusions of persecution and unprovoked violence. If injected in large doses, amphetamines produce a feeling of intense pleasure, followed by sensations of vigor and euphoria that last for several hours. As these feelings wear off, they are replaced by feelings of irritability and vague uneasiness. Long-term use of amphetamines at high doses can cause paranoia, hallucinations, delusions, and incoherence. Methamphetamine users have signs of brain damage similar to those seen in Parkinson's disease patients that appear to persist even after drug use ceases, causing impaired memory and motor coordination. Withdrawal symptoms may include muscle aches and tremors, along with profound fatigue, deep depression, despair, and apathy. Chronic high-dose use is often associated with pronounced psychological cravings and obsessive drug-seeking behavior.

Women who use amphetamines during pregnancy risk premature birth, stillbirth, low birth weight, and early infant death. Babies born to amphetamine-using mothers have a higher incidence of cleft palate, cleft lip, and deformed limbs. They may also experience symptoms of withdrawal from amphetamines.

Ritalin

A stimulant with amphetamine-like effects, Ritalin (methylphenidate) is used to treat attention-deficit/hyperactivity disorder (ADHD). When taken orally at prescribed levels, it has little potential for abuse. When injected or snorted, however, dependence and tolerance can rapidly result. Ritalin abuse among high school and college students began to be reported in the 1990s; in a 2005 survey, 3% of college students reported having used Ritalin in the previous year.

Ephedrine

Amphetamine was made in the 1920s by modifying the chemical ephedrine, which was originally isolated from a Chinese herbal tea. Although somewhat less potent than amphetamine, ephedrine does produce stimulant effects. Ephedrine has been linked to heart arrhythmia, stroke, psychotic reactions, seizures, and some deaths, and it may be particularly dangerous at high doses or when combined with another stimulant such as caffeine. Until 2004, ephedrine was a common ingredient in over-the-counter dietary supplements for weight loss. But following the publication of studies about its dangers, the FDA banned the sale of ephedrine; the ban was upheld by a U.S. Court of appeals in 2006.

Caffeine

Caffeine is probably the most popular psychoactive drug and also one of the most ancient. It is found in coffee, tea, cocoa, soft drinks, headache remedies, and OTC preparations like NōDōz. In ordinary doses, caffeine produces greater alertness and a sense of well-being. It also decreases feelings of fatigue or boredom; using caffeine may enable a person to keep at physically exhausting or repetitive tasks longer. Such use is usually followed, however, by a sudden letdown. Caffeine does not noticeably influence a person's ability to perform complex mental tasks unless fatigue, boredom, or other factors have already affected normal performance.

Caffeine mildly stimulates the heart and respiratory system, increases muscular tremor, and enhances gastric

Terms

state dependence A situation in which information learned in a drug-induced state is difficult to recall when the effect of the drug wears off.

psychosis A severe mental disorder characterized by a distortion of reality; symptoms might include delusions or hallucinations.

Vw

secretion. Higher doses may cause nervousness, anxiety, irritability, headache, disturbed sleep, and gastric irritation or peptic ulcers. In people with high blood pressure, caffeine can cause blood pressure to rise even further above normal; in people with type 2 diabetes, caffeine may cause glucose and insulin levels to rise after meals. Some people, especially children, are quite vulnerable to the adverse effects of caffeine. They become wired: hyperactive and overly sensitive to any stimulation in their environment. In rare instances, the disturbance is so severe that there is misperception of their surroundings—a toxic psychosis.

Drinks containing caffeine are rarely harmful for most individuals, but some tolerance develops, and withdrawal symptoms of irritability, headaches, and even mild depression do occur. Thus, although we don't usually think of caffeine as a dependence-producing drug, for some people it is. People can usually avoid problems by simply decreasing their daily intake of caffeine (Figure 9-4); if intake is decreased gradually, withdrawal symptoms can be reduced or avoided. About 80–90% of American adults consume caffeine regularly; the average daily intake is about 280 mg.

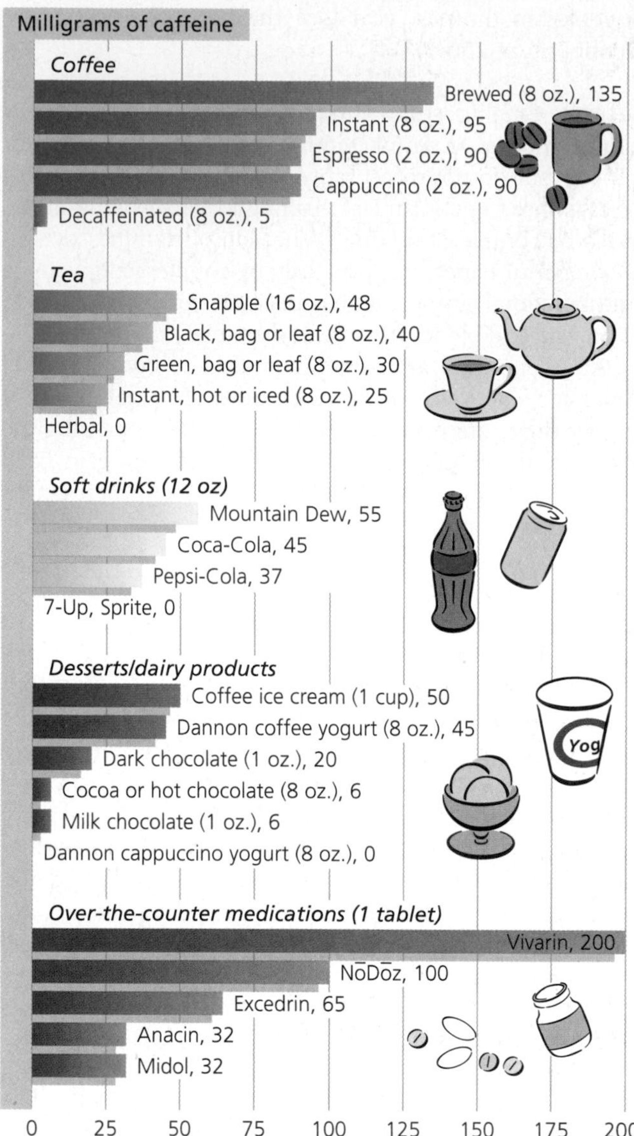

Figure 9-4 Common sources of caffeine. The caffeine content of products varies with the brand and preparation method; the values shown here are averages. SOURCES: McCusker, R. R., B. A. Goldberger, and E. J. Cone. 2006. Caffeine content of energy drinks, carbonated sodas, and other beverages. *Journal of Analytic Toxicology* 30(2): 112–114; Become a bean counter. 2000. *Prevention,* July; International Food Information Council. 1998. *Everything You Need to Know About Caffeine* (http://ific.org/publications/brochures/caffeinebroch.cfm; retrieved August 16, 2006).

Marijuana and Other Cannabis Products

Marijuana is the most widely used illegal drug in the United States (cocaine is second). More than 40% of Americans—more than 90 million—have tried marijuana at least once; among 21–25-year-olds, more than 50% have tried marijuana. In recent surveys, more than 17% of college students report using marijuana within the past month.

Marijuana is a crude preparation of various parts of the Indian hemp plant *Cannabis sativa,* which grows in most parts of the world. THC (tetrahydrocannabinol) is the main active ingredient in marijuana. Based on THC content, the potency of marijuana preparations varies widely. Marijuana plants that grow wild often have less than 1% THC in their leaves, whereas when selected strains are cultivated by separation of male and female plants (*sinsemilla*), the bud leaves from the flowering tops may contain 7–8% THC. Hashish, a potent preparation made from the thick resin that exudes from the leaves, may contain up to 14% THC. These various preparations have all been known and used for centuries, so the frequently heard claim that today's marijuana is more potent than the marijuana of the 1970s is not strictly true. However, a greater proportion of the marijuana sold today is the higher-potency (and more expensive) sinsemilla; hence, the average potency of street marijuana has increased.

Marijuana is usually smoked, but it can also be ingested. The classification of marijuana is a matter of some debate. For this reason, it is treated separately here.

Short-Term Effects and Uses As is true with most psychoactive drugs, the effects of a low dose of marijuana are strongly influenced both by the user's expectations and by past experiences. At low doses, marijuana users typically experience euphoria, a heightening of subjective sensory experiences, a slowing down of the perception of passing time, and a relaxed, laid-back attitude. These pleasant effects are the reason this drug is so widely used. With moderate doses, these effects become stronger, and the user can also expect to have impaired memory function, disturbed thought patterns, lapses of attention, and feelings of **depersonalization,** in which the mind seems to be separated from the body.

The effects of marijuana in higher doses are determined mostly by the drug itself rather than by the user's expectations and setting. Very high doses produce feelings of depersonalization, as well as marked sensory distortion and changes in body image (such as a feeling that the body is very light). Inexperienced users sometimes think these sensations mean they are going crazy and become anxious or even panicky. Such reactions resemble a bad trip on LSD, but they happen much less often, are less severe, and do not last as long. However, unexpected reactions are the leading reason for emergency room visits by users of marijuana or hashish.

Physiologically, marijuana increases heart rate and dilates certain blood vessels in the eyes, which creates the characteristic bloodshot eyes. The user may also feel less inclined toward physical exertion and may feel particularly hungry or thirsty. THC affects parts of the brain controlling balance, coordination, and reaction time; thus marijuana use reduces driving performance. The combination of alcohol and marijuana is even more dangerous: Even a low dose of marijuana, when combined with alcohol, significantly impairs driving performance and increases crash risk.

In 1999, the Institute of Medicine determined that some compounds in marijuana may have legitimate medical use. For example, marijuana has been shown to ease pain, reduce nausea, and increase appetite. These benefits led several states to approve the use of "medical marijuana" by extremely ill patients, with physician monitoring. However, because growing, selling, or possessing marijuana is a federal crime, the Supreme Court has held that state laws permitting medical marijuana use cannot supersede federal law. This means anyone who uses marijuana for medical reasons—even in a state that approves such use—can still be prosecuted under federal drug laws. The ethical debates over medical marijuana use continue, as do court cases.

Long-Term Effects The most probable long-term effect of smoking marijuana is respiratory damage, including impaired lung function and chronic bronchial irritation. Although there is no evidence linking marijuana use to lung cancer, it may cause changes in lung tissue that promote cancer growth. Marijuana users may be at increased risk for emphysema and cancer of the head and neck; among people with chronic conditions like cancer and AIDS, marijuana use is associated with increased risk of fatal lung infections. (These negative effects from smoking marijuana are key reasons why the Institute of Medicine report on medical marijuana recommended the development of alternative methods of delivering the potentially beneficial compounds in marijuana.) Heavy users may experience learning problems, as well as subtle impairments of attention and memory that may or may not be reversible following long-term abstinence. Long-term use may also decrease testosterone levels and sperm counts and increase sperm abnormalities.

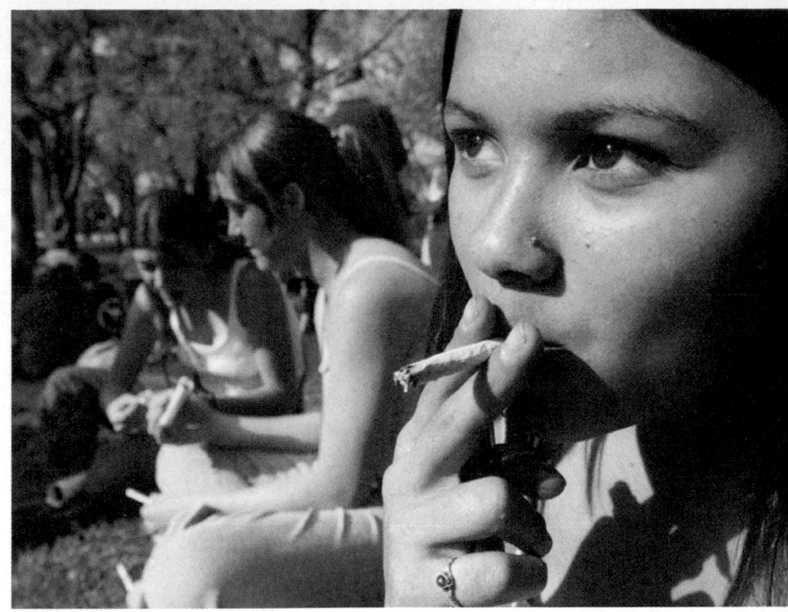

Marijuana is the most widely used illegal drug in the United States. At low doses, marijuana users experience euphoria and a relaxed attitude.

Heavy marijuana use during pregnancy may cause impaired fetal growth and development, low birth weight, and increased risk of ectopic pregnancy. Marijuana may act synergistically with alcohol to increase the damaging effects of alcohol on the fetus. THC rapidly enters breast milk and may impair an infant's early motor development.

Dependence Regular users of marijuana can develop tolerance; some develop dependence, and researchers estimate that 1.5% of Americans meet the APA criteria for marijuana dependence. Withdrawal symptoms may occur in the majority of dependent or heavy users; common symptoms include anger or aggression, irritability, nervousness or restlessness, sleep difficulties, and decreased appetite or weight loss.

Hallucinogens

Hallucinogens are a group of drugs whose predominant pharmacological effect is to alter the user's perceptions, feelings, and thoughts. Hallucinogens include LSD (lysergic acid diethylamide), mescaline, psilocybin, STP (4-methyl-2,5-dimethoxyamphetamine), DMT (dimethyltryptamine), MDMA (3,4-methylene-dioxymethamphetamine), ketamine, and PCP (phencyclidine). These drugs are most commonly ingested or smoked.

Terms

depersonalization A state in which a person loses the sense of his or her reality or perceives his or her body as unreal.

hallucinogen Any of several drugs that alter perception, feelings, or thoughts; examples are LSD, mescaline, and PCP.

In the News

The Meth Epidemic

As its name suggests, methamphetamine is similar to the stimulant amphetamine. Meth, however, is more addictive and dangerous than most forms of amphetamine because it is more toxic and its effects last longer. Methamphetamine is highly addictive; many casual users rapidly become regular users.

Methamphetamine has several street names, including "speed" and "chalk." One form of meth—methamphetamine hydrochloride—is known as "ice," "crystal," and "glass." Meth is available in powder and crystal form and can be swallowed, snorted, smoked, or injected. Once taken, the drug causes the brain to release high amounts of dopamine, a key neurotransmitter.

What Are Meth's Effects?

By stimulating dopamine activity in the brain, meth increases the user's ability to stay awake and perform physical activity. Meth's other short-term effects can include euphoria, rapid breathing, increased body temperature (hyperthermia), insomnia, tremors, anxiety, and convulsions.

In the long term, methamphetamine's effects can be devastating. Severe weight loss, heart attack, stroke, hallucinations, violence, paranoia, and psychotic behavior have all been linked to meth addiction. Brain damage similar to that found in Parkinson's disease and Alzheimer's disease has been reported in long-term meth users. Meth use causes extensive tooth decay and tooth loss, a condition referred to as "meth mouth." The drug takes a severe toll on the user's heart, increasing heart rate and blood pressure, damaging blood vessels, and causing irregular heartbeat. Such cardiovascular damage can be fatal.

Who Uses Meth?

The National Survey on Drug Use and Health reported that more than half a million Americans aged 12 and older were current users of methamphetamine in 2005. The researchers warned that this number is probably an underestimate due to survey wording; other estimates put the number of regular meth users closer to 1.5 million. The highest rates of use are among young adults aged 18–25.

Although methamphetamine is often called "poor man's cocaine," its users are not all poor or poorly educated; rather, they span the socioeconomic spectrum. The drug spread east from the West Coast and is now found in all 50 states, in rural, suburban, and urban areas. Many drug enforcement and government officials say methampethamine is the number-one drug problem in the United States today.

Related Issues

Along with the physical problems suffered by meth users, the drug has led to a growing array of social and emotional problems. For example, because meth diminishes the user's judgment, many meth addicts engage in unsafe sex—often with injection drug users—when they're high. As a result, meth users face an increased risk of infection from a variety of transmittable diseases, especially HIV and hepatitis C. Meth use is also associated with domestic violence and family breakdown.

Another problem unique to meth is its do-it-yourself appeal to users and dealers. The drug is relatively easy to make, using commonly available chemicals, and clandestine meth labs in residential living rooms and basements have sprung up across the country. One of the chemicals used in making meth is pseudoephedrine, a drug found in products used to relive nasal or sinus congestion, such as Sudafed and other cold and allergy medications. To limit access to this drug, Congress passed the Combat Methamphetamine Epidemic Act of 2005 as part of the Patriot Act, requiring behind-the-counter sale of products containing pseudoepinehprine and two other drugs used to make meth. Quantities that can be purchased are limited, and customers must show a photo ID and sign a logbook. Cold and allergy products containing ingredients not used in meth production are still available on the shelves, such as Sudafed PE.

Methamphetamine production is also very dangerous. The use of caustic and highly explosive chemicals puts meth "cooks" at risk for injury and death from explosion and fire.

Treatment Options

At this time, there are few treatment options for meth addiction. Cognitive behavioral therapy is widely viewed as the best approach; therapy helps users identify the root causes of their addiction and teaches them skills needed to effectively quit using the drug. In some cases, antidepressants or antianxiety medications are prescribed, but there currently is no single effective pharmacological treatment for methamphetamine addiction. In studies, the drug Prometa has been effective in helping meth addicts break their addiction. Further studies are under way.

LSD LSD is one of the most powerful psychoactive drugs. Tiny doses will produce noticeable effects in most people, such as an altered sense of time, visual disturbances, an improved sense of hearing, mood changes, and distortions in how people perceive their bodies. Dilation of the pupils and slight dizziness, weakness, and nausea may also occur. With larger doses, users may experience a phenomenon known as **synesthesia,** feelings of depersonalization, and other alterations in the perceived relationship between the self and external reality.

Many hallucinogens induce tolerance so quickly that after only one or two doses their effects decrease substantially. The user must then stop taking the drug for several days before his or her system can be receptive to it again. These drugs cause little drug-seeking behavior and no physical dependence or withdrawal symptoms.

The immediate effects of low doses of hallucinogens are largely determined by expectations and setting. Many effects are hard to describe because they involve subjective and unusual dimensions of awareness—the **altered states of consciousness** for which these drugs are famous. For this reason, hallucinogens have acquired a certain aura not associated with other drugs. People have taken LSD in search of a religious or mystical experience or in the hope of exploring new worlds. During the 1960s, some psychiatrists gave LSD to their patients to help them talk about their repressed feelings.

A severe panic reaction, which can be terrifying in the extreme, can result from taking any dose of LSD. It is impossible to predict when a panic reaction will occur. Some LSD users report having had hundreds of pleasurable and ecstatic experiences before having a bad trip, or bummer. If the user is already in a serene mood and feels no anger or hostility and if he or she is in secure surroundings with trusted companions, a bad trip may be less likely, but a tranquil experience is not guaranteed.

Even after the drug's chemical effects have worn off, spontaneous flashbacks and other psychological disturbances can occur. **Flashbacks** are perceptual distortions and bizarre thoughts that occur after the drug has been entirely eliminated from the body. Although they are relatively rare phenomena, flashbacks can be extremely distressing. They are often triggered by specific psychological cues associated with the drug-taking experience, such as certain mood states or even types of music.

During the 1970s, researchers claimed that LSD damages chromosomes. But later evidence indicates that LSD in moderate doses, at least the pure LSD produced in the laboratory, does not damage chromosomes, cause detectable genetic damage, or produce birth defects.

Other Hallucinogens Most other hallucinogens have the same general effects as LSD, but there are some variations. For example, a DMT or ketamine high does not last as long as an LSD high; an STP high lasts longer. MDMA has both hallucinogenic and amphetamine-like properties. Tolerance to MDMA develops quickly, and high doses can cause anxiety, delusions, and paranoia. (See the box "Club Drugs" on p. 251 for more on MDMA.)

PCP, also known as "angel dust," "hog," and "peace pill," reduces and distorts sensory input, especially **proprioception,** the sensation of body position and movement; it creates a state of sensory deprivation. PCP was initially used as an anesthetic but was unsatisfactory because it caused agitation, confusion, and delirium (loss of contact with reality). Because it can be easily made, PCP is often available illegally and is sometimes used as an inexpensive replacement for other psychoactive drugs. The effects of ketamine are similar to those of PCP—confusion, agitation, aggression, and lack of coordination—but they tend to be less predictable. Tolerance to either drug can develop rapidly.

Mescaline, derived from the peyote cactus, is the ceremonial drug of the Native American Church. It causes effects similar to LSD, including altered perception and feeling; increased body temperature, heart rate, and blood pressure; weakness and trembling; and sleeplessness. Obtaining mescaline is expensive, so most street mescaline is diluted LSD or a mixture of other drugs. Hallucinogenic effects can be obtained from certain mushrooms (*Psilocybe mexicana,* or "magic mushrooms"), certain morning glory seeds, nutmeg, jimsonweed, and other botanical products, but unpleasant side effects, such as dizziness, have limited the popularity of these products.

Inhalant use is difficult to monitor and control because inhalants are found in many inexpensive and legal products. Low doses of inhalants may cause a user to feel slightly stimulated; higher concentrations can cause a loss of consciousness, heart failure, and death.

Inhalants

Inhaling certain chemicals can produce effects ranging from heightened pleasure to delirium and death. Inhalants fall into several major groups: (1) volatile solvents, which are found in products such as paint thinner, glue, and gasoline; (2) aerosols, which are sprays that contain propellants and solvents; (3) nitrites, such as butyl nitrite and amyl nitrite; and (4) anesthetics, which include nitrous oxide, or laughing gas. Inhalant use tends to be highest among younger adolescents and declines with age; in surveys, about 4% of eighth graders, 2% of twelfth graders, and 0.6% of college students report using inhalants in the past month.

Inhalant use is difficult to control because inhalants are easy to obtain. They are present in a variety of seemingly

Terms

VW

synesthesia A condition in which a stimulus evokes not only the sensation appropriate to it but also another sensation of a different character, such as when a color evokes a specific smell.

altered states of consciousness Profound changes in mood, thinking, and perception.

flashback A perceptual distortion or bizarre thought that recurs after the chemical effects of a drug have worn off.

proprioception The sensation of body position and movement, from muscles, joints, and skin.

harmless products, from dessert-topping sprays to underarm deodorants, that are both inexpensive and legal. Using the drugs also requires no illegal or suspicious paraphernalia. Inhalant users get high by sniffing, snorting, "bagging" (inhaling fumes from a plastic bag), or "huffing" (placing an inhalant-soaked rag in the mouth).

Although different in makeup, nearly all inhalants produce effects similar to those of anesthetics, which slow down body functions. Low doses may cause users to feel slightly stimulated; at higher doses, users may feel less inhibited and less in control. Sniffing high concentrations of the chemicals in solvents or aerosol sprays can cause a loss of consciousness, heart failure, and death. High concentrations of any inhalant can also cause death from suffocation by displacing the oxygen in the lungs and central nervous system. Deliberately inhaling from a bag or in a closed area greatly increases the chances of suffocation. Other possible effects of the excessive or long-term use of inhalants include damage to the nervous system (impaired perception, reasoning, memory, and muscular coordination); hearing loss; increased risk of cancer; and damage to the liver, kidneys, and bone marrow.

DRUG USE: THE DECADES AHEAD

Drug research will undoubtedly provide new information, new treatments, and new chemical combinations in the decades ahead. New psychoactive drugs may present unexpected possibilities for therapy, social use, and abuse. Making honest and unbiased information about drugs available to everyone, however, may cut down on their abuse. Misinformation about the dangers of drugs—using scare tactics—can lead some people to disbelieve any reports of drug dangers, no matter how soundly based and well documented they are.

Although the use of some drugs, both legal and illegal, has declined dramatically since the 1970s, the use of others has held steady or increased. Mounting public concern has led to great debate and a wide range of opinions about what should be done. Efforts to combat the problem include workplace drug testing, tougher law enforcement and prosecution, and treatment and education. With drugs entering the country on a massive scale from South America, Southeast Asia, and elsewhere and being distributed through tightly controlled drug-smuggling organizations and street gangs, it remains to be seen how effective any program will be.

Drugs, Society, and Families

The economic cost of drug use is staggering. Each year, Americans spend over $50 billion on illegal drugs, with an additional $100 billion going to cover enforcement, prevention, treatment, lost wages, and drug-related injuries and crime. But the costs are more than just financial; they are also paid in human pain and suffering.

The relationship between drugs and crime is complex. The criminal justice system is inundated with people accused of crimes related to drug possession, sale, or use. More than 2 million arrests are made each year for drug and alcohol violations, and over 100,000 people are in jail for violating drug laws. Many assaults and murders are committed when people try to acquire or protect drug territories, settle disputes about drugs, or steal from dealers. Violence and the use of guns are more common in neighborhoods where drug trafficking is prevalent. Addicts commit more robberies and burglaries than criminals not on drugs. People under the influence of drugs, especially alcohol, are more likely to commit violent crimes like rape and murder than people who do not use drugs. Although often associated with poor inner-city areas and ethnic minorities, drug-related problems affect all groups and every area of the country (see the box "Drug Use and Ethnicity: Risk Factors and Protective Factors").

Drug use is also a health care issue for society. In the United States, illegal drug use leads to more than 500,000 emergency room admissions and nearly 20,000 deaths annually. Although it is in the best interest of society to treat addicts who want help, there is not nearly enough space in treatment facilities to help the estimated 5 million Americans in need of immediate treatment. Drug addicts who want to quit, especially those among the urban poor, often have to wait a year or more for acceptance into a residential care or other treatment program.

Drug abuse also takes a toll on individuals and families. Children born to women who use drugs such as alcohol, tobacco, or cocaine may have long-term health problems. Drug use in families can become a vicious cycle. Observing adults around them using drugs, children assume it is an acceptable way to deal with problems. Problems such as abuse, neglect, lack of opportunity, and unemployment become contributing factors to drug use and serve to perpetuate the cycle.

Legalizing Drugs

Pointing out that many of the social problems associated with drugs are related to prohibition rather than to the effects of the drugs themselves, some people have argued for various forms of drug legalization or decriminalization. Proposals range from making drugs such as marijuana and heroin available by prescription to allowing licensed dealers to sell some of these drugs to adults. Proponents argue that crimes by drug users are usually committed to buy drugs that cost relatively more than alcohol and tobacco because they are produced illegally and that making some currently illicit drugs legal—but putting controls on them similar to those used for alcohol, tobacco, and prescription drugs—could eliminate many of the problems related to drug use.

Opponents of drug legalization argue that allowing easier access to drugs would expose many more people to

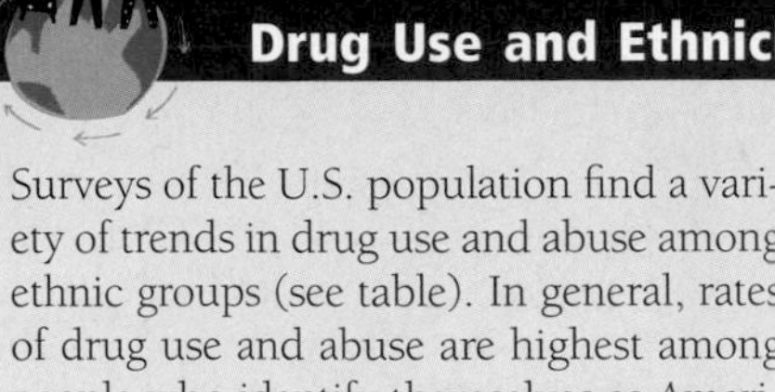

Drug Use and Ethnicity: Risk Factors and Protective Factors

Surveys of the U.S. population find a variety of trends in drug use and abuse among ethnic groups (see table). In general, rates of drug use and abuse are highest among people who identify themselves as American Indians or Alaska Natives or as being of two races; rates are lowest among Asian Americans. In addition to the general trends shown in the table, there are also trends relating to specific drugs; for example, hallucinogen use is relatively prevalent among whites and Latinos, inhalant use among Native Hawaiians and Pacific Islander Americans.

However, as is true for many areas of health, ethnic trends are influenced by a complex interplay of other factors:

- *Educational status*: Adults with four or more years of college are more likely to have *tried* illicit drugs than are people of the same age who never finished high school, but *current* drug use is lower among college graduates than among people with less education. Among teens, poor school performance is associated with increased risk for illicit drug use.
- *Employment status:* Most adult drug users are employed, but rates of current drug use are much higher among people who are unemployed or who work part-time compared with those who are employed full-time.
- *Parental education and socioeconomic status:* Students from poor families have higher rates of *early* drug use compared with students from wealthier families, but by the twelfth grade, the differences disappear. Socioeconomic status and parental education are closely linked.
- *Geographic area:* Current drug use in the United States is highest in the West and Northeast; drug use is also somewhat higher in metropolitan and urban areas compared with more rural areas. People living in communities with high rates of poverty, crime, and unemployment have higher than average rates of drug use and abuse. Specific drugs may also be more available—and their abuse more prevalent—in certain regions or communities.

Strong cultural identity is associated with reduced risk of drug use and abuse among all groups. Researchers hope to learn more about other protective factors by studying groups that have relatively low rates of drug use and abuse, especially Asian Americans of all ages and African American adolescents. Some factors believed to contribute to lower rates of drug use among these groups include the following:

- *Parental and community disapproval of drug and alcohol use:* Parents of African American and Asian American children tend to have more restrictive drug and alcohol use norms than white parents, and black parents tend to monitor their children's activities and friendships more closely than white parents. Parental disapproval of drug use is often tied to greater perceived risk of drug use—and lower rates of drug use—among teens.
- *Close family ties:* Asian American teens are the likeliest to come from intact homes. Black teens, although least likely to come from intact homes, often come from single-parent households with close extended family ties. Respect for authority and family loyalty are strongly valued among many Asian American populations. Teens from cohesive and stable families are less likely to use drugs.
- *Focus on schooling and education:* Teens from families who value education and where parents help with homework and limit weeknight time with friends have lower rates of drug use. Asian Americans have twice the rate of college graduation compared with other groups.

SOURCES: Johnston, L. D., et al. 2006. *Monitoring the Future: National Results on Adolescent Drug Use: Overview of Key Findings, 2005.* Bethesda, Md.: National Institute on Drug Abuse; Office of Applied Studies, Substance Abuse and Mental Health Services Administration. 2006. *Results from the 2005 National Survey on Drug Use and Health* (http://www.oas.samhsa.gov, retrieved November 17, 2006); Drug Policy Alliance. 2006. *Race and the Drug War: Affected Communities* (http://www.drugpolicy.org/communities/race/; retrieved August 8, 2006); National Asian Pacific American Families Against Substance Abuse. 2006. *Fact Sheet: Multiracial Asian American and Pacific Islander Alcohol, Tobacco & Other Drugs* (http://www.napafasa.org/resources/doc/Multiracial AAPI Fact Sheet.pdf; retrieved August 8, 2006); National Center on Addiction and Substance Abuse at Columbia University. 2003. *The Formative Years: Pathways to Substance Abuse Among Girls and Young Women Ages 8–22* (http://www.casacolumbia.org/Absolutenm/articlefiles/151006.pdf; retrieved August 8, 2006).

National Survey Results

	Lifetime Drug Use	Past Year Drug Use	Past Month Drug Use: Age 12–17	Past Month Drug Use: Age 18–25	Past Month Drug Use: Age 26 and Older	Past Month Drug Use: All Ages	Past Year Illicit Drug Dependence
Whites	49.1	15.0	10.1	21.6	5.7	8.1	4.9
African Americans	43.3	14.6	11.0	18.7	6.3	9.7	4.8
Latinos	35.4	12.9	9.4	14.1	4.7	7.6	5.1
Asian Americans	24.3	6.9	3.3	8.1	1.7	3.1	1.6
American Indians and Alaska Natives	58.4	26.2	19.2	24.2	7.9	12.8	12.7
Native Hawaiians and Pacific Islander Americans*	51.0	18.5	n/a	n/a	n/a	8.7	5.6
Two or more races	54.9	20.1	9.7	30.7	10.1	12.2	8.7

*2003 data; no data available for 2004.

possible abuse and dependence. Drugs would be cheaper and easier to obtain, and drug use would be more socially acceptable. Legalizing drugs could cause an increase in drug use among children and teenagers. Opponents point out that alcohol and tobacco are major causes of disease and death in our society and that they should not be used as models for other practices.

Drug Testing

One of the most controversial issues in American politics is drug testing in the workplace. It has been estimated that as many as 10% of workers use psychoactive drugs on the job. For some occupations, such as air traffic controllers, truck drivers, and train engineers, drug use can create significant hazards, sometimes involving hundreds of people. Some people believe that the dangers are so great that all workers should be tested and that anyone found with traces of drugs in the blood or urine should be either fired or treated. Others insist that this would violate people's right to privacy and to freedom from unreasonable search, guaranteed by the Fourth Amendment. Opponents point out that most jobs do not involve hazards, so employees who take drugs are not any more dangerous than employees who do not.

Despite the expense, many employers now test their employees, and the U.S. armed forces test military personnel regularly. People in jobs involving transportation—truck drivers, bus drivers, train engineers, airline pilots—are required by federal law to be tested regularly to ensure public safety. The primary criterion leading most companies to use drug testing is the company's liability if an employee under the influence of a drug makes a mistake that could potentially harm others.

Most drug testing involves a urine test; a test for alcohol involves a blood test or a breath test. The accuracy of these tests has improved in recent years, so there are fewer opportunities for people to cheat or for the tests to yield inaccurate results. If a person tests positive for drugs, the employer may provide drug counseling or treatment, suspend the employee until he or she tests negative, or fire the individual.

The FDA has approved several over-the-counter home drug testing kits designed to allow parents to check their children for drug use. Urine samples are collected at home; preliminary results may be available immediately, but final results require that the sample be sent to a laboratory for analysis. Many experts, including the American Academy of Pediatrics, advise against the use of home tests in cases of suspected drug use; instead, they recommend a comprehensive evaluation by a qualified health professional.

Treatment for Drug Dependence

A variety of programs is available to help people break their drug habits, but there is no single best method of treatment. The relapse rate is high for all types of treatment but is similar to the rate of relapse seen in people being treated for diabetes, high blood pressure, and asthma. Numerous studies have shown that being treated is better than not being treated. To be successful, treatment must deal with the reasons behind people's drug abuse and help them develop behaviors, attitudes, and a social support system that will help them remain drug-free.

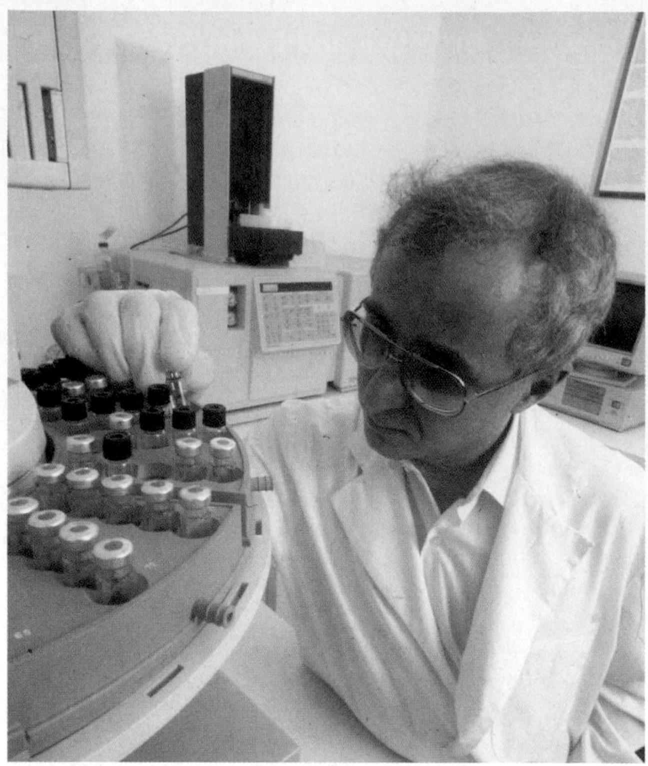

Many companies test current and prospective employees for drug use. Most drug testing involves a urine test that can detect recent use of marijuana, heroin, cocaine, amphetamines, codeine, and many other psychoactive drugs.

Medication-Assisted Treatment Medications are increasingly being used in addiction treatment—to reduce the craving for the abused drug or to block or oppose its effects. Perhaps the best-known medication for drug abuse is methadone, a synthetic drug used as a substitute for heroin. Use of methadone prevents withdrawal reactions and reduces the craving for heroin; it enables dependent people to function normally in social and vocational activities, although they remain dependent on methadone. The narcotic buprenorphine, approved in 2002 for treatment of opioid addiction, also reduces cravings; researchers are studying long-acting forms of this drug, which may be even more effective than use of a daily pill. Many other medications are under study; drugs used specifically in the treatment of nicotine and alcohol dependence are discussed in Chapters 10 and 11.

Medication therapy is relatively simple and inexpensive and is therefore popular among patients, health care providers, and insurance companies. However, the relapse rate is high. Combining drug therapy with psychological and social services improves success rates, underscoring the importance of psychological factors in drug dependence.

Treatment Centers Treatment centers offer a variety of short-term and long-term services, including hospitalization, detoxification, counseling, and other mental health services. The therapeutic community is a specific type of center, a residential program run in a completely drug-free atmosphere. Administered by ex-addicts, these programs use confrontation, strict discipline, and unrelenting peer pressure to attempt to resocialize the addict with a different set of values. Halfway houses, transitional settings between a 24-hour-a-day program and independent living, are an important phase of treatment for some people. Strategies for evaluating programs are given in the box "Choosing a Drug-Treatment Program" on page 262.

Self-Help Groups and Peer Counseling Groups such as Alcoholics Anonymous (AA) and Narcotics Anonymous (NA) have helped many people. People treated in drug substitution programs or substance-abuse treatment centers are often urged or required to join a self-help group as part of their recovery. These groups follow a 12-step program. Group members' first step is to acknowledge that they have a problem over which they have no control. Peer support is a critical ingredient of these programs, and members usually meet at least once a week. Each member is paired with a sponsor to call on for advice and support if the temptation to relapse becomes overwhelming. With such support, thousands of substance-dependent people have been able to recover, remain abstinent, and reclaim their lives. Chapters of AA and NA meet on some college campuses; community-based chapters are listed in the phone book and in local newspapers. (Also see the For More Information section at the end of the chapter.)

Many colleges also have peer counseling programs, in which students are trained to help other students who have drug problems. A peer counselor's role may be as limited as referring a student to a professional with expertise in substance dependence for an evaluation or as involved as helping arrange a leave of absence from school for participation in a drug-treatment program. Most peer counseling programs are founded on principles of strict confidentiality. Peer counselors may also be able to help students who are concerned about a classmate or loved one with an apparent drug problem (see the box "If Someone You Know Has a Drug Problem . . ." on p. 263). Information about peer counseling programs is usually available from the student health center.

Harm Reduction Strategies Recognizing that many attempts at treatment are at first unsuccessful and that a drug-free society may be an unobtainable goal, some experts advocate the use of harm reduction strategies. The goal of harm reduction is to minimize the negative effects of drug use and abuse; a common example is the use of designated drivers to reduce alcohol-related motor vehicle crashes. In terms of illicit drugs, drug substitution programs such as methadone maintenance are one form of harm reduction; although participants remain drug dependent, the negative individual and social consequences of their drug use is reduced. Syringe exchange programs, designed to reduce transmission of HIV and hepatitis C, are another harm reduction approach. Some experts have also suggested free testing of street drugs for purity and potency to help users avoid unintentional toxicity or overdose. Harm reduction strategies are controversial, in part because they measure success not in terms of overall levels of drug use and dependence but rather in terms of the harm caused by drug use in terms of illness, death, and crime.

Codependency Many treatment programs also offer counseling for those who are close to drug abusers. Drug abuse takes a toll on friends and family members, and counseling can help people work through painful feelings of guilt and powerlessness. **Codependency,** in which a person close to the drug abuser is controlled by the abuser's behavior, sometimes develops. Codependent people may come to believe that love, approval, and security are contingent on their taking care of the abuser. People can become codependent naturally because they want to help when someone they love becomes dependent on a drug. They may assume that their good intentions will persuade the drug user to stop.

Codependent people often engage in behaviors that remove or soften the effects of the drug use on the user—so-called *enabling* behaviors. However, the habit of enabling can inhibit a drug-dependent person's recovery because the person never has to experience the consequences of his or her behavior. Often, the enabler is dependent, too—on the patterns of interaction in the relationship. People who need to take care of people often marry people who need to be taken care of. Children in these families often develop the same behavior pattern as one of their parents, by either becoming helpless or becoming a caregiver. For this reason, many treatment programs involve the whole family.

Term

codependency A relationship in which a non–substance-abusing partner or family member is controlled by the abuser's behavior; codependent people frequently engage in enabling behaviors.

Vw

Critical Consumer

Choosing a Drug-Treatment Program

When evaluating different facilities or programs for drug treatment, consider the following issues:

- *What type of treatment or facility is most appropriate?* Intensive outpatient treatment is available through many community mental health centers, as well as through specialized drug-treatment facilities. Such programs typically require several sessions per week, combining individual therapy, group counseling, and attendance at 12-step meetings. Residential, or inpatient, facilities may be associated with a medical facility such as a hospital, or they may be freestanding programs that focus solely on substance-abuse treatment. Some residential treatment programs last longer or cost more per week than many health insurance plans will cover.
- *How will treatment be paid for?* Many health insurance plans limit residential treatment to a maximum of 3 weeks or less. They may also require that you first attempt a less expensive form of treatment before they will approve coverage for a residential facility.
- *Is there likely to be a need for medical support?* Chronic alcoholics or abusers of other CNS depressants may experience life-threatening seizures or other withdrawal symptoms during the first few days of detoxification. Malnutrition is common among substance abusers, and injection drug users may suffer from local infections and bloodborne diseases such as hepatitis or HIV infection. Medical problems such as these are best handled in an inpatient program with good medical support.
- *What is the level of professional training of the staff?* Is there a medical doctor on-site or making frequent visits? Are there trained nurses? Licensed psychologists or social workers? Many successful programs are staffed primarily by recovering alcoholics or drug users. Do those staff members have training and certification as addiction specialists or some other license or certificate?
- *Does the program provide related services, such as family and job counseling and post-treatment follow-up?* These types of services are extremely important for the long-term success of drug-abuse treatment.
- *Can you visit the facility and speak with the staff and clients?* A prospective client and his or her family should be allowed to visit any treatment center or program.

Have you ever been an enabler in a relationship? You may have, if you've ever done any of the following:

- Given someone one more chance to stop abusing drugs, then another, and another . . .
- Made excuses or lied for someone to his or her friends, teachers, or employer
- Joined someone in drug use and blamed others for your behavior
- Loaned money to someone to continue drug use
- Stayed up late waiting for or gone out searching for someone who uses drugs
- Felt embarrassed or angry about the actions of someone who uses drugs
- Ignored the drug use because the person got defensive when you brought it up
- Not confronted a friend or relative who was obviously intoxicated or high on a drug

If you come from a codependent family or see yourself developing codependency relationships or engaging in enabling behaviors, consider acting now to make changes in your patterns of interaction. Remember, you cannot cause or cure drug dependence in another person.

Preventing Drug Abuse

Obviously, the best solution to drug abuse is prevention. Government attempts at controlling the drug problem tend to focus on stopping the production, importation, and distribution of illegal drugs. Creative effort also has to be put into stopping the demand for drugs. Developing persuasive antidrug educational programs offers the best hope for solving the drug problem in the future. Indirect approaches to prevention involve building young people's self-esteem, improving their academic skills, and increasing their recreational opportunities. Direct approaches involve giving information about the adverse effects of drugs and teaching tactics that help students resist peer pressure to use drugs in various situations. Developing strategies for resisting peer pressure is one of the more effective techniques.

Prevention efforts need to focus on the different motivations individuals have for using and abusing specific drugs at different ages. For example, grade-school children seem receptive to programs that involve their parents or well-known adults such as professional athletes. Adolescents in junior or senior high school are often more responsive to peer counselors. Many young adults tend to be influenced by efforts that focus on health education. For all ages, it is important to provide nondrug alternatives—such as recreational facilities, counseling, greater opportunities for leisure activities, and places to socialize—that speak to the individual's or group's specific reasons for using drugs. Reminding young people that most people, no matter what age, are *not* users of illegal drugs, do *not* smoke cigarettes, and do *not* get drunk frequently is a critical part of preventing substance abuse.

Take Charge

If Someone You Know Has a Drug Problem . . .

Changes in behavior and mood in someone you know may signal a growing dependence on drugs. Signs that a person's life is beginning to focus on drugs include the following:

- Sudden withdrawal or emotional distance
- Rebellious or unusually irritable behavior
- A loss of interest in usual activities or hobbies
- A decline in school performance
- A sudden change in the chosen group of friends
- Changes in sleeping or eating habits
- Frequent borrowing of money or stealing
- Secretive behavior about personal possessions, such as a backpack or the contents of a drawer
- Deterioration of physical appearance

If you believe a family member or friend has a drug problem, obtain information about resources for drug treatment available on your campus or in your community. Communicate your concern, provide him or her with information about treatment options, and offer your support during treatment. If the person continues to deny having a problem, you may want to talk with an experienced counselor about setting up an intervention—a formal, structured confrontation designed to end denial by having family, friends, and other caring individuals present their concerns to the drug user. Participants in an intervention would indicate the ways in which the individual is hurting others as well as himself or herself. If your friend or family member agrees to treatment, encourage him or her to attend a support group such as Narcotics Anonymous or Alcoholics Anonymous. And finally, examine your relationship with the abuser for signs of codependency. If necessary, get help for yourself; friends and family of drug users can often benefit from counseling.

The Role of Drugs in Your Life

Where do you fit into this complex picture of drug use and abuse? Chances are that you've had experience with OTC and prescription drugs, and you may or may not have had experience with one or more of the drugs described in this chapter. You probably know someone who has used or abused a psychoactive drug. Whatever your experience has been up to now, it's likely that you will encounter drugs at some point in your life. To make sure you'll have the inner resources to resist peer pressure and make your own decision, cultivate a variety of activities you enjoy doing, realize that you are entitled to have your own opinion, and don't neglect your self-esteem.

Issues to Consider Before you try a psychoactive drug, consider the following questions:

- *What are the risks involved?* Many drugs carry an immediate risk of injury or death. Most involve the longer-term risk of abuse and dependence.
- *Is using the drug compatible with your goals?* Consider how drug use will affect your education and career objectives, your relationships, your future happiness, and the happiness of those who love you.
- *What are your ethical beliefs about drug use?* Consider whether using a drug would cause you to go against your personal ethics, religious beliefs, social values, or family responsibilities.
- *What are the financial costs?* Many drugs are expensive, especially if you become dependent on them.
- *Are you trying to solve a deeper problem?* Drugs will not make emotional pain go away; in the long run, they will only make it worse. If you are feeling depressed or anxious, seek help from a mental health professional instead of self-medicating with drugs.

Like all aspects of health-related behavior, making responsible decisions about drug use depends on information, knowledge, and insight into yourself. Many choices are possible; making the ones that are right for you is what counts.

What to Do Instead of Drugs If you have used or considered using drugs, think carefully about your reasons for doing so. Consider trying healthier strategies for dealing with difficult emotions and peer pressure. For ideas, look over the following list of reasons for drug use and suggested alternative activities:

- *Bored?* Go for a walk or a run; stimulate your senses at a museum or a movie; challenge your mind with a new game or book; introduce yourself to someone new.
- *Stressed?* Practice relaxation or visualization; try to slow down and open your senses to the natural world; get some exercise.
- *Shy or lonely?* Talk to a counselor; enroll in a shyness clinic; learn and practice communication techniques.
- *Feeling low on self-esteem?* Focus on the areas in which you are competent; give yourself credit for the things you do well. A program of regular exercise can also enhance self-esteem.

- *Depressed or anxious?* Talk to a friend, parent, or counselor.
- *Apathetic or lethargic?* Force yourself to get up and get some exercise to energize yourself; assume responsibility for someone or something outside yourself; volunteer.
- *Searching for meaning?* Try yoga or meditation; explore spiritual experiences through religious groups, church, prayer, or reading.
- *Afraid to say no?* Take a course in assertiveness training; get support from others who don't want to use drugs; remind yourself that you have the right and the responsibility to make your own decisions.
- *Still feeling peer pressure?* Begin to look for new friends or roommates. Take a class or join an organization that attracts other health-conscious people.

Tips for Today

The essence of wellness is taking charge of your life. Dependence on drugs or compulsive activities is the very opposite of wellness, because it involves relinquishing control over your life to chemical substances or forces outside yourself. The best treatment for dependence is prevention—not starting in the first place—but it's never too late to regain control of your life.

Right now you can

- Go outside and sit on a park bench, or walk around outside at half your normal pace, opening all your senses to the beauty of nature. If you can't get to a beautiful place, close your eyes and visualize one. See if you can experience a "natural high."
- Substitute some bottled water for your caffeinated soda, and make your next cup of coffee half decaf.
- Consider whether someone you love has a drug problem; if so, consider how you can best help that person face and solve the problem.
- Plan to get enough sleep this week, so you won't feel the need for stimulants to be awake and alert.
- Examine what you've been doing lately to see if you are truly making your own decisions—or if some substance or out-of-control behavior has you in its power; if so, start thinking about how to regain control.

SUMMARY

- Addictive behaviors are reinforcing. Addicts experience a strong compulsion for the behavior and a loss of control over it; an escalating pattern of abuse with serious negative consequences may result.
- The sources or causes of addiction include heredity, personality, lifestyle, and environmental factors. People may use an addictive behavior as a means of alleviating stress or painful emotions.
- Many common behaviors are potentially addictive, including gambling, shopping, sexual activity, Internet use, eating, and working.
- Drug abuse is a maladaptive pattern of drug use that persists despite adverse social, psychological, or medical consequences.
- Drug dependence involves taking a drug compulsively, which includes neglecting constructive activities because of it and continuing to use it despite experiencing adverse effects resulting from its use. Tolerance and withdrawal symptoms are often present.
- Reasons for using drugs include the lure of the illicit; curiosity; rebellion; peer pressure; and the desire to alter one's mood or escape boredom, anxiety, depression, or other psychological problems.
- Psychoactive drugs affect the mind and body by altering brain chemistry. The effect of a drug depends on the properties of the drug and how it's used (drug factors), the physical and psychological characteristics of the user (user factors), and the physical and social environment surrounding the drug use (social factors).
- Opioids relieve pain, cause drowsiness, and induce euphoria; they reduce anxiety and produce lethargy, apathy, and an inability to concentrate.
- CNS depressants slow down the overall activity of the nerves; they reduce anxiety and cause mood changes, impaired muscular coordination, slurring of speech, and drowsiness or sleep.
- CNS stimulants speed up the activity of the nerves, causing acceleration of the heart rate, a rise in blood pressure, dilation of the pupils and bronchial tubes, and an increase in gastric and adrenal secretions.
- Marijuana usually causes euphoria and a relaxed attitude at low doses; very high doses produce feelings of depersonalization and sensory distortion. The long-term effects may include chronic bronchitis and cancer; use during pregnancy may impair fetal growth.
- Hallucinogens alter perception, feelings, and thought and may cause an altered sense of time, visual disturbances, and mood changes.
- Inhalants are present in a variety of harmless products; they can cause delirium. Their use can lead to loss of consciousness, heart failure, suffocation, and death.
- Economic and social costs of drug abuse include the financial costs of law enforcement, treatment, and health care and the social costs of crime, violence, and family problems. Drug testing and drug legalization have been proposed to address some of the problems related to drug abuse.
- Approaches to treatment include medication, treatment centers, self-help groups, and peer counseling; many programs also offer counseling to family members.

Behavior Change Strategy

Changing Your Drug Habits

This behavior change strategy focuses on one of the most commonly used drugs—caffeine. If you are concerned about your use of a different drug or another type of addictive behavior, you can devise your own plan based on this one and on the steps outlined in Chapter 1.

Because caffeine supports certain behaviors that are characteristic of our culture, such as sedentary, stressful work, you may find yourself relying on coffee (or tea, chocolate, or cola) to get through a busy schedule. Such habits often begin in college. Fortunately, it's easier to break a habit before it becomes entrenched as a lifelong dependency.

When you are studying for exams, the forced physical inactivity and the need to concentrate even when fatigued may lead you to overuse caffeine. But caffeine doesn't help unless you are already sleepy. And it does not relieve any underlying condition (you are just more tired when it wears off). How can you change this pattern?

Self-Monitoring

Keep a log of how much caffeine you eat or drink. Use a measuring cup to measure coffee or tea. Using Figure 9-4, convert the amounts you eat or drink into an estimate expressed in milligrams of caffeine. Be sure to include all forms, such as chocolate bars and OTC medications, as well as caffeine candy, colas, cocoa or hot chocolate, chocolate cake, tea, and coffee.

Self-Assessment

At the end of the week, add up your daily totals and divide by 7 to get your daily average in milligrams. How much is too much? At more than 250 mg per day, you may well be experiencing some adverse symptoms. If you are experiencing at least five of the following symptoms, you may want to cut down.

- Restlessness
- Nervousness
- Excitement
- Insomnia
- Flushed face
- Excessive sweating
- Gastrointestinal problems
- Muscle twitching
- Rambling thoughts and speech
- Irregular heartbeat
- Periods of inexhaustibility
- Excessive pacing or movement

Set Limits

Can you restrict your caffeine intake to a daily total, and stick to this contract? If so, set a cutoff point, such as one cup of coffee. Pegging it to a specific time of day can be helpful, because then you won't confront a decision at any other point (and possibly fail). If you find you cannot stick to your limit, you may want to cut out caffeine altogether; abstinence can be easier than moderation for some people. If you experience caffeine withdrawal symptoms (headache, fatigue), you may want to cut your intake more gradually.

Find Other Ways to Keep Up Your Energy

If you are fatigued, it makes sense to get enough sleep or exercise more, rather than drowning the problem in coffee or tea. Different people need different amounts of sleep; you may also need more sleep at different times, such as during a personal crisis or an illness. Also, exercise raises your metabolic rate for hours afterward—a handy fact to exploit when you want to feel more awake and want to avoid an irritable caffeine jag. And if you've been compounding your fatigue by not eating properly, try filling up on complex carbohydrates such as whole-grain bread or crackers instead of candy bars.

Tips on Cutting Out Caffeine Here are some more ways to decrease your consumption of caffeine:

- Keep some noncaffeinated drinks on hand, such as decaffeinated coffee, herbal teas, mineral water, bouillon, or hot water.
- Alternate between hot and very cold liquids.
- Fill your coffee cup only halfway.
- Avoid the office or school lunchroom or cafeteria and the chocolate sections of the grocery store. (Often people drink coffee or tea and eat chocolate simply because they're available.)
- Read labels of over-the-counter medications to check for hidden sources of caffeine.

Take Action

1. **Research local addiction services:** Find out what types of services are available on your campus or in your community to handle drug dependence and other addictive behaviors. If there are none, what services are needed? Locate the school official and public health agency responsible for your campus and community, and ask why these needs aren't being met.

2. **Survey attitudes:** Survey three older adults and three young students about their attitudes toward legalizing marijuana. Are there any differences? If so, what accounts for these differences? What kinds of reasons do they give for their positions?

3. **Analyze media portrayals:** Look at a current movie or television program, paying special attention to how drug use is portrayed. What messages are being conveyed? If possible, compare a recent movie with one made 10–20 years ago. Has the presentation of drug use changed? If so, how?

4. **Be a mentor or role model:** Consider volunteering at your local YMCA or with Boys and Girls Clubs or Big Brothers Big Sisters. By providing positive role models and activities, such organizations help keep young people away from drugs and other unhealthy behaviors. You can also just take time out to talk with the young people in your life about making smart choices.

For More Information

Books

Aue, P. W. 2006. *Teen Drug Abuse: Opposing Viewpoints*. San Diego: Greenhaven Press. *Explores key issues relating to drug use and abuse by teenagers.*

Hanson, G. R., et al. 2006. *Drugs and Society*, 9th ed. Boston: Jones & Bartlett. *Discusses the impact of drug abuse on individuals' lives and on the broader society.*

Karch, S. B. 2006. *Drug Abuse Handbook*, 2nd ed. London: CRC Press. *Explores drug abuse from a variety of perspectives, including clinical and criminological.*

Ksir, C., C. L. Hart, and O. S. Ray. 2008. *Drugs, Society, and Human Behavior*, 12th ed. New York: McGraw-Hill. *Examines drugs and behavior from the behavioral, pharmacological, historical, social, legal, and clinical perspectives.*

Lessa, N. R., et al. 2006. *Wiley Concise Guides to Mental Health: Substance Use Disorders*. New York: Wiley. *A clearly written introduction to the diagnosis and treatment of various kinds of substance abuse.*

Murphy, P. J. M., and M. Shlafer. 2006. *Over-the-Counter Drugs of Abuse*. New York: Chelsea House Publications. *An up-to-date discussion of nonprescription medicines and their abuse.*

Rosen Publishing. 2006. *Drug Abuse and Society Series*. New York: Rosen Publishing. *A series of short books, each exploring a different type of drugs—from prescription medicine to club drugs—and their use and abuse.*

WW Organizations, Hotlines, and Web Sites

Addiction: Close to Home. Created to accompany a PBS television series on addiction, this site provides information about prevention, treatment, and public policy; it also includes animated illustrations of how drugs affect the brain.
http://www.pbs.org/wnet/closetohome/home.html

Center for On-Line Addiction. Contains information about Internet and cybersex addiction.
http://netaddiction.com

ClubDrugs.Org. Provides information on drugs commonly classified as "club drugs."
http://www.clubdrugs.org

Do It Now Foundation. Provides youth-oriented information about drugs.
http://www.doitnow.org

Drug Enforcement Administration: Drugs of Abuse. Provides basic facts about major drugs of abuse, including penalties for drug trafficking.
http://www.dea.gov/concern/concern.htm

Frontline: Drug Wars. Includes information on key drugs, drug abusers, and the issues surrounding America's "war on drugs."
http://www.pbs.org/wgbh/pages/frontline/shows/drugs

Gamblers Anonymous. Includes questions to help diagnose gambling problems and resources for getting help.
http://www.gamblersanonymous.org

Habitsmart. Contains information about addictive behavior, including tips for effectively managing problematic habitual behaviors, a self-scoring alcohol checkup, and links.
http://www.habitsmart.com

Higher Eduction Center for Alcohol and Other Drug Prevention. Gives information about alcohol and drug abuse on campus and links to related sites.
http://www.edc.org/hec

Indiana Prevention Resource Center. A clearinghouse of information and links on substance-abuse topics, including specific psychoactive drugs and issues such as drug testing and drug legalization.
http://www.drugs.indiana.edu

Narcotics Anonymous (NA). Similar to Alcoholics Anonymous, NA sponsors 12-step meetings and provides other support services for drug abusers.
818-773-9999
http://www.na.org

There are also 12-step programs that focus on specific drugs:
Cocaine Anonymous
http://www.ca.org
Marijuana Anonymous
http://www.marijuana-anonymous.org

National Center on Addiction and Substance Abuse (CASA) at Columbia University. Provides information about the costs of substance abuse to individuals and society.
http://www.casacolumbia.org

National Clearinghouse for Alcohol and Drug Information. Provides statistics, information, and publications on substance abuse, including resources for people who want to help friends and family members overcome substance-abuse problems.
http://www.health.org

National Council on Problem Gambling. Provides information and help for people with gambling problems and their families, including a searchable directory of counselors.
800-522-4700
http://www.ncpgambling.org

National Drug Information, Treatment, and Referral Hotlines. Sponsored by the SAMHSA Center for Substance Abuse Treatment, these hotlines provide information on drug abuse and on HIV infection as it relates to substance abuse; referrals to support groups and treatment programs are available.
800-662-HELP
800-729-6686 (Spanish)
800-487-4889 (TDD for hearing impaired)

National Institute on Drug Abuse. Develops and supports research on drug-abuse prevention programs; fact sheets on drugs of abuse are available on the Web site or via recorded phone messages, fax, or mail.
http://www.drugabuse.gov

Office of National Drug Control Policy (ONDCP). Provides information on national and international drug-related topics, including U.S. policies related to prevention, education, treatment, and enforcement.
http://www.whitehousedrugpolicy.gov

Society for the Advancement of Sexual Health. Provides information, resources, and a self-quiz relating to sexual addiction.
http://www.ncsac.org

Substance Abuse and Mental Health Services Administration (SAMHSA). Provides statistics, information, and other resources related to substance-abuse prevention and treatment.
http://www.samhsa.gov

See also the listings for Chapters 10 and 11.

Selected Bibliography

American Psychiatric Association. 2000. *Diagnostic and Statistical Manual of Mental Disorders*, Fourth Edition, Text Revision. *(DSM-IV-TR)*. Washington, D.C.: American Psychiatric Association.

Beers, M. H., et. al. 2006. *The Merck Manual of Diagnosis and Therapy*, 18th ed. New York: John Wiley & Sons.

Braine, N. 2004. Long-term effects of syringe exchange on risk behavior and HIV prevention. *AIDS Education and Prevention* 16(3): 264–275.

Budney, A. J., et al. 2004. Review of the validity and significance of cannabis withdrawal syndrome. *American Journal of Psychiatry* 161(11): 1967–1977.

Centers for Disease Control and Prevention. 2005. *HIV/AIDS Surveillance Report, 2004: Vol. 16* (http://www.cdc.gov/hiv/topics/surveillance/resources/reports/2004report/default.htm; retrieved August 7, 2006).

Centers for Disease Control and Prevention. 2006. Methamphetamine Use and HIV Risk Behaviors Among Heterosexual Men. *Morbidity and Mortality Weekly Report* (55)10: 273–277.

Centers for Disease Control and Prevention, National Center for HIV, STD, and TP Prevention. 2006. *Viral Hepatitis C* (http://www.cdc.gov/ncidod/diseases/hepatitis/c/index.htm; retrieved August 8, 2006).

Colfax, G., et al. 2005. Longitudinal patterns of methamphetamine, popper (amyl nitrite), and cocaine use and high-risk sexual behavior among a cohort of San Francisco men who have sex with men. *Journal of Urban Health*, epub February 28.

Compton, W. M., et al. 2004. Prevalence of marijuana use disorder in the United States. *Journal of the American Medical Association* 291(17): 2114–2121.

Delaney-Black, V., et al. 2004. Prenatal cocaine: Quantity of exposure and gender moderation. *Journal of Developmental and Behavioral Pediatrics* 25(4): 254–263.

Grant, J. E., et al. 2006. Multicenter investigation of the opioid antagonist nalmefene in the treatment of pathological gambling. *American Journal of Psychiatry* 163(2): 303–312.

Hurd, Y. L., et al. 2005. Marijuana impairs growth in mid-gestation fetuses. *Neurotoxicology and Teratology* 27(2): 221–229.

Iannone, M., et al. 2006. Electrocortical effects of MDMA are potentiated by acoustic stimulation in rats. *BMC Neuroscience* 7: 13.

Jefferson, D. J. 2005. America's most dangerous drug. *Newsweek*, 8 August, 41–48.

Johnston, L. D., et al. 2004. *Monitoring the Future: National Survey Results on Drug Use, 1975–2003. Volume I: Secondary School Students* (NIH Publication No. 04-5507). Bethesda, Md.: National Institute on Drug Abuse.

Johnston, L. D., et al. 2004. *Monitoring the Future: National Survey Results on Drug Use, 1975–2003. Volume II: College Students and Adults Ages 19–45* (NIH Publication No. 04-5508). Bethesda, Md.: National Institute on Drug Abuse.

Johnston, L. D., et al. 2006. *Monitoring the Future: National Results on Adolescent Drug Use: Overview of Key Findings, 2005*. Bethesda, Md.: National Institute on Drug Abuse.

Juliano, L. M., and R. R. Griffiths. 2004. A critical review of caffeine withdrawal: Empirical validation of symptoms and signs, incidence, severity, and associated features. *Psychopharmacology* 176(1): 1–29.

Kim, S. W., et al. 2006. Pathological gambling and mood disorders: Clinical associations and treatment implications. *Journal of Affective Disorders* 92(1): 109–116.

Lane, J. D., et al. 2004. Caffeine impairs glucose metabolism in type 2 diabetes. *Diabetes Care* 27(8): 2047–2048.

Lynch, W. J., P. K. Maciejewski, and M. N. Potenza. 2004. Psychiatric correlates of gambling in adolescents and young adults grouped by age at gambling onset. *Archives of General Psychiatry* 61(11): 1116–1122.

Maglione, M., et al. 2005. Psychiatric effects of ephedra use: An analysis of Food and Drug Administration reports of adverse events. *American Journal of Psychiatry* 162(1): 189–191.

Mahowald, M. L., J. A. Singh, and P. Majeski. 2005. Opioid use by patients in an orthopedics spine clinic. *Arthritis and Rheumatology* 52(1): 312–321.

McBride, B. F., et al. 2004. Electrocardiographic and hemodynamic effects of a multicomponent dietary supplement containing ephedra and caffeine. *Journal of the American Medical Association* 291(4): 216–221.

McCusker, R. R., et al. 2006. Caffeine content of energy drinks, carbonated sodas, and other beverages. *Journal of Analytical Toxicology* 30(2): 112–114.

Messinis, L., et al. 2006. Neuropsychological deficits in long-term frequent cannabis users. *Neurology* 66(5): 737–739.

National Clearinghouse for Alcohol and Drug Information. 2006. *Drugs of Abuse* (http://www.health.org/govpubs/rpo926; retrieved August 7, 2006).

National Institute on Drug Abuse. 2005. *Research Report Series: Inhalant Abuse* (http://www.drugabuse.gov/PDF/RRInhalants.pdf; retrieved August 8, 2006).

Office of Applied Studies, Substance Abuse and Mental Health Services Administration. 2006. *Results from the 2005 National Survey on Drug Use and Health: National Findings* (http://oas.samhsa.gov/; retrieved November 17, 2006).

Office of Applied Studies, Substance Abuse and Mental Health Services Administration. 2006. *Treatment Episode Data Set (TEDS). Highlights—2004. National Admissions to Substance Abuse Treatment Services* (http://wwwdasis.samhsa.gov/teds04/tedshigh2k4.pdf; retrieved August 7, 2006).

Office of National Drug Control Policy. 2006. *Women and Drugs* (http://whitehousedrugpolicy.gov/drugfact/women/index.html; retrieved August 7, 2006).

Opioid abuse. 2004. *Journal of the American Medical Association* 291(11): 1394.

Parrott, A. C. 2005. Chronic tolerance to recreational MDMA (3,4-methylenedioxymethamphetamine) or ecstasy. *Journal of Psychopharmacology* 19(1): 71–83.

The Partnership for a Drug-Free America. 2006. *Drug Guide: Inhalants* (http://www.drugfree.org/Portal/Drug_Guide/Inhalants; retrieved August 9, 2006).

Preidt, R. 2006. *Heavy Pot Smoking Doesn't Increase Lung Cancer Risk: Study* (http://www.healthday.com/view.cfm?id=532865; retrieved August 7, 2006).

Ramaekers, J. G., et al. 2004. Dose-related risk of motor vehicle crashes after cannabis use. *Drug and Alcohol Dependence* 73(2): 109–119.

Ren, S., et al. 2006. Effect of long-term cocaine use on regional left ventricular function as determined by magnetic resonance imaging. *American Journal of Cardiology* 97(7): 1085–1088.

Savoca, M. R., et al. 2005. Association of ambulatory blood pressure and dietary caffeine in adolescents. *American Journal of Hypertension* 18(1): 116–120.

Singer, L. T., et al. 2004. Cognitive outcomes of preschool children with prenatal cocaine exposure. *Journal of the American Medical Association* 291(20): 2448–2456.

Substance Abuse and Mental Health Services Administration. 2005 Nonmedical oxycodone users: A comparison with heroin users. *The NSDUH Report*, January.

Wareing, M., et al. 2005. Visuo-spatial working memory deficits in current and former users of MDMA ('ecstasy'). *Human Psychopharmacology* 20(2): 115–23.

Waska, R. 2006. Addictions and the quest to control the object. *American Journal of Psychoanalysis* 66(1): 43–62.

World Health Organization. 2006. *Management of Substance Abuse* (http://www.who.int/substance_abuse/en; retrieved August 9, 2006).

Zakzanis, K. K., and Z. Campbell. 2006. Memory impairment in now abstinent MDMA users and continued users: A longitudinal follow-up. *Neurology* 66(5): 740–741.

Looking AHEAD

After reading this chapter, you should be able to

- Explain how alcohol is absorbed and metabolized by the body
- Describe the immediate and long-term effects of drinking alcohol
- Define alcohol abuse, binge drinking, and alcoholism and discuss their effects on the drinker and others
- Evaluate the role of alcohol in your life, and list strategies for using it responsibly

The Responsible Use of Alcohol

Test Your Knowledge

1. **"Moderate drinking" is having three or fewer drinks per day.**
   True or false?
2. **How many adults in the United States do not drink any alcohol?**
   a. 1 in 10
   b. 1 in 5
   c. 1 in 3
3. **If a man and a woman of the same weight drink the same amount of alcohol, the woman will become intoxicated more quickly than the man.**
   True or false?
4. **Drinking too much alcohol in too short a time can cause death from alcohol poisoning.**
   True or false?
5. **Drinking coffee will help you sober up.**
   True or false?
6. **About 10,000 college students between the ages of 18 and 24 are victims of alcohol-related sexual assault or date rape each year.**
   True or false?

ANSWERS

1. FALSE. Moderate drinking is no more than one drink per day for women and no more than two drinks per day for men.
2. C. Most other adults drink lightly and occasionally; a small number of heavy drinkers, about 7% of adults, consume more than half of all the alcohol in the United States. Overall, college students drink more alcohol and are more likely to binge drink than young adults who are not in college, but nonstudents are more likely to be dependent on alcohol.
3. TRUE. Women usually have a higher percentage of body fat than men and a less active form of a stomach enzyme that breaks down alcohol. Both factors cause them to become intoxicated more quickly and to a greater degree.
4. TRUE. Consuming a number of drinks over a period of several hours is likely to cause intoxication, followed by a hangover; chugging the same amount in an hour or less can be lethal.
5. FALSE. Once alcohol has been absorbed by the body, nothing speeds its metabolism.
6. FALSE. The figure is more than 97,000 students; each year, a half million students report having unsafe sex while drunk or having sex when they are too intoxicated to know whether they have consented.

Visit the *Core Concepts in Health* Online Learning Center (www.mhhe.com/insel10e) for study aids and many additional resources.

Alcohol has been used in religious ceremonies, in feasts and celebrations, and as a medicine for thousands of years. Throughout history, alcohol has been more popular than any other drug in the Western world, despite numerous prohibitions against it. Alcohol has a somewhat contradictory role in human life. Most of us think of alcohol the way it is portrayed in advertisements, on television, and in movies—as part of good times at the beach, social occasions, and elegant gatherings. Used in moderation, alcohol can enhance social occasions by loosening inhibitions and creating a pleasant feeling of relaxation. But the use of alcohol can also be unhealthy. Like other drugs, alcohol has definite physiological effects on the body that can impair functioning in the short term and cause devastating damage in the long term. For some people, alcohol becomes an addiction, leading to a lifetime of recovery or, for a few, to debilitation and death. Many of our slang expressions for intoxication reflect its less positive aspects; we say we're "smashed," "bombed," or "wasted."

In the report *Health, United States, 2006,* the Centers for Disease Control and Prevention estimate that 55% of adult Americans (age 18 and older) currently drink; about 14% are former drinkers, and the remaining 31% are lifetime abstainers. About 79% of adult American drinkers are light drinkers, 14% are moderate drinkers, and 7% are heavy drinkers. These estimates are based on the number of days per year people reported having five or more drinks. According to the *National Survey on Drug Abuse and Health* for 2005, 3.5% of Americans were dependent on alcohol; another 4.3% were classified as alcohol abusers. Heavy drinkers account for over half of all the alcohol consumed, as well as a disproportionate amount of the social, economic, and medical costs of alcohol abuse (estimated at over $180 billion per year). Alcohol is responsible for about 85,000 deaths per year among Americans and is the third leading actual cause of death. It is the leading cause of death among people aged 15–24.

The use of alcohol is a complex issue, one that demands conscious thought and informed decisions. In our society, some people choose to drink in moderation, some choose not to drink at all, and others realize too late that they've made an unwise choice—when they become dependent on alcohol, are involved in an alcohol-related car crash, or simply wake up to discover they've done something they regret. This chapter discusses the complexities of alcohol use and provides information that will help you make the choices that are right for you.

THE NATURE OF ALCOHOL

How does alcohol affect people? Does it affect some people differently than others? Can some people handle alcohol? Is it possible to drink a safe amount of alcohol? Many of the misconceptions about the effects of alcohol can be cleared up by taking a closer look at the chemistry of alcohol and how it is absorbed and metabolized by the body.

The Chemistry of Alcohol

Ethyl alcohol is the psychoactive ingredient in all alcoholic beverages. Beer, a mild intoxicant brewed from a mixture of grains, usually contains 3–6% alcohol by volume. Ales and malt liquors are 6–8% alcohol by volume. Wines are made by *fermenting* the juices of grapes or other fruits. The concentration of alcohol in table wines is about 9–14%. *Fortified wines,* so named because alcohol has been added to them, contain about 20% alcohol; these include sherry, port, and Madeira. Stronger alcoholic beverages, called *hard liquors,* are made by *distilling* brewed or fermented grains or other products. These beverages, including gin, whiskey, brandy, rum, tequila, vodka, and liqueurs, usually contain 35–50% alcohol.

The concentration of alcohol in a beverage is indicated by the **proof value,** which is two times the percentage concentration. For example, if a beverage is 100 proof, it contains 50% alcohol. Two ounces of 100-proof whiskey contain 1 ounce of pure alcohol. The proof value of hard liquors can usually be found on the bottle labels. When alcohol consumption is discussed, "one drink" refers to a 12-ounce bottle of beer, a 5-ounce glass of table wine, or a cocktail with 1.5 ounces of 80-proof liquor. Each of these different drinks contains approximately the same amount of alcohol: 0.5–0.6 ounce.

Alcohol provides 7 calories per gram, and the alcohol in one drink (14–17 grams) supplies about 100–120 calories. Most alcoholic beverages also contain some carbohydrate, so, for example, one beer provides about 150 total calories. The "light" in light beer refers to calories; a light beer typically has close to the same alcohol content as a regular beer and about 100 calories. A 5-ounce glass of red wine has 100 calories; white wine has 96. A 3-ounce margarita supplies 157 calories, a 6-ounce cosmopolitan has 143 calories, and a 6-ounce rum and Coke contains about 180 calories.

There are a number of different kinds of alcohol. In this book, the term **alcohol** refers to ethyl alcohol, which is the only kind of alcohol that can be consumed. Other kinds of alcohol such as methanol (wood alcohol) and isopropyl alcohol (rubbing alcohol) are highly toxic and can cause blindness and other serious problems when consumed even in low doses.

Absorption

When a person ingests alcohol, about 20% is rapidly absorbed from the stomach into the bloodstream. About 75% is absorbed through the upper part of the small intestine. Any remaining alcohol enters the bloodstream further along the gastrointestinal tract. Once in the bloodstream, alcohol

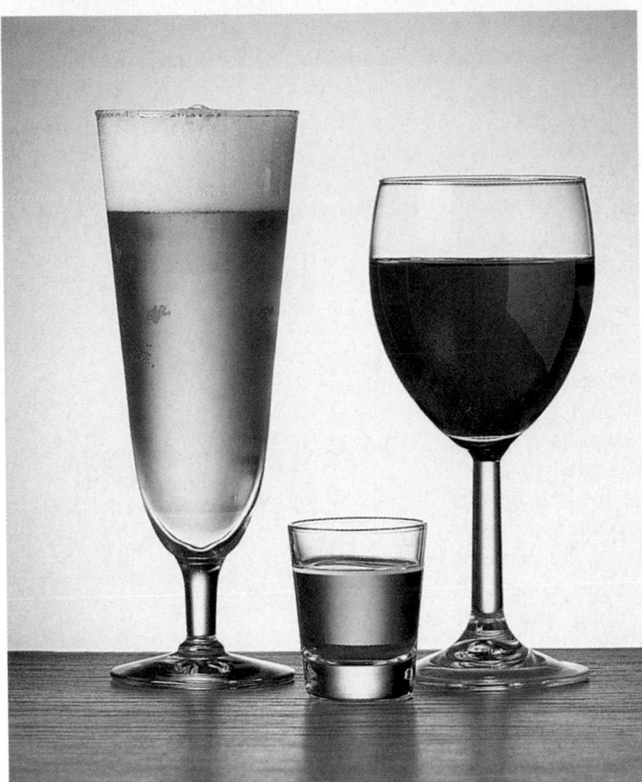

Ethyl alcohol is the common psychoactive drug found in all alcoholic beverages. One drink—a 12-ounce beer, a 1.5-ounce cocktail, or a 5-ounce glass of wine—contains about 0.5–0.6 ounce of ethyl alcohol.

produces feelings of intoxication. The rate of absorption is affected by a variety of factors. For example, the carbonation in a beverage like champagne increases the rate of alcohol absorption. Artificial sweeteners (commonly used in drink mixers) have been shown to have the same effect. Food in the stomach slows the rate of absorption, as does the drinking of highly concentrated alcoholic beverages such as hard liquor. But remember: *All* alcohol a person consumes is eventually absorbed.

Metabolism and Excretion

Alcohol is quickly transported throughout the body by the blood. Because alcohol easily moves through most biological membranes, it is rapidly distributed throughout most body tissues. The main site of alcohol **metabolism** is the liver, though a small amount of alcohol is metabolized in the stomach. (See the box "Metabolizing Alcohol: Our Bodies Work Differently" on p. 272.)

About 2–10% of ingested alcohol is not metabolized in the liver or other tissues but is excreted unchanged by the lungs, kidneys, and sweat glands. Excreted alcohol causes the telltale smell on a drinker's breath and is the basis of breath and urine analyses for alcohol levels. Although such analyses do not give precise measurements of alcohol concentrations in the blood, they do provide a reasonable approximation if done correctly.

Alcohol Intake and Blood Alcohol Concentration

Blood alcohol concentration (BAC), a measure of intoxication, is determined by the amount of alcohol consumed in a given amount of time and by individual factors:

- *Body weight:* In most cases, a smaller person develops a higher BAC than a larger person after drinking the same amount of alcohol. A smaller person has less overall body tissue into which alcohol can be distributed.
- *Percent body fat:* A person with a higher percentage of body fat will usually develop a higher BAC than a more muscular person of the same weight. Alcohol does not concentrate as much in fatty tissue as in muscle and most other tissues, in part because fat has fewer blood vessels.
- *Sex:* Women metabolize less alcohol in the stomach than men do because the stomach enzyme that breaks down alcohol before it enters the bloodstream is four times more active in men than in women. This means that more unmetabolized alcohol is released into the bloodstream in women. Because women are also generally smaller than men and have a higher percentage of body fat, women will have a higher BAC than men after consuming the same amount of alcohol. Hormonal fluctuations may also affect the rate of alcohol metabolism, making a woman more susceptible to high BACs at certain times during her menstrual cycle (usually just prior to the onset of menstruation).

BAC also depends on the balance between the rate of alcohol absorption and the rate of alcohol metabolism. A man who weighs 150 pounds and has normal liver function metabolizes about 0.3 ounce of alcohol per hour, the equivalent of about half a 12-ounce bottle of beer or a 5-ounce glass of wine.

The rate of alcohol metabolism varies among individuals and is largely determined by genetic factors and drinking behavior. (Chronic drinking activates enzymes that metabolize alcohol in the liver, so people who drink frequently metabolize alcohol at a more rapid rate than nondrinkers.)

Terms

Vw

proof value Two times the percentage of alcohol by volume; a beverage that is 50% alcohol by volume is 100 proof.

alcohol The intoxicating ingredient in fermented liquors; a colorless, pungent liquid.

metabolism The chemical transformation of food and other substances in the body into energy and wastes.

blood alcohol concentration (BAC) The amount of alcohol in the blood in terms of weight per unit volume; used as a measurement of intoxication.

Dimensions of Diversity

Metabolizing Alcohol: Our Bodies Work Differently

Do you notice that you react differently to alcohol than some of your friends do? If so, you may be noticing genetic differences in alcohol metabolism that are associated with ethnicity. Alcohol is metabolized mainly in the liver, where it is broken down by an enzyme called alcohol dehydrogenase, producing a by-product called acetaldehyde (see the figure). Acetaldehyde is responsible for many of the unpleasant effects of alcohol abuse. Another enzyme, acetaldehyde dehydrogenase, breaks this product down further.

Some people, including many of Asian descent or of certain Jewish population groups, have genes that cause them to produce somewhat different forms of the two enzymes that metabolize alcohol. The result is high concentrations of acetaldehyde in the brain and other tissues, producing a host of unpleasant symptoms. When people with these enzymes drink alcohol, they experience a physiological reaction referred to as *flushing syndrome*. Their skin feels hot, their heart and respiration rates increase, and they may get a headache, vomit, or break out in hives. Drinking makes some people so uncomfortable that it's unlikely they could ever become addicted to alcohol.

The body's response to acetaldehyde is the basis for treating alcohol abuse with the drug disulfiram (Antabuse), which inhibits the action of acetaldehyde dehydrogenase. When a person taking disulfiram ingests alcohol, acetaldehyde levels increase rapidly, and he or she develops an intense flushing reaction along with weakness, nausea, vomiting, and other disagreeable symptoms.

How people behave in relation to alcohol is influenced in complex ways by many factors, including social and cultural ones. But in this case at least, individual choices and behavior are strongly influenced by a specific genetic characteristic.

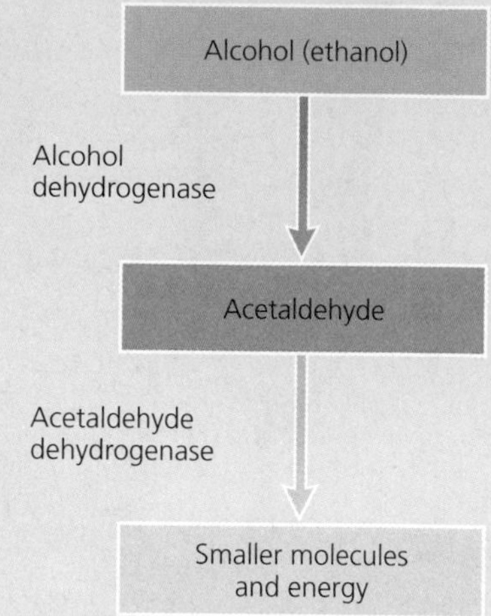

Contrary to popular myths, this metabolic rate *cannot* be influenced by exercise, breathing deeply, eating, drinking coffee, or taking other drugs. The rate of alcohol metabolism is the same whether a person is asleep or awake.

If a person absorbs slightly less alcohol each hour than he or she can metabolize in an hour, the BAC remains low. People can drink large amounts of alcohol this way over a long period of time without becoming noticeably intoxicated; however, they do run the risk of significant long-term health hazards (described later in the chapter). If a person is absorbing alcohol more quickly than it can be metabolized, the BAC will steadily increase, and he or she will become more and more drunk (Table 10-1). How fast you drink makes a big difference in how high your BAC will be. Consuming several drinks over a period of 2 or 3 hours is likely to cause intoxication, followed on the next day by a hangover; chugging the same amount of alcohol in an hour or less could be lethal.

Table 10-1 The Effects of Alcohol

BAC (%)	Common Behavioral Effects	Hours Required to Metabolize Alcohol
0.00–0.05	Slight change in feelings, usually relaxation and euphoria. Decreased alertness.	2–3
0.05–0.10	Emotional instability, with exaggerated feelings and behavior. Reduced social inhibitions. Impairment of reaction time and fine motor coordination. Increasingly impaired during driving. Legally drunk at 0.08%.	3–6
0.10–0.15	Unsteadiness in standing and walking. Loss of peripheral vision. Driving is extremely dangerous.	6–10
0.15–0.30	Staggering gait. Slurred speech. Pain and other sensory perceptions greatly impaired.	10–24
More than 0.30	Stupor or unconsciousness. Anesthesia. Death possible at 0.35% and above. Can result from rapid or binge drinking with few earlier effects.	More than 24

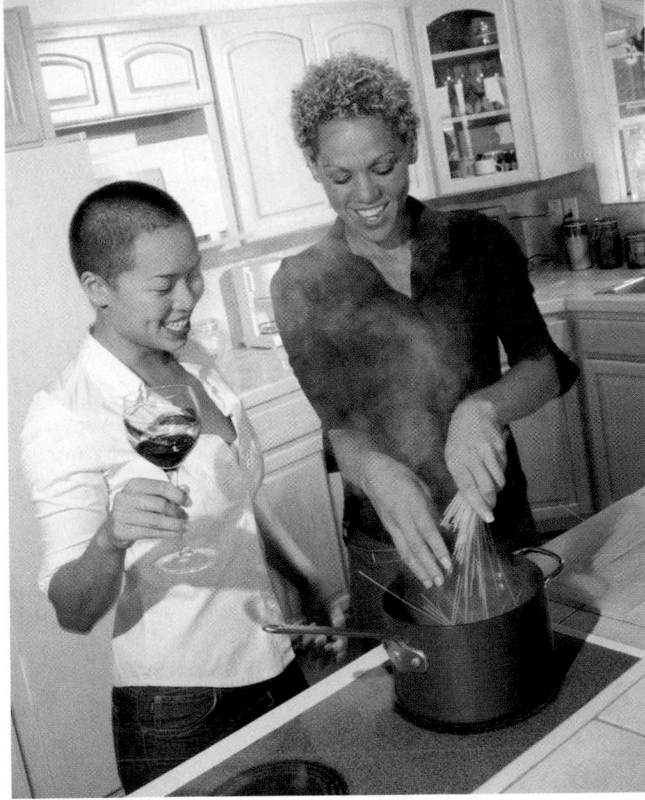

Alcohol loosens inhibitions; when used in moderation, it tends to make people feel more relaxed and sociable.

ALCOHOL AND HEALTH

The effects of alcohol consumption on health depend on the individual, the circumstances, and the amount of alcohol consumed.

The Immediate Effects of Alcohol

BAC is a primary factor determining the effects of alcohol (see Table 10-1). At low concentrations, alcohol tends to make people feel relaxed and jovial, but at higher concentrations people are more likely to feel angry, sedated, or sleepy. Alcohol is a CNS depressant, and its effects vary because body systems are affected to different degrees at different BACs. At any given BAC, the effects of alcohol are more pronounced when the BAC is rapidly increasing than when it is slowly increasing, steady, or decreasing. The effects of alcohol are more pronounced if a person drinks on an empty stomach, because alcohol is absorbed more quickly and the BAC rises more quickly.

Low Concentrations of Alcohol The effects of alcohol can first be felt at a BAC of about 0.03–0.05%. These effects may include light-headedness, relaxation, and a release of inhibitions. Most drinkers experience mild euphoria and become more sociable. When people drink in social settings, alcohol often seems to act as a stimulant, enhancing conviviality or assertiveness. This apparent stimulation occurs because alcohol depresses inhibitory centers in the brain. A new study suggests, however, that even one drink can significantly impair a person's vision and ability to judge visual information.

Higher Concentrations of Alcohol At higher concentrations, the pleasant effects tend to be replaced by more negative ones: interference with motor coordination, verbal performance, and intellectual functions. The drinker often becomes irritable and may be easily angered or given to crying. When the BAC reaches 0.1%, most sensory and motor functioning is reduced, and many people become sleepy. Vision, smell, taste, and hearing become less acute. At 0.2%, most drinkers are completely unable to function, either physically or psychologically, because of the pronounced depression of the central nervous system, muscles, and other body systems. Coma usually occurs at a BAC of 0.35%, and any higher level can be fatal.

Shakespeare accurately described the effects of alcohol on sexual functioning. He said (in *Macbeth*) that "it stirs up desire, but it takes away the performance." Small doses may improve sexual functioning for individuals who are especially anxious or self-conscious, but higher doses usually have a negative effect. Excessive alcohol use can result in reduced erection response and reduced vaginal lubrication. Testicular atrophy (shrinking) may result from the long-term overuse of alcohol.

Alcohol causes blood vessels near the skin to dilate, so drinkers often feel warm; their skin flushes, and they may sweat more. Flushing and sweating contribute to heat loss, and so the internal body temperature falls. High doses of alcohol may impair the body's ability to regulate temperature, causing it to drop sharply, especially if the surrounding temperature is low. Drinking alcoholic beverages to keep warm in cold weather does not work and can even be dangerous.

Drinking alcohol, particularly in large amounts, disturbs normal sleep patterns. Alcohol may facilitate falling asleep more quickly, but the sleep is often light, punctuated with awakenings, and unrefreshing. Even after the habitual drinker stops drinking, his or her sleep may be altered for weeks or months.

Alcohol Hangover Despite all the jokes about hangovers, anyone who has experienced a severe hangover knows they are no laughing matter. The symptoms include headache, shakiness, nausea, diarrhea, fatigue, and impaired mental functioning. It is estimated that hangovers cost the U.S. economy billions of dollars each year because of absenteeism and poor job performance.

A hangover is probably caused by a combination of the toxic products of alcohol breakdown, dehydration, and hormonal effects. During a hangover, heart rate and blood

Take Charge

Dealing with an Alcohol Emergency

Remember: Being very drunk is potentially life-threatening. Helping a drunken friend could save a life.

- Be firm but calm. Don't engage the person in an argument or discuss her drinking behavior while she is intoxicated.
- Get the person out of harm's way—don't let her drive or wander outside. Don't let her drink any more alcohol.
- If the person is unconscious, don't assume she is just "sleeping it off." Place her on her side with her knees up. This position will help prevent choking if the person should vomit.
- Stay with the person—you need to be ready to help if she vomits or stops breathing.
- Don't try to give the person anything to eat or drink, including coffee or other drugs. Don't give cold showers or try to make her walk around. None of these things help anyone to sober up, and they can be dangerous.

Call 911 immediately in any of the following instances:

- You can't wake the person even with shouting or shaking.
- The person is taking fewer than 8 breaths per minute or her breathing seems shallow or irregular.
- You think the person took other drugs in addition to alcohol.
- The person has had an injury, especially a blow to the head.
- The person drank a large amount of alcohol within a short period of time and then became unconscious. Death caused by alcohol poisoning most often occurs when the blood alcohol level rises very quickly due to rapid ingestion of alcohol.

If you aren't sure what to do, call 911. You may save a life.

pressure increase, making some individuals more vulnerable to heart attacks. Electroencephalography (brain wave measurement) shows diffuse slowing of brain waves for up to 16 hours after BAC drops to zero. Studies of pilots, drivers, and skiers all indicate that coordination and cognition are impaired in a person with a hangover, increasing the risk of injury.

The best treatment for hangover is prevention. Nearly all men can expect a hangover if they drink more than five or six drinks; for women, the number is three or four drinks. Drinking less, drinking at a slower pace, and consuming plenty of nonalcoholic liquids decrease the risk of hangover. If you do get a hangover, remember that your ability to drive is definitely impaired, even after your BAC has returned to zero.

Alcohol Poisoning Acute alcohol poisoning occurs much more frequently than most people realize, and all too often it causes death. Drinking large amounts of alcohol over a short period of time can rapidly raise the BAC into the lethal range. Alcohol, either alone or in combination with other drugs, is responsible for more toxic overdose deaths than any other drug. A common scenario for alcohol poisoning is that inexperienced drinkers try to outdo each other by consuming glass after glass of alcohol as rapidly as possible. Coma and death can result before the participants in this game have any awareness of how dangerous it can be. Children are at especially high risk for alcohol poisoning. Even a partially empty glass of liquor carelessly left out after a party can result in serious poisoning, or even death, if consumed by a toddler or small child.

Death from alcohol poisoning may be caused either by central nervous system and respiratory depression or by inhaling fluid or vomit into the lungs. The amount of alcohol it takes to make a person unconscious is dangerously close to a fatal dose. Special care should be taken to ensure the safety of anyone who has been drinking heavily, especially if the person becomes unconscious (see the box "Dealing with an Alcohol Emergency").

Using Alcohol with Other Drugs Alcohol-drug combinations are one of the leading causes of drug-related deaths in this country. Using alcohol while taking any other drug that can cause CNS depression increases the effects of both drugs, potentially leading to coma, respiratory depression, and death. Examples of common drugs that can result in oversedation when combined with alcohol include barbiturates, Valium-like drugs, narcotics such as codeine, and OTC antihistamines such as Benadryl. For people who consume three or more drinks per day, use of OTC pain relievers like aspirin, ibuprofen, or acetaminophen increases the risk of stomach bleeding or liver damage. Some antibiotics and diabetes medications can also interact dangerously with alcohol.

Many illegal drugs are especially dangerous when combined with alcohol. Life-threatening overdoses occur at much lower doses when heroin and other narcotics are combined with alcohol. When cocaine and alcohol are used together, a toxic substance called cocaethylene is formed; this substance is responsible for more than half of all cocaine-related deaths.

The safest strategy is to avoid combining alcohol with any other drug—prescription, over-the-counter, or illegal. If in doubt, ask your pharmacist or physician before using any drug in combination with alcohol, or just don't do it.

Alcohol-Related Injuries and Violence The combination of impaired judgment, weakened sensory perception, reduced inhibitions, impaired motor coordination, and, often, increased aggressiveness and hostility that characterizes alcohol intoxication can be dangerous or even deadly. According to the 2004 *National Hospital Ambulatory Medical Care Survey,* alcohol and drug use accounted for 1.6 million emergency room visits in the United States in 2004. Through homicide, suicide, automobile crashes, and other incidents, alcohol use was linked to more than 75,000 American deaths in 2001. A 2006 study found that more than 3000 minors die each year as a result of alcohol abuse. Alcohol use contributes to over 50% of all murders, assaults, and rapes, and alcohol is frequently found in the bloodstream of both perpetrators and victims. The majority of people who attempt suicide have been drinking, and about half of all successful suicides are alcoholics. Alcohol use more than triples the chances of fatal injuries during leisure activities such as swimming and boating, and more than half of all fatal falls and serious burns happen to people who have been drinking.

Alcohol and Sexual Decision Making Alcohol seriously affects a person's ability to make wise decisions about sex. A recent survey of college students revealed that frequent binge drinkers were five times more likely to engage in unplanned sexual activity and five-and-a-half times more likely to have unprotected sex than non–binge drinkers. Heavy drinkers are also more likely to have multiple sex partners and to engage in other forms of high-risk sexual behavior. For all these reasons, rates of sexually transmitted diseases and unwanted pregnancy are higher among people who drink heavily than among people who drink moderately or not at all. A study comparing rates of gonorrhea (a sexually transmitted disease) in states with varying minimum drinking ages and beer taxes found that gonorrhea rates dropped significantly among young people when beer taxes were increased and the minimum drinking age was raised.

Women who binge-drink are at increased risk for rape and other forms of nonconsensual sex. The laws regarding sexual consent are clear: A person who is very drunk or passed out cannot consent to sex. If you have sex with a person who is drunk or unconscious, you are committing sexual assault. Claiming that you were drunk at the time won't absolve you of your legal and moral responsibility for this serious crime.

Drinking and Driving

Despite recent improvements, drunk driving continues to be one of the most serious public health and safety problems in the United States. In 2004, nearly 250,000 people were injured in alcohol-related automobile crashes—an average of 1 person injured every 2 minutes. Nearly 40% of the more than 42,000 crash fatalities in 2004 were alcohol-related, down from about 50% in 1990. Increased public education about drunk driving and stiffer drunk driving laws are primarily responsible for this improvement. Still, in the 2005 *National Survey on Drug Use and Health,* 13% of U.S. drivers admitted to having used alcohol or another drug before driving a vehicle.

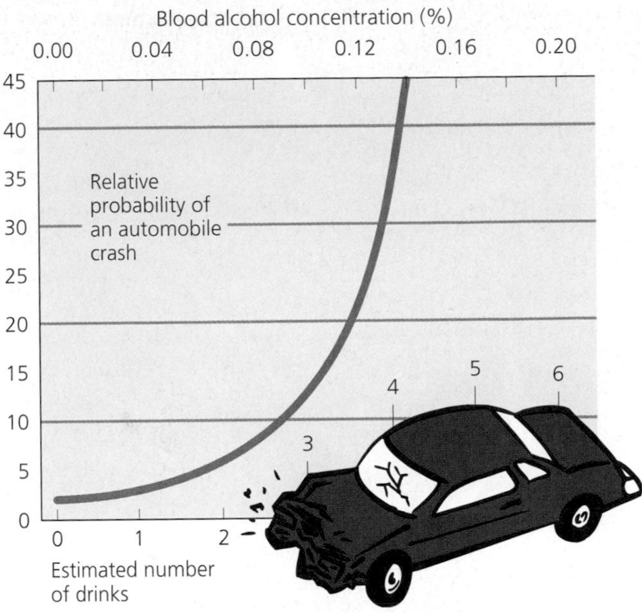

Figure 10-1 The dose-response relationship between BAC and automobile crashes.

The *dose-response function* (see Chapter 9) is the relationship between the amount of alcohol or drug consumed and the type and intensity of the resulting effect. Higher doses of alcohol are associated with a much greater probability of automobile crashes (Figure 10-1). A person driving with a BAC of 0.14% is more than 40 times more likely to be involved in a crash than someone with no alcohol in his or her blood. For those with a BAC above 0.14%, the risk of a fatal crash is estimated to be 380 times higher. The risks for young drivers are even greater than indicated in Figure 10-1, even at very low BACs. Younger drivers have less experience with both driving and alcohol, which results in significant impairment with BACs as low as 0.02%.

In addition to an increased risk of injury and death, driving while intoxicated can have serious legal consequences. Drunk driving is against the law. In 2006, the legal limit for BAC was 0.08% in all states and the District of Columbia. Under current zero-tolerance laws in many states, drivers under age 21 who have consumed *any* alcohol may have their licenses suspended. There are stiff penalties for drunk driving, including fines, loss of license, confiscation of vehicle, and jail time. Many cities have checkpoints where drivers are stopped and checked for intoxication.

Alcohol interferes with judgment, perception, coordination, and other areas of mental and physical functioning, and it is a factor in a majority of all fatal automobile crashes. This driver is lucky that he was stopped by a suspicious police officer before a crash occurred. He is being given a breath test to determine his blood alcohol concentration.

Numerous studies have shown that alcohol-related highway deaths fall when states lower the legal BAC. Many developed countries have lower BAC limits than the United States. The most common BAC limit is 0.05%, a level used by Australia, Belgium, Denmark, France, Germany, Greece, Spain, and many other countries; Sweden and Russia have BAC limits of 0.02%.

People who drink and drive are unable to drive safely because their judgment is impaired, their reaction time is slower, and their coordination is reduced. The number of drinks it takes the average person to reach various BACs is shown in Figure 10-2. However, some driving skills are affected at BACs of 0.02% and lower; at 0.05%, visual perception, reaction time, and certain steering tasks are all impaired. Any amount of alcohol impairs your ability to drive safely, and fatigue augments alcohol's effects.

If you are out of your home and drinking, find an alternative means of transportation or follow the practice of having a *designated driver,* an individual who refrains from drinking in order to provide safe transportation home for others in the group. The responsibility can be rotated for different occasions. Remember, you risk more than your own life when you drink and drive. Causing serious injury or death results in lifelong feelings of sadness and guilt for the driver and tremendous grief for the friends and families of victims.

It's more difficult to protect yourself against someone else who drinks and drives. Learn to be alert to the erratic driving that signals an impaired driver. Warning signs include wide, abrupt, and illegal turns; straddling the center line or lane marker; driving against traffic; driving on the shoulder; weaving, swerving, or nearly striking an object or another vehicle; following too closely; erratic speed; driving with headlights off at night; and driving with the window down in very cold weather. If you see any of these signs, try the following strategies:

- If the driver is ahead of you, maintain a safe following distance. Don't try to pass.
- If the driver is behind you, turn right at the nearest intersection, and let the driver pass.
- If the driver is approaching your car, move to the shoulder and stop. Avoid a head-on collision by sounding your horn or flashing your lights.
- When approaching an intersection, slow down and stay alert for vehicles that don't appear to be slowing in preparation for stopping at a stop sign or red light.

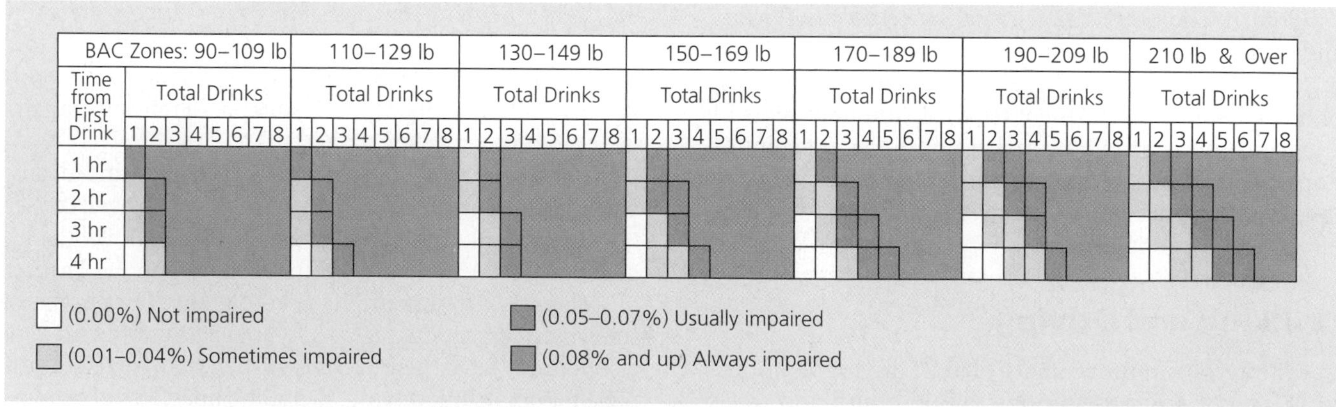

Figure 10-2 Approximate blood alcohol concentration and body weight. This chart illustrates the BAC an average person of a given weight would reach after drinking the specified number of drinks in the time shown. The legal limit for BAC is 0.08%; for drivers under 21 years of age, many states have zero-tolerance laws that set BAC limits of 0.01% or 0.02%.

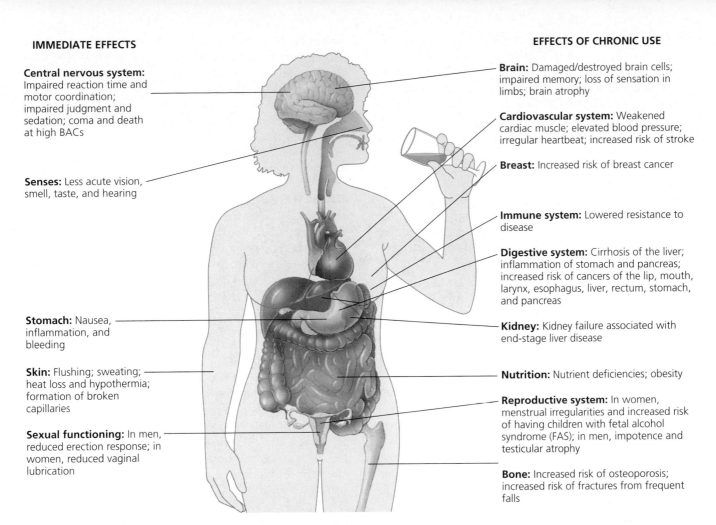

IMMEDIATE EFFECTS

Central nervous system: Impaired reaction time and motor coordination; impaired judgment and sedation; coma and death at high BACs

Senses: Less acute vision, smell, taste, and hearing

Stomach: Nausea, inflammation, and bleeding

Skin: Flushing; sweating; heat loss and hypothermia; formation of broken capillaries

Sexual functioning: In men, reduced erection response; in women, reduced vaginal lubrication

EFFECTS OF CHRONIC USE

Brain: Damaged/destroyed brain cells; impaired memory; loss of sensation in limbs; brain atrophy

Cardiovascular system: Weakened cardiac muscle; elevated blood pressure; irregular heartbeat; increased risk of stroke

Breast: Increased risk of breast cancer

Immune system: Lowered resistance to disease

Digestive system: Cirrhosis of the liver; inflammation of stomach and pancreas; increased risk of cancers of the lip, mouth, larynx, esophagus, liver, rectum, stomach, and pancreas

Kidney: Kidney failure associated with end-stage liver disease

Nutrition: Nutrient deficiencies; obesity

Reproductive system: In women, menstrual irregularities and increased risk of having children with fetal alcohol syndrome (FAS); in men, impotence and testicular atrophy

Bone: Increased risk of osteoporosis; increased risk of fractures from frequent falls

Figure 10-3 The immediate and long-term effects of alcohol use.

- Make sure your safety belt is fastened and children are in approved safety seats.
- Report suspected impaired drivers to the nearest police station by phone. Give a description of the vehicle, license number, location, and direction the vehicle is headed.

The Effects of Chronic Use

Because alcohol is distributed throughout most of the body, it can affect many different organs and tissues (Figure 10-3). Problems associated with chronic, or habitual, use of alcohol include diseases of the digestive and cardiovascular systems and some cancers. Drinking during pregnancy risks the health of both the woman and the developing fetus.

The Digestive System Even in relatively small amounts, alcohol can alter the normal functioning of the liver. Within just a few days of heavy alcohol consumption, fat begins to accumulate in liver cells, resulting in the development of "fatty liver." If drinking continues, inflammation of the liver can occur, resulting in alcoholic hepatitis, a frequent cause of hospitalization and death in alcoholics. Both fatty liver and alcoholic hepatitis are potentially reversible if the person stops drinking. With continued alcohol use, however, liver cells are progressively damaged and then permanently destroyed. The destroyed cells are replaced by fibrous scar tissue, a condition known as **cirrhosis.** As cirrhosis develops, a drinker may gradually lose his or her capacity to tolerate alcohol, because there are fewer and fewer healthy cells remaining in the liver to metabolize it. In 2004, alcohol-precipitated cirrhosis was the twelfth leading cause of death in the United States.

As with most health hazards, the risk of cirrhosis depends on an individual's susceptibility, largely genetically

Term

cirrhosis A disease in which the liver is severely damaged by alcohol, other toxins, or infection.

determined, and the amount of alcohol consumed over time. Some people show signs of cirrhosis after a few years of consuming three or four drinks per day. Women generally develop cirrhosis at lower levels of alcohol consumption than men. Alcoholics are especially susceptible to infection with hepatitis C virus (HCV); the combination of alcohol abuse and HCV infection greatly increases the risk for cirrhosis and liver cancer.

Signs of cirrhosis can include jaundice (a yellowing of the skin and white part of the eyes) and the accumulation of fluid in the abdomen and lower extremities. Some people with cirrhosis have no obvious outward signs of the disease. Treatment for cirrhosis includes a balanced diet and complete abstinence from alcohol. People with cirrhosis who continue to drink have only a 50% chance of surviving 5 or more years.

Alcohol can inflame the pancreas, causing nausea, vomiting, abnormal digestion, and severe pain. Acute alcoholic pancreatitis generally occurs in binge drinkers. Unlike cirrhosis, which usually occurs after years of fairly heavy alcohol use, pancreatitis can occur after just one or two severe binge-drinking episodes. Acute pancreatitis is often fatal and can also develop into a chronic condition.

Overuse of alcohol is a common cause of bleeding in the gastrointestinal tract. Vomiting after an alcohol binge can result in tearing of esophageal blood vessels. Chronic alcohol use with cirrhosis frequently results in the development of enlarged, fragile esophageal and rectal veins, which can easily burst with potentially fatal results. Even a relatively small amount of alcohol can cause painful irritation of the lining of the stomach.

The Cardiovascular System The effects of alcohol on the cardiovascular system depend on the amount of alcohol consumed. Moderate doses of alcohol—less than one drink a day for women and two drinks a day for men—may reduce the risk of heart disease and heart attack in some people. (The possible health benefits of alcohol are discussed later in this chapter.) However, higher doses of alcohol have harmful effects on the cardiovascular system. In some people, more than two drinks a day will elevate blood pressure, making stroke and heart attack more likely. Some alcoholics show a weakening of the heart muscle, a condition known as **cardiac myopathy.** Binge drinking can cause "holiday heart," a syndrome characterized by serious abnormal heart rhythms, which usually appear within 24 hours of a binge episode.

Although the relationships between alcohol and cardiovascular disease are multiple and complex, it is clear that excessive drinking increases the risk of disease. These health risks progressively increase as the amount of excessive drinking increases.

Cancer Alcoholics have a cancer rate about ten times higher than that of the general population. They are particularly vulnerable to cancers of the throat, larynx, esophagus, upper stomach, liver, and pancreas. Drinking three or more alcoholic beverages per day doubles a woman's risk of developing breast cancer. Some studies have linked even moderate drinking to increased risk for cancers of the breast, mouth, throat, and esophagus. In May 2000, the U.S. Department of Health and Human Services added alcoholic beverages to the list of known human carcinogens.

Brain Damage Heavy social drinkers and alcoholics show evidence of brain damage. Men who have 100 or more drinks per month and women who have 80 or more drinks per month experience impairment of memory, processing speed, attention, and balance. Brain shrinkage has also been found among heavy drinkers; slight reduction in brain volume has been seen even in moderate drinkers, although it is unclear whether this indicates the death of nerve cells.

Mortality As an ancient proverb states, "Those who worship Bacchus [the god of wine] die young." Excessive alcohol consumption is a factor in several of the leading causes of death for Americans. Average life expectancy among alcoholics is about 15 years less than among nonalcoholics; heavy drinkers may die in their twenties or thirties. About half the deaths caused by alcohol are due to chronic conditions such as cirrhosis and cancer; the other half are due to acute conditions or events such as car crashes, falls, and suicide. Because many deaths from acute conditions occur in youths and young adults, alcohol is responsible for 2.3 million years of potential life lost each year.

The Effects of Alcohol Use During Pregnancy

Alcohol ingested during pregnancy is harmful to the developing fetus. Alcohol and its metabolic product, acetaldehyde, readily cross the placenta. Damage to the fetus depends on the stage of pregnancy and the amount of alcohol consumed. Alcohol use in early pregnancy can cause a miscarriage. Moderate to heavy alcohol use can cause a collection of birth defects known as **fetal alcohol syndrome (FAS).** Children with FAS have a characteristic mixture of deformities that include a small head, abnormal facial structure, heart defects, and other physical abnormalities; most are mentally impaired, and their physical and mental growth is slower than normal.

FAS is a permanent, incurable condition that causes lifelong disability; it is by far the most common preventable cause of mental retardation in the Western world. Full-blown FAS occurs in 1 or 2 out of every 1000 live births in the United States. Many more babies are born with **alcohol-related neurodevelopmental disorder (ARND).** Children with ARND appear physically normal but often

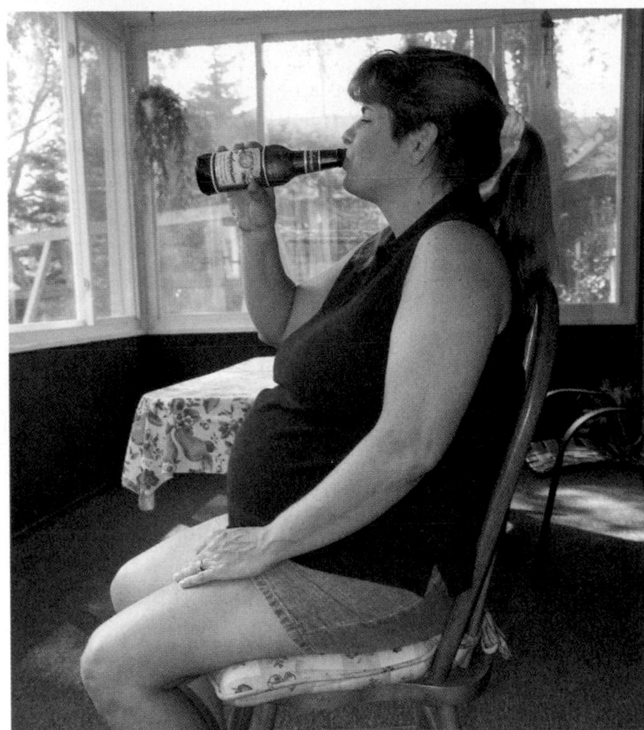

A high level of alcohol consumption during pregnancy is associated with miscarriage, stillbirth, and a cluster of birth defects known as fetal alcohol syndrome. Total abstinence from alcohol during pregnancy is recommended.

have significant learning and behavioral disorders and are, as adults, more likely to develop substance-abuse problems and to have criminal records.

Heavy drinking early in pregnancy is responsible for most of the physical abnormalities associated with FAS. Binge drinking among women of childbearing age is thus of particular concern because women may drink heavily during the first few days and weeks of gestation before they become aware that they are pregnant. Fetal alcohol exposure later in pregnancy is more likely to cause brain damage without obvious external signs. Getting drunk just one time during the final 3 months of pregnancy, when brain cells are developing rapidly, can cause fetal brain damage.

No one is sure exactly how much alcohol use is required to cause FAS, but no amount of alcohol during pregnancy is considered safe. A 2002 study found that children born to mothers who drank as little as one-and-a-half drinks per week during their pregnancy weighed less and were shorter at age 14 than children of mothers who did not drink at all during pregnancy. This is one of the first studies to show a significant difference between the children of nondrinkers and those of light drinkers. The children in this study did not have FAS, but their smaller size may be a marker for subtle, persistent alcohol damage. The adverse effects of alcohol are especially pronounced when women drink early in pregnancy. For this reason, women who are trying to conceive or who are sexually active without using effective contraception should abstain from alcohol in order to avoid inadvertently harming their fetus before they even know they are pregnant. Experts agree that the safest course of action is complete abstinence from alcohol during pregnancy. Despite this, about 10% of pregnant women do consume alcohol, and about 4% are binge drinkers. In 2005, the Surgeon General released an advisory to raise awareness about the dangers of drinking during pregnancy.

Any alcohol consumed by a nursing mother quickly enters the breast milk. What impact this has on the child or on the mother's milk production is a matter of controversy. Dosage may again be the key issue. However, many physicians advise nursing mothers to abstain from drinking alcohol because of the belief that any amount may have negative effects on the baby's brain development.

Possible Health Benefits of Alcohol

The relationship between alcohol use and health is complex and still under investigation. Numerous studies have shown that, on average, light to moderate drinkers live longer than either abstainers or heavy drinkers. Based on this and other research on the health benefits of alcohol, some have begun to think of alcohol—in particular, red wine—as the latest health drink. But although moderate alcohol consumption may provide some health benefits for a given individual, for many people the dangers of alcohol are much greater than the potential benefits.

A recent large-scale study found that the risks and benefits of drinking alcohol vary considerably with the age of the drinker. If you are 35 or younger, your odds of dying *increase* in direct proportion to the amount of alcohol you drink. Among people under age 35, even light drinkers have slightly higher mortality rates than nondrinkers. In other words, young adults who drink *any* amount of alcohol are more likely to die than nondrinkers of the same age. Alcohol consumption appears to confer health benefits primarily to older individuals, with the greatest benefits seen in people age 65 and older.

Moderate drinking may also benefit people who currently have or are at high risk for certain diseases such as

Terms

cardiac myopathy Weakening of the heart muscle through disease.

fetal alcohol syndrome (FAS) A characteristic group of birth defects caused by excessive alcohol consumption by the mother, including facial deformities, heart defects, and physical and mental impairments.

alcohol-related neurodevelopmental disorder (ARND) Cognitive and behavioral problems seen in people whose mothers drank alcohol during pregnancy.

coronary heart disease. In a 2006 study of men age 50 and over, those who drank moderately each day reduced their risk of heart disease by about 40%, compared to men who never drank. The difference was not as great in women. Moderate drinking may improve heart health by raising blood levels of HDL (the beneficial form of cholesterol), by thinning the blood, and by reducing inflammation and the risk of dangerous blood clots, all of which can contribute to the risk of a heart attack. Individuals with heart disease or with strong risk factors should talk with their doctors about the possible health benefits of moderate drinking. Some evidence also suggests that moderate drinkers may be less likely to develop a variety of other conditions, including diabetes, strokes, arterial blockages in the legs, Alzheimer's disease, and benign prostate enlargement. Moderate wine consumption may also lower blood glucose levels, possibly reducing the risk of heart disease in some people.

Research is under way to determine whether the apparent health benefits of wine are due to the alcohol or to some other substance found in wine. Some experts believe that the apparent benefit of wine may merely reflect the fact that wine drinkers tend to be more affluent and to have healthier lifestyles than non–wine drinkers.

Moderate drinking is not without risk, however. It increases the risk of dying from unintentional injuries, violence, and certain types of cancer. In women, even moderate drinking may increase the risk of breast cancer; those who are at risk for breast cancer should discuss the potential risks and benefits of alcohol with their physician. There is also a risk that moderate drinking will not stay moderate. People who avoid alcohol because they or family members have had problems with dependence in the past should not start drinking for their health. People with conditions such as depression that are worsened by alcohol use should probably avoid even moderate drinking. Nor should drinkers use this information as an excuse to overindulge; any health benefits of alcohol are negated by heavy use. In addition, there are many situations in which consuming any amount of alcohol is unwise, including during pregnancy, while taking medication that may interact with alcohol, and when driving or engaging in another activity that requires attention, skill, or coordination. Sexually active women who are not consistently using effective contraception should also not drink.

The bottom line is that limited, regular consumption of alcohol may be beneficial for some adults, but there is a narrow window of benefit, and excessive drinking causes serious health problems. The *Dietary Guidelines for Americans* recommends that if you drink alcoholic beverages, you should do it in moderation, with meals, at times when consumption does not put you or others at risk. Moderate drinking means no more than one drink a day for women and two drinks a day for men.

ALCOHOL ABUSE AND DEPENDENCE

Abuse of and dependence on alcohol affect more than just the drinker. Friends, family members, coworkers, strangers that drinkers encounter on the road, and society as a whole pay the physical, emotional, and financial costs of the misuse of alcohol.

Alcohol Abuse

As explained in Chapter 9, the American Psychiatric Association's *Diagnostic and Statistical Manual of Mental Disorders* makes a distinction between substance abuse and substance dependence. **Alcohol abuse** is recurrent alcohol use that has negative consequences, such as drinking in dangerous situations (before driving, for instance), or drinking patterns that result in academic, professional, interpersonal, or legal difficulties. **Alcohol dependence,** or **alcoholism,** involves more extensive problems with alcohol use, usually involving physical tolerance and withdrawal. Alcoholism is discussed in greater detail later in the chapter.

Other authorities use different definitions to describe problems associated with drinking. The important point is that one does not have to be an alcoholic to have problems with alcohol. The person who drinks only once a month, perhaps after an exam, but then drives while intoxicated is an alcohol abuser.

How can you tell if you are beginning to abuse alcohol or if someone you know is doing so? Look for the following warning signs:

- Drinking alone or secretively
- Using alcohol deliberately and repeatedly to perform or get through difficult situations
- Feeling uncomfortable on certain occasions when alcohol is not available
- Escalating alcohol consumption beyond an already established drinking pattern
- Consuming alcohol heavily in risky situations, such as before driving
- Getting drunk regularly or more frequently than in the past
- Drinking in the morning or at other unusual times

Binge Drinking

A common form of alcohol abuse on college campuses is **binge drinking.** In surveys of students on over 100 college campuses, 44% reported binge drinking, defined as having five drinks in a row for men or four in a row for women on at least one occasion in the 2 weeks prior to the survey. Some 23% of all students were found to be frequent binge drinkers, defined as having at least three binges during the 2-week period. Students living at fraternity

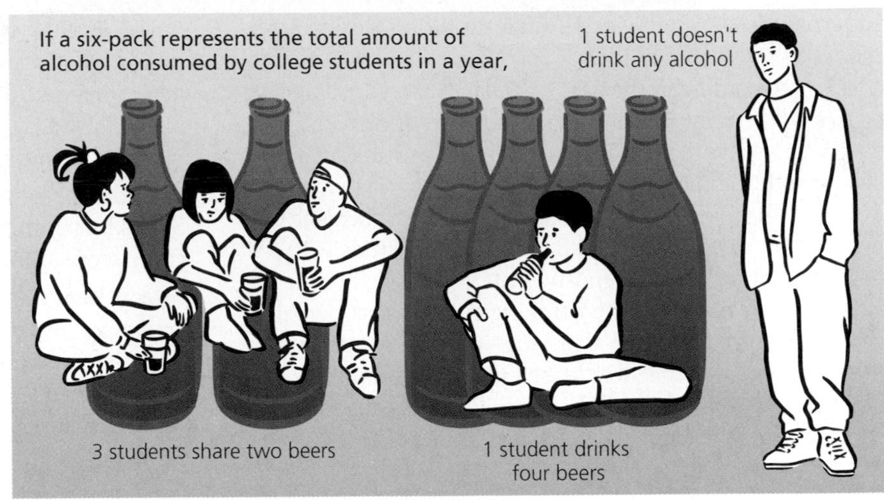

If a six-pack represents the total amount of alcohol consumed by college students in a year,
1 student doesn't drink any alcohol
3 students share two beers
1 student drinks four beers

Figure 10-4 Alcohol consumption by college students. Alcohol consumption by students varies considerably, with some abstaining and some drinking large amounts. Only one in five college students is a frequent binge drinker, but this group accounts for nearly three-fourths of all the alcohol consumed by college students each year and causes or experiences the majority of alcohol-related problems. SOURCE: Wechsler, H., et al. 2000. *From Knowledge to Action: How Harvard's College Alcohol Study Can Help Your Campus Design a Campaign Against Student Alcohol Abuse* (http://www.hsph.harvard.edu/cas/test/articles/change2.html; retrieved August 9, 2006).

houses had the highest rate of binge drinking, up to 80%. Men were more likely to binge than women, and white students had higher rates of binge drinking than students of other ethnicities. Nineteen percent of students abstained from alcohol (Figure 10-4).

Binge drinking has a profound effect on students' lives. Frequent binge drinkers were found to be three to seven times more likely than non–binge drinkers to engage in unplanned or unprotected sex, to drive after drinking, and to get hurt or injured (Table 10-2). Binge drinkers were also more likely to miss classes, get behind in schoolwork, and argue with friends. The more frequent the binges, the more problems the students encountered. Despite their experiences, fewer than 1% of the binge drinkers identified themselves as problem drinkers.

Binge drinking kills dozens of American college students each year. Some die from acute alcohol poisoning. The typical scenario involves a hazing ritual, a competition, or a bet that involves drinking a large amount of alcohol very quickly. This kind of fast, heavy drinking can result in unconsciousness and death very quickly, before anyone realizes that something is seriously wrong. Many other students die from alcohol-related injuries, including those from motor vehicle crashes.

Binge drinking also affects nonbingeing students. At schools with high rates of binge drinking, the nonbingers were up to twice as likely to report being bothered by the alcohol-related behaviors of others than were students at schools with lower rates of binge drinking. These problems included having sleep or studying disrupted; having to take care of a drunken student; being insulted or humiliated; experiencing unwanted sexual advances; and being pushed, hit, or assaulted.

The *Healthy People 2010* report sets the goal of reducing the rate of binge drinking to 20% among college students. Binge drinking is a difficult problem to address because many students arrive at college with drinking

VITAL STATISTICS

Table 10-2 The Effects of Binge Drinking on College Students

	Percentage of Students Experiencing Problems	
Alcohol-Related Problem	Non–Binge Drinkers	Frequent Binge Drinkers
Drove after drinking alcohol	18	58
Did something they regretted	17	62
Argued with friends	10	43
Engaged in unplanned sex	9	41
Missed a class	9	60
Got behind in schoolwork	9	42
Had unprotected sex	4	21
Got hurt or injured	4	28
Got into trouble with police	2	14
Had five or more of these problems since school year began	4	48

SOURCE: Wechsler, H., and B. Wuethrich. 2003. *Dying to Drink: Confronting Binge Drinking on College Campuses*, reprint ed. Emmaus, Pa.: Rodale.

Terms

alcohol abuse The use of alcohol to a degree that causes physical damage, impairs functioning, or results in behavior harmful to others.

alcohol dependence A pathological use of alcohol or impairment in functioning due to alcohol; characterized by tolerance and withdrawal symptoms; alcoholism.

alcoholism A chronic psychological disorder characterized by excessive and compulsive drinking.

binge drinking Periodically drinking alcohol to the point of severe intoxication.

patterns already established (binge drinking during high school is a strong predictor of binge drinking during college). According to the 2005 *National Survey on Drug Use and Health,* nearly 3 million children and adolescents between ages 12 and 17 had engaged in binge drinking in the past month. Studies show that the earlier a person begins drinking, the more likely he or she will abuse or become dependent on alcohol as an adult. In one such study, 47% of respondents met the diagnostic criteria for alcoholism by age 21. Many colleges have drinking cultures that perpetuate the pattern of binge drinking. On many campuses, drinking behavior that would be classified as abuse in another setting may be viewed as socially acceptable or even attractive (see the box "College Binge Drinking").

Alcoholism

As mentioned earlier, alcoholism, or alcohol dependence, is usually characterized by tolerance to alcohol and withdrawal symptoms. Everyone who drinks—even nonalcoholics—develops tolerance after repeated alcohol use. As described in Chapter 9, *tolerance* means that a drinker needs more alcohol to achieve intoxication or the desired effect, that the effects of continued use of the same amount of alcohol are diminished, or that the drinker can function adequately at doses or a BAC that would produce significant impairment in a casual user. Heavy users of alcohol may need to consume about 50% more than they originally needed in order to experience the same degree of intoxication.

Withdrawal occurs when someone who has been using alcohol heavily for several days or more suddenly stops drinking or markedly reduces intake. Symptoms of withdrawal include trembling and nervousness and sometimes even **hallucinations** and seizures.

Patterns and Prevalence Alcoholism occurs among people of all ethnic groups and at all socioeconomic levels. The stereotype of the alcoholic skid-row bum actually accounts for fewer than 5% of all alcohol-dependent people and usually represents the final stage of a drinking career that began years earlier. There are different patterns of alcohol dependence, including these four common ones:

1. *Regular daily intake of large amounts.* This continuous pattern is the most common adult pattern of excessive consumption in most countries.

2. *Regular heavy drinking limited to weekends.* This pattern of binge drinking is often followed by teenagers and college students.

3. *Long periods of sobriety interspersed with binges of daily heavy drinking lasting for weeks or months.* This episodic, or bender, pattern is common in the United States but quite uncommon in France, although the per capita consumption of alcohol is higher in France.

4. *Heavy drinking limited to periods of stress.* This reactive pattern is associated with periods of anxiety or depression, such as at times of test anxiety or of other performance fears, interpersonal problems, or school or work pressures.

Once established, alcoholism often exhibits a pattern of exacerbations and remissions. The person may stop drinking and abstain from alcohol for days or months after a frightening problem develops. After a period of abstinence, an alcoholic often attempts controlled drinking, which almost inevitably leads to an escalation in drinking and more problems. Alcoholism is not hopeless, however; many alcoholics do achieve permanent abstinence.

According to the 2005 *National Survey on Drug Use and Health,* more than 16.5 million Americans are heavy drinkers and nearly 55 million are binge drinkers. Studies suggest that the lifetime risk of alcoholism in the United States is about 10% for men and about 3% for women. The risk for women has been increasing in recent years as women's roles in our society have expanded.

Health Effects Tolerance and withdrawal can have a serious impact on health. An alcoholic requires increasing amounts of alcohol to produce the desired effects, and these larger doses increase the chance of adverse physical effects. When alcoholics stop drinking or sharply decrease their intake, they experience withdrawal. Symptoms include trembling hands (shakes, or jitters), a rapid pulse and accelerated breathing rate, insomnia, nightmares, anxiety, and gastrointestinal upset. These symptoms usually begin 5–10 hours after alcohol intake is decreased and improve after 4–5 days. After a week, most people feel much better, but occasionally anxiety, insomnia, and other symptoms persist for 6 months or more.

More severe withdrawal symptoms occur in about 5% of alcoholics. These include seizures (sometimes called rum fits), confusion, and hallucinations. Still less common is **DTs (delirium tremens),** a medical emergency characterized by severe disorientation, confusion, epileptic-like seizures, and vivid hallucinations, often of vermin and small animals. The mortality rate from DTs can be as high as 15%, especially in very debilitated people with preexisting medical illnesses.

Because alcohol is distributed throughout the body's organs and tissues, alcoholism takes a heavy physical and psychological toll. Alcoholics face all the physical health risks associated with intoxication and chronic drinking

Terms

VW

hallucination A false perception that does not correspond to external reality, such as seeing visions or hearing voices that are not there.

DTs (delirium tremens) A state of confusion brought on by the reduction of alcohol intake in an alcohol-dependent person; other symptoms are sweating, trembling, anxiety, hallucinations, and seizures.

College Binge Drinking

College binge drinking, a serious problem for more than 30 years, finally began receiving national attention in the past decade, due in part to alcohol-related tragedies. Highly publicized cases of deaths caused by alcohol overdose, alcohol-related injuries (including motor vehicle crashes) and violent crimes, student riots, and serious vandalism have all drawn attention to the epidemic of heavy drinking on college campuses.

An estimated 1700 college students age 18–24 die from alcohol-related injuries and alcohol overdoses each year. To many people, heavy drinking is considered a normal and integral part of college life. But research has shown that the pattern of excessive binge drinking common on many of today's college campuses has had a devastating impact on far too many students, as well as on their families and communities.

Much of the current data on college drinking comes from the ongoing Harvard School of Public Health College Alcohol Study, the first large-scale national study of college drinking habits. Since 1993, studies of college students across the United States have confirmed that nearly half (44%) of all college students binge-drink. The statistics have shocked many students, college administrators, and parents into demanding a change in our attitudes and policies regarding alcohol use on campus.

In response to this increased awareness of the college alcohol problem, the Task Force of the National Advisory Council on Alcohol Abuse and Alcoholism was formed. Its report documents the extent of the alcohol problem and is a call to action for colleges and their surrounding communities to reexamine their alcohol policies.

What are some of the facts about college drinking? A recent survey of 14,000 students at U.S. 4-year colleges found that 31% of college students meet the medical criteria for a diagnosis of alcohol abuse and 6% for a diagnosis of alcohol dependence. More students drink alcohol than use cigarettes, marijuana, or cocaine combined. Alcohol use and abuse are linked to many serious problems on campus; the annual toll includes the following:

- Nearly 600,000 students between 18 and 24 are unintentionally injured in alcohol-related incidents (motor vehicle crashes, fights, falls, and so on).
- College students currently spend $5.5 billion a year on alcohol, more than they spend on textbooks, soft drinks, tea, milk, juice, and coffee combined.
- About 700,000 students are assaulted by another student who has been drinking.
- Nearly 100,000 students are victims of alcohol-related sexual assault, including date rape. Nearly 75% of female rape victims were raped while intoxicated.
- Hundreds of thousands of students engage in unsafe sex while intoxicated, resulting in dramatically increased risk for STDs and unwanted pregnancy.
- As many as 2.1 million students drive while under the influence of alcohol.
- About 1.2–1.5% of college students attempt suicide because of drinking or drug use.
- Among students who live on campus and don't binge-drink, 61% say that drinkers have disrupted their study or sleep time, 50% say they have had to take care of a drunken student, and 29% say they have been insulted or humiliated by a drunken student.

Heavy alcohol use detracts from the college experience of drinkers and nondrinkers alike. The National Advisory Council Task Force calls for an overhaul of the campus drinking culture. Unfortunately, drinking to excess has been a college tradition for decades. Changing long-entrenched campus drinking habits will require effort on the part of students, college administrators, parents, and communities alike. According to the Task Force, changes must occur on three levels:

1. Ultimately, *individual students* must take responsibility for their own behavior. Motivating and encouraging students to develop a new, healthier relationship to alcohol is the focus of this part of the Task Force's recommendation. Students who enter college as nonbingers should be supported, and treatment should be readily available to problem drinkers. Groups at special risk for increasing or established problem drinking behavior include first-year students, Greek organization members, and athletes.

2. The *student body as a whole* must work to discourage alcohol abuse. This effort might include promoting alcohol-free activities for students, reducing the availability of alcohol, and avoiding the social and commercial promotion of alcohol on campus. Fraternities and sororities must be involved in these changes, as the most serious binge drinking tends to occur among their members.

3. *Colleges and surrounding communities* must cooperate to discourage excessive drinking. A 2006 study shows that violence is greater in areas where alcohol is more easily obtained, and researchers believe this is true of other alcohol-related problems. College administrators, law enforcement, bar and liquor store owners, residents who live near the campus, and the court system all must work together to reduce the availability of cheap alcohol. Laws that prohibit excessive and underage drinking must be fairly enforced. Students who commit crimes while under the influence must receive appropriate punishment, including restitution to any victims. College administrators must find other funding sources to replace the financial support that currently flows in from the alcohol industry in exchange for advertising and promotion of their products on college campuses.

Excessive binge drinking undermines the quality of colleges. Solutions to the problem of alcohol overuse are complex, but change is possible. Individual students can find out about the alcohol problems on their campus and work together with their college administrators and the community to find solutions. Colleges can say no to the alcohol industry when it comes to alcohol promotion on campus, even if it means a loss of substantial revenue. Working together, students, faculty, administrators, parents, and the community can put an end to the destructive culture of heavy drinking on college campuses.

SOURCES: White, A. M., C. L. Kraus, and H. Swartzwelder. 2006. Many college freshmen drink at levels far beyond the binge threshold. *Alcoholism, Clinical and Experimental Research* 30(6): 1006–1010; Harvard College Alcohol Study. 2005. *Binge Drinking on Campus Lower in States with Fewer Adult Binge Drinkers and Stronger Alcohol Control Laws* (http://www.hsph.harvard.edu/cas/Documents/state/state_pr.html; retrieved August 10, 2006); Hingson, R., et al. 2005. Magnitude of alcohol-related mortality and morbidity among U.S. college students ages 18–24. *Annual Review of Public Health* 26: 259–279; Mohler-Kuo, M., et al. 2004. Correlates of rape while intoxicated in a national sample of college women. *Journal of Studies on Alcohol* 65(1): 37–45; National Institute on Alcohol Abuse and Alcoholism. 2002. *A Call to Action: Changing the Culture of Drinking at U.S. Colleges* (http://www.collegedrinkingprevention.gov/Reports/TaskForce/TaskForce_TOC.aspx; retrieved August 10, 2006).

In Focus

Children of Alcoholics

About one out of eight Americans grows up in an alcoholic household. For these children, life is a struggle to deal with constant stress, anxiety, and embarrassment. They may be victims of violence, abuse, or neglect in the home. Family life centers on the drinking parent, and children's needs are often ignored.

Children in alcoholic households often cope by learning patterns of interaction that help them survive childhood but that don't support their own healthy development. Many adult children of alcoholics fear losing control, and they try to control their own feelings and behavior and those of people around them. They may fear emotions, even pleasant feelings such as happiness and joy. They avoid conflict and are easily upset by criticism from authority figures. Other common traits include an overdeveloped sense of responsibility and hypersensitivity to the needs of others. Children of alcoholics often feel guilty if they stand up for themselves and acknowledge their own needs. All these characteristics can be stumbling blocks to forming healthy relationships.

Children of alcoholics are more likely than other children to become alcoholic themselves and to marry alcoholics. An estimated 13–25% of children of alcoholics will become alcoholic at some point in their lives. They are more likely to abuse other drugs and develop an eating disorder. They are also particularly prone to stress-related medical illnesses.

If you are the child of an alcoholic, be aware, first, that you are not alone. Millions of people have been through the same problem and have dreamed of having a happy family life in which drinking is not an issue. Realize, too, that other people can understand what you have been through and can help. Find a person you can trust, and confide in her or him. It may seem safer to keep your feelings secret, but talking about the problem is the first step toward a healthy readjustment. Many adult children of alcoholics benefit greatly from therapy with a counselor who is experienced in treating people who have been affected by an alcoholic family. Individual or group therapy can be a critical step in recovery. (The For More Information section at the end of this chapter lists agencies that can provide help and referrals.)

Finally, acknowledge that your parent's alcoholism is not your fault. Many children of alcoholics carry a burden of guilt from early childhood, when they could not understand that they weren't the cause of their parent's behavior. This unexamined assumption is often part of the emotional pain experienced by children of alcoholics.

described earlier in the chapter. Some of the damage is compounded by nutritional deficiencies that often accompany alcoholism. A mental problem associated with alcohol use is profound memory gaps (commonly known as blackouts), which are sometimes filled by conscious or unconscious lying.

The specific health effects of alcoholism tend to vary from person to person. For example, one individual may suffer from problems with memory and CNS defects and have no liver or gastrointestinal problems. Another person with a similar drinking and nutritional history may have advanced liver disease but no memory gaps.

Social and Psychological Effects Alcohol use causes more serious social and psychological problems than all other forms of drug abuse combined. For every person who is an alcoholic, another three or four people are directly affected (see the box "Children of Alcoholics"). In a 2004 Gallup poll, about a third of Americans reported that alcohol had been a source of trouble in their family.

Alcoholics frequently suffer from mental disorders in addition to their substance dependence. Alcoholics are much more likely than nonalcoholics to suffer from clinical depression, panic disorder, schizophrenia, and antisocial personality disorders. People with anxiety or panic attacks may try to use alcohol to lessen their anxiety, even though alcohol often makes these disorders worse. Alcoholics also often have other substance-abuse problems.

An estimated 3 million Americans age 14–17 show signs of potential alcohol dependence. These numbers are far greater than those associated with cocaine, heroin, or marijuana use. The social and psychological consequences of excessive drinking in young people are more difficult to measure than the risks to physical health. One consequence is that excessive drinking interferes with learning the interpersonal and job-related skills required for adult life. Excessive drinkers sometimes narrow their circle of friends to other heavy drinkers and thus limit the range of people they can learn from. Perhaps most important is that people who were excessive drinkers in college are more likely to have social, occupational, and health problems 20 years later. Despite media attention on cocaine and other drugs, alcohol abuse remains our society's number-one drug-abuse problem.

Causes of Alcoholism The precise causes of alcoholism are unknown, but many factors are probably involved. Studies of twins and adopted children clearly demonstrate the importance of genetics. If one of a pair of fraternal twins is alcoholic, then the other has about twice the chance of becoming alcoholic. For the identical twin of an alcoholic, the risk of alcoholism is about four times that of the general population. These risks persist even when the twins have little contact with each other or their biological parents. Similarly, adoption studies show an increased risk among children of alcoholics, even if they were adopted at birth into nondrinking families. Alcoholism in adoptive parents, contrarily, doesn't make individuals more or less likely to become alcoholic. Some studies suggest that as much as 50–60% of a person's risk for alcoholism is determined by genetic factors. Many genes are thought to be involved in shaping the risk for alcoholism.

Not all children of alcoholics become alcoholic, however, and it is clear that other factors are involved. A person's risk of developing alcoholism may be increased by certain personality disorders, having grown up in a violent or otherwise troubled household, and imitating the alcohol abuse of peers and other role models. People who begin drinking excessively in their teens are especially prone to binge drinking and alcoholism later in life. Common psychological features of individuals who abuse alcohol are denial ("I don't have a problem") and rationalization ("I drink because I need to socialize with my customers"). Certain social factors have also been linked with alcoholism, including urbanization, disappearance of the extended family, a general loosening of kinship ties, increased mobility, and changing values.

Treatment Some alcoholics recover without professional help. How often this occurs is unknown, but possibly as many as one-third stop drinking on their own or reduce their drinking enough to eliminate problems. Often these spontaneous recoveries are linked to an alcohol-related crisis, such as a health problem or the threat of being fired. Not all alcoholics must hit bottom before they are motivated to stop. People vary markedly in what induces them to change their behavior. For some, the first blackout or alcohol-related automobile crash fosters abstinence.

Most alcoholics, however, require a treatment program of some kind in order to stop drinking. Many different kinds of programs exist. No single treatment works for everyone, so a person may have to try different programs before finding the right one. More than 750,000 Americans sought treatment for alcohol abuse in 2004.

Although treatment is not successful for all alcoholics, considerable optimism has replaced the older view that nothing could be done. Many alcoholics have patterns of drinking that fluctuate widely over time. These fluctuations indicate that their alcohol abuse is a response to environmental factors, such as life stressors or social pressures, and therefore may be influenced by treatment.

One of the oldest and best-known recovery programs is Alcoholics Anonymous (AA). AA consists of self-help groups that meet several times each week in most communities and follow a 12-step program. Important steps for people in these programs include recognizing that they are "powerless over alcohol" and must seek help from a "higher power" in order to regain control of their lives. By verbalizing these steps, the alcoholic directly addresses the denial that is often prominent in alcoholism and other addictions. Many AA members have a sponsor of their choosing who is available by phone 24 hours a day for individual support and crisis intervention. AA convincingly shows the alcoholic that abstinence can be achieved and also provides a sober peer group of people who share the same identity—that of recovering alcoholics.

Alcoholics Anonymous is generally recognized as an effective mutual help program, but not everyone responds to its style and message, and other recovery approaches are available. Some, like Rational Recovery and Women for Sobriety, deliberately avoid any emphasis on higher spiritual powers. Even people who are helped by AA often find that it works best in combination with counseling and medical care. A more controversial approach to problem drinking is offered by the group Moderation Management, which encourages people to manage their drinking behavior by limiting intake or abstaining.

Al-Anon is a companion program to AA that consists of groups for families and friends of alcoholics. In Al-Anon, spouses and others explore how they enabled the alcoholic to drink by denying, rationalizing, or covering up his or her drinking and how they can change this codependent behavior.

Employee assistance programs and school-based programs represent another approach to alcoholism treatment that works for some people. One of the advantages of these programs is that they can deal directly with work and campus issues, often important sources of stress for the alcohol abuser. These programs sometimes encourage learning effective coping responses for internal and external sources of distress. Individuals might also benefit from learning new cognitive concepts, such as a self-identity that does not involve drinking.

Inpatient hospital rehabilitation is useful for some alcoholics, especially if they have serious medical or mental problems or if life stressors threaten to overwhelm them. When the person returns to the community, however, it is critical that there be some form of active, continuing, long-term treatment. Patients who return to a spouse or family often require ongoing treatment on issues involving those significant others, such as establishing new routines and planning shared recreational activities that do not involve drinking.

There are also some pharmacological treatments for alcoholism:

- *Disulfiram* (Antabuse) inhibits the metabolic breakdown of acetaldehyde and causes patients to flush and feel ill when they drink, thus theoretically inhibiting impulse drinking. However, it is potentially dangerous if the user does also drink. Antabuse can help alcoholics abstain from drinking in the long run; it works best combined with ongoing therapy.

- *Naltrexone* reduces the craving for alcohol and decreases the pleasant, reinforcing effects of alcohol without making the user ill. It also works most effectively in combination with counseling and other forms of psychosocial treatment.
- *Acamprosate* (Campral), approved by the FDA in 2005, helps people maintain alcohol abstinence after they have stopped drinking. It is unclear precisely how it works, but it appears to act on the brain pathways related to alcohol abuse.

Research is currently under way on other medications, including topiramate, baclofen, and gabapentin.

In people who abuse alcohol and have significant depression or anxiety, the use of antidepressant or antianxiety medication can improve both mental health and drinking behavior. In addition, drugs such as diazepam (Valium) are sometimes prescribed to replace alcohol during initial stages of withdrawal. Such chemical substitutes are usually useful for only a week or so, because alcoholics are at particularly high risk for developing dependence on other drugs. Counseling and peer-group support are generally the most essential elements of alcoholism treatment, with or without drugs.

Alcohol-treatment programs are successful in achieving an extended period of sobriety for about half of those who participate. Success rates of conventional treatment programs are about the same for men and women and for people from different ethnic groups. Women, minorities, and the poor often face major economic and social barriers to receiving treatment. Most inpatient treatment programs are financially out of reach for people of low income or those without insurance coverage. AA remains the mainstay of treatment for most people and is often a component of even the most expensive treatment programs. Special AA groups exist in many communities for young people, women, gay men and lesbians, non–English speakers, and a variety of interest groups. You can find out about AA meetings in your community by looking in the phone book or consulting the For More Information section at the end of the chapter.

Gender and Ethnic Differences

Alcohol abusers come from all socioeconomic levels and cultural groups, but there are notable differences in patterns of drinking between men and women and among different ethnic groups (Table 10-3).

Men Among white American men, excessive drinking often begins in the teens or twenties and progresses gradually through the thirties until the individual is clearly identifiable as an alcoholic by the time he is in his late thirties or early forties. Other men remain controlled drinkers until later in life, sometimes becoming alcoholic in association with retirement, the inevitable losses of aging, boredom, illness, or psychological disorders. (See the box "Gender and Alcohol Use and Abuse.")

VITAL STATISTICS

Table 10-3 Prevalence of Alcohol Abuse and Dependence

	Past Year Prevalence (Percentage)	
	Alcohol Abuse	Alcohol Dependence
Gender		
Men	6.1	4.6
Women	2.6	2.4
Ethnicity		
White	4.6	3.5
African American	2.9	3.4
American Indians and Alaska Natives	4.4	10.4
Native Hawaiians and other Pacific Islanders	1.9	n/a
Asian Americans	2.7	1.0
Latinos	4.5	3.6
Total population	**4.3**	**3.5**

SOURCE: Office of Applied Studies, Substance Abuse and Mental Health Services Administration. 2006. *Results from the 2005 National Survey on Drug Use and Health: National Findings.* (http://oas.samhsa.gov; retrieved November 17, 2006).

Women The progression of alcoholism in women is usually different. Women tend to become alcoholic at a later age and with fewer years of heavy drinking. It is not unusual for women in their forties or fifties to become alcoholic after years of controlled drinking. Women alcoholics develop cirrhosis and other medical complications somewhat more often than men. Women alcoholics may have more medical problems because they are less likely to seek early treatment. In addition, there may be an inherently greater biological risk for women who drink.

African Americans Alcohol abuse is a serious problem for African Americans. Although as a group they use less alcohol than most other groups (including whites), they face disproportionately high levels of alcohol-related birth defects, cirrhosis, cancer, hypertension, and other medical problems. In addition, blacks are more likely than members of other ethnic groups to be victims of alcohol-related homicides, criminal assaults, and injuries. African American women are more likely to abstain from

Gender Matters

Gender and Alcohol Use and Abuse

Men are more likely than women to drink alcohol, to abuse alcohol, and to have alcohol dependency. Men account for the majority of alcohol-related deaths and injuries in the United States, the greater proportion occurring in men age 35 and younger. Most alcohol-related deaths and injuries among men result from acute conditions related to intoxication, such as motor vehicle crashes, falls, drowning, suicide, and homicide.

A variety of factors contributes to the higher rates of alcohol use and abuse among men. Traditional or stereotypic gender roles and ideas regarding masculinity and drinking behavior may promote excessive alcohol consumption among men. Young men in particular are also more likely to engage in all types of risky health behaviors. Men drive more miles, drive more dangerously, and are more likely to drive while intoxicated. They tend to have greater access to firearms, contributing to their increased rates of suicide and homicide. Men may also be more likely than women to use alcohol to cope with stress and other life challenges.

Women are not immune to alcohol problems, however, and rates of alcohol abuse and dependence among women have increased in the past decade. Whether a woman is a "social drinker," a binge drinker, or a heavy daily user, the impact of alcohol on her will be different from and generally greater than the impact of comparable use on a man. And because of the social stigma attached to problem drinking, particularly among women, women are less likely to seek early treatment.

Women become intoxicated at lower doses of alcohol than men, and they tend to experience the adverse physical effects of chronic drinking sooner and at lower levels of alcohol consumption than men. Female alcoholics have higher death rates than male alcoholics, including death rates from cirrhosis. They develop alcohol liver disease and alcohol-related brain damage after a comparatively shorter period of heavy drinking and a lower level of drinking than men. Some alcohol-related health problems are unique to women, including an increased risk of breast cancer, menstrual disorders, infertility, and, in pregnant women, giving birth to a child with FAS.

Women from all walks of life and all ethnic groups can develop alcohol problems, but those who have never married or are divorced are more likely to drink heavily than married or widowed women. Women who have multiple life roles, such as parent, worker, and spouse, are less vulnerable to alcohol problems than women who have fewer roles.

Both men and women are likely to be the perpetrator or victim of a crime when they have been drinking. Sexual assaults of all types, and date rape in particular, are more likely to occur when people are intoxicated. Alcohol use also makes men and women much less likely to practice safer sex, leaving them vulnerable to significant and lasting health problems as the result of sexually transmitted diseases and, for women, to unintended pregnancy.

alcohol use than white women, but among black women who drink there is a higher percentage of heavy drinkers. Urban black males commonly start drinking excessively and develop serious neurological illnesses at an earlier age than urban white males. They also have a higher rate of alcoholism-related suicide.

AA groups of predominantly African Americans have been shown to provide effective treatment, perhaps because essential elements of AA—sharing common experiences, mutual acceptance of one another as human beings, and trusting a higher power—are already a part of African American culture. Treatment efforts that use the extended family and include occupational training are also especially effective.

Latinos Drinking patterns among Latinos vary significantly, depending on their specific cultural background and how long they and their families have lived in the United States. Drunk driving and cirrhosis are the most common causes of alcohol-related death and injury among Hispanic men. Hispanic women are more likely to abstain from alcohol than white or black women, but those who do drink are at special risk for problems. Treating the entire family as a unit is an important part of treatment because family pride, solidarity, and support are important aspects of Latino culture. Some Hispanics do better during treatment if treatment efforts are integrated with the techniques of *curanderos* (folk healers) and *espiritistas* (spiritists).

Asian Americans As a group, Asian Americans have lower-than-average rates of alcohol abuse. However, acculturation may somewhat weaken the generally strong Asian taboos and community sanctions against alcohol use. For many Asian Americans, though, the genetically based physiological aversion to alcohol remains a deterrent to abuse. For those needing treatment, ethnic agencies, health care professionals, and ministers seem to be the most effective sources.

American Indians and Alaska Natives Alcohol abuse is one of the most widespread and severe health problems among American Indians and Alaska Natives, especially for adolescents and young adults. Excessive drinking varies from tribe to tribe but is generally high in both men and women. The rate of alcoholism among American Indians is twice that of the general population, and the death rate from alcohol-related causes is about eight times higher. Treatment may be more effective if it reflects tribal values. Some healers have incorporated aspects of American Indian religions into the therapeutic process, using traditional sweat houses, prayers, and dances.

Helping Someone with an Alcohol Problem

Helping a friend or relative with an alcohol problem requires skill and tact. One of the first steps is making sure you are not an enabler or codependent, perhaps unknowingly allowing someone to continue excessively using alcohol. Enabling takes many forms. One of the most common is making excuses or covering up for the alcohol abuser—for example, saying "he has the flu" when it is really a hangover. Whenever you find yourself minimizing or lying about someone's drinking behavior, a warning bell should sound. Another important step is open, honest labeling—"I think you have a problem with alcohol." Such explicit statements usually elicit emotional rebuttals and may endanger a relationship. In the long run, however, you are not helping your friends by allowing them to deny their problems with alcohol or other drugs. Taking action shows that you care.

Even when problems are acknowledged, there is usually reluctance to get help. You can't cure a friend's drinking problem, but you can guide him or her to appropriate help. Your best role might be to obtain information about the available resources and persistently encourage their use. Consider making an appointment for your friend at the student health center and then go with him or her to the appointment. Most student health centers will be able to recommend local options for self-help groups and formal treatment; the counseling center is another excellent source for help. You can also check the phone book and the Internet for local chapters of AA and other groups (see For More Information at the end of the chapter). And don't underestimate the power of families to help. An honest phone call to your friend's parents could save a life if your friend is in serious trouble with alcohol.

DRINKING BEHAVIOR AND RESPONSIBILITY

The responsible use of alcohol means drinking in such a way that you keep your BAC low, so that your behavior is always under your control. In addition to controlling your own drinking, there are things you can do to promote responsible alcohol use in others.

Examine Your Attitudes About Alcohol Use

Think about how you really feel about drinking. Is it of little consequence to you or perhaps even an intrusion into your college experience? Or is alcohol the key ingredient for any and all fun activities? Can you imagine having a good time at a party or at the beach without alcoholic beverages? How do you perceive nondrinkers at a party where others are drinking? Do they seem mature or odd? What do your answers to these questions say about your attitude about alcohol and the role of alcohol in your life?

Attitudes toward drinking are usually based on a multitude of experiences, including your family background. Consider how alcohol was used in your family when you were growing up. Was it used for family celebrations? Was alcohol a big deal in your family, or was it treated as a relatively unimportant occasional addition to dinner? Was alcohol a source of problems, with a parent or relative becoming dependent on alcohol and/or abusive when drunk? Do you think that alcohol problems run in your family? Understanding the source of some of your beliefs and feelings about alcohol may give you insight into your current drinking habits as well as your feelings about other people's use of alcohol.

Also examine your ideas about alcohol use on your college campus. Does it seem to you as if everyone at your college drinks? Do you feel pressure to drink or use illegal drugs, even if you don't really feel like it? Who pressures you? Why do you think some people push others to engage in heavy drinking? A recent survey of college students found that over half felt pressured to use alcohol or illegal drugs and that this pressure hampered their schoolwork. Even though it may seem that everyone drinks, about one in five college students is a nondrinker, with a higher percentage of abstainers at many schools. Remember that the majority of American adults drink moderately or not at all. Frequent binge drinking is far outside the norm in the adult world.

Examine Your Drinking Behavior

When you want to drink responsibly, it's helpful to know, first of all, why you drink. The following are common reasons given by college students:

- "It lets me go along with my friends."
- "It makes me less self-conscious and more social."
- "It makes me less inhibited in thinking, saying, or doing certain things."
- "It relieves depression, anxiety, tension, or worries."
- "It enables me to experience a different state of consciousness."

If you drink alcohol, what are your reasons for doing so? Are you attempting to meet underlying needs that could best be addressed by other means?

After examining your reasons for drinking, take a closer look at your drinking behavior. Is it moderate and responsible? Or do you frequently overindulge and suffer negative consequences? The Behavior Change Strategy at the end of the chapter explains how to keep and analyze

Assess Yourself

Do You Have a Problem with Alcohol?

For each question, choose the answer that best describes your behavior. Then total your scores.

Questions	Points 0	1	2	3	4	Your Score
1. How often do you have a drink containing alcohol?	Never	Monthly or less	2–4 times a month	2–3 times a week	4 or more times a week	____
2. How many drinks containing alcohol do you have on a typical day when you are drinking?	1 or 2	3 or 4	5 or 6	7–9	10 or more	____
3. How often do you have 6 or more drinks on one occasion?	Never	Less than monthly	Monthly	Weekly	Daily or almost daily	____
4. How often during the past year have you found that you were not able to stop drinking once you had started?	Never	Less than monthly	Monthly	Weekly	Daily or almost daily	____
5. How often during the past year have you failed to do what was normally expected because of drinking?	Never	Less than monthly	Monthly	Weekly	Daily or almost daily	____
6. How often during the past year have you needed a first drink in the morning to get yourself going after a heavy drinking session?	Never	Less than monthly	Monthly	Weekly	Daily or almost daily	____
7. How often during the past year have you had a feeling of guilt or remorse after drinking?	Never	Less than monthly	Monthly	Weekly	Daily or almost daily	____
8. How often during the past year have you been unable to remember what happened the night before because you had been drinking?	Never	Less than monthly	Monthly	Weekly	Daily or almost daily	____
9. Have you or someone else been injured as a result of your drinking?	No	Yes, but not in the past year (2 points)		Yes, during the past year (4 points)		____
10. Has a relative, friend, doctor, or other health worker been concerned about your drinking or suggested you cut down?	No	Yes, but not in the past year (2 points)		Yes, during the past year (4 points)		____
					Total	____

A total score of 8 or more indicates a strong likelihood of hazardous or harmful alcohol consumption. Even if you score below 8, if you are encountering drinking-related problems with your academic performance, job, relationships, health, or the law, you should consider seeking help. The effects of alcohol abuse can be extremely serious—even fatal—both to you and to others.

SOURCE: Babor, T. F., J. C. Higgins-Biddle, J. B. Saunders, and M. G. Monteiro. 2001. *AUDIT: The Alcohol Use Disorders Identification Test: Guidelines for Use in Primary Care,* 2nd ed. Geneva: World Health Organization.

a record of your drinking. The CAGE screening test can help you determine whether you, or someone close to you, may have a drinking problem. Answer yes or no to the following questions:

Have you ever felt you should
Cut down on your drinking?
Have people
Annoyed you by criticizing your drinking?
Have you ever felt bad or
Guilty about your drinking?
Have you ever had an
Eye-opener (a drink first thing in the morning to steady your nerves or get rid of a hangover)?

One "yes" response suggests a possible alcohol problem; if you answered yes to more than one question, it is highly likely that a problem exists. For a more detailed evaluation of your drinking habits, complete the questionnaire in the box "Do You Have a Problem with Alcohol?" If the results of either assessment test indicate a potential problem, get help right away.

People who choose to drink should do so responsibly—in moderation and when doing so does not put themselves or others in danger. By choosing a designated driver, these men help ensure a safe trip home.

Drink Moderately and Responsibly

Sometimes people lose control when they misjudge how much they can drink. At other times, they set out deliberately to get drunk. Following are some strategies for keeping your drinking and your behavior under control.

Drink Slowly Learn to sip your drinks rather than gulp them. Do not drink alcoholic beverages to quench your thirst. Avoid drinks made with carbonated mixers, especially if you're thirsty; you'll be more likely to gulp them down.

Space Your Drinks Learn to drink nonalcoholic drinks at parties, or alternate them with alcoholic drinks. Learn to refuse a round: "I've had enough for right now." Parties are easier for some people if they hold a glass of something nonalcoholic that has ice and a twist of lime floating in it so it looks like an alcoholic drink.

Eat Before and While Drinking Avoid drinking on an empty stomach. Food in your stomach will not prevent the alcohol from eventually being absorbed, but it will slow down the rate somewhat and thus often lower the peak BAC. In restaurants, order your food before you order a drink. Try to have something to eat before you go out to a party where alcohol will be served.

Know Your Limits and Your Drinks Learn how different BACs affect you. In a safe setting such as your home, with your roommate or a friend, see how a set amount—say, two drinks in an hour—affects you. A good test is walking heel to toe in a straight line with your eyes closed or standing with your feet crossed and trying to touch your finger to your nose with your eyes closed.

But be aware that in different settings your performance, and especially your ability to judge your behavior, may change. At a given BAC, you will perform less well when surrounded by activity and boisterous companions than you will in a quiet test setting with just one or two other people. This impairment results partially because alcohol reduces your ability to perform when your brain is bombarded by multiple stimuli. It is useful to discover the rate at which you can drink without increasing your BAC. Be able to calculate the approximate amount a given drink increases your BAC.

Promote Responsible Drinking in Others

Although you cannot completely control the drinking behavior of others, there are things you can do to help promote responsible drinking.

Encourage Responsible Attitudes Our society teaches us attitudes toward drinking that contribute to alcohol-related problems. Many of us have difficulty expressing disapproval about someone who has drunk too much, and we are amused by the antics of a funny drunk. We accept the alcohol industry's linkage of drinking with virility or sexuality (see the box "Alcohol Advertising"). And many people treat nondrinkers as nonconformists in social settings. Recognize that the choice to abstain is neither odd nor unusual. More than one-third of adults do not drink at all or drink very infrequently. Most adults are capable of enjoying their leisure time without alcohol or drugs. In hazardous situations,

Critical Consumer

Alcohol Advertising

VW

To be a careful and informed health consumer, you need to consider the effects that advertisements have on you. Are alcohol ads, such as those featuring young musicians, talking frogs, or football games between beer bottles, harmless fun? Or can they have more serious effects? How do such ads affect you?

Alcohol manufacturers spend $6 billion every year on advertising and promotions. They claim that the purpose of their advertising is to persuade adults who already drink to choose a certain brand. But in reality, ads cleverly engage young people and children—never overtly suggesting that young people should drink, but clearly linking alcohol and good times.

Alcohol ads are common during televised sporting events and other shows popular with teenagers. By age 18, the average American teen will have seen 100,000 TV beer commercials, and teens are more likely than adults to see alcohol ads in their favorite magazines. Studies show that the more TV adolescents watch, the more likely they are to take up drinking in their teens. New alcoholic drinks geared to the tastes of young people are heavily promoted. "Hard lemonade" and other fruity or sweetened drinks ("alcopops" or "low-alcohol refreshers") have been described by teens as a way to get drunk without suffering the bitter taste of most alcoholic beverages. Though only recently introduced, these drinks have been tried by almost half of 14–18-year-olds.

Alcohol manufacturers also reach out to young people at youth-oriented activities like concerts and sporting events. Product logos are heavily marketed through sales of T-shirts, hats, and other items. Many colleges allow alcohol manufacturers to advertise at campus events in exchange for sponsorship.

What is the message of all these advertisements? Think about the alcohol ads you've seen. Many give the impression that drinking alcohol is a normal part of everyday life and good times. This message seems to work well on the young, many of whom believe that heavy-duty drinking at parties is normal and fun. The use of famous musicians, athletes, or actors in commercials increases the appeal of alcohol by associating it with fame, wealth, sex, and popularity. Many beer advertisements, for example, portray beer drinking as a critical part of one's success in finding an attractive mate.

What ads don't show is the darker side of drinking. You never see hangovers, car crashes, slipping grades, or violence. Although some ads include a brief message such as "know when to say when," the impact of such cautions is small compared to that of the image of happy, attractive young people having fun while drinking.

The next time you see an advertisement for alcohol, take a critical look. What is the message of the ad? What audience is being targeted, and what is the ad implying about alcohol use? Be aware of its effect on you.

such as driving or operating machinery, abstinence is the only appropriate choice.

Be a Responsible Host When you are the host, serve nonalcoholic beverages as well as alcohol. Popular nonalcoholic choices include soft drinks, sparkling water, fruit juice, and alcohol-free wine, beer, and mixers. Serve only enough alcohol for each guest to have a moderate number of drinks. Don't put out large kegs of beer, as these invite people to overindulge. For parties hosted by a dorm, fraternity, or other campus group, don't allow guests to have unlimited drinks for a single admission fee, as this also encourages binge drinking.

Always serve food along with alcohol, and stop serving alcohol an hour or more before people will leave. If possible, arrange carpools with designated nondrinking drivers in advance. Remind your guests who are under 21 about the new zero-tolerance laws in many states—even a single drink can result in an illegal BAC. Insist that guests who drink too much take a taxi, ride with someone else, or stay overnight rather than drive.

Plan social functions with no alcohol at all. Outdoor parties, hikes, and practically every other type of social occasion can be enjoyable without alcohol. If that doesn't seem possible to you, then examine your drinking patterns and attitudes toward alcohol. If you can't have fun without drinking, you may have a problem with alcohol.

Hold the Drinker Responsible The individual who consumes alcohol must take full responsibility for his or her behavior. Pardoning unacceptable behavior fosters the attitude that the behavior is caused by the drug. The drinker is thereby excused from responsibility and learns to expect minimal adverse consequences for his or her behavior. The opposite approach—holding the individual fully accountable for his or her behavior—is a more effective policy. For example, alcohol-impaired drivers who receive legal penalties have fewer subsequent rearrests than those who receive only mandatory treatment. Restrictions on public smoking gained momentum after nonsmokers learned about the dangers that environmental tobacco smoke posed to them. Other people's drunkenness can impinge on your living or study environment. Speak up against this behavior—and insist on your rights.

Learn About Prevention Programs What alternatives are being developed on your campus or in your community to keg parties and other events where heavy drinking occurs? Does your campus have dormitories, fraternities, or sororities where members agree to abstain from alcohol or drug use? Are programs available for students who are at high risk for alcohol abuse, such as those whose parents abused alcohol? Are counseling or self-help programs like AA available?

Take Community Action Consider joining an action group such as Students Against Destructive Decisions (SADD). The goal of SADD is to address the issues of drinking, impaired driving, drug use, and other destructive decisions and killers of young people. Lesson plans, peer counseling, and the promotion of better communication between students and parents are all used to help protect students from the dangers of drinking, drug use, and impaired driving.

Tips for Today

Alcohol has a paradoxical place in our culture. Sometimes it's associated with pleasure and celebration, and sometimes it's associated with disease and death. The key is how people use or misuse it. The responsible use of alcohol means drinking in moderation or not at all.

Right now you can

- Consider whether you have a history of alcohol abuse or dependence in your family; if you do, ask yourself if you are making good decisions about alcohol right now, ones that will not cause you problems later in your life.
- If you drink, put some sodas in your refrigerator and have one the next time you reach for a beer; offer your friends sodas, too.
- If you drink, plan ahead for the next party you attend, figuring out how you can limit yourself to one or two drinks.
- Ask your roommates or friends if they know that binge drinking can be fatal; if they don't know, give them the facts about it; also share with them the information in this chapter about how to deal with an alcohol emergency.

SUMMARY

- Although alcohol has been a part of human celebrations for a long time, it is a psychoactive drug capable of causing addiction.
- After being absorbed into the bloodstream in the stomach and small intestine, alcohol is transported throughout the body. The liver metabolizes alcohol as blood circulates through it.
- If people drink more alcohol each hour than the body can metabolize, blood alcohol concentration (BAC) increases. The rate of alcohol metabolism depends on a variety of individual factors.
- Alcohol is a CNS depressant. At low doses, it tends to make people feel relaxed.
- At higher doses, alcohol interferes with motor and mental functioning; at very high doses, alcohol poisoning, coma, and death can occur. Effects may be increased if alcohol is combined with other drugs.
- Alcohol use increases the risk of injury and violence; drinking before driving is particularly dangerous, even at low doses.
- Continued alcohol use has negative effects on the digestive and cardiovascular systems and increases cancer risk and overall mortality.
- Pregnant women who drink risk giving birth to children with a cluster of birth defects known as fetal alcohol syndrome (FAS). Even occasional drinking during pregnancy can cause brain injury in the fetus.
- Moderate drinking may decrease the risk of coronary heart disease in some people.
- Alcohol abuse involves drinking in dangerous situations or drinking to a degree that causes academic, professional, interpersonal, or legal difficulties.
- Alcohol dependence, or alcoholism, is characterized by more extensive problems with alcohol, usually involving tolerance and withdrawal.
- Binge drinking is a common form of alcohol abuse on college campuses that has negative effects on both drinking and nondrinking students.
- Physical consequences of alcoholism include the direct effects of tolerance and withdrawal, as well as all the problems associated with chronic drinking. Psychological problems include memory loss and additional mental disorders such as depression.
- Treatment approaches include mutual support groups like AA, job- and school-based programs, inpatient hospital programs, and pharmacological treatments.
- Helping someone who abuses alcohol means avoiding being an enabler and obtaining information about available resources and persistently encouraging their use.
- Strategies for keeping drinking under control include examining attitudes about drinking and drinking behavior, drinking slowly, spacing drinks, eating before and while drinking, and knowing one's limits.
- Strategies for promoting responsible drinking in others include encouraging responsible attitudes, being a responsible host, holding the drinker responsible for his or her actions, learning about prevention programs, and taking community action.

Developing Responsible Drinking Habits

How much do you drink? Is it the right amount for you? You may know the answer to this question already, or you may not have given it much thought. Many people learn through a single unpleasant experience how alcohol affects them. Others suffer ill effects but choose to ignore or deny them.

To make responsible and informed choices about using alcohol, consider, first, whether there is any history of alcohol abuse in your family. If someone in your family is dependent on alcohol, you have a higher-than-average likelihood of becoming dependent too. Second, consider whether you are dependent on other substances or behaviors. Do you smoke, drink strong coffee every day, or use other drugs regularly? Does some habit control your life? Some people have more of a tendency to become addicted than others, and a person with one addiction is often likely to have other addictions as well. If this is the case for you, again you may need to be more cautious with alcohol.

Keep a Record

Once you have answered these questions, find out more about your alcohol-related behavior by keeping track of your drinking for 2 weeks in your health journal. Keep a daily alcohol behavior record like the one illustrated in Chapter 1 for eating behavior. Include information on

- *The drinking situation,* including type of drink, time of day, how fast you drank it, where you were, and what else you were doing.
- *Your internal state,* including what made you want to drink and your feelings, thoughts, and concerns at the time. Note how others influenced you.
- *The consequences of drinking,* including any changes in your feelings or behavior while or after you were drinking, such as silliness, assertiveness, aggressiveness, or depression.

Analyze Your Record

Next, analyze your record to detect patterns of feelings and environmental cues. Do you always drink when you're at a certain place or with certain people? Do you sometimes drink just to be sociable, when you don't really want a drink and would be satisfied with a nonalcoholic beverage? Refer to the list of warning signs of alcohol abuse given in the text. Are any of them true for you? For example, do you feel uncomfortable in a social situation if alcohol is *not* available?

Set Goals

Now that you've analyzed your record, think about whether you want to change any of your behaviors. Would you do better academically if you drank less? Has drinking had a negative impact on any of your relationships? Have you risked infection and unplanned pregnancy by having unprotected sex while drunk? Do you depend on alcohol in order to have a good time? Have you been injured while drinking? If you drink and drive or if you feel you are becoming dependent on alcohol, it is time to change your drinking behavior. Decide on goals that will give you the best health and safety returns, such as a beer or a glass of wine with dinner, one drink per hour at a party, or no alcohol at all.

Devise a Plan

Refer to your health journal to see what kinds of patterns your drinking falls into and where you can intervene to break the behavior chain. If you have determined that your life would be improved if you changed your drinking habits, now is the time to make changes. For some people, simple changes in the environment such as stocking the refrigerator with alternative beverages like juices or sparkling water can be helpful. If you feel self-conscious about ordering a nonalcoholic drink when you're out with a group, try recruiting a friend to do the same. If it's too difficult to avoid drinking in some situations, such as at a bar or a beer party, you may decide to avoid those situations for a period of time.

Examine your friendships. If drinking is becoming a problem for you and some of your friends drink heavily, you may need to think about letting those relationships go. If you find support groups helpful, check with your college counseling center or health clinic; most schools sponsor peer group activities for those who are working to change their drinking habits. Local chapters of AA and other organizations may have groups geared toward college-age people.

Instead of drinking, you can try other activities that produce the same effect. For example, if you drink to relieve anxiety or tension, try adding 20–30 minutes of exercise to your schedule to help you manage stress. Or try doing a relaxation exercise or going for a brisk walk to help reduce anxiety before a party or date. If you drink to relieve depression or to stop worrying, consider finding a trustworthy person (perhaps a professional counselor) to talk to about the problem that's bothering you. If you drink to feel more comfortable sexually, consider ways to improve communication with your partner so you can deal with sexual issues more openly. When these activities are successful, they will reinforce your responsible drinking decisions and make it more likely that you'll make the same decisions again in the future.

For other ways to monitor and control your drinking behavior, see the suggestions in the section "Drinking Behavior and Responsibility."

Reward Yourself and Monitor Your Progress

If changing your drinking behavior turns out to be difficult, it may be a clue that drinking was becoming a problem for you—all the more reason to get it under control now. Be sure to reward yourself as you learn to drink responsibly (or not at all). You may lose weight, look better, feel better, and have higher self-esteem as a result of limiting your drinking. Keep track of your progress in your health journal, and use the strategies described in Chapter 1 for maintaining your program. Remember, when you establish sensible drinking habits, you're planning not just for this week or month—but for your whole life.

Take Action

1. **Interview peers:** Interview some of your fellow students about their drinking habits. How much do they drink, and how often? Are they more likely to drink on certain days or in certain circumstances? Are there any habits that seem to be common to most students? How do your own drinking habits compare to those of people you interviewed?

2. **Visit a local AA or Al-Anon group:** Some AA groups encourage visitors. If your local chapter does so, attend a meeting to see how the organization functions. What behavioral techniques are used to help people stop drinking? How effective do these techniques seem to be? If there is a local codependent or Al-Anon group, attend one of the group's meetings. What themes are emphasized? Do any themes apply to your relationships?

3. **Plan an alcohol-free party:** What would you serve to eat and drink? What would you tell people about the party when you invite them?

4. **Identify alcohol ads and points of sale in your community:** Look around your neighborhood and note the types of alcohol advertisements you find. How many are there, and what groups are being targeted—for example, young people, college students, or people of a particular ethnic group? Also identify where alcohol is sold: in what types of stores, and in how many locations? Is there a cluster of bars in a particular location? If you notice patterns that suggest marketing or sales targeted at particular groups, consider bringing your findings to the attention of community leaders.

For More Information

Books

Herrick, C. 2006. 100 *Questions & Answers About Alcoholism & Drug Addiction*. Boston: Jones & Bartlett Publishers. *Answers a range of specific questions about alcohol abuse, dependence, and treatment options.*

Kinney, J. 2009. *Loosening the Grip: A Handbook of Alcohol Information*, 9th ed. New York: McGraw-Hill. *A fascinating book about alcohol, including information on physical effects, abuse, alcoholism, and cultural aspects of alcohol use.*

Lu, K. 2006. *Media and College Binge-Drinking: Direct and Indirect Media Influences on Drinking Norm*. Ann Arbor: ProQuest/UMI. *A quantitative review of the effect of the media on students' perceptions about drinking.*

Seaman, B. 2006. *Binge: Campus Life in an Age of Disconnection and Excess*. New York: Wiley. *An exploration of campus life at 12 residential colleges and universities, with discussions on the effects of student isolation, peer pressure, and drinking on today's students.*

Zailckas, K. 2006. *Smashed: Story of a Drunken Girlhood* (reprint ed.). New York: Penguin. *A young woman writes about her experiences of drinking through high school and college; also includes information from surveys and research into the effects of alcohol use.*

Organizations, Hotlines, and Web Sites

Al-Anon Family Group Headquarters. Provides information and referrals to local Al-Anon and Alateen groups. The Web site includes a self-quiz to determine if you are affected by someone's drinking.
888-4AL-ANON
http://www.al-anon.alateen.org

Alcoholics Anonymous (AA) World Services. Provides general information on AA, literature on alcoholism, and information about AA meetings and related 12-step organizations.
212-870-3400
http://www.alcoholics-anonymous.org

AlcoholScreening.Org. Provides information about alcohol and health, referrals for treatment and support groups, and a drinking self-assessment.
http://www.alcoholscreening.org

Alcohol Treatment Referral Hotline. Provides referrals to local intervention and treatment providers.
800-ALCOHOL

American Psychiatric Association: College Mental Health. Covers a wide variety of mental health issues affecting college students, including alcohol abuse and treatment.
http://www.healthyminds.org/collegementalhealth.cfm

Bacchus and Gamma Peer Education Network. An association of college- and university-based peer education programs that focus on prevention of alcohol abuse.
http://www.bacchusgamma.org

The College Alcohol Study. Harvard School of Public Health. Provides information about and results from the recent studies of binge drinking on college campuses.
http://www.hsph.harvard.edu/cas

College Drinking Prevention. Includes information about alcohol, including myths about alcohol use and an interactive look at how alcohol affects the body.
http://www.collegedrinkingprevention.gov/students

Facts on Tap. Provides information about alcohol and college life, sex and alcohol, and children of alcoholics, as well as suggestions for students who have been negatively affected by other students' alcohol use.
http://www.factsontap.org

Habitsmart. Contains an online self-scoring alcohol-use assessment, tips for outsmarting cravings, and links to related sites.
http://www.habitsmart.com

HadEnough.Org. Provides information and a self-quiz on binge drinking among college students.
http://www.hadenough.org

Higher Education Center for Alcohol and Other Drug Prevention. Provides support for campus alcohol and illegal drug prevention efforts; a Web site gives information about alcohol and drug abuse on campus and links to related sites.
http://www.edc.org/hec

Intoximeters Drink Wheel Blood Alcohol Test. Calculate your approximate BAC based on body weight, gender, and amount of alcohol consumed.
http://www.intox.com/wheel/drinkwheel.asp

Moderation Management Network. Controversial self-help program designed to help early problem drinkers limit their drinking; not intended for serious alcohol abusers or alcoholics.
http://www.moderation.org

Mothers Against Drunk Driving (MADD). Supports efforts to develop solutions to the problems of drunk driving and underage drinking; provides news, information, and brochures about many topics, including a guide for giving a safe party.
http://www.madd.org

National Association for Children of Alcoholics (NACoA). Provides information and support for children of alcoholics.
888-554-COAS
http://www.nacoa.net

National Clearinghouse for Alcohol and Drug Information/ Prevention Online. Provides statistics and information on alcohol abuse, including resources for people who want to help friends and family members overcome alcohol-abuse problems.
800-729-6686
http://www.health.org

National Council on Alcoholism and Drug Dependence (NCADD). Provides information and counseling referrals.
212-269-7797; 800-NCA-CALL (24-hour Hope Line)
http://www.ncadd.org

National Institute on Alcohol Abuse and Alcoholism (NIAAA). Provides booklets and other publications on a variety of alcohol-related topics, including fetal alcohol syndrome, alcoholism treatment, and alcohol use and minorities.
http://www.niaaa.nih.gov

Rational Recovery. A free self-help program that offers an alternative to 12-step programs; the emphasis is on learning the skill of abstinence.
http://www.rational.org

See also the listings for Chapter 9.

Selected Bibliography

Addolorato, G., et al. 2006. Baclofen: A new drug for the treatment of alcohol dependence. *International Journal of Clinical Practice* 60(8): 1003–1008.

Aetna InteliHealth. 2005. *Health A to Z: Alcohol Dependence (Alcoholism)* (http://www.intelihealth.com/IH/ihtIH/EM/9339/32060.html; retrieved August 9, 2006).

Anton, R. F., et al. 2006. Combined pharmacotherapies and behavioral interventions for alcohol dependence: The COMBINE study: A randomized controlled trial. *Journal of the American Medical Association* 295(17): 2003–2017.

Callahan, M. 2006. Cocktail confidential. *Health,* June, 169–171.

Centers for Disease Control and Prevention. 2004. Alcohol-attributable deaths and years of potential life lost, United States, 2001. *Morbidity and Mortality Weekly Report* 53(37): 866–870.

Clifasefi, S. L., et al. 2006. Blind drunk: The effects of alcohol on inattentional blindness. *Applied Cognitive Psychology* 20(5): 697–704.

College Drinking Prevention. 2005. *A Snapshot of Annual High-Risk College Drinking Consequences* (http://www.collegedrinkingprevention.gov/StatsSummaries/snapshot.aspx; retrieved August 8, 2006).

Collins, G. B., et al. 2006. Drug adjuncts for treating alcohol dependence. *Cleveland Clinic Journal of Medicine* 73(7): 641–644.

Costello, R. M. 2006. Long-term mortality from alcoholism: A descriptive analysis. *Journal of Studies on Alcohol* 67(5): 694–699.

Dawson, D. A., et al. 2005. Recovery from DSM-IV alcohol dependence: United States, 2001–2002. *Addiction* 100(3): 281–292.

Edelson, E. 2006. *Daily Drinking Cuts Heart Disease Risk for Men. HealthDay 26 May* (http://www.healthday.com/view.cfm?id=532938; retrieved August 10, 2006).

Gruenewald, P. J., and L. Remer. 2006. Changes in outlet densities affect violence rates. *Alcoholism: Clinical and Experimental Research* 30(7): 1184–1193.

Heilig, M., and M. Egli. 2006. Pharmacological treatment of alcohol dependence: Target symptoms and target mechanisms. *Pharmacology and Therapeutics* 111(3): 855–876.

Hingson, R., et al. 2005. Magnitude of alcohol-related mortality and morbidity among U.S. college students ages 18–24. *Annual Review of Public Health* 26: 259–279.

Hingson, R. W., et al. 2006. Age at drinking onset and alcohol dependence: Age at onset, duration, and severity. *Archives of Pediatrics and Adolescent Medicine* 160(7): 739–746.

Insurance Institute for Highway Safety. 2006. *DUI/DWI Laws as of June 2006* (http://www.iihs.org/laws/state_laws/dui.html; retrieved August 11, 2006).

Krampe, H., et al. 2006. Follow-up of 180 alcoholic patients for up to 7 years after outpatient treatment: Impact of alcohol deterrents on outcome. *Alcohol: Clinical and Experimental Research* 30(1): 86–95.

The Marin Institute. 2005. *Health Care Costs of Alcohol* (http://www.marininstitute.org/alcohol_policy/health_care_costs.htm; retrieved August 9, 2006).

Mayo Clinic. 2006. Pain relievers and alcohol: A potentially risky combination. *Mayo Clinic Health Letter,* 6, May.

McCaig, L. F., and E. N. Nawar. 2006. National Hospital Ambulatory Medical Care Survey: 2004 emergency department summary. *Advance Data from Vital and Health Statistics* No. 372. Hyattsville, Md.: National Center for Health Statistics.

Miller, T. R., et al. 2006. Societal costs of underage drinking. *Journal of Studies on Alcohol* 67(4): 519–528.

Minino, A. M., et al. 2006. Deaths: Preliminary Data for 2004. *National Vital Statistics Reports* 54(19).

Monti, P. M., et al. 2005. Adolescence: Booze, brains, and behavior. *Alcoholism: Clinical and Experimental Research* 29(2): 207–220.

National Center for Health Statistics. 2006. *Health, United States, 2005, with Chartbook on Trends in the Health of Americans.* Hyattsville, Md.: National Center for Health Statistics.

National Highway Transportation Safety Administration. 2005. *Alcohol-Related Fatalities in 2004* (http://www-nrd.nhtsa.dot.gov/pdf/nrd-30/NCSA/RNotes/2005/809904.pdf; retrieved August 9, 2006).

National Highway Transportation Safety Administration. 2006. *Driver Alcohol Involvement in Fatal Crashes by Age Group and Vehicle Type* (http://www-nrd.nhtsa.dot.gov/pdf/nrd-30/NCSA/RNotes/2006/810598.pdf; retrieved August 9, 2006).

National Institute on Alcohol Abuse and Alcoholism. 2006. *Young Adult Drinking.* Alcohol Alert No. 68. Bethesda, Md.: National Institute on Alcohol Abuse and Alcoholism.

Nelson, T. F., et al. 2005. The state sets the rate: The relationship of college binge drinking rates and selected state alcohol control policies. *American Journal of Public Health* 95(3): 441–446.

Office of Applied Studies, Substance Abuse and Mental Health Services Administration. 2006. *Results from the 2005 National Survey on Drug Use and Health: National Findings,* September 2006 (http://oas.samhsa.gov/ retrieved November 17, 2006).

Office of Applied Studies, Substance Abuse and Mental Health Services Administration. 2006. *Treatment Episode Data Set (TEDS): Highlights—2004* (http://www.oas.samhsa.gov; EDS/2k4TEDS/TEDShi2k4toc.htm; retrieved August 11, 2006).

Perreira, K. M., and K. E. Cortes. 2006. Explaining Race/Ethnicity and Nativity Differences in Alcohol and Tobacco Use During Pregnancy. *American Journal of Public Health,* 27 July, epub.

Slutska, W. S. 2005. Alcohol use disorders among US college students and their non-college-attending peers. *Archives of General Psychiatry* 62(3): 321–327.

U.S. Surgeon General. 2005. *U.S. Surgeon General Releases Advisory on Alcohol Use in Pregnancy* (http://www.hhs.gov/surgeongeneral/pressreleases/sg02222005.html; retrieved August 11, 2006).

Willford, J., et al. 2006. Moderate prenatal alcohol exposure and cognitive status of children at age 10. *Alcoholism: Clinical and Experimental Research* 30(6): 1051–1059.

FILTER CIGARETTES

Emphysema
Ultra Lights!

LOW TAR & NICOTINE

Got Emphysema?

Looking AHEAD

After reading this chapter, you should be able to

- List the reasons people start using tobacco and why they continue to use it
- Explain the short- and long-term health risks associated with tobacco use
- Discuss the effects of environmental tobacco smoke on nonsmokers
- Describe the social costs of tobacco, and list actions that have been taken to combat smoking in the public and private sectors
- Prepare plans to stop using tobacco and to avoid environmental tobacco smoke

Toward a Tobacco-Free Society

Test Your Knowledge

1. **People who smoke "light" or low-tar cigarettes reduce their risk of smoking-related diseases compared to people who smoke other cigarettes.**
   True or false?
2. **Which of the following substances is found in tobacco smoke?**
   a. acetone (nail polish remover)
   b. ammonia (cleaner)
   c. hexamine (lighter fluid)
   d. toluene (industrial solvent)
3. **Every day in the United States, about 1000 children and adolescents between the ages of 12 and 17 start smoking.**
   True or false?
4. **Cigarette smoking increases the risk for which of the following conditions?**
   a. facial wrinkling
   b. miscarriage
   c. impotence
   d. automobile crashes
5. **A person who quits smoking now will reduce his or her risk of lung cancer within 10 years.**
   True or false?
6. **Every cigarette a person smokes reduces life expectancy by about 1 minute.**
   True or false?

ANSWERS

1. FALSE. Smokers who choose "light" or low-tar cigarettes do not reduce tar intake or smoking-related disease risks, nor is there any evidence that switching to "light" cigarettes helps smokers quit.
2. ALL FOUR. Tobacco contains thousands of chemical substances, including many that are poisonous or linked to the development of cancer.
3. FALSE. The number is closer to 4000 children and adolescents. The average age of a first-time smoker is 13.
4. ALL FOUR. Cigarette smoking reduces the quality of life and is the greatest preventable cause of death in the United States.
5. TRUE. The lung cancer rate of a former smoker is 50% of that of a continuing smoker within 10 years of quitting.
6. FALSE. Every cigarette reduces life expectancy by about 11 minutes; one carton represents a day and a half of lost life.

Visit the *Core Concepts in Health* Online Learning Center (www.mhhe.com/insel10e) for study aids and many additional resources.

Once considered a glamorous and sophisticated habit, smoking is now viewed with increasing disapproval. The recognition of the health risks of smoking is a primary cause of this change in public opinion, and it has led to significant changes in the behavior of many Americans. Over the past four decades, the proportion of cigarette smoking among adults in the United States has dropped 30%. Private businesses and all levels of government have jumped on the nonsmoking bandwagon: Almost every state now restricts smoking in public places, and several have introduced statewide smoking bans for indoor workplaces. The U.S. Surgeon General has proposed that America become completely smoke-free.

Despite such progress, tobacco use is still widespread. In 2005, 29.4% of Americans age 12 and older reported having used tobacco in some form during the past 30 days; although the rate of tobacco use declined slightly from 2002 to 2005, it remained unchanged from 2004 to 2005. Smoking is the leading cause of preventable death in the United States and has negative health effects on people at all stages of life, from unborn babies to seniors. Each year 440,000 Americans die prematurely from tobacco-related causes (Figure 11-1). This accounts for nearly one in every five adult deaths each year. Male and female smokers lose an average of 13.2 and 14.5 years of life, respectively. Nonsmokers, particularly children whose parents smoke, also suffer. Exposure to environmental tobacco smoke (ETS) causes more than 35,000 deaths annually among nonsmokers. Smoking by pregnant women is responsible for about 1000 infant deaths each year in this country. Children exposed to ETS suffer higher rates of asthma, bronchitis, and pneumonia. Spit (smokeless) tobacco and cigars are regaining popularity: The use of spit tobacco products has tripled since 1972, and cigar smoking has increased 50% since 1993.

Given the overwhelming evidence against tobacco, why would anyone today begin using it? How does it exercise its hold over users? In this chapter, we explore answers to these and other questions about nicotine addiction.

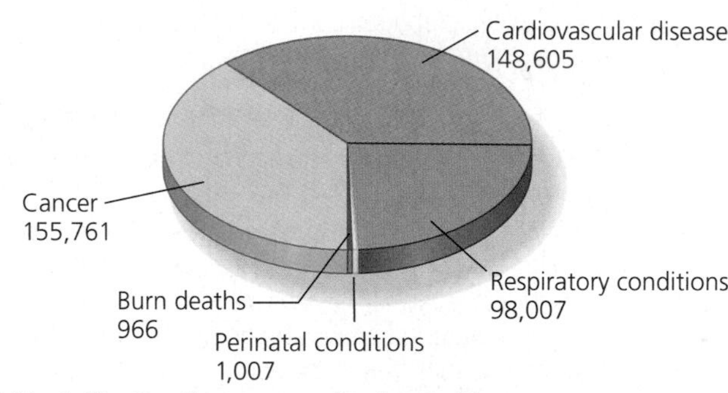

(a) Mortality: Deaths per year due to smoking

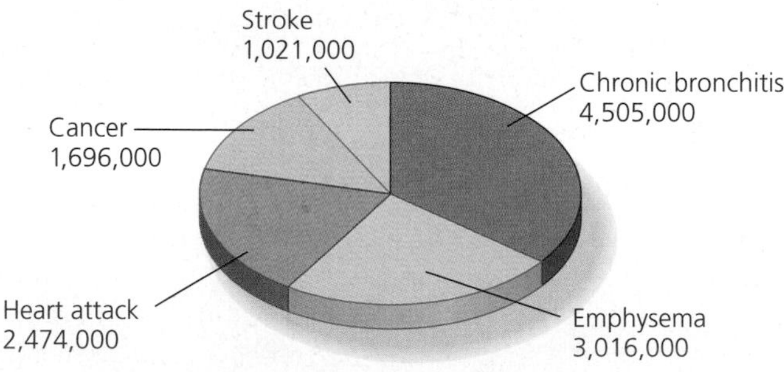

(b) Morbidity: Number of people with chronic illnesses due to smoking

VITAL STATISTICS

Figure 11-1 Annual mortality and morbidity among smokers attributable to smoking. SOURCES: Centers for Disease Control and Prevention. 2003. Cigarette smoking attributable morbidity—United States, 2000. *Morbidity and Mortality Weekly Report* 52(35): 842–844; Centers for Disease Control and Prevention. 2002. Annual smoking-attributable mortality, years of potential life lost, and economic costs. *Morbidity and Mortality Weekly Report* 51(14): 300–303.

WHY PEOPLE USE TOBACCO

An estimated 71.5 million Americans, including nearly 4 million adolescents, use tobacco. Each day more than 2000 teenagers become regular smokers, and at least one-third of them will die prematurely because of tobacco. Most smokers understand the risks of tobacco use: More than 80% of adult smokers believe tobacco will shorten their life and would like to quit. Each year roughly 40% of smokers quit for at least a day, but 9 out of 10 of them are smoking again within a year.

Nicotine Addiction

The primary reason people continue to use **tobacco** is that they have become addicted to a powerful psychoactive drug: **nicotine.** Although the tobacco industry long maintained that nicotine had not been proved to be addictive, scientific evidence overwhelmingly shows that nicotine is highly addictive. Many researchers consider nicotine to be the most physically addictive of all the psychoactive drugs. According to a 2006 study by the Massachusetts Department of Public Health, the amount of nicotine in cigarettes increased by 10% between 1998 and 2004.

Some neurological studies indicate that nicotine acts on the brain in much the same way as cocaine and heroin. Nicotine reaches the brain via the bloodstream seconds after it is inhaled or, in the case of spit tobacco, absorbed through membranes of the mouth or nose. It triggers the release of powerful chemical messengers in the brain, including epinephrine, norepinephrine, and dopamine. But unlike street drugs, most of which are used to achieve a high, nicotine's primary attraction seems to lie in its ability to modulate everyday emotions.

At low doses, nicotine acts as a stimulant: It increases heart rate and blood pressure and, in adults, can enhance

Assess Yourself

Nicotine Dependence: Are You Hooked?

Answer each question in the list below, giving yourself the appropriate number of points.

_____ 1. How soon after you wake up do you have your first cigarette?
  a. within 5 minutes (3)
  b. 6–30 minutes (2)
  c. 31–60 minutes (1)
  d. after 60 minutes (0)

_____ 2. Do you find it difficult to refrain from smoking in places where it is forbidden, such as the library, a theater, or a doctor's office?
  a. yes (1)
  b. no (0)

_____ 3. Which cigarette would you most hate to give up?
  a. the first one in the morning (1)
  b. any other (0)

_____ 4. How many cigarettes a day do you smoke?
  a. 10 or less (0)
  b. 11–20 (1)
  c. 21–30 (2)
  d. 31 or more (3)

_____ 5. Do you smoke more frequently during the first hours after waking than during the rest of the day?
  a. yes (1)
  b. no (0)

_____ 6. Do you smoke if you are so ill that you are in bed most of the day?
  a. yes (1)
  b. no (0)

_____ TOTAL

A total score of 7 or more indicates that you are very dependent on nicotine and are likely to experience withdrawal symptoms when you stop smoking. A score of 6 or less indicates low to moderate dependence.

SOURCE: Heatherton, T. F., et al. 1991. The Fagerstrom Test for Nicotine Dependence: A revision of the Fagerstrom Tolerance Questionnaire. *British Journal of Addictions* 86(9): 1119–1127.

alertness, concentration, rapid information processing, memory, and learning. People type faster on nicotine, for instance. The opposite effect occurs in teens who smoke, however; they show impairment in memory and other cognitive functions.

In some circumstances, nicotine acts as a mild sedative. Most commonly, nicotine relieves symptoms such as anxiety, irritability, and mild depression in tobacco users who are experiencing withdrawal. Some studies have shown that high doses of nicotine and rapid smoking cause increases in levels of glucocorticoids and endorphins, chemicals that act in the brain to moderate moods and reduce stress. Tobacco users are able to fine-tune nicotine's effects and regulate their moods by increasing or decreasing their intake of the drug. Studies have shown that smokers experience milder mood variation than nonsmokers while performing long, boring tasks or while watching emotional movies, for example.

All tobacco products contain nicotine, and the use of any of them can lead to addiction (see the box "Nicotine Dependence: Are You Hooked?"). Nicotine addiction fulfills the criteria for substance dependence described in Chapter 9, including loss of control, tolerance, and withdrawal.

Loss of Control Three out of four smokers want to quit but find they cannot. Although 60–80% of people who attend stop-smoking clinics are able to quit, three-quarters of them start smoking again within a year—a relapse rate similar to rates for alcoholics and heroin addicts. Quitting may be even harder for smokeless users: In one study, only 1 of 14 spit tobacco users who participated in a tobacco-cessation clinic was able to stop for more than 4 hours.

Regular tobacco users live according to a rigid cycle of need and gratification. On average, they can go no more than 40 minutes between doses of nicotine; otherwise, they begin feeling edgy and irritable and have trouble concentrating. If ignored, nicotine cravings build until getting a cigarette or some spit tobacco becomes a paramount concern, crowding out other thoughts. Tobacco users may plan their daily schedule around opportunities to satisfy their nicotine cravings; this loss of control and personal freedom can affect all the dimensions of wellness (see the box "Tobacco Use and Religion: Global Views" on p. 300).

Tobacco users become adept, therefore, at keeping a steady amount of nicotine circulating in the blood and going to the brain. In one experiment, smokers were given cigarettes that looked and tasted alike but varied in nicotine content. The subjects automatically adjusted their rate and depth of inhalation so that they absorbed

Terms

tobacco The leaves of cultivated tobacco plants prepared for smoking, chewing, or use as snuff.

nicotine A poisonous, addictive substance found in tobacco and responsible for many of the effects of tobacco.

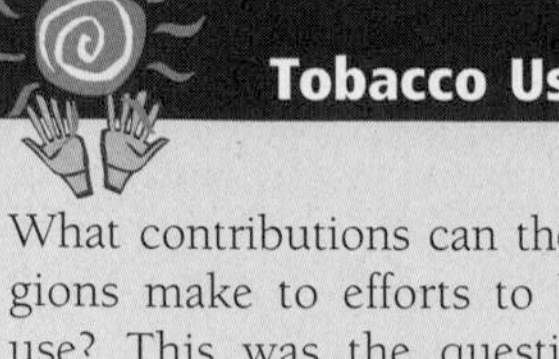

Tobacco Use and Religion: Global Views

What contributions can the world's religions make to efforts to limit tobacco use? This was the question behind a meeting attended by representatives of the major religions of the world at the headquarters of the World Health Organization (WHO).

Tobacco Use as a Violation of Religious Principles

A primary thread among all the religions is a condemnation of tobacco use for its damaging effects on the body. Most religions regard the human body as the dwelling place of the spirit; as such, it deserves care and respect.

The Baha'i faith, for example, strongly discourages smoking as unclean and unhealthy. Some Protestant churches consider tobacco use a violation of the body. For Hindus, smoking goes against one of the primary spiritual practices, the care of the body. The Roman Catholic Church endorses the age-old adage "a sound mind in a sound body." For Muslims, one of the five essential principles on which religious law is based is the protection of the integrity of the individual. In Judaism, people are urged to "choose life" and to choose whatever strengthens the capacity to live. Buddhists believe that the body doesn't belong to the person at all—even suicide is considered murder—and one must do nothing to harm it.

A second thread common to most religions is the notion that dependence and addiction run counter to ideas of freedom, choice, and human dignity. Buddhism teaches a path of freedom—a way of life without dependence on anything. Hindus regard tobacco use as a *vyasana,* a dependence that is not necessary for the preservation of health. Protestant churches caution that any form of dependence is contrary to the notion of Christian freedom.

A third argument against tobacco use is the immorality of imposing secondhand smoke on nonsmokers, which is seen as inflicting harm on others. In Hinduism, harming others is sinful. In the Jewish tradition, those who force nonsmokers to breathe smoke jeopardize the lives of others, and to do so is to jeopardize the whole universe.

The Role of Individual Responsibility

Most religions focus on the role of individual responsibility in overcoming dependence on tobacco. In Buddhism, for example, people must assume responsibility for their habits; they practice introspection to understand the cause of problems within themselves and the effects of their actions on others. The principles of Islam are based on notions of responsibility and protection; a fundamental message is that you are responsible for your body and for your health.

Religion and Tobacco Control

Common threads again emerged in discussions of how the problem of tobacco use should be approached. The Islamic view is that the campaign to control tobacco use must be based on awareness, responsibility, and justice. Developing awareness means providing information on the global problem. Fostering responsibility means helping people understand what they need to do to attain well-being. Emphasizing social and human justice means helping the farmers and societies that depend on tobacco cultivation to find alternative crops.

According to the representative from the Geneva Interreligious Platform (a project involving Hindus, Buddhists, Jews, Christians, Muslims, and Baha'is), the best approach is prevention. Here, the rights of nonsmokers clearly prevail over the freedom of smokers. In support of this position, the common religious exhortation not to do unto others what you would not have them do unto you can be invoked. Further, adequate information should be provided to counter the deceptive images projected by tobacco industry advertising, especially where minors are concerned. Protection of the weak and denunciation of dishonesty are underlying values of all religious traditions.

Religious traditions can best assist adult smokers by reminding them of two principles: one, the value of liberation from any form of slavery, and two, respect for life out of deference to the source of all life, which religions call by different names—God, ultimate reality, and so on—but which is the supreme value of any religious commitment.

SOURCE: World Health Organization. 2006. *Tobacco Free Initiative* (http://www.who.int/tobacco/en/; retrieved August 12, 2006).

their usual amount of nicotine. In other studies, heavy smokers were given nicotine without knowing it, and they cut down on their smoking without a conscious effort. Spit tobacco users maintain blood nicotine levels as high as those of cigarette smokers.

Tolerance and Withdrawal Using tobacco builds up tolerance. Where one cigarette may make a beginning smoker nauseated and dizzy, a long-term smoker may have to chain-smoke a pack or more to experience the same effects. For most regular tobacco users, sudden abstinence from nicotine produces predictable withdrawal symptoms as well. These symptoms, which come on several hours after the last dose of nicotine, can include severe cravings, insomnia, confusion, tremors, difficulty concentrating, fatigue, muscle pains, headache, nausea, irritability, anger, and depression. Users undergo measurable changes in brain waves, heart rate, and blood pressure, and they perform poorly on tasks requiring sustained attention. Although most of these symptoms of physical dependence pass in 2 or 3 days, the craving associated with addiction persists. Many ex-smokers report intermittent, intense urges to smoke for years after quitting.

Many teenagers believe they will be able to stop smoking when they want. In fact, adolescents are more vulnerable to nicotine than are older tobacco users. Compared with older smokers, adolescents become heavy smokers and develop dependence after fewer cigarettes. Nicotine addiction can start within a few days of smoking and after just a few cigarettes. Over half of teenagers who try cigarettes progress to daily use, and about half of those who ever smoke daily progress to nicotine dependence. In polls, about 75% of smoking teens state they wish they had never started. Another survey revealed that only 5% of high school smokers predicted they would definitely be smoking in 5 years; in fact, close to 75% were smoking 7–9 years later.

Social and Psychological Factors

Why do tobacco users have such a hard time quitting even when they want to? Social and psychological forces combine with physiological addiction to maintain the tobacco habit. Many people, for example, have established habits of smoking while doing something else—while talking, working, drinking, and so on. The spit tobacco habit is also associated with certain situations—studying, drinking coffee, or playing sports. It is difficult for these people to break their habits because the activities they associate with tobacco use continue to trigger their urge. Such activities are called **secondary reinforcers;** they act together with the physiological addiction to keep the user dependent on tobacco.

Genetic Factors

Genetic makeup does not guarantee protection against nicotine dependence or make addiction inevitable. But inherited characteristics do play an important role in some aspects of tobacco use. Studies that look for differences in behavior among twins and other sibling pairs suggest that genetic factors are more important than social and environmental factors in smoking initiation and in the development of nicotine dependence when people do start to smoke.

Scientists have begun to identify specific genes associated with biological response to tobacco use. For example, a gene that influences the way in which nicotine is metabolized, or broken down in the body, helps regulate the activity of an enzyme called CYP2A6. When people with slow CYP2A6 metabolism use tobacco, the nicotine remains in their blood longer than in people who have the gene for a faster metabolizing form of the enzyme. The slow metabolizers are more likely to feel nausea or dizziness when they first use tobacco, are less likely to continue smoking if they try it, and find it easier to quit if they do become regular smokers. Further research will likely identify other genes involved in nicotine dependence.

The average age of new smokers is 13, and most adult smokers began as teenagers. In 2005, about 55% of high school–age smokers said they wish they had never started.

Why Start in the First Place?

A junior high school girl takes up smoking in an attempt to appear older. A high school boy uses spit tobacco in the bullpen, emulating the major league ball players he admires. An overweight first-year college student turns to cigarettes, hoping they will curb her appetite. Smoking rates among American youth rose steadily through the 1990s but have begun to decline. Between 2002 and 2005, use of cigarettes among youths aged 12–17 declined from 13% to 10.8%, and use of cigars, bidis, and kreteks also dropped. Moreover, use of spit tobacco and pipes among high school students held steady, suggesting that high school students were not just switching from cigarettes to other tobacco products. There was no similar drop in tobacco use among middle school students, however.

It is not clear why middle school and high school students appear to respond differently to the current

Term

secondary reinforcers Stimuli that are not necessarily pleasurable in themselves but that are associated with other stimuli that are pleasurable.

Vw

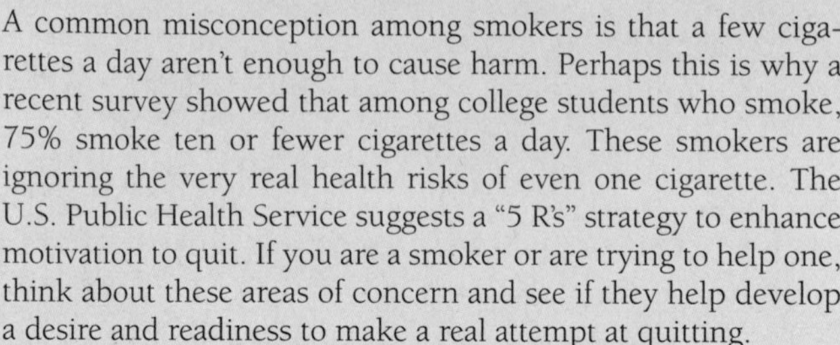

Take Charge

Building Motivation to Quit Smoking

A common misconception among smokers is that a few cigarettes a day aren't enough to cause harm. Perhaps this is why a recent survey showed that among college students who smoke, 75% smoke ten or fewer cigarettes a day. These smokers are ignoring the very real health risks of even one cigarette. The U.S. Public Health Service suggests a "5 R's" strategy to enhance motivation to quit. If you are a smoker or are trying to help one, think about these areas of concern and see if they help develop a desire and readiness to make a real attempt at quitting.

Relevance: Think about the personal relevance of quitting tobacco use. What would the effects be on your family and friends? How would your daily life improve? What is the most important way that quitting would change your life?

Risks: There are immediate risks, such as shortness of breath, infertility, and impotence, and long-term risks, including cancer, heart disease, and respiratory problems. Remember, smoking is harmful both to you and to anyone exposed to your smoke.

Rewards: The list of the rewards of quitting is almost endless, including improving immediate and long-term health, saving money, and feeling better about yourself. You can also stop worrying about quitting and set a good example for others.

Roadblocks: What are the potential obstacles to quitting? Are you worried about withdrawal symptoms, weight gain, or lack of support? How can these barriers be overcome?

Repetition: Revisit your reasons for quitting and strengthen your resolve until you are ready to prepare a plan. Most people make several attempts to quit before they succeed. Relapsing once does not mean that you will never succeed.

SOURCES: Rigotti, N. A., J. E. Lee, and H. Wechsler. 2000. U.S. college students' use of tobacco products. *Journal of the American Medical Association* 284(6): 699–705; Fiore, M. C., et al. 2000. *Treating Tobacco Use and Dependence.* Clinical Practice Guidelines. Rockville, Md.: U.S. Department of Health and Human Services.

anti-smoking environment, which includes increases in cigarette prices; more widespread smoke-free laws and policies; restrictions on tobacco advertising; and local, state, and national anti-tobacco campaigns such as the truth® campaign. However, promotional spending by the tobacco industry has increased substantially, and industry-sponsored media efforts may be diluting the impact of public health campaigns.

Children and teenagers constitute 90% of all new smokers in this country. Every day, more than 4000 children and adolescents between the ages of 12 and 17 start smoking, while hundreds of others take up snuff or chewing tobacco. The average age for starting smokers is 13; for spit tobacco users, 10. Meanwhile, children—especially girls—are beginning to experiment with tobacco at ever-younger ages. The earlier people begin smoking, the more likely they are to become heavy smokers—and to die of tobacco-related disease.

Rationalizing the Dangers Making the decision to smoke requires minimizing or denying both the health risks of tobacco use and the tremendous pain, disability, emotional trauma, family stress, and financial expense involved in tobacco-related diseases such as cancer and emphysema. A sense of invincibility, characteristic of many adolescents and young adults, also contributes to the decision to use tobacco. Young people may persuade themselves they are too intelligent, too lucky, or too healthy to be vulnerable to tobacco's dangers (see the box "Building Motivation to Quit Smoking"). "I'm not dumb enough to get hooked," they may argue. "I'll be able to quit before I do myself any real harm." Other typical rationalizations: "My grandmother smoked and she lived to be 80" and "You can get killed just by crossing the street."

Listening to Advertising Advertising is a powerful influence. In 2003, the tobacco industry spent more than $15 billion on advertising that links tobacco products with desirable traits such as confidence, popularity, sexual attractiveness, and slenderness. The American public responded that year by consuming 400 billion cigarettes. Young people are a prime target of such ads. Once a teen begins smoking, nicotine addiction can lead to a lifetime of smoking. As one teenager said, "It may have been my decision to smoke my first cigarette, and maybe even my second. But now *needing* to smoke is no longer a choice."

The tobacco industry has perfected techniques that target young people, for it is young smokers who are the likeliest to purchase familiar brands. Thus, the most heavily advertised cigarettes—Marlboro, Camel, and Newport—are the choice of 90% of teen smokers. Only a third of adult smokers, who prefer less expensive generic cigarettes, choose these brands. R. J. Reynolds Tobacco Company's promotion of the Camel brand, the most notorious tobacco campaign ever aimed at young people, recruited millions of new smokers and quadrupled Camel's share of tobacco companies' most coveted demographic—the FUBYAS, or "first usual brand younger adult smoker." To tobacco companies, "younger adult" means 14 or older, and Joe Camel became as familiar to children as Mickey Mouse. In surveys, more than 90% of 6-year-olds recognized the character.

Young people are not the only group targeted. Certain brands are designed to appeal primarily to men, women, or particular ethnic groups. For example, Virginia Slims tries to appeal to women by associating the brand with confidence and sexual attractiveness. Magazines that are targeted at African American audiences receive proportionately more revenues from cigarette advertising than do other consumer magazines. Billboards advertising tobacco products are placed in black communities four or five times more often than in primarily white communities.

The government began regulating tobacco advertising in 1967. Under the Fairness Doctrine, the Federal Communications Commission (FCC) required broadcasters to air anti-smoking messages along with industry-sponsored cigarette advertisements on television and radio. Anti-smoking ads featuring unattractive older people smoking or cigarettes used as coffin nails effectively counteract the glamorous images that appear in tobacco ads. Between 1967 and 1971, when anti-smoking messages were first broadcast, per capita cigarette consumption declined by 7%—one of the largest declines ever. Cigarette advertising on television and radio was banned altogether in 1971. In 1996, the FDA issued strict advertising regulations designed to reduce minors' exposure and access to tobacco advertising and products; however, the Supreme Court ruled in March 2000 that the FDA does not have the authority to regulate tobacco. Debate continues over legislation that would give the FDA regulatory authority.

In November 1998, controls on advertising were enacted as part of the $206 billion deal to settle lawsuits brought against the tobacco industry by the attorneys general of 39 states (see pp. 315–317 for more information). This settlement limits or bans billboard and transit advertising of tobacco products; cartoon characters in advertisements and packaging; tobacco logos on T-shirts, hats, and other promotional items; brand-name sponsorship of sporting events; and payments for product placement in movies, television, and concerts.

The 1998 advertising limits changed the environment but not the intensity of tobacco marketing. According to the Federal Trade Commission (FTC), the amount spent by the tobacco industry on advertising and product promotion in 2003—$15.15 billion—was the highest ever reported and represented an increase of 22% over 2002. About 71% ($10.8 billion) of the expenditure went for cost discounts that allowed retailers to keep cigarette prices low in the face of increasing taxes on tobacco products. Other point-of-sale expenditures ("buy two, get one free," give-away discount coupons, and payments for preferential placement of displays) accounted for an additional $1.4 billion of the overall marketing budget. The concentration of the industry's promotional effort is most apparent in neighborhood convenience stores, where tobacco products and promotional displays are prominently placed—often at child's eye-level—at the store's most-visited location, the checkout counter. In this carefully engineered setting, tobacco products are presented as a colorful and commonplace part of the neighborhood retail environment—as acceptable as a candy bar or quart of milk.

Emulating Smoking Onscreen Tobacco companies agreed to end paid product placement in movies as part of the 1998 settlement; a voluntary ban had been in effect since 1990. This ban does not appear to be having the intended effect, however. Researchers have found that smoking in movies has actually increased significantly since 1990, to levels not seen since 1960. In the 2 years following the settlement, smoking in PG-13 movies increased by 50%. Half the tobacco shots in the top movies from 2002 to 2003 were in G, PG, and PG-13 movies.

The portrayal of smoking in films does not reflect U.S. patterns of tobacco use. The prevalence of smoking among lead characters is three to four times that among comparable Americans. Films typically show the smoker as white, male, well educated, successful, and attractive. In reality, smokers tend to be poor and to have less education. In the top-grossing films in 2002–2003, smoking was portrayed in more than 73% of the films, including 82% of PG-13 films; smoking was often shown positively as a means to relieve tension or as something to do while socializing. Negative consequences resulting from tobacco use were depicted for only 3% of the major characters who used tobacco. By showing smoking in an unrealistically positive light, films may be acting as advertisement.

Does smoking on-screen affect real-life smoking habits? Studies of adolescents have consistently found a strong association between seeing tobacco use in films and trying cigarettes. Adolescents who see more smoking in films or whose favorite movie stars frequently use tobacco on-screen have more positive attitudes about smoking and are as much as three times more likely to have tried smoking than teens with less exposure to films. Teens may be particularly sensitive to on-screen portrayals of smoking be cause they are in the process of developing adult identities; during this period, they may try out different personas, including those of their favorite movie stars.

Some groups equate seeing a favorite actor smoke on-screen with now-banned celebrity television advertisements for cigarettes. They suggest an automatic R rating for any film that shows tobacco use, equating smoking with violence, strong language, sexuality, and nudity in determining a film's rating. The debate over the prevalence and effects of smoking is likely to continue.

Who Uses Tobacco?

Not all young people are equally vulnerable to the lure of tobacco. Research suggests that the more of the following characteristics that apply to a child or adolescent, the more likely he or she is to use tobacco:

- A parent or sibling uses tobacco.
- Peers use tobacco.

VITAL STATISTICS

Table 11-1 Who Smokes?

	Percentage of Smokers		
	Men	Women	Total
Ethnic group (age ≥ 18)			
White	24.0	20.0	21.9
Black	26.7	17.3	21.5
Asian	20.6	6.1	13.3
American Indian/ Alaska Native	37.5	26.8	32.0
Latino	21.1	11.1	16.2
Education (age ≥ 25)			
≤8 years	21.0	13.4	17.1
9–11 years	36.8	29.0	32.6
12 years (no diploma)	30.2	22.2	26.0
GED diploma	47.5	38.8	43.2
12 years (diploma)	28.8	20.7	24.6
Associate degree	26.1	17.1	20.9
Undergraduate degree	11.9	9.6	10.7
Graduate degree	6.9	7.4	7.1
Total	**23.9**	**18.1**	**20.9**

SOURCE: Centers for Disease Control and Prevention. 2006. Tobacco use among adults—United States, 2005. *Morbidity and Mortality Weekly Report* 55(42): 1145–1148.

- The child comes from a blue-collar family.
- The child comes from a low-income home.
- The family is headed by a single parent.
- The child performs poorly in school.
- The child drops out of school.
- The child has positive attitudes about tobacco use.

In 2005, 23.9% of men and 18.1% of women smoked cigarettes (Table 11-1). Rates of smoking varied, based on gender, age, ethnicity, and education level (see the box "Smoking Among U.S. Ethnic Populations"). Adults with less than a twelfth-grade education were much more likely to smoke cigarettes than those with a college degree. The reverse is true for cigars: Cigar smoking is most common among the affluent and those with high educational attainment.

Between 1996 and 2001 the percentage of smokers who said they smoked only occasionally rose in 38 states and the District of Columbia, and recent surveys indicate the trend is continuing. Most of those who describe themselves as occasional smokers (smoke on some days but not daily) are young adults age 18–25 who say they smoke only at parties or when they are with friends who smoke. Health officials warn that occasional smokers are as vulnerable as other smokers to developing dependence and addiction to nicotine. They are also less likely to try to quit.

Although all states ban the sale of tobacco to anyone under 18 years of age, at least 500 million packs of cigarettes and 26 million containers of chewing tobacco are consumed by minors each year. In 2004, about 5% of 13-year-old Americans said they had used tobacco products in the last month. Among high school students, about 23% smoke cigarettes at least occasionally and 14% smoke cigars. An estimated 8%, including 10% of white male students, use spit tobacco. Male college athletes and professional baseball players report even higher rates of spit tobacco use.

Men and women with other drug-abuse problems frequently use tobacco. For example, studies show that roughly 80% of alcoholics and more than 90% of heroin addicts are heavy smokers. Smoking also is more prevalent among people with mental disorders than among the rest of the population: 40% of people with major depression, social phobias, and generalized anxiety disorder—and eight out of ten people with schizophrenia—are smokers. Such findings suggest that underlying psychological or physiological traits may predispose people to drug use, including tobacco.

HEALTH HAZARDS

Tobacco adversely affects nearly every part of the body, including the brain, stomach, mouth, and reproductive organs.

Tobacco Smoke: A Toxic Mix

Tobacco smoke contains hundreds of damaging chemical substances, including acetone (nail polish remover), ammonia, hexamine (lighter fluid), and toluene (industrial solvent). Smoke from a typical unfiltered cigarette contains about 5 billion particles per cubic millimeter—50,000 times as many as are found in an equal volume of smoggy urban air. These particles, when condensed, form the brown, sticky mass called **cigarette tar.**

Carcinogens and Poisons At least 43 chemicals in tobacco smoke are linked to the development of cancer. Some, such as benzo(a)pyrene and urethane, are **carcinogens;** that is, they directly cause cancer. Other chemicals, such as formaldehyde, are **cocarcinogens;** they do not themselves cause cancer but combine with other chemicals to stimulate the growth of certain cancers, at least in laboratory animals. Other substances in

Terms

cigarette tar A brown, sticky mass created when the chemical particles in tobacco smoke condense.

carcinogen Any substance that causes cancer.

cocarcinogen A substance that works with a carcinogen to cause cancer.

Dimensions of Diversity

Smoking Among U.S. Ethnic Populations

The overall rate of tobacco use among Americans age 12 and older was 29.4% in 2005. That means on average that any group of a dozen people is likely to include three or four who use tobacco. But averages include wide variations among populations, and ethnic differences appear in the earliest stages of tobacco use.

About 23% of all U.S. high school students described themselves as "current cigarette users" in 2005. African American students (13%) were less likely than either whites (26%) or Latinos (22%) to smoke in high school. Similarly, far more white students (11%) described themselves as "frequent" smokers than did Latinos (8%) or blacks (5%). Use of smokeless tobacco shows an even greater disparity. White high school students are nearly 10 times more likely to use spit tobacco than are African American students, and about 5 times more likely than Latino students. White students (14.9%) smoke cigars only slightly more often than Latino students (14.6%) or black students (10.3%).

Wide ethnic variations also exist among smokers over 18 years old. More than 33% of American Indian and Alaska Native adults are smokers; among Asian Americans, only 11% of adults smoke, about half the rate for the general population. Within the broad ethnic categories even greater variation occurs: Among people grouped under the broad category Latinos, 30% of Puerto Ricans but only 19% of Central or South Americans are smokers. There are higher smoking rates among population groups who trace their origins to Southeast Asia (for example, Vietnam, Cambodia, or Laos) than among other population groups within the general Asian American grouping (for example, people from the Philippines, China, or Japan). Time in the United States, English proficiency, and level of educational attainment also influence smoking rates.

In populations of Asian and Pacific Islander Americans, rates of smoking are much higher among men than among women, regardless of country of origin. Although smoking among women decreases with age in the general population, smoking rates among Asian and Pacific Islander women increase with age. Asian and Pacific Islander Americans, male and female, who do smoke tend to smoke fewer cigarettes per day (a half a pack daily or less) than whites who smoke.

The variations between and within ethnic populations reflect a complex interplay of social, environmental, and cultural factors. For example, in some Latino populations, strong parental disapproval of smoking, particularly for girls, holds down the rate of smoking initiation; for other groups, smoking may have a mature and masculine aura, thereby promoting smoking. In some populations, socioeconomic factors may limit access to stop-smoking programs; prevention programs may also not be available to non–English speaking groups.

Tobacco companies understand the value of marketing strategies based on ethnic, cultural, age, and other differences. In 2004, a New York Supreme Court justice ruled that Brown & Williamson Tobacco Company was illegally appealing to young people with its "Kool MIXX" marketing campaign, which focused on hip-hop music and culture. R. J. Reynolds Tobacco Company (RJRT) is continuing an extensive marketing effort for "Exotic Blends"—fruit- and spice-flavored, premium-priced, and imaginatively packaged versions of Camel cigarettes—in minority communities and to women. To increase Camel cigarette sales in the gay and lesbian community, RJRT developed a marketing plan designated Project Sub Culture Urban Marketing, or "Project SCUM." The campaign identified gays, "rebellious generation X," and street people as markets where "opportunity exists for a cigarette manufacturer to dominate." (A memo describing Camel's SCUM strategy is available at http://www.projectscum.org.)

Examine your own attitudes toward smoking and smokers—where do your ideas come from? Also consider the tobacco advertising you encounter: What groups are being targeted and how are they being targeted? As a smoker, a parent, or a concerned member of your community, it is important to be aware of the amount and type of tobacco advertising that you encounter and how your own background may influence your smoking attitudes and behavior.

SOURCES: Office of Applied Studies, Substance Abuse and Mental Health Services Administration. 2006. *Results from the 2005 National Survey on Drug Use and Health: National Findings*, September 2006 (http://oas.samhsa.gov/; retrieved; November 17, 2006). Centers for Disease Control and Prevention. 2004. Prevalence of cigarette use among 14 racial/ethnic populations—United States, 1990–2001. *Morbidity and Mortality Weekly Report* 53(3): 49–52; Centers for Disease Control and Prevention. 2006. Youth Risk Behavior Surveillance—United States, 2005. *Morbidity and Mortality Weekly Report* 55(SS05): 1–108.

tobacco cause health problems because they damage the lining of the respiratory tract or decrease the lungs' ability to fight off infection.

Tobacco also contains poisonous substances, including arsenic and hydrogen cyanide. In addition to being an addictive psychoactive drug, nicotine is also a poison and can be fatal in high doses. Many cases of nicotine poisoning occur each year in toddlers and infants who pick up and eat cigarette butts they find at home or on the playground.

Cigarette smoke contains carbon monoxide, the deadly gas in automobile exhaust, in concentrations 400 times greater than is considered safe in industrial workplaces. Not surprisingly, smokers often complain of breathlessness when they require a burst of energy to run across campus for their next class. Carbon monoxide displaces oxygen in red blood cells, depleting the body's supply of life-giving oxygen for extra work. Carbon monoxide also impairs visual acuity, especially at night.

Additives Tobacco manufacturers use additives to manipulate the taste and effect of cigarettes and other

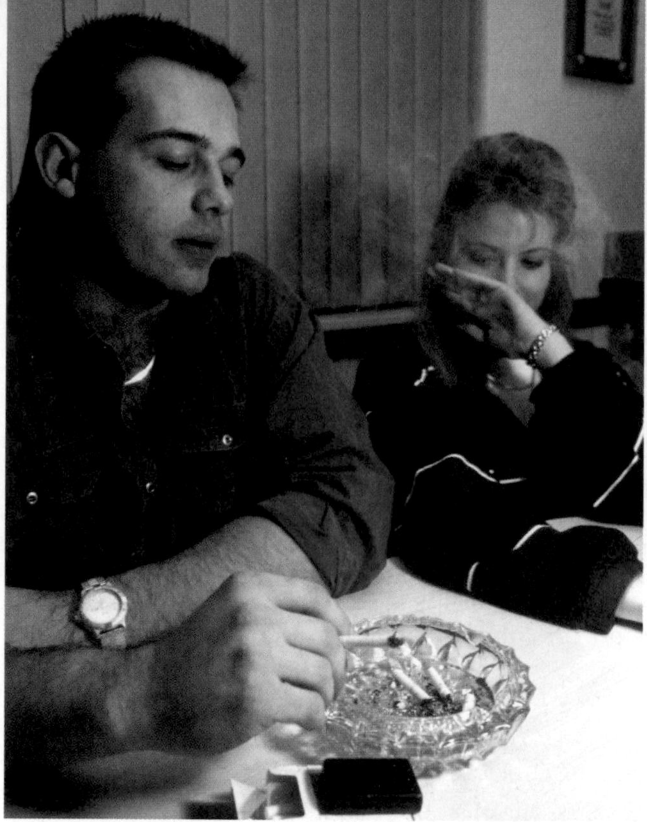

Cigarette smoke contains many toxic and carcinogenic chemicals that affect both the person smoking and the people breathing the environmental tobacco smoke. A growing body of evidence links ETS with lung cancer and respiratory and cardiovascular diseases.

tobacco products. Nearly 600 chemicals, approved as safe when used as food additives, are used in manufacturing cigarettes. In 1994, U.S. cigarette manufacturers submitted a list of tobacco additives to the Department of Health and Human Services, which made the list public and accompanied it with the notice that "although these ingredients are regarded as safe when ingested in foods, some may form carcinogens when heated or burned."

Additives account for roughly 10%, by weight, of a cigarette, and include sugars and other flavoring agents, humectants (compounds that keep tobacco from drying out), and chemicals that enhance the addicting properties of nicotine. The added sugars—including licorice, cocoa, and honey—have a dual role. As flavor enhancers, sugars mask the harsh, bitter taste of tobacco, making it possible for smokers, particularly first-time smokers, to inhale larger volumes of smoke and therefore absorb more nicotine. When sugars burn, they produce acetaldehyde, a chemical that enhances the addictive effect of nicotine and is a carcinogen. Other flavor components, such as the theobromine found in cocoa and the glycyrrhizin in licorice, share one of the properties of menthol—they act as bronchodilators, opening the lungs' airways and making it easier for nicotine to get into the bloodstream. (Menthol cigarettes are discussed on p. 307.)

Ammonia plays a complex role in tobacco products, but its chief purpose is to boost the amount of addictive nicotine delivered by cigarettes. Ammonia reduces the acidity of tobacco smoke and releases nicotine in the form of a base (alkaline) rather than a salt (acid) bound to other acid components of smoke. As a free base, nicotine is more readily absorbed into the blood.

Ammonia and other additives are essential to the technology of reconstituted tobacco, which enables manufacturers to make cigarettes from leaf scraps and stems of tobacco plants (high in nicotine but harsh and bitter tasting). Flavor additives improve the taste, and ammonia delivers higher levels of nicotine. Cigarettes made from reconstituted tobacco treated with flavor enhancers and ammonia contain nearly twice as much available nicotine as cigarettes made from tobacco leaf. A study of free-base nicotine content in 11 brands of cigarettes available in the United States found that some contained 10–20 times higher percentages of free-base nicotine than experts had previously believed. Content ranged from less than 2% in some brands to as high as 36% for the specialty brand American Spirit. Marlboro brands contained up to 9.6% free-base nicotine.

Some additives are intended to make sidestream smoke (the uninhaled smoke from a burning cigarette) less obvious and objectionable. For example, potassium citrate, aluminum and other metal hydroxides, and clay are added to cigarette wrappers to convert particulate ash into an invisible gas with less irritating odor than would be given off by a conventional paper wrapper. These additives serve no purpose in making cigarettes more desirable and addicting to the smoker; instead, they are intended to reduce social pressures from nonsmokers.

Effects of Smoking Behavior All smokers absorb some gases, tar, and nicotine from cigarette smoke, but smokers who inhale bring most of these substances into their bodies and keep them there. In 1 year, a typical pack-a-day smoker takes in 50,000–70,000 puffs. Smoke from a cigarette, pipe, or cigar directly assaults the mouth, throat, and respiratory tract. The nose, which normally filters about 75% of foreign matter we breathe, is completely bypassed.

In a cigarette, the unburned tobacco itself acts as a filter. As a cigarette burns down, there is less and less filter. Thus, more chemicals are absorbed into the body during the last third of a cigarette than during the first. A smoker can cut down on the absorption of harmful chemicals by not smoking cigarettes down to short butts. Any gains, of course, will be offset by smoking more cigarettes, inhaling more deeply, or puffing more frequently.

"Light" and Low-Tar Cigarettes Some smokers switch to low-tar, low-nicotine, or filtered cigarettes because they believe them to be healthier alternatives. But there is no such thing as a safe cigarette, and smoking behavior is a more important factor in tar and nicotine intake than the type of cigarette smoked. Smokers who switch to a low-nicotine brand often compensate by smoking more cigarettes, inhaling more deeply, taking larger or more frequent puffs, or blocking ventilation holes with lips or fingers to offset the effects of filters. Studies have found that people who smoke "light" cigarettes inhale up to eight times as much tar and nicotine as printed on the label. Studies also show that smokers of light cigarettes are less likely to quit than smokers of regular cigarettes, probably due to the misperception that light cigarettes are safer. Use of "light" and low-tar cigarettes does not reduce the risk of smoking-related illnesses. In 2006 tobacco companies were ordered by a federal judge to stop using deceptive labels like "light," "ultra-light," and "low-tar" on their products, but appeals continue.

Menthol Cigarettes Concerns have also been raised about menthol cigarettes. About 70% of African American smokers smoke these cigarettes, as compared to 30% of whites. Studies have found that blacks absorb more nicotine than other groups and metabolize it more slowly; they also have lower rates of successful quitting. The anesthetizing effect of menthol, which may allow smokers to inhale more deeply and hold smoke in their lungs for a longer period, may be partly responsible for these differences. Research is needed to determine if effects of menthol and differences in smoking behavior can help explain the higher rates of smoking-related diseases seen among blacks.

The Immediate Effects of Smoking

The beginning smoker often has symptoms of mild nicotine poisoning: dizziness; faintness; rapid pulse; cold, clammy skin; and sometimes nausea, vomiting, and diarrhea. The seasoned smoker occasionally suffers these effects of nicotine poisoning, particularly after quitting and then returning to a previous level of consumption. The effects of nicotine on smokers vary, depending greatly on the size of the nicotine dose and how much tolerance previous smoking has built up. Nicotine can either excite or tranquilize the nervous system, depending on dosage.

Nicotine has many other immediate effects. It stimulates the part of the brain called the **cerebral cortex.** It also stimulates the adrenal glands to discharge adrenaline. And it inhibits the formation of urine; constricts the blood vessels, especially in the skin; accelerates the heart rate; and elevates blood pressure. Higher blood pressure, faster heart rate, and constricted blood vessels require the heart to pump more blood. In healthy people, the heart can usually meet this demand, but in people whose coronary arteries are damaged enough to interfere with the flow of blood, the heart muscle may be strained.

Smoking depresses hunger contractions and dulls the taste buds; smokers who quit often notice that food tastes much better. Smoking is not useful for weight loss, however. Smoking for decades may lessen or prevent age-associated weight gain for some smokers, but for people under 30, smoking is not associated with weight loss. Figure 11-2 (p. 308) summarizes these immediate effects.

The Long-Term Effects of Smoking

Smoking is linked to many deadly and disabling diseases. Research indicates that the total amount of tobacco smoke inhaled is a key factor contributing to disease. People who smoke more cigarettes per day, inhale deeply, puff frequently, smoke cigarettes down to the butts, or begin smoking at an early age run a greater risk of disease than do those who smoke more moderately or who do not smoke at all. Many diseases have already been linked to smoking, and as more research is done, even more diseases associated with smoking are being uncovered. The costliest ones—to society as well as to the individual—are cardiovascular diseases, respiratory diseases such as emphysema and lung cancer, and other cancers.

Cardiovascular Disease Although lung cancer tends to receive the most publicity, one form of cardiovascular disease, **coronary heart disease (CHD),** is actually the most widespread single cause of death for cigarette smokers. CHD often results from **atherosclerosis,** a condition in which fatty deposits called **plaques** form on the inner walls of heart arteries, causing them to narrow and stiffen. Smoking and exposure to environmental tobacco smoke (ETS) permanently accelerate the rate of plaque accumulation in the coronary arteries—50% for smokers, 25% for ex-smokers, and 20% for people regularly exposed to ETS. The crushing chest pain of **angina pectoris,** a primary symptom of CHD, results when the heart muscle, or *myocardium,* does not get enough oxygen. Sometimes a plaque forms at a narrow point in a main coronary artery. If the plaque completely blocks the flow of blood to a portion of the heart, that portion may die. This type of heart attack is called a **myocardial infarction.**

CHD can also interfere with the heart's electrical activity, resulting in disturbances of the normal heartbeat rhythm.

Terms

Vw

cerebral cortex The outer layer of the brain, which controls complex behavior and mental activity.

coronary heart disease (CHD) Cardiovascular disease caused by hardening of the arteries that supply oxygen to the heart muscle; also called *coronary artery disease.*

atherosclerosis Cardiovascular disease caused by the deposit of fatty substances in the walls of the arteries.

plaque A deposit on the inner wall of blood vessels; blood can coagulate around plaque and form a clot.

angina pectoris Chest pain due to coronary heart disease.

myocardial infarction A heart attack caused by the complete blockage of a main coronary artery.

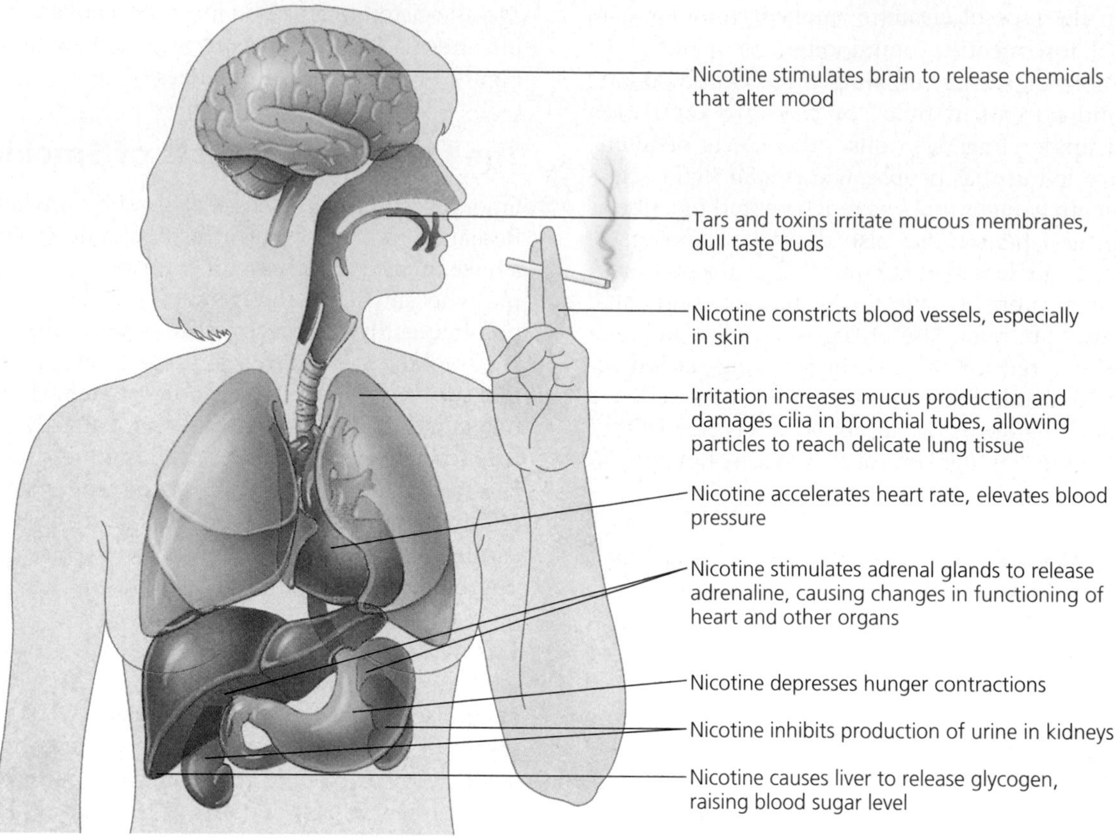
Nicotine stimulates brain to release chemicals that alter mood
Tars and toxins irritate mucous membranes, dull taste buds
Nicotine constricts blood vessels, especially in skin
Irritation increases mucus production and damages cilia in bronchial tubes, allowing particles to reach delicate lung tissue
Nicotine accelerates heart rate, elevates blood pressure
Nicotine stimulates adrenal glands to release adrenaline, causing changes in functioning of heart and other organs
Nicotine depresses hunger contractions
Nicotine inhibits production of urine in kidneys
Nicotine causes liver to release glycogen, raising blood sugar level

Figure 11-2 The short-term effects of smoking a cigarette.

Sudden and unexpected death is a common result of CHD, particularly among smokers. (See Chapter 15 for a more extensive discussion of cardiovascular disease.)

Smokers have a death rate from CHD that is 70% higher than that of nonsmokers. Deaths from CHD associated with cigarette smoking are most common in people age 40–50. (In contrast, deaths from lung cancer caused by smoking are most likely to occur in 60–70-year-olds.) Among people *under* age 40, smokers are five times more likely than nonsmokers to have a heart attack. Cigar and pipe smokers run a lower risk than cigarette smokers.

We do not completely understand how cigarette smoking increases the risk of CHD, but researchers are beginning to shed light on the process. Smoking reduces the amount of "good" cholesterol (high-density lipoprotein, or HDL) in the blood, thereby promoting plaque formation in artery walls. Smoking may also increase tension in heart muscle walls, speeding up the rate of muscular contraction and accelerating the heart rate. The workload of the heart thus increases, as does its need for oxygen and other nutrients. Carbon monoxide produced by cigarette smoking combines with hemoglobin in the red blood cells, displacing oxygen and thus providing less oxygen to the heart. One study showed that the additional blood supply available to the heart during stress was 21% less in smokers than in nonsmokers. This reduced blood flow is an early indicator of future heart attacks or strokes.

The risks of CHD decrease rapidly when a person stops smoking; this is particularly true for younger smokers, whose coronary arteries have not yet been extensively damaged. Cigarette smoking has also been linked to other cardiovascular diseases, including the following:

- *Stroke,* a sudden interference with the circulation of blood in a part of the brain, resulting in the destruction of brain cells
- *Aortic aneurysm,* a bulge in the aorta caused by a weakening in its walls
- *Pulmonary heart disease,* a disorder of the right side of the heart, caused by changes in the blood vessels of the lungs

Lung Cancer and Other Cancers Cigarette smoking is the primary cause of lung cancer. A recent study identified the precise mechanism: Benzo(a)pyrene, a chemical found in tobacco smoke, causes genetic mutations in lung cells that are identical to those found in many patients with lung cancer. Those who smoke two or more packs of cigarettes a day have lung cancer death rates 12–25 times greater than those of nonsmokers. The dramatic rise in lung cancer rates among women in the past 40 years clearly parallels the increase of smoking in this group; lung cancer now exceeds breast cancer as the leading cause of cancer deaths among women. The risk of developing lung cancer increases with the number of cigarettes smoked each day, the number of years of smoking, and the age at which the person started smoking.

While cigar and pipe smokers have a higher risk of lung cancer than nonsmokers do, the risk is lower than that for cigarette smokers. Smoking filter-tipped cigarettes slightly reduces health hazards, unless the smoker compensates by smoking more, as is often the case.

Evidence suggests that after 1 year without smoking, the risk of lung cancer decreases substantially. After 10 years, the risk of lung cancer among ex-smokers is 50% of that of continuing smokers. The sooner one quits, the better: If smoking is stopped before cancer has started, lung tissue tends to repair itself, even if cellular changes that can lead to cancer are already present.

Research has also linked smoking to cancers of the trachea, mouth, pharynx, esophagus, larynx, pancreas, bladder, kidney, breast, cervix, stomach, liver, colon, and skin. For more information on cancer, see Chapter 16.

Chronic Obstructive Lung Disease

The lungs of a smoker are constantly exposed to dangerous chemicals and irritants, and they must work harder to function adequately. The stresses placed on the lungs by smoking can permanently damage lung function and lead to *chronic obstructive lung disease (COLD)*, also known as chronic obstructive pulmonary disease (COPD) or chronic lower respiratory disease. COLD is the fourth leading cause of death in the United States. This progressive and disabling disorder consists of several different but related diseases; emphysema and chronic bronchitis are two of the most common.

Cigarette smokers are up to 18 times more likely than nonsmokers to die from emphysema and chronic bronchitis. (Pipe and cigar smokers are more likely to die from COLD than are nonsmokers, but they have a smaller risk than cigarette smokers.) A 2006 study found that one in four heavy smokers develops COLD. The risk rises with the number of cigarettes smoked and falls when smoking ceases. For most Americans, cigarette smoking is a more important cause of COLD than air pollution, but exposure to both is more dangerous than exposure to either by itself.

EMPHYSEMA Smoking is the primary cause of **emphysema,** a particularly disabling condition in which the walls of the air sacs in the lungs lose their elasticity and are gradually destroyed. The lungs' ability to obtain oxygen and remove carbon dioxide is impaired. A person with emphysema is breathless, is constantly gasping for air, and has the feeling of drowning. The heart must pump harder and may become enlarged. People with emphysema often die from a damaged heart. There is no known way to reverse this disease. In its advanced stage, the victim is bedridden and severely disabled.

CHRONIC BRONCHITIS Persistent, recurrent inflammation of the bronchial tubes characterizes **chronic bronchitis.** When the cell lining of the bronchial tubes is irritated, it secretes excess mucus. Bronchial congestion is followed by a chronic cough, which makes breathing more and more difficult. If smokers have chronic bronchitis, they face a greater risk of lung cancer, no matter how old they are or how many (or few) cigarettes they smoke. Chronic bronchitis seems to be a shortcut to lung cancer.

Other Respiratory Damage

Even when the smoker shows no signs of lung impairment or disease, cigarette smoking damages the respiratory system. Normally the cells lining the bronchial tubes secrete mucus, a sticky fluid that collects particles of soot, dust, and other substances in inhaled air. Mucus is carried up to the mouth by the continuous motion of the cilia, hairlike structures that protrude from the inner surface of the bronchial tubes (Figure 11-3 on p. 310). If the cilia are destroyed or impaired, or if the pollution of inhaled air is more than the system can remove, the protection provided by cilia is lost.

Cigarette smoke first slows and then stops the action of the cilia. Eventually it destroys them, leaving delicate membranes exposed to injury from substances inhaled in cigarette smoke or from the polluted air in which the person lives or works. Special cells, *macrophages,* a type of white blood cell, also work to remove foreign particles from the respiratory tract by engulfing them. Smoking appears to make macrophages work less efficiently. This interference with the functioning of the respiratory system often leads rapidly to the conditions known as smoker's throat and smoker's cough, as well as to shortness of breath. Even smokers of high school age show impaired respiratory function, compared with nonsmokers of the same age. Other respiratory effects of smoking include a worsening of allergy and asthma symptoms and an increase in the smoker's susceptibility to colds.

Although cigarette smoking can cause many respiratory disorders and diseases, the damage is not always permanent. Once a person stops smoking, steady improvement in overall lung function usually takes place. Chronic coughing subsides, mucus production returns to normal, and breathing becomes easier. The likelihood of lung disease drops sharply. People of all ages, even those who have been smoking for decades, improve after they stop smoking. If given a chance, the human body has remarkable powers of restoring itself.

Terms

emphysema A disease characterized by a loss of lung tissue elasticity and breakup of the air sacs, impairing the lungs' ability to obtain oxygen and remove carbon dioxide.

chronic bronchitis Recurrent, persistent inflammation of the bronchial tubes.

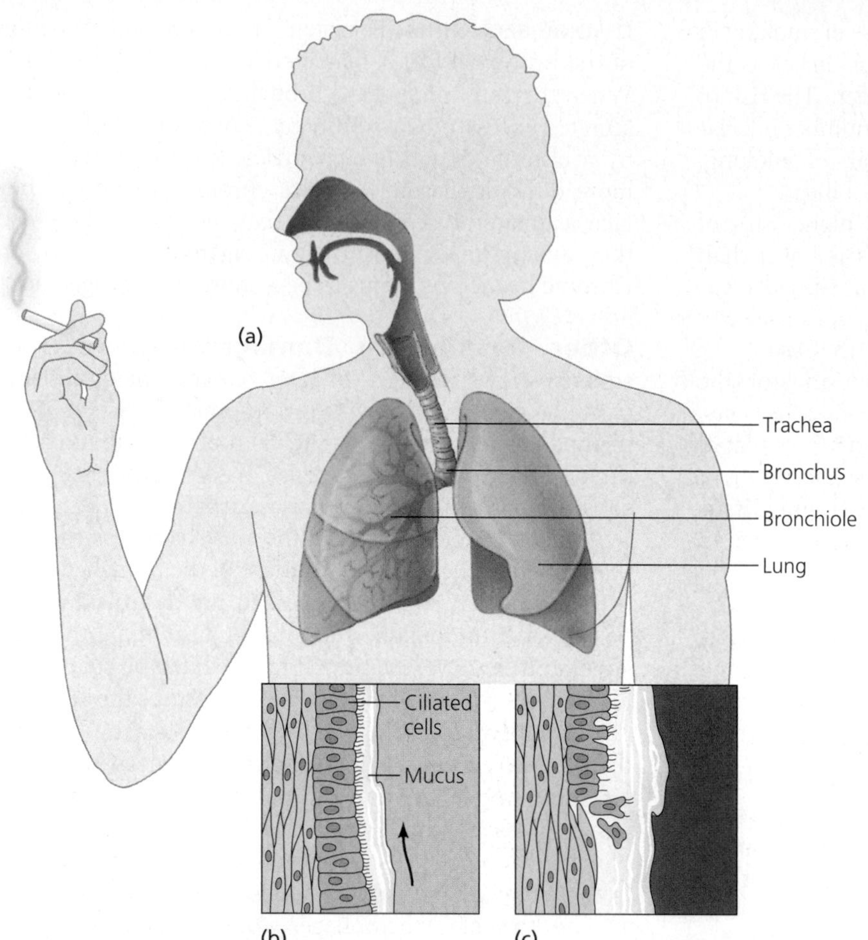

Figure 11-3 Damage to the lungs caused by smoking. (a) The respiratory system. (b) The inside of a bronchiole of a nonsmoker. Foreign particles are collected by a thin layer of sticky mucus and transported out of the lungs, up toward the mouth, by the action of cilia. (c) The inside of a bronchiole of a smoker. Smoking irritates the lung tissue and causes increased mucus production, which can overwhelm the action of the cilia. A smoker develops a chronic cough as the lungs try to rid themselves of foreign particles and excess mucus. Eventually the cilia are destroyed, leaving the delicate lung tissue exposed to injury from foreign substances.

Additional Health, Cosmetic, and Economic Concerns

- *Ulcers.* People who smoke are more likely to develop peptic ulcers and are more likely to die from them (especially stomach ulcers), because smoking impairs the body's healing ability. Smoking also increases the risk of gastroesophageal reflux, which causes heartburn and can, if severe, raise the risk of esophageal cancer.
- *Impotence.* Smoking affects blood flow in the veins and arteries of the penis, and it is an independent risk factor for impotence. In one recent study, smokers were twice as likely as nonsmokers to experience erectile dysfunction (impotence).
- *Reproductive health problems.* Smoking is linked to reduced fertility in both men and women. A study of 18-year-old smoking men found that they had a significantly higher proportion of abnormally shaped sperm and sperm with genetic defects than nonsmokers. In women, smoking can contribute to menstrual disorders, early menopause, and complications of pregnancy. See the box "Gender and Tobacco Use."
- *Dental diseases.* Smokers are at increased risk for tooth decay and gum and periodontal diseases, with symptoms appearing by the mid-20s.
- *Diminished physical senses.* Smoking dulls the senses of taste and smell. Over time, it increases the risk for hearing loss, and for macular degeneration and cataracts (both serious eye conditions that can result in partial or total blindness).
- *Injuries.* Smokers have higher rates of motor vehicle crashes, fire-related injuries, and back pain.
- *Cosmetic concerns.* Smoking can cause premature skin wrinkling, premature baldness, stained teeth, discolored fingers, and a persistent tobacco odor in clothes and hair.
- *Economic costs.* In 2003, the average per-pack price of cigarettes was $4.04. A pack-a-day habit costs nearly $1500 each year for cigarettes alone. Other costs include higher health and home insurance premiums; more frequent cleaning of clothes, teeth, home, office, and car; and repair of burnt clothing, upholstery, and carpeting—for a cost of $3000 per year. A study by researchers at Duke University estimated that the total cost for a 24-year-old—including cigarettes, lost earnings, insurance costs, and harm done by environmental tobacco smoke—is nearly $40 per pack.

Gender Matters: Gender and Tobacco Use

American men are currently more likely than women to smoke, but women younger than age 23 are becoming smokers at a faster rate than any other population segment. As the rate of smoking among women approaches that of men, so do rates of tobacco-related illness and death. Lung cancer, emphysema, and cardiovascular diseases sicken and kill both men and women who smoke, and more American women now die each year from lung cancer than from breast cancer.

Although overall risks of tobacco-related illness are similar for women and men, sex appears to make a difference in some diseases. Women, for example, are more at risk for smoking-related blood clots and strokes than are men, and the risk is even greater for women using oral contraceptives. Among men and women with the same smoking history, the odds for developing three major types of cancer, including lung cancer, is 1.2–1.7 times higher in women than in men. One possible explanation for this difference is that women are more likely to use low-tar cigarettes and thus engage in compensatory behaviors such as deep inhalation, which is linked to increased respiratory damage. Women may also have a greater biological vulnerability to lung cancer.

For both men and women, tobacco use is associated with increased incidence of sex-specific health problems. Men who smoke increase their risk of erectile dysfunction and infertility due to reduced sperm density and motility. Women who smoke have higher rates of osteoporosis (a bone-thinning disease that can lead to fractures), thyroid-related diseases, and depression.

Women who smoke also have risks associated with reproduction and the reproductive organs. Smoking is associated with greater menstrual bleeding, greater duration of painful menstrual cramps, and more variability in menstrual cycle length. Smokers have a more difficult time becoming pregnant, and they reach menopause on average a year or two earlier than nonsmokers. When women smokers become pregnant, they face increased chances of miscarriage or placental disorders that lead to bleeding and premature delivery; rates of ectopic pregnancy, preeclampsia, and stillbirth are also higher among women who smoke. Smoking is a risk factor for cervical cancer.

When women decide to try to stop smoking, they are more likely than men to join a support group. Overall, though, women are less successful than men in quitting. Women report more severe withdrawal symptoms when they stop smoking and are more likely than men to report cravings in response to social and behavioral cues associated with smoking. For men, relapse to smoking is often associated with work or social pressure; women are more likely to relapse when sad or depressed or concerned about weight gain. Women and men also respond differently to medications: Nicotine replacement therapy appears to work better for men, whereas the non-nicotine medication bupropion appears to work better for women.

In addition, smoking contributes to osteoporosis, increases the risk of complications from diabetes, and accelerates the course of multiple sclerosis. Further research may link tobacco use to still other disorders.

Cumulative Effects The cumulative effects of tobacco use fall into two general categories. The first category is reduced life expectancy. A male who takes up smoking before age 15 and continues to smoke is only half as likely to live to age 75 as a male who never smokes. If he inhales deeply, he risks losing a minute of life for every minute of smoking. Females who have similar smoking habits also have a reduced life expectancy. Smoking reduces their life expectancy by more than 10 years.

The second category involves quality of life. A national health survey begun in 1964 shows that smokers spend one-third more time away from their jobs because of illness than nonsmokers. Female smokers spend 17% more days sick in bed than female nonsmokers. Lost work days due to smoking number in the millions.

Both men and women smokers show a greater rate of acute and chronic disease than people who have never smoked. Smokers become disabled at younger ages than nonsmokers and have more years of unhealthy life in addition to a shorter life span. The U.S. Public Health Service estimates that if all people had the same rate of disease as those who never smoked, there would be 1 million fewer cases of chronic bronchitis, 1.8 million fewer cases of **sinusitis**, and 1 million fewer cases of peptic ulcers in the country every year.

Other Forms of Tobacco Use

Many smokers have switched from cigarettes to other forms of tobacco, such as spit (smokeless) tobacco, cigars and pipes, and clove cigarettes and bidis. However, each of these alternatives is far from safe.

Spit (Smokeless) Tobacco More than 6.5 million adults and about 8% of all high school students are current spit tobacco users. Spit tobacco use has increased in recent years and is especially common among Native Americans, adolescent males (especially white males),

Term VW

sinusitis Inflammation of the sinus cavities; symptoms include headache, fever, and pain.

Cigars contain more tobacco than cigarettes and so produce more tar when smoked. Cigar smokers face an increased risk of cancer even if they don't inhale the smoke.

male college athletes, and professional baseball players. About 80% of users start by the ninth grade.

Spit tobacco comes in two major forms: snuff and chewing tobacco (chew). In snuff, the tobacco leaf is processed into a coarse, moist powder and mixed with flavorings. Snuff is usually sold in small tins. Users place a "pinch," "dip," or "quid" between the lower lip or cheek and gum and suck on it. In chewing tobacco, the tobacco leaf may be shredded ("leaf"), pressed into bricks or cakes ("plugs"), or dried and twisted into rope-like strands ("twists"). Chew is usually sold in pouches. Users place a wad of tobacco in their mouth and then chew or suck it to release the nicotine. All types of smokeless tobacco cause an increase in saliva production, and the resulting tobacco juice is spit out or swallowed.

The nicotine in spit tobacco—along with flavorings and additives—is absorbed through the gums and lining of the mouth. Holding an average-size dip in the mouth for 30 minutes delivers about the same amount of nicotine as two or three cigarettes. Because of its nicotine content, spit tobacco is highly addictive. Some users keep it in their mouth even while sleeping.

Although not as dangerous as smoking cigarettes, the use of spit tobacco carries many health risks. Changes can occur in the mouth after only a few weeks of use: Gums and lips become dried and irritated and may bleed. White or red patches may appear inside the mouth; this condition, known as *leukoplakia,* can lead to oral cancer. A study of major league baseball players found dangerous mouth lesions in 83 out of the 141 spit tobacco users who were examined. Other studies have found even higher rates of oral sores. About 25% of regular spit tobacco users have *gingivitis* (inflammation) and recession of the gums and bone loss around the teeth, especially where the tobacco is usually placed. The senses of taste and smell are usually dulled. In addition, other people find the presence of wads of tobacco in the mouth, stained teeth, bad breath, and behaviors such as frequent spitting to be unpleasant.

One of the most serious effects of spit tobacco is an increased risk of oral cancer—cancers of the lip, tongue, cheek, throat, gums, roof and floor of the mouth, and larynx. Spit tobacco contains at least 28 chemicals known to cause cancer, and long-term snuff use may increase the risk of oral cancer by as much as 50 times. Surgery to treat oral cancer is often disfiguring and may involve removing parts of the face, tongue, cheek, or lip.

Data on the incidence of heart disease among spit tobacco users have not yet been collected. But it is known that dipping and chewing tobacco produce blood levels of nicotine similar to those in cigarette smokers. High blood levels of nicotine have dangerous effects on the cardiovascular system, including elevation of blood pressure, heart rate, and blood levels of certain fats. Other chemicals in spit tobacco are believed to pose risks to developing fetuses.

Cigars and Pipes After more than two decades of decline, cigar smoking has increased by nearly 50% since 1993. The popularity of cigars is highest among white males age 18–44 with higher-than-average income and education, but women are also smoking cigars in record numbers. Cigar use is also growing among young people: In government surveys, nearly 10% of 16- and 17-year-old students reported having smoked at least one cigar in the previous month. Less than 1% of Americans, mostly males who also smoke cigarettes, are pipe smokers.

Cigars are made from rolled whole tobacco leaves; pipe tobacco is made from shredded leaves and often flavored. Because cigar and pipe smoke are more alkaline than cigarette smoke, users of cigars and pipes do not need to inhale in order to ingest nicotine; instead, they absorb nicotine through the gums and lining of the mouth. Cigars contain more tobacco than cigarettes and so contain more nicotine and produce more tar when smoked. Large cigars may contain as much tobacco as a whole pack of cigarettes and take 1–2 hours to smoke.

The smoke from cigars contains many of the same toxins and carcinogens as the smoke from cigarettes, some in much higher quantities. The health risks of cigars depend on the number of cigars smoked and whether the smoker inhales. Because most cigar and pipe users do not inhale, they have a lower risk of cancer and cardiovascular and respiratory diseases than cigarette smokers. However, their risks are substantially higher than those of nonsmokers. For example, compared to nonsmokers, people who smoke one or two cigars per day without inhaling have 6 times the risk of cancer of the larynx. The risks are much higher for cigar smokers who do inhale: They have 27 times the risk of oral cancer and 53 times the risk of cancer of the larynx compared to nonsmokers, and their risk of heart and lung diseases approaches that of cigarette smokers. Smoking a cigar immediately impairs the ability of blood vessels to dilate, reducing the amount of oxygen delivered to tissues, including heart muscle, especially during times of stress. Pipe and cigar smoking are also risk factors for pancreatic cancer, which is almost always fatal.

Nicotine addiction is another concern. Most adults who smoke cigars do so only occasionally, and there is little evidence that use of cigars by adults leads to addiction. The recent rise in cigar use among teens has raised concerns, however, because nicotine addiction almost always develops in the teen or young adult years. More research is needed to determine if cigar use by teens will develop into nicotine addiction and frequent use of either cigarettes or spit tobacco. In June of 2000 the FTC announced an agreement to put warning labels on cigar packages, 34 years after warning labels first appeared on cigarette packages.

Clove Cigarettes and Bidis Clove cigarettes, also called "kreteks" or "chicartas," are made of tobacco mixed with chopped cloves; they are imported primarily from Indonesia and Pakistan. Clove cigarettes contain almost twice as much tar, nicotine, and carbon monoxide as conventional cigarettes and so have all the same health hazards. Some chemical constituents of cloves may also be dangerous. For example, eugenol, an anesthetic compound found in cloves, may impair the respiratory system's ability to detect and defend against foreign particles. There have been a number of serious respiratory injuries and deaths from the use of clove cigarettes.

Bidis, or "beadies," are small cigarettes imported from India that contain species of tobacco different from those used by U.S. cigarette manufacturers. The tobacco in bidis is hand-rolled in Indian ebony leaves (tendu) and then often flavored; clove, mint, chocolate, and fruit varieties are available. Bidis contain up to four times more nicotine than and twice as much tar as U.S. cigarettes. Use of bidis has been growing among teens, possibly because of the flavorings they contain or because they look and smell somewhat like marijuana cigarettes (joints); they do not have the same effects as marijuana, however.

Currently, an estimated 3% of high school students use clove cigarettes or bidis (Figure 11-4). Neither is a safe or healthy alternative to conventional tobacco cigarettes.

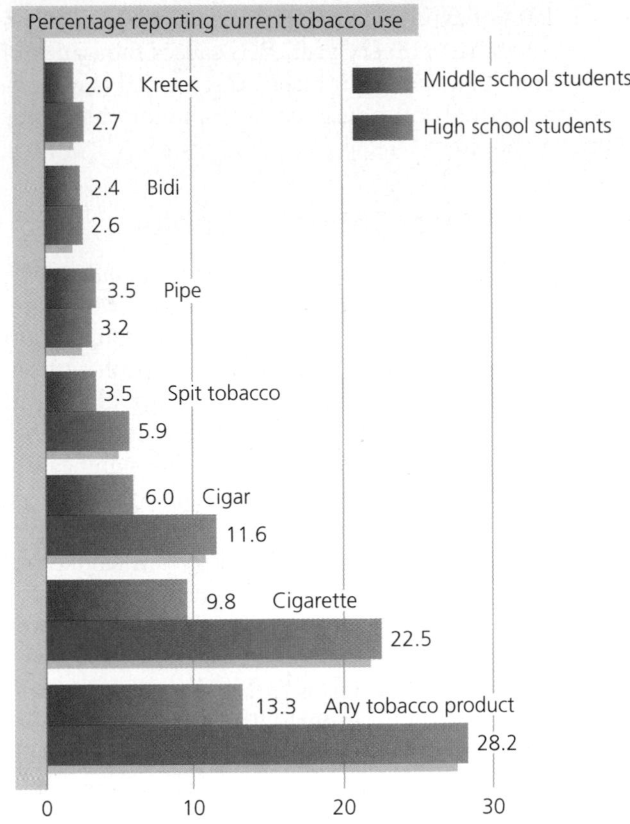

Figure 11-4 Tobacco use among middle school and high school students. Although it is illegal for those under age 18 to purchase tobacco, 13.3% of middle school and 28.2% of high school students report having used some form of tobacco within the past month.

SOURCE: Centers for Disease Control and Prevention. 2006. Tobacco use among middle and high school students—United States, 2004. *Morbidity and Mortality Weekly Report* 54(12)—Corrected (http://www.cdc.gov/tobacco/nyts/correctionnotice.htm; retrieved August 13, 2006).

THE EFFECTS OF SMOKING ON THE NONSMOKER

In a watershed decision in 1993, the U.S. Environmental Protection Agency (EPA) designated **environmental tobacco smoke (ETS)** a Class A carcinogen—an agent known to cause cancer in humans. In 2000, the Department of Health and Human Services' National Toxicology Program classified ETS as a "known human carcinogen." These designations put ETS in the same category as notorious cancer-causing agents like asbestos. In 2006, the Surgeon General issued a report concluding that there is

Term

environmental tobacco smoke (ETS) Smoke that enters the atmosphere from the burning end of a cigarette, cigar, or pipe, as well as smoke that is exhaled by smokers; also called *secondhand smoke*.

no safe level of exposure to ETS; even brief exposure can cause serious harm. Every year, ETS causes thousands of deaths from lung cancer and heart disease and is responsible for hundreds of thousands of respiratory infections in young children.

Environmental Tobacco Smoke

Environmental tobacco smoke, or *secondhand smoke,* consists of mainstream smoke and sidestream smoke. Smoke exhaled by smokers is referred to as **mainstream smoke. Sidestream smoke** enters the atmosphere from the burning end of a cigarette, cigar, or pipe. Undiluted sidestream smoke, because it is not filtered through either a cigarette filter or a smoker's lungs, has significantly higher concentrations of the toxic and carcinogenic compounds found in mainstream smoke. For example, compared to mainstream smoke, sidestream smoke has (1) twice as much tar and nicotine; (2) three times as much benzo(a)pyrene, a carcinogen; (3) almost three times as much carbon monoxide, which displaces oxygen from red blood cells and forms *carboxyhemoglobin,* a dangerous compound that seriously limits the body's ability to use oxygen; and (4) three times as much ammonia.

Nearly 85% of the smoke in a room where someone is smoking comes from sidestream smoke. Of course, sidestream smoke is diffused through the air, so nonsmokers don't inhale the same concentrations of toxic chemicals that the smoker does. Still, the concentrations can be high. In rooms where people are smoking, levels of carbon monoxide, for instance, can exceed those permitted by Federal Air Quality Standards for outside air. In a typical home with the windows closed, it takes about 6 hours for 95% of the airborne cigarette smoke particles to clear.

The secondhand smoke from a cigar can be even more dangerous than that from cigarettes. The EPA has found that the output of carcinogenic particles from a cigar exceeds that of three cigarettes, and cigar smoke contains up to 30 times more carbon monoxide.

ETS Effects Studies show that up to 25% of nonsmokers subjected to ETS develop coughs, 30% develop headaches and nasal discomfort, and 70% suffer from eye irritation. Other symptoms range from breathlessness to sinus problems. People with allergies tend to suffer the most. The odor of tobacco smoke clings to skin and clothes—another unpleasant effect of ETS.

Terms

Ww

mainstream smoke Smoke that is inhaled by a smoker and then exhaled into the atmosphere.

sidestream smoke Smoke that comes from the burning end of a cigarette, cigar, or pipe.

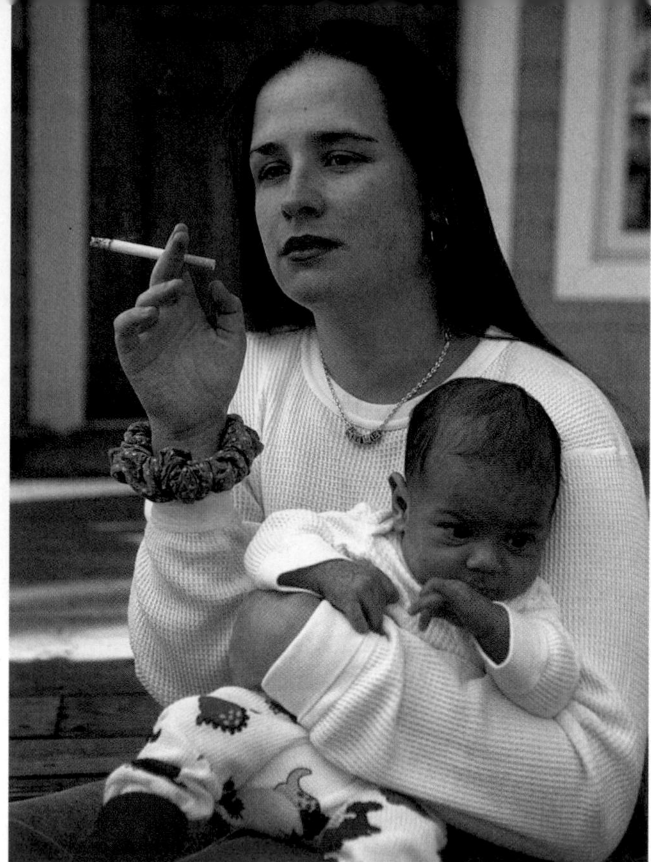

It is estimated that 19 million American infants and children are regularly exposed to environmental tobacco smoke. ETS can cause SIDS, trigger respiratory infections, cause or aggravate asthma, contribute to middle-ear infections, and impair development.

But ETS causes more than just annoyance and discomfort; it causes 3000 lung cancer deaths annually. People who live, work, or socialize among smokers face a 24–50% increase in lung cancer risk. ETS is responsible for about 35,000 deaths overall each year. As described earlier, exposure to ETS is associated with a 20% increase in the progression of atherosclerosis. ETS also aggravates asthma, an increasing cause of sudden death in otherwise healthy adults, and increases the risk for breast and cervical cancers. Scientists have been able to measure changes that contribute to lung tissue damage and potential tumor promotion in the bloodstreams of healthy young test subjects who spend just 3 hours in a smoke-filled room. After just 30 minutes of exposure to ETS, the endothelial function in the coronary arteries of healthy nonsmokers is reduced to the same level as that of smokers. And nonsmokers can still be affected by the harmful effects of ETS hours after they have left a smoky environment. Carbon monoxide, for example, lingers in the bloodstream 5 hours later.

Infants, Children, and ETS Recent studies have shown that infants exposed to smoke from more than 21 cigarettes a day are more than 23 times more likely to die of sudden infant death syndrome (SIDS) than babies not exposed to ETS. The National Cancer Institute recently estimated that ETS causes up to 18,600 cases of low birth weight each year. Children under 5 whose primary caregiver smokes 10 or more cigarettes per day have measurable blood levels of nicotine and tobacco carcinogens. Chemicals in tobacco smoke also show up in breast milk, and breastfeeding may pass more chemicals to the infant of a smoking mother than direct exposure to ETS.

ETS triggers 150,000–300,000 cases of bronchitis, pneumonia, and other respiratory infections in infants and toddlers up to age 18 months each year, resulting in 7,500–15,000 hospitalizations. Older children suffer, too. ETS is a risk factor for asthma in children who have not previously displayed symptoms of the disease, and it aggravates the symptoms of the 200,000 to 1 million children who already have asthma. ETS is also linked to reduced lung function and fluid buildup in the middle ear, a contributing factor in middle-ear infections, a leading reason for childhood surgery. Children and teens exposed to ETS score lower on tests of reading and reasoning. Later in life, people exposed to ETS as children are at increased risk for lung cancer, emphysema, and chronic bronchitis.

Why are infants and children so vulnerable? Because they breathe faster than adults, they inhale more air—and more of the pollutants in the air. Because they also weigh less, they inhale three times more pollutants per unit of body weight than adults do. And because their young lungs are still growing, this intake can impair optimal development. The problem is widespread: About 19 million American children are exposed to ETS.

Avoiding ETS Given the health risks of exposure to ETS, try these strategies to keep the air around you safe:

- *Speak up tactfully.* Smokers may not know the dangers they are causing or may not know it bothers you.
- *Display reminders.* Put up signs asking smokers to refrain in your home, work area, and car.
- *Don't allow smoking in your home or room.* Get rid of ashtrays and ask smokers to light up outside.
- *Open a window.* If you cannot avoid being in a room with a smoker, at least try to provide some ventilation.
- *Sit in the nonsmoking section in restaurants and other public areas.* Complain to the manager if none exists.
- *Fight for a smoke-free work environment.* Join with your coworkers to either eliminate all smoking indoors or confine it to certain areas.
- *Discuss quitting strategies.* Social pressure is a major factor in many former smokers' decisions to quit. Help the smokers in your life by sharing quitting strategies with them.

Smoking and Pregnancy

Smoking almost doubles a pregnant woman's chance of having a miscarriage, and it significantly increases her risk of ectopic pregnancy. Maternal smoking causes an estimated 4600 infant deaths in the United States each year, primarily due to premature delivery and smoking-related problems with the placenta. Maternal smoking is a major factor in low birth weight, which puts newborns at high risk for infections and other serious problems. If a nonsmoking mother is regularly exposed to ETS, her infant is also at greater risk for low birth weight. Recent studies have also shown that babies whose mothers smoked during pregnancy had higher rates of colic, clubfoot, cleft lip and palate, and impaired lung function; they may also have genetic damage.

Babies born to mothers who smoke more than two packs a day perform poorly on developmental tests in the first hours after birth, compared to babies of nonsmoking mothers. Later in life, obesity, hyperactivity, short attention span, and lower scores on spelling and reading tests all occur more frequently in children whose mothers smoked during pregnancy than in those born to nonsmoking mothers. Prenatal tobacco exposure has also been associated with behavioral problems in children, including immaturity, emotional instability, physical aggression, and hyperactivity. Other research shows that teenagers whose mothers smoked during pregnancy have lower scores on tests of general intelligence and poorer performance on tasks requiring auditory memory than do children who were not exposed to cigarette smoke before birth. Males born to smoking mothers have higher rates of adolescent and adult criminal activity, suggesting that maternal smoking may cause brain damage that increases the risk of criminal behavior. Nevertheless, about 11% of pregnant women smoke and only about 14% of female smokers quit while pregnant; *Healthy People 2010* sets a goal of increasing this to 30%.

The Cost of Tobacco Use to Society

The health care costs associated with smoking exceed $75 billion per year. If the cost of lost productivity from sickness, disability, and premature death is included, the total is closer to $157 billion. This works out to $7.18 per pack of cigarettes, far more than the average $0.84 per pack tax collected by states to offset tobacco-related medical costs.

In order to recoup public health care expenditures, 43 state attorneys general filed suit against tobacco companies. In March 1997, Liggett Group settled its part of the suit by agreeing to turn over internal documents and to pay a portion of its profits to cover tobacco-related medical expenses and anti-smoking campaigns. In November 1998, an agreement was reached that settled 39 state lawsuits and applied to seven states that never filed suit. (Four states—Florida, Minnesota, Mississippi, and Texas—settled their suits separately for a total of $40 billion.) The 1998 Master Settlement Agreement (MSA) requires the tobacco companies to pay states $206 billion over 25 years; it also limits or bans certain types of advertising, promotions, and lobbying. Many of the provisions of the deal are designed to limit youth exposure and access to tobacco. In exchange, the tobacco industry settled the state lawsuits and is protected

In the News

After the Master Settlement Agreement

WWW

In the 1998 Master Settlement Agreement (MSA), the tobacco industry agreed to pay states more than $200 billion over 25 years as compensation for tobacco-related health care costs and as a penalty for deceptive marketing of their addictive and dangerous products. The legal, economic, and social impact of the MSA continues to influence tobacco use and control. Since the settlement, tobacco use has begun declining, acceptance of smoking—in public buildings and private workplaces—is decreasing, and quit-smoking programs are becoming more widely available.

Tobacco companies are fighting these trends. In 2004, industry lobbying contributed to the decision by Congress to abandon legislative efforts to permit the FDA to regulate tobacco—the only legal product that kills at least a third of those who use it regularly—in the same way that the agency now regulates products such as breakfast cereal or lip gloss. Industry expenditures on marketing have increased, emphasizing discounts, promotion of existing brands, and the introduction of new products—still addictive and dangerous but promoted as stylish or less harmful.

Recent reductions in smoking rates are in part the result of actions by state governments. Legislatures passed increases in tobacco taxes, driving up the price of smoking. Research suggests that a 10% increase in the price of cigarettes reduces youth smoking by 7% and overall cigarette sales by 3–5%. States have also used settlement funds to pay for educational campaigns that reduce the number of new smokers and encourage quitting. This spending, too, pays dividends: Each dollar spent to control tobacco yields a savings of $3 in smoking-related health costs.

In recent years, however, states have shifted settlement money from tobacco control to other budget obligations, such as funding Medicaid and capital projects and covering general budget shortfalls. A study issued by the Campaign for Tobacco-Free Kids estimated that states would take in more than $21 billion in revenues from the tobacco settlement and taxes on tobacco products during 2006 but would spend only about $550 million on tobacco control and use-prevention programs—about one-third of the amount recommended by the Centers for Disease Control and Prevention (CDC).

Meanwhile, the tobacco industry has stepped up its advertising and marketing campaigns. It is estimated that the industry spends nearly $30 in marketing for every dollar the states spend on tobacco control programs. Tobacco companies increased cigarette promotions during the implementation of the MSA and continue to do so whenever state taxes on tobacco products are raised. They have also exploited loopholes in the MSA to keep tobacco products visible on televised sports programs.

Tobacco use will soon become the leading cause of death worldwide. According to the World Health Organization (WHO), globally 4.9 million deaths per year are attributable to tobacco. Deaths are projected to nearly double by 2020, with 70% taking place in developing countries. The tobacco industry—faced with increased regulation, growing awareness of the health risks of smoking, and declining sales in Europe and North America—has stepped up activities to establish and expand markets in the developing world. The poor will be increasingly victimized by tobacco and its burden of disease.

To help protect health worldwide, WHO developed the Framework Convention on Tobacco Control (FCTC), a global public health treaty designed to reduce tobacco-related deaths and disease. FCTC sets international standards on tobacco price and tax increases, tobacco advertising and sponsorship, health warnings and labeling, illicit trade, and secondhand smoke. FCTC attained the status of international law in 2004, and by 2006 113 countries had signed the treaty. The first Conference of the Parties met in February 2006 in support of the goal of defeating the tobacco epidemic. The United States signed the treaty in 2004, but the treaty has not yet been ratified by the Senate and written into U.S. law.

SOURCES: Zwarun, L. 2006. Ten years and 1 Master Settlement Agreement later: The nature and frequency of alcohol and tobacco promotion in televised sports, 2000 through 2002. *American Journal of Public Health* 96(8): 1492–1497; Loomis, B. R., et al. 2006. Point of purchase cigarette promotions before and after the Master Settlement Agreement. *Tobacco Control* 15(2): 140–142; World Health Organization. 2006. *Framework Convention on Tobacco Control*. Geneva: World Health Organization; Krugman, D. M., et al. 2005. Understanding the role of cigarette promotion and youth smoking in a changing marketing environment. *Journal of Health Communication* 10(3): 261–178; Sloan, F. A., C. A. Matthews, and J. G. Trogdon. 2004. Impacts of the Master Settlement Agreement on the tobacco industry. *Tobacco Control* 13(4): 356–361.

from future suits by states, counties, towns, and other public entities. Tobacco companies passed the costs of the settlement on to smokers, increasing the average price of a pack of cigarettes by approximately 45 cents.

The governors involved in the MSA unanimously declared themselves "committed to spending a significant portion of the tobacco settlement funds on smoking cessation programs, health care, education, and programs benefiting children." A report prepared on the fifth anniversary of the settlement found that only four states—Maine, Delaware, Mississippi, and Arkansas—fund tobacco prevention and cessation programs at minimum levels recommended by the CDC. In a survey by the U.S. General Accounting Office, only nine states reported plans to spend more than 10% of their settlement money on tobacco control programs in 2004; nine planned to spend more than half on budget deficits (see the box "After the Master Settlement Agreement").

In March 2000 the Supreme Court ruled that the FDA lacks the authority to regulate tobacco products, stopping the FDA's efforts to prevent tobacco sales and marketing to minors. Among the FDA's guidelines affected is the requirement that retailers ask for identification from tobacco purchasers who appear to be under age 27.

In July 2000, a Florida jury ordered tobacco companies to pay $145 billion in punitive damages in a class-action lawsuit filed on behalf of some 700,000 Florida smokers. A Florida appeals court later ruled that the MSA did not allow punitive damages; the plaintiffs appealed that decision to the Florida Supreme Court. In July 2006, the Florida Supreme Court eliminated the $145 billion punitive award, but it also overturned the appeals court's entire ruling for a variety of reasons. The court held that plaintiffs *could* seek both compensatory and punitive damages from tobacco companies. Legal experts say the court's decision could open the floodgates to thousands of lawsuits against tobacco companies.

The industry was dealt another potential blow in August 2006, when a U.S. District Court judge ordered tobacco companies to stop marketing cigarettes with labels like "light" and "low-tar." The judge found that tobacco companies had violated racketeering laws by conspiring for years to deceive the public about the health risks of smoking. At the same time, the judge said that she did not have the power to order the industry to pay billions of dollars to fund anti-smoking and education programs. Both anti-smoking advocates and tobacco companies claimed the ruling as a victory, and litigation and court cases continue. For current information on political and legal activities, visit the Web site of one of the tobacco control advocacy groups listed in the For More Information sections at the end of the chapter.

WHAT CAN BE DONE?

There are many ways to act against this public health threat.

Action at the Local Level

Before the EPA issued its report declaring ETS to be a carcinogen, most efforts to limit smoking focused on enacting local laws and ordinances. Tobacco interests have been able to block actions at the national and state levels through lobbying and political contributions. However, during the 1980s and 1990s, tobacco restrictions were passed by local school boards, town councils, and county boards of supervisors, over which the tobacco industry has little or no influence.

There are now thousands of local ordinances across the nation that restrict or ban smoking in restaurants, stores, workplaces, and even public outdoor areas. Since the EPA classification of environmental tobacco smoke as a carcinogen, local governments and businesses have become bolder about protecting nonsmokers. As local nonsmoking laws proliferate, evidence mounts that environmental restrictions are effective in encouraging smokers to quit. In some states, however, the tobacco industry has responded by lobbying state legislatures to pass preemptive legislation making it illegal for local jurisdictions to pass laws regulating tobacco use.

Action at the State and Federal Levels

The EPA report fundamentally changed the politics of tobacco by declaring that smokers not only shorten their own lives but also kill innocent bystanders. It became harder for politicians who are sympathetic to the tobacco industry—and who often accept sizable contributions from tobacco interests—to argue that anti-tobacco laws constitute unwarranted intrusions into voters' private lives.

State legislatures have passed many tough new anti-tobacco laws. California has one of the most aggressive—and successful—tobacco control programs, combining taxes on cigarettes, graphic advertisements, and bans on smoking in bars and restaurants. In the past decade, per-capita cigarette consumption fell by 50% in California, lung cancer cases dropped 14%, and heart disease deaths were reduced by more than 30,000. California now has the second lowest rate of smoking among U.S. states. Utah, with a smoking rate of 12%, is the first (and only) state to meet the *Healthy People 2010* target. Kentucky has the highest rate, 31%.

California, Delaware, New York, Connecticut, Maine, Massachusetts, and Rhode Island have smoke-free workplace laws that cover all workers. Florida, Idaho, and Utah have passed similar legislation, excluding stand-alone bars. Other states are considering similar protection for their citizens. An assessment made in 2006 found that 42% of Americans live in municipalities with smoke-free restaurants and 30% live in locations with smoke-free workplaces. Hundreds of colleges and universities now have totally smoke-free campuses or prohibit smoking in residential buildings.

The federal government is also acting to protect nonsmokers from ETS. Smoking has been banned on virtually all domestic airplane flights, and the U.S. Defense Department has banned smoking at all military work sites. And the U.S. Occupational Safety and Health Administration considered nationwide rules that would, in effect, ban smoking on the job except in specially ventilated areas.

International Action

Many countries are following the United States' lead in restricting smoking. Smoking is now banned on many international air flights, as well as in many restaurants and hotels and on public transportation in some countries. The World Health Organization has taken the lead in international anti-tobacco efforts by sponsoring the Framework Convention on Tobacco Control. Another international activity is the annual commemoration of World No Tobacco Day (May 31), on which smokers are encouraged to stop smoking for 1 day. (This is similar to the American Cancer Society's Great American Smokeout®, held each November.) The smoker who successfully takes the first step of quitting for a day may be encouraged enough to

Take Charge

Helping a Friend or Partner Stop Using Tobacco

The U.S. Public Health Service recommends a "Five A's" approach for physicians to help patients quit tobacco use. If someone you care about uses tobacco, you can try the same strategies to help them quit.

1. **Ask** about tobacco use. How many cigarettes does your girlfriend smoke each day? How long has your roommate been dipping snuff?
2. **Advise** tobacco users to stop. Express your concern over the tobacco user's habit. "When we're close, the smell of smoke on your hair and breath bothers me. I've noticed you cough a lot and your voice is raspy. I'm worried about your health. You should stop."
3. **Assess** the tobacco user's willingness to quit. "Next week would be a good time to try to quit. Would you be willing to give it a try?"
4. **Assist** the tobacco user who is willing to stop. To coincide with your partner's quit date, take him away for a romantic weekend far from the places he associates with smoking. Offer to be an exercise partner. Call once a day to offer support and help. Bring gifts of low-calorie snacks or projects that occupy the hands. If the quitter lapses, be encouraging. A lapse doesn't have to become a relapse.
5. **Arrange** follow-up. Maintaining abstinence is an ongoing process. Celebrate milestones of 1 week, 1 month, 1 year without tobacco. Note how much better your friend's or partner's car, room, and person smell, how much healthier he or she is, and how much you appreciate not having to breathe tobacco smoke.

Keep in mind the special influence that a partner or loved one can have on someone who is trying to quit using tobacco. Recent research has shown that certain kinds of behavior by a partner are consistently related to successful quitting, whereas other behaviors are related to relapse. Behaviors linked to success include expressing pleasure at the smoker's efforts to quit, actively rewarding the smoker's efforts (for example, giving a small gift), helping to calm the smoker when he or she is feeling stressed or irritable, and actively sharing in an activity such as dancing, jogging, or hiking that serves as a distraction from smoking.

Sometimes a tobacco user's partner does things that are intended to be helpful but actually interfere with the user's efforts to quit. These behaviors include hiding ashtrays, keeping track of the amount of tobacco used, hiding or throwing out the smoker's cigarettes, frequently mentioning the health risks associated with tobacco, ignoring the smoker during efforts to quit, downplaying the difficulty of quitting, and complaining about the partner's irritability during attempts to quit.

If your partner is trying to quit and you are uncertain how to help, ask what would be most helpful. Recognize that tobacco use is your partner's problem, and although there may be things you can do to help, your partner is ultimately in control of his or her own body. If your partner asks you to back off, then do so within the limits you have established in your relationship. If your partner gets angry or irritable, recognize that this hypersensitivity is a normal but temporary side effect of nicotine withdrawal and remind yourself that it will pass. Listen to your partner, communicate your feelings as clearly as possible, and do what you can to reduce your partner's stress level, such as temporarily taking over a household chore. If you smoke, you can help your partner by not smoking in open view and by providing positive support. Even better, take inspiration from your partner's efforts and quit.

SOURCE: "Five A's" from Fiore, E. M. C., et al. 2000. *Treating Tobacco Use and Dependence.* Clinical Practice Guideline. Rockville, Md.: U.S. Department of Health and Human Services.

follow through on the commitment and become a permanent nonsmoker. With more than 1 billion smokers worldwide, addressing the global impact of tobacco use will require a massive coordinated effort.

Action in the Private Sector

The EPA report also shook up the private sector, giving employers reason to fear worker's compensation claims based on exposure to workplace smoke. The year after the report was issued, businesses including McDonald's and Taco Bell banned smoking in thousands of their restaurants across the country. The number of smoke-free restaurants has increased dramatically in recent years, and the vast majority of the nation's shopping malls now prohibit smoking.

Such local, state, national, and international efforts represent progress, but health activists warn that tobacco industry influence remains strong. The tobacco industry contributes heavily to sympathetic legislative officeholders and candidates. Many states have relatively weak antismoking laws that are backed by the tobacco industry and include clauses that prevent the passage of stricter local ordinances. Since 1999, tobacco interests have spent more than $112 million on federal lobbying activities. During the 2003–2004 election cycle, the industry gave nearly $2.8 million to federal candidates, political parties, and political committees.

Individual Action

When a smoker violates a no-smoking designation, complain. If your favorite restaurant or shop doesn't have a nonsmoking policy, ask the manager to adopt one. If you see children buying tobacco, report this illegal activity to the facility manager or the police. Learn more about addiction and tobacco cessation so you can better support the tobacco users you know (see the box "Helping a Friend or Partner Stop Using Tobacco"). Vote for candidates who support anti-tobacco measures; contact local, state, and national representatives to express your views.

Cancel your subscriptions to magazines that carry tobacco advertising; send a letter to the publisher explaining your decision. Voice your opinion about other positive representations of tobacco use. (A recent study found that more than two-thirds of children's animated feature films have featured tobacco or alcohol use with no clear message that such practices were unhealthy.) Volunteer with the American Lung Association, the American Cancer Society, or the American Heart Association.

These are just some of the many ways in which individuals can help support tobacco prevention and stop-smoking efforts. Nonsmokers have the right not only to breathe clean air but also to take action to help solve one of society's most serious public health threats.

Controlling the Tobacco Companies

With their immensely profitable industry shrinking, tobacco companies are concentrating on appealing to narrower and narrower market segments with an ever-increasing array of brands and styles—over 350 in all. As tobacco use has declined among better-educated, wealthier segments of the American population, tobacco companies have redirected their marketing efforts toward minorities, the poor, and young women, populations among whom smoking rates are still high. This practice of targeting specific segments of the market has become controversial, especially when the segment has an unusually high risk for fatal diseases caused by tobacco use.

With cigarette sales falling in the United States, tobacco companies have begun focusing on increasing the export of cigarettes, particularly to developing nations. As companies compete for customers in the years ahead, the need to exercise public pressure to keep the powerful tobacco companies in check will persist.

HOW A TOBACCO USER CAN QUIT

Since 1964, over 50% of all adults who have ever smoked have quit. Giving up tobacco is a long-term, intricate process. Heavy smokers who say they have just stopped cold turkey don't tell of the thinking and struggling and other mental processes that contributed to their final conquest over this powerful addiction. Olympic diver Greg Louganis, who began smoking at the age of 8, has said that he considers quitting, at the age of 23, the greatest accomplishment of his life.

Research shows that tobacco users move through predictable stages—from being uninterested in stopping, to thinking about change, to making a concerted effort to stop, to finally maintaining abstinence. But most attempt to quit several times before they finally succeed. Relapse is a normal part of the process.

The Benefits of Quitting

Giving up tobacco provides immediate health benefits to men and women of all ages (Table 11-2). People who quit smoking find that food tastes better. Their sense of smell is

Table 11-2 Benefits of Quitting Smoking

Within 20 minutes of your last cigarette:
- You stop polluting the air
- Blood pressure drops to normal
- Pulse rate drops to normal
- Temperature of hands and feet increases to normal

8 hours:
- Carbon monoxide level in blood drops to normal
- Oxygen level in blood increases to normal

24 hours:
- Chance of heart attack decreases

48 hours:
- Nerve endings start regrowing
- Ability to smell and taste is enhanced

2–3 months:
- Circulation improves
- Walking becomes easier
- Lung function increases up to 30%

1–9 months:
- Coughing, sinus congestion, fatigue, and shortness of breath all decrease

1 year:
- Heart disease death rate is half that of a smoker

5 years:
- Stroke risk drops nearly to the risk for nonsmokers

10 years:
- Lung cancer death rate drops to 50% of that of continuing smokers
- Incidence of other cancers (mouth, throat, larynx, esophagus, bladder, kidney, and pancreas) decreases
- Risk of ulcer decreases

15 years:
- Risk of lung cancer is about 25% of that of continuing smokers
- Risks of heart disease and death are close to those for nonsmokers

SOURCES: American Lung Association. 2002. *Benefits of Quitting* (http://www.lungusa.org/tobacco/quit_ben.html; retrieved August 18, 2006); American Cancer Society. 2000. *Quitting Smoking* (http://www.cancer.org/tobacco/quitting.html; retrieved August 18, 2006).

Quitting smoking improves the quality of life. In addition to reducing his long-term disease risks, this ex-smoker has more energy and an improved capacity for exercise.

sharper. Circulation improves, heart rate and blood pressure drop, and lung function and heart efficiency increase. Ex-smokers can breathe more easily, and their capacity for exercise improves. Many ex-smokers report feeling more energetic and alert. They experience fewer headaches. Even their complexion may improve. Quitting also has a positive effect on long-term disease risk. From the first day without tobacco, ex-smokers begin to decrease their risk of cancer of the lung, larynx, mouth, pancreas, bladder, cervix, and other sites. Risk of heart attack, stroke, and other cardiovascular diseases drops quickly, too.

The younger people are when they stop smoking, the more pronounced the health improvements. And these improvements gradually but invariably increase as the period of nonsmoking lengthens. It's never too late to quit, though. According to a U.S. Surgeon General's report, people who quit smoking, regardless of age, live longer than people who continue to smoke. Even smokers who have already developed chronic bronchitis or emphysema may show some improvement when they quit.

Options for Quitting

Most tobacco users—76% in a recent survey—want to quit, and half of those who want to quit will make an attempt this year. What are their options? No single method works for everyone, but each does work for some people some of the time. In June 2000, the U.S. Public Health Service issued new guidelines for medical professionals on how to help their patients quit smoking, emphasizing the benefits of both behavioral and pharmacological interventions.

Choosing to quit requires developing a strategy for success. Some people quit cold turkey, whereas others taper off slowly. There are over-the-counter and prescription products that help many people (see the box "Smoking Cessation Products" for more on these options). Behavioral factors that have been shown to increase the chances of a smoker's permanent smoking cessation are support from others and regular exercise. Support can come from friends and family and/or formal group programs sponsored by organizations such as the American Cancer Society, the American Lung Association, and the Seventh-Day Adventist Church or by your college health center or community hospital. Programs that combine group support with nicotine replacement therapy have rates of continued abstention as high as 35% after 1 year.

Free telephone quitlines are emerging as a popular and effective strategy to help stop smoking. Quitlines are staffed by trained counselors who help each caller plan a personal quitting strategy, usually including a combination of nicotine replacement therapy, changes in daily habits, and emotional support. Counselors provide printed materials that match the smoker's needs and schedule phone counseling sessions for key days after a smoker quits. Smokers can schedule sessions to fit their schedule, and some quitlines may provide stop-smoking medications at reduced prices. Almost all smokers make more than one attempt to stop before they succeed in quitting for good; and quitline counselors can help smokers understand what leads to relapse, review their reasons for wanting to quit, and make a better plan for the next attempt. The goal is for smokers to find a support system and techniques that work for them.

Critical Consumer

Smoking Cessation Products

VW

Each year, millions of Americans visit their doctors in the hope of finding a drug that can help them stop smoking. Although pharmacological options are limited, the few available drugs have proved successful.

Chantix (Varinicline)

The newest smoking cessation drug, marketed under the name Chantix, received approval from the FDA in May 2006. The active ingredient in Chantix, varinicline tartrate, works in two ways: It reduces nicotine cravings, easing the withdrawal process, and it blocks the pleasant effects of nicotine. The drug acts on neurotransmitter receptors in the brain.

Six clinical trials, which included more than 3600 long-term, chronic smokers, demonstrated that Chantix is an effective smoking cessation aid. In one of the studies, nearly 25% of Chantix users stopped smoking for a full year. Results varied with the dosage and duration of treatment.

Unlike most smoking cessation products currently on the market, Chantix is not a nicotine replacement. For this reason, smokers may be advised to continue smoking for the first few days of treatment, to avoid withdrawal and to allow the drug to build up in their system. The approved course of treatment is 12 weeks, but the duration and recommended dosage depend on several factors, including the smoker's general health and the length and severity of his or her nicotine addiction.

Side effects reported with Chantix include nausea, headache, vomiting, sleep disruptions, and change in taste perception. People with kidney problems or who take certain medications should not take Chantix, and it is not recommended for women who are pregnant or nursing.

Zyban (Bupropion)

Bupropion is an antidepressant (prescribed under the name Wellbutrin) as well as a smoking cessation aid (prescribed under the name Zyban). As a smoking cessation aid, bupropion eases the symptoms of nicotine withdrawal and reduces the urge to smoke. Like Chantix, it acts on neurotransmitter receptors in the brain. Scientists are not certain how the drug works in relation to nicotine, but it has been successfully used in smoking cessation programs.

Bupropion is not a nicotine replacement, so the user may need to continue smoking for the first few days of treatment. A nicotine replacement product, such as a patch or gum, may be recommended to further ease withdrawal symptoms after the user stops smoking.

Bupropion users have reported an array of side effects, but they are rare. Side effects may be reduced by changing the dosage, taking the medicine at a different time of day, or taking it with or without food. Bupropion is not recommended for people with specific physical conditions or who take certain drugs. Zyban and Wellbutrin should not be taken together.

Nicotine Replacement Products

The most widely used smoking cessation products replace the nicotine that the user would normally get from tobacco. The user continues to get nicotine, so withdrawal symptoms and cravings are reduced. Although still harmful, nicotine replacement products provide a cleaner form of nicotine, without the thousands of poisons and tars produced by burning tobacco. Less of the product is used over time, as the need for nicotine decreases.

Nicotine replacement products come in several forms, including patches, gum, lozenges, nasal sprays, and inhalers. They are available in a variety of strengths and can be worked into many different smoking cessation strategies. Most are available without a prescription.

The nicotine patch is popular because it can be applied and forgotten until it needs to be removed or changed, usually every 16 or 24 hours. Placed on the upper arm or torso, it releases a steady stream of nicotine, which is absorbed through the skin. The main side effects are skin irritation and redness. Nicotine gum and nicotine lozenges have the advantage of allowing the smoker to use them whenever he or she craves nicotine. Side effects of nicotine gum include mouth sores and headaches; nicotine lozenges can cause nausea and heartburn. Nicotine nasal sprays and inhalers are available only by prescription.

Although all these products have proved to be effective in helping users stop smoking, experts recommend them only as one part of a complete smoking cessation program. Such a program should include regular professional counseling and physician monitoring.

In 2004, the Department of Health and Human Services established a national toll-free number, 1-800-QUITNOW (1-800-784-8669), to serve as a single access point for smokers seeking information and assistance in quitting. Callers are routed to their state's smoking cessation quitline or, in states that have not established quitlines, to one maintained by the National Cancer Institute.

Most smokers in the process of quitting experience both physical and psychological effects of nicotine withdrawal, and exercise can help with both. For many smokers, their tobacco use is associated with certain times and places—following a meal, for example. Resolving to walk after dinner instead of lighting up provides a distraction from cravings and eliminates the cues that trigger a desire to smoke. In addition, many people worry about weight gain associated with quitting. Although most ex-smokers do gain a few pounds, at least temporarily, incorporating exercise into a new tobacco-free routine lays the foundation for healthy weight management. The health risks of adding a few pounds are far outweighed by the risks of continued smoking; it's estimated that a smoker would have to gain 75–100 pounds to equal the health risks of smoking a pack a day.

As with any significant change in health-related behavior, giving up tobacco requires planning, sustained effort, and support. It is an ongoing process, not a one-time event. The Behavior Change Strategy describes the steps that successful quitters follow.

Behavior Change Strategy

Kicking the Tobacco Habit

You can look forward to a longer and healthier life if you join the 47 million Americans who have quit using tobacco. The steps for quitting described below are discussed in terms of the most popular tobacco product in the United States—cigarettes—but they can be adapted for all forms of tobacco.

Gather Information

Collect personal smoking information in a detailed journal about your smoking behavior. Write down the time you smoke each cigarette of the day, the situation you are in, how you feel, where you smoke, and how strong your craving for the cigarette is, plus any other information that seems relevant. Part of the job is to identify patterns of smoking that are connected with routine situations (for example, the coffee break smoke, the after-dinner cigarette, the tension-reduction cigarette). Use this information to discover the behavior patterns involved in your smoking habit.

Make the Decision to Quit

Choose a date in the near future when you expect to be relatively stress-free and can give quitting the energy and attention it will require. Don't choose a date right before or during finals week, for instance. Consider making quitting a gift: Choose your birthday as your quit date, for example, or make quitting a Father's Day or Mother's Day present. You might also want to coordinate your quit date with a buddy—a fellow tobacco user who wants to quit or a nonsmoker who wants to give up another bad habit or begin an exercise program. Tell your friends and family when you plan to quit. Ask them to offer encouragement and help hold you to your goal.

Decide what approach to quitting will work best for you. Will you go cold turkey, or will you taper off? Will you use nicotine patches or gum? Will you join a support group or enlist the help of a buddy? Prepare a contract for quitting, as discussed in Chapter 1. Set firm dates and rewards, and sign the contract. Post it in a prominent place.

Prepare to Quit

One of the most important things you can do to prepare to quit is to develop and practice nonsmoking relaxation techniques. Many smokers find that they use cigarettes to help them unwind in tense situations or to relax at other times. If this is true for you, you'll need to find and develop effective substitutes. It takes time to become proficient at relaxation techniques, so begin practicing before your quit date. Refer to the detailed discussion of relaxation techniques in Chapter 2.

Other things you can do to help prepare for quitting include the following:

- Make an appointment to see your physician. Ask about OTC and prescription aids for tobacco cessation and whether one or more might be appropriate for you.
- Make a dentist's appointment to have your teeth cleaned the day after your target quit date.
- Start an easy exercise program, if you're not exercising regularly already.
- Buy some sugarless gum. Stock your kitchen with low-calorie snacks.
- Clean out your car, and air out your house. Send your clothes out for dry cleaning.
- Throw away all your cigarette-related paraphernalia (ashtrays, lighters, etc.).
- The night before your quit day, get rid of all your cigarettes. Have fun with this—get your friends or family to help you tear them up.
- Make your last few days of smoking inconvenient: Smoke only outdoors and when alone. Don't do anything else while you smoke.

Quitting

Your first few days without cigarettes will probably be the most difficult. It's hard to give up such a strongly ingrained habit, but remember that millions of Americans have done it—and you can, too. Plan and rehearse the steps you will take when you experience a powerful craving. Avoid or control situations that you know from your journal are powerfully associated with your smoking (see the table). If your hands feel empty without a cigarette, try holding or fiddling with a small object such as a paper clip or pencil.

Social support can also be a big help. Arrange with a buddy to help you with your weak moments, and call him or her whenever you feel overwhelmed by an urge to smoke. Tell people you've just quit. You may discover many inspiring former smokers who can encourage you and reassure you that it's possible to quit and lead a happier, healthier life. Find a formal support group to join if you think it will help.

Maintaining Nonsmoking

The lingering smoking urges that remain once you've quit should be carefully

Tips for Today

Smoking is the leading preventable cause of death in the United States. Most smokers get hooked before they realize it, providing a market of millions to the tobacco industry. For most smokers, quitting is one of the hardest things they'll ever do. The best choice is never to start.

Right now you can

- If you smoke, put your cigarette out and go brush your teeth. Throw the pack and matches away.
- If you smoke, think about the next time you'll want a cigarette, such as while talking on the phone this afternoon or relaxing after dinner tonight. Visualize yourself enjoying this activity without a cigarette in your hand. Imagine yourself as a healthier, more robust person. See if you get pleasure or satisfaction from thinking of yourself as a nonsmoker, as an ex-smoker, or as someone liberated from dependence on cigarettes.
- If you use tobacco, go outside for a short walk or a stretch to limber up. Breathe deeply. Tell a friend you've just decided to quit.
- Resolve to talk to someone you know who uses tobacco, offering support and assistance if the person is interested in quitting.

tracked and controlled because they can cause relapses if left unattended. Keep track of these urges in your journal to help you deal with them. If certain situations still trigger the urge for a cigarette, change something about the situation to break past associations. If stress or boredom causes strong smoking urges, use a relaxation technique, take a brisk walk, have a stick of gum, or substitute some other activity for smoking.

Don't set yourself up for a relapse. If you allow yourself to get overwhelmed at school or work or to gain weight, it will be easier to convince yourself that now isn't the right time to quit. This *is* the right time. Continue to practice time-management and relaxation techniques. Exercise regularly, eat sensibly, and get enough sleep. These habits will not only ensure your success at remaining tobacco-free but also serve you well in stressful times throughout your life. In fact, former smokers who have quit for at least 3 months report reduced stress levels, probably because quitting smoking lowers overall arousal.

Watch out for patterns of thinking that can make nonsmoking more difficult. Focus on the positive aspects of not smoking, and give yourself lots of praise—you deserve it. Stick with the schedule of rewards you developed for your contract.

Keep track of the emerging benefits that come from having quit. Items that might appear on your list include improved stamina, an increased sense of pride at having kicked a strong addiction, a sharper sense of taste and smell, no more smoker's cough, and so on. Keep track of the money you're saving by not smoking, and spend it on things you really enjoy. And if you do lapse, be gentle with yourself. Lapses are a normal part of quitting. Forgive yourself, and pick up where you left off.

Strategies for Dealing with High-Risk Smoking Situations

Cues and High-Risk Situations	Suggested Strategies
Awakening in morning	Brush your teeth as soon as you wake up. Take a shower or bath.
Drinking coffee	Do something else with your hands. Drink tea or another beverage instead.
Eating meals	Sit in nonsmoking sections of restaurants. Get up from the table right after eating, and start another activity. Brush your teeth right after eating.
Driving a car	Have the car cleaned when you quit smoking. Chew sugarless gum or eat a low-calorie snack. Take public transportation or ride your bike. Turn on the radio and sing along.
Socializing with friends who smoke	Suggest nonsmoking events (movies, theater, shopping). Tell friends you've quit and ask them not to smoke around you, offer you cigarettes, or give you cigarettes if you ask for them.
Drinking at a bar, restaurant, or party	Try to take a nonsmoker with you, or associate with nonsmokers. Let friends know you've just quit. Moderate your intake of alcohol (it can weaken your resolve).
Encountering stressful situations	Practice relaxation techniques. Take some deep breaths. Get out of your room or house. Go somewhere that doesn't allow smoking. Take a shower, chew gum, call a friend, or exercise.

SOURCES: Strategies adapted with permission from *Postgraduate Medicine* 90(1), July 1991; Antonuccio, D. O. 1993. *Butt Out, The Smoker's Book: A Compassionate Guide to Helping Yourself Quit Smoking, With or Without a Partner.* Saratoga, Calif.: R & E.

SUMMARY

- Smoking is the largest preventable cause of ill health and death in the United States. Nevertheless, millions of Americans continue to use tobacco.
- Regular tobacco use causes physical dependence on nicotine, characterized by loss of control, tolerance, and withdrawal. Habits can become associated with tobacco use and trigger the urge for a cigarette.
- People who begin smoking are usually imitating others or responding to seductive advertising. Smoking is associated with low education level and the use of other drugs.
- Tobacco smoke is made up of hundreds of different chemicals, including some that are carcinogenic or poisonous or that damage the respiratory system.
- Nicotine acts on the nervous system as a stimulant or a depressant. It can cause blood pressure and heart rate to increase, straining the heart.
- Cardiovascular disease is the most widespread cause of death for cigarette smokers. Cigarette smoking is the primary cause of lung cancer and is linked to many other cancers and respiratory diseases.
- Cigarette smoking is linked to ulcers, impotence, reproductive health problems, dental diseases, and other

conditions. Tobacco use leads to lower life expectancy and to a diminished quality of life.

- The use of spit tobacco leads to nicotine addiction and is linked to oral cancers.
- Cigars, pipes, clove cigarettes, and bidis are not safe alternatives to cigarettes.
- Environmental tobacco smoke (ETS) contains high concentrations of toxic chemicals and can cause headaches, eye and nasal irritation, and sinus problems. Long-term exposure to ETS can cause lung cancer and heart disease.
- Infants and young children take in more pollutants than adults do; children whose parents smoke are especially susceptible to respiratory diseases.
- Smoking during pregnancy increases the risk of miscarriage, stillbirth, congenital abnormalities, premature birth, and low birth weight. SIDS, behavior problems, and long-term impairments in development are also risks.
- The overall cost of tobacco use to society includes the cost of both medical care and lost worker productivity.
- There are many avenues individuals and groups can take to act against tobacco use. Nonsmokers can use social pressure and legislative channels to assert their rights to breathe clean air.
- Giving up smoking is a difficult and long-term process. Although most ex-smokers quit on their own, some smokers benefit from stop-smoking programs, OTC and prescription medications, and support groups.

Take Action

1. **Interview successful quitters:** Interview one or two former tobacco users about their experiences with tobacco and the methods they used to quit. Why did they start smoking or using tobacco, how old were they when they started, and how long did their habit continue? What made them decide to quit? How did they quit? What could a current tobacco user learn from their experience of quitting?

2. **Identify community smoking restrictions:** Make a tour of the public facilities in your community and on your campus, such as movie theaters, auditoriums, business and school offices, and classrooms. What kinds of restrictions on smoking do these places have? In your opinion, are they appropriate? If you feel more or different restrictions are in order, write a letter to the editor of your school or local newspaper, and state your case. Support it with convincing arguments and appropriate facts.

For More Information

Books

Dean, Michael. 2007. *Empty Cribs: The Impact of Smoking on Child Health.* New York: Arts & Sciences Publishing. *Examines the effects of smoking on children, both before and after delivery, with a special focus on SIDS.*

Gilman, S. L., ed. 2004. *Smoke: A Global History of Smoking.* London: Reaktion Books. *A look at smoking and its effects, including history and issues related to culture, art, and gender.*

Jeorgensen, N. A., ed. 2006. *Passive Smoking and Health Research.* Hauppauge, N.Y.: Nova Science Publishers. *A scientific look at the health effects of environmental tobacco smoke.*

Sloan, F. A., et al. 2006. *The Price of Smoking,* New ed. Cambridge, Mass.: MIT Press. *A careful examination of the economic and social consequences of smoking.*

Self-help books designed to help smokers quit:

Carr, A. 2005. *The Easy Way to Stop Smoking.* New York: Sterling.

How to Quit Smoking Without Gaining Weight. 2004. New York: American Lung Association.

Kicking Butts: Quit Smoking and Take Charge of Your Health. 2002. Atlanta: American Cancer Society.

Organizations, Hotlines, and Web Sites

Action on Smoking and Health (ASH). An advocacy group that provides statistics, news briefs, and other information.
202-659-4310
http://ash.org

American Cancer Society (ACS). Sponsor of the annual Great American Smokeout; provides information on the dangers of tobacco, as well as tools for prevention and cessation for both smokers and users of spit tobacco.
800-ACS-2345
http://www.cancer.org

American Lung Association. Provides information on lung diseases, tobacco control, and environmental health.
800-LUNG-USA; 212-315-8700
http://www.lungusa.org

CDC's Tobacco Information and Prevention Source (TIPS). Provides research results, educational materials, and tips on how to quit smoking; Web site includes special sections for kids and teens.
800-CDC-INFO
http://www.cdc.gov/tobacco

Environmental Protection Agency Indoor Air Quality/ETS. Provides information and links about secondhand smoke.
866-SMOKE-FREE
http://www.epa.gov/smokefree

Nicotine Anonymous. A 12-step program for tobacco users.
http://www.nicotine-anonymous.org

Quitnet. Provides interactive tools and questionnaires, support groups, a library, news on tobacco issues, and quitting programs for both smokers and spit tobacco users.
http://www.quitnet.com

Smokefree.Gov. Provides step-by-step strategies for quitting as well as expert support via telephone or instant messaging.
http://www.smokefree.gov
1-800-QUITNOW (1-800-784-8669)
http://www.cancer.gov (additional information)

Tobacco BBS. A resource center on tobacco and smoking issues that includes news and information, assistance for smokers who want to quit, and links to related sites.
http://www.tobacco.org

Tobacco Control Resource Center and Tobacco Products Liability Project (TPLP). Provides current information about tobacco-related court cases and legislation.

http://www.tobacco.neu.edu

World Health Organization Tobacco Free Initiative. Promotes the goal of a tobacco-free world.

http://www.who.int/tobacco/en

World No Tobacco Day (WNTD). Provides information on the annual worldwide event to encourage people to quit smoking; includes general information about tobacco use and testimonials of ex-smokers.

http://www.worldnotobaccoday.com

See also the listings for Chapters 9, 15, and 16.

Selected Bibliography

American Cancer Society. 2005. *Cancer Facts and Figures, 2005.* Atlanta, Ga.: American Cancer Society.

American Nonsmokers' Rights Foundation. 2006. *Colleges and Universities with Smokefree Air Policies: July 1, 2006* (http://www.no-smoke.org/pdf/smokefreecollegesuniversities.pdf; retrieved August 14, 2006).

American Nonsmokers' Rights Foundation. 2006. *Summary of 100% Smokefree State Laws and Population Protected by State and Local Laws: July 1, 2006* (http://www.no-smoke.org/pdf/SummaryUSPopList.pdf; retrieved August 14, 2006).

Anthonisen, N. R., et al. 2005. The effects of a smoking cessation intervention on 14.5-year mortality: A randomized clinical trial. *Annals of Internal Medicine* 142(4): 233–239.

Campaign for Tobacco-Free Kids. 2004. *State Cigarette Excise Tax Rates and Rankings* (http://tobaccofreekids.org/research/factsheets/pdf/0097.pdf; retrieved December 19, 2004).

Centers for Disease Control and Prevention. 2006. Cigarette use among high school students—United States, 1991–2005. *Morbidity and Mortality Weekly Report* 55(26): 724–726.

Centers for Disease Control and Prevention. 2006. Tobacco use among middle and high school students—United States, 2004. *Morbidity and Mortality Weekly Report* 54(12)—Corrected (http://www.cdc.gov/tobacco/nyts/correctionnotice.htm; retrieved August 13, 2006).

Centers for Disease Control and Prevention. 2006. Youth Risk Behavior Surveillance—United States, 2005. *Morbidity and Mortality Weekly Report* 55(SS05): 1–108.

Collins, S. L., and S. Izenwasser. 2004. Chronic nicotine differentially alters cocaine-induced locomotor activity in adolescent vs. adult male and female rats. *Neuropharmacology* 46(3): 349–362.

de la Chica, R. A., et al. 2005. Chromosomal instability in amniocytes from fetuses of mothers who smoke. *Journal of the American Medical Association* 293(10): 1212–1222.

Distefan, J. M., J. P. Pierce, and E. A. Gilpin. 2004. Do favorite movie stars influence adolescent smoking initiation? *American Journal of Public Health* 94(7): 1239–1244.

Doll, R., et al. 2004. Mortality in relation to smoking: 50 years' observations on male British doctors. *British Medical Journal* 328(7455): 1519.

Ezzati, M., and A. D. Lopez. 2004. Regional, disease specific patterns of smoking-attributable mortality in 2000. *Tobacco Control* 13(4): 388–395.

Farrelly, M. C., et al. 2005. Evidence of a dose-response relationship between "truth" antismoking ads and youth smoking prevalence. *American Journal of Public Health* 95(3): 425–431.

Federal Trade Commission. 2005. *Federal Trade Commission Cigarette Report for 2003* (http://www.ftc.gov/reports/cigarette05/050809cigrpt.pdf; retrieved August 13, 2006).

Food and Drug Administration. 2006. *FDA Approves Novel Medication for Smoking Cessation* (http://www.fda.gov/bbs/topics/NEWS/2006/NEW01370.html; retrieved August 19, 2006).

Gades, N. M., et al. 2005. Association between smoking and erectile dysfunction: A population-based study. *American Journal of Epidemiology* 161(4): 346–351.

Giovino, G. A., et al. 2004. Epidemiology of menthol cigarette use. *Nicotine & Tobacco Research* 6(Suppl 1): 67–81.

Government Accountability Office. 2004. *Tobacco Settlement: States' Allocations of Fiscal Year 2003 and Expected Fiscal Year 2004 Payments.* GAO 04–518. Washington, D.C.: Government Accountability Office.

Hanaoka, T., et al. 2005. Active and passive smoking and breast cancer risk in middle-aged Japanese women. *International Journal of Cancer* 114(2): 317–322.

Henschke, C. I., and O. S. Miettinen. 2004. Women's susceptibility to tobacco carcinogens. *Lung Cancer* 43(1): 1–5.

Jacobsen, L. K., et al. 2005. Effects of smoking and smoking abstinence on cognition in adolescent tobacco smokers. *Biological Psychiatry* 57(1): 56–66.

Lerman, C., et al. 2004. Interacting effects of the serotonin transporter gene and neuroticism in smoking practices and nicotine dependence. *Molecular Psychiatry.* In press.

Mahonen, M. S., et al. 2004. Current smoking and the risk of non-fatal myocardial infarction in the WHO MONICA Project populations. *Tobacco Control* 13(3): 244–250.

McCabe, R. E., et al. 2004. Smoking behaviors across anxiety disorders. *Journal of Anxiety Disorders* 18(1): 7–18.

Moran, S., H. Wechsler, and N. A. Rigotti. 2004. Social smoking among U.S. college students. *Pediatrics* 114(4): 1028–1034.

National Cancer Institute. 2004. *The Truth About "Light" Cigarettes: Questions and Answers* (http://cis.nci.nih.gov/fact/3_74.htm; retrieved September 3, 2004).

National Center for Health Statistics. 2006. Deaths: Preliminary Data for 2004. *National Vital Statistics Reports* 54(19).

The Nemours Foundation. 2005. *Smoking Stinks!* (http://www.kidshealth.org/kid/watch/house/smoking.html; retrieved August 12, 2006).

Office of Applied Studies, Substance Abuse and Mental Health Services Administration. 2006. *Results from the 2005 National Survey on Drug Use and Health: National Findings, September 2006* (http://oas.samhsa.gov/; retrieved November 17, 2006).

O'Loughlin, J., et al. 2004. Genetically decreased CYP2A6 and the risk of tobacco dependence: A prospective study of novice smokers. *Tobacco Control* 13(4): 422–428.

Prochazka, A. J., et al. 2004. A randomized trial of nortriptyline combined with transdermal nicotine for smoking cessation. *Archives of Internal Medicine* 164(20): 2229–2233.

Schroeder, S. A. 2004. Tobacco control in the wake of the 1998 Master Settlement Agreement. *New England Journal of Medicine* 350(3): 293–301.

Shiffman, S., M. E. Di Marino, and J. L. Pillitteri. 2005. The effectiveness of nicotine patch and nicotine lozenge in very heavy smokers. *Journal of Substance Abuse Treatment* 28(1): 49–55.

Sloan, F. A., et al. 2004. *The Price of Smoking.* Cambridge, Mass.: MIT Press.

Smoke Free Movies. 2004. *Now Showing* (http://smokefreemovies.ucsf.edu/problem/now_showing.html; retrieved December 20, 2004).

Tobacco Products Liability Project. 2006. *Despite headlines, Florida Supreme Court's decision in Engle case will prove to be an enormous blow to cigarette companies* (http://www.tobacco.neu.edu/litigation/cases/pressreleases/englevflsupct2006.htm; retrieved August 14, 2006).

Trimble, C. L., et al. 2005. Active and passive cigarette smoking and the risk of cervical neoplasia. *Obstetrics and Gynecology* 105(1):174–81.

U.S. Surgeon General. 2006. *The Health Consequences of Involuntary Exposure to Tobacco Smoke* (http://www.surgeongeneral.gov/library/secondhandsmoke/report/; retrieved August 13, 2006).

Vineis, P., et al. 2005. Environmental tobacco smoke and risk of respiratory cancer and chronic obstructive pulmonary disease in former smokers and never smokers in the EPIC prospective study. *British Medical Journal* 330(7486): 277.

WebMD. 2006. *Smoking Cessation Health Center* (http://www.webmd.com/diseases_and_conditions/smoking_cessation.htm; retrieved August 14, 2006).

Yolton, K., et al. 2005. Exposure to environmental tobacco smoke and cognitive abilities among U.S. children and adolescents. *Environmental Health Perspectives* 113(1): 98–103.

Zhang, X., et al. 2005. Association of passive smoking by husbands with prevalence of stroke among Chinese women nonsmokers. *American Journal of Epidemiology* 161(3): 213–218.

12

Looking AHEAD

After reading this chapter, you should be able to

- List the essential nutrients, and describe the functions they perform in the body
- Describe the guidelines that have been developed to help people choose a healthy diet, avoid nutritional deficiencies, and reduce their risk of diet-related chronic diseases
- Discuss nutritional guidelines for vegetarians and for special population groups
- Explain how to use food labels and other consumer tools to make informed choices about foods
- Put together a personal nutrition plan based on affordable foods that you enjoy and that will promote wellness, today as well as in the future

Nutrition Basics

Test Your Knowledge

1. It is recommended that all adults consume one to two servings each of fruits and vegetables every day.
True or false?

2. How many french fries are considered to be one ½-cup serving?
a. 10
b. 15
c. 25

3. Candy is the leading source of added sugars in the American diet.
True or false?

4. Which of the following is not a whole grain?
a. brown rice
b. wheat flour
c. popcorn

5. Nutritionists advise reduced intake of saturated and trans fats for which of the following reasons?
a. They increase levels of low-density lipoproteins (LDL), or "bad" cholesterol.
b. They provide more calories than other types of fat.
c. They increase the risk of heart disease.

ANSWERS

1. FALSE. For someone consuming 2000 calories, a minimum of nine servings per day—four of fruits and five of vegetables—is recommended, the equivalent of 4½ cups per day. The majority of Americans fail to meet this goal; half of all the vegetables we *do* eat are potatoes—and half of those are french fried.
2. A. Many people underestimate the size of the portions they eat, leading to overconsumption of calories and fat.
3. FALSE. Regular (nondiet) sodas are the leading source of sugar and of calories, with an average of 55 gallons consumed per person per year. Each 12-ounce soda supplies about 10 teaspoons of sugar, or nearly 10% of the calories in a 2000-calorie diet.
4. B. Unless labeled *whole* wheat, wheat flour is processed to remove the bran and the germ and is not a whole grain.
5. A AND C. High intake of saturated and trans fats raises LDL levels and the risk of heart disease. Saturated and trans fats provide the same number of calories as other types of fat—9 calories per gram (compared to 4 calories per gram for protein and carbohydrate).

Ww Visit the *Core Concepts in Health* Online Learning Center (www.mhhe.com/insel10e) for study aids and many additional resources.

In your lifetime, you'll spend about 6 years eating—about 70,000 meals and 60 tons of food. What you choose to eat can have profound effects on your health and well-being. Of particular concern is the connection between lifetime nutritional habits and the risk of major chronic diseases, including heart disease, cancer, stroke, and diabetes. Choosing foods that provide adequate amounts of the nutrients you need while limiting the substances linked to disease should be an important part of your daily life. The food choices you make will significantly influence your health—both now and in the future.

Choosing a healthy diet that supports maximum wellness and protects against disease is a two-part process. First, you have to know which nutrients are necessary and in what amounts. Second, you have to translate those requirements into a diet consisting of foods you like to eat that are both available and affordable. Once you have an idea of what constitutes a healthy diet for you, you may want to make adjustments in your current diet to bring it into line with your goals.

This chapter provides the basic principles of **nutrition.** It introduces the six classes of essential nutrients, explaining their roles in the functioning of the body. It also provides different sets of guidelines that you can use to design a healthy diet plan. Finally, it offers practical tools and advice to help you apply the guidelines to your own life. Diet is an area of your life in which you have almost total control. Using your knowledge and understanding of nutrition to create a healthy diet plan is a significant step toward wellness.

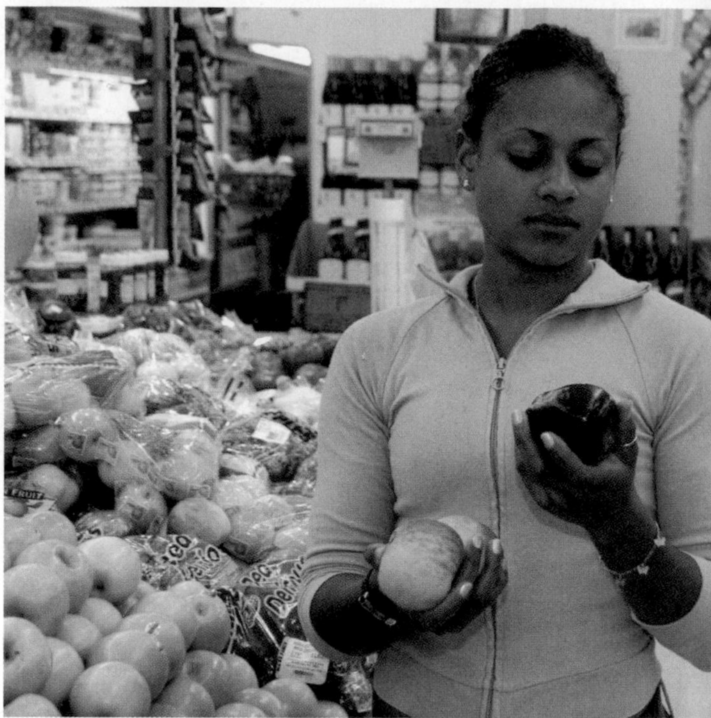

Our bodies require adequate amounts of all essential nutrients—water, proteins, carbohydrates, fats, vitamins, and minerals—in order to grow and function properly. Choosing foods to satisfy these nutritional requirements is an important part of a healthy lifestyle.

NUTRITIONAL REQUIREMENTS: COMPONENTS OF A HEALTHY DIET

When you think about your diet, you probably do so in terms of the foods you like to eat—a turkey sandwich and a glass of milk or black beans and rice. What's important for your health, though, are the nutrients contained in those foods. Your body requires proteins, fats, carbohydrates, vitamins, minerals, and water—about 45 **essential nutrients.** The word *essential* in this context means that you must get these substances from food because your body is unable to manufacture them at all, or at least not fast enough to meet your physiological needs. Plants obtain all the chemicals they need from air, water, soil, and sunlight. Animals, including humans, must eat foods to obtain the nutrients necessary to keep their bodies growing and functioning properly. Your body obtains these nutrients through the process of **digestion,** in which the foods you eat are broken down into compounds your gastrointestinal tract can absorb and your body can use (Figure 12-1). A diet containing adequate amounts of all essential nutrients is vital because various nutrients provide energy, help build and maintain body tissues, and help regulate body functions (see the box "Eating Habits and Total Wellness" on p. 330).

The energy in foods is expressed as **kilocalories.** One kilocalorie represents the amount of heat it takes to raise the temperature of 1 liter of water 1°C. A person needs about 2000 kilocalories per day to meet his or her energy needs. In common usage, people usually refer to kilocalories as *calories,* which is technically a much smaller energy unit: (1 kilocalorie contains 1000 calories). We use the familiar word *calorie* in this chapter to stand for the larger energy unit; you'll also find the word *calorie* used on food labels.

Of the six classes of essential nutrients, three supply energy:

- Fat = 9 calories per gram
- Protein = 4 calories per gram
- Carbohydrate = 4 calories per gram

Alcohol, though not an essential nutrient, also supplies energy, providing 7 calories per gram. (One gram equals a little less than .04 ounce.) The high caloric content of fat is one reason experts often advise against high fat consumption; most of us do not need the extra calories to meet energy needs. Regardless of their source, calories consumed in excess of energy needs are converted to fat and stored in the body.

But just meeting energy needs is not enough; our bodies require adequate amounts of all the essential nutrients to

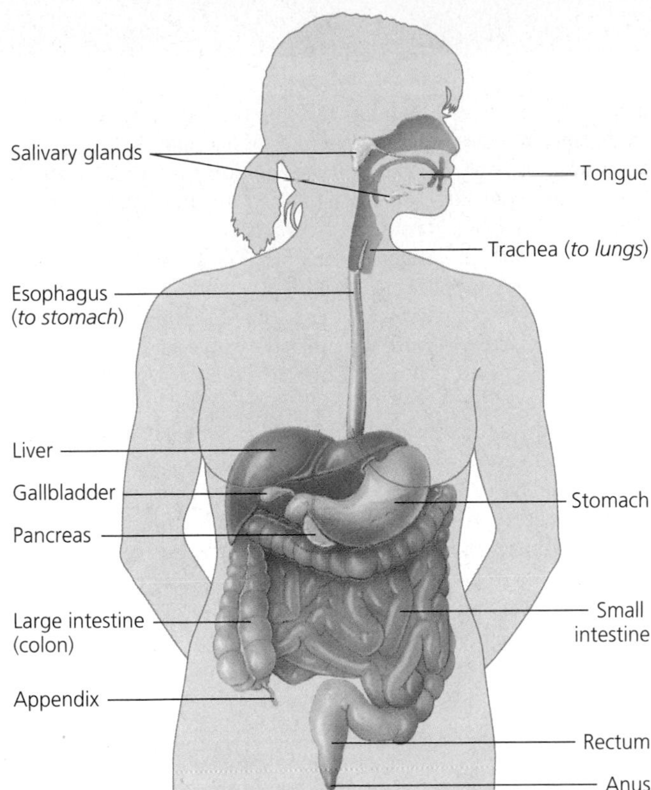

Figure 12-1 The digestive system. Food is partially broken down by being chewed and mixed with saliva in the mouth. After traveling to the stomach via the esophagus, food is broken down further by stomach acids and other secretions. As food moves through the digestive tract, it is mixed by muscular contractions and broken down by chemicals. Most absorption of nutrients occurs in the small intestine, aided by secretions from the pancreas, gallbladder, and intestinal lining. The large intestine reabsorbs excess water; the remaining solid wastes are collected in the rectum and excreted through the anus.

grow and function properly. Practically all foods contain mixtures of nutrients, although foods are commonly classified according to the predominant nutrient; for example, spaghetti is thought of as a carbohydrate. Let's take a closer look at the function and sources of each class of nutrients.

Proteins—The Basis of Body Structure

Proteins form important parts of the body's main structural components: muscles and bones. Proteins also form important parts of blood, enzymes, some hormones, and cell membranes. As mentioned earlier, proteins also provide energy (4 calories per gram) for the body.

Amino Acids The building blocks of proteins are called **amino acids.** Twenty common amino acids are found in food; nine of these are essential: histidine, isoleucine, leucine, lysine, methionine, phenylalanine, threonine, tryptophan, and valine. The other eleven amino acids can be produced by the body, given the presence of the needed components supplied by foods.

Complete and Incomplete Proteins Individual protein sources are considered *complete* if they supply all the essential amino acids in adequate amounts and *incomplete* if they do not. Meat, fish, poultry, eggs, milk, cheese, and soy provide complete proteins. Incomplete proteins, which come from other plant sources such as **legumes** and nuts, are good sources of most essential amino acids but are usually low in one or two.

Certain combinations of vegetable proteins, such as wheat and peanuts in a peanut butter sandwich, allow each vegetable protein to make up for the amino acids missing in the other protein. The combination yields a complete protein. Many traditional food pairings, such as beans and rice or corn and beans, emerged as dietary staples because they are complementary proteins. It was once believed that vegetarians had to complement their proteins at each meal in order to receive the benefit of a complete protein. It is now known, however, that proteins consumed throughout the course of the day can complement each other to form a pool of amino acids the body can draw from to produce the necessary proteins. Vegetarians should include a variety of vegetable protein sources in their diets to make sure they get all the essential amino acids in adequate amounts. (Healthy vegetarian diets are discussed later in the chapter.) About two-thirds of the protein in the American diet comes from animal sources (red meat and milk); therefore, the American diet is rich in essential amino acids.

Recommended Protein Intake Adequate daily intake of protein for adults is 0.8 gram per kilogram (0.36 gram per pound) of body weight, corresponding to 50 grams of protein per day for someone who weighs 140 pounds and 65 grams of protein for someone who weighs 180 pounds. This amount of protein is easily obtained from popular foods: 3 ounces of lean

Terms

Vw

nutrition The science of food and how the body uses it in health and disease.

essential nutrients Substances the body must get from foods because it cannot manufacture them at all or fast enough to meet its needs. These nutrients include proteins, fats, carbohydrates, vitamins, minerals, and water.

digestion The process of breaking down foods in the gastrointestinal tract into compounds the body can absorb.

kilocalorie A measure of energy content in food; 1 kilocalorie represents the amount of heat needed to raise the temperature of 1 liter of water 1°C; commonly referred to as *calorie.*

protein An essential nutrient; a compound made of amino acids that contain carbon, hydrogen, oxygen, and nitrogen.

amino acids The building blocks of proteins.

legumes Vegetables such as peas and beans that are high in fiber and are also important sources of protein.

Mind/Body/Spirit

Eating Habits and Total Wellness

Healthy eating does more than nourish your body—it enhances your ability to enjoy life to the fullest by improving overall wellness, both physical and mental. One study examined a group of adults who followed a healthy eating plan for four years. At the end of this period, the study subjects were more confident with their food choices and more satisfied with their lives in general than their peers who did not make any dietary changes. The reverse is also true—when people overeat they often have feelings of guilt, anger, discouragement, and even self-loathing. Out-of-control eating can erode self-confidence and lead to depression. How we eat is a reflection of how we feel about ourselves. Enjoying food and eating well is a major part of a healthy and happy life.

Can individual foods affect the way we feel? Limited scientific evidence points to some correlation between certain foods and one's mood. Many people, especially women, seem to crave chocolate when they are "blue." Studies show that chocolate, in small quantities, may indeed give you a lift. Sugary foods tend to temporarily raise serotonin levels in the brain, which can improve mood (serotonin is a neurotransmitter associated with a calm, relaxed state). The fat found in chocolate acts to increase endorphins, brain chemicals that reduce pain and increase feelings of well-being. Chocolate also contains caffeine, theobromine, phenylethylamine, and a variety of other less studied chemicals that may have a positive influence on mood.

A commonly held belief about the connection between food and the mind is that eating sugary foods makes people (especially children) hyperactive. Parents often comment on the wild behavior observed at parties and festive events where lots of sweets are consumed. However, several carefully controlled studies showed no correlation between behavior and the consumption of sugary foods. Researchers speculate that high-sugar foods tend to be eaten at birthday parties and other exciting occasions when children tend to be highly stimulated regardless of what they eat.

Some recent research shows that eating certain carbohydrate-rich foods, such as a plain baked potato or a bagel with jelly, can have a temporary calming effect. Scientists postulate that this occurs because carbohydrates stimulate insulin release, which improves the transport of the amino acid tryptophan (the major building block for serotonin) into the brain. This effect is most pronounced when rapidly digestible carbohydrates are consumed alone, with no fats or proteins in the meal. The practical implications of this research are uncertain.

If you are looking for a mental boost, some scientists think that eating a meal consisting primarily of protein-rich foods may be helpful. The theory is that proteins contain the amino acid tyrosine, which is used by the body to manufacture the neurotransmitters dopamine and norepinephrine. Some researchers postulate that eating protein-containing foods could increase the synthesis of these neurotransmitters, which can speed reaction time and increase alertness. Whether this really works, especially in well-nourished individuals who have not been lacking these nutrients to begin with, remains to be seen. In the meantime, it wouldn't hurt, and might even help, to include some protein in the meal you eat prior to your next big exam.

What we know about how food affects mood remains limited. But evidence points to the commonsense conclusion that enjoying reasonable portions of a variety of healthy and tasty foods is a great way to optimize your physical and mental health.

SOURCE: Fahey, T. D., P. M. Insel, and W. T. Roth. 2007. *Fit and Well,* 7th ed. New York: McGraw-Hill.

meat, poultry, or fish or ½ cup of tofu contains about 20–25 grams of protein; 1 cup of dry beans (legumes such as pinto and kidney beans), 15–20 grams; 1 cup of milk or yogurt or 1½ ounces of cheese, 8–12 grams; and cereals, grains, nuts, and vegetables, about 2–4 grams of protein per serving.

Most Americans meet or exceed the protein intake needed for adequate nutrition. Protein consumed beyond what the body needs is synthesized into fat for energy storage or burned for energy requirements. Consuming somewhat above daily needs is not harmful, but it can contribute fat to the diet because protein-rich foods are often fat-rich as well. A very high protein intake can also strain the kidneys. A fairly broad range of protein intakes is associated with good health, and the Food and Nutrition Board recommends that the amount of protein adults eat should fall within the range of 10–35% of total daily calorie intake, depending on the individual's age. The average American diet includes about 15–16% of total daily calories as protein.

Fats—Essential in Small Amounts

Fats, also known as *lipids,* are the most concentrated source of energy, at 9 calories per gram. The fats stored in your body represent usable energy, they help insulate your body, and they support and cushion your organs. Fats in the diet help your body absorb fat-soluble vitamins, as well as add important flavor and texture to foods. Fats are the major fuel for the body during rest and light activity. Two fats, linoleic acid and alpha-linolenic acid, are essential components of the diet. They are used to make compounds that are key regulators of such body functions as the maintenance of blood pressure and the progress of a healthy pregnancy.

Types and Sources of Fats Most of the fats in food are in the form of triglycerides, which are composed of a glycerol molecule (an alcohol) plus three fatty acids. A fatty acid is made up of a chain of carbon atoms with oxygen attached at one end and hydrogen atoms attached

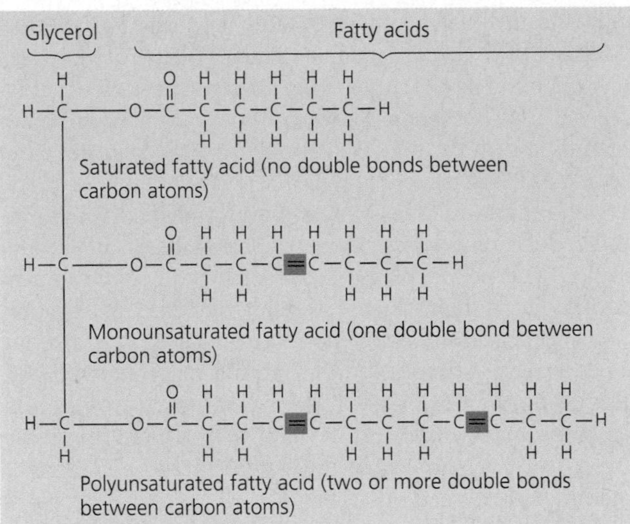

Figure 12-2 Chemical structures of saturated and unsaturated fatty acids. This example of a triglyceride consists of a molecule of glycerol with three fatty acids attached. Fatty acids can differ in the length of their carbon chains and their degree of saturation.

along the length of the chain. Fatty acids differ in the length of their carbon atom chains and in their degree of saturation (the number of hydrogens attached to the chain). If every available bond from each carbon atom in a fatty acid chain is attached to a hydrogen atom, the fatty acid is said to be **saturated** (Figure 12-2). If not all the available bonds are taken up by hydrogens, the carbon atoms in the chain will form double bonds with each other. Such fatty acids are called *unsaturated fats.* If there is only one double bond, the fatty acid is called **monounsaturated.** If there are two or more double bonds, the fatty acid is called **polyunsaturated.** The essential fatty acids, linoleic and alpha-linolenic acids, are both polyunsaturated. The different types of fatty acids have different characteristics and different effects on your health.

Food fats are usually composed of both saturated and unsaturated fatty acids; the dominant type of fatty acid determines the fat's characteristics. Food fats containing large amounts of saturated fatty acids are usually solid at room temperature; they are generally found naturally in animal products. The leading sources of saturated fat in the American diet are red meats (hamburger, steak, roasts), whole milk, cheese, hot dogs, and lunch meats. Food fats containing large amounts of monounsaturated and polyunsaturated fatty acids are usually from plant sources and are liquid at room temperature. Olive, canola, safflower, and peanut oils contain mostly monounsaturated fatty acids. Soybean, corn, and cottonseed oils contain mostly polyunsaturated fatty acids.

There are notable exceptions to these generalizations. When unsaturated vegetable oils undergo the process of **hydrogenation,** a mixture of saturated and unsaturated fatty acids is produced. Hydrogenation turns many of the double bonds in unsaturated fatty acids into single bonds, increasing the degree of saturation and producing a more solid fat from a liquid oil. Hydrogenation also changes some unsaturated fatty acids to **trans fatty acids,** unsaturated fatty acids with an atypical shape that affects their behavior in the body. Food manufacturers use hydrogenation to increase the stability of an oil so it can be reused for deep frying, to improve the texture of certain foods (to make pastries and pie crusts flakier, for example), and to extend the shelf life of foods made with oil. Hydrogenation is also used to transform a liquid oil into margarine or vegetable shortening.

Many baked and fried foods are prepared with hydrogenated vegetable oils, so they can be relatively high in saturated and trans fatty acids. Leading sources of trans fats in the American diet are deep-fried fast foods such as french fries and fried chicken (typically fried in vegetable shortening rather than oil); baked and snack foods such as pot pies, cakes, cookies, pastries, doughnuts, and chips; and stick margarine. In general, the more solid a hydrogenated oil is, the more saturated and trans fats it contains; for example, stick margarines typically contain more saturated and trans fats than do tub or squeeze margarines. Small amounts of trans fatty acids are found naturally in meat and milk.

Hydrogenated vegetable oils are not the only plant fats that contain saturated fats. Palm and coconut oils, although derived from plants, are also highly saturated. However, fish oils, derived from an animal source, are rich in polyunsaturated fats.

Fats and Health Different types of fats have very different effects on health. Many studies have examined the effects of dietary fat intake on blood **cholesterol** levels and the risk of heart disease. Saturated and trans fatty acids

Terms

saturated fat A fat with no carbon-carbon double bonds; usually solid at room temperature.

monounsaturated fat A fat with one carbon-carbon double bond; liquid at room temperature.

polyunsaturated fat A fat containing two or more carbon-carbon double bonds; liquid at room temperature.

hydrogenation A process by which hydrogens are added to unsaturated fats, increasing the degree of saturation and turning liquid oils into solid fats. Hydrogenation produces a mixture of saturated fatty acids and standard and trans forms of unsaturated fatty acids.

trans fatty acid A type of unsaturated fatty acid produced during the process of hydrogenation; trans fats have an atypical shape that affects their chemical activity.

cholesterol A waxy substance found in the blood and cells and needed for synthesis of cell membranes, vitamin D, and hormones.

raise blood levels of **low-density lipoprotein (LDL),** or "bad" cholesterol, thereby increasing a person's risk of heart disease. Unsaturated fatty acids lower LDL. Monounsaturated fatty acids, such as those found in olive and canola oils, may also increase levels of **high-density lipoproteins (HDL),** or "good" cholesterol, providing even greater benefits for heart health. In large amounts, trans fatty acids may lower HDL. Saturated fats have been found to impair the ability of HDLs to prevent inflammation of the blood vessels, one of the key factors in vascular disease; they have also been found to reduce the ability of the blood vessels to react normally to stress. Thus, to reduce the risk of heart disease, it is important to choose unsaturated fats instead of saturated and trans fats. (See Chapter 15 for more on cholesterol.)

Most Americans consume more saturated fat than trans fat (12% versus 2–4% of total daily calories). However, health experts are particularly concerned about trans fats because of their double negative effect on heart health—they both raise LDL and lower HDL—and because there is less public awareness of trans fats. Since January 2006, food labels have included trans fat content. Consumers can also check for the presence of trans fats by examining the ingredient list of a food for partially hydrogenated oil or vegetable shortening.

For heart health, it's important to minimize your consumption of both saturated and trans fats. The best way to reduce saturated fat in your diet is to lower your intake of meat and full-fat dairy products (whole milk, cream, butter, cheese, yogurt, ice cream). To lower trans fats, decrease your intake of deep-fried foods and crackers, cookies, and other baked goods made with hydrogenated vegetable oils; use liquid oils for cooking; and favor tub or squeeze margarines over stick margarines. Remember, the softer or more liquid a fat is, the less saturated and trans fat it is likely to contain.

Although saturated and trans fats pose health hazards, other fats can be beneficial. When used in place of saturated fats, monounsaturated fatty acids, as found in avocados, most nuts, and olive, canola, peanut, and safflower oils, improve cholesterol levels and may help protect against some cancers. **Omega-3 fatty acids,** a form of polyunsaturated fat found primarily in fish, may be even more healthful. An omega-3 fatty acid has its endmost double bond three carbons from the end of the fatty acid chain. (The polyunsaturated fatty acid shown in Figure 12-2 is an omega-3 form.) Omega-3s and the compounds the body makes from them have a number of heart-healthy effects: They reduce the tendency of blood to clot, inhibit inflammation and abnormal heart rhythms, and reduce blood pressure and risk of heart attack and stroke in some people. Because of these benefits, nutritionists recommend that Americans increase the proportion of omega-3s in their diet by eating fish two or more times a week. Salmon, tuna, trout, mackerel, herring, sardines, and anchovies are all good sources of omega-3s; lesser amounts are found in plant foods, including dark-green leafy vegetables; walnuts; flaxseeds; and canola, walnut, and flaxseed oils.

Another form of polyunsaturated fat, omega-6 fatty acid, has its endmost double bond at the sixth carbon atom. Most of the polyunsaturated fats currently consumed by Americans are omega-6s, primarily from corn oil and soybean oil. Foods rich in omega-6s are important because they contain the essential nutrient linoleic acid. However, some nutritionists recommend that people reduce the proportion of omega-6s they consume in favor of omega-3s. To make this adjustment, use canola oil rather than corn oil in cooking, and check for corn, soybean, or cottonseed oil in products such as mayonnaise, margarine, and salad dressing.

In addition to its effects on heart disease risk, dietary fat can affect health in other ways. Diets high in fatty red meat are associated with an increased risk of certain forms of cancer, especially colon cancer. A high-fat diet can also make weight management more difficult. Because fat is a concentrated source of calories (9 calories per gram versus 4 calories per gram for protein and carbohydrate), a high-fat diet is often a high-calorie diet that can lead to weight gain. In addition, there is some evidence that calories from fat are more easily converted to body fat than calories from protein or carbohydrate.

Although more research is needed on the precise effects of different types and amounts of fat on overall health, a great deal of evidence points to the fact that most people benefit from keeping their overall fat intake at recommended levels and choosing unsaturated fats instead of saturated and trans fats. The types of fatty acids and their effects on health are summarized in Figure 12-3.

Recommended Fat Intake To meet the body's demand for essential fats, adult men need about 17 grams per day of linoleic acid and 1.6 grams per day of alpha-linolenic acid; adult women need 12 grams of linoleic acid and 1.1 grams of alpha-linolenic acid. It takes only 3–4 teaspoons (15–20 grams) of vegetable oil per day incorporated into your diet to supply the essential fats. Most Americans consume sufficient amounts of the essential

Terms

VW

low-density lipoprotein (LDL) Blood fat that transports cholesterol to organs and tissues; excess amounts result in the accumulation of deposits on artery walls.

high-density lipoprotein (HDL) Blood fat that helps transport cholesterol out of the arteries, thereby protecting against heart disease.

omega-3 fatty acids Polyunsaturated fatty acids commonly found in fish oils that are beneficial to cardiovascular health; the endmost double bond occurs three carbons from the end of the fatty acid chain.

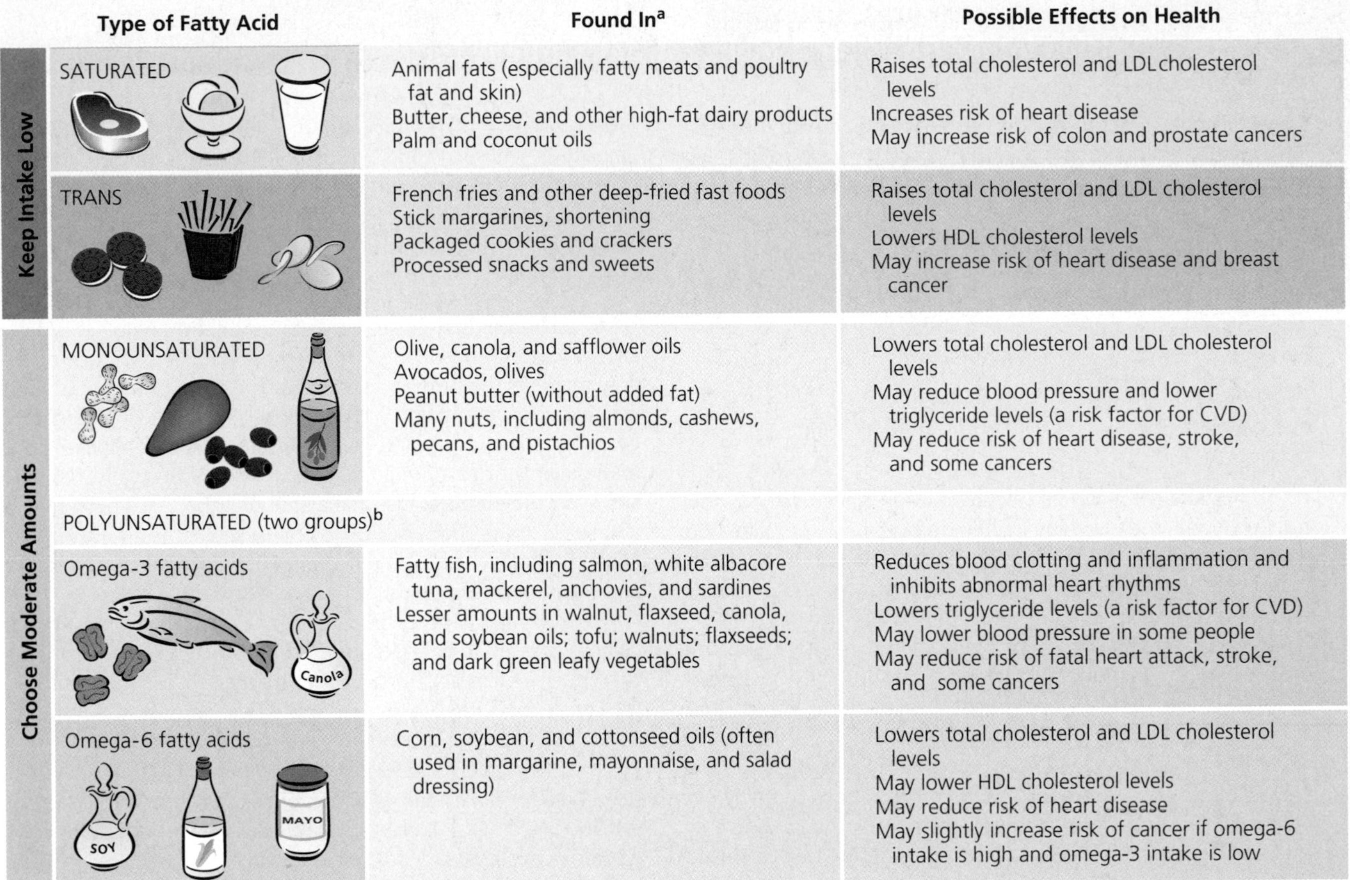

	Type of Fatty Acid	Found In[a]	Possible Effects on Health
Keep Intake Low	SATURATED	Animal fats (especially fatty meats and poultry fat and skin) Butter, cheese, and other high-fat dairy products Palm and coconut oils	Raises total cholesterol and LDL cholesterol levels Increases risk of heart disease May increase risk of colon and prostate cancers
	TRANS	French fries and other deep-fried fast foods Stick margarines, shortening Packaged cookies and crackers Processed snacks and sweets	Raises total cholesterol and LDL cholesterol levels Lowers HDL cholesterol levels May increase risk of heart disease and breast cancer
Choose Moderate Amounts	MONOUNSATURATED	Olive, canola, and safflower oils Avocados, olives Peanut butter (without added fat) Many nuts, including almonds, cashews, pecans, and pistachios	Lowers total cholesterol and LDL cholesterol levels May reduce blood pressure and lower triglyceride levels (a risk factor for CVD) May reduce risk of heart disease, stroke, and some cancers
	POLYUNSATURATED (two groups)[b]		
	Omega-3 fatty acids	Fatty fish, including salmon, white albacore tuna, mackerel, anchovies, and sardines Lesser amounts in walnut, flaxseed, canola, and soybean oils; tofu; walnuts; flaxseeds; and dark green leafy vegetables	Reduces blood clotting and inflammation and inhibits abnormal heart rhythms Lowers triglyceride levels (a risk factor for CVD) May lower blood pressure in some people May reduce risk of fatal heart attack, stroke, and some cancers
	Omega-6 fatty acids	Corn, soybean, and cottonseed oils (often used in margarine, mayonnaise, and salad dressing)	Lowers total cholesterol and LDL cholesterol levels May lower HDL cholesterol levels May reduce risk of heart disease May slightly increase risk of cancer if omega-6 intake is high and omega-3 intake is low

[a] Food fats contain a combination of types of fatty acids in various proportions; for example, canola oil is composed mainly of monounsaturated fatty acids (62%) but also contains polyunsaturated (32%) and saturated (6%) fatty acids. Food fats are categorized here according to their predominant fatty acid.

[b] The essential fatty acids are polyunsaturated: Linoleic acid is an omega-6 fatty acid and alpha-linolenic acid is an omega-3 fatty acid.

Figure 12-3 Types of fatty acids and their possible effects on health. The health effects of dietary fats are still being investigated. In general, nutritionists recommend that we consume a diet moderate in fat overall and that we choose unsaturated fats instead of saturated and trans fats. Monounsaturated fats and omega-3 polyunsaturated fats may be particularly good choices for promoting health. Eating lots of fat of any type can provide excess calories because all types of fats are rich sources of energy (9 calories per gram).

fats; limiting unhealthy fats is a much greater health concern.

Limits for total fat, saturated fat, and trans fat intake have been set by a number of government and research organizations. In 2002, the Food and Nutrition Board of the Institute of Medicine released recommendations for the balance of energy sources in a healthful diet. These new recommendations, called Acceptable Macronutrient Distribution Ranges (AMDRs), are based on ensuring adequate intake of essential nutrients while also reducing the risk of chronic diseases such as heart disease and cancer. As with protein, a range of levels of fat consumption is associated with good health; the AMDR for total fat is 20–35% of total calories. Although more difficult for consumers to monitor, AMDRs have also been set for omega-6 fatty acids (5–10%) and omega-3 fatty acids (0.6–1.2%) as part of total fat intake. Because any amount of saturated and trans fats increases the risk of heart disease, the Food and Nutrition Board recommends that saturated fat and trans fat intake be kept as low as possible; most fat in a healthy diet should be unsaturated. American adults currently consume about 33% of total calories as fat, including 11–12% of calories as saturated fat and 2–4% as trans fat.

For advice on setting individual intake goals, see the box "Setting Intake Goals for Protein, Fat, and Carbohydrate" on page 334. To determine how close you are to meeting your personal intake goals for fat, keep a running total over the course of the day. For prepared foods, food labels list the number of grams of fat, protein, and carbohydrate; the breakdown for popular fast-food items can be found in Appendix A. Nutrition information is also available in many grocery stores, in inexpensive published nutrition guides, and online (see For More Information at the end of the chapter). By checking these resources, you can keep track of the total grams of fat, protein, and carbohydrate you eat and assess your current diet.

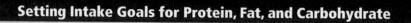

Setting Intake Goals for Protein, Fat, and Carbohydrate

Take Charge

Goals have been established by the Food and Nutrition Board to help ensure adequate intake of the essential amino acids, fatty acids, and carbohydrate. The daily goals for adequate intake for adults are as follow:

	Men	Women
Protein	56 grams	46 grams
Fat: Linoleic acid	17 grams	12 grams
Alpha-linolenic acid	1.6 grams	1.1 grams
Carbohydrate	130 grams	130 grams

Protein intake goals can be calculated more specifically by multiplying your body weight in kilograms by 0.8 or your body weight in pounds by 0.36. (Refer to the Nutrition Resources section at the end of the chapter for information for specific age groups and life stages.)

To meet your daily energy needs, you need to consume more than the minimally adequate amounts of the energy-providing nutrients listed above, which alone supply only about 800–900 calories. The Food and Nutrition Board provides additional guidance in the form of Acceptable Macronutrient Distribution Ranges (AMDRs). The ranges can help you balance your intake of the energy-providing nutrients in ways that ensure adequate intake while reducing the risk of chronic disease. The AMDRs for protein, total fat, and carbohydrate are as follow:

Protein	10–35% of total daily calories
Total fat	20–35% of total daily calories
Carbohydrate	45–65% of total daily calories

To set individual goals, begin by estimating your total daily energy (calorie) needs; if your weight is stable, your current energy intake is the number of calories you need to maintain your weight at your current activity level. Next, select percentage goals for protein, fat, and carbohydrate. You can allocate your total daily calories among the three classes of macronutrients to suit your preferences; just make sure that the three percentages you select total 100% and that you meet the minimum intake goals listed. Two samples reflecting different total energy intake and nutrient intake goals are shown in the table below.

To translate your own percentage goals into daily intake goals expressed in calories and grams, multiply the appropriate percentages by total calorie intake and then divide the results by the corresponding calories per gram. For example, a fat limit of 35% applied to a 2200-calorie diet would be calculated as follows: $0.35 \times 2200 = 770$ calories of total fat; $770 \div 9$ calories per gram $= 86$ grams of total fat. (Remember that, fat has 9 calories per gram and that protein and carbohydrate have 4 calories per gram.)

Two Sample Macronutrient Distributions

		Sample 1		Sample 2	
Nutrient	AMDR	Individual Goals	Amounts for a 1600-Calorie Diet	Individual Goals	Amounts for a 2800-Calorie Diet
Protein	10–35%	15%	240 calories = 60 grams	30%	840 calories = 210 grams
Fat	20–35%	30%	480 calories = 53 grams	25%	700 calories = 78 grams
Carbohydrate	45–65%	55%	880 calories = 220 grams	45%	1260 calories = 315 grams

SOURCE: Food and Nutrition Board, Institute of Medicine, National Academies. 2002. *Dietary Reference Intakes: Applications in Dietary Planning*, Washington, D.C.: National Academies Press.

For most Americans, meeting recommendations for fat intake means lowering intake of saturated and trans fats and maintaining total fat intake within the healthy range (see Figure 12-3). You can still eat high-fat foods, but it makes good sense to limit the size of your portions and to balance your intake with low-fat foods. For example, peanut butter is high in fat, with 8 grams (72 calories) of fat in each 90-calorie tablespoon. Two tablespoons of peanut butter eaten on whole-wheat bread and served with a banana, carrot sticks, and a glass of fat-free milk makes a nutritious lunch—high in protein and carbohydrate, and relatively low in fat (500 calories, 18 grams of total fat, 4 grams of saturated fat). Four tablespoons of peanut butter on high-fat crackers with potato chips, cookies, and whole milk is a less healthy combination (1000 calories, 62 grams of total fat, 15 grams of saturated fat). So although it's important to evaluate individual food items for their fat content, it is more important to look at them in the context of your overall diet.

Carbohydrates—An Ideal Source of Energy

Carbohydrates are needed in the diet primarily to supply energy for body cells. Some cells, such as those found in the brain and other parts of the nervous system and in blood, use only carbohydrates for fuel. During high-intensity exercise, muscles also use primarily carbohydrates for fuel. When we don't eat enough carbohydrates to satisfy the needs of the brain and red blood cells, our bodies synthesize carbohydrates from proteins. In situations of extreme deprivation, when the diet lacks a sufficient amount of both carbohydrates and proteins, the body turns to its own organs and tissues, breaking down proteins in muscles, the heart, kidneys, and other vital organs to supply carbohydrate needs. This rarely occurs, however, because consuming the equivalent of just three or four slices of bread supplies the body's daily minimum need for carbohydrates.

Simple and Complex Carbohydrates Carbohydrates are classified into two groups: simple and complex. Simple carbohydrates contain only one or two sugar units in each molecule; they include sucrose (table sugar), fructose (fruit sugar, honey), maltose (malt sugar), and lactose (milk sugar). Simple carbohydrates provide much of the sweetness in foods and are found naturally in fruits and milk and are added to soft drinks, fruit drinks, candy, and sweet desserts. There is no evidence that any type of simple sugar is more nutritious than others.

Complex carbohydrates consist of chains of many sugar molecules; they include starches and most types of dietary fiber. Starches are found in a variety of plants, especially grains (wheat, rye, rice, oats, barley, millet), legumes (dry beans, peas, and lentils), and tubers (potatoes and yams). Most other vegetables contain a mixture of starches and simple carbohydrates. Fiber, discussed in the next section, is found in grains, fruits, and vegetables.

During digestion in the mouth and small intestine, your body breaks down starches and double sugars into single sugar molecules, such as **glucose,** for absorption. Once glucose is in the bloodstream, the pancreas releases the hormone insulin, which allows cells to take up glucose and use it for energy. The liver and muscles also take up glucose to provide carbohydrate storage in the form of **glycogen.** Some people have problems controlling blood glucose levels, a disorder called diabetes mellitus (see Chapter 14 for more on diabetes). Carbohydrates consumed in excess of the body's energy needs can be changed into fat and stored. Whenever calorie intake exceeds calorie expenditure, fat storage can lead to weight gain. This is true whether the excess calories come from carbohydrates, proteins, fat, or alcohol.

Refined Carbohydrates Versus Whole Grains Complex carbohydrates can be further divided between refined, or processed, carbohydrates and unrefined carbohydrates, or whole grains. Before they are processed, all grains are **whole grains,** consisting of an inner layer, germ; a middle layer, the endosperm; and an outer layer, bran. During processing, the germ and bran are often removed, leaving just the starchy endosperm. The refinement of whole grains transforms whole-wheat flour to white flour, brown rice to white rice, and so on.

Refined carbohydrates usually retain all the calories of their unrefined counterparts, but they tend to be much lower in fiber, vitamins, minerals, and other beneficial compounds. (Many refined grain products are enriched or fortified with vitamins and minerals, but often the nutrients lost in processing are not replaced.) Unrefined carbohydrates tend to take longer to chew and digest than refined ones; they also enter the bloodstream more slowly. This slower digestive pace tends to make people feel full sooner and for a longer period. Also, a slower rise in blood glucose levels following consumption of complex carbohydrates may help in the management of diabetes. Whole grains are also high in dietary fiber and so have all the benefits of fiber. Consumption of whole grains has been linked to a reduced risk of heart disease, diabetes, high blood pressure, stroke, and certain forms of cancer. For all these reasons, whole grains are recommended over those that have been refined. This does not mean that you should never eat refined carbohydrates such as white bread or white rice, simply that whole-wheat bread, brown rice, and other whole grains are healthier choices. See the box "Choosing More Whole-Grain Foods" (p. 336) for tips on increasing your intake of whole grains.

Glycemic Index and Glycemic Response Insulin and glucose levels rise and fall following a meal or snack containing any type of carbohydrate. Some foods cause a quick and dramatic rise in glucose and insulin levels; others have a slower, more moderate effect. A food that has a rapid effect on blood glucose levels is said to have a high **glycemic index.** Research findings have been mixed, but some studies have found that consuming a meal containing high glycemic index foods may increase appetite, and that over the long term, diets rich in these foods may increase risk of diabetes and heart disease for some people. High glycemic index foods do not, as some popular diets claim, directly cause weight gain beyond the calories they contain.

Attempting to base food choices on glycemic index can be a difficult task, however. Although unrefined complex

Terms

VW

carbohydrate An essential nutrient; sugars, starches, and dietary fiber are all carbohydrates.

glucose A simple sugar that is the body's basic fuel.

glycogen An animal starch stored in the liver and muscles.

whole grain The entire edible portion of a grain such as wheat, rice, or oats, consisting of the germ, endosperm, and bran. During milling or processing, parts of the grain are removed, often leaving just the endosperm.

glycemic index A measure of how the ingestion of a particular food affects blood glucose levels.

Take Charge

Choosing More Whole-Grain Foods

Whole-grain foods are good weapons against heart disease, diabetes, high blood pressure, stroke, and certain cancers. They are also low in fat and so can be a good choice for managing weight. Federal dietary guidelines recommend 6 or more total servings of grain products every day, with at least half of these servings from whole grains. However, Americans currently average less than 1 serving of whole grains per day.

What Are Whole Grains?

The first step in increasing your intake of whole grains is to correctly identify them. The following are whole grains:

whole wheat	whole-grain corn
whole rye	popcorn
whole oats	brown rice
oatmeal	whole-grain barley

More unusual choices include bulgur (cracked wheat), millet, kasha (roasted buckwheat kernels), quinoa, wheat and rye berries, amaranth, wild rice, graham flour, whole-grain kamut, whole-grain spelt, and whole-grain triticale.

Wheat flour, unbleached flour, enriched flour, and degerminated corn meal are not whole grains. Wheat germ and wheat bran are also not whole grains, but they are the constituents of wheat typically left out when wheat is processed and so are healthier choices than regular wheat flour, which typically contains just the endosperm.

Reading Food Packages to Find Whole Grains

To find packaged foods rich in whole grains, read the list of ingredients and check for special health claims related to whole grains. The *first* item on the list of ingredients should be one of the whole grains listed above. In addition, the FDA allows manufacturers to include special health claims for foods that contain 51% or more whole-grain ingredients. Such products may contain a statement such as the following on their packaging: "Rich in whole grain," "Made with 100% whole grain," or "Diets rich in whole-grain foods may help reduce the risk of heart disease and certain cancers." However, many whole-grain products will not carry such claims. Product names and food color can be misleading. *When in doubt, always check the list of ingredients, looking for "whole" as the first word on the list.*

Incorporating Whole Grains into Your Daily Diet

- *Bread:* Look for sandwich breads, bagels, English muffins, buns, and pita breads with a whole grain listed as the first ingredient.
- *Breakfast cereals:* Check the ingredient list for whole grains. Whole-grain choices include oatmeal, muesli, shredded wheat, and some types of raisin bran, bran flakes, wheat flakes, toasted oats, and granola.
- *Rice:* Choose brown rice or rice blends that include brown rice.
- *Pasta:* Look for whole-wheat, whole-grain kamut, or whole-grain spelt pasta.
- *Tortillas:* Choose whole-wheat or whole-corn tortillas.
- *Crackers and snacks:* Some varieties of crackers are made from whole grains, including some flatbreads or crispbreads, woven wheat crackers, and rye crackers. Other whole-grain snack possibilities include popcorn, popcorn cakes, brown rice cakes, whole-corn tortilla chips, and whole-wheat fig cookies. Be sure to check food labels for fat content, as many popular snacks are high in fat.
- *Mixed-grain dishes:* Combine whole grains with other foods to create healthy mixed dishes. Possibilities include tabouli; soups made with hulled barley or wheat berries; and pilafs, casseroles, and salads made with brown rice, whole-wheat couscous, kasha, millet, wheat bulgur, or quinoa.

If your grocery store doesn't carry all of these items, try your local health food store.

carbohydrates and high-fiber foods generally tend to have a low glycemic index, patterns are less clear for other types of foods and do not follow a easy distinction such as that of simple versus complex carbohydrates. For example, some fruits with fairly high levels of simple carbohydrates have only a moderate effect on blood glucose levels, whereas white rice, potatoes, and white bread, which are rich in complex carbohydrates, have a high glycemic index. Watermelon has a glycemic index more than twice that of strawberries, and the glycemic index of a banana changes dramatically as it ripens. The body's response to carbohydrates also depends on many other factors, such as how foods are combined and prepared and the fitness status of the individual.

This complexity is one reason major health organizations have not issued specific guidelines for glycemic index. For people with particular health concerns, glycemic index may be an important consideration; however, it should not be the sole criterion for food choices. For example, ice cream has a lower glycemic index than brown rice or carrots—but that doesn't make it a healthier choice overall. Glycemic index is discussed further in Chapters 14 and 15. For now, remember that most unrefined grains, fruits, vegetables, and legumes are rich in nutrients, have a relatively low energy density, and have a low to moderate glycemic index. Choose a variety of vegetables daily, and avoid heavy consumption of white potatoes. Limit foods that are high in added sugars but provide few other nutrients. Some studies have singled out regular soda, with its large dose of rapidly absorbable sugar, as specifically linked to increased diabetes risk.

Recommended Carbohydrate Intake On average, Americans consume 200–300 grams of carbohydrate per day, well above the 130 grams needed to meet the body's requirement for essential carbohydrate. A range of intakes is associated with good health, and experts recommend that adults consume 45–65% of total daily calories as carbohydrate, about 225–325 grams of carbohydrate for someone consuming 2000 calories per day. The focus should be on consuming a variety of foods rich in complex carbohydrates, especially whole grains.

Although the Food and Nutrition Board set an AMDR for added sugars of 25% or less of total daily calories, many health experts recommend an even lower intake. World Health Organization guidelines suggested a limit of 10% of total daily calories from added sugars; limits set by the USDA in 2005 are even lower, with a maximum of about 8 teaspoons (32 grams) suggested for someone consuming 2000 calories per day. Foods high in added sugar are generally high in calories and low in nutrients and fiber, thus providing empty calories. To reduce your intake of added sugars, limit soft drinks, candy, sweet desserts, and sweetened fruit drinks. The simple carbohydrates in your diet should come mainly from fruits, which are excellent sources of vitamins and minerals, and from low-fat or fat-free milk and other dairy products, which are high in protein and calcium.

Athletes in training can especially benefit from high-carbohydrate diets (60–70% of total daily calories), which enhance the amount of carbohydrates stored in their muscles (as glycogen) and therefore provide more carbohydrate fuel for use during endurance events or long workouts. In addition, high glycemic index carbohydrates consumed during prolonged athletic events can help fuel muscles and extend the availability of the glycogen stored in muscles. Caution is in order, however, because overconsumption of carbohydrates can lead to fatigue and underconsumption of other nutrients.

Fiber—A Closer Look

Fiber is the term given to nondigestible carbohydrates provided by plants. Instead of being digested, like starch, fiber passes through the intestinal tract and provides bulk for feces in the large intestine, which in turn facilitates elimination. In the large intestine, some types of fiber are broken down by bacteria into acids and gases, which explains why consuming too much fiber can lead to intestinal gas. Because humans cannot digest fiber, it is not a source of carbohydrate in the diet; however, the consumption of fiber is necessary for good health.

Types of Fiber The Food and Nutrition Board has defined two types of fiber: dietary fiber and functional fiber. **Dietary fiber** refers to the nondigestible carbohydrates (and the noncarbohydrate substance lignin) that are present naturally in plants such as grains, legumes, and vegetables. **Functional fiber** refers to nondigestible carbohydrates that have been either isolated from natural sources or synthesized in a lab and then added to a food product or dietary supplement. **Total fiber** is the sum of dietary and functional fiber.

Fibers have different properties that lead to different physiological effects in the body. For example, viscous fibers such as those found in oat bran or legumes can delay stomach emptying, slow the movement of glucose into the blood after eating, and reduce absorption of cholesterol. Other types of fiber, such as those found in wheat bran or psyllium seed, increase fecal bulk and help prevent constipation, hemorrhoids, and **diverticulitis.** A diet high in fiber can help reduce the risk of type 2 diabetes and heart disease as well as improve gastrointestinal health. Some studies have linked high-fiber diets with reduced risk of colon and rectal cancer; other studies have suggested that other characteristics of diets rich in fruits, vegetables, and whole grains may be responsible for this reduction in risk (see Chapter 16 for more on cancer and diet).

Sources of Fiber All plant foods contain some dietary fiber. Fruits, legumes, oats (especially oat bran), and barley all contain the viscous types of fiber that help lower blood glucose and cholesterol levels. Wheat (especially wheat bran), other grains and cereals, and vegetables are good sources of cellulose and other fibers that help prevent constipation. Psyllium, which is often added to cereals or used in fiber supplements and laxatives, improves intestinal health and also helps control glucose and cholesterol levels. The processing of packaged foods can remove fiber, so it is important to rely on fresh fruits and vegetables and foods made from whole grains as your main sources of fiber.

Recommended Fiber Intake To reduce the risk of chronic disease and maintain intestinal health, the Food and Nutrition Board recommends a daily fiber intake of 38 grams for adult men and 25 grams for adult women. Americans currently consume about half this amount. Fiber should come from foods, not supplements, which should be used only under medical supervision. To

Terms

Vw

dietary fiber Nondigestible carbohydrates and lignin that are intact in plants.

functional fiber Nondigestible carbohydrates either isolated from natural sources or synthesized; these may be added to foods and dietary supplements.

total fiber The total amount of dietary fiber and functional fiber in the diet.

diverticulitis A digestive disorder in which abnormal pouches form in the walls of the intestine and become inflamed.

increase the amount of fiber in your daily diet to recommended levels, try the following strategies:

- Choose whole-grain foods instead of those made from processed grains. Select high-fiber breakfast cereals (those with 5 or more grams of fiber per serving).
- Eat whole, unpeeled fruits rather than drinking fruit juice. Top cereals, yogurt, and desserts with berries, unpeeled apple slices, or other fruit.
- Include legumes in soups and salads. Combine raw vegetables with pasta, rice, or beans in salads.
- Substitute bean dip for cheese-based or sour cream–based dips or spreads. Use raw vegetables rather than chips for dipping.

Vitamins—Organic Micronutrients

Vitamins are organic (carbon-containing) substances required in small amounts to regulate various processes within living cells (Table 12-1). Humans need 13 vitamins; 4 are fat-soluble (A, D, E, and K), and 9 are water-soluble (C, and the 8 B-complex vitamins: thiamin, riboflavin, niacin, vitamin B-6, folate, vitamin B-12, biotin, and pantothenic acid). Solubility affects how a vitamin is absorbed, transported, and stored in the body. The water-soluble vitamins are absorbed directly into the bloodstream, where they travel freely; excess water-soluble vitamins are detected and removed by the kidneys and excreted in urine. Fat-soluble vitamins require a more complex absorptive process; they are usually carried in the blood by special proteins and are stored in the liver and in fat tissues rather than excreted.

Functions of Vitamins Many vitamins help chemical reactions take place. They provide no energy to the body directly but help unleash the energy stored in carbohydrates, proteins, and fats. Vitamins are critical in the production of red blood cells and the maintenance of the nervous, skeletal, and immune systems. Some vitamins act as **antioxidants,** which help preserve healthy cells in the body. Key vitamin antioxidants include vitamin E, vitamin C, and the vitamin A precursor beta-carotene. (Antioxidants are described later in the chapter.)

Terms

vitamins Carbon-containing substances needed in small amounts to help promote and regulate chemical reactions and processes in the body.

antioxidant A substance that can lessen the breakdown of food or body constituents by free radicals; actions include binding oxygen, donating electrons to free radicals, and repairing damage to molecules.

scurvy A disease caused by a lack of vitamin C, characterized by bleeding gums, loosening teeth, and poor wound healing.

Sources of Vitamins The human body does not manufacture most of the vitamins it requires and must obtain them from foods. Vitamins are abundant in fruits, vegetables, and grains. In addition, many processed foods, such as flour and breakfast cereals, contain added vitamins. A few vitamins are made in certain parts of the body: The skin makes vitamin D when it is exposed to sunlight, and intestinal bacteria make vitamin K. Nonetheless, you still need to obtain vitamin D and vitamin K from foods.

Vitamin Deficiencies and Excesses If your diet lacks sufficient amounts of a particular vitamin, characteristic symptoms of deficiency develop (see Table 12-1.) For example, vitamin A deficiency can cause blindness, and vitamin B-6 deficiency can cause seizures. The best-known deficiency disease is probably **scurvy,** caused by vitamin C deficiency. In the eighteenth century, it killed many sailors on long ocean voyages, until people realized that eating citrus fruits could prevent it. Even today people develop scurvy; its presence suggests a very poor intake of fruits and vegetables, which are rich sources of vitamin C.

Vitamin deficiency diseases are most often seen in developing countries; they are relatively rare in the United States because vitamins are readily available from our food supply. People suffering from alcoholism and malabsorption disorders probably run the greatest risk of vitamin deficiencies. However, intakes below recommended levels can have adverse effects on health even if they are not low enough to cause a deficiency disease. For example, low intake of folate and vitamins B-6 and B-12 has been linked to increased heart disease risk. Many Americans consume less-than-recommended amounts of several vitamins, including vitamins A, C, and D; vitamin E intake is also low among some groups, especially African Americans. Table 12-1 lists good food sources of vitamins.

Extra vitamins in the diet can also be harmful, especially when taken as supplements. High doses of vitamin A are toxic and increase the risk of birth defects, for example. Vitamin B-6 can cause irreversible nerve damage when taken in large doses. Megadoses of fat-soluble vitamins are particularly dangerous because the excess will be stored in the body rather than excreted, increasing the risk of toxicity. Even when vitamins are not taken in excess, relying on supplements for an adequate intake of vitamins can be a problem. There are many substances in foods other than vitamins and minerals, and some of these compounds may have important health effects. Later in the chapter we discuss specific recommendations for vitamin intake and when a vitamin supplement is advisable. For now, keep in mind that it's best to obtain most of your vitamins from foods rather than supplements.

Table 12-1 Facts About Vitamins

Vitamin	Important Dietary Sources	Major Functions	Signs of Prolonged Deficiency	Toxic Effects of Megadoses
Fat-Soluble				
Vitamin A	Liver, milk, butter, cheese, and fortified margarine; carrots, spinach, and other orange and deep-green vegetables and fruits	Maintenance of vision, skin, linings of the nose, mouth, digestive and urinary tracts, immune function	Night blindness; dry, scaling skin; increased susceptibility to infection; loss of appetite; anemia; kidney stones	Liver damage, miscarriage and birth defects, headache, vomiting and diarrhea, vertigo, double vision, bone abnormalities
Vitamin D	Fortified milk and margarine, fish oils, butter, egg yolks (sunlight on skin also produces vitamin D)	Development and maintenance of bones and teeth, promotion of calcium absorption	Rickets (bone deformities) in children; bone softening, loss, and fractures in adults	Kidney damage, calcium deposits in soft tissues, depression, death
Vitamin E	Vegetable oils, whole grains, nuts and seeds, green leafy vegetables, asparagus, peaches	Protection and maintenance of cellular membranes	Red blood cell breakage and anemia, weakness, neurological problems, muscle cramps	Relatively nontoxic, but may cause excess bleeding or formation of blood clots
Vitamin K	Green leafy vegetables; smaller amounts widespread in other foods	Production of factors essential for blood clotting and bone metabolism	Hemorrhaging	None reported
Water-Soluble				
Biotin	Cereals, yeast, egg yolks, soy flour, liver; widespread in foods	Synthesis of fat, glycogen, and amino acids	Rash, nausea, vomiting, weight loss, depression, fatigue, hair loss	None reported
Folate	Green leafy vegetables, yeast, oranges, whole grains, legumes, liver	Amino acid metabolism, synthesis of RNA and DNA, new cell synthesis	Anemia, weakness, fatigue, irritability, shortness of breath, swollen tongue	Masking of vitamin B-12 deficiency
Niacin	Eggs, poultry, fish, milk, whole grains, nuts, enriched breads and cereals, meats, legumes	Conversion of carbohydrates, fats, and protein into usable forms of energy	Pellagra (symptoms include diarrhea, dermatitis, inflammation of mucous membranes, dementia)	Flushing of the skin, nausea, vomiting, diarrhea, liver dysfunction, glucose intolerance
Pantothenic acid	Animal foods, whole grains, broccoli, potatoes; widespread in foods	Metabolism of fats, carbohydrates, and proteins	Fatigue, numbness and tingling of hands and feet, gastrointestinal disturbances	None reported
Riboflavin	Dairy products, enriched breads and cereals, lean meats, poultry, fish, green vegetables	Energy metabolism; maintenance of skin, mucous membranes, and nervous system structures	Cracks at corners of mouth, sore throat, skin rash, hypersensitivity to light, purple tongue	None reported
Thiamin	Whole-grain and enriched breads and cereals, organ meats, lean pork, nuts, legumes	Conversion of carbohydrates into usable forms of energy, maintenance of appetite and nervous system function	Beriberi (symptoms include muscle wasting, mental confusion, anorexia, enlarged heart, nerve changes)	None reported
Vitamin B-6	Eggs, poultry, fish, whole grains, nuts, soybeans, liver, kidney, pork	Metabolism of amino acids and glycogen	Anemia, convulsions, cracks at corners of mouth, dermatitis, nausea, confusion	Neurological abnormalities and damage
Vitamin B-12	Meat, fish, poultry, fortified cereals	Synthesis of blood cells; other metabolic reactions	Anemia, fatigue, nervous system damage, sore tongue	None reported
Vitamin C	Peppers, broccoli, spinach, brussels sprouts, citrus fruits, strawberries, tomatoes, potatoes, cabbage, other fruits and vegetables	Maintenance and repair of connective tissue, bones, teeth, and cartilage; promotion of healing; aid in iron absorption	Scurvy, anemia, reduced resistance to infection, loosened teeth, joint pain, poor wound healing, hair loss, poor iron absorption	Urinary stones in some people, acid stomach from ingesting supplements in pill form, nausea, diarrhea, headache, fatigue

SOURCES: Food and Nutrition Board, Institute of Medicine. 2006. *Dietary Reference Intakes: The Essential Guide to Nutrient Requirements.* Washington, D.C.: The National Academies Press. The complete Dietary Reference Intake reports are available from the National Academy Press (http://www.nap.edu); Shils, M. E., et al., eds. 2005. *Modern Nutrition in Health and Disease,* 10th ed. Baltimore: Lippincott Williams & Wilkins.

Keeping the Nutrient Value in Food Vitamins and minerals can be lost or destroyed during the storage and cooking of foods. To retain nutrients, consume or process vegetables as soon as possible after purchasing. Store fruits and vegetables in the refrigerator in covered containers or plastic bags to minimize moisture loss; freeze foods that won't be eaten within a few days. (Frozen and canned vegetables are usually as high in nutrients as fresh vegetables because nutrients are locked in when produce is frozen or canned.) To reduce nutrient losses during food preparation, minimize the amount of water used and the total cooking time. Develop a taste for a crunchier texture in cooked vegetables. Baking, steaming, broiling, grilling, and microwaving are all good methods of preparing vegetables.

Minerals—Inorganic Micronutrients

Minerals are inorganic (non–carbon-containing) elements you need in relatively small amounts to help regulate body functions, aid in the growth and maintenance of body tissues, and help release energy (Table 12-2). There are about 17 essential minerals. The major minerals, those that the body needs in amounts exceeding 100 milligrams per day, include calcium, phosphorus, magnesium, sodium, potassium, and chloride. The essential trace minerals, those that you need in minute amounts, include copper, fluoride, iodide, iron, selenium, and zinc.

Characteristic symptoms develop if an essential mineral is consumed in a quantity too small or too large for good health. The minerals commonly lacking in the American diet are iron, calcium, potassium, and magnesium. Focus on good food choices for these (see Table 12-2). Lean meats are rich in iron, whereas low-fat or fat-free dairy products are excellent choices for calcium. Potassium is found in green leafy vegetables, white and sweet potatoes, bananas, and other fruits and vegetables. Plant foods such as whole grains and leafy vegetables are good sources of magnesium. Iron-deficiency **anemia** is a problem in many age groups, and researchers fear poor calcium intakes in childhood are sowing the seeds for future **osteoporosis**, especially in women. See Chapter 19 for more information on osteoporosis; the box "Eating for Healthy Bones" (p. 342) has tips for building and maintaining bone density.

Terms

Vw

minerals Inorganic compounds needed in relatively small amounts for regulation, growth, and maintenance of body tissues and functions.

anemia A deficiency in the oxygen-carrying material in the red blood cells.

osteoporosis A condition in which the bones become extremely thin and brittle and break easily.

free radical An electron-seeking compound that can react with fats, proteins, and DNA, damaging cell membranes and mutating genes in its search for electrons; produced through chemical reactions in the body and by exposure to environmental factors such as sunlight and tobacco smoke.

Water—Vital but Often Ignored

Water is the major component in both foods and the human body: You are composed of about 50–60% water. Your need for other nutrients, in terms of weight, is much less than your need for water. You can live up to 50 days without food, but only a few days without water.

Water is distributed all over the body, among lean and other tissues and in blood and other body fluids. Water is used in the digestion and absorption of food and is the medium in which most of the chemical reactions take place within the body. Some water-based fluids, like blood, transport substances around the body, whereas other fluids serve as lubricants or cushions. Water also helps regulate body temperature.

Water is contained in almost all foods, particularly in liquids, fruits, and vegetables. The foods and fluids you consume provide 80–90% of your daily water intake; the remainder is generated through metabolism. You lose water each day in urine, feces, and sweat and through evaporation from your lungs.

Most people can maintain a healthy water balance by consuming beverages at meals and drinking fluids in response to thirst. Water and other beverages typically make up about 80% of your fluid intake; the remainder comes from foods, especially fruits and vegetables. In 2004, the Food and Nutrition Board set levels of adequate water intake to maintain hydration; all fluids, including those containing caffeine, can count toward your total daily fluid intake. Under these guidelines, men need to consume about 3.7 total liters of water, with 3.0 liters (about 13 cups) coming from beverages; women need 2.7 total liters, with 2.2 liters (about 9 cups) coming from beverages. (See Table 1 in the Nutrition Resources section at the end of the chapter for information on specific age groups.) If you exercise vigorously or live in a hot climate, you need to consume additional fluids to maintain a balance between water consumed and water lost. Severe dehydration causes weakness and can lead to death.

Other Substances in Food

Many substances in food are not essential nutrients but may influence health.

Antioxidants When the body uses oxygen or breaks down certain fats or proteins as a normal part of metabolism, it gives rise to substances called **free radicals.** Environmental factors such as cigarette smoke, exhaust

Table 12-2 Facts About Selected Minerals

Mineral	Important Dietary Sources	Major Functions	Signs of Prolonged Deficiency	Toxic Effects of Megadoses
Calcium	Milk and milk products, tofu, fortified orange juice and bread, green leafy vegetables, bones in fish	Formation of bones and teeth, control of nerve impulses, muscle contraction, blood clotting	Stunted growth in children, bone mineral loss in adults; urinary stones	Kidney stones, calcium deposits in soft tissues, inhibition of mineral absorption, constipation
Fluoride	Fluoridated water, tea, marine fish eaten with bones	Maintenance of tooth and bone structure	Higher frequency of tooth decay	Increased bone density, mottling of teeth, impaired kidney function
Iodine	Iodized salt, seafood, processed foods	Essential part of thyroid hormones, regulation of body metabolism	Goiter (enlarged thyroid), cretinism (birth defect)	Depression of thyroid activity, hyperthyroidism in susceptible people
Iron	Meat and poultry, fortified grain products, dark green vegetables, dried fruit	Component of hemoglobin, myoglobin, and enzymes	Iron-deficiency anemia, weakness, impaired immune function, gastrointestinal distress	Nausea, diarrhea, liver and kidney damage, joint pains, sterility, disruption of cardiac function, death
Magnesium	Widespread in foods and water (except soft water); especially found in grains, legumes, nuts, seeds, green vegetables, milk	Transmission of nerve impulses, energy transfer, activation of many enzymes	Neurological disturbances, cardiovascular problems, kidney disorders, nausea, growth failure in children	Nausea, vomiting, diarrhea, central nervous system depression, coma; death in people with impaired kidney function
Phosphorus	Present in nearly all foods, especially milk, cereal, peas, eggs, meat	Bone growth and maintenance, energy transfer in cells	Impaired growth, weakness, kidney disorders, cardiorespiratory and nervous system dysfunction	Drop in blood calcium levels, calcium deposits in soft tissues, bone loss
Potassium	Meats, milk, fruits, vegetables, grains, legumes	Nerve function and body water balance	Muscular weakness, nausea, drowsiness, paralysis, confusion, disruption of cardiac rhythm	Cardiac arrest
Selenium	Seafood, meat, eggs, whole grains	Defense against oxidative stress, regulation of thyroid hormone action	Muscle pain and weakness, heart disorders	Hair and nail loss, nausea and vomiting, weakness, irritability
Sodium	Salt, soy sauce, salted foods, tomato juice	Body water balance, acid-base balance, nerve function	Muscle weakness, loss of appetite, nausea, vomiting; deficiency is rarely seen	Edema, hypertension in sensitive people
Zinc	Whole grains, meat, eggs, liver, seafood (especially oysters)	Synthesis of proteins, RNA, and DNA; wound healing; immune response; ability to taste	Growth failure, loss of appetite, impaired taste acuity, skin rash, impaired immune function, poor wound healing	Vomiting, impaired immune function, decline in blood HDL levels, impaired copper absorption

SOURCES: Food and Nutrition Board, Institute of Medicine. 2006. *Dietary Reference Intakes: The Essential Guide to Nutrient Requirements.* Washington, D.C.: The National Academies Press. The complete Dietary Reference Intake reports are available from the National Academy Press (http://www.nap.edu); Shils, M. E., et al., eds. 2005. *Modern Nutrition in Health and Disease,* 10th ed. Baltimore: Lippincott Williams & Wilkins.

fumes, radiation, excessive sunlight, certain drugs, and stress can increase free radical production. A free radical is a chemically unstable molecule that reacts with fats, proteins, and DNA, damaging cell membranes and mutating genes. Free radicals have been implicated in aging, cancer, cardiovascular disease, and other degenerative diseases like arthritis.

Antioxidants found in foods can help protect the body from damage by free radicals in several ways. Some prevent or reduce the formation of free radicals; others remove free radicals from the body; still others repair some types of free radical damage after it occurs. Some antioxidants, such as vitamin C, vitamin E, and selenium, are also essential nutrients; others, such as carotenoids, found in yellow, orange, and deep-green vegetables, are not. Researchers recently identified the top antioxidant-containing foods and beverages as blackberries, walnuts, strawberries, artichokes, cranberries, brewed coffee, raspberries, pecans, blueberries, cloves, grape juice, unsweetened baking chocolate, sour cherries, and red

Take Charge

Eating for Healthy Bones

Osteoporosis is a condition in which bones become dangerously thin and fragile over time. An estimated 10 million Americans over age 50 have osteoporosis, and another 34 million are at risk. Most bone mass is built by age 18, and after bone density peaks between ages 25 and 35, bone mass is slowly lost over time. To prevent osteoporosis, the best strategy is to build as much bone as possible during your youth and then do everything you can to maintain it as you age. Up to 50% of bone loss is determined by controllable lifestyle factors, especially diet and exercise habits. Key nutrients include the following:

Calcium Consuming an adequate amount of calcium is important throughout life to build and maintain bone mass. Americans average 600–800 mg of calcium per day, only about half of what is recommended. Milk, yogurt, and calcium-fortified orange juice, bread, and cereals are all good sources. Nutritionists suggest that you obtain calcium from foods first and then take supplements only if needed to make up the difference.

Vitamin D Vitamin D is necessary for bones to absorb calcium; a daily intake of 5 μg is recommended for adults age 19–50. Vitamin D can be obtained from foods and is manufactured by the skin when it is exposed to sunlight. Candidates for vitamin D supplements include people who don't eat many foods rich in vitamin D; those who have dark skin or who don't expose their face, arms, and hands to the sun (without sunscreen) for 5–15 minutes a few times each week; and people who live north of an imaginary line roughly between Boston and the Oregon–California border (the sun is weaker in northern latitudes).

Vitamin K Vitamin K promotes the synthesis of proteins that help keep bones strong. Broccoli and leafy green vegetables are rich in vitamin K.

Other Nutrients Several other nutrients may play an important role in bone health.

- *Vitamin C* works with calcium and other minerals to build bone; it also helps produce the connective tissue collagen, which forms the scaffolding in bones.
- *Magnesium* aids in bone formation.
- *Potassium* helps bones retain calcium.
- *Manganese* may help lessen calcium losses.
- *Zinc* and *copper* help maintain collagen.
- *Boron* may increase calcium absorption.

Several dietary substances may have a *negative* effect on bone health. Alcohol reduces the body's ability to absorb calcium and may interfere with the bone-protecting effects of the hormone estrogen. High sodium intake increases calcium loss in the urine, and thus may lead to loss of calcium from the skeleton. Caffeine may also cause small losses of urinary calcium, and experts often recommend that heavy caffeine consumers take special care to include calcium-rich foods in their diet. Adding milk to coffee or tea may offset the effect of caffeine on calcium loss. Protein can help build bone if intake of calcium and vitamin D is adequate; however, if calcium and vitamin D intake is low, high protein intake may lead to calcium loss. Chronic excess intake of retinol, one form of vitamin A, is associated with decreased bone density; if you consume a vitamin supplement or vitamin A–fortified foods, try to limit your daily intake of retinol to no more than 100% of the RDA. (You may need to check labels to determine what form of vitamin A is present; beta-carotene, which the body can convert to vitamin A, is not associated with problems.) Drinking lots of soda, which often replaces milk in the diet and which is high in phosphorus (a mineral that may interfere with calcium absorption), has been shown to increase the risk of bone fracture in teenage girls. For healthy bones, then, it is important to be moderate in your consumption of alcohol, protein, sodium, caffeine, retinol, and sodas.

Finally, it is important to combine a healthy diet with regular exercise. Weight-bearing aerobic activities, if performed regularly, help build and maintain bone mass throughout life. Strength training improves bone density, muscle mass, strength, and balance, protecting against both bone loss and falls, a major cause of fractures. See Chapter 13 for tips on creating a complete, personalized exercise program.

wine. Also high in antioxidants are Brussels spouts, kale, cauliflower, and pomegranates.

Phytochemicals Antioxidants fall into the broader category of **phytochemicals,** substances found in plant foods that may help prevent chronic disease. Researchers have just begun to identify and study all the different compounds found in foods, and many preliminary findings are promising. For example, certain substances found in soy foods may help lower cholesterol levels. Sulforaphane, a compound isolated from broccoli and other **cruciferous vegetables,** may render some carcinogenic compounds harmless. Allyl sulfides, a group of chemicals found in garlic and onions, appear to boost the activity of cancer-fighting immune cells. Further research on phytochemicals may extend the role of nutrition to the prevention and treatment of many chronic diseases.

If you want to increase your intake of phytochemicals, it is best to obtain them by eating a variety of fruits, vegetables, and grains rather than relying on supplements. Like many vitamins and minerals, isolated phytochemicals may be harmful if taken in high doses. In addition, it is likely that their health benefits are the result of chemical substances working in combination. The role of phytochemicals in disease prevention is discussed further in Chapters 15 and 16.

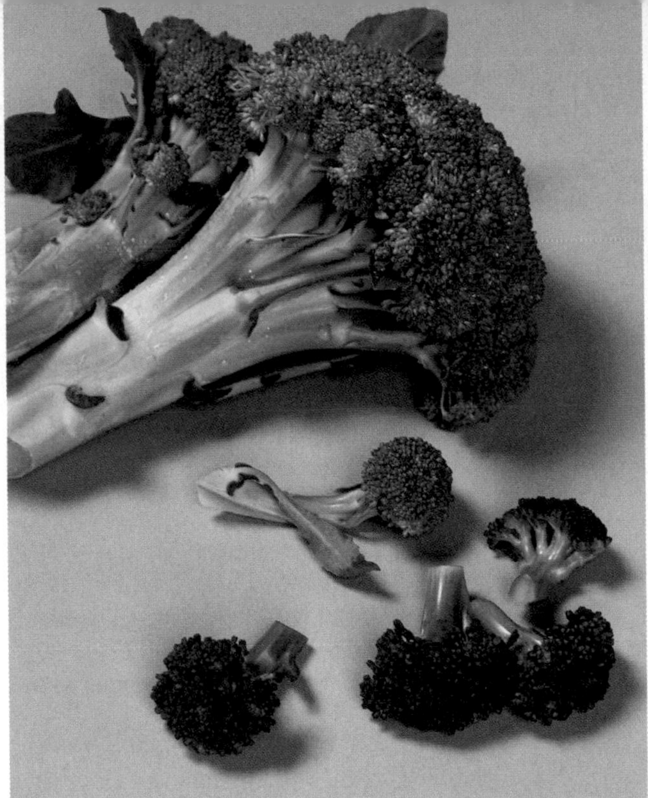

Cruciferous vegetables like broccoli are rich in phytochemicals and essential vitamins and minerals. Most Americans can obtain adequate amounts of essential nutrients as well as other beneficial compounds by consuming a healthy, varied diet that favors nutrient-dense foods.

NUTRITIONAL GUIDELINES: PLANNING YOUR DIET

The second part of putting together a healthy food plan—after you've learned about necessary nutrients—is choosing foods that satisfy nutritional requirements and meet your personal criteria. Various tools have been created by scientific and government groups to help people design healthy diets. The **Dietary Reference Intakes (DRIs)** are standards for nutrient intake designed to prevent nutritional deficiencies and reduce the risk of chronic disease. **Dietary Guidelines for Americans** have been established to promote health and reduce the risk for major chronic diseases through diet and physical activity. Further guidance symbolized by **MyPyramid** provides daily food intake patterns that meet the DRIs and are consistent with the Dietary Guidelines for Americans.

Dietary Reference Intakes (DRIs)

How much vitamin C, iron, calcium, and other nutrients do you need to stay healthy? The Food and Nutrition Board establishes dietary standards, or recommended intake levels, for Americans of all ages. The current set of standards, called Dietary Reference Intakes (DRIs), is relatively new, having been introduced in 1997. The DRIs are frequently reviewed and are updated as new nutrition-related information becomes available. The DRIs present different categories of nutrients in easy-to-read table format. An earlier set of standards, called the Recommended Dietary Allowances (RDAs), focused on preventing nutritional deficiency diseases such as anemia. The DRIs have a broader focus because of research that looked not just at the prevention of nutrient deficiencies but also at the role of nutrients in promoting optimal health and preventing chronic diseases such as cancer, osteoporosis, and heart disease.

The DRIs include standards for both recommended intakes and maximum safe intakes. The recommended intake of each nutrient is expressed as either a *Recommended Dietary Allowance (RDA)* or *Adequate Intake (AI)*. An AI is set when there is not enough information available to set an RDA value; regardless of the type of standard used, however, the DRI represents the best available estimate of intake for optimal health. The *Tolerable Upper Intake Level (UL)* sets the maximum daily intake that is unlikely to cause health problems in a healthy person. For example, the RDA for calcium for an 18-year-old female is 1300 mg per day; the UL is 2500 mg per day. Because of lack of data, ULs have not been set for all nutrients. This does not mean that people can tolerate chronic intakes of these vitamins and minerals above recommended levels. Like all chemical agents, nutrients can produce adverse effects if intakes are excessive. There is no established benefit from consuming nutrients at levels above the RDA or AI. The DRIs can be found in the Nutrition Resources section at the end of the chapter. (For more information, visit the Web site of the National Academies' Food and Nutrition Board; see For More Information at the end of the chapter.)

Should You Take Supplements? The aim of the DRIs is to guide you in meeting your nutritional needs primarily with food, rather than with vitamin and mineral supplements. Supplements lack potentially beneficial

Terms

VW

phytochemical A naturally occurring substance found in plant foods that may help prevent and treat chronic diseases like cancer and heart disease; *phyto* means plant.

cruciferous vegetables Vegetables of the cabbage family, including cabbage, broccoli, brussels sprouts, kale, and cauliflower; the flower petals of these plants form the shape of a cross, hence the name.

Dietary Reference Intakes (DRIs) An umbrella term for four types of nutrient standards: Adequate Intake (AI), Estimated Average Requirement (EAR), and Recommended Dietary Allowance (RDA) set levels of intake considered adequate to prevent nutrient deficiencies and reduce the risk of chronic disease; Tolerable Upper Intake Level (UL) sets the maximum daily intake that is unlikely to cause health problems.

Dietary Guidelines for Americans General principles of good nutrition intended to help prevent certain diet-related diseases.

MyPyramid A food-group plan that provides practical advice to ensure a balanced intake of the essential nutrients.

phytochemicals and fibers that are found only in whole foods. Most Americans can obtain the vitamins and minerals they need to prevent deficiencies by consuming a varied, nutritionally balanced diet. The use of supplements to reduce heart disease or cancer risk remains controversial; intake levels above the UL should be avoided.

The question of whether to take supplements is a serious one. Some vitamins and minerals are dangerous when ingested in excess, as shown in Tables 12-1 and 12-2. Large doses of particular nutrients can also cause health problems by affecting the absorption of other vitamins and minerals. For these reasons, think carefully about whether to take high-dose supplements; consider consulting a physician or registered dietitian.

In setting the DRIs, the Food and Nutrition Board recommended supplements of particular nutrients for the following groups:

- Women who are capable of becoming pregnant should obtain 400 μg per day of folic acid (the synthetic form of the vitamin folate) from fortified foods and/or supplements in addition to folate from a varied diet. Research indicates that this level of folate intake will reduce the risk of neural tube defects. (This defect occurs early in pregnancy, before most women know they are pregnant; therefore, the recommendation for the folate intake applies to all women of reproductive age rather than only to pregnant women.) Since 1998, enriched breads, flours, cornmeals, rice, noodles, and other grain products have been fortified with small amounts of folic acid. Folate is found naturally in leafy green vegetables, legumes, oranges and orange juice, and strawberries.
- People over age 50 should consume foods fortified with vitamin B-12, B-12 supplements, or a combination of the two in order to meet the majority of the RDA of 2.4 μg of B-12 daily. Up to 30% of people over 50 may have problems absorbing protein-bound B-12 in foods. Vitamin B-12 in supplements and fortified foods is more readily absorbed and can help prevent a deficiency.

Because of the oxidative stress caused by smoking, the Food and Nutrition Board also recommends that smokers consume 35 mg *more* vitamin C per day than the RDA set for their age and sex (for adults, recommended daily vitamin C intakes for nonsmokers are 90 mg for men and 75 mg for women). However, supplements are not usually needed because this extra vitamin C can easily be obtained from foods. For example, one cup of orange juice has about 100 mg of vitamin C.

Supplements may also be recommended in other cases. Women with heavy menstrual flows may need extra iron to compensate for the monthly loss. The elderly, people with dark skin, and people exposed to little sunlight may need extra vitamin D from vitamin D–fortified foods and/or supplements that contain vitamin D. Some vegetarians may need supplemental calcium, iron, zinc, and vitamin B-12, depending on their food choices. Newborns need a single dose of vitamin K, which must be administered under the direction of a physician. People who consume few calories, who have certain diseases, or who take certain medications may need specific vitamin and mineral supplements; such supplement decisions must be made by a physician because some vitamins and minerals counteract the actions of certain medications.

In deciding whether to take a vitamin and mineral supplement, consider whether you already regularly consume a fortified breakfast cereal. Many breakfast cereals contain almost as many nutrients as a multivitamin pill. If you do decide to take a supplement, choose a balanced formulation that contains 50–100% of the Daily Value (see below) for vitamins and minerals. Avoid supplements containing large doses of particular nutrients. See page 361 for more on choosing and using supplements.

Daily Values Because the DRIs are too cumbersome to use as a basis for food labels, the U.S. Food and Drug Administration uses another set of dietary standards, the **Daily Values.** The Daily Values are based on several different sets of guidelines and include standards for fat, cholesterol, carbohydrate, dietary fiber, and selected vitamins and minerals. The Daily Values represent appropriate intake levels for a 2000-calorie diet. The percent Daily Value shown on a food label shows how well that food contributes to your recommended daily intake. Food labels are described in detail later in the chapter.

Dietary Guidelines for Americans

To provide general guidance for choosing a healthy diet, the U.S. Department of Agriculture (USDA) and the U.S. Department of Health and Human Services (DHHS) have jointly issued Dietary Guidelines for Americans, most recently in 2005. These guidelines are intended for healthy children age 2 and older and adults of all ages. Key recommendations include the following:

- Consume a variety of nutrient-dense foods within and among the basic food groups, while staying within energy needs.
- Control calorie intake to manage body weight.
- Be physically active every day.
- Increase daily intake of foods from certain groups: fruits and vegetables, whole grains, and fat-free or low-fat milk and milk products.
- Choose fats wisely for good health, limiting intake of saturated and trans fats.
- Choose carbohydrates wisely for good health, limiting intake of added sugars.
- Choose and prepare foods with little salt, and consume potassium-rich foods.
- If you drink alcoholic beverages, do so in moderation.
- Keep foods safe to eat.

Following these guidelines promotes health and reduces risk for chronic diseases, including heart disease, cancer, diabetes, stroke, osteoporosis, and obesity. Each of the recommendations in the 2005 Dietary Guidelines for Americans is supported by an extensive review of scientific and medical evidence. What follows is a brief summary of the guidelines.

Adequate Nutrients within Calorie Needs Many people consume more calories than they need while failing to meet recommended intakes for all nutrients. Meeting the DRIs provides a foundation not only for current health but also for reducing chronic disease risk. Many adults don't eat enough calcium, potassium, fiber, magnesium, and vitamins A, C, and E; many children don't get enough calcium, potassium, fiber, magnesium, and vitamin E. Most people need to choose meals and snacks that are high in nutrients but low to moderate in calories.

Two eating plans that translate nutrient recommendations into food choices are the USDA's MyPyramid and the DASH eating plan. MyPyramid is described in detail in the next section (pp. 350–354); the DASH plan appears in the Nutrition Resources section at the end of the chapter. You can obtain all the nutrients and other substances you need by choosing the recommended number of daily servings from basic food groups and following the advice about selecting nutrient-dense foods within the groups. Following these plans would mean that many Americans would have to make some general dietary changes:

- Eat more dark green vegetables, orange vegetables, legumes, fruits, whole grains, and low-fat and fat-free milk and milk products.
- Eat less refined grains, saturated fat, trans fat, cholesterol, added sugars, and calories.

Your nutrients should come primarily from foods that contain not only the essential vitamins and minerals but also hundreds of naturally occurring substances that may benefit health, such as antioxidants. Situations in which a supplement might be recommended were described earlier in the chapter.

For maximum nutrition, it is important to consume foods from all the food groups daily and to consume a variety of nutrient-dense foods within the groups. Nutrient-dense foods are those that provide substantial amounts of vitamins and minerals and relatively few calories. Americans currently consume many foods and beverages that are low in nutrient density, making it difficult or impossible to meet nutrient needs without overconsuming calories. Selecting nutrient-dense foods—low-fat forms of foods in each group and those free of added sugars—allows you to meet your nutrient needs without overconsuming calories and unhealthy food components such as saturated and trans fats.

People's food choices can be affected by individual and cultural preferences, moral beliefs, the cost and availability of food, and food intolerances and allergies. But healthy eating is possible no matter how foods are prepared or combined (see the box "Ethnic Foods" on p. 346). If you avoid most or all foods from any of the major food groups, be sure to get enough nutrients from the other groups. MyPyramid can be applied to vegetarian diets.

Weight Management Overweight and obesity are a major public health problem in the United States. Calorie intake and physical activity (see next section) work together to influence body weight. Most Americans need to reduce the amount of calories they consume, increase their level of physical activity, and make wiser food choices. Many adults gain weight slowly over time, but even small changes in behavior can help avoid weight gain.

Evaluate your body weight in terms of body mass index (BMI), a measure of relative body weight that also takes height into account (see Chapter 14 for instructions on how to determine your BMI). If your current weight is healthy, aim to avoid weight gain. Do so by increasing physical activity and making small cuts in calorie intake. Choose nutrient-dense foods and sensible portion sizes. Avoiding weight gain is easier than losing weight: For example, for most adults, a reduction of 50 to 100 calories per day may prevent gradual weight gain, whereas a reduction of 500 calories or more per day may be needed initially for weight loss.

Monitoring weight regularly helps people know if they need to adjust their food intake or physical activity to maintain a healthy weight. Those who need to lose weight should aim for slow, steady weight loss by decreasing calorie intake, maintaining adequate nutrient intake, and increasing physical activity. In terms of macronutrient intake, use the AMDR ranges described earlier in the chapter for dietary planning; within these healthy ranges, total calorie intake is what counts for weight management rather than specific percentages of particular macronutrients.

Physical Activity Regular physical activity improves fitness, helps manage weight, promotes psychological well-being, and reduces risk of heart disease, high blood pressure, cancer, and diabetes. Become active if you are inactive, and maintain or increase physical activity if you are already active. The amount of daily physical activity recommended for you depends on your current health status and goals.

- To reduce the risk of chronic disease, aim to accumulate at least 30 minutes (adults) or 60 minutes (children) of moderate physical activity—the equivalent of brisk walking at a pace of 3–4 miles per hour—beyond your usual activity at work, home, and school. Greater health benefits can be obtained by engaging in more vigorous activity or activity of longer duration.

Term

VW

Daily Values A simplified version of the RDAs used on food labels; also included are values for nutrients with no RDA per se.

Ethnic Foods

There is no one ethnic diet that clearly surpasses all others in providing people with healthful foods. However, every diet has its advantages and disadvantages and, within each cuisine, some foods are better choices. The dietary guidelines described in this chapter can be applied to any ethnic cuisine. For additional guidance, refer to the table below.

	Choose More Often	**Choose Less Often**
Chinese	Dishes that are steamed, poached (jum), boiled (chu), roasted (kow), barbecued (shu), or lightly stir-fried Hoisin sauce, oyster sauce, wine sauce, plum sauce, velvet sauce, or hot mustard Fresh fish and seafood, skinless chicken, tofu Mixed vegetables, Chinese greens Steamed rice, steamed spring rolls, soft noodles	Fried wontons or egg rolls Crab rangoon Crispy (Peking) duck or chicken Sweet-and-sour dishes made with breaded and deep-fried meat, poultry, or fish Fried rice Fried or crispy noodles
French	Dishes prepared au vapeur (steamed), en brochette (skewered and broiled), or grillé (grilled) Fresh fish, shrimp, scallops, or mussels or skinless chicken, without sauces Clear soups	Dishes prepared à la crème (in cream sauce), au gratin or gratinée (baked with cream and cheese), or en croûte (in pastry crust) Drawn butter, hollandaise sauce, and remoulade (mayonnaise-based sauce)
Greek	Dishes that are stewed, broiled, or grilled, including shish kebabs (souvlaki) Dolmas (grape leaves) stuffed with rice Tzatziki (yogurt, cucumbers, and garlic) Tabouli (bulgur-based salad) Pita bread, especially whole wheat	Moussaka, saganaki (fried cheese) Vegetable pies such as spanakopita and tyropita Baba ghanoush (eggplant and olive oil) Deep-fried falafel (chickpea patties) Gyros stuffed with ground meat Baklava
Indian	Dishes prepared masala (curry), tandoori (roasted in a clay oven), or tikke (pan roasted); kebabs Raita (yogurt and cucumber salad) and other yogurt-based dishes and sauces Dal (lentils), pullao or pilau (basmati rice) Chapati (baked bread)	Ghee (clarified butter) Korma (meat in cream sauce) Samosas, pakoras (fried dishes) Molee and other coconut milk–based dishes Poori, bhatura, or paratha (fried breads)
Italian	Pasta primavera or pasta, polenta, risotto, or gnocchi with marinara, red or white wine, white or red clam, or light mushroom sauce Dishes that are grilled or prepared cacciatore (tomato-based sauce), marsala (broth and wine sauce), or piccata (lemon sauce) Cioppino (seafood stew) Vegetable soup, minestrone or fagioli (beans)	Antipasto (cheese, smoked meats) Dishes that are prepared alfredo, frito (fried), crema (creamed), alla panna (with cream), or carbonara Veal scaloppini Chicken, veal, or eggplant parmigiana Italian sausage, salami, and prosciutto Buttered garlic bread Cannoli
Japanese	Dishes prepared nabemono (boiled), shabu-shabu (in boiling broth), mushimono (steamed), nimono (simmered), yaki (broiled), or yakimono (grilled) Sushi or domburi (mixed rice dish) Steamed rice or soba (buckwheat), udon (wheat), or rice noodles	Tempura (battered and fried) Agemono (deep fried) Katsu (fried pork cutlet) Sukiyaki Fried tofu
Mexican	Soft corn or wheat tortillas Burritos, fajitas, enchiladas, soft tacos, and tamales filled with beans, vegetables, or lean meats Refried beans, nonfat or low-fat; rice and beans Ceviche (fish marinated in lime juice) Salsa, enchilada sauce, and picante sauce Gazpacho, menudo, or black bean soup Fruit or flan for dessert	Crispy, fried tortillas Dishes that are fried, such as chile relleños, chimichangas, flautas, and tostadas Nachos and cheese, chili con queso, and other dishes made with cheese or cheese sauce Guacamole, sour cream, and extra cheese Refried beans made with lard Fried ice cream
Thai	Dishes that are barbecued, sautéed, broiled, boiled, steamed, braised, or marinated Sâté (skewered and grilled meats) Fish sauce, basil sauce, chili or hot sauces Bean thread noodles, Thai salad	Coconut milk soup Peanut sauce or dishes topped with nuts Mee-krob (crispy noodles) Red, green, and yellow curries, which typically contain coconut milk

SOURCES: National Heart, Lung and Blood Institute. 2006. *Guidelines on Overweight and Obesity: Electronic Textbook* (http://www.nhlbi.nih.gov/guidelines/obesity/e_txtbk/appndx/6a3b.htm; retrieved June 24, 2006). Duyff, R. L. 2006. *The American Dietetic Association's Complete Food and Nutrition Guide*, 2nd ed. Hoboken, N.J.: Wiley.

- To help manage body weight and prevent gradual, unhealthy weight gain, engage in 60 minutes of moderately to vigorously intense activity on most days of the week.
- To sustain weight loss in adulthood, engage daily in at least 60–90 minutes of moderate physical activity.

You can do the activity all at once or spread it out over several 10-minute or longer bouts during the day; choose activities you enjoy and can do regularly. You can boost fitness by engaging in exercises specifically designed for the health-related fitness components: cardiorespiratory endurance exercises, stretching exercises for flexibility, and resistance training for muscular strength and endurance. See Chapter 13 for advice on increasing daily physical activity and creating a complete fitness program.

Food Groups to Encourage Many Americans do not consume the recommended amounts of fruits, vegetables, whole grains, and low-fat or fat-free milk products—all of which have health benefits.

FRUITS AND VEGETABLES Fruits and vegetables are important sources of dietary fiber, vitamins, and minerals. For a 2000-calorie diet, about 4½ cups or the equivalent (9 servings) of fruits and vegetables each day is recommended. Eat a variety of fruits—fresh, frozen, canned, or dried—rather than fruit juice for most of your fruit choices. For vegetables, choose a variety of colors and kinds. Eat more of the following types of vegetables:

- Dark green vegetables, such as broccoli, kale, and other dark leafy greens
- Orange vegetables, such as carrots, sweet potatoes, pumpkin, and winter squash
- Legumes, such as pinto beans, kidney beans, black beans, garbanzo beans, split peas, and lentils

Other fruits and vegetables that are important sources of nutrients of concern include tomatoes and tomato products, red sweet peppers, cabbage and other cruciferous vegetables, bananas, citrus fruits, berries, and melons. See the discussion of MyPyramid for more advice on choosing fruits and vegetables.

WHOLE GRAINS Whole grains provide more fiber and nutrients than refined grains, and intake of whole grains reduces the risk of chronic disease and helps with weight maintenance. For a 2000-calorie diet, 6 ounce-equivalents (6 servings) of grains each day are recommended; at least half of these servings should be whole grains. (One ounce is about 1 slice of bread, 1 cup of breakfast cereal flakes, or ½ cup of cooked pasta or rice.) The remaining grain servings should be from enriched or whole-grain products. Refer back to p. 336 for information on identifying whole-grain products.

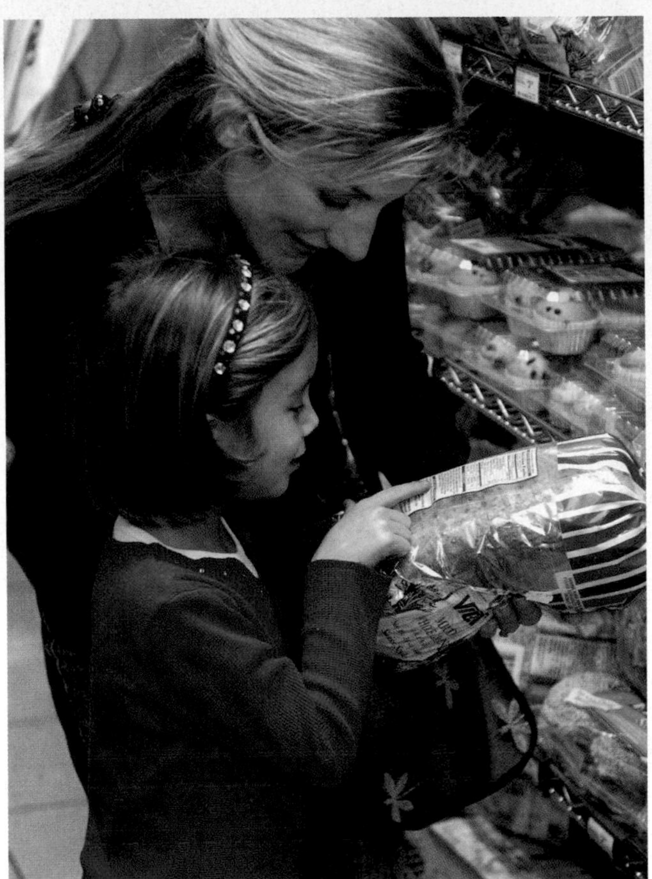

Whole grains provide more nutrients and fiber than refined grains, and they may help reduce the risk of chronic disease. Half of your daily grain servings should come from whole grains. To check if a food contains whole grains, read the ingredient list on the food label.

LOW-FAT AND FAT-FREE MILK AND MILK PRODUCTS Milk and other dairy products are important sources of calcium and other nutrients. Regular consumption of milk and milk products can reduce the risk of low bone mass throughout life. Choosing low-fat and fat-free dairy products helps to control calorie intake and reduce intake of saturated fat and cholesterol. For adults, the equivalent of 3 daily cups of fat-free or low-fat milk or milk products is recommended; 1½ ounces of cheese is the equivalent of 1 cup of milk. Yogurt and lactose-free milk are options for people who are lactose intolerant, as is use of the enzyme lactase prior to the consumption of milk products. For individuals who avoid all milk products, nondairy calcium sources include fortified cereals and beverages, tofu prepared with calcium sulfate, green leafy vegetables, soybeans, and certain types of fish.

Fats Fats and oils provide the essential fatty acids needed for a healthy diet, but, as described earlier in the chapter, the type and amount of fats consumed can make a difference for health. A diet low in saturated fat, trans fat, and cholesterol helps keep blood cholesterol low and reduces the risk for heart disease; a diet containing

Take Charge

Reducing the Saturated and Trans Fats in Your Diet

Your overall goal is to limit total fat intake to no more than 35% of total calories. Within that limit, favor unsaturated fats from vegetable oils, nuts, and fish over saturated and trans fats from animal products and foods made with hydrogenated vegetable oils or shortening. Saturated and trans fat intake should be kept as low as possible within a nutritionally adequate diet.

- Be moderate in your consumption of foods high in fat, including fast food, commercially prepared baked goods and desserts, deep-fried foods, meat, poultry, nuts and seeds, and regular dairy products.
- When you do eat high-fat foods, limit your portion sizes, and balance your intake with other foods that are low in fat.
- Choose lean cuts of meat, and trim any visible fat from meat before and after cooking. Remove skin from poultry before or after cooking.
- Drink fat-free or low-fat milk instead of whole milk, and use lower-fat varieties in puddings, soups, and baked products. Substitute plain low-fat yogurt, blender-whipped low-fat cottage cheese, or buttermilk for sour cream.
- Use vegetable oil instead of butter or margarine. Use tub or squeeze margarine instead of stick margarine. Look for margarines that are free of trans fats. Minimize intake of coconut or palm oil.
- Season vegetables, seafood, and meats with herbs and spices rather than with creamy sauces, butter, or margarine.
- Try lemon juice on salad, or use a yogurt-based salad dressing instead of mayonnaise or sour cream dressings.
- Steam, boil, bake, or microwave vegetables, or stir-fry them in a small amount of vegetable oil.
- Roast, bake, or broil meat, poultry, or fish so that fat drains away as the food cooks.
- Use a nonstick pan for cooking so that added fat will be unnecessary; use a vegetable spray for frying. Kitchen stores sell non-aerosol spray bottles to use with regular cooking oils.
- Chill broths from meat or poultry until the fat becomes solid. Spoon off the fat before using the broth.
- Substitute egg whites for whole eggs when baking; limit the number of egg yolks when scrambling eggs.
- Choose fruits as desserts most often.
- Eat a low-fat vegetarian main dish at least once a week.

omega-3 fats from fish also reduces the risk for heart disease. Goals for fat intake for most adults are as follows:

Total fat: 20–35% of total daily calories

Saturated fat: Less than 10% of total daily calories

Trans fat: As little as possible

Cholesterol: Less than 300 mg per day

Most fats in the diet should come from sources of unsaturated fats, such as fish, nuts, and vegetable oils. When selecting and preparing meat, poultry, dry beans, and milk or milk products, make choices that are lean, low-fat, or fat-free. To reduce trans fat intake, limit intake of foods made with hydrogenated vegetable oils. Refer to the box "Reducing the Saturated and Trans Fats in Your Diet" for additional specific suggestions.

Cholesterol is found only in animal foods. If you need to reduce your cholesterol intake, limit your intake of foods that are particularly high in cholesterol, including egg yolks, dairy fats, certain shellfish, and liver and other organ meats; watch your serving sizes of animal foods. Food labels list the fat and cholesterol content of foods.

Two servings per week of fish rich in heart-healthy omega-3 fatty acids are also recommended for people at high risk for heart disease. However, for certain groups, intake limits are set for varieties of fish that may contain mercury; see page 364 for more information. Fish rich in omega-3 fatty acids include salmon, mackerel, and trout.

Carbohydrates Carbohydrates are an important energy source in a healthy diet. Foods rich in carbohydrates may also be rich in dietary fiber, which promotes healthy digestion and helps reduce the risk of type 2 diabetes and heart disease. Fruits, vegetables, whole grains, and fat-free or low-fat milk can provide the recommended amount of carbohydrate. Choose fiber-rich foods often—for example, whole fruits, whole grains, and legumes.

People who consume foods and beverages high in added sugars tend to consume more calories but smaller amounts of vitamins and minerals than those who limit their intake of added sugars. A food is likely high in sugar if one of the following appears first or second in the list of ingredients or if several are listed: sugar (any type, including beet, brown, invert, raw, and cane), corn syrup or sweetener, fruit juice concentrate, honey, malt syrup, molasses, syrup, cane juice, or dextrose, fructose, glucose, lactose, maltose, or sucrose.

To reduce added sugar consumption, cut back on soft drinks, candies, sweet desserts, fruit drinks, and other foods high in added sugars. Watch out for specialty drinks like café mochas, chai tea, smoothies, and sports drinks, which can contain hundreds of extra calories from sugar. Drink water rather than sweetened drinks, and don't let sodas and other sweets crowd out more nutritious foods, such as low-fat milk. Regular soda is the leading source of both added sugars and calories in the American diet, but it provides little in the way of nutrients except sugar (Figure 12-4). The 10 teaspoons of sugar in a 12-ounce soda can exceed the

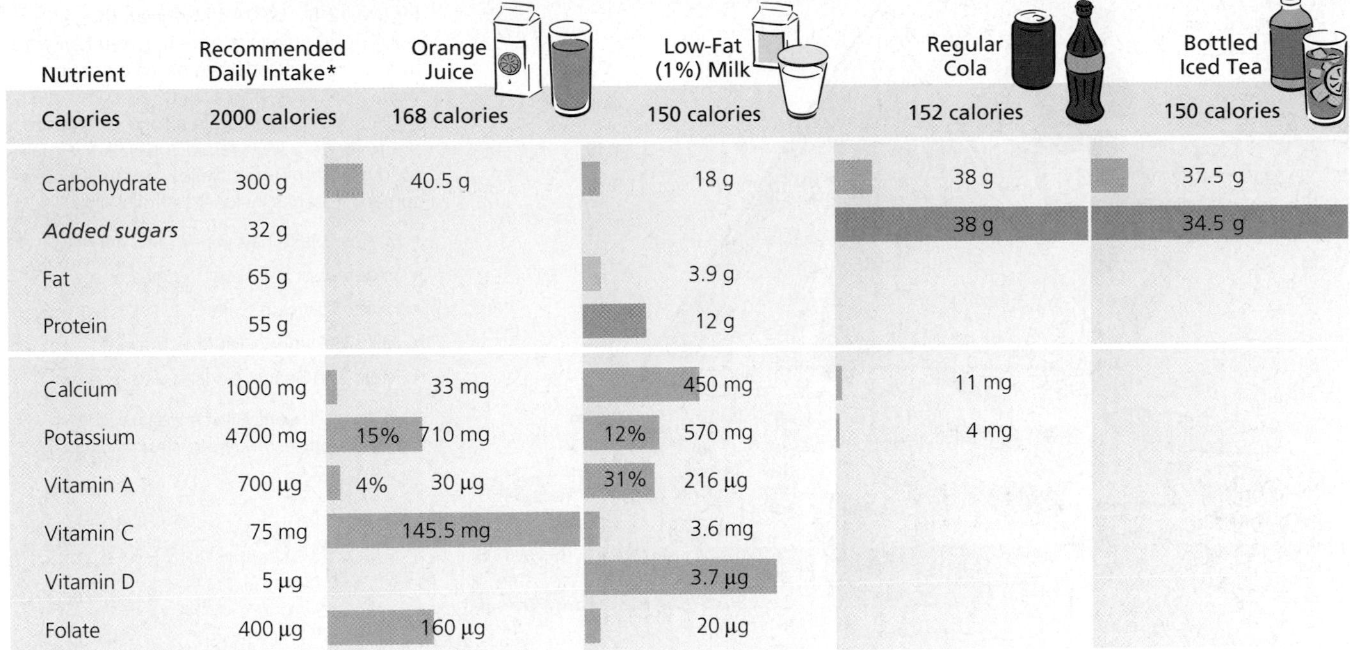

Nutrient	Recommended Daily Intake*	Orange Juice	Low-Fat (1%) Milk	Regular Cola	Bottled Iced Tea
Calories	2000 calories	168 calories	150 calories	152 calories	150 calories
Carbohydrate	300 g	40.5 g	18 g	38 g	37.5 g
Added sugars	32 g			38 g	34.5 g
Fat	65 g		3.9 g		
Protein	55 g		12 g		
Calcium	1000 mg	33 mg	450 mg	11 mg	
Potassium	4700 mg	15% 710 mg	12% 570 mg	4 mg	
Vitamin A	700 µg	4% 30 µg	31% 216 µg		
Vitamin C	75 mg	145.5 mg	3.6 mg		
Vitamin D	5 µg		3.7 µg		
Folate	400 µg	160 µg	20 µg		

*Recommended intakes and limits appropriate for a 20-year-old woman consuming 2000 calories per day.

Figure 12-4 Nutrient density of 12-ounce portions of selected beverages. The four beverages shown have approximately the same number of calories in a 12-ounce serving. However, regular cola and iced tea provide few nutrients besides added sugars; both contain more than the total daily recommended limit of added sugars (about 8 teaspoons). Orange juice is rich in potassium, vitamin C, and folate; low-fat milk is an excellent source of protein, calcium, potassium, vitamin A, and vitamin D. (Color bars represent percentage of recommended daily intake or limit for each nutrient.)

recommended daily limit for added sugars for someone consuming 2000 calories per day; for more on added sugar limits, see the discussion of MyPyramid.

Keep your teeth and gums healthy by limiting consumption of sweet or starchy foods between meals and brushing and flossing regularly; drinking fluoridated water also reduces the risk of dental caries.

Sodium and Potassium Many people can reduce their chance of developing high blood pressure or lower already elevated blood pressure by consuming less salt; reducing blood pressure lowers the risk for stroke, heart disease, and kidney disease. Salt is made up of the minerals sodium and chloride, and although both of these minerals are essential for normal body function, we need only small amounts (1500 mg per day for adults). Most Americans consume much more salt than they need. The goal is to reduce sodium intake to less than 2300 milligrams per day, the equivalent of about 1 teaspoon of salt. Certain groups, including people with hypertension, African Americans, and older adults, benefit from an even lower sodium intake (no more than 1500 mg per day).

Salt is found mainly in processed and prepared foods; smaller amounts may also be added during cooking or at the table. To lower your intake of salt, choose fresh or plain frozen meat, poultry, seafood, and vegetables most often; these are lower in salt than processed forms are. Check and compare the sodium content in processed foods, including frozen dinners, cheeses, soups, salad dressings, sauces, and canned mixed dishes. Add less salt during cooking and at the table, and limit your use of high-sodium condiments like soy sauce, ketchup, mustard, pickles, and olives. Use lemon juice, herbs, and spices instead of salt to enhance the flavor of foods.

Along with lowering salt intake, increasing potassium intake helps lower blood pressure. Fruits, vegetables, and most milk products are available in forms that contain no salt, and many of these are sources of potassium. Potassium-rich foods include leafy green vegetables, sweet and white potatoes, winter squash, soybeans, tomato sauce, bananas, peaches, apricots, cantaloupes, and orange juice.

Alcoholic Beverages Alcoholic beverages supply calories but few nutrients. Drinking in moderation—that is, no more than one drink per day for women and no more than two drinks per day for men—is associated with mortality reduction among some groups, primarily males age 45 and older and women age 55 and older. Among younger people, alcohol use provides little if any health benefit, and heavy drinking is associated with motor vehicle injuries and deaths, liver disease, stroke, violence, and other health problems (see Chapter 10 for more on the health risks and potential benefits of alcohol use).

People who should not drink at all include individuals who cannot restrict their drinking to moderate levels; women who are pregnant or breastfeeding or who may become pregnant; children and adolescents; people with specific health conditions; individuals who plan to drive or

Figure 12-5 USDA's MyPyramid. The USDA food guidance system, called MyPyramid, can be personalized based on an individual's sex, age, and activity level; visit MyPyramid.gov to obtain a food plan appropriate for you. MyPyramid contains five main food groups plus oils (yellow band). Key consumer messages include the following:

- Grains: Make half your grains whole
- Vegetables: Vary your veggies
- Fruits: Focus on fruits
- Milk: Get your calcium-rich foods
- Meat and Beans: Go lean with protein

SOURCE: U.S. Department of Agriculture. 2005. *MyPyramid* (http://www.mypyramid.gov; retrieved August 15, 2006).

operate machinery or engage in any activity that requires attention, skill, or coordination; and individuals taking prescription or over-the-counter medications that can interact with alcohol. If you choose to drink alcoholic beverages, do so sensibly, moderately, and with meals. Never drink in situations where it may put you or others at risk.

Food Safety Safe foods are those that pose little risk from harmful bacteria, viruses, parasites, toxins, or chemical or physical contaminants. Foodborne diseases affect about 76 million Americans each year. Actions by consumers can reduce the occurrence of foodborne illness significantly. It is especially important to be careful with perishable foods such as poultry, meats, eggs, shellfish, milk products, and fresh fruits and vegetables. Refer to the section "Protecting Yourself Against Foodborne Illness" (pp. 360–363) for specific food safety tips.

Some organizations, such as the American Cancer Society (ACS), have additional recommendations to reduce cancer risk, including not smoking and limiting intake of salt-cured, smoked, and nitrite-cured foods such as bacon or sausage. Curing and smoking of foods help make food safer, but nitrites have been associated with an increased risk of colon and other gastrointestinal cancers in some people. The addition of vitamin C and other antioxidants to cured meats cuts the risk, but these foods should still be consumed in moderation because they are often high in saturated fat, cholesterol, and sodium. The latest ACS guidelines on nutrition and physical activity for cancer prevention are discussed in Chapter 16.

USDA's MyPyramid

When the first USDA daily food guide was published, in 1916, it emphasized the importance of getting enough calories from fats and sugars to support daily activity. Today, the guidelines stress the importance of limiting fats and sugars to control calorie intake. Many Americans are familiar with the USDA Food Guide Pyramid, the food guidance system that was first released in 1992. Since the initial release of the Pyramid, scientists have updated both nutrient recommendations (the DRIs) and the Dietary Guidelines for Americans. So, as the 2005 Dietary Guidelines were prepared, the USDA reassessed its overall food guidance system and released MyPyramid in April 2005 (Figure 12-5).

A variety of experts have proposed other food-group plans. Some of these address perceived shortcomings in the USDA plans, and some adapt the basic 1992 Pyramid to special populations. Two alternative food plans appear in the Nutrition Resources section at the end of the chapter: The DASH eating plan and the Harvard Healthy Eating Pyramid. The USDA Center for Nutrition Policy and Promotion (www.usda.gov/cnpp) has more on alternative food plans for special populations such as young children, older adults, and people choosing particular ethnic diets. MyPyramid is available in Spanish, and there is a special adaptation of MyPyramid for children age 6–11, called MyPyramid for Kids. (www.mypyramid.gov/kids).

Another food plan that has received attention in recent years is the Mediterranean diet, which emphasizes vegetables, fruits, and whole grains; daily servings of beans, legumes, and nuts; moderate consumption of fish, poultry, and dairy products; and the use of olive oil over other types of fat, especially saturated fat. The Mediterranean diet has been associated with lower rates of heart disease and cancer, and a 2006 study found a link between the diet and a greatly reduced risk of Alzheimer's disease.

Key Messages of MyPyramid The new MyPyramid symbol (see Figure 12-5) has been developed to remind consumers to make healthy food choices and to be active every day. Consuming a balance of servings from each food group will not only meet nutrient needs but also help to reduce chronic disease risk. Key messages include the following:

- *Personalization* is represented by the person on the steps and the MyPyramid.gov site, which includes individualized recommendations, interactive assessments of food intake and physical activity, and tips for success.
- *Daily physical activity*, represented by the person climbing the steps, is important for maintaining a healthy weight and reducing the risk of chronic disease.
- *Moderation* of food intake is represented by the narrowing of each food group from bottom to top. The wider base stands for foods with little or no solid fats or added sugars, which should be selected more often; the narrower top represents food containing more solid fats and added sugars, which should be limited.
- *Proportionality* is represented by the different widths of the food group bands. The widths provide a general guide for how much food a person should choose from each group.
- *Variety* is represented by the six color bands representing the five food groups of MyPyramid and oils. Foods from all groups are needed daily for good health.
- *Gradual improvement* is a good strategy; people can benefit from taking small steps to improve their diet and activity habits each day.

The MyPyramid chart in Figure 12-6 (p. 352) shows the food intake patterns recommended for different levels of calorie intake; Table 12-3 (p. 353) provides guidance for determining an appropriate calorie intake for weight maintenance. Use the table to identify an energy intake that is about right for you; then refer to the appropriate column in Figure 12-6. A personalized version of MyPyramid recommendations can also be obtained by visiting MyPyramid.gov. Each food group is described briefly below. Past experiences have shown that many Americans have trouble identifying serving sizes, so recommended daily intakes from each group are now given in terms of cups and ounces; see the box "Judging Portion Sizes" (p. 353) for additional advice.

Grains Foods from this group are usually low in fat and rich in complex carbohydrates, dietary fiber (if grains are unrefined), and many vitamins and minerals, including thiamin, riboflavin, iron, niacin, folic acid (if enriched or fortified), and zinc. Someone eating 2000 calories a day should include 6 ounce-equivalents each day, with half of those servings from whole grains such as whole-grain bread, whole-wheat pasta, high-fiber cereal, and brown rice. The following count as 1 ounce-equivalent:

- 1 slice of bread
- 1 small (2½-inch diameter) muffin
- 1 cup ready-to-eat cereal flakes
- ½ cup cooked cereal, rice, grains, or pasta
- 1 6-inch tortilla

Choose foods that are typically made with little fat or sugar (bread, rice, pasta) over those that are high in fat and sugar (croissants, chips, cookies, doughnuts).

Vegetables Vegetables contain carbohydrates, dietary fiber, vitamin A, vitamin C, folate, potassium, and other nutrients. They are also naturally low in fat. In a 2000-calorie diet, 2½ cups (5 servings) of vegetables should be included daily. Each of the following counts as 1 serving (½ cup or equivalent) of vegetables:

- ½ cup raw or cooked vegetables
- 1 cup raw leafy salad greens
- ½ cup vegetable juice

Because vegetables vary in the nutrients they provide, it is important to consume a variety of types of vegetables to obtain maximum nutrition. Many Americans consume only a few types of vegetables, with white potatoes (baked or served as french fries) being the most popular. To help boost variety, MyPyramid recommends servings from five different subgroups within the vegetables group; try to consume vegetables from several subgroups each day. (For clarity, Figure 12-6 shows servings from the subgroups in terms of weekly consumption.)

- Dark green vegetables like spinach, chard, collards, bok choy, broccoli, kale, romaine, and turnip and mustard greens
- Orange and deep yellow vegetables like carrots, winter squash, sweet potatoes, and pumpkin
- Legumes like pinto beans, kidney beans, black beans, lentils, chickpeas, soybeans, split peas, and tofu; legumes can be counted as servings of vegetables *or* as alternatives to meat
- Starchy vegetables like corn, green peas, and white potatoes
- Other vegetables; tomatoes, bell peppers (red, orange, yellow, or green), green beans, and cruciferous vegetables like cauliflower are good choices

Fruits Fruits are rich in carbohydrates, dietary fiber, and many vitamins, especially vitamin C. For someone eating a 2000-calorie diet, 2 cups (4 servings) of fruits are recommended daily. The following each count as 1 serving (½ cup or equivalent) of fruit:

- ½ cup fresh, canned, or frozen fruit
- ½ cup fruit juice (100% juice)
- 1 small whole fruit
- ¼ cup dried fruit

Good choices from this group are citrus fruits and juices, melons, pears, apples, bananas, and berries. Choose

Daily Amount of Food from Each Group

Food group amounts shown in cups (c) or ounce-equivalents (oz-eq), with number of daily servings (srv) shown in parentheses; vegetable subgroup amounts are per week

Calorie level	1600	1800	2000	2200	2400	2600	2800	3000
Grains	5 oz-eq	6 oz-eq	6 oz-eq	7 oz-eq	8 oz-eq	9 oz-eq	10 oz-eq	10 oz-eq
Whole grains	3 oz-eq	3 oz-eq	3 oz-eq	3.5 oz-eq	4 oz-eq	4.5 oz-eq	5 oz-eq	5 oz-eq
Other grains	2 oz-eq	3 oz-eq	3 oz-eq	3.5 oz-eq	4 oz-eq	4.5 oz-eq	5 oz-eq	5 oz-eq
Vegetables	2 c (4 srv)	2.5 c (5 srv)	2.5 c (5 srv)	3c (6 srv)	3 c (6 srv)	3.5 c (7 srv)	3.5 c (7 srv)	4 c (8 srv)
Dark green	2 c/wk	3 c/wk	3 c/wk	3 c/wk	3 c/wk	3 c/wk	3 c/wk	3 c/wk
Orange	1.5 c/wk	2 c/wk	2 c/wk	2 c/wk	2 c/wk	2.5 c/wk	2.5 c/wk	2.5 c/wk
Legumes	2.5 c/wk	3 c/wk	3 c/wk	3 c/wk	3 c/wk	3.5 c/wk	3.5 c/wk	3.5 c/wk
Starchy	2.5 c/wk	3 c/wk	3 c/wk	6 c/wk	6 c/wk	7 c/wk	7 c/wk	9 c/wk
Other	5.5 c/wk	6.5 c/wk	6.5 c/wk	7 c/wk	7 c/wk	8.5 c/wk	8.5 c/wk	10 c/wk
Fruits	1.5 c (3 srv)	1.5 c (3 srv)	2 c (4 srv)	2 c (4 srv)	2 c (4 srv)	2 c (4 srv)	2.5 c (5 srv)	2.5 c (5 srv)
Milk	3 c	3 c	3 c	3 c	3 c	3 c	3 c	3 c
Lean meat and beans	5 oz-eq	5 oz-eq	5.5 oz-eq	6 oz-eq	6.5 oz-eq	6.5 oz-eq	7 oz-eq	7 oz-eq
Oils	5 tsp	5 tsp	6 tsp	6 tsp	7 tsp	8 tsp	8 tsp	10 tsp

The discretionary calorie allowances shown below are the calories remaining at each level after nutrient-dense foods in each food group are selected. Those trying to lose weight may choose not to use discretionary calories. For those wanting to maintain weight, discretionary calories may be used to increase the amount of food from each food group; to consume foods that are not in the lowest fat form or that contain added sugars; to add oil, fat, or sugars to foods; or to consume alcohol. The amounts below show how discretionary calories may be divided between solid fats and added sugars.

Discretionary calories	132	195	267	290	362	410	426	512
Solid fats	11 g	15 g	18 g	19 g	22 g	24 g	24 g	29 g
Added sugars	12 g (3 tsp)	20 g (5 tsp)	32 g (8 tsp)	38 g (9 tsp)	48 g (12 tsp)	56 g (14 tsp)	60 g (15 tsp)	72 g (18 tsp)

Figure 12-6 MyPyramid food intake patterns. To determine an appropriate amount of food from each group, find the column with your approximate daily energy intake. That column lists the daily recommended intake from each food group. Visit MyPyramid.gov for a personalized intake plan and for intakes for other calorie levels. SOURCE: U.S. Department of Health and Human Services and U.S. Department of Agriculture. 2005. *Dietary Guidelines for Americans*, 2005, *Appendix A. Eating Patterns* (http://www.health.gov/dietaryguidelines/dga2005/document/html/appendixA.htm; retrieved August 15, 2006).

whole fruits often—they are higher in fiber and often lower in calories than fruit juices. Fruit *juices* typically contain more nutrients and less added sugar than fruit *drinks*. For canned fruits, choose those packed in 100% fruit juice or water rather than in syrup.

Milk This group includes all milk and milk products, such as yogurt, cheeses (except cream cheese), and dairy desserts, as well as lactose-free and lactose-reduced products. Foods from this group are high in protein, carbohydrate, calcium, riboflavin, and vitamin D (if fortified). Those consuming 2000 calories per day should include 3 cups of milk or the equivalent daily. Each of the following counts as the equivalent of 1 cup:

- 1 cup milk or yogurt
- ½ cup ricotta cheese
- 1½ ounces natural cheese
- 2 ounces processed cheese

Take Charge

Judging Portion Sizes

Studies have shown that most people underestimate the size of their food portions, in many cases by as much as 50%. If you need to retrain your eye, try using measuring cups and spoons and an inexpensive kitchen scale when you eat at home. With a little practice, you'll learn the difference between 3 and 8 ounces of chicken or meat, and what a half-cup of rice really looks like. For quick estimates, use the following equivalents:

- 1 teaspoon of margarine = the tip of your thumb
- 1 ounce of cheese = your thumb, four dice stacked together, or an ice cube
- 3 ounces of chicken or meat = a deck of cards or an audiocassette tape
- 1 cup of pasta = a small fist or a tennis ball
- ½ cup of rice or cooked vegetables = an ice cream scoop or one-third of a can of soda
- 2 tablespoons of peanut butter = a ping-pong ball or large marshmallow
- 1 medium potato = a computer mouse
- 1–2-ounce muffin or roll = plum or large egg
- 2-ounce bagel = hockey puck or yo-yo
- 1 medium fruit (apple or orange) = baseball
- ¼ cup nuts = golf ball
- Small cookie or cracker = poker chip

Table 12-3 MyPyramid Daily Calorie Intake Levels

Age (years)	Sedentary[a]	Moderately Active[b]	Active[c]
Child			
2–3	1000	1000–1400	1000–1400
Female			
4–8	1200–1400	1400–1600	1400–1800
9–13	1400–1600	1600–2000	1800–2200
14–18	1800	2000	2400
19–30	1800–2000	2000–2200	2400
31–50	1800	2000	2200
51+	1600	1800	2000–2200
Male			
4–8	1200–1400	1400–1600	1600–2000
9–13	1600–2000	1800–2200	2000–2600
14–18	2000–2400	2400–2800	2800–3200
19–30	2400–2600	2600–2800	3000
31–50	2200–2400	2400–2600	2800–3000
51+	2000–2200	2200–2400	2400–2800

[a]A lifestyle that includes only the light physical activity associated with typical day-to-day life.
[b]A lifestyle that includes physical activity equivalent to walking about 1.5 to 3 miles per day at 3 to 4 miles per hour (30–60 minutes a day of moderate physical activity), in addition to the light physical activity associated with typical day-to-day life.
[c]A lifestyle that includes physical activity equivalent to walking more than 3 miles per day at 3 to 4 miles per hour (60 or more minutes a day of moderate physical activity), in addition to the light physical activity associated with typical day-to-day life.

SOURCE: U.S. Department of Agriculture. 2005. *MyPyramid Food Intake Pattern Calorie Levels* (http://www.mypyramid.gov/downloads/MyPyramid_Calorie_Levels.pdf; retrieved August 16, 2006).

Cottage cheese is lower in calcium than most other cheeses; ½ cup is equivalent to ¼ cup milk. Ice cream is also lower in calcium and higher in sugar and fat than many other dairy products; one scoop counts as ⅓ cup milk. To limit calories and saturated fat in your diet, it is best to choose servings of low-fat and fat-free items from this group.

Meat and Beans This group includes meat, poultry, fish, dry beans and peas, eggs, nuts, and seeds. These foods provide protein, niacin, iron, vitamin B-6, zinc, and thiamin; the animal foods in the group also provide vitamin B-12. For someone consuming a 2000-calorie diet, 5½ ounce-equivalents is recommended. Each of the following counts as equivalent to 1 ounce:

- 1 ounce cooked lean meat, poultry, or fish
- ¼ cup cooked dry beans (legumes) or tofu
- 1 egg
- 1 tablespoon peanut butter
- ½ ounce nuts or seeds

One egg at breakfast, ½ cup of pinto beans at lunch, and a 3-ounce (cooked weight) hamburger at dinner would add up to the equivalent of 6 ounces of lean meat for the day. To limit your intake of fat and saturated fat, choose lean cuts of meat and skinless poultry, and watch your serving sizes carefully. Choose at least one serving of plant proteins, such as black beans, lentils, or tofu, every day.

Oils The Oils group represents the oils that are added to foods during processing, cooking, or at the table; oils and soft margarines include vegetable oils and soft vegetable oil table spreads that have no trans fats. These are major sources of vitamin E and unsaturated fatty acids, including the essential fatty acids. For a 2000-calorie diet, 6 teaspoons of oils per day are recommended. One teaspoon is the equivalent of the following:

- 1 teaspoon vegetable oil or soft margarine
- 1 tablespoon salad dressing or light mayonnaise

Foods that are mostly oils include nuts, olives, avocados, and some fish. The following portions include about 1 teaspoon of oil: 8 large olives, 1/6 medium avocado, 1/2 tablespoon peanut butter, and 1/3 ounce roasted nuts. Food labels can help consumers identify the type and amount of fat in various foods.

Discretionary Calories, Solid Fats, and Added Sugars The suggested intakes from the basic food groups in MyPyramid assume that nutrient-dense forms are selected from each group; nutrient-dense forms are those that are fat-free or low-fat and that contain no added sugars. If this pattern is followed, then a small amount of additional calories can be consumed—the *discretionary calorie allowance.* Figure 12-6 shows the discretionary calorie allowance at each calorie level in MyPyramid.

People who are trying to lose weight may choose not to use discretionary calories. For those wanting to maintain weight, discretionary calories may be used to increase the amount of food from a food group; to consume foods that are not in the lowest fat form or that contain added sugars; to add oil, fat, or sugars to foods; or to consume alcohol. The amounts shown in Figure 12-6 show how discretionary calories may be divided between solid fats and added sugars. The values for additional fat target no more than 30% of total calories from fat and less than 10% of calories from saturated fat. Examples of discretionary solid fat calories include choosing higher-fat meats such as sausages, or chicken with skin, or whole milk instead of fat-free milk and topping foods with butter. For example, a cup of whole milk has 60 calories more than a cup of fat-free milk; these 60 calories would be counted as discretionary calories.

As described earlier in the chapter, added sugars are the sugars added to foods and beverages in processing or preparation, not the naturally occurring sugars in fruits or milk. The suggested amounts of added sugars may be helpful limits for including some sweetened foods or beverages in the daily diet without exceeding energy needs or underconsuming other nutrients. For example, in a 2000-calorie diet, MyPyramid lists 32 grams (8 teaspoons) for discretionary intake of added sugars. In the American diet, added sugars are often found in sweetened beverages (regular soda, sweetened teas, fruit drinks), dairy products (ice cream, some yogurts), and grain products (bakery goods). For example, a 20-ounce regular soda has 260 calories from added sugars that would be counted as discretionary calories. The current American diet includes higher-than-recommended levels of sugar intake.

Remember, the amounts listed in Figure 12-6 for solid fats and added sugars assume that you selected foods in nutrient-dense forms from the major foods groups; don't just add fats and sugars to your diet. To control weight and obtain adequate amounts of essential nutrients, it is important to choose nutrient-dense forms of foods for most of your daily servings.

For an evaluation of your diet, complete the activity in the box "Your Diet Versus MyPyramid Recommendations."

The Vegetarian Alternative

Some people choose a diet with one essential difference from the diets we've already described—foods of animal origin (meat, poultry, fish, eggs, milk) are eliminated or restricted. Many do so for health reasons; vegetarian diets tend to be lower in saturated fat, cholesterol, and animal protein and higher in complex carbohydrates, dietary fiber, folate, vitamins C and E, carotenoids, and phytochemicals. Some people adopt a vegetarian diet out of concern for the environment, for financial considerations, or for reasons related to ethics or religion.

Types of Vegetarian Diets There are various vegetarian styles; the wider the variety of the diet eaten, the easier it is to meet nutritional needs. **Vegans** eat only plant foods. **Lacto-vegetarians** eat plant foods and dairy products. **Lacto-ovo-vegetarians** eat plant foods, dairy products, and eggs. According to recent polls, over 5 million American adults never eat meat, poultry, or fish and fall into one of these three groups. Others can be categorized as **partial vegetarians, semivegetarians,** or **pescovegetarians;** these individuals eat plant foods, dairy products, eggs, and usually a small selection of poultry, fish, and other seafood. Many other people choose vegetarian meals frequently but are not strictly vegetarian. Including some animal protein (such as dairy products) in a vegetarian diet makes planning easier, but it is not necessary.

A Food Plan for Vegetarians MyPyramid can be adapted for use by vegetarians with only a few key modifications. For the meat and beans group, vegetarians can focus on the nonmeat choices of dry beans (legumes), nuts, seeds, eggs, and soy foods like tofu (soybean curd) and tempeh (a cultured soy product). Vegans and other vegetarians who do not consume any dairy products must

Terms

VW

vegan A vegetarian who eats no animal products at all.

lacto-vegetarian A vegetarian who includes milk and cheese products in the diet.

lacto-ovo-vegetarian A vegetarian who eats no meat, poultry, or fish but does eat eggs and milk products.

partial vegetarian, semivegetarian, or pescovegetarian A vegetarian who includes eggs, dairy products, and/or small amounts of poultry and seafood in the diet.

Your Diet Versus MyPyramid Recommendations

1. **Keep a food record:** To evaluate your daily diet, begin by keeping a record of everything you eat on a typical day. To help with your analysis, break down each food item into its component parts and note your portion sizes; for example, a turkey sandwich might be listed as 2 slices sourdough bread, 3 ounces turkey, 1 tomato, 1 tablespoon mayonnaise, and so on.
2. **Compare your servings to the recommendations of MyPyramid:** Complete the chart below to compare your daily diet to MyPyramid. See Figure 12-6 for the recommended daily intake for your calorie level.

Food Group	Recommended Daily Amounts/Servings for Your Energy Intake	Your Actual Daily Intake (Amounts/Servings)	Serving Sizes and Equivalents
Grains (*total*)			1 oz equivalents = 1 slice of bread; 1 small muffin; 1 cup ready-to-eat cereal flakes; or ½ cup cooked cereal, rice, grains, or pasta
Whole grains			
Other grains			
Vegetables (*total*)			½ cup or equivalent (1 serving) = ½ cup raw or cooked vegetables; 1 cup raw leafy salad greens; or ½ cup vegetable juice
*Dark green**			
*Deep yellow**			
*Legumes**			
*Starchy**			
*Other**			
Fruits			½ cup or equivalent (1 serving) = ½ cup fresh, canned, or frozen fruit; ½ cup fruit juice; 1 small whole fruit; or ¼ cup dried fruit
Milk			1 cup or equivalent = 1 cup milk or yogurt; 1-½ oz natural cheese; or 2 oz processed cheese
Meat and Beans			1 oz equivalents = 1 oz lean meat, poultry, or fish; ¼ cup cooked dry beans or tofu; 1 egg; 1 tablespoon peanut butter; or ½ oz nuts or seeds
Oils			1 teaspoon or equivalent = 1 teaspoon vegetable oil or 1 tablespoon light mayonnaise or salad dressing
Solid Fats			
Added Sugars			

*Compare your daily intake with the approximate daily intake derived from the weekly pattern given in MyPyramid (Figure 12-6).

It may be difficult to track values for added sugars and, especially, oils and fats, but be as accurate as you can. Check food labels for information on fat and sugar. (NOTE: For a more complete and accurate analysis of your diet, keep food records for 3 days and then average the results.) MyPyramid.gov has additional guidelines for counting discretionary calories.

3. **Further evaluate your food choices within the groups:** Based on the data you collected and what you learned in the chapter, what were the especially healthy choices you made (for example, whole grains and citrus fruits) and what were your less healthy choices? Identify and list foods in the latter category, as these are areas where you can make changes to improve your diet. In particular, you may want to limit your intake of the following: processed, sweetened grains; high-fat meats and poultry skin; deep-fried fast foods; full-fat dairy products; regular sodas, sweetened teas, fruit drinks; alcoholic beverages; other foods that primarily provide sugar and fat and few other nutrients.
4. **Make healthy changes:** Bring your diet in line with MyPyramid by adding servings from food groups for which you fall short of the recommendations. To maintain a healthy weight, you may need to balance these additions by reductions in other areas—by eliminating some of the fats, oils, sweets, and alcohol you consume; by cutting extra servings from food groups for which your intake is more than adequate; or by making healthier choices within the food groups. Make a list of foods to add and a list of foods to eliminate; post your lists in a prominent location.

For a more detailed analysis of your current diet, including intakes of specific nutrients, use the online MyPyramid Tracker tool available at MyPyramid.gov.

Gender Matters

How Different Are the Nutritional Needs of Women and Men?

When it comes to nutrition, men and women have a lot in common. Both sexes need the same essential nutrients, and the Dietary Guidelines for Americans apply equally to both. But beyond the basics, men and women need different amounts of essential nutrients and have different nutritional concerns.

Women tend to be smaller and weigh less than men, and thus have lower energy requirements and need to consume fewer calories than men to maintain a healthy weight. For most nutrients, women need the same or slightly lower amounts than men. But because women consume fewer calories, they may have more difficulty getting adequate amounts of all essential nutrients and need to focus on nutrient-dense foods.

Two nutrients of special concern to women are calcium and iron. Low calcium intake may be linked to the development of osteoporosis in later life. The *Healthy People 2010* report sets a goal of increasing from 40% to 75% the proportion of women age 20–49 who meet the dietary recommendation for calcium. Fat-free and low-fat dairy products and fortified cereal, bread, and orange juice are good choices for calcium-rich foods.

Menstruating women also have higher iron needs than other groups, and low iron intake can lead to iron-deficiency anemia. Lean red meat, green leafy vegetables, and fortified breakfast cereals are good sources of iron. As discussed earlier, all women capable of becoming pregnant should consume adequate folic acid from fortified foods and/or supplements.

Men are seldom thought of as having nutritional deficiencies because they generally have high-calorie diets. However, many men have a diet that does not follow recommended food intake patterns and includes more red meat and fewer fruits, vegetables, and whole grains than recommended. This dietary pattern is linked to heart disease and some types of cancer. A high intake of calories can lead to weight gain over time if a man's activity level decreases as he ages. To reduce chronic disease risk, men should focus on increasing their consumption of fruits, vegetables, and whole grains to obtain vitamins, minerals, fiber, and phytochemicals.

The "Eat 5 to 9 a Day for Better Health" program was created by the National Cancer Institute and U.S. Department of Health and Human Services to promote increased intake of fruits and vegetables. For strategies and guidelines for consuming more fruits and vegetables, visit http://www.5aday.gov. The program has been expanded to include dietary options for both men and women.

find other rich sources of calcium (see below). Fruits, vegetables, and whole grains are healthy choices for people following all types of vegetarian diets.

A healthy vegetarian diet emphasizes a wide variety of plant foods. Although plant proteins are generally of lower quality than animal proteins, choosing a variety of plant foods will supply all of the essential amino acids. Choosing minimally processed and unrefined foods will maximize nutrient value and provide ample dietary fiber. Daily consumption of a variety of plant foods in amounts that meet total energy needs can provide all needed nutrients, except vitamin B-12 and possibly vitamin D. Strategies for obtaining nutrients of concern include the following:

- *Vitamin B-12* is found naturally only in animal foods; if dairy products and eggs are limited or avoided, B-12 can be obtained from fortified foods such as ready-to-eat cereals, soy beverages, meat substitutes, and special yeast products or from supplements.
- *Vitamin D* can be obtained by spending 5–15 minutes a day in the sun, by consuming vitamin D–fortified products like ready-to-eat cereals and soy or rice milk, or by taking a supplement.
- *Calcium* is found in legumes, tofu processed with calcium, dark green leafy vegetables, nuts, tortillas made from lime-processed corn, and fortified orange juice, soy milk, bread, and other foods.
- *Iron* can be obtained from whole grains, fortified bread and breakfast cereals, dried fruits, green leafy vegetables, nuts and seeds, legumes, and soy foods. The iron in plant foods is more difficult for the body to absorb than is the iron from animal sources; consuming a good source of vitamin C with most meals is helpful because vitamin C improves iron absorption.
- *Zinc* is found in whole grains, nuts, legumes, and soy foods.

It takes a little planning and common sense to put together a good vegetarian diet. If you are a vegetarian or considering becoming one, devote some extra time and thought to your diet. It's especially important to eat as wide a variety of foods as possible to ensure that all your nutritional needs are satisfied. Consulting with a registered dietitian will make your planning even easier. Vegetarian diets for children, teens, and pregnant and lactating women warrant professional guidance.

Dietary Challenges for Special Population Groups

The Dietary Guidelines for Americans and MyPyramid provide a basis that everyone can use to create a healthy diet. However, some population groups face special dietary challenges (see the box "How Different Are the Nutritional Needs of Women and Men?").

Children and Teenagers Young people often simply need to be encouraged to eat. Perhaps the best thing a parent can do for younger children is to provide them with a variety of foods. Add vegetables to casseroles and fruit to cereal; offer fruit and vegetable juices or homemade yogurt or fruit shakes instead of sugary drinks. Allowing children to help prepare meals is another good way to increase overall food consumption and variety. Many children and teenagers enjoy eating at fast-food restaurants; they should be encouraged to select the healthiest choices from fast-food menus (see Appendix A) and to complete the day's diet with low-fat, nutrient-rich foods.

College Students Foods that are convenient for college students are not always the healthiest choices. It is easy for students who eat in buffet-style dining halls or food courts to overeat, and the foods offered are not necessarily high in essential nutrients and low in fat. The same is true of meals at fast-food restaurants, another convenient source of quick and inexpensive meals for busy students. Although no food is entirely bad, consuming a wide variety of foods is critical for a healthy diet. See the box "Eating Strategies for College Students" on page 358 for tips on making healthy eating convenient and affordable.

Older Adults Nutrient needs do not change much as people age; but because older adults tend to become less active, they require fewer calories to maintain body weight. At the same time, the absorption of nutrients tends to be lower in older adults because of age-related changes in the digestive tract. Thus, they must consume nutrient-dense foods in order to meet their nutritional requirements. As discussed earlier, foods fortified with vitamin B-12 and/or B-12 supplements are recommended for people over age 50. Because constipation is a common problem, consuming foods high in fiber and getting adequate fluids are important goals.

Athletes Key dietary concerns for athletes are meeting their increased energy requirements and drinking enough fluids during practice and throughout the day to remain fully hydrated. Endurance athletes may also benefit from increasing the amount of carbohydrate in the diet to 60–70% of total daily calories; this increase should come in the form of complex, rather than simple, carbohydrates. Athletes for whom maintaining low body weight and body fat is important—such as skaters, gymnasts, and wrestlers—should consume adequate nutrients and avoid falling into unhealthy patterns of eating. Eating for exercise is discussed in more detail in Chapter 13; refer to Chapter 14 for information on eating disorders.

People with Special Health Concerns Many Americans have special health concerns that affect their dietary needs. For example, women who are pregnant or breastfeeding require extra calories, vitamins, and minerals (see Chapter 8). People with diabetes benefit from a well-balanced diet that is low in simple sugars, high in complex carbohydrates, and relatively rich in monounsaturated fats. People with high blood pressure need to control their weight and limit their sodium consumption. If you have a health problem or concern that may require a special diet, discuss your situation with a physician or registered dietitian.

A PERSONAL PLAN: MAKING INFORMED CHOICES ABOUT FOOD

Now that you understand the basis of good nutrition and a healthy diet, you can put together a diet that works for you. Focus on the likely causes of any health problems in your life, and make specific dietary changes to address them. You may also have some specific areas of concern, such as interpreting food labels and dietary supplement labels, avoiding foodborne illnesses and environmental contaminants, and understanding food additives. We turn to these and other topics next.

Reading Food Labels

Food labels can help consumers in applying the principles of the Dietary Guidelines for Americans. Since 1994, all processed foods regulated by either the FDA or the USDA have included standardized nutrition information on their labels. Every food label shows serving sizes and the amount of fat, saturated fat, trans fat, cholesterol, sodium, total carbohydrate, dietary fiber, sugars, and protein in each serving. To make intelligent choices about food, learn to read and *understand* food labels (see the box "Using Food Labels" on p. 359).

Fresh meat, poultry, fish, fruits, and vegetables are not required to have food labels, and many of these products are not packaged. You can obtain information on the nutrient content of these items from basic nutrition books, registered dietitians, nutrient analysis computer software, the World Wide Web, and the companies that produce or distribute these foods. Also, supermarkets often have large posters or pamphlets listing the nutrient contents of these foods.

Reading Dietary Supplement Labels

Dietary supplements include vitamins, minerals, amino acids, herbs, glandular extracts, enzymes, and other compounds. They may come in the form of tablets, capsules, liquids, or powders. Surveys indicate that over half of American adults use dietary supplements at least occasionally, and sales have more than quadrupled since 1990, to over $15 billion per year. Although dietary supplements are often thought to be safe and "natural," they contain powerful, bioactive chemicals that have the potential for harm. About one-quarter of all pharmaceutical drugs are derived from botanical sources—morphine from poppies and digoxin from foxglove, for example.

Take Charge

Eating Strategies for College Students

General Guidelines

- Eat slowly, and enjoy your food. Set aside a separate time to eat, and don't eat while you study.
- Eat a colorful, varied diet. The more colorful your diet is, the more varied and rich in fruits and vegetables it will be. Many Americans eat few fruits and vegetables, despite the fact that these foods are typically inexpensive, delicious, rich in nutrients, and low in fat and calories.
- Eat breakfast. You'll have more energy in the morning and be less likely to grab an unhealthy snack later on.
- Choose healthy snacks—fruits, vegetables, grains, and cereals—as often as you can.
- Drink water more often than soft drinks or other sweetened beverages. Rent a mini-refrigerator for your dorm room and stock up on healthy beverages.
- Pay attention to portion sizes.
- Combine physical activity with healthy eating. You'll feel better and have a much lower risk of many chronic diseases. Even a little exercise is better than none.

Eating in the Dining Hall

- Choose a meal plan that includes breakfast, and don't skip it.
- Accept that dining hall food is not going to taste the same as home cooking. Find healthy dishes that you like.
- If menus are posted or distributed, decide what you want to eat before you get in line, and stick to your choices. Consider what you plan to do and eat for the rest of the day before making your choices.
- Ask for large servings of vegetables and small servings of meat and other high-fat main dishes. Build your meals around grains and vegetables.
- Try whole grains like brown rice, whole-wheat bread, and whole-grain cereals.
- Choose leaner poultry, fish, or bean dishes rather than high-fat meats and fried entrees.
- Ask that gravies and sauces be served on the side; limit your intake.
- Choose broth-based or vegetable soups rather than cream soups.
- At the salad bar, load up on leafy greens, beans, and fresh vegetables. Avoid mayonnaise-coated salads, bacon, croutons, and high-fat dressings. Put dressing on the side, and dip your fork into it rather than pouring it over the salad.
- Drink nonfat milk, water, mineral water, or 100% fruit juice rather than heavily sweetened fruit drinks, whole milk, or soft drinks.
- Choose fruit for dessert rather than pastries, cookies, or cakes.
- Do some research about the foods and preparation methods used in your dining hall or cafeteria. Discuss any suggestions you have with your food-service manager.

Eating in Fast-Food Restaurants

- Most fast-food chains can provide a brochure with a nutritional breakdown of the foods on the menu. Ask for it. (See also the information in Appendix A.)
- Order small single burgers with no cheese instead of double burgers with many toppings. If possible, ask for them broiled instead of fried.
- Ask for items to be prepared without mayonnaise, tartar sauce, sour cream, or other high-fat sauces. Ketchup, mustard, and fat-free mayonnaise or sour cream are better choices and are available at many fast-food restaurants.
- Choose whole-grain buns or bread for burgers and sandwiches.
- Choose chicken items made from chicken breast, not processed chicken.
- Order vegetable pizzas without extra cheese.
- If you order french fries or onion rings, get the smallest size, and/or share them with a friend. Better yet, get a salad or fruit cup instead.

Eating on the Run

Are you chronically short of time? Pack these items for a quick snack or meal: fresh or dried fruit, fruit juices, raw fresh vegetables like carrots, plain bagels, bread sticks, whole-wheat fig bars, low-fat cheese sticks or cubes, low-fat crackers or granola bars, fat-free or low-fat yogurt, snack-size cereal boxes, pretzels, rice or corn cakes, plain popcorn, soup (if you have access to a microwave), or water.

And, as described earlier, even essential vitamins and minerals can have toxic effects if consumed in excess.

In the United States, supplements are not legally considered drugs and are not regulated the way drugs are. Before they are approved by the FDA and put on the market, drugs undergo clinical studies to determine safety, effectiveness, side effects and risks, possible interactions with other substances, and appropriate dosages. The FDA does not authorize or test dietary supplements, and supplements are not required to demonstrate either safety or effectiveness prior to marketing. Although dosage guidelines exist for some of the compounds in dietary supplements, dosages for many are not well established.

Food labels are designed to help consumers make food choices based on the nutrients that are most important to good health. In addition to listing nutrient content by weight, the label puts the information in the context of a daily diet of 2000 calories that includes no more than 65 grams of fat (approximately 30% of total calories). For example, if a serving of a particular product has 13 grams of fat, the label will show that the serving represents 20% of the daily fat allowance. If your daily diet contains fewer or more than 2000 calories, you need to adjust these calculations accordingly.

Food labels contain uniform serving sizes. This means that if you look at different brands of salad dressing, for example, you can compare calories and fat content based on the serving amount. (Food label serving sizes may be larger or smaller than MyPyramid serving size equivalents, however.) Regulations also require that foods meet strict definitions if their packaging includes the terms *light, low-fat,* or *high-fiber* (see below). Health claims such as "good source of dietary fiber" or "low in saturated fat" on packages are signals that those products can wisely be included in your diet. Overall, the food label is an important tool to help you choose a diet that conforms to MyPyramid and the Dietary Guidelines.

Selected Nutrient Claims and What They Mean

Healthy A food that is low in fat, is low in saturated fat, has no more than 360–480 mg of sodium and 60 mg of cholesterol, *and* provides 10% or more of the Daily Value for vitamin A, vitamin C, protein, calcium, iron, or dietary fiber.

Light or lite One-third fewer calories or 50% less fat than a similar product.

Reduced or fewer At least 25% less of a nutrient than a similar product; can be applied to fat ("reduced fat"), saturated fat, cholesterol, sodium, and calories.

Extra or added 10% or more of the Daily Value per serving when compared to what a similar product has.

Good source 10–19% of the Daily Value for a particular nutrient per serving.

High, rich in, or excellent source of 20% or more of the Daily Value for a particular nutrient per serving.

Low calorie 40 calories or less per serving.

High fiber 5 g or more of fiber per serving.

Good source of fiber 2.5–4.9 g of fiber per serving.

Fat-free Less than 0.5 g of fat per serving.

Low-fat 3 g of fat or less per serving.

Saturated fat-free Less than 0.5 g of saturated fat and 0.5 g of trans fatty acids per serving.

Low saturated fat 1 g or less of saturated fat per serving and no more than 15% of total calories.

Cholesterol-free Less than 2 mg of cholesterol and 2 g or less of saturated fat per serving.

Low cholesterol 20 mg or less of cholesterol and 2 g or less of saturated fat per serving.

Low sodium 140 mg or less of sodium per serving.

Very low sodium 35 mg or less of sodium per serving.

Lean Cooked seafood, meat, or poultry with less than 10 g of fat, 4.5 g or less of saturated fat, and less than 95 mg of cholesterol per serving.

Extra lean Cooked seafood, meat, or poultry with less than 5 g of fat, 2 g of saturated fat, and 95 mg of cholesterol per serving.

Note: As of June 2005, the FDA had not yet defined nutrient claims relating to carbohydrate, so foods labeled low- or reduced-carbohydrate do not conform to any approved standard.

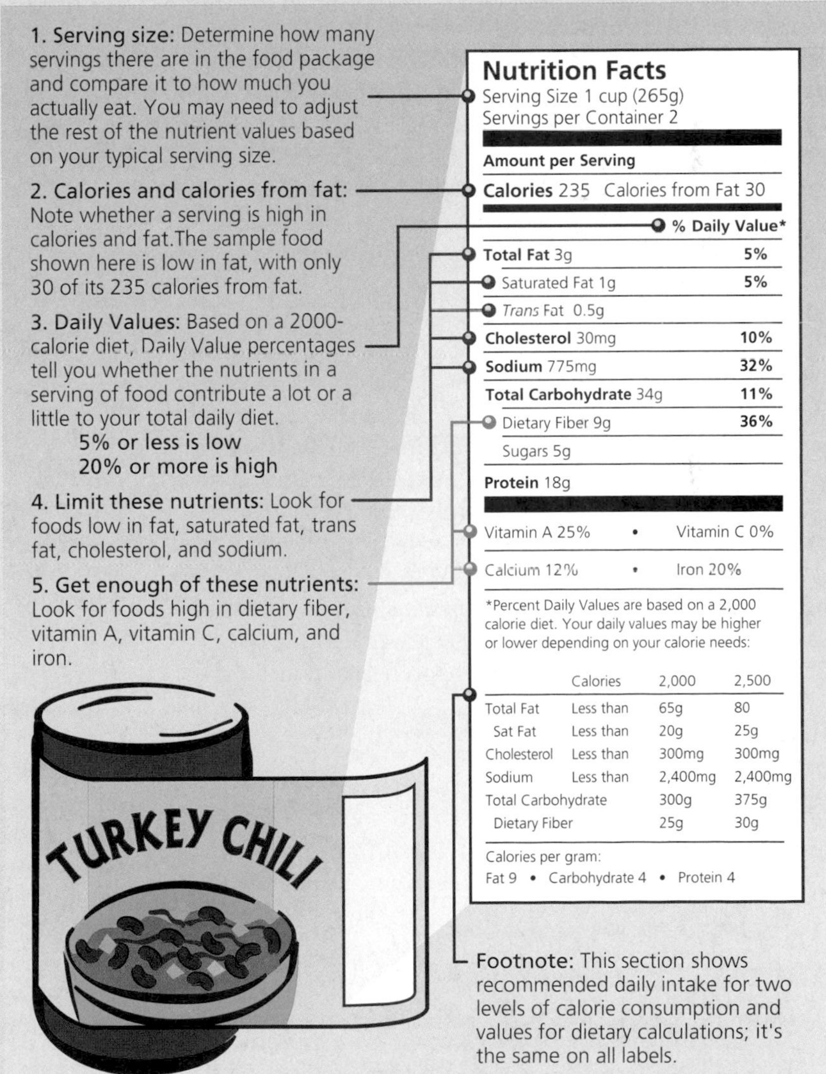

1. Serving size: Determine how many servings there are in the food package and compare it to how much you actually eat. You may need to adjust the rest of the nutrient values based on your typical serving size.
2. Calories and calories from fat: Note whether a serving is high in calories and fat. The sample food shown here is low in fat, with only 30 of its 235 calories from fat.
3. Daily Values: Based on a 2000-calorie diet, Daily Value percentages tell you whether the nutrients in a serving of food contribute a lot or a little to your total daily diet.
5% or less is low
20% or more is high
4. Limit these nutrients: Look for foods low in fat, saturated fat, trans fat, cholesterol, and sodium.
5. Get enough of these nutrients: Look for foods high in dietary fiber, vitamin A, vitamin C, calcium, and iron.
TURKEY CHILI
Footnote: This section shows recommended daily intake for two levels of calorie consumption and values for dietary calculations; it's the same on all labels.

Nutrition Facts
Serving Size 1 cup (265g)
Servings per Container 2

Amount per Serving
Calories 235 Calories from Fat 30

	% Daily Value*
Total Fat 3g	**5%**
Saturated Fat 1g	**5%**
Trans Fat 0.5g	
Cholesterol 30mg	**10%**
Sodium 775mg	**32%**
Total Carbohydrate 34g	**11%**
Dietary Fiber 9g	**36%**
Sugars 5g	
Protein 18g	

Vitamin A 25% • Vitamin C 0%
Calcium 12% • Iron 20%

*Percent Daily Values are based on a 2,000 calorie diet. Your daily values may be higher or lower depending on your calorie needs:

	Calories	2,000	2,500
Total Fat	Less than	65g	80
Sat Fat	Less than	20g	25g
Cholesterol	Less than	300mg	300mg
Sodium	Less than	2,400mg	2,400mg
Total Carbohydrate		300g	375g
Dietary Fiber		25g	30g

Calories per gram:
Fat 9 • Carbohydrate 4 • Protein 4

Although many ingredients in dietary supplements have been used for centuries in Eastern or European herbal medicine, some have been found to be dangerous or to interact with prescription or over-the-counter drugs in dangerous ways. Garlic supplements, for example, can cause bleeding if taken with anticoagulant ("blood thinning") medications. Even products that are generally considered safe can have side effects—St. John's wort, for example, increases the skin's sensitivity to sunlight and may decrease the effectiveness of oral contraceptives, drugs used to treat HIV infection, and other medications.

There are also key differences in how drugs and supplements are manufactured. FDA-approved medications are standardized for potency, and quality control and proof of purity are required. Dietary supplement manufacture is not as closely regulated, and there is no guarantee that a product even contains a given ingredient, let alone in the appropriate amount. The potency of herbal supplements tends to vary widely due to differences in growing and harvesting conditions, preparation methods, and storage. Some manufacturers attempt to standardize their products by isolating the compounds believed to be responsible for an herb's action. However, potency is often still highly variable, and when several compounds are thought to be responsible for an herb's effect, often only one is standardized. In addition, herbs can be contaminated or misidentified at any stage from harvest to packaging. The FDA has recalled several products due to the presence of dangerous contaminants, including heavy metals and pharmaceutical drugs.

With increased consumer knowledge and demand, it is likely that both the research base and the manufacturing standards for supplements will improve. (The FDA proposed manufacturing standards in 2003.) To provide consumers with more reliable and consistent information about supplements, the FDA requires supplements to have labels similar to those found on foods (see the box "Using Dietary Supplement Labels" for more information). Label statements and claims about supplements are also regulated.

Finally, it is important to remember that dietary supplements are no substitute for a healthy diet. Supplements do not provide all the known—or yet-to-be-discovered—benefits of whole foods. Supplements should also not be used as a replacement for medical treatment for serious illnesses. (See Chapter 21 for more on herbal remedies.)

Protecting Yourself Against Foodborne Illness

Many people worry about additives or pesticide residues in their food, but a greater threat comes from microorganisms that cause foodborne illnesses. Raw or undercooked animal products, such as chicken, hamburger, and oysters, pose the greatest threat, although in recent years contaminated fruits and vegetables have been catching up. The CDC estimates that about 76 million illnesses, 325,000 hospitalizations, and 5000 deaths occur each year in the United States due to foodborne illness. Symptoms include diarrhea, vomiting, fever, and weakness. Although the effects of foodborne illnesses are usually not serious, some groups, such as children, pregnant women, and the elderly, are more at risk for severe complications such as rheumatic diseases, seizures, blood poisoning, other ailments, and death.

Causes of Foodborne Illnesses Most cases of foodborne illness are caused by **pathogens,** disease-causing microorganisms. Food can be contaminated with pathogens through improper handling; pathogens can grow if food is prepared or stored improperly. Causes of foodborne illness in the United States include the following pathogens:

- *Campylobacter jejuni* causes more cases of foodborne illness than any other bacteria. It is most commonly found in contaminated water, raw milk, and raw or undercooked poultry, meat, or shellfish; the majority of chickens sold in the United States test positive for the presence of *C. jejuni.* Symptoms of infection include diarrhea, fever, abdominal and muscle pain, and headache, which resolve in 7–10 days. However, in about 1 in 1000 cases, *Campylobacter* infection triggers Guillain-Barré syndrome, a neurological disease that can cause numbness, weakness, and (usually temporary) paralysis.
- *Salmonella* bacteria are most often found in raw or undercooked eggs, poultry, and meat; milk and dairy products; seafood; fruits and vegetables, including sprouts; and inadequately refrigerated and reheated leftovers. The recent identification of an antibiotic-resistant strain of *Salmonella* has raised concerns about a potential increase in serious illness from *Salmonella.*
- *Shigella* bacteria are found in the human intestinal tract and usually transmitted via fecal contamination of food and water. Outbreaks are typically traced to foods, especially salads, that have been handled by people using poor personal hygiene. Contaminated water, milk, and dairy products are other possible sources of infection.
- *Escherichia coli* bacteria, found in the intestinal tracts of humans and animals, most commonly contaminate water, raw milk, raw to rare ground beef, unpasteurized juices, and fruits and vegetables. A certain strain, known as *E. coli* O157:H7, is of particular concern because it produces a toxin that causes serious illness and sometimes death. Children are particularly at risk for developing hemolytic uremic syndrome, which causes kidney failure. A September 2006 outbreak of *E. coli* O157:H17 in spinach made more than 200 people sick in 26 states and left three dead. The outbreak was traced to a spinach field in Central California contaminated by cattle and wildlife.

VW **Term**

pathogen A microorganism that causes disease.

Using Dietary Supplement Labels

Since 1999, specific types of information have been required on the labels of dietary supplements. In addition to basic information about the product, labels include a "Supplement Facts" panel, modeled after the "Nutrition Facts" panel used on food labels (see the label below). Under the Dietary Supplement Health and Education Act (DSHEA) and food labeling laws, supplement labels can make three types of health-related claims.

- *Nutrient-content claims,* such as "high in calcium," "excellent source of vitamin C," or "high potency." The claims "high in" and "excellent source of" mean the same as they do on food labels. A "high potency" single-ingredient supplement must contain 100% of its Daily Value; a "high potency" multi-ingredient product must contain 100% or more of the Daily Value of at least two-thirds of the nutrients present for which Daily Values have been established.
- *Health claims,* if they have been authorized by the FDA or another authoritative scientific body. The association between adequate calcium intake and lower risk of osteoporosis is an example of an approved health claim. Since 2003, the FDA has also allowed so-called *qualified* health claims for situations in which there is emerging but as yet inconclusive evidence for a particular claim. Such claims must include qualifying language such as "scientific evidence suggests but does not prove" the claim.
- *Structure-function claims,* such as "antioxidants maintain cellular integrity" or "this product enhances energy levels." Because these claims are not reviewed by the FDA, they must carry a disclaimer (see the sample label).

Tips for Choosing and Using Dietary Supplements

- Check with your physician before taking a supplement. Many are not meant for children, elderly people, women who are pregnant or breast-feeding, people with chronic illnesses, or people taking prescription or OTC medications.
- Choose brands made by nationally known food and drug manufacturers or house brands from large retail chains. Due to their size and visibility, such sources are likely to have high manufacturing standards.
- Look for the USP verification mark on the label, indicating that the product meets minimum safety and purity standards developed under the Dietary Supplement Verification Program by the United States Pharmacopeia (USP). The USP mark means that the product (1) contains the ingredients stated on the label, (2) has the declared amount and strength of ingredients, (3) will dissolve effectively, (4) has been screened for harmful contaminants, and (5) has been manufactured using safe, sanitary, and well-controlled procedures. The National Nutritional Foods Association (NNFA) has a self-regulatory testing program for its members; other, smaller associations and labs, including ConsumerLab.Com, also test and rate dietary supplements.
- Follow the cautions, instructions for use, and dosage given on the label.
- If you experience side effects, discontinue use of the product and contact your physician. Report any serious reactions to the FDA's MedWatch monitoring program (800-FDA-1088; http://www.fda.gov/medwatch).

For More Information About Dietary Supplements

ConsumerLab.Com: http://www.consumerlab.com

Food and Drug Administration: http://vm.cfsan.fda.gov/~dms/supplmnt.html

National Institutes of Health, Office of Dietary Supplements: http://dietary-supplements.info.nih.gov

Natural Products Association: http://www.naturalproductsassoc.org

U.S. Department of Agriculture: http://www.nal.usda.gov/fnic/etext/000015.html

U.S. Pharmacopeia: http://www.usp.org/uspverified/dietarysupplements

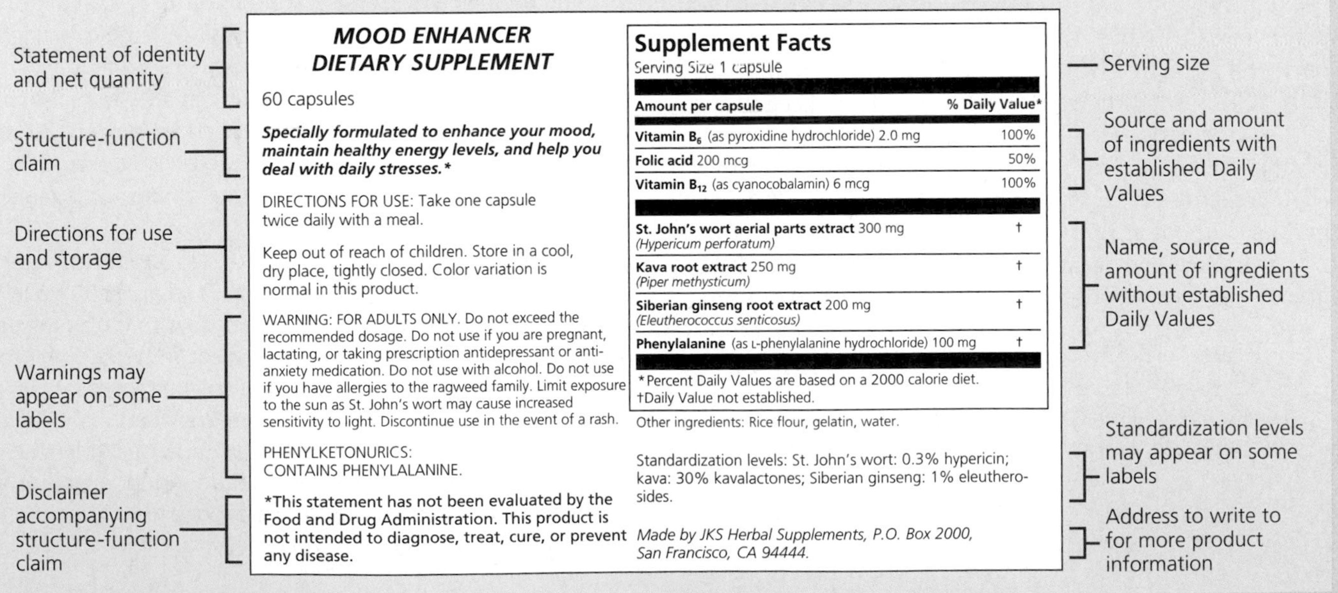

- *Listeria monocytogenes* sickens about 2300 Americans a year, causing death in about 20% of cases. It is found in soft cheeses, raw milk, improperly processed ice cream, raw leafy vegetables, hot dogs and lunch meats, and other meat, poultry, and processed foods. *Listeria* is particularly dangerous for pregnant women and their fetuses, babies and children, older adults, and people with weakened immune systems.
- *Staphylococcus aureus* lives mainly in nasal passages and skin sores; it is transferred to food when people handle food or sneeze or cough over food. Foods contaminated with *S. aureus* may include cooked hams, egg and potato salads, cheese, seafood, whipped cream, and milk. *S. aureus* multiplies rapidly at room temperature to produce a toxin that causes illness.
- *Clostridium botulinum* is widely distributed in nature, but it grows only in environments with little or no oxygen; it produces a toxin that causes illness. Potential sources of *C. botulinum* include improperly canned foods, garlic in oil, sausages and other meat products, and vacuum-packed and tightly wrapped foods. Although rare, botulism is potentially fatal if untreated because the toxin affects the nervous system.
- *Norovirus,* the most common viral cause of foodborne illness, may be found in contaminated water, raw or insufficiently cooked shellfish, and salads contaminated by food handlers. Noroviruses typically cause vomiting, diarrhea, and abdominal pain, lasting 1–3 days.

Other causes of foodborne illness include the bacteria *Clostridium perfringens, Vibrio vulnificus,* and *Yersinia enterocolytica;* the hepatitis A virus; the parasites *Trichinella spiralis* (found in pork and wild game), *Anisakis* (found in raw fish), *Giardia lamblia, Cyclospora cayetanensis,* and tapeworms; and certain molds.

A potential new threat from food is bovine spongiform encephalopathy (BSE), or "mad cow disease," a fatal degenerative neurological disease caused by an abnormal protein that forms deposits in the brain. A variant form of the human version of this disease, known as Creutzfeldt-Jakob disease (CJD), is believed to be caused by eating beef contaminated with central nervous system tissue from BSE-infected cows. To date, there have been about 150 confirmed cases worldwide of this variant CJD among the hundreds of thousands of people who may have consumed BSE-contaminated products. In December 2003, the first BSE-infected cow in the United States was identified; no meat or organs from this animal had made it into the food supply. Although the USDA states that the risk to human health from BSE is extremely low, additional steps are being taken to prevent the BSE protein from entering the food supply; visit the USDA Web site for more information (www.usda.gov).

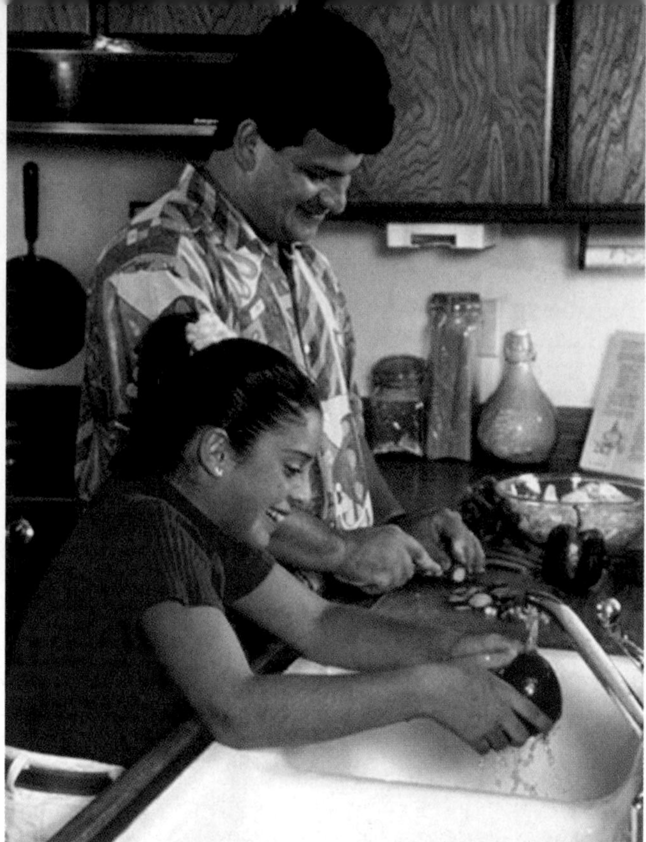

Careful food handling greatly reduces the risk of foodborne illness. Helpful strategies include washing hands and all fruits and vegetables, using separate cutting boards for meat and for foods that will be eaten raw, cooking meat thoroughly, and refrigerating leftovers promptly.

Term

polychlorinated biphenyl (PCB) An industrial chemical used as an insulator in electrical transformers and linked to certain human cancers.

Preventing and Treating Foodborne Illnesses

Because every teaspoon of the soil that our food grows in contains about 2 billion bacteria (only some of them pathogenic), we are always exposed to the possibility of a foodborne illness. You can't tell by taste, smell, or sight whether a food is contaminated. Some studies have revealed high levels of contamination. In 2003, *Consumer Reports* tested 484 chickens purchased in grocery stores and found that half were contaminated with *Campylobacter* and/or *Salmonella;* many of the strains of bacteria found were resistant to antibiotics.

Although pathogens are usually destroyed during cooking, the U.S. government is taking steps to bring down levels of contamination. In addition to new microbiological testing methods for inspection of meat and poultry processing plants, raw meat and poultry products are now sold with safe handling and cooking instructions, and all packaged, unpasteurized fresh fruit and vegetable juices carry warnings about potential contamination. Foodborne illness outbreaks associated with food-processing plants

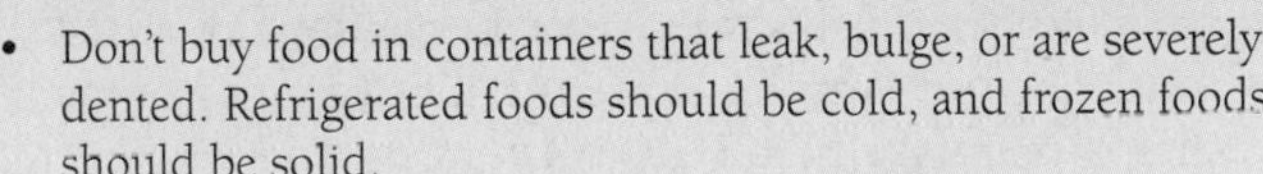

Take Charge

Safe Food Handling

- Don't buy food in containers that leak, bulge, or are severely dented. Refrigerated foods should be cold, and frozen foods should be solid.
- Refrigerate perishable items as soon as possible after purchase. Use or freeze fresh meats within 3–5 days and fresh poultry, fish, and ground meat within 1–2 days.
- Store raw meat, poultry, fish, and shellfish in containers in the refrigerator so that the juices don't drip onto other foods. Keep these items away from other foods, surfaces, utensils, or serving dishes to prevent cross-contamination.
- Thaw frozen food in the refrigerator or in the microwave oven, not on the kitchen counter. Cook foods immediately after thawing.
- Thoroughly wash your hands with warm soapy water for 20 seconds before and after handling food, especially raw meat, fish, shellfish, poultry, or eggs.
- Make sure counters, cutting boards, dishes, utensils, and other equipment are thoroughly cleaned before and after use using hot soapy water. Wash dishcloths and kitchen towels frequently.
- If possible, use separate cutting boards for meat, poultry, and seafood and for foods that will be eaten raw, such as fruits and vegetables. Replace cutting boards once they become worn or develop hard-to-clean grooves.
- Thoroughly rinse and scrub fruits and vegetables with a brush, if possible, or peel off the skin.
- Cook foods thoroughly, especially beef, poultry, fish, pork, and eggs; cooking kills most microorganisms. Use a food thermometer to ensure that foods are cooked to a safe temperature. Hamburgers should be cooked to 160°F. Turn or stir microwaved food to make sure it is heated evenly throughout. When eating out, order hamburger cooked well-done and make sure foods are served piping hot.
- Cook stuffing separately from poultry; or wash poultry thoroughly, stuff immediately before cooking, and transfer the stuffing to a clean bowl immediately after cooking. The temperature of cooked stuffing should reach 165°F.
- Keep hot foods hot (140°F or above) and cold foods cold (40°F or below); harmful bacteria can grow rapidly between these two temperatures. Refrigerate foods within 2 hours of purchase or preparation, and within 1 hour if the air temperature is above 90°F. Refrigerate foods at or below 40°F and freeze at or below 0°F. Use refrigerated leftovers within 3–4 days.
- Don't eat raw animal products, including raw eggs in homemade hollandaise sauce or eggnog. Use only pasteurized milk and juice, and look for pasteurized eggs, which are now available in some states.
- Cook eggs until they're firm, and fully cook foods containing eggs. Store eggs in the coldest part of the refrigerator, not in the door, and use them within 3–5 weeks.
- Because of possible contamination with *E. coli* O157:H7 and *Salmonella,* avoid raw sprouts. Even sprouts grown under clean conditions in the home can be risky because bacteria may be present in the seeds. Cook sprouts before eating them.
- Read the food label and package information, and follow safety instructions such as "Keep Refrigerated" and the "Safe Handling Instructions."
- According to the USDA, "When in doubt, throw it out." Even if a food looks and smells fine, it may not be safe. If you aren't sure that a food has been prepared, served, and stored safely, don't eat it.

Additional precautions are recommended for people at particularly high risk for foodborne illness—pregnant women, young children, older persons, and people with weakened immune systems or certain chronic illnesses. If you are a member of one of these groups, don't eat or drink any of the following products: unpasteurized juices; raw sprouts; unpasteurized (raw) milk and products made from unpasteurized milk; raw or undercooked meat, poultry, eggs, fish, and shellfish; and soft cheeses such as feta, Brie, Camembert, or blue-veined cheeses. To protect against *Listeria,* it's also important to avoid ready-to-eat foods such as hot dogs, luncheon meats, and cold cuts unless they are reheated until they are steaming hot.

make headlines, but most cases of illness trace back to poor food handling in the home or in food-service establishments. To decrease your risk of foodborne illness, follow the guidelines in the box "Safe Food Handling."

If you think you may be having a bout of foodborne illness, drink plenty of clear fluids to prevent dehydration and rest to speed recovery. To prevent further contamination, wash your hands often, and always before handling food. A fever higher than 102°F, blood in the stool, or dehydration deserves a physician's evaluation, especially if the symptoms persist for more than 2–3 days. In cases of suspected botulism—characterized by symptoms such as double vision, paralysis, dizziness, and vomiting—consult a physician immediately to receive an antitoxin.

Environmental Contaminants and Organic Foods

Contaminants are also present in the food-growing environment, but few of them ever enter the food and water supply in amounts sufficient to cause health problems. Environmental contaminants include various minerals, antibiotics, hormones, pesticides, the industrial chemicals known as **PCBs (polychlorinated biphenyls)**, and naturally occurring substances such as cyanogenic glycosides (found in lima beans and the pits of some fruits) and certain molds. Their effects depend on many factors, including concentration, length of exposure, and the age and health status of the person involved. Safety regulations attempt to keep our exposure to contaminants at safe levels, but monitoring is difficult and many substances (such as pesticides) persist in the environment long after being banned from use.

Organic Foods Some people who are concerned about pesticides and other environmental contaminants choose to buy foods that are **organic.** To be certified as organic by the USDA, foods must meet strict production, processing, handling, and labeling criteria. Organic crops must meet limits on pesticide residues; for meat, milk, eggs, and other animal products to be certified organic, animals must be given organic feed and access to the outdoors and may not be given antibiotics or growth hormones. The use of genetic engineering, ionizing radiation, and sewage sludge is prohibited. Products can be labeled "100% organic" if they contain all organic ingredients and "organic" if they contain at least 95% organic ingredients; all such products may carry the USDA organic seal. A product with at least 70% organic ingredients can be labeled "made with organic ingredients" but cannot use the USDA seal.

USDA ORGANIC

Organic foods are not necessarily chemical-free, however. They may be contaminated with pesticides used on neighboring lands or on foods transported in the same train or truck. However, they do tend to have lower levels of pesticide residues than conventionally grown crops. Some experts recommend that consumers who want to buy organic fruits and vegetables spend their money on those that carry higher pesticide residues than their conventional counterparts (the "dirty dozen"): apples, bell peppers, celery, cherries, imported grapes, nectarines, peaches, pears, potatoes, red raspberries, spinach, and strawberries. Experts also recommend buying organic beef, poultry, eggs, dairy products, and baby food. Fruits and vegetables that carry little pesticide residue whether grown conventionally or organically include asparagus, avocadoes, bananas, broccoli, cauliflower, corn, kiwi, mangoes, onions, papaya, pineapples, and peas. All foods are subject to strict pesticide limits; the debate about the health effects of small amounts of residue is ongoing.

Whether organic foods are better for your health or not, organic farming is better for the environment. It helps maintain biodiversity of crops and replenish the earth's resources; it is less likely to degrade soil, contaminate water, or expose farm workers to toxic chemicals. As multinational food companies get into the organic food business, however, consumers who want to support environmentally friendly farming methods should look for foods that are not only organic but locally grown.

Guidelines for Fish Consumption A specific area of concern has been possible mercury contamination in fish. Overall, fish and shellfish are healthy sources of protein, omega-3 fats, and other nutrients; and prudent choices can minimize the risk of any possible negative health effects. High mercury concentrations are most likely to be found in predator fish—large fish that eat smaller fish. Mercury can cause brain damage to fetuses and young children. In 2004, the FDA and Environmental Protection Agency (EPA) released an advisory with specific guidelines for certain groups. To reduce exposure to the harmful effects of mercury, women who are or who may become pregnant and nursing mothers should follow these guidelines:

- Do not eat shark, swordfish, king mackerel, or tilefish.
- Eat up to 12 ounces a week of a variety of fish and shellfish that is lower in mercury, such as shrimp, canned light tuna, salmon, pollock, and catfish. Limit consumption of albacore tuna to 6 ounces per week.
- Check advisories about the safety of recreationally caught fish from local lakes, rivers, and coastal areas; if no information is available, limit consumption to 6 ounces per week.

The same FDA/EPA guidelines apply to children, although they should consume smaller servings.

Some experts have also expressed concern about the presence of toxins such as PCBs in farmed fish, especially farmed salmon. Although no federal guidelines have been set, some researchers suggest that consumers limit themselves to 8 ounces of farmed salmon per month. Fish should be labeled with its country of origin and whether it is wild or farmed; most canned salmon is wild.

Additives in Food

Today, some 2800 substances are intentionally added to foods for one or more of the following reasons: (1) to maintain or improve nutritional quality, (2) to maintain freshness, (3) to help in processing or preparation, or (4) to alter taste or appearance. Additives make up less than 1% of our food. The most widely used are sugar, salt, and corn syrup; these three plus citric acid, baking soda,

Terms

Vw

organic A designation applied to foods grown and produced according to strict guidelines limiting the use of pesticides, nonorganic ingredients, hormones, antibiotics, irradiation, genetic engineering, and other practices.

food irradiation The treatment of foods with gamma rays, X rays, or high-voltage electrons to kill potentially harmful pathogens and increase shelf life.

genetically modified (GM) organism A plant, animal, or microorganism in which genes have been added, rearranged, or replaced through genetic engineering.

vegetable colors, mustard, and pepper account for 98% by weight of all food additives used in the United States.

Some additives may be of concern for certain people, either because they are consumed in large quantities or because they cause some type of reaction. Additives having potential health concerns include the following:

- *Nitrates and nitrites:* Used to protect meats from contamination with botulism. Their consumption is associated with the synthesis of cancer-causing agents in the stomach, but the cancer risk appears to be low, except for people with low stomach acid output (such as some elderly people).
- *BHA and BHT:* Used to help maintain the freshness of foods. Some studies indicate a potential link between BHT and an increased risk of certain cancers, but any risk from these agents is considered to be low. Some manufacturers have stopped using BHT and BHA.
- *Sulfites:* Used to keep vegetables from turning brown. They can cause severe reactions in some people. The FDA severely limits the use of sulfites and requires any foods containing sulfites to be clearly labeled.
- *Monosodium glutamate (MSG):* Typically used as a flavor enhancer. MSG may cause some people to experience episodes of increased blood pressure and sweating. If you are sensitive to MSG, check food labels when shopping, and ask to have it left out of dishes you order at restaurants.

Food additives pose no significant health hazard to most people because the levels used are well below any that could produce toxic effects. To avoid potential problems, eat a variety of foods in moderation. If you are sensitive to an additive, check food labels when you shop, and ask questions when you eat out.

Food Irradiation

Food irradiation is the treatment of foods with gamma rays, X rays, or high-voltage electrons to kill potentially harmful pathogens, including bacteria, parasites, insects, and fungi that cause foodborne illness. It also reduces spoilage and extends shelf life. For example, irradiated strawberries stay unspoiled in the refrigerator up to 3 weeks, versus only 3–5 days for untreated berries. Since 1963, the government has allowed the irradiation of certain foods; this growing list includes wheat and flour (1963); white potatoes (1964); pork, herbs and spices, and fruits and vegetables (1986); raw poultry (1992); and red meat (1999). The same irradiation process has also been used for decades on such items as plastic wrap, milk cartons, teething rings, contact lenses, and medical supplies.

Even though irradiation has been generally endorsed by agencies such as the World Health Organization, the Centers for Disease Control and Prevention, and the American Medical Association, few irradiated foods are currently on the market due to consumer resistance and skepticism. Studies haven't conclusively identified any harmful effects of food irradiation, and the newer methods of irradiation involving electricity and X rays do not require the use of any radioactive materials. Some irradiated foods may taste slightly different, just as pasteurized milk tastes slightly different than unpasteurized milk.

Studies indicate that when consumers are given information about the process of irradiation and the benefits of irradiated foods, most want to purchase them. Without such information, many remain skeptical. All primary irradiated foods (meat, vegetables, and so on) are labeled with the flowerlike radura symbol and a brief information label; spices and foods that are merely ingredients do not have to be so labeled. It is important to remember that although irradiation kills most pathogens, it does not completely sterilize foods. Proper handling of irradiated foods is still critical for preventing foodborne illness.

Genetically Modified Foods

Genetic engineering involves altering the characteristics of a plant, animal, or microorganism by adding, rearranging, or replacing genes in its DNA; the result is a **genetically modified (GM) organism.** New DNA may come from related species or from entirely different types of organisms. Many GM crops are already grown in the United States: About 75% of the current U.S. soybean crop has been genetically modified to be resistant to an herbicide used to kill weeds, and about 34% of the U.S. corn crop carries genes for herbicide resistance or pest resistance. Products made with GM organisms include juice, soda, nuts, tuna, frozen pizza, spaghetti sauce, canola oil, chips, salad dressings, and soup.

The potential benefits of GM foods cited by supporters include improved yields overall and in difficult growing conditions, increased disease resistance, improved nutritional content, lower prices, and less pesticide use. Critics of biotechnology argue that unexpected effects may occur: Gene manipulation could elevate levels of naturally occurring toxins or allergens, permanently change the gene pool and reduce biodiversity, and produce pesticide-resistant insects through the transfer of genes. Experience has shown that GM products are difficult to keep separate from non-GM products; animal escapes, cross-pollination, and contamination during processing are just a few ways GM organisms could potentially appear unexpectedly in the food supply or the environment.

According to the National Academy of Sciences, there is currently no proof that the GM food already on the market is unsafe. However, experts have recommended regulatory changes and further study of key issues, particularly the environmental effects of the escape of GM animals. Labeling has been another major concern, with surveys indicating that most Americans want to know if their food contains GM ingredients. Under current rules, the FDA requires special labeling only when a food's composition is changed significantly or when a known allergen such as a peanut gene is introduced into a food. The only foods guaranteed not to contain GM ingredients are those certified as organic.

Food Allergies and Food Intolerances

For some people, consuming a particular food causes symptoms such as itchiness, swollen lips, or abdominal pain. Adverse reactions like these may be due to a food allergy or a food intolerance, and symptoms may range from annoying to life-threatening. If you've had an adverse reaction to a food, it's important to determine whether your symptoms are due to an allergy or an intolerance so that you can take appropriate action.

Food Allergies A true **food allergy** is a reaction of the body's immune system to a food or food ingredient, usually a protein. The immune system perceives the reaction-provoking substance, or allergen, as foreign and acts to destroy it. This immune reaction can occur within minutes of ingesting the food, resulting in symptoms that affect the skin (hives), gastrointestinal tract (cramps or diarrhea), respiratory tract (asthma), or mouth (swelling of the lips or tongue). The most severe response is a systemic reaction called anaphylaxis, which involves a potentially life-threatening drop in blood pressure.

Food allergies affect only about 2% of the adult population and about 4–6% of infants; many infants outgrow food allergies. Although numerous food allergens have been identified, just eight foods account for more than 90% of the food allergies in the United States: cow's milk, eggs, peanuts, tree nuts (walnuts, cashews, and so on), soy, wheat, fish, and shellfish. Food labels are now required to state the presence of the eight most common allergens in plain language in the ingredient list. Individuals with food allergies, especially those prone to anaphylaxis, must diligently avoid trigger foods. This involves carefully reading food labels and asking questions about ingredients when eating out. People at risk are usually advised to carry medications to treat anaphylaxis, such as injectable epinephrine. Refer to Chapter 17 for more on allergies.

Terms

VW

food allergy An adverse reaction to a food or food ingredient in which the immune system perceives a particular substance (allergen) as foreign and acts to destroy it.

food intolerance An adverse reaction to a food or food ingredient that doesn't involve the immune system; intolerances are often due to a problem with metabolism.

Food Intolerances Many people who believe they have food allergies may actually suffer from a much more common source of adverse food reactions, a **food intolerance.** In the case of a food intolerance, the problem usually lies with metabolism rather than with the immune system. Typically, the body cannot adequately digest a food or food component, often because of some type of chemical deficiency; in other cases, the body reacts to a particular compound in a food. Lactose intolerance is a fairly common food intolerance. A more serious condition is intolerance of gluten, a protein component of some grains; in affected individuals, consumption of gluten damages the lining of the small intestine. Sulfite, a common food additive, can produce severe asthmatic reactions in sensitive individuals. Food intolerances have also been attributed to tartrazine (a yellow food coloring), MSG, and the sweetener aspartame.

Food intolerance reactions often produce symptoms similar to food allergies, such as diarrhea or cramps, but reactions are typically localized and not life-threatening. Many people with food intolerances can consume small amounts of the food that affects them; exceptions are gluten and sulfite, which must be avoided by sensitive individuals. Through trial and error, most people with food intolerances can adjust their intake of the trigger food to an appropriate level.

If you suspect that you have a food allergy or intolerance, a good first step is to keep a food diary. Note everything you eat or drink, any symptoms you develop, and how long after eating the symptoms appear. Then make an appointment with your physician to go over your diary and determine if any additional tests are needed.

Staying Committed to a Healthy Diet

You've learned about nutrition, how to interpret labels, and how to avoid food-related illness. With this foundation, you can now put together a diet that works for you. You can customize a food plan based on your age, sex, weight, activity level, medical risk factors—and, of course, personal tastes.

Sticking to a healthy diet is usually easiest when people choose and prepare their own food at home (see the box "America's Poor Eating Habits"). For meals prepared at home, advance planning is the key: Map out meals and shop appropriately, cook in advance when possible, and prepare enough food for leftovers later in the week. A tight budget need not make it more difficult to eat healthy meals. It makes good health sense and good budget sense to use only small amounts of meat and to have a few meatless meals each week.

Healthy eating becomes more challenging when you dine out. Portion sizes in restaurants are often far larger than the portion sizes used in MyPyramid. Try eating only

America's Poor Eating Habits

The typical American diet has changed significantly in recent decades—and not for the better. The top ten sources of calories in the American diet, which together account for more than 30% total energy intake, do not reflect healthy eating habits (see table). Americans now consume too many calories, often in the form of added sugars and fats, but too few vitamins and minerals, in part because intake of fruits, vegetables, and milk products is relatively low.

Consumption of regular sodas and sweetened fruit drinks has nearly doubled since 1970, and Americans consume an average of 152 pounds of added sugars each year. Milk consumption has dropped 40% since 1970 as children and young adults have switched to sodas, which now account for nearly 10% of daily calories for 12–19-year-olds. Americans now eat out much more than in the past—more than 40% of Americans eat out at least once on a typical day—and foods eaten outside the home tend to be higher in calories and lower in nutrients than foods prepared at home.

Individual Choice

Individual choice is certainly a key component in recent dietary shifts. Low prices and convenience are valued by American consumers, and there has been a rapid increase in the availability of affordable, convenient, and tasty foods. Many foods with these characteristics do not have a healthy nutritional profile; they tend to be energy-dense and nutrient-poor. American consumers know they should make better choices—but they frequently fail to do so.

Environmental Influences

While acknowledging the role of personal responsibility, some experts also point to environmental factors. Convenience foods are now widely available for purchase, and in many urban neighborhoods in particular, it is easier to buy fast food than fruits and vegetables. In part because sugar is inexpensive, many foods high in added sugars are inexpensive. (Federal subsidies for corn make high-fructose corn syrup, which is found in a wide variety of processed foods, very inexpensive.)

The food industry spends over $30 billion a year on advertising, special promotions, and supermarket slotting fees, with $10 billion of this directed at children. McDonald's alone spends over $1 billion each year on ads, compared to just $1 million spent by the National Cancer Institute for its "5 to 9 a Day" fruits and vegetables campaign.

Many ads target children under age 10, who researchers have found cannot distinguish between advertising and informational programming. (A study of Australian children age 9–10 found that more than half believed that Ronald McDonald "knows best" when it comes to what children should eat.) Most ads during children's programming feature large portions of sweetened breakfast cereals, fruit-flavored drinks, and fast food. Teen programming features three times as many ads for soft drinks as for milk, a ratio that mirrors consumption patterns.

And young people can now consume fast food at school: About 30% of public high schools offer some type of brand-name fast food, and food ads are featured in television programming shown in schools. (Some school districts have raised money by accepting marketing deals with brand-name soda and fast-food companies.)

What Can Be Done?

Several different strategies have been proposed to promote personal responsibility and combat negative environmental forces:

- Change the price structure of food. Add small taxes on soft drinks, fast food, and other nutrient-poor foods to subsidize (and lower) the costs of healthy foods and to fund campaigns to promote healthy diet and activity habits.
- Prominently print or post basic nutrition information for meals ordered in restaurants and for convenience foods and fast foods. For example, the calorie, sugar, and fat content of sodas and popcorn could be printed on the cups in which they are served at schools, restaurants, and movie theaters.
- Restrict food advertising aimed at children, and ban commercials for unhealthy foods on school television programs.

Top Ten Sources of Calories in the American Diet

Food	Percent of Total Calories
Regular soft drinks	7.1
Cake, sweet rolls, doughnuts, pastries	3.6
Hamburgers, cheeseburgers, meatloaf	3.1
Pizza	3.1
Potato chips, corn chips, popcorn	2.9
Rice	2.7
Rolls, buns, English muffins, bagels	2.7
Cheese or cheese spread	2.6
Beer	2.6
French fries, fried potatoes	2.2

- Require that all meals sold on school grounds meet federal nutrition recommendations; ban paid marketing agreements between schools and fast-food and soft-drink companies.
- Increase public awareness of factors that promote unhealthy food choices, including low cost, accessibility, convenience, and taste (added sugars and fats).

If you're concerned about your own eating habits and those of people in your community, speak with your consumer dollars. Make it a priority to purchase healthy foods when they are offered. In addition, be aware of outside influences on your food choices. This chapter—and the resources listed at the end of the chapter—provide many suggestions for choosing delicious, convenient, and healthy foods.

SOURCES: Block, G. 2004. Foods contributing to energy intake in the US: Data from NHANES III and NHANES 1999–2000. *Journal of Food Composition and Analysis* 17(2004): 439–447; Brownell, K. D. 2004. *Food Fight*. New York: McGraw-Hill; Liebman, B. 2002. The changing American diet. *Nutrition Action HealthLetter,* December; Nestle, M., and M. F. Jacobson. 2000. Halting the obesity epidemic: A public health policy approach. *Public Health Reports* 115: 12–24.

part of your meal and take the rest home for a meal later in the week. Don't hesitate to ask questions about how menu selections are prepared and to ask for adjustments, such as salad dressings or sauces served on the side. To limit your fat and calorie intake, order dishes that have been broiled or grilled rather than fried, choose rice or a plain baked potato over french fries, and select a clear soup rather than a creamy one. Desserts that are irresistible can, at least, be shared.

Strategies like these can be helpful, but small changes cannot change a fundamentally high-fat, high-calorie meal into a moderate, healthful one. Often, the best advice is to bypass the sweet-and-sour pork with fried rice for an equally flavorful but low-fat entrée. Fast-food meals are often particularly high in calories, fat, sodium, and sugar and low in fiber and some vitamins and minerals. If you do eat at a fast-food restaurant, make sure the rest of your meals that day include healthier choices.

The information provided in this chapter should give you the tools you need to design and implement a diet that you enjoy and that promotes long-term health and well-being. If you need additional information or have questions about nutrition, be sure the source you consult is reliable.

Tips for Today

Eating is one of life's great pleasures. There are many ways to satisfy your nutrient needs, so you can create a healthy diet that takes into account your personal preferences and favorite foods. If your current eating habits are not as healthy as they could be, you can choose equally delicious foods that offer both short-term and long-term health benefits. Opportunities to improve your diet present themselves every day, and small changes add up.

Right now you can

- Substitute a healthy snack—an apple, a banana, or popcorn—for a bag of chips or cookies.
- Drink a glass of water, and put a bottle of water in your backpack for tomorrow.
- Plan to make healthy selections when you go to dinner, such as grilled or steamed vegetables instead of french fries or salmon instead of steak.
- Study the box on ethnic foods in this chapter and plan to order a healthy selection the next time you eat at your favorite ethnic restaurant. Do the same with the fast-food restaurants listed in Appendix A.

SUMMARY

- To function at its best, the human body requires about 45 essential nutrients in specific proportions. People get the nutrients needed to fuel their bodies and maintain tissues and organ systems from foods; the body cannot synthesize most of them.
- Proteins, made up of amino acids, form muscles and bones and help make up blood, enzymes, hormones, and cell membranes. Foods from animal sources provide complete proteins; plants provide incomplete proteins.
- Fats, a concentrated source of energy, also help insulate the body and cushion the organs; 1 tablespoon of vegetable oil per day supplies the essential fats. Dietary fat intake should be 20–35% of total daily calories. Unsaturated fats should be favored over saturated and trans fats.
- Carbohydrates supply energy to the brain and other parts of the nervous system as well as to red blood cells. The body needs about 130 grams of carbohydrates a day, but more is recommended.
- Fiber includes nondigestible carbohydrates provided mainly by plants. Adequate intake of fiber (38 grams per day for men and 25 grams per day for women) can help people manage diabetes and high cholesterol levels and improve intestinal health.
- The 13 vitamins needed in the diet are organic substances that promote specific chemical and cell processes within living tissue. Deficiencies or excesses can cause serious illnesses and even death.
- The approximately 17 minerals needed in the diet are inorganic substances that regulate body functions, aid in the growth and maintenance of body tissues, and help in the release of energy from foods.
- Water is used to digest and absorb food, transport substances around the body, lubricate joints and organs, and regulate body temperature.
- Foods contain other substances such as phytochemicals, which may not be essential nutrients but which reduce chronic disease risk.
- Dietary Reference Intakes (DRIs) are recommended intakes for essential nutrients that meet the needs of healthy people.
- The Dietary Guidelines for Americans address the prevention of diet-related diseases such as CVD, cancer, and diabetes. The guidelines advise us to consume a variety of foods while staying within calorie needs; manage body weight through calorie control and regular physical activity; eat more fruits, vegetables, whole grains, and reduced-fat dairy products; choose fats and carbohydrates wisely; eat less salt and more potassium; be moderate with alcohol intake; and handle foods safely.
- Choosing foods from each group in MyPyramid every day helps ensure the appropriate amounts of necessary nutrients.
- A vegetarian diet can meet human nutritional needs.
- Almost all foods have labels that show how much fat, cholesterol, protein, fiber, and sodium they contain. Serving sizes are standardized, and health claims are carefully regulated. Dietary supplements also have uniform labels.
- Foodborne illnesses are a greater threat to health than additives and environmental contaminants. Other dietary issues of concern to some people include organic foods, food irradiation, genetic modification of foods, and food allergies and intolerances.

Behavior Change Strategy

Improving Your Diet by Choosing Healthy Beverages

After reading this chapter and completing the dietary assessment on p. 355, you can probably identify several changes you could make to improve your diet. Here, we focus on choosing healthy beverages to increase intake of nutrients and decrease intake of empty calories from added sugars and fat. However, this model of dietary change can be applied to any modification you'd like to make to your diet. Additional specific plans for improving diet can be found in the Behavior Change Strategies in Chapter 15 (decreasing saturated and trans fat intake) and Chapter 16 (increasing intake of fruits and vegetables).

Gather Data and Establish a Baseline

Begin by tracking your beverage consumption in your health journal. Write down the types and amounts of beverages you drink, including water. Also note where you were at the time and whether you obtained the beverage there or brought it with you. At the same time, investigate your options. Find out what other beverages you can easily obtain over the course of your daily routine. For example, what drinks are available in the dining hall where you eat lunch or at the food court where you often grab snacks? How many drinking fountains do you walk by over the course of the day? This information will help you put together a successful plan for change.

Analyze Your Data and Set Goals

Evaluate your beverage consumption by dividing your typical daily consumption between healthy and less healthy choices. Use the following guide as a basis, and add other beverages to the lists as needed.

Choose less often:

- Regular soda
- Sweetened bottled iced tea
- Fruit beverages made with little fruit juice (usually labeled fruit drinks, punches, beverages, blends, or ades)
- Whole milk

Choose more often:

- Water—plain, mineral, and sparkling
- Low-fat or fat-free milk
- Fruit juice (100% juice)
- Unsweetened herbal tea

How many beverages do you consume daily from each category? What would be a healthy and realistic goal for change? For example, if your beverage consumption is currently evenly divided between the "choose more often" and "choose less often" categories (four from each list), you might set a final goal for your behavior change program of increasing your healthy choices by two (to six from the "more often" list and two from the "less often" list).

Develop a Plan for Change

Once you've set your goal, you need to develop strategies that will help you choose healthy beverages more often. Consider the following possibilities:

- Keep healthy beverages on hand; if you live in a student dorm, rent a small refrigerator or keep bottled water, juice, fat-free milk, and other healthy choices in the dorm kitchen's refrigerator.
- Plan ahead, and put a bottle of water or 100% juice in your backpack every day.
- Check food labels on beverages for serving sizes, calories, and nutrients; comparison shop to find the healthiest choices, and watch your serving sizes. Use this information to make your "choose more often" list longer and more specific.
- If you eat out frequently, examine all the beverages available at the places you typically eat your meals. You'll probably find that healthy choices are available; if not, bring along your own drink or find somewhere else to eat.
- For a snack, try water and a piece of fruit rather than a heavily sweetened beverage.
- Create healthy beverages that appeal to you; for example, try adding slices of citrus fruit to water or mixing 100% fruit juice with sparkling water.

You may also need to make some changes in your routine to decrease the likelihood that you'll make unhealthy choices. For example, you might discover from your health journal that you always buy a soda after class when you pass a particular vending machine. If this is the case, try another route that allows you to avoid the machine. And try to guard against impulse buying by carrying water or a healthy snack with you every day.

To complete your plan, try some of the other behavior change strategies described in Chapter 1: Develop and sign a contract, set up a system of rewards, involve other people in your program, and develop strategies for challenging situations. Once your plan is complete, take action. Keep track of your progress in your health journal by continuing to monitor and evaluate your beverage consumption.

Take Action

1. **Examine ingredients and nutrient content:** Read the list of ingredients on three or four canned or packaged foods that you enjoy eating. If any ingredients are unfamiliar to you, find out what they are and why they have been used. A nutrition textbook from the library may be a helpful resource. Also examine and compare nutrient content using the food label. Are you surprised by the energy or nutrient content of any of the foods you examine?

2. **Investigate nutritional and dietary guidelines:** What guidelines are used to prepare the food served in your school? Are they consistent with what you've learned in this chapter? If not, try to find out more about the guidelines that have been used and why they were chosen.

3. **Prepare a flavorful low-fat vegetarian and/or ethnic meal.** Use the suggestions in the chapter, and check your local

library for appropriate cookbooks. How do the foods included in the meal and the preparation methods differ from what you're used to?

4. **Keep a journal:** A nutrition journal is useful for evaluating and improving your diet. The very act of recording everything you eat may improve your dietary habits—you'll find yourself thinking before you eat and avoiding some unhealthy choices so that you don't have to record them in your journal. Keeping a journal boosts your awareness of your food choices and your portion sizes, and it reinforces your commitment to improving your diet.

5. **Volunteer in your community:** There are many opportunities for improving the nutritional status of members of your community. Consider volunteering at a food bank or a kitchen at a homeless shelter. Or find a community garden program for schoolchildren or low-income families—working in a vegetable garden increases your own connection to the food you eat and improves your community.

For More Information

Books

Duyff, R. L. 2006. *ADA Complete Food and Nutrition Guide,* 3rd ed. Hoboken, N.J.: Wiley. *An excellent review of current nutrition information.*

Insel, P., R. E. Turner, and D. Ross. 2006. *Nutrition,* 3rd ed. Sudbury, Mass.: Jones & Bartlett. *An introductory nutrition textbook covering a variety of key topics.*

Katz, D., and M. Gonzalez. 2004. *The Way to Eat.* Chicago, Ill.: American Dietetic Association. *Guide to a lifetime of eating well and promoting good health, weight control, and enjoyment of food.*

Melina, V., and B. Davis. 2003. *The New Becoming Vegetarian: The Essential Guide to a Healthy Vegetarian Diet.* Summertown, Tn.: Healthy Living Publications. *Provides information on the health benefits of vegetarian diets and how to plan healthy meals.*

Selkowitz, A. 2005. *The College Student's Guide to Eating Well on Campus,* revised ed. Bethesda, Md.: Tulip Hill Press. *Provides practical advice for students, including how to make healthy choices when eating in a dorm or restaurant and how to stock a first pantry.*

Wardlaw, G. M., and A. M. Smith. 2006. *Contemporary Nutrition,* 6th ed. New York: McGraw-Hill. *A review of major concepts in nutrition.*

Newsletters

Environmental Nutrition (800-424-7887; http://www.environmentalnutrition.com)

Nutrition Action Health Letter (202-332-9110; http://www.cspinet.org/nah)

Tufts University Health & Nutrition Letter (800-274-7581; http://www.healthletter.tufts.edu)

Organizations, Hotlines, and Web Sites

American Dietetic Association. Provides a wide variety of nutrition-related educational materials.
800-877-1600
http://www.eatright.org

American Heart Association: Delicious Decisions. Provides basic information about nutrition, tips for shopping and eating out, and heart-healthy recipes.
http://www.deliciousdecisions.org

FDA Center for Food Safety and Applied Nutrition. Offers information about topics such as food labeling, food additives, dietary supplements, and foodborne illness.
http://vm.cfsan.fda.gov

Food Safety Hotlines. Provide information on safe purchase, handling, cooking, and storage of food.
888-SAFEFOOD (FDA)
800-535-4555 (USDA)

Gateways to Government Nutrition Information. Provide access to government resources relating to food safety and nutrition.
http://www.foodsafety.gov
http://www.nutrition.gov

Harvard School of Public Health Nutrition Source. Provides recent key research findings, including advice on interpreting news on nutrition; an overview of the Healthy Eating Pyramid, an alternative to the basic USDA pyramid; and suggestions for building a healthy diet.
http://www.hsph.harvard.edu/nutritionsource

International Food Information Council. Provides information on food safety and nutrition for consumers, journalists, and educators.
http://www.ific.org

MyPyramid.Gov. Provides personalized dietary plans and interactive food and activity tracking tools.
http://www.mypyramid.gov

National Academies' Food and Nutrition Board. Provides information about the Dietary Reference Intakes and related guidelines.
http://www.iom.edu/CMS/3788.aspx

National Cancer Institute: Eat 5 to 9 a Day for Better Health. Provides tips and recipes to help consumers increase their intake of fruits and vegetables.
http://5aday.nci.nih.gov

Tufts University Nutrition Navigator. Provides descriptions and ratings for many nutrition-related Web pages.
http://navigator.tufts.edu

USDA Center for Nutrition Policy and Promotion. Includes information on the Dietary Guidelines and MyPyramid.
http://www.usda.gov/cnpp

USDA Food and Nutrition Information Center. Provides a variety of materials and extensive links relating to the Dietary Guidelines, food labels, MyPyramid, and many other topics.
http://www.nal.usda.gov/fnic

Vegetarian Resource Group. Information and links for vegetarians and people interested in learning more about vegetarian diets.
http://www.vrg.org

You can obtain nutrient breakdowns of individual food items from the following sites:

Nutrition Analysis Tool, University of Illinois, Urbana/Champaign
http://nat.crgq.com

USDA Nutrient Data Laboratory
http://www.ars.usda.gov/main/site_main.htm?modecode=12354500

See also the resources listed in the dietary supplements box on page 361 and in the For More Information sections in Chapters 13–16 and 19.

Selected Bibliography

Aldana, S. G., et al. 2005. Effects of an intensive diet and physical activity modification program on the health risks of adults. *Journal of the American Dietetic Association* 105(3): 371–381.

American Heart Association. 2006. *Our 2006 Diet and Lifestyle Recommendations* (http://www.americanheart.org/presenter.jhtml?identifier=851; retrieved August 15, 2006).

Block, G. 2004. Foods contributing to energy intake in the US: Data from NHANES III and NHANES 1999–2000. *Journal of Food Composition and Analysis* 17(2004): 439–447.

Briefel, R. R., and C. I. Johnson. 2004. Secular trends in dietary intake in the United States. *Annual Review of Nutrition 2004* 24: 401–431.

Centers for Disease Control and Prevention. 2006. *Nutrition for Everyone: Quick Tips* (http://www.cdc.gov/nccdphp/dnpa/nutrition/nutrition_for_everyone/quick_tips/index.htm; retrieved August 16, 2006).

Clifton, P. M., J. B. Keogh, and M. Noakes. 2004. Trans fatty acids in adipose tissue and the food supply are associated with myocardial infarction. *Journal of Nutrition* 134: 874–879.

Cotton, P. A., et al. 2004. Dietary sources of nutrients among U.S. adults, 1994 to 1996. *Journal of the American Dietetic Association* 104: 921–930.

Ervin, R. B., et al. 2004. Dietary intake of selected minerals for the United States population: 1999–2000. *Advance Data from Vital and Health Statistics* No. 341.

Food and Drug Administration. 2004. *Backgrounder for the 2004 FDA/EPA Consumer Advisory: What You Need to Know About Mercury in Fish and Shellfish* (http://www.fda.gov/oc/opacom/hottopics/mercury/backgrounder.html; retrieved August 16, 2006).

Food and Drug Administration. 2004. *Fact Sheet: Carbohydrates* (http://www.fda.gov/oc/initiatives/obesity/factsheet.html; retrieved August 16, 2006).

Food and Drug Administration, Center for Food Safety and Applied Nutrition. 2006. *Trans Fat Now Listed with Saturated Fat and Cholesterol on the Nutrition Facts Label* (http://www.cfsan.fda.gov/~dms/transfat.html; retrieved August 16, 2006).

Food and Nutrition Board, Institute of Medicine. 2005. *Dietary Reference Intakes for Energy, Carbohydrate, Fiber, Fat, Fatty Acids, Cholesterol, Protein, and Amino Acids.* Washington, D.C.: National Academy Press.

Food and Nutrition Board, Institute of Medicine. 2005. *Dietary Reference Intakes for Water, Potassium, Sodium, Chloride, and Sulfate.* Washington, D.C.: National Academy Press.

Foote, J. A., et al. 2004. Dietary variety increases the probability of nutrient adequacy among adults. *Journal of Nutrition* 134: 1779–1784.

Gilroy, C. M., et al. 2003. Echinacea and truth in labeling. *Archives of Internal Medicine* 163(6): 699–704.

A guide to the best and worst drinks. 2006. *Consumer Reports on Health,* July, 8–9.

Hanley, D. A., and K. S. Davison. 2005. Vitamin D insufficiency in North America. *Journal of Nutrition* 135(2): 332–337.

Harvard School of Public Health, Department of Nutrition. 2006. *The Nutrition Source: Knowledge for Healthy Eating* (http://www.hsph.harvard.edu/nutritionsource/index.html; retrieved August 16, 2006).

He, K., et al. 2004. Accumulated evidence on fish consumption and coronary heart disease mortality: A meta-analysis of cohort studies. *Circulation* 109: 2705–2711.

Hites, R. A., et al. 2004. Global assessment of organic contaminants in farmed salmon. *Science* 303(5655): 225–229.

Houston, D. K., et al. 2005. Dairy, fruit, and vegetable intakes and functional limitations and disability in a biracial cohort. *American Journal of Clinical Nutrition* 81(2): 515–522.

Joint WHO/FAO Expert Consultation. 2003. *Diet, Nutrition, and the Prevention of Chronic Diseases* (http://whqlibdoc.who.int/trs/WHO_TRS_916.pdf; retrieved August 16, 2006).

Kranz, S., et al. 2005. Adverse effect of high added sugar consumption on dietary intake in American preschoolers. *Journal of Pediatrics* 46(1): 105–111.

Lichtenstein, A. H., et al. 2006. Diet and Lifestyle Recommendations, Revision 2006. A Scientific Statement from the American Heart Association Nutrition Committee. *Circulation* 114(1): 82–96.

Liebman, B. 2006. Whole Grains: The Inside Story. *Nutrition Action Health Letter* 33(4): 1–5.

Liu, S., et al. 2003. Is intake of breakfast cereals related to total and cause-specific mortality in men? *American Journal of Clinical Nutrition* 77(3): 594–599.

McKeown, N. M., et al. 2002. Whole-grain intake is favorably associated with metabolic risk factors for type 2 diabetes and cardiovascular disease in the Framingham Offspring Study. *American Journal of Clinical Nutrition* 76(2): 390–398.

Ma, Y., et al. 2005. Association between dietary carbohydrates and body weight. *American Journal of Epidemiology* 161(4): 359–367.

Mayo Clinic. 2006. *Healthy diet basics: Using a food pyramid* (http://www.mayoclinic.com/health/healthy-diet/NU00190; retrieved August 16, 2006).

Michaelsson, K., et al. 2003. Serum retinol levels and the risk of fracture. *New England Journal of Medicine* 348(4): 287–294.

Mosaffarian, D., et al. 2006. Trans fatty acids and cardiovascular disease. *New England Journal of Medicine* 354(15): 1601–1613.

Nanney, M. S., et al. 2004. Rationale for a consistent "powerhouse" approach to vegetable and fruit messages. *Journal of the American Dietetic Association* 104(3): 352–356.

National Academy of Sciences, Institute of Medicine, Food and Nutrition Board. 2005. *Dietary Reference Intakes: Recommended Intakes for Individuals* (http://www.iom.edu/Object.File/Master/7/300/Webtablemacro.pdf; retrieved August 15, 2006).

National Center for Health Statistics. 2003. Dietary intake of ten key nutrients for public health, United States: 1999–2000. *Advance Data from Vital and Health Statistics* No. 334.

Nicholls, S. J., et al. 2006. Consumption of saturated fat impairs the anti-inflammatory properties of high-density lipoproteins and endothelial function. *Journal of the American College of Cardiology* 48(4): 715–720.

Of birds and bacteria. 2003. *Consumer Reports,* January.

Opotowsky, A. R., et al. 2004. Serum vitamin A concentration and the risk of hip fracture among women 50 to 74 years old in the United States. *American Journal of Medicine* 117(3): 169–174.

Palmer, M. E., et al. 2003. Adverse events associated with dietary supplements: An observational study. *Lancet* 361(9352): 101–106.

Pereira, M. A., et al. 2004. Dietary fiber and risk of coronary heart disease: A pooled analysis of cohort studies. *Archives of Internal Medicine* 164(4): 370–376.

Tirodkar, M. A., and A. Jain. 2003. Food messages on African American television shows. *American Journal of Public Health* 93(3): 439–441.

U.S. Department of Agriculture. 2006. *Inside the Pyramid* (http://www.mypyramid.gov/pyramid.index.html; retrieved August 15, 2006).

U.S. Department of Agriculture, Food Safety and Inspection Service. 2005. *Fact Sheet: Bovine Spongiform Encephalopathy — "Mad Cow Disease"* (http://www.fsis.usda.gov/Fact_Sheets/Bovine_Spongiform_Encephalopathy_Mad_Cow_Disease/index.asp; retrieved August 16, 2006).

U.S. Department of Health and Human Services and U.S. Department of Agriculture. 2005. *Dietary Guidelines for Americans 2005* (http://www.healthierus.gov/dietaryguidelines/index.html; retrieved August 15, 2006).

U.S. Department of Health and Human Services and U.S. Department of Agriculture. 2005. *Finding Your Way to a Healthier You: Based on the Dietary Guidelines for Americans.* Home and Garden Bulletin No. 232-CP.

U.S. Department of Health and Human Services and U.S. Environmental Protection Agency. 2006. *Mercury Levels in Commercial Fish and Shellfish* (http://www.cfsan.fda.gov/~frf/sea-mehg.html; retrieved August 16, 2006).

Vieth, R. 2006. What is the optimal vitamin D status for health? *Progress in Biophysics and Molecular Biology* 92(1): 26–32.

Nutrition Resources

Table 1 Dietary Reference Intakes (DRIs): Recommended Levels for Individual Intake

Life Stage	Group	Biotin (µg/day)	Choline (mg/day)[a]	Folate (µg/day)[b]	Niacin (mg/day)[c]	Pantothenic Acid (mg/day)	Riboflavin (mg/day)	Thiamin (mg/day)	Vitamin A (µg/day)[d]	Vitamin B-6 (mg/day)	Vitamin B-12 (µg/day)	Vitamin C (mg/day)[e]	Vitamin D (µg/day)[f]	Vitamin E (mg/day)[g]
Infants	0–6 months	5	125	65	2	1.7	0.3	0.2	400	0.1	0.4	40	5	4
	7–12 months	6	150	80	4	1.8	0.4	0.3	500	0.3	0.5	50	5	5
Children	1–3 years	8	200	**150**	**6**	2	**0.5**	**0.5**	**300**	**0.5**	**0.9**	**15**	5	**6**
	4–8 years	12	250	**200**	**8**	3	**0.6**	**0.6**	**400**	**0.6**	**1.2**	**25**	5	**7**
Males	9–13 years	20	375	**300**	**12**	4	**0.9**	**0.9**	**600**	**1.0**	**1.8**	**45**	5	**11**
	14–18 years	25	550	**400**	**16**	5	**1.3**	**1.2**	**900**	**1.3**	**2.4**	**75**	5	**15**
	19–30 years	30	550	**400**	**16**	5	**1.3**	**1.2**	**900**	**1.3**	**2.4**	**90**	5	**15**
	31–50 years	30	550	**400**	**16**	5	**1.3**	**1.2**	**900**	**1.3**	**2.4**	**90**	5	**15**
	51–70 years	30	550	**400**	**16**	5	**1.3**	**1.2**	**900**	**1.7**	**2.4**[h]	**90**	10	**15**
	>70 years	30	550	**400**	**16**	5	**1.3**	**1.2**	**900**	**1.7**	**2.4**[h]	**90**	15	**15**
Females	9–13 years	20	375	**300**	**12**	4	**0.9**	**0.9**	**600**	**1.0**	**1.8**	**45**	5	**11**
	14–18 years	25	400	**400**[i]	**14**	5	**1.0**	**1.0**	**700**	**1.2**	**2.4**	**65**	5	**15**
	19–30 years	30	425	**400**[i]	**14**	5	**1.1**	**1.1**	**700**	**1.3**	**2.4**	**75**	5	**15**
	31–50 years	30	425	**400**[i]	**14**	5	**1.1**	**1.1**	**700**	**1.3**	**2.4**	**75**	5	**15**
	51–70 years	30	425	**400**[i]	**14**	5	**1.1**	**1.1**	**700**	**1.5**	**2.4**[h]	**75**	10	**15**
	>70 years	30	425	**400**	**14**	5	**1.1**	**1.1**	**700**	**1.5**	**2.4**[h]	**75**	15	**15**
Pregnancy	≤18 years	30	450	**600**[i]	**18**	6	**1.4**	**1.4**	**750**	**1.9**	**2.6**	**80**	5	**15**
	19–30 years	30	450	**600**[j]	**18**	6	**1.4**	**1.4**	**770**	**1.9**	**2.6**	**85**	5	**15**
	31–50 years	30	450	**600**[j]	**18**	6	**1.4**	**1.4**	**770**	**1.9**	**2.6**	**85**	5	**15**
Lactation	≤18 years	35	550	**500**	**17**	7	**1.6**	**1.4**	**1200**	**2.0**	**2.8**	**115**	5	**19**
	19–30 years	35	550	**500**	**17**	7	**1.6**	**1.4**	**1300**	**2.0**	**2.8**	**120**	5	**19**
	31–50 years	35	550	**500**	**17**	7	**1.6**	**1.4**	**1300**	**2.0**	**2.8**	**120**	5	**19**
Tolerable Upper Intake Levels for Adults (19–70)			*3500*	*1000*[k]	*35*[k]				*3000*	*100*		*2000*	*50*	*1000*[k]

NOTE: The table includes values for the type of DRI standard—Adequate Intake (AI) or Recommended Dietary Allowance (RDA)—that has been established for that particular nutrient and life stage; RDAs are shown in **bold type.** The final row of the table shows the Tolerable Upper Intake Levels (ULs) for adults; refer to the full DRI report for information on other ages and life stages. A UL is the maximum level of daily nutrient intake that is likely to pose no risk of adverse effects. There is insufficient data to set ULs for all nutrients, but this does not mean that there is no potential for adverse effects; source of intake should be from food only to prevent high levels of intake of nutrients without established ULs. In healthy individuals, there is no established benefit from nutrient intakes above the RDA or AI.

[a]Although AIs have been set for choline, there are few data to assess whether a dietary supply of choline is needed at all stages of the life cycle, and it may be that the choline requirement can be met by endogenous synthesis at some of these stages.

[b]As dietary folate equivalents (DFE): 1 DFE = 1 µg food folate = 0.6 µg folate from fortified food or as a supplement consumed with food = 0.5 µg of a supplement taken on an empty stomach.

[c]As niacin equivalents (NE): 1 mg niacin = 60 mg tryptophan.

Table 1 Dietary Reference Intakes (DRIs): Recommended Levels for Individual Intake (*Continued*)

Life Stage	Group	Vitamin K (μg/day)	Calcium (mg/day)	Chromium (μg/day)	Copper (μg/day)	Fluoride (mg/day)	Iodine (μg/day)	Iron (mg/day)[l]	Magnesium (mg/day)	Manganese (mg/day)	Molybdenum (μg/day)	Phosphorus (mg/day)	Selenium (μg/day)	Zinc (mg/day)[m]
Infants	0–6 months	2.0	210	0.2	200	0.01	110	0.27	30	0.003	2	100	15	2
	7–12 months	2.5	270	5.5	220	0.5	130	11	75	0.6	3	275	20	3
Children	1–3 years	30	500	11	340	0.7	90	7	80	1.2	17	460	20	3
	4–8 years	55	800	15	440	1	90	10	130	1.5	22	500	30	5
Males	9–13 years	60	1300	25	700	2	120	8	240	1.9	34	1250	40	8
	14–18 years	75	1300	35	890	3	150	11	410	2.2	43	1250	55	11
	19–30 years	120	1000	35	900	4	150	8	400	2.3	45	700	55	11
	31–50 years	120	1000	35	900	4	150	8	420	2.3	45	700	55	11
	51–70 years	120	1200	30	900	4	150	8	420	2.3	45	700	55	11
	>70 years	120	1200	30	900	4	150	8	420	2.3	45	700	55	11
Females	9–13 years	60	1300	21	700	2	120	8	240	1.6	34	1250	40	8
	14–18 years	75	1300	24	890	3	150	15	360	1.6	43	1250	55	9
	19–30 years	90	1000	25	900	3	150	18	310	1.8	45	700	55	8
	31–50 years	90	1000	25	900	3	150	18	320	1.8	45	700	55	8
	51–70 years	90	1200	20	900	3	150	8	320	1.8	45	700	55	8
	>70 years	90	1200	20	900	3	150	8	320	1.8	45	700	55	8
Pregnancy	≤18 years	75	1300	29	1000	3	220	27	400	2.0	50	1250	60	13
	19–30 years	90	1000	30	1000	3	220	27	350	2.0	50	700	60	11
	31–50 years	90	1000	30	1000	3	220	27	360	2.0	50	700	60	11
Lactation	≤18 years	75	1300	44	1300	3	290	10	360	2.6	50	1250	70	14
	19–30 years	90	1000	45	1300	3	290	9	310	2.6	50	700	70	12
	31–50 years	90	1000	45	1300	3	290	9	320	2.6	50	700	70	12
Tolerable Upper Intake Levels for Adults (19–70)			*2500*		*10,000*	*10*	*1100*	*45*	*350*[k]	*11*	*2000*	*4000*	*400*	*40*

[d]As retinol activity equivalents (RAEs): 1 RAE = 1 μg retinol, 12 μg β-carotene, or 24 μg α-carotene or β-cryptoxanthin. Preformed vitamin A (retinol) is abundant in animal-derived foods; provitamin A carotenoids are abundant in some dark yellow, orange, red, and deep-green fruits and vegetables. For preformed vitamin A and for provitamin A carotenoids in supplements, 1RE = 1 RAE; for provitamin A carotenoids in foods, divide the REs by 2 to obtain RAEs. The UL applies only to preformed vitamin A.

[e]Individuals who smoke require an additional 35 mg/day of vitamin C over that needed by nonsmokers; nonsmokers regularly exposed to tobacco smoke should ensure they meet the RDA for vitamin C.

[f]As cholecalciferol: 1 μg cholecalciferol = 40 IU vitamin D. DRI values are based on the absence of adequate exposure to sunlight.

[g]As α-tocopherol. Includes naturally occurring RRR-α-tocopherol and the 2R-stereoisomeric forms from supplements; does not include the 2S-stereoisomeric forms from supplements.

[h]Because 10–30% of older people may malabsorb food-bound B-12, those over age 50 should meet their RDA mainly with supplements or foods fortified with B-12.

[i]In view of evidence linking folate intake with neural tube defects in the fetus. It is recommended that all women capable of becoming pregnant consume 400 μg from supplements or fortified foods in addition to consuming folate from a varied diet.

[j]It is assumed that women will continue consuming 400 μg from supplements or fortified food until their pregnancy is confirmed and they enter prenatal care, which ordinarily occurs after the end of the periconceptional period—the critical time for formation of the neural tube.

[k]The UL applies only to intake from supplements, fortified foods, and/or pharmacological agents and not to intake from foods.

[l]Because the absorption of iron from plant foods is low compared to that from animal foods, the RDA for strict vegetarians is approximately 1.8 times higher than the values established for omnivores (14 mg/day for adult male vegetarians; 33 mg/day for premenopausal female vegetarians). Oral contraceptives (OCs) reduce menstrual blood losses, so women taking them need less daily iron; the RDA for premenopausal women taking OCs is 10.9 mg/day. For more on iron requirements for other special situations, refer to *Dietary Reference Intakes for Vitamin A, Vitamin K, Arsenic, Boron, Chromium, Copper, Iodine, Iron, Manganese, Molybdenum, Nickel, Silicon, Vanadium, and Zinc* (visit http://www.nap.edu for the complete report).

[m]Zinc absorption is lower for those consuming vegetarian diets so the zinc requirement for vegetarians is approximately twofold greater than for those consuming a nonvegetarian diet.

Table 1 Dietary Reference Intakes (DRIs): Recommended Levels for Individual Intake (*continued*)

					Carbohydrate		Total Fiber	Total Fat	Linoleic Acid		Alpha-linolenic Acid		Protein[n]		
Life Stage	Group	Potassium (g/day)	Sodium (g/day)	Chloride (g/day)	RDA/AI (g/day)	AMDR[o] (%)	RDA/AI (g/day)	AMDR[o] (%)	RDA/AI (g/day)	AMDR[o] (%)	RDA/AI (g/day)	AMDR[o] (%)	RDA/AI (g/day)	AMDR[o] (%)	Water[p] (L/day)
Infants	0–6 months	0.4	0.12	0.18	60	ND[q]	ND	[r]	4.4	ND[q]	0.5	ND[q]	9.1	ND[q]	0.7
	7–12 months	0.7	0.37	0.57	95	ND[q]	ND	[r]	4.6	ND[q]	0.5	ND[q]	**13.5**	ND[q]	0.8
Children	1–3 years	3.0	1.0	1.5	**130**	45–65	19	30–40	7	5–10	0.7	0.6–1.2	**13**	5–20	1.3
	4–8 years	3.8	1.2	1.9	**130**	45–65	25	25–35	10	5–10	0.9	0.6–1.2	**19**	10–30	1.7
Males	9–13 years	4.5	1.5	2.3	**130**	45-65	31	25–35	12	5–10	1.2	0.6–1.2	**34**	10–30	2.4
	14–18 years	4.7	1.5	2.3	**130**	45–65	38	25–35	16	5–10	1.6	0.6–1.2	**52**	10–30	3.3
	19–30 years	4.7	1.5	2.3	**130**	45–65	38	20–35	17	5–10	1.6	0.6–1.2	**56**	10–35	3.7
	31–50 years	4.7	1.5	2.3	**130**	45–65	38	20–35	17	5–10	1.6	0.6–1.2	**56**	10–35	3.7
	51–70 years	4.7	1.3	2.0	**130**	45–65	30	20–35	14	5–10	1.6	0.6–1.2	**56**	10–35	3.7
	>70 years	4.7	1.2	1.8	**130**	45–65	30	20–35	14	5–10	1.6	0.6–1.2	**56**	10-35	3.7
Females	9–13 years	4.5	1.5	2.3	**130**	45–65	26	25–35	10	5–10	1.0	0.6–1.2	**34**	10–30	2.1
	14–18 years	4.7	1.5	2.3	**130**	45–65	26	25–35	11	5–10	1.1	0.6–1.2	**46**	10–30	2.3
	19–30 years	4.7	1.5	2.3	**130**	45–65	25	20–35	12	5–10	1.1	0.6–1.2	**46**	10–35	2.7
	31–50 years	4.7	1.5	2.3	**130**	45–65	25	20–35	12	5–10	1.1	0.6–1.2	**46**	10–35	2.7
	51–70 years	4.7	1.3	2.0	**130**	45–65	21	20–35	11	5–10	1.1	0.6–1.2	**46**	10–35	2.7
	>70 years	4.7	1.2	1.8	**130**	45–65	21	20–35	11	5–10	1.1	0.6–1.2	**46**	10–35	2.7
Pregnancy	≤18 years	4.7	1.5	2.3	**175**	45–65	28	20–35	13	5–10	1.4	0.6–1.2	**71**	10–35	3.0
	19–30 years	4.7	1.5	2.3	**175**	45–65	28	20–35	13	5–10	1.4	0.6–1.2	**71**	10–35	3.0
	31–50 years	4.7	1.5	2.3	**175**	45–65	28	20–35	13	5–10	1.4	0.6–1.2	**71**	10–35	3.0
Lactation	≤18 years	5.1	1.5	2.3	**210**	45–65	29	20–35	13	5–10	1.3	0.6–1.2	**71**	10–35	3.8
	19–30 years	5.1	1.5	2.3	**210**	45–65	29	20–35	13	5–10	1.3	0.6–1.2	**71**	10–35	3.8
	31–50 years	5.1	1.5	2.3	**210**	45–65	29	20–35	13	5–10	1.3	0.6–1.2	**71**	10-35	3.8
Tolerable Upper Intake Level for Adults (19–70)			2.3	3.6											

[n]Daily protein recommendations are based on body weight for reference body weights. To calculate for a specific body weight, use the following values: 1.5 g/kg for infants, 1.1 g/kg for 1–3 years, 0.95 g/kg for 4–13 years, 0.85 g/kg for 14–18 years, 0.8 g/kg for adults, and 1.1 g/kg for pregnant (using prepregnancy weight) and lactating women.

[o]Acceptable Macronutrient Distribution Range (AMDR), expressed as a percent of total daily calories, is the range of intake for a particular energy source that is associated with reduced risk of chronic disease while providing intakes of essential nutrients. If an individual consumes in excess of the AMDR, there is a potential for increasing the risk of chronic diseases and/or insufficient intakes of essential nutrients.

[p]Total water intake from fluids and food.

[q]Not determinable due to lack of data of adverse effects in this age group and concern with regard to lack of ability to handle excess amounts. Source of intake should be from food only to prevent high levels of intake.

[r]For infants, Adequate Intake of total fat is 31 grams/day (0–6 months) and 30 grams per day (7–12 months) from breast milk and, for infants 7–12 months, complementary food and beverages.

SOURCE: Food and Nutrition Board, Institute of Medicine, National Academies. 2004. *Dietary Reference Intakes Tables* (http://www.iom.edu/file.asp?id=21372; retrieved December 21, 2004). The complete Dietary Reference Intake reports are available from the National Academies Press (http://www.nap.edu).

Nutrition Resources

Food groups	1600 calories	2000 calories	2600 calories	3100 calories	Serving sizes and notes
	Number of servings per day (or per week, as noted)				
Grains	6	6–8	10–11	12–13	1 slice bread, 1 oz dry cereal, 1/2 cup cooked rice, pasta, or cereal; choose whole grains
Vegetables	3–4	4–5	5–6	6	1 cup raw leafy vegetables, 1/2 cup cooked vegetables, 1/2 cup vegetable juice
Fruits	4	4–5	5–6	6	1/2 cup fruit juice, 1 medium fruit, 1/4 cup dried fruit, 1/2 cup fresh, frozen, or canned fruit
Low-fat or fat-free dairy foods	2–3	2–3	3	3–4	1 cup milk; 1 cup yogurt, 1-1/2 oz cheese; choose fat-free or low-fat types
Meat, poultry, fish	3–6	6 or less	6	6–9	1 oz cooked meats, poultry, or fish: select only lean; trim away visible fats; broil, roast, or boil instead of frying; remove skin from poultry
Nuts, seeds, legumes	3 servings/ week	4–5 servings/ week	1	1	1/3 cup or 1-1/2 oz nuts, 2 Tbsp or 1/2 oz seeds, 1/2 cup cooked dry beans/peas, 2 Tbsp peanut butter
Fats and oils	2	2–3	3	4	1 tsp soft margarine; 1 Tbsp low-fat mayonnaise, 2 Tbsp light salad dressing, 1 tsp vegetable oil; DASH has 27% of calories as fat (low in saturated fat)
Sweets	0	5 servings/ week or less	2	2	1 Tbsp sugar, 1 Tbsp jelly or jam, 1/2 cup sorbet, 1 cup lemonade; sweets should be low in fat

Figure 1 The DASH Eating Plan. SOURCE: National Institutes of Health, National Heart, Lung, and Blood Institute. 2006. *Your Guide to Lowering Your Blood Pressure with DASH: How Do I Make the Dash?* (http://www.nhlbi.nih.gov/health/public/heart/hbp/dash/how_make_dash.html; retrieved August 16, 2006).

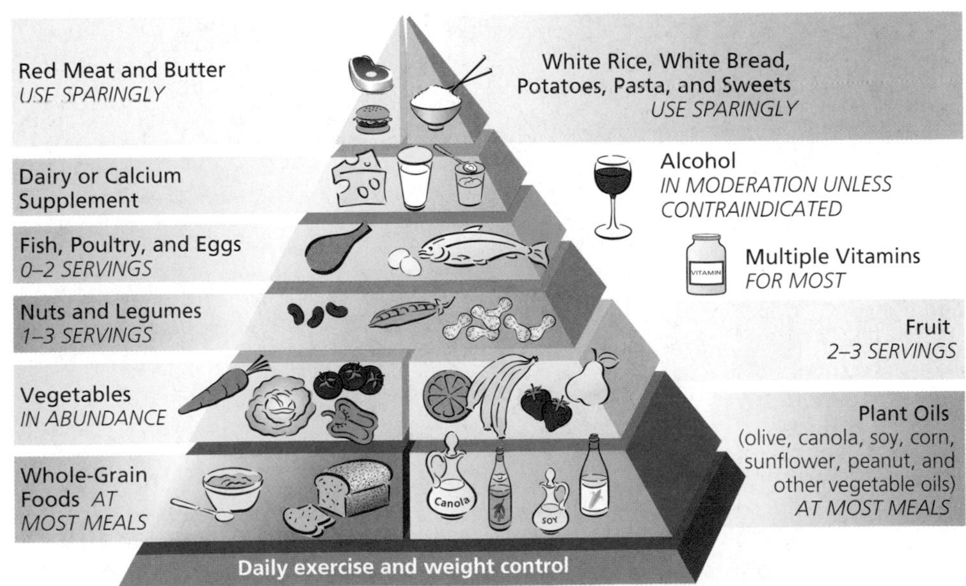

Figure 2 Healthy Eating Pyramid. The Healthy Eating Pyramid is an alternative food-group plan developed by researchers at the Harvard School of Public Health; this pyramid reflects many major research studies that have looked at the relationship between diet and long-term health. The Healthy Eating Pyramid differentiates between the various dietary sources of fat, protein, and carbohydrate, and it emphasizes whole grains, vegetable oils, fruits and vegetables, nuts, and dry peas and beans. SOURCE: Reprinted by permission of Simon & Schuster Adult Publishing Group from *Eat, Drink, and Be Healthy: The Harvard Medical School Guide to Healthy Eating* by Walter C Willett, M.D. Copyright © 2001 by the President and Fellows of Harvard College.

13

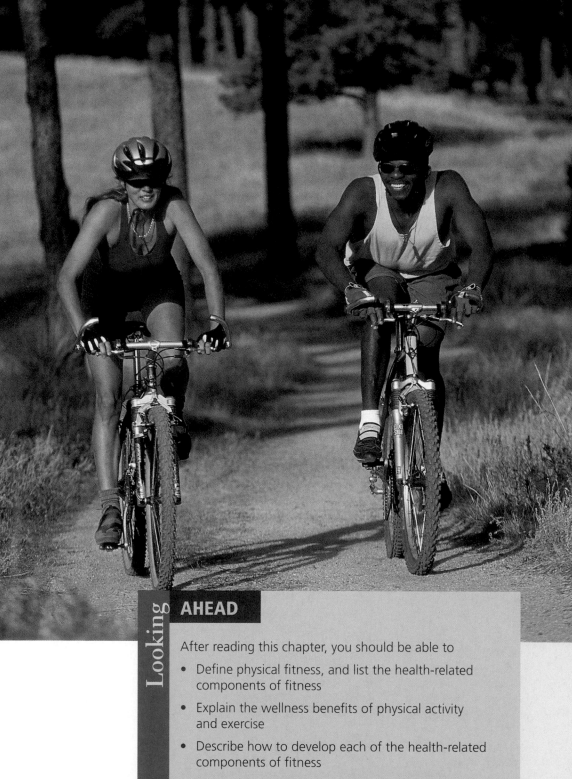

Looking AHEAD

After reading this chapter, you should be able to

- Define physical fitness, and list the health-related components of fitness
- Explain the wellness benefits of physical activity and exercise
- Describe how to develop each of the health-related components of fitness
- Discuss how to choose appropriate exercise equipment, how to eat and drink for exercise, how to assess fitness, and how to prevent and manage injuries
- Put together a personalized exercise program that you enjoy and that will enable you to achieve your fitness goals

Exercise for Health and Fitness

Test Your Knowledge

1. About what percentage of short trips (less than one mile) do American adults make by walking?
a. 15%
b. 25%
c. 50%

2. Compared to sedentary people, those who engage in regular moderate exercise are likely to
a. have fewer colds.
b. be less anxious and depressed.
c. fall asleep more quickly and sleep better.
d. be more alert and creative.

3. For women, weight training typically results in which of the following?
a. bulky muscles
b. significant increases in body weight
c. improved body image

4. If you want to lose fat around your middle to have a flat stomach, you should do sit-ups.
True or false?

5. Which of the following is a symptom of metabolic syndrome?
a. abdominal fat deposits
b. type 2 diabetes
c. high blood pressure
d. insulin resistance

ANSWERS

1. A. The vast majority of short trips are made in automobiles. Most people have many opportunities to incorporate more physical activity into their daily routine.
2. ALL FOUR. Exercise has many immediate benefits that affect all the dimensions of wellness and improve overall quality of life.
3. C. Because women have lower levels of testosterone than men, they do not develop large muscles or gain significant amounts of weight in response to a moderate weight training program.
4. FALSE. The energy burned by sit-ups comes from fat stores throughout the body, not just from the abdomen, so sit-ups are no better at trimming fat from your stomach than any other calisthenic exercise.
5. ALL FOUR. Metabolic syndrome is linked to several lifestyle factors that can lead to cardiovascular disease. People who get little or no exercise have a much higher than normal risk of developing metabolic syndrome and heart disease.

Visit the Core Concepts in Health Online Learning Center (www.mhhe.com/insel10e) for study aids and many additional resources.

Your body is a wonderful moving machine. Your bones, joints, and ligaments provide a support system for movement; your muscles perform the motions of work and play; your heart and lungs nourish your cells as you move through your daily life. But your body is made to work best when it is physically active. It readily adapts to practically any level of activity and exercise: The more you ask of your body—your muscles, bones, heart, lungs—the stronger and more fit it becomes. The opposite is also true. Left unchallenged, bones lose their density, joints stiffen, muscles become weak, and cellular energy systems begin to degenerate. To be truly healthy, human beings must be active.

The benefits of physical activity are both physical and mental, immediate and far-reaching. Being physically fit makes it easier to do everyday tasks, such as lifting; it provides reserve strength for emergencies; and it helps people look and feel good. Over the long term, physically fit individuals are less likely to develop heart disease, cancer, high blood pressure, diabetes, and many other degenerative diseases. Their cardiorespiratory systems tend to resemble those of people 10 or more years younger than themselves. As they get older, they may be able to avoid weight gain, muscle and bone loss, fatigue, memory loss, dementia, and other problems associated with aging. With a healthy heart, strong muscles, a lean body, and a repertoire of physical skills they can call on for recreation and enjoyment, fit people can maintain their physical and mental well-being throughout their entire lives.

Unfortunately, modern life for most Americans provides few built-in occasions for vigorous activity. Technological advances have made our lives increasingly sedentary: We drive cars, ride escalators, watch television, and push papers around at school and work. A 2005 study reported that 33% of American adolescents and 14% of adults aged 20 to 49 were unable to meet cardiorespiratory fitness standards. According to *Healthy People 2010,* levels of physical activity remain low for all populations of Americans (Figure 13-1). In 1996, the U.S. Surgeon General published *Physical Activity and Health,* a report designed to reverse these trends and get Americans moving. The report's conclusions include the following:

- People of all ages, both male and female, benefit from regular physical activity.
- People can obtain significant health benefits by including a moderate amount of physical activity on most, if not all, days of the week. Through a modest increase in daily activity, most Americans can improve their health and quality of life.
- Additional health benefits can be gained through more vigorous or longer duration physical activity.
- Physical activity reduces the risk of premature mortality, improves psychological health, and is important for the health of muscle, bones, and joints.

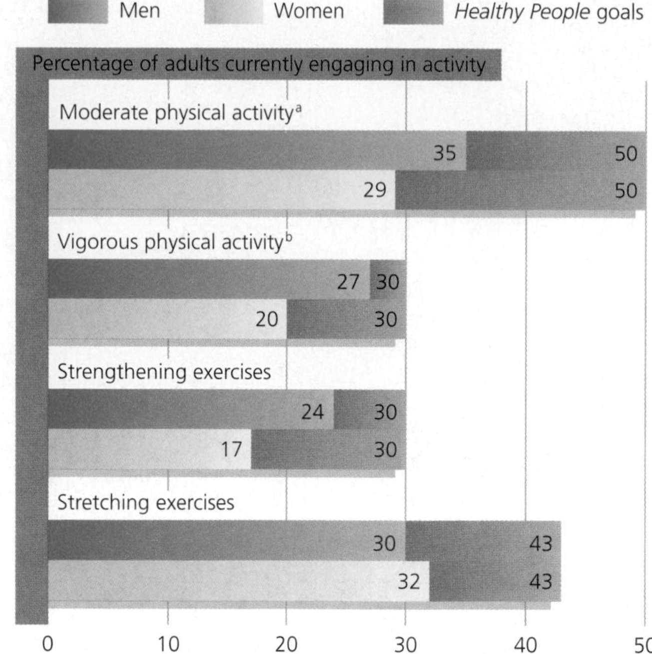

[a]Moderate physical activity for 30 or more minutes on 5 or more days per week.
[b]Vigorous physical activity for 20 or more minutes on 3 or more days per week.

VITAL STATISTICS

Figure 13-1 Current levels of physical activity among American adults. SOURCE: National Center for Health Statistics. 2004. *DATA2010: The Healthy People 2010 Database* (http://wonder.cdc.gov/data2010; retrieved August 21, 2006).

Are you one of the 54% of Americans who are not regularly active? Or one of the 15% who are not active at all? This chapter will give you the basic information you need to put together a physical fitness program that will work for you. If approached correctly, physical activity can contribute immeasurably to overall wellness, add fun and joy to life, and provide the foundation for a lifetime of fitness.

WHAT IS PHYSICAL FITNESS?

Physical fitness is a set of physical attributes that allows the body to respond or adapt to the demands and stress of physical effort—that is, to perform moderate-to-vigorous levels of physical activity without becoming overly tired. Physical fitness has many components, some related to general health and others related more specifically to particular sports or activities. The five components of fitness most important for health are cardiorespiratory endurance, muscular strength, muscular endurance, flexibility, and body composition (proportion of fat to fat-free mass).

Cardiorespiratory Endurance

Cardiorespiratory endurance is the ability to perform prolonged, large-muscle, dynamic exercise at moderate-

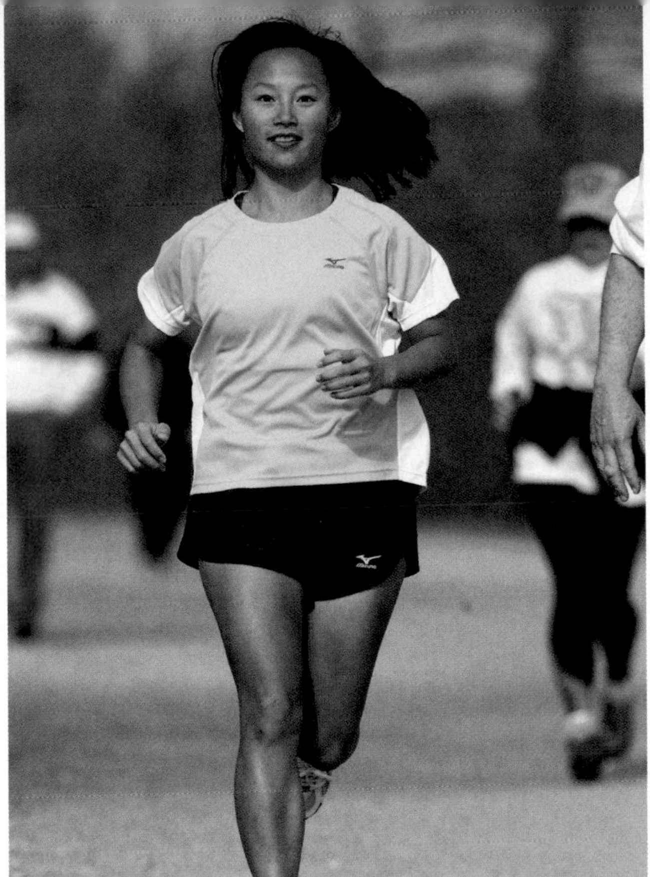

Cardiorespiratory endurance exercise conditions the heart, improves the function of the entire cardiorespiratory system, and has many other health benefits. An effective personal fitness program should be built around an activity like running, walking, biking, swimming, or group exercises such as aerobic dance or martial arts workouts.

to-high levels of intensity. It depends on factors such as the ability of the lungs to deliver oxygen from the environment to the bloodstream, the heart's capacity to pump blood, the ability of the nervous system and blood vessels to regulate blood flow, the muscles' capacity to generate power, and the capability of the body's chemical systems to use oxygen and process fuels for exercise.

When levels of cardiorespiratory fitness are low, the heart has to work very hard during normal daily activities and may not be able to work hard enough to sustain high-intensity physical activity in an emergency. As cardiorespiratory fitness improves, the heart begins to function more efficiently. It doesn't have to work as hard at rest or during low levels of exercise. The heart pumps more blood per heartbeat, resting heart rate slows down, blood volume increases, blood supply to the tissues improves, the body is better able to cool itself, and resting blood pressure decreases. A healthy heart can better withstand the strains of everyday life, the stress of occasional emergencies, and the wear and tear of time. Endurance training also improves the functioning of biochemical systems, particularly in the muscles and liver, thereby enhancing the ability to use stored energy and energy supplied by food and to do more exercise with less effort from the oxygen transport system.

Cardiorespiratory endurance is a critically important component of health-related fitness because the functioning of the heart and lungs is so essential to overall wellness. A person simply cannot live very long or very well without a healthy heart. Low levels of cardiorespiratory fitness are linked with heart disease, the leading cause of death in the United States. Cardiorespiratory endurance is developed by activities that involve continuous rhythmic movements of large-muscle groups like those in the legs—for example, walking, jogging, cycling, and aerobic dance.

Muscular Strength

Muscular strength is the amount of force a muscle can produce with a single maximum effort. Strong, powerful muscles are important for the smooth and easy performance of everyday activities, such as carrying groceries, lifting boxes, and climbing stairs, as well as for emergency situations. They help keep the skeleton in proper alignment, preventing back and leg pain and providing the support necessary for good posture. Muscular strength has obvious importance in recreational activities. Strong people can hit a tennis ball harder, kick a soccer ball farther, and ride a bicycle uphill more easily.

Muscle tissue is an important element of overall body composition. Greater muscle mass makes possible a higher rate of metabolism and faster energy use, which help to maintain a healthy body weight. Maintaining strength and muscle mass is vital for healthy aging. Older people tend to lose muscle cells (a condition called sarcopenia), and many of the remaining muscle cells become nonfunctional because they lose their attachment to the nervous system. Strength training helps maintain muscle mass, function, and balance in older people, which greatly enhances their quality of life and prevents life-threatening injuries. Strength training has also been shown to benefit cardiovascular health. Muscular strength can be developed by training with weights or by using the weight of the body for resistance during calisthenic exercises such as push-ups and curl-ups.

Terms

VW

physical fitness A set of physical attributes that allows the body to respond or adapt to the demands and stress of physical effort.

cardiorespiratory endurance The ability of the body to perform prolonged, large-muscle, dynamic exercise at moderate-to-high levels of intensity.

muscular strength The amount of force a muscle can produce with a single maximum effort.

Muscular Endurance

Muscular endurance is the ability to resist fatigue and sustain a given level of muscle tension—that is, to hold a muscle contraction for a long period of time or to contract a muscle over and over again. Muscular endurance is important for good posture and for injury prevention. For example, if abdominal and back muscles are not strong enough or don't have the endurance to hold the spine correctly, the chances of low-back pain and back injury are increased. Muscular endurance helps people cope with the physical demands of everyday life and enhances performance in sports and work. It is also important for most leisure and fitness activities. Like muscular strength, muscular endurance is developed by stressing the muscles with a greater load (weight) than they are used to. The degree to which strength or endurance develops depends on the type and amount of stress that is applied.

Flexibility

Flexibility is the ability to move the joints through their full range of motion. Although range of motion is not a significant factor in everyday activities for most people, inactivity causes the joints to become stiffer with age. Stiffness often causes older people to assume unnatural body postures, and it can lead to back, shoulder, or neck pain. Stretching exercises can help ensure a normal range of motion and pain-free joints.

Body Composition

Body composition refers to the proportion of fat and fat-free mass (muscle, bone, and water) in the body. Healthy body composition involves a high proportion of fat-free mass and an acceptably low level of body fat. A person with excessive body fat is more likely to experience a variety of health problems, including heart disease, high blood pressure, stroke, joint problems, diabetes, gallbladder disease, cancer, and back pain. The best way to lose fat is through a lifestyle that includes a sensible diet and exercise. The best way to add muscle mass is through resistance training such as weight training. (Body composition is discussed in more detail in Chapter 14.)

Terms

VW

muscular endurance The ability of a muscle or group of muscles to remain contracted or to contract repeatedly for a long period of time.

flexibility The range of motion in a joint or group of joints; flexibility is related to muscle length.

body composition The proportion of fat and fat-free mass (muscle, bone, and water) in the body.

In addition to these five health-related components of physical fitness, physical fitness for a particular sport or activity might include any or all of the following: coordination, speed, reaction time, agility, balance, and skill. Sport-specific skills are best developed through practice. The skill and coordination needed to play basketball, for example, are developed by playing basketball.

THE BENEFITS OF EXERCISE

As mentioned earlier, the human body is very adaptable. The greater the demands made on it, the more it adjusts to meet the demands—it becomes fit. Over time, immediate, short-term adjustments translate into long-term changes and improvements (Figure 13-2). For example, when breathing and heart rate increase during exercise, the heart gradually develops the ability to pump more blood with each beat. Then, during exercise, it doesn't have to beat as fast to meet the body's demand for oxygen. The goal of regular physical activity is to bring about these kinds of long-term changes and improvements in the body's functioning.

Scientists have found that exercise is one of the most important things you can do to improve your level of wellness. Regular exercise increases energy levels, improves emotional and psychological well-being, and boosts the immune system. It prevents heart disease, some types of cancer, stroke, high blood pressure, insulin resistance, type 2 diabetes, obesity, and osteoporosis. At any age, people who exercise are less likely to die from all causes than are their sedentary peers. Worldwide, it is estimated that physical inactivity causes 1.9 million deaths per year.

Improved Cardiorespiratory Functioning

Every time you take a breath, oxygen in the air enters your lungs and is picked up by red blood cells and transported to your heart. From there, the heart pumps oxygenated blood throughout the body to organs and tissues that use it. During exercise, the cardiorespiratory system (heart, lungs, and circulatory system) must work harder to meet the body's increased demand for oxygen. Regular endurance exercise improves the functioning of the heart and the ability of the cardiorespiratory system to carry oxygen to body tissues. Exercise directly affects the health of your arteries, keeping them from stiffening or clogging with plaque and reducing the risk of cardiovascular disease. Exercise also improves sexual function and general vitality.

More Efficient Metabolism

Endurance exercise improves metabolism, the process that converts food to energy and builds tissue. This process involves oxygen, nutrients, hormones, and enzymes. A physically fit person is better able to generate

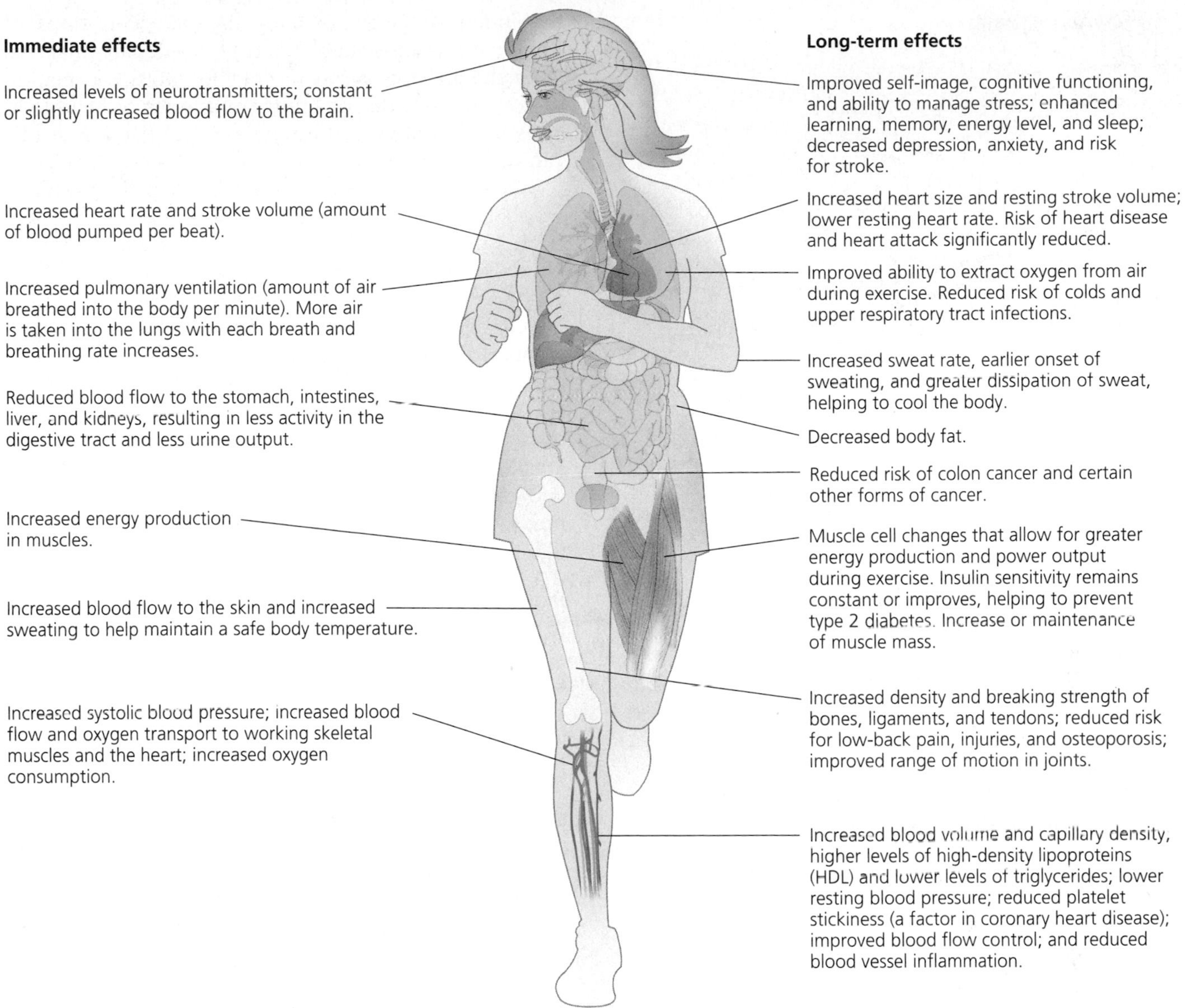

Immediate effects
Increased levels of neurotransmitters; constant or slightly increased blood flow to the brain.
Increased heart rate and stroke volume (amount of blood pumped per beat).
Increased pulmonary ventilation (amount of air breathed into the body per minute). More air is taken into the lungs with each breath and breathing rate increases.
Reduced blood flow to the stomach, intestines, liver, and kidneys, resulting in less activity in the digestive tract and less urine output.
Increased energy production in muscles.
Increased blood flow to the skin and increased sweating to help maintain a safe body temperature.
Increased systolic blood pressure; increased blood flow and oxygen transport to working skeletal muscles and the heart; increased oxygen consumption.
Long-term effects
Improved self-image, cognitive functioning, and ability to manage stress; enhanced learning, memory, energy level, and sleep; decreased depression, anxiety, and risk for stroke.
Increased heart size and resting stroke volume; lower resting heart rate. Risk of heart disease and heart attack significantly reduced.
Improved ability to extract oxygen from air during exercise. Reduced risk of colds and upper respiratory tract infections.
Increased sweat rate, earlier onset of sweating, and greater dissipation of sweat, helping to cool the body.
Decreased body fat.
Reduced risk of colon cancer and certain other forms of cancer.
Muscle cell changes that allow for greater energy production and power output during exercise. Insulin sensitivity remains constant or improves, helping to prevent type 2 diabetes. Increase or maintenance of muscle mass.
Increased density and breaking strength of bones, ligaments, and tendons; reduced risk for low-back pain, injuries, and osteoporosis; improved range of motion in joints.
Increased blood volume and capillary density, higher levels of high-density lipoproteins (HDL) and lower levels of triglycerides; lower resting blood pressure; reduced platelet stickiness (a factor in coronary heart disease); improved blood flow control; and reduced blood vessel inflammation.

Figure 13-2 Immediate and long-term effects of regular exercise. When exercise is performed regularly, short-term changes in the body develop into more permanent adaptations; these long-term effects include improved ability to exercise, reduced risk of many chronic diseases, improved psychological and emotional well-being, and increased life expectancy.

energy, to use carbohydrates and fats for energy, and to regulate hormones. Exercise may also protect cells from damage from free radicals, which are destructive chemicals produced during normal metabolism (see Chapter 12), and from inflammation caused by high blood pressure or cholesterol, nicotine, and overeating. Training activates antioxidant enzymes that prevent free radical damage and maintain the health of the body's cells.

Improved Body Composition

Healthy body composition means that the body has a high proportion of fat-free mass and a relatively small proportion of fat. Too much body fat, particularly abdominal fat, is linked to a variety of health problems, including heart disease, cancer, and diabetes. Healthy body composition can be difficult to achieve and maintain because a diet that contains all essential nutrients can be relatively high in calories, especially for someone who is sedentary. Excess calories are stored in the body as fat.

Exercise can improve body composition in several ways. Endurance exercise significantly increases daily calorie expenditure; it can also slightly raise *metabolic rate,* the rate at which the body burns calories, for several hours after an exercise session. Strength training increases muscle mass, thereby tipping the body composition ratio toward fat-free mass and away from fat. It can also help with losing fat because metabolic rate is directly proportional to fat-free mass: The more muscle mass, the higher the metabolic rate.

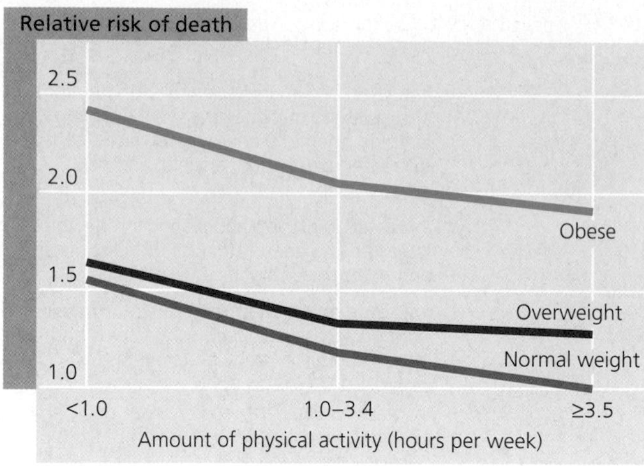

Figure 13-3 Relationship among amount of physical activity, body weight, and risk of death. Physical activity reduces the risk of death for people at all levels of body fatness. SOURCE: Hu, F. B., et al. 2004. Adiposity compared with physical activity in predicting mortality among women. *New England Journal of Medicine* 351(26): 2694–2703.

Physical activity reduces the risk of death regardless of its effect on body composition. That is, greater levels of activity are associated with lower death rates among people who are overweight or obese as well as people who are at a healthy weight (Figure 13-3). Physical activity does not eliminate the health risks associated with overweight, but it reduces its effects.

Disease Prevention and Management

Regular physical activity lowers your risk of many chronic, disabling diseases.

Cardiovascular Disease A sedentary lifestyle is one of the six major risk factors for **cardiovascular disease (CVD),** including heart attack and stroke. The other major risk factors are smoking, abnormal blood fats, high blood pressure, diabetes, and obesity. Most of these risk factors are linked by a group of symptoms that scientists call the *metabolic syndrome.* These symptoms include insulin resistance, high blood pressure, abnormal blood fats, abdominal fat deposits, type 2 diabetes, blood clotting abnormalities, and blood vessel inflammation (see Chapter 15 for more on metabolic syndrome). People who are sedentary have CVD death rates significantly higher than those of fit individuals. Physical inactivity increases the risk of CVD by 50–240%. The benefit of physical activity occurs at moderate levels of activity and increases with increasing levels of activity. Exercise positively affects the risk factors for CVD, including cholesterol levels and high blood pressure. Exercise also directly interferes with the disease process itself, directly lowering risk of heart disease and stroke.

BLOOD FAT LEVELS Endurance exercise and strength training have a positive effect on the balance of lipids that circulate in the blood. High concentrations of lipids such as cholesterol and triglycerides are linked to heart disease because they contribute to the formation of fatty deposits on the linings of arteries. When blood clots block a narrowed artery, a heart attack or stroke can occur.

Cholesterol is carried in the blood by **lipoproteins,** which are classified according to size and density. Cholesterol carried by low-density lipoproteins (LDLs) sticks to the walls of coronary arteries. High-density lipoproteins (HDLs) pick up excess cholesterol in the bloodstream and carry it back to the liver for excretion from the body. High LDL levels and low HDL levels increase the risk of cardiovascular disease. High levels of HDL and low levels of LDL are associated with lower risk.

Heart disease is covered in Chapter 15. For our purposes in this chapter, it is important to know only that endurance exercise and strength training influence blood lipids in a positive way, by increasing HDL and decreasing LDL and triglycerides—reducing the risk of CVD.

HIGH BLOOD PRESSURE Regular endurance exercise tends to reduce high blood pressure (hypertension), a contributing factor in diseases such as coronary heart disease, stroke, kidney failure, and blindness. Intense, long-duration exercise works best, but even moderate exercise can produce significant improvements. Strength training also reduces blood pressure.

CORONARY HEART DISEASE Coronary heart disease (CHD), also called coronary artery disease (CAD), involves blockage of one of the coronary arteries. These blood vessels supply the heart with oxygenated blood, and an obstruction in one of them can cause a heart attack. Exercise directly interferes with the disease process that causes coronary artery blockage. It also enhances the function of cells lining the arteries that help regulate blood flow. Finally, exercise minimizes other risk factors—such as obesity, high blood pressure, and blood fat levels—that contribute to CHD.

STROKE A stroke occurs when a blood vessel leading to the brain is blocked, often through the same disease process that leads to heart attacks. Regular exercise reduces the risk of stroke.

Cancer Studies have shown a relationship between increased physical activity and a reduced risk of cancer, but these findings are not conclusive. There is evidence that exercise reduces the risk of colon cancer and promising data that it reduces the risk of cancer of the breast and reproductive organs in women and prostate cancer in men. Exercise may decrease the risk of colon cancer by speeding the movement of food through the gastrointestinal tract (quickly eliminating potential carcinogens), lowering blood insulin levels, enhancing immune function, and reducing blood fats. The protective mechanism in the case of reproductive system cancers is less clear, but physical activity during the high school and college years may be particularly important for preventing breast cancer later in life. Some studies have also found that regular physical activity reduces the risk of pancreatic cancer.

Osteoporosis A special benefit of exercise, especially for women, is protection against osteoporosis, a disease that results in loss of bone density and poor bone strength. Weight-bearing exercise, which includes almost everything except swimming, helps build bone during childhood and the teens and twenties. Older people with denser bones can better endure the bone loss that occurs with aging. Strength training and impact exercises such as jumping rope can increase bone density throughout life. With stronger bones and muscles and better balance, fit people are less likely to experience debilitating falls and bone fractures. Along with exercise, a well-balanced diet containing adequate calcium and vitamin D and normal hormone function are also essential for strong bones. (One caution: Too much exercise can depress levels of estrogen, which helps maintain bone density, thereby leading to bone loss, even in young women.)

Type 2 Diabetes People with diabetes are prone to heart disease, blindness, and severe problems of the nervous and circulatory systems. Exercise prevents the development of type 2 diabetes, the most common form of the disease. Exercise burns excess sugar and makes cells more sensitive to insulin. Exercise also helps keep body fat at healthy levels. (Obesity is a key risk factor for type 2 diabetes.) For people who have diabetes, physical activity is an important part of treatment. See Chapter 14 for more on diabetes.

Improved Psychological and Emotional Wellness

The joy of a well-hit cross-court backhand, the euphoria of a walk through the park, or the rush of a downhill schuss through deep powder snow provides pleasure that transcends health benefits alone. People who are physically active experience many social, psychological, and emotional benefits. For example,

- *Reduced stress.* In response to stressors, physically fit people experience milder physical responses and less emotional distress than sedentary individuals. Physical activity also provides protection against the effects of stress that have been linked to poor cardiorespiratory health. Psychological stress causes increased secretion of epinephrine and norepinephrine, compounds associated with the fight-or-flight reaction, which are thought to speed the development of atherosclerosis (hardening of the arteries). Excessive hostility is also associated with a risk of heart disease. Endurance exercise decreases the secretion of hormones and neurotransmitters triggered by emotional stress. It also can diffuse hostility and alleviate feelings of stress and anxiety by providing an emotional outlet and inducing feelings of relaxation. Regular exercise can also relieve sleeping problems.
- *Reduced anxiety and depression.* Sedentary adults are much more likely to feel fatigue and depression than those who are physically active. Exercise is an effective treatment for people with depression and improves mood in nondepressed people who feel fine or who feel a little bit down.
- *Improved self-image.* Performing physical activities provides proof of skill and self-control, thus enhancing your self-concept. Sticking with an exercise program increases people's belief in their ability to be active, thereby boosting self-efficacy. Exercise also helps you look and feel better, boosting self-confidence and body image.
- *Learning and memory.* Exercise enhances the formation and survival of new nerve cells and the connections between nerves, which in turn improve memory and learning. Physical activity helps maintain mental functioning in older adults and may ward off dementia.
- *Enjoyment.* Exercise is fun. It offers an arena for harmonious interaction with other people, as well as opportunities to strive and excel. Physically fit people can perform everyday tasks—such as climbing stairs and carrying books or groceries—with ease. They have plenty of energy and can lead lives that are full and varied.

For more on the psychological benefits of physical activity, see the box "Exercise and the Mind" on page 384.

Improved Immune Function

Exercise can have either positive or negative effects on the immune system, the physiological processes that protect us from disease. It appears that moderate endurance exercise boosts immune function, whereas excessive training depresses it. Physically fit people get fewer colds and upper respiratory tract infections than people who are not fit. The immune system—and ways to strengthen it—is discussed further in Chapter 17.

Prevention of Injuries and Low-Back Pain

Increased muscle strength provides protection against injury because it helps people maintain good posture and appropriate body mechanics when carrying out everyday

Terms

VW

cardiovascular disease (CVD) A collective term for diseases of the heart and blood vessels.

lipoproteins Substances in blood, classified according to size, density, and chemical composition, that transport fats.

Mind/Body/Spirit

Exercise and the Mind

If you've ever gone for a long, brisk walk after a hard day's work, you know how refreshing exercise can be. Exercise can improve mood, stimulate creativity, clarify thinking, relieve anxiety, and provide an outlet for anger or aggression. But why does exercise make you feel good? Does it simply take your mind off your problems? Or does it cause a physical reaction that affects your mental state?

Current research indicates that exercise triggers many physical changes in the body that can alter mood. Scientists are now trying to explain how and why exercise affects the mind. One theory has to do with the physical structure of the brain. The area of the brain responsible for the movement of muscles is near the area responsible for thought and emotion. As muscles work vigorously, the resulting stimulation in the muscle center of the brain may also stimulate the thought and emotion center, producing improvements in mood and cognitive functions.

Other researchers suggest that exercise stimulates the release of brain chemicals that affect mood. Exercise increases levels of **endorphins,** brain chemicals that can suppress fatigue, decrease pain, and produce euphoria. Levels of a chemical called anandamide are increased in people who exercise at a moderate intensity for an extended period. Anandamide produces effects similar to those of THC, the psychoactive chemical found in marijuana. The "runner's high" often experienced after running several miles may be due to the action of endorphins or anandamide.

Another area of research focuses on changes in brain activity during and after exercise. One change is an increase in alpha brain wave activity. Alpha waves indicate a highly relaxed state; meditation also induces alpha wave activity. Another change is an alteration in the levels of **neurotransmitters,** brain chemicals that increase alertness and reduce stress.

Higher levels of neurotransmitters such as serotonin may explain how exercise improves mild to moderate cases of depression. Researchers have found that exercise can be as effective as psychotherapy in treating depression and even more effective when used in conjunction with other therapies. In addition to boosting neurotransmitter activity, exercise provides a distraction from stressful stimuli, enhances self-esteem, and may provide an opportunity for positive social interactions.

Another benefit of regular exercise is improved self-esteem and body image. According to a recent study, women who worked out on a regular basis rated their bodies as more attractive and healthier than did sedentary women. They actually weighed an average of 11–12 pounds more than the less active women, suggesting that active women are more comfortable bucking cultural ideals of body shape. Other studies have found that athletes tend to have more positive images of their bodies than nonathletes, regardless of gender, sport, or level of expertise.

Although most people don't associate exercise with mental skills, physical activity has been shown to have positive effects on cognitive functioning in both the short term and the long term. Exercise improves alertness and memory and can help you perform cognitive tasks at your peak level. Exercise may also help boost creativity. In a study of college students, those who ran regularly or took aerobic dance classes scored significantly higher on standard psychological tests of creativity than sedentary students. Over the long term, exercise can slow and possibly even reverse certain age-related declines in cognitive performance, including slowed reaction time and loss of short-term memory and nonverbal reasoning skills.

The message from this research is that exercise is a critical factor in developing *all* the dimensions of wellness, not just physical health. Even moderate exercise like walking briskly a few times per week can significantly improve your well-being. A lifetime of physical activity can leave you with a healthier body and a sharper, happier, more creative mind.

activities such as walking, lifting, and carrying. Good muscle endurance in the abdomen, hips, lower back, and legs support the back in proper alignment and help prevent low-back pain, which afflicts a significant majority of Americans at some time in their lives.

Improved Wellness over the Life Span

Although people differ in the maximum levels of fitness they can achieve through exercise, the wellness benefits of exercise are available to everyone (see the box "Exercise for People with Disabilities and Other Special Health Concerns"). Exercising regularly may be the single most important thing you can do now to improve the quality of your life in the future. All the benefits of exercise continue to accrue but gain new importance as the resilience of youth begins to wane. Simply stated, exercising can help you live a longer and healthier life.

Terms

Vw

endorphins Brain chemicals that seem to be involved in modulating pain and producing euphoria.

neurotransmitters Brain chemicals that transmit nerve impulses.

DESIGNING YOUR EXERCISE PROGRAM

The best exercise program has two primary characteristics: It promotes your health, and it's fun for you to do. Exercise does not have to be a chore. On the contrary, it can provide some of the most pleasurable moments of your day, once you make it a habit. A little thought and planning will help you achieve these goals.

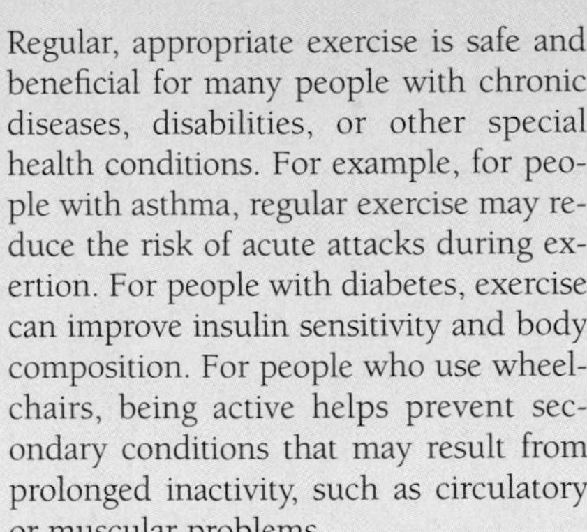

Exercise for People with Disabilities and Other Special Health Concerns

Regular, appropriate exercise is safe and beneficial for many people with chronic diseases, disabilities, or other special health conditions. For example, for people with asthma, regular exercise may reduce the risk of acute attacks during exertion. For people with diabetes, exercise can improve insulin sensitivity and body composition. For people who use wheelchairs, being active helps prevent secondary conditions that may result from prolonged inactivity, such as circulatory or muscular problems.

For everyone, activity provides an emotional boost that helps support a positive attitude as well as opportunities to make new friends, increase self-confidence, and gain a sense of accomplishment. For many people with special health concerns, the risks associated with *not* exercising are far greater than those associated with a moderate program of regular exercise.

If you have a special health concern and have hesitated becoming more active, one helpful strategy is to take a class or join an exercise group specifically designed for your condition. Many health centers and support groups sponsor specially tailored activity programs. For example, health clubs may have modified aerobics classes, special weight training machines, and classes involving mild exercise in warm water; popular sports and recreational activities include adapted golf, swimming, and skiing and wheelchair tennis, hockey, and basketball. Such a class or group activity can provide you with both expert advice and exercise partners who share your concerns and goals. If you prefer to exercise at home, exercise videos are available for people with a variety of conditions.

The fitness recommendations for the general population presented in this chapter can serve as general guidelines for any exercise program. However, for people with special health concerns, certain precautions and monitoring may be required. *Anyone with special health concerns should consult a physician before beginning an exercise program.* Guidelines and cautions for some common conditions are described below:

Asthma

- Carry medication during workouts and avoid exercising alone. Use your inhaler before exercise, if recommended by your physician.
- Exercise regularly, and warm up and cool down slowly to reduce the risk of acute attacks.
- When starting a fitness program, choose self-paced endurance activities, especially those involving interval training (short bouts of exercise followed by rest periods).
- When possible, avoid circumstances that may trigger an asthma attack, including cold, dry air or pollen or dust. Drink water to keep your airways moist, and in cold weather, cover your mouth with a mask or scarf to warm and humidify the air you breathe. Swimming is a good activity choice for people with asthma.

Diabetes

- Don't exercise alone; wear a bracelet identifying yourself as having diabetes.
- If you are taking insulin or another medication, you may need to adjust the timing and amount of each dose as you learn to balance your energy intake and output and your medication dosage.
- To prevent abnormally rapid absorption of injected insulin, inject it over a muscle that won't be exercised and wait at least an hour before exercising.
- Check blood sugar levels before, during, and after exercise, and adjust your diet or insulin dosage if needed. Avoid exercise if your blood sugar level is above 250 mg/dl, and ingest carbohydrates prior to exercise if your blood sugar level is below 100 mg/dl. Have high-carbohydrate foods available during a workout.
- Check your skin regularly for blisters and abrasions, especially on your feet.

Obesity

- For maximum benefit and minimum risk, begin with low- to moderate-intensity activities and increase intensity slowly as your fitness improves.
- To lose weight or maintain lost weight, exercise moderately 60 minutes or more every day; you can exercise all at once or divide your total activity time into sessions of 10 or more minutes.
- At first choose non- or low-weight-bearing activities like swimming, water exercises, cycling, or walking.
- Stay alert for symptoms of heat-related problems during exercise.
- Try to include as much lifestyle physical activity in your daily routine as possible.
- Include strength training in your program to build or maintain muscle mass.

Heart Disease and Hypertension

- Warm-up and cool-down sessions should be gradual and last at least 10 minutes.
- Exercise at a moderate rather than a high intensity; monitor your heart rate during exercise, and stop if you experience dizziness or chest pain.
- Increase exercise frequency, intensity, and time very gradually.
- Don't hold your breath when exercising as this can cause sudden, steep increases in blood pressure.
- Discuss the effects of your medication with your physician; for example, certain drugs for hypertension affect heart rate. If your physician has prescribed nitroglycerine, carry it with you during exercise.

Arthritis

- Begin an exercise program as early as possible in the course of the disease.
- Warm up thoroughly before each workout to loosen stiff muscles and lower the risk of injury.
- Avoid high-impact activities that may damage arthritic joints; consider swimming or water aerobics.
- In strength training, pay special attention to muscles that support and protect affected joints; add weight very gradually.
- Perform flexibility exercises regularly.

Osteoporosis

- If possible, choose low-impact, weight-bearing activities to help safely maintain bone density.
- To prevent fractures, avoid any activity or movement that stresses the back or carries a risk of falling.
- Weight train to improve strength and balance and reduce the risk of falls and fractures, but avoid lifting heavy weights.

No matter what your level of ability or disability, you can make physical activity an integral part of your life.

Physical Activity and Exercise for Health and Fitness

Physical activity can be defined as any body movement carried out by skeletal muscles and requiring energy. Different types of physical activity can be arranged on a continuum based on the amount of energy they require. Quick, easy movements such as standing up or walking down a hallway require little energy or effort; more intense, sustained activities such as cycling 5 miles or running in a race require considerably more.

The term *exercise* is commonly used to refer to a subset of physical activity—planned, structured, repetitive movement of the body designed specifically to improve or maintain physical fitness. As described earlier, levels of fitness depend on physiological factors such as the heart's ability to pump blood. To develop fitness, a person must perform a sufficient amount of physical activity to stress the body and cause long-term physiological changes. The precise type and amount of activity required to develop fitness is discussed in greater detail later in the chapter. For now, just remember that only some types of physical activity—those usually referred to as exercise—will develop fitness. This distinction is important for setting goals and developing a program.

Washing and waxing a car for 45–60 minutes
Washing windows or floors for 45–60 minutes
Playing volleyball for 45 minutes
Playing touch football for 30–45 minutes
Gardening for 30–45 minutes
Wheeling self in wheelchair for 30–40 minutes
Walking 1¾ miles in 35 minutes (20 min/mile)
Basketball (shooting baskets) for 30 minutes
Bicycling 5 miles in 30 minutes
Dancing fast (social) for 30 minutes
Pushing a stroller 1½ miles in 30 minutes
Raking leaves for 30 minutes
Walking 2 miles in 30 minutes (15 min/mile)
Water aerobics for 30 minutes
Swimming laps for 20 minutes
Wheelchair basketball for 20 minutes
Basketball (playing a game) for 15–20 minutes
Bicycling 4 miles in 15 minutes
Jumping rope for 15 minutes
Running 1½ miles in 15 minutes (10 min/mile)
Shoveling snow for 15 minutes
Stairwalking for 15 minutes

Less Vigorous, More Time ↕ ***More Vigorous, Less Time***

Figure 13-4 Examples of moderate amounts of physical activity. A moderate amount of physical activity is roughly equivalent to physical activity that uses approximately 150 calories of energy per day, or 1000 calories per week. Some activities can be performed at various intensities; the suggested durations correspond to expected intensity of effort. SOURCE: U.S. Department of Health and Human Services. 1996. *Physical Activity and Health. A Report of the Surgeon General: At-a-Glance.* Washington, D.C.: U.S. Department of Health and Human Services.

Lifestyle Physical Activity for Health Promotion The Surgeon General's report and joint guidelines from the CDC and the American College of Sports Medicine (ACSM) recommend that all Americans include a moderate amount of physical activity on most, preferably all, days of the week. The report suggests a goal of expending 150 calories per day, or about 1000 calories per week, in physical activity. Because energy expenditure is a function of both intensity and duration of activity, the same amount of benefit can be obtained in longer sessions of moderate-intensity activities as in shorter sessions of high-intensity activities. Thus, 15 minutes of running is equivalent to 30 minutes of brisk walking (Figure 13-4).

In this lifestyle approach to physical activity, the daily total of activity can be accumulated in multiple short bouts—for example, two 10-minute bicycle rides to and from class and a brisk 15-minute walk to the post office. Everyday tasks at school, work, and home can be structured to contribute to the daily activity total (see the box "Becoming More Active"). In addition to recommending moderate-intensity physical activity, the Surgeon General's report recommends that people perform resistance training (exercising against an opposing force such as a weight) at least twice a week to build and maintain strength.

By increasing lifestyle physical activity in accordance with the guidelines given in the Surgeon General's report, people can expect to significantly improve their health and well-being. Such a program may not, however, increase physical fitness. A program of 30 minutes of lifestyle activity per day may also not be enough activity for some people to achieve and maintain a healthy body weight.

Lifestyle Physical Activity for Health Promotion and Weight Management Since the publication of the physical activity guidelines from the Surgeon General and the CDC/ACSM, other organizations have released physical activity recommendations that focus on specific health concerns. Because more than half of all U.S. adults are overweight, guidelines that focus on weight management are of particular interest. Guidelines from the Institute of Medicine, the 2005 Dietary Guidelines for Americans, and the World Health Organization/FAO Expert Report—all of which focus on weight control in addition to general health promotion—set higher daily goals for physical activity than the Surgeon General's report. These guidelines recognize that for people who need to prevent weight gain, to lose weight, or to maintain weight loss, 30 minutes per day of physical activity may not be enough—and so they recommend 60–90 or more minutes per day of physical activity. The different recommendations may seem confusing and contradictory, but all major health organizations have the same message: People can improve their health by becoming more active.

Take Charge

Becoming More Active

"Too little time" is a common excuse for not being physically active. Learning to manage your time successfully is crucial if you are to maintain a wellness lifestyle. You can begin by keeping a record of how you are currently spending your time; in your health journal, use a grid broken into blocks of 15, 20, or 30 minutes to track your daily activities. Then analyze your record: List each type of activity and the total time you engaged in it on a given day—for example, sleeping, 7 hours; eating, 1.5 hours; studying, 3 hours; and so on. Take a close look at your list of activities and prioritize them according to how important they are to you, from essential to somewhat important to not important at all.

Based on the priorities you set, make changes in your daily schedule by subtracting time from some activities in order to make time for physical activity. Look particularly carefully at your leisure time activities and your methods of transportation; these are areas where it is easy to build in physical activity. Make changes using a system of tradeoffs. For example, you may choose to reduce the total amount of time you spend playing computer games, listening to the radio, and chatting on the telephone in order to make time for an after-dinner bike ride or walk with a friend. You may decide to watch 10 fewer minutes of television in the morning in order to change your 5-minute drive to class into a 15-minute walk. In making these kinds of changes in your schedule, don't feel that you have to miss out on anything you enjoy. You can get more from less time by focusing on what you are doing and by combining activities. The following are just a few ways to become more active:

- Take the stairs instead of the elevator or escalator.
- Walk to the mailbox, post office, store, bank, or library whenever possible.
- Park your car a mile or even just a few blocks from your destination, and walk briskly.
- Do at least one chore every day that requires physical activity: wash the windows or your car, clean your room or house, mow the lawn, rake the leaves.
- Take study or work breaks to avoid sitting for more than 30 minutes at a time. Get up and walk around the library, your office, or your home or dorm; go up and down a flight of stairs.
- Stretch when you stand in line or watch TV.
- When you take public transportation, get off one stop down the line and walk to your destination.
- Go dancing instead of to a movie.
- Walk to visit a neighbor or friend rather than calling him or her on the phone. Go for a walk while you chat.
- Put your remote controls in storage; when you want to change TV channels or radio stations, get up and do it by hand.
- Take the dog for a walk (or an extra walk) every day.
- Play actively with your children or go for a walk pushing a stroller.
- If weather or neighborhood safety rule out walking outside, look for alternate locations—an indoor track, enclosed shopping mall, or even a long hallway. Look for locations near or on the way between your campus, workplace, or residence.
- Remember, being busy isn't the same thing as being active. Seize every opportunity to get up and walk around. Move more and sit less.

Exercise Programs to Develop Physical Fitness

The Surgeon General's report also summarized the benefits of more formal exercise programs. It concluded that people can obtain even greater health benefits by increasing the duration and intensity of activity. Thus, a person who engages in a structured, formal exercise program designed to measurably improve physical fitness will obtain even greater improvements in quality of life and greater reductions in disease and mortality risk (Figure 13-5 on p. 388).

How Much Physical Activity Is Enough?

Some experts believe that people get most of the health benefits of a formal exercise program simply by becoming more active over the course of the day. Others think that the lifestyle approach sets too low an activity goal; they argue that people should exercise long and intensely enough to improve the body's capacity for exercise—that is, to improve physical fitness. There is probably truth in both positions.

Most experts agree that some physical activity is better than none but that more—as long as it does not result in injury or become obsessive—is probably better than some. Regular physical activity, regardless of intensity, makes you healthier and can help protect you against many chronic diseases. However, exercising at low intensities does little to improve physical fitness. Although you get many of the health benefits of exercise by simply being more active, you obtain even more benefits when you are physically fit. In addition to long-term health benefits, fitness also significantly contributes to quality of life. Fit people have more energy and better body control. They can enjoy a more active lifestyle—cycling, hiking, skiing, and so on—than their more sedentary counterparts. Even if you don't like sports, you need physical energy and stamina in your daily life and for many nonsport leisure activities—visiting museums, playing with children, gardening, and so on.

A physical activity pyramid to guide you in meeting goals for physical activity is shown in Figure 13-6 on p. 388. If you are sedentary, start at the bottom of the pyramid and gradually increase the moderate-intensity physical activity in your daily life. You don't have to exercise

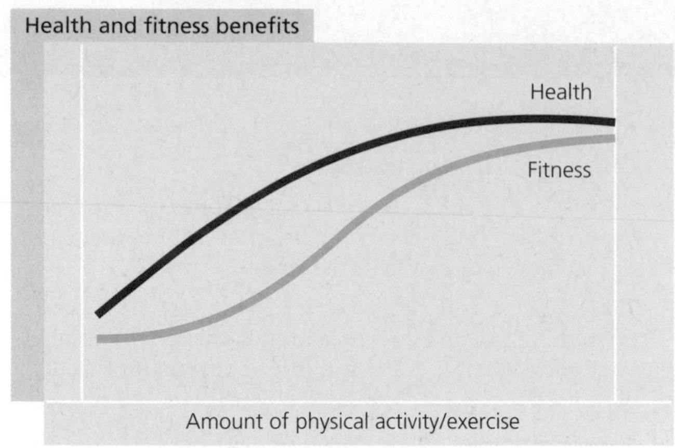

Figure 13-5 Relationship between amount of activity and health and fitness benefits. The health benefits of physical activity and exercise exist along a continuum. A fairly low level of physical activity (burning 1000 calories per week) can provide substantial health benefits, although it does little to increase fitness. Engaging in exercise that is more intense or of longer duration (burning 2000 calories per week) leads to greater health benefits and significant increases in fitness. Optimal fitness may require expending 3000 calories or more per week. SOURCE: American College of Sports Medicine. 2006. *ACSM's Resource Manual for Guidelines for Exercise Testing and Prescription,* 5th ed. Philadelphia: Lippincott Williams & Wilkins.

vigorously, but you should experience a moderate increase in your heart and breathing rates; appropriate activities include walking, climbing stairs, doing yard work, and washing your car. As mentioned earlier, your activity time can be broken up into small blocks over the course of a day. Work up to meeting the goal set by the Surgeon General's report of using about 150 calories a day in physical activity. Choose to be active whenever you can. If weight management is a concern for you, begin by achieving the goal of 30 minutes per day and then gradually raise your activity level to 60 minutes per day or more.

For even greater benefits, move up to the next two levels of the pyramid, which illustrate parts of a formal exercise program. The American College of Sports Medicine has established guidelines for creating an exercise program that includes **cardiorespiratory endurance (aerobic) exercise,** strength training, and flexibility training (Table 13-1). Such a program will develop all the health-related components of physical fitness. The following sections of this chapter will show you how to develop a personalized exercise program. For a summary of the health and fitness benefits of different levels of physical activity, see Figure 13-7 on page 390.

First Steps

Are you thinking about starting a formal exercise program? A little planning can help make it a success.

Medical Clearance Previously inactive men over 40 and women over 50 should get a medical examination

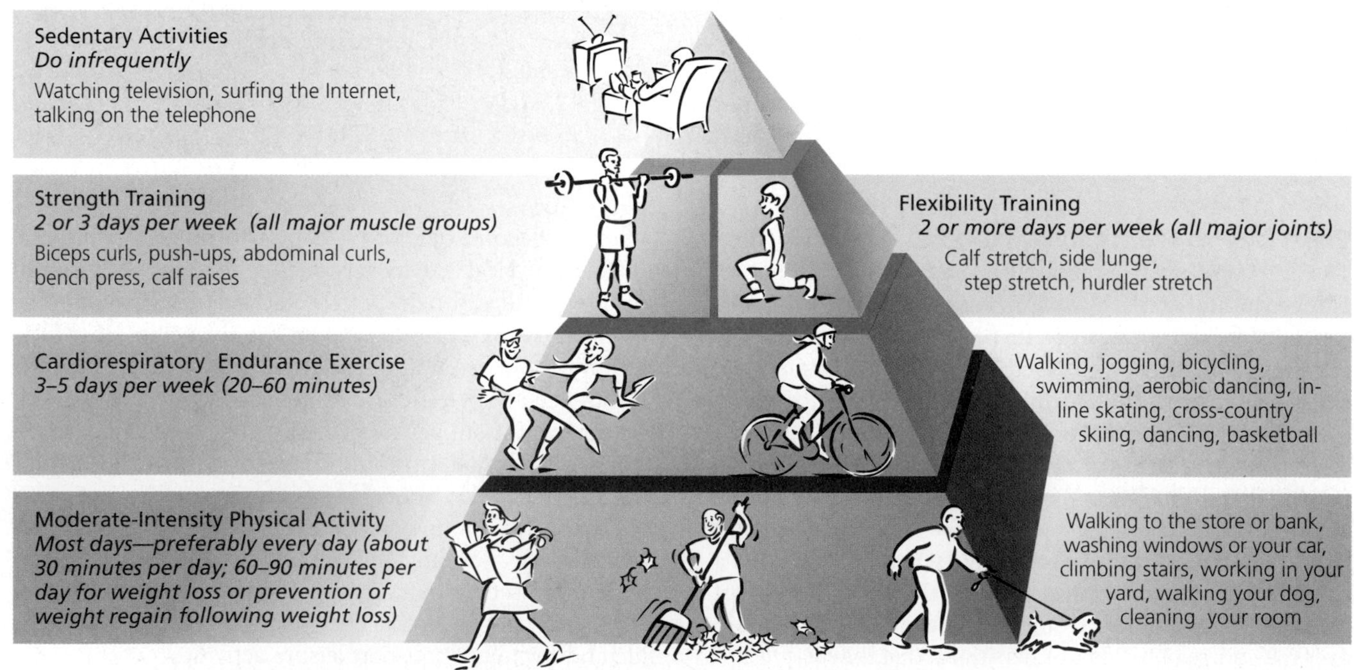

Sedentary Activities
Do infrequently
Watching television, surfing the Internet, talking on the telephone
Strength Training
2 or 3 days per week (all major muscle groups)
Biceps curls, push-ups, abdominal curls, bench press, calf raises
Flexibility Training
2 or more days per week (all major joints)
Calf stretch, side lunge, step stretch, hurdler stretch
Cardiorespiratory Endurance Exercise
3–5 days per week (20–60 minutes)
Walking, jogging, bicycling, swimming, aerobic dancing, in-line skating, cross-country skiing, dancing, basketball
Moderate-Intensity Physical Activity
Most days—preferably every day (about 30 minutes per day; 60–90 minutes per day for weight loss or prevention of weight regain following weight loss)
Walking to the store or bank, washing windows or your car, climbing stairs, working in your yard, walking your dog, cleaning your room

Figure 13-6 Physical activity pyramid. This physical activity pyramid is designed to help people become more active. If you are currently sedentary, begin at the bottom of the pyramid and gradually increase the amount of moderate-intensity physical activity in your life. If you are already moderately active, begin a formal exercise program that includes cardiorespiratory endurance exercise, flexibility training, and strength training to help you develop all the health-related components of fitness.

Table 13-1 Exercise Recommendations for Fitness Development in Healthy Adults

Exercise to Develop and Maintain Cardiorespiratory Endurance and Body Composition	
Frequency of training	3–5 days per week.
Intensity of training	55/65–90% of maximum heart rate or 40/50–85% of heart rate reserve or maximum oxygen uptake reserve. The lower intensity values (55–64% of maximum heart rate and 40–49% of heart rate reserve) are most applicable to individuals who are quite unfit. For average individuals, intensities of 70–85% of maximum heart rate or 60–80% of heart rate reserve are appropriate; see page 392 for instructions for determining target heart rate.
Time (duration) of training	20–60 total minutes of continuous or intermittent (in sessions lasting 10 or more minutes) aerobic activity. Duration is dependent on the intensity of activity; thus, low-intensity activity should be conducted over a longer period of time (30 minutes or more). Low-to-moderate-intensity activity of longer duration is recommended for nonathletic adults.
Type (mode) of activity	Any activity that uses large-muscle groups, can be maintained continuously, and is rhythmic and aerobic in nature—for example, walking-hiking, running-jogging, cycling-bicycling, cross-country skiing, aerobic dance, stair climbing, swimming, and skating.
Exercise to Develop and Maintain Muscular Strength and Endurance, Flexibility, and Body Composition	
Resistance training	One set of 8–10 exercises that condition the major muscle groups should be performed 2–3 nonconsecutive days per week. Most people should complete 8–12 repetitions of each exercise to the point of fatigue; practicing other repetition ranges (for example, 3–5 or 12–15) also builds strength and endurance; for older and frailer people (approximately 50–60 and older), 10–15 repetitions with a lighter weight may be more appropriate. Multiple-set regimens will provide greater benefits if time allows. Any mode of exercise that is comfortable throughout the full range of motion is appropriate (for example, free weights, bands, or machines).
Flexibility training	Static stretches should be performed for the major muscle groups at least 2–3 days per week, ideally 5–7 days per week. Stretch to the point of tightness, holding each stretch for 15–30 seconds; perform 2–4 repetitions of each stretch.

SOURCE: Adapted from American College of Sports Medicine. 2006. *ACSM's Guidelines for Exercise Testing and Prescription*, 7th ed. Philadelphia: Lippincott Williams & Wilkins.

before beginning an exercise program. Diabetes, asthma, heart disease, and extreme obesity are conditions that may call for a modified program. If you have an increased risk of heart disease because of smoking, high blood pressure, or obesity, get a physical checkup, including an **electrocardiogram (ECG or EKG)**, before beginning an exercise program. To evaluate your readiness for exercise, you can complete a questionnaire developed by the Canadian Society for Exercise Physiology at their Web site (www.csep.ca/forms.asp).

Basic Principles of Physical Training

To put together an effective exercise program, you should first understand the basic principles of physical training.

SPECIFICITY To develop a fitness component, you must perform exercises that are specifically designed for that component. This is the principle of *specificity*. Weight training, for example, develops muscular strength, but is less effective for developing flexibility. Specificity also applies to the skill-related fitness components and to the different parts of the body. A well-rounded exercise program includes exercises geared to each component of fitness, to different parts of the body, and to specific activities or sports.

PROGRESSIVE OVERLOAD Your body adapts to the demands of exercise by improving its functioning. When the amount of exercise, also called **overload**, is progressively increased, fitness continues to improve. Too little exercise will have no effect on fitness; too much may cause injury. The appropriate amount depends on your current level of fitness, your fitness goals, and the fitness components being developed. A novice, for example, might experience

Terms

cardiorespiratory endurance (aerobic) exercise Rhythmical, large-muscle exercise for a prolonged period of time; partially dependent on the ability of the cardiovascular system to deliver oxygen to tissues.

electrocardiogram (ECG or EKG) A recording of the changes in electrical activity of the heart.

overload The amount of stress placed on the body; a gradual increase in the amount of overload causes adaptations that improve fitness.

Vw

	Lifestyle physical activity 	Moderate exercise program 	Vigorous exercise program 
Description	Moderate physical activity—an amount of activity that uses about 150 calories per day	Cardiorespiratory endurance exercise (20–60 minutes, 3–5 days per week); strength training (2–3 days per week) and stretching exercises (2 or more days per week)	Cardiorespiratory endurance exercise (20–60 minutes, 3–5 days per week); interval training; strength training (3–4 days per week); and stretching exercises (5–7 days per week)
Sample activities or program	*One of the following:* • Walking to and from work, 15 minutes each way • Cycling to and from class, 10 minutes each way • Yard work for 30 minutes • Dancing (fast) for 30 minutes • Playing basketball for 20 minutes	• Jogging for 30 minutes, 3 days per week • Weight training, 1 set of 8 exercises, 2 days per week • Stretching exercises, 3 days per week	• Running for 45 minutes, 3 days per week • Intervals: running 400 m at high effort, 4 sets, 2 days per week • Weight training, 3 sets of 10 exercises, 3 days per week • Stretching exercises, 6 days per week
Health and fitness benefits	Better blood cholesterol levels, reduced body fat, better control of blood pressure, improved metabolic health, and enhanced glucose metabolism; improved quality of life; reduced risk of some chronic diseases Greater amounts of activity can help prevent weight gain and promote weight loss	All the benefits of lifestyle physical activity, plus improved physical fitness (increased cardiorespiratory endurance, muscular strength and endurance, and flexibility) and even greater improvements in health and quality of life and reductions in chronic disease risk	All the benefits of lifestyle physical activity and a moderate exercise program, with greater increases in fitness and somewhat greater reductions in chronic disease risk Participating in a vigorous exercise program may increase risk of injury and overtraining

Figure 13-7 Health and fitness benefits of different amounts of physical activity and exercise.

fitness benefits from jogging a mile in 10 minutes, but this level of exercise would cause no physical adaptations in a trained distance runner.

The amount of overload needed to maintain or improve a particular level of fitness is determined in four dimensions, represented by the acronym FITT:

Frequency

Intensity

Time

Type

• *Frequency, or how often.* Optimum exercise frequency, expressed in number of days per week, varies with the component being developed and your goals. A frequency of 3–5 days per week is recommended for cardiorespiratory endurance exercise, 2 or 3 days per week for strength training, and 2 to 3 days per week, ideally 5 to 7 days per week, for stretching.

• *Intensity, or how hard.* Fitness benefits occur when you exercise harder than your normal level of activity. To develop cardiorespiratory endurance, you must raise your heart rate above normal; to develop muscular strength, you must lift a heavier weight than you normally do; to develop flexibility, you must stretch your muscles beyond their normal length. A gradual increase in intensity is recommended to avoid injury.

• *Time (duration), or how long.* If fitness benefits are to occur, exercise sessions must last for an extended period of time. Depending on the component being developed and your intensity level, a duration of 20–60 minutes is usually recommended.

• *Type, or mode of activity.* The type of exercise in which you should engage varies with each fitness component and with your personal fitness goals. To develop cardiorespiratory endurance, you need to engage in continuous activities involving large-muscle groups—walking, cycling, or swimming, for example. Resistive exercises develop muscular strength and endurance; stretching exercises build flexibility. The frequency, intensity, and time of exercise will be different for each type of activity.

These dimensions of overload are described individually as they apply to the health-related components of fitness discussed in this chapter.

REVERSIBILITY The body adjusts to lower levels of physical activity in the same way it adjusts to higher levels—

the principle of *reversibility.* When you stop exercising, you can lose up to 50% of fitness improvements within 2 months. Try to exercise consistently, and don't quit if you miss a few workouts. If a training schedule must be curtailed temporarily, fitness improvements are best maintained if exercise intensity is kept constant and frequency and/or time is reduced.

INDIVIDUAL DIFFERENCES Anyone watching the Olympics can see that, from a physical standpoint, we are not all created equal. There are limits to the potential for improvement and large individual differences in our ability to improve fitness, achieve a desirable body composition, and perform and learn sports skills. Scientists have identified specific genes that influence the capacity to alter body fat, strength, and endurance. In addition, men tend to have higher endurance capacity than women due to higher testosterone levels (which affect oxygen transport and cellular metabolism) and lower levels of body fat. However, men and women have the same capacity for improvement when gains are expressed as a percent of initial fitness. Although genetics and gender may place certain limits on your level of fitness and skill, physical training improves fitness and wellness regardless of heredity.

Selecting Activities

If you have been inactive, you should begin slowly by gradually increasing the amount of moderate physical activity in your life (the bottom of the activity pyramid). Once your body has adjusted to your new level of activity, you will be ready to choose additional activities for your exercise program.

Consider your choices carefully. First, be sure the activities you choose contribute to your overall wellness. Choose activities that make sense for you. Are you competitive? If so, try racquetball, basketball, or squash. Do you prefer to exercise alone? Then consider cross-country skiing or road running. Have you been sedentary? A walking program may be a good place to start.

If you think you may have trouble sticking with an exercise program, find a structured activity that you can do with a buddy or a group. If you don't have any favorite sports or activities, try something new. Take a physical education class, join a health club, or sign up for jazz dancing. You're sure to find an activity that's both enjoyable and good for you.

Be realistic about the constraints presented by some sports, such as accessibility, expense, and time. For example, if you have to travel for hours to get to a ski area, skiing may not be a good choice for your regular exercise program. If you don't have large blocks of time available, you may have trouble squeezing in 18 holes of golf. And if you've never played tennis, it will probably take you a fair amount of time to reach a reasonable skill level; you may be better off with a program of walking or jogging to get good workouts while you're improving your tennis game.

A general fitness program that supports an active lifestyle and promotes good health should contain the following components: cardiorespiratory endurance exercises, muscular strength and endurance exercises, flexibility exercises, and training in specific skills.

Cardiorespiratory Endurance Exercises

Exercises that condition your heart and lungs should have a central role in your fitness program. The best exercises for developing cardiorespiratory endurance stress a large portion of the body's muscle mass for a prolonged period of time. These include walking, jogging, running, swimming, bicycling, and aerobic dancing. Many popular sports and recreational activities, such as racquetball, tennis, basketball, and soccer, are also good if the skill level and intensity of the game are sufficient to provide a vigorous workout.

Frequency

The optimal workout schedule for endurance training is 3–5 days per week. Beginners should start with 3 and work up to 5 days. Training more than 5 days a week often leads to injury for recreational athletes. Although you do get health benefits from exercising very vigorously only 1 or 2 days per week, you risk injury because your body never gets a chance to adapt fully to regular exercise training.

Intensity

The most misunderstood aspect of conditioning, even among experienced athletes, is training intensity. Intensity is the crucial factor in attaining a significant training effect—that is, in increasing the body's cardiorespiratory capacity. A primary purpose of endurance training is to increase **maximal oxygen consumption (VO_{2max})**. VO_{2max} represents the maximum ability of the cells to use oxygen and is considered the best measure of cardiorespiratory capacity. Intensity of training is the crucial factor in improving VO_{2max}.

However, it's not true that the harder you work, the better it is for you. Working too hard can cause injury, just as not working hard enough provides less benefit. One of the easiest ways to determine exactly how intensely you should work involves measuring your heart rate. It is not necessary or desirable to exercise at your maximum heart rate—the fastest heart rate possible before exhaustion sets in—in order to improve your cardiorespiratory capacity. Beneficial effects occur at lower heart rates with a much lower risk of injury. **Target heart rate range** is the range of rates at which you should exercise to obtain cardiorespiratory

Terms

maximal oxygen consumption (VO_{2max}) The body's maximum ability to transport and use oxygen.

target heart rate range The range of heart rates at which exercise yields cardiorespiratory benefits.

Vw

Take Charge

Determining Your Target Heart Rate Range

Your target heart rate is the range of rates at which you should exercise to experience cardiorespiratory benefits. Your target heart rate range is based on your maximum heart rate, which can be estimated from your age. (If you are a serious athlete or face possible cardiovascular risks from exercise, you may want to have your maximum heart rate determined more accurately through a treadmill test in a physician's office, hospital, or sports medicine laboratory.) Your target heart rate is a range: The lower value corresponds to moderate-intensity exercise, and the higher value is associated with high-intensity exercise. Target heart rate ranges are shown in the table.

You can monitor the intensity of your workouts by measuring your pulse either at your wrist or at one of your carotid arteries, located on either side of your Adam's apple. Your pulse rate drops rapidly after exercise, so begin counting immediately after you have finished exercising. You will obtain the most accurate results by counting beats for 10 seconds and then multiplying by 6 to get your heart rate in beats per minute (bpm). The 10-second counts corresponding to each target heart rate range are also shown in the table.

Age (years)	Target Heart Rate Range (bpm)*	10-Second Count (beats)*
20–24	127–180	21–30
25–29	124–176	20–29
30–34	121–171	20–28
35–39	118–167	19–27
40–44	114–162	19–27
45–49	111–158	18–26
50–54	108–153	18–25
55–59	105–149	17–24
60–64	101–144	16–24
65+	97–140	16–23

*Target heart rates lower than those shown here are appropriate for individuals who are quite unfit. Ranges are based on the following formula: Target heart rate = 0.65 to 0.90 of maximum heart rate, assuming maximum heart rate = 220 − age.

benefits. To find out how you can determine the intensity at which you should exercise, refer to the box "Determining Your Target Heart Rate Range."

After you begin your fitness program, you may improve quickly because the body adapts readily to new exercises; the rate of improvement may slow after the first month or so. The more fit you become, the harder you will have to work to improve. By monitoring your heart rate, you will always know if you are working hard enough to improve, not hard enough, or too hard. For most people, a fitness program involves attaining an acceptable level of fitness and then maintaining that level. There is no need to keep working indefinitely to improve; doing so only increases the chance of injury. After you have reached the level you want, you can maintain fitness by exercising at the same intensity at least 3 nonconsecutive days per week.

Time (Duration) A total time of 20–60 minutes is recommended; exercise can take place in a single session or several sessions lasting 10 or more minutes. The total duration of exercise depends on its intensity. To improve cardiorespiratory endurance during a low- to moderate-intensity activity such as walking or slow swimming, you should exercise for 45–60 minutes. For high-intensity exercise performed at the top of your target heart rate zone, a duration of 20 minutes is sufficient. It is usually best to start off with less vigorous activities and only gradually increase intensity.

You can use these three dimensions of cardiorespiratory endurance training—frequency, intensity, and time—to develop a fitness program that strengthens your heart and lungs and provides all the benefits described earlier in this chapter. Build your program around at least 20 minutes of endurance exercise at your target heart rate 3 to 5 days a week. Then add exercises that develop the other components of fitness.

The Warm-Up and Cool-Down It is always important to warm up before you exercise and to cool down afterward. Warming up enhances your performance and decreases your chances of injury. Your muscles work better when their temperature is elevated slightly above resting level. Warming up helps your body's physiology gradually progress from rest to exercise. Blood needs to be redirected to active muscles, and your heart needs time to adapt to the increased demands of exercise. A warm-up helps spread **synovial fluid** throughout the joints, which helps protect joint surfaces from wear and tear. (It's like warming up a car to spread oil through the engine parts before shifting into gear.)

A warm-up session should include low-intensity movements similar to those in the activity that will follow. For example, hit forehands and backhands before a tennis game or jog slowly for 400 meters before progressing to an 8-minute mile. Some people like to include stretching exercises in their warm-up. Experts recommend that you stretch *after* the active part of your warm-up, when your body temperature has been elevated. Studies have found that stretching prior to exercise can temporarily decrease muscle strength and power, so if a high-performance workout is

Gender Matters

Gender Differences in Muscular Strength

Men are generally stronger than women because they typically have larger bodies overall and a larger proportion of their total body mass is made up of muscle. But when strength is expressed per unit of muscle tissue, men are only 1–2% stronger than women in the upper body and about equal to women in the lower body. Individual muscle cells are larger in men, but the functioning of the cells is the same in both sexes.

Two factors that help explain these disparities are testosterone levels and the speed of nervous control of muscle. Testosterone promotes the growth of muscle tissue in both males and females, but testosterone levels are about 6–10 times higher in men than in women, so men develop larger muscles. Also, because the male nervous system can activate muscles faster, men tend to have more power.

Some women are concerned that they will develop large muscles from strength training. Because of hormonal differences, most women do not develop large muscles unless they train intensely over many years or take steroids. Women do gain muscle and improve body composition through strength training, but they don't develop bulky muscles or gain significant amounts of weight. A study of average women who weight trained 2–3 days per week for 8 weeks found that the women gained about 1.75 pounds of muscle and lost about 3.5 pounds of fat. Another study followed women who trained with weights for 2 years. Not only did the women reduce their overall body fat levels but they ended up with less fat around their midsection. This "belly fat" is associated with several diseases, including diabetes and CVD.

Losing muscle over time is a much greater health concern for women than small gains in muscle weight in response to strength training, especially as any gains in muscle weight are typically more than balanced with loss of fat weight. Both men and women lose muscle mass and power as they age, but because men start out with more muscle when they are young and don't lose power as quickly as women, older women tend to have greater impairment of muscle function than older men. This may partially explain the higher incidence of life-threatening falls in older women.

The bottom line is that both men and women can benefit from strength training. *Healthy People 2010* sets a national health objective of increasing to 30% the proportion of adults who perform strength training exercises on 2 or more days per week, a goal also endorsed by the American College of Sports Medicine. In 2006, however, the CDC reported that only 21% of men and 17.5% of women met this goal, underscoring the need for additional programs and campaigns that promote this form of exercise.

SOURCES: Fahey, T. D. 2007. *Basic Weight Training for Men and Women*, 6th ed. New York: McGraw-Hill; Centers for Disease Control and Prevention. 2006. Trends in strength training—United States, 1998–2004. *Morbidity and Mortality Weekly Report* 55(28): 769–772.

your goal, it is best to stretch after a workout. See pages 395–397 for more on stretching.

Cooling down after exercise is important to restore the body's circulation to its normal resting condition. When you are at rest, a relatively small percentage of your total blood volume is directed to muscles, but during exercise, as much as 85% of the heart's output is directed to them. During recovery from exercise, it is important to continue exercising at a low level to provide a smooth transition to the resting state. Cooling down helps regulate the return of blood to your heart.

Developing Muscular Strength and Endurance

Any program designed to promote health should include exercises that develop muscular strength and endurance. Your ability to maintain correct posture and move efficiently depends in part on adequate muscle fitness. Strengthening exercises also increase muscle tone, which improves the appearance of your body. A lean, healthy-looking body is certainly one of the goals and one of the benefits of an overall fitness program (see the box "Gender Differences in Muscular Strength").

Types of Strength Training Exercises Muscular strength and endurance can be developed in many ways, from weight training to calisthenics. Common exercises such as curl-ups, push-ups, pull-ups, and wall-sitting (leaning against a wall in a seated position and supporting yourself with your leg muscles) maintain the muscular strength of most people if they practice them several times a week. To condition and tone your whole body, choose exercises that work the major muscles of the shoulders, chest, back, arms, abdomen, and legs.

To increase muscular strength and endurance, you must do **resistance exercise**—exercises in which your muscles must exert force against a significant amount of resistance. Resistance can be provided by weights, exercise machines, or your own body weight. **Isometric (static) exercises** involve applying force without movement, such as when you contract your abdominal muscles. This static type of exercise is valuable for toning and strengthening muscles. Isometrics can be practiced anywhere and do not require

Terms

VW

synovial fluid Fluid found within many joints that provides lubrication and nutrition to the cells of the joint surface.

resistance exercise Exercise that forces muscles to contract against increased resistance; also called *strength training*.

isometric (static) exercise The application of force without movement.

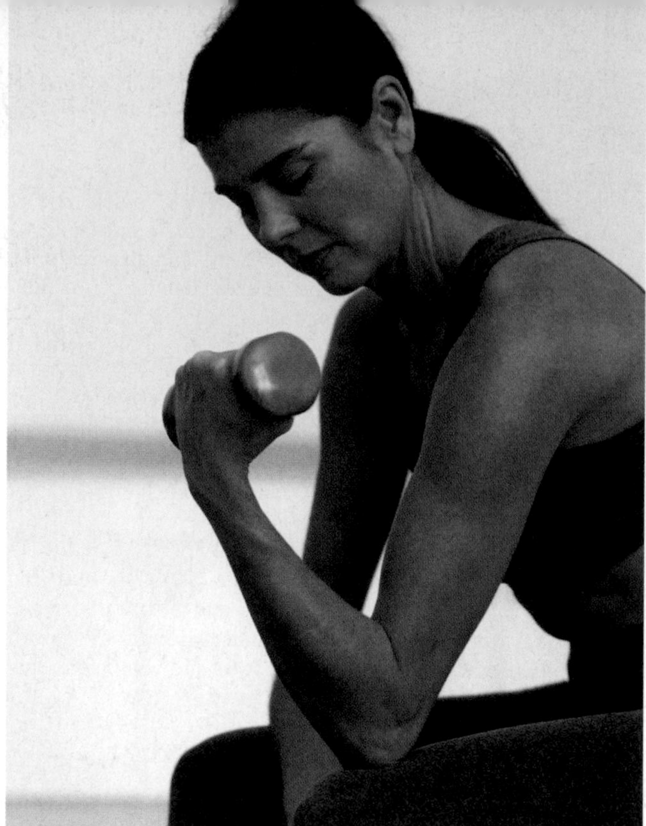

Building muscular strength is a key component of a fitness program. Weight training is just one way to increase strength, improve muscle tone, and enhance the overall appearance of the body.

any equipment. For maximum strength gains, hold an isometric contraction maximally for 6 seconds; do five to ten repetitions. Don't hold your breath—that can restrict blood flow to your heart and brain. Within a few weeks, you will notice the effect of this exercise. Isometrics are particularly useful when recovering from an injury.

Isotonic (dynamic) exercises involve applying force with movement, as, for example, in weight training exercises such as the bench press. These are the most popular type of exercises for increasing muscle strength and seem to be most valuable for developing strength that can be transferred to other forms of physical activity. They include exercises using barbells, dumbbells, weight machines, and body weight, as in push-ups or curl-ups.

Choosing Equipment Weight machines are preferred by many people because they are safe, convenient, and easy to use. You just set the resistance (usually by placing a pin in the weight stack), sit down at the machine, and start working. Machines make it easy to isolate and work specific muscles. Free weights require more care, balance, and coordination to use, but they strengthen your body in ways that are more adaptable to real life. When using free weights, you need to use a spotter, someone who stands by to assist in case you lose control over a weight (see the box "Safe Weight Training").

Choosing Exercises A complete weight training program works all the major muscle groups: neck, upper back, shoulders, arms, chest, abdomen, lower back, thighs, buttocks, and calves. Different exercises work different muscles, so it usually takes about eight to ten exercises to get a complete workout for general fitness—for example, bench presses to develop the chest, shoulders, and upper arms; pull-ups to work the biceps and upper back; squats to develop the legs and buttocks; toe raises to work the calves; and so on. If you are also training for a particular sport, include exercises to strengthen the muscles important for optimal performance and those most likely to be injured.

Refer to the Online Learning Center (www.mhhe.com/insel10e) for a sample recommended program for strength training. A sample workout card for monitoring your progress and video clips of selected exercises are also included.

Frequency For general fitness, the American College of Sports Medicine recommends a frequency of 2 or 3 nonconsecutive days per week. This allows your muscles a day of rest between workouts to avoid soreness and injury. If you enjoy weight training and would like to train more often, try working different muscle groups on alternate days.

Intensity and Time The amount of weight (resistance) you lift in weight training exercises is equivalent to intensity in cardiorespiratory endurance training; the number of repetitions of each exercise is equivalent to time. In order to improve fitness, you must do enough repetitions of each exercise to temporarily fatigue your muscles. The number of repetitions needed to cause fatigue depends on the amount of resistance: the heavier the weight, the fewer repetitions to reach fatigue. In general, a heavy weight and a low number of repetitions (1–5) build strength, whereas a light weight and a high number of repetitions (20–25) build endurance. For a general fitness program to build both strength and endurance, try to do 8–12 repetitions of each exercise; a few exercises, such as abdominal crunches and calf raises, may require more. (For people who are 50–60 years of age and older, 10–15 repetitions of each exercise using a lighter weight is recommended.)

The first few sessions of weight training should be devoted to learning the exercises. To start, choose a weight that you can move easily through 8–12 repetitions. Add weight when you can do more than 12 repetitions of an exercise. If adding weight means you can do only 7 or 8 repetitions before your muscles fatigue, stay with that weight until you can again complete 12 repetitions. If you can do only 4–6 repetitions after adding weight, or if you can't maintain good form, you've added too much and should

Term

VW **isotonic (dynamic) exercise** The application of force with movement.

Take Charge

Safe Weight Training

General Strategies

- Lift weights from a stabilized body position. Protect your back from dangerous positions. Don't twist your body while lifting.
- Don't lift beyond the limits of your strength.
- Be aware of what's going on around you so that you don't bump into someone or get too close to a moving weight stack.
- Don't use defective equipment; report any equipment problems immediately.
- Don't chew gum when exercising.
- *Don't hold your breath while doing weight training exercises.* Exhale when exerting the greatest force, and inhale when moving the weight into position. (Holding your breath raises blood pressure and causes a decrease in blood returning to the heart; it can make you become dizzy and faint.)
- Rest between lifts.
- Always warm up before training and cool down afterward.

Free Weights

- Use spotters to avoid injury. A spotter can help you if you cannot complete a lift or if the weight tilts.
- Secure weight plates to barbells with a collar to prevent them from sliding off.
- Keep weights as close to your body as possible. Do most of your lifting with your legs; keep your hips and buttocks tucked in.
- Lift weights smoothly and slowly; don't bounce or jerk them. Control the weight through the entire range of motion.
- When holding barbells and dumbbells, wrap your thumbs around the bar when gripping it.

Weight Machines

- Stay away from moving parts of the machine that could pinch your skin or crush your fingers.
- Adjust each machine for your body so that you don't have to work in an awkward position.
- Beware of broken bolts, frayed cables, broken chains, or loose cushions that can give way and cause serious injury.
- Make sure the machines are clean. Carry a towel with you, and place it on the machine where you will sit or lie down.

take some off. As a general guideline, try increases of approximately ½ pound of additional weight for each 10 pounds you are currently lifting.

For developing strength and endurance for general fitness, a single set (group) of each exercise is sufficient, provided you use enough resistance (weight) to fatigue your muscles. Doing more than one set of each exercise may increase strength development, and most serious weight trainers do at least three sets of each exercise. If you do more than one set of an exercise, rest long enough between sets to allow your muscles to recover.

As with cardiorespiratory endurance exercise, you should warm up before every weight training session and cool down afterward. You can expect to improve rapidly during the first 6–10 weeks of training; gains will then come more slowly. Factors such as age, motivation, gender, and heredity will affect your program. Your ultimate goal depends on you. After you have achieved the level of strength and muscularity that you want, you can maintain your gains by training 2–3 nonconsecutive days per week.

A Caution About Supplements No nutritional supplement or drug will change a weak person into a strong person. Those changes require regular training that stresses the body and causes physiological adaptations. Supplements or drugs that promise quick, large gains in strength usually don't work and are often either dangerous, expensive, or both (see the box "Drugs and Supplements for Improved Athletic Performance" on p. 396). Over-the-counter supplements are not carefully regulated, and their long-term effects have not been systematically studied. The International Olympic Committee recently issued a warning after researchers tested hundreds of nutritional supplements and found that 15% contained substances that would cause an athlete to fail a drug test. Use your critical thinking skills to evaluate claims about supplements, and stay with the proven method of a steady, progressive fitness program to build strength.

Flexibility Exercises

Flexibility, or stretching, exercises are important for maintaining the normal range of motion in the major joints of the body. Some exercises, such as running, can actually decrease flexibility because they require only a partial range of motion. Like a good weight training program, a good stretching program includes exercises for all the major muscle groups and joints of the body: neck, shoulders, back, hips, thighs, hamstrings, and calves. Refer to the Online Learning Center (www.mhhe.com/insel10e) for a sample recommended program for flexibility training.

Proper Stretching Technique Stretching should be performed statically. Ballistic stretching (known as

In the News

Drugs and Supplements for Improved Athletic Performance

In 2006, doping scandals snared athletes in sports as diverse as cycling, baseball, and track and field. Cyclist Floyd Landis fought charges that he used synthetic testosterone to help him win the 2006 Tour de France. Giants hitter Barry Bonds continued to deny that he knowingly used steroids provided by BALCO (Bay Area Laboratory Cooperative), while his trainer served prison time for refusing to testify against him and BALCO's founder faced federal charges. Though implicated in the BALCO scandal, Olympic sprinter Marion Jones was cleared of doping changes. In the wake of these and other events, the U.S. Congress, professional sports leagues, and anti-doping agencies all sought ways to rid sports of banned substances.

Drugs intended to enhance athletic performance are used not only by elite Olympic and professional athletes but also by active individuals of all fitness levels. About 2–6% of high school and college students report having used anabolic steroids, and over-the-counter dietary supplements are much more popular. Many such substances are ineffective and expensive, and many are also dangerous. For example, supplements marketed to bodybuilders containing gamma butyrolactone or butanediol, CNS depressants related to the illegal drug gamma hydroxybutyrate (GHB), may cause vomiting, seizures, coma, and potentially fatal withdrawal reactions (see Chapter 9). A few of the most widely used compounds are described below.

Anabolic Steroids These synthetic derivatives of testosterone are taken to increase strength, power, speed, endurance, muscle size, and aggressiveness. **Anabolic steroids** have dangerous side effects, including disruption of the body's hormone system, liver disease, acne, breast development and testicular shrinkage in males, masculinization in women and children, and increased risk of heart disease and cancer. A 2006 study found a link between steroid use and risk of heart attack, stroke, and sudden death.

Steroid users who inject the drugs face the same health risks as other injection drug users, including increased risk of HIV infection. Steroids have been found to be a gateway to the use of other drugs.

Adrenal Androgens This group of drugs, which includes dehydroepiandrosterone (DHEA) and androstenedione, are typically taken to stimulate muscle growth and aid in weight control. The few studies of these agents done on humans show that they are of very little value in improving athletic performance, and they have side effects similar to those of anabolic steroids, especially when taken in high doses.

Ephedra and Other Stimulants These drugs may be taken to increase training intensity, to suppress hunger, to reduce fatigue, and to promote weight loss. They raise heart rate and blood pressure and, at high doses, may increase the risk of heart attack, stroke, and heat-related illness. Several stimulants, including ephedra and phenylpropanolamine, have been banned by the FDA. The 2004 ban on ephedra was challenged by manufacturers of dietary supplements, but the ban was upheld in a U.S. Court of Appeals in 2006.

Erythropoietin (EPO) A naturally occurring hormone that boosts the concentration of red blood cells, EPO is used by endurance athletes to improve performance. EPO can cause blood clots and death.

Creatine Monohydrate Creatine is thought to improve performance in short-term, high-intensity, repetitive exercise and decrease the risk of injury. A 2006 study, however, showed that the drug provided no performance boost to athletes who took creatine for several weeks. The long-term effects of creatine use, especially among young people, are not well established.

Protein, Amino Acid, and Polypeptide Supplements Little research supports the use of such supplements, even in athletes on extemely heavy training regimens. The protein requirements of athletes are not much higher than those of sedentary individuals, and most people take in more than enough protein in their diets. By substituting supplements for food sources of protein, people may risk deficiencies in other key nutrients typically found in such foods, including iron and B vitamins.

Chromium Picolinate Sold over the counter, chromium picolinate is a more easily digested form of the trace mineral chromium. Although often marketed as a means to build muscle and reduce fat, most studies have found no positive effects. Long-term use of high dosages may have serious health consequences.

"bouncing") is dangerous and counterproductive. In active stretching, a muscle is stretched under a person's own power by contracting the opposing muscles. In passive stretching, an outside force or resistance provided by yourself, a partner, gravity, or a weight helps elongate the targeted muscle. You can achieve a greater range of motion and a more intense stretch using passive stretching, but there is a greater risk of injury. The safest and most convenient technique may be active static stretching with a passive assist. For example, you might do a seated stretch of your calf muscles both by contracting the muscles on the top of your shin and by grabbing your feet and pulling them toward you.

Frequency Do stretching exercises at least 2–3 days per week, ideally 5–7 days per week. If you stretch after cardiorespiratory endurance exercise or strength training, during your cool-down, you may develop more flexibility,

Term

anabolic steroids Synthetic male hormones used to increase muscle size and strength.

When performed regularly, stretching exercises help maintain or improve the range of motion in joints. For each exercise, stretch to the point of tightness in the muscle and hold the position for 15–30 seconds.

because your muscles are warmer then and can be stretched farther.

Intensity and Time For each exercise, stretch to the point of tightness in the muscle, and hold the position for 15–30 seconds. Rest for 30–60 seconds, and then repeat, trying to stretch a bit farther. Relax and breathe easily as you stretch. You should feel a pleasant, mild stretch as you let the muscles relax; stretching should not be painful. Do 2–4 repetitions of each exercise. A complete flexibility workout usually takes about 20–30 minutes.

Increase your intensity gradually over time. Improved flexibility takes many months to develop. There are large individual differences in joint flexibility. Don't feel you have to compete with others during stretching workouts.

Training in Specific Skills

The final component in your fitness program is learning the skills required for the sports or activities in which you choose to participate. Taking the time and effort to acquire competence means that instead of feeling ridiculous, becoming frustrated, and giving up in despair, you achieve a sense of mastery and add a new physical activity to your repertoire.

The first step in learning a new skill is getting help. Sports like tennis, golf, sailing, and skiing require mastery of basic movements and techniques, so instruction from a qualified teacher can save you hours of frustration and increase your enjoyment of the sport. Skill is also important in conditioning activities such as jogging, swimming, and cycling. Even if you learned a sport as a child, additional instruction now can help you refine your technique, get over stumbling blocks, and relearn skills that you may have learned incorrectly.

Putting It All Together

Now that you know the basic components of a fitness program, you can put them all together in a program that works for you. Remember to include the following:

- *Cardiorespiratory endurance exercise:* Do at least 20 minutes of aerobic exercise at your target heart rate 3 to 5 days a week.
- *Muscular strength and endurance:* Work the major muscle groups (one or more sets of eight to ten exercises) 2 or 3 nonconsecutive days a week.
- *Flexibility exercise:* Do stretches at least 2 or 3 days a week, ideally 5 to 7 days a week, preferably after exercise, when your muscles are warm.
- *Skill training:* Incorporate some or all of your aerobic or strengthening exercise into an enjoyable sport or physical activity.

Refer to Figure 13-8 for a summary of the FITT principle for the health-related fitness components; the fitness

	Cardiorespiratory endurance training	Strength training	Flexibility training
Frequency	3–5 days per week	2–3 nonconsecutive days per week	2–3 days per week (minimum); 5–7 days per week (ideal)
Intensity	55/65–90% of maximum heart rate	Sufficient resistance to fatigue muscles	Stretch to the point of tension
Time	20–60 minutes in sessions lasting 10 minutes or more	8–12 repetitions of each exercise, 1 or more sets	2–4 repetitions of each exercise, held for 15–30 seconds
Type	Continuous rhythmic activities using large muscle groups	Resistance exercises for all major muscle groups	Stretching exercises for all major joints

Figure 13-8 A summary of the FITT principle for the health-related components of fitness

Table 13-2 A Summary of Sports and Fitness Activities

This table classifies sports and activities as high (H), moderate (M), or low (L) in terms of their ability to develop each of the five components of physical fitness: cardiorespiratory endurance (CRE), muscular strength (MS), muscular endurance (ME), flexibility (F), and body composition (BC). The skill level needed to obtain fitness benefits is noted: Low (L) means little or no skill is required to obtain fitness benefits, moderate (M) means average skill is needed to obtain fitness benefits, and high (H) means much skill is required to obtain fitness benefits. The fitness prerequisite, or conditioning needs of a beginner, is also noted: Low (L) means no fitness prerequisite is required, moderate (M) means some preconditioning is required, and high (H) means substantial fitness is required. The last two columns list the calorie cost of each activity when performed moderately and vigorously. To determine how many calories you burn, multiply the value in the appropriate column by your body weight and then by the number of minutes you exercise. Work up to using 300 or more calories per workout.

Sports and Activities	Components					Skill Level	Fitness Prerequisite	Approximate Calorie Cost (cal/lb/min)	
	CRE	*MS**	*ME**	*F**	*BC*			*Moderate*	*Vigorous*
Aerobic dance	H	M	H	H	H	L	L	.046	.062
Backpacking	H	M	H	M	H	L	M	.032	.078
Badminton, skilled, singles	H	M	M	M	H	M	M	—	.071
Ballet (floor combinations)	M	M	H	H	M	M	L	—	.058
Ballroom dancing	M	L	M	L	M	M	L	.034	.049
Baseball (pitcher and catcher)	M	M	H	M	M	H	M	.039	—
Basketball, half court	H	M	H	M	H	M	M	.045	.071
Bicycling	H	M	H	M	H	M	L	.049	.071
Bowling	L	L	L	L	L	L	L	—	—
Calisthenic circuit training	H	M	H	M	H	L	L	—	.060
Canoeing and kayaking (flat water)	M	M	H	M	M	M	M	.045	—
Cheerleading	M	M	M	M	M	M	L	.033	.049
Fencing	M	M	H	H	M	M	L	.032	.078
Field hockey	H	M	H	M	H	M	M	.052	.078
Folk and square dancing	M	L	M	L	M	L	L	.039	.049
Football, touch	M	M	M	M	M	M	M	.049	.078
Frisbee, ultimate	H	M	H	M	H	M	M	.049	.078
Golf (riding cart)	L	L	L	M	L	L	L	—	—
Handball, skilled, singles	H	M	H	M	H	M	M	—	.078
Hiking	H	M	H	L	H	L	M	.051	.073
Hockey, ice and roller	H	M	H	M	H	M	M	.052	.078
Horseback riding	M	M	M	L	M	M	M	.052	.065
Interval circuit training	H	H	H	M	H	L	L	—	.062
Jogging and running	H	M	H	L	H	L	L	.060	.104
Judo	M	H	H	M	M	M	L	.049	.090

benefits of a variety of activities are provided in Table 13-2 to help you plan your program.

GETTING STARTED AND STAYING ON TRACK

Once you have a program that fulfills your basic fitness needs and suits your personal tastes, adhering to a few basic principles will help you improve at the fastest rate, have more fun, and minimize the risk of injury. These principles include buying appropriate equipment, eating and drinking properly, and managing your program so it becomes an integral part of your life.

Selecting Instructors, Equipment, and Facilities

Once you've chosen the activities for your program, you may need to obtain appropriate information, instruction, and equipment or find an appropriate facility.

Finding Help and Advice About Exercise

One of the best places to get help is an exercise class, where an expert instructor can help you learn the basics of training and answer your questions. A qualified personal trainer can also get you started on an exercise program or a new form of training. Make sure that your instructor or trainer has proper qualifications, such as a

Sports and Activities	Components					Skill Level	Fitness Prerequisite	Approximate Calorie Cost (cal/lb/min)	
	CRE	*MS**	*ME**	*F**	*BC*			*Moderate*	*Vigorous*
Karate	H	M	H	H	H	L	M	.049	.090
Lacrosse	H	M	H	M	H	H	M	.052	.078
Modern dance (moving combinations)	M	M	H	H	M	L	L	—	.058
Orienteering	H	M	H	L	H	L	M	.049	.078
Outdoor fitness trails	H	M	H	M	H	L	L	—	.060
Popular dancing	M	L	M	M	M	M	L	—	.049
Racquetball, skilled, singles	H	M	M	M	H	M	M	.049	.078
Rock climbing	M	H	H	H	M	H	M	.033	.033
Rope skipping	H	M	H	L	H	M	M	.071	.095
Rowing	H	H	H	H	H	L	L	.032	.097
Rugby	H	M	H	M	H	M	M	.052	.097
Sailing	L	L	M	L	L	M	L	—	—
Skating, ice, roller, and in-line	M	M	H	M	M	H	M	.049	.095
Skiing, alpine	M	H	H	M	M	H	M	.039	.078
Skiing, cross-country	H	M	H	M	H	M	M	.049	.104
Soccer	H	M	H	M	H	M	M	.052	.097
Squash, skilled, singles	H	M	M	M	H	M	M	.049	.078
Stretching	L	L	L	H	L	L	L	—	—
Surfing (including swimming)	M	M	M	M	M	H	M	—	.078
Swimming	H	M	H	M	H	M	L	.032	.088
Synchronized swimming	M	M	H	H	M	H	M	.032	.052
Table tennis	M	L	M	M	M	M	L	—	.045
Tennis, skilled, singles	H	M	M	M	H	M	M	—	.071
Volleyball	M	L	M	M	M	M	M	—	.065
Walking	H	L	M	L	H	L	L	.029	.048
Water polo	H	M	H	M	H	H	M	—	.078
Water skiing	M	M	H	M	M	H	M	.039	.055
Weight training	L	H	H	H	M	L	L	—	—
Wrestling	H	H	H	H	H	H	H	.065	.094
Yoga	L	L	M	H	L	H	L	—	—

*Ratings are for the muscle groups involved.

SOURCE: Kusinitz, I., and M. Fine. 1995. *Your Guide to Getting Fit,* 3rd ed. Mountain View, Calif.: Mayfield. Copyright © 1995 by Consumers Union of U.S., Inc. Yonkers, NY 10703-1057, a nonprofit organization. Originally published in *Physical Fitness for Practically Everybody* by Kusinitz and Fine. Reprinted with permission for educational purposes only. No commercial use or reproduction permitted. www.ConsumerReports.org.

college degree in exercise physiology or physical education and certification by the American College of Sports Medicine (ACSM), National Strength and Conditioning Association (NSCA), or another professional organization. Don't seek out a person for advice simply because he or she looks fit. You can further your knowledge by reading articles by experts in fitness magazines.

Many Web sites provide fitness programs, including ongoing support and feedback via e-mail. Many of these sites charge a fee, so it is important to review the sites, decide which ones seem most appropriate, and if possible go through a free trial period before subscribing. Also remember to consider the reliability of the information at fitness Web sites, especially those that also advertise or sell products. A few popular sites are listed in For More Information at the end of the chapter.

Selecting Equipment Try to purchase the best equipment you can afford. Good equipment will enhance your enjoyment and decrease your risk of injury. Appropriate safety equipment, such as pads and helmets for in-line skating, is particularly important. If you shop around, you can often find bargains through mail-order companies and discount or used equipment stores.

Before you invest in a new piece of equipment, investigate it. Is it worth the money? Does it produce the results its proponents claim for it? Is it safe? Does it fit properly, and is it in good working order? Does it provide a genuine workout? Will you really use it? Before you buy an expensive piece of equipment, try it out at a local gym to make sure that you'll use it regularly. Also check whether you have space to use and store it at home. Ask the experts (coaches, physical educators, and sports instructors) for their opinion. Better yet, educate yourself. Every sport, from running to volleyball, has its own magazine. Expending a little effort to educate yourself will be well rewarded. Footwear is an important piece of equipment for almost any activity; see the box "Choosing Exercise Footwear" for shopping strategies.

Choosing a Fitness Center Are you thinking of becoming a member of a health club or fitness center? Be sure to choose one that has the right programs and equipment available at the times you will use them. You should feel comfortable with the classes and activities available; the age, fitness level, and dress of others in the club; and the types of music used in classes. The facility and equipment should be clean and well maintained, including the showers and lockers; the staff should be well trained and helpful. Ask for a free trial workout, a 1-day pass, or an inexpensive 1- to 2-week trial membership before committing to a long-term contract. Be wary of promotional gimmicks and high-pressure sales tactics. Also make sure the facility is certified; look for the displayed names American College of Sports Medicine (ACSM); National Strength and Conditioning Association (NSCA); American Council on Exercise (ACE); Aerobics and Fitness Association of America (AFAA); or International Health, Racquet, and Sportsclub Association (IHRSA). These trade associations have established standards to help protect consumer health, safety, and rights. Find a facility that you feel comfortable with and that meets your needs.

Eating and Drinking for Exercise

Most people do not need to change their eating habits when they begin a fitness program. Many athletes and other physically active people are lured into buying aggressively advertised vitamins, minerals, and protein supplements; but, in almost every case, a well-balanced diet contains all the energy and nutrients needed to sustain an exercise program (see Chapter 12).

A balanced diet is also the key to improving your body composition when you begin to exercise more. One of the promises of a fitness program is a decrease in body fat and an increase in muscular body mass. As mentioned earlier, the control of body fat is determined by the balance of energy in the body. If more calories are consumed than are expended through metabolism and exercise, then fat increases. If the reverse is true, fat is lost. The best way to control body fat is to follow a diet containing adequate but not excessive calories and to be physically active.

One of the most important principles to follow when exercising is to drink enough water. Your body depends on water to sustain many chemical reactions and to maintain correct body temperature. Sweating during exercise depletes the body's water supply and can lead to dehydration if fluids are not replaced. Serious dehydration can cause reduced blood volume, accelerated heart rate, elevated body temperature, muscle cramps, heat stroke, and other serious problems.

Drinking fluids before and during exercise is important to prevent dehydration and enhance performance. Thirst receptors in the brain make you want to drink fluids, but during heavy or prolonged exercise or exercise in hot weather, thirst alone isn't a good indication of how much fluid you need to drink. As a rule of thumb, drink at least 2 cups (16 ounces) of fluid 2 hours before exercise and then drink enough during exercise to match fluid loss in sweat—at least 1 cup of fluid every 20–30 minutes of exercise, more in hot weather or if you sweat heavily. To determine if you're drinking the right amount of fluid, weigh yourself before and after an exercise session: Any weight loss is due to fluid loss that needs to be replaced. Any weight gain is due to overconsumption of fluid.

Bring a bottle of water when you exercise so you can replace your fluids when they're depleted. For exercise sessions lasting less than 60–90 minutes, cool water is an excellent fluid replacement. For longer workouts, a sports drink that contains water and small amounts of electrolytes (sodium, potassium, and magnesium) and simple carbohydrates (sugar, usually in the form of sucrose or glucose) is recommended.

Managing Your Fitness Program

How can you tell when you're in shape? When do you stop improving and start maintaining? How can you stay motivated? If your program is going to become an integral part of your life, and if the principles behind it are going to serve you well in the future, these are key questions.

Consistency: The Key to Physical Improvement It is important to be able to recognize when you have achieved the level of fitness that is appropriate for you. This level will vary, of course, depending on your goals, the intensity of your program, and your natural ability. Your body gets into shape by adapting to increasing levels of physical stress. If you don't push yourself by increasing the intensity of your workout—by adding weight or running a little faster or a little longer—no change will occur in your body.

But if you subject your body to severe stress, it will break down and become distressed or injured. Overtraining (overdoing exercise) is just as bad as not exercising hard enough. No one can become fit overnight. Your body needs time to adapt to increasingly higher levels of stress. The process of improving fitness involves a countless number of stresses and adaptations. If you feel

Choosing Exercise Footwear

Footwear is perhaps the most important item of equipment for most activities. Shoes protect and support your feet and improve your traction. When you jump or run, you place as much as six times more force on your feet than when you stand still. Shoes can help cushion against the stress that this additional force places on your lower legs, thereby preventing injuries. Some athletic shoes are also designed to help prevent ankle rollover, another common source of injury.

General Guidelines

When choosing athletic shoes, first consider the activity you've chosen for your exercise program. Shoes appropriate for different activities have very different characteristics. For example, running shoes typically have highly cushioned midsoles, rubber outsoles with elevated heels, and a great deal of flexibility in the forefoot. The heels of walking shoes tend to be lower, less padded, and more beveled than those designed for running. For aerobic dance, shoes must be flexible in the forefoot and have straight, nonflared heels to allow for safe and easy lateral movements. Court shoes also provide substantial support for lateral movements; they typically have outsoles made from white rubber that will not damage court surfaces.

Also consider the location and intensity of your workouts. If you plan to walk or run on trails, choose shoes with water-resistant, highly durable uppers and more outsole traction. If you work out intensely or have a relatively high body weight, you'll need thick, firm midsoles to avoid bottoming-out the cushioning system of your shoes.

Foot type is another important consideration. If your feet tend to roll inward excessively, you may need shoes with additional stability features on their inner side to counteract this movement. If your feet tend to roll outward excessively, you may need highly flexible and cushioned shoes that promote foot motion. For aerobic dancers with feet that tend to roll inward or outward, mid-cut to high-cut shoes may be more appropriate than low-cut aerobic shoes or cross-trainers (shoes designed to be worn for several different activities). Compared with men, women have narrower feet overall and narrower heels relative to the forefoot. Most women will get a better fit if they choose shoes that are specifically designed for women's feet rather than those that are downsized versions of men's shoes.

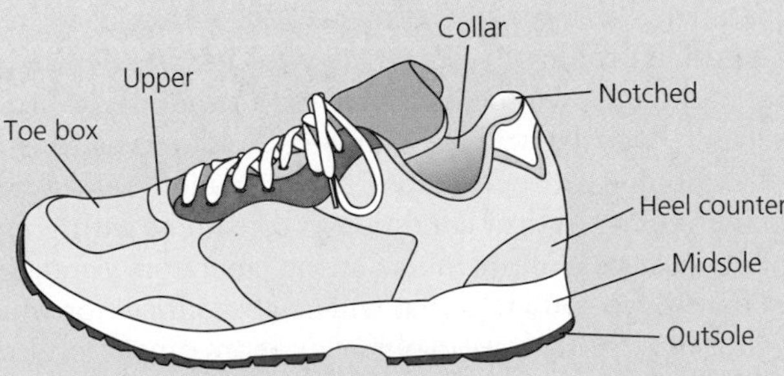

Successful Shopping

For successful shoe shopping, keep the following strategies in mind:

- Shop at an athletic shoe or specialty store that has personnel trained to fit athletic shoes and a large selection of styles and sizes.
- Shop late in the day or, ideally, following a workout. Your foot size increases over the course of the day and as a result of exercise.
- Wear socks like those you plan to wear during exercise. If you have an old pair of athletic shoes, bring them with you. The wear pattern on your old shoes can help you select a pair with extra support or cushioning in the places you need it the most.
- Ask for help. Trained salespeople know which shoes are designed for your foot type and your level of activity. They can also help fit your shoes properly.
- Don't insist on buying shoes in what you consider to be your typical shoe size. Sizes vary from shoe to shoe. In addition, foot sizes change over time, and many people have one foot that is larger or wider than the other. Try several sizes in several widths, if necessary. Don't buy shoes that are too small.
- Try on both shoes, and wear them for 10 or more minutes. Try walking on a noncarpeted surface. Approximate the movements of your activity: walk, jog, run, jump, and so on.
- Check the fit and style carefully:

  Is the toe box roomy enough? Your toes will spread out when your foot hits the ground or you push off. There should be at least one thumb's width of space from the longest toe to the end of the toe box.

  Do the shoes have enough cushioning? Do your feet feel supported when you bounce up and down? Try bouncing on your toes and on your heels.

  Do your heels fit snugly into the shoe? Do they stay put when you walk, or do they rise up?

  Are the arches of your feet right on top of the shoes' arch supports?

  Do the shoes feel stable when you twist and turn on the balls of your feet? Try twisting from side to side while standing on one foot.

  Do you feel any pressure points?
- If the shoes are not comfortable in the store, don't buy them. Don't expect athletic shoes to stretch over time in order to fit your feet properly.
- Replace athletic shoes about every 3 months or 300–500 miles of jogging or walking.

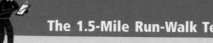

The 1.5-Mile Run-Walk Test

You can obtain a general rating of your cardiorespiratory fitness by taking the 1.5-mile run-walk test. Don't attempt this test unless you have completed at least 6 weeks of some type of conditioning activity. Also, if you are over age 35 or have questions about your health, check with your physician before taking this test.

You'll need a stopwatch, clock, or watch with a second hand and a running track or course that is flat and provides measurements of up to 1.5 miles. You may want to practice pacing yourself prior to taking the test to avoid going too fast at the start and becoming fatigued before you finish. Allow yourself a day or two to recover from a practice run before taking the test.

Warm up before taking the test with some walking, easy jogging, and stretching exercises. The idea is to cover the distance as fast as possible, at a pace that is comfortable for you. You can run or walk the entire distance or use some combination of running and walking. If possible, monitor your own pace, or have someone call out your time at various intervals to help you determine whether your pace is correct. When you have completed the test, refer to the table for your cardiorespiratory fitness rating. Be sure to cool down by walking or jogging slowly for about 5 minutes.

Standards for the 1.5-Mile Run-Walk Test (minutes:seconds)

	Superior	Excellent	Good	Fair	Poor	Very Poor
Women						
Age: 18–29	11:00 or less	11:15–12:45	13:00–14:15	14:30–15:45	16:00–17:30	17:45 or more
30–39	11:45 or less	12:00–13:30	13:45–15:15	15:30–16:30	16:45–18:45	19:00 or more
40–49	12:45 or less	13:00–14:30	14:45–16:30	16:45–18:30	18:45–20:45	21:00 or more
50–59	14:15 or less	14:30–16:30	16:45–18:30	18:45–20:30	20:45–23:00	23:15 or more
60 and over	14:00 or less	14:15–17:15	17:30–20:15	20:30–22:45	23:00–24:45	25:00 or more
Men						
Age: 18–29	9:15 or less	9:30–10:30	10:45–11:45	12:00–12:45	13:00–14:00	14:15 or more
30–39	9:45 or less	10:00–11:00	11:15–12:15	12:30–13:30	13:45–14:45	15:00 or more
40–49	10:00 or less	10:15–11:45	12:00–13:00	13:15–14:15	14:30–16:00	16:15 or more
50–59	10:45 or less	11:00–12:45	13:00–14:15	14:30–15:45	16:00–17:45	18:00 or more
60 and over	11:15 or less	11:30–13:45	14:00–15:45	16:00–17:45	18:00–20:45	21:00 or more

SOURCES: Formula for maximal oxygen consumption taken from McArdle, W. D., F. I. Katch, and V. L. Katch. 1991. *Exercise Physiology: Energy, Nutrition, and Human Performance*. Philadelphia: Lea & Febiger, pp. 225–226. Ratings based on norms from The *Physical Fitness Specialist Certification Manual*, The Cooper Institute, Dallas, TX, revised 2005. Used with permission.

extremely sore and tired the day after exercising, then you have worked too hard. Injury will slow you down just as much as a missed workout.

Consistency is the key to getting into shape without injury. Steady fitness improvement comes when you overload your body consistently over a long period of time. The best way to ensure consistency is to keep a training journal in which you record the details of your workouts: how far you ran, how much weight you lifted, how many laps you swam, and so on. This record will help you evaluate your progress and plan your workout sessions intelligently. Don't increase your exercise volume by more than 5–10% per week.

Assessing Your Fitness When are you in shape? It depends. One person may be out of shape running a mile in 5 minutes; another may be in shape running a mile in 12 minutes. As mentioned earlier, your ultimate level of fitness depends on your goals, your program, and your natural ability. The important thing is to set goals that make sense for you.

If you are interested in finding out exactly how fit you are before you begin a program, the best approach is to get an assessment from a sports medicine laboratory. Such laboratories can be found in university physical education departments and medical centers. Here you will receive an accurate profile of your capacity to exercise. Typically, your endurance will be measured on a treadmill or bicycle, your body fat will be estimated, and your strength and flexibility will be tested. This evaluation will reveal whether your physical condition is consistent with good health, and the staff members at the laboratory can suggest an exercise program that will be appropriate for your level of fitness. To assess your own approximate level of cardiorespiratory endurance, take the test in the box "The 1.5-Mile Run-Walk Test."

Table 13-3 Care of Common Exercise Injuries and Discomforts

Injury	Symptoms	Treatment
Blister	Accumulation of fluid in one spot under the skin	Don't pop or drain it unless it interferes too much with your daily activities. If it does pop, clean the area with antiseptic and cover with a bandage. Do not remove the skin covering the blister.
Bruise (contusion)	Pain, swelling, and discoloration	R-I-C-E: rest, ice, compression, elevation.
Joint sprain	Pain, tenderness, swelling, discoloration, and loss of function	R-I-C-E; apply heat when swelling has disappeared. Stretch and strengthen the affected area.
Muscle cramp	Painful, spasmodic muscle contractions	Gently stretch for 15–30 seconds at a time, and/or massage the cramped area. Drink fluids.
Muscle soreness or stiffness	Pain and tenderness in the affected muscle	Stretch the affected muscle gently; exercise at a low intensity; apply heat.
Muscle strain	Pain, tenderness, swelling, and loss of strength in the affected muscle	R-I-C-E; apply heat when swelling has disappeared. Stretch and strengthen the affected area.
Shin splints	Pain and tenderness on the front of the lower leg; sometimes also pain in the calf muscle	Rest; apply ice to the affected area several times a day and before exercise; wrap with tape for support. Stretch and strengthen muscles in the lower legs. Purchase good-quality footwear, and run on soft surfaces.
Side stitch	Pain on the side of the abdomen	Stretch the arm on the affected side as high as possible; if that doesn't help, try bending forward while tightening the abdominal muscles.

SOURCE: Fahey, T. D., P. M. Insel, and W. T. Roth. 2007. *Fit and Well: Core Concepts and Labs in Physical Fitness and Wellness*, 7th ed. New York: McGraw-Hill.

Preventing and Managing Athletic Injuries

Although annoying, most injuries are neither serious nor permanent. However, an injury that is not cared for properly can escalate into a chronic problem. It is important to learn how to deal with injuries so they don't derail your fitness program (Table 13-3).

Some injuries require medical attention. Consult a physician for head and eye injuries, possible ligament injuries, broken bones, and internal disorders such as chest pain, fainting, and intolerance to heat. Also seek medical attention for apparently minor injuries that do not get better within a reasonable amount of time.

For minor cuts and scrapes, stop the bleeding and clean the wound with soap and water. Treat soft tissue injuries (muscles and joints) with the R-I-C-E principle:

Rest: Stop using the injured area as soon as you experience pain, protect it from further injury, and avoid any activity that causes pain.

Ice: Apply ice to the injured area to reduce swelling and alleviate pain. Apply ice immediately for 10–20 minutes, and repeat every few hours until the swelling disappears. Let the injured part return to normal temperature between icings, and do not apply ice to one area for more than 20 minutes (10 minutes if you are using a cold gel pack).

Compression: Wrap the injured area with an elastic or compression bandage between icings. If the area starts throbbing or begins to change color, the bandage may be wrapped too tightly. Do not sleep with the bandage on.

Elevation: Raise the injured area above heart level to decrease the blood supply and reduce swelling.

After about 36–48 hours, apply heat, if the swelling has completely disappeared, to help relieve pain, relax muscles, and reduce stiffness. Immerse the affected area in warm water or apply warm compresses, a hot water bottle, or a heating pad.

After a minor athletic injury, gradually reintroduce the stress of the activity until you are capable of returning to full intensity. Before returning to full exercise participation, you should have a full range of motion in your joints; normal strength and balance among your muscles;

no injury-compensation movements, such as limping; and little or no pain.

To prevent injuries in the future, follow a few basic guidelines:

1. Stay in condition; haphazard exercise programs invite injury.
2. Warm up thoroughly before exercise.
3. Use proper body mechanics when lifting objects or executing sports skills.
4. Don't exercise when you're ill or overtrained (experiencing extreme fatigue due to overexercising).
5. Use the proper equipment.
6. Don't return to your normal exercise program until athletic injuries have healed.

You can minimize the risk of injury by following safety guidelines, using proper technique and equipment, respecting signals from your body that something may be wrong, and treating any injuries that occur. Warm up, cool down, and drink plenty of fluids before, during, and after exercise. Use special caution in extreme heat or humidity (over 80°F and/or 60% humidity): Exercise slowly, rest frequently in the shade, wear clothing that "breathes," and drink plenty of fluids; slow down or stop if you begin to feel uncomfortable. During hot weather, it's best to exercise in the early morning or evening, when temperatures are lowest.

It makes sense to choose activities that will add enjoyment to your life for years to come. In this group of older people, we can see the rewards of a lifetime of fitness and smart exercise habits.

Staying with Your Program Once you have attained your desired level of fitness, you can maintain it by exercising regularly at a consistent intensity, 3 to 5 days a week. You must work at the intensity that brought you to your desired fitness level. If you don't, your body will become less fit because less is expected of it. In general, if you exercise at the same intensity over a long period, your fitness will level out and can be maintained easily.

Adapt your program to changes in environment or schedule. Don't use wet weather or a new job as an excuse to give up your fitness program. If you walk in the summer, dress appropriately and walk in the winter as well. (Exercise is usually safe even in very cold temperatures as long as you dress warmly in layers and don't stay out too long.) If you can't go out because of darkness or an unsafe neighborhood, walk in a local shopping mall or on campus or join a gym and walk on a treadmill. Changes in your job or family situation can also affect your exercise program. Remember that physical activity is important for your energy level, self-esteem, and well-being. You owe it to yourself to include physical activity in your day. Try to exercise before going to work or to do some physical activity during your lunch hour—even if it's only a short walk or a few trips up and down the stairs.

What if you run out of steam? Although good health is an important *reason* to exercise, it's a poor *motivator* for consistent adherence to an exercise program. A variety of specific suggestions for staying with your program are given in the box "Maintaining Your Exercise Program" and in the Behavior Change Strategy at the end of the chapter. It's a good idea to have a meaningful goal, anything from fitting into the same-size jeans you used to wear to successfully skiing down a new slope.

Varying your program is another key strategy. Some people alternate two or more activities—swimming and jogging, for example—to improve a particular component of fitness. The practice, called **cross-training,** can help prevent boredom and overuse injuries. Explore many exercise options. Consider competitive sports at the recreational level: swimming, running, racquetball, volleyball, golf, and so on. Find out how you can participate in an activity you've never done before: canoeing, hang gliding, windsurfing, backpacking. Try new activities, especially ones that you will be able to do for the rest of your life. Get maps of the recreational or wilderness areas near you, and go exploring. Fill a canteen, pack a good lunch, and take along a wildflower or bird book. Every step you take will bring you closer to your ultimate goal—fitness and wellness that last a lifetime.

Term

cross-training Participating in two or more activities to develop a particular component of fitness.

Take Charge

Maintaining Your Exercise Program

- *Set realistic goals.* Unrealistically high goals will only discourage you.
- *Sign a contract and keep a fitness journal.* A journal can help keep your program on track, identify sources of problems, and give you a continuing sense of accomplishment.
- *Start slowly, and increase your intensity and duration gradually.* Overzealous exercising can result in discouraging discomforts and injuries. Your program is meant to last a lifetime. The important first step is to break your established pattern of inactivity.
- *Make your program fun.* Participate in a variety of different activities that you enjoy. Vary the routes you take walking, running, or biking.
- *Exercise with a friend.* The social side of exercise is an important factor for many regular exercisers.
- *Focus on the positive.* Concentrate on the improvements you obtain from your program, how good you feel during and after exercise.
- *Revisit and revise.* If your program turns out to be unrealistic, revise it. Expect to make many adjustments in your program along the way.
- *Expect fluctuation.* On some days your progress will be excellent, whereas on others you'll barely be able to drag yourself through your scheduled activities.
- *Expect lapses.* Don't let lapses discourage you or make you feel guilty. Instead, feel a renewed commitment to your exercise program.
- *Plan ahead for difficult situations.* Think about what circumstances might make it tough to keep up with your fitness routine, and develop strategies for sticking with your program. For example, devise a plan for your program during vacation, travel, bad weather, and so on.
- *Reward yourself.* Give yourself frequent rewards for sticking with your program.
- *Renew your attitude.* If you notice you're slacking off, try to list the negative thoughts and behaviors that are causing noncompliance. Devise a strategy to decrease the frequency of negative thoughts and behaviors. Make changes in your program plan and reward system to help renew your enthusiasm and commitment.
- *Review your goals.* Visualize what it will be like to reach them, and keep these pictures in your mind as an incentive to stick to your program.

Tips for Today

Physical activity and exercise offer benefits in nearly every area of wellness, helping you generate energy, manage stress, control your weight, improve your mood, and, of course, become physically stronger and healthier. Building a program of regular exercise into your life is well worth the effort, even if it seems complicated or difficult at first. Even a low-to-moderate level of activity provides valuable health benefits. The important thing is to get moving: When in doubt, exercise!

Right now you can

- Get up and stretch.
- Go outside and take a brisk walk.
- Look at your calendar for the rest of the week and write in some physical activity—such as walking, running, biking, skating, swimming, hiking, or playing Frisbee—on as many days as you can; schedule the activity for a specific time, and stick to it.
- If you don't yet use the gym or fitness facility on your campus, go there now and begin planning how to use it.
- Call a friend and invite him or her to start a regular exercise program with you.

SUMMARY

- The five components of physical fitness most important to health are cardiorespiratory endurance, muscular strength, muscular endurance, flexibility, and body composition.
- Exercise improves the functioning of the heart and the ability of the cardiorespiratory system to carry oxygen to the body's tissues. It also increases the efficiency of the body's metabolism and improves body composition.
- Exercise lowers the risk of cardiovascular disease by improving blood fat levels, reducing high blood pressure, and interfering with the disease process that causes coronary artery blockage.
- Exercise reduces the risk of cancer, osteoporosis, and diabetes. It improves immune function and psychological health and helps prevent injuries and low-back pain.
- Everyone should accumulate at least 30–60 minutes per day of moderate endurance-type physical activity. Additional health and fitness benefits can be achieved through longer or more vigorous activity.
- Cardiorespiratory endurance exercises stress a large portion of the body's muscle mass. Endurance exercise should be performed 3–5 days per week for a total of 20–60 minutes per day. Intensity can be evaluated by measuring the heart rate.

Planning a Personal Exercise Program

Behavior Change Strategy

Although most people recognize the importance of incorporating exercise into their lives, many find it difficult to do. No single strategy will work for everyone, but the general steps outlined here should help you create an exercise program that fits your goals, preferences, and lifestyle. A carefully designed contract and program plan can help you convert your vague wishes into a detailed plan of action. And the strategies for program compliance outlined here and in Chapter 1 can help you enjoy and stick with your program for the rest of your life.

Step 1: Set Goals

Setting specific goals to accomplish by exercising is an important first step in a successful fitness program because it establishes the direction you want to take. Your goals might be specifically related to health, such as lowering your blood pressure and risk of heart disease, or they might relate to other aspects of your life, such as improving your tennis game or the fit of your clothes. If you can decide why you're starting to exercise, it can help you keep going.

Think carefully about your reasons for incorporating exercise into your life, and then fill in the goals portion of the Personal Fitness Contract.

Step 2: Select Activities

As discussed in the chapter, the success of your fitness program depends on the consistency of your involvement. Select activities that encourage your commitment: The right program will be its own incentive to continue; poor activity choices provide obstacles and can turn exercise into a chore.

When choosing activities for your fitness program, consider the following:

- Is this activity fun? Will it hold my interest over time?
- Will this activity help me reach the goals I have set?
- Will my current fitness and skill level enable me to participate fully in this activity?
- Can I easily fit this activity into my daily schedule? Are there any special requirements (facilities, partners, equipment, etc.) that I must plan for?
- Can I afford any special costs required for equipment or facilities?
- If you have special exercise needs due to a particular health problem: Does this activity conform to those exercise needs? Will it enhance my ability to cope with my specific health problem?

Refer to Table 13-2, which summarizes the fitness benefits and other characteristics of many activities. Using the guidelines listed above, select a number of sports and activities. Fill in the Program Plan portion of the Fitness Contract, using Table 13-2 to include the fitness components your choices will develop and the frequency, intensity, and time standard you intend to meet for each activity. Does your program meet the criteria of a complete fitness program discussed in the chapter?

Step 3: Make a Commitment

Complete your Fitness Contract and Program Plan by signing your contract and having it witnessed and signed by someone who can help make you accountable for your progress. By completing a written contract, you will make a firm commitment and will be more likely to follow through until you meet your goals.

Step 4: Begin and Maintain Your Program

Start out slowly to allow your body time to adjust. Be realistic and patient—meeting your goals will take time. The following guidelines may help you start and stick with your program:

- Set aside regular periods for exercise. Choose times that fit in best with your schedule, and stick to them. Allow an adequate amount of time for warm-up, cool-down, and a shower.
- Take advantage of any opportunity for exercise that presents itself (for example, walk to class, take the stairs instead of the elevator).
- Do what you can to avoid boredom. Do stretching exercises or jumping jacks to music, or watch the evening news while riding your stationary bicycle.
- Exercise with a group that shares your goals and general level of competence.
- Vary the program. Change your activities periodically. Alter your route or distance if biking or jogging. Change racquetball partners, or find a new volleyball court.
- Establish minigoals or a point system, and work rewards into your program. Until you reach your main goals, a series of small rewards will help you stick with your program. Rewards should be things you enjoy that are easily obtainable.

- Warming up before exercising and cooling down afterward improve your performance and decrease your chances of injury.
- Exercises that develop muscular strength and endurance involve exerting force against a significant resistance. A strength training program for general fitness typically involves one set of 8–12 repetitions of 8–10 exercises, 2 or 3 nonconsecutive days per week.
- A good stretching program includes exercises for all the major muscle groups and joints of the body. Do a series of active, static stretches (possibly with a passive assist) 2–3 days per week, ideally 5–7 days per week. Hold each stretch for 15–30 seconds; do two to four repetitions. Stretch when muscles are warm.
- Instructors, equipment, and facilities should be chosen carefully to enhance enjoyment and prevent injuries.
- A well-balanced diet contains all the energy and nutrients needed to sustain a fitness program. When exercising, remember to drink enough fluids.
- Rest, ice, compression, and elevation (R-I-C-E) are treatments for muscle and joint injuries.
- A desired level of fitness can be maintained by exercising 3 to 5 days a week at a consistent intensity.
- Strategies for maintaining an exercise program over the long term include having meaningful goals, varying the program, and trying new activities.

Personal Fitness Contract

I, ______________________, am contracting with myself to follow an exercise program to work at the following goals. I will begin my program on ______________________.

Fitness Goals

1. ______________________	4. ______________________
2. ______________________	5. ______________________
3. ______________________	6. ______________________

Program Plan

	Components (Check ✔)					Frequency (Check ✔)								
Activities	CRE	MS	ME	F	BC	M	Tu	W	Th	F	Sa	Su	Intensity	Time
1.														
2.														
3.														
4.														
5.														

Note: You should conduct activities for achieving CRE goals at your target heart rate.

I agree to maintain a record of my activity, assess my progress periodically, and, if necessary, revise my goals.

Signed ______________________ Date ______________________

Witness ______________________

Step 5: Record and Assess Your Progress

Keeping a record that notes the daily results of your program will help remind you of your ongoing commitment to your program and give you a sense of accomplishment. Create daily and weekly program logs that you can use to track your progress. Record the activity frequency, intensity, time, and type. Keep your log handy, and fill it in immediately after each exercise session. Post it in a visible place to remind you of your activity schedule and to provide incentive for improvement.

SOURCE: Adapted from Kusinitz, I., and M. Fine. 1995. *Your Guide to Getting Fit,* 3rd ed. Mountain View, Calif.: Mayfield.

Take Action

1. **Investigate campus resources:** Go to your school's physical education office and ask for a comprehensive listing of all the exercise and fitness facilities available on your campus. Visit the facilities you haven't yet seen, and investigate the activities that take place there. If there are sports or activities you'd like to try, consider doing so.

2. **Investigate community resources:** Investigate the fitness clubs in your community. How do they compare with one another? How do they measure up in terms of the guidelines provided in this chapter?

3. **Count your steps:** Wear a pedometer to count your daily steps. (Experts suggest avoiding the cheapest pedometers, which tend to be inaccurate.) To begin, wear the pedometer for a week and determine your typical level of activity (average steps per day). Then record the number of steps you take during 10 minutes of brisk walking; three times that number represents the Surgeon General's minimum recommendation of 30 minutes of brisk walking per day. Set a daily goal and continue to track and record your steps. For information on the Shape Up America! 10,000 Steps Program, visit www.shapeup.org/10000steps.html.

For More Information

Books

Anderson, B., and J. Anderson. 2003. *Stretching*, 20th anniv. ed. Bolinas, Calif.: Shelter Publications. *Updated edition of a classic, with more than 200 stretches for 60 sports and activities.*

Bahrke, M., and C. Yesalis. 2002. *Performance-Enhancing Substances in Sport Exercise.* Champaign, Ill.: Human Kinetics. *Provides up-to-date coverage of the issues surrounding supplements as well as the current state of research on major types of supplements and their effects on athletic performance.*

Fahey, T. 2007. *Basic Weight Training for Men and Women*, 6th ed. New York: McGraw-Hill. *Weight training and plyometric exercises for fitness, weight control, and improved sports performance.*

Fahey, T., P. Insel, and W. Roth. 2007. *Fit and Well: Core Concepts and Labs in Physical Fitness and Wellness*, 7th ed. New York: McGraw-Hill. *A comprehensive guide to developing a complete fitness program.*

Nieman, D. C. 2007. *Exercise Testing and Prescription. A Health-Related Approach*, 6th ed. New York: McGraw-Hill. *A comprehensive discussion of the effects of exercise and exercise testing and prescription.*

U.S. Department of Health and Human Services. 1996. *Physical Activity and Health: A Report of the Surgeon General.* Atlanta, Ga.: Department of Health and Human Services. (Also available online: http://www.cdc.gov/nccdphp/sgr/sgr.htm.) *Provides a summary of the evidence for the benefits of physical activity as well as recommendations for activity and exercise.*

Organizations, Hotlines, and Web Sites

American Academy of Orthopaedic Surgeons. Provides fact sheets on many fitness and sports topics, including how to begin a program, how to choose equipment, and how to prevent and treat many types of injuries.
http://orthoinfo.aaos.org

American College of Sports Medicine. Provides brochures, publications, and audio- and videotapes on the positive effects of exercise.
317-637-9200
http://www.acsm.org

American Council on Exercise. Promotes exercise and fitness for all Americans; the Web site features fact sheets on many consumer topics, including choosing shoes, cross-training, steroids, and getting started on an exercise program.
800-825-3636
http://www.acefitness.org

American Heart Association: Just Move. Provides practical advice for people of all fitness levels plus an online fitness diary.
http://www.justmove.org

Canada's Physical Activity Guide. Offers many suggestions for incorporating physical activity into everyday life; also includes the Physical Activity Readiness Questionnaire (PAR-Q) to assess safety of exercise.
http://www.phac-aspc.gc.ca/guide/index_e.html

CDC Physical Activity Information. Provides information on the benefits of physical activity and suggestions for incorporating moderate physical activity into daily life.
http://www.cdc.gov/nccdphp/dnpa

Disabled Sports USA. Provides sport and recreation services to people with physical or mobility disorders.
http://www.dsusa.org

Exercise: A Guide from the National Institute on Aging and the National Aeronautics and Space Administration. Provides practical advice on fitness for seniors; includes animated instructions for specific weight training and flexibility exercises.
http://weboflife.ksc.nasa.gov/exerciseandaging/toc.html

Federal Trade Commission: Consumer Protection—Diet, Health, and Fitness. Provides several brochures with consumer advice about purchasing exercise equipment.
http://www.ftc.gov/bcp/menu-health.htm

Georgia State University: Exercise and Physical Fitness Page. Provides information about the benefits of exercise and how to get started on a fitness program.
http://www.gsu.edu/~wwwfit

Mayo Clinic Healthy Living Centers. Select the Fitness and Sports Medicine Health Living Center for more information on incorporating physical activity and exercise into your daily life.
http://www.MayoClinic.com/health/HealthyLivingIndex/HealthyLivingIndex

MedlinePlus: Exercise and Physical Fitness. Provides links to news and reliable information about fitness and exercise from government agencies and professional associations.
http://www.nlm.nih.gov/medlineplus/exerciseandphysicalfitness.html

National Institute on Drug Abuse: Anabolic Steroid Abuse. Provides information and links about the dangers of anabolic steroids.
http://www.steroidabuse.org

President's Council on Physical Fitness and Sports (PCPFS). Provides information on PCPFS programs and publications.
http://www.fitness.gov
http://www.presidentschallenge.org

SmallStep.Gov. Provides resources for increasing activity and improving diet through small changes in daily habits.
http://www.smallstep.gov

World Health Organization (WHO): Move for Health. Provides information about the WHO initiative to promote increased physical activity.
http://www.who.int/moveforhealth/en/

Commercial Web sites that feature fitness and nutrition programs include the following:

iShape
http://www.ishape.com
My Exercise Plan
http://www.myexerciseplan.com
Popular Fitness
http://www.popularfitness.com

Web sites with links to information on a wide variety of activities and fitness issues include the following:

Fitness Partner Connection Jumpsite
http://www.primusweb.com/fitnesspartner
NetSweat: The Internet's Fitness Resource
http://www.netsweat.com
Yahoo! Fitness
http://dir.yahoo.com/Health/Fitness

See also the listings for Chapters 12, 14, and 15.

Selected Bibliography

American Cancer Society. 2006. *Cancer Prevention and Early Detection: Facts and Figures 2006.* Atlanta, Ga.: American Cancer Society.

American College of Sports Medicine. 2006. *ACSM's Guidelines for Exercise Testing and Prescription,* 7th ed. Philadelphia: Lippincott Williams & Wilkins.

American College of Sports Medicine. 2006. *ACSM's Resource Manual for Guidelines for Exercise Testing and Prescription,* 5th ed. Philadelphia: Lippincott Williams & Wilkins.

American Heart Association. 2006. *Heart Disease and Stroke Statistics—2006 Update.* Dallas: American Heart Association.

Bertoli, S., et al. 2006. Nutritional status and dietary patterns in disabled people. *Nutrition Metabolism and Cardiovascular Diseases* 16(2): 100–112.

Brooks, G. A., et al. 2005. *Exercise Physiology: Human Bioenergetics and Its Applications,* 4th ed. New York: McGraw-Hill.

Brownson, R. C., T. K. Boehmer, and D. A. Luke. 2005. Declining rates of physical activity in the United States: What are the contributors? *Annual Review of Public Health* 26: 421–443.

Burke, L. M., et al. 2006. Energy and carbohydrate for training and recovery. *Journal of Sports Science* 24(7): 675–685.

Carnathon, M.R., M. Gulati, and P. Greenland. 2006. Prevalence and cardiovascular disease correlates of low cardiorespiratory fitness in adolescents and adults. *Journal of the American Medical Association* 294(23): 2981–2988.

Centers for Disease Control and Prevention. 2005. Adult participation in recommended levels of physical activity—United States, 2001 and 2003. *Morbidity and Mortality Weekly Report* 54(47): 1208–1212.

Centers for Disease Control and Prevention. 2004. *Improving Nutrition and Increasing Physical Activity* (http://www.cdc.gov/nccdphp/bb_nutrition/index.htm; retrieved August 21, 2006).

Colbert, L. H., et al. 2004. Physical activity, exercise, and inflammatory markers in older adults: Findings from the health, aging and body composition study. *Journal of the American Geriatrics Society* 52: 1098–1104.

Cooper, C. B. 2006. Exercise testing does not have to be complicated. *Chronic Respiratory Disease* 3(2): 107–108.

Cussler, E. C., et al. 2003. Weight lifted in strength training predicts bone change in postmenopausal women. *Medicine and Science in Sports and Exercise* 35(1): 10–17.

Dal Maso, L., et al. 2006. Lifetime occupational and recreational physical activity and risk of benign prostatic hyperplasia. *International Journal of Cancer* 118(10): 2632–2635.

Dietrich A., and W. F. McDaniel. 2004. Endocannabinoids and exercise. *British Journal of Sports Medicine* 38: 536–541.

Dishman, R. K., et al. 2006. Neurobiology of exercise. *Obesity* (Silver Spring) 14(3): 345–356.

Dugan, S. 2005. Safe exercise for women. *ACSM Fit Society Page,* Winter.

Dunn, A. L., et al. 2005. Exercise treatment for depression: Efficacy and dose response. *American Journal of Preventive Medicine* 28(1): 1–8.

Fahey, T. D., P. M. Insel, and W. T. Roth. 2007. *Fit and Well: Core Concepts and Labs in Physical Fitness and Wellness,* 7th ed. New York: McGraw-Hill.

Fenicchia, L. M., et al. 2004. Influence of resistance exercise training on glucose control in women with type 2 diabetes. *Metabolism* 53(3): 284–289.

Food and Drug Administration. 2004. *Questions and Answers: Androstenedione* (http://cfsan.fda.gov/~androqa.html; retrieved August 21, 2006).

Food and Nutrition Board, Institute of Medicine, National Academies. 2002. *Dietary Reference Intakes for Energy, Carbohydrates, Fiber, Fat, Protein and Amino Acids (Macronutrients).* Washington, D.C.: National Academy Press.

Franco, O. H., et al. 2005. Effects of physical activity on life expectancy with cardiovascular disease. *Archives of Internal Medicine* 165(20): 2355–2360.

Gunter, M. J., and M. F. Leitzmann. 2006. Obesity and colorectal cancer: Epidemiology, mechanisms and candidate genes. *Journal of Nutritional Biochemistry* 17(3): 145–156.

Hambrecht, R., and S. Gielen. 2005. Essay: Hunter-gatherer to sedentary lifestyle. *Lancet* 366 (Suppl 1): S60–S61.

Hart, L. 2006. Exercise therapy for nonspecific low-back pain: A meta-analysis. *Clinical Journal of Sports Medicine* 16(2): 189–190.

Is it okay to be fat if you're fit? 2005. *Harvard Health Letter,* March, 4.

John, E. M., P. L. Horn-Ross, and J. Koo. 2004. Lifetime physical activity and breast cancer risk in a multiethnic population. *Cancer Epidemiology, Biomarkers & Prevention* 12(11 Pt 1): 1143–1152.

Kelly, C. W. 2005. Commitment to Health Scale. *Journal of Nursing Measurement* 13(3): 219–229.

Lakka, T. A., and C. Bouchard. 2005. Physical activity, obesity and cardiovascular diseases. *Handbook of Experimental Pharmacology* 2005(170): 137–163.

Larson, E.B., et al. 2006. Exercise is associated with reduced risk for incident dementia among persons 65 years of age and older. *Annals of Internal Medicine* 144(2): 73–81.

LaRoche, D. P., and D. A. Connolly. 2006. Effects of stretching on passive muscle tension and response to eccentric exercise. *American Journal of Sports Medicine* 34(6): 1000–1007.

Parsons, T. J., et al. 2006. Physical activity and change in body mass index from adolescence to mid-adulthood in the 1958 British cohort. *International Journal of Epidemiology* 35(1): 197–204.

Pescatello, L. S., et al. 2004. American College of Sports Medicine Position Stand: Exercise and hypertension. *Medicine and Science in Sports and Exercise* 36(3): 533–553.

Ricciardi, R. 2005. Sedentarism: A concept analysis. *Nursing Forum* 40(3): 79–87.

Sato, T., et al. 2005. Quantification of relationship between health status and physical fitness in middle-aged and elderly males and females. *Journal of Sports Medicine and Physical Fitness* 45(4): 561–569.

Sawka, M. N., et al. 2005. Human water needs. *Nutritional Reviews* 63(6 Pt 2): S30–S39.

Sheel, A. W., et al. 2004. Sex differences in respiratory exercise physiology. *Sports Medicine* 34: 567–579.

Shehab, R., et al. 2006. Pre-exercise stretching and sports-related injuries: Knowledge, attitudes and practices. *Clinical Journal of Sports Medicine* 16(3): 228–231.

Shetty, P. 2005. Energy requirements of adults. *Public Health Nutrition* 8(7A): 994–1009.

U.S. Department of Health and Human Services. 2005. *Dietary Guidelines for Americans, 2005* (http://www.healthierus.gov/dietaryguidelines; retrieved August 21, 2006).

Vaz, M., et al. 2005. A compilation of energy costs of physical activities. *Public Health Nutrition* 8(7A): 1153–1183.

Weuve, J., et al. 2004. Physical activity, including walking, and cognitive function in older women. *Journal of the American Medical Association* 292(12): 1454–1461.

Wong, S. L., et al. 2004. Cardiorespiratory fitness is associated with lower abdominal fat independent of body mass index. *Medicine and Science in Sports and Exercise* 36(2): 286–291.

World Health Organization. 2004. *Physical Activity* (http://www.who.int/dietphysicalactivity/publications/facts/pa/en; retrieved August 21, 2006).

14

Looking AHEAD

After reading this chapter, you should be able to

- Discuss different methods for assessing body weight and body composition
- Explain the health risks associated with overweight and obesity
- Explain factors that may contribute to a weight problem, including genetic, physiological, lifestyle, and psychosocial factors
- Describe lifestyle factors that contribute to weight gain and loss, including the roles of diet, exercise, and emotional factors
- Identify and describe the symptoms of eating disorders and the health risks associated with them
- Design a personal plan for successfully managing body weight

Weight Management

Test Your Knowledge

1. About what percentage of American adults are overweight?
a. 15%
b. 35%
c. 65%

2. Genetic factors explain most cases of obesity.
True or false?

3. The consumption of low-calorie sweeteners has helped Americans control their weight.
True or false?

4. Approximately how many female high school and college students have either anorexia or bulimia?
a. 0%
b. 1%
c. 2%

5. Which of the following is the most significant risk factor for type 2 diabetes (the most common type of diabetes)?
a. smoking
b. low-fiber diet
c. overweight or obesity
d. inactivity

6. People who are overweight get less sleep than people who are at a healthy body weight.
True or false?

ANSWERS

1. C. About 66% of American adults are overweight, including approximately 32% who are obese. The rate of obesity among adults has increased more than 75% since 1990.
2. FALSE. Genetic factors may increase an individual's tendency to gain weight, but lifestyle is the key contributing factor.
3. FALSE. Since the introduction of low-calorie sweeteners, both total calorie intake and total sugar intake have increased, as has the proportion of Americans who are overweight.
4. C. About 2–4% of female students suffer from bulimia or anorexia, and many more occasionally engage in behaviors associated with anorexia or bulimia.
5. C. All four are risk factors for diabetes, but overweight or obesity is the most significant. It's estimated that 90% of cases of type 2 diabetes could be prevented if people adopted healthy lifestyle behaviors.
6. TRUE. It is unclear if there is a cause-and-effect relationship between lack of sleep and increased body weight, but insufficient sleep may affect hormones, metabolism, and appetite. Adequate sleep may also help prevent eating in response to feelings of stress and low energy.

Visit the *Core Concepts in Health* Online Learning Center (www.mhhe.com/insel10e) for study aids and many additional resources.

Achieving and maintaining a healthy body weight is a serious public health challenge in the United States and a source of distress for many Americans. Under standards developed by the National Institutes of Health, about 66% of American adults are overweight, including more than 32% who are obese (Figure 14-1). This is almost 20% more than just 20 years ago. The number of severely obese people has nearly tripled in the past decade. At this rate, by 2030, it is estimated that the entire American adult population will be overweight or obese. Lifestyle changes may be at the root of this increase (see the box "The Growing American Waistline"). And while millions struggle to lose weight, others fall into dangerous eating patterns such as binge eating or self-starvation.

Although not completely understood, managing body weight is not a mysterious process. It's simply balancing calories consumed with calories expended in daily activities—in other words, eating a moderate diet and exercising regularly. Unfortunately, this is not as exciting as the latest fad diet or "scientific breakthrough" that promises slimness without effort. Many people fail in their efforts to manage their weight because they emphasize short-term weight loss rather than permanent changes in lifestyle. Successful weight management requires the long-term coordination of many aspects of a wellness lifestyle, including proper nutrition, adequate physical activity, and stress management.

This chapter explores the factors that contribute to the development of overweight and to eating disorders. It also takes a closer look at weight management through lifestyle behaviors and suggests specific strategies for reaching and maintaining a healthy weight.

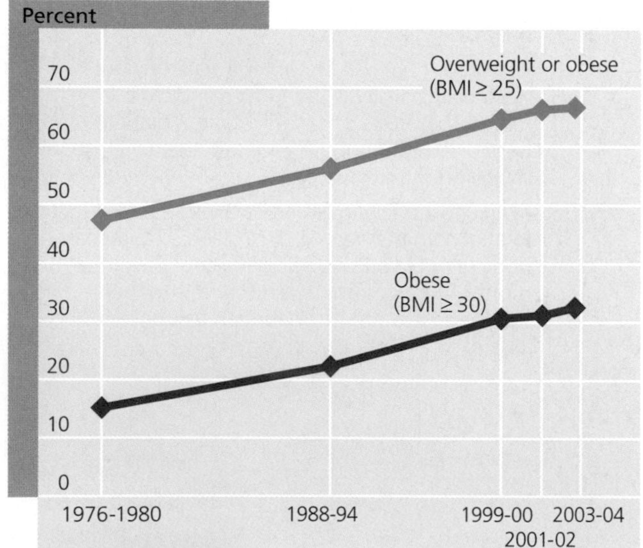

Figure 14-1 Prevalence of overweight and obesity among American adults age 20–74. SOURCE: National Center for Health Statistics. 2006. *2003–2004 National Health and Nutrition Examination Survey (NHANES).* Hyattsville, Md.: National Center for Health Statistics.

BASIC CONCEPTS OF WEIGHT MANAGEMENT

How many times have you or one of your friends said, "I'm too fat; I need to lose weight"? If you are like most people, you are concerned about what you weigh. But how do you decide if you are overweight? At what point does being overweight present a health risk? And how thin is too thin?

Body Composition

The human body can be divided into fat-free mass and body fat. Fat-free mass is composed of all the body's nonfat tissues: bone, water, muscle, connective tissue, organ tissues, and teeth. Body fat includes both essential and nonessential body fat. Remember that 1 pound of body fat is equal to 3500 calories. This means that having only an extra 10 calories a day will equal a 1-pound weight gain over a year; in just 10 years, this would amount to a 10-pound weight gain. **Essential fat** includes *lipids,* or fats, incorporated in the nerves, brain, heart, lungs, liver, and mammary glands. These fat deposits, crucial for normal body functioning, make up approximately 3–5% of total body weight in men and 8–12% in women. The larger percentage in women is due to fat deposits in the breasts, uterus, and other sites specific to females. Women naturally have more body fat than men because of their ability to bear children. Women tend to deposit fat in the lower body and thus develop a pear-shaped body. Men tend to deposit fat around their stomachs or abdomens, thus developing an apple-shaped body. As discussed later in the chapter, the accumulation of fat around the waist has an adverse effect on health.

Nonessential (storage) fat exists primarily within *adipose tissue,* or fat cells, often located just below the skin and around major organs. The amount of storage fat varies from person to person based on many factors, including gender, age, heredity, metabolism, diet, and activity level. When we talk about wanting to lose weight, most of us are referring to storage fat.

What is most important for health is not total weight but rather the proportion of the body's total weight that is fat—the **percent body fat.** For example, two women may both be 5 feet, 5 inches tall and weigh 130 pounds. But one woman, an endurance runner, may have only 15% of her body weight as fat, whereas the other, sedentary, woman may have 34% body fat. Although 130 pounds is not considered overweight for women of this height by most standards, the sedentary woman may be overfat. (Methods for measuring and evaluating percent body fat are presented later in this chapter.) Because most people use the word "overweight" to describe the condition of having too much body fat, we use it in this chapter, although "overfat" is actually a more accurate term.

In the News

The Growing American Waistline

For several decades, and especially since 1990, the prevalence of overweight and obesity has been increasing in the United States. Despite widespread media attention and public health campaigns, the trend shows little sign of abating. A 2006 study reported that during the 6-year period from 1999 to 2004, the prevalence of overweight in children and adolescents increased significantly, as did the prevalence of obesity in men. There was no increase in the prevalence of obesity in women, however, suggesting that body weight increases may be leveling off in at least one segment of the population.

Along with rising rates of obesity come increased rates of obesity-related health problems, including a more than 60% rise in rates of type 2 diabetes since 1990. Inactivity and overweight may account for as many as 112,000 premature deaths annually in the United States, second only to tobacco-related deaths.

Contributing Factors

The basic facts of energy balance help explain the expanding American waistline: According to the USDA, average calorie intake among Americans increased by more than 500 calories per day between 1970 and 2003, and levels of physical activity have declined. What are some of the factors underlying this change?

- *More meals eaten outside the home, especially fast-food meals:* Studies of adults have found that the more people eat out, the more calories they consume and the more body fat they have. The average American consumes 40%–50% of meals and snacks away from home. One-third of American children eat fast food on any given day, and children who eat fast food consume almost 200 more calories per day than those who don't.
- *Increased portion sizes:* The average fast-food burger, which weighed about 1 ounce in 1957, now weighs up to 6 ounces. The typical serving of soda was 8 fluid ounces in 1957; now it is 32–64 ounces. The average movie theater serving of popcorn was 3 cups in 1957; today, it is 16 cups.
- *Increased consumption of soda:* Regular soft drinks are the leading source of calories in the American diet. Since 35 million U.S. public school students are plagued with obesity, soda distributors have recently agreed to stop most soda sales in public schools. The plan will go into effect in most schools by 2009 and in the rest by 2010. The William J. Clinton Foundation and the American Heart Association combined to broker the agreement.
- *Lack of sleep:* Most adult Americans get less than the recommended 7–8 hours of sleep per night, and evidence is mounting that insufficient sleep contributes to weight gain. Scientists believe this is because sleeplessness leads to an imbalance between two hormones involved in regulating the urge to eat. To combat this problem, researchers suggest that people simply get more sleep.
- *More time spent in sedentary activities:* Americans now spend far more time watching television and movies, sitting in cars, playing video games, and in other sedentary activities than they do in activities requiring more energy.

Possible Solutions

Some possible strategies for improving America's food choices include making healthy foods more attractive from a price perspective, placing consumer-friendly nutrition and serving-size information in prominent locations, restricting food advertising aimed at children, and improving food options sold on school grounds. Changes are needed at individual, family, school, community, and national levels.

Clear messages about physical activity and healthy food choices are needed from all sources, including public information campaigns, physicians, and school programs. Restaurants and food manufacturers should be encouraged to provide not only more information but healthier choices and portion sizes. Support is also needed to get healthy food and activity options into communities that currently lack them, especially low-income communities.

As officials debate potential solutions, there are many actions you can take to manage your own weight, as described in this chapter and Chapters 12 and 13.

SOURCES: Ogden, C. L., et al. 2006. Prevalence of overweight and obesity in the United States, 1999–2004. *Journal of the American Medical Association* 295(13): 1549–1555; Centers for Disease Control and Prevention. 2006. Overweight and Obesity: U.S. Obesity Trends, 1985–2004 (http://www.cdc.gov/nccdphp/dnpa/obesity/trend/maps; retrieved September 8, 2006); Centers for Disease Control and Prevention. 2006. Overweight and Obesity: Contributing Factors (http://www.cdc.gov/nccdphp/ dnpa/obesity/contributing_factors.htm; retrieved September 8, 2006); U.S. Department of Agriculture, Economic Research Service. 2005. U.S. Food Consumption Up 16 Percent Since 1970 (http://www.ers.usda.gov/AmberWaves/November05/Findings/USFoodConsumption.htm; retrieved November 17, 2005).

Energy Balance

The key to keeping a healthy ratio of fat to fat-free mass is maintaining an energy balance (Figure 14-2). You take in energy (calories) from the food you eat. Your body uses energy (calories) to maintain vital body functions (resting metabolism), to digest food, and to fuel physical activity. When energy in equals energy out, you maintain your current weight. To change your

Terms

essential fat The fat in the body necessary for normal body functioning.

nonessential (storage) fat Extra fat or fat reserves stored in the body.

percent body fat The percentage of total body weight that is composed of fat.

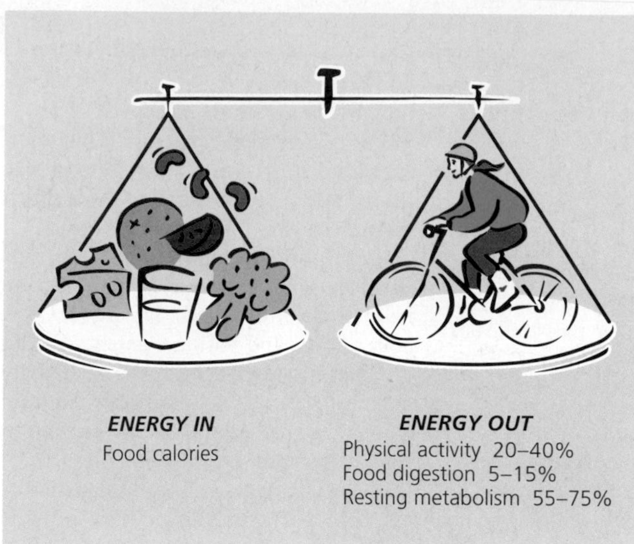

Figure 14-2 The energy balance equation. In order to maintain your current weight, you must burn as many calories as you take in as food each day.

weight and body composition, you must tip the energy balance equation in a particular direction. If you take in more calories daily than your body burns, the excess calories will be stored as fat, and you will gain weight over time. If you eat fewer calories than you burn each day, you will lose some of that storage fat and probably lose weight.

If we look at the energy balance equation today as expressed for the general American population, the equation is tipped heavily toward the energy-in side. Our environment is rich in large portion sizes; high-fat, high-calorie foods; and palatable, easily available, and inexpensive foods. Unfortunately, the energy-out side of the equation has not compensated for increased energy intake; instead, we've decreased work-related physical activity, decreased activity associated with daily living, and increased time spent in sedentary behaviors like TV watching and computer use.

The two parts of the energy balance equation over which you have the most control are the energy you take in as food and the energy you burn during physical activity. To create a negative energy balance and lose weight and body fat, you can increase the amount of energy you burn by increasing your level of physical activity and/or decrease the amount of energy you take in by consuming fewer calories. Specific strategies for altering energy balance are discussed later in the chapter.

Evaluating Body Weight and Body Composition

Overweight is usually defined as total body weight above the recommended range for good health (as determined by large-scale population surveys). **Obesity** is defined as a more serious degree of overweight. Many methods are available for measuring and evaluating body weight and percent body fat; the cutoff points for defining overweight and obesity vary with the method chosen.

Height-Weight Charts In the past, many people relied on height-weight charts to evaluate body weight. Based on insurance company statistics, these charts list a range of ideal or recommended body weights associated with the lowest mortality for people of a particular sex, age, and height. Although easy to use, height-weight charts can be highly inaccurate for some people, and they provide only an indirect measure of body fat.

Body Mass Index **Body mass index (BMI)** is a measure of body weight that is useful for classifying the health risks of body weight if you don't have access to more sophisticated methods. Though more accurate than height-weight tables, BMI is also based on the concept that weight should be proportional to height. Easy to calculate and rate, BMI is a fairly accurate measure of the health risks of body weight for average people. Researchers frequently use BMI in conjunction with waist circumference in studies that examine the health risks associated with body weight.

However, because BMI doesn't distinguish between fat weight and fat-free weight, it can be very inaccurate for some groups, including people of short stature (under 5 feet), muscular athletes, and older adults with little muscle mass due to inactivity or an underlying disease. If you are in one of these groups, use one of the methods described in the next section for estimating percent body fat to assess whether your current weight and body composition are healthy. BMI is also not particularly useful for tracking changes in body composition—gains in muscle mass and losses of fat. Women are likely to have more body fat for a given BMI than men.

BMI is defined as body weight (in kilograms) divided by the square of height (in meters). You can determine your BMI by referring to Figure 14-3, or you can use the following short-cut formula to calculate it more precisely. The example below is for a person who is 5 feet, 6 inches tall (66 inches) and weighs 150 pounds:

1. Multiply weight (in pounds) by 704
   150 × 704 = 105,600
2. Multiply height (in inches) by height (in inches)
   66 × 66 = 4,356
3. Divide the answer in step 1 by the answer in step 2 to obtain a value for BMI.
   BMI = 105,600 ÷ 4,356 = 24.2

Under standards issued by the National Institutes of Health (NIH), a BMI between 18.5 and 24.9 is considered healthy; a person with a BMI of 25 or above is classified as overweight, and a person with a BMI of 30 or above is classified as obese. A person with a BMI below 18.5 is

	<18.5 Underweight		18.5–24.9 Normal						25–29.9 Overweight					30–34.9 Obesity (Class I)					35–39.9 Obesity (Class II)					≥40 Extreme obesity
BMI	17	18	19	20	21	22	23	24	25	26	27	28	29	30	31	32	33	34	35	36	37	38	39	40
Height									Body Weight (pounds)															
4' 10"	81	86	91	96	101	105	110	115	120	124	129	134	139	144	148	153	158	163	168	172	177	182	187	192
4' 11"	84	89	94	99	104	109	114	119	124	129	134	139	144	149	154	159	163	168	173	178	183	188	193	198
5'	87	92	97	102	108	113	118	123	128	133	138	143	149	154	159	164	169	174	179	184	190	195	200	205
5' 1"	90	95	101	106	111	117	122	127	132	138	143	148	154	159	164	169	175	180	185	191	196	201	207	212
5' 2"	93	98	104	109	115	120	126	131	137	142	148	153	159	164	170	175	181	186	191	197	202	208	213	219
5' 3"	96	102	107	113	119	124	130	136	141	147	153	158	164	169	175	181	186	192	198	203	209	215	220	226
5' 4"	99	105	111	117	122	128	134	140	146	152	157	163	169	175	181	187	192	198	204	210	216	222	227	233
5' 5"	102	108	114	120	126	132	138	144	150	156	162	168	174	180	186	192	198	204	210	216	222	229	235	241
5' 6"	105	112	118	124	130	136	143	149	155	161	167	174	180	186	192	198	205	211	217	223	229	236	242	248
5' 7"	109	115	121	128	134	141	147	153	160	166	173	179	185	192	198	204	211	217	224	230	236	243	249	256
5' 8"	112	118	125	132	138	145	151	158	165	171	178	184	191	197	204	211	217	224	230	237	244	250	257	263
5' 9"	115	122	129	136	142	149	156	163	169	176	183	190	197	203	210	217	224	230	237	244	251	258	264	271
5' 10"	119	126	133	139	146	153	160	167	174	181	188	195	202	209	216	223	230	237	244	251	258	265	272	279
5' 11"	122	129	136	143	151	158	165	172	179	187	194	201	208	215	222	230	237	244	251	258	265	273	280	287
6'	125	133	140	148	155	162	170	177	184	192	199	207	214	221	229	236	243	251	258	266	273	280	288	295
6' 1"	129	137	144	152	159	167	174	182	190	197	205	212	220	228	235	243	250	258	265	273	281	288	296	303
6' 2"	132	140	148	156	164	171	179	187	195	203	210	218	226	234	242	249	257	265	273	281	288	296	304	312
6' 3"	136	144	152	160	168	176	184	192	200	208	216	224	232	240	248	256	264	272	280	288	296	304	312	320
6' 4"	140	148	156	164	173	181	189	197	206	214	222	230	238	247	255	263	271	280	288	296	304	312	321	329

Figure 14-3 Body mass index (BMI). To determine your BMI, find your height in the left column. Move across the appropriate row until you find the weight closest to your own. The number at the top of the column is the BMI at that height and weight. SOURCE: Ratings from National Heart, Lung, and Blood Institute. 1998. *Clinical Guidelines on the Identification, Evaluation, and Treatment of Overweight and Obesity in Adults: The Evidence Report.* Bethesda, Md.: National Institutes of Health.

classified as underweight, although low BMI values may be healthy in some cases if they are not the result of smoking, an eating disorder, or an underlying disease; a BMI of 17.5 or less is sometimes used as a diagnostic criterion for the eating disorder anorexia nervosa.

Body Composition Analysis The most accurate and direct way to evaluate body composition is to determine percent body fat; a variety of methods are available. Refer to Table 14-1 for body composition ratings based on percent body fat; as with BMI, the percent body fat ratings indicate cutoff points for health risks associated with underweight and obesity.

HYDROSTATIC (UNDERWATER) WEIGHING AND BOD POD One of the most accurate techniques is hydrostatic weighing. In this method, a person is submerged and weighed under water. Percent body fat can be calculated from body density. Muscle has a higher density and fat a lower density than water, so people with more fat tend to float and weigh less under water, while lean people tend to sink and weigh more under water. The Bod Pod uses air instead of water. A person sits in a chamber, and computerized pressure sensors determine the amount of air displaced by the person's body.

SKINFOLD MEASUREMENTS The skinfold thickness technique measures the thickness of fat under the skin. Measurements are taken at several sites and plugged into formulas that predict body fat percentages.

ELECTRICAL IMPEDANCE ANALYSIS In this method, electrodes are attached to the body and a harmless electrical current is transmitted from electrode to electrode. The electrical conduction through the body favors the path of the fat-free tissues over the fat tissues. A computer can calculate fat percentages from measurements of current.

SCANNING PROCEDURES High-tech scanning procedures are highly accurate means of assessing body composition, but they require expensive equipment. These procedures include computed tomography (CT), magnetic resonance imaging (MRI), dual-energy X-ray absorptiometry (DEXA), and dual-photon absorptiometry. Other procedures include infrared reactance (Futrex 1100) and total body electrical conductivity (TOBEC).

Terms

overweight Body weight that falls above the range associated with minimum mortality.

obesity The condition of having an excess of nonessential body fat; having a body mass index of 30 or greater or having a percent body fat greater than about 24% for men and 38% for women.

body mass index (BMI) A measure of relative body weight that takes height into account and is highly correlated with more direct measures of body fat; calculated by dividing total body weight (in kilograms) by the square of height (in meters).

Table 14-1 Percent Body Fat Classification

	Percent Body Fat (%)		
	20–39 Years	40–59 Years	60–79 Years
Women			
Essential[a]	8–12	8–12	8–12
Low/athletic[b]	13–20	13–22	13–23
Recommended	21–32	23–33	24–35
Overfat[c]	33–38	34–39	36–41
Obese[c]	≥39	≥40	≥42
Men			
Essential[a]	3–5	3–5	3–5
Low/athletic[b]	6–7	6–10	6–12
Recommended	8–19	11–21	13–24
Overfat[c]	20–24	22–27	25–29
Obese[c]	≥25	≥28	≥30

The cutoffs for recommended, overfat, and obese ranges in this table are based on a study that linked body mass index classifications from the National Institutes of Health with predicted percent body fat (measured using dual energy X-ray absorptiometry).

[a]Essential body fat is necessary for the basic functioning of the body.
[b]Percent body fat in the low/athletic range may be appropriate for some people as long as it is not the result of illness or disordered eating habits.
[c]Health risks increase as percent body fat exceeds the recommended range.

SOURCES: Gallagher, D., et al. 2000. Healthy percentage body fat ranges: An approach for developing guidelines based on body mass index. *American Journal of Clinical Nutrition* 72: 694–701; American College of Sports Medicine. 2006. *ACSM's Resource Manual for Guidelines for Exercise Testing and Prescription,* 5th ed. Philadelphia: Lippincott Williams & Wilkins.

Excess Body Fat and Wellness

The amount of fat in the body—and its location—can have profound effects on health.

The Health Risks of Excess Body Fat Obesity doubles mortality rates and can reduce life expectancy by 10–20 years. In fact, if the current trends in overweight and obesity (and their related health problems) continue, scientists believe that the average American's life expectancy will soon decline by 5 years. Obese individuals have a 50–100% increased risk of death from all causes, compared with normal weight persons. Obesity is associated with unhealthy cholesterol and triglyceride levels, impaired heart function, and death from cardiovascular disease. Other health risks include hypertension, many kinds of cancer, impaired immune function, gallbladder and kidney diseases, skin problems, impotence, sleep and breathing disorders, back pain, arthritis, and other bone and joint disorders. Obesity is also associated with complications of pregnancy, menstrual irregularities, urine leakage (stress incontinence), increased surgical risk, and psychological disorders and problems (such as depression, low self-esteem, and body dissatisfaction).

There is a strong association between excess body fat and diabetes mellitus, a disease that causes a disruption of normal metabolism. The pancreas normally secretes the hormone insulin, which stimulates cells to take up glucose to produce energy (Figure 14-4). In diabetes, this process is disrupted, causing a buildup of glucose in the bloodstream. Diabetes is associated with kidney failure; nerve damage; circulation problems and amputations; retinal damage and blindness; and increased rates of heart attack, stroke, and hypertension. Excess body fat is a major risk factor for type 2 diabetes (the most common form of diabetes). Obese people are more than three times as likely to develop diabetes, and the incidence of diabetes among Americans has increased dramatically as the rate of obesity has climbed. Diabetes is currently the sixth leading cause of death in the United States (see the box "Diabetes" on p. 418 for more information).

The risks from obesity increase with its severity, and they are much more likely to occur in people who are more than twice their desirable body weight. Controversy exists about the precise degree of risk at lower levels of overweight, particularly among overweight individuals who are physically active. The health risks associated with overweight depend in part on an individual's overall health and other risk factors, such as high blood pressure, unhealthy cholesterol levels, body fat distribution, and tobacco use. The NIH recommends weight loss for people whose BMI places them in the obese category and for those who are overweight *and* have two or more major risk factors for disease. If your BMI is 25 or above, consult a physician for help in determining a healthy BMI for you.

Many people who are overweight have some of the risk factors associated with obesity. The Nurses' Health Study, in which Harvard researchers have followed more than 120,000 women since 1976, has found that even mildly to moderately overweight women have an 80% increased risk of developing CHD compared to leaner women. This study also confirmed that to reduce the risk of dying prematurely of any cause, maintaining a desirable body weight is important. This conclusion was supported by a 10-year study that ended in 2006 after following a half-million Americans in their fifties. Researchers concluded that subjects who were even slightly overweight were up to 40% more likely to die within the next decade, compared to age-matched people who had a desirable weight. But it is also important to realize that small weight losses—5% to 10% of total body weight—can lead to significant health improvements.

Symptoms of diabetes

- Frequent urination
- Extreme thirst and hunger
- Unexplained weight loss
- Extreme fatigue
- Blurred vision
- Frequent infections
- Slow wound healing
- Tingling or numbness in hands and feet
- Dry, itchy skin

Note: In the early stages, diabetes often has no symptoms.

Esophagus

Stomach

Pancreas

Small intestine

Normal
Insulin binds to receptors on the surface of a cell and signals special transporters in the cell to transport glucose inside.

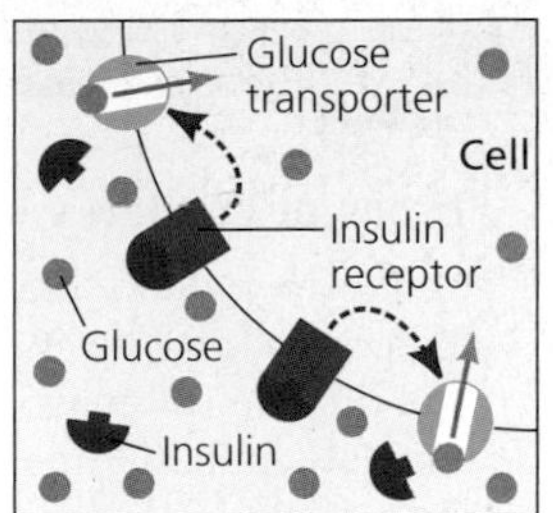

Type 1 diabetes
The pancreas produces little or no insulin. Thus, no signal is sent instructing the cell to transport glucose, and glucose builds up in the bloodstream.

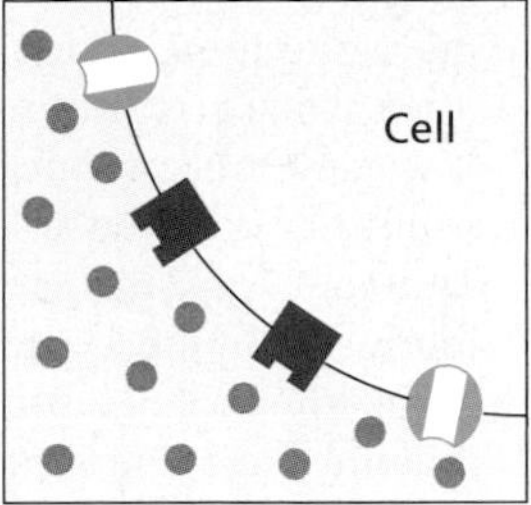

Type 2 diabetes
The pancreas produces too little insulin and/or the body's cells are resistant to it. Some insulin binds to receptors on the cell's surface, but the signal to transport glucose is blocked. Glucose builds up in the bloodstream.

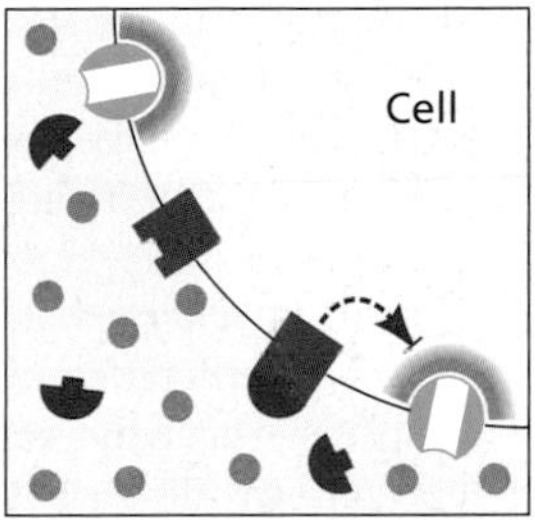

Figure 14-4 Diabetes mellitus. During digestion, carbohydrates are broken down in the small intestine into glucose, a simple sugar that enters the bloodstream. The presence of glucose signals the pancreas to release insulin, a hormone that helps cells take up glucose; once inside a cell, glucose can be converted to energy. In diabetes, this process is disrupted, resulting in a buildup of glucose in the bloodstream.

Body Fat Distribution and Health The distribution of body fat is also an important indicator of health. Men and postmenopausal women tend to store fat in the upper regions of their bodies, particularly in the abdominal area (the apple shape). Premenopausal women usually store fat in hips, buttocks, and thighs (the pear shape). Excess fat in the abdominal area increases risk of high blood pressure, diabetes, early-onset heart disease, stroke, certain types of cancer, and mortality. This risk is independent of a person's BMI. The reason for this increase in risk is not entirely clear, but it appears that abdominal fat is more easily mobilized and sent into the bloodstream, increasing disease-related blood fat levels.

The risks from body fat distribution are usually assessed by measuring waist circumference (the distance around the abdomen at the level of the hip bone, known as the iliac crest). Waist circumference can be used as a measure of abdominal obesity, an indicator of disease risk, and to monitor changes in body composition over time. More research is needed to determine the precise degree of risk associated with specific values for waist measurement. However, a total waist measurement of more than 40 inches for men and 35 inches for women is associated with a significantly increased risk of disease.

A person doesn't have to be technically overfat to have fat distribution be a risk factor, nor do all overfat people face this increased risk. The NIH BMI guidelines state that large waist circumference can be a marker for increased risk of diabetes, high blood pressure, and CVD even in people with a BMI in the normal range. And at any given level of overweight, people with a large waist circumference and/or additional disease risk factors are at greater risk for health problems. For example, a man with a BMI of 27, a waist circumference above 40 inches, and diabetes is at greater risk for health problems than another man who has a BMI of 27 but has a smaller waist and no other risk factors. Abdominal obesity and any two other risk factors associated with cardiovascular health put an individual at risk for metabolic syndrome. Abdominal obesity (as measured by waist circumference) is a primary component of metabolic syndrome and a forewarning of diabetes and heart disease.

Weight Cycling It has been hypothesized that repeatedly losing and regaining weight, known as weight

Diabetes

Types of Diabetes

About 21 million Americans (or 7% of the population) have diabetes. By 2050, the prevalence may increase to more than 48 million Americans, or 12% of the population, according to the CDC. About 5–10% of people with diabetes have the more serious form, known as type 1 diabetes. In this type of diabetes, the pancreas produces little or no insulin, so daily doses of insulin are required. Type 1 diabetes occurs when the body's immune system, triggered by a viral infection or some other environmental factor, mistakenly destroys the insulin-producing cells in the pancreas. It usually strikes before age 30.

The remaining 90–95% of Americans with diabetes have type 2 diabetes, and the prevalence is rising dramatically. This condition can develop slowly, and about a third of affected individuals are unaware of their condition. In type 2 diabetes, the pancreas doesn't produce enough insulin, cells are resistant to insulin, or both. This condition is usually diagnosed in people over age 40, although there has been a tenfold increase in type 2 diabetes in children in the past two decades. About one-third of people with type 2 diabetes must take insulin; others may take medications that increase insulin production or stimulate cells to take up glucose.

A third type of diabetes occurs in about 7% of women during pregnancy. *Gestational diabetes* usually disappears after pregnancy, but more than half of women who experience it eventually develop type 2 diabetes.

The term *pre-diabetes* describes blood glucose levels that are higher than normal but not high enough for a diagnosis of full-blown diabetes. About 41 million Americans have pre-diabetes, and most people with the condition will develop type 2 diabetes unless they adopt preventive lifestyle measures. Pre-diabetes poses a risk to health beyond just the development of diabetes: Blood glucose levels in the pre-diabetes range increase the risk of heart attack or stroke by 50%. The insulin resistance and elevated glucose levels associated with pre-diabetes (and diabetes) are one of the five defining risk factors of metabolic syndrome (see Chapter 15).

The major factors involved in the development of diabetes are age, obesity, physical inactivity, a family history of diabetes, and lifestyle. Excess body fat is a key risk factor because the cells of obese people are less responsive to insulin, and insulin resistance is almost always a precursor of type 2 diabetes. Ethnic background also plays a role. African Americans and Hispanics are 55% more likely than non-Hispanic whites to develop type 2 diabetes; more than 20% of Hispanics over age 65 have diabetes. Native Americans also have a higher-than-average incidence of diabetes.

Prevention

It is estimated that 90% of cases of type 2 diabetes could be prevented if people adopted healthy lifestyle behaviors, including regular physical activity, a moderate diet, and modest weight loss. For people with pre-diabetes, lifestyle measures are more effective than medication for delaying or preventing the development of diabetes. Studies of people with pre-diabetes show that just a 5–7% weight loss can lower diabetes onset by nearly 60%. Exercise (endurance and/or strength training) makes cells more sensitive to insulin and helps stabilize blood glucose levels; it also helps keep body fat at healthy levels.

A moderate diet to control body fat is perhaps the most important dietary recommendation for the prevention of diabetes. However, the composition of the diet may also be important. Studies have linked diets low in fiber and high in sugar, refined carbohydrates, saturated fat, red meat, and high-fat dairy products to increased risk of diabetes; diets rich in whole grains, fruits, vegetables, legumes, fish, and poultry may be protective. The overall pattern of a person's diet is most important, but specific foods linked to higher risk of diabetes include regular (nondiet) soft drinks, white bread, white rice, french fries, processed meats (bacon, sausage, hot dogs), and sugary desserts.

Treatment

There is no cure for diabetes, but it can be successfully managed. Treatment involves keeping blood sugar levels within safe limits through diet, exercise, and, if necessary, medication. Blood sugar levels can be monitored using a home test; close monitoring and control of glucose levels can significantly reduce the rate of serious complications. New drug therapies include inhibitors known as DDP-4, which lower blood sugar without causing weight gain.

Nearly 90% of people with type 2 diabetes are overweight when diagnosed, including 55% who are obese. An important step in treatment is to lose weight; even a small amount of weight loss can be beneficial. People with diabetes should obtain carbohydrate from whole grains, fruits, vegetables, and low-fat dairy products; carbohydrate and monounsaturated fat together should provide 60–70% of total daily calories. Regular exercise and a healthy diet are often sufficient to control type 2 diabetes.

Warning Signs and Testing

A wellness lifestyle that includes a healthy diet and regular exercise is the best strategy for preventing diabetes. If you do develop diabetes, the best way to avoid complications is to recognize the symptoms and get early diagnosis and treatment. Be alert for the warning signs listed in Figure 14-4. Pre-diabetes and type 2 diabetes are often asymptomatic in the early stages, and routine screening is recommended for people over age 45 and anyone younger who is at high risk, including anyone who is obese.

The American Diabetes Association's Web site (http://www.diabetes.org) includes an interactive diabetes risk assessment. Screening involves a blood test to check glucose levels after either a period of fasting or the administration of a set dose of glucose. A fasting glucose level of 126 mg/dl or higher indicates diabetes; a level of 100–125 mg/dl indicates pre-diabetes. If you are concerned about your risk for diabetes, talk with your physician about being tested.

cycling or yo-yo dieting, might be harmful both to overall health and to efforts at weight loss. Weight cycling, it was thought, might make the body more efficient at extracting and storing calories from food; thus, with each successive diet, it would become more difficult to lose weight. Most studies, however, have not supported this idea or found weight cycling to be harmful to the health of an obese person. Most researchers believe that obese individuals should continue to try to control their weight. Losing even a few pounds brings substantial health benefits that appear to exceed any potential risks that might be incurred from weight loss or weight cycling.

Body Image The collective picture of the body as seen through the mind's eye, **body image** consists of perceptions, images, thoughts, attitudes, and emotions. A negative body image is characterized by dissatisfaction with the body in general or some part of the body in particular. Recent surveys indicate that the majority of Americans, many of whom are not actually overweight, are unhappy with their body weight or with some aspect of their appearance.

Losing weight or getting cosmetic surgery does not necessarily improve body image. However, improvements in body image may occur in the absence of changes in weight or appearance. Many experts now believe that body image issues must be dealt with as part of treating obesity and eating disorders. See pages 437–440 for more information on body image and eating disorders.

Problems Associated with Very Low Levels of Body Fat Health experts have generally viewed very low levels of body fat—less than 8–12% for women and 3–5% for men—as a threat to wellness. Extreme leanness has been linked with reproductive, circulatory, and immune system disorders. Extremely lean people may experience muscle wasting and fatigue; they are also more likely to suffer from dangerous eating disorders.

In physically active women and girls, particularly those involved in sports where weight and appearance are important (ballet, gymnastics, skating, and distance running, for example), a condition called the **female athlete triad** may develop. The triad consists of three interrelated disorders: abnormal eating patterns (and excessive exercising), followed by **amenorrhea** (absence of menstruation), followed by decreased bone density (premature osteoporosis). Prolonged amenorrhea can cause bone density to erode to a point that a woman in her twenties will have the bone density of a woman in her sixties. Left untreated, the triad can lead to decreased physical performance, increased incidence of bone fractures, disturbances of heart rhythm and metabolism, and even death.

What Is the Right Weight for You?

For most of us, body weight and percentage of body fat fall somewhere below the levels associated with significant health risks. For us, these assessment tests do not really answer the question How much should I weigh? BMI, percent body fat, and waist circumference measurement can best serve as general guides or estimates for body weight (Table 14-2, p. 420).

To answer the question of what you should weigh, let your lifestyle be your guide. Don't focus on a particular weight as your goal. Instead, focus on living a lifestyle that includes eating moderate amounts of healthful foods, getting plenty of exercise, thinking positively, and learning to cope with stress. Then let the pounds fall where they may. For most people, the result will be close to the recommended weight ranges discussed earlier. For some, their weight will be somewhat higher than societal standards—but right for them. By letting a healthy lifestyle determine your weight, you can avoid developing unhealthy patterns of eating and a negative body image.

FACTORS CONTRIBUTING TO EXCESS BODY FAT

Much research has been done in an effort to pinpoint the cause of overweight and obesity. It appears, however, that body weight and body composition are determined by multiple factors that may vary with each individual. These factors can be grouped into genetic, physiological, lifestyle, and psychosocial factors.

Genetic Factors

Estimates of the genetic contribution to obesity vary widely, from about 25% to 40% of an individual's body fat. More than 300 genes have been linked to obesity, but their actions are still under study. Genes influence body size and shape, body fat distribution, and metabolic rate. Genetic factors also affect the ease with which weight is gained as a result of overeating and where on the body extra weight is added. If both parents are obese, their children have an 80% risk of being obese; children with only one obese parent face a 40% risk of becoming obese. In studies that compared adoptees and their biological parents, the

Terms

VW

body image The mental representation a person holds about his or her body at any given moment in time, consisting of perceptions, images, thoughts, attitudes, and emotions about the body.

female athlete triad A condition consisting of three interrelated disorders: abnormal eating patterns (and excessive exercising) followed by lack of menstrual periods (amenorrhea) and decreased bone density (premature osteoporosis).

amenorrhea The absence of menstruation.

Table 14-2	Body Mass Index (BMI) Classification and Disease Risk			
			Disease Risk Relative to Normal Weight and Waist Circumference[a]	
Classification	BMI (kg/m^2)	Obesity Class	Men ≤ 40 in. (102 cm) Women ≤ 35 in. (88 cm)	> 40 in. (102 cm) > 35 in. (88 cm)
Underweight[b]	<18.5		—	—
Normal[c]	18.5–24.9		—	—
Overweight	25.0–29.9		Increased	High
Obesity	30.0–34.9	I	High	Very high
	35.0–39.9	II	Very high	Very high
Extreme obesity	≥ 40.0	III	Extremely high	Extremely high

[a]Disease risk for type 2 diabetes, hypertension, and cardiovascular disease. The waist circumference cutoff points for increased risk are 40 inches (102 cm) for men and 35 inches (88 cm) for women.
[b]Research suggests that a low BMI can be healthy in some cases, as long as it is not the result of smoking, an eating disorder, or an underlying disease process. A BMI of 17.5 or less is sometimes used as a diagnostic criterion for the eating disorder anorexia nervosa.
[c]Increased waist circumference can also be a marker for increased risk, even in persons of normal weight.

SOURCE: Adapted from National Heart, Lung, and Blood Institute. 1998. *Clinical Guidelines on the Identification, Evaluation, and Treatment of Overweight and Obesity in Adults: The Evidence Report.* Bethesda, Md.: National Institutes of Health.

weights of the adoptees were found to be more like those of the biological parents than the adoptive parents, again indicating a strong genetic link.

Research thus suggests a genetic component in the determination of body weight. However, hereditary influences must be balanced against the contribution of environmental factors. Not all children of obese parents become obese, and normal-weight parents may have overweight children. In a study comparing men born and raised in Ireland with their biological brothers who lived in the United States, the American men were found to weigh, on average, 6% more than their Irish brothers. Environmental factors like diet and exercise are probably responsible for this difference. Thus, the *tendency* to develop obesity may be inherited, but the expression of this tendency is affected by environmental influences.

The message you should take from this research is that genes are not destiny. It is true that some people have a harder time losing weight and maintaining weight loss than others. However, with increased exercise and attention to diet, even those with a genetic tendency toward obesity can maintain a healthy body weight. And regardless of genetic factors, lifestyle choices remain the cornerstone of successful weight management.

Term

Ww

resting metabolic rate (RMR) The energy required to maintain vital body functions, including respiration, heart rate, body temperature, and blood pressure, while the body is at rest.

Physiological Factors

Metabolism is a key physiological factor in the regulation of body fat and body weight; hormones also play a role. Other factors that have been proposed as contributing to obesity include fat cells and carbohydrate craving.

Metabolism Metabolism is the sum of all the vital processes by which food energy and nutrients are made available to and used by the body. The largest component of metabolism, **resting metabolic rate (RMR)**, is the energy required to maintain vital body functions, including respiration, heart rate, body temperature, and blood pressure, while the body is at rest. As shown in Figure 14-2, RMR accounts for about 55–75% of daily energy expenditure. The energy required to digest food accounts for an additional 5–15% of daily energy expenditure. The remaining 20–40% is expended during physical activity.

Both heredity and behavior affect metabolic rate. Men, who have a higher proportion of muscle mass than women, have a higher RMR (muscle tissue is more metabolically active than fat). Also, some individuals inherit a higher or lower RMR than others. A higher RMR means that a person burns more calories while at rest and can therefore take in more calories without gaining weight.

Weight loss or gain also affects metabolic rate. When a person loses weight, both RMR and the energy required to perform physical tasks decrease. The reverse occurs when weight is gained. One of the reasons exercise is so important during a weight-loss program is that exercise, especially resistance training, helps maintain muscle mass and metabolic rate.

Exercise has a positive effect on metabolism. When people exercise, they slightly increase their RMR—the number of calories their bodies burn at rest. They also increase their muscle mass, which is associated with a higher metabolic rate. The exercise itself also burns calories, raising total energy expenditure. The higher the energy expenditure, the more the person can eat without gaining weight. (The role of exercise in weight management is discussed in greater detail later in the chapter.)

Hormones Hormones clearly play a role in the accumulation of body fat, especially for females. Hormonal changes at puberty, during pregnancy, and at menopause contribute to the amount and location of fat accumulation. For example, during puberty, hormones cause the development of secondary sex characteristics, including larger breasts, wider hips, and a fat layer under the skin.

One hormone thought to be linked to obesity is leptin. Secreted by the body's fat cells, leptin is carried to the brain, where it appears to let the brain know how big or small the body's fat stores are. With this information, the brain can regulate appetite and metabolic rate accordingly. Other hormones that may be involved in the regulation of appetite are cholecystokinin (CCK), peptide YY, grelin, and gluconlike peptide-1 (GLP-1). Researchers hope to use these hormones to develop treatments for obesity based on appetite control; however, as most of us will admit, hunger is often *not* the primary reason we overeat. Cases of obesity based solely or primarily on hormone abnormalities do exist, but they are rare. Lifestyle choices still account for the largest proportion of the differences in body weight and body composition among individuals.

Fat Cells The amount of fat the body can store is a function of the number and size of fat cells. These fat cells are like little compartments that can be inflated to hold body fat; when all or nearly all the fat cells are filled, the body makes more, thereby increasing its ability to store fat. Some people are born with an above-average number of fat cells and thus have the potential for storing more energy as body fat. Overeating at critical times, such as in childhood, can cause the body to expand the number of fat cells. It has been hypothesized that having more or larger fat cells creates biological pressure to keep eating to fill all the fat cells; however, this has not been substantiated by research. If a person loses weight, fat cell content is depleted, but it is unclear whether the number of fat cells can be decreased.

Carbohydrate Craving It has been hypothesized that carbohydrate craving may cause overeating and thus lead to overweight and obesity. Animal studies have suggested that consuming carbohydrates increases brain levels of serotonin, a neurotransmitter that induces calmness. People with low levels of serotonin thus might crave and consume carbohydrates because they experience improved mood and reduced fatigue after eating foods such as bread, pasta, and candy. However, research in humans supporting this hypothesis remains incomplete.

The typical American lifestyle does not lead naturally to healthy weight management. Labor-saving devices such as escalators help reinforce our sedentary habits.

A number of popular diets have been based on the idea that carbohydrates in general or foods with a high glycemic index cause weight gain (see Chapter 12 for a description of glycemic index). Carbohydrates do affect levels of glucose and insulin in the blood, but there is no real data that consumption of foods containing carbohydrates increases appetite and/or body weight beyond the effects of the calories contained in the foods. There are many other influences on appetite and caloric intake. In Asian nations such as China and Japan, people consume diets very high in carbohydrate and have low rates of obesity. Experts suggest that people follow the carbohydrate and calorie intake levels recommended by the Dietary Guidelines for Americans. It is most important to manage overall calorie intake and to choose healthy sources of carbohydrate.

Lifestyle Factors

Although genetic and physiological factors may increase risk for excess body fat, they are not sufficient to explain the increasingly high rate of obesity seen in the United States. The gene pool has not changed dramatically in the past 40 years, during which time the rate of obesity among Americans has more than doubled (see the box "Overweight and Obesity Among U.S. Ethnic Populations"). Clearly, other factors are at work—particularly lifestyle factors such as increased energy intake and decreased physical activity.

Eating Americans have access to an abundance of highly palatable and calorie-dense foods, and many have eating habits that contribute to weight gain. Most overweight adults will admit to eating more than they should

Dimensions of Diversity

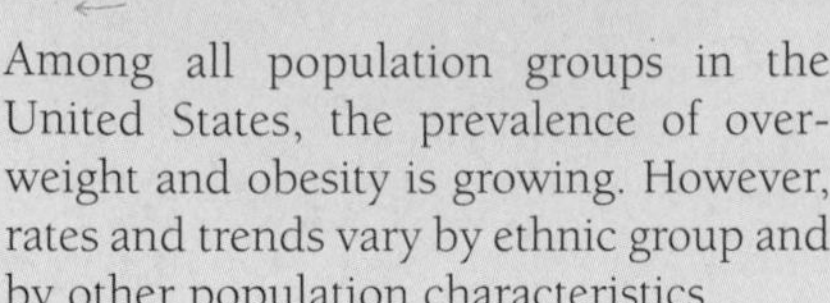

Overweight and Obesity Among U.S. Ethnic Populations

Among all population groups in the United States, the prevalence of overweight and obesity is growing. However, rates and trends vary by ethnic group and by other population characteristics.

- Certain groups, including African Americans, Latinos, and American Indians and Alaska Natives, have higher-than-average rates of obesity. Asian Americans have a low rate of obesity.
- There is considerable variation within populations grouped into general ethnic categories. For example, Asian Americans, Vietnamese Americans, and Chinese Americans have very low rates of obesity, and Asian Indians have much higher rates of obesity.
- Within all groups, women have higher rates of overweight and obesity than men.
- Low socioeconomic status is associated with higher rates of overweight and obesity. Researchers theorize that people living in poor communities are more greatly affected by a toxic food and exercise environment—meaning there are fewer opportunities to purchase healthy foods and safely engage in regular physical activity. In addition, many foods low in price are high in calorie density (fast food, for example).
- Higher or increasing socioeconomic status is associated with lower rates of obesity among some groups and constant or increased rates of obesity among other groups. Groups that are transitioning from poverty, food scarcity, and jobs that require significant energy expenditure may not have good family or community models of reducing energy intake and increasing leisure-time physical activity.
- Acculturation boosts body weight. The longer a foreign-born person lives in the United States, the more likely she or he is to become obese. BMI among immigrants begins to climb after about 10 years of U.S. residence, and after 15 years, it approaches the national average.
- Cultural factors that influence dietary and exercise behaviors appear to play a role in the development of obesity. There are also cultural differences in acceptance of larger body size and in body image perception. For example, one study found that African Americans were more likely to think they were thinner than they really were and whites were more likely to think they were fatter than they really were.
- Some studies have found that African Americans, on average, have lower resting metabolic rates than whites; in addition, weight loss may cause greater declines in RMR among African Americans. Further research is needed to determine the influence RMR differences may have on rates of obesity and successful weight loss among African Americans.
- The health consequences of obesity affect ethnic populations in different ways. At a given level of BMI, Latinos are significantly more likely to have type 2 diabetes. Obesity in African Americans is associated with increased risk of developing hypertension at a younger age and in a more severe form.
- For Asian Americans or persons of Asian descent, waist circumference is a better indicator of relative disease risk than BMI, and disease risk goes up at a lower level of BMI than for individuals of other groups. For Asian populations, WHO guidelines have a lower BMI cutoff for defining overweight (BMI > 23).

SOURCES: Centers for Disease Control and Prevention. 2006. Racial and Ethnic Approaches to Community Health (REACH 2010): Addressing Disparities in Health (http://www.cdc.gov/nccdphp/publications/aag/reach.htm; retrieved September 10, 2006); Chou, J., and H. S. Juon. 2006. Assessing overweight and obesity risk among Korean Americans in California using World Health Organization body mass index criteria for Asians. *Preventing Chronic Disease* 3(3): A79; Kumanyika, S., and S. Grier. 2006. Targeting interventions for ethnic minority and low-income populations. *The Future of Children* 16(1): 187–207; Whitaker, R. C., and S. M. Orzol. 2006. Obesity among US urban preschool children: Relationships to race, ethnicity, and socioeconomic status. *Archives of Pediatric and Adolescent Medicine* 160(6): 578–584; Goel, M. S., et al. 2004. Obesity among U.S. immigrant subgroups by duration of residence. *Journal of the American Medical Association* 292(23): 2860–2867; Centers for Disease Control and Prevention. 2004. Prevalence of diabetes among Hispanics. *Morbidity and Mortality Weekly Report* 53(40): 941–944.

of high-fat, high-sugar, high-calorie foods. Americans eat out more frequently now than in the past, and we rely more heavily on fast food and packaged convenience foods. Restaurant and convenience food portion sizes tend to be large, and the foods themselves are likely to be high in fat, sugar, and calories and low in nutrients. Studies have consistently found that people underestimate portion sizes by as much as 25%.

The average calorie intake by Americans has increased by about 300 calories per day since 1970. Many of those extra calories come from carbohydrates, such as refined sugars. Levels of physical activity declined during this period. The net result has been a substantial increase in the number of Americans who are overweight and obese. Eating for weight management is discussed later in this chapter.

Physical Activity Research has shown that activity levels among Americans are declining, beginning in childhood and continuing throughout the life cycle. Many schools have cut back on physical education classes and recess. Most adults drive to work, sit all day, and then relax in front of the TV at night. During leisure time, both children and adults surf the Internet, play video games, or watch TV rather than bicycle, participate in sports, or just do yardwork or chores around the house. One study found that 60% of the incidence of overweight can be linked to excessive television viewing. On average, Americans exercise 15 minutes per day and watch 170 minutes of TV and movies. Modern conveniences such as remote controls, elevators, and power mowers have also reduced daily physical activity.

Psychosocial Factors

Many people have learned to use food as a means of coping with stress and negative emotions. Eating can provide a powerful distraction from difficult feelings—loneliness, anger, boredom, anxiety, shame, sadness, inadequacy. It can be used to combat low moods, low energy levels, and low self-esteem (see the box "What Triggers Your Eating?" on p. 424). When food and eating become the primary means of regulating emotions, binge eating or other disturbed eating patterns can develop.

Obesity is strongly associated with socioeconomic status. The prevalence of obesity goes down as income level goes up. More women than men are obese at lower income levels, but men are somewhat more obese at higher levels. These differences may reflect the greater sensitivity and concern for a slim physical appearance among upper-income women, as well as greater access to information about nutrition, to low-fat and low-calorie foods, and to opportunities for physical activity. It may also reflect the greater acceptance of obesity among certain ethnic groups, as well as different cultural values related to food choices.

In some families and cultures, food is used as a symbol of love and caring. It is an integral part of social gatherings and celebrations. In such cases, it may be difficult to change established eating patterns because they are linked to cultural and family values.

ADOPTING A HEALTHY LIFESTYLE FOR SUCCESSFUL WEIGHT MANAGEMENT

When all the research has been assessed, it is clear that most weight problems are lifestyle problems. Even though more and more young people are developing weight problems, most arrive at early adulthood with the advantage of having a normal body weight—neither too fat nor too thin. In fact, many young adults get away with terrible eating and exercise habits and don't develop a weight problem. But as the rapid growth of adolescence slows and family and career obligations increase, maintaining a healthy weight becomes a greater challenge. Slow weight gain is a major cause of overweight and obesity, so weight management is important for everyone, not just for people who are currently overweight. A good time to develop a lifestyle for successful weight management is during early adulthood, when healthy behavior patterns have a better chance of taking a firm hold.

Permanent weight loss is not something you start and stop. You need to adopt healthy behaviors that you can maintain throughout your life. Lifestyle factors that are critical for successful long-term weight management include eating habits, level of physical activity, an ability to think positively and manage your emotions effectively, and the coping strategies you use to deal with the stresses and challenges in your life.

Diet and Eating Habits

In contrast to dieting, which involves some form of food restriction, diet refers to your daily food choices. Everyone has a diet, but not everyone is dieting. You need to develop a diet that you enjoy and that enables you to maintain a healthy body composition. Use MyPyramid or DASH as the basis for a healthy diet (see Chapter 12). For weight management, pay special attention to total calories, portion sizes, energy density, fat and carbohydrate intake, and eating habits.

Total Calories MyPyramid suggests approximate daily energy intakes based on gender, age, and activity level (see Table 12-3). However, energy balance may be a more important consideration for weight management than total calories consumed (see Figure 14-2). To maintain your current weight, the total number of calories you eat must equal the number you burn. To lose weight, you must decrease your calorie intake and/or increase the number of calories you burn; to gain weight, the reverse is true. (One pound of body fat represents 3500 calories.)

The best approach for weight loss is combining an increase in physical activity with moderate calorie restriction. Don't go on a crash diet. To maintain weight loss, you will probably have to maintain some degree of the calorie restriction you used to lose the weight. Therefore, you need to adopt a level of food intake that provides all the essential nutrients that you can live with over the long term. For most people, maintaining weight loss is more difficult than losing the weight in the first place.

Portion Sizes Overconsumption of total calories is closely tied to portion sizes. Many Americans are unaware that the portion sizes of packaged foods and of foods served at restaurants have increased in size, and most of us significantly underestimate the amount of food we eat. One 2006 study found that the larger the meal, the greater the underestimation of calories. Limiting portion sizes is critical for maintaining good health. For many people, concentrating on portion sizes is easier than counting calories.

To counteract portion distortion, weigh and measure your food at home for a few days every now and then. In addition, check the serving sizes listed on packaged foods. With practice, you'll learn to judge portion sizes more accurately. When eating out, try to order the smallest-sized items on the menu. When a small isn't small enough, take half home or share it with a friend. It is especially important to limit serving sizes of foods that are high in calories and low in nutrients. Don't supersize your meals and snacks; although huge servings may seem like the best deal, it is more important to order just what you

What Triggers Your Eating?

Hunger isn't the only reason people eat. Efforts to maintain a healthy body weight can be sabotaged by eating related to other factors, including emotions, environment, and patterns of thinking. This quiz is designed to provide you with a score for five factors that describe many people's eating habits. This information will put you in a better position to manage your eating behavior and control your weight. Circle the number that indicates to what degree each situation is likely to make you start eating.

	Very Unlikely									Very Likely
Social										
1. Arguing or having a conflict with someone	1	2	3	4	5	6	7	8	9	10
2. Being with others when they are eating	1	2	3	4	5	6	7	8	9	10
3. Being urged to eat by someone else	1	2	3	4	5	6	7	8	9	10
4. Feeling inadequate around others	1	2	3	4	5	6	7	8	9	10
Emotional										
5. Feeling bad, such as being anxious or depressed	1	2	3	4	5	6	7	8	9	10
6. Feeling good, happy, or relaxed	1	2	3	4	5	6	7	8	9	10
7. Feeling bored or having time on my hands	1	2	3	4	5	6	7	8	9	10
8. Feeling stressed or excited	1	2	3	4	5	6	7	8	9	10
Situational										
9. Seeing an advertisement for food or eating	1	2	3	4	5	6	7	8	9	10
10. Passing by a bakery, cookie shop, or other enticement to eat	1	2	3	4	5	6	7	8	9	10
11. Being involved in a party, celebration, or special occasion	1	2	3	4	5	6	7	8	9	10
12. Eating out	1	2	3	4	5	6	7	8	9	10
Thinking										
13. Making excuses to myself about why it's OK to eat	1	2	3	4	5	6	7	8	9	10
14. Berating myself for being fat or unable to control my eating	1	2	3	4	5	6	7	8	9	10
15. Worrying about others or about difficulties I'm having	1	2	3	4	5	6	7	8	9	10
16. Thinking about how things should or shouldn't be	1	2	3	4	5	6	7	8	9	10
Physiological										
17. Experiencing pain or physical discomfort	1	2	3	4	5	6	7	8	9	10
18. Experiencing trembling, headache, or light-headedness associated with no eating or too much caffeine	1	2	3	4	5	6	7	8	9	10
19. Experiencing fatigue or feeling overtired	1	2	3	4	5	6	7	8	9	10
20. Experiencing hunger pangs or urges to eat, even though I've eaten recently	1	2	3	4	5	6	7	8	9	10

Scoring

Total your scores for each category, and enter them below. Then rank the scores by marking the highest score 1, next highest score 2, and so on. Focus on the highest-ranked categories first, but any score above 24 is high and indicates that you need to work on that category.

Category	Total Score	Rank Order
Social (Items 1–4)	_____	_____
Emotional (Items 5–8)	_____	_____
Situational (Items 9–12)	_____	_____
Thinking (Items 13–16)	_____	_____
Physiological (Items 17–20)	_____	_____

What Your Score Means

Social A high score here means you are very susceptible to the influence of others. Work on better ways to communicate more assertively, handle conflict, and manage anger. Challenge your beliefs about the need to be polite and the obligations you feel you must fulfill.

Emotional A high score here means you need to develop effective ways to cope with emotions. Work on developing skills in stress management, time management, and communication. Practicing positive but realistic self-talk can help you handle small daily upsets.

Situational A high score here means you are especially susceptible to external influences. Try to avoid external cues and respond differently to those you cannot avoid. Control your environment by changing the way you buy, store, cook, and serve food. Anticipate potential problems, and have a plan for handling them.

Thinking A high score here means that the way you think—how you talk to yourself, the beliefs you hold, your memories, and your expectations—have a powerful influence on your eating habits. Try to be less self-critical, less perfectionistic, and more flexible in your ideas about the way things ought to be. Recognize when you're making excuses or rationalizations that allow you to eat.

Physiological A high score here means that the way you eat, what you eat, or medications you are taking may be affecting your eating behavior. You may be eating to reduce physical arousal or deal with physical discomfort. Try eating three meals a day, supplemented with regular snacks if needed. Avoid too much caffeine. If any medication you're taking produces adverse physical reactions, switch to an alternative, if possible. If your medications may be affecting your hormone levels, discuss possible alternatives with your physician.

SOURCE: Adapted from Nash, J. D. 1997. *The New Maximize Your Body Potential.* Boulder, Colorado: Bull. Reprinted with permission from Bull Publishing Company.

Large portions can make it more difficult to consume a moderate diet and manage weight. Many people significantly underestimate the amount of food they eat.

need. Refer to Chapter 12 and the Online Learning Center for more information on choosing appropriate portion sizes.

Energy (Calorie) Density Experts also recommend that you pay attention to energy density—the number of calories per ounce or gram of weight in a food. Studies suggest that it isn't consumption of a certain amount of fat or calories in food that reduces hunger and leads to feelings of fullness and satisfaction; rather, it is consumption of a certain weight of food. Foods that are low in energy density have more volume and bulk—that is, they are relatively heavy but have few calories. For example, for the same 100 calories, you could consume 21 baby carrots or 4 pretzel twists; you are more likely to feel full after eating the serving of carrots because it weighs 10 times that of the serving of pretzels (10 ounces versus 1 ounce).

To cut back on calories and still feel full, then, you should favor foods with a low energy density. Fresh fruits and vegetables, with their high water and fiber content, are low in energy density, as are whole-grain foods. Fresh fruits contain less calories and more fiber than fruit juices or drinks. Meat, ice cream, potato chips, croissants, crackers, and low-fat cakes and cookies are examples of foods high in energy density. Strategies for lowering the energy density of your diet include the following:

- Eat fruit with breakfast and for dessert.
- Add extra vegetables to sandwiches, casseroles, stir-fry dishes, pizza, pasta dishes, and fajitas.
- Start meals with a bowl of broth-based soup; include a green salad or fruit salad.
- Snack on fresh fruits and vegetables rather than crackers, chips, or other energy-dense snack foods.
- Limit serving sizes of energy-dense foods such as butter, mayonnaise, cheese, chocolate, fatty meats, croissants, and snack foods that are fried, high in added sugars (including reduced-fat products), or contain trans fats.

Fat Calories Although some fat is needed in the diet to provide essential nutrients, you should avoid overeating fatty foods. There is some evidence that fat calories are more easily converted to body fat than calories from protein or carbohydrate. Limiting fat in the diet can also help you limit your total calories. As described in Chapter 12, fat should supply 20–35% of your average total daily calories, which translates into no more than 78 grams of fat in a 2000-calorie diet each day. Most of the fat in your diet should be in the form of unsaturated fats from plant and fish sources. Saturated and trans fats should be limited for weight control and disease prevention. In 2006, the American Heart Association recommended limiting trans fats to less than 1% of total calories. Foods high in unhealthy fats include full-fat dairy products, fatty meats, stick margarine, deep-fried foods, and other processed and fast foods.

As Chapter 12 made clear, moving toward a diet strong in complex carbohydrates and fresh fruits and vegetables, and away from a reliance on meat and processed foods, is an effective approach to reducing fat consumption. In fact, a vegetarian—or even vegan—diet may be the solution for many people who need to greatly reduce their calories from fat. A recent study of overweight women showed that those who followed a strict vegetarian diet lost nearly twice as much weight as women who followed a standard low-cholesterol diet. Watch out for processed foods labeled "fat-free" or "reduced fat," as they may be high in calories (see the box "Evaluating Fat and Sugar Substitutes"). In addition, researchers have found that many Americans compensate for a lower-fat diet by consuming more calories overall. A low-fat diet that is high in calories will not lead to weight loss.

Carbohydrate Most experts agree that people should consume about 45–65% of total daily calories as carbohydrate, with special emphasis on whole grains, vegetables, fruits, and other foods high in fiber. Americans currently consume most of their carbohydrate calories in the form of foods high in refined carbohydrates and added sugars—soft drinks and heavily sweetened fruit drinks, white rice, white potatoes, and breads, cereals, and snack foods made with refined grains. Such foods are typically high in calories and low in other essential nutrients; they also often cause dramatic swings in blood glucose and insulin levels and have been implicated in the development of type 2 diabetes and heart disease.

Foods high in whole grains and fiber are typically lower in calorie density, saturated fat, and added sugars and may promote feelings of satiety (fullness)—all characteristic features of a dietary pattern for successful weight management. They also help maintain normal

Evaluating Fat and Sugar Substitutes

Critical Consumer

For successful weight management, some people find it helpful to limit their intake of foods high in fat and simple sugars. Foods made with fat and sugar substitutes are often promoted for weight loss. But just what are fat and sugar substitutes? And can they really contribute to weight management?

Fat Substitutes

A variety of substances are used to replace fats in processed foods and other products. Some contribute calories, protein, fiber, and/or other nutrients, whereas others do not. Fat replacers fall into three general categories:

- *Carbohydrate-based fat replacers* include starch, fibers, gums, cellulose, polydextrose, and fruit purees. They are the oldest and most widely used form of fat replacer and are found in dairy and meat products, baked goods, salad dressings, and many other prepared foods. Newer types such as Oatrim, Z-trim, and Nu-trim are made from types of dietary fiber that may actually lower cholesterol levels. Carbohydrate-based fat replacers contribute 0–4 calories per gram.
- *Protein-based fat replacers* are typically made from milk, egg whites, soy, or whey; trade names include Simplesse, Dairy-lo, and Supro. They are used in cheese, sour cream, mayonnaise, margarine spreads, frozen desserts, salad dressings, and baked goods. Protein-based fat replacers typically contribute 1–4 calories per gram.
- *Fat-based fat replacers* include glycerides, olestra, and other special types of fatty acids. Some of these compounds are not absorbed well by the body and so provide fewer calories per gram (5 calories compared with the standard 9 for fats); others are impossible for the body to digest and so contribute no calories at all. Olestra, marketed under the trade name Olean and used in fried snack foods, is an example of the latter type of compound. Concerns have been raised about the safety of olestra because it reduces the absorption of fat-soluble nutrients and certain antioxidants and because it causes gastrointestinal distress in some people.

Nonnutritive Sweeteners and Sugar Alcohols

Sugar substitutes are often referred to as nonnutritive sweeteners because they provide no calories or essential nutrients. By 2005, five types of nonnutritive sweeteners had been approved for use in the United States: acesulfame-K (Sunett, Sweet One), aspartame (NutraSweet, Equal, NatraTaste), saccharin (Sweet 'N Low), sucralose (Splenda), and neotame. They are used in beverages, desserts, baked goods, yogurt, chewing gum, and products such as toothpaste, mouthwash, and cough syrup. Another sweetener, stevia, is an extract of a South American shrub; it is classified as a dietary supplement and so is not regulated by the FDA.

Sugar alcohols are made by altering the chemical form of sugars extracted from fruits and other plant sources; they include erythritol, isomalt, lactitol, maltitol, mannitol, sorbitol, and zylitol. Sugar alcohols provide 0.2–2.5 calories per gram, compared to 4 calories per gram in standard sugar. They have typically been used to sweeten sugar-free candies but are now being added to many sweet foods promoted as low-carbohydrate products, often combined with other sweeteners. Sugar alcohols are digested in a way that can create gas, cramps, and diarrhea if they are consumed in large amounts—more than about 10 grams in one meal. To avoid problems, check ingredient lists to determine if a food contains sugar alcohols.

Fat and Sugar Substitutes in Weight Management

Whether fat and sugar substitutes help you achieve and maintain a healthy weight depends on your lifestyle—your overall eating and activity habits. The increase in the availability of fat-free and sugar-free foods in the United States has *not* been associated with a drop in calorie consumption. When evaluating foods with fat and sugar substitutes, consider these issues:

- *Is the food lower in calories or just lower in fat?* Reduced-fat foods often contain extra sugar to improve the taste and texture lost when fat is removed, so such foods may be as high or even higher in total calories than their fattier counterparts. Limiting fat intake is an important goal for weight management, but so is controlling total calories.
- *Are you choosing foods with fat and/or sugar substitutes instead of foods you typically eat or in addition to foods you typically eat?* If you consume low-fat, no-sugar-added ice cream instead of regular ice cream, you may save calories. But if you add such ice cream to your daily diet simply because it is lower in fat and sugar, your overall calorie consumption—and your weight—may increase.
- *How many foods containing fat and sugar substitutes do you consume each day?* Although the FDA has given at least provisional approval to all the fat and sugar substitutes currently available, health concerns about some of these products linger. One way to limit any potential adverse effects is to read labels and monitor how much of each product you consume.
- *Is an even healthier choice available?* Many of the foods containing fat and sugar substitutes are low-nutrient snack foods. Although substituting a lower-fat or lower-sugar version of the same food may be beneficial, fruits, vegetables, and whole grains are healthier snack choices.

blood glucose and insulin levels and reduce the risk of heart disease. For weight management and overall health, choose a diet rich in complex carbohydrates from whole grains, vegetables, and fruits; avoid high-fat toppings, added sugars (especially sugary soft drinks, fruit drinks, and desserts), and refined carbohydrates.

Protein The typical American consumes more than an adequate amount of protein. Special dietary supplements that provide extra protein are unnecessary for most people, and protein not needed by the body for growth and tissue repair may be stored as fat. Foods high in protein are often also high in fat. Stick to the recommended protein intake of

10–35% of total daily calories. High-protein diets promoted for weight loss are discussed later in the chapter.

Eating Habits Equally important to weight management is eating small, frequent meals—four to five meals per day, including breakfast and snacks—on a dependable, regular schedule. Skipping meals leads to excessive hunger, feelings of deprivation, and increased vulnerability to binge eating or snacking on high-calorie, high-fat, or sugary foods. A regular pattern of eating, along with some personal rules governing food choices, is a way of thinking about and then internalizing the many details that go into a healthy, low-fat diet. (For effective weight management, it is better to consume the majority of calories during the day rather than in the evening.) Rules for breakfast might be these, for example: Choose a sugar-free, high-fiber cereal with fat-free milk on most days; have a hard-boiled egg (no more than 3 per week); save pancakes and waffles for special occasions, unless they are whole-grain.

Decreeing some foods off-limits generally sets up a rule to be broken. The better principle is "everything in moderation." If a particular food becomes troublesome, it might be placed off-limits temporarily until control over it is regained. The ultimate goal is to eat in moderation; no foods need to be entirely off-limits, though some should be eaten judiciously.

Physical Activity and Exercise

Regular physical activity is another important lifestyle factor in weight management. Physical activity and exercise burn calories and keep the metabolism geared to using food for energy instead of storing it as fat. Making significant cuts in food intake in order to lose weight is a difficult strategy to maintain; increasing your physical activity is a much better approach. Regular physical activity also protects against weight gain and is essential for maintaining weight loss.

As described in Chapter 13, the first step in becoming more active is to incorporate more physical activity into your daily life. Accumulate 30 minutes or more of moderate-intensity physical activity—walking, gardening, housework, and so on—on most, or preferably all, days of the week. Moderate-intensity physical activities are equal, in effort, to walking briskly—1 mile in 15–20 minutes; other moderate-intensity activities include bicycling (10–12 mph), dancing, hiking, golfing (without a cart), raking leaves, vacuuming a carpet, playing volleyball, and washing a car. Take advantage of routine opportunities to be more active; in the long term, even a small increase in activity level can help maintain your current weight or help you lose a modest amount of weight. In fact, research suggests that fidgeting—stretching, squirming, standing up, and so on—may help prevent weight gain after overeating in some people. If you simply walked around during TV commercials while watching 2 hours of prime-time programming, you'd accumulate more than 30 minutes of physical activity. Short bouts of activity spread throughout the day can produce many of the same health benefits as continuous physical activity.

If you are overweight or obese and want to lose weight and keep it off, a greater amount of physical activity is necessary. People who lose weight and don't regain it typically burn at least 2800 calories per week in physical activity—the equivalent of about 1 hour of brisk walking per day. The 2005 Dietary Guidelines for Americans recommend at least 60 minutes of daily physical activity to avoid slow weight gain in adulthood, and at least 60–90 minutes of activity to lose weight or to prevent weight regain after losing weight.

Once you become more active every day, consider beginning a formal exercise program that includes cardiorespiratory endurance exercise, resistance training, and stretching exercises. Moderate cardiorespiratory endurance exercise, sustained for 45 minutes to 1 hour, can help trim body fat permanently. Strength training helps increase fat-free mass, which results in more calorie burning even outside of exercise periods.

The message about exercise is that regular exercise, maintained throughout life, makes weight management easier and improves quality of life (see the box "Exercise, Body Image, and Self-Esteem" on p. 428). The sooner you establish good habits, the better. The key to success is making exercise an integral part of the lifestyle you can enjoy now and in the future. Chapter 13 contains many suggestions for becoming a more active, physically fit person.

Thinking and Emotions

What goes on in your head is another factor in a healthy lifestyle and successful weight management. The way you think about yourself and your world influences and is influenced by how you feel and how you act. Certain kinds of thinking produce negative emotions, which can undermine a healthy lifestyle.

Research on people who have a weight problem indicates that low self-esteem and the negative emotions that accompany it are significant problems. This often results in part from mentally comparing the actual self to an internally held picture of an ideal self. The greater the discrepancy, the larger the impact on self-esteem and the more likely the presence of negative emotions.

Often our internalized ideal self is the result of having adopted perfectionistic goals and beliefs about how we and others should be. Examples of such beliefs are "If I don't do things perfectly, I'm a failure" and "It's terrible if I'm not thin." These irrational beliefs may cause stress and emotional pain. The remedy is to challenge such beliefs and replace them with more realistic ones.

The beliefs and attitudes you hold give rise to self-talk, an internal dialogue about events that happen to and around you. Positive self-talk includes leading yourself through the steps of a job and then praising yourself when it's successfully completed. Negative self-talk takes

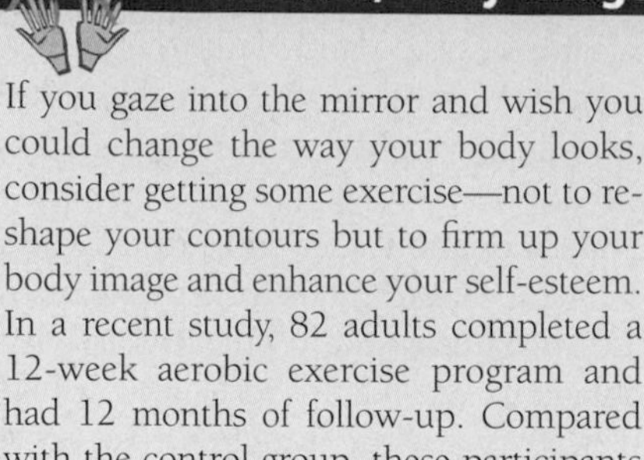

Mind/Body/Spirit

Exercise, Body Image, and Self-Esteem

If you gaze into the mirror and wish you could change the way your body looks, consider getting some exercise—not to reshape your contours but to firm up your body image and enhance your self-esteem. In a recent study, 82 adults completed a 12-week aerobic exercise program and had 12 months of follow-up. Compared with the control group, these participants improved their fitness and also benefited psychologically in tests of mood, anxiety, and self-concept. These same physical and psychological benefits were still significant at the 1-year follow-up.

One reason for the findings may be that people who exercise regularly often gain a sense of mastery and competence that enhances their self-esteem and body image. In addition, exercise contributes to a more toned look, which many adults prefer. Research suggests that physically active people are more comfortable with their body and their image than sedentary people are. In one workplace study, 60 employees were asked to complete a 36-session stretching program whose main purpose was to prevent muscle strains at work. At the end of the program, besides the significant increase by all participants in measurements of flexibility, their perceptions of their bodies improved and so did their overall sense of self-worth.

Similar results were obtained in a Norwegian study, in which 219 middle-aged people at risk for heart disease were randomly assigned to one of four groups: diet, diet plus exercise, exercise, and no intervention. The greater the participation of individuals in the exercise component of the program, the higher were their scores in perceived competence/self-esteem and coping.

SOURCES: DiLorenzo, T. M., et al. 1999. Long-term effects of aerobic exercise on psychological outcomes. *Preventive Medicine* 28(1): 75–85; Sorensen, M., et al. 1999. The effect of exercise and diet on mental health and quality of life in middle-aged individuals with elevated risk factors for cardiovascular disease. *Journal of Sports Science* 17(5): 369–377; Moore, T. M. 1998. A workplace stretching program. *AAOHN Journal* 46(12): 563–568.

the form of self-deprecating remarks, self-blame, and angry and guilt-producing comments. Negative self-talk can undermine efforts at self-control and lead to feelings of anxiety and depression (see Chapter 3).

Your beliefs and attitude influence how you interpret what happens to you and what you can expect in the future, as well as how you feel and react. A healthy lifestyle is supported by having realistic beliefs and goals and by engaging in positive self-talk and problem-solving efforts.

Coping Strategies

Adequate and appropriate coping strategies for dealing with the stresses and challenges of life are another lifestyle factor in weight management. One strategy that some people adopt for coping is eating. (Others use drugs, alcohol, smoking, spending, gambling, and so on, to cope.) When boredom occurs, eating can provide entertainment. Food may be used to alleviate loneliness or as a pickup for fatigue. Eating provides distraction from difficult problems and is a means of punishing the self or others for real or imagined transgressions.

People with a healthy lifestyle have more effective ways to get their needs met. Having learned to communicate assertively and to manage interpersonal conflict effectively, they don't shrink from problems or overreact. The person with a healthy lifestyle knows how to create and maintain relationships with others and has a solid network of friends and loved ones. Food is used appropriately—to fuel life's activities and gain personal satisfaction, not to manage stress.

Obtaining adequate amounts of sleep is important for stress management and may be a key component of successful weight management. A recent study found a link between sleep and body mass index: People with a healthy BMI slept more than people who were overweight and obese. A cause-and-effect relationship is not yet established, but it is possible that insufficient sleep may affect hormones, metabolism, and appetite.

The healthy lifestyle that naturally and easily results in a reasonable body weight is one characterized by good nutrition, adequate exercise, positive thinking and emotions, and effective coping strategies and behavior patterns (see the box "Strategies for Successful Weight Management").

APPROACHES TO OVERCOMING A WEIGHT PROBLEM

Each year, Americans spend more than $40 billion on various weight-loss plans and products. What should you do if you are overweight? You have several options.

Doing It Yourself

If you need to lose weight, focus on adopting the healthy lifestyle described throughout this book. The right weight for you will naturally evolve. Combine modest cuts in energy intake with exercise, and avoid very-low-calorie diets. (In general, a low-calorie diet should have 1200–1500 calories per day.) By producing a negative energy balance of 250–1000 calories per day, you will produce the recommended weight loss of 0.5–2.0 pounds per week. Don't try to lose weight more rapidly. Realize that most low-calorie diets cause a rapid loss of body water at first. When this phase passes, weight loss declines. As a result, dieters are often misled into believing that their efforts are not working.

Strategies for Successful Weight Management

Food Choices

- Follow the recommendations in MyPyramid for eating a moderate, varied diet.
- Pay attention to the energy density and nutrient density of your food choices. Favor foods with a low energy density and a high nutrient density.
- Emphasize variety, adequacy, and balance in your food choices.
- Check food labels for serving sizes, calories, and nutrient levels.
- Watch for hidden calories. Reduced-fat foods often have as many calories as their full-fat versions. Fat-based condiments like butter, margarine, mayonnaise, and salad dressings provide about 100 calories per tablespoon; added sugars such as jams, jellies, and syrup are also packed with calories.
- Drink fewer calories. Many Americans consume high-calorie beverages such as soda, fruit drinks, sports drinks, alcohol, and specialty coffees and teas.
- For problem foods, try eating small amounts under controlled conditions. Go out for a scoop of ice cream, for example, rather than buying a half gallon for your freezer.

Planning and Serving

- Keep a log of what you eat. Before you begin your program, your log will provide a realistic picture of your current diet and what changes you can make. Once you start your program, a log will keep you focused on your food choices and portion sizes. Consider tracking the following:
  - food eaten
  - hunger level
  - circumstances (location, other activities)
  - outside influences (environment, other people)
  - thoughts and emotions
- Eat four to five meals/snacks daily, including breakfast, to distribute calories throughout your day. In studies, people who eat breakfast consume fewer calories overall over the course of the day. Keep low-calorie snacks on hand to combat the munchies: baby carrots, popcorn, and fresh fruits and vegetables are good choices.
- When shopping, make a list and stick to it. Don't shop when you're hungry. Avoid aisles that contain problem foods.
- Consume the majority of your daily calories during the day, not in the evening.
- Pay special attention to portion sizes. Use measuring cups and spoons and a food scale to become more familiar with appropriate portion sizes.
- Serve meals on small plates and in small bowls to help you eat smaller portions without feeling deprived.
- Eat only in specifically designated spots. Remove food from other areas of your house or apartment.
- When you eat, just eat—don't do anything else, such as read or watch TV.
- Eat more slowly. It takes time for your brain to get the message that your stomach is full. Take small bites and chew food thoroughly. Pay attention to every bite, and enjoy your food. Between bites, try putting down your fork or spoon and taking sips of water or another beverage.
- When you're done eating, remove your plate. Cue yourself that the meal is over—drink a glass of water, suck on a mint, chew gum, or brush your teeth.

Special Occasions

- When you eat out, choose a restaurant where you can make healthy food choices. Ask the server not to put bread and butter on the table before the meal, and request that sauces and salad dressings be served on the side. If portion sizes are large, take half your food home for a meal later in the week.
- If you cook a large meal for friends, send leftovers home with your guests.
- If you're eating at a friend's, eat a little and leave the rest. Don't eat to be polite; if someone offers you food you don't want, thank the person and decline firmly: "No thank you, I've had enough" or "It's delicious, but I'm full."
- Take care during the winter holidays. Research indicates that people gain less than they think during the winter holidays (about a pound) but that the weight isn't lost during the rest of the year, leading to slow, steady weight gain.

Physical Activity and Stress Management

- Increase your level of daily physical activity. If you have been sedentary for a long time or are seriously overweight, increase your level of activity slowly. Start by walking 10 minutes at a time, and work toward 30–60 minutes or more of moderate physical activity per day.
- Begin a formal exercise program that includes cardiorespiratory endurance exercise, strength training, and stretching (see Chapter 13).
- Develop techniques for handling stress—go for a walk or use a relaxation technique. Practice positive self-talk. Get adequate sleep.
- Develop strategies for coping with nonhunger cues to eat, such as boredom, sleepiness, or anxiety. Try calling a friend, taking a shower, or reading a magazine.
- Tell family members and friends that you're making some changes in your eating and exercise habits. Ask them to be supportive.

For additional tips, visit the Department of Health and Human Services Small Steps Web site (www.smallstep.gov), which includes many specific suggestions to encourage individuals and families to take steps toward a healthier lifestyle.

They then give up, not realizing that smaller, mostly fat, losses later in the diet are actually better than the initial larger, mostly fluid losses. Reasonable weight loss is 8–10% of body weight over 6 months. A registered dietitian or nutritionist can recommend an appropriate plan for you when you want to lose weight on your own. For more tips, refer to the Behavior Change Strategy at the end of the chapter.

For many Americans, maintaining weight loss is a bigger challenge than losing weight. Most weight lost during a period of dieting is regained. When planning a weight management program, it is extremely important to include strategies that you can maintain over the long term, both for food choices and for physical activity. Weight management is a lifelong project.

Diet Books

Many people who try to lose weight by themselves fall prey to one or more of the dozens of diet books on the market. Although some contain useful advice and tips for motivation, most make empty promises. Some guidelines for evaluating and choosing a diet book follow:

- Reject books that advocate an unbalanced way of eating. These include books advocating a high-carbohydrate-only diet or those advocating low-carbohydrate, high-protein diets. Also reject books promoting a single food, such as cabbage or grapefruit.
- Reject books that claim to be based on a "scientific breakthrough" or to have the "secret to success."
- Reject books that use gimmicks, such as matching eating to blood type, hyping insulin resistance as the single cause of obesity, combining foods in special ways to achieve weight loss, rotating levels of calories, or purporting that a weight problem is due to food allergies, food sensitivities, yeast infections, or hormone imbalances.
- Reject books that promise quick weight loss or that limit the selection of foods.
- Accept books that advocate a balanced approach to diet plus exercise and sound nutrition advice.

Many diets can cause weight loss if maintained; the real difficulty is finding a safe and healthy pattern of food choices and physical activity that results in long-term maintenance of a healthy body weight and reduced risk of chronic disease (see the box "Is Any Diet Best for Weight Loss?"). Check the Online Learning Center for worksheets that can help you evaluate diet books and commercial weight-loss programs.

Dietary Supplements and Diet Aids

The number of dietary supplements and other weight-loss aids on the market has also increased in recent years.

There are many plans and supplements promoted for weight loss, but few have any research supporting their effectiveness for long-term weight management. Developing lifelong healthy eating and exercise habits is the best approach for achieving and maintaining a healthy body composition.

Weight-loss supplements represent about $2 billion in sales; in a recent survey of over-the-counter (OTC) weight-loss pill users, more than 25% were young obese women and 8% were normal-weight women. Promoted in advertisements, magazines, direct mail campaigns, infomercials, and Web sites, these products typically promise a quick and easy path to weight loss. Most of these products are marketed as dietary supplements and so are subject to fewer regulations than OTC medications. A 2002 report from the Federal Trade Commission stated that more than half of advertisements for weight-loss products made representations that are likely to be false. In addition, use of OTC products doesn't help in the adoption of lifestyle behaviors that can help people achieve and maintain a healthy weight over the long term.

The bottom line on nonprescription diet aids is caveat emptor—let the buyer beware. There is no quick and easy way to lose weight. The most effective approach is to develop healthy diet and exercise habits and make them a permanent part of your lifestyle. Some commonly marketed OTC products for weight loss are described below.

Formula Drinks and Food Bars Canned diet drinks, powders used to make shakes, and diet food bars and snacks are designed to achieve weight loss by substituting for some or all of a person's daily food intake. However, most people find it difficult to use these products for long periods, and muscle loss and other serious health problems may result if they are used as the sole source of nutrition for an extended period. Use of such products

Is Any Diet Best for Weight Loss?

Experts agree that reducing energy (calorie) intake promotes weight loss. However, many popular commercial and published weight-loss plans include a special hook and promote specific food choices and macronutrient (protein, fat, carbohydrate) combinations as best for weight loss. Research findings have been mixed, but two points are clear: Total calorie intake matters, and the best diet is probably the one that an individual can stick with.

Low-Carbohydrate Diets

Some low-carb diets advocate fewer than 10% of total calories from carbohydrate, compared with the 45–65% recommended by the Food and Nutrition Board. Some suggest daily carbohydrate intake below the 130 grams needed to provide essential carbohydrate in the diet. Small studies have found that low-carbohydrate diets can help with short-term weight loss and be safe for relatively short periods of time—although unpleasant effects such as bad breath, constipation, and headache are fairly common.

Some low-carb diets tend to be very high in protein and saturated fat and low in fiber, whole grains, vegetables, and fruits (and thus lacking in some vitamins and minerals). Diets high in protein and saturated fat have been linked to increased risk of heart disease, high blood pressure, and cancer. Other low-carb diets, though still emphasizing protein, limit saturated fats, allow most vegetables after an initial period, and advocate switching to "healthy carbs." These diets are healthier than the more extreme versions.

Low-Fat Diets

Many experts advocate diets that are relatively low in fat, high in carbohydrate, and moderate in protein. Critics of these diets blame them for rising rates of obesity and note that very-low-fat, very-high-carbohydrate diets can increase triglyceride levels and lower levels of good (HDL) cholesterol in some people. However, these negative effects can be counteracted with moderate-intensity exercise, and low-fat diets combined with physical activity can be safe and effective for many people.

Few experts take the position that low-fat, high-carbohydrate diets, apart from overall diet and activity patterns, are responsible for the increase in obesity among Americans. However, the debate has highlighted the importance of total calorie intake and the quality of carbohydrate choices. Most Americans consume large amounts of refined carbohydrates and added sugars from energy-dense, nutrient-poor foods; they do not consume the recommended whole grains, vegetables, and fruits. A low-fat diet is not a license to consume excess calories, even in low-fat foods.

How Do Popular Diets Measure Up?

In one recent study, obese people on a very-low-carbohydrate, high-fat diet lost more weight over a 6-month period than people following a moderate-fat diet. However, after a year, the difference in weight loss between the two groups was no longer significant, and the dropout rate from both groups was high.

A 2005 study followed participants in four popular diets that emphasize different strategies—Weight Watchers (restricted portion sizes and calories), Atkins (low-carbohydrate, high-fat), Zone (relatively high protein, moderate fat and carbohydrate), and Ornish (very low fat). Each of these diets modestly reduced body weight and heart disease risk factors. There was no significant difference in weight loss at 1 year among the diets, and the more closely people adhered to each diet, the more weight they lost. The dropout rates were high—about 50% for Atkins and Ornish and about 35% for Weight Watchers and Zone. The message from this study? Finding a dietary approach that you can stick to is key to long-term success.

Energy Balance Counts: The National Weight Control Registry

Future research may determine that certain macronutrient patterns may be somewhat more helpful for disease reduction in people with particular risk profiles. However, in terms of weight loss, such differences among diets are likely overshadowed by the importance of total calorie intake and physical activity. Important lessons about energy balance can be drawn from the National Weight Control Registry, an ongoing study of people who have lost significant amounts of weight and kept it off. The average participant in the registry has lost 71 pounds and kept the weight off for more than 5 years. Nearly all participants use a combination of diet and exercise to manage their weight. Most consumed diets moderate in calories and relatively low in fat and fried foods; they monitor their body weight and their food intake frequently. Participants engage in an average of 60 minutes of moderate physical activity daily. The National Weight Control Registry study illustrates that to lose weight and keep it off, you must decrease daily calorie intake and/or increase daily physical activity—and continue to do so over your lifetime.

A Balanced Approach

Long-term maintenance of healthy body weight and reduction of chronic disease risk requires permanent changes in lifestyle. Diets advocating strict limits on any nutrient or food groups may be impractical and difficult to maintain over the long term. The latest USDA guidelines provide a good model for healthy food and activity choices. Basic guidelines for weight loss and risk reduction advocated by many experts include the following:

- Set reasonable goals; even small amounts of weight loss benefit health.
- Reduce your intake of saturated and trans fats, refined carbohydrates, and added sugars. Favor mono- and polyunsaturated fats, lean protein sources, fat-free and low-fat dairy foods, whole grains, vegetables, and fruits. Select nutrient-dense choices within each food group.
- Incorporate 60 or more minutes of physical activity into your daily routine; begin a formal exercise program for even greater health and fitness benefits.
- Choose a healthy dietary pattern that works for you over the long term.

SOURCES: Battle of the diet books II. 2006. *Nutrition Action Healthletter,* July/August; Dansinger, M. L., et al. 2005. Comparison of the Atkins, Ornish, Weight Watchers, and Zone diets for weight loss and heart disease risk reduction. *Journal of the American Medical Association* 293(1): 43–53; Hays, N. P., et al. 2004. Effects of an ad libitum low-fat, high-carbohydrate diet on body weight, body composition, and fat distribution in older men and women. *Archives of Internal Medicine* 164(2): 210–217; Hill, J., and R. Wing. 2003. The National Weight Control Registry. *Permanente Journal* 7(3): 34–37; Bravata, D. M., et al. 2003. Efficacy and safety of low-carbohydrate diets. *Journal of the American Medical Association* 289: 1837–1850; Foster, G. D., et al. 2003. A randomized trial of low-carbohydrate diet for obesity. *New England Journal of Medicine* 348: 2082–2090.

Table 14-3 Ingredients Commonly Found in Weight-Loss Products

Common Name	Use/Claim	Evidence/Efficacy	Safety Issues
Bitter orange extract (*Citrus aurantium*)	CNS stimulant	Limited evidence	Highly concentrated extracts may increase blood pressure; should not be used by people with cardiac problems
Caffeine	CNS stimulant; increases fat metabolism	Amplifies effects of ephedra	Generally considered safe; caution advised in caffeine-sensitive individuals
Garcinia cambogia	May interfere with fat metabolism or suppress appetite	Inconclusive evidence	Short-term use (<12 weeks) generally considered safe when used as directed
Green tea extract	Diuretic; increases metabolism	Limited evidence	Generally considered safe
Guarana	CNS stimulant; diuretic	Few clinical trials	Same as for caffeine; overdose can cause painful urination, abdominal spasms, and vomiting
Senna, cascara, aloe, buckthorn berries	Stimulant, laxative	Not effective for weight loss	Chronic use decreases muscle tone in large intestine, causes electrolyte imbalances, and leads to dependence on laxatives
Tea, kola, dandelion, bucho, uva-ursi, damiana, juniper	Diuretic	Not effective for weight loss	Chronic use can cause possible electrolyte imbalance in some people
Yerba mate	Stimulant, laxative, diuretic	Limited evidence	Long-term use as a beverage may increase risk of oral cancer

SOURCE: Adapted from Leslie, K. K. 2003. Herbal weight-loss products: Effective and appropriate? *Today's Dietician* 5(8).

sometimes results in rapid short-term weight loss, but the weight is typically regained because users don't learn to change their eating and lifestyle behaviors.

Herbal Supplements As described in Chapter 12, herbs are marketed as dietary supplements, so there is little information about effectiveness, proper dosage, drug interactions, and side effects. In addition, labels may not accurately reflect the ingredients and dosages present, and safe manufacturing practices are not guaranteed. For example, the substitution of a toxic herb for another compound during the manufacture of a Chinese herbal weight-loss preparation caused more than 100 cases of kidney damage and cancer among users in Europe.

In 2004, the FDA banned the sale of ephedra (*ma huang*), stating that it presented a significant and unreasonable risk to human health. Although challenged by lawsuits, the ban was upheld in 2006 by a U.S. Court of Appeals. Ephedrine, the active ingredient in ephedra, is structurally similar to amphetamine and was widely used in weight-loss supplements. It may suppress appetite, but adverse effects have included elevated blood pressure, panic attacks, seizures, insomnia, and increased risk of heart attack or stroke, particularly when combined with another stimulant, such as caffeine. The synthetic stimulant phenylpropanolamine was banned in 2000 for similar reasons. Other herbal stimulants still on the market are described in Table 14-3.

Dietary Supplements Fiber is another common ingredient in OTC diet aids, promoted for appetite control. However, dietary fiber acts as a bulking agent in the large intestine, not the stomach, so it doesn't have a pronounced effect on appetite. In addition, many diet aids contain only 3 or fewer grams of fiber, which does not contribute much toward the recommended daily intake of 25–38 grams. Other popular dietary supplements include conjugated linoleic acid, carnitine, chromium, pyruvate, calcium, B vitamins, chitosan, and a number of products labeled "fat absorbers," "fat blockers," and "starch blockers." Research has not found these products to be effective, and many have potentially adverse side effects.

Weight-Loss Programs

Weight-loss programs come in a variety of types, including noncommercial support organizations, commercial programs, Web sites, and clinical programs.

Noncommercial Weight-Loss Programs Noncommercial programs such as TOPS (Take Off Pounds Sensibly) and Overeaters Anonymous (OA) mainly provide group support. They do not advocate any particular diet but do recommend seeking professional advice for creating an individualized plan. Like Alcoholics Anonymous, OA is a 12-step program with a spiritual orientation that promotes abstinence from compulsive overeating. These types of programs are generally free. Your physician or a registered dietitian can also provide information and support for weight loss.

Commercial Weight-Loss Programs Commercial weight-loss programs typically provide group support, nutrition education, physical activity recommendations, and behavior modification advice for changing habits. Some also make available packaged foods to assist in following dietary advice. A 2005 study evaluated major commercial weight-loss programs, including Weight Watchers, NutriSystem, Jenny Craig, and L A Weight Loss for 12 weeks or more with a 1-year follow-up assessment. Results showed Weight Watchers to be the only moderately priced commercial program with a mean loss of 5% of initial weight.

Commercial programs can work, but only if you are motivated to decrease calorie intake and increase physical activity. A responsible and safe weight-loss program should have the following features:

1. The recommended diet should be safe and balanced, include all the food groups, and meet the DRIs for all nutrients. Physical activity and exercise should be strongly encouraged.
2. The program should promote slow, steady weight loss averaging 0.5–2.0 pounds per week. (There may be some greater weight loss initially due to fluid loss.)
3. If a participant plans to lose more than 20 pounds, has any health problems, or is taking medication on a regular basis, physician evaluation and monitoring should be recommended. The staff of the program should include qualified counselors and health professionals.
4. The program should include plans for weight maintenance after the weight-loss phase is over.
5. The program should provide information on all fees and costs, including those of supplements and prepackaged foods, as well as data on risks and expected outcomes of participating in the program.

In addition, you should consider whether a program fits your lifestyle and whether you are truly ready to make a commitment to it. A strong commitment and a plan for maintenance are especially important because only about 10–15% of program participants maintain their weight loss—the rest gain back all or more than they had lost. One study of participants found that regular exercise was the best predictor of maintaining weight loss, whereas frequent television viewing was the best predictor of weight gain.

Online Weight-Loss Programs A recent addition to the weight-loss program scene is the Internet-based program. Most such Web sites include a cross between self-help and group support through chat rooms, bulletin boards, and e-newsletters. Many sites offer online self-assessment for diet and physical activity habits as well as a meal plan; some provide access to a staff professional for individualized help. Many are free, but some charge a small weekly or monthly fee. Preliminary research suggests that this type of program provides an alternative to in-person diet counseling and can lead to weight loss for some people. One site, eDiets, published data on 46 women with 1.1% weight loss at 1 year. Studies found that people who logged on to Internet programs more frequently tended to lose more weight; weekly online contact in terms of behavior therapy proved most successful for weight loss. The criteria used to evaluate commercial programs can also be applied to Internet-based programs. In addition, check whether a program offers member-to-member support and access to staff professionals.

Clinical Weight-Loss Programs Medically supervised clinical programs are usually located in a hospital or other medical setting. Designed to help those who are severely obese, these programs typically involve a closely monitored very-low-calorie diet. The cost of a clinical program is usually high, but insurance will often cover part of the fee.

Prescription Drugs

For a medicine to cause weight loss, it must reduce energy consumption, increase energy expenditure, and/or interfere with energy absorption. The medications most often prescribed for weight loss are appetite suppressants that reduce feelings of hunger or increase feelings of fullness. Appetite suppressants usually work by increasing levels of catecholamine or serotonin, two brain chemicals that affect mood and appetite. All prescription weight-loss drugs have potential side effects. Those that affect catecholamine levels, including phentermine (Ionamin, Obenix, Fastin, and Adipex-P), diethylpropion (Tenuate), and mazindol (Sanorex), may cause sleeplessness, nervousness, and euphoria. Sibutramine (Meridia) acts on both the serotonin and catecholamine systems; it may trigger increases in blood pressure and heart rate. Headaches, constipation or diarrhea, dry mouth, and insomnia are other side effects.

Most appetite suppressants are approved by the FDA only for short-term use. Two drugs, however, are approved for longer-term use: sibutramine and orlistat (Xenical). Sibutramine's safety and efficacy record is good, but regular monitoring of blood pressure is required during therapy. Orlistat lowers calorie consumption by blocking fat absorption in the intestines; it prevents about 30% of the fat in food from being digested. Similar to the fat substitute olestra, orlistat reduces the absorption of fat-soluble vitamins and antioxidants. Therefore, taking a vitamin supplement is highly recommended if taking orlistat. Side effects include diarrhea, cramping, and other gastrointestinal problems if users do not follow a low-fat diet. If you have pizza and ice cream, for example, you will probably experience severe diarrhea.

A new drug, rimonabant (Acomplia) has been used successfully in Europe and is now awaiting FDA approval for use in the United States. Rimonabant suppresses appetite by acting on certain brain receptors. Studies show that rimonabant may lead to greater weight loss than other drugs and may help users keep weight off for a longer time. Side effects include mild diarrhea, dizziness, and nausea. Using weight-loss medications in combination or for long periods of time is considered off-label use; this means that although it is legal, the FDA has not approved such use.

These medications work best in conjunction with behavior modification. Studies have generally found that appetite suppressants produce modest weight loss—about 5–22 pounds above the loss expected with nondrug obesity treatments. Individuals respond very differently, however, and some experience more weight loss than others. Unfortunately, weight loss tends to level off or reverse after 4–6 months on a medication, and many people regain the weight they've lost when they stop taking the drug.

Side effects and risks are other concerns. In 1997, the FDA removed from the market two prescription weight-loss drugs, fenfluramine (Pondimin) and dexfenfluramine (Redux), after their use was linked to potentially life-threatening heart valve problems. (Fenfluramine was used most often in combination with phentermine, an off-label combination referred to as "fen/phen.") It appears that people who took these drugs over a long period or at high dosages are at greatest risk for problems, but the FDA recommends that anyone who has taken either of these drugs be examined by a physician.

Prescription weight-loss drugs are not for people who just want to lose a few pounds. The latest federal guidelines advise people to try lifestyle modification for at least 6 months before trying drug therapy. Prescription drugs are recommended only in certain cases: for people who have been unable to lose weight with nondrug options and who have a BMI over 30 (or over 27 if two or more additional risk factors such as diabetes and high blood pressure are present). For severely obese people who have been unable to lose weight by other methods, prescription drugs may provide a good option. Even modest weight loss provides significant health benefits for obese individuals.

Surgery

Almost 5% of Americans are severely obese, meaning they have a BMI of 40 or higher or are 100 pounds or more over recommended weight. The number of severely obese people has nearly tripled in the past decade. Severe obesity is a serious medical condition that is often complicated by other health problems such as diabetes, sleep disorders, heart disease, and arthritis. Surgical intervention may be necessary as a treatment of last resort. According to a National Institutes of Health (NIH) Consensus Conference, gastric bypass surgery is recommended for patients with a BMI greater than 40, or greater than 35 with obesity-related illnesses.

In 2002, nearly 72,000 people underwent gastric bypass surgery. Due to the increasing prevalence of severe obesity and the reduction of premature deaths, surgical treatment of obesity is growing worldwide. Obesity-related health conditions, as well as risk of premature death, generally improve after surgical weight loss. However, surgery is not without risks. A 2006 study found that patients with poor cardiorespiratory fitness prior to surgery experienced more postoperative complications, including stroke, kidney failure, and even death, than patients with higher fitness levels.

Gastric bypass surgery modifies the gastrointestinal tract by changing either the size of the stomach or how the intestine drains, thereby reducing food intake. The two most common surgeries are the Roux-en-Y gastric bypass and the vertical banded gastroplasty (VBG/Lap-Band). In the *Roux-en-Y gastric bypass* procedure, the stomach is separated into two pouches, one large and one small. A "Y" segment of the small intestine is attached to the smaller pouch. The small stomach pouch restricts food intake, and the bypass of the lower stomach and part of the small intestine results in the absorption of fewer calories (and nutrients). Side effects include fat intolerance, nutritional deficiencies, and dumping syndrome, which involves gastrointestinal distress.

In *vertical banded gastroplasty (VBG)*, a small gastric pouch is created in the upper part of the stomach by applying a double row of staples that essentially elongates the esophagus. This small pouch empties into the remaining stomach through an outlet that is restricted with a band. The procedure controls the gastric emptying of food and the volume of foods eaten. Common complications associated with this kind of surgery are nausea, vomiting, band slippage, gastroesophageal reflux, and stenosis (constriction of the outlet). When compared with Roux-en-Y gastric bypass, VBG has a lower initial weight loss and a greater weight regain.

In a variation of VGB, called Lap-Band, an adjustable band is placed around the stomach. The band is implanted laparoscopically, via a tube inserted through a small incision in the abdomen. The band ties off a portion of the stomach, creating a small pouch similar to that created in VGB surgery. The band is filled with saline and can be tightened or loosened by adding or removing saline through a small tube that exits through the patient's abdomen. The Lap-Band procedure has about the same success rate as VGB and is generally considered to be safe.

Weight loss from surgery generally ranges between 40% and 70% of total body weight over the course of a year. In a 2006 study that included mild to moderately obese (BMI 30–35) adults, gastric banding surgery was significantly more effective in reducing weight and improving quality of life than nonsurgical methods, even after 2 years. For surgical procedures, the key to success is to have adequate follow-up and to stay motivated so that lifestyle behaviors and eating patterns are changed permanently.

Another procedure, *liposuction,* has become popular for removing localized fat deposits. This cosmetic procedure does not improve health the way weight loss does and involves considerable pain and discomfort.

The image of the ideal body promoted by the fashion and fitness industries doesn't reflect the wide range of body shapes and sizes that are associated with good health. An overconcern with body image can contribute to low self-esteem and the development of eating disorders.

Psychological Help

When concern about body weight has developed into an eating disorder, the help of a professional is recommended. In choosing a therapist, be sure to ask about credentials and experience (see Chapter 3). The therapist should have experience working with weight management, body image issues, eating disorders, addictions, and abuse issues.

BODY IMAGE

As described earlier in the chapter, body image consists of perceptions, images, thoughts, attitudes, and emotions. Developing a positive body image is an important aspect of psychological wellness and an important component of successful weight management. See the box "Gender, Ethnicity, and Body Image" on page 436 for suggestions on how to develop a healthy body image.

Severe Body Image Problems

Poor body image can cause significant psychological distress. A person can become preoccupied with a perceived defect in appearance, thereby damaging self-esteem and interfering with relationships. Adolescents and adults who have a negative body image are more likely to diet restrictively, eat compulsively, or develop some other form of disordered eating.

When dissatisfaction becomes extreme, the condition is called *body dysmorphic disorder (BDD).* BDD affects about 2% of Americans, males and females in equal numbers; BDD usually begins before age 18 but can begin in adulthood. Sufferers are overly concerned with physical appearance, often focusing on slight flaws that are not obvious to others. Low self-esteem is common. Individuals with BDD may spend hours every day thinking about their flaws and looking at themselves in mirrors; they may desire and seek repeated cosmetic surgeries. BDD is related to obsessive-compulsive disorder and can lead to depression, social phobia, and suicide if left untreated. An individual with BDD needs to get professional evaluation and treatment; medication and therapy can help people with BDD.

In some cases, body image may bear little resemblance to fact. A person suffering from the eating disorder anorexia nervosa typically has a severely distorted body image—she believes herself to be fat even when she has become emaciated (see the next section for more on anorexia). Distorted body image is also a hallmark of *muscle dysmorphia,* a disorder experienced by some bodybuilders and other active people in which they see themselves as small and out of shape despite being very muscular. Those who suffer from muscle dysmorphia may let obsessive bodybuilding interfere with their work and relationships. They may also use steroids and other potentially dangerous muscle-building drugs.

Gender Matters

Gender, Ethnicity, and Body Image

Body Image and Gender

Women are much more likely than men to be dissatisfied with their bodies, often wanting to be thinner than they are. In one study, only 30% of eighth-grade girls reported being content with their bodies, while 70% of their male classmates expressed satisfaction with their looks. Girls and women are much more likely than boys and men to diet, develop eating disorders, and be obese.

One reason that girls and women are dissatisfied with their bodies is that they are influenced by the media—particularly advertisements and women's fashion magazines. Most teen girls report that the media influence their idea of the perfect body and their decision to diet. In a study of adult women, viewing pictures of thin models in magazines had an immediate negative effect on their mood. In another study, 68% of female college students felt worse about their own appearance after looking through women's magazines. Some 75% of normal-weight women think they are overweight, and 90% overestimate their body size. Clearly, media images affect women's self-image and self-esteem. For American women of all ages, success is still too often equated with how we look rather than who we are.

It is important to note that the image of the ideal woman presented in the media is often unrealistic and even unhealthy. In a review of BMI data for Miss America pageant winners since 1922, researchers noted a significant decline in BMI over time, with an increasing number of recent winners having BMIs in the underweight category. The average fashion model is 4–7 inches taller and more than 25 pounds lighter than the average American woman. Most fashion models are thinner than 98% of American women.

Our culture may be promoting an unattainable masculine ideal as well. Researchers surveying male undergraduates found that media consumption was positively associated with a desire for thinness and muscularity. Researchers studying male action figures such as GI Joe from the past 40 years noted that they have become increasingly muscular. A recent Batman action figure, if projected onto a man of average height, would result in someone with a 30-inch waist, 57-inch chest, and 27-inch biceps. Such media messages can be demoralizing, and, although not as commonly, boys and men do also suffer from body image problems.

Body Image and Ethnicity

The thin, toned look as a feminine ideal is just a fashion, one that is not shared by all cultures. Although some groups espouse thinness as an ideal body type, others do not. In many traditional African societies, for example, full-figured women's bodies are seen as symbols of health, prosperity, and fertility. African American teenage girls have a much more positive body image than do white girls; in one survey, two-thirds of them defined beauty as "the right attitude," whereas white girls were more preoccupied with weight and body shape.

A study of college students found that white and Latina students tend to have more body image problems than African American and Asian American students; black students had the most positive general body image among the groups of students in the study. Nevertheless, recent evidence indicates that African American women are as likely to engage in disordered eating behavior, especially binge eating and vomiting, as their Latina, American Indian, and white counterparts. These findings underscore the complex nature of eating disorders and body image.

Avoiding Body Image Problems

To minimize your risk of developing a body image problem, keep the following strategies in mind:

- Focus on healthy habits and good physical health. Eat a moderate, balanced diet, and choose physical activities you enjoy. Avoid chronic or repetitive dieting.
- Focus on good psychological health and put concerns about physical appearance in perspective. Your worth as a human being is not dependent on how you look.
- Practice body acceptance. You can influence your body size and type to some degree through lifestyle, but the basic fact is that some people are genetically designed to be bigger or heavier than others. Focus on healthy lifestyle behaviors and accept your body as it is.
- Find things to appreciate in yourself besides an idealized body image. Men and women whose self-esteem is based primarily on standards of physical attractiveness can find it difficult to age gracefully. Those who can learn to value other aspects of themselves are more accepting of the physical changes that occur naturally with age.
- View food choices as morally neutral—eating dessert isn't bad and doesn't make you a bad person. Healthy eating habits are an important part of a wellness lifestyle, but the things you really care about and do are more important in defining who you are.
- Don't judge yourself or others based on appearance. Watch your attitudes toward people of differing body sizes and shapes, and don't joke about someone's body type. Take people seriously for what they say and do, not for their appearance. Body size is just one external characteristic; millions of happy and successful people also just happen to have a weight problem.
- See the beauty and fitness industries for what they are. Realize that one of their goals is to prompt dissatisfaction with yourself so that you will buy their products.

Acceptance and Change

Most Americans, young and old, are unhappy with some aspect of their appearance, often their weight. The can-do attitude of Americans, together with the belief that there is a solution to this dissatisfaction, leads to more problems with body image, as well as to dieting, disordered eating, and the desire for cosmetic surgery to fix perceived defects.

In fact, there are limits to the changes that can be made to body weight and body shape, both of which are influenced by heredity. The changes that can and should be made are lifestyle changes—engaging in regular physical activity, obtaining adequate nutrition, and maintaining healthy eating habits. With these changes, the body weight and shape that develop will be natural and appropriate for an individual's particular genetic makeup.

Knowing when the limits to healthy change have been reached—and learning to accept those limits—is crucial for overall wellness. Women in particular tend to measure self-worth in terms of their appearance; when they don't measure up to an unrealistic cultural ideal, they see themselves as defective and their self-esteem falls. The result can be negative body image, disordered eating, or even a full-blown eating disorder. Women who view their bodies positively tend to be more intuitive eaters, relying on internal hunger and fullness cues to regulate what and how much they eat. They think more about how their bodies feel and function than how they appear to others.

Weight management needs to take place in a positive and realistic atmosphere. For an obese person, losing as few as 10 pounds can reduce blood pressure and improve mood. The hazards of excessive dieting and overconcern about body weight need to be countered by a change in attitude. A reasonable weight must take into account a person's weight history, social circumstances, metabolic profile, and psychological well-being.

EATING DISORDERS

Problems with body weight and weight control are not limited to excessive body fat. A growing number of people, especially adolescent girls and young women, experience **eating disorders,** characterized by severe disturbances in body image, eating patterns, and eating-related behaviors. The major eating disorders are anorexia nervosa, bulimia nervosa, and binge-eating disorder. Disordered eating affects an estimated 10 million American females and 1 million males. Many more people have abnormal eating habits and attitudes about food that, although not meeting the criteria for a major eating disorder, do disrupt their lives.

Anorexia nervosa is characterized by a refusal to maintain a minimally normal body weight. **Bulimia nervosa** is characterized by repeated episodes of binge eating followed by compensatory behaviors such as self-induced vomiting, the misuse of laxatives or diuretics, fasting, or excessive exercise. **Binge-eating disorder** is characterized by binge eating without regular use of compensatory behaviors. Eating disorders are associated with depression, anxiety, low self-esteem, and increased health risks, including, in some cases, increased risk of premature death.

Eating disorders are more prevalent in developed countries than in developing ones. At any given time, 0.5–2.0% of Americans suffer from anorexia and have bulimia. Research suggests that about 10% of college-aged women suffer from clinical or borderline eating disorders and about 5% have bulimia. Binge-eating disorder may affect 2–5% of all adults and 8% of those who are obese. In the United States, anorexia and bulimia affect far more women than men: Of the 1 million Americans who develop anorexia or bulimia each year, 90% are female. Of those with binge-eating disorder, 60% are female. Eating disorder rates are increasing among males and females of all socioeconomic and cultural groups.

Factors in Developing an Eating Disorder

Many factors are probably involved in the development of an eating disorder. Although wildly different explanations have been proposed, they share one central feature: a dissatisfaction with body image and body weight. Such dissatisfaction is created by distorted thinking, including perfectionistic beliefs, unreasonable demands for self-control, and excessive self-criticism. Dissatisfaction with body weight leads to dysfunctional attitudes about eating, such as fear of fat and preoccupation with food, and problematic eating behaviors, including excessive dieting, constant calorie counting, and frequent weighing.

Heredity appears to play a role in the development of eating disorders, accounting for more than 50% of the risk. But as with other conditions, only the tendency to develop an eating disorder is explained by heredity; the expression of this tendency is affected by other factors. The home environment is one factor: Families in which there is hostility, abuse, or lack of cohesion provide fertile ground for the development of an eating disorder; a rigid or overprotective parent can also increase risk. Cultural messages, as well as family, friends, and peers, shape attitudes toward the self and others. Comparing oneself negatively with others can damage self-esteem and increase vulnerability. Young people who see themselves as lacking control over their lives are also at high risk for eating disorders. About 90% of eating disorders begin during adolescence. In recent years, however, cases of eating disorders have increased among children as young as 8.

Certain turning points in life, such as leaving home for college, often trigger an eating disorder. How a person copes

Terms

Ww

eating disorder A serious disturbance in eating patterns or eating-related behavior, characterized by a negative body image and concerns about body weight or body fat.

anorexia nervosa An eating disorder characterized by a refusal to maintain body weight at a minimally healthy level and an intense fear of gaining weight or becoming fat; self-starvation.

bulimia nervosa An eating disorder characterized by recurrent episodes of binge eating and purging—overeating and then using compensatory behaviors such as vomiting, laxatives, and excessive exercise to prevent weight gain.

binge-eating disorder An eating disorder characterized by binge eating and a lack of control over eating behavior in general.

with such stresses can influence risk, particularly in individuals who have few stress-management skills. An eating disorder may become a means of coping: The abnormal eating behavior—starvation, **purging,** or binge eating—reduces anxiety by producing numbness and alleviating emotional pain. Restrictive dieting is another possible trigger for the development of eating disorders.

Anorexia Nervosa

A person with anorexia nervosa does not eat enough food to maintain a reasonable body weight. Anorexia affects 1% of Americans, or about 3 million people, 95% of them female. Although it can occur later, anorexia typically develops between the ages of 12 and 18.

Characteristics of Anorexia Nervosa People with anorexia have an intense fear of gaining weight or becoming fat. Their body image is so distorted that even when emaciated they think they are fat. People with anorexia may engage in compulsive behaviors or rituals that help keep them from eating, though some may also binge and purge. They often use vigorous and prolonged exercise to reduce body weight as well. Although they may express a great interest in food, even taking over the cooking responsibilities for the rest of the family, their own diet becomes more and more extreme. People with anorexia often hide or hoard food without eating it.

Anorexic people are typically introverted, emotionally reserved, and socially insecure. They are often model children who rarely complain and are anxious to please others and win their approval. Although school performance is typically above average, they are often critical of themselves and not satisfied with their accomplishments. For people with anorexia nervosa, their entire sense of self-esteem may be tied up in their evaluation of their body shape and weight.

Health Risks of Anorexia Nervosa Because of extreme weight loss, females with anorexia often stop menstruating, become intolerant of cold, and develop low blood pressure and heart rate. They develop dry skin that is often covered by fine body hair like that of an infant. Their hands and feet may swell and take on a blue tinge.

Anorexia nervosa has been linked to a variety of medical complications, including disorders of the cardiovascular, gastrointestinal, endocrine, and skeletal systems. When body fat is virtually gone and muscles are severely wasted, the body turns to its own organs in a desperate search for protein. Death can occur from heart failure caused by electrolyte imbalances. About one in ten women with anorexia dies of starvation, cardiac arrest, or other medical complications—the highest death rate for any psychiatric disorder. Depression is also a serious risk, and about half the fatalities related to anorexia are suicides.

Bulimia Nervosa

A person suffering from bulimia nervosa engages in recurrent episodes of binge eating followed by purging. Bulimia is often difficult to recognize because sufferers conceal their eating habits and usually maintain a normal weight, although they may experience weight fluctuations of 10–15 pounds. Although bulimia usually begins in adolescence or young adulthood, it has begun to emerge at increasingly younger (11–12 years) and older (40–60 years) ages.

Characteristics of Bulimia Nervosa During a binge, a bulimic person may rapidly consume anywhere from 1000 to 60,000 calories. This is followed by an attempt to get rid of the food by purging, usually by vomiting or using laxatives or diuretics. During a binge, bulimics feel as though they have lost control and cannot stop or limit how much they eat. Some binge and purge only occasionally; others do so many times every day.

People with bulimia may appear to eat normally, but they are rarely comfortable around food. Binges usually occur in secret and can become nightmarish—ravaging the kitchen for food, going from one grocery store to another to buy food, or even stealing food. During the binge, food acts as an anesthetic, and all feelings are blocked out. Afterward, bulimics feel physically drained and emotionally spent. They usually feel deeply ashamed and disgusted with both themselves and their behavior and terrified that they will gain weight from the binge.

Major life changes such as leaving for college, getting married, having a baby, or losing a job can trigger a binge-purge cycle. At such times, stress is high and the person may have no good outlet for emotional conflict or tension. As with anorexia, bulimia sufferers are often insecure and depend on others for approval and self-esteem. They may hide difficult emotions such as anger and disappointment from themselves and others. Binge eating and purging become a way of dealing with feelings.

Health Risks of Bulimia Nervosa The binge-purge cycle of bulimia places a tremendous strain on the body and can have serious health effects. Contact with vomited stomach acids erodes tooth enamel. Bulimic people often develop tooth decay because they binge on foods that contain large amounts of simple sugars. Repeated vomiting or the use of laxatives, in combination with deficient calorie intake, can damage the liver and kidneys and cause cardiac arrhythmia. Chronic hoarseness and esophageal tearing

Term

VW

purging The use of vomiting, laxatives, excessive exercise, restrictive dieting, enemas, diuretics, or diet pills to compensate for food that has been eaten and that the person fears will produce weight gain.

with bleeding may also result from vomiting. More rarely, binge eating can lead to rupture of the stomach. Although many bulimic women maintain normal weight, even a small weight loss to lower-than-normal weight can cause menstrual problems. And although less often associated with suicide or premature death than anorexia, bulimia is associated with increased depression, excessive preoccupation with food and body image, and sometimes disturbances in cognitive functioning.

Binge-Eating Disorder

Binge-eating disorder affects about 2% of American adults. It is characterized by uncontrollable eating, usually followed by feelings of guilt and shame with weight gain. Common eating patterns are eating more rapidly than normal, eating until uncomfortably full, eating when not hungry, and preferring to eat alone. Binge eaters may eat large amounts of food throughout the day, with no planned mealtimes. Many people with binge-eating disorder mistakenly see rigid dieting as the only solution to their problem. However, rigid dieting usually causes feelings of deprivation and a return to overeating.

Compulsive overeaters rarely eat because of hunger. Instead, food is used as a means of coping with stress, conflict, and other difficult emotions or to provide solace and entertainment. People who do not have the resources to deal effectively with stress may be more vulnerable to binge-eating disorder. Inappropriate overeating often begins during childhood. In some families, eating may be used as an activity to fill otherwise empty time. Parents may reward children with food for good behavior or withhold food as a means of punishment, thereby creating distorted feelings about the use of food.

Binge eaters are almost always obese, so they face all the health risks associated with obesity. In addition, binge eaters may have higher rates of depression and anxiety. To overcome binge eating, a person must learn to put food and eating into proper perspective and develop other ways of coping with stress and painful emotions.

Borderline Disordered Eating

Eating habits and body image run a continuum from healthy to seriously disordered. Where each of us falls along that continuum can change depending on life stresses, illnesses, and many other factors. People with borderline disordered eating have some symptoms of eating disorders but do not meet the full diagnostic criteria for anorexia, bulimia, or binge-eating disorder. Behaviors such as excessive dieting, occasional bingeing or purging, or the inability to control eating turn food into the enemy and create havoc in the lives of millions of Americans.

How do you know if you have disordered eating habits? When thoughts about food and weight dominate your life, you have a problem. If you're convinced that your worth as a person hinges on how you look and how much you weigh, it's time to get help. Other danger signs include frequent feelings of guilt after a meal or snack, any use of vomiting or laxatives after meals, or overexercising or severely restricting your food intake to compensate for what you've already eaten.

If you suspect you have an eating problem, don't go it alone or delay getting help, as disordered eating habits can develop into a full-blown eating disorder. Check with your student health or counseling center—nearly all colleges have counselors and medical personnel who can help you or refer you to a specialist if needed. If you are concerned about eating habits of a family member or friend, refer to the suggestions in the box "If Someone You Know Has an Eating Disorder . . ." on page 440.

Treating Eating Disorders

The treatment of eating disorders must address both problematic eating behaviors and the misuse of food to manage stress and emotions. Anorexia nervosa treatment first involves averting a medical crisis by restoring adequate body weight; then the psychological aspects of the disorder can be addressed. The treatment of bulimia nervosa or binge-eating disorder involves first stabilizing the eating patterns, then identifying and changing the patterns of thinking that led to disordered eating, and then improving coping skills. Concurrent problems, such as depression or anxiety, must also be addressed.

In 2006, a study published in the *Journal of the American Medical Association* showed that the antidepressant Prozac, which is widely used to treat anorexia, worked no better than a placebo in preventing recurrence in women recovering from the disorder. However, the anti-seizure drug topiramate has shown promise in the treatment of bulimia, reducing the urges to binge and purge.

Treatment of eating disorders usually involves a combination of psychotherapy and medical management. The therapy may be carried out individually or in a group; sessions involving the entire family may be recommended. A support or self-help group can be a useful adjunct to such treatment. Medical professionals, including physicians, dentists, gynecologists, and registered dietitians, can evaluate and manage the physical damage caused by the disorder. If a patient is severely depressed or emaciated, hospitalization may be necessary.

Today's Challenge

Although most people don't succumb to irrational or distorted ideas about their bodies, many do become obsessed with dieting. The challenge facing Americans today is achieving a healthy body weight without excessive dieting—by adopting and maintaining sensible eating habits, an active lifestyle, realistic and positive attitudes and emotions, and creative ways of handling stress.

Take Charge

If Someone You Know Has an Eating Disorder . . .

- Educate yourself about eating disorders and their risks and about treatment resources in your community. (See the For More Information section for suggestions.)
- Write down specific ways the person's eating problem is affecting you or others in the household. Call a house meeting to talk about how others are affected by the problem and how to take action.
- Consider consulting a professional about the best way to approach the situation. Research how and where your friend can get help. Attend a local support group.
- Arrange to speak privately with the person, along with other friends or family members. Let one person lead the group and do most of the talking. Discuss specific incidents and the consequences of disordered eating.
- If you are going to speak with your friend, write down ahead of time what your concerns are and what you would like to say. Expect that the person you are concerned about will deny there is a problem, minimize it, or become angry with you. Remain calm and nonjudgmental, and continue to express your concern.
- Avoid giving simplistic advice about eating habits. Gently encourage your friend to eat properly.
- Take time to listen to your friend, and express your support and understanding. Encourage honest communication. Emphasize your friend's good characteristics and compliment all her or his successes.
- Help maintain the person's sense of dignity by encouraging personal responsibility and decision making. Be patient and realistic; recovery is a long process. Continue to love and support your friend.
- If the situation is an emergency—if the person has fainted or attempted suicide, for example—take immediate action. Call 911 for help.
- If you feel very upset about the situation, seek professional help. Remember, you are not to blame for another person's eating disorder.

Tips for Today

Maintaining a healthy weight means balancing calories in with calories out. Many forces and factors in contemporary society work against a healthy balance, so it's imperative that individuals take active control of managing their weight. Many approaches work, but the simplest formula is moderate food intake coupled with regular exercise.

Right now you can

- Drink a glass of water instead of a soda.
- Throw away any high-calorie, low-nutrient snack foods in your kitchen and buy fruits and vegetables as snacks instead.
- Put a sign on your refrigerator reminding you of your weight-management goals.
- Go outside and walk or jog for 15 minutes or take a 15-minute bike ride.
- Review the information on portion sizes in Chapter 12 and consider whether the portions you usually take at meals are larger than they need to be.

SUMMARY

- Body composition is the relative amounts of fat-free mass and fat in the body. *Overweight* and *obesity* refer to body weight or the percentage of body fat that exceeds what is associated with good health.
- The key to weight management is maintaining a balance of calories in (food) and calories out (resting metabolism, food digestion, and physical activity).
- Standards for assessing body weight and body composition include body mass index (BMI) and percent body fat.
- Too much or too little body fat is linked to health problems; the distribution of body fat can also be a significant risk factor.
- An inaccurate or negative body image is common and can lead to psychological distress.
- Genetic factors help determine a person's weight, but the influence of heredity can be overcome with attention to lifestyle factors.
- Physiological factors involved in the regulation of body weight and body fat include metabolic rate, hormonal influences, and the size and number of fat cells.
- Nutritional guidelines for weight management include consuming a moderate number of calories; limiting portion sizes, energy density, and the intake of fat, simple sugars, refined carbohydrates, and protein to recommended levels; and developing an eating schedule and rules for food choices.
- Activity guidelines for weight management emphasize daily physical activity and regular sessions of cardiorespiratory endurance exercise and strength training.
- Weight management requires developing positive, realistic self-talk and self-esteem and a repertoire of appropriate techniques for handling stress and other emotional and physical challenges.

Behavior Change Strategy

A Weight-Management Program

The behavior management plan described in Chapter 1 provides an excellent framework for a weight-management program. Following are some suggestions about specific ways you can adapt that general plan to controlling your weight.

Motivation and Commitment

Make sure you are motivated and committed before you begin. Failure at weight loss is a frustrating experience that can make it more difficult to lose weight in the future. Think about why you want to lose weight. Self-focused reasons, such as to feel good about yourself or to have a greater sense of well-being, are often associated with success. Trying to lose weight for others or out of concern for how others view you is a poor foundation for a weight-loss program. Make a list of your reasons for wanting to lose weight, and post it in a prominent place.

Setting Goals

Choose a reasonable weight you think you would like to reach over the long term, and be willing to renegotiate it as you get further along. Break down your long-term weight and behavioral goals into a series of short-term goals. Develop a new way of behaving by designing small, manageable steps that will get you to where you want to go.

Creating a Negative Energy Balance

When your weight is constant, you are burning approximately the same number of calories as you are taking in. To tip the energy balance toward weight loss, you must either consume fewer calories, or burn more calories through physical activity, or both. One pound of body fat represents 3500 calories. To lose weight at the recommended rate of 0.5–2.0 pounds per week, you must create a negative energy balance of 1750–7000 calories per week or 250–1000 calories per day. To generate a negative energy balance, it's usually best to begin by increasing activity level rather than decreasing your calorie consumption.

Physical Activity

Consider how you can increase your energy output simply by increasing routine physical activity, such as walking or taking the stairs. (Figure 13-4 shows activities that use about 150 calories.) If you are not already involved in a regular exercise routine aimed at increasing endurance and building or maintaining muscle mass, seek help from someone who is competent to help you plan and start an appropriate exercise routine. If you are already doing regular physical exercise, evaluate your program according to the guidelines in Chapter 13.

Don't try to use exercise to spot reduce. Leg lifts, for example, contribute to fat loss only to the extent that they burn calories; they don't burn fat just from your legs. You can make parts of your body appear more fit by exercising them, but the only way you can reduce fat in any specific part of your body is to create an overall negative energy balance.

Diet and Eating Habits

If you can't generate a large enough negative energy balance solely by increasing physical activity, you may want to supplement exercise with modest cuts in your calorie intake. Don't think of this as going on a diet; your goal is to make small changes in your diet that you can maintain for a lifetime. Focus on cutting your intake of saturated and trans fats and added sugars and on eating a variety of nutritious foods in moderation. Don't skip meals, fast, or go on a very-low-calorie diet or a diet that is unbalanced.

Making changes in eating habits is another important strategy for weight management. If your program centers on a conscious restriction of certain food items, you're likely to spend all your time thinking about the forbidden foods. Focus on *how* to eat rather than *what* to eat. Refer to the box "Strategies for Successful Weight Management" for suggestions.

Self-Monitoring

Keep a record of your weight and behavior change progress. Try keeping a record of everything you eat. Write down what you plan to eat, in what quantity, *before* you eat. You'll find that just having to record something that is not OK to eat is likely to stop you from eating it. If you also note what seems to be triggering your urges to eat (for example, you feel bored, or someone offered you something), you'll become more aware of your weak spots and be better able to take corrective action. Also, keep track of your daily activities and your formal exercise program so you can monitor increases in physical activity.

Putting Your Plan into Action

- Examine the environmental cues that trigger poor eating and exercise habits, and devise strategies for dealing with them. For example, you may need to remove problem foods from your house temporarily or put a sign on the refrigerator reminding you to go for a walk instead of having a snack. Anticipate problem situations, and plan ways to handle them more effectively.
- Create new environmental cues that will support your new healthy behaviors. Put your walking shoes by the front door. Move fruits and vegetables to the front of the refrigerator.
- Get others to help. Talk to friends and family members about what they can do to support your efforts. Find a buddy to join you in your exercise program.
- Give yourself lots of praise and rewards. Think about your accomplishments and achievements and congratulate yourself. Plan special nonfood treats for yourself, such as a walk or a movie. Reward yourself often and for anything that counts toward success.
- If you do slip, tell yourself to get back on track immediately, and don't waste time on self-criticism. Think positively instead of getting into a cycle of guilt and self-blame. Don't demand too much of yourself.
- Don't get discouraged. Be aware that although weight loss is bound to slow down after the first loss of body fluid, the weight loss at this slower rate is more permanent than earlier, more dramatic, losses.
- Remember that weight management is a lifelong project. You need to adopt reasonable goals and strategies that you can maintain over the long term.

- People can be successful at long-term weight loss on their own, by combining diet and exercise.
- Diet books, OTC diet aids and supplements, and formal weight-loss programs should be assessed for safety and efficacy.
- Professional help is needed in cases of severe obesity; medical treatments include prescription drugs, surgery, and psychological therapy.
- Dissatisfaction with weight and shape are common to all eating disorders. Anorexia nervosa is characterized by self-starvation, distorted body image, and an intense fear of gaining weight. Bulimia nervosa is characterized by recurrent episodes of uncontrolled binge eating and frequent purging. Binge-eating disorder involves binge eating without regular use of compensatory purging.

Take Action

1. **Interview a successful dieter:** Identify some people who have successfully lost weight and kept it off, and interview them. What were their strategies and techniques? In what ways did they change their exercise and eating habits? Do you think their approach would work for others?

2. **Assess your body composition:** Find out what percentage of your body weight is fat by taking one of the tests described in this chapter at your campus health clinic, sports medicine clinic, or health club. If you have too high or too low a proportion of body fat, consider taking steps to change it.

3. **Critique advertisements:** Leaf through a few fashion and fitness magazines, and evaluate the "ideal" body types presented for women and men. Are they realistic? Are they healthy? How does looking at them affect you? Consider writing letters to advertisers; voice your opinion (positive or negative) about the body types and images they present.

For More Information

Books

Beck, C. 2004. *Anorexia and Bulimia for Dummies*. Hoboken, N.J.: John Wiley & Sons. *An easy-to-understand guide to eating disorders.*

Critser, G. 2004. *Fat Land: How Americans Became the Fattest People in the World*. Boston: Mariner Books. *A look at the many factors in American life that have contributed to the rapid increase in obesity rates.*

Dillon, E. 2006. *Issues That Concern You: Obesity*. New York: Greenhaven Press. *A collection of perspectives on the causes of obesity, its management, and its impact on individuals and society.*

Ferguson, J. M., and C. Ferguson. 2003. *Habits Not Diets*, 4th ed. Boulder, Colo.: Bull. *A behavior-change approach to changing diet and activity habits that includes many helpful practical tips, assessment worksheets, and tracking forms.*

Gaesser, G. A., and K. Kratina. 2006. *It's the Calories, Not the Carbs*. Victoria, B.C.: Trafford Publishing. *Provides a detailed look at the facts behind successful weight loss by shunning fad diets and practicing sound energy balance.*

Hensrud, D. D. 2005. *Mayo Clinic Healthy Weight for Everyone*. Rochester, Minn.: Mayo Clinic. *Provides guidelines for successful weight management.*

Ihde, G. M. 2006. *Considering Weight-Loss Surgery: The Facts You Need to Know for a Healthy Recovery*. Victoria, B.C.: Trafford. *An easy-to-read guide to the benefits and risks of weight-loss surgery.*

Milchovich, S. K., and B. Dunn-Long. 2003. *Diabetes Mellitus: A Practical Handbook*, 8th. ed. Boulder, Colo.: Bull. *A user-friendly guide to diabetes.*

Organizations, Hotlines, and Web Sites

American Diabetes Association. Provides information, a free newsletter, and referrals to local support groups; the Web site includes an online diabetes risk assessment.
800-342-2383
http://www.diabetes.org

Calorie Control Council. Site includes a variety of interactive calculators, including an Exercise Calculator that estimates the calories burned from various forms of physical activity.
http://www.caloriecontrol.org

Cyberdiet. Provides a variety of assessment and planning tools as well as practical tips for adopting a healthy lifestyle.
http://www.cyberdiet.com

FDA Center for Food Safety and Applied Nutrition: Dietary Supplements. Provides background facts and information on the current regulatory status of dietary supplements, including compounds marketed for weight loss.
http://www.cfsan.fda.gov/~dms/supplmnt.html

Federal Trade Commission (FTC): Project Waistline. Provides advice for evaluating advertising about weight-loss products.
http://www.ftc.gov/bcp/conline/edcams/waistline/index.html

National Heart, Lung, and Blood Institute (NHLBI): Aim for a Healthy Weight. Provides information and tips on diet and physical activity, as well as a BMI calculator.
http://www.nhlbi.nih.gov/health/public/heart/obesity/lose_wt

National Institute of Diabetes and Digestive and Kidney Diseases (NIDDK). Provides information and referrals for problems related to obesity, weight control, and nutritional disorders.
877-946-4627
http://win.niddk.nih.gov/

Partnership for Healthy Weight Management. Provides information on evaluating weight-loss programs and advertising claims.
http://www.consumer.gov/weightloss

SmallStep.Gov. Provides resources for increasing activity and improving diet through small changes in daily habits.
http://www.smallstep.gov

U.S. Consumer Gateway: Health—Dieting and Weight Control. Provides links to government sites with advice on evaluating claims about weight-loss products and programs.
http://www.consumer.gov/health.htm

USDA Food and Nutrition Information Center: Weight and Obesity. Provides links to recent reports and studies on the issue of obesity among Americans.
http://www.nal.usda.gov/fnic/reports/obesity.html

Resources for people concerned about eating disorders:

Eating Disorder Referral and Information Center
http://www.edreferral.com
Eating Disorders Shared Awareness
http://www.something-fishy.org
MedlinePlus: Eating Disorders
http://www.nlm.nih.gov/medlineplus/eatingdisorders.html
National Association of Anorexia Nervosa and Associated Disorders
847-831-3438 (referral line)
http://www.anad.org
National Eating Disorders Association
800-931-2237
http://www.nationaleatingdisorders.org

See also the listings in Chapters 12 and 13.

Selected Bibliography

Adams, K. F., et al. 2006. Overweight, obesity, and mortality in a large prospective cohort of persons 50 to 71 years old. *The New England Journal of Medicine* 355(8): 763–778.

American College of Sports Medicine. 2006. *ACSM's Resource Manual for Guidelines for Exercise Testing and Prescription,* 5th ed. Philadelphia: Lippincott Williams & Wilkins.

American Diabetes Association. 2004. *How to Tell if You Have Pre-Diabetes* (http://www.diabetes.org/pre-diabetes/pre-diabetes-symptoms.jsp; retrieved August 22, 2006).

American Dietetic Association. 2006. *Evidence Based Guidelines: Adult Weight Management* (http://www.eatright.org; retrieved August 22, 2006).

Baker, B. 2006. Weight loss and diet plans. *American Journal of Nursing* 106(6): 52–59.

Behn, A., and E. Ur. 2006. The obesity epidemic and its cardiovascular consequences. *Current Opinions in Cardiology* 21(4): 353–360.

Bowman, S. A., et al. 2004. Effects of fast-food consumption on energy intake and diet quality among children in a national household survey. *Pediatrics* 113(1 Pt 1): 112–118.

Buchwald, H., et al. 2004. Bariatric surgery: A systematic review and meta-analysis. *Journal of the American Medical Association* 292(14): 1724–1737.

Centers for Disease Control and Prevention. 2004. *Overweight and Obesity: Economic Consequences* (http://www.cdc.gov/nccdphp/dnpa/obesity/economic_consequences.htm; retrieved January 3, 2005).

Centers for Disease Control and Prevention. 2004. Prevalence of diabetes among Hispanics—selected areas, 1998–2002. *Morbidity and Mortality Weekly Report* 53(40): 941–944.

Centers for Disease Control and Prevention. 2006. *Diabetes Care.* Atlanta, Ga.: U.S. Department of Health and Human Services, Centers for Disease Control and Prevention.

Dong, L., G. Block, and S. Mandel. 2004. Activities contributing to total energy expenditure in the United States: Results from the NHAPS Study. *International Journal of Behavioral Nutrition and Physical Activity* 1(4).

Farshchi, H. R., M. A. Taylor, and I. A. Macdonald. 2005. Deleterious effects of omitting breakfast on insulin sensitivity and fasting lipid profiles in healthy lean women. *American Journal of Clinical Nutrition* 81(2): 388–396.

Flegal, K. M., et al. 2005. Excess deaths associated with underweight, overweight, and obesity. *Journal of the American Medical Association* 293(15): 1861–1867.

Fenicchia, L. M., et al. 2004. Influence of resistance exercise training on glucose control in women with type 2 diabetes. *Metabolism* 53(3): 284–289.

Fung, T. T., et al. 2004. Dietary patterns, meat intake, and the risk of type 2 diabetes in women. *Archives of Internal Medicine* 164(20): 2235–2240.

Graves, B. S., and R. L. Welsh. 2004. Recognizing the signs of body dysmorphic disorder and muscle dysmorphia. *ACSM's Health and Fitness Journal,* January/February.

Hu, F. B., et al. 2004. Adiposity as compared with physical activity in predicting mortality among women. *New England Journal of Medicine* 351(26): 2694–2703.

Kaiser Family Foundation. 2004. The role of media in childhood obesity. *Issue Brief,* February.

Ma, Y., et al. 2005. Association between dietary carbohydrates and body weight. *American Journal of Epidemiology* 161(4): 359–367.

McBride, B. F., et al. 2004. Electrocardiographic and hemodynamic effects of a multicomponent dietary supplement containing ephedra and caffeine. *Journal of the American Medical Association* 291(4): 216–221.

McCullough, P. A., et al. 2006. Cardiorespiratory fitness and short-term complications after bariatric surgery. *CHEST* 130: 517–525.

Mokdad, A. H., et al. 2005. Correction: Actual causes of death in the United States, 2000. *Journal of the American Medical Association* 293(3): 293–294.

Muenning, P., et al. 2006. Gender and the burden of disease attributable to obesity. *American Journal of Public Health* 96(9): 1662–1668.

Nicklas, B. J., et al. 2004. Association of visceral adipose tissue with incident myocardial infarction in older men and women: The Health, Aging and Body Composition Study. *American Journal of Epidemiology* 160(8): 741–749.

O'Brien, P., et al. 2006. Treatment of mild to moderate obesity with laparoscopic adjustable gastric banding or an intensive medical program. *Annals of Internal Medicine* 144(9): 625–633.

Ogden, C. L., et al. 2006. Prevalence of overweight and obesity in the United States, 1999–2004. *Journal of the American Medical Association* 295(13): 1549–1555.

Olshansky, S. J., et al. 2005. A potential decline in life expectancy in the United States in the 21st century. *New England Journal of Medicine* 352(11): 1138–1145.

Schulze, M. B., et al. 2004. Sugar-sweetened beverages, weight gain, and incidence of type 2 diabetes in young and middle-aged women. *Journal of the American Medical Association* 292(8): 927–934.

Scott, B. J. 2002. Frame size, circumference and skinfolds. *Handbook of Nutrition and Food.* Boca Raton, Fla.: CRC Press.

Sweeteners can sour your health. 2005. *Consumer Reports on Health,* January.

Taylor, E. N., et al. 2005. Obesity, weight gain, and risk of kidney stones. *Journal of the American Medical Association* 293(4): 455–462.

Tsai, A. G., and T. A. Wadden. 2005. Systematic review: An evaluation of major commercial weight loss programs in the United States. *Annals of Internal Medicine* 142(1): 56–66.

U.S. Department of Health and Human Services. 2005. *Dietary Guidelines for Americans* (http://www.healthierus.gov/dietaryguidelines; retrieved August 22, 2006).

van Dam, R. M., et al. 2006. The relationship between overweight in adolescence and premature death in women. *Annals of Internal Medicine* 145(2): 91–97.

Vorona, R. D., et al. 2005. Overweight and obese patients in a primary care population report less sleep than patients with a normal body mass index. *Archives of Internal Medicine* 165: 25–30.

Walsh, T. B., et al. 2006. Fluoxetine after weight restoration in anorexia nervosa. *Journal of the American Medical Association* 295(22): 2605–2612.

Wansink, B., and P. Chandon. 2006. Meal size, not body size, explains errors in estimating calorie content of meals. *Annals of Internal Medicine* 145: 326–332.

Weinstein, A. R., et al. 2004. Relationship of physical activity vs. body mass index with type 2 diabetes in women. *Journal of the American Medical Association* 292(10): 1188–1194.

Weinstein, P. K. 2006. A review of weight loss programs delivered via the Internet. *Journal of Cardiovascular Nursing* 21(4): 251–258.

Wong, S. L., et al. 2004. Cardiorespiratory fitness is associated with lower abdominal fat independent of body mass index. *Medicine and Science in Sports and Exercise* 36(2): 286–291.

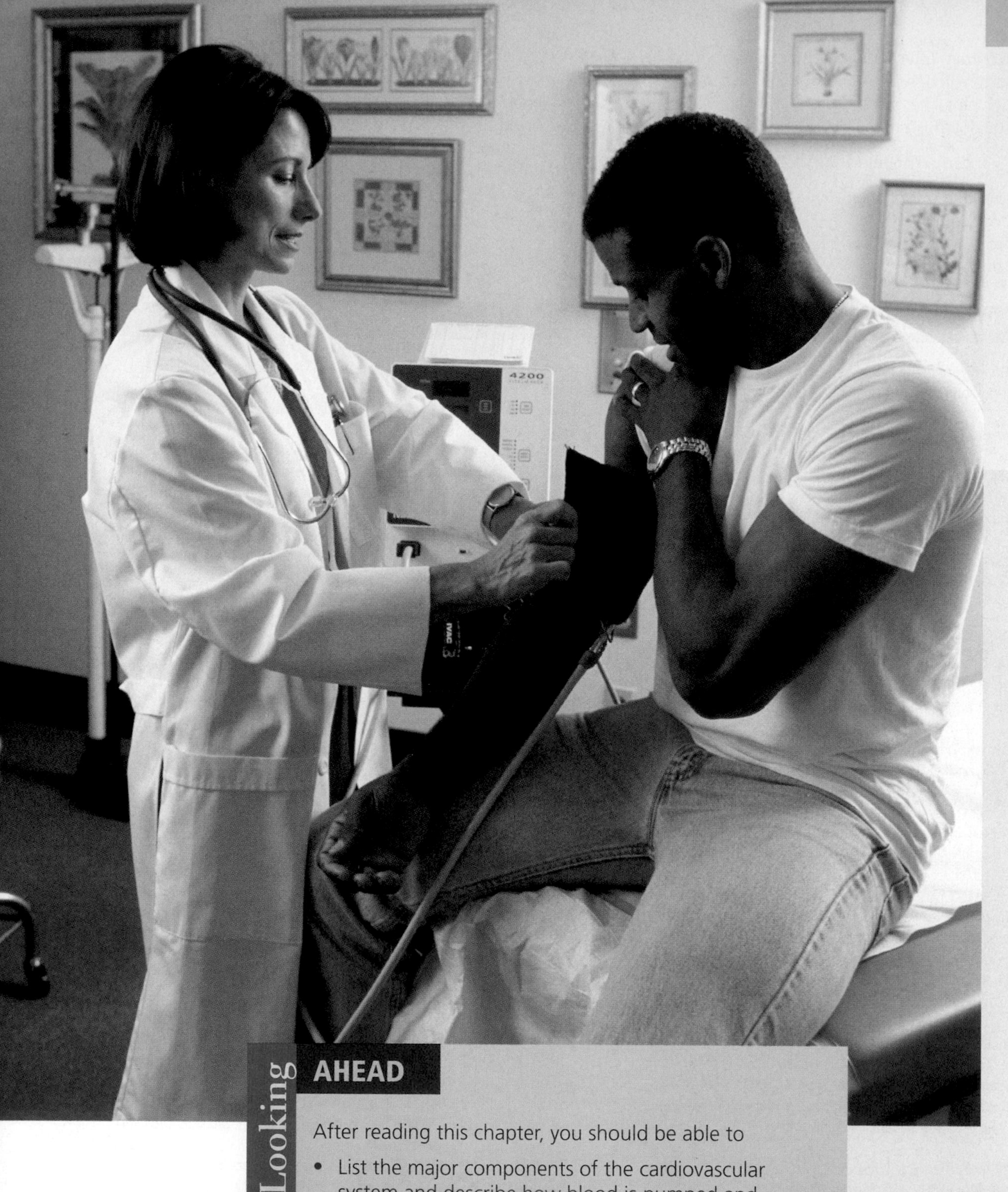

15

Looking AHEAD

After reading this chapter, you should be able to

- List the major components of the cardiovascular system and describe how blood is pumped and circulated throughout the body
- Describe the controllable and uncontrollable risk factors associated with cardiovascular disease
- Discuss the major forms of cardiovascular disease and how they develop
- List the steps you can take to lower your personal risk of developing cardiovascular disease

Cardiovascular Health

Test Your Knowledge

1. **Reducing the amount of cholesterol you eat is the most important dietary change you can make to improve your blood cholesterol levels.**
   True or false?
2. **Women are about as likely to die of cardiovascular disease as they are to die of breast cancer.**
   True or false?
3. **On average, how much earlier does heart disease develop in people who don't exercise regularly than in people who do?**
   a. 6 months
   b. 2 years
   c. 6 years
4. **Healthy teenagers have no signs of cardiovascular disease.**
   True or false?
5. **Which of the following foods would be a good choice for promoting heart health?**
   a. brown rice
   b. salmon
   c. bananas

ANSWERS

1. FALSE. Limiting your intake of saturated and trans fats, which promote the production of cholesterol by the liver, is the key dietary change for improving blood cholesterol levels; dietary cholesterol has much less of an effect on blood cholesterol.
2. FALSE. Cardiovascular disease kills far more. Among American women, about 1 in 2 deaths is due to cardiovascular disease and about 1 in 30 is due to breast cancer.
3. C. Both aerobic exercise and strength training significantly improve cardiovascular health.
4. FALSE. Autopsy studies of young trauma victims show that narrowing of the arteries that supply the heart with blood begins in adolescence in many people.
5. ALL THREE. Whole grains (such as whole wheat, oatmeal, rye, barley, and brown rice), foods with omega-3 fatty acids (salmon), and foods high in potassium and low in sodium (bananas) all improve cardiovascular health.

Visit the *Core Concepts in Health* Online Learning Center (www.mhhe.com/insel10e) for study aids and many additional resources.

Cardiovascular disease (CVD) affects more than 71 million Americans and is the leading cause of death in the United States, claiming one life every 35 seconds—about 2500 Americans every day. Nearly half of all Americans alive today will die from CVD. Heart attacks and strokes are the most common life-threatening manifestations of CVD. Though we typically think of CVD as primarily affecting men and older adults, heart attack is the number-one killer of American women, and nearly a third of heart attacks occur in people under age 65.

CVD is largly due to our way of life. Too many Americans eat an unhealthy diet, are overweight and sedentary, smoke, manage stress ineffectively, have uncontrolled high blood pressure or high cholesterol levels, and don't know the signs of CVD. Not all the risk factors for CVD are controllable—for example, the older you are, the greater your risk for CVD. But many key risk factors can be treated or modified, and you can reduce your risk for CVD.

Exactly what is CVD, and how does it do its damage? More important, what steps can you take now to keep your heart healthy throughout your life? This chapter will provide some answers to these questions.

THE CARDIOVASCULAR SYSTEM

The cardiovascular system consists of the heart and blood vessels; together, they move blood throughout the body.

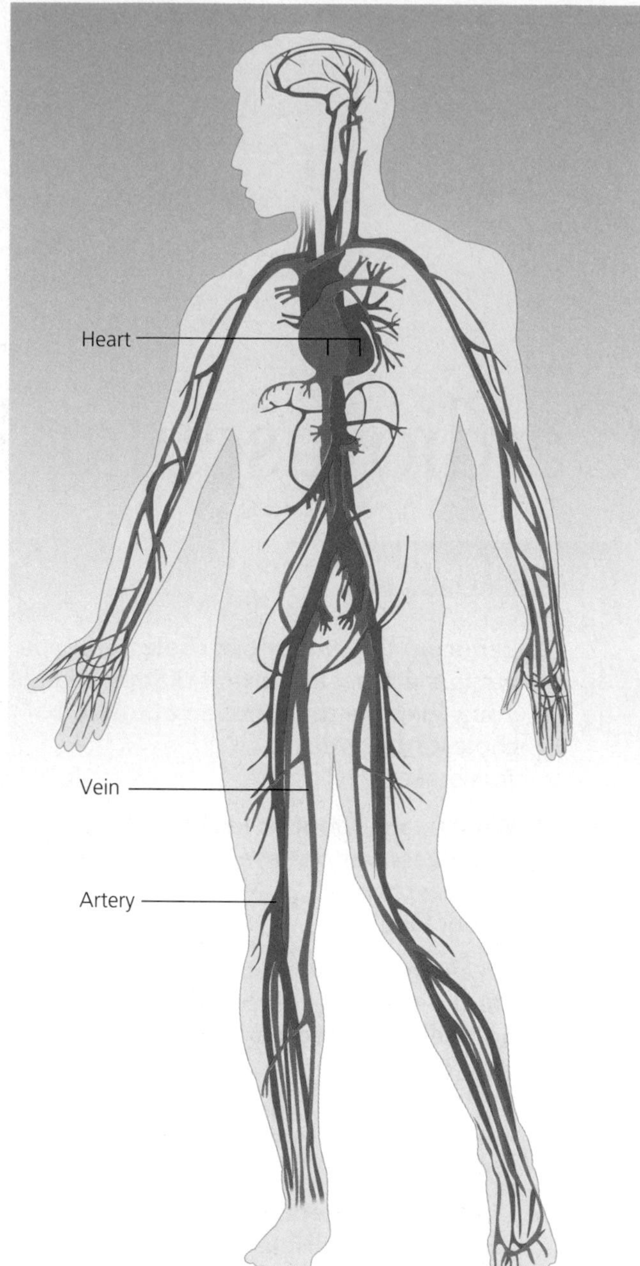

Figure 15-1 The cardiovascular system.

A 150-pound person has about 5 quarts of blood, which circulates about once every minute.

The heart is a four-chambered, fist-size muscle located just beneath the ribs under the left breast (Figure 15-1). It pumps deoxygenated (oxygen-poor) blood to the lungs and oxygenated (oxygen-rich) blood to the rest of the body. There are two circulatory systems. Deoxygenated blood from the body enters the right side of the heart, which pumps blood to the lungs in a process called **pulmonary circulation.** After going through the lungs, oxygenated blood enters the left side of the heart and is pumped to the rest of the body through **systemic circulation.**

Terms

Vw

cardiovascular disease (CVD) The collective term for various forms of diseases of the heart and blood vessels.

pulmonary circulation The part of the circulatory system governed by the right side of the heart; the circulation of blood between the heart and the lungs.

systemic circulation The part of the circulatory system governed by the left side of the heart; the circulation of blood between the heart and the rest of the body.

atria The two upper chambers of the heart in which blood collects before passing to the ventricles.

vena cava The large vein through which blood is returned to the right atrium of the heart.

ventricles The two lower chambers of the heart that pump blood through arteries to the lungs and other parts of the body.

aorta The large artery that receives blood from the left ventricle and distributes it to the body.

systole Contraction phase of the heart.

diastole Relaxation phase of the heart.

sinus node A collection of specialized cells in the right atrium that serves as the pacemaker of the heart.

veins Vessels that carry blood to the heart.

arteries Vessels that carry blood away from the heart.

coronary arteries A system of arteries branching from the aorta that provides blood to the heart muscle.

capillaries Very small blood vessels that serve to exchange oxygen and nutrients between the blood and the tissues.

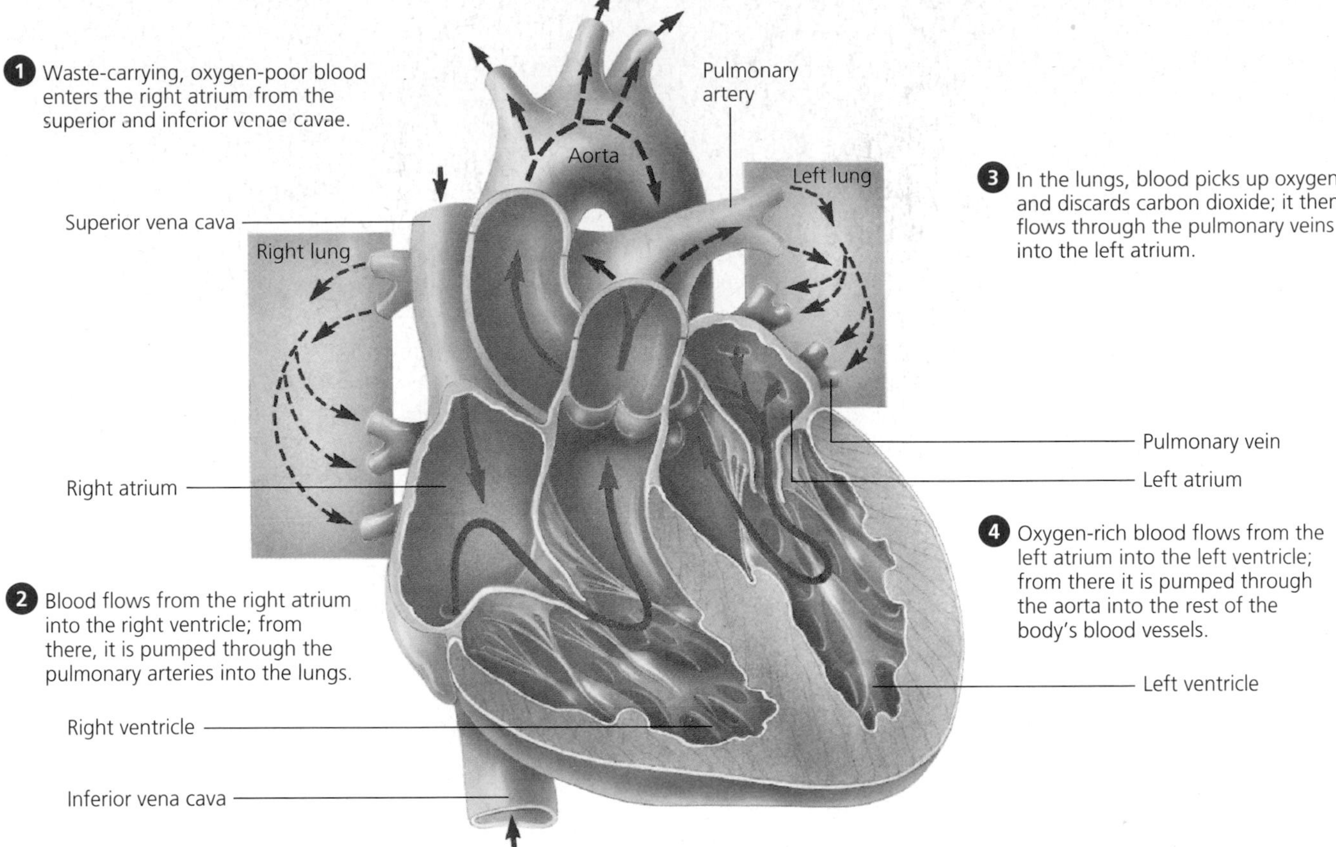

1 Waste-carrying, oxygen-poor blood enters the right atrium from the superior and inferior venae cavae.
Aorta
Pulmonary artery
Left lung
3 In the lungs, blood picks up oxygen and discards carbon dioxide; it then flows through the pulmonary veins into the left atrium.
Superior vena cava
Right lung
Pulmonary vein
Left atrium
Right atrium
4 Oxygen-rich blood flows from the left atrium into the left ventricle; from there it is pumped through the aorta into the rest of the body's blood vessels.
2 Blood flows from the right atrium into the right ventricle; from there, it is pumped through the pulmonary arteries into the lungs.
Left ventricle
Right ventricle
Inferior vena cava

Figure 15-2 Circulation in the heart.

Used, oxygen-poor blood enters the right upper chamber, or **atrium,** of the heart through the **vena cava,** the largest vein in the body (Figure 15-2). Valves prevent the blood from flowing the wrong way. As the right atrium fills, it contracts and pumps blood into the right lower chamber, or **ventricle,** which then contracts and pumps blood through the pulmonary artery into the lungs. There, blood picks up oxygen and discards carbon dioxide. Cleaned, oxygenated blood then flows through the pulmonary veins into the left atrium. As this chamber fills, it contracts and pumps blood into the powerful left ventricle, which pumps the blood through the **aorta,** the body's largest artery, to be fed into the rest of the body's blood vessels. The period of the heart's contraction is called **systole;** the period of relaxation is called **diastole.**

The heartbeat—the split-second sequence of contractions of the heart's four chambers—is controlled by electrical impulses. These signals originate in a bundle of specialized cells in the right atrium called the **sinus node.** Unless the pace is sped up or slowed down by the brain in response to stimuli such as danger or exhaustion, the heart produces electrical impulses at a steady rate.

Blood vessels are classified by function and size. **Veins** carry blood to the heart; **arteries** carry blood away from the heart. Veins have thin walls; arteries have thick elastic walls that enable them to expand or contract with the volume of the blood being pumped through them. After leaving the heart, the aorta branches into smaller and smaller vessels. Two vital arteries, the left and right **coronary arteries,** branch off the aorta to carry blood back to the heart muscle itself (Figure 15-3).

The smallest arteries branch further into **capillaries,** tiny vessels only one cell thick. The capillaries deliver oxygen and nutrient-rich blood to the tissues and receive oxygen-poor, waste-carrying blood. From the capillaries, this blood empties into small veins and then into larger veins that eventually return it to the heart. From there the cycle is repeated.

RISK FACTORS FOR CARDIOVASCULAR DISEASE

Researchers have identified a variety of factors associated with an increased risk of developing cardiovascular disease. They are grouped into two categories: major risk factors and contributing risk factors. Some risk factors, such as diet, exercise habits, and use of tobacco, are linked to controllable aspects of lifestyle and can therefore be changed. Others, such as age, sex, and heredity, are beyond an individual's control.

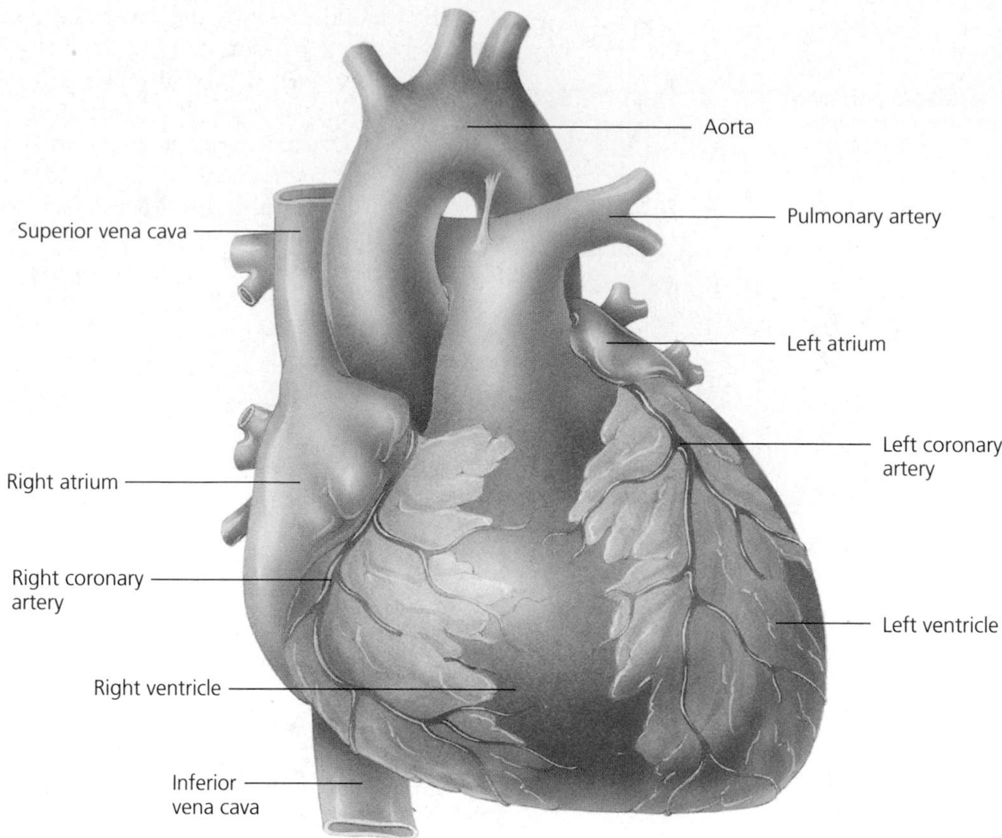

Figure 15-3 Blood supply to the heart.

Major Risk Factors That Can Be Changed

The American Heart Association (AHA) has identified six major risk factors for CVD that can be changed: tobacco use, high blood pressure, unhealthy blood cholesterol levels, physical inactivity, obesity, and diabetes.

Tobacco Use About one in five deaths from CVD is attributable to smoking. Despite a 47% decline in smoking since 1965, it remains the number-one preventable cause of CVD in the United States. People who smoke a pack of cigarettes a day have twice the risk of heart attack as nonsmokers; smoking two or more packs a day triples the risk. And when smokers do have heart attacks, they are 2 to 4 times more likely than nonsmokers to die from them. Cigarette smoking also doubles the risk of stroke. Women who smoke heavily and use oral contraceptives are up to 32 times more likely to have a heart attack and up to 20 times more likely to have a stroke than women who don't smoke and take the pill.

Smoking raises the risk for CVD in several ways. Nicotine increases blood pressure and heart rate; the carbon monoxide in cigarette smoke displaces oxygen in the blood, reducing the oxygen available to the heart and other parts of the body. Smoking damages the linings of arteries, reduces levels of high-density lipoproteins (HDL), and raises levels of triglycerides and low-density lipoproteins (LDL). It causes the **platelets** in blood to become sticky and cluster, promoting clotting. Smoking also speeds the development of fatty deposits in arteries.

You don't have to smoke to be affected. The risk of death from coronary heart disease increases up to 30% among those exposed to environmental tobacco smoke (ETS) at home or at work. Researchers estimate that as many as 35,000 nonsmokers die from CVD each year as a result of exposure to ETS. A 2006 Surgeon General's report concluded that there is no safe level of exposure to secondhand smoke.

High Blood Pressure High blood pressure, or **hypertension,** is a risk factor for many forms of cardiovascular disease, including heart attacks and strokes, and is itself considered a form of CVD. Hypertension can also cause kidney failure and damage to nearly every organ in the body. Blood pressure, the force exerted by the blood on the vessel walls, is created by the pumping action of the heart. When the heart contracts (systole), blood pressure increases. When the heart relaxes (diastole), pressure decreases. High blood pressure occurs when too much force is exerted against the walls of the arteries. Many

Table 15-1 Blood Pressure Classification for Healthy Adults

Category[a]	Systolic (mm Hg)		Diastolic (mm Hg)
Normal[b]	below 120	and	below 80
Prehypertension	120–139	or	80–89
Hypertension[c]			
Stage 1	140–159	or	90–99
Stage 2	160 and above	or	100 and above

[a]When systolic and diastolic pressure fall into different categories, the higher category should be used to classify blood pressure status.
[b]The risk of death from heart attack and stroke begins to rise when blood pressure is above 115/75.
[c]Based on the average of two or more readings taken at different physician visits. In persons older than 50 years, systolic blood pressure greater than 140 is a much more significant CVD risk factor than diastolic blood pressure.

SOURCE: *The Seventh Report of the Joint National Committee on Prevention, Detection, Evaluation, and Treatment of High Blood Pressure.* 2003. Bethesda, Md.: National Heart, Lung, and Blood Institute. National Institutes of Health (NIH Publication No. 03-5233).

factors affect blood pressure, such as exercise or excitement. Short periods of high blood pressure are normal, but chronic high blood pressure is a health risk.

Blood pressure is measured with a stethoscope and an instrument called a sphygmomanometer. It is expressed as two numbers—for example, 120 over 80—and measured in millimeters of mercury. The first number is the systolic blood pressure; the second is the diastolic blood pressure. A normal blood pressure reading for a healthy adult is 115 systolic over 75 diastolic; CVD risk increases when blood pressure rises above this level. High blood pressure in adults is defined as equal to or greater than 140 over 90 (Table 15-1).

High blood pressure results from an increased output of blood by the heart or from increased resistance to blood flow in the arteries. The latter condition can be caused by constriction of smooth muscle surrounding the arteries or by **atherosclerosis,** a disease process that causes arteries to become clogged and narrowed. High blood pressure also scars and hardens arteries, making them less elastic and further increasing blood pressure. When a person has high blood pressure, the heart must work harder than normal to force blood through the narrowed and stiffened arteries, straining both the heart and arteries. Eventually, the strained heart weakens and tends to enlarge, which weakens it even more.

High blood pressure is often called a silent killer, because it usually has no symptoms. A person may have high blood pressure for years without realizing it. But during that time, it damages vital organs and increases the risk of heart attack, congestive heart failure, stroke, kidney failure, and blindness. In about 90% of people with high blood pressure, the cause is unknown. This type of high blood pressure is called primary (or essential) hypertension and is probably due to a mixture of genetic and environmental factors, including obesity, stress, excessive alcohol intake, inactivity, and a high-fat, high-salt diet. In the remaining 10% of people, the condition is caused by an underlying illness and is referred to as secondary hypertension.

Hypertension is common, occurring in nearly one in three adults. Overall, about 30% of adults (65 million people) have hypertension, and 30% have prehypertension. The incidence of high blood pressure increases with age; however, it can occur among children and young adults, and women sometimes develop hypertension during pregnancy (blood pressure usually returns to normal following the pregnancy). High blood pressure is two to three times more common in women taking oral contraceptives, especially in obese and older women; this risk increases with the duration of use. The risk of developing hypertension is highest in African Americans, in whom, compared with other groups, the disorder is often more severe, more resistant to treatment, and more likely to be fatal at an early age. Among people age 20–39, African Americans also have higher rates of prehypertension.

Primary hypertension cannot be cured, but it can be controlled. Because hypertension has no early warning signs, it's crucial to have your blood pressure tested at least once every 2 years (more often if you have other CVD risk factors). Follow your physician's advice about lifestyle changes and medication. Unfortunately, only about 63% of Americans with hypertension are aware that they have it, and only about 34% with hypertension have it under control.

Lifestyle changes are recommended for everyone with prehypertension and hypertension. These changes include weight reduction, regular exercise, a healthy diet, and moderation of alcohol use. The DASH diet (see Chapter 12) is recommended; it emphasizes eating more fruits, vegetables, and whole grains and increasing potassium and fiber intake. A 2006 study showed that even small increases in fruit and vegetable intake created measurable drops in blood pressure. Reducing salt intake is also recommended. Many people are salt-sensitive, meaning that their blood pressure will decrease significantly when salt intake is restricted. Salt restriction has less impact on those who are not salt-sensitive, but it may still be beneficial.

Terms

platelets Microscopic disk-shaped cell fragments in the blood that activate on contact with foreign objects and release chemicals that are necessary for the formation of blood clots.

hypertension Sustained abnormally high blood pressure.

atherosclerosis A form of CVD in which the inner layers of artery walls are made thick and irregular by plaque deposits; arteries become narrow, and blood supply is reduced.

African Americans, in particular, can reduce their blood pressure by lowering their salt intake, getting more potassium, and following the DASH diet. The 2005 Dietary Guidelines for Americans recommend restricting sodium consumption to less than 2300 mg (about 1 teaspoon of salt) per day. People with hypertension, African Americans, and middle-aged and older adults should aim to consume no more than 1500 mg of sodium per day. Adequate potassium intake is also important. The recommended intake is 4.7 grams per day, which should be obtained through food. Supplements should be taken only when recommended by a physician; excessively high levels of potassium can be lethal.

For people whose blood pressure isn't adequately controlled with lifestyle changes, medication is prescribed. Many different types of antihypertensive drugs are available; the right one usually lowers blood pressure effectively with few side effects.

Recent research has shed new light on the importance of lowering blood pressure to improve cardiovascular health. Death rates from CVD begin to rise when blood pressure is above 115 over 75, well below the traditional 140 over 90 cutoff for hypertension. People with blood pressures in the prehypertension range are at increased risk of heart attack and stroke as well as at significant risk of developing full-blown hypertension; preventive lifestyle measures are strongly recommended for people with prehypertension. Lowering your blood pressure is beneficial, even if your current blood pressure is already below 140 over 90.

High Levels of Cholesterol Cholesterol is a fatty, waxlike substance that circulates through the bloodstream and is an important component of cell membranes, sex hormones, vitamin D, the fluid that coats the lungs, and the protective sheaths around nerves. Adequate cholesterol is essential for the proper functioning of the body. However, excess cholesterol can clog arteries and increase the risk of cardiovascular disease. Our bodies obtain cholesterol in two ways: from the liver, which manufactures it, and from the foods we eat.

GOOD VERSUS BAD CHOLESTEROL Cholesterol is carried in the blood in protein-lipid packages called lipoproteins (Figure 15-4). **Low-density lipoproteins (LDLs)** shuttle cholesterol from the liver to the organs and tissues that require it. LDL is known as bad cholesterol because if there is more than the body can use, the excess is deposited in the blood vessels. LDL that accumulates and becomes trapped in artery walls may be oxidized by free radicals, speeding inflammation and damage to artery walls and increasing the likelihood of a blockage. If coronary arteries are blocked, the result may be a heart attack; if an artery carrying blood to the brain is blocked, a stroke may occur. **High-density lipoproteins (HDLs),** or good cholesterol, shuttle unused cholesterol back to the liver for recycling. By removing cholesterol from blood vessels, HDL helps protect against atherosclerosis.

RECOMMENDED BLOOD CHOLESTEROL LEVELS The risk for cardiovascular disease increases with higher blood cholesterol levels, especially LDL (Table 15-2). The National Cholesterol Education Program (NCEP) recommends lipoprotein testing at least once every 5 years for all adults, beginning at age 20. The recommended test is

Terms

VW

low-density lipoprotein (LDL) Blood fat that transports cholesterol from the liver to organs and tissues; excess is deposited on artery walls, where it can eventually block the flow of blood to the heart and brain; "bad" cholesterol.

high-density lipoprotein (HDL) Blood fat that helps transport cholesterol out of the arteries and thus protects against heart diseases; "good" cholesterol.

Table 15-2 Cholesterol Guidelines

LDL cholesterol (mg/dl)*	
Less than 100	Optimal
100–129	Near optimal/above optimal
130–159	Borderline high
160–189	High
190 or more	Very high
Total cholesterol (mg/dl)	
Less than 200	Desirable
200–239	Borderline high
240 or more	High
HDL cholesterol (mg/dl)	
Less than 40	Low (undesirable)
60 or more	High (desirable)
Triglycerides (mg/dl)	
Less than 150	Normal
150–199	Borderline high
200–499	High
500 or more	Very high

*These are general goals for LDL; specific LDL goals depend on a person's other risk factors; for people at very high risk, an LDL goal of less than 70 mg/dl may be appropriate.

SOURCES: Grundy, S. M., et al. 2004. Implications of recent clinical trials for the National Cholesterol Education Program Adult Treatment Panel III Guidelines. *Circulation* 110: 227–239; Expert Panel on Detection, Evaluation, and Treatment of High Blood Cholesterol in Adults. 2001. Executive Summary of the Third Report of the National Cholesterol Education Program (NCEP) Expert Panel on Detection, Evaluation, and Treatment of High Blood Cholesterol in Adults (Adult Treatment Panel III). *Journal of the American Medical Association* 285(19).

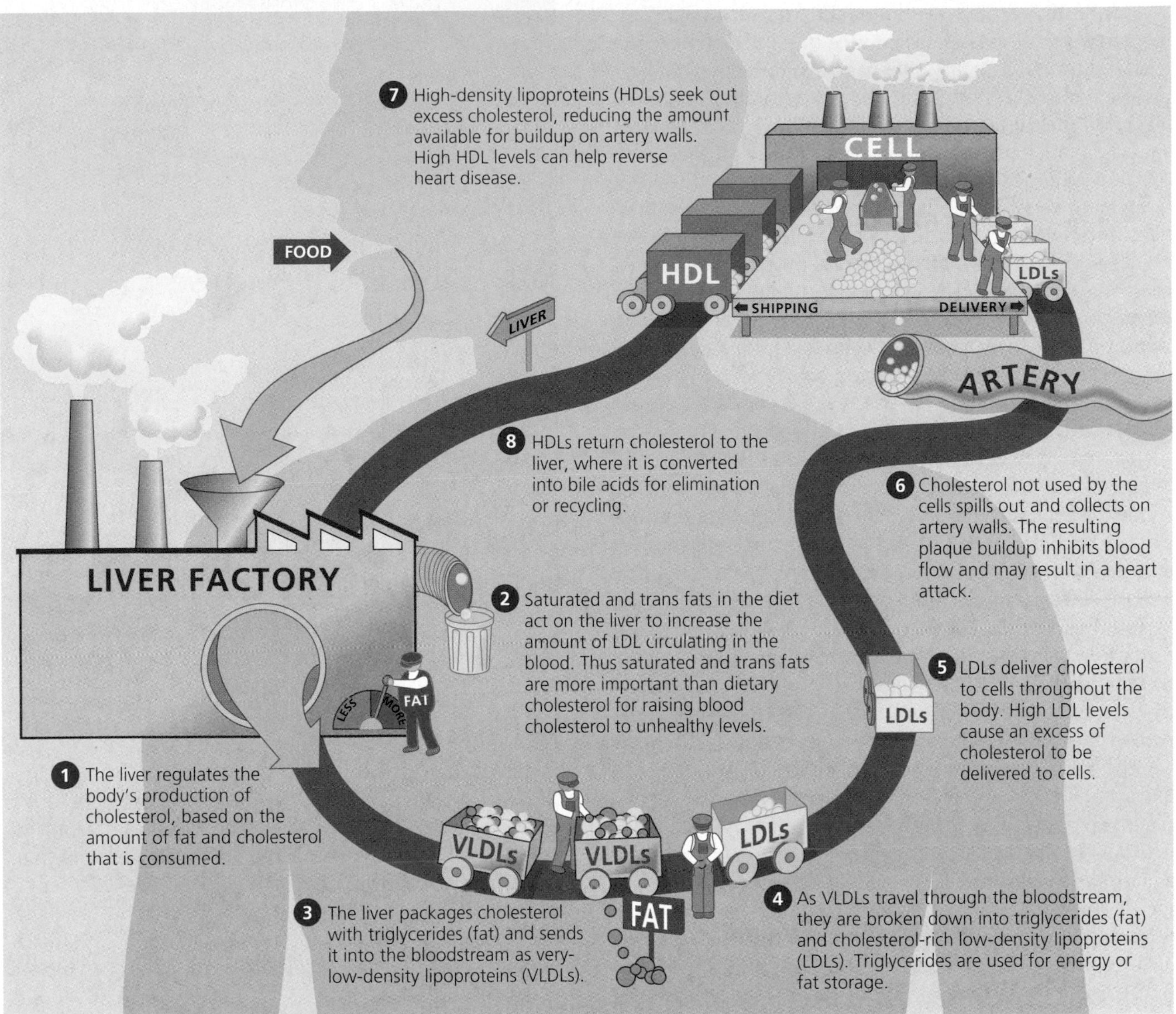

7 High-density lipoproteins (HDLs) seek out excess cholesterol, reducing the amount available for buildup on artery walls. High HDL levels can help reverse heart disease.
CELL
FOOD
HDL
LDLs
SHIPPING
DELIVERY
LIVER
ARTERY
8 HDLs return cholesterol to the liver, where it is converted into bile acids for elimination or recycling.
6 Cholesterol not used by the cells spills out and collects on artery walls. The resulting plaque buildup inhibits blood flow and may result in a heart attack.
LIVER FACTORY
2 Saturated and trans fats in the diet act on the liver to increase the amount of LDL circulating in the blood. Thus saturated and trans fats are more important than dietary cholesterol for raising blood cholesterol to unhealthy levels.
LESS
MORE
FAT
LDLs
5 LDLs deliver cholesterol to cells throughout the body. High LDL levels cause an excess of cholesterol to be delivered to cells.
1 The liver regulates the body's production of cholesterol, based on the amount of fat and cholesterol that is consumed.
VLDLs
VLDLs
LDLs
FAT
3 The liver packages cholesterol with triglycerides (fat) and sends it into the bloodstream as very-low-density lipoproteins (VLDLs).
4 As VLDLs travel through the bloodstream, they are broken down into triglycerides (fat) and cholesterol-rich low-density lipoproteins (LDLs). Triglycerides are used for energy or fat storage.

Figure 15-4 Travels with cholesterol.

a fasting lipoprotein profile that measures total cholesterol, LDL cholesterol, HDL cholesterol, and triglycerides (another blood fat). In general, high LDL, total cholesterol, and triglyceride levels and low HDL levels are associated with a higher risk for CVD; lowering LDL, total cholesterol, and triglycerides can lower risk. Raising HDL is important because a high HDL level seems to offer protection from CVD even in cases where total cholesterol is high. This seems to be especially true for women.

As shown in Table 15-2, LDL levels below 100 mg/dl (milligrams per deciliter) and total cholesterol levels below 200 mg/dl are desirable. An estimated 100 million American adults—about half the adult population—have total cholesterol levels of 200 mg/dl or higher. The CVD risk associated with elevated cholesterol levels also depends on other factors. For example, an above-optimal level of LDL would be of more concern for an individual who also smokes and has high blood pressure than for an individual without these additional CVD risk factors, and it is especially a concern for diabetics. Specific NCEP guidelines for cholesterol based on risk factors are presented later in the chapter.

BENEFITS OF CONTROLLING CHOLESTEROL People can cut their heart attack risk by about 2% for every 1% that they reduce their total blood cholesterol levels. People who lower their total cholesterol from 250 to 200 mg/dl, for example, reduce their risk of heart attack by 40%. In addition, studies indicate that improving LDL and HDL levels not only reduces the likelihood that arteries will become clogged but may also reverse deposits on artery walls, thereby actually helping clean out diseased arteries.

How can you improve your cholesterol levels? Your primary goal should be to reduce your LDL to healthy levels. Important dietary changes for reducing LDL levels include substituting unsaturated for saturated and trans fats and increasing fiber intake. Decreasing your intake of saturated and trans fats is particularly important because they promote the production of cholesterol by the liver. Exercising regularly and eating more fruits, vegetables, fish, and whole grains also help. Many experts believe cholesterol-lowering foods may be most effective when eaten in combination, rather than separately. You can raise your HDL levels by exercising regularly, losing weight if you are overweight, quitting smoking, and altering the amount and type of fat you consume.

Physical Inactivity A sedentary lifestyle is a known major risk factor for CVD, but despite an increasing awareness of the risks of inactivity, only about 30% of American adults are getting the recommended amount of physical activity. People, especially females, become less active as they age, and rates of activity are particularly low among certain ethnic populations and people who have little education and low incomes and who live in the north-central and southern states.

Regular physical activity has direct and indirect benefits on the heart. Directly, it lowers heart rate and blood pressure, while improving the strength with which the heart pumps blood to the body and the ability of the tissues to extract oxygen from that blood. Indirectly, physical activity positively affects almost every risk factor for CVD. Exercise is thought to be the closest thing we have to a magic bullet against heart disease. It lowers CVD risk by helping decrease blood pressure, increase HDL levels, maintain desirable weight, and prevent or control diabetes; exercise also improves the functioning of the endothelial cells that line coronary arteries and decreases platelet aggregation, which can lead to clot formation in the coronary arteries.

In general, the more physical activity you engage in, the more cardiovascular benefit you derive. A minimum of 30 minutes per day of moderate-intensity physical activity is recommended. For those attempting to manage weight, prevent gradual weight gain, or maintain weight loss, 60–90 minutes per day are recommended. One recent study found that women who accumulated at least 3 hours of brisk walking each week cut their risk of heart attack and stroke by more than half. More intense or longer-duration exercise has even greater health benefits.

Terms

endothelial cells Cells lining the inside of arteries; they help regulate blood flow and prevent platelets from sticking.

hypertrophy Abnormal enlargement of an organ secondary to an increase in cell size.

A diet high in fiber and low in saturated and trans fats can help lower levels of total cholesterol and LDL. This young woman is eating a vegetable sandwich on whole-grain bread with fresh fruit for lunch.

Obesity As your weight increases, your risk of CVD increases. The risk of death from CVD is two to three times more likely in obese people (BMI ≥ 30) than it is in lean people (BMI 18.5–24.9), and for every 5-unit increment of BMI, a person's risk of death from coronary heart disease increases by 30%. BMI at age 18 predicts mortality due to CVD—the higher your BMI at age 18, the more likely you are to eventually die from CVD. Maintaining a healthy weight is also important. Researchers found that middle-aged women who had gained 22 pounds or more since age 18 had a significantly higher risk of subsequent death from CVD than those who were able to maintain their weight over time.

The increased risk of CVD associated with overweight is present even if a person has no other risk factors, but, unfortunately, overweight people usually do have other CVD risk factors. Excess body fat is strongly associated with hypertension, high cholesterol levels, insulin resistance, diabetes, physical inactivity, and increasing age. It is also associated with endothelial cell dysfunction and increased inflammatory markers, such as CRP (discussed later in this chapter). **Endothelial cells** line the inside of arteries, including the coronary arteries, and they help regulate blood flow to the heart and keep platelets and other cells from sticking to artery walls. When the endothelial cells are healthy, the coronary arteries dilate (widen) when the heart needs more blood, but when the cells are dysfunctional, the coronary arteries instead constrict, limiting blood flow to the heart. With excess weight, there is also more blood to pump and the heart has to work harder. This causes chronically elevated pressures within the heart chambers that can lead to ventricular **hypertrophy,** and eventually the heart muscle can start to fail.

As discussed in Chapter 14, the distribution of body fat is significant: Fat that collects around the abdomen is more dangerous than fat that collects around the hips. Obesity in general, and abdominal obesity in particular, is significantly associated with narrowing of the coronary arteries, even in young adults in their twenties. Abdominal obesity can increase your risk even if your weight is normal. The ratio of your waist-to-hip measurements is a good indicator of your risk for heart disease. A waist-to-hip ratio of 85% or lower is optimal for women; 90% or lower is optimal for men.

Physical activity and physical fitness also have a strong positive influence on cardiovascular health in those who are overweight and obese. People who are obese but have at least moderate cardiorespiratory fitness may have lower rates of cardiovascular disease than their normal-weight but unfit peers. For someone who is overweight, even modest weight reduction—5–10% of body weight—can reduce CVD risk.

Diabetes As described in Chapter 14, diabetes is a disorder characterized by elevated blood glucose levels due to an insufficient supply or inadequate action of insulin. Diabetes doubles the risk of CVD for men and triples the risk for women. The most common cause of death in adults with diabetes is CVD, and they usually die at younger ages than people without diabetes. There is an estimated loss of 5–10 years of life in those with diabetes. The reason for the increased CVD risk among people with diabetes is complex. Diabetics have higher rates of other CVD risk factors, including hypertension, obesity, and unhealthy blood lipid levels (typically, high triglyceride levels and low HDL levels). The elevated blood glucose and insulin levels that occur in diabetes can damage the endothelial cells that line the arteries, making them more vulnerable to atherosclerosis; diabetics also often have platelet and blood coagulation abnormalities that increase the risk of heart attacks and strokes. People with pre-diabetes also face a significantly increased risk of CVD.

The number of people with diabetes (14.1 million) and pre-diabetes (14.7 million) continues to climb and is closely linked to obesity. It is estimated that for every kilogram increase in weight, the risk of diabetes increases by approximately 9%. The largest increase in prevalence of type 2 diabetes over the past decade has been among people age 30–39, and there has also been an alarming increase among children and adolescents. Children who are diagnosed with diabetes typically develop complications in their twenties or thirties. Complications of diabetes mainly affect the arteries. When small arteries are affected, the result can be problems with vision (retinopathy that can lead to blindness), kidney function (nephropathy that can require dialysis), and the nervous system (neuropathy that can lead to amputation). When the larger arteries are affected, all forms of CVD result, including heart attacks, strokes, and peripheral vascular disease. Having diabetes is considered to be a heart disease risk equivalent, meaning that your CVD morbidity and mortality risk is the same as if you already had coronary artery disease. And diabetics who do have CAD fare even worse; they have accelerated atherosclerosis and derive less benefit from common forms of treatment than nondiabetics.

Routine screening for diabetes is not currently recommended unless a person has symptoms of diabetes or other CVD risk factors. In people with pre-diabetes, a healthy diet and exercise are more effective than medication at preventing diabetes. For people with diabetes, a healthy diet, exercise, and careful control of glucose levels are recommended to decrease chances of developing complications. Unfortunately, even people whose diabetes is under control face a high risk of CVD, so control of other risk factors is critical.

Contributing Risk Factors That Can Be Changed

Various other factors that can be changed have been identified as contributing to CVD risk, including triglyceride levels and psychological and social factors.

High Triglyceride Levels Like cholesterol, triglycerides are blood fats that are obtained from food and manufactured by the body. High triglyceride levels are a reliable predictor of heart disease, especially if associated with other risk factors, such as low HDL levels, obesity, and diabetes. Factors contributing to elevated triglyceride levels include excess body fat, physical inactivity, cigarette smoking, type 2 diabetes, excess alcohol intake, very high carbohydrate diets, and certain diseases and medications.

Much of the picture regarding triglycerides remains unclear, however. Studies have yet to show whether lowering triglyceride levels will actually decrease heart disease. Elevated triglyceride levels are most often seen in people with other lipid abnormalities; and the lifestyle modifications that help lower cholesterol also help decrease triglycerides, making it difficult to identify any potential independent benefit of lowering triglyceride levels.

A full lipid profile should include testing and evaluation of triglyceride levels (see Table 15-2). For people with borderline high triglyceride levels, increased physical activity, reduced intake of added sugars, and weight reduction can help bring levels down into the healthy range; for people with high triglyceride levels, drug therapy may be recommended. Being moderate in the use of alcohol and quitting smoking are also important.

Psychological and Social Factors Many of the psychological and social factors that influence other areas of wellness are also important risk factors for CVD. The idea that the mind and the body are connected certainly seems to be true when it comes to the heart. When you become excited or stressed or angry, you can probably feel your heart pounding harder and faster. The cardiovascular system is affected by both sudden, acute episodes of mental stress and the more chronic, underlying emotions of anger, anxiety, and depression.

STRESS Excessive stress can strain the heart and blood vessels over time and contribute to CVD. When you experience stress, the brain tells the adrenal glands to secrete cortisol and **catecholamines,** which in turn activate the sympathetic nervous system. As described in Chapter 2, the sympathetic nervous system causes the fight-or-flight response; this response increases heart rate and blood pressure so that more blood is distributed to the heart and other muscles in anticipation of physical activity. Blood glucose concentrations and cholesterol also increase to provide a source of energy, and the platelets become activated so that they will be more likely to clot in case of injury. Such a response can be adaptive if you're being chased by a hungry lion but may be more detrimental than useful if you're sitting at a desk taking an exam.

If you are healthy, you can tolerate the cardiovascular responses that take place during stress, but if you already have CVD, stress can lead to adverse outcomes such as abnormal heart rhythms (arrhythmias), heart attacks, and sudden cardiac death. It has long been known that an increase in heart rhythm problems and deaths is associated with acute mental stress. For example, the rate of potentially life-threatening arrhythmias in patients who already had underlying heart disease doubled during the month after the September 11 World Trade Center terrorist attacks; interestingly, this increase was not limited to people in close proximity to Manhattan.

Because avoiding all stress is impossible, having healthy mechanisms to cope with it is your best defense. Instead of adopting unhealthy habits such as smoking or overeating, use healthier coping strategies such as exercising, getting enough sleep, and talking to others.

CHRONIC HOSTILITY AND ANGER Certain traits in the hard-driving Type A personality—hostility, cynicism, and anger—are associated with increased risk of heart disease. Men prone to anger have two to three times the heart attack risk of calmer men and are much more likely to develop CVD at young ages. In a 10-year study of young adults age 18–30 years, those with high hostility levels were more than twice as likely to develop coronary artery calcification (a marker of early atherosclerosis) as those with low hostility levels. See the box "Anger, Hostility, and Heart Disease" for more information.

SUPPRESSING PSYCHOLOGICAL DISTRESS Consistently suppressing anger and other negative emotions may also be hazardous to a healthy heart. People who hide psychological distress appear to have higher rates of heart disease than people who experience similar distress but share it with others. People with such "Type D" personalities tend to be pessimistic, negative, and unhappy and to suppress these feelings. Researchers are not yet certain why the Type D trait is dangerous. It may have physical effects, or it may lead to social isolation and poor communication with physicians.

DEPRESSION In both men and women, depression appears to increase the risk of CVD in healthy individuals, and it definitely increases the risk of adverse cardiac events in those who already have heart disease. You do not need to have a major depressive disorder to be affected: For each depressive symptom you have, the risk seems to increase in a linear fashion (see Chapter 3 for symptoms of depression).

Depression is common in people with coronary heart disease (CHD), and patients who are depressed tend to have worse outcomes than those who are not. Up to a third of patients experience major depression within 1 year of having a heart attack, and those who are depressed after having a heart attack are more likely to have another heart attack or die of a cardiac cause. Even in those with CHD who have not had a recent cardiac event, up to 20% have depression, and this number may be even higher in women. Major depressive disorder at the time of treatment for coronary artery disease is associated with both short- and long-term complications, including subsequent heart attack and death.

The relationship between depression and CHD is complex and not fully understood. Those who are depressed may engage in unhealthy behaviors such as smoking and inactivity that lead to heart disease. They may not consistently take prescribed medications, and they may not cope well with having an illness or undergoing a medical procedure. Depression also causes physiologic changes; for example, it elevates basal levels of catecholamines and cortisol, which, as described earlier, increases blood pressure, blood glucose levels, cholesterol levels, and platelet aggregation.

ANXIETY Chronic anxiety and anxiety disorders (such as phobias and panic disorder) are associated with up to a threefold increased risk of coronary heart disease, heart attack, and sudden cardiac death. There is some evidence that, similar to people with depression, people with anxiety are more likely to have a subsequent adverse cardiac event after having a heart attack. At the same time, people with anxiety and depression often have medically unexplained chest pain, meaning that no evidence of coronary artery disease can be found. This can create difficulties in diagnosis and disease management, but it is important to

Term

Vw **catecholamines** A group of chemically similar hormones and neurotransmitters that are active during the fight-or-flight response; includes epinephrine and norepinephrine.

Anger, Hostility, and Heart Disease

Current research suggests that people with a quick temper, a persistently hostile outlook, and a cynical, mistrusting attitude toward life are more likely to develop heart disease than those with a calmer, more trusting attitude. People who are angry frequently, intensely, and for long periods experience the stress response—and its accompanying boosts in heart rate, blood pressure, and stress hormone levels—much more often than more relaxed individuals. Over the long term, these effects may damage arteries and promote CVD.

Are You Too Hostile?

To help answer that question, Duke University researcher Redford Williams, M.D., has devised a short self-test. It's not a scientific evaluation, but it does offer a rough measure of hostility. Are the following statements true or false for you?

1. I often get annoyed at checkout cashiers or the people in front of me when I'm waiting in line.
2. I usually keep an eye on the people I work or live with to make sure they do what they should.
3. I often wonder how homeless people can have so little respect for themselves.
4. I believe that most people will take advantage of you if you let them.
5. The habits of friends or family members often annoy me.
6. When I'm stuck in traffic, I often start breathing faster and my heart pounds.
7. When I'm annoyed with people, I really want to let them know it.
8. If someone does me wrong, I want to get even.
9. I'd like to have the last word in any argument.
10. At least once a week, I have the urge to yell at or even hit someone.

According to Williams, five or more "true" statements suggest that you're excessively hostile and should consider taking steps to mellow out.

Managing Your Anger

Begin by monitoring your angry responses and looking for triggers—people or situations that typically make you angry. Familiarize yourself with the patterns of thinking that lead to angry or hostile feelings, and then try to head them off before they develop into full-blown anger. If you feel your anger starting to build, try reasoning with yourself by asking the following questions:

1. *Is this really important enough to get angry about?* For example, is having to wait an extra 5 minutes for a late bus so important that you should stew about it for the entire 15-minute ride?
2. *Am I really justified in getting angry?* Is the person in front of you really driving slowly, or are you trying to speed?
3. *Is getting angry going to make a real and positive difference in this situation?* Will yelling and slamming the door really help your friend find the concert tickets he misplaced?

If you answer yes to all three questions, then calm but assertive communication may be an appropriate response. If your anger isn't reasonable, try distracting yourself or removing yourself from the situation. Exercise, humor, social support, and other stress-management techniques can also help (see Chapter 3 for additional anger-management tips). Your heart—and the people around you—will benefit from your calmer, more positive outlook.

SOURCES: Boyle, S. H., et al. 2005. Hostility, age, and mortality in a sample of cardiac patients. *American Journal of Cardiology* 96(1): 64–66; Heart disease: It's partly in your head. 2005. *Harvard Heart Letter,* June. QUIZ SOURCE: Williams, Virginia, and Redford Williams. *Life Skills.* New York: Times Books. Reprinted by permission of the authors.

always seek medical attention if you are unsure about the cause of your chest pain.

SOCIAL ISOLATION Social isolation and low social support (living alone, having few friends or family members, and not belonging to organizations, clubs, or churches) are associated with an increased incidence of CHD and poorer outcomes after the first diagnosis of CHD. Elderly men and women who report less emotional support from others before they have a heart attack are almost three times more likely to die in the first 6 months after the attack. This is particularly true for men. A strong social support network is a major antidote to stress. Friends and family members can also promote and support a healthy lifestyle.

LOW SOCIOECONOMIC STATUS Low socioeconomic status and low educational attainment also increase risk for CVD. These associations are probably due to a variety of factors, including lifestyle and access to health care.

Alcohol and Drugs Although moderate drinking may have health benefits for some people, drinking too much alcohol raises blood pressure and can increase the risk of stroke and heart failure. Stimulant drugs, particularly cocaine, can also cause serious cardiac problems, including heart attack, stroke, and sudden cardiac death. Cocaine stimulates the nervous system, promotes platelet aggregation, and can cause spasm in the coronary arteries. The effect of cocaine on heart attack risk is unrelated to the amount ingested, the route of administration, or the frequency of use; the risk increases if cocaine use is combined with use of tobacco or another drug. Injection drug use can cause infection of the heart and stroke.

Major Risk Factors That Can't Be Changed

A number of major risk factors for CVD cannot be changed: heredity, aging, being male, and ethnicity.

Stress and social isolation can increase the risk of cardiovascular disease. A strong social support network improves both heart health and overall wellness.

Heredity CVD is considered a genetically complex disease because there is no one gene that causes it. Instead, multiple genes contribute to the development of CVD and its associated risk factors, such as high cholesterol, hypertension, diabetes, and obesity. Having a favorable set of genes decreases your risk of developing CVD; having an unfavorable set of genes increases your risk. Risk, however, is modifiable by lifestyle factors such as whether you smoke, exercise, or eat a healthy diet.

Because of the genetic complexity of CVD, genetic screening is usually recommended for only a few specific conditions (for example, certain cholesterol disorders), but you can learn more about your personal risk just by assessing your family history. If you have a first-degree relative (parent, sibling, child) with CAD, you have a twofold increased risk of someday developing CAD yourself. Genetics seem to play an especially strong role in early CAD, which occurs before age 60. Having a family member diagnosed with early CAD increases the risk of experiencing early CAD as much as sevenfold; the risk is even higher if the affected relative is female, and the earlier the onset of the CAD, the higher the risk.

Don't forget the role of lifestyle factors, however. Coronary artery disease is usually the result of the interaction of several unfavorable genetic and lifestyle factors, and people with the greatest number of genetic and lifestyle risk factors will face the highest risks. People with favorable genes may not develop CAD despite having an unhealthy lifestyle, and people with many healthy habits may still develop CAD because they have an unfavorable genetic makeup. But it's important to remember that people who inherit a tendency for CVD are not destined to develop it. They may, however, have to work harder than other people to prevent CVD.

Aging About 70% of all heart attack victims are age 65 or older, and more than four out of five who suffer fatal heart attacks are over 65. For people over 55, the incidence of stroke more than doubles in each successive decade. However, even people in their thirties and forties, especially men, can have heart attacks.

Being Male Although CVD is the leading killer of both men and women in the United States, men face a greater risk of heart attack than women, especially earlier in life. Until age 55, men also have a greater risk of hypertension. Estrogen production, which is highest during the childbearing years, may protect premenopausal women against CVD (see the box "Women and CVD"). By age 75, the gender gap nearly disappears.

Ethnicity Death rates from heart disease vary among ethnic groups in the United States, with African Americans having much higher rates of hypertension, heart disease, and stroke than other groups (see the box "Ethnicity and CVD" on p. 458). In 2005, the FDA approved the first-ever drug for a specific racial group; the drug BiDil reduces the symptoms associated with heart failure. BiDil proved very effective in African American patients but showed little or no benefit in patients of other races. Puerto Rican Americans, Cuban Americans, and Mexican Americans are also more likely to suffer from high blood pressure and angina (a warning sign of heart disease) than non-Hispanic white Americans. Asian Americans historically have had far lower rates of CVD than white Americans.

Possible Risk Factors Currently Being Studied

In recent years, a number of other possible risk factors for cardiovascular disease have been identified. These include homocysteine, specific types of cholesterol, infectious agents, inflammation, and others.

Inflammation and C-Reactive Protein Inflammation plays a key role in the development of CVD. When an artery is injured by smoking, cholesterol, hypertension, or other factors, the body's response is to produce inflammation. A substance called C-reactive protein (CRP) is released into the bloodstream during the inflammatory response, and studies suggest that high levels of CRP indicate a substantially elevated risk of heart attack and stroke. CRP may also be harmful to the coronary arteries themselves.

In 2003, the CDC and the American Heart Association jointly recommended testing of CRP levels for people at intermediate risk for CVD because people in this risk category who are found to also have high CRP levels may benefit from additional CVD testing or treatment. (This guideline assumes that people at high risk for CVD are already receiving treatment.) Lifestyle changes and

Gender Matters: Women and CVD

CVD has traditionally been thought of as a man's disease, and until recently, this has been the justification for carrying out almost all CVD research on men. It is true that men have a higher incidence of cardiovascular problems than women, especially before age 50. On average, women live 10–15 more years free of coronary heart disease than men do. But heart disease is the leading cause of death among women, and it has killed more women than men every year since 1984.

Polls indicate that women vastly underestimate their risk of dying of a heart attack and, in turn, overestimate their risk of dying of breast cancer. In reality, nearly 1 in 2 women dies of CVD, whereas 1 in 30 dies of breast cancer. Minority women face the highest risk of developing CVD, but their awareness of heart disease as a killer of women is lower than that of white women. To help raise awareness of CVD in women, the American Heart Association launched the "Go Red for Women" campaign; visit their Web site for more information (http://www.goredforwomen.org/).

Risk factors for CVD are similar for men and women and include age, family history, smoking, hypertension, high cholesterol, and diabetes. There are some gender differences, however. HDL appears to be an even more powerful predictor of CAD risk in women than it is in men. Also, women with diabetes have a greater risk of having CVD events like heart attack and stroke than men with diabetes, so much so that diabetes appears to eliminate the 10- to 15-year advantage women traditionally have had over men for CVD.

Estrogen: A Heart Protector?

The hormone estrogen, produced naturally by a woman's ovaries until menopause, improves blood lipid concentrations and other CVD risk factors. For the past several decades, many U.S. physicians encouraged menopausal women to take hormone replacement therapy (HRT) to relieve menopause symptoms and presumably reduce the risk of CVD. However, studies found that HRT may actually *increase* a woman's risk for heart disease and certain other health problems, including breast cancer. Some newer studies have found a reduced risk of CVD in women who start HRT in the early stages of menopause (usually the mid-40s), suggesting that outcomes may depend on several factors, including the timing of hormone use. The U.S. Preventive Services Task Force and the American Heart Association currently recommend that HRT not be used to protect against CVD.

For younger women, the most common form of hormonal medication is oral contraceptives (OCs). Typical OCs contain estrogen and progestin in relatively low doses and are generally considered safe for most nonsmoking women. But women who smoke and use OCs are up to 32 times more likely to have a heart attack than nonsmoking OC users.

Postmenopausal Women: At Risk

When women do have heart attacks, they are more likely than men to die within a year. One reason is that because women develop heart disease at older ages, they are more likely to have other health problems that complicate treatment. Women have smaller hearts and arteries than men, possibly making diagnosis and treatment more difficult. There may also be unknown biological or psychosocial risk factors contributing to women's mortality.

Also, medical personnel appear to evaluate and treat women less aggressively than men. Women with positive stress tests and those whose evaluation raises concern about a heart attack are less likely to be referred to cardiac catheterization than are men and, therefore, are less likely to receive coronary angiography. When women do have coronary angiography, they are more likely than men to have normal test results. The explanation for this phenomenon of chest pain with normal coronary arteries (called *Syndrome X*) is unknown, but it is thought that women may have damage to coronary microcirculation (the heart's microscopic vessels) that is not detected by the test. In addition, studies of heart attack patients have found that women usually have to wait longer than men to receive clot-dissolving drugs in an emergency room.

Women presenting with CHD are just as likely as men to report chest pain, but are also likely to report non-chest-pain symptoms, which may obscure their diagnosis. These additional symptoms include fatigue, weakness, shortness of breath, nausea, vomiting, and pain in the abdomen, neck, jaw, and back. Women are also more likely to have pain at rest, during sleep, or with mental stress. A woman who experiences these symptoms should be persistent in seeking accurate diagnosis and appropriate treatment.

Careful diagnosis of cardiac symptoms is also key in cases of stress-induced cardiomyopathy ("broken heart syndrome"), which occurs much more commonly in women. In this condition, a severe stress response stuns the heart, producing heart-attack-like symptoms and decreased pumping function of the heart, but no damage to the heart muscle. Typically, the condition reverses quickly, and correct diagnosis is important to avoid unnecessary invasive procedures.

certain drugs can reduce CRP levels. Statin drugs, widely prescribed to lower cholesterol, also decrease inflammation and reduce CRP levels; this may be one reason that statin drugs seem to lower CVD risk even in people with normal blood lipid levels. Studies published in 2005 found that patients who received intensive statin treatment, which lowered both LDL cholesterol and CRP levels, fared better than patients who received less aggressive treatment that primarily targeted LDL levels. The reduction in risk from decreased CRP levels was independent of changes in LDL. Further research may help clarify who can benefit most from testing and treatment for CRP levels.

Insulin Resistance and Metabolic Syndrome

When you consume carbohydrate, your blood glucose level increases. This stimulates the pancreas to secrete insulin, which allows body cells to pick up glucose to use for energy (see Figure 14-4 on p. 417). The function of insulin is to maintain proper glucose levels in

Dimensions of Diversity

Ethnicity and CVD

Although cardiovascular disease is the leading cause of death for all Americans, there is a higher prevalence of CVD and its associated risk factors in adult African Americans and Mexican Americans than in whites and Asian Americans. The reasons for these disparities likely include both genetic and environmental factors.

African Americans are at substantially higher risk for death from CVD than other groups. The rate of hypertension among African Americans is among the highest of any group in the world. Blacks tend to develop hypertension at an earlier age than whites, and their average blood pressures are much higher. African Americans have a higher risk of stroke, have strokes at younger ages, and, if they survive, have more significant stroke-related disabilities. Some experts recommend that blacks be treated with antihypertensive drugs at an earlier stage—when blood pressure reaches 130/80 rather than the typical 140/90 cutoff for hypertension.

A number of genetic and biological factors may contribute to CVD in African Americans. They may be more sensitive to dietary sodium, leading to greater blood pressure elevation in response to a given amount of sodium. African Americans may also experience less dilation of blood vessels in response to stress, an attribute that also raises blood pressure.

Heredity also plays a large role in the tendency to develop diabetes, another important CVD risk factor that is more common in blacks than whites. However, Latinos are even more likely to develop diabetes and insulin resistance, and at a younger age, than African Americans. There is variation within the Latino population, however, with a higher prevalence of diabetes occurring among Mexican Americans and Puerto Ricans and a relatively lower prevalence among Cuban Americans.

Another factor that likely contributes to the high incidence of CVD among ethnic minority groups is low income. Economic deprivation usually means reduced access to adequate health care and health insurance. Also associated with low income is low educational attainment, which often means less information about preventive health measures, such as diet and stress management. And people with low incomes tend to smoke more, use more salt, and exercise less than those with higher incomes.

Discrimination may also play a role in CVD. Physicians and hospitals may treat the medical problems of ethnic minorities differently than those of whites. Discrimination, along with low income and other forms of deprivation, may also increase stress, which is linked with hypertension and CVD. In terms of access to care, factors such as insurance coverage and availability of high-tech cardiac equipment in hospitals used most often by minorities may also play a role.

CVD risk in ethnic groups is further affected by immigration and one's place of birth. Upon immigration to the United States, an Asian's risk for CVD tends to increase and reflect that of a typical American more than a typical Asian, perhaps in part because Asian immigrants often abandon their traditional (and healthier) diets.

However, birthplace (and its associated lifestyle factors) also seems to be a strong determinant of risk. One study found that among New Yorkers born in the Northeast, blacks and whites have nearly identical risk of CVD. But black New Yorkers who were born in the South have a sharply higher risk, and black New Yorkers born in the Caribbean have a significantly lower risk. Researchers speculate that instead of abandoning their traditional diets and lifestyles, blacks from the South instead bring these traditions with them. Some risk factors for CVD, including smoking and a high-fat diet, are more common in the South. When combined with urban stress, these factors create a lifestyle that is far from heart-healthy.

All Americans are advised to have their blood pressure checked regularly, exercise, eat a healthy diet, manage stress, and avoid smoking. These general preventive strategies may be particularly helpful for ethnic minorities. Tailoring your lifestyle to your particular ethnic risk may also be helpful in some cases. For example, studies have found that diets high in potassium and calcium may be particularly helpful in improving blood pressure in African Americans; fruits, vegetables, grains, and nuts are rich in potassium, and dairy products are high in calcium. Latinos, who are at greater risk for insulin resistance, may benefit from lifestyle strategies targeting metabolic syndrome. Discuss your particular risk profile with your physician to help identify lifestyle changes most appropriate for you.

the body, which it does by affecting the uptake of glucose from the blood by muscle and fat tissue and by limiting the liver's production of glucose. As people gain weight and engage in less physical activity, their muscles, fat, and liver become less sensitive to the effect of insulin—a condition known as insulin resistance (or pre-diabetes). As the body becomes increasingly insulin resistant, the pancreas must secrete more and more insulin (hyperinsulinemia) to keep glucose levels within a normal range. Eventually, however, even high levels of insulin may become insufficient, and blood glucose levels will also start to rise (hyperglycemia), resulting in type 2 diabetes.

Those who have insulin resistance tend to have several other related risk factors; as a group, this cluster of abnormalities is called metabolic syndrome or insulin resistance syndrome (Table 15-3). Having metabolic syndrome significantly increases the risk of CVD—up to three times in men and six times in women. It is estimated that nearly 25% of the U.S. population has metabolic syndrome. Rates are highest among Mexican Americans, especially women. Among whites, the prevalence is similar in men and women, but among African Americans, the prevalence among women is 57% higher than in men. Some people are genetically predisposed, and among this

Table 15-3 Defining Characteristics of Metabolic Syndrome*

Abdominal obesity (waist circumference)	
Men	>40 in (>102 cm)
Women	>35 in (>88 cm)
Triglycerides	≥150 mg/dl
HDL cholesterol	
Men	<40 mg/dl
Women	<50 mg/dl
Blood pressure	≥130/≥85 mm Hg
Fasting glucose	≥110 mg/dl

*A person is diagnosed with metabolic syndrome if she or he has three or more of the risk factors listed here.

SOURCE: National Cholesterol Education Program. 2001. *ATP III Guidelines At-A-Glance Quick Desk Reference.* Bethesda, Md.: National Heart, Lung, and Blood Institute. NIH Publication No. 01-3305.

group, factors such as excess body fat and inactivity can elicit insulin resistance. However, metabolic syndrome is not limited to obese people.

To reduce your risk for metabolic syndrome, choose a healthy diet and get plenty of exercise. Regular physical activity increases your body's sensitivity to insulin in addition to improving cholesterol levels and decreasing blood pressure. Reducing calorie intake to prevent weight gain or losing weight if needed will also reduce insulin resistance. The amount and type of carbohydrate intake is also important: Diets high in carbohydrates, especially high-glycemic-index foods, can raise levels of glucose and triglycerides and lower HDL, thus contributing to the development or worsening of metabolic syndrome and CVD, particularly in people who are already sedentary and overweight. For people prone to insulin resistance, eating more unsaturated fats, protein, vegetables, and fiber while limiting added sugars and starches may be beneficial.

Homocysteine Elevated levels of homocysteine, an amino acid circulating in the blood, are associated with an increased risk of CVD. Homocysteine appears to damage the lining of blood vessels, resulting in inflammation and the development of fatty deposits in artery walls. These changes can lead to the formation of clots and blockages in arteries, which in turn can cause heart attacks and strokes. High homocysteine levels are also associated with cognitive impairment, such as memory loss.

Men generally have higher homocysteine levels than women, as do individuals with diets low in folic acid, vitamin B-12, and vitamin B-6. Many genes may cause elevated homocysteine levels, and some genes associated with small-to-moderate elevations are quite common in the general population. A recent study showed that taking folic acid will decrease homocysteine levels, but it does not lower the risk of CVD and may actually be harmful. Therefore, taking folic acid beyond the dose found in a multivitamin is not recommended. Instead, it may be more helpful to follow a diet rich in fruits, vegetables, and whole grains. Also, if your homocysteine level is high, aggressively controlling your other cardiac risk factors is that much more important.

Infectious Agents Several infectious agents have been identified as possible culprits in the development of CVD. *Chlamydia pneumoniae,* a common cause of flu-like respiratory infections, has been found in sections of clogged, damaged arteries but not in sections of healthy arteries. It does not appear that antibiotic treatment for *C. pneumoniae* reduces risk, but further research is needed. Other infectious agents may also play a role in CVD.

Lipoprotein(a) A high level of a specific type of LDL called lipoprotein(a), or Lp(a), may be a risk factor for CHD, especially when associated with high LDL or low HDL levels. Lp(a) is thought to contribute to CVD by promoting clots and by delivering cholesterol to a site of vascular injury. Lp(a) levels have a strong genetic component and are difficult to treat. Lp(a) levels tend to increase with age and vary by race, with higher levels found in African Americans than in whites. About 25% of the U.S. population has elevated lipoprotein(a) levels. Lifestyle modifications such as diet, exercise, and weight loss appear to have little effect in lowering Lp(a). High-dose niacin has been shown to decrease Lp(a), but studies are still needed to see if lower levels actually reduce the risk of CVD. In the meantime, if you have elevated Lp(a), any other cholesterol abnormalities—such as elevated LDL—should be treated even more aggressively.

LDL Particle Size Research has shown that LDLparticles differ in size and density and that the concentrations of different particles vary among individuals. LDL cholesterol profiles can be divided into three general types: People with pattern A have mostly large, buoyant LDL particles; people with pattern B have mostly small, dense LDL particles; and people with pattern C have a mixture of particle types. Small, dense LDL particles pose a greater CVD risk than large particles; thus, people with LDL pattern B are at greater risk for CVD. Exercise, a low-fat diet, and certain lipid-lowering drugs may help lower CVD risk in people with LDL pattern B. In a recent study of men who walked or jogged 12–20 miles per week, total cholesterol and LDL levels were often unchanged, but the LDL particles became larger and less dense.

Fibrinogen Fibrinogen is a protein that is essential for the formation of blood clots. High levels of fibrinogen are linked to increased risk of coronary heart disease and stroke. Elevated fibrinogen levels may be one way traditional risk factors such as smoking, obesity, diabetes, and elevated blood lipids cause CVD. Improvement in these risk factors, especially quitting smoking, tends to decrease fibrinogen levels. Fibrates and niacin can also lower fibrinogen levels. Currently, experts do not recommend routine measurement of fibrinogen for prediction of CVD.

Blood Viscosity and Iron High blood viscosity (thickness) may increase the risk of CVD; excess iron stores have also been linked to higher risk, especially for men and postmenopausal women (iron stores are usually lower in younger women because of menstrual blood loss). Regular blood donation, which reduces iron stores and blood viscosity, is associated with lower CVD risk in men. Drinking five or more glasses of water a day may also reduce risk by reducing blood viscosity. On the flip side, high consumption of heme iron—found in meat, fish, and poultry—is associated with an increased risk of heart attack. Men and postmenopausal women should consult a physician before taking iron supplements.

Uric Acid Recent research suggests a link between high blood levels of uric acid and CVD mortality, particularly among postmenopausal women and African Americans. Uric acid may raise CVD risk by increasing inflammation and platelet aggregation or by influencing the development of hypertension; high uric acid levels also cause gout (a type of arthritis), kidney stones, and certain forms of kidney disease. Medications to lower uric acid levels are available, but it is not yet known if they will be useful in preventing CVD.

Time of Day and Time of Year More heart attacks and sudden cardiac deaths occur in the morning hours between 6:00 A.M. and noon than during other times of the day. This trend may be explained by the natural increase in adrenaline and cortisol levels that occurs in the morning and by an increase in the sympathetic nervous system activity as people hurry around at the beginning of their day. Blood pressure is often lowest during sleep and highest in the morning, and endothelial function may be impaired in the early morning.

There is also a seasonal pattern of heart attacks, with up to 50% more occurring in winter months than in summer months. Heart attacks that occur in winter also tend to be more often fatal than those that occur during summer. Possible explanations include low temperature, which can constrict blood vessels; bursts of exertion, such as snow shoveling; increased rates of smoking; increased stress and depression, including seasonal affective disorder (see Chapter 3); holiday-related episodes of high-fat eating and binge drinking; and physiological factors, including levels of cholesterol and C-reactive protein, which appear to rise in winter. People who have symptoms of heart trouble may also be more reluctant to seek help during the holidays.

MAJOR FORMS OF CARDIOVASCULAR DISEASE

Collectively, the various forms of CVD kill more Americans than the next four leading causes of death combined (Figure 15-5). The financial burden of CVD, including the costs of medical treatments and lost productivity, is more than $400 billion annually.

The main forms of CVD are atherosclerosis, heart disease and heart attack, stroke, peripheral arterial disease (PAD), congestive heart failure, congenital heart disease, rheumatic heart disease, and heart valve problems. Many forms are interrelated and have elements in common; we treat them separately here for the sake of clarity. Hypertension, which is both a major risk factor and a form of CVD, was described earlier in the chapter.

Atherosclerosis

Atherosclerosis is a form of arteriosclerosis, or thickening and hardening of the arteries. In atherosclerosis, arteries become narrowed by deposits of fat, cholesterol, and other substances. The process begins when the endothelial cells (cells that line the arteries) become damaged, most likely through a combination of factors such as smoking, high blood pressure, high insulin or glucose levels, and deposits of oxidized LDL particles. The body's response to this damage results in inflammation and changes in the artery lining that create a sort of magnet for LDL, platelets, and other cells; these cells build up and cause a bulge in the wall of the artery. As these deposits, called **plaques**, accumulate on artery walls, the arteries lose their elasticity and their ability to expand and contract, restricting blood flow. Once narrowed by a plaque, an artery is vulnerable to blockage by blood clots (Figure 15-6, p. 462). The risk of life-threatening clots and heart attacks increases if the fibrous cap covering a plaque ruptures.

If the heart, brain, and/or other organs are deprived of blood, and thus the vital oxygen it carries, the effects of atherosclerosis can be deadly. Coronary arteries, which supply the heart with blood, are particularly susceptible to plaque buildup, a condition called **coronary heart disease (CHD),** or *coronary artery disease (CAD).* The blockage of a coronary artery causes a heart attack. If a cerebral artery (leading to the brain) is blocked, the result is a stroke. If an artery in a limb becomes narrowed or blocked, it causes *peripheral arterial disease,* a condition that causes pain and sometimes loss of the affected limb.

The main risk factors for atherosclerosis are cigarette smoking, physical inactivity, high levels of blood

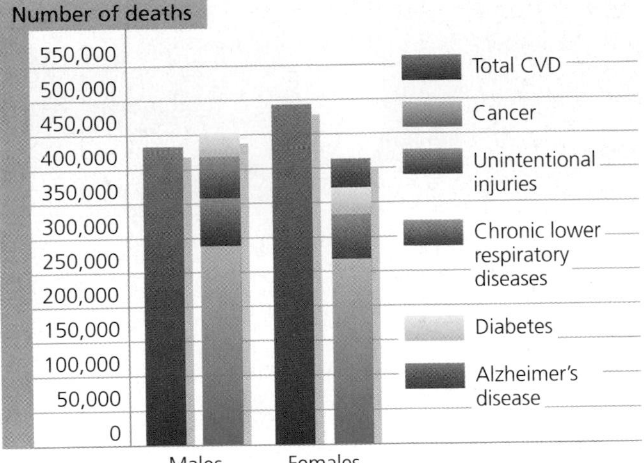

(a) Leading causes of death

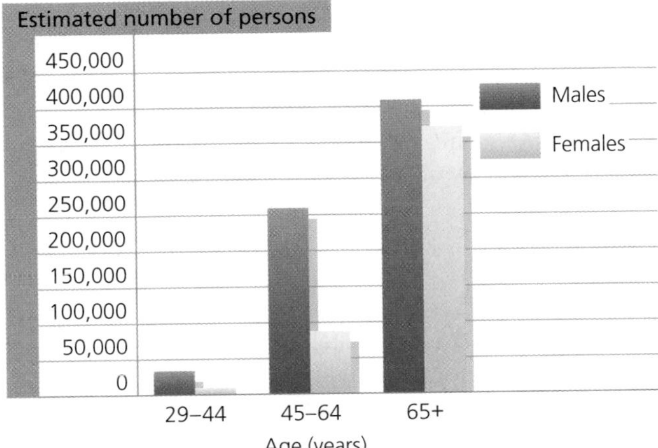

(b) Annual incidence of heart attack

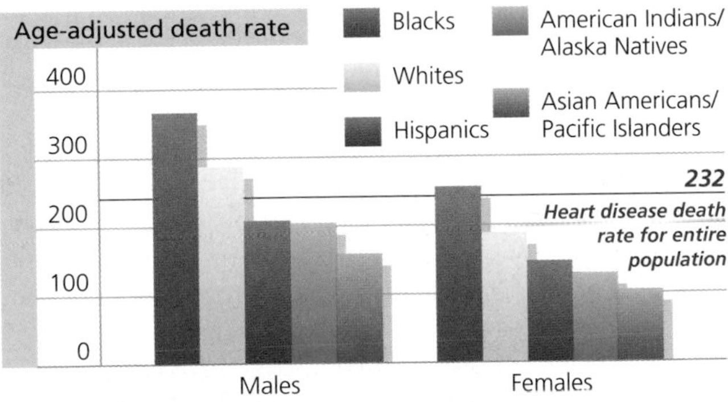

(c) Heart disease death rates

VITAL STATISTICS

Figure 15-5 A statistical look at cardiovascular disease in the United States. (a) The leading causes of death. CVD causes more deaths than the next four causes combined. (b) Estimated numbers of Americans who have a heart attack each year. Among heart attack victims under age 65, men significantly outnumber women; after age 65, women start to catch up. (c) Heart disease death rates by gender and ethnicity. SOURCES: American Heart Association. 2006. *Heart Disease and Stroke Statistics—2006 Update*. Dallas, Tex.: American Heart Association; National Center for Health Statistics. 2006. *Health, United States, 2006*. Hyattsville, Md.: U.S. Public Health Service.

cholesterol, high blood pressure, and diabetes. Atherosclerosis often begins in childhood.

Heart Disease and Heart Attack

The most common form of heart disease is coronary artery disease caused by atherosclerosis. When one of the coronary arteries, the arteries that branch off the aorta and supply blood directly to the heart muscle, becomes blocked, a heart attack results. A heart attack caused by a clot is called a **coronary thrombosis.** Every year, about 1.2 million Americans have a heart attack (see Figure 15-5). Although a **heart attack,** or *myocardial infarction (MI)*, may come without warning, it is usually the end result of a long-term disease process. During a heart attack, part of the myocardium (heart muscle) may die from lack of blood flow.

Symptoms of MI may include chest pain or pressure; arm, neck, or jaw pain; difficulty breathing; excessive sweating; nausea and vomiting; and loss of consciousness. Although chest pain occurs in the majority of MI victims, a recent study of over 750,000 MI patients revealed that about one-third of people having a heart attack do not experience chest pain. Women, ethnic minorities, older adults, and people with diabetes were the most likely groups to experience heart attack without chest pain or to have several other accompanying symptoms (see the box "Women and CVD" on p. 457). Because symptoms can vary so widely, it is estimated that 40% of heart attacks go undiagnosed.

Angina Arteries narrowed by disease may still be open enough to deliver blood to the heart. At times, however—during stress or exertion, for example—the heart needs more oxygen than can flow through narrowed arteries. When the need for oxygen exceeds the supply, chest pain, called **angina pectoris,** may occur. Angina pain is usually felt as an extreme tightness in the chest and heavy pressure behind the breastbone or in the shoulder, neck, arm, hand, or back. This pain, although not actually a heart attack, is a warning that the load on the heart must be reduced. The symptoms of

Terms

plaque A deposit of fatty (and other) substances on the inner wall of the arteries.

coronary heart disease (CHD) Heart disease caused by atherosclerosis in the arteries that supply blood to the heart muscle; also called *coronary artery disease.*

coronary thrombosis A clot in a coronary artery.

heart attack Damage to, or death of, heart muscle, resulting from a failure of the coronary arteries to deliver enough blood to the heart; also known as *myocardial infarction (MI).*

angina pectoris Pain in the chest, and often in the left arm and shoulder, caused by the heart muscle not receiving enough blood.

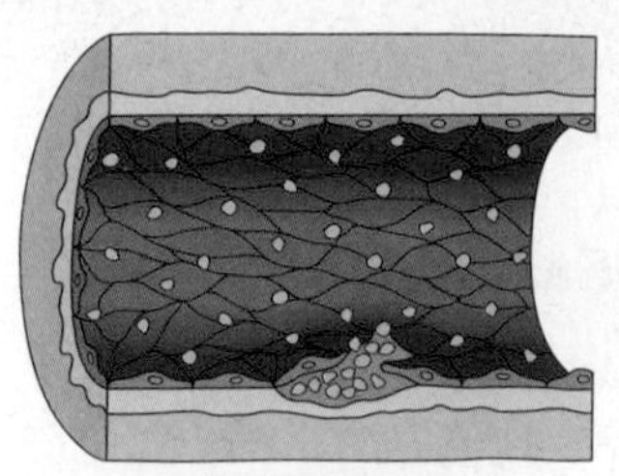

Plaque buildup begins when endothelial cells lining the arteries are damaged by smoking, high blood pressure, oxidized LDL, and other causes; excess cholesterol particles collect beneath these cells.

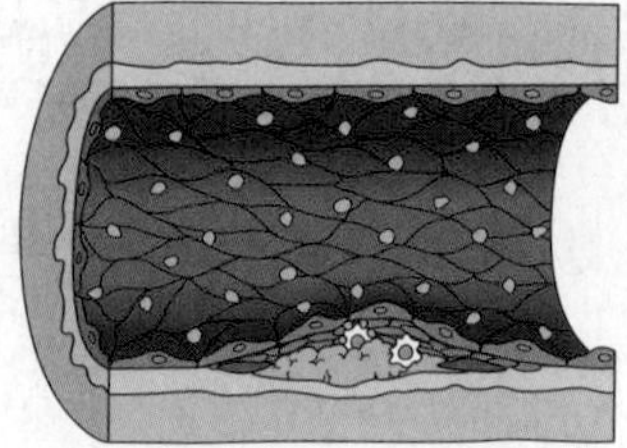

In response to the damage, platelets and other types of cells collect at the site; a fibrous cap forms, isolating the plaque within the artery wall. An early-stage plaque is called a fatty streak.

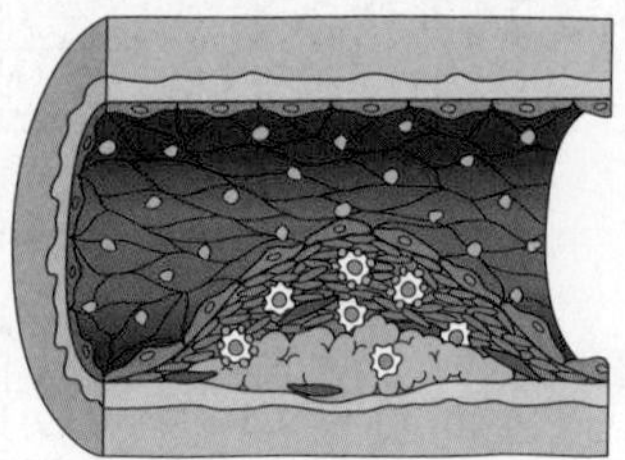

Chemicals released by cells in and around the plaque cause further inflammation and buildup; an advanced plaque contains LDL, white blood cells, connective tissue, smooth muscle cells, platelets, and other compounds.

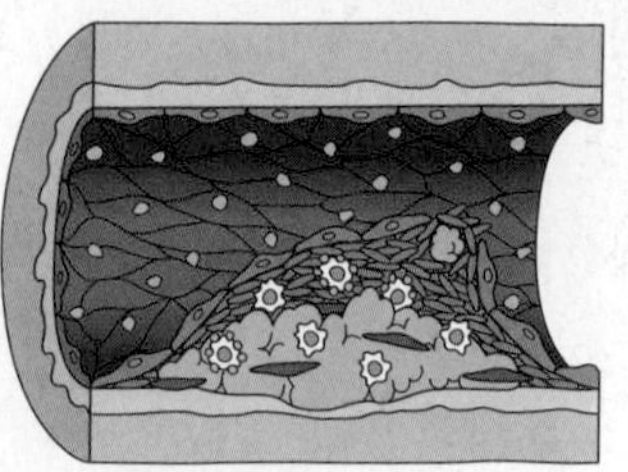

The narrowed artery is vulnerable to blockage by clots. The risk of blockage and heart attack rises if the fibrous cap cracks (probably due to destructive enzymes released by white blood cells within the plaque).

Figure 15-6 Stages of plaque development.

angina are often very difficult to distinguish from a heart attack. Any severe chest pain that lasts more than a few minutes should be considered life-threatening, and emergency medical help should be obtained immediately. Angina may be controlled in a number of ways (with drugs and surgical or nonsurgical procedures), but its course is unpredictable. Over a period ranging from hours to years, the narrowing may go on to full blockage and a heart attack.

Arrhythmias and Sudden Cardiac Death The pumping of the heart is controlled by electrical impulses from the sinus node that maintain a regular heartbeat of 60–100 beats per minute. If this electrical conduction system is disrupted, the heart may beat too quickly, too slowly, or in an irregular fashion, a condition known as **arrhythmia.** Arrhythmia can cause symptoms ranging from imperceptible to severe and even fatal.

Sudden cardiac death, also called cardiac arrest, is most often caused by an arrhythmia called ventricular fibrillation, a kind of quivering of the ventricle that makes it ineffective in pumping blood. If ventricular fibrillation continues for more than a few minutes, it is generally fatal. Cardiac defribrillation, in which an electrical shock is delivered to the heart, can be effective in jolting the heart into a more efficient rhythm. Emergency personnel typically carry defibrillators, and automated external defibrillators (AEDs) are becoming increasingly available in public places for use by the general public. AEDs monitor the heart's rhythm and, if appropriate, deliver an electrical shock. (Training in the use of AEDs is available from organizations such as the American Red Cross and the American Heart Association.) Sudden cardiac death most often occurs in people with coronary heart disease. Serious arrhythmias frequently develop during or after a heart attack and are often the actual cause of death in cases of a fatal MI.

Other potential causes of arrhythmia include congenital heart abnormalities, infections, drug use, chest trauma, and congestive heart failure. Some arrhythmias cause no problems and resolve without treatment; more serious arrhythmias are usually treated with medication or a surgically implanted pacemaker or defibrillator that delivers electrical stimulation to the heart to create a more normal rhythm.

Helping a Heart Attack Victim Most people who die from a heart attack do so within 2 hours from the time they experience the first symptoms. Unfortunately, half of all heart attack victims wait more than 2 hours before getting help. If you or someone you are with has any of the warning signs of heart attack listed in the box "What to Do in Case of a Heart Attack, Stroke, or Cardiac Arrest," take immediate action. Get help even if the person denies there is something wrong. One additional step recommended by many experts is for the affected individual to chew and swallow one adult aspirin tablet (325 mg); aspirin has an immediate anticlotting effect.

If the person loses consciousness, emergency **cardiopulmonary resuscitation (CPR)** should be initiated by a qualified person. Damage to the heart muscle increases with time. If the person receives emergency care quickly enough, a clot-dissolving agent can be injected to break up a clot in the coronary artery.

Terms

VW

arrhythmia A change in the normal pattern of the heartbeat.

sudden cardiac death A nontraumatic, unexpected death from sudden cardiac arrest, most often due to arrhythmia; in most instances, victims have underlying heart disease.

cardiopulmonary resuscitation (CPR) A technique involving mouth-to-mouth breathing and chest compression to keep oxygen flowing to the brain.

electrocardiogram (ECG or EKG) A test to detect abnormalities by evaluating the electrical activity in the heart.

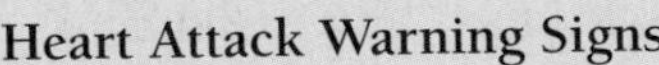

What to Do in Case of a Heart Attack, Stroke, or Cardiac Arrest

Heart Attack Warning Signs

Some heart attacks are sudden and intense—the "movie heart attack," where no one doubts what's happening. But most heart attacks start slowly, with mild pain or discomfort. Often people affected aren't sure what's wrong and wait too long before getting help. Here are signs that can mean a heart attack is happening:

- **Chest discomfort.** Most heart attacks involve discomfort in the center of the chest that lasts more than a few minutes, or that goes away and comes back. It can feel like uncomfortable pressure, squeezing, fullness, or pain.
- **Discomfort in other areas of the upper body.** Symptoms can include pain or discomfort in one or both arms, the back, neck, jaw, or stomach.
- **Shortness of breath.** May occur with or without chest discomfort.
- **Other signs:** These may include breaking out in a cold sweat, nausea, vomiting, or lightheadedness.

If you or someone you're with has chest discomfort, especially with one or more of the other signs, don't wait longer than a few minutes (no more than 5) before calling for help.

Calling 9-1-1 is almost always the fastest way to get lifesaving treatment. Emergency medical services staff can begin treatment when they arrive—up to an hour sooner than if someone gets to the hospital by car. The staff are also trained to revive someone whose heart has stopped. Patients with chest pain who arrive by ambulance usually receive faster treatment at the hospital, too.

If you can't access the emergency medical services (EMS), have someone drive you to the hospital right away. If you're the one having symptoms, don't drive yourself, unless you have absolutely no other option.

Stroke Warning Signs

The American Stroke Association says these are the warning signs of stroke:

- Sudden numbness or weakness of the face, arm, or leg, especially on one side of the body
- Sudden confusion, trouble speaking or understanding
- Sudden trouble seeing in one or both eyes
- Sudden trouble walking, dizziness, or loss of balance or coordination
- Sudden, severe headache with no known cause

If you or someone with you has one or more of these signs, don't delay! Immediately call 9-1-1 or the emergency medical services (EMS) number so an ambulance (ideally with advanced life support) can be sent for you. Also, check the time so you'll know when the first symptoms appeared. It's very important to take immediate action. If given within 3 hours of the start of symptoms, a clot-busting drug can reduce long-term disability for the most common type of stroke.

Signs of Cardiac Arrest

Cardiac arrest strikes immediately and without warning. Here are the signs:

- Sudden loss of responsiveness. No response to gentle shaking. No movement or coughing.
- No normal breathing. The victim does not take a normal breath for several seconds.
- No signs of circulation. No pulse or blood pressure.

If cardiac arrest occurs, call 9-1-1 and begin CPR immediately. If an automated external defibrillator (AED) is available and someone trained to use it is nearby, involve her or him.

SOURCE: American Heart Association. 2005. Heart Attack, Stroke, and Cardiac Arrest Warning Signs. Reproduced with permission. www.americanheart.org.

Detecting and Treating Heart Disease Physicians have an expanding array of tools to evaluate the condition of the heart and its arteries. Currently, the most common initial screening tool for CAD is the stress, or exercise, test, in which a patient runs or walks on a treadmill or pedals a stationary cycle while being monitored for abnormalities with an **electrocardiogram (ECG or EKG).** Certain characteristic changes in the heart's electrical activity while under stress can reveal particular heart problems, such as restricted blood flow. Exercise testing can also be performed in conjunction with imaging techniques such as nuclear medicine or echocardiography that provide pictures of the heart, which can help pinpoint problems.

Other tests for evaluating CHD are

- Electron-beam computed tomography (EBCT) uses a sweeping electron beam to produce computerized cross-sectional images; it can detect calcium in the arteries, a marker for atherosclerosis.
- Echocardiography utilizes sound waves to examine the heart's pumping function and valves.
- Multi-slice computed tomography (MSCT) is another type of CT that produces very thinly sliced images of the heart, allowing physicians to see very small structures such as the coronary arteries.
- **Magnetic resonance imaging (MRI)** uses powerful magnets to look inside the body and generate pictures of the heart and blood vessels.

If symptoms or non-invasive tests suggest coronary artery disease, the next step is usually a coronary **angiogram,** performed in a cardiac catheterization lab. In this test, a catheter (small plastic tube) is threaded into an artery, usually in the groin, and advanced through the aorta to the coronary arteries. The catheter is then placed into the opening of the coronary artery and a special dye is injected. The dye can be seen moving through the arteries under moving X ray, and any narrowings or blockages can be identified. If a problem is found, it is commonly treated with **balloon angioplasty,** which is performed by specially trained cardiologists. Over 650,000 of the procedures are performed each year. This technique involves placing a small wire in the artery and feeding a deflated balloon over it. The balloon is advanced to the site of the narrowing and then inflated, flattening the fatty plaque and widening the arterial opening. This is generally followed by placement of a stent, a small metal tube that helps keep the artery open. Repeat clogging of the artery, known as restenosis, can occur, but the introduction of stents coated with medication, which is slowly released over a few months, significantly decreases the chance of restenosis.

Other treatments, ranging from medication to major surgery, are also available. Along with a low-fat diet, regular exercise, and smoking cessation, one frequent recommendation for people at high risk for CVD is to take an aspirin tablet every day. Aspirin has an anticlotting effect, discouraging platelets in the blood from sticking to arterial plaques and forming clots; it also reduces inflammation. (Low-dose aspirin therapy appears to help prevent first heart attacks in men, second heart attacks in men and women, and strokes in women over age 65.) Prescription drugs can help control heart rate, dilate arteries, lower blood pressure, and reduce the strain on the heart—raising both quality and length of life in heart patients. In patients with coronary artery disease, a class of cholesterol-lowering drugs called statins is effective in preventing heart attacks; statins also have beneficial anti-inflammatory effects.

Every year, **coronary bypass surgery** is performed on over 250,000 people, about half of whom are under age 65. Cardiothoracic surgeons remove a healthy blood vessel, usually a vein from one of the patient's legs, and graft it from the aorta to one or more coronary arteries to bypass a blockage.

Whatever treatment is used, the person with heart disease is also advised to make behavior and lifestyle changes. Otherwise, the arteries simply become clogged again, and the same problems recur a few years later.

Terms

Vw

magnetic resonance imaging (MRI) A computerized imaging technique that uses a strong magnetic field and radio frequency signals to examine a thin cross section of the body.

angiogram A picture of the arterial system taken after injecting a dye that is opaque to X rays; also called *arteriogram.*

balloon angioplasty A technique in which a catheter with a deflated balloon on the tip is inserted into an artery; the balloon is then inflated at the point of obstruction in the artery, pressing the plaque against the artery wall to improve blood supply; also known as *percutaneous transluminal coronary angioplasty (PTCA).*

coronary bypass surgery Surgery in which a vein is grafted from a point above to a point below an obstruction in a coronary artery, improving the blood supply to the heart.

stroke An impeded blood supply to some part of the brain resulting in the destruction of brain cells; also called *cerebrovascular accident.*

ischemic stroke Impeded blood supply to the brain caused by the obstruction of a blood vessel by a clot.

hemorrhagic stroke Impeded blood supply to the brain caused by the rupture of a blood vessel.

thrombus A blood clot in a blood vessel that usually remains at the point of its formation.

embolus A blood clot that breaks off from its place of origin in a blood vessel and travels through the bloodstream.

aneurysm A sac formed by a distention or dilation of the artery wall.

transient ischemic attack (TIA) A small stroke; usually a temporary interruption of blood supply to the brain, causing numbness or difficulty with speech.

Stroke

For brain cells to function as they should, they must have a continuous and ample supply of oxygen-rich blood. If brain cells are deprived of blood for more than a few minutes, they die. A **stroke,** also called a *cerebrovascular accident (CVA),* occurs when the blood supply to the brain is cut off. One study found that about 2 million brain cells died per minute during a stroke and the brain aged about 3.5 years each hour. In the past, not much could be done for stroke victims; today, however, prompt treatment of stroke can greatly decrease the risk of permanent disability. Everyone should know the warning signs of a stroke and seek immediate medical help, just as they would at the first sign of a heart attack.

Types of Strokes There are two major types of strokes: **ischemic strokes,** which are caused by blockages in blood vessels, and **hemorrhagic strokes,** which are caused by rupture of blood vessels, leading to bleeding into the brain (Figure 15-7). One type of ischemic stroke, the *thrombotic stroke,* is caused by a **thrombus,** a blood clot that forms in a cerebral artery that has been narrowed or damaged by atherosclerosis. The other type of ischemic stroke, called an *embolic stroke,* is caused by an **embolus,** a wandering blood clot that is carried in the bloodstream and may become wedged in one of the cerebral arteries. Many embolic strokes are linked to a type of abnormal heart rhythm called atrial fibrillation; when this arrhythmia occurs, blood may pool in an atrium and form a clot. Ischemic

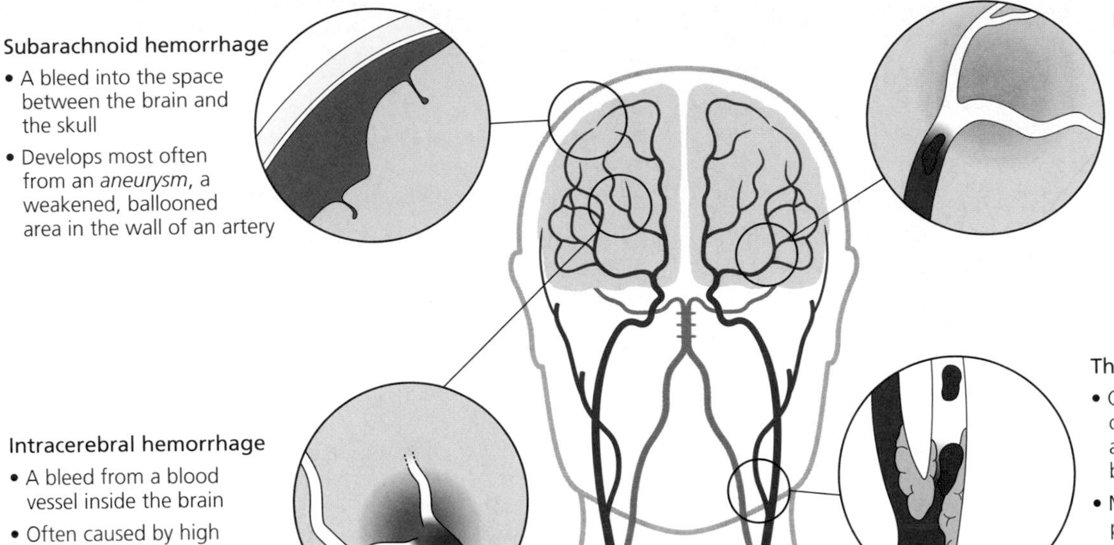

HEMORRHAGIC STROKE
• 20% of strokes
• Caused by ruptured blood vessels followed by blood leaking into tissue
• Usually more serious than ischemic stroke
ISCHEMIC STROKE
• 80% of strokes
• Caused by blockages in brain blood vessels; potentially treatable with clot-busting drugs
• Brain tissue dies when blood flow is blocked
Subarachnoid hemorrhage
• A bleed into the space between the brain and the skull
• Develops most often from an *aneurysm*, a weakened, ballooned area in the wall of an artery
Embolic stroke
• Caused by *emboli*, blood clots that travel from elsewhere in the body to the brain blood vessels
• 25% of embolic strokes are related to atrial fibrillation
Intracerebral hemorrhage
• A bleed from a blood vessel inside the brain
• Often caused by high blood pressure and the damage it does to arteries
Thrombotic stroke
• Caused by *thrombi*, blood clots that form where an artery has been narrowed by atherosclerosis
• Most often develops when part of a thrombus breaks away and causes a blockage in a downstream artery

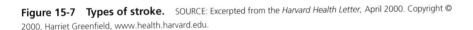

Figure 15-7 Types of stroke. SOURCE: Excerpted from the *Harvard Health Letter,* April 2000. Copyright © 2000, Harriet Greenfield, www.health.harvard.edu.

strokes, which account for 80% of all strokes, are potentially treatable with clot-busting drugs, so obtaining immediate medical help is critical to improving chances for recovery.

The other type of stroke, less common but more severe, is the hemorrhagic stroke. It occurs when a blood vessel in the brain bursts, spilling blood into the surrounding tissue. Cells normally nourished by the artery are deprived of blood and cannot function. In addition, accumulated blood from the burst vessel may put pressure on surrounding brain tissue, causing damage and even death. In a *subarachnoid hemorrhage,* a blood vessel on the brain's surface ruptures and bleeds into the space between the brain and the skull; a ruptured vessel within the brain causes an *intracerebral hemorrhage.* Hemorrhages can be caused by head injuries or the bursting of a malformed blood vessel or an **aneurysm,** a blood-filled pocket that bulges out from a weak spot in an artery wall. Aneurysms in the brain may remain stable and never break. But when they do, the result is a stroke. Aneurysms may be caused or worsened by high blood pressure.

The Effects of a Stroke The interruption of the blood supply to any area of the brain prevents the nerve cells there from functioning—in some cases causing death. Of the 700,000 Americans who have strokes each year, nearly one-third die within a year. Those who survive usually have some lasting disability. Which parts of the body are affected depends on the area of the brain that has been damaged. Nerve cells control sensation and most of our body movements, and a stroke may cause paralysis, walking disability, speech impairment, memory loss, and changes in behavior. The severity of the stroke and its long-term effects depend on which brain cells have been injured, how widespread the damage is, how effectively the body can restore the blood supply, and how rapidly other areas of the brain can take over. Early treatment can significantly reduce the severity of disability resulting from a stroke.

Detecting and Treating Stroke Death rates from stroke have declined significantly over the past decades—from nearly 90% in 1950 to about 33% today. Effective treatment requires the prompt recognition of symptoms and correct diagnosis of the type of stroke. Signs of a stroke are listed in the box on page 463; also see the box "Three Simple Ways to Recognize a Stroke" on page 466.

Some stroke victims have a **transient ischemic attack (TIA),** or ministroke, days, weeks, or months before they have a full-blown stroke. A TIA produces temporary stroke-like symptoms, such as weakness or numbness in an arm or a leg, speech difficulty, or dizziness; but these symptoms are brief, often lasting just a few minutes, and do not cause permanent damage. However, TIAs should be taken as warning signs of a stroke, and anyone with a suspected TIA should get immediate medical help.

Strokes should be treated with the same urgency as heart attacks. A person with stroke symptoms should be

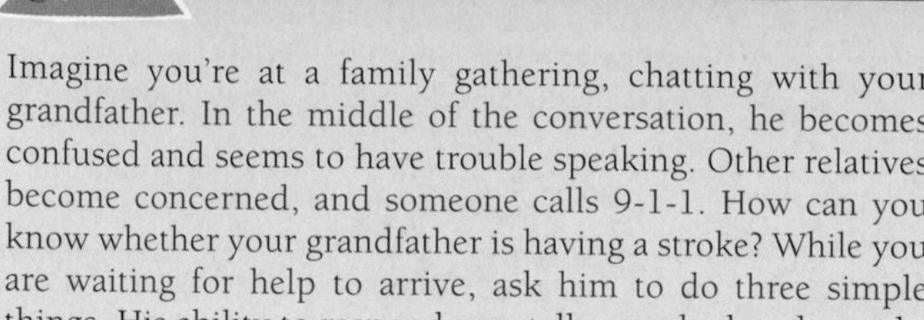

Three Simple Ways to Recognize a Stroke

Take Charge

Imagine you're at a family gathering, chatting with your grandfather. In the middle of the conversation, he becomes confused and seems to have trouble speaking. Other relatives become concerned, and someone calls 9-1-1. How can you know whether your grandfather is having a stroke? While you are waiting for help to arrive, ask him to do three simple things. His ability to respond may tell you whether the problem is a stroke.

"Give me a smile."

Ask your grandfather to smile, or just to show his teeth. If his smile droops on one side or if he is unable to move or open one side of his mouth, he may be having a stroke.

"Hold your arms out."

Ask your grandfather to close his eyes and hold his arms straight out for just a few seconds. If he cannot move one arm, or if he cannot hold one arm still, it may be a sign of a stroke.

"Say this for me."

Ask your grandfather to repeat a short, simple sentence (not a tongue-twister), like "Take me out to the ballgame." If he has difficulty speaking or cannot speak, then a stroke is possible.

If someone has trouble performing any one of these three tests, he or she may be suffering a stroke. Follow the steps for helping a stroke victim in the box "What to Do in Case of a Heart Attack, Stroke, or Cardiac Arrest" on page 463.

rushed to the hospital. A **computed tomography (CT)** scan, which uses a computer to construct an image of the brain from X rays, can assess brain damage and determine the type of stroke. Newer techniques using MRI and ultrasound are becoming increasingly available and should improve the speed and accuracy of stroke diagnosis.

If tests reveal that a stroke is caused by a blood clot—and if help is sought within a few hours of the onset of symptoms—the person can be treated with the same kind of clot-dissolving drugs that are used to treat coronary artery blockages. If the clot is dissolved quickly enough, brain damage is minimized and symptoms may disappear. (The longer the brain goes without blood, the greater the risk of permanent damage.) Drugs that help protect healthy brain cells from the effects of stroke are currently being tested. People who have had TIAs or who are at high risk for stroke due to narrowing of the carotid arteries may undergo a surgical procedure called *carotid endarterectomy,* in which plaque is removed. There is also a nonsurgical procedure, similar to coronary angioplasty and stenting, that can be done in the carotid arteries.

If tests reveal that a stroke was caused by a cerebral hemorrhage, drugs may be prescribed to lower the blood pressure, which will usually be high. Careful diagnosis is crucial, because administering clot-dissolving drugs to a person suffering a hemorrhagic stroke would cause more bleeding and potentially more brain damage.

If detection and treatment of stroke come too late, rehabilitation is the only treatment. Although damaged or destroyed brain tissue does not normally regenerate, nerve cells in the brain can make new pathways, and some functions can be taken over by other parts of the brain. Some spontaneous recovery starts immediately after a stroke and continues for a few months.

Rehabilitation consists of physical therapy, which helps strengthen muscles and improve balance and coordination; speech and language therapy, which helps those whose speech has been damaged; and occupational therapy, which helps improve hand-eye coordination and everyday living skills. Some people recover completely in a matter of days or weeks, but most stroke victims who survive must adapt to some disability.

Terms

Vw

computed tomography (CT) The use of computerized X ray images to create a cross-sectional depiction (scan) of tissue density.

peripheral arterial disease (PAD) Atherosclerosis in arteries in the legs (or, less commonly, arms) that can impede blood flow and lead to pain, infection, and loss of the affected limb.

pulmonary edema The accumulation of fluid in the lungs.

congestive heart failure A condition resulting from the heart's inability to pump out all the blood that returns to it; blood backs up in the veins leading to the heart, causing an accumulation of fluid in various parts of the body.

congenital heart disease A defect or malformation of the heart or its major blood vessels, present at birth.

hypertrophic cardiomyopathy (HCM) An inherited condition in which there is an enlargement of the heart muscle, especially between the two ventricles.

murmur An abnormal heart sound indicating turbulent blood flow through a valve or hole in the heart.

rheumatic fever A disease, mainly of children, characterized by fever, inflammation, and pain in the joints; often damages the heart valves and muscle, a condition called rheumatic heart disease.

Peripheral Arterial Disease

Peripheral arterial disease (PAD) refers to atherosclerosis in the leg (or arm) arteries, which can eventually limit or completely obstruct blood flow. The same process that occurs in the heart arteries can occur in any artery of the body. In fact, patients with PAD frequently also have coronary artery disease and cerebrovascular disease, and they have an increased risk of death from CVD. Approximately 10 million people in the United States have PAD.

The risk factors associated with coronary atherosclerosis, such as smoking, diabetes, hypertension, and high cholesterol, also contribute to atherosclerosis in the peripheral circulation. The risk of PAD is significantly increased in people with diabetes and people who smoke. The likelihood of needing an amputation is increased in those who continue to smoke, and PAD in people with diabetes tends to be extensive and severe.

Symptoms of PAD include claudication and rest pain. *Claudication* is aching or fatigue in the affected leg with exertion, particularly walking, which resolves with rest. Claudication occurs when leg muscles do not get adequate blood and oxygen supply. *Rest pain* occurs when the limb artery is unable to supply adequate blood and oxygen even when the body is not physically active. This occurs when the artery is significantly narrowed or completely blocked. If blood flow is not restored quickly, cells and tissues die; in severe cases, amputation may be needed. PAD is the leading cause of amputation in people over age 50.

Congestive Heart Failure

A number of conditions—high blood pressure, heart attack, atherosclerosis, alcoholism, viral infections, rheumatic fever, birth defects—can damage the heart's pumping mechanism. When the heart cannot maintain its regular pumping rate and force, fluids begin to back up. When extra fluid seeps through capillary walls, edema (swelling) results, usually in the legs and ankles, but sometimes in other parts of the body as well. Fluid can collect in the lungs and interfere with breathing, particularly when a person is lying down. This condition is called **pulmonary edema,** and the entire process is known as **congestive heart failure.**

Congestive heart failure can be controlled. Treatment includes reducing the workload on the heart, modifying salt intake, and using drugs that help the body eliminate excess fluid. Drugs used to treat congestive heart failure improve the pumping action of the heart, lower blood pressure so the heart doesn't have to work as hard, and help the body eliminate excess salt and water. When medical therapy is ineffective, heart transplant is a solution for some patients with severe heart failure, but the need greatly exceeds the number of hearts available. There are about 2200 heart transplants performed each year.

The risk of heart failure increases with age, and being overweight is a significant independent risk factor. Experts fear that the incidence of heart failure will increase dramatically over the next few decades as our population ages and becomes increasingly obese.

Other Forms of Heart Disease

Other, less common, forms of heart disease include congenital heart disease, rheumatic heart disease, and heart valve disorders.

Congenital Heart Disease About 40,000 children born each year in the United States have a defect or malformation of the heart or major blood vessels. These conditions are collectively referred to as **congenital heart disease,** and they cause about 4200 deaths a year. The most common congenital defects are holes in the wall that divides the chambers of the heart. Such defects cause the heart to produce a distinctive sound, making diagnosis relatively simple. Another defect is *coarctation of the aorta,* a narrowing, or constriction, of the aorta. Heart failure may result unless the constricted area is repaired by surgery.

Most of the common congenital defects can now be accurately diagnosed and treated with medication or surgery. Early recognition of possible heart disease in a newborn is important in saving lives.

Hypertrophic cardiomyopathy (HCM) occurs in 1 out of every 500 people and is the most common cause of sudden death among athletes younger than age 35 (see the box "Sudden Death in Young Athletes" on p. 468). It generally is an inherited condition that causes the heart muscle to become hypertrophic (enlarged), primarily in the septum, which is the area between the two ventricles. Young children with this disorder usually have no obvious symptoms; the hypertrophy generally develops gradually between ages 5 and 15. People with hypertrophic cardiomyopathy are at high risk for sudden death, mainly due to serious arrhythmias. Hypertrophic cardiomyopathy may be identified by a **murmur,** diagnosed using echocardiography. Researchers are trying to identify the genes that cause this disease so that one day it may be diagnosed and treated very early, perhaps even before the hypertrophy develops.

Possible treatments include medication and a pacemaker or internal defibrillator. If the hypertrophy is mainly in the septum, some of the septum can be surgically removed or a nonsurgical procedure can be done to kill off the extra muscle. In either case, symptoms are significantly reduced, but the risk of arrhythmia and sudden death remains. The mortality rate is approximately 3% per year in adults and up to 6% per year in children. Individuals with hypertrophic cardiomyopathy should usually not participate in competitive sports because of the high risk of sudden death. In addition, if one person in a family is diagnosed with HCM, it is generally advised that all immediate family members get an echocardiogram. Children of an affected parent need an echocardiogram every 3 years until puberty and then once a year until age 20.

Rheumatic Heart Disease **Rheumatic fever,** a consequence of certain types of untreated streptococcal throat infections (group A beta-hemolytic), is a leading cause of heart trouble worldwide. Rheumatic fever can permanently damage the heart muscle and heart valves, a condition called rheumatic heart disease (RHD). Many of the approximately 100,000 operations on heart valves performed annually are related to RHD, and about 3500 Americans die each year from RHD. Fortunately, the incidence of rheumatic fever has declined significantly in the United

In the News

Sudden Death in Young Athletes

Although the sudden death of a young athlete (under age 35) tends to attract a lot of attention, it is an uncommon event, occurring in about 1 out of 200,000 athletes per year. The majority of these deaths are due to congenital cardiovascular conditions that are usually without prior symptoms and are therefore unlikely to be diagnosed during life without specific screening. These conditions also occur in the general population but may be more lethal during intense physical activity. Indeed, most young athletes who die suddenly do so during or immediately after training or competition.

The most common cardiovascular cause of sudden death in young athletes is hypertrophic cardiomyopathy, accounting for about one-third of cases. In this condition, the heart muscle becomes very thick, which can impede the outflow of blood and cause fatal arrhythmias, especially during physical activity. Some people have a mild form that is hard to distinguish during screening tests from a normal athletic heart, which like any other muscle becomes bigger from physical activity.

The second most common cardiovascular cause of sudden death in athletes is congenital coronary artery anomalies, which account for about 20% of cases. In this condition, a coronary artery is malformed or doesn't arise from its normal position on the aorta; for example, if the left coronary artery originates from the right side of the aorta, near the right coronary artery, it may then have an unusual bend or shape. During physical activity, the anomalous artery may be unable to provide adequate blood flow to the heart muscle, leading to damage to the heart cells or to fatal arrhythmia.

Congenital malformations, including problems with the heart valves and the electrical conduction system, account for most other sudden deaths among athletes. Coronary artery disease is a more common cause in older athletes but rarely occurs in younger athletes. In about 2% of deaths, no cause can be identified. Some of these deaths may be due to noncardiac factors, including substance abuse (for example, cocaine) or use of the supplement ephedra. Use of anabolic steroids is associated with an increase in LDL cholesterol and early coronary artery disease, as well as risk of sudden cardiac death.

The majority (90%) of young athletes who have sudden cardiac death are male. Possible explanations are that men are more likely than women to participate in organized sports, to be exposed to more intensive training demands, and to participate in the sports most associated with sudden deaths (basketball, football). Men also have higher rates of certain cardiovascular problems, including hypertrophic cardiomyopathy. Ethnicity may also play a role, with the majority of reported sudden deaths in competitive athletes occuring in whites (52%) and African Americans (44%).

In most cases, underlying cardiovascular disease was completely unsuspected in affected individuals: Fewer than 20% report cardiovascular symptoms in the 36 months preceding their deaths.

There has been an effort to reduce the number of sudden deaths in young athletes by implementing preparticipation screening programs, although such programs are not foolproof. The American Heart Association has developed guidelines for screening high school and collegiate athletes. Those with a history of cardiovascular symptoms, a family history of sudden death, a murmur, or other worrisome physical findings should be referred to a cardiovascular specialist for further evaluation. If a cardiovascular condition that could lead to sudden cardiac death is identified, recommendations will be outlined for determining eligibility for continued participation in competitive sports.

States since the introduction of antibiotics; rates are highest among African Americans, Latinos, and American Indians.

Symptoms of strep throat include the sudden onset of a sore throat, painful swallowing, fever, swollen glands, headache, nausea, and vomiting. Careful laboratory diagnosis is important because strep throat is treated with antibiotics, which are not useful in the treatment of far more common viral sore throats. Rheumatic fever primarily affects children between the ages of 5 and 15. The symptoms generally occur about 3 weeks after the strep infection. They tend to be vague but may include weight loss or failure to gain weight, fever, poor appetite, repeated nosebleeds, jerky body movements, fatigue, weakness, and pain in the arms, legs, or abdomen. If left untreated, up to 3% of strep infections progress into rheumatic fever.

Term

mitral valve prolapse (MVP) A condition in which the mitral valve billows out during ventricular contraction, possibly allowing leakage of blood from the left ventricle into the left atrium.

Heart Valve Disorders Congenital defects and certain types of infections can cause abnormalities in the valves between the chambers of the heart. Heart valve problems generally fall into two categories—the valve fails to open fully, or it fails to close completely. In either case, blood flow through the heart is impaired. Treatment for heart valve disorders depends on their location and severity; serious problems may be treated with surgery to repair or replace a valve. People with certain types of heart valve defects are advised to take antibiotics prior to some types of dental and surgical procedures in order to prevent bacteria, which may be dislodged into the bloodstream during the procedure, from infecting the defective valve.

Do More

- Eat a diet rich in fruits, vegetable, whole grains, and low-fat or fat-free dairy products. Eat 7–13 servings of fruits and vegetables each day.
- Eat several servings of high-fiber foods each day.
- Eat 2 or more servings of fish per week; try a few servings of nuts and soy foods each week.
- Choose unsaturated fats rather than saturated and trans fats.
- Be physically active; do both aerobic exercise and strength training on a regular basis.
- Achieve and maintain a healthy weight.
- Develop effective strategies for handling stress and anger. Nurture old friendships and family ties, and make new friends; pay attention to your spiritual side.
- Obtain recommended screening tests and follow your physician's recommendations.

Do Less

- Don't use tobacco in any form: cigarettes, spit tobacco, cigars and pipes, bidis and clove cigarettes.
- Avoid exposure to environmental tobacco smoke.
- Limit consumption of fats, especially trans fats and saturated fats.
- Limit consumption of cholesterol, added sugars, and refined carbohydrates.
- Avoid excessive alcohol consumption—no more than one drink per day for women and two drinks per day for men.
- Limit consumption of salt to no more than 2300 mg of sodium per day (1500 mg if you have or are at high risk for hypertension).
- Avoid excess stress, anger, and hostility.

Figure 15-8 Strategies for reducing your risk of cardiovascular disease.

The most common heart valve disorder is **mitral valve prolapse (MVP)**, which occurs in about 4% of the population. MVP is characterized by a billowing of the mitral valve, which separates the left ventricle and left atrium, during ventricular contraction; in some cases, blood leaks from the ventricle into the atrium. Most people with MVP have no symptoms; they have the same ability to exercise and live as long as people without MVP. The condition is often diagnosed during a routine medical exam when an extra heart sound (a click) or murmur is heard; the diagnosis can be confirmed with echocardiography. Treatment is usually unnecessary, although surgery may be needed in the rare cases where leakage through the faulty valve is severe. Experts disagree over whether patients with MVP should take antibiotics prior to dental procedures; most often, only those patients with significant leakage of blood from the valve are advised to take antibiotics.

PROTECTING YOURSELF AGAINST CARDIOVASCULAR DISEASE

There are several important steps you can take now to lower your risk of developing CVD (Figure 15-8). CVD can begin very early in life. For example, fatty streaks (very early atherosclerosis) can be seen on the aorta in children younger than age 10. Also, young adults with relatively low cholesterol levels go on to live substantially longer than those with higher levels. Reducing CVD risk factors when you are young can pay off with many extra years of life and health (see the box "Are You at Risk for CVD?" on p. 470).

Eat Heart-Healthy

For most Americans, eating a heart-healthy diet involves many of the changes suggested in the 2005 Dietary Guidelines for Americans: cutting total fat intake, substituting unsaturated fats for saturated and trans fats, and increasing intake of whole grains and fiber. Such changes can lower blood levels of total cholesterol, LDL cholesterol, and triglycerides. Reducing salt intake and obtaining adequate potassium can help lower blood pressure. A moderate amount of alcohol may also be beneficial for some people.

Decreased Fat and Cholesterol Intake The National Cholesterol Education Program (NCEP) recommends that all Americans over age 2 adopt a diet in which total fat consumption is no more than 30% of total daily calories, with no more than one-third of total fat calories (10% of total daily calories) coming from saturated fat. The American Heart Association now recommends that no more than 7% of daily calories come from saturated fats; this recommendation applies to everyone. For people with heart disease or high LDL levels, the NCEP recommends a total fat intake of 25–35% of total daily calories and a saturated fat intake of less than 7% of total calories. (As described earlier, the higher total fat allowance is for people with insulin resistance who need to decrease their carbohydrate intake.

Saturated fats are found in animal products, palm and coconut oil, and hydrogenated vegetable oils, which are also high in trans fats. Saturated and trans fats influence the production and excretion of cholesterol by the liver, so decreasing saturated and trans fat intake is the most

Are You at Risk for CVD?

Your chances of suffering an early heart attack or stroke depend on a variety of factors, many of which are under your control. The best time to identify your risk factors and change your behavior to lower your risk is when you are young. You can significantly affect your future health and quality of life if you adopt healthy behaviors. To help identify your risk factors, circle the response for each risk category that best describes you:

1. Gender and Age

0 Female age 55 or younger; male age 45 or younger
2 Female age 55 or older or male age 45 or older

2. Heredity

0 Neither parent suffered a heart attack or stroke before age 60.
3 One parent suffered a heart attack or stroke before age 60.
7 Both parents suffered a heart attack or stroke before age 60.

3. Smoking

0 Never smoked
3 Quit more than 2 years ago and lifetime smoking is less than 5 pack-years*
6 Quit less than 2 years ago and/or lifetime smoking is greater than 5 pack-years*
8 Smoke less than ½ pack per day
13 Smoke more than ½ pack per day
15 Smoke more than 1 pack per day

4. Environmental Tobacco Smoke

0 Do not live or work with smokers
2 Exposed to ETS at work
3 Live with a smoker
4 Both live and work with smokers

5. Blood Pressure

If available, average your last three readings:

0 120/80 or below
1 121/81–130/85
3 Don't know
5 131/86–150/90
9 151/91–170/100
13 Above 170/100

6. Total Cholesterol (mg/dl)

0 Lower than 190
1 190–210
2 Don't know
3 211–240
4 241–270
5 271–300
6 Over 300

7. HDL Cholesterol (mg/dl)

0 Over 60
1 55–60
2 Don't know
3 45–54
5 35–44
7 25–34
12 Lower than 25

8. Exercise

0 Exercise three times a week
1 Exercise once or twice a week
2 Occasional exercise less than once a week
7 Rarely exercise

9. Diabetes

0 No personal or family history
2 One parent with diabetes
6 Two parents with diabetes
9 Non–insulin-dependent diabetes
13 Insulin-dependent diabetes

10. Body Mass Index (kg/m^2)

0 <23.0
1 23.0–24.9
2 25.0–28.9
3 29.0–34.9
5 35.0–39.9
7 ≥40

11. Stress

0 Relaxed most of the time
1 Occasional stress and anger
2 Frequently stressed and angry
3 Usually stressed and angry

Scoring

Total your risk factor points. Refer to the list below to get an approximate rating of your risk of suffering an early heart attack or stroke.

Score	Estimated Risk
Less than 20	Low risk
20–29	Moderate risk
30–45	High risk
Over 45	Extremely high risk

*Pack-years can be calculated by multiplying the number of packs you smoked per day by the number of years you smoked. For example, if you smoked a pack and a half a day for 5 years, you would have smoked the equivalent of 1.5 × 5 = 7.5 pack-years.

important dietary change you can make to achieve and maintain healthy cholesterol levels. Choose unsaturated fats, especially monounsaturated fats, and omega-3 polyunsaturated fats, over saturated and trans fats. The American Heart Association recommends that less than 1% of total calories come from trans fats.

Animal products contain cholesterol as well as saturated fat; vegetable products do not contain cholesterol. The NCEP recommends that most Americans limit dietary cholesterol intake to no more than 300 mg per day; for people with heart disease or high LDL levels, the suggested daily limit is 200 mg. The cholesterol content of packaged foods is stated on food labels, along with their total, saturated, and trans fat content.

Increased Fiber Intake Fiber traps the bile acids the liver needs to manufacture cholesterol and carries them to the large intestine, where they are excreted. It slows the production of proteins that promote blood clotting. Fiber may also interfere with the absorption of dietary fat and may help you cut total food intake because foods rich in fiber tend to be filling. Studies have shown that a high-fiber diet is associated with a 40–50% reduction in the risk of heart attack and stroke. To obtain the recommended 25–38 grams of dietary fiber per day, choose a diet rich in whole grains, fruits, and vegetables. Good sources of fiber include oatmeal, some breakfast cereals, barley, legumes, and most fruits and vegetables.

Decreased Sodium Intake and Increased Potassium Intake Reducing sodium intake to recommended levels, while also increasing potassium intake, can help reduce blood pressure for many people. The recommended limit for sodium intake is 2300 mg per day; for population groups at special risk, including those with hypertension, middle-aged and older adults, and African Americans, the recommended limit is 1500 mg per day. About 10% of the sodium in the American diet occurs naturally in food, and another 10% is added during cooking or at the table; the remainder is added during processing. To limit sodium intake, read food labels carefully, and avoid foods particularly high in sodium; instead, choose foods that are fresh, less processed, and less sodium-dense.

Adequate potassium intake is also important in control of blood pressure, and many Americans consume less than recommended amounts of the mineral. Good food sources include leafy green vegetables like spinach and beet greens, root vegetables like white and sweet potatoes, vine fruits like cantaloupe and honeydew melon, winter squash, bananas, many dried fruits, and tomato sauce.

Moderate Alcohol Consumption (For Some) The Dietary Guidelines for Americans state that moderate alcohol consumption may lower the risk of CHD among middle-aged and older adults. (Moderate means no more than one drink per day for women and two drinks per day for men.) Moderate alcohol use may increase HDL cholesterol; it may also reduce stroke risk, possibly by dampening the inflammatory response or by affecting blood clotting. For most people under age 45, however, the risks of alcohol use probably outweigh any health benefit. Excessive alcohol consumption increases the risk of a variety of serious health problems, including hypertension, stroke, some cancers, liver disease, alcohol dependence, and injuries (see Chapter 10). If you do drink, do so moderately, with food, and at times when drinking will not put you or others at risk.

Other Dietary Factors Researchers have identified other dietary factors that may affect CVD risk:

- *Omega-3 fatty acids.* Found in fish, shellfish, and some plant foods (nuts and canola, soybean, and flaxseed oils), omega-3 fatty acids may reduce clotting, abnormal heart rhythms, and inflammation and have other heart-healthy effects, such as lowering triglycerides. The American Heart Association recommends eating fish two or more times a week; fish oil capsules may be appropriate for some people who won't eat fish or who have certain CVD risk factors. Note that omega-3 fatty acids may raise LDL levels and some fish sources may be high in mercury. Plant sources of omega-3 fatty acids are also a good choice.
- *Plant stanols and sterols.* Plant stanols and sterols, found in some types of trans fat–free margarines and other products, reduce the absorption of cholesterol in the body and help lower LDL levels. For people with high LDL levels that do not respond to changes in fat intake, the NCEP suggests an intake of 2 grams per day of plant stanols or sterols.
- *Folic acid, vitamin B-6, and vitamin B-12.* These vitamins lower homocysteine levels, and folic acid has also been found to reduce the risk of hypertension.
- *Calcium.* Diets rich in calcium may help prevent hypertension and possibly stroke by reducing insulin resistance and platelet aggegration. Good sources of calcium are low-fat and fat-free dairy products (see Chapter 12).
- *Soy protein.* Although soy itself doesn't seem to have much effect on cholesterol, replacing some animal proteins with soy protein (e.g., tofu) may help lower LDL cholesterol.
- *Healthy carbohydrates.* Most of the carbohydrates in the current American diet come from added sugars, refined grains, and starchy foods, including soft drinks, sweets, white potatoes (including french fries and chips), white bread, and refined ready-to-eat cereals; these foods are often relatively low in nutrients and have a high glycemic index. Healthier carbohydrates choices, including

whole grains, fruits, and nonstarchy vegetables, typically provide more nutrients and have a lower glycemic index. Choosing healthy carbohydrates is important for people with insulin resistance, pre-diabetes, or diabetes.

• *Total calories.* Some studies have found that reducing energy intake can improve cholesterol and triglyceride levels as much as reducing fat intake does. Reduced calorie intake also helps control body weight, an extremely important risk factor for CVD.

Although nutrition is important, most experts recommend against taking nutritional supplements (especially extra folic acid and B vitamins) as a way to prevent heart disease. If you are concerned about your heart health and may not be getting the nutrition you need, ask your physician or a registered dietician for advice.

DASH A diet plan that reflects many of the recommendations described above was released as part of a study called Dietary Approaches to Stop Hypertension, or DASH (see Chapter 12). The DASH study found that a diet low in fat and high in fruits, vegetables, and low-fat dairy products reduces blood pressure. (It also follows the recommendations for lowering the risk of heart disease, cancer, and osteoporosis.) For people on a diet of 2000 calories per day, the DASH diet plan is as follows:

- 6–8 servings per day of grains and grain products
- 4–5 servings per day of vegetables
- 4–5 servings per day of fruits
- 2–3 servings per day of low-fat or fat-free dairy products
- 6 or fewer 1-ounce servings per day of meats, poultry, and fish
- 4–5 servings per *week* of nuts, seeds, and legumes
- 2–3 servings per day of added fats, oils, and salad dressings
- 5 or fewer servings per *week* of snacks and sweets

Remember not to focus on one particular food. Success depends on the collective effects of your entire diet. Eat a varied, moderate diet rich in fruits, vegetables, and whole grains, and use your common sense. For example, substituting olive oil or canola oil for butter is a helpful change because it lowers saturated fat intake. But adding a new oil to your diet—without subtracting fat elsewhere—will add calories and fat and not be nearly as beneficial.

Exercise Regularly

You can significantly reduce your risk of CVD with a moderate amount of physical activity. Follow the guidelines for physical activity and exercise described in Chapter 13. The American Heart Association recommends strength training in addition to aerobic exercise for building and maintaining cardiovascular health. Strength training helps lower blood pressure, reduce body fat, and improve lipid levels and glucose metabolism.

Avoid Tobacco

Remember: The number-one risk factor for CVD that you can control is smoking. If you smoke, quit. If you don't, don't start. The majority of people who start don't believe they will become hooked, but most do. If you live or work with people who smoke, encourage them to quit—for their sake and yours. Exposure to ETS raises your risk of CVD, and there is no safe level of exposure. If you find yourself breathing in smoke, take steps to prevent or stop the exposure.

Until recently, many experts believed that 5 or more years after quitting smoking, a former smoker's CVD risk would drop to about that of a person who had never smoked. However, research now indicates that the rate of plaque formation in arteries is significantly greater in former smokers than in those who have never smoked. What seems to matter most for CVD risk is the total amount of smoking over a lifetime rather than whether a person is currently smoking. The same study also showed that people exposed to environmental tobacco smoke have a significantly higher rate of plaque formation than nonsmokers who are not exposed to ETS.

The bottom line? Not smoking is highly beneficial. If you stop smoking, your risk of CVD will decrease, regardless of the age at which you quit. But abstaining from cigarette smoking and avoiding ETS throughout your entire life is even better.

Know and Manage Your Blood Pressure

Currently, only about 34% of Americans with hypertension have their blood pressure under control; the *Healthy People 2010* report sets the goal of increasing this number to 50%. If you have no CVD risk factors, have your blood pressure measured by a trained professional at least once every 2 years; yearly tests are recommended if you have other risk factors. If your blood pressure is high, follow your physician's advice on how to lower it. For those with hypertension that is not readily controlled with lifestyle changes, an array of antihypertension medications are available.

Know and Manage Your Cholesterol Levels

All people age 20 and over should have their cholesterol checked at least once every 5 years. The NCEP recommends a fasting lipoprotein profile that measures total cholesterol, HDL, LDL, and triglyceride levels. Once you know your baseline numbers, you and your physician can develop an LDL goal and lifestyle plan. Your LDL goal

Religion and Wellness

In the past decade, numerous observational studies have shown a link between religious or spiritual factors and health. Regardless of why or how this relationship happens, the evidence clearly connects religion and wellness along several dimensions.

- *Reduced risk of disease and faster recovery.* Researchers have found that people who attend religious services regularly have especially low rates of heart disease, lung disease, cirrhosis of the liver, and some kinds of cancer. Older adults who attend religious services have healthier immune systems and recover from surgery more quickly. One study found that "positive religious coping styles" in cardiac patients contributed to better overall functioning after surgery.
- *Improved emotional health.* Religion also seems to aid in recovery from depression. Participating in religious activities, listening to religious programs on the radio, and watching religious programs on television are all associated with fewer symptoms of depression.
- *Longer life expectancy.* One study found that people who attend religious services one or more times a week live about 8 years longer than people who never attend services. How involved people are in their faith may be more important than was previously believed.

Although researchers are not sure why religion or spirituality seems to improve health, several explanations have been offered:

- *Social support.* Attending religious services helps people feel they are part of a community with similar values. It promotes social support and caring.
- *Healthy habits.* Religion may encourage healthy habits—such as eating less meat, drinking less alcohol, or eating a vegetarian diet—and also may discourage behavior that is harmful to health, such as smoking and indiscriminate sex.
- *Positive attitude.* Having a sense of meaning and purpose in life results in a positive attitude and a sense of hope. This outlook may help patients participate more in their own care.
- *Moments of relaxation.* Deep relaxation during prayer may invoke benefits by eliciting the relaxation response.

SOURCES: Ai, A. L., et al. 2006. Depression, faith-based coping, and short-term postoperative global functioning in adult and older patients undergoing cardiac surgery. *Journal of Psychosomatic Research* 60(1): 21–28; Strawbridge, W. J., et al. 2001. Religious attendance increases survival by improving and maintaining good health behaviors, mental health, and social relationships. *Annals of Behavioral Medicine* 23(1): 68–74; Hummer, R. A., et al. 1999. Religious involvement and U.S. adult mortality. *Demography* 36: 273–285.

depends in part on how many of the following major risk factors you have:

- Cigarette smoking
- High blood pressure
- Low HDL cholesterol (less than 40 mg/dl)
- A family history of heart disease
- Age (≥45 for men, ≥55 years for women)

An HDL level of 60 mg/dl or higher is protective and counts as a negative risk factor, meaning it removes one risk factor from your total count of risk factors. Depending on your LDL level and other risk factors, your physician may recommend changes in lifestyle alone or lifestyle changes in combination with drug therapy. The lifestyle modifications recommended by the 2001 NCEP guidelines, known collectively as "Therapeutic Lifestyle Changes" (TLC), include the TLC diet, weight management, and increased physical activity. The TLC diet includes total fat intake of 25–35% of total daily calories, saturated fat intake of less than 7% of total calories, and, for some people, 10–25 grams per day of viscous (soluble) fiber and 2 grams per day of plant stanols and sterols.

- If you have one or no risk factors, the NCEP sets an LDL goal of less than 160 mg/dl. If your LDL is below that level, maintain a healthy lifestyle by eating a heart-healthy diet, getting regular exercise, maintaining a healthy body weight, and not smoking. If your LDL is 160 mg/dl or higher, you should begin TLC; you may also need medication to bring your LDL into the healthy range.
- If you have two or more risk factors for heart disease, the NCEP sets an LDL goal of less than 130 mg/dl. If your LDL level is 130 or above, begin TLC; if your LDL level remains above the goal and your risk for CVD is fairly high, your physician may recommend medication.
- If you have heart disease or a condition such as diabetes that the NCEP considers the risk equivalent of heart disease, your goal for LDL is less than 100 mg/dl. For very-high-risk patients, the goal is less than 70 mg/dl. TLC is recommended for all people in this risk category. In addition, a variety of medications are available to lower LDL and improve other blood fat levels.

Develop Effective Ways to Handle Stress and Anger

To reduce the psychological and social risk factors for CVD, develop effective strategies for handling the stress in your life. Shore up your social support network, and try some of the techniques described in Chapter 2 for managing stress (see also the box "Religion and Wellness").

Manage Other Risk Factors and Medical Conditions

Know your CVD risk factors and follow your physician's advice for testing, lifestyle changes, and drug treatments.

If you are at high risk for CVD, consult a physician about taking small doses of aspirin. Aspirin reduces inflammation and the blood's tendency to clot, thereby reducing the risk of CVD for some people. Low doses of aspirin (50–325 mg) may be recommended to treat TIA, stroke, angina, heart attack, and certain other cardiovascular problems. A 2006 study found that regular aspirin intake significantly reduced the risk of heart attack in men but not in women. Aspirin use lowered the risk of stroke in women but not in men. Regular aspirin use carries possible side effects, such as gastrointestinal bleeding.

Tips for Today

Risk factors for cardiovascular disease fall into two categories—those you can do something about, such as physical activity and levels of stress, and those you can't, such as age and ethnicity. Because cardiovascular disease is a long-term process that can begin when you're young, it's important to develop heart-healthy habits early in life.

Right now you can

- Plan to have fish for dinner two times this week.
- Practice time management by prioritizing your day's activities; work on accomplishing the most important tasks first.
- Resolve to address any nagging interpersonal issue that's been causing you stress.
- Go to the gym or fitness facility on your campus and get started on an aerobic exercise program.

SUMMARY

- The cardiovascular system pumps and circulates blood throughout the body. The heart pumps blood to the lungs via the pulmonary artery and to the body via the aorta.
- The exchange of nutrients and waste products takes place between the capillaries and the tissues.
- The six major risk factors for CVD that can be changed are smoking, high blood pressure, unhealthy cholesterol levels, inactivity, obesity, and diabetes.
- Effects of smoking include lower HDL levels, increased blood pressure and heart rate, accelerated plaque formation, and increased risk of blood clots.
- Hypertension occurs when blood pressure exceeds normal limits most of the time. It weakens the heart, scars and hardens arteries, and can damage the eyes and kidneys.
- High LDL and low HDL cholesterol levels contribute to clogged arteries and increase the risk of CVD.
- Physical inactivity, obesity, and diabetes are interrelated and are associated with high blood pressure and unhealthy cholesterol levels.
- Contributing risk factors that can be changed include high triglyceride levels and psychological and social factors.
- Risk factors for CVD that can't be changed include being over 65, being male, being African American, and having a family history of CVD.
- Atherosclerosis is a progressive hardening and narrowing of arteries that can lead to restricted blood flow and even complete blockage.
- Heart attacks are usually the result of a long-term disease process. Warning signs of a heart attack include chest discomfort, shortness of breath, nausea, and sweating.
- A stroke occurs when the blood supply to the brain is cut off by a blood clot or hemorrhage. A transient ischemic attack (TIA) is a warning sign of stroke.
- Congestive heart failure occurs when the heart's pumping action becomes less efficient and fluid collects in the lungs or in other parts of the body.
- Dietary changes that can protect against CVD include decreasing your intake of fat, especially saturated and trans fats, and cholesterol, and increasing your intake of fiber by eating more fruits, vegetables, and whole grains.
- CVD risk can also be reduced by engaging in regular exercise, avoiding tobacco and environmental tobacco smoke, knowing and managing your blood pressure and cholesterol levels, developing effective ways of handling stress and anger, and managing other risk factors and medical conditions.

Take Action

1. **Learn CPR:** The CPR courses given by the American Red Cross and other groups provide invaluable training that may help you save a life some day. Anyone can take these courses and become qualified to perform CPR and use AED equipment. Investigate CPR courses in your community, and sign up to take one.

2. **Investigate your family's CVD history:** Do some research into your family medical history. Is there CVD in your family, as indicated by premature deaths from heart attack, stroke, or heart failure? Is there a family history of diabetes? Keep your family health history in mind as you consider whether you need to make lifestyle changes to avoid CVD.

Behavior Change Strategy

Reducing the Saturated and Trans Fats in Your Diet

No more than 7% of the calories in your diet should come from saturated fats, and no more than 1% should come from trans fats. Foods high in saturated fat include meat, poultry skin, full-fat dairy products, coconut and palm oils, and hydrogenated vegetable oils. Hydrogenated fats and products such as snack foods that are made with them and deep-fried fast food are high in trans fats.

Monitor Your Current Diet

To see how your diet measures up, keep track of everything you eat for 3 days in your health journal. Information about the calorie and saturated fat content of foods is available on many food labels, in books, and on the Internet. The list below gives a few average values for foods that are rich sources of trans fats in the American diet. However, food companies are trying to reduce or eliminate trans fats from their products, so it's important to read the labels.

	Grams of trans fat/serving
Pot pie	6
French fries (large)	5
Pound cake	5
Fish sticks	5
Doughnut	4
Biscuit	4
Fried, breaded chicken	3
Danish pastry	3
Vegetable shortening	3
Margarine (stick)	2
Microwave popcorn	2
Sandwich cookies	2
Snack crackers	2
Margarine (tub)	1

At the end of the monitoring period, write in the calories and grams of saturated and trans fat for as many as possible of the foods you've eaten. Determine the percentage of daily calories as fat that you consumed for each day: multiply grams of saturated and trans fats by 9 (fat has 9 calories per gram) and then divide by total calories. For example, if you consumed 30 grams of saturated and trans fats and 2100 calories on a particular day, then your saturated and trans fat consumption as a percentage of total calories would be $30 \times 9 = 270$ calories of fat $\div$ 2100 total calories $= 0.13$, or 13%. If you have trouble obtaining all the data you need to do the calculations, you can still estimate whether your diet is high in saturated and trans fats by seeing how many servings of foods high in unhealthy fats you typically consume on a daily basis (see the list).

Making Heart-Healthy Changes

To reduce your intake of unhealthy fats, you may want to set a limit on the number of servings of foods high in saturated and trans fats that you consume each day. Or you may want to set a more precise goal and then continue to monitor your daily consumption. The 7% limit set by the American Heart Association and the NCEP corresponds to 12 grams of saturated and trans fats in a 1600-calorie diet, 17 grams in a 2200-calorie diet, and 22 grams in a 2800-calorie diet.

To plan healthy changes, take a close look at your food record. Do you choose many foods high in saturated and trans fats? Do you limit your portion sizes to those recommended by MyPyramid? Try making healthy substitutions. Do you have a salami and cheese sandwich for lunch? Try turkey for a change. Do you always order french fries when you eat out? Try half a plain baked potato or a different vegetable next time. Do you snack on pastries, cookies, doughnuts, chips, or fatty crackers? Try fresh fruits and vegetables instead. If you frequently eat in fast-food restaurants or other places where the majority of the menu is heavy in saturated and trans fats, trying finding an appealing alternative—and recruit some friends to join you.

When you do choose foods that are rich in saturated and trans fats, *watch your portion sizes carefully*. Choose cuts of meat that have the least amount of visible fat, and trim off what you see. And try to balance your choices throughout the day: For example, if your lunch includes a hamburger and fries, choose broiled fish or poultry or a vegetarian pasta dish for dinner. There are plenty of delicious choices that are low in saturated and trans fats. Plan your diet around a variety of whole grains, vegetables, legumes, and fruits, which are nearly always low in fats and high in nutrients.

(continued)

For More Information

Books

Freeman, M. W., and C. E. Junge. 2005. *Harvard Medical School Guide to Lowering Your Cholesterol.* New York: McGraw-Hill. *Information about cholesterol, including lifestyle changes and medication for improving cholesterol levels.*

Moore, T., et al. 2003. *The DASH Diet for Hypertension.* New York: Pocket Books. *Provides background information and guidelines for adopting the DASH diet; also includes recipes.*

Nelson, M. E., and A. Lichtenstein. 2006. *Strong Women, Strong Hearts.* New York: Perigee Trade. *Lifestyle advice for women to prevent heart disease.*

Phibbs, B. 2007. *The Human Heart: A Basic Guide to Heart Disease.* Philadelphia: Lippincott Williams & Wilkins. *Provides information about heart disease, treatments, and recovery for patients and their families.*

Reaven, G. M., et al. 2001. *Syndrome X, the Silent Killer: The New Heart Disease Risk.* St. Louis, Mo.: Fireside. *Provides information about metabolic syndrome and insulin resistance, including lifestyle strategies for affected individuals.*

Romaine, D. S., and O. S. Randall. 2005. *The Encyclopedia of Heart and Heart Disease.* New York: Facts on File. *Includes entries on the functioning of the cardiovascular system, types and causes of heart disease, and prevention and treatment.*

Instead of . . .	Try . . .
Butter, stick margarine, vegetable shortening, coconut and palm oils	Vegetable oils, trans fat–free tub or squeeze margarines
Whole or 2% milk; regular cheese, mayonnaise, and sour cream	Fat-free or 1% milk, low-fat cheese, fat-free or low-fat sour cream, yogurt, or mayonnaise
Chips, cheese puffs, crackers, buttered popcorn	Fruits, vegetables, rice cakes, plain popcorn, pretzels, fat-free chips, baked crackers
Cakes, cookies, pastries, doughnuts, cinnamon rolls, pie, regular ice cream	Fruit or a *small* serving of a low-fat sweet (angel food cake; fat-free ice cream, frozen yogurt, sherbet, or sorbet)
Biscuits, croissants, fried tortillas, regular granola, muffins, coffee cake	Whole-grain breads and rolls, baked tortillas, low-fat granola or cold cereal, English muffin, or bagel
Creamy or cheesy sauces and soups	Tomato- and other vegetable-based sauces, clam sauce, clear soups
Ground beef, hamburger patty, meatloaf, ribs, T-bone or flank steak, prime grades of beef	Ground turkey, veggie burger, extra lean ground beef, round steak, sirloin, choice or select grades of beef
Pork chops, roast, or ribs; bone-in ham; lamb chops or ribs	Pork sirloin or tenderloin, boneless ham, veal chops and cutlets, leg of lamb
Bacon, sausage, lunch meats, hot dogs	Canadian bacon; turkey ham or pastrami, other low-fat lunch meats
Poultry with skin; fried chicken or fish	Skinless poultry, especially breast or drumstick; baked, broiled, grilled, or roasted poultry or fish; ground turkey
French fries, onion rings	Baked potato or other nonfried vegetable, rice
Pizza, pot pie, macaroni and cheese, and other high-fat convenience foods	Vegetarian or turkey chili, pasta with vegetables, grilled poultry and fish dishes

SOURCES: New heart dos and don'ts. 2006. *Consumer Reports Health,* March, 49; American Heart Association. 2000. *An Eating Plan for Healthy Americans: The New 2000 Food Guidelines.* Dallas, Tex.: American Heart Association; U.S. Department of Agriculture and U.S. Department of Health and Human Services. 2000. *Nutrition and Your Health: Dietary Guidelines for Americans,* 5th ed. Home and Garden Bulletin No. 232.

Organizations, Hotlines, and Web Sites

American Heart Association. Provides information on hundreds of topics relating to the prevention and control of cardiovascular disease; sponsors a general Web site as well as several sites focusing on specific topics.

800-AHA-USA1 (800-242-8721; general information)
http://www.americanheart.org (general information)
http://www.deliciousdecisions.org (dietary advice)
http://www.justmove.org (fitness advice)

Dietary Approaches to Stop Hypertension (DASH). Provides information about the design, diets, and results of the DASH study, including tips on how to follow the DASH diet at home.

http://www.nhlbi.nih.gov/health/public/heart/hbp/dash

Franklin Institute Science Museum/The Heart: An On-Line Exploration. An online museum exhibit containing information on the structure and function of the heart, how to monitor your heart's health, and how to maintain a healthy heart.

http://www.fi.edu/biosci/heart.html

HeartInfo—Heart Information Network. Provides information for heart patients and others interested in learning how to identify and reduce their risk factors for heart disease; includes links to many related sites.

http://www.heartinfo.org

MedlinePlus: Blood, Heart, and Circulation Topics. Provides links to reliable sources of information on many topics relating to cardiovascular health.

http://www.nlm.nih.gov/medlineplus/heartandcirculation.html

National Heart, Lung, and Blood Institute. Provides information on and interactive applications for a variety of topics relating to cardiovascular health and disease, including cholesterol, smoking, obesity, hypertension, and the DASH diet.

800-575-WELL
http://www.nhlbi.nih.gov
http://rover.nhlbi.nih.gov/chd

National Stroke Association. Provides information and referrals for stroke victims and their families; the Web site has a stroke risk assessment.

800-STROKES
http://www.stroke.org

See also the listings for Chapters 2, 3, and 12–14.

Selected Bibliography

Ajani, U. A., et al. 2004. Body mass index and mortality among US male physicians. *Annals of Epidemiology* 14(10): 731–739.

American Heart Association. 2006. *Heart Disease and Stroke Statistics—2006 Update.* Dallas: American Heart Association.

Barrett-Connor, E., et al. 2004. Women and heart disease: The role of diabetes and hyperglycemia. *Archives of Internal Medicine* 164: 934–942.

Berger, J. S., et al. 2006. Aspirin for the primary prevention of cardiovascular events in women and men: A sex-specific meta-analysis of randomized controlled trials. *Journal of the American Medical Association* 295(3): 306–313.

Bonaa, K. H., et al. 2006. Homocysteine lowering and cardiovascular events after acute myocardial infarction. *New England Journal of Medicine* 354(15): 1578–1588.

Bradley, E. H., et al. 2004. Racial and ethnic differences in time to acute reperfusion therapy for patients hospitalized with myocardial infarction. *Journal of the American Medical Association* 292(13): 1563–1572.

Cardiopulmonary resuscitation (CPR). 2005. *Journal of the American Medication Association* 293(3): 388.

Centers for Disease Control and Prevention. 2005. Differences in disability among black and white stroke survivors—United States, 2000–2001. *Morbidity and Mortality Weekly Report* 54(1): 3–9.

Centers for Disease Control and Prevention. 2005. Health disparities experienced by black or African Americans—United States. *Morbidity and Mortality Weekly Report* 54(1): 1–3.

Cooper, R. S., et al. 2005. An international comparative study of blood pressure in populations of European vs. African descent. *BMC Medicine* 3(1): 2.

Daviglus, M. L., et al. 2004. Favorable cardiovascular risk profile in young women and long-term risk of cardiovascular and all-cause mortality. *Journal of the American Medical Association* 292(13): 1588–1592.

de Torbal, A., et al. 2006. Incidence of recognized and unrecognized myocardial infarction in men and women aged 55 and older: The Rotterdam Study. *European Heart Journal* 27(6): 729–736.

Eaker, E., et al. 2004. Anger and hostility predict the development of atrial fibrillation in men in the Framingham Offspring Study. *Circulation* 109: 1267–1271.

Elliott, P., et al. 2006. Association between protein intake and blood pressure: The INTERMAP study. *Archives of Internal Medicine* 166(1): 79–87.

Forman, J. P., et al. 2005. Folate intake and risk of incident hypertension among U.S. women. *Journal of the American Medical Association* 293(3): 320–329.

Geerts, S. O., et al. 2004. Further evidence of the association between periodontal conditions and coronary artery disease. *Journal of Periodontology* 75(9): 1274–1280.

Jenkins, D. J., et al. 2006. Assessment of the longer-term effects of a dietary portfolio of cholesterol-lowering foods in hypercholesterolemia. *American Journal of Clinical Nutrition* 83(3): 582–591.

Jensen, M. K., et al. 2004. Intakes of whole grains, bran, and germ and the risk of coronary heart disease in men. *American Journal of Clinical Nutrition* 80(6): 1492–1499.

Kastrati, A., et al. 2005. Sirolimus-eluting stent or paclitaxel-eluting stent vs. balloon angioplasty for prevention of recurrences in patients with coronary in-stent restenosis. *Journal of the American Medical Association* 293(2): 165–171.

Kelemen, L. E., et al. 2005. Associations of dietary protein with disease and mortality in a prospective study of postmenopausal women. *American Journal of Epidemiology* 161(3): 239–249.

Koton, S., et al. 2004. Triggering risk factors for ischemic stroke. *Neurology* 63(11): 2006–2010.

Lloyd-Jones, D. M., et al. 2004. Parental cardiovascular disease as a risk factor for cardiovascular disease in middle-aged adults. *Journal of the American Medical Association* 291(18): 2204–2211.

Meadows, M. 2005. Brain attack: A look at stroke prevention and treatment. *FDA Consumer,* March/April.

Mosca, L., et al. 2004. Evidence-based guidelines for cardiovascular disease prevention in women. *Circulation* 109: 672–693.

Mozaffarian, D., et al. 2005. Interplay between different polyunsaturated fatty acids and risk of coronary heart disease in men. *Circulation* 111(2): 157–164.

Mukamal, K. J., et al. 2005. Alcohol and risk of ischemic stroke in men: The role of drinking patterns and usual beverage. *Annals of Internal Medicine* 142(1): 11–19.

Nissen, S. E., et al. 2005. Statin therapy, LDL cholesterol, C-reactive protein, and coronary artery disease. *New England Journal of Medicine* 352(1): 29–38.

O'Meara, J. G., et al. 2004. Ethnic and sex differences in the prevalence, treatment, and control of dyslipidemia among hypertensive adults in the GENOA study. *Archives of Internal Medicine* 164: 1313–1318.

Pereira, M. A., et al. 2004. Effects of a low-glycemic load diet on resting energy expenditure and heart disease risk factors during weight loss. *Journal of the American Medical Association* 292(20): 2482–2490.

Phillips, D. P., et al. 2004. Cardiac mortality is higher around Christmas and New Year's than at any other time. *Circulation* 110(25): 3781–3788.

Refsum, H., et al. 2006. The Hordaland Homocysteine Study: A community-based study of homocysteine, its determinants, and associations with disease. *Journal of Nutrition* 136(6 Suppl): 1731S–1740S.

Ridker, P. M., et al. 2005. C-reactive protein levels and outcomes after statin therapy. *New England Journal of Medicine* 352(1): 20–28.

Ridker, P. M., et al. 2005. A randomized trial of low-dose aspirin in the primary prevention of cardiovascular disease in women. *New England Journal of Medicine,* epub, March 7.

Rothwell, P. M., and C. P. Warlow. 2005. Timing of TIAs preceding stroke: Time window for prevention is very short. *Neurology* 64(5): 817–820.

Rozanski, A. S., et al. 2005. The epidemiology, pathophysiology, and management of psychosocial risk factors in cardiac practice: The emerging field of behavioral cardiology. *Journal of the American College of Cardiology* 45(5): 637–651.

Shai, I., et al. 2004. Homocysteine as a risk factor for coronary heart diseases and its association with inflammatory biomarkers, lipids and dietary factors. *Atherosclerosis* 177(2): 375–381.

Shai, I., et al. 2004. Multivariate assessment of lipid parameters as predictors of coronary heart disease among postmenopausal women. *Circulation* 110(18): 2824–2830.

St.-Onge, M. P., I. Janssen, and S. B. Heymsfield. 2004. Metabolic syndrome in normal-weight Americans: New definition of the metabolically obese, normal-weight individual. *Diabetes Care* 27(9): 2222–2228.

Timing is everything: Fluctuations in cardiac risk. 2004. *Harvard Men's health watch,* December.

Tufts University. 2006. Pendulum swings on estrogen and women's heart health risk. *Health & Nutrition Newsletter* 24(3): 1–2.

Turhan, H., et al. 2005. High prevalence of metabolic syndrome among young women with premature coronary artery disease. *Coronary Artery Disease* 16(1): 37–40.

Webb, D. 2005. Supplements for a healthy heart: What works, what doesn't. *Environmental Nutrition* 28(12): 1, 4.3

Willingham, S. A., and E. S. Kilpatrick. 2005. Evidence of gender bias when applying the new diagnostic criteria for myocardial infarction. *Heart* 91(2): 237–238.

Wittstein, I. S., et al. 2005. Neurohumoral features of myocardial stunning due to sudden emotional stress. *New England Journal of Medicine* 352(6): 539–548.

Yusuf, S., et al. 2005. Obesity and the risk of myocardial infarction in 27,000 participants from 52 countries: A case-control study. *Lancet* 366(9497): 1640–1649.

Zhu, S., et al. 2004. Lifestyle behaviors associated with lower risk of having the metabolic syndrome. *Metabolism* 53(11): 1503–1511.

16

Looking AHEAD

After reading this chapter, you should be able to

- Explain what cancer is and how it spreads
- List and describe common cancers—their risk factors, signs and symptoms, treatments, and approaches to prevention
- Discuss some of the causes of cancer and how they can be avoided or minimized
- Describe how cancer can be detected, diagnosed, and treated
- List specific actions you can take to lower your risk of cancer

Cancer

Test Your Knowledge

1. Which type of cancer kills the most women each year?
a. breast cancer
b. lung cancer
c. ovarian cancer

2. Which type of cancer kills the most men each year?
a. prostate cancer
b. lung cancer
c. colon cancer

3. Testicular cancer is the most common cancer in men under age 30.
True or false?

4. The use of condoms during sexual intercourse can prevent cervical cancer in women.
True or false?

5. Now that most people know of the dangers of tanning lamps and tanning beds—including premature skin aging and increased risk of skin cancer—college students are using them less.
True or false?

6. Eating which of these foods may help prevent cancer?
a. chili peppers
b. broccoli
c. oranges

ANSWERS

1. B. There are more cases of breast cancer each year, but lung cancer kills more women. Smoking is the primary risk factor for lung cancer.
2. B. There are more cases of prostate cancer, but lung cancer kills about three times as many men as prostate cancer does each year.
3. TRUE. Although rare, testicular cancer is the most common cancer in men under age 30. Regular self-exams may aid in its detection.
4. TRUE. The primary cause of cervical cancer is infection with human papillomavirus (HPV), a sexually transmitted pathogen. The use of condoms helps prevent HPV infection.
5. FALSE. Nearly half of all college students report using tanning lamps within the past year, and more than 90% of the users knew of the dangers.
6. ALL THREE. These and many other fruits and vegetables are rich in phytochemicals, naturally occurring substances that may have anti-cancer effects.

Visit the *Core Concepts in Health* Online Learning Center (www.mhhe.com/insel10e) for study aids and many additional resources.

Cancer is derived from the Greek word for crab, *karkinos.* The early Greek physicians who first described cancerous tumors had no notion of their cause or true nature, but they were struck by the resemblance of some invasive tumors to crabs: a hard mass with clawlike extensions and an aggressive nature. Today, though we know a great deal about cancer, the old metaphor still has power; cancer has maintained its reputation as an alien presence in the body, capable of causing pain, great harm, even death. Cancer causes about 565,000 deaths in the United States each year and is the leading cause of disease-related death among people under age 65. Overall, cancer is the second most common cause of death, after heart disease. According to the National Institutes of Health (NIH), cancer costs Americans nearly $175 billion annually.

While medical science struggles to find cures for the various cancers that plague us, evidence indicates that more than half of all cancers could be prevented by simple changes in lifestyle like those described in earlier chapters. Tobacco use is responsible for about one-third of all cancer deaths (Figure 16-1). Poor diet and exercise habits, including their effect on obesity, account for another one-third of cancer deaths. Your behavior now will determine your cancer risk in the future.

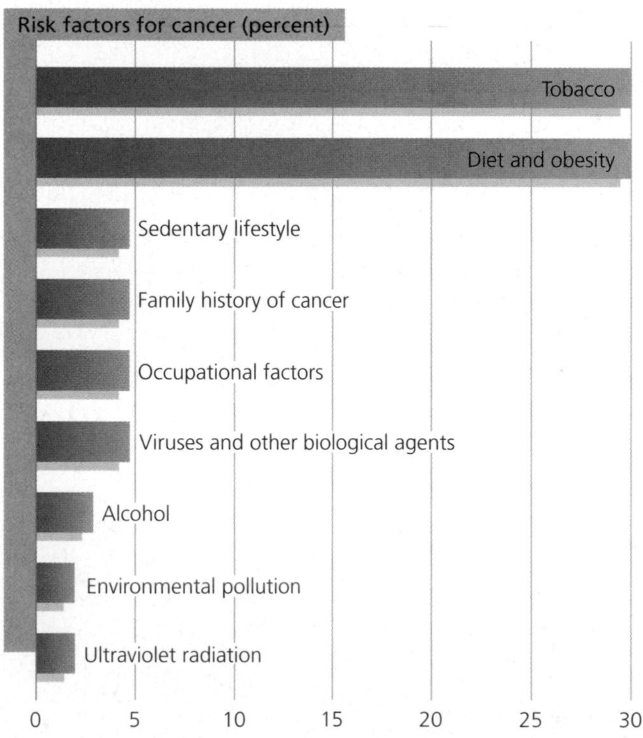

VITAL STATISTICS

Figure 16-1 Percentage of all cancer deaths linked to risk factors. SOURCE: Harvard Center for Cancer Prevention. 1996. Harvard Report on Cancer Prevention. Vol. 1: Human Causes of Cancer. *Cancer Causes and Control* 7(Suppl).

WHAT IS CANCER?

Cancer is the abnormal, uncontrolled growth of cells, which, if left untreated, can ultimately cause death.

Benign Versus Malignant Tumors

Most cancers take the form of tumors, although not all tumors are cancerous. A tumor is simply a mass of tissue that serves no physiological purpose. It can be benign, like a wart, or malignant, like most lung cancers.

Benign tumors are made up of cells similar to the surrounding normal cells and are enclosed in a membrane that prevents them from penetrating neighboring tissues. They are dangerous only if their physical presence interferes with body functions. A benign brain tumor, for example, can cause death if it blocks the blood supply to the brain.

The term **malignant tumor** (or *neoplasm*) is synonymous with cancer. A malignant tumor is capable of invading surrounding structures, including blood vessels, the **lymphatic system,** and nerves. It can also spread to distant sites via the blood and lymphatic circulation, thereby producing invasive tumors in almost any part of the body. A few cancers, like leukemia, or cancer of the blood, do not produce a mass. Because leukemia cells do have the fundamental property of rapid, uncontrolled growth, they are still malignant and therefore cancers.

Every case of cancer begins as a change in a cell that allows it to grow and divide when it should not. Normally (in adults), cells divide and grow at a rate just sufficient to replace dying cells. When you cut your finger, for example, the cells around the wound divide more rapidly to heal the wound. When the wound is healed, the rate of cell growth and division returns to normal. In contrast, a malignant cell divides without regard for normal control mechanisms and gradually produces a mass of abnormal cells, or a tumor. It takes about a billion cells to make a mass the size of a pea, so a single tumor cell must go through many divisions, often taking years, before the tumor grows to a noticeable size (Figure 16-2).

Eventually a tumor produces a sign or symptom that is determined by its location in the body. In the breast, for example, a tumor may be felt as a lump and diagnosed as cancer by an X ray or **biopsy.** In less accessible locations, like the lung, ovary, or intestine, a tumor may be noticed only after considerable growth has taken place and may then be detected only by an indirect symptom—for instance, a persistent cough or unexplained bleeding or pain. In the case of leukemia, there is no lump, but the changes in the blood will eventually be noticed as increasing fatigue, infection, or abnormal bleeding.

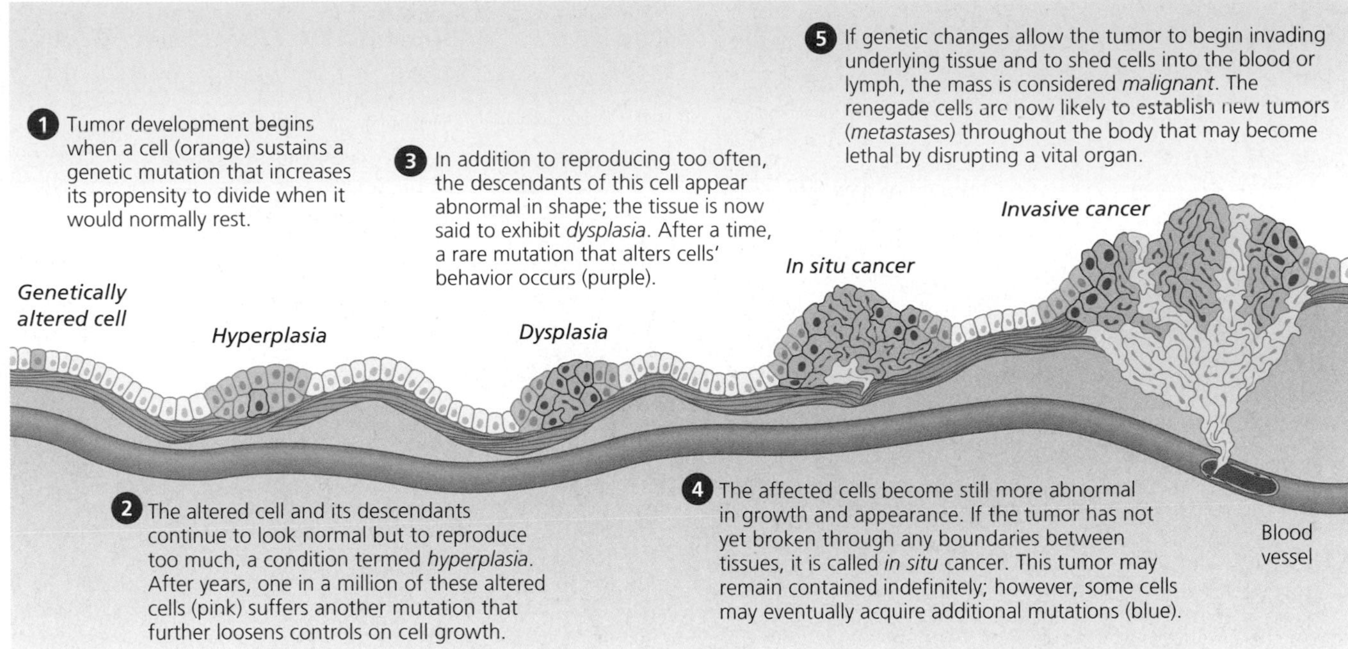

1 Tumor development begins when a cell (orange) sustains a genetic mutation that increases its propensity to divide when it would normally rest.
3 In addition to reproducing too often, the descendants of this cell appear abnormal in shape; the tissue is now said to exhibit dysplasia. After a time, a rare mutation that alters cells' behavior occurs (purple).
5 If genetic changes allow the tumor to begin invading underlying tissue and to shed cells into the blood or lymph, the mass is considered malignant. The renegade cells are now likely to establish new tumors (metastases) throughout the body that may become lethal by disrupting a vital organ.
Invasive cancer
In situ cancer
Genetically altered cell
Hyperplasia
Dysplasia
2 The altered cell and its descendants continue to look normal but to reproduce too much, a condition termed hyperplasia. After years, one in a million of these altered cells (pink) suffers another mutation that further loosens controls on cell growth.
4 The affected cells become still more abnormal in growth and appearance. If the tumor has not yet broken through any boundaries between tissues, it is called in situ cancer. This tumor may remain contained indefinitely; however, some cells may eventually acquire additional mutations (blue).
Blood vessel

Figure 16-2 Tumor development occurs in stages. SOURCE: Weinberg, R. A. 1996. How cancer arises. *Scientific American,* September. Copyright © 1996 by Dana Burns-Pizer. Reprinted with permission.

How Cancer Spreads: Metastasis

Metastasis, the spreading of cancer cells, occurs because cancer cells do not stick to each other as strongly as normal cells do and therefore may not remain at the site of the *primary tumor,* the original location. They break away and can pass through the lining of lymph or blood vessels to invade nearby tissue. Once it is established, the tumor can recruit normal cells—such as bone marrow cells—modify them, and use them as "envoys" to travel to different parts of the body and prepare other sites to receive traveling cancer cells. The envoy cells work by creating proteins that attract the free-floating cancer cells, allowing them to gather at a new site and resume replicating. This traveling and seeding process is called *metastasizing,* and the new tumors are called *secondary tumors,* or *metastases.*

The ability of cancer cells to metastasize makes early cancer detection critical. To control the cancer, every cancerous cell must be removed. Once cancer cells enter either the lymphatic system or the bloodstream, it is extremely difficult to stop their spread to other organs of the body. In fact, counting the number of lymph nodes that contain cancer cells is one of the principal methods of predicting the outcome of the disease; the probability of a cure is much greater when the lymph nodes do not contain cancer cells.

Types of Cancer

The behavior of tumors arising in different body organs is characteristic of the tissue of origin. (Figure 16-3 on p. 482 shows the major cancer sites and the incidence of each type.) Because each cancer begins as a single (altered) cell with a specific function in the body, the cancer retains some of the properties of the normal cell for a time. For instance, cancer of the thyroid gland may produce too much thyroid hormone and cause hyperthyroidism as well as cancer. Usually, however, cancer cells lose their resemblance to normal tissue as they continue to divide, becoming groups of rogue cells with increasingly unpredictable behavior.

Malignant tumors are classified according to the types of cells that give rise to them:

- **Carcinomas** arise from **epithelia,** tissues that cover external body surfaces, line internal tubes and

Terms

cancer Abnormal, uncontrolled cellular growth.

malignant tumor A tumor that is cancerous and capable of spreading.

benign tumor A tumor that is not cancerous.

lymphatic system A system of vessels that returns proteins, lipids, and other substances from fluid in the tissues to the circulatory system.

biopsy The removal and examination of a small piece of body tissue; a needle biopsy uses a needle to remove a small sample; some biopsies require surgery.

metastasis The spread of cancer cells from one part of the body to another.

carcinoma Cancer that originates in epithelial tissue (skin, glands, and lining of internal organs).

epithelial layer A layer of tissue that covers a surface or lines a tube or cavity of the body, enclosing and protecting other parts of the body.

Vw

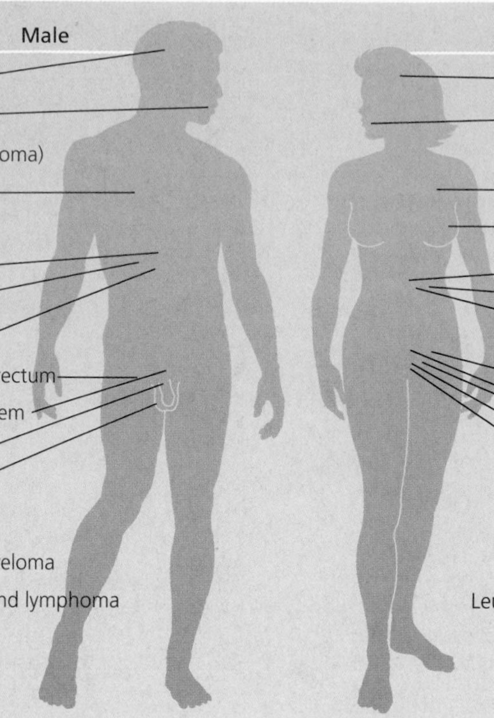

New cases	Deaths	Male	Female	New cases	Deaths
10,700	7,300	Brain	Brain	8,100	5,600
20,200	5,100	Oral	Oral	10,800	2,400
34,300	5,000	Skin (melanoma)	Skin (melanoma)	27,900	2,900
92,700	90,300	Lung	Lung	81,800	72,100
			Breast	212,900	41,000
13,400	6,700	Stomach	Stomach	8,900	4,700
12,600	10,800	Liver	Liver	5,900	5,400
17,200	16,100	Pancreas	Pancreas	16,600	16,200
72,800	27,900	Colon and rectum	Colon and rectum	75,800	27,300
70,900	17,500	Urinary system	Urinary system	31,800	9,100
234,500	27,400	Prostate	Ovary	20,200	15,300
8,300	400	Testes	Uterus	41,200	7,400
			Cervix	9,700	3,700
9,300	5,700	Multiple myeloma	Multiple myeloma	7,300	5,600
54,900	23,300	Leukemia and lymphoma	Leukemia and lymphoma	46,900	19,400
68,500	47,800	Other	Other	73,700	35,500
720,300	**291,300**	Total	**Total**	**679,500**	**273,600**

VW VITAL STATISTICS

Figure 16-3 Cancer cases and deaths by site and sex. The New Cases column indicates the number of cancers that occurred in each site; the Deaths column indicates the number of cancer deaths that were attributed to each type. SOURCE: American Cancer Society. 2006. *Cancer Facts and Figures, 2006*. Atlanta: American Cancer Society.

cavities, and form the secreting portion of glands. They are the most common type of cancers; major sites include the skin, breast, uterus, prostate, lungs, and gastrointestinal tract.

- **Sarcomas** arise from connective and fibrous tissues such as muscle, bone, cartilage, and the membranes covering muscles and fat.
- **Lymphomas** are cancers of the lymph nodes, part of the body's infection-fighting system.
- **Leukemias** are cancers of the blood-forming cells, which reside chiefly in the **bone marrow.**

There is a great deal of variation in how easily different cancers can be detected and how well they respond to treatment. For example, certain types of skin cancer are easily detected, grow slowly, and are very easy to remove; virtually all of the 1 million cases of these types of skin cancer that occur each year in the United States are cured. Cancer of the pancreas, on the other hand, is very difficult to detect or treat, and very few patients survive the disease. In general, it is very difficult for an **oncologist** to predict how a specific tumor will behave, because every tumor arises from a unique set of changes in a single cell.

Terms

VW

sarcoma Cancer arising from bone, cartilage, or striated muscle.

lymphoma A tumor originating from lymphatic tissue.

leukemia Cancer of the blood or the blood-forming cells.

bone marrow Soft vascular tissue in the interior cavities of bones that produces blood cells.

oncologist A specialist in the study of tumors.

The Incidence of Cancer

Each year, about 1.4 million people in the United States are diagnosed with cancer. Most will be cured, but about 36% will die as a result of their cancer within 5 years of diagnosis. These grim statistics exclude more than 1 million cases of the curable types of skin cancer. At current U.S. rates, nearly 1 in 2 men and more than 1 in 3 women will develop cancer at some point in their lives (see the box "Gender and Cancer").

Are cancer deaths increasing in the United States? Until 1991, the answer was yes, largely due to a wave of lethal lung cancers among men caused by smoking. In 1991, the death rate stopped increasing and began to fall slowly; it has dropped more than 10% since 1990. This is a very promising trend, as it suggests that efforts at prevention, early detection, and improved therapy are

Gender Matters

Gender and Cancer

Men and women share most major risk factors for cancer, but they do have a different experience because more than a third of all cancers occur in sex organs (prostate, testes, breast, ovary, uterus, cervix). For women, this means that in addition to lifestyle factors such as smoking, diet, and exercise, hormonal factors relating to their menstrual and childbearing history are also important risk considerations. Women may also have a greater biological vulnerability to certain carcinogens, such as those in cigarettes.

Overall, however, men are more likely than women to have cancer and to die of cancer. For some cancers, the differences are especially significant. For example, men are much more likely than women to die from oral cancer, skin cancer, lung cancer, liver cancer, and urinary cancer. Here are some of the factors underlying the higher death rates among men:

- *Higher rates of tobacco use:* Particularly in the past, men had significantly higher rates of smoking than women, leading to much higher rates of the many cancers linked to smoking. Men also have much higher rates of spit tobacco and cigar use.

The graphs clearly show the powerful effects of smoking on cancer death rates since 1930. Lung cancer rates among men increased dramatically following significantly increased smoking rates beginning in the early 1900s (inexpensive machine-produced cigarettes were developed in the late1800s). The lung cancer rate leveled off and (for men) started to decline after smoking rates began dropping. The smoking-related increase in lung cancer among women occurred about 20–30 years after that seen in men, as smoking among women became more socially acceptable and widespread beginning in the 1930s and 1940s.

- *Higher rates of alcohol use and abuse:* Alcohol abuse is more common in men and is a risk factor for several cancers, including oral and liver cancers.
- *Greater occupational exposure to carcinogens:* Men are more likely to work in jobs where they are exposed to chemicals—including asbestos, arsenic, coal tar, pitch, and dyes—or radiation, and such exposure is a risk factor for cancers of the bladder, lung, and skin. Men are also more likely to have outdoor jobs involving frequent sun exposure.
- *Less use of preventive measures and less contact with health care providers:* Traditional gender roles may make men more likely to minimize symptoms and less likely to seek help or to discuss cancer-related worries with a health care provider. Men may place a low status on preventive care or screenings, such as using sunscreen and wearing hats to protect the skin from the sun or performing self-exams.

Many of the factors underlying men's greater risk for cancer are controllable. It is important for both men and women to remember that there are many concrete steps they can take to significantly reduce their risk of cancer.

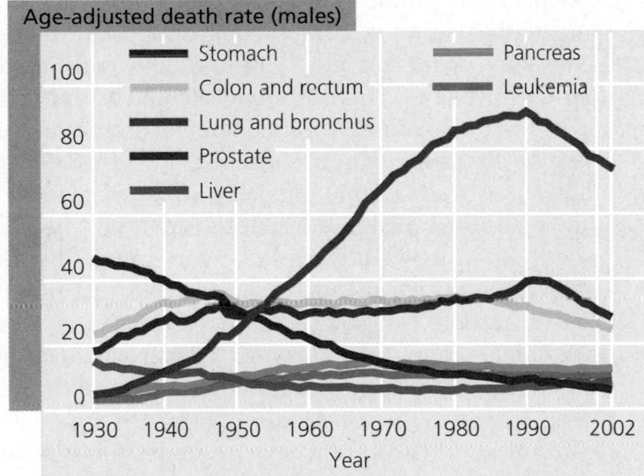

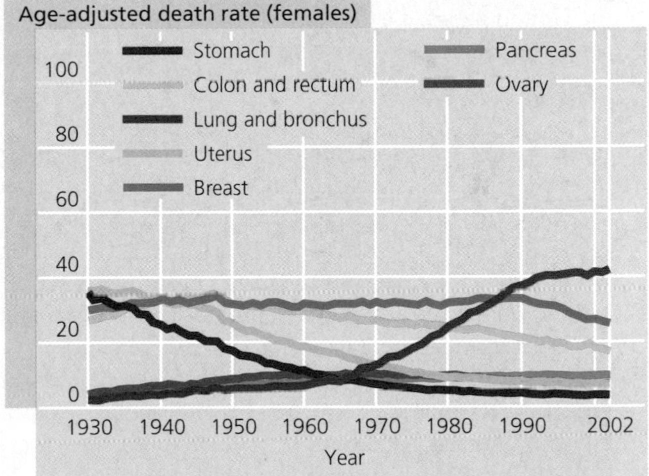

Change in cancer death rates since 1930 SOURCE: American Cancer Society's *Cancer Facts and Figures 2006*, © 2006 American Cancer Society, Inc. www.cancer.org. Reprinted with permission.

all bearing fruit. However, death rates from cancer are not declining as fast as those from heart disease, in large part because of the differing effects that quitting smoking has on disease risk: Heart-related damage of smoking reverses more quickly and more significantly than the cancer-related damage from smoking; smoking-related gene mutations cannot be reversed, although other mechanisms can sometimes control cellular changes. (Heart disease also has other risk factors like high cholesterol and blood pressure that can be tested for and controlled.) If heart disease death rates continue to decline faster than cancer death rates, cancer may overtake heart disease as the leading cause of death among Americans of all ages. Cancer kills more people under age 65 than does heart disease.

Could more people be saved from cancer? The American Cancer Society (ACS) estimates that 90% of skin cancer could be prevented by protecting the skin from the rays of the sun and 87% of lung cancer could be prevented by avoiding exposure to tobacco smoke. Thousands of cases of colon, breast, and uterine cancer could be prevented by improving the diet and controlling body weight. Regular screenings and self-examinations have the potential to save an additional 100,000 lives per year. Although cancer may seem like a mysterious disease, there are many concrete strategies you can adopt to reduce your risk.

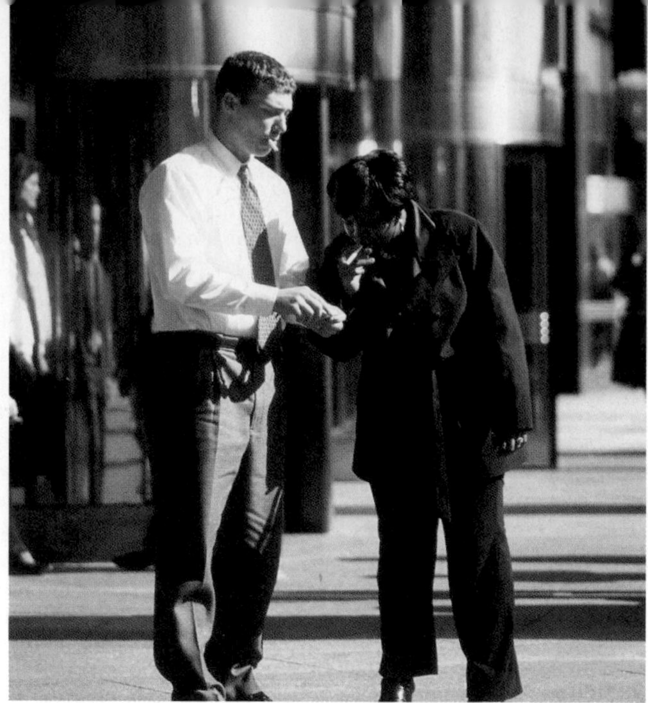

Smoking is responsible for about 30% of all cancer deaths. The benefits of quitting are substantial: Lung cancer risk decreases significantly after 1 smoke-free year and drops to half that of continuing smokers after 10 smoke-free years.

COMMON CANCERS

A discussion of all types of cancer is beyond the scope of this book. In this section we look at some of the most common cancers and their causes, prevention, and treatment.

Lung Cancer

Lung cancer is the most common cause of cancer death in the United States; it is responsible for about 162,000 deaths each year. Since 1987 lung cancer has surpassed breast cancer as the leading cause of cancer death in women.

Risk Factors The chief risk factor for lung cancer is tobacco smoke, which accounts for 87% of lung cancer cases. (Other negative effects of tobacco smoke on the lungs were discussed in Chapter 11.) When smoking is combined with exposure to other **carcinogens,** such as asbestos particles or certain pollutants, the risk of cancer can be multiplied by a factor of 10 or more.

The smoker is not the only one at risk. In 1993, the U.S. Environmental Protection Agency (EPA) classified environmental tobacco smoke (ETS) as a human carcinogen. In 2006, the Surgeon General issued a report concluding that there is no safe level of exposure to ETS; even brief exposure can cause serious harm. Long-term exposure to ETS increases the risk of lung cancer. Secondhand smoke, the smoke from the burning end of the cigarette, has significantly higher concentrations of the toxic and carcinogenic compounds found in mainstream smoke. It is estimated that ETS causes about 3000 lung cancer deaths each year.

Detection and Treatment Lung cancer is difficult to detect at an early stage and hard to cure even when detected early. Symptoms of lung cancer do not usually appear until the disease has advanced to the invasive stage. Signals such as a persistent cough, chest pain, or recurring bronchitis may be the first indication of a tumor's presence. Studies suggest that spiral CT (computed tomography) scans, a computer-assisted body imaging technique, can detect lung cancer significantly earlier than chest X rays. This screening method is expensive and often not covered by insurance, but further evaluation may determine that it is beneficial for high-risk individuals, such as chronic smokers. In cases where CT scanning is not available, a diagnosis can usually be made by chest X ray or by studying the cells in sputum. Because almost all lung cancers arise from the cells that line the bronchi, tumors can sometimes be visualized by fiber-optic bronchoscopy, a test in which a flexible lighted tube is inserted into the windpipe and the surfaces of the lung passages are directly inspected.

Treatment for lung cancer depends on the type and stage of the cancer. If caught early, localized cancers can be treated with surgery. But because only about 16% of lung cancers are detected before they spread, radiation and **chemotherapy** are often used in addition to surgery. For cases detected early, 50% of patients are alive 5 years after diagnosis; but overall, the survival rate is only 15%. Phototherapy, gene therapy, and immunotherapy (a vaccine) are being studied in the hope of improving these statistics. In addition, one form of lung cancer, known as small-cell lung cancer and accounting for about 20% of cases, can be treated fairly successfully with chemotherapy—alone or in combination with radiation. A large percentage of cases go into **remission,** which in some cases lasts for years.

Colon and Rectal Cancer

Another common cancer in the United States is colon and rectal cancer (also called colorectal cancer). Although there are effective screening methods for colorectal cancer, it is the second leading cause of cancer death.

Risk Factors Age is a key risk factor for colon and rectal cancer, with more than 90% of cases diagnosed in people age 50 and older. Heredity also plays a role: Many cancers arise from preexisting **polyps,** small growths on the wall of the colon that may gradually develop into malignancies. The tendency to form colon polyps appears to be determined by specific genes, and 15–30% of colon cancers may be due to inherited gene mutations. Chronic inflammation of the colon as a result of disorders such as ulcerative colitis also increases the risk of colon cancer. Type 2 diabetes raises colon cancer risk by about 40%.

Lifestyle is also a risk factor for colon and rectal cancer. Regular physical activity appears to reduce a person's risk, whereas obesity increases risk. A diet rich in red and processed meats increases risk, although it is unclear whether fat or some other component of meat is the culprit. A diet rich in fruits, vegetables, and whole grains is associated with lower risk. However, research findings on whether dietary fiber prevents colon cancer have been mixed. Further investigation of different types and sources of fiber and other properties of plant-based diets may help clarify the relationship between diet and colon cancer. Studies have suggested a protective role for folic acid, magnesium, vitamin D, and calcium; in contrast, high intake of refined carbohydrates, simple sugars, and smoked meats and fish may increase risk. A plant-based, high-fiber diet is still recommended because it is associated with a lower risk of cancer overall and also helps prevent heart disease, hypertension, and diabetes.

Excessive alcohol use and smoking may increase the risk of colorectal cancer. Use of oral contraceptives or hormone replacement therapy may reduce risk in women. Regular use of nonsteroidal anti-inflammatory drugs such as aspirin and ibuprofen may decrease the risk of colon cancer and other cancers of the digestive tract.

Detection and Treatment If identified early, precancerous polyps and early-stage cancers can be removed before they become malignant or spread. Because polyps may bleed as they progress, the standard warning signs of colon cancer are bleeding from the rectum and a change in bowel habits. Regular screening tests are recommended beginning at age 50 (earlier for people with a family history of the disease). A yearly stool blood test can detect small amounts of blood in the stool long before obvious bleeding would be noticed. More involved screening tests are recommended at 5- or 10-year intervals. In sigmoidoscopy or colonoscopy, a flexible fiber-optic device is inserted through the rectum; the colon can be examined and polyps can be biopsied or removed without major surgery. Screening is effective; studies show it could reduce the occurrence of colorectal cancer by 80%. Still, only about one-half of adults have undergone any of these tests.

Surgery is the primary treatment for colon and rectal cancer. Radiation and chemotherapy may be used before surgery to shrink a tumor or after surgery to destroy any remaining cancerous cells. For advanced cancer, treatment with bevacizumab (Avastin), a monoclonal antibody, in combination with chemotherapy is an option (see p. 487 for an explanation of monoclonal antibodies). This treatment inhibits the growth of new blood vessels (angiogenesis) in tumors. The survival rate is 90% for colon and rectal cancers detected early and 64% overall.

Breast Cancer

Breast cancer is the most common cancer in women and causes almost as many deaths in women as lung cancer. In men, breast cancer occurs only rarely. In the United States, about 1 woman in 7 will develop breast cancer during her lifetime, and 1 woman in 30 will die from the disease. About 213,000 American women are diagnosed with breast cancer each year. About 41,000 women die from breast cancer each year.

Less then 1% of breast cancer cases occur in women under age 30, but a woman's risk doubles every 5 years between ages 30 and 45 and then increases more slowly, by 10–15% every 5 years after age 45. More than 75% of breast cancers are diagnosed in women over 50.

Risk Factors There is a strong genetic factor in breast cancer. A woman who has two close relatives with breast cancer is four to six times more likely to develop the disease than a woman who has no close relatives with it. However, even though genetic factors are important, only about 15% of cancers occur in women with a family history of breast cancer.

Other risk factors include early onset of menstruation, late onset of menopause, having no children or having a first child after age 30, current use of hormone replacement therapy (HRT), obesity, and alcohol use. Estrogen may be a unifying element for many of these risk factors. Estrogen circulates in a woman's body in high concentrations between puberty and menopause. Fat cells also produce estrogen, and estrogen levels are higher in obese women. Alcohol can interfere with estrogen metabolism in the liver and increase estrogen levels in the blood. Estrogen promotes

Terms

carcinogen Any substance that causes cancer.

chemotherapy The treatment of cancer with chemicals that selectively destroy cancerous cells.

remission A period during the course of cancer in which there are no symptoms or other evidence of disease.

polyp A small, usually harmless, mass of tissue that projects from the inner surface of the colon or rectum.

Vw

the growth of cells in responsive sites, including the breast and the uterus, so any factor that increases estrogen exposure may raise breast cancer risk. A dramatic drop of 7.2% in rates of breast cancer in 2003 was attributed at least in part to reduced use of HRT by women over 50 beginning in July 2002. Millions of women stopped taking the hormones after research linked HRT with an increased risk of breast cancer and heart disease.

Breast cancer incidence is high in industrialized Western countries but low in developing non-Western countries. Differences in diet and exercise habits may explain this pattern, but the connections are still being investigated. Monounsaturated fats have been linked with reduced risk, and certain types of polyunsaturated fat may increase risk. A diet rich in vegetables may also have a protective effect. Regular exercise is extremely important: A study of more than 25,000 women found that those who exercised regularly had a 37% lower risk of breast cancer than those who did not exercise. Vigorous exercise may reduce estrogen levels in the blood, and physical activity of all intensities helps control body weight. Both obesity and significant weight gain during adulthood are linked to increased risk of breast cancer.

A recent study found an interesting association between antibiotic use and increased breast cancer risk; however, this association may not be causal and could be related to other factors such as the patient's reasons for antibiotic use and her overall immune function. Antibiotics should be used only when prescribed and exactly as directed. Some research has also found that long-term use of aspirin and other nonsteroidal anti-inflammatory drugs reduces risk, possibly by affecting estrogen synthesis.

Although some of the risk factors for breast cancer cannot be changed, important lifestyle risk factors can be controlled. Eating a low-fat, vegetable-rich diet, exercising regularly, limiting alcohol intake, and maintaining a healthy body weight can minimize the chance of developing breast cancer, even for women at risk from family history or other factors.

Early Detection A cure is most likely if breast cancer is detected early, so regular screening is a good investment, even for younger women. The ACS advises a three-part personal program for the early detection of breast cancer:

- *Mammography:* The ACS recommends a **mammogram** (low-dose breast X ray) every year for women over 40. Mammography is especially valuable as an early detection tool because it can identify breast abnormalities that may be cancer at an early stage, before physical symptoms develop. Studies show that magnetic resonance imaging (MRI) may be better than mammography at detecting breast abnormalities in some women. Digital mammography has proved better than standard mammography in spotting tumors in women with dense breasts.
- *Clinical breast exam:* Women between ages 20 and 39 should have a clinical breast exam every 3 years, and women age 40 and older should have one every year before their scheduled mammogram.
- *Breast self-exams:* Breast self-exam (BSE) allows a woman to become familiar with her breasts, so she can alert her health care provider to any changes. Women who choose to do breast self-exams should begin at age 20 (see the box "Breast Self-Examination").

Breast pain or tenderness is usually associated with benign conditions such as menstruation rather than breast cancer. The first physical signs of breast cancer are more likely to be a lump, swelling, or thickening; skin irritation or dimpling; or nipple pain, scaliness, or retraction. Although most breast lumps are benign, any breast lump should be brought to the attention of a health care provider.

Treatment If a lump is detected, it may be scanned by **ultrasonography** and biopsied to see if it is cancerous. The biopsy may be done either by needle in the physician's office or surgically. In 90% of cases, the lump is found to be a cyst or other harmless growth, and no further treatment is needed. If the lump does contain cancer cells, a variety of surgeries may be called for, ranging from a lumpectomy (removal of the lump and surrounding tissue) to a mastectomy (removal of the breast). For small tumors, lumpectomy is as effective as mastectomy. To determine whether the cancer has spread, lymph nodes from the armpit may be removed and examined. If cancer cells are found, tumor cells remaining in the body can often be slowed or killed by additional therapy, such as radiation, chemotherapy, or both.

Survival of breast cancer varies, depending on the nature of the tumor and whether it has metastasized. If the tumor is discovered before it has spread to the adjacent lymph nodes, the patient has about a 98% chance of surviving more than 5 years. The survival rate for all stages is 88% at 5 years and 80% at 10 years.

New Strategies for Treatment and Prevention A number of new drugs have been developed for the treatment or prevention of breast cancer. A family of drugs called selective estrogen-receptor modulators, or SERMs, act like estrogen in some tissues of the body but block estrogen's effects in others. One SERM, tamoxifen, has long been used in breast cancer treatment because it blocks the action of estrogen in breast tissue. In 1998, the

Terms

Vw

mammograms Low-dose X rays of the breasts used to check for early signs of breast cancer.

ultrasonography An imaging method in which sound waves are bounced off body structures to create an image on a TV monitor; also called *ultrasound.*

Take Charge

Breast Self-Examination

The best time for a woman to examine her breasts is when the breasts are not tender or swollen. Women who are pregnant or breastfeeding or have breast implants can also choose to examine their breasts regularly. Women who examine their breasts should have their technique reviewed during their periodic health examinations by their health care professional. It is acceptable for women to choose not to do BSE or to do BSE occasionally. If you choose not to do BSE, you should still be familiar with your breasts and report any changes without delay to your doctor.

How to Examine Your Breasts

- Lie down and place your right arm behind your head. The exam is done while lying down, not standing up, because the breast tissue then spreads evenly over the chest wall and is as thin as possible, making it much easier to feel all the breast tissue.
- Use the finger pads of the three middle fingers on your left hand to feel for lumps in the right breast. Use overlapping dime-size circular motions of the finger pads to feel the breast tissue.

- Use three different levels of pressure to feel all the breast tissue. Light pressure is needed to feel the tissue closest to the skin; medium pressure to feel a little deeper; and firm pressure to feel the tissue closest to the chest and ribs. A firm ridge in the lower curve of each breast is normal. If you're not sure how hard to press, talk with your doctor or nurse. Use each pressure level to feel the breast tissue before moving on to the next spot.
- Move around the breast in an up-and-down pattern starting at an imaginary line drawn straight down your side from the underarm and moving across the breast to the middle of the chest bone (the sternum, or breastbone). Be sure to check the entire breast area, going down until you feel only ribs and going up to the neck or collar bone (clavicle).
- Repeat the exam on your left breast, using the finger pads of the right hand. Some evidence suggests that the up-and-down pattern (sometimes called the vertical pattern) is the most effective pattern for covering the entire breast, without missing any breast tissue.

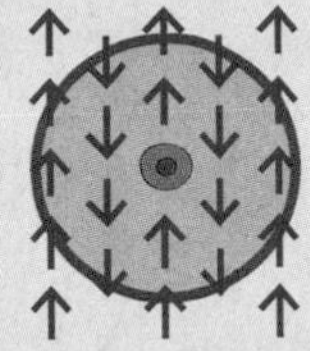

- While standing in front of a mirror with your hands pressing firmly down on your hips, look at your breasts for any changes of size, shape, contour, or dimpling. (Pressing down on the hips contracts the chest wall muscles and enhances any breast changes.)
- Examine each underarm while sitting up or standing and with your arm only slightly raised so you can easily feel in this area. Raising your arm straight up tightens the tissue in this area and makes it difficult to examine.

SOURCE: American Cancer Society's Web site www.cancer.org, 2005.

FDA approved the use of tamoxifen to reduce the risk of breast cancer in healthy women who are at high risk for the disease. However, the drug has serious potential side effects, including increased risk of blood clots and uterine cancer, and its long-term effects are unknown. Another SERM currently being tested as a potential preventive agent is raloxifene, an osteoporosis drug that has fewer side effects than tamoxifen. Although still controversial, the use of SERMs in the prevention of breast cancer is a major breakthrough.

Women may take tamoxifen, anastrozole, or other drugs or undergo chemotherapy to help reduce the risk of recurrence. A genetic test can help predict the risk of breast cancer recurrence and help identify women who will benefit most from chemotherapy; women can then make more informed treatment decisions. For advanced cancer, treatment with trastuzumab (Herceptin), a monoclonal antibody, is an option for some women. Antibodies, discussed in Chapter 17, are proteins produced by the immune system that recognize and bind to foreign substances such as bacteria; monoclonal antibodies are a special type of antibody that is produced in the laboratory and designed to bind to a specific cancer-related target. About 30% of metastatic breast cancer tumors produce excess amounts of a growth-promoting protein called HER2. Herceptin binds to the excess HER2, thus blocking its action and slowing tumor growth. Herceptin is typically used alone or in combination with paclitaxel (Taxol), a drug that interferes with cell division.

Prostate Cancer

The prostate gland is situated at the base of the bladder in men. It produces seminal fluid; if enlarged, it can block the flow of urine. Prostate cancer is the most common cancer in men and, after lung cancer, the cause of the most cancer-related deaths. Nearly 235,000 new cases are diagnosed each year, and more than 27,000 American men die from the disease each year.

Risk Factors Age is the strongest predictor of the risk, with about 75% of cases of prostate cancer diagnosed in men over age 65. Inherited genetic predisposition may be responsible for 5–10% of cases, and men with a family history of the disease should be particularly vigilant about screening. African American men have the highest rate of prostate cancer of any group in the world; both genetic and lifestyle factors may be involved. Diets high in calories, dairy products, and animal fats and low in plant foods have also been implicated as possible culprits, as have obesity, inactivity, and a history of sexually transmitted diseases. Type 2 diabetes and insulin resistance are also associated with prostate cancer. Soy foods, tomatoes, and cruciferous vegetables are being investigated for their possible protective effects.

Detection Early prostate cancer usually has no symptoms. Warning signs of prostate cancer can include changes in urinary frequency, weak or interrupted urine flow, painful urination, and blood in the urine. Techniques for early detection include a digital rectal examination and the **prostate-specific antigen (PSA) blood test.** The American Cancer Society recommends that men be provided information about the benefits and limitations of the tests and that both the exam and the PSA test be offered annually, beginning at age 50 for men at average risk and age 45 for men at high risk, including African Americans and those with a family history of the disease.

During a digital rectal exam, a physician feels the prostate gland through the rectum to determine if the gland is enlarged or if lumps are present. The PSA blood test may detect an elevated level or a rapid increase in PSA: The PSA test can help catch early prostate cancer, but it also can register benign conditions (more than half of men over 50 have benign prostate disease) and very slow-growing cancers that are unlikely to kill affected individuals. Further, it is not rare for men with normal PSA levels to have prostate cancer.

Terms

Ww

prostate-specific antigen (PSA) blood test A diagnostic test for prostate cancer that measures blood levels of prostate-specific antigen (PSA).

incontinence The inability to control the flow of urine.

impotence Erectile dysfunction—the inability to have an erection or ejaculate; an inability to perform sexual intercourse.

Pap test A scraping of cells from the cervix for examination under a microscope to detect cancer.

endometrium The layers of tissue lining the uterus.

Some experts contend that PSA testing should not be performed on all men or should be used only in conjunction with other tests. Because PSA tests can yield false-positive results, they may lead men to receive further testing or treatment that is not needed. Researchers are looking for ways to make the PSA test more sensitive. One strategy is to repeat the test over time to chart a rate of change. A newer approach involves measuring the percentage of PSA that is free-floating in the blood. PSA made by cancer cells is more likely to circulate bound to other proteins, whereas PSA from healthy prostate cells is more likely to be unbound. Thus, a low proportion of unbound, or free PSA indicates greater risk, while a high proportion of free PSA is associated with lower risk.

Ultrasound is used increasingly as a follow-up, to detect lumps too small to be felt and to determine their size, shape, and properties. A needle biopsy of suspicious lumps can be performed relatively painlessly, and whether the biopsied cells are malignant or benign can be determined by examining them under a microscope.

Treatment Treatments vary based on the stage of the cancer and the age of the patient. A small, slow-growing tumor in an older man may be treated with watchful waiting because he is more likely to die from another cause before his cancer becomes life threatening; however, a recent study shows that older men who undergo treatment live longer than those who don't. More aggressive treatment would be indicated for younger men or those with more advanced cancers. Treatment usually involves radical prostatectomy, in which the prostate is removed surgically. Although radical surgery has an excellent cure rate, it is major surgery and often results in **incontinence** and/or **impotence.**

A less-invasive alternative involves surgical implantation of radioactive seeds. Radiation from the seeds destroys the tumor and much of the normal prostate tissue but leaves surrounding tissue relatively untouched. Alternative or additional treatments include external radiation, hormones that shrink tumors, cryotherapy, and anti-cancer drugs. Survival rates for all stages of this cancer have improved steadily since 1940; the 5-year survival rate is now nearly 100%.

Cancers of the Female Reproductive Tract

Because the uterus, cervix, and ovaries are subject to similar hormonal influences, the cancers of these organs can be discussed as a group.

Cervical Cancer Cervical cancer is at least in part a sexually transmitted disease. Most cases of cervical cancer stem from infection by the human papillomavirus (HPV), a group of about 100 related viruses that cause both common warts and genital warts. When certain types of HPV are introduced into the cervix, usually by an infected sex partner, the virus infects cervical cells, causing the cells to divide and grow. If unchecked, this growth can develop into cervical cancer. Cervical cancer is associated with multiple sex partners and is extremely rare in women who have not had heterosexual intercourse. The regular use of condoms can reduce the risk of transmitting HPV. Studies also suggest that women whose sexual partners are circumcised may be at reduced risk because circumcised men are less likely to be infected with HPV and to pass it to their partners.

Because only a very small percentage of HPV-infected women ever get cervical cancer, other factors must be involved. Two of the most important seem to be smoking and infection with genital herpes (discussed in Chapter 18 with other STDs). Both smoking and herpes infection can cause cancerous changes in cells in the laboratory and can speed and intensify the cancerous changes begun by HPV. Exposure to environmental tobacco smoke also appears to increase risk. Research suggests that women with high levels of HPV 16, a specific form of HPV, are at particularly high risk for the infection to develop into cancer. Some studies show that past exposure to the bacterium that causes the STD chlamydia may be a risk factor for cervical cancer that operates independently of HPV.

Screening for the changes in cervical cells that precede cancer is done chiefly by means of the **Pap test.** During a pelvic exam, loose cells are scraped from the cervix, spread on a slide, stained for easier viewing, and examined under a microscope to see whether they are normal in size and shape. If cells are abnormal, a condition commonly referred to as *cervical dysplasia,* the Pap test is repeated at intervals. Sometimes cervical cells spontaneously return to normal, but in about one-third of cases, the cellular changes progress toward malignancy. If this happens, the abnormal cells must be removed, either surgically or by destroying them with a cryoscopic (ultracold) probe or localized laser treatment. When the abnormal cells are in a precancerous state, the small patch of dangerous cells can be completely removed.

Without timely surgery, the malignant patch of cells goes on to invade the wall of the cervix and spreads to adjacent lymph nodes and to the uterus. At this stage, chemotherapy may be used with radiation to kill the fast-growing cancer cells, but chances for a complete cure are lower. Even when a cure can be achieved, it often means surgical removal of the uterus.

Because the Pap test is highly effective, all sexually active women and women between ages 18 and 65 should be tested. The recommended schedule for testing depends on risk factors, the type of Pap test performed, and whether the Pap test is combined with HPV testing. Unlike most cancers, which occur most often after the age of 60, cancer of the cervix occurs frequently in women in their thirties or even twenties. In the United States, more than 10,000 women are diagnosed with cervical cancer each year; the disease kills more than 3000 annually.

In 2006, the federal government approved a vaccine that protects against four types of HPV viruses, including two that cause about 70% of cervical cancer cases. Studies show the vaccine also protects against cancers of the vagina and vulva. The HPV/cervical cancer vaccine, named Gardasil, is given in three doses over a 6-month period, at a cost of about $360. The vaccine is recommended for all girls age 11–12; the recommendation also allows for vaccination of girls as young as 9 and women through age 26. The drug is not yet known to be effective in recommended for boys or men, but it may be recommended when more information becomes available.

Uterine, or Endometrial, Cancer Cancer of the lining of the uterus, or **endometrium,** most often occurs after the age of 55. The risk factors are similar to those for breast cancer: prolonged exposure to estrogen, early onset of menstruation, late menopause, never having been pregnant, and obesity; type 2 diabetes is also associated with increased risk. The use of oral contraceptives, which combine estrogen and progestin, appears to provide protection.

Endometrial cancer is usually detectable by pelvic examination. It is treated surgically, commonly by hysterectomy, or removal of the uterus; radiation treatment, hormones, and chemotherapy may be used in addition to surgery. When the tumor is detected at an early stage, about 96% of patients are alive and disease-free 5 years later. When the disease has spread beyond the uterus, the 5-year survival rate is less than 67%.

Ovarian Cancer Although ovarian cancer is rare compared with cervical or uterine cancer, it causes more deaths than the other two combined. It cannot be detected by Pap tests or any other simple screening method and is often diagnosed only late in its development, when surgery and other therapies are unlikely to be successful. The risk factors are similar to those for breast and endometrial cancer: increasing age (most ovarian cancer occurs after age 60), never having been pregnant, a family history of breast or ovarian cancer, obesity, and specific genetic mutations. A high number of ovulations appears to increase the chance that a cancer-causing genetic mutation will occur, so anything that lowers the number of lifetime ovulation cycles—pregnancy, breastfeeding, or use of oral contraceptives—reduces a woman's risk of ovarian cancer. A diet rich in fruits and vegetables may be associated with reduced risk.

There are often no warning signs of developing ovarian cancer. Early clues may include increased abdominal size and bloating, urinary urgency, and pelvic pain. Women with symptoms or who are at high risk because of family history or because they harbor a mutant gene should have thorough pelvic exams at regular intervals, as recommended by their physician. Pelvic exams may include the use of ultrasound to view the ovaries. Blood tests for a tumor marker called CA-125 and for a group of protein markers are being investigated as possible screening tests.

Ovarian cancer is treated by surgical removal of both ovaries, the fallopian tubes, and the uterus. Radiation and chemotherapy are sometimes used in addition to surgery. When the tumor is localized to the ovary, the survival rate after 5 years is 94%. But for all stages, the survival rate is only 44%, reflecting the difficulty of early detection.

Other Female Reproductive Tract Cancers

From 1938 to 1971, millions of women were given a synthetic hormone called DES (diethylstilbestrol), which was thought to help prevent miscarriage. It was later discovered that DES daughters (daughters born to these women) have an increased risk, about 1 in 1000, of a vaginal or cervical cancer called clear cell cancer. This cancer is extremely rare in unexposed women. DES daughters may also have an anatomically abnormal reproductive tract and have problems with fertility or miscarriage. Though this is primarily a health threat for daughters, there is also some risk to DES sons, who may have an increased risk of abnormalities of the reproductive tract, including undescended testicles, a risk factor for testicular cancer.

If you suspect you may be a DES daughter or son, you should ask your mother if she took any medications while pregnant and, if possible, review her medical records for that time. A DES daughter should find a physician who is familiar with the problems of DES exposure; more frequent and more thorough pelvic exams are recommended. A recent animal study suggested the possibility of an increased third-generation cancer risk from DES, but further research is needed to determine if the finding applies to DES granddaughters.

The UVA radiation emitted by most tanning-salon beds doesn't usually cause an immediate sunburn or readily visible skin damage, but it does cause premature wrinkling and aging of the skin and skin cancer.

Skin Cancer

Skin cancer is the most common cancer of all when cases of the highly curable forms are included in the count. (Usually these forms are not included, precisely because they are easily treated.) Of the more than 1 million cases of skin cancer diagnosed each year, 62,000 are of the most serious type, **melanoma.** Treatments are usually simple and successful when the cancers are caught early.

Risk Factors Almost all cases of skin cancer can be traced to excessive exposure to **ultraviolet (UV) radiation** from the sun, including longer-wavelength ultraviolet A (UVA) and shorter-wavelength ultraviolet B (UVB) radiation. UVB radiation causes sunburns and can damage the eyes and the immune system. UVA is less likely to cause an immediate sunburn, but by damaging connective tissue it leads to premature aging of the skin, giving it a wrinkled, leathery appearance. (Tanning lamps and tanning-salon beds emit mostly UVA radiation.) Both UVA and UVB radiation have been linked to the development of skin cancer, and the National Toxicology Program has declared both solar and artificial sources of UV radiation, including sunlamps and tanning beds, to be known human carcinogens.

Both severe, acute sun reactions (sunburns) and chronic low-level sun reactions (suntans) can lead to skin cancer. People with fair skin have less natural protection against skin damage from the sun and a higher risk of developing skin cancer; people with naturally dark skin have a considerable degree of protection (see the box "What's Your UV Risk?"). Caucasians are about 20 times more likely than African Americans to develop melanoma, but African Americans and Latinos are still at risk. Severe sunburns in childhood have been linked to a greatly increased risk of skin cancer in later life, so children in particular should be protected. According to the American Academy of Dermatology, the risk of skin cancer doubles in people who have had five or more sunburns in their lifetime. Because of damage to the ozone layer of the atmosphere (discussed in Chapter 24), there is a chance that we may all be exposed to increasing amounts of UV radiation in the future.

Other risk factors for skin cancer include having many moles, particularly large ones; spending time at high altitudes; and a family history of the disease. Skin cancer

Terms

VW

melanoma A malignant tumor of the skin that arises from pigmented cells, usually a mole.

ultraviolet (UV) radiation Light rays of a specific wavelength emitted by the sun; most UV rays are blocked by the ozone layer in the upper atmosphere.

basal cell carcinoma Cancer of the deepest layers of the skin.

squamous cell carcinoma Cancer of the surface layers of the skin.

sunscreen A substance used to protect the skin from UV rays; usually applied as an ointment or a cream.

Assess Yourself

What's Your UV Risk?

Your risk of skin cancer from the ultraviolet radiation in sunlight depends on several factors. Take the quiz below to see how sensitive you are. The higher your UV-risk score, the greater your risk of skin cancer—and the greater your need to take precautions against too much sun.

Score 1 point for each true statement:

_____ 1. I have blond or red hair.
_____ 2. I have light-colored eyes (blue, gray, green).
_____ 3. I freckle easily.
_____ 4. I have many moles.
_____ 5. I had two or more blistering sunburns as a child.
_____ 6. I spent lots of time in a tropical climate as a child.
_____ 7. I have a family history of skin cancer.
_____ 8. I work outdoors.
_____ 9. I spend a lot of time in outdoor activities.
_____ 10. I like to spend as much time in the sun as I can.
_____ 11. I sometimes go to a tanning parlor or use a sunlamp.
_____ Total score

Score	Risk of skin cancer from UV radiation
0	Low
1–3	Moderate
4–7	High
8–11	Very high

For self-assessments for other types of cancer, visit the Harvard Center for Cancer Prevention's Your Disease Risk Web site (www.yourdiseaserisk.harvard.edu).

SOURCE: Adapted from Shear, N. 1996. What's your UV-risk score? *Consumer Reports on Health,* June.

may also be caused by exposure to coal tar, pitch, creosote, arsenic, and radioactive materials; but compared to sunlight, these agents account for only a small proportion of cases.

Types of Skin Cancer There are three main types of skin cancer, named for the types of skin cells from which they develop. **Basal cell** and **squamous cell carcinomas** together account for about 95% of the skin cancers diagnosed each year. They are usually found in chronically sun-exposed areas, such as the face, neck, hands, and arms. They usually appear as pale, waxlike, pearly nodules or red, scaly, sharply outlined patches. These cancers are often painless, although they may bleed, crust, and form an open sore on the skin.

Melanoma is by far the most dangerous skin cancer because it spreads so rapidly. Since 1980, the incidence of melanoma has increased by about 3% per year. It is the most common cancer among women age 25–29. It can occur anywhere on the body, but the most common sites are the back, chest, abdomen, and lower legs. A melanoma usually appears at the site of a preexisting mole. The mole may begin to enlarge, become mottled or varied in color (colors can include blue, pink, and white), or develop an irregular surface or irregular borders. Tissue invaded by melanoma may also itch, burn, or bleed easily.

Prevention One of the major steps you can take to protect yourself against all forms of skin cancer is to avoid lifelong overexposure to sunlight. Blistering, peeling sunburns from unprotected sun exposure are particularly dangerous, but suntans—whether from sunlight or tanning lamps—also increase your risk of developing skin cancer later in life. People of every age, especially babies and children, need to be protected from the sun with **sunscreens** and protective clothing. For a closer look at sunlight and skin cancer, see the box "Choosing and Using Sunscreens and Sun-Protective Clothing" on page 492.

Detection and Treatment The only sure way to avoid a serious outcome from skin cancer is to make sure it is recognized and diagnosed early. More than half of all melanomas are brought to a physician's attention by patients themselves. Make it a habit to examine your skin regularly. Most of the spots, freckles, moles, and blemishes on your body are normal; you were born with some of them, and others appear and disappear throughout your life. But if you notice an unusual growth, discoloration, sore that does not heal, or mole that undergoes a sudden or progressive change, see your physician or a dermatologist immediately.

The characteristics that may signal that a skin lesion is a melanoma—asymmetry, border irregularity, color change, and a diameter greater than ¼ inch—are illustrated in Figure 16-4 on page 493. A mole that changes in size, shape, or color is also of concern. In addition, if someone in your family has had numerous skin cancers or melanomas, consult a dermatologist for a complete skin examination and discussion of your particular risk.

If you have an unusual skin lesion, your physician will examine it and possibly perform a biopsy. If the lesion is cancerous, it is usually removed surgically, a

Choosing and Using Sunscreens and Sun-Protective Clothing

With consistent use of the proper clothing, sunscreens, and common sense, you can lead an active outdoor life *and* protect your skin against most sun-induced damage. Clothing should be your first and best line of defense. Sun-protective clothing can effectively block nearly all UVA and UVB rays. Sunscreens do provide protection, but many allow considerable UVA radiation to pass through to your skin. And even the best sunscreens are effective only when applied properly and reapplied frequently—something most people fail to do.

Clothing

- Wear long-sleeved shirts and long pants. Dark-colored, tightly woven fabrics provide reasonable protection from the sun. Another good choice is clothing made from special sun-protective fabrics; these garments have an Ultraviolet Protection Factor (UPF) rating, similar to the SPF for sunscreens. For example, a fabric with a UPF rating of 20 allows only one-twentieth of the sun's UV radiation to pass through. There are three categories of UPF protection: A UPF of 15–24 provides "good" UV protection, a UPF of 25–39 provides "very good" protection, and a UPF of 40–50 provides "excellent" protection. By comparison, typical shirts provide a UPF of only 5–9, a value that drops when clothing is wet.
- Consider washing some extra sun protection into your clothing. A new laundry additive adds UV protection to ordinary fabrics and is recommended by the Skin Cancer Foundation.
- Wear a hat. Your face, ears, neck, and scalp are especially vulnerable to the sun's harmful effects, making hats an essential weapon in the battle against sun damage. A good choice is a broad-brimmed hat or a legionnaire-style cap that covers the ears and neck. Wear sunscreen on your face even if you are wearing a hat.
- Wear sunglasses. Exposure to UV rays can damage the eyes and cause cataracts.

Sunscreen

- Use a sunscreen and lip balm with a sun protection factor (SPF) of 15 or higher. (An SPF rating refers to the amount of time you can stay out in the sun before you burn, compared with not using sunscreen; for example, a product with an SPF of 15 would allow you to remain in the sun without burning 15 times longer, on average, than if you didn't apply sunscreen.) If you're fair-skinned, have a family history of skin cancer, are at high altitude, or will be outdoors for many hours, use a sunscreen with a high SPF (30+).
- Choose a broad-spectrum sunscreen that protects against both UVA and UVB radiation. The SPF rating of a sunscreen currently applies only to UVB, but a number of ingredients, especially titanium dioxide and zinc oxide, are effective at blocking most UVA radiation. You can also look for an FDA-approved sunscreen called Anthelios SX, which contains the ingredient Mexoryl (ecamsule). Mesoryl blocks both UVA and UVB and has been found to be more protective against UVA than any other sunscreen ingredient. Use a water-resistant sunscreen if you swim or sweat quite a bit. If you have acne, look for a sunscreen that is labeled "noncomedogenic," which means that it will not cause pimples.
- Shake sunscreen before applying. Apply it 30 minutes before exposure to allow it time to penetrate the skin. Reapply sunscreen frequently and generously to all sun-exposed areas (many people overlook their temples, ears, and sides and backs of their necks). Most people use less than half as much as they need to attain the full SPF rating. One ounce of sunscreen—one-fourth of a 4-ounce container—is about enough to provide one application for an average-size adult in a swimsuit. Reapply sunscreen 15–30 minutes after sun exposure begins and then every few hours after that and/or following activities such as swimming that could remove sunscreen.
- If you're taking medications, ask your physician or pharmacist about possible reactions to sunlight or interactions with sunscreens. Medications for acne, allergies, and diabetes are just a few of the products that can trigger reactions. If you're using sunscreen and an insect repellent containing DEET, use extra sunscreen (DEET may decrease sunscreen effectiveness).
- Don't let sunscreens give you a false sense of security. Most of the sunscreens currently on the market allow considerable UVA radiation to penetrate the skin, with the potential for causing skin cancers (especially melanoma) as well as wrinkles and other forms of skin damage.

Time of Day and Location

- Avoid sun exposure between 10 A.M. and 4 P.M., when the sun's rays are most intense. Clouds allow as much as 80% of UV rays to reach your skin. Stay in the shade when you can.
- Consult the day's UV Index, which predicts UV levels on a 0–10+ scale, to get a sense of the amount of sun protection you'll need; take special care on days with a rating of 5 or above. UV Index ratings are available in local newspapers, from the weather bureau, or from certain Web sites.
- UV rays can penetrate at least 3 feet in water, so swimmers should wear water-resistant sunscreens. Snow, sand, water, concrete, and white-painted surfaces are also highly reflective.

Tanning Salons and Sunless Tanning Products

- Stay away from tanning salons! Despite advertising claims to the contrary, the lights used in tanning parlors are damaging to your skin. Tanning beds and lamps emit mostly UVA radiation, which penetrates more deeply than UVB and increases your risk of premature skin aging (such as wrinkles) and skin cancer.
- If you must have a tan, consider a sunless tanning product. Lotions, creams, and sprays containing the color additive dihydroxyacetone (DHA) are approved by the FDA for tanning. (So-called tanning accelerators and tanning pills have not been shown to be safe and effective and are not approved by the FDA.) DHA is for external use only and should not be inhaled, ingested, or used around the eyes. Tanning salons that offer spraying or misting with DHA need to ensure that customers are protected from exposure to the eyes, lips, and mucous membranes as well as internal exposure. Most sunless tanning products do not contain sunscreen, so if you use them in the sun, also wear sunscreen.

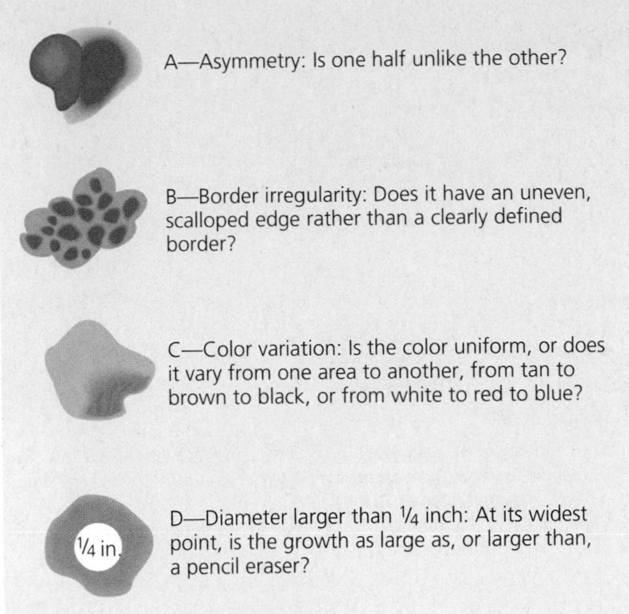

A—Asymmetry: Is one half unlike the other?
B—Border irregularity: Does it have an uneven, scalloped edge rather than a clearly defined border?
C—Color variation: Is the color uniform, or does it vary from one area to another, from tan to brown to black, or from white to red to blue?
1/4 in.
D—Diameter larger than 1/4 inch: At its widest point, is the growth as large as, or larger than, a pencil eraser?

Figure 16-4 The ABCD test for melanoma. To see a variety of photos of melanoma and benign moles, visit the National Cancer Institute's Visuals Online site (http://visualsonline.cancer.gov).

procedure that can almost always be performed in the physician's office using a local anesthetic. Occasionally, other forms of treatment may be used. Even for melanoma, the outlook after removal in the early stages is good, with a 5-year survival rate of 98% if the tumor is localized but only 60% if the cancer has spread to adjacent lymph nodes. Since prevention requires a minimum of time and attention, it pays to be alert.

Oral Cancer

Oral cancer—cancers of the lip, tongue, mouth, and throat—can be traced principally to cigarette, cigar, or pipe smoking, the use of spit tobacco, and the excessive consumption of alcohol. These risk factors work together to multiply a person's risk of oral cancer. The incidence of oral cancer is twice as great in men as in women and most frequent in men over 40. Some prominent sufferers of oral cancer have included Sigmund Freud and Fidel Castro, both notorious cigar smokers. Sports figures who have cultivated a taste for spit tobacco are now also increasingly being diagnosed with oral cancer. Among long-term snuff users, the excess risk of cancers of the cheek, tongue, and gum is nearly 50-fold (see Chapter 11 for more on cigars and spit tobacco).

Oral cancers do have the virtue of being fairly easy to detect, but they are often hard to cure. Furthermore, among those who survive, a significant number will develop another primary cancer of the head and neck. The primary methods of treatment are surgery and radiation. The overall survival rate is about 59%.

Testicular Cancer

Testicular cancer is relatively rare, accounting for only 1% of cancer in men (about 8300 cases per year), but it is the most common cancer in men age 20–35. It is much more common among white Americans than Latinos, Asian Americans, or African Americans and among men whose fathers had testicular cancer. Men with undescended testicles are at increased risk for testicular cancer, and for this reason the condition should be corrected in early childhood. Men whose mothers took DES during pregnancy have an increased risk of undescended testicles and other genital anomalies. Thus, they may have a higher risk of testicular cancer.

Self-examination may help in the early detection of testicular cancer (see the box "Testicle Self-Examination" on p. 494). Tumors are treated by surgical removal of the testicle and, if the tumor has spread, by chemotherapy. The 5-year survival rate for testicular cancer is 96%.

Other Cancers

Several other cancers affect a significant number of people each year. Some have identifiable risk factors, particularly smoking and obesity, that are controllable; causes of others are still under investigation.

Pancreatic Cancer The pancreas, a gland found deep within the abdomen behind the stomach, produces both digestive enzymes and insulin. Because of the gland's hidden location, pancreatic cancer is usually well advanced before symptoms become noticeable. No effective cure is available, and it is the fifth leading cause of cancer death in the United States: Each year there are about 34,000 new cases and about 32,000 deaths. About 3 out of 10 cases are linked to smoking. Other risk factors include being male, African American, obese, sedentary, or over age 60; having a family history of pancreatic cancer; having diabetes; and eating a diet high in fat and meat and low in vegetables.

Stomach Cancer In many parts of the world, stomach cancer is the most common form of cancer. It is relatively unusual in the United States, with about 22,300 new cases and 11,400 deaths each year. It tends to occur after the age of 50 and is almost twice as common in men as in women. Risk factors include infection with the bacterium *Helicobacter pylori,* which has also been linked to the development of ulcers, and a diet high in smoked, salted, or pickled fish or meat. Bacteria, including *H. pylori,* can convert the nitrites in preserved foods into carcinogenic amines, and salt can break down the normal protective stomach coating, allowing these carcinogenic compounds access to the cells of the stomach wall. However, the great majority of people with *H. pylori* infection do not develop stomach cancer, particularly if they

Take Charge

Testicle Self-Examination

The best time to perform a testicular self-exam is after a warm shower or bath, when the scrotum is relaxed. First, stand in front of a mirror and look for any swelling of the scrotum. Then examine each testicle with both hands. Place the index and middle fingers under the testicle and the thumbs on top; roll the testicle gently between the fingers and thumbs. Don't worry if one testicle seems slightly larger than the other—that's common. Also, expect to feel the epididymis, the soft, sperm-carrying tube at the rear of the testicle.

Perform the self-exam each month. If you find a lump, swelling, or nodule, consult a physician right away. The abnormality may not be cancer, but only a physician can make a diagnosis. Other possible signs of testicular cancer include a change in the way a testicle feels, a sudden collection of fluid in the scrotum, a dull ache in the lower abdomen or groin, a feeling of heaviness in the scrotum, or pain in a testicle or the scrotum.

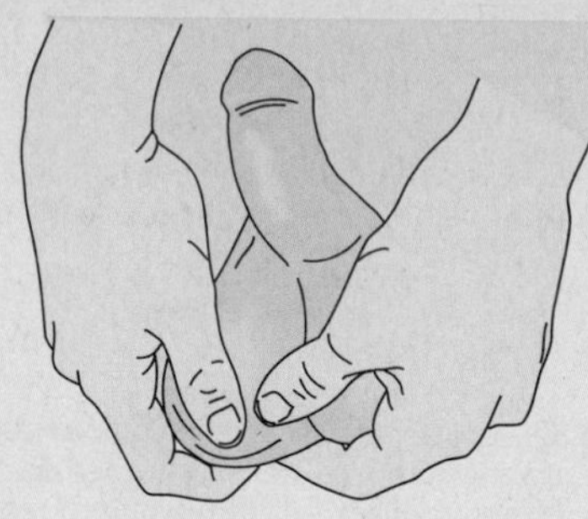

SOURCES: Testicular Cancer Resource Center. 2004. *How to Do a Testicular Self Examination* (http://www.acor.org/TCRC/tcexam.html; retrieved August 30, 2006); National Cancer Institute. 2005. *Questions and Answers About Testicular Cancer* (http://www.cancer.gov/cancertopics/factsheet/Sites-Types/testicular; retrieved August 30, 2006).

maintain a low-salt diet with adequate amounts of fruits, vegetables, and whole grains. There is no screening test for stomach cancer; it is usually recognized only after it has spread, and the 5-year survival rate is only 23% for all stages.

Bladder Cancer This cancer is almost three times as common in men as in women, and smoking is the key risk factor. People living in urban areas and workers exposed to chemicals used in the dye, rubber, and leather industries are also at increased risk. There is no screening test for it; the first symptoms are likely to be blood in the urine and/or increased frequency of urination. These symptoms can also signal a urinary infection but should trigger a visit to a physician, who can evaluate the possibility of cancer. With early detection, more than 90% of cases are curable. There are about 61,400 new cases and about 13,000 deaths each year.

Kidney Cancer Although this cancer usually occurs in people over 50, anyone can develop it, and there are few controllable risk factors. Smoking and obesity are mild risk factors, as is a family history of the disease. Symptoms may include fatigue, pain in the side, and blood in the urine. Kidney cancer has been difficult to treat, with a 5-year survival rate of only 65% for all stages. Recently, immune cell therapies have shown some promise in the disease's advanced stage. There are about 39,000 new cases each year and about 12,800 deaths.

Brain Cancer Tumors can arise from most of the many types of cells that are found in the brain. The vast majority of brain cancers develop for no apparent reason; one of the few established risk factors is ionizing radiation, such as X rays. Before the risks were recognized, children with ringworm of the scalp (a fungal infection) often received low-dose radiation therapy, which substantially increased their risk of brain tumors later in life. Symptoms are often nonspecific and include headaches, fatigue, behavioral changes, and sometimes seizures. There has been a slight increase in the incidence of tumors over the past 20 years, but this may be due to improved methods of diagnosis. Some brain tumors are curable by surgery or by radiation and chemotherapy, but most are not. Survival time varies, depending on the type of the tumor, from 1 to 8 years. In the United States each year there are about 18,800 new cases and 13,000 deaths.

Leukemia Leukemia, cancer of the white blood cells, can affect both children and adults. It starts in the bone marrow but can then spread to the lymph nodes, spleen, liver, other organs, and central nervous system. Like brain cancer, it is a complex disease with many different types and subtypes. Most people with leukemia have no known risk factors. About 20% of cases of adult leukemia are related to smoking; other possible risk factors include radiation and certain chemicals and infections. Most symptoms occur because leukemia cells crowd out the production of normal blood cells; the result can be fatigue, anemia, weight loss, and increased risk of infection. Treatment and survival rates vary, depending on the exact type and other factors. There are about 35,000 new cases and 22,300 deaths each year.

Lymphoma Arising from the lymph cells, lymphoma begins in the lymph nodes and then may spread to almost any part of the body. There are two types—Hodgkin's disease and non-Hodgkin's lymphoma (NHL). NHL is the more common and more deadly form of the disease. It is the sixth most common cancer in the United States, with about 66,700 people diagnosed annually; about half of all patients will eventually die from the disease. Risk factors for NHL are not well understood, but people with compromised immune systems are at much greater risk, especially when exposed to radiation or certain infections and chemicals. A new therapy based on the use of antibodies has shown promise in treating patients. Rates of Hodgkin's disease have fallen by more than 50% since the early 1970s, and there are now about 7800 cases and 1500 deaths each year.

Multiple Myeloma Normal plasma cells play an important role in the immune system, producing antibodies. Malignant plasma cells may produce tumors in several sites, particularly in the bone marrow; when they grow in multiple sites, they are referred to as multiple myeloma (MM). By crowding out normal bone marrow cells, MM can lead to anemia, excessive bleeding, and decreased resistance to infection. Age is the most significant risk factor: The average age at diagnosis is about 70. Other risk factors are not well understood, although MM is about twice as common among African Americans as among whites. Obesity has been associated with MM in women. Although treated with chemotherapy and slow in its progression, the disease is usually fatal. New therapies have been developed, and their impact on survival is being assessed.There are about 16,600 new cases each year and 11,300 deaths.

THE CAUSES OF CANCER

Although scientists do not know everything about what causes cancer, they have identified genetic, environmental, and lifestyle factors. (For information on possible factors involved in cancer incidence, see the box "Ethnicity, Poverty, and Cancer" on p. 496). There are usually several steps in the transformation of a normal cell into a cancer cell, and in many cases several factors may work together in the development of cancer.

The Role of DNA

Heredity and genetics are becoming increasingly important factors in assessing a person's risk of cancer. The inheritance of certain genes may predispose some people to develop cancers at a younger age, and various DNA techniques are used to identify specific genetic mutations associated with such cancers.

DNA Basics The nucleus of each cell in your body contains 23 pairs of **chromosomes,** which are made up of tightly packed coils of **DNA** (deoxyribonucleic acid). DNA consists of two long strands wound around each other in a spiral structure, like a twisted ladder; scientists refer to this spiral as a double helix. The rungs of the ladder are made from four different nucleotide bases: adenine, thymine, cytosine, and guanine, or A, T, C, and G. The arrangement of nucleotide bases along the double helix constitutes the genetic code. You can think of this code as a set of instructions for building, operating, and repairing your body.

A **gene** is a smaller unit of DNA made up of a specific sequence of nucleotide bases. Each chromosome contains hundreds, and in some cases thousands, of genes; you have about 25,000 genes in all. Each of your genes controls the production of a particular protein. The makeup of each protein—which amino acids it contains and in what sequence—is determined by its precise sequence of A, T, C, and G. Proteins build cells and make them work: They serve both as the structural material for your body and as the regulators of all chemical reactions and metabolic processes. By making different proteins at different times, genes can act as switches to alter the ways a cell works.

Except for sperm and egg cells, every cell in your body contains two copies of each gene, one on each of a pair of chromosomes. You inherit one copy of each gene from your mother and one from your father. Every cell contains a copy of the complete DNA sequence with all the genes. What makes the cells in your body different from one another in both structure and function—one a nerve cell and one a muscle cell, for example—is not which genes they contain, but which genes are expressed. Some genes are active and produce proteins all the time; others are expressed rarely.

Cells reproduce by dividing in two, and your body makes billions of new cells every day. When a cell divides, the DNA replicates itself so that each new cell has a complete set of chromosomes. Through the proteins for which they code, some genes are responsible for controlling the rate of cell division, and some types of cells divide much more rapidly than others. Genes that control the rate of cell division often play a critical role in the development of cancer.

DNA Mutations and Cancer A mutation is any change in the normal sequence of nucleotide bases in a

Terms VW

chromosomes The threadlike bodies in a cell nucleus that contain molecules of DNA; most human cells contain 23 pairs of chromosomes.

DNA Deoxyribonucleic acid, a chemical substance that carries genetic information.

gene A section of a chromosome that contains the nucleotide base sequence for making a particular protein; the basic unit of heredity.

Dimensions of Diversity

Ethnicity, Poverty, and Cancer

Rates of cancer have declined among all U.S. ethnic groups in recent years, but significant disparities still exist.

- Among U.S. ethnic groups, African Americans have the highest incidence of and death rates from cancer.
- White women have a higher incidence of breast cancer, but African American women have the highest death rate. Black women are less likely to receive regular mammograms and more likely to experience delays in follow-up.
- African American men have a higher rate of prostate cancer than any other U.S. group and more than twice the death rate of other groups. However, black men are less likely than white men to undergo PSA testing for prostate cancer.
- Latinas have the highest incidence of cervical cancer, but African American women have the highest death rate. Language barriers and problems accessing screening services are thought to particularly affect Latinas, who have relatively low rates of Pap testing.
- Asian Americans and Pacific Islander Americans have the highest rates of liver and stomach cancers. Recent immigration helps explain these higher rates, as these cancers are usually caused by infections that are more prevalent in the recent immigrant's country of origin.
- Significant disparities also exist within broad ethnic categories; for example, Vietnamese American women have a rate of cervical cancer four times higher than the overall rate among Asian American and Pacific Islander women.

Some of the disparities in cancer risks and rates may be influenced by genetic or cultural factors. For example, certain genetic/molecular features of aggressive breast cancer are more common among African American women with the disease; they are more likely to be diagnosed at a later stage and with more aggressive tumors. Genetic factors may also help explain the high rate of prostate cancer among black men. Women from cultures where early marriage and motherhood is common are likely to have a lower risk of breast cancer. People who don't smoke or who are vegetarians for religious or cultural reasons may have lower rates of many cancers.

Most of the differences in cancer rates and deaths, however, are thought to be the result of socioeconomic inequities, which influence the prevalence of many underlying cancer risk factors as well as access to early detection and quality treatment. People of low socioeconomic status are more likely to smoke, abuse alcohol, eat unhealthy foods, and be sedentary and overweight—all of which are associated with cancer. High levels of stress associated with poverty may impair the immune system, the body's first line of defense against cancer.

People with low incomes are more likely to live in unhealthy environments. For example, Latinos and Asian and Pacific Islander Americans are more likely than other groups to live in areas that do not meet federal air quality standards. Low-income people may also have jobs in which they come into daily contact with carcinogenic chemicals. They may face similar risks in their homes and schools, where they may be exposed to asbestos or other carcinogens.

People with low incomes also have less exposure to information about cancer, are less aware of the early warning signs of cancer, and are less likely to seek medical care when they have such symptoms. Lack of health insurance is a key factor explaining higher death rates among people with low incomes. A study comparing low-income Americans and Canadians found that the Canadians were more likely to survive cancer, possibly due to Canada's system of universal health care, which ensures access to treatment regardless of income. Discrimination and language and cultural barriers can also affect patients' use of the health care system.

Public education campaigns that encourage healthy lifestyle habits, routine cancer screening, and participation in clinical trials may be one helpful strategy to reduce cancer disparities. But the effects of poverty are more difficult to overcome. Some medical scientists look to policymakers for solutions and maintain that living and working conditions in the inner cities must be improved and that access to quality health care must be assured for all Americans. Then, even without new miracle drugs or medical breakthroughs, the United States could see a real decrease in cancer rates in low-income populations.

SOURCES: American Cancer Society. 2006. *Cancer Facts and Figures 2006*. Atlanta: American Cancer Society; Chlebowski, R. T., et al. 2005. Ethnicity and breast cancer: Factors influencing differences in incidence and outcome. *Journal of the National Cancer Institute* 97(6): 439–448; CDC Office of Minority Health. 2006. *Eliminate Disparities in Cancer Screening and Management* (http://www.cdc.gov/omh/AMH/factsheets/cancer.htm; retrieved August 30, 2006); National Cancer Institute. 2005. *Cancer Health Disparities: Fact Sheet* (http://www.cancer.gov/newscenter/healthdisparities; retrieved August 30, 2006).

gene. Like a typographical error, it may involve a deletion or a substitution of a certain base—for example, CAA may become CA or CTA. Some mutations are inherited: If the egg or sperm cell that produces a child contains a mutation, so will every one of the child's 30 trillion cells. Environmental agents can also produce mutational damage; these **mutagens** include radiation, certain viruses, and chemical substances in the air we breathe. (When a mutagen also causes cancer, it is called a carcinogen.) Some mutations are the result of copying errors that occur when DNA replicates itself as part of cell division.

A mutated gene no longer contains the proper code for producing its protein. Because a cell has two copies of each gene, it can sometimes get by with only one functioning version. In this case, the mutation may have no effect on health. However, if both copies of a gene are damaged or if the cell needs two normal copies to function properly, then the cell will cease to behave normally.

It requires several mutational changes over a period of years before a normal cell takes on the properties of a cancer cell. Genes in which mutations are associated with the conversion of a normal cell into a cancer cell are known as **oncogenes.** In their undamaged form, many oncogenes play a role in controlling or restricting cell growth; these are **tumor suppressor genes.** Mutational damage to these genes releases the brake on growth and leads to rapid and uncontrolled cell division—a precondition for the development of cancer.

A good example of how a series of mutational changes can produce cancer is provided by the p53 gene, located on chromosome 17. In its normal form, the protein that is coded for by this gene actually helps prevent cancer: If a cell's DNA is damaged, the p53 protein can either kill the cell outright or stop it from replicating until the damaged DNA is repaired. For example, if a skin cell's DNA is mutated by exposure to sunlight, the p53 protein activates the cell's "suicide" machinery. (The scientific term for this programmed cell death is **apoptosis.**) By thus preventing the replication of damaged DNA, the p53 protein keeps cells from progressing toward cancer. However, if the p53 gene itself undergoes a mutation, these controls are lost, and the cell can become cancerous. In fact, the damaged version of p53 can actually promote cell division and the spread of cancer.

A damaged p53 gene can be inherited, but carcinogenic damage or DNA copying errors are more common causes of p53 mutations. The carcinogen benzo(a)pyrene, found in tobacco smoke, causes a particular mutation in p53 that is linked to many cases of lung cancer. Other agents contribute to cancer by interfering with the p53 protein after it is produced. For example, human papillomavirus, the infectious agent linked to cervical cancer, neutralizes the p53 protein. Researchers believe that damage to the p53 gene and protein may be involved, directly and indirectly, in as many as 50–60% of all cancers.

Hereditary Cancer Risks One way to obtain a mutated oncogene is to inherit it. Using information from the Human Genome Project, scientists have been able to identify the genes responsible for some conditions. One example is BRCA1 (breast cancer gene 1): Women who inherit a damaged copy of this suppressor gene face a significantly increased risk of breast and ovarian cancer.

It is important to remember, however, that most cancers are not linked to heredity; mutational damage usually occurs after birth. New studies have led some researchers to believe that the gene–cancer link has been oversold to the medical community and to the public. Although some specific genes do increase the risk for some cancers, they say, it is unlikely that science will identify genes that increase the risk of cancer in general. For example, only about 5–10% of breast cancer cases can be traced to inherited copies of a damaged BRCA1 gene. Lifestyle decisions are still important even for those who have inherited a damaged suppressor gene.

Testing and identification of hereditary cancer risks can be helpful for some people, especially if it leads to increased attention to controllable risk factors and better medical screening. For more on hereditary cancer risks and the issues involved in genetic testing, see the box "Genetic Testing for Breast Cancer" on page 498.

Cancer Promoters Substances known as cancer promoters make up another important piece of the cancer puzzle. Carcinogenic agents such as UV radiation that cause mutational changes in the DNA of oncogenes are known as cancer *initiators*. Cancer *promoters*, on the other hand, don't directly produce DNA mutations. Instead, they accelerate the growth of cells without damaging or permanently altering their DNA. However, a faster growth rate means less time for a cell to repair DNA damage caused by initiators, so errors are more likely to be passed on. Estrogen, which stimulates cellular growth in the female reproductive organs, is an example of a cancer promoter. Cigarette smoke is a complete carcinogen because it acts as both an initiator and a promoter.

Colon cancer provides a good example of how the combination of initiators and promoters contributes to the development of cancer. Colon cells may divide more rapidly if the diet is high in red meat. Under these circumstances of growth promotion, a cell with a preexisting mutation in an oncogene has an increased chance of progressing toward cancer. Increasing intake of fruits, vegetables, and calcium may reverse this effect and slow the growth of cells that line the colon, thereby decreasing the possibility of cancer developing.

Although much still needs to be learned about the role of genetics in cancer, it's clear that minimizing mutation damage to our DNA will lower our risk of many cancers. Unfortunately, a great many substances produce cancer-causing mutations, and we can't escape them all. By

Terms

VW

mutagen Any environmental factor that can cause mutation, such as radiation and atmospheric chemicals.

oncogene A gene involved in the transformation of a normal cell into a cancer cell.

tumor suppressor gene A type of oncogene that normally functions to restrain cellular growth.

apoptosis Genetically programmed cell death, in which the cell undergoes shrinkage, condensation of the nucleus, and fragmentation. Many cancer cells lose their ability to respond to the normal apoptosis triggers, such as DNA damage.

In Focus

Genetic Testing for Breast Cancer

Linda's mother, sister, and grandmother all developed breast cancer at around age 40. Now Linda is wondering if she should be tested for mutations in the breast cancer genes, BRCA1 and BRCA2. She is not alone. Recent discoveries of disease-related genes are opening up a host of issues related to genetic testing and associated legal, financial, and ethical concerns. Tests for hereditary mutations in breast cancer genes are now commercially available, but who should be tested?

Researchers identified BRCA1 in 1994 and BRCA2 in 1995. About 1 or 2 in 1000 women in the general population carry a mutant copy of BRCA1 or BRCA2, but in certain groups, most notably women of Ashkenazi (Eastern European) Jewish descent, as many as 3 in 100 may carry an altered gene. Defects in these genes cause breast cancer in as many as 50–80% of affected women; they also increase the risk of ovarian cancer and, in men, prostate cancer. Women with an altered BRCA gene tend to develop breast cancer at younger ages than other women, and the cancers that develop are more malignant. The situation is complex, however, because hundreds of different mutations of BRCA1 and BRCA2 have been identified, and not all of them carry the same risks. Additional genes influencing risk have been identified—TSG101 in 1997, BRAF35 in 2001, BASE in 2003, CHEK2 in 2005—and others will no doubt be found in the future.

Genetic analysis of DNA from a blood sample can identify mutant copies of BRCA1 and BRCA2. The tests can be expensive, however, ranging from $350 to more than $2000. (Searching for a mutation on a large gene is a bit like looking for a single typo in a novel.) Good news from a genetic test is reassuring, but it doesn't guarantee freedom from disease. Only 5–10% of all cases of breast cancer occur among women who inherit an altered version of BRCA1 or BRCA2. And a woman with a family history of breast cancer must still be monitored closely, even if she carries normal versions of BRCA1 and BRCA2; the cancer-causing genetic defect in her family could be located on another gene.

What about women who test positive for an altered copy of the gene? Options include close monitoring, drug treatment with a SERM such as tamoxifen, and surgical removal of currently healthy breasts or ovaries. None of these strategies completely eliminates risk, and they may expose a woman to a dangerous or drastic treatment that is actually unnecessary. And those who test positive can face problems in addition to an uncertain medical future. Some health insurers may use the results of a genetic test to justify canceling coverage. Although currently rare, such genetic discrimination could become a major problem as more and more disease-related genes are identified. Recent legislation has attempted to protect people from losing coverage due to the results of genetic tests.

The U.S. Preventive Services Task Force recommends that genetic screen be offered only to women with a definite family history of breast or ovarian cancer. The group also says no woman should undergo screening without first receiving genetic counseling. If you think you are at high risk for a genetic abnormality because of your family or ethnic background, consider genetic counseling. A counselor can help you consider all the issues related to testing and can guide you in making the decision that is right for you.

identifying the important carcinogens and understanding how they produce their effects, we can help keep our DNA intact and avoid activating sleeping oncogenes. The careful study of oncogenes should also lead to more precise methods of assessing cancer risk and to new methods of diagnosis and treatment.

Dietary Factors

Diet is one of the most important factors in cancer prevention, but it is also one of the most complex and controversial. Diets high in meat, fast food, refined carbohydrates, and simple sugars and low in fruits and vegetables are associated with a higher risk of cancer than are plant-based diets rich in whole grains, fruits, and vegetables. The picture becomes less clear, however, when researchers attempt to identify the particular constituents of foods that affect cancer risk. The foods you eat contain many biologically active compounds, and your food choices affect your cancer risk by both exposing you to potentially dangerous compounds and depriving you of potentially protective ones. For example, snacking on a doughnut instead of an apple means that you consume more fat and simple sugars *and* less fiber and fewer vitamins. Research into particular food components can help guide you in making dietary choices, but keep in mind that the overall quality of your diet is most important.

Let's take a look at some of the dietary factors that may affect cancer risk.

Dietary Fat and Meat In general, diets high in fat and meat have been associated with higher rates of certain cancers, including those of the colon, esophagus, stomach, and prostate. Dietary fat may promote colon cancer by stimulating the production of bile acids, which are necessary to break down and digest material in the colon. Once produced, these bile acids remove layers of cells from the intestinal epithelium, which in turn are replaced by new cells. Newly formed and rapidly growing cells are particularly susceptible to carcinogens. Diets high in animal fats and low in plant fats may also increase the risk of aggressive forms of prostate cancer, possibly by affecting hormone levels.

As is the case for heart disease, certain types of fats may be riskier than others. Some studies suggest that diets favoring omega-6 polyunsaturated fats over the omega-3 forms commonly found in fish may be associated with a higher risk of certain cancers, and that monounsaturated fats may have a protective effect. Omega-3 fatty acids appear to slow the growth of colon cancer cells and may have protective factors against breast, prostate, and pancreatic cancers (see Chapter 12 for more on different types of fatty acids). The association between meat and cancer may be linked to the particular mix of fatty acids found in meat and how those fats are digested; in addition, high consumption of the iron in meat may promote the formation of free radicals. Curing, smoking, and grilling and other cooking methods utilizing a direct flame or high temperatures may also produce carcinogenic compounds such as polycyclic aromatic hydrocarbons. Grilling vegetables does not produce these compounds.

Alcohol Alcohol is associated with an increased incidence of several cancers. An average alcohol intake of three drinks per day is associated with a doubling in the risk of breast cancer. Alcohol and tobacco interact as risk factors for oral cancer, and heavy users of both alcohol and tobacco have a risk of oral cancer up to 15 times greater than that of people who don't drink or smoke. Alcohol also increases the risk of colon cancer.

Fried Foods In 2002, scientists in Sweden reported finding high levels of the chemical acrylamide in starch-based foods that had been fried or baked at high temperatures. Other labs have confirmed this finding and found substantial amounts of acrylamide in a variety of foods, especially french fries and certain types of snack chips and crackers. At high doses, acrylamide is toxic to humans and can induce mutations and cancer in lab animals; it is classified as a probable human carcinogen.

Studies are ongoing, but in 2005, WHO urged food companies to work to lower the acrylamide content of foods to reduce any risk to public health. Acrylamide levels vary widely in foods, and there are currently no warnings against eating specific foods. The wisest course may be to consume a variety of foods and avoid overindulging in any single class of foods, particularly foods like french fries and potato chips, which may contain other unhealthy substances such as saturated and trans fats. You can also limit your exposure to acrylamide by not smoking—you would likely get much more of the chemical from smoking than from food.

Fiber Determining the effects of fiber intake on cancer risk is complicated by the fact that fiber is found in foods that also contain many other potential anti-cancer agents—fruits, vegetables, and whole grains. Various potential cancer-fighting actions have been proposed for fiber, but none of these actions has been firmly established. Further study is needed to clarify the relationship between fiber intake and cancer risk, and experts still recommend a high-fiber diet for its overall positive effect on health.

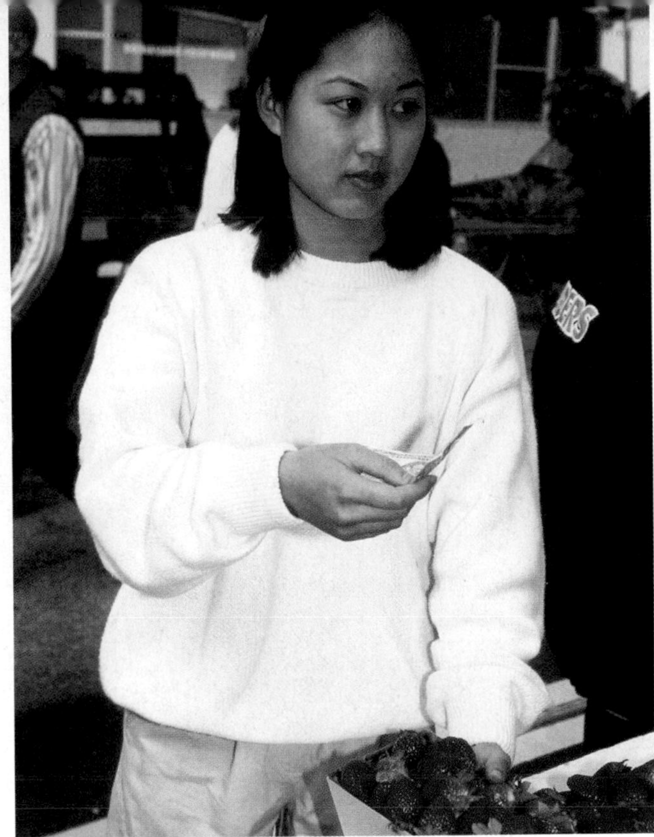

Your food choices significantly affect your risk of cancer. By consuming the recommended number of servings of fruits and vegetables per day, this young woman ensures that her diet is high in fiber and rich in cancer-fighting phytochemicals.

Fruits and Vegetables Exactly which constituents of fruits and vegetables are responsible for reducing cancer risk is not clear, but researchers have identified many mechanisms by which food components may act against cancer: Some may prevent carcinogens from forming in the first place or block them from reaching or acting on target cells. Others boost enzymes that detoxify carcinogens and render them harmless. Still other anti-cancer agents act on cells that have already been exposed to carcinogens, slowing the development of cancer or starving cancer cells of oxygen and nutrients by cutting off their blood supply.

Some essential nutrients act as **anticarcinogens.** For example, vitamin C, vitamin E, selenium, and the **carotenoids** (vitamin A precursors) may help block the

Terms

VW

anticarcinogen An agent that destroys or otherwise blocks the action of carcinogens.

carotenoid Any of a group of yellow-to-red plant pigments that can be converted to vitamin A by the liver; many act as antioxidants or have other anti-cancer effects. The carotenoids include beta-carotene, lutein, lycopene, and zeaxanthin.

Table 16-1 Choosing Foods with Phytochemicals

Food	Phytochemical and Its Potential Anti-Cancer Effects
Chili peppers (Note: Hotter peppers contain more capsaicin.)	Capsaicin: Neutralizes the effect of nitrosamines; may block carcinogens in cigarette smoke from acting on cells
Citrus fruits (oranges, lemons, limes), onions, apples, berries, eggplant	Flavonoids: Act as antioxidants; block access of carcinogens to cells; suppress malignant changes in cells; prevent cancer cells from multiplying
Citrus fruits, cherries	Monoterpenes: Help detoxify carcinogens; inhibit spread of cancer cells
Cruciferous vegetables (broccoli, cabbage, bok choy, cauliflower, kale, brussels sprouts, collards)	Isothiocyanates: Boost production of cancer-fighting enzymes; suppress tumor growth; block effects of estrogen on cell growth
Garlic, onions, leeks, shallots, chives	Allyl sulfides: Increase levels of enzymes that break down potential carcinogens; boost activity of cancer-fighting immune cells
Grapes, red wine, peanuts	Resveratrol: Acts as an antioxidant; suppresses tumor growth
Green, oolong, and black teas (Note: Drinking tea that is burning hot may *increase* cancer risk.)	Polyphenols: Increase antioxidant activity; prevent cancer cells from multiplying; help speed excretion of carcinogens from the body
Orange or deep yellow, red or pink, and dark green vegetables and some fruits	Carotenoids: Act as anitoxidants; reduce levels of cancer-promoting enzymes; inhibit spread of cancer cells
Soy foods, whole grains, flax seeds, nuts	Phytoestrogens: Block effects of estrogen on cell growth; lower blood levels of estrogen; inhibit angiogenesis
Whole grains, legumes	Phytic acid: Binds iron, which may prevent it from creating cell-damaging free radicals

initiation of cancer by acting as **antioxidants.** As described in Chapter 12, antioxidants prevent **free radicals** from damaging DNA. Vitamin C may also block the conversion of nitrites (food preservatives) into cancer-causing agents. Folic acid may inhibit the transformation of normal cells into malignant cells and strengthen immune function. Calcium inhibits the growth of cells in the colon and may slow the spread of potentially cancerous cells.

Many other anti-cancer agents in the diet fall under the broader heading of **phytochemicals,** substances in plants that help protect against chronic diseases. One of the first to be identified was **sulforaphane,** a potent anticarcinogen found in broccoli. Sulforaphane induces the cells of the liver and kidney to produce higher levels of protective enzymes, which then neutralize dietary carcinogens. Most fruits and vegetables contain beneficial phytochemicals, and researchers are just beginning to identify them. Some of the most promising are listed in Table 16-1.

To increase your intake of these potential cancer fighters, eat a wide variety of fruits, vegetables, legumes, and grains. Don't try to rely on supplements. Many of these compounds are not yet available in supplement form, and optimal intakes have not been determined. Like many vitamins and minerals, isolated phytochemicals may be harmful if taken in high doses. Beta-carotene pills, for example, may increase smokers' risk of lung cancer. In addition, it is likely that the anti-cancer effects of many foods are the result of many chemical substances working in combination. Some practical suggestions for maximizing your intake of anti-cancer agents are included in the Behavior Change Strategy at the end of the chapter.

Inactivity and Obesity

Several common types of cancer are associated with an inactive lifestyle, and research has shown a relationship between increased physical activity and a reduction in cancer risk. There is good evidence that exercise reduces the risk of colon cancer, perhaps by speeding the movement of food through the digestive tract, strengthening immune function, and decreasing blood fat levels. When young girls get adequate exercise, they tend to gain weight more slowly, menstruation begins later, and their risk of breast and ovarian cancers is reduced.

In addition, exercise is important because it helps prevent obesity, an independent risk factor for cancer (Figure 16-5). A high percentage of body fat appears to increase the risk of cancers of the prostate, breast, female reproductive tract, and kidney and possibly the colon and gallbladder. Obesity may affect hormone levels in the blood, slow the transit time of food through the colon, change the way the body metabolizes fat, and generally promote cell growth. All of these actions have the potential to increase cancer risk. Obesity is also associated with pre-diabetes and diabetes, and high blood sugar levels have also been linked to increased risk of cancer.

In the United States, about 170,000 cancer deaths per year appear to be due to a combination of dietary habits

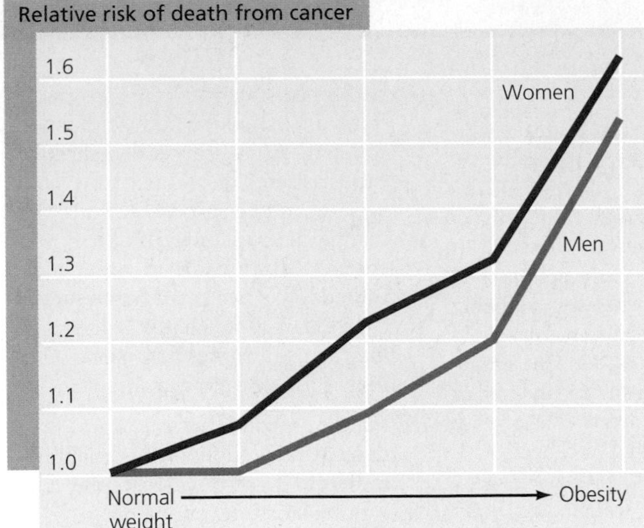

Figure 16-5 Body weight and cancer mortality. For both men and women, overweight and obesity are associated with significantly higher rates of death from cancer. SOURCE: Data from Calle, E. E., et al. 2003. Overweight, obesity, and mortality from cancer in a prospectively studied cohort of U.S. adults. *New England Journal of Medicine* 34(17): 1625–1638; illustration from Fahey, T. D., P. M. Insel, and W. T. Roth. 2007. *Fit & Well*, 7th ed., Fig. 12-4, p. 372. New York: McGraw-Hill. Copyright © 2007 The McGraw-Hill Companies, Inc. Reprinted with permission.

and a sedentary lifestyle. Alarmingly, however, only 8% of Americans are aware that being overweight increases one's cancer risk (see the box "Cancer Myths and Misperceptions" on p. 502). One expert estimates that if we were all to exercise for 20 minutes each day and make the dietary changes discussed in this chapter, about 40,000 cancer deaths could be prevented each year.

Microbes

It is estimated that about 15% of the world's cancers are caused by microbes, including viruses, bacteria, and parasites, although the percentage is much lower in developed countries like the United States. As discussed earlier, certain types of human papillomavirus cause many cases of cervical cancer, and the *Helicobacter pylori* bacterium has been definitely linked to stomach cancer.

Viruses seem to be the main cancer causers. The Epstein-Barr virus, best known for causing mononucleosis, is also suspected of contributing to Hodgkin's disease, cancer of the pharynx, and some stomach cancers. Human herpesvirus 8 has been linked to Kaposi's sarcoma and certain types of lymphoma. Hepatitis viruses B and C together cause as many as 80% of the world's liver cancers. Hepatitis B is spread mainly through sexual intercourse, though it can be passed through contact with any body fluid or with contaminated needles. A vaccine for hepatitis B is available. Hepatitis C is most commonly acquired through blood transfusions or injection drug use, but it, too, can be spread sexually. Although most people who develop hepatitis recover, up to 10% of people with hepatitis B and 85% of people with hepatitis C become chronic carriers of the virus and are at high risk for liver cancer. The best way to avoid contracting these viruses is to limit the number of sex partners you have, practice safer sex, and avoid sharing needles.

Carcinogens in the Environment

Some carcinogens occur naturally in the environment, like the sun's UV rays. Others are manufactured or synthetic substances that show up occasionally in the general environment but more often in the work environments of specific industries.

Ingested Chemicals The food industry uses preservatives and other additives to prevent food from becoming spoiled or stale (see Chapter 12). Some of these compounds are antioxidants and may actually decrease any cancer-causing properties the food might have. Other compounds, like the nitrates and nitrites found in processed meat, are potentially more dangerous.

Nitrates and nitrites are added to foods like beer and ale, ham, bacon, hot dogs, and lunch meats. The nitrites inhibit the growth of bacteria, which could otherwise cause food poisoning. They also preserve the pink color of the meat, which has no bearing on taste but looks more appetizing to many people. While nitrates and nitrites are not themselves carcinogenic, they can combine with dietary substances in the stomach and be converted to **nitrosamines**, which are highly potent carcinogens. Foods cured with nitrites, as well as those cured by salt or smoke, have been linked to esophageal and stomach cancer, and they should be eaten only in modest amounts.

Environmental and Industrial Pollution Pollutants in urban air have long been suspected of contributing to the incidence of lung cancer. Fossil fuels and

Terms

VW

antioxidant A substance that can lessen the breakdown of food or body constituents; actions include binding oxygen and donating electrons to free radicals.

free radicals Electron-seeking compounds that can react with fats, proteins, and DNA, damaging cell membranes and mutating genes in their search for electrons; produced through chemical reactions in the body and by exposure to environmental factors such as sunlight and tobacco smoke.

phytochemical A naturally occurring substance found in plant foods that may help prevent chronic diseases such as cancer and heart disease; *phyto* means "plant."

sulforaphane A compound found in cruciferous vegetables that can activate the body's detoxifying enzyme system.

nitrosamine A carcinogen made in the stomach from nitrates and nitrites.

Cancer Myths and Misperceptions

Almost daily, cancer receives wide-ranging media coverage as it affects the lives of its victims and as breakthroughs create new hope for a cure. During regular checkups, doctors and dentists routinely look for signs of cancer and are quick to discuss the risks of being stricken by cancer.

Remarkably, even as we are being inundated with information about cancer, studies show that most Americans do not understand basic facts about the disease. Indeed, many still believe myths about cancer that were disproved long ago. Such misperceptions are leading Americans to ignore good advice on cancer prevention and to continue lifestyle habits that increase the risk of cancer.

Healthier Cigarettes?

Scientists have concluded that "low-tar," "low-nicotine," and "light" cigarettes are no safer than regular cigarettes. In fact, some brands of light cigarettes contain just as much nicotine and additives as regular cigarettes. Further, users of light cigarettes tend to smoke more frequently and inhale more deeply than smokers of regular cigarettes—often in the misguided belief that their chosen brand won't hurt them. In a 2006 survey, 72% of women and 63% of men said they believed light cigarettes were not as harmful as regular cigarettes. Meantime, smoking remains the leading preventable cause of cancer and is responsible for nearly 90% of all lung cancer deaths.

Similarly, many smokers have switched to smokeless tobacco products (such as chewing tobacco), thinking they pose no health risks. Not so, say the experts. Smokeless tobacco products pack a big nicotine punch and contribute to head, throat, and oral cancers.

Obesity and Cancer

A 2006 survey conducted for the American Cancer Society showed that only 8% of Americans are aware of the link between obesity and cancer. (Only about 15% of respondents knew their own BMI; most overweight and obese people surveyed did not view themselves as being too heavy.) The lack of awareness extends beyond the United States; a recent survey of European and South American women revealed that only 5% knew that obesity and poor diet were linked to cancer.

As is the case with heart disease, maintaining a healthy weight and body composition can help reduce the risk of cancer. Although scientists aren't sure how body fat works to increase cancer risk, there is bountiful evidence that overweight and obese people are in greater danger of breast, prostate, colorectal, and other cancers. In fact, obesity is the second most preventable cause of death.

Prevailing Myths

In light of such findings, it may not be surprising to learn that many Americans accept some myths about cancer, such as the following:

- *Supplements prevent cancer.* Scientists say there is no evidence that any single vitamin, mineral, or herb can boost the immune system enough to ward off cancer. The best dietary advice, they say, is to eat a wide variety of foods daily, emphasizing whole grains, fruits, and vegetables.
- *Surgery causes cancer to spread.* For generations, physicians did not have the means to detect cancer until it was advanced. As a result, doctors often performed surgery to remove a tumor from one part of the body without realizing that the cancer had already metastasized. When cancer was found again in another part of the body, many patients assumed that their surgery had "disturbed" the cancer and caused it to spread. This myth prevails even today, although it was disproved long ago. Surgery, in fact, is one of the most effective cancer treatments.
- *Cancer cannot be prevented.* As described throughout this chapter, individuals can do a lot to prevent cancer. Most preventive measures are simple, commonsense practices such as eating a healthy diet, exercising, controlling weight, and not smoking.
- *Stress causes cancer.* Stress has been linked to a variety of illnesses, but there is no evidence that it causes cancer. Some very recent surveys, in fact, indicate that stress may actually help prevent certain cancers.
- *Cancer cannot be cured.* There are more than 10 million cancer survivors in the United States who can dispute this myth. Treatments are more powerful than ever, and although some types of cancer are more lethal than others, there is hope for anyone whose cancer is detected early and who takes steps to get rid of it.

Surveys show that a significant percentage of Americans still believe these myths (more than 40%, in some cases). Such thinking is both wrongheaded and dangerous. The first step in preventing and treating cancer is finding good sources of reliable information and following a qualified physician's advice.

their combustion products, such as complex hydrocarbons, have been of special concern, and most gas stations are now required to provide special nozzles to reduce the amount of gasoline vapor released when you fill your tank. The effect of air pollutants has been difficult to study because of the overwhelmingly greater influence of smoking on lung cancer rates. Urban air pollution appears to have a measurable but limited role in causing lung cancer. (Chapter 24 has more information on air pollution.)

The best available data indicate that less than 2% of cancer deaths are caused by general environmental pollution, such as substances in our air and water (see the box "Cancer Myths and Misperceptions"). Exposure to carcinogenic materials in the workplace is a more serious problem. Occupational exposure to specific carcinogens may account for up to 5% of cancer deaths. For example, diesel exhaust may contribute to lung cancer in truck operators and railroad workers, soot may cause skin cancer in firefighters and bricklayers, and hair dyes have been linked to bladder cancer in hairdressers and barbers. With increasing industry and government regulation, we can anticipate that the industrial sources of cancer risk will continue to diminish, at least in the United States. In contrast, in the former Soviet Union and Eastern European countries, where environmental concerns were sacrificed to industrial productivity for decades, cancer rates from industrial pollution continue to climb.

Radiation All sources of radiation are potentially carcinogenic, including medical X rays, radioactive substances (radioisotopes), and UV rays from the sun. Striking examples of the effects of radiation can be seen in the survivors of the atomic bombings of Hiroshima and Nagasaki in 1945 and in residents of the area surrounding the Chernobyl nuclear reactor that blew up in 1986. In Japan, new cancers, especially leukemias, are still occurring over 50 years after the bombings. In Belarus, Russia, and Ukraine, the areas most affected by the radioactive debris from Chernobyl, rates of thyroid cancer in children are as much as 30 times higher than before the explosion. People living near Chernobyl suffered genetic damage that is being passed on to their children.

The continuing cancer cases in survivors of Hiroshima, Nagasaki, and Chernobyl are a warning to us that any unnecessary exposure to ionizing radiation should be avoided. Most physicians and dentists are quite aware of the risk of radiation, and successful efforts have been made to reduce the amount of radiation needed for mammograms, dental X rays, and other necessary medical X rays. Full-body CT scans are sometimes advertised for routine screening in otherwise well individuals in order to look for tumors. Such screening is not recommended; it is typically expensive and may have false-positive findings that lead to unnecessary and invasive additional tests. Also, the radiation in these full-body X rays may itself raise the risk of cancer; the radiation dose of one full-body CT scan is nearly 100 times that of a typical mammogram.

Another source of environmental radiation is radon gas. Radon is a radioactive decomposition product of radium, which is found in small quantities in some rocks and soils. Radon is inhaled with the air we breathe, so it comes into intimate contact with the cells of the lungs, where its radiation can produce mutations. Radon and smoking together create a more-than-additive risk of lung cancer. In most of our homes and classrooms, radon is rapidly dissipated into the atmosphere, and very low levels of radon do not appear to increase cancer risk. But in certain kinds of enclosed spaces, such as mines, some basements, and airtight houses built of brick or stone, it can rise to dangerous levels (see Chapter 24).

Sunlight is a very important source of radiation, but because its rays penetrate only a millimeter or so into the skin, it could be considered a surface carcinogen. Most cases of skin cancer are the relatively benign and highly curable basal cell carcinomas, but a substantial minority are the potentially deadly malignant melanomas. As discussed earlier, all types of skin cancer are increased by early and excessive exposure to the sun, and severe sunburn early in childhood appears to carry with it an added risk of melanoma later in life.

Cell phones generate low levels of non-ionizing radiation, a different type of radiation from that used for medical X rays (see Chapter 24). Studies of the effects of exposure to non-ionizing radiation from cell phones have had mixed results, and researchers have found no conclusive link between cell phone use and brain cancer. Research is ongoing, however, and until the effects of such radiation exposure have been determined, some health professionals suggest discouraging children from using mobile phones excessively because their brains are more susceptible to radiation than are those of adults.

DETECTING, DIAGNOSING, AND TREATING CANCER

Early cancer detection often depends on our willingness to be aware of changes in our own body and to make sure we keep up with recommended diagnostic tests. Although treatment success varies with individual cancers, cure rates have increased—sometimes dramatically—in this century.

Detecting Cancer

Unlike those of some other diseases, early signs of cancer are usually not apparent to anyone but the person who has them. Even pain is not a reliable guide to early detection, because the initial stages of cancer may be painless. Self-monitoring is the first line of defense, and the American Cancer Society recommends that you watch for the seven major warning signs shown in Figure 16-6. Remember them by the acronym CAUTION.

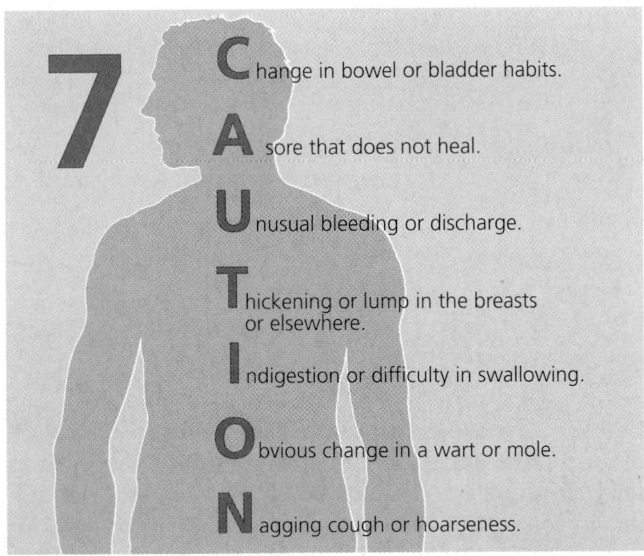

7
Change in bowel or bladder habits.
A sore that does not heal.
Unusual bleeding or discharge.
Thickening or lump in the breasts or elsewhere.
Indigestion or difficulty in swallowing.
Obvious change in a wart or mole.
Nagging cough or hoarseness.

Figure 16-6 The seven major warning signs of cancer.

Table 16-2 Screening Guidelines for the Early Detection of Cancer in Asymptomatic People

Site	Recommendation
Breast	• Yearly mammograms are recommended starting at age 40. The age at which screening should be stopped should be individualized by considering the potential risks and benefits of screening in the context of overall health status and longevity. • Clinical breast exam should be part of a periodic health exam, about every 3 years for women in their twenties and thirties, and every year for women age 40 and older. • Women should know how their breasts normally feel and report any breast change promptly to their health care providers. Breast self-exam is an option for women starting in their twenties. • Women at increased risk (e.g., family history, genetic tendency, past breast cancer) should talk with their doctors about the benefits and limitations of starting mammography screening earlier, having additional tests (i.e., breast ultrasound and MRI), or having more frequent exams.
Colon and rectum	Beginning at age 50, men and women should begin screening with one of the examination schedules below: • A fecal occult blood test (FOBT) or fecal immunochemical test (FIT) every year • A flexible sigmoidoscopy (FSIG) every 5 years • Annual FOBT or FIT and flexible sigmoidoscopy every 5 years* • A double-contrast barium enema every 5 years • A colonoscopy every 10 years **Combined testing is preferred over either annual FOBT or FIT, or FSIG every 5 years, alone. People who are at moderate or high risk for colorectal cancer should talk with a doctor about a different testing schedule.*
Prostate	The PSA test and the digital rectal examination should be offered annually, beginning at age 50, to men who have a life expectancy of at least 10 years. Men at high risk (African American men and men with a strong family history of one or more first-degree relatives diagnosed with prostate cancer at an early age) should begin testing at age 45. For men at both average risk and high risk, information should be provided about what is known and what is uncertain about the benefits and limitations of early detection and treatment of prostate cancer so that they can make an informed decision about testing.
Uterus	***Cervix:*** Screening should begin approximately 3 years after a woman begins having vaginal intercourse, but no later than age 21. Screening should be done every year with regular Pap tests or every 2 years using liquid-based tests. At or after age 30, women who have had three normal test results in a row may get screened every 2 to 3 years. Alternatively, cervical cancer screening with HPV DNA testing and conventional or liquid-based cytology could be performed every 3 years. However, doctors may suggest a woman get screened more often if she has certain risk factors, such as HIV infection or a weak immune system. Women 70 years and older who have had three or more consecutive normal Pap tests in the past 10 years may choose to stop cervical cancer screening. Screening after total hysterectomy (with removal of the cervix) is not necessary unless the surgery was done as a treatment for cervical cancer. ***Endometrium:*** The American Cancer Society recommends that at the time of menopause all women should be informed about the risks and symptoms of endometrial cancer, and strongly encouraged to report any unexpected bleeding or spotting to their physicians. Annual screening for endometrial cancer with endometrial biopsy beginning at age 35 should be offered to women with or at risk for hereditary nonpolyposis colon cancer (HNPCC).
Cancer-related checkup	For individuals undergoing periodic health examinations, a cancer-related checkup should include health counseling and, depending on a person's age and gender, might include examinations for cancers of the thyroid, oral cavity, skin, lymph nodes, testes, and ovaries, as well as for some nonmalignant diseases.

SOURCE: American Cancer Society's *Cancer Facts and Figures 2006*. Copyright © 2006 American Cancer Society, Inc. www.cancer.org. Reprinted with permission.

Although none of the warning signs is a sure indication of cancer, the appearance of any one should send you to see your physician. By being aware yourself of the risk factors in your own life, including the cancer history of your immediate family and your own past history, you can often bring a problem to the attention of a physician long before it would have been detected at a routine physical.

In addition to self-monitoring, the ACS recommends routine cancer checkups, as well as specific screening tests for certain cancers (Table 16-2).

Diagnosing Cancer

Detection of a cancer by physical examination is only the beginning. Methods for determining the exact location, type, and degree of malignancy of a cancer continue to improve. Knowledge of the exact location and size of a tumor is necessary for precise and effective surgery or radiation therapy. This is especially true in cases where the tumor may be hard to reach, as in the brain.

Imaging studies or exploratory surgery may be performed to identify a cancer's *stage*—a designation based on a tumor's size, location, and spread that helps determine appropriate treatment. A biopsy may be performed to confirm the type of tumor. Several diagnostic imaging techniques have replaced exploratory surgery for some patients. In **magnetic resonance imaging (MRI)**, a huge electromagnet is used to detect hidden tumors by mapping, on a computer screen, the vibrations of different atoms in the body. **Computed tomography (CT)** scanning uses X rays to examine the brain and other parts of the body. The process allows the construction of cross sections, which show a tumor's shape and location more accurately than is possible with conventional X rays. For patients undergoing radiation therapy, CT scanning enables the therapist to pinpoint the tumor more precisely, thereby providing more accurate radiation dosage while sparing normal tissue.

Ultrasonography has also been used increasingly in the past few years to view tumors. It has several advantages: It can be used in the physician's office, it is less expensive than other imaging methods, and it is completely safe. Prostate ultrasound (a rectal probe using ultrasonic waves to produce an image of the prostate gland) is being investigated for its ability to detect small, hidden tumors that would be missed by a digital rectal exam.

Treating Cancer

The ideal cancer therapy would kill or remove all cancerous cells while leaving normal tissue untouched. Sometimes this is almost possible, as when a surgeon removes a small superficial tumor of the skin. Usually the tumor is less accessible, and some combination of surgery, radiation therapy, and chemotherapy must be applied instead. Some patients choose to combine conventional therapies with alternative treatments (see the box "Avoiding Cancer Quackery" on p. 506).

Surgery For most cancers, surgery is the most useful treatment. In many cases, the organ containing the tumor is not essential for life and can be partially or completely removed. This is true especially for localized breast, prostate, or testicular cancer, where the surgical removal of one breast, the prostate gland, or one testicle may give a long-lasting cure. Surgery is less effective when the tumor involves cells of the immune system, which are widely distributed throughout the body, or when the cancer has already metastasized. In such cases, surgery must be combined with other techniques.

Chemotherapy Chemotherapy, or the use of cell-killing drugs to destroy rapidly growing cancer cells, has been in use since the 1940s. Many of these drugs work by interfering with DNA synthesis and replication in rapidly dividing cells. Normal cells, which usually grow slowly, are not destroyed by these drugs. However, some normal tissues such as intestinal, hair, and blood-forming cells are always growing, and damage to these tissues produces the unpleasant side effects of chemotherapy, including nausea, vomiting, diarrhea, and hair loss.

Chemotherapy drugs are often used in combinations or with surgery. Recently, in a procedure called **induction chemotherapy,** physicians have begun to use chemotherapy before surgery, both to shrink the tumor and to kill any existing small metastases as soon as possible.

Radiation In cancer radiation therapy, a beam of X rays or gamma rays is directed at the tumor, and the tumor cells are killed. Occasionally, when an organ is small enough, radioactive seeds are surgically placed inside the cancerous organ to destroy the tumor and then removed later if necessary. Radiation destroys both normal and cancerous cells, but because it can be precisely directed at the tumor it is usually less toxic for the patient than either surgery or chemotherapy, and it can often be performed on an outpatient basis. Radiation may be used as an exclusive treatment or in combination with surgery and/or chemotherapy.

New and Experimental Techniques Many new and exciting possibilities for cancer therapy promise alternatives to the options of surgery, radiation, and chemotherapy. Although it is impossible to predict which of these new approaches will be most successful, researchers hope that cancer therapy overall will become increasingly safer and more effective.

- *Gene therapy.* Completion of the sequencing of the human genome in 2000 opened a treasure chest of new insights into cancer. Scientists have already

Terms

magnetic resonance imaging (MRI) A computerized imaging technique that uses a strong magnetic field and radio frequency signals to examine a thin cross section of the body; also known as *nuclear magnetic resonance imaging (NMR).*

computed tomography (CT) The use of computerized X ray images to create a cross-sectional depiction of tissue density.

induction chemotherapy The use of chemotherapy prior to surgery to shrink a cancerous tumor and prevent metastasis; sometimes eliminates the need for radical surgery.

Vw

Critical Consumer

Avoiding Cancer Quackery

VW

Sometimes conventional treatments for cancer are simply not enough. A patient may be told that there is little conventional therapy can do, other than providing medication to ease pain. When therapy is available, it may be painful and even intolerable to some people. Not surprisingly, many cancer patients look for complementary and alternative therapies. As many as 80% of cancer patients report combining conventional treatments with some type of mind-body technique. A much smaller number of patients look for alternatives to the more conventional therapies. These may be therapies within the bounds of legitimate medical practice that have not yet proven themselves in clinical trials. Or, at the extreme, alternative therapies may be scientifically unsound and dangerous, as well as expensive.

Complementary therapies such as yoga, massage, meditation, music therapy, t'ai chi, and prayer can have positive physical and psychological benefits for patients and help them improve their quality of life as they deal with illness and the often difficult treatments for cancer. Mind-body practices can reduce pain and anxiety, improve sleep, and give people a sense of control and participation in their treatment; such practices may also enhance the immune system. (See Chapter 2 for more on stress and relaxation techniques.) Mind-body practices typically can be used in combination with conventional cancer therapies.

For other types of therapies, the National Cancer Institute suggests that patients and their families consider the following questions when making decisions about cancer treatment:

- *Has the treatment been evaluated in clinical trials?* Advances in cancer treatment are made through carefully monitored clinical trials. If a patient wants to try a new therapy, participation in a clinical trial may be a treatment option. (See For More Information at the end of the chapter for more on clinical trials.)
- *Do the practitioners of an approach claim that the medical community is trying to keep their cure from the public?* No one genuinely committed to finding better ways to treat a disease would knowingly keep an effective treatment secret or try to suppress such a treatment.
- *Does the treatment rely on nutritional or diet therapy as its main focus?* Although diet can be a key risk factor in the development of cancer, there is no evidence that diet alone can get rid of cancerous cells in the body.
- *Do those who endorse the treatment claim that it is harmless and painless and that it produces no unpleasant side effects?* Reputable researchers are working to develop less toxic cancer therapies, but because effective treatments for cancer must be powerful, they frequently have unpleasant side effects.
- *Does the treatment have a secret formula that only a small group of practitioners can use?* Scientists who believe they have developed an effective treatment routinely publish their results in reputable journals so they can be evaluated by other researchers.

Use special caution when evaluating cancer remedies promoted online; one recent study found that as many as one-third of cancer-related alternative medicine sites offered advice that was harmful or potentially dangerous.

One danger of alternative medicine is the very real possibility that proven therapies will be neglected while unproven, faddish alternative approaches are pursued; if alternate therapies delay proven therapies, lives may be lost. Another danger is that complementary therapies may counteract or affect conventional therapies; for example, some herbal supplements have been found to affect how cancer drugs are absorbed and used by the body. A recent study revealed that 70% of patients using complementary therapies do not inform their physicians. However, it is essential for physicians to have this information so any side effects or harmful interactions can be prevented.

SOURCES: American Cancer Society. 2006. *Complementary and Alternative Therapies* (http://www.cancer.org/docroot/ETO/ETO_5.asp; retrieved August 30, 2006); National Cancer Institute. 2006. *Complementary and Alternative Medicine in Cancer Treatment: Questions and Answers* (http://www.cancer.gov/cancertopics/factsheet/therapy/CAM; retrieved August 30, 2006).

discovered important new subtypes of tumors for breast cancer, melanoma, leukemia, and lymphomas based on patterns of gene expression. **Gene therapy** is the manipulation of gene expression in human cells. Gene therapy offers a potential treatment or cure for cancer, as well as for various genetic diseases. For gene therapy to succeed, new genes must be delivered to defective cells without disturbing the overall functioning of the cells. In the treatment of cancer, gene therapy would "turn off" the genes responsible for causing cells to divide rapidly and become malignant. Using this approach, researchers hope to develop targeted therapies for specific cancers.

- *Bone marrow and stem cell transplants.* In cancers of the blood-forming cells or lymph cells, a patient's own bone marrow may have to be eliminated by radiation or chemotherapy to rid the body of cancer cells. Bone marrow can then be restored by transplanting healthy bone marrow cells from a compatible donor. Transplant incompatibility can be a problem, but progress on this front has been made recently through the use of **stem cells.** These unique, unspecialized cells can divide and produce more specialized cell types, including bone marrow cells (see Chapter 19). These stem cells can be identified, purified, and grown outside the body and then transplanted back into the cancer patient. This technique would allow for safe repopulation of bone marrow after radiation.

- *Biological therapies.* Biological therapies are based on enhancing the immune system's reaction to a tumor. Techniques include cancer vaccines, genetic modification of the body's immune cells, and the use of genetically engineered **cytokines**, which enhance immune cell function. Melanomas seem particularly susceptible to these biological approaches. Cancer vaccines are also under study for kidney cancer, lymphoma, lung cancer, and other cancers.
- *Proteasome inhibitors.* Proteasomes help control the *cell cycle*—the process through which cells divide. If proteasomes malfunction, as is often the case in cancer cells, then cells may begin multiplying out of control. Proteasome inhibitors block the action of proteasomes, halting cell division and killing the cells. One proteasome inhibitor is now being used against certain cancers, and other such drugs are in development.
- *Anti-angiogenesis drugs.* To obtain nutrients, cancer cells signal the body to produce new blood vessels, a process called angiogenesis. Drugs that block angiogenesis could keep tumors from growing and spreading.
- *Enzyme activators/blockers.* Normal cells die after dividing a given number of times. Scientists believe that the enzyme caspase triggers the death of normally functioning cells. In cancer cells, caspase activity may be blocked. Conversely, if the enzyme telomerase becomes active in cancer cells, the life/death cycle stops and the cells duplicate indefinitely. In effect, inactive caspase or active telomerase may make cancer cells "immortal." Researchers are studying compounds that can either activate caspase or deactivate telomerase; either type of drug might lead cancer cells to self-destruct. No such drugs are now in clinical use.

Living with Cancer

There are about 10 million cancer survivors in the United States. The fear of cancer never disappears, however; there is always the risk of a recurrence.

Cancer survivors may suffer economic prejudice from insurers, who can refuse to issue or renew health coverage. This sort of problem can be devastating to a cancer survivor who may be struggling both psychologically and financially to restore a normal existence. Several states have passed legislation to prevent such discrimination.

Psychological support is an important factor during treatment for cancer (see the box "Coping with Cancer" on p. 508). For some patients, family and friends plus a caring physician or nurse provide all the support that is necessary. For many people, an organized support group can help provide needed social and psychological support.

Social support can play a crucial role in cancer treatment for these patients. Studies indicate that support group participants have lower levels of anxiety and depression, and manage pain more successfully.

PREVENTING CANCER

Your lifestyle choices can radically lower your cancer risks, so you *can* take a very practical approach to cancer prevention (Figure 16-7).

Avoiding Tobacco

Smoking is responsible for 80–90% of all lung cancers and for about 30% of all cancer deaths. People who smoke two or more packs of cigarettes a day have lung cancer mortality rates 15–25 times greater than those of nonsmokers. The carcinogenic chemicals in smoke are transported throughout the body in the bloodstream, making smoking a carcinogen for many forms of cancer other than lung cancer. ETS is dangerous to nonsmokers.

Terms

gene therapy The manipulation of gene expression in human cells; offers a potential treatment or cure for cancer by "turning off" the genes responsible for causing cells to divide rapidly and become malignant.

stem cells Unspecialized cells that can divide and produce cells that differentiate into the many different types of specialized cells in the body (brain cells, muscle cells, skin cells, blood cells, and so on).

cytokine A chemical messenger produced by a variety of cell types that helps regulate many cell functions; immune system cells release cytokines that help amplify and coordinate the immune response.

VW

A cancer diagnosis was once viewed as the equivalent of a death sentence, and individuals and families were often left to face their fears alone. People were sometimes reluctant to admit to the diagnosis of cancer or share it with others because of feelings of hopelessness or irrational guilt. Since about the 1970s, a cultural shift has taken place. Improved diagnostic methods and therapies have resulted in longer survival times and an increasing percentage of cures. Media attention on positive developments has created a better understanding of the scientific basis of cancer. Some of the mystery and dread of cancer has begun to abate, leading to a more positive atmosphere for cancer patients and their families.

If You Are the Patient

Each person's experience with cancer is unique, based on his or her own personality and values. Some people turn to their friends and family members for support, whereas others prefer help from other cancer patients, professional counselors, or faith-based groups. If you are a cancer patient, it is important to do what is right for you. Strategies for dealing with difficult emotions such as fear, anxiety, depression, and loss of control include the following:

- Remember that cancer doesn't always mean death. Many cancers are curable or controllable for long periods, and survivors may return to a normal, healthy life. Hope and optimism are important elements in cancer survival.
- Focus on controlling what you can. Be informed and involved with your medical care, keep your appointments, and make healthy changes in your lifestyle.
- Work toward having a positive attitude, but don't feel guilty if you can't maintain it all the time. Having cancer is difficult, and low moods will occur no matter how good you are at coping. If they become frequent or severe, seek help.
- Use strategies that have helped you solve problems and manage your emotions in the past. Some people respond to information gathering, talking with others, and prayer or meditation. Physical activity, music, art, and sharing personal stories may help lessen stress.
- Confide feelings and worries to someone close to you. Don't bottle up your feelings to spare your loved ones. If you don't feel comfortable sharing with others, consider expressing your emotions in a journal.
- Explore groups that can help you get through this difficult time. There are many support groups for people who have cancer or who have survived it.

Finding a Support Group

Support groups may be led by cancer survivors, group members, or trained professionals. These groups typically present information, teach coping skills, and give cancer patients a place to share common concerns and obtain emotional support. Support groups may focus on education, behavioral training, or group interaction. Behavioral training can involve meditation and other techniques to reduce stress or the effects of chemotherapy or radiation therapy.

Research has shown that support groups can enhance quality of life in very practical ways. For instance, patients in breast cancer support groups were found to have improved psychological symptoms, less pain, and improved family relationships compared with patients in a control group. Some early studies even suggested a longer survival time for cancer patients in support groups, but more recent studies have cast doubt on this result.

Support groups vary in quality, and people with cancer may find that a support group fails to discuss topics relevant to their personal situation. Some people may find a support group upsetting because it stirs up too many uncomfortable feelings or because the leader is not skilled. Find a group that is right for you. Online support groups can be very helpful for people living in rural areas or confined to their homes. However, medical information on the Internet is highly variable in quality, and you should check with your physician before making any treatment changes based on online information.

Supporting a Person with Cancer

There is no one right way to act with a person facing cancer. Reassure the person of your love, and let him or her know that you are available for both practical and emotional support. A person with cancer may want you to be very involved in treatment or coping, or he or she may want your help in maintaining a more normal routine. Guidelines for visiting a cancer patient include the following:

- Before you visit, call to ask if it's a good time. Surprise visits are often not welcome. Don't overstay your welcome.
- Be a good listener. Allow the person to express all his or her feelings, and don't discount fears or minimize the seriousness of the situation. Let the patient decide whether the two of you talk about the illness. It's human to want to laugh and talk about other things sometimes.
- Ask "What can I get you?" or "How can I help?" instead of saying "Let me know if I can help." Make specific offers: to clean the bathroom, go grocery shopping, do laundry, or give caregivers a break.
- Refrain from offering advice. You may have heard about the latest treatment or hottest physician, but unless you are asked for suggestions, keep them to yourself.
- If you want to take food, ask about dietary restrictions ahead of time. Use a disposable container so the person won't have to return it.
- Don't be put off if your first visit gets a lukewarm reception. Many cancer victims are on an emotional roller coaster, and their feelings and needs will change over time.

If you find yourself struggling with difficult emotions or challenging new roles and responsibilities, remember that support groups also exist for friends and family members of cancer patients. These groups give people a place to express their fears about issues such as relationship changes, financial problems, and providing emotional support for the cancer patient.

SOURCES: Kissane, D. W., et al. 2004. Effect of cognitive-existential group therapy on survival in early-stage breast cancer. *Journal of Clinical Oncology* 22(21): 4255–4260; National Cancer Institute. 2002. *Your Mind and Your Feelings After Cancer Treatment* (http://www.cancer.gov/cancerinfo/life-after-treatment/page6; retrieved August 30, 2006); Goodwin, P. J., et al. 2001. The effect of group psychosocial support on survival in metastatic breast cancer. *New England Journal of Medicine* 345(24): 1719–1726; Life with cancer: How to provide support. 1996. *Women's Health Advocate*, September; Holland, J. C. 1996. Cancer's psychological challenges. *Scientific American*, September.

Do More

- Eat a varied, plant-based diet that is high in fiber-rich foods such as legumes and whole grains
- Eat 7–13 servings of fruits and vegetables every day, favoring foods from the following categories:
  - Cruciferous vegetables
  - Citrus fruits
  - Berries
  - Dark green leafy vegetables
  - Dark yellow, orange, or red fruits and vegetables
- Be physically active
- Maintain a healthy weight
- Practice safer sex (to avoid HPV infection)
- Protect your skin from the sun with appropriate clothing and sunscreen
- Perform regular self-exams (breast self-exam, testicular self-exam, skin self-exam)
- Obtain recommended screening tests and discuss with your physician any family history of cancer.

Do Less

- Don't use tobacco in any form:
  - Cigarettes
  - Spit tobacco
  - Cigars and pipes
  - Bidis and clove cigarettes
- Avoid exposure to environmental tobacco smoke
- Limit consumption of fatty meats and other sources of saturated fat
- Avoid excessive alcohol consumption
- Limit consumption of salt
- Don't eat charred foods, and limit consumption of cured and smoked meats and meat and fish grilled in a direct flame
- Limit exposure to UV radiation from sunlight or tanning lamps or beds
- Avoid occupational exposure to carcinogens

Figure 16-7 Strategies for reducing your risk of cancer.

If you smoke, stop. If you don't smoke, avoid breathing the smoke from other people's cigarettes.

The use of spit tobacco, highly habit-forming because of its nicotine content, is also dangerous because it increases the risk of cancers of the mouth, larynx, throat, and esophagus.

Controlling Diet and Weight

The 2006 American Cancer Society (ACS) Nutrition and Physical Activity Guidelines for Cancer Prevention encourage individuals to eat a plant-based diet containing five or more servings of a variety of vegetables and fruits every day, to choose whole grains over processed grains, and to limit consumption of processed and red meats. The ACS recommends maintaining a healthy weight throughout life by balancing caloric intake with physical activity and achieving and maintaining a healthy weight if currently overweight or obese. Being overweight or obese is linked with increased risk of several kinds of cancer, including breast and colon cancer. Also recommended is drinking alcohol in moderation, if at all. Alcohol is a cause of cancers of the mouth, pharynx, larynx, esophagus, liver, and breast and may increase the risk of colorectal cancer.

Regular Exercise

The ACS Guidelines encourage everyone to adopt a physically active lifestyle. For adults, at least 30 minutes of moderate to vigorous physical activity, above usual activities, on 5 or more days per week are recommended; 45 to 60 minutes of intentional physical activity are preferable. For children and adolescents, at least 60 minutes of moderate to vigorous physical activity at least 5 days per week are recommended.

Protecting Skin from the Sun

Almost all cases of nonmelanoma skin cancer are considered to be sun-related, and sun exposure is a major factor in the development of melanoma as well. Wear protective clothing when you're out in the sun, and use a sunscreen with an SPF rating of 15 or higher. Don't go to tanning salons; they do not provide safe tans.

Avoiding Environmental and Occupational Carcinogens

Most medical X rays are adjusted to deliver the lowest dose of radiation possible without sacrificing image quality. Radiation from radon may pose a threat in some homes; remedial steps should be taken if tests indicate high levels of radon. A number of industrial agents that some people are exposed to on the job are associated with cancer, including nickel, chromate, asbestos, and vinyl chloride. Avoid occupational exposure to carcinogens, and don't smoke; the cancer risks of many of these agents increase greatly when combined with smoking.

Recommended Screening Tests

Your first line of defense against cancer involves the lifestyle changes described above that help you avoid cancer-causing agents. Your second line of defense involves having any cancers that do develop discovered as quickly as possible through regular self-exams and medical screening tests. Stay alert for the signs and symptoms that could indicate cancer (see Figure 16-6), and follow the American Cancer Society screening guidelines listed in Table 16-2. Both lifestyle changes and a program of early detection are important to your long-term health.

Tips for Today

Our knowledge about the causes of cancer has grown exponentially in the past few decades, and research in biology and genetics offers the hope of better cancer therapies in the future. A growing body of research also suggests that we can take an active role in preventing many cancers by adopting a wellness lifestyle. Exercise, diet, and awareness are three important keys to cancer prevention.

Right now you can

- Do a breast self-exam, if you are a woman, or a testicular self-exam, if you are a man.
- Plan to have two vegetables with dinner tonight, one of them broccoli, cauliflower, brussels sprouts, or kale.
- Put your sunscreen by the front door so you'll remember to apply it the next time you go out in the sun, or put a brimmed hat by the door or in the car.
- Memorize the seven major warning signs of cancer represented by the acronym CAUTION.

SUMMARY

- A malignant tumor can invade surrounding structures and spread to distant sites via the blood and lymphatic system, producing additional tumors.
- A malignant cell divides without regard for normal growth. As tumors grow, they produce signs or symptoms that are determined by their location in the body.
- One in two men and one in three women will develop cancer, but more than half will be cured.
- Lung cancer kills more people than any other type of cancer. Tobacco smoke is the primary cause.
- Colon and rectal cancer is linked to age, heredity, obesity, and a diet rich in red meat and low in fruits and vegetables. Most colon cancers arise from preexisting polyps.
- Breast cancer affects about one in seven women in the United States. Although there is a genetic component to breast cancer, diet and hormones are also risk factors.
- Prostate cancer is chiefly a disease of aging; diet and lifestyle probably are factors in its occurrence. Early detection is possible through rectal examinations, PSA blood tests, and sometimes ultrasound.
- Cancers of the female reproductive tract include cervical, uterine, and ovarian cancer. The Pap test is an effective screening test for cervical cancer.
- Abnormal cellular changes in the epidermis, often a result of exposure to the sun, cause skin cancer, as does chronic exposure to certain chemicals. Skin cancers occur as basal cell carcinoma, squamous cell carcinoma, and melanoma.
- Oral cancer is caused primarily by smoking, excess alcohol consumption, and use of spit tobacco. Oral cancers are easy to detect but often hard to treat.
- Testicular cancer can be detected early through self-examination.
- Mutational damage to a cell's DNA can lead to rapid and uncontrolled growth of cells; mutagens include radiation, viral infection, and chemical substances in food and air.
- Cancer-promoting dietary factors include meat, certain types of fats, and alcohol.
- Diets high in fruits and vegetables are linked to a lower risk of cancer.
- Other possible causes of cancer include inactivity and obesity, certain types of infections and chemicals, and radiation.
- Self-monitoring and regular screening tests are essential to early cancer detection; early signs can be remembered by using the acronym CAUTION.
- Methods of cancer diagnosis include magnetic resonance imaging, computed tomography, and ultrasound.
- Treatment methods usually consist of some combination of surgery, chemotherapy, and radiation. Gene therapy, bone marrow and stem cell transplants, proteasome inhibitors, biological therapies, and drugs that inhibit angiogenesis or telomerase also hold promise as effective treatments.
- Strategies for preventing cancer include avoiding tobacco; eating a varied, moderate diet and controlling weight; exercising regularly; protecting skin from the sun; avoiding exposure to environmental and occupational carcinogens; and getting recommended cancer screening tests.

Take Action

1. **Try some cancer-fighting foods:** Look through the foods listed in Table 16-1 and the Behavior Change Strategy and choose four or five that you don't typically eat. During the next week, make a point of trying each of the foods you've chosen.

2. **Do a self-exam:** Devise a plan for incorporating regular self-examinations for cancer (breast self-examination or testicle self-examination) into your life. What strategies will help you remember to do your monthly exam? How can you keep yourself motivated?

Behavior Change Strategy

Incorporating More Fruits and Vegetables into Your Diet

When we think about the health benefits of fruits and vegetables, we usually focus on the fact that they are rich in carbohydrates, dietary fiber, and vitamins and low in fat. A benefit that we may overlook is that they contain specific cancer-fighting compounds, phytochemicals, that help slow, stop, or even reverse the process of cancer. The National Cancer Institute (NCI) reports that people who eat five or more servings a day of fruits and vegetables have half the risk of cancer of those who eat less than two; according to the NCI, seven to nine servings or more per day is optimal. The NCI, along with industry groups, has developed a program to help more Americans increase their intake of fruits and vegetables to health-promoting levels—the "Eat 5 to 9 a Day for Better Health" program.

Most Americans need to double the amount of fruits and vegetables they eat every day. Begin by monitoring your diet for 1–2 weeks to assess your current intake; then look for ways to incorporate these foods into your diet in easy and tasty ways. Here are some tips to get you started.

Breakfast

- Drink 100% juice every morning.
- Add raisins, berries, or sliced fruit to cereal, pancakes, or waffles. Top bagels with tomato slices.
- Try a fruit smoothie made from fresh or frozen fruit and orange juice or low-fat yogurt.

Lunch

- Choose vegetable soup or salad with your meal.
- Replace potato chips or french fries with cut-up vegetables.
- Add extra chunks of fruits or vegetables to salads.
- Try adding vegetables such as roasted peppers, cucumber slices, shredded carrots, avocado, or salsa to sandwiches.
- Drink tomato or vegetable juice instead of soda (watch for excess sodium).

Dinner

- Choose a vegetarian main course, such as stir-fry or vegetable stew. Have at least two servings of vegetables with every dinner.
- Microwave vegetables and sprinkle them with a little bit of Parmesan cheese.
- Substitute vegetables for meat in casseroles and pasta and chili recipes.
- At the salad bar, pile your plate with healthy vegetables and use low-fat or nonfat dressing.

Snacks and On the Go

- Keep ready to-eat-fruits and vegetables on hand (apples, plums, pears, and carrots).
- Keep small packages of dried fruit in the car (try dried apricots, peaches, and pears and raisins).
- Make ice cubes from 100% fruit juice and drop them into regular or sparkling water.
- Freeze grapes for a cool summer treat.

In the Grocery Store

- Stock up on canned, frozen, and dried fruits and vegetables when they go on sale. Buy fresh fruits and vegetables in season; they'll taste best and be less expensive.
- To save on preparation time, buy presliced vegetables and fruits and prepackaged salads.
- Try a new fresh fruit or vegetable every week.

The All-Stars

Different fruits and vegetables contribute different vitamins, phytochemicals, and other nutrients, so be sure to get a variety. The following types of produce are particularly rich in nutrients and phytochemicals:

- Cruciferous vegetables (broccoli, cauliflower, cabbage, bok choy, brussels sprouts, kohlrabi, turnips, etc.)
- Citrus fruits (oranges, lemons, limes, grapefruit, tangerines, etc.)
- Berries (strawberries, raspberries, blueberries, etc.)
- Dark green leafy vegetables (spinach, chard, collards, beet greens, kale, mustard greens, romaine and other dark lettuces, etc.)
- Deep yellow, orange, and red fruits and vegetables (carrots, pumpkin, sweet potatoes, winter squash, red and yellow bell peppers, apricots, cantaloupe, mangoes, papayas, etc.)

SOURCES: National Cancer Institute. 2005. *Eat 5 to 9 A Day for Better Health* (http://www.5aday.gov; retrieved August 30, 2006); The produce prescription. 2000. *Consumer Reports on Health*, December; Welland, D. 1999. Fruits and vegetables: Easy ways to five-a-day. *Environmental Nutrition*, June.

3. **Construct a family cancer health history:** Interview your parents or grandparents about your family medical history. Are there any cases of cancer in your family, and has anyone died of cancer? Do you see any patterns? Be sure to discuss your family history with your physician.

4. **Participate in a cancer fundraiser:** Many local and national cancer organizations sponsor events such as walkathons to help raise money for cancer research and treatment. Consider volunteering at such an event.

For More Information

Books

American Cancer Society. 2003. *Cancer: What Causes It. What Doesn't.* Atlanta: American Cancer Society. *Provides basic background information about cancer and its causes.*

American Institute for Cancer Research. 2005. *The New American Plate Cookbook.* Berkeley, Calif.: U.C. Berkeley Press. *Provides guidelines and recipes for healthy eating to prevent cancer and other chronic diseases.*

Hartmann, L. C., C. L. Loprinzi, and B. S. Gostout. 2005. *Mayo Clinic: Guide to Women's Cancers.* New York: Kensington Publishing. *Provides information about a variety of women's cancers.*

Johns Hopkins Consumer Health. 2005. *Prostate Disorders.* Redding, Conn.: Medletter Associates. *Provides information about the diagnosis and treatment options for benign prostate problems and prostate cancer.*

McKinnell, R. G., et al. 2006. *The Biological Basis of Cancer,* 2nd ed. Boston: Cambridge University Press. *Examines the underlying causes of cancer and discusses actual cases of the disease and its impact on patients and families.*

Turkington, C., and W. LiPera. 2005. *The Encyclopedia of Cancer.* New York: Facts on File. *Includes entries on a variety of topics relating to cancer causes, prevention, diagnosis, and treatment.*

WW Organizations, Hotlines, and Web Sites

American Academy of Dermatology. Provides information on skin cancer prevention.
866-503-SKIN
http://www.aad.org

American Cancer Society. Provides a wide range of free materials on the prevention and treatment of cancer.
800-ACS-2345
http://www.cancer.org

American Institute for Cancer Research. Provides information on lifestyle and cancer prevention, especially nutrition.
800-843-8114
http://www.aicr.org

Cancer Guide: Steve Dunn's Cancer Information Page. Links to many good cancer resources on the Internet and advice about how to make best use of information.
http://www.cancerguide.org

Cancer News. Provides links to news and information on many types of cancer.
http://www.cancernews.com

Centers for Disease Control and Prevention: DES Update. Provides information about drugs containing DES and advice for exposed women and DES daughters and sons.
http://www.cdc.gov/DES

Clinical Trials. Information about clinical trials for new cancer treatments can be accessed at the following sites:
http://www.cancer.gov/clinicaltrials
http://www.centerwatch.com

Dole 5-A-Day/Nutrition Education. Provides resources for parents, children, and educators, including extensive nutrition information about fruits and vegetables.
http://www.dole5aday.com

EPA/Sunwise. Information about the UV Index and the effects of sun exposure, with links to sites with daily UV Index ratings for cities in the United States and other countries.
http://www.epa.gov/sunwise/uvindex.html

Food and Drug Administration, Center for Drug Evaluation and Research: Oncology Tools. Provides information about types of cancer, treatments, and clinical trials.
http://www.fda.gov/cder/cancer

Harvard Center for Cancer Prevention: Your Disease Risk. Includes interactive risk assessments as well as tips for preventing common cancers.
http://www.yourcancerrisk.harvard.edu

MedlinePlus Cancer Information. Provides news and links to reliable information on a variety of cancers and cancer treatment.
http://www.nlm.nih.gov/medlineplus/cancers.html

National Cancer Institute. Provides information on treatment options, screening, and clinical trials and on the national "Eat 5 to 9 Servings of Fruits and Vegetables A Day for Better Health Program" that promotes greater consumption of fruits and vegetables.
800-4-CANCER
http://www.cancer.gov
http://www.5aday.gov/

National Comprehensive Cancer Network (NCCN). Presents treatment guidelines for physicians and patients related to the treatment of various cancers; these guidelines were developed by a group of leading cancer centers.
http://www.nccn.org

National Toxicology Program. The federal program that creates regular reports listing those substances that are known or reasonably assumed to cause cancer in humans.
http://ntp-server.niehs.nih.gov

New York Online Access to Health (NOAH)/Cancer. Provides information about cancer—causes, symptoms, types, treatments, clinical trials—and links to related sites.
http://www.noah-health.org/en/cancer

Oncolink/The University of Pennsylvania Cancer Center Resources. Contains information on different types of cancer and answers to frequently asked questions.
http://www.oncolink.org

See also the listings in Chapters 10–14.

Selected Bibliography

Abbasi, N. R., et al. 2004. Early diagnosis of cutaneous melanoma. *Journal of the American Medical Association* 292(22): 2771–2776.

Agency for Healthcare Research and Quality. 2006. *Noninvasive Tests May Miss Breast Cancer, AHRQ Study Finds* (http://www.ahrq.gov/news/press/pr2006/effbrancpr.htm; retrieved August 29, 2006).

American Cancer Society. 2005. *Many Still Buy Into Common Cancer Myths* (http://www.cancer.org/docroot/NWS/content/NWS_2_1x_Many_Still_Buy_Into_Common_Cancer_Myths.asp; retrieved August 30, 2006).

American Cancer Society. 2006. *Cancer Facts and Figures 2006.* Atlanta: American Cancer Society.

American Cancer Society. 2006. *Few Americans Know Connection Between Excess Weight and Cancer Risk, Survey Finds* (http://www.cancer.org/docroot/MED/content/MED_2_1x_Few_Americans_Know_Connection_Between_Excess_Weight_and_Cancer_Risk_Survey_Finds.asp; retrieved August 30, 2006).

Baker, S., and J. Kaprio. 2006. Common susceptibility genes for cancer: Search for the end of the rainbow. *British Medical Journal* 332(7550): 1150–1152.

Bjorge, T., S. Tretli, and A. Engeland. 2004. Relation of height and body mass index to renal cell carcinoma in two million Norwegian men and women. *American Journal of Epidemiology* 160(12): 1168–1176.

Brand, T. C., et al. 2006. Prostate cancer detection strategies. *Current Urology Reports* 7(3): 181–185.

Brenner, D. J., et al. 2004. Estimated radiation risks potentially associated with full-body CT screening. *Radiology* 232(3): 735–738.

Chao, A., et al. 2005. Meat consumption and risk of colorectal cancer. *Journal of the American Medical Association* 293(2): 172–182.

Chia, K. S., et al. 2005. Profound changes in breast cancer incidence may reflect changes into a Westernized lifestyle: A comparative population-based study in Singapore and Sweden. *International Journal of Cancer* 113(2): 302–306.

de Vries, S. H., et al. 2004. Prostate cancer characteristics and prostate specific antigen changes in screening detected patients initially treated with a watchful waiting policy. *Journal of Urology* 172(6 Pt 1): 2193–2196.

Elmore, J. G., et al. 2005. Screening for breast cancer. *Journal of the American Medical Association* 293(10): 1245–1256.

Flood, A., et al. 2005. Calcium from diet and supplements is associated with reduced risk of colorectal cancer in a prospective cohort of women. *Cancer Epidemiology, Biomarkers and Prevention* 14(1): 126–132.

Food and Agriculture Organization and World Health Organization. 2005. *Joint FAO/WHO Expert Committee on Food Additives: Summary and Conclusions* (http://www.who.int/ipcs/food/jecfa/summaries/en; retrieved March 29, 2005).

Garland, S. 2006. Efficacy of a quadrivalent HPV (types 6, 11, 16, 18) L1 VLP vaccine against external genital disease: Future 1 analysis. *European Journal of Obstetrics, Gynecology, and Reproductive Biology*, August 16.

Genetics and breast cancer. 2004. *Journal of the American Medical Association* 292(4): 522.

Goff, B. A., et al. 2004. Frequency of symptoms of ovarian cancer in women presenting to primary care clinics. *Journal of the American Medical Association* 291(22): 2705–2712.

Harper, D. M., et al. 2004. Efficacy of a bivalent L1 virus-like particle vaccine in prevention of infection with human papillomavirus types 16 and 18 in young women: A randomised controlled trial. *Lancet* 364(9447): 1757–1765.

Hou, L., et al. 2004. Computing physical activity and risk of colon cancer in Shanghai, China. *American Journal of Epidemiology* 160(9): 860–867.

Jee, S. H., et al. 2005. Fasting serum glucose level and cancer risk in Korean men and women. *Journal of the American Medical Association* 293(2): 194–202.

Jemal, A., et al. 2005. Cancer Statistics, 2005. *CA: A Cancer Journal for Clinicians* 55(1): 10–30.

Kaplan, R. N., et al. 2005. VEGFR1-positive haematopoietic bone marrow progenitors initiate the pre-metastatic niche. *Nature* 438(7069): 820–827.

Kroenke, C. H., et al. 2005. Weight, weight gain, and survival after breast cancer diagnosis. *Journal of Clinical Oncology* 23(7): 1370–1378.

Laaksonen, D. E., et al. 2004. Serum linoleic and total polyunsaturated fatty acids in relation to prostate and other cancers: A population-based cohort study. *International Journal of Cancer* 111(3): 444–450.

Martinez, M. E. 2005. Primary prevention of colorectal cancer: Lifestyle, nutrition, exercise. *Recent Results in Cancer Research* 166: 177–211.

Mayo Clinic. 2006. Skin cancer epidemic. Take steps to avoid sun damage. *Mayo Clinic Health Letter* 24(4): 1–3.

Meadows, M. 2004. Cancer vaccines: Training the immune system to fight cancer. *FDA Consumer*, September/October.

Melanoma. 2004. *Journal of the American Medical Association* 292(22): 2800.

Mor, G., et al. 2005. Serum protein markers for early detection of ovarian cancer. *Proceedings of the National Academy of Sciences USA*, epub May 12.

National Cancer Institute. 2005. *Cancer Trends Progress Report—2005 Update* (http://progressreport.cancer.gov; retrieved August 29, 2006).

National Toxicology Program. 2005. *Report on Carcinogens*, Eleventh Edition. Research Triangle Park, N. C.: National Toxicology Program.

New treatments for colorectal cancer. 2004. *FDA Consumer*, May/June.

Osborn, N. K., and D. A. Ahlquist. 2005. Stool screening for colorectal cancer: Molecular approaches. *Gastroenterology* 128(1): 192–206.

Paik, S., et al. 2004. A multigene assay to predict recurrence of tamoxifen-treated, node-negative breast cancer. *New England Journal of Medicine* 351(27): 2817–2826.

Pelucchi, C., et al. 2004. Fibre intake and prostate cancer risk. *International Journal of Cancer* 109(2): 278–280.

Prostate cancer: Should you still have a PSA test? 2005. *University of California, Berkeley Wellness Letter*, January.

Putt, K. S., et al. 2006. Small-molecule activation of procaspase-3 to caspase-3 as a personalized anticancer strategy. *Nature Chemical Biology*, August.

Roden, R. B., et al. 2004. Vaccination to prevent and treat cervical cancer. *Human Pathology* 35(8): 971–982.

Seeff, L. C., et al. 2004. How many endoscopies are performed for colorectal cancer screening? Results from CDC's survey of endoscopic capacity. *Gastroenterology* 127(6): 1670–1677.

Terry, M. B., et al. 2004. Association of frequency and duration of aspirin use and hormone receptor status with breast cancer risk. *Journal of the American Medical Association* 291(20): 2433–2440.

Thompson, I. M., et al. 2004. Prevalence of prostate cancer among men with prostate-specific antigen level $<$ or $=4.0$ ng per milliliter. *New England Journal of Medicine* 350(22): 2239–2246.

Trimble, C. L., et al. 2005. Active and passive cigarette smoking and the risk of cervical neoplasia. *Obstetrics and Gynecology* 105(1): 174–181.

University of California, Berkeley, School of Public Health. 2006. Wellness Facts. *Wellness Letter* 22(5): 1.

Van Gils, C. H., et al. 2005. Consumption of vegetables and fruits and risk of breast cancer. *Journal of the American Medical Association* 293(3): 183–193.

Velicer, C. M., et al. 2004. Antibiotic use in relation to the risk of breast cancer. *Journal of the American Medical Association* 291(7): 827–835.

Weinstein, S. J., et al. 2005. Serum alpha-tocopherol and gamma-tocopherol in relation to prostate cancer risk in a prospective study. *Journal of the National Cancer Institute* 97(5): 396–399.

World Health Organization. 2005. *Cancer: Diet and Physical Activity's Impact* (http://www.who.int/dietphysicalactivity/publications/facts/cancer/en/; retrieved January 20, 2005).

17

Looking AHEAD

After reading this chapter, you should be able to

- Describe the step-by-step process by which infectious diseases are transmitted
- List the body's physical and chemical barriers to infection
- Explain how the immune system responds to an invading microorganism
- List the major types of pathogens and describe the common diseases they cause
- Discuss steps you can take to prevent infections and strengthen your immune system

Immunity and Infection

Test Your Knowledge

1. A person with an infectious disease is not contagious unless he or she exhibits symptoms.
True or false?

2. First-year college students, particularly those who live in dormitories or residence halls, are at moderately increased risk for contracting meningitis compared with others their age.
True or false?

3. When taking a prescription antibiotic, you should stop taking the medicine as soon as your infection clears up.
True or false?

4. Which of the following is most likely to increase your risk of catching a cold?
a. getting chilled or overheated
b. talking to someone who may have a cold
c. shaking hands with someone who may have a cold

5. Because medical facilities are sanitary, patients rarely catch bacterial infections in hospitals.
True or false?

6. You can lower your chances of getting sick by doing which of the following?
a. washing your hands frequently
b. obtaining all recommended immunizations
c. getting adequate sleep

ANSWERS

1. FALSE. A person can be contagious before exhibiting any symptoms and may cease to be contagious before symptoms disappear.
2. TRUE. The Centers for Disease Control and Prevention recommend the meningococcal vaccine for first-year college students living in dormitories and others at risk.
3. FALSE. More than 50% of people fail to take all their medication, leading to relapses and the development of antibiotic-resistant bacteria.
4. C. Most cold viruses are transmitted through hand-to-hand contact; frequent, thorough hand washing can decrease the risk of contracting a cold.
5. FALSE. About 2 million Americans get bacterial infections in hospitals each year, and about 90,000 people die from those illnesses.
6. ALL THREE. Frequent hand washing prevents the transmission of many disease-causing agents. Immunizations prime the body to tackle an invading organism; adequate sleep helps support a healthy immune system.

Visit the *Core Concepts in Health* Online Learning Center (www.mhhe.com/insel10e) for study aids and many additional resources.

Most of the time, we go about our daily lives without thinking of the countless microscopic organisms that live around, on, and in us. Although most microbes are beneficial, many of them can cause human disease. But the constant vigilance of our immune system keeps them at bay and our bodies intact and healthy. The immune system works to keep the body from being overwhelmed, not just by external invaders that cause **infections**, but also by internal changes such as cancer.

Most people don't notice these internal skirmishes unless they become sick and find themselves deprived of their usual feelings of well-being. But many people today are more knowledgeable about the complexities of immunity because they have heard about, or had experience with, HIV infection, which directly attacks the immune system. The rise in other infections has caught the public's attention, too. Annually, 2 million Americans get bacterial infections in hospitals; about 90,000 die from those illnesses. Old scourges like tuberculosis are making comebacks, too—in stronger, drug-resistant forms.

This chapter provides information that will help you understand immunity, infection, and how to keep yourself well in a world of disease-causing microorganisms.

THE CHAIN OF INFECTION

Infectious diseases are transmitted from one person to another through a series of steps—a chain of infection (Figure 17-1). New infections can be prevented by interfering with any step in this process.

Links in the Chain

The chain of infection has six major links: the pathogen, its reservoir, a portal of exit, a means of transmission, a portal of entry, and a new host.

Terms

Ww

infection Invasion of the body by a microorganism.

pathogen A microorganism that causes disease.

toxin A poisonous substance produced by a microorganism.

reservoir A natural environment in which a pathogen typically lives.

vector An insect, rodent, or other organism that carries and transmits a pathogen from one host to another.

lymphatic system A system of vessels and organs that picks up excess fluid, proteins, lipids, and other substances from the tissues; filters out pathogens and other waste products; and returns the cleansed fluid to the general circulation.

systemic infection An infection spread by the blood or lymphatic system to large portions of the body.

Pathogen The infectious disease cycle begins with a **pathogen,** a microorganism that causes disease. HIV, the virus that causes AIDS, and the tuberculosis bacterium are examples of pathogens. Many pathogens cause illness because they produce **toxins** that harm human tissue; others do so by directly invading body cells.

Reservoir The pathogen has a natural environment—called a **reservoir**—in which it typically lives. This reservoir can be a person, an animal, or an environmental component like soil or water. A person who is the reservoir for a pathogen may be ill or may be an asymptomatic carrier who, although having no symptoms, is capable of spreading infection.

Portal of Exit To transmit infection, the pathogen must leave the reservoir through some portal of exit. In the case of a human reservoir, portals of exit include saliva (for mumps, for example), the mucous membranes (for many sexually transmitted diseases), blood (for HIV and hepatitis), feces (for intestinal infections), and nose and throat discharges (for colds and influenza).

Means of Transmission Transmission can occur directly or indirectly. In direct transmission, the pathogen is passed from one person to another without an intermediary. Direct transmission usually requires fairly close association with an infected host, but not necessarily physical contact. For example, sneezing and coughing can discharge infectious particles into the air, where they can be inhaled by someone nearby. Most common respiratory infections are passed directly: A person with a cold blows her nose and gets some infectious droplets on her hands; she then shakes hands with someone, who later touches his nose and passes the pathogen into his own body. Many intestinal infections are also transmitted hand-to-hand; the initial contamination may result from a failure to wash hands after using the toilet or changing a diaper. Other means of direct transmission include sexual contact and contact with blood.

Transmission can also occur indirectly. Animals or insects such as rats, ticks, and mosquitoes can serve as **vectors,** carrying the pathogen from one host to another. Pathogens can also be transmitted via contaminated soil, food, or water or from inanimate objects, such as eating utensils, doorknobs, and handkerchiefs. Some pathogens float in the air for long periods, suspended on tiny particles of dust or droplets that can travel long distances before they are inhaled and cause infection.

Portal of Entry To infect a new host, a pathogen must have a portal of entry into the body. Pathogens can enter in one of three general ways:

1. Direct contact with or penetration of the skin.
2. Inhalation through the mouth or nose.
3. Ingestion of contaminated food or water.

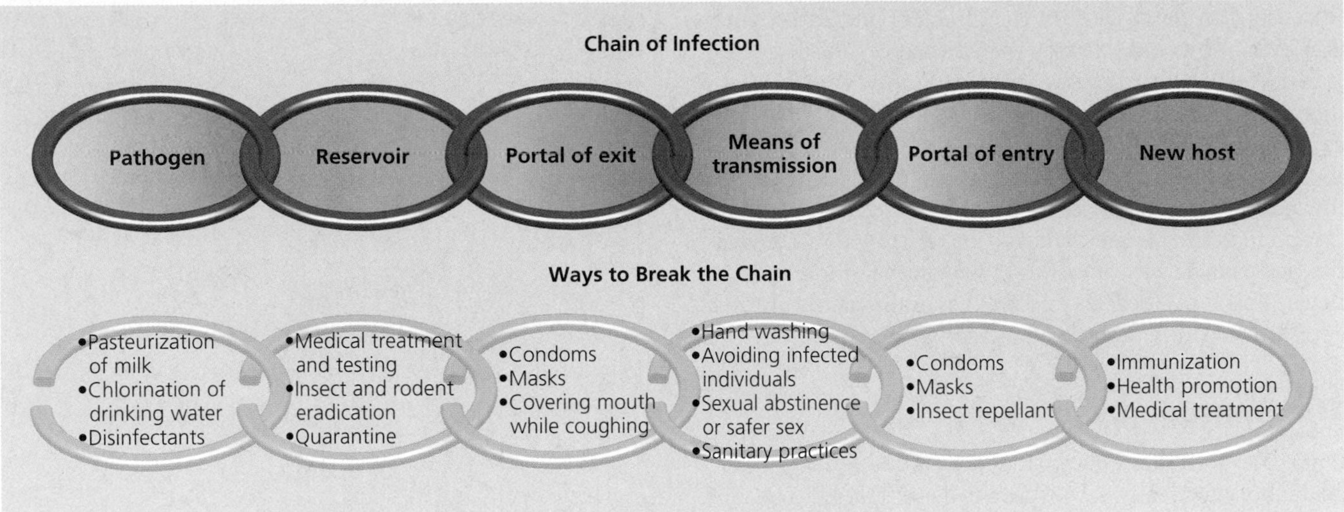

Figure 17-1 The chain of infection. Any break in the chain of infection can prevent disease.

Pathogens that enter the skin or mucous membranes can cause a local infection of the tissue, or they may penetrate into the bloodstream or **lymphatic system,** thereby causing a more extensive **systemic infection.** Agents that cause STDs usually enter the body through the mucous membranes lining the urethra (in males) or the cervix (in females). Organisms that are transmitted via respiratory secretions may cause upper respiratory infections or pneumonia, or they may enter the bloodstream and cause systemic infection. Foodborne and waterborne organisms enter the mouth and travel to the location that will best support their reproduction. They may attack the cells of the small intestine or the colon, causing diarrhea, or they may enter the bloodstream via the digestive system and travel to other parts of the body.

The New Host Once in the new host, a variety of factors determine whether the pathogen will be able to establish itself and cause infection. People with a strong immune system or resistance to a particular pathogen will be less likely to become ill than people with poor immunity (the concept of immunity will be discussed later in the chapter). The number of pathogens that enter the new host is also important; the body's defenses may be able to overcome a few bacteria, for example, but may be overwhelmed by thousands. If conditions are right, the pathogen will multiply and produce disease in the new host. In such a case, the new host may become a reservoir from which a new chain of infection can be started.

Breaking the Chain

Interruption of the chain of infection at any point can prevent disease. Strategies for breaking the chain include a mix of public health measures and individual action. For example, a pathogen's reservoir can be isolated or destroyed, as when a sick individual is placed under quarantine or when insects or animals carrying pathogens are killed. Public sanitation practices, such as sewage treatment and the chlorination of drinking water, can also kill pathogens. Transmission can be disrupted through strategies like hand washing and the use of facemasks. Immunization and the treatment of infected hosts can stop the pathogen from multiplying, producing a serious disease, and being passed on to a new host. Some methods of breaking the chain of infection are listed in Figure 17-1.

THE BODY'S DEFENSE SYSTEM

Our bodies have very effective ways of protecting themselves against invasion by foreign organisms, especially pathogens. The body's first line of defense is a formidable array of physical and chemical barriers. When these barriers are breached, the body's immune system comes into play. Together, these defenses provide an effective response to nearly all the challenges and invasions our bodies will ever experience.

Physical and Chemical Barriers

The skin, the body's largest organ, prevents many microorganisms from entering the body. Although many bacterial and fungal organisms live on the surface of the skin, very few can penetrate it except through a cut or break. Wherever there is an opening in the body, or an area without skin, other barriers exist. The mouth, the main entry to the gastrointestinal system, is lined with mucous membranes, which contain cells designed to prevent the passage of unwanted organisms and particles. Body openings and the fluids that cover them (for example, tears, saliva, and vaginal secretions) are rich in antibodies (discussed in detail later in the chapter) and in enzymes that break down and destroy many microorganisms.

The respiratory tract is lined not only with mucous membranes but also with cells having hairlike protrusions called cilia. The cilia sweep foreign matter up and out of the respiratory tract. Particles that are not caught by this mechanism may be expelled from the system by a cough. If the ciliated cells are damaged or destroyed, a cough is the body's only way of ridding the airways of foreign particles. This is one reason smokers generally have a chronic cough—to compensate for damaged airways.

The Immune System

Once the body has been invaded by a foreign organism, an elaborate system of responses is activated. The immune system operates through a remarkable information network involving billions of cellular defenders who rush to protect the body when a threat arises. We discuss here two of the body's responses: the inflammatory response and the immune response. But before we cover these specific defenses, we briefly describe the defenders themselves and the mechanisms by which they work.

Immunological Defenders The immune response is carried out by different types of white blood cells, all of which are continuously being produced in the bone marrow. **Neutrophils,** one type of white blood cell, travel in the bloodstream to areas of invasion, attacking and ingesting pathogens. **Macrophages,** or "big eaters," take up stations in tissues and act as scavengers, devouring pathogens and worn-out cells. **Natural killer cells** directly destroy virus-infected cells and cells that have turned cancerous. **Dendritic cells,** which reside in tissues, eat pathogens and activate lymphocytes. **Lymphocytes,** of which there are several types, are white blood cells that travel in both the bloodstream and the lymphatic system. At various places in the lymphatic system there are lymph nodes (or glands), where macrophages and dendritic cells congregate and filter bacteria and other substances from the lymph (Figure 17-2). When these nodes are actively involved in fighting an invasion of microorganisms, they fill with cells; physicians use the location of swollen lymph nodes as a clue to the location and cause of an infection.

The two main types of lymphocytes are known as **T cells** and **B cells.** T cells are further differentiated into **helper T cells, killer T cells,** and **suppressor T cells.** B cells are lymphocytes that produce **antibodies.** The first time T cells and B cells encounter a specific invader, some of them are reserved as **memory T and B cells,** enabling the body to mount a rapid response should the same invader appear again in the future. These cells and cell products—macrophages, natural killer cells, dendritic cells, T cells, B cells and antibodies, and memory cells—are the primary players in the body's immune response.

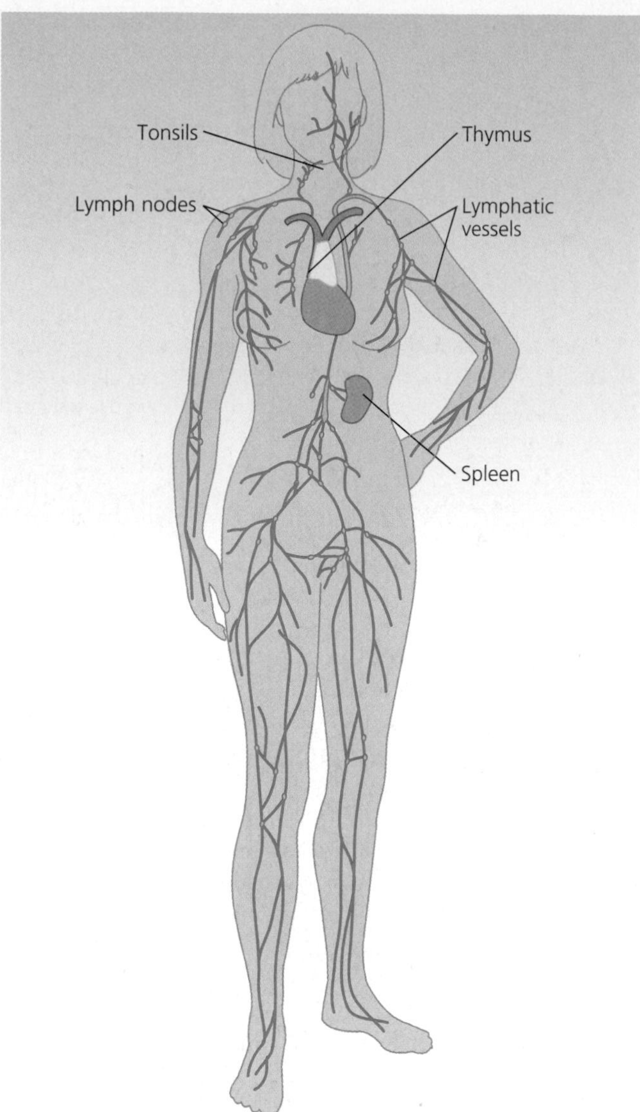

Figure 17-2 The lymphatic system. The lymphatic system consists of a network of vessels and organs, including the spleen, lymph nodes, thymus, and tonsils. The vessels pick up excess fluid and proteins, lipids, and other particles from body tissues. These pass through the lymph nodes, where macrophages and dendritic cells help clear the lymph (fluid) of debris and bacteria and other pathogens. The cleansed lymph is then returned to the bloodstream. The lymphatic organs are production centers for infection-fighting cells and sites for some immune responses.

The immune system is built on a remarkable feature of these defenders: the ability to distinguish foreign cells from the body's own cells. Because lymphocytes are capable of great destruction, it is essential that they not attack the body itself. When they do, they cause **autoimmune diseases,** such as lupus and rheumatoid arthritis.

How do lymphocytes know when they have encountered foreign substances? All the cells of an individual's body display markers on their surfaces—tiny molecular shapes—that identify them as "self" to lymphocytes that encounter them. Invading microorganisms also display markers on their surface; lymphocytes identify these as foreign, or "nonself." Nonself markers that trigger the immune response are known as **antigens.**

Antibodies have complementary surface markers that work with antigens like a lock and key. When an antigen appears in the body, it eventually encounters an antibody with a complementary pattern; the antibody locks onto the antigen, triggering a series of events designed to destroy the invading pathogen. The truly astonishing thing is that the body does not synthesize the appropriate antibody lock after it comes into contact with the antigen key. Rather, antibodies already exist for millions, if not billions, of possible antigens.

The Inflammatory Response When the body has been injured or infected, one of the body's responses is the inflammatory response. Special cells in the area of invasion or injury release **histamine** and other substances that cause blood vessels to dilate and fluid to flow out of capillaries into the injured tissue. This produces increased heat, swelling, and redness in the affected area. White blood cells, including neutrophils, dendritic cells, and macrophages, are drawn to the area and attack the invaders—in many cases, destroying them. At the site of infection there may be pus, a collection of dead white blood cells and debris resulting from the encounter.

The Immune Response The immune system makes two types of responses to invading pathogens: natural (innate) and acquired (adaptive). Neutrophils, macrophages, dendritic cells, and natural killer cells are part of the natural response. They recognize pathogens as "foreign" but have no memory of past infections; they respond the same way no matter how many times a pathogen invades. These cells essentially eat the invaders, destroying them internally. Natural killer cells also destroy infected body cells, breaking the chain of reproduction of a pathogen and helping to stop an infection. T and B cells are part of the acquired response. They change after one contact with the pathogen, developing a memory for the antigen. If the body is invaded again, they recognize the pathogen and mount a much more potent response.

For convenience, we can think of the immune response as having four phases: (1) recognition of the invading pathogen, (2) amplification of defenses, (3) attack, and (4) slowdown (Figure 17-3, p. 520). In each phase, crucial actions occur that are designed to destroy the invader and restore the body to health.

- *Phase 1.* Dendritic cells are drawn to the site of the injury and consume the foreign cells; they then provide information about the pathogen by displaying its antigen on their surfaces. Helper T cells read this information and rush to respond.
- *Phase 2.* Helper T cells multiply rapidly and trigger the production of killer T cells and B cells in the spleen and lymph nodes. **Cytokines,** chemical messengers secreted by lymphocytes, help regulate and coordinate the immune response; *interleukins* and *interferons* are two examples of cytokines. They stimulate increased production of T cells, B cells, and antibodies; promote the activities of natural killer cells; produce fever; and have special antipathogenic properties themselves.
- *Phase 3.* Killer T cells strike at foreign cells and body cells that have been invaded and infected, identifying them by the antigens displayed on the cell surfaces. Puncturing the cell membrane, they sacrifice body cells in order to destroy the foreign organism within. This type of action is known as a *cell-mediated immune response,* because the attack is carried out by cells. Killer T cells also trigger an amplified inflammatory response and recruit more macrophages to help clean up the site.

Terms

VW

neutrophil A type of white blood cell that engulfs foreign organisms and infected, damaged, or aged cells; particularly prevalent during the inflammatory response.

macrophage A large phagocytic (cell-eating) cell that devours foreign particles.

natural killer cell A type of white blood cell that directly destroys virus-infected cells and cancer cells.

dendritic cell A white blood cell specialized to activate T and B cells.

lymphocyte A white blood cell continuously made in lymphoid tissue as well as in bone marrow.

T cell A lymphocyte that arises in bone marrow and matures in the thymus (thus its name).

B cell A lymphocyte that matures in the bone marrow and produces antibodies.

helper T cell A lymphocyte that helps activate other T cells and may help B cells produce antibodies.

killer T cell A lymphocyte that kills body cells that have been invaded by foreign organisms; also can kill cells that have turned cancerous.

suppressor T cell A lymphocyte that inhibits the growth of other lymphocytes.

antibody A specialized protein, produced by white blood cells, that can recognize and neutralize specific microbes.

memory T and B cells Lymphocytes generated during an initial infection that circulate in the body for years, remembering the specific antigens that caused the infection and quickly destroying them if they appear again.

autoimmune disease A disease in which the immune system attacks the person's own body.

antigen A marker on the surface of a foreign substance that immune system cells recognize as nonself and that triggers the immune response.

histamine A chemical responsible for the dilation and increased permeability of blood vessels in allergic reactions.

cytokine A chemical messenger produced by a variety of cell types that helps regulate many cell functions; immune system cells release cytokines that help amplify and coordinate the immune response.

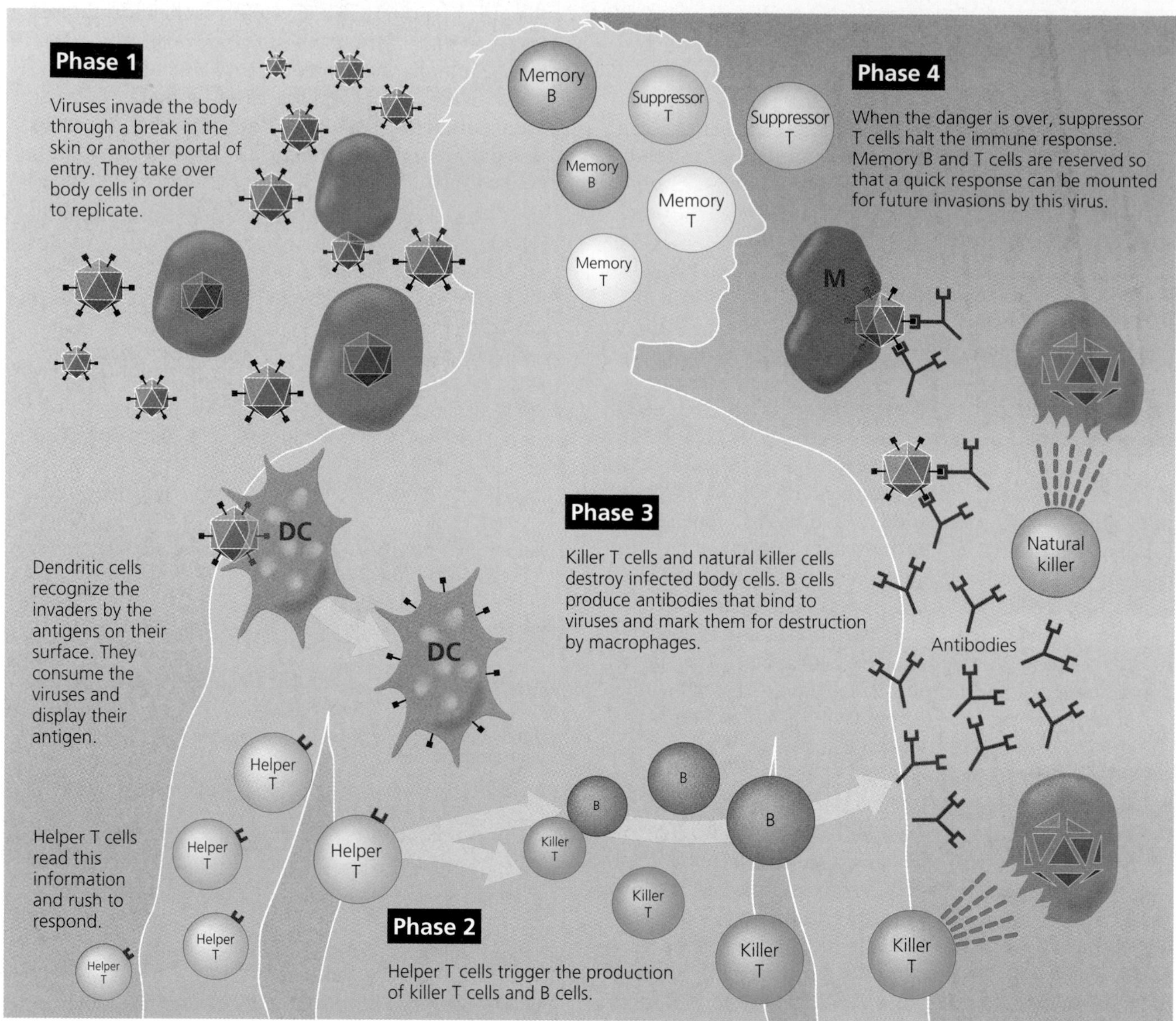

Phase 1
Viruses invade the body through a break in the skin or another portal of entry. They take over body cells in order to replicate.
Memory B
Suppressor T
Memory B
Memory T
Memory T
Suppressor T
Phase 4
When the danger is over, suppressor T cells halt the immune response. Memory B and T cells are reserved so that a quick response can be mounted for future invasions by this virus.
M
DC
Dendritic cells recognize the invaders by the antigens on their surface. They consume the viruses and display their antigen.
DC
Phase 3
Killer T cells and natural killer cells destroy infected body cells. B cells produce antibodies that bind to viruses and mark them for destruction by macrophages.
Natural killer
Antibodies
Helper T
Helper T cells read this information and rush to respond.
Helper T
Helper T
Helper T
Helper T
B
B
B
Killer T
Killer T
Phase 2
Helper T cells trigger the production of killer T cells and B cells.
Killer T
Killer T

Figure 17-3 The immune response. Once invaded by a pathogen, the body mounts a complex series of reactions to eliminate the invader. Pictured here are the principal elements of the immune response to a virus; not shown are the many types of cytokines that help coordinate the actions of different types of defenders.

B cells work in a different way. Stimulated to multiply by helper T cells, they produce large quantities of antibody molecules, which are released in the bloodstream and tissues. Antibodies are Y-shaped protein molecules that bind to antigen-bearing targets and mark them for destruction by macrophages. This type of response is known as an *antibody-mediated immune response*. Antibodies work against bacteria and against viruses and other substances when they are in the body but outside cells. They do not work against infected body cells or viruses that are replicating inside cells.

- *Phase 4.* The last phase of the immune response is a slowdown of activity. When the danger is over, suppressor T cells halt the immune response and restore homeostasis, or stability. The dead cells, killed pathogens, and other debris that result from the immune response are scavenged by certain types of white blood cells; filtered out of circulation by the liver, spleen, and kidneys; and excreted from the body.

Immunity After an infection, survival often confers **immunity;** that is, an infected person will never get the same illness again. This is because some of the lymphocytes created during the amplification phase of the immune response are reserved as memory T and B cells. As part of the acquired immune response, they continue to

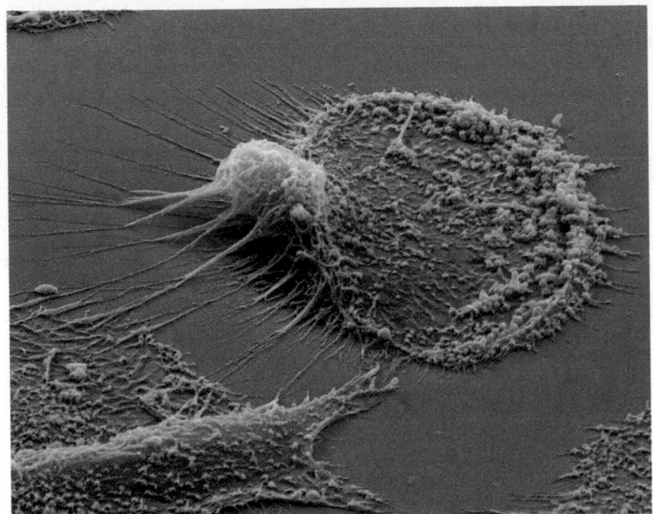

Dendritic cells are white blood cells that engulf foreign cells and display their antigens, thereby activating T and B cells. The dendritic cell shown in this scanning electron micrograph is magnified 2700 times.

circulate in the blood and lymphatic system for years or even for the rest of the person's life. If the same antigen enters the body again, the memory T and B cells recognize and destroy it before it can cause illness. This subsequent response takes only a day or two, whereas the original response lasted several days, during which time the individual suffered the symptoms of illness. The ability of memory lymphocytes to remember previous infections is known as **acquired immunity.**

Symptoms and Contagion The immune system is operating at the cellular level at all times, maintaining its vigilance when you're well and fighting invaders when you're sick. How does it all feel to you, the host for these activities? How do your symptoms relate to the course of the infection and the immune response?

During **incubation,** when viruses are multiplying in the body or when bacteria are actively multiplying before the immune system has gathered momentum, you may not have any symptoms of the illness, but you may be contagious. During the second and third phases of the immune response, you may still be unaware of the infection, or you may "feel a cold coming on." Symptoms first appear during the **prodromal period,** which follows incubation. If the infected host has acquired immunity, the infection may be eradicated during the incubation period or the prodromal period. In this case, although you may have felt you were coming down with a cold, for example, it does not develop into a full-blown illness.

Many symptoms of an illness are actually due to the immune response of the body rather than to the actions or products of the invading organism. For example, fever is caused by the release and activation of certain cytokines in macrophages and other cells during the immune response. These cytokines travel in the bloodstream to the brain and cause the body's thermostat to be reset to a higher level. The resulting elevated temperature helps the body in its fight against pathogens by enhancing immune responses. (During an illness, it is necessary to lower a fever only if it is uncomfortably high [over 101.5°F] or if it occurs in an infant who is at risk for seizures from fever.)

Similarly, you get a runny nose when your lymphocytes destroy infected mucosal cells, leading to increased mucus production. You get a sore throat when your lymphocytes destroy infected throat cells, and the malaise and fatigue of the flu may be caused by interferons.

You are contagious when there are infectious microbes in your body and they can gain access to another person. This may be before a vigorous immune response has occurred, so at times you may be contagious before experiencing any symptoms. This means that you can transmit an illness without knowing you're infected or catch an illness from someone who doesn't appear to be sick. On the other hand, your symptoms may continue after the pathogens have been mostly destroyed, when you are no longer infectious.

Immunization

The ability of the immune system to remember previously encountered organisms and retain its strength against them is the basis for immunization. When a person is immunized, the immune system is primed with an antigen similar to the pathogenic organism but not as dangerous. The body responds by producing antibodies, which prevent serious infection when and if the person is exposed to the disease organism itself. These preparations used to manipulate the immune system are known as **vaccines** (Table 17-1, p. 522).

Terms

Vw

immunity Mechanisms that defend the body against infection; specific defenses against specific pathogens.

acquired immunity The body's ability to mobilize the cellular memory of an attack by a pathogen to throw off subsequent attacks; acquired through vaccination as well as the normal immune response.

incubation The period when bacteria or viruses are actively multiplying inside the body's cells; usually a period without symptoms of illness.

prodromal period The stage of an infection, following incubation, during which initial symptoms begin to appear but the host does not feel ill; a highly contagious period.

vaccine A preparation of killed or weakened microorganisms, inactivated toxins, or components of microorganisms that is administered to stimulate an immune response; a vaccine protects against future infection by the pathogen.

Table 17-1 Immunizations for Children and Adults

Vaccine	People for Whom Immunization Is Recommended
Diphtheria	All children; booster shot recommended at 11–12 years or 13–18 years and thereafter every 10 years
H. influenzae type b (Hib)	All children (protects against meningitis); older children and adults who have had a splenectomy or bone marrow transplant, have sickle cell disease or HIV/AIDS, or are undergoing immunosuppressant drug therapy
Hepatitis A	All children at age 1 year; injection drug users, men who have sex with men, people with chronic hepatitis, and others at risk
Hepatitis B	All children and unvaccinated adolescents; adults at risk, including health care workers, household contacts and sex partners of infected people, injection drug users, people with STDs, and adults who have more than one sex partner in a 6-month period
Human papillomamvirus (HPV)	Girls age 11-12; may be given to girls as young as 9 and women through age 26
Influenza	Annual vaccination for all children age 6–59 months and their caregivers; adults age 50 and older; nursing home residents; anyone with heart, lung, or other chronic disorders (including asthma and diabetes) and others at high risk; women who will be in the second or third trimester of pregnancy during the influenza season; children aged 6 months and over with certain risk factors; anyone over age 6 months who wishes to reduce risk of influenza; people who are immunosuppressed.
Measles and mumps	All children; unvaccinated adults born after 1956 who are not immune (those who received only one dose or were vaccinated between 1963 and 1967 may need revaccination)
Meningococcal conjugate	All children at age 11–12 years or at high-school entry, first-year college students living in dormitories, military recruits, and others at increased risk
Pertussis (whooping cough)	All children; booster shot recommended at 11–12 years or 13–18 years and thereafter every 10 years
Pneumococcal polysaccharide	Adults age 65 and older; anyone with chronic heart or lung disease or with no functional spleen; others at high risk, including Alaska Natives and certain American Indian groups
Pneumococcal conjugate	All children; people with chronic illness, including chronic heart, lung, kidney, or liver disease, diabetes, HIV/AIDS, sickle cell disease; anyone with a suppressed immune system
Polio	All children; adults at risk, including certain laboratory and health care workers
Rabies	Anyone at risk from a bite, scratch, or mucous membrane exposure to a potentially rabid animal or from any direct contact with a bat (unless the person can be certain that exposure did not occur); people who work with animals may need preexposure immunization
Rubella (German measles)	All children; unvaccinated adults who are not immune, especially women
Tetanus (lockjaw)	All children; booster shot recommended at 11–12 years or 13–18 years and thereafter every 10 years (sooner if more than 5 years has elapsed since the previous booster and the individual has a contaminated wound)
Varicella-zoster (chicken pox)	Children over age 12 months; unvaccinated adolescents and adults who have not had chicken pox, especially health care workers and others at high risk for exposure; a vaccine for shingles, also caused by varicella-zoster, is available for adults 60 and older.

For international travelers, all standard childhood immunizations should be up to date and additional vaccines considered. Further information is available from the CDC's National Immunization Program (800-232-2522; http://www.cdc.gov/nip) and the CDC's Travel Information (877-394-8747; http://www.cdc.gov/travel).

SOURCES: Centers for Disease Control and Prevention. 2006. Recommended Childhood and Adolescent Immunization Schedule—United States, 2006. *Morbidity and Mortality Weekly Report* 54(52): Q1–Q4; Centers for Disease Control and Prevention. 2006. Recommended Adult Immunization Schedule—United States, October 2006–September 2007. *Morbidity and Mortality Weekly Report* 55(40): Q1–Q4.

Types of Vaccines Vaccines can be made in several ways. In some cases, microbes are cultured in the laboratory in a way that attenuates (weakens) them. These live, attenuated organisms are used in vaccines against diseases such as measles, mumps, and rubella (German measles). In other cases, when it is not possible to breed attenuated organisms, vaccines are made from pathogens that have been killed in the laboratory but that still retain their ability to stimulate the production of antibodies. Vaccines composed of killed viruses are used against influenza viruses, among others.

Vaccines confer what is known as *active immunity*—that is, the vaccinated person produces his or her own antibodies to the microorganism. Another type of injection confers *passive immunity.* In this case, a person exposed to a disease is injected with the antibodies themselves, produced by other human beings or animals who have recovered from the disease. Injections of gamma globulin—a product made from the blood plasma of many individuals containing all the antibodies they have ever made—are sometimes given to people to create a rapid but temporary immunity to a particular disease. Gamma globulin is also sometimes used to treat antibody deficiency syndromes.

Immunization Issues

Potential shortages and safety issues are areas of concern related to vaccines.

VACCINE SHORTAGES IN THE UNITED STATES Periodic shortages of influenza vaccine make the headlines, but flu vaccine is not the only one occasionally in short supply. There have been temporary shortages of most childhood vaccines in the past 5 years. Contributing factors include insufficient vaccine stockpiles, manufacturing and production problems, and the limited number of companies involved in vaccine production. Vaccines are expensive to develop and produce, carry high liability, and return relatively low profits. The influenza vaccine, which must be changed each year to match the viral strains in circulation and takes months to produce, may be particularly vulnerable to supply problems.

DEATHS FROM VACCINE-PREVENTABLE DISEASES WORLDWIDE The number of illnesses and deaths from vaccine-preventable diseases are at near record low levels in the United States. But worldwide, more than 4 million people—most of them infants and children in developing countries—die each year from vaccine-preventable diseases. Factors such as unsanitary and crowded living conditions, poor nutritional status, and limited access to health care make a child more likely to acquire infections and become seriously ill. The WHO and other organizations and governments are working to vaccinate as many children as possible. Challenges include not only funding for sufficient vaccine supplies but also overcoming problems related to storage, transportation, and delivery of multiple doses of vaccines. Infection rates around the world highlight the importance of immunization in the United States; if vaccination rates fall, an epidemic of measles or diphtheria may be just one airline passenger away.

VACCINE SAFETY Side effects from immunization are usually mild, such as soreness at the injection site. It is estimated that an allergic reaction may occur in 1 in 1.5 million doses. Any risk from vaccines must be balanced against the risk posed by the diseases they prevent; for example, the death rate from diphtheria is about 5–10%. The CDC monitors reports of adverse reactions to vaccines, and new formulations or types of vaccines are being developed to increase safety. For example, oral polio vaccine, which contains live but weakened polio virus, has been replaced by inactivated polio virus, which contains killed virus. The oral vaccine is somewhat more effective, but in about 1 in 2.4 million cases, it causes polio; because of the low risk for polio in the United States, the oral vaccine is no longer used.

A possible link has also been proposed between immunization and autism, a severe developmental disorder characterized by behavioral problems and impaired social and communication skills. However, a 2004 Institute of Medicine report concluded that evidence does not support such a link; a large 2006 study confirmed this conclusion. Thimerosol, a mercury-containing preservative, was withdrawn from pediatric vaccines beginning in 1999. Although no clear link has been found between thimerosol-containing vaccines and autism, removing thimerosol from vaccines reduces children's exposure to mercury, a neurotoxin.

Allergy: The Body's Defense System Gone Haywire

Are you among the estimated 50 million Americans affected by **allergies?** Allergies result from a hypersensitive and overactive immune system. The immune system typically defends the body against only genuinely harmful pathogens such as viruses and bacteria. However, in someone with an allergy, the immune system also mounts a response to a harmless substance such as pollen or animal dander. Allergy symptoms—stuffy nose, sneezing, wheezing, skin rashes, and so on—result primarily from the immune response rather than from the substances that provoke the response.

Allergens

Substances that provoke allergies are known as **allergens;** they may cause a response if they are inhaled or swallowed or if they come in contact with the skin. Different people have allergic reactions to different substances, but more than half of Americans age 6–59 react to at least one common allergen. Common allergens include the following:

- *Pollen:* Referred to as hay fever or allergic rhinitis, pollen allergies are widespread; weeds, grasses, and trees are common producers of allergenic pollen.
- *Animal dander:* People with animal allergies are usually allergic not to fur but to dander (dead skin flakes), urine, or a protein found in saliva; allergies to mice, dogs, and/or cats are common.
- *Dust mites and cockroaches:* The droppings of cockroaches and microscopic dust mites can trigger

Terms

VW

allergy A disorder caused by the body's exaggerated response to foreign chemicals and proteins; also called *hypersensitivity*.

allergen A substance that triggers an allergic reaction.

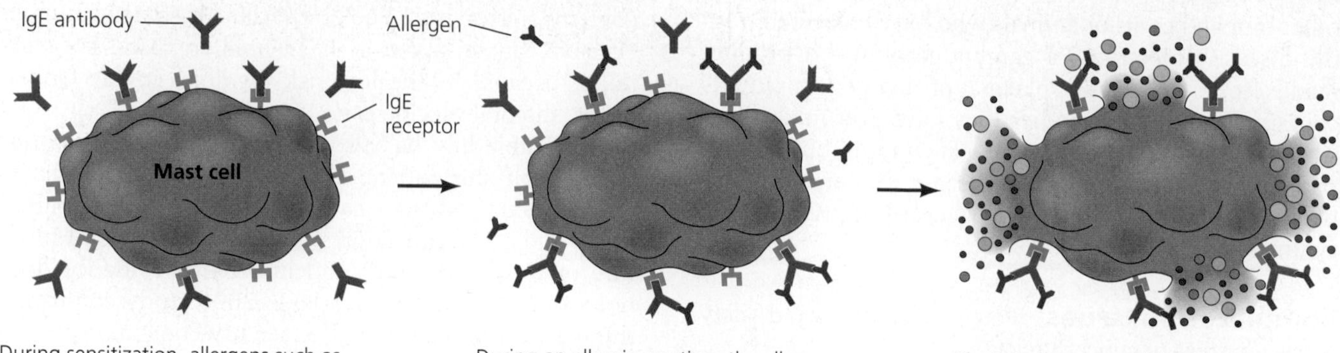

IgE antibody
Allergen
IgE receptor
Mast cell
During sensitization, allergens such as pollen trigger the production of IgE antibodies, which bind to mast cells.
During an allergic reaction, the allergens enter the bloodstream and are recognized and bound by the IgE antibodies.
The IgE-allergen combination causes mast cells to release histamine and other compounds into surrounding tissue, producing allergy symptoms.

Figure 17-4 The allergic response.

allergies; mites live in carpets, upholstered furniture, and bedding.

- *Molds and mildew:* The small spores produced by these fungi can trigger allergy symptoms; molds and mildew thrive in damp areas of buildings.
- *Foods:* The most common food allergens in adults include peanuts, tree nuts, fish, and shellfish.
- *Insect stings:* The venom of insects such as yellow jackets, honeybees, hornets, paper wasps, and fire ants causes allergic reactions in some people.

People may also be allergic to certain medications, plants such as poison oak, latex, metals such as nickel, and compounds found in cosmetics.

The Allergic Response Most allergic reactions are due to the production of a special type of antibody known as immunoglobulin E (IgE). Initial exposure to a particular allergen may cause little response, but it sensitizes the immune system by causing the production of allergen-specific IgE, which binds to mast cells (Figure 17-4). When the body is subsequently exposed to the allergen, the allergen binds to IgE, causing the mast cells to release large amounts of histamine and other compounds into surrounding tissues.

Histamine has many effects, including increasing the inflammatory response and stimulating mucus production. The precise symptoms depend on what part of the body is affected. In the nose, histamine may cause congestion and sneezing; in the eyes, itchiness and tearing; in the skin, redness, swelling, and itching; in the intestines, bloating and cramping; and in the lungs, coughing, wheezing, and shortness of breath. In some people, an allergen can trigger an asthma attack (see the box "Poverty, Ethnicity, and Asthma"). Symptoms often occur immediately, within minutes of exposure, but inflammatory reactions may take hours or days to develop and then may persist for several days.

The most serious, but rare, kind of allergic reaction is **anaphylaxis,** which results from a release of histamine throughout the body. Anaphylactic reactions can be life-threatening because symptoms may include swelling of the throat, extremely low blood pressure, fainting, heart arrhythmia, and seizures. Anaphylaxis is a medical emergency, and treatment requires immediate injection of epinephrine. People at risk for anaphylaxis should wear medical alert identification and keep self-administrable epinephrine readily available.

Term

VW **anaphylaxis** A severe systemic hypersensitive reaction to an allergen characterized by difficulty breathing, low blood pressure, heart arrhythmia, seizure, and sometimes death.

Dealing with Allergies If you suspect you might have an allergy, visit your physician or an allergy specialist. You may be asked to keep a diary to help identify allergens to which you are susceptible, or you may undergo allergy skin tests or blood tests. Your physician can help you put together a plan for your condition. There are three general strategies for dealing with allergies:

- *Avoidance:* You may be able to avoid or minimize exposure to allergens by making changes in your environment or behavior. For example, removing carpets from the bedroom and using special bedding can reduce dust mite contact. Pollen exposure can be limited by avoiding outdoor activities during peak pollination times, keeping windows shut, and showering and changing clothes following outdoor activities. If you can't part with a pet, keep pets out of bedrooms and frequently vacuum or damp-mop floors.
- *Medication:* A variety of medications are available for allergy sufferers. Many over-the-counter (OTC) antihistamines are effective at controlling symptoms such as blocked nasal, sinus, or middle ear passages.

Dimensions of Diversity

Poverty, Ethnicity, and Asthma

What Is Asthma?

The symptoms of asthma—wheezing, tightness in the chest, and shortness of breath—may be mild and occur only occasionally, or they may be severe and occur daily. Asthma is caused by both inflammation of the airways and spasm of the muscles surrounding the airways. The spasm causes constriction, and the inflammation causes the airway linings to swell and secrete extra mucus, which further obstructs the passages. The inflammation can become chronic, making airways even more sensitive to triggers.

An attack begins when something sets off inflammation of the bronchial tubes. Usually it's an allergic reaction to an inhaled allergen, most commonly dust mites, mold, animal dander, or pollen. Anything that irritates or overtaxes the bronchial airways can also trigger spasms: exercise, cold air, pollutants, tobacco smoke, infection, or stress. In female asthmatics, hormonal changes that occur as menstruation starts may increase vulnerability to attacks.

Patterns and Prevalence

Asthma can be disabling and even fatal—and the prevalence of asthma is increasing. In the United States, more than 22 million adults and 9 million children have asthma; each year, asthma is responsible for almost 2 million emergency department visits and more than 4200 deaths. Since 1980, the number of Americans with asthma has more than doubled, and despite better treatment options, the death rate has nearly tripled.

The tendency to develop asthma may be hereditary, but some patterns appear to link it to ethnicity and socioeconomic status. Particularly affected are African Americans, American Indians, and Alaska Natives; people living in inner cities; children; and people older than age 65. Asian and Pacific Islander Americans have a relatively low incidence of asthma. African Americans' risk of being hospitalized with asthma is four times greater than that of other ethnic groups; blacks are five times more likely to die from asthma. From 1980 to 2001, asthma-related deaths among African Americans rose by about 30%.

Much of the difference between ethnic groups disappears when poverty is factored in. People with low incomes are more often exposed to underlying risk factors and to attack triggers—higher levels of indoor air pollutants and allergens—in part because they may live in poorly ventilated housing and spend more time indoors. Higher levels of outdoor air pollution are also typically found in poor neighborhoods. Cockroach and mouse allergies are important causes of asthma-related illness among children in inner-city areas.

Treatment and Prevention of Attacks

Inhaling a muscle-relaxing medication from a bronchodilator can relieve an asthma attack immediately by opening the bronchial tubes. Inhaling an anti-inflammatory drug can treat the underlying inflammation. Both types of treatments may be needed to get asthma under control. Other medications for asthma block the actions of molecules involved in the body's inflammatory response. Asthmatics can monitor their condition by self-testing their peak air flow several times a day; a drop in peak air flow can signal an upcoming attack.

It's also a good idea to avoid allergens when possible. A recent study of urban children found that relatively small changes can reduce asthma symptoms and health care visits. In this study, allergen exposures were reduced by covering the mattresses and pillows with special covers; by using HEPA filters in vacuum cleaners and room air purifiers; and by employing professional pest control. Other researchers have found that many children with asthma live in households in which simple allergen-control methods haven't been taken, including closing windows to keep pollen out, avoiding environmental tobacco smoke, and reducing or eliminating exposure to pets.

SOURCES: Morgan, W. J., et al. 2004. Results of a home-based environmental intervention among urban children with asthma. *New England Journal of Medicine* 351: 1068–1080; Centers for Disease Control and Prevention. 2004. Asthma prevalence and control characteristics by race/ethnicity—United States, 2002. *Morbidity and Mortality Weekly Report* 53(7): 145–148; Cabana, M. D., et al. 2004. Parental management of asthma triggers within a child's environment. *Journal of Allergy and Clinical Immunology* 114(2): 352–357; National Institute of Allergy and Infectious Disease. 2001. *Asthma: A Concern for Minority Populations* (http://www.niaid.nih.gov/factsheets/asthma.htm; retrieved September 5, 2006).

Prescription corticosteroids markedly reduce allergy symptoms, but they have significant side effects, including reduced bone density, if used for long periods. Drug manufacturers have designed aerosol delivery systems for corticosteroids that help limit systemic absorption and side effects.

- *Immunotherapy:* Referred to as "allergy shots," immunotherapy desensitizes a person to a particular allergen through the administration of gradually increasing doses of the allergen over a period of months or years. Allergy symptoms often diminish markedly during the period in which the person receives the injections and sometimes for years afterward.

THE TROUBLEMAKERS: PATHOGENS AND DISEASE

Now that we've discussed the intricate system that protects us from disease, let's consider some pathogens, the disease-producing organisms that live within us and around us. When they succeed in gaining entry to body tissue, they can cause illness and sometimes death to the unfortunate host. Worldwide, infectious diseases are responsible for more than 11 million deaths each year (Table 17-2, p. 526).

Pathogens include bacteria, viruses, fungi, protozoa, parasitic worms, and prions (Figure 17-5, p. 527). Infections

VITAL STATISTICS

Table 17-2 Top Infectious Diseases Worldwide

Disease	Approximate Number of Deaths per Year
Pneumonia	3,884,000
HIV/AIDS	2,777,000
Diarrheal diseases	1,798,000
Tuberculosis	1,566,000
Malaria	1,272,000
Measles	611,000
Pertussis (whooping cough)	294,000
Tetanus	214,000
Meningitis	173,000
Syphilis	157,000

Many of the 618,000 deaths from liver cancer each year can be traced to viral hepatitis. Overall, infectious diseases kill more than 11 million people each year, representing nearly 19% of all deaths.

SOURCE: World Health Organization. 2004. *The World Health Report 2004*. Geneva: World Health Organization.

can occur almost anywhere in or on the body; common types of infection include bronchitis, infection of the airways (bronchi); meningitis, infection of the tissue surrounding the brain and spinal cord; conjunctivitis, infection of the layer of cells surrounding the eyes; pharyngitis, or sore throat; pneumonia, infection of the lung; gastroenteritis, infection of the gastrointestinal tract; cellulitis, infection of the soft tissues; osteomyelitis, infection of the bones; and so on, for every tissue and organ.

Bacteria

The most abundant living things on earth are **bacteria,** single-celled organisms that usually reproduce by splitting in two to create a pair of identical cells. Many species of bacteria feed on dead matter and play an important role in the recycling of nutrients for other organisms; other species feed on living things and may cause disease. Bacteria are often classified according to their shape: they may be bacilli (rod-shaped), cocci (spherical), spirochete (spiral-shaped), or vibrios (comma-shaped).

We harbor both helpful and harmful bacteria on our skin and in our gastrointestinal and reproductive tracts. The human colon contains friendly bacteria that produce certain vitamins and help digest nutrients. (A large portion of feces consists of bacteria.) Friendly bacteria also keep harmful bacteria in check by competing for food and resources and secreting substances toxic to pathogenic bacteria. For example, *Lactobacillus acidophilus* resides in the vagina and produces chemicals that kill yeast and bacteria that cause vaginal infections.

Not all bacteria found in the body are beneficial, however. If they gain access to the gastrointestinal tract via food or drink, unfriendly bacteria can disrupt the normal harmony in the intestines by invading cells or producing damaging toxins. Sexual activity can introduce pathogenic bacteria into the reproductive tract. Within the bloodstream, tissues, and organs, the human body is usually aseptic—devoid of bacteria. If bacteria find their way into these areas, infection may result. It is here that the immune system keeps up its constant surveillance, seeking out and destroying any invaders. Some bacterial infections of concern are described on the following pages.

Terms

bacterium (plural, **bacteria)** A microscopic single-celled organism; about 100 bacterial species can cause disease in humans.

pneumonia Inflammation of the lungs, typically caused by infection or exposure to chemical toxins or irritants.

mycoplasma A small bacterium with an incomplete cell wall that may cause sore throats, ear infections, and pneumonia.

meningitis Infection of the meninges (membranes covering the brain and spinal cord).

streptococcus Any of a genus (*Streptococcus*) of spherical bacteria; streptococcal species can cause skin infections, strep throat, rheumatic fever, pneumonia, scarlet fever, and other diseases.

Pneumonia Inflammation of the lungs, called **pneumonia,** may be caused by infection with bacteria, viruses, or fungi or by contact with chemical toxins or irritants. Pneumonia can be serious if the alveoli (air sacs) become clogged with fluid, thus preventing oxygen from reaching the bloodstream. Pneumonia often follows another illness, such as a cold or the flu, but the symptoms are typically more severe—fever, chills, shortness of breath, increased mucus production, and cough. Pneumonia ranks seventh among the leading causes of death for Americans; people most at risk for severe infection include those under age 2 and over age 75 and those with chronic health problems such as heart disease, asthma, or HIV. Bacterial pneumonia can be treated with antibiotics.

Pneumococcus bacteria are the most common cause of bacterial pneumonia; a vaccine is available and recommended for all adults age 65 and older and others at risk. Other bacteria that may cause pneumonia include *Streptococcus pneumoniae, Chlamydia pneumoniae,* and **mycoplasmas.** Outbreaks of infection with mycoplasmas are relatively common among young adults, especially in crowded settings such as dormitories.

Meningitis Infection of the *meninges,* the membranes covering the brain and spinal cord, is called **meningitis.** Viral meningitis is usually mild and goes away on its own; bacterial meningitis, however, can be life-threatening and requires immediate treatment with antibiotics. Symptoms of meningitis include fever, a severe

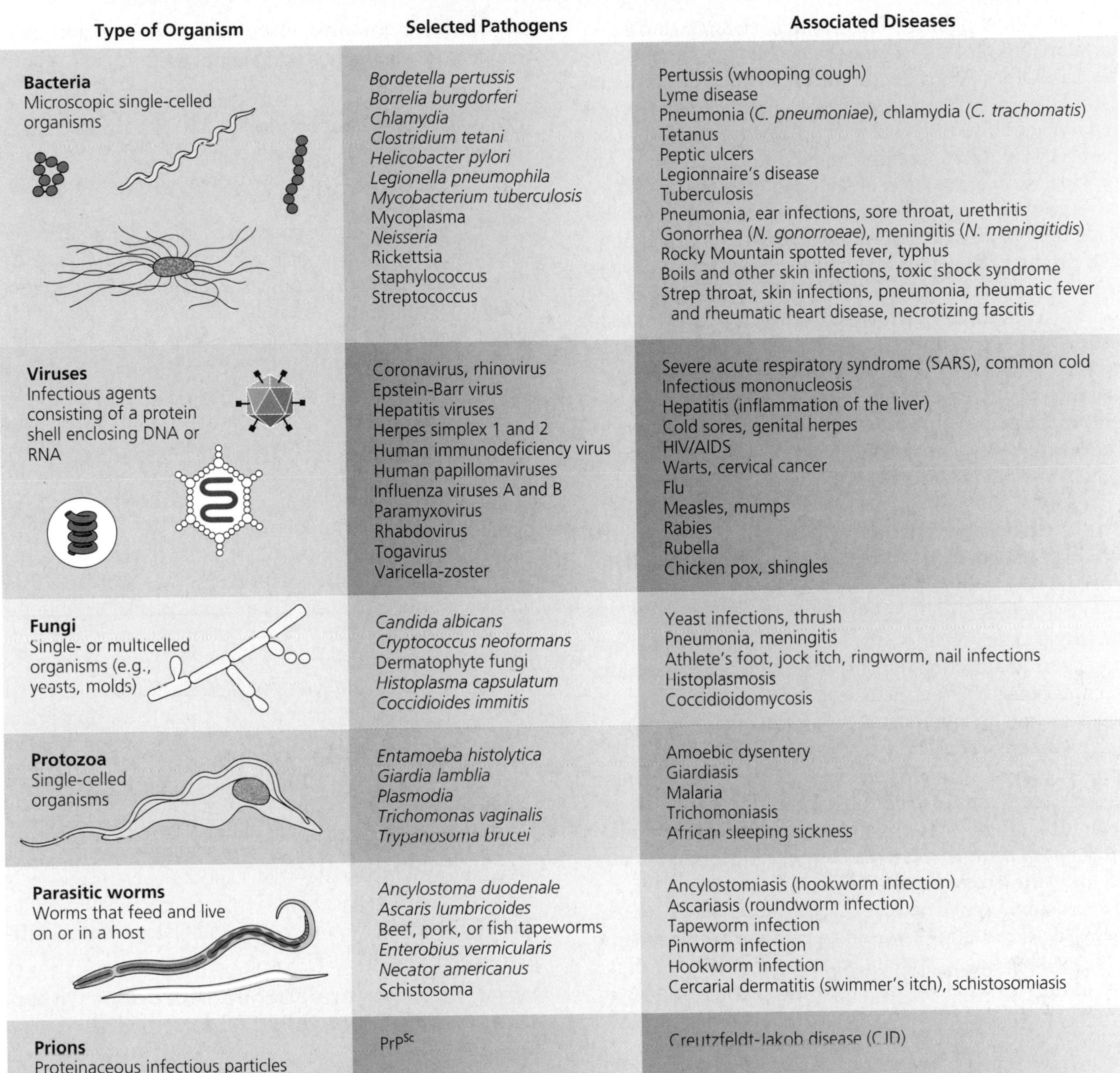

Type of Organism	Selected Pathogens	Associated Diseases
Bacteria Microscopic single-celled organisms	*Bordetella pertussis*	Pertussis (whooping cough)
	Borrelia burgdorferi	Lyme disease
	Chlamydia	Pneumonia (*C. pneumoniae*), chlamydia (*C. trachomatis*)
	Clostridium tetani	Tetanus
	Helicobacter pylori	Peptic ulcers
	Legionella pneumophila	Legionnaire's disease
	Mycobacterium tuberculosis	Tuberculosis
	Mycoplasma	Pneumonia, ear infections, sore throat, urethritis
	Neisseria	Gonorrhea (*N. gonorroeae*), meningitis (*N. meningitidis*)
	Rickettsia	Rocky Mountain spotted fever, typhus
	Staphylococcus	Boils and other skin infections, toxic shock syndrome
	Streptococcus	Strep throat, skin infections, pneumonia, rheumatic fever and rheumatic heart disease, necrotizing fascitis
Viruses Infectious agents consisting of a protein shell enclosing DNA or RNA	Coronavirus, rhinovirus	Severe acute respiratory syndrome (SARS), common cold
	Epstein-Barr virus	Infectious mononucleosis
	Hepatitis viruses	Hepatitis (inflammation of the liver)
	Herpes simplex 1 and 2	Cold sores, genital herpes
	Human immunodeficiency virus	HIV/AIDS
	Human papillomaviruses	Warts, cervical cancer
	Influenza viruses A and B	Flu
	Paramyxovirus	Measles, mumps
	Rhabdovirus	Rabies
	Togavirus	Rubella
	Varicella-zoster	Chicken pox, shingles
Fungi Single- or multicelled organisms (e.g., yeasts, molds)	*Candida albicans*	Yeast infections, thrush
	Cryptococcus neoformans	Pneumonia, meningitis
	Dermatophyte fungi	Athlete's foot, jock itch, ringworm, nail infections
	Histoplasma capsulatum	Histoplasmosis
	Coccidioides immitis	Coccidioidomycosis
Protozoa Single-celled organisms	*Entamoeba histolytica*	Amoebic dysentery
	Giardia lamblia	Giardiasis
	Plasmodia	Malaria
	Trichomonas vaginalis	Trichomoniasis
	Trypanosoma brucei	African sleeping sickness
Parasitic worms Worms that feed and live on or in a host	*Ancylostoma duodenale*	Ancylostomiasis (hookworm infection)
	Ascaris lumbricoides	Ascariasis (roundworm infection)
	Beef, pork, or fish tapeworms	Tapeworm infection
	Enterobius vermicularis	Pinworm infection
	Necator americanus	Hookworm infection
	Schistosoma	Cercarial dermatitis (swimmer's itch), schistosomiasis
Prions Proteinaceous infectious particles	PrP^{Sc}	Creutzfeldt-Jakob disease (CJD)

Figure 17-5 Pathogens and associated infectious diseases.

headache, stiff neck, sensitivity to light, and confusion. Before the 1990s, *Haemophilus influenzae* type b (Hib) was the leading cause of bacterial meningitis, but routine vaccination of children has reduced the occurrence of Hib meningitis. Today, *Neisseria meningitidis* and *Streptococcus pneumoniae* are the leading causes of bacterial meningitis.

In the United States, about 2700 cases of meningitis are reported each year, although the actual number is probably higher. The disease is fatal in 10% of cases, and about 10–20% of people who recover have permanent hearing loss or other serious effects. Worldwide, meningitis kills about 170,000 people each year, particularly in the so-called meningitis belt in sub-Saharan Africa.

A vaccine is available, but it is not effective against all strains of meningitis-causing bacteria. The CDC recommends routine vaccination of children 11–12 years old, previously unvaccinated adolescents at high school entry, and first-year college students who live in dormitories.

Strep Throat and Other Streptococcal Infections The **streptococcus** bacterium is spherical-shaped and often grows in chains. Streptococcal pharyngitis, or strep throat, is characterized by a red, sore throat with white patches on the tonsils, swollen lymph nodes, fever, and headache. It is typically spread through close contact with an infected person via respiratory droplets (sneezing or coughing). If left untreated, strep throat can develop into the more serious rheumatic fever (see Chapter 15). Other streptococcal infections include scarletina (scarlet fever), characterized by a sore throat, fever, bright red tongue, and a rash over the upper body; impetigo, a superficial skin infection most common among children; and erysipelas, inflammation of skin and underlying tissues.

A particularly virulent type of streptococcus can invade the bloodstream, spread to other parts of the body, and produce dangerous systemic illness. It can also cause a serious but rare infection of the deeper layers of the skin, a condition called necrotizing fascitis, or "flesh-eating strep." This dangerous infection is characterized by tissue death and is treated with antibiotics and removal of the infected tissue or limb. Other species of streptococci are implicated in pneumonia, endocarditis (infection of the heart lining and valves), and serious infections in pregnant women and newborns.

Toxic Shock Syndrome and Other Staphylococcal Infections The spherical-shaped **staphylococcus** bacterium often grows in small clusters. It is commonly found on the skin and in the nasal passages of healthy people. Occasionally, staphylococci enter the body and cause an infection, ranging from minor skin infections such as boils to very serious conditions such as blood infections and pneumonia. A particular strain known as methicillin-resistant *Staphylococcus aureus* (MRSA) has become the most common cause of skin infections treated in emergency rooms. This antibiotic-resistant strain causes painful skin lesions that resemble infected spider bites.

Staphylococcus aureus is also responsible for many cases of **toxic shock syndrome (TSS).** In this condition, the bacteria produce a deadly toxin that causes shock (potentially life-threatening low blood pressure), high fever, a peeling skin rash, and inflammation of several organ .systems. TSS was first diagnosed in women using highly absorbent tampons, which appear to allow the growth of staphylococci; however, about half of all cases occur in men and in women not using tampons.

Tuberculosis Caused by the bacterium *Mycobacterium tuberculosis,* **tuberculosis (TB)** is a chronic bacterial infection that usually affects the lungs. TB is spread via the respiratory route. Symptoms include coughing, fatigue, night sweats, weight loss, and fever.

Ten to 15 million Americans have been infected with, and therefore continue to carry, *M. tuberculosis.* Only about 10% of people with latent TB infections actually develop an active case of the disease; their immune system prevents the disease from becoming active. In the United States, active TB is most common among people infected with HIV, recent immigrants from countries where TB is **endemic,** and those who live in the inner cities. Worldwide, about 2 billion people—one-third of the population—are infected with TB, and each year about 8.9 million develop active TB and more than 1.7 million die.

Many strains of tuberculosis respond to antibiotics, but only over a course of treatment lasting 6–12 months. Failure to complete treatment can lead to relapse and the development of strains of antibiotic-resistant bacteria. The increase in multidrug-resistant TB has alarmed public health officials and led to new strategies to ensure that infected individuals receive and complete appropriate treatment. Of particular concern is the emergence of *M. tuberculosis* with extensive resistance to second-line drugs. These drugs are more toxic than first-line drugs—the drugs primarily used against bacterial infections. From 2000 to 2004, 20% of TB bacteria isolated in labs were multidrug resistant (MDR) and 2% were extensively drug resistant (XDR). XDR TB is geographically widespread, occurring even in the United States, and is a serious threat to public health.

Lyme Disease and Other Tickborne Infections As described earlier, one method of disease transmission is via insect vectors. Lyme disease is one such infection, and it accounts for more than 95% of all reported vectorborne illness in the United States—more than 23,000 cases per year. It is spread by the bite of a tick of the genus *Ixodes* that is infected with the spiral-shaped bacterium *Borrelia burgdorferi.* Ticks acquire the spirochete by ingesting the blood of an infected animal; they may then transmit the microbe to their next host. The deer tick is responsible for transmitting Lyme disease bacteria to humans in the northeastern and north-central United States; on the Pacific Coast, the culprit is the western black-legged tick. Lyme disease has been reported in 48 states, but significant risk of infection is found in only about 100 counties in 10 states located in the northeastern and mid-Atlantic seaboard, the upper north-central region, and parts of northern California.

Symptoms of Lyme disease vary but typically occur in three stages. In the first stage, about 80% of affected

Terms

Ww

staphylococcus Any of a genus (*Staphylococcus*) of spherical, clustered bacteria commonly found on the skin or in the nasal passages; staphylococcal species may enter the body and cause conditions such as boils, pneumonia, and toxic shock syndrome.

toxic shock syndrome (TSS) Sudden onset of fever, aches, vomiting, and peeling rash, followed in some cases by shock and inflammation of multiple organs; often caused by a toxin produced by *Staphylococcus aureus.*

tuberculosis (TB) A chronic bacterial infection that usually affects the lungs.

endemic Persistent and relatively widespread in a given population.

rickettsia A bacterium that can reproduce only inside living cells, transmitted by ticks, fleas, and lice; causes Rocky Mountain spotted fever and typhus.

Protecting Yourself Against Tickborne and Mosquitoborne Infections

Take Charge

Avoid Tick Habitat

When possible, avoid areas that are likely to be infested with ticks, particularly in spring and summer, when the immature ticks, called nymphs, are most likely to feed. Ticks favor moist, shaded habitats, especially as provided by leaf litter and low-lying vegetation in wooded, brushy, or overgrown grassy habitats. Don't sit on logs or lean against trees. State and local health departments, park personnel, and agricultural extension services can provide information on the distribution of ticks in your area.

Avoid Mosquitoes

Dawn, dusk, and early evening are times of major mosquito activity, so limit your outdoor activities during these periods or take special care to wear appropriate clothing and use insect repellent. Installing or repairing window and door screens can help keep insects outside. Place mosquito netting over infant carriers when you are outdoors with infants.

Eliminate any standing water near your home to prevent mosquitoes from breeding. Drain or upend containers (flower pots, pet dishes, and so on), change birdbath water weekly, and drill holes in the bottom of containers and tire swings that are left outside. Report dead birds to state and local health departments; birds are particularly susceptible to West Nile virus, and dead ones may indicate local infection.

Wear Protective Clothing and Apply Insect Repellent

Wear light-colored clothing so that insects can be spotted more easily. Wear long-sleeved shirts and tuck pants into socks or the tops of boots to help keep ticks from reaching your skin. Ticks are usually located close to the ground, so wearing high boots may provide additional protection. In 2005, the CDC expanded its list of recommended mosquito repellents to include DEET (n,n-diethyl-m-toluamide), picaridin (KBR 3023), and oil of lemon eucalyptus (PMD); the repellent permethrin can be applied to clothing but not skin. All repellents should be used carefully and as described on the product label.

Remove Attached Ticks

Transmission of an infectious agent is unlikely to occur until a tick has fed on you for several hours (36 hours in the case of Lyme disease), so daily checks for ticks and their prompt removal will help prevent infection. Search your entire body for ticks, using a handheld or full-length mirror; also check children and pets. Ticks are small; in the nymph phase, they may resemble poppy seeds (see figure).

Deer tick (actual size)

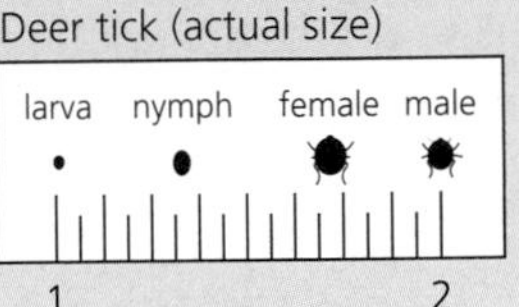

To remove a tick, use blunt-tipped tweezers and shield your fingers with rubber gloves or a paper towel. Grasp the tick as close to the skin surface as possible and pull upward (away from the skin) with steady, even pressure. Do not twist or jerk the tick, as this may cause the mouthparts to break off and remain in the skin. If this happens, remove the mouthparts with tweezers. Do not squeeze, crush, or puncture the body of the tick because its fluids may contain infectious organisms. After removing the tick, disinfect the bite site and wash your hands with soap and water. Save ticks for identification in case you become ill. Place the tick in a plastic bag in your freezer, and note the date of the bite.

SOURCES: Centers for Disease Control and Prevention. 2005. *Updated Information Regarding Mosquito Repellents* (http://www.cdc.gov/ncidod/dvbid/westnile/RepellentUpdates.htm; retrieved May 13, 2005). West Nile: Behind the buzz. 2004. *UC Berkeley Wellness Letter,* July; Centers for Disease Control and Prevention. 2003. *West Nile Virus Prevention* (http://www.cdc.gov/ncidod/dvbid/westnile/qa/prevention.htm; retrieved January 31, 2005); Centers for Disease Control and Prevention. 2002. *Lyme Disease: Prevention and Control* (http://www.cdc.gov/ncidod/dvbid/lyme; retrieved December 10, 2002).

individuals develop a bull's-eye-shaped red rash expanding from the area of the bite, usually about 2 weeks after the bite occurs. The second stage occurs weeks to months later in 10–20% of untreated patients; symptoms may involve the nervous and cardiovascular systems and can include impaired coordination, partial facial paralysis, and heart rhythm abnormalities. These symptoms usually disappear on their own within a few weeks. The third stage, which occurs in about half of untreated people, can develop months or years after the tick bite and usually consists of chronic or recurring arthritis. Lyme disease can also cause fetal damage or death at any stage of pregnancy. Lyme disease is preventable by avoiding contact with ticks or by removing a tick before it has had the chance to transmit the infection (see the box "Protecting Yourself Against Tickborne and Mosquitoborne Infections"). Lyme disease is treatable at all stages, although arthritis symptoms may not completely resolve.

Rocky Mountain spotted fever and typhus are caused by **rickettsias** and are also transmitted via tick bites. Rocky Mountain spotted fever is characterized by sudden onset of fever, headache, and muscle pain, followed by development of a spotted rash. Prior to the development of antibiotics, as many as 30% of affected individuals died; the death rate has now dropped to 3–5%. Ehrlichiosis, another tickborne disease, typically causes less severe symptoms. As with Lyme disease, the risk of acquiring Rocky Mountain spotted fever and ehrlichiosis is greater in areas where specific bacteria-carrying tick species are common.

Ulcers About 25 million Americans suffer from ulcers, sores or holes in the lining of the stomach or the first part of the small intestine (duodenum). It used to be thought that spicy food and stress were major causes of ulcers, but it is now known that as many as 90% of ulcers are caused by infection with *Helicobacter pylori.* Ulcer symptoms include gnawing or burning pain in the abdomen, nausea, and loss of appetite. If tests show the presence of *H. pylori,* antibiotics often cure the infection and the ulcers.

Other Bacterial Infections The following are a few of the many other infections caused by bacteria:

- *Tetanus:* Also known as lockjaw, tetanus is caused by the bacterium *Clostridium tetani,* which thrives in deep puncture wounds and produces a deadly toxin. The toxin causes muscular stiffness and spasms, and infection is fatal in about 30% of cases. Due to widespread vaccination, tetanus is rare in the United States. Worldwide, however, more than 200,000 people die from tetanus each year, primarily newborns infected through the unsterile cutting of the umbilical cord.
- *Pertussis:* Also known as whooping cough, pertussis is a highly contagious respiratory illness caused by a toxin produced by the bacterium *Bordetella pertussis.* Pertussis is characterized by bursts of rapid coughing, followed by a long attempt at inhalation that is often accompanied by a high-pitched whoop; symptoms may persist for 2–8 weeks. The number of U.S. cases has risen steadily over the past two decades, to more than 11,000 cases per year. Those at high risk include infants and children who are too young to be fully vaccinated and those who have not completed the primary vaccination series. Adolescents and adults become susceptible when immunity from vaccination decreases over time, so a booster shot is recommended at 11–12 years or during adolescence and thereafter every 10 years. Adults account for about 28% of whooping cough cases.
- *Urinary tract infections (UTIs):* Infection of the bladder and urethra is most common among sexually active women but can occur in anyone. The bacterium *Escherichi coli* is the most common infectious agent, responsible for about 80% of all UTIs. Infection most often occurs when bacteria from the digestive tract that live on the skin around the anus get pushed toward the opening of the urethra during sexual intercourse; then, the bacteria travel up the urethra and into the bladder. Women who are particularly susceptible may be given a supply of antibiotics to use after intercourse or at the first sign of infection; urinating before and after intercourse may also help prevent UTIs.

Bacteria responsible for foodborne illness were described in Chapter 12; Chapter 18 discusses sexually transmitted bacterial infections such as chlamydia.

Antibiotic Treatments The body's immune system can fight off many, if not most, bacterial infections. However, while the body musters its defenses, some bacteria can cause a great deal of damage: Inflammation, caused by the gathering of white blood cells, may lead to scarring and permanently damaged tissues. To help the body deal with these infections, science and medicine have made a considerable contribution: antibiotics.

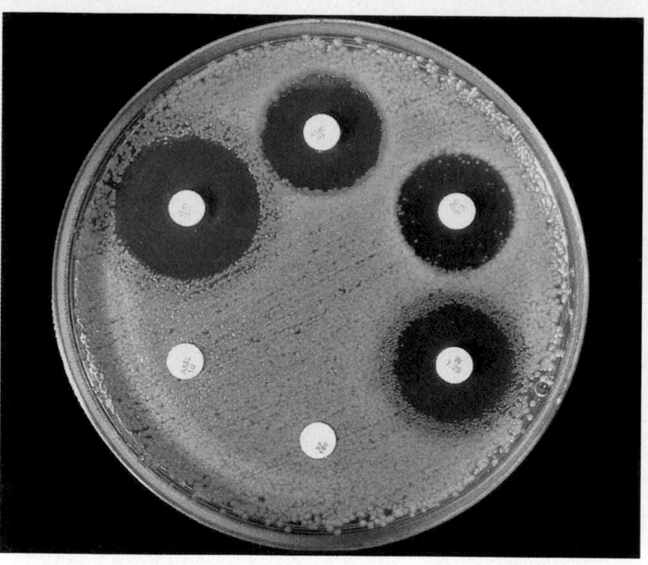

One of the dangers of antibiotic overuse is the development of bacteria resistant to drugs. Cultures of *E. coli* (a bacterium normally present in the human intestine) in this laboratory dish are sensitive to four different types of antibiotics, as indicated by the wide circles where no bacteria are growing, but they are resistant to two other types, which have no effect on their growth.

ACTIONS OF ANTIBIOTICS Antibiotics are both naturally occurring and synthetic substances having the ability to kill bacteria. Most antibiotics work in a similar fashion: They interrupt the production of new bacteria by damaging some part of their reproductive cycle or by causing faulty parts of new bacteria to be made. Penicillins inhibit the formation of the cell wall when bacteria divide to form new cells. Other antibiotics inhibit the production of certain proteins by the bacteria, and still others interfere directly with the reading of genetic material (DNA) during the process of bacterial reproduction. Antibiotics are among the most widely prescribed and effective drugs.

ANTIBIOTIC RESISTANCE When antibiotics are misused or overused, the pathogens they are designed to treat can become resistant to their effects. A bacterium can become resistant from a chance genetic mutation or through the transfer of genetic material from one bacterium to another. When exposed to antibiotics, resistant bacteria can grow and flourish, while the antibiotic-sensitive bacteria die off. Eventually, an entire colony of bacteria can become resistant to one or more antibiotics and can become very difficult to treat. Antibiotic-resistant strains of many common bacteria have developed, including strains of gonorrhea (an STD) and salmonellosis (a foodborne illness). One strain of tuberculosis is resistant to seven different antibiotics.

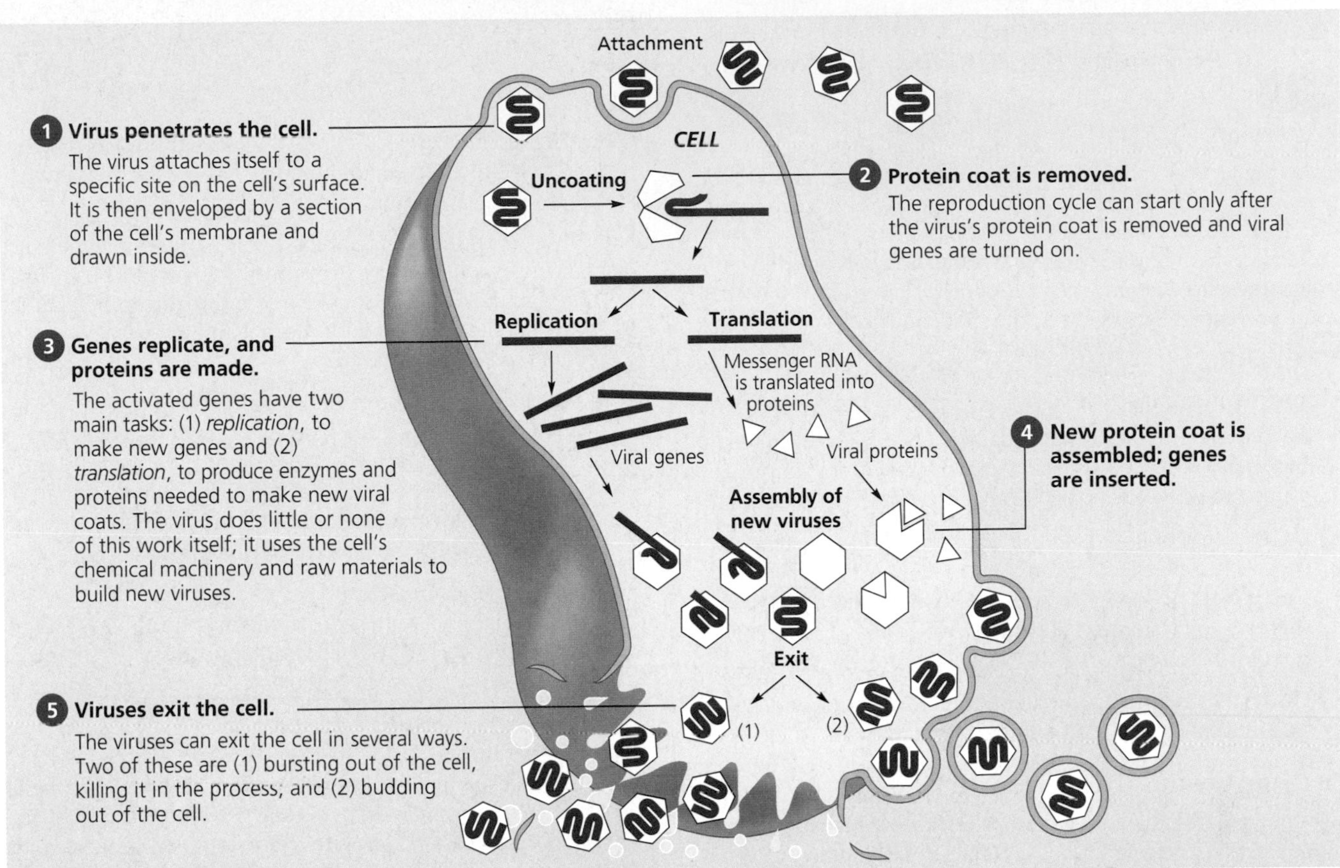

Attachment
CELL
1 Virus penetrates the cell.
The virus attaches itself to a specific site on the cell's surface. It is then enveloped by a section of the cell's membrane and drawn inside.
Uncoating
2 Protein coat is removed.
The reproduction cycle can start only after the virus's protein coat is removed and viral genes are turned on.
Replication
Translation
3 Genes replicate, and proteins are made.
The activated genes have two main tasks: (1) replication, to make new genes and (2) translation, to produce enzymes and proteins needed to make new viral coats. The virus does little or none of this work itself; it uses the cell's chemical machinery and raw materials to build new viruses.
Messenger RNA is translated into proteins
Viral genes
Viral proteins
4 New protein coat is assembled; genes are inserted.
Assembly of new viruses
Exit
(1)
(2)
5 Viruses exit the cell.
The viruses can exit the cell in several ways. Two of these are (1) bursting out of the cell, killing it in the process; and (2) budding out of the cell.

Figure 17-6 Life cycle of a virus.

Antibiotic resistance is a major factor contributing to the recent rise in problematic infectious diseases.

The more often bacteria encounter antibiotics, the more likely they are to develop resistance. Resistance is promoted when people fail to take the full course of an antibiotic or when they inappropriately take antibiotics for viral infections. Another possible source of resistance is the use of antibiotics in agriculture, which is estimated to account for 50–80% of the 25,000 tons of antibiotics used annually in the United States. At least four species of antibiotic-resistant bacteria are documented to have been transmitted from food animals to humans. In 2002, the FDA issued guidelines to the pharmaceutical industry regarding the use of new antibiotics in food-producing animals. Limits may be placed on the use in animals of drugs used in human medicine as last resorts for serious or life-threatening disease.

You can help prevent the development of antibiotic-resistant strains of bacteria by using antibiotics properly:

- Don't take an antibiotic every time you get sick. They are mainly helpful for bacterial infections; they are ineffective against viruses.
- Use antibiotics as directed, and finish the full course of medication even if you begin to feel better. This helps ensure that all targeted bacteria are killed off.
- Never take an antibiotic without a prescription. If you take an antibiotic for a viral infection, take the wrong one, or take an insufficient dose, your illness will not improve, and you'll give bacteria the opportunity to develop resistance.

Viruses

Visible only with an electron (high-magnification) microscope, **viruses** are on the borderline between living and nonliving matter. Viruses lack all the enzymes essential to energy production and protein synthesis in normal animal cells, and they cannot grow or reproduce by themselves. Viruses are **parasites;** they take what they need for growth and reproduction from the cells they invade. Once a virus is inside the host cell, it sheds its protein covering, and its genetic material takes control of the cell and manufactures more viruses like itself (Figure 17-6).

Terms

Vw

virus A very small infectious agent composed of nucleic acid (DNA or RNA) surrounded by a protein coat; lacks an independent metabolism and reproduces only within a host cell.

parasite An organism that lives on or within a living host; the relationship benefits the parasite and harms the host.

Critical Consumer

Preventing and Treating the Common Cold

VW

Prevention

Colds are usually spread by hand-to-hand contact with another person or with objects such as doorknobs and telephones, which an infected person may have handled. The best way to avoid transmission is to wash your hands frequently with warm water and soap. Keeping your immune system strong is another good prevention strategy (see the guidelines provided later in the chapter).

Home Treatments

- Get some extra rest. It isn't usually necessary to stay home in bed, but you will need to slow down a little from your usual routine to give your body a chance to fight the infection.
- Drink plenty of liquids to prevent dehydration. Hot liquids such as herbal tea and clear chicken soup will soothe a sore throat and loosen secretions; gargling with a glass of slightly salty water may also help. Avoid alcoholic beverages when you have a cold.
- Hot showers or the use of a humidifier can help eliminate nasal stuffiness and soothe inflamed membranes.

Over-the-Counter Treatments

Avoid multisymptom cold remedies. Because these products include drugs to treat symptoms you may not even have, you risk suffering from side effects from medications you don't need. It's better to treat each symptom separately:

- *Analgesics*—aspirin, acetaminophen (Tylenol), ibuprofen (Advil or Motrin), and naproxen sodium (Aleve)—all help lower fever and relieve muscle aches. Use of aspirin is associated with an increased risk of a serious condition called Reye's syndrome in children and teenagers; for this reason, aspirin should be given only to adults.
- *Decongestants* shrink nasal blood vessels, relieving swelling and congestion. However, they may dry out mucous membranes in the throat and make a sore throat worse. Nasal sprays shouldn't be used for more than 2–3 days to avoid rebound congestion.
- *Cough medicines* may be helpful when your cough is nonproductive (not bringing up mucus) or if it disrupts your sleep or work. Expectorants make coughs more productive by increasing the volume of mucus and decreasing its thickness, thereby helping remove irritants from the respiratory airways. Suppressants (antitussives) reduce the frequency of coughing.
- *Antihistamines* decrease nasal secretions caused by the effects of histamine, so they are much more useful in treating allergies than colds. *Caution:* Many antihistamines can make you drowsy.

Antibiotics will not help a cold unless a bacterial infection such as strep throat is also present, and overuse of antibiotics leads to the development of drug resistance. The jury is still out on whether other remedies, including zinc gluconate lozenges, echinacea, and vitamin C, will relieve symptoms or shorten the duration of a cold. Researchers are also studying antiviral drugs that target the most common types of cold viruses.

Sometimes a cold leads to a more serious complication, such as bronchitis, pneumonia, or strep throat. If a fever of 102°F or higher persists, or if cold symptoms don't get better after 2 weeks, see your physician.

The normal functioning of the host cell is thereby disrupted. In order to fight viruses, the cellular immunity system produces substances such as interferon; unfortunately, these same substances are also responsible for most of the symptoms of a viral illness.

Illnesses caused by viruses are the most common forms of **contagious disease.** Different viruses affect different kinds of cells, and the seriousness of the disease they cause depends greatly on which kind of cell is affected. The viruses that cause colds, for example, attack upper respiratory tract cells, which are constantly cast off and replaced; the disease is therefore mild. Poliovirus, in contrast, attacks nerve cells that cannot be replaced, and the consequences, such as paralysis, are severe. HIV infection, a viral illness that destroys immune system cells, can destroy the body's ability to fight infectious diseases (see Chapter 18).

The Common Cold Although generally brief, lasting only 4–7 days, colds are nonetheless irritating and often interfere with one's normal activities. A cold may be caused by any of more than 200 different viruses that attack the lining of the nasal passages; rhinoviruses and coronaviruses cause a large percentage of all colds among adults. Cold viruses are almost always transmitted by hand-to-hand contact. To lessen your risk of contracting a cold, wash your hands frequently; if you touch someone else, avoid touching your face until after you've washed your hands. Colds are not caused by exposure to cold weather or by being chilled or overheated; more colds do occur in the fall and winter months, probably because of the opening of school season (children contract more colds than adults) and because people spend more time indoors in the fall and winter months, making person-to-person transmission of viruses more likely.

If you do catch a cold, over-the-counter cold remedies may help treat your symptoms but do not directly attack the viral cause (see the box "Preventing and Treating the Common Cold"). Sometimes it is difficult to determine whether your symptoms are due to a virus (as for colds, flu, and some sinus infections), a bacterium (as for other sinus infections), or an allergy, but this information is

Table 17-3 What's Causing My Symptoms?

Symptoms	Influenza	Common Cold	Allergy	Sinusitis
Headache	Usually	Occasionally	Occasionally	Usually
Muscle aches	Usually (severe)	Usually (mild)	Rarely	Rarely
Fatigue, weakness	Usually (severe; sudden onset; may last several weeks)	Usually (mild)	Rarely	Rarely
Fever	Usually (high, typically 102–104°F; sudden onset; lasts 3–4 days)	Occasionally (mild)	Never	Occasionally
Cough	Usually (often severe)	Occasionally	Occasionally	Usually
Runny, stuffy nose	Occasionally	Usually	Usually	Usually (stuffy)
Nasal discharge	Occasionally	Usually (thick, clear to yellowish green)	Usually (watery, clear)	Usually (thick, yellowish green)
Sneezing	Occasionally	Occasionally	Usually	Rarely
Sore throat	Occasionally	Usually	Occasionally	Rarely
Itchy eyes, nose, throat	Rarely	Rarely	Usually	Never

SOURCE: Is it the flu? 2000. *Consumer Reports,* November. www.ConsumerReports.org, www.ConsumerReportsOnHealth.org.

important for appropriate treatment (Table 17-3). For example, antibiotics will not help treat a cold but will help treat a bacterial sinus infection.

Influenza Commonly called the flu, **influenza** is an infection of the respiratory tract caused by the influenza virus. (Many people use the term "stomach flu" to describe gastrointestinal illnesses, but these infections are actually caused by organisms other than influenza viruses). Compared to the common cold, influenza is a more serious illness, usually including a fever and extreme fatigue. Most people who get the flu recover within 1–2 weeks, but some develop potentially life-threatening complications, such as pneumonia. The highest rates of infection occur in children. Influenza is associated with more than 100,000 hospitalizations and 36,000 deaths each year, primarily among people over age 50 and those with chronic health problems. Influenza is highly contagious and is spread via respiratory droplets (see the box "The Next Influenza Pandemic—When, Not If?").

The most effective way of preventing the flu is through annual vaccination. The influenza vaccine consists of killed virus and provides protection against the strains of the virus currently circulating; it is updated each year in response to changes in the virus. Vaccination can be appropriate for anyone age 6 months or older who wants to reduce his or her risk of the flu. The CDC strongly recommands vaccination for all children age 6 to 59 months, people age 50 or older, anyone age 6 months and older with long-term health conditions, anyone with a weakened immune system, women who will be pregnant during the flu season, residents of nursing homes and long-term care facilities, age 6 months to 18 years on long-term aspirin treatment, health care workers, and household contacts and caregivers of children up to 5 years old and persons at high risk.

A number of medications are used to treat influenza, but in most cases they can shorten the duration of illness by little more than a day and then only if treatment begins within 1–2 days after onset of symptoms. Several medications are also effective in reducing the risk of illness from influenza; however, they are less effective than the vaccine.

Measles, Mumps, and Rubella Three childhood viral illnesses that have waned in the United States due to effective vaccines are measles, mumps, and rubella (German measles). Measles and rubella are generally characterized by rash and fever. Measles can occasionally cause more severe illness, including liver or brain infection or pneumonia; worldwide, more than 600,000 people die each year from measles. Measles is a highly contagious disease, and prior to the introduction of vaccines, more than 90% of Americans contracted measles by age 15. Rubella, if it infects a

Terms

Vw

contagious disease A disease that can be transmitted from one person to another; most are viral diseases, such as the common cold and flu.

influenza Infection of the respiratory tract by the influenza virus, which is highly infectious and adaptable; the form changes so easily that every year new strains arise, making treatment difficult; commonly known as the flu.

In the News

The Next Influenza Pandemic—When, Not If?

WWW

Influenza Virus Basics

There are three main types of influenza viruses, designated A, B, and C. Influenza C usually causes only mild illness and has not been associated with widespread outbreaks. Types A and B, however, are responsible for **epidemics** of respiratory illness that occur almost every winter. Influenza A viruses are further divided into subtypes, based on differences in two surface antigens: hemagglutinin (H) and neuraminidase (N).

Influenza A viruses also differ from types B and C in that they can infect a variety of animals in addition to humans. Aquatic birds, such as ducks, are a natural reservoir for influenza A; they carry and can spread the virus but do not themselves become ill. Avian strains can infect and cause serious illness in domestic poultry and may also infect pigs, humans, and other mammals.

Antigenic Drift and Shift

Through replication errors and gene sharing, influenza viruses undergo constant change, enabling them to evade the immune system and thereby make people susceptible to influenza throughout life. A person infected with influenza does develop antibodies, but as the H and N antigens change, the antibodies no longer recognize the virus, and reinfection can occur.

Small changes in H and N antigens are referred to as *antigenic drift;* these changes are why the flu vaccine is reformulated each year. Fortunately, if the changes in H and N are small, the immune system may at least partially recognize the virus, giving many people some immune protection against the new strain.

Occasionally, an influenza A virus undergoes a sudden, dramatic change, called *antigenic shift*. If this occurs and the new virus spreads easily from person to person, a worldwide epidemic, called a **pandemic**, can occur because few people have any antibody protection against the virus. Antigenic shift occurs when an avian influenza virus mixes and exchanges genes with a human virus; this mixing may occur when a human or an animal such as a pig is simultaneously infected by both human and avian strains of influenza A.

Influenza pandemics usually occur about every 30 years or so. During the twentieth century, three major influenza pandemics occurred in humans:

- 1918–1919 ("Spanish flu"): About 20–40% of the world's population became ill, and as many as 40 million people died, including more than 500,000 Americans.
- 1957–1958 ("Asian flu")
- 1968–1969 ("Hong Kong flu")

The Next Pandemic

Many experts believe that an influenza pandemic is overdue, inevitable, and possibly imminent. Conditions that allow the mingling of flu viruses—including wild and domestic birds, humans, and other flu carriers living in crowded conditions and close proximity—exist in many parts of the world.

Scientists have been monitoring the progress of a strain of avian influenza A(H5N1) in Asia that has caused a small but deadly number of cases in humans. The initial outbreak in 1997–1998 killed 6 people in Hong Kong. Local authorities contained the outbreak quickly by tracing its source to infected chickens, ducks, and geese and then ordering the slaughter of all domestic poultry. Many experts believe that this quick action probably averted a pandemic.

The H5N1 strain doesn't pass easily to or between humans; the only case of human-to-human transmission involved a mother caring for a dying child. However, when it infects humans, it is deadly. Through mid-2006, outbreaks of H5N1 avian influenza were reported among migratory birds and poultry flocks in several countries in Asia, Africa, the Middle East, and Europe. Where those outbreaks occurred, people who came into close contact with infected birds became ill or died. As of mid-June 2006, 225 people worldwide were diagnosed with H5N1 infection and 128 of those victims died.

The more people who are infected, the greater the chance that avian and human strains will mix, producing an influenza virus that is easily transmitted between people. It is hoped that the resulting strain will be less lethal than the avian strain; human strains tend to be less deadly, and the quick death of avian hosts prevents the virus from being transmitted. However, one lesson from the 1918–1919 pandemic is that crowded human conditions—such as the army trenches, military hospitals, and troop transport ships associated with World War I—promote the development of lethal human flu strains.

Scientists are studying the virus to determine how many mutations it would take to allow H5N1 to pass easily between humans. In July 2006, drug manufacturer GlaxoSmithKline reported the development of a new vaccine that is more effective than current drugs against H5N1 influenza A. About 80% of persons immunized with the new drug developed antibodies after two low-dose injections. That compares to a 50% efficacy rate for previous drugs given at higher doses. The vaccine, which hasn't been shown to protect against mutated H5N1 viruses, is awaiting FDA approval.

pregnant woman, can be transmitted to a fetus, causing miscarriage, stillbirth, and severe birth defects, including deafness, eye and heart defects, and mental impairment. Mumps generally causes swelling of the parotid (salivary) glands, located just below and in front of the ears. This virus can also cause meningitis and, in males, inflammation of the testes.

Chicken Pox, Cold Sores, and Other Herpesvirus Infections The **herpesviruses** are a large group of viruses. Once infected, the host is never free of the virus. The virus lies latent within certain cells and becomes active periodically, producing symptoms. Herpesviruses are particularly dangerous for people with a depressed immune system, as in the case of

In Focus

Are All Diseases Infectious?

Are all diseases infectious? Probably not, although researchers have recently been identifying infectious bases for more and more diseases—even diseases that have long been thought to be caused by other factors. Some scientists feel that the role of infectious agents in the major killers of today—CVD, cancer, diabetes, and so on—has been greatly underestimated. The following are just a few examples:

- **Ulcers.** Although long believed to be caused by spicy food, stress, and smoking, most cases of ulcers are now known to be caused by infection with *Helicobacter pylori*.
- **Type 1 diabetes.** A viral infection is thought to trigger the immune system to destroy insulin-producing cells in the pancreas; when this occurs, the pancreas is no longer able to produce enough insulin to metabolize glucose.
- **Multiple sclerosis (MS).** Infection with a virus, possibly human herpesvirus 6, has been proposed as the precipitating cause of MS, a condition characterized by damage to nerve fiber coverings and progressive muscle weakness.
- **Schizophrenia.** Some studies have found that people with schizophrenia are more likely than unaffected individuals to have elevated antibodies to the Borna virus. The Borna virus may be one of several infectious agents that trigger changes in the brain leading to schizophrenia.
- **Childhood obsessive-compulsive disorder (OCD).** Some cases of OCD that begin in early childhood have been found to follow infection with streptococcus bacteria. It is thought that antibodies produced to fight the infection, rather than the infection itself, may cause OCD. Some affected children improve when they are given intravenous immunoglobulin or undergo plasma exchange to remove the antibodies from their blood.
- **Heart disease.** Several infectious agents have been implicated in the inflammatory processes underlying atherosclerosis, including *Chlamydia pneumoniae* and *Cytomegalovirus*. Research is under way to determine if antibiotics can lessen the risk of heart attack in infected individuals.
- **Cancer.** A number of infections have been linked to specific types of cancer: human papillomavirus and cervical cancer; Epstein-Barr virus and Burkitt's lymphoma, nasopharyngeal cancer and some B-cell lymphomas; hepatitis B and C viruses and liver cancer; HTLV-1 and T-cell leukemia; *Helicobacter pylori* and stomach cancer; and human herpesvirus 8 and Kaposi's sarcoma.

HIV infection. The family of herpesviruses includes the following:

- *Varicella-zoster virus,* which causes chicken pox and shingles. Chicken pox is a highly contagious childhood disease characterized by an itchy rash made up of small blisters; the infection is usually mild, although complications are more likely to occur in young infants and adults. After the rash resolves, the virus becomes latent, living in sensory nerves. Many years later, the virus may reactivate and cause shingles; symptoms of shingles include pain in the affected nerves and a rash on the skin that follows the pattern of the nerve pathways (often a band over the ribs on one side of the body). A vaccine is available that prevents chicken pox in the majority of cases and results in milder illness if the disease does occur. In 2006, the FDA approved the vaccine Zostavax for people aged 60 and older; in studies, the vaccine reduced the risk of shingles in older adults by up to 64%.
- *Herpes simplex virus (HSV) types 1 and 2,* which cause cold sores and the STD herpes (Chapter 18). Herpes infections are characterized by small, painful ulcers in the area around the mouth or genitals, at the site where a person first contracts the virus. Following the initial infection, HSV becomes latent and may reactivate again and again over time. Many infected people do not know they are infected, and the virus can be transmitted even when sores are not apparent. Antiviral medications are available to prevent recurrences of genital herpes.
- *Epstein-Barr virus (EBV),* which causes infectious mononucleosis. Mono, as it is commonly called, is characterized by fever, sore throat, swollen lymph nodes, and fatigue. It is usually spread by intimate contact with the saliva of an infected person—hence the name "kissing disease." Mono most often affects adolescents and young adults; by age 40, nearly 90% of Americans have become infected with EBV. Although EBV does reactivate throughout life, it generally does not cause any further symptoms. In a few people, especially those with HIV infection, EBV is associated with the development of cancers of the lymph system (see the box "Are All Diseases Infectious?").

At one time, EBV was implicated as a cause of *chronic fatigue syndrome (CFS),* a disorder characterized by severe chronic fatigue, impaired memory or concentration, and physical symptoms such as persistent sore throat or muscle pain. However, CFS has not been linked to any single infectious agent; other possible causes of CFS

Terms

Vw

epidemic The occurrence in a particular community or region of more than the expected number of cases of a particular disease.

pandemic A disease epidemic that is unusually severe or widespread; often used to refer to worldwide epidemics affecting a large proportion of the population.

herpesvirus A family of viruses responsible for cold sores, mononucleosis, chicken pox, and the STD known as herpes; frequently causes latent infections.

include abnormalities in immunity, hormone levels, and the regulation of blood pressure.

Two herpesviruses that can cause severe infections in people with a suppressed immune system are cytomegalovirus (CMV), which infects the lungs, brain, colon, and eyes, and human herpesvirus 8 (HHV-8), which has been linked to Kaposi's sarcoma.

Viral Encephalitis HSV type 1 is a possible cause of viral **encephalitis,** inflammation of brain tissue due to a viral infection. Other possible causes include HIV and several mosquitoborne viruses, including Japanese encephalitis virus, equine encephalomyelitis virus, and West Nile virus. Mild cases of encephalitis may cause fever, headache, nausea, and lethargy; severe cases are characterized by memory loss, delirium, diminished speech function, and seizures, and they may result in permanent brain damage or death.

Viral Hepatitis Viral **hepatitis** is a term used to describe several different infections that cause inflammation of the liver. Hepatitis is usually caused by one of the three most common hepatitis viruses. Hepatitis A virus (HAV) causes the mildest form of the disease and is usually transmitted by food or water contaminated by sewage or an infected person. Hepatitis B virus (HBV) is usually transmitted sexually; it is discussed in detail in Chapter 18. Hepatitis C virus (HCV) can also be transmitted sexually, but it is much more commonly passed through direct contact with infected blood via injection drug use or, prior to the development of screening tests, blood transfusions. HBV and, to a lesser extent, HCV can also be passed from a pregnant woman to her child. There are effective vaccines for hepatitis A and B, but more than 150,000 new cases of hepatitis occur in the United States each year.

Symptoms of acute hepatitis infection can include fatigue, **jaundice,** abdominal pain, loss of appetite, nausea, and diarrhea. Most people recover from hepatitis A within a month or so. However, 5–10% of people infected with HBV and 85–90% of people infected with HCV become chronic carriers of the virus, capable of infecting others for the rest of their lives. Some chronic carriers remain asymptomatic, while others slowly develop chronic liver disease, cirrhosis, or liver cancer. An estimated 4 million Americans and 500 million people worldwide may be chronic carriers of hepatitis. Each year in the United States, HBV and HCV are responsible for more than 15,000 deaths, and these numbers are expected to climb as more people infected in the 1970s and 1980s develop problems. HCV infection is already the most frequent reason for liver transplants among U.S. adults, and it is thought to be a major factor in the 70% increase in U.S. liver cancer rates since the 1970s.

The extent of HCV infection has only recently been recognized, and most infected people are unaware of their condition. To ensure proper treatment and prevention, testing for HCV may be recommended for people at risk, including people who have ever injected drugs (even once), who received a blood transfusion or a donated organ prior to July 1992, who have engaged in high-risk sexual behavior, or who have had body piercing, tattoos, or acupuncture involving unsterile equipment. (See the box "Tattoos and Body Piercing" for information on improving safety and satisfaction related to body art.) Antiviral drugs are available to treat chronic hepatitis, but they are not completely effective and may have significant side effects.

Poliomyelitis An infectious viral disease that affects the nervous system, **poliomyelitis** can cause irreversible paralysis and death in some affected individuals. As with other vaccine-preventable diseases, the incidence of polio declined dramatically in the United States following the introduction of the vaccine, and North and South America are now considered free of the disease. In 1998, the WHO set the goal of eradicating polio from the world; in April 2006, the Centers for Disease Control and Prevention announced that polio remained endemic in only 4 countries: Afghanistan, India, Nigeria, and Pakistan.

Rabies Caused by a rhabdovirus, rabies is a potentially fatal infection of the central nervous system that is most often transmitted through an animal bite. U.S. rabies-related deaths among humans declined dramatically during the twentieth century due to the widespread vaccination of domestic animals and the development of a highly effective vaccine regimen that provides immunity following exposure (post-exposure prophylaxis, or PEP). Although rabies is rare in the United States, most recent cases have been traced to bats. The CDC recommends that PEP be considered for anyone who has had direct physical contact with a bat, including someone who has been in the same room with a bat and who might be unaware that contact has occurred (a sleeping child, for example). PEP consists of one dose of immunoglobulin and five doses of rabies vaccine over a 28-day period.

Human Papillomavirus (HPV) The more than 100 different types of HPV cause a variety of warts (moncancerous skin tumors), including common warts on the hands, plantar warts on the soles of the feet, and genital warts

Terms

Vw

encephalitis Inflammation of the brain; fever, headache, nausea, and lethargy are common initial symptoms, followed in some cases by memory loss, seizures, brain damage, and death.

hepatitis Inflammation of the liver, which can be caused by infection, drugs, or toxins.

jaundice Increased bile pigment levels in the blood, characterized by yellowing of the skin and the whites of the eyes.

poliomyelitis A disease of the nervous system, sometimes crippling; vaccines now prevent most cases of polio.

fungus A single-celled or multicelled organism that absorbs food from living or dead organic matter; examples include molds, mushrooms, and yeasts. Fungal diseases include yeast infections, athlete's foot, and ringworm.

Tattoos and Body Piercing

Careful selection of a body artist and attention to aftercare instructions can help improve safety and satisfaction following tattooing or piercing.

Tattoos

Tattoos are permanent marks or designs applied with an electrically powered instrument that injects dye into the second layer of the skin with an action that resembles that of a sewing machine. Needles in the machine are connected to tubes containing different colors of dye. Pain and a small amount of bleeding are common; a tattoo typically takes a week or two to heal. Tattoos need to be protected from sun exposure until completely healed.

Body Piercing

Piercing is usually done with plierslike equipment that pushes a needle or other sharp device through the skin; the piercing is kept open by a piece of jewelry. Earlobe piercing is the most common, but people may also pierce the upper ear, eyebrow, tongue, lip, nose, navel, nipples, or genitals. Healing time may vary from several weeks to a year depending on the site of the piercing and other factors. Some pain and swelling are common; there may be prolonged bleeding following oral piercing due to the high degree of vascularization of the tongue.

Potential Health Issues

- ***Infection:*** There is a risk of transmission of bloodborne infectious agents, including hepatitis B and C and HIV, if instruments are not sterilized properly; however, no cases of HIV infection have been traced to tattooing or piercing. In June, 2006, the CDC reported an outbreak of methicillin-resistant *Staphylococcus aureus* (MRSA) among customers of tattoo parlors in several states. In most cases, investigators found that the tattooists did not follow proper hygiene procedures, such as changing gloves between customers. MRSA is commonly called a "superbug"; it can cause necrotizing fasciitis, also known as the "flesh-eating disease." The highly drug-resistant bacterium can be deadly if it becomes entrenched deep beneath the skin. Any unexpected degree of pain or swelling should be promptly evaluated by a physician. Due to the potential risks, people currently cannot donate blood for 12 months following application of body art, including tattoos and some body piercings. People with heart valve problems should check with a physician prior to body piercing to determine if they should take antibiotics in advance of the procedure in order to prevent infection of the heart.
- ***Allergic reactions:*** Some people may be allergic to pigments used in tattooing or to metals used in body-piercing jewelry. All jewelry should be of noncorrosive materials such as stainless steel or titanium; avoid jewelry that contains nickel.
- ***Nodules and scars:*** Some people may develop granulomas (nodules) or keloids (a type of scar) following tattooing or body piercing.
- ***Problems relating to placement:*** Tattoos may become swollen or burned if people undergo magnetic resonance imaging (MRI), and tattoos may also interfere with the quality of MRI images. Oral ornaments may obscure dental problems in dental X rays; they may also damage teeth and fillings and interfere with speech and chewing. Navel piercings may become infected more easily because tight-fitting clothes allow moisture to collect in the area.

Tattoos are meant to be permanent and so are expensive and very difficult (or impossible) to remove completely. Tattoo removal may involve scraping or cutting off the layers of tattooed skin or using laser surgery to break up the pigment in the tattoo; some scarring can occur. Body piercings may close and heal once the jewelry is removed, but they may leave a permanent scar.

Choosing a Body Artist and Studio

Ask about experience and infection-control procedures. A body art studio should be clean and have an autoclave for sterilizing instruments. Needles should be sterilized and disposable; piercing guns should not be used, as they cannot be adequately sterilized. The body artist should wear disposable latex gloves throughout the procedure. Leftover tattoo ink should be thrown away and not reused. Ask to see references and aftercare instructions beforehand.

Some states and local health departments regulate body art facilities. In addition, you can ask if the studio and/or artist are members of the Alliance for Professional Tattooists (http://www.safe-tattoos.com) or the Association of Professional Piercers (http://www.safepiercing.org); these organizations have developed infection-control and other guidelines for their members to follow.

around the genitalia. Depending on their location, warts may be removed using over-the-counter preparations or professional methods such as laser surgery or cryosurgery. Because HPV infection is chronic, warts can reappear despite treatment. As described in Chapter 16, HPV causes the majority of cases of cervical cancer. A vaccine was approved in 2006 and is recommended for girls age 11–12; it may be given to girls as young as 9 and women through age 26.

Treating Viral Illnesses Although many viruses cannot be treated medically, researchers have recently begun to develop antiviral drugs. These typically work by interfering with some part of the viral life cycle; for example, they may prevent a virus from entering body cells or from successfully reproducing within cells. Antivirals are currently available to fight infections caused by HIV, influenza, herpes simplex, varicella-zoste, HBV, and HVC. Most other viral diseases must simply run their course.

Fungi

A **fungus** is an organism that absorbs food from organic matter. Fungi may be multicellular (like molds) or

Hand washing is one of the best ways to prevent the spread of infectious diseases. Always wash your hands before, during, and after preparing food; before eating; and after using the bathroom. Wet your hands, apply soap, and rub vigorously for 10–20 seconds.

unicellular (like yeasts). Mushrooms and the molds that form on bread and cheese are all fungi. Only about 50 fungi out of many thousands of species cause disease in humans, and these diseases are usually restricted to the skin, mucous membranes, and lungs. Some fungal diseases are extremely difficult to treat because some fungi form spores, an especially resistant dormant stage of the organism.

Candida albicans is a common fungus found naturally in the vagina of most women. In normal amounts, it causes no problems, but when excessive growth occurs, the result is itching and discomfort, commonly known as a yeast infection. Factors that increase the growth of *C. albicans* include the use of antibiotics, clothing that keeps the vaginal area excessively warm and moist, pregnancy, oral contraceptive use, and certain diseases, including diabetes and HIV infection. The most common symptom is usually a thick white or yellowish discharge. Treatment consists of OTC antifungal creams and suppositories or prescription oral antifungal medication. Women should not self-treat unless they are certain from a past medical diagnosis that they have a yeast infection. (Misdiagnosis could mean that a different and more severe infection goes untreated.) *C. albicans* overgrowth can occur in other areas of the body, especially in the mouth in infants (a condition known as thrush).

Other common fungal conditions, including athlete's foot, jock itch, and ringworm, affect the skin. These three mild conditions are usually easy to cure and rarely cause major problems.

Fungi can also cause systemic diseases that are severe, life-threatening, and extremely difficult to treat. Histoplasmosis, or valley fever, causes pulmonary and sometimes systemic disease and is most common in the Mississippi and Ohio River Valleys. Coccidioidomycosis is also known as valley fever because it is most frequent in the San Joaquin Valley of California. Fungal infections can be especially deadly in people with an impaired immune system.

Protozoa

Another group of pathogens is single-celled organisms known as **protozoa.** Hundreds of millions of people in developing countries suffer from protozoal infections.

Malaria, caused by a protozoan of the genus *Plasmodium,* is characterized by recurrent attacks of severe flu-like symptoms (chills, fever, headache, nausea, and vomiting) and may cause anemia. The protozoan is injected into the bloodstream via a mosquito bite. Although relatively rare in the United States, malaria is a major killer worldwide; each year, there are 350–500 million new cases of malaria and more than 1 million deaths, mostly among infants and children. Drugs are available to prevent and treat malaria, but in the poorest, most remote areas, conditions make it difficult to distribute drugs. Further, drug-resistant strains of malaria have emerged, requiring treatment with multiple new medicines.

Giardiasis is caused by *Giardia lamblia,* a single-celled parasite that lives in the intestines of humans and animals. Giardiasis is characterized by nausea, diarrhea, bloating, and abdominal cramps, and it is among the most common waterborne diseases in the United States. People may become infected with *Giardia* if they consume contaminated food or water or pick up the parasite from the contaminated surface of an object such as a bathroom fixture, diaper pail, or toy. People at risk include child care workers, children who attend day care, international travelers, and hikers and campers who drink untreated water. Giardiasis is rarely serious and can be treated with prescription medications.

Other protozoal infections include the following:

- *Trichomoniasis,* a common vaginal infection. Although usually mild and treatable, trich may increase the risk of HIV transmission (see Chapter 18).
- *Trypanosomiasis* (African sleeping sickness), which is transmitted through the bite of an infected tsetse fly and causes extreme fatigue, fever, rash, severe headache, central nervous system damage, and death.
- *Amoebic dysentery,* a severe form of amebiasis, infection of the intestines with the parasite *Entamoeba histolytica.* It is characterized by bloody diarrhea, stomach pain, and fever.

Parasitic Worms

The **parasitic worms** are the largest organisms that can enter the body to cause infection. The tapeworm, for example, can grow to a length of many feet. Worms, including intestinal parasites such as the tapeworm and hookworm, cause a great variety of relatively mild infections. Pinworm, the most common worm infection in the United States, primarily affects young children. Pinworms are white and about the size of a staple and live in the rectum of humans; they can cause itching and difficulty sleeping. Smaller worms known as flukes infect organs such as the liver and lungs and, in large numbers, can be deadly. Generally speaking, worm infections originate from contaminated food or drink and can be controlled by careful attention to hygiene.

Prions

In recent years, several fatal degenerative disorders of the central nervous system have been linked to **prions,** or proteinaceous infectious particles. Unlike all other infectious agents, prions appear to lack DNA or RNA and to consist only of protein; their presence in the body does not trigger an immune response. Prions have an abnormal shape and form deposits in the brain. They may spread by triggering normal proteins to change their structure to the abnormal, damaging, form.

Prions are associated with a class of diseases known as *transmissible spongiform encephalopathies (TSEs),* which are characterized by spongelike holes in the brain; symptoms of TSEs include loss of coordination, weakness, dementia, and death. Known prion diseases include Creutzfeldt-Jakob disease (CJD) in humans; bovine spongiform encephalopathy (BSE), or mad cow disease, in cattle; and scrapie in sheep. Some prion diseases are inherited or the result of spontaneous genetic mutations, whereas others are the result of eating infected tissue or being exposed to prions during medical procedures such as organ transplants. A variant form of CJD referred to as vCJD occurs in humans who are infected by eating beef from cows with BSE. (Researchers are investigating the possible role of prions in other brain disorders such as Alzheimer's disease.)

Many countries have reported cows infected with BSE; the first U.S. BSE case was identified in 2003 (see Chapter 12). Several steps have been taken or proposed to reduce the number of BSE-infected cows and the likelihood of meat from an infected animal entering the human food supply. These include increased surveillance, limiting or banning the use of cattle products in feed for other cattle, prohibiting meat imports from countries with BSE-infected cattle, restricting certain people from giving blood, and banning the use of downer (nonambulatory disabled) cattle for food for human consumption. Prions present special challenges because they are resistant to heat, radiation, and chemicals that kill other pathogens and because the diseases they cause have a long incubation period. In fact, experts say BSE can take 50 years to incubate. Authorities are now concerned that many more people may harbor BSE than estimated, leading to an epidemic of vCJD in coming decades. Scientists are working to develop new tests that would detect low levels of dangerous prions in asymptomatic cattle.

Emerging Infectious Diseases

The reduction in deaths from infectious diseases in the United States is one of the major public health achievements of the past century. Improvements in sanitation, hygiene, and water quality and the development of antibiotics all contributed to reduced death rates from tuberculosis, pneumonia, diarrhea, and other infections. However, after decades of decline, the U.S. death rate from infectious diseases began to climb in 1981, largely due to the HIV/AIDS epidemic. Globally, infectious diseases remain a major killer, and new concerns such as antibiotic resistance and bioterrorism have emerged in the past 20 years. Emerging infectious diseases are those infections whose incidence in humans has increased or threatens to increase in the near future. They include both known diseases that have experienced a resurgence, such as tuberculosis and cholera, and diseases that were previously unknown or confined to specific areas, such as the Ebola and West Nile viruses.

Selected Infections of Concern Although the chances of the average American contracting an exotic infection are very low, emerging infections are a concern to public health officials and represent a challenge to all nations in the future.

WEST NILE VIRUS A mini-outbreak of encephalitis in New York in 1999 led to identification of this virus, which had previously been restricted to Africa, the Middle East, and parts of Europe. Between 1999 and 2005, the virus spread across the United States and caused more than

Terms

VW

protozoan (plural, **protozoa)** A microscopic single-celled organism that often produces recurrent, cyclical attacks of disease.

malaria A severe, recurrent, mosquitoborne infection caused by the protozoan *Plasmodium*.

giardiasis An intestinal disease caused by the protozoan *Giardia lamblia*.

parasitic worm A pathogen that causes intestinal and other infections; includes tapeworms, hookworms, pinworms, and flukes.

prion Proteinaceous infectious particles thought to be responsible for a class of neurodegenerative diseases known as transmissible spongiform encephalopathies; Creutzfeldt-Jakob disease (CJD) in humans and bovine spongiform encephalopathy (BSE, or mad cow disease) are prion diseases.

19,500 illnesses and 770 deaths. West Nile virus is carried by birds and then passed to humans when mosquitoes bite first an infected bird and then a person. Most people who are bitten have few or no symptoms, but the virus can cause permanent brain damage or death in some. Vaccines are being developed for West Nile virus, but it is important to protect yourself from mosquito bites.

SEVERE ACUTE RESPIRATORY SYNDROME (SARS) In late 2002, SARS appeared in southern China and quickly spread to more than 15 countries; it is a form of pneumonia that is fatal in about 5–15% of cases. SARS is caused by a new type of coronavirus found in wildlife that may have crossed the species barrier when certain wildlife species were consumed as delicacies. It has reemerged several times since 2002, and by 2005 had been responsible for more than 8000 illnesses and 800 deaths.

ROTAVIRUS The leading viral cause of gastroenteritis, an intestinal inflammation that results in vomiting and diarrhea, rotavirus infects almost every child at one time or another. Worldwide, the virus kills about 600,000 children each year, mostly in developing countries. Left untreated, rotavirus-induced diarrhea can become severe and lead to dehydration, which can be fatal. Rotavirus spreads through poor hygiene and sanitation practices. In 2006, the FDA approved the first vaccine (RotaTeq) to prevent the disease in infants.

ESCHERICHIA COLI O157:H7 This potentially deadly strain of *E. coli*, transmitted in contaminated food, can cause bloody diarrhea and kidney damage. The first major outbreak occurred in 1993, when over 600 people became ill and 4 children died after eating contaminated and undercooked fast-food hamburgers. In 2006, more than 200 people became ill and 3 died from eating spinach from a field in California contaminated by cattle and wildlife. Other outbreaks have been linked to lettuce, alfalfa sprouts, unpasteurized juice, petting zoos, and contaminated public swimming pools. An estimated 70,000 cases and 6 deaths occur in the United States each year.

HANTAVIRUS Since first being recognized in 1993, over 300 cases of hantavirus pulmonary syndrome (HPS) have been reported in the United States. HPS is caused by the rodentborne Sin Nombre virus (SNV) and is spread primarily through airborne viral particles from rodent urine, droppings, or saliva. It is characterized by a dangerous fluid buildup in the lungs and is fatal in about 45% of cases.

EBOLA So far, outbreaks of the often fatal Ebola hemorrhagic fever (EHF) in humans have occurred only in Africa. The Ebola virus is transmitted by direct contact with infected blood or other body secretions, and many cases of EHF have been linked to unsanitary conditions in medical facilities. Because symptoms appear quickly and 70% of victims die, usually within a few days, the virus tends not to spread widely.

Factors Contributing to Emerging Infections

What's behind this rising tide of infectious diseases? Contributing factors are complex and interrelated.

DRUG RESISTANCE New or increasing drug resistance has been found in organisms that cause malaria, tuberculosis, gonorrhea, influenza, AIDS, and pneumococcal and staphylococcal infections. Infections caused by drug-resistant organisms prolong illness, and—if not treated in time with more effective, expensive drugs—they can cause death. Some bacterial strains now appear to be resistant to all available antibiotics. The cost of drug resistance exceeds $25 billion each year and is increasing.

POVERTY More than 1 billion people live in extreme poverty, and half the world's population have no regular access to essential drugs. Population growth, urbanization, overcrowding, and migration (including the movement of refugees) also spread infectious diseases.

BREAKDOWN OF PUBLIC HEALTH MEASURES A poor public health infrastructure is often associated with poverty and social upheaval, but problems such as contaminated water supplies can occur even in industrial countries. Inadequate vaccination has led to the reemergence of diseases such as diphtheria and pertussis. Natural disasters such as hurricanes also disrupt the public health infrastructure, leaving survivors with contaminated water and food supplies and no shelter from disease-carrying insects.

ENVIRONMENTAL CHANGES Changes in land use—deforestation, the damming of rivers, the spread of ranching and farming—alter the distribution of disease vectors and bring people into contact with new pathogens. A shift in rainfall patterns caused by global warming may allow mosquitoborne diseases such as malaria to spread from the tropics into the temperate zones.

TRAVEL AND COMMERCE More than 500 million travelers cross national borders each year, and international tourism and trade open the world to infectious agents. SARS was quickly spread throughout the world by infected air travelers. The reintroduction of cholera into the Western Hemisphere is thought to have occurred through the discharge of bilge water from a Chinese freighter into the waters off Peru.

MASS FOOD PRODUCTION AND DISTRIBUTION Food now travels long distances to our table, and microbes are transmitted along with it. Mass production of food increases the likelihood that a chance contamination can lead to mass illness.

HUMAN BEHAVIORS Changes in patterns of human behavior also influence the spread of infectious diseases. The widespread use of injectable drugs rapidly transmits HIV infection and hepatitis. Changes in sexual behavior over the past 30 years have led to a proliferation of old and new STDs. The use of day-care facilities for children has led to increases in the incidence of several infections that cause diarrhea.

Gender Matters: Women and Autoimmune Diseases

Although the immune systems of men and women are essentially the same, women have much higher rates of many autoimmune diseases. The reason is somewhat of a mystery. One clue may come from pregnancy: In order to conceive and carry a baby to term, a woman's body must temporarily suppress its immune response so it doesn't attack the sperm or the fetus. Another factor seems to be related to estrogen. Estrogen receptors have been found on suppressor T cells, pointing to a possible link between the glands controlling immunity and those controlling sex hormones. The expression of certain kinds of immune response genes is also linked to some autoimmune diseases, as are certain infections. Women also appear to have somewhat enhanced immunity compared to men, a factor that could be linked to both longer life spans and higher rates of autoimmune disorders.

Systemic lupus erythematosus is an autoimmune disease in which the immune system attacks the body's normal tissue, causing inflammation of the joints, blood vessels, heart, lungs, brain, and kidneys. Its symptoms include painful swollen joints, a rash on the nose and cheeks, sensitivity to sunlight, chest pain, fatigue, and dizziness. There are about 1.4–2.0 million Americans with lupus, 80% of them women; the disorder is especially common among Native American and African American women. Lupus usually begins before menopause and may flare up during pregnancy; for some women, symptoms also increase in severity during menstruation or with the use of oral contraceptives. A link between these exacerbating factors is increased levels of estrogen, but this connection is not well understood. Researchers have also identified genetic mutations that may be associated with lupus.

In rheumatoid arthritis, the body's immune system attacks the membranes lining the joints, causing pain and swelling. Among the estimated 1% of American adults with rheumatoid arthritis, women outnumber men 3 to 1. The causes of the disease are not well understood. Researchers have hypothesized that an as-yet-unidentified virus may stimulate the immune system and trigger the disease. When the disease is present in younger women, symptoms often improve during pregnancy, when estrogen levels are higher, the opposite of what is seen in the case of lupus. Therefore, although estrogen levels may play a role in these disorders, its effects appear to be influenced by many other factors.

Other autoimmune disorders more common among women than men include multiple sclerosis, a neurological disease caused by the destruction of the protective coating around nerves; scleroderma, a connective tissue disease characterized by thickening, hardening, and tightening of the skin; and Graves' disease, characterized by an increase in the production of thyroid hormone, which affects metabolism and many body systems. Continued scientific investigation will help pinpoint the causes and triggers of autoimmune disorders and explain their higher incidence among women.

BIOTERRORISM The deliberate release of deadly infectious agents is an ongoing concern. In 2001, infectious anthrax spores sent through the mail sickened 11 and killed 5 people in the United States. Potential bioterrorism agents that the CDC categorizes as a highest concern are those that can be easily disseminated or transmitted from person to person and that have a high mortality rate and the potential for a major public health impact; these include anthrax, smallpox, plague, botulism, and viral hemorrhagic fevers such as Ebola.

International efforts at monitoring, preventing, and controlling the spread of emerging infections are under way. Microbes do not respect national borders, so only a global response can make the world a safer and healthier place for everyone.

Other Immune Disorders: Cancer and Autoimmune Diseases

The immune system has evolved to protect the body from invasion by foreign microorganisms. Sometimes, as in the case of cancer, the body comes under attack by its own cells. As explained in Chapter 16, cancer cells cease to cooperate normally with the rest of the body and multiply uncontrollably. The immune system can often detect cells that have recently become cancerous and then destroy them just as it would a foreign microorganism. But if the immune system breaks down, as it may when people get older, when they have certain immune disorders (including HIV infection), or when they are receiving chemotherapy for other diseases, the cancer cells may multiply out of control before the immune system recognizes the danger. By the time the immune system gears up to destroy the cancerous cells, it may be too late.

Another immune disorder occurs when the body confuses its own cells with foreign organisms. As described earlier, the immune system must recognize many thousands of antigens as foreign and then be able to recognize the same antigens again and again. Our own tissue cells also are antigenic; that is, they would be recognized by another person's immune system as foreign. A delicate balance must be maintained to ensure that one's immune system recognizes only truly foreign antigens as enemies; erroneous recognition of one's own cells as foreign produces havoc.

This is what happens in autoimmune diseases such as rheumatoid arthritis and systemic lupus erythematosus. In this type of malady, the immune system seems to be a bit too sensitive and begins to misapprehend itself as nonself. For reasons not well understood, these conditions are much more common in women than in men (see the box "Women and Autoimmune Diseases").

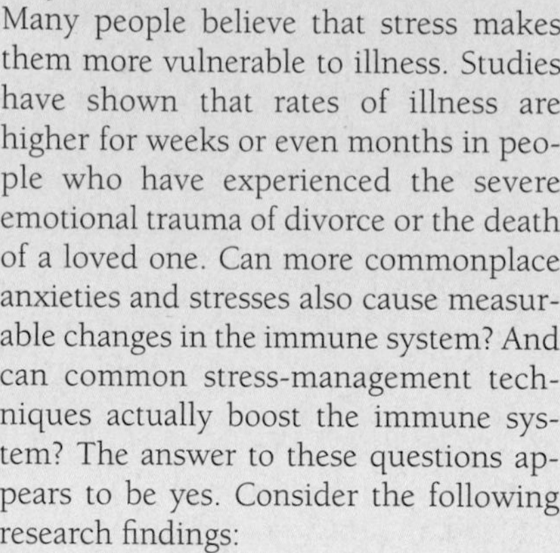

Mind/Body/Spirit

Immunity and Stress

Many people believe that stress makes them more vulnerable to illness. Studies have shown that rates of illness are higher for weeks or even months in people who have experienced the severe emotional trauma of divorce or the death of a loved one. Can more commonplace anxieties and stresses also cause measurable changes in the immune system? And can common stress-management techniques actually boost the immune system? The answer to these questions appears to be yes. Consider the following research findings:

- Medical students taking final exams showed a much weaker immune response to a hepatitis vaccination than unstressed students. In other studies, stress was associated with lower T-cell responses and antibody levels following influenza vaccinations.
- Individuals who had higher levels of stress and who had a negative or pessimistic outlook developed more colds over the course of a yearlong study than individuals with lower levels of stress and a more positive outlook.
- In a study of caregivers, relaxation sessions were associated with increased secretion of cytokines in minor wounds, thus speeding healing. Relaxation and imagery have also been shown to increase T-cell levels in some people.
- A study comparing parents of children with cancer (who presumably had high stress levels) with parents of healthy children found that stress appears to interfere with the body's ability to shut down the inflammatory response after it gets started. Continuing high levels of cytokines and inflammation could harm health. The same study found that social support improves the immune response.

In seeking to explain these effects, researchers are looking at the connections between stress, hormones, and immunity. Some hormones, such as cortisol, appear to impair the ability of immune cells to multiply and function. Others, such as prolactin, seem to give immune cells a boost. By matching stress levels and hormonal changes to the ups and downs of immune function, researchers hope to gain a better grasp of the shifting chemistry of mind and immunity.

SOURCES: Miller, G. E., S. Cohen, and A. K. Ritchey. 2002. Chronic psychological stress and the regulation of pro-inflammatory cytokines: A glucocorticoid-resistance model. *Health Psychology* 21(6): 531–541; Takkouche, B., et al. 2001. A cohort study of stress and the common cold. *Epidemiology* 12: 345–349; Bauer, M. E., et al. 2000. Chronic stress in caregivers of dementia patients is associated with reduced lymphocyte sensitivity to glucocorticoids. *Journal of Neuroimmunology* 103(1): 84–92; Cohen, S., W. J. Doyle, and D. P. Skoner. 1999. Psychological stress, cytokine production, and severity of upper respiratory illness. *Psychosomatic Medicine* 61(2): 175–180.

GIVING YOURSELF A FIGHTING CHANCE: HOW TO SUPPORT YOUR IMMUNE SYSTEM

Pathogens pose a formidable threat to wellness, but you can take many steps to prevent them from getting control of your body and compromising your health. Public health measures protect people from many diseases that are transmitted via water, food, or insects. A clean water supply and adequate sewage treatment help control typhoid fever and cholera, for example, and mosquito eradication programs control malaria and encephalitis. Proper food inspection and preparation prevent illness caused by foodborne pathogens (see Chapter 12).

What can you do to strengthen your immune system to help prevent infection? The most important thing you can do is to take good care of your body, with adequate nutrition, exercise, rest, and moderation in lifestyle. Medical science has not come up with anything that can improve on the millions of years of evolution that have culminated in your immune system. Of course, once infection has begun, some diseases can be fought with the aid of antibiotics and antiviral drugs. But these medications are not helpful in *preventing* infection, except in circumstances where normal immunity is breached, such as in surgery.

Scientists have discovered, however, that even the strongest immune system (as measured by the number of helper T cells) fluctuates throughout a person's life. You are most susceptible to disease at the extremes of life—when first born, before you have developed active immunity against most pathogens, and in old age, when the immune system, like the rest of the body, starts to deteriorate. You can't avoid being young or old, but you can make sure you get appropriate vaccinations to help the immune system in case of invasion by specific pathogens (see Table 17-1).

Stress, affected by lifestyle and attitudes, influences the immune response. Research has shown that the actual number of helper T cells rises and falls inversely with stress; that is, the higher the stress, the lower the T-cell count (see the box "Immunity and Stress"). As described in Chapter 2, stress encompasses many variables, ranging from emotional stressors, such as anger, anxiety, depression, and grief, to physical stressors, such as poor nutrition, sleep deprivation, overexertion, and substance abuse. Developing effective ways of coping with stress can improve many of the dimensions of wellness.

In addition to managing the stress in your life and getting all your immunizations, you can help your body defend itself against disease by following the guidelines in the box "How to Keep Yourself Well." As is the case with all your body systems, your immune system works best when you support it with a healthy lifestyle.

Take Charge

How to Keep Yourself Well

- Eat a balanced diet, and maintain a healthy weight. Consume a variety of nutrient-dense foods to obtain the recommended amount of nutrients every day (see Chapter 12).
- Get enough sleep, 6–8 hours every night. Sleep is extremely important in helping the body replenish itself. Adequate sleep allows the proper production and performance of all immune system cells and functions. Insufficient sleep predisposes you to a great number of illnesses and more severe infections.
- Exercise (but not while you're sick). Moderate endurance exercise is an excellent way to reduce stress and strengthen the body, thereby preventing infection. However, exercising vigorously while you are sick may actually decrease your immunity and can prolong the infection, probably by facilitating the replication of the viruses.
- Don't smoke, and drink alcohol only in moderation. Smoking decreases the levels of some immune cells, and heavy and long-term drinking interferes with the normal functioning of the immune system.
- Wash your hands frequently. Remove your rings, and rub all surfaces of your hands with lather for at least 10–20 seconds; rinse thoroughly. Antibacterial soaps have not been found to reduce the risk of infection, and some experts are concerned that widespread use of antibacterial products may contribute to the development of drug-resistant bacteria. Although they don't work any better than plain soap and water, alcohol-based hand sanitizers are a good option when hand washing facilities aren't available. It's a good idea to keep a bottle of sanitizer with you for such occasions; just make sure that the product is at least 60% alcohol.
- Avoid contact with people who are contagious with infectious diseases transmitted via the respiratory route, such as influenza, chicken pox, and tuberculosis.
- Handle and prepare foods safely (see Chapter 12); don't drink water from streams or lakes, even in seemingly pristine wilderness areas.
- Avoid contact with mosquitoes and ticks. (See p. 530.)
- Avoid contact with rodents and other disease carriers. Don't touch or feed wild rodents or any wild animals. Air out unused cabins before occupying them, and avoid stirring up dust when cleaning rodent-infested areas by first wetting the areas with disinfectant.
- Practice safer sex (see Chapter 18) and don't inject drugs.
- Get all appropriate immunizations, and use antibiotics appropriately. If you have a heart valve disorder and are at increased risk for infection (see Chapter 15), check with your physician about antibiotic use before dental or surgical procedures and before body piercing.
- If you do become ill, allow yourself time to recover. Be courteous to others by washing your hands frequently and covering your nose and mouth when you sneeze or cough.

Tips for Today

The immune system is a remarkable information network; it operates continuously on the cellular level to keep you well. You can support your immune system by practicing a wellness lifestyle—getting enough sleep, managing stress, eating well, exercising, and protecting yourself against infectious agents.

Right now you can

- Go wash your hands, and count out 20 seconds while doing so; you can estimate 20 seconds by singing "Twinkle, Twinkle, Little Star" slowly or "Happy Birthday" twice.
- Plan to move up your bedtime by 15 minutes, starting tonight.
- Put a small pack of tissues in your bag or coat pocket to use when you sneeze or cough, to avoid transmitting infection to others.
- Contribute a bar of soap or liquid hand soap to a public washroom you use frequently, such as in a common living area, in an academic building, or at work.

SUMMARY

- The step-by-step process by which infections are transmitted from one person to another involves the pathogen, its reservoir, a portal of exit, a means of transmission, a portal of entry, and a new host.
- Infection can be prevented by breaking the chain at any point. Strategies include public health measures such as treatment of drinking water and individual actions such as hand washing.
- Physical and chemical barriers to microorganisms include skin, mucous membranes, and the cilia lining the respiratory tract.
- The immune response is carried out by white blood cells that are continuously produced in the bone marrow. These include neutrophils, macrophages, dendritic cells, natural killer cells, and lymphocytes.
- The immune response has four stages: recognition of the invading pathogen; rapid replication of killer T cells and B cells; attack by killer T cells and macrophages; suppression of the immune response.

- Immunization is based on the body's ability to remember previously encountered organisms and retain its strength against them.
- Allergic reactions occur when the immune system responds to harmless substances as if they were dangerous antigens.
- Bacteria are single-celled organisms; some cause disease in humans. Bacterial infections include pneumonia, meningitis, strep throat, toxic shock syndrome, tuberculosis, Lyme disease, and ulcers.
- Most antibiotics work by interrupting the production of new bacteria; they do *not* work against viruses. Bacteria can become resistant to antibiotics.
- Viruses cannot grow or reproduce themselves; different viruses cause the common cold, influenza, measles, mumps, rubella, chicken pox, cold sores, mononucleosis, encephalitis, hepatitis, polio, and warts.
- Other diseases are caused by certain types of fungi, protozoa, parasitic worms, and prions.
- Autoimmune diseases occur when the body identifies its own cells as foreign.
- The immune system needs little help other than adequate nutrition and rest, a moderate lifestyle, and protection from excessive stress. Vaccinations also help protect against disease.

Take Action

1. **Create an immunization record:** Find out from your parents or your health records which immunizations you have had, including when you last had a tetanus shot. Are your immunizations up to date? If they aren't, or if you're not sure, check with your school health center for recommendations.

2. **Compare cold remedies:** Go to your local pharmacy and examine the cold and cough remedies. Exactly which symptoms does each one claim to alleviate and with what active ingredient? If possible, ask the pharmacist which ones he or she recommends for various symptoms.

For More Information

Books

Barry, J. 2005. *The Great Influenza: The Epic Story of the Deadliest Plague in History*. New York: Penguin. *A compelling account of the medical, social, and political aspects of the influenza epidemic of 1918–1919.*

Bollet, A. J. 2004. *Plagues and Poxes: The Impact of Human History on Epidemic Disease*. New York: Demos Medical. *Describes how human activity affects diseases.*

Roitt, I. M., et al. 2006. *Roitt's Essential Immunology*, 11th ed. London: Blackwell Publishing. *A highly readable introduction to the science of immunology.*

Siegel, M. 2006. *Bird Flu: Everything You Need to Know About the Next Pandemic*. New York: Wiley. *A practicing physician and teacher examines the potential threat of an avian flu outbreak and explains the measures we can take to protect ourselves.*

Sompayrac, L. M. 2003. *How the Immune System Works*. 2nd ed. Malden, Mass.: Blackwell Science. *A highly readable overview of basic concepts of immunity.*

WW Organizations, Hotlines, and Web Sites

Alliance for the Prudent Use of Antibiotics. Provides information on the proper use of antibiotics and tips for avoiding infections.
http://www.tufts.edu/med/apua

American Academy of Allergy, Asthma, and Immunology. Provides information and publications; pollen counts are available from the Web site.
800-822-2762
http://www.aaaai.org

American Autoimmune-Related Diseases Association. Provides background information, coping tips, and an online knowledge quiz about autoimmune diseases.
http://www.aarda.org

American College of Allergy, Asthma, and Immunology. Provides information for patients and physicians; Web site includes an extensive glossary of terms related to allergies and asthma.
http://www.acaai.org

American Society for Microbiology. Includes a library of images and an introduction to microbes.
http://www.microbeworld.org (Microbe World online)
http://www.washup.org (Clean Hands Campaign)

Bugs in the News! Provides information about microbiology—allergies, antibodies, antibiotics, mad cow disease, and more—in easy-to-understand language.
http://people.ku.edu/~jbrown/bugs.html

CDC National Center for Infectious Diseases. Provides extensive information on a wide variety of infectious diseases.
http://www.cdc.gov/ncidod

CDC National Immunization Program. Information and answers to frequently asked questions about immunizations.
800-CDC-SHOT
877-FYI-TRIP (international travel information)
http://www.cdc.gov/nip
http://www.cdc.gov/travel

Cells Alive! Includes micrographs of immune cells and pathogens at work.
http://www.cellsalive.com

National Foundation for Infectious Diseases. Provides information about a variety of diseases and disease issues.
http://www.nfid.org

National Institute of Allergy and Infectious Diseases. Includes fact sheets about many topics relating to allergies and infectious diseases, including tuberculosis and STDs.
http://www.niaid.nih.gov

World Health Organization: Infectious Diseases. Provides fact sheets about many emerging and tropical diseases as well as information about current outbreaks.
http://www.who.int/topics/infectious_diseases/en/

See also the listings in Chapter 12 (food safety), Chapter 18, and Appendix B.

Selected Bibliography

Andries, K., et al. 2005. A diarylquinoline drug active on the ATP synthetase of *Mycobacterium tuberculosis. Science* 307(5707): 223–227.

Arbes, S. J., et al. 2005. Prevalences of positive skin test responses to 10 common allergens in the US population: Results from the third National Health and Nutrition Examination Survey. *Journal of Allergy and Clinical Immunology* 116(2): 377–383.

Cashman, N. R., and B. Caughey. 2004. Prion diseases—Close to an effective therapy? *Nature Reviews: Drug Discovery* 3(12): 874–884.

Centers for Disease Control and Prevention. 2004. *Basic Facts About Asthma* (http://www.cdc.gov/asthma/faqs.htm; retrieved September 5, 2006).

Centers for Disease Control and Prevention. 2004. Bovine spongiform encephalopathy in a dairy cow—Washington state, 2003. *Morbidity and Mortality Weekly Report* 52(53): 1280–1285.

Centers for Disease Control and Prevention. 2004. Trends in tuberculosis—United States, 1998–2003. *Morbidity and Mortality Weekly Report* 53(10): 209–214.

Centers for Disease Control and Prevention. 2004. Update: West Nile virus screening of blood donations and transfusion-associated transmission. *Morbidity and Mortality Weekly Report* 53(13): 281–284.

Centers for Disease Control and Prevention. 2005. Recommended adult immunization schedule—United States, October 2005–September 2006. *Morbidity and Mortality Weekly Report* 54(40): Q1–Q4.

Centers for Disease Control and Prevention. 2006. Emergence of *Mycobacterium tuberculosis* with extensive resistance to second-line drugs worldwide, 2000–2004. *Morbidity and Mortality Weekly Report* 55(11): 301–305.

Centers for Disease Control and Prevention. 2006. Methicillin-resistant *Staphylococcus aureus* skin infections among tattoo recipients—Ohio, Kentucky, and Vermont, 2004–2005. *Morbidity and Mortality Weekly Report* 55(24): 667–669.

Centers for Disease Control and Prevention. 2006. Pertussis—United States, 2001–2003. *Morbidity and Mortality Weekly Report* 54(50): 1283–1286.

Centers for Disease Control and Prevention. 2006. Preventing tetanus, diphtheria, and pertussis among adolescents: Use of tetanus toxoid, reduced diphtheria toxoid and acellular pertussis vaccine. *Morbidity and Mortality Weekly Report* 55(RR03): 1–34.

Centers for Disease Control and Prevention. 2006. Progress toward interruption of wild poliovirus transmission—Worldwide, January 2005–March 2006. *Morbidity and Mortality Weekly Report* 55(16): 458–462.

Centers for Disease Control and Prevention. 2006. Recommended childhood and adolescent immunization schedule—United States, 2006. *Morbidity and Mortality Weekly Report* 54(51 & 52): Q1–Q4.

Centers for Disease Control and Prevention. 2006. *2005–2006 U.S. Influenza Season Summary* (http://www.cdc.gov/flu/weekly/weeklyarchives2005-2006/05-06summary.htm; retrieved September 10, 2006).

Centers for Disease Control and Prevention, National Center for Health Statistics. 2006. *Asthma Prevalence, Health Care Use and Mortality, 2002* (http://www.cdc.gov/nchs/products/pubs/pubd/hestats/asthma/asthma.htm; retrieved September 5, 2006).

Cieslak, P. R., K. Hedberg, and L. E. Lee. 2004. Chickenpox outbreak in a highly vaccinated school population: In reply. *Pediatrics* 114(4): 1131.

Fairweather, D., and N. R. Rose. 2004. Women and autoimmune diseases. *Emerging Infectious Diseases* 10(11): 2005–2011.

Fauci, A. S. 2004. Emerging infectious diseases: A clear and present danger to humanity. *Journal of the American Medical Association* 292(15): 1887–1888.

Gupta, R. S., et al. 2006. The widening black/white gap in asthma hospitalizations and mortality. *Journal of Allergy and Clinical Immunology* 117(2): 351–358.

Immunization Safety Review Committee. 2004. *Immunization Safety Review: Vaccines and Autism.* Washington, D.C.: National Academy Press.

Keene, W. E., A. C. Markum, and M. Samadpour. 2004. Outbreak of *Pseudomonas aeruginosa* infections caused by commercial piercing of upper ear cartilage. *Journal of the American Medical Association* 291(8): 981–985.

Larson, E. L., et al. 2004. Effect of antibacterial home cleaning and handwashing products on infectious disease symptoms: A randomized, double-blind trial. *Annals of Internal Medicine* 140(5): 321–329.

Lee, G. M., et al. 2005. Illness transmission in the home: A possible role for alcohol-based hand gels. *Pediatrics* 115(4): 852–860.

Levy, S. B., and B. Marshall. 2004. Antibacterial resistance worldwide. Causes, challenges, and responses. *Nature Medicine* 10(12 Suppl): S122–S129.

National Immunization Program. 2005. *Epidemiology and Prevention of Vaccine-Preventable Diseases,* 8th ed. Rev. Waldorf, Md.: Public Health Foundation.

Oren, W. 2005. Worrying about killer flu. *Discover,* February.

Parker, S. K., et al. 2004. Thimerosal-containing vaccines and autistic spectrum disorder: A critical review of published original data. *Pediatrics* 114(3): 793–804.

Prusiner, S. B. 2004. Detecting mad cow disease. *Scientific American,* July.

Samandari, T., B. P. Bell, and G. L. Armstrong. 2004. Quantifying the impact of hepatitis A immunization in the United States, 1995–2001. *Vaccine* 22(31–32): 4342–4350.

Smeeth, L., et al. 2004. MMR vaccination and pervasive developmental disorders: A case-control study. *Lancet* 364(9438): 963–969.

Snow, R. W., et al. 2005. The global distribution of clinical episodes of *Plasmodium falciparum malaria. Nature* 434: 214–217.

Vazquez, M., et al. 2004. Effectiveness over time of varicella vaccine. *Journal of the American Medical Association* 291(7): 851–855.

World Health Organization. 2004. *WHO Guidelines for the Global Surveillance of Severe Acute Respiratory Syndrome (SARS), Updated Recommendations, October 2004.* Geneva: World Health Organization.

World Health Organization. 2004. *The World Health Report 2004: Changing History.* Geneva: World Health Organization.

18

Looking AHEAD

After reading this chapter, you should be able to

- Explain how HIV infection affects the body and how it is transmitted, diagnosed, and treated
- Discuss the symptoms, risks, and treatments for the other major STDs
- List strategies for protecting yourself from STDs

Sexually Transmitted Diseases

Test Your Knowledge

1. If you have a sexually transmitted disease (STD), you will know it.
True or false?

2. Worldwide, HIV infection is spread primarily via which of the following?
a. injection drug use
b. sex between men
c. mother-to-child transmission
d. heterosexual sex

3. Of the developed countries, which one has the highest rate of sexually transmitted diseases?
a. Germany
b. United States
c. Canada
d. France

4. A man with an STD is more likely to transmit the infection to a female partner than vice versa.
True or false?

5. After you have had an STD once, you become immune to that disease and cannot get it again.
True or false?

ANSWERS

1. FALSE. Many people with STDs have no symptoms and do not know they are infected; however, they can still pass an infection to their partners.
2. D. The vast majority of HIV infection cases worldwide result from heterosexual contact, and nearly two-thirds of all new cases occur in teenage girls and young women.
3. B. The United States has the highest rate of STDs of any developed nation. If current trends continue, 50% of all Americans will contract a sexually transmitted disease by age 25.
4. TRUE. For many STDs, infected men are at least twice as likely as infected women to transmit an STD to their partner. And many STDs are more physically damaging to women than to men.
5. FALSE. Reinfection with STDs is very common. For example, if you are treated and cured of chlamydia and then you have sex with your untreated partner, the chances are very good that you will be infected again.

Visit the *Core Concepts in Health* Online Learning Center (www.mhhe.com/insel10e) for study aids and many additional resources.

Acquired immunodeficiency syndrome (AIDS) is a leading cause of death in many parts of the world. By 2030, AIDS may become the third leading cause of death worldwide (following heart disease and stroke), displacing respiratory infections from that ranking. Most of the approximately 40 million people around the world who are infected with **human immunodeficiency virus (HIV),** the virus that causes AIDS, will likely die within the next 10 years. Although the death rate from AIDS in the United States began to decline in 1996, more than 500,000 of the approximately 1.5 million Americans who have been infected with HIV have died from the disease, and it remains a major killer of Americans. Worldwide, AIDS is the leading cause of death for people age 15–59.

Although recent public education campaigns have focused primarily on HIV infection, all the **sexually transmitted diseases (STDs)**—gonorrhea, HPV infection (genital warts), chlamydia, herpes, syphilis, and others—continue to have a high incidence among Americans (Table 18-1). The United States has the highest rate of STDs of any developed nation; at current U.S. rates, half of all young people will acquire an STD by age 25. Worldwide, more than 400 million people are affected by STDs each year.

STDs are a particularly insidious group of diseases because a person can be infected and able to transmit the disease yet not look or feel sick. The cost of unprotected sex may not become apparent for many years. Then a person may find that an undiagnosed STD has led to infertility, contributed to the development of cancer, or caused a birth defect in a child. In the case of HIV infection, the immune system becomes weakened and can no longer provide protection against disease.

It is important that everyone have a clear understanding of what STDs are, how they are transmitted, and how they can be prevented. The crucial message is that they *can* be prevented. And many can also be cured if they are treated early and properly. This chapter provides information about healthy, safer sexual behavior to help you understand what you can do to reduce the further spread of these diseases.

VITAL STATISTICS

Table 18-1 Estimated Incidence and Prevalence of STDs in the United States

	Estimated Annual Incidence	Estimated Prevalence[a]
Trichomoniasis	7,400,000	n/a
HPV infection	6,200,000	20,000,000
Chlamydia	2,800,000	1,900,000
Genital herpes	1,600,000	45,000,000
Gonorrhea	718,000	n/a
Hepatitis B[b]	81,000	1,250,000
Syphilis (all stages)[c]	61,000	n/a
HIV infection[b]	40,000	1,000,000

n/a = not available.

[a]Because the viral STDs are persistent and incurable, the number of currently infected people capable of transmitting the infection (prevalence) greatly exceeds the annual number of new cases (incidence) of the viral STDs. Chlamydia prevalence remains high because most cases are asymptomatic and undiagnosed.

[b]Hepatitis B and HIV infection can be transmitted in a variety of ways; about half of all cases of HIV and 30–60% of cases of hepatitis B are transmitted sexually.

[c]Total includes about 8,000 cases of primary- and secondary-stage syphilis, the stages of the disease during which it can be easily transmitted to others.

SOURCES: Weinstock; H., S. Berman, and W. Cates. 2004. Sexually transmitted diseases among American youth: Incidence and prevalence estimates, 2000. *Perspectives on Sexual and Reproductive Health* 36(1): 6–10. Additional data from the Centers for Disease Control and Prevention and the Kaiser Family Foundation.

THE MAJOR STDS

In general, seven different STDs pose major health threats: HIV/AIDS, hepatitis, syphilis, chlamydia, gonorrhea, herpes, and HPV infection (genital warts). These diseases are considered major because they are serious in themselves, cause serious complications if left untreated, and/or pose risks to a fetus or newborn. In addition, pelvic inflammatory disease (PID) is a common complication of gonorrhea and chlamydia and merits discussion as a separate disease. The pathogens responsible for these and other STDs are listed in Table 18-2.

The bacterial STDs, including chlamydia, gonorrhea, and syphilis, are curable with antibiotics. Unfortunately, previous infection does not confer immunity, so a person can be reinfected despite treatment. The viral STDs—herpes, genital HPV infection (warts), hepatitis, and HIV infection—are not curable with current therapies. Although antiviral drugs and other medications can reduce the effects of these STDs, the virus remains in the body and may cause chronic or recurrent infection. A further risk of all STDs is that they can substantially contribute to the spread of HIV. The sores and inflammation caused by STDs allow HIV to pass more easily from one person to another.

HIV Infection and AIDS

HIV infection is one of the most serious and challenging problems facing the United States and the world today. Worldwide, it is estimated that more than 65 million people have been infected since the epidemic began—nearly 1% of the world's population—and that more than 25 million have died (see the box "HIV Infection Around the World" on p. 550). An estimated 4.3 million adults

Table 18-2 Sexually Transmitted Pathogens and Associated Diseases

Pathogen	Disease
Bacteria	
Chlamydia trachomatis	Chlamydia, pelvic inflammatory disease, epididymitis, urethritis
Gardnerella vaginalis	Bacterial vaginosis
Haemophilus ducreyi	Chancroid
Neisseria gonorrhoeae	Gonorrhea, pelvic inflammatory disease, epididymitis, urethritis
Treponema pallidum	Syphilis
Viruses	
Hepatitis B virus (HBV)	Hepatitis, cirrhosis, liver cancer
Herpes simplex viruses (HSV)	Genital herpes, oral-labial herpes (cold sores)
Human immunodeficiency virus (HIV)	HIV infection/AIDS
Human papillomavirus (HPV)	Genital warts, cervical cancer
Protozoa	
Trichomonas vaginalis	Trichomoniasis
Ectoparasites	
Phthirus pubis	Pubic lice
Sarcoptes scabiei	Scabies

and children were newly infected in 2006, and 40% of these new infections were in young people age 15–24. By 2006, about 1 million Americans were believed to be living with HIV. More than one-quarter of HIV-infected Americans are unaware they are infected.

HIV is thought to be a relatively new disease in humans. In 2006, researchers discovered a group of wild chimpanzees in Cameroon that carry SIVspc, a virus very similar to the pandemic strain of HIV seen around the world in humans. Genetic evidence shows that SIV first spread from chimpanzees to humans in the 1930s, when the trapping and butchering of chimpanzees was common. SIV is fairly benign in chimps, but as it "made the jump" to humans, it became more virulent and deadly. Poverty, the harsh environment, crowded living conditions, and unsound vaccination practices contributed to the disease's spread through local populations. Eventually, global travel allowed the disease to spread to the rest of the world.

Why do SIV and HIV, which are almost identical viruses, have such different effects on the immune systems of chimpanzees and their genetically similar "cousins," human beings? Some experts believe that the answer to this mystery may provide clues that can help make humans less vulnerable to HIV.

What Is HIV Infection? **HIV infection** is a chronic disease that progressively damages the body's immune system, making an otherwise healthy person less able to resist a variety of infections and disorders. Normally, when a virus or other pathogen enters the body, it is targeted and destroyed by the immune system. But the human immunodeficiency virus (HIV) attacks the immune system itself, invading and taking over **CD4 T cells,** monocytes, and macrophages, which are essential elements of the immune system. HIV enters a human cell and converts its own genetic material, RNA, into DNA. It then inserts this DNA into the chromosomes of the host cell. The viral DNA takes over the CD4 cell, causing it to produce new copies of HIV; it also makes the CD4 cell incapable of performing its immune functions. HIV primarily affects the T-cell part of the immune system (see Chapter 17).

Immediately following infection with HIV, billions of infectious particles are produced every day. For a time, the immune system keeps pace, also producing billions of new cells. Unlike the virus, however, the immune system cannot make new cells indefinitely; as long as the virus keeps replicating, it wins in the end. The destruction of the immune system is signaled by the loss of CD4 T cells

Terms

acquired immunodeficiency syndrome (AIDS) A generally fatal, incurable, sexually transmitted viral disease.

human immunodeficiency virus (HIV) The virus that causes HIV infection and AIDS.

sexually transmitted disease (STD) A disease that can be transmitted by sexual contact; some STDs can also be transmitted by other means.

HIV infection A chronic, progressive viral infection that damages the immune system.

CD4 T cell A type of white blood cell that helps coordinate the activity of the immune system; the primary target for HIV infection. A decrease in the number of these cells correlates with the risk and severity of HIV-related illness.

HIV Infection Around the World

In 2006, the world marked the twenty-fifth year since AIDS, a previously unknown disease, was diagnosed in 5 young gay men in Los Angeles. We now know that HIV originated in Africa about five decades earlier. HIV is now a worldwide scourge, with 65 million people infected and 25 million deaths since the epidemic began. Although some developments in efforts to address the epidemic have been promising, the number of people living with AIDS increased in every region of the world between 2004 and 2006.

The vast majority of cases—95%—have occurred in developing countries, where heterosexual contact is the primary means of transmission, responsible for 85% of all adult infections. In the developed world, HIV is increasingly becoming a disease that disproportionately affects the poor and ethnic minorities. Worldwide, women are the fastest-growing group of newly infected people; nearly half (48%) of adults living with HIV in 2006 were women. In addition, an estimated 2.3 million children are living with HIV infection and about 15 million children are AIDS orphans.

Sub-Saharan Africa remains the hardest hit of all areas of the world. Two-thirds of all adults and children with HIV live in this region, and three-quarters of all deaths due to AIDS in 2006 occurred here. However, because the epidemic started about 10 years later in Asia than in Africa, experts expect an explosion of new cases in Asia. And because Asia accounts for more than 50% of the world's population, the pool of people at risk is much larger than in Africa. India has overtaken South Africa as the country with the largest number of people living with HIV infection. HIV is also spreading rapidly in Eastern Europe, and former Soviet countries have seen a fifty-fold increase in HIV infection in 8 years.

Efforts to combat AIDS are complicated by political, economic, and cultural barriers. Education and prevention programs are often hampered by resistance from social and religious institutions and by the taboo on openly discussing sexual issues. Condoms are unfamiliar in many countries, and women in many societies do not have sufficient control over their lives to demand that men use condoms during sex. Prevention approaches that have had success include STD treatment and education, public education campaigns about safer sex, and syringe exchange programs for injection drug users.

In countries where there is a substantial imbalance in the social power of men and women, empowering women is a crucial priority in reducing the spread of HIV. In particular, reducing sexual violence against women, allowing women property and inheritance rights, and increasing women's access to education and employment are essential.

International efforts are under way to make condoms more available by lowering their price and to develop effective antiviral creams that women can use without the knowledge of their partners. Other potential strategies for fighting the spread of HIV include the widespread use of drugs to suppress genital herpes simplex, an extremely common STD that can dramatically increase transmission of HIV. Also, the practice of male circumcision might be useful in reducing the spread of HIV (and chlamydia, discussed later in this chapter). Recent research has shown a 60% reduction in HIV transmission among circumcised men compared with uncircumcised men, even when controlling for other factors.

In developed nations such as the United States, new drugs are easing AIDS symptoms and lowering viral levels dramatically for some patients. In the past few years, a small but growing number of people in poor countries have gained access to antiviral drugs because of the introduction of inexpensive generic drugs and increasing international funding for HIV treatment. Still, the vast majority of people with HIV remain untreated. Until vaccines or a low-cost cure is developed, efforts must continue to focus on prevention through educational campaigns and behavior change.

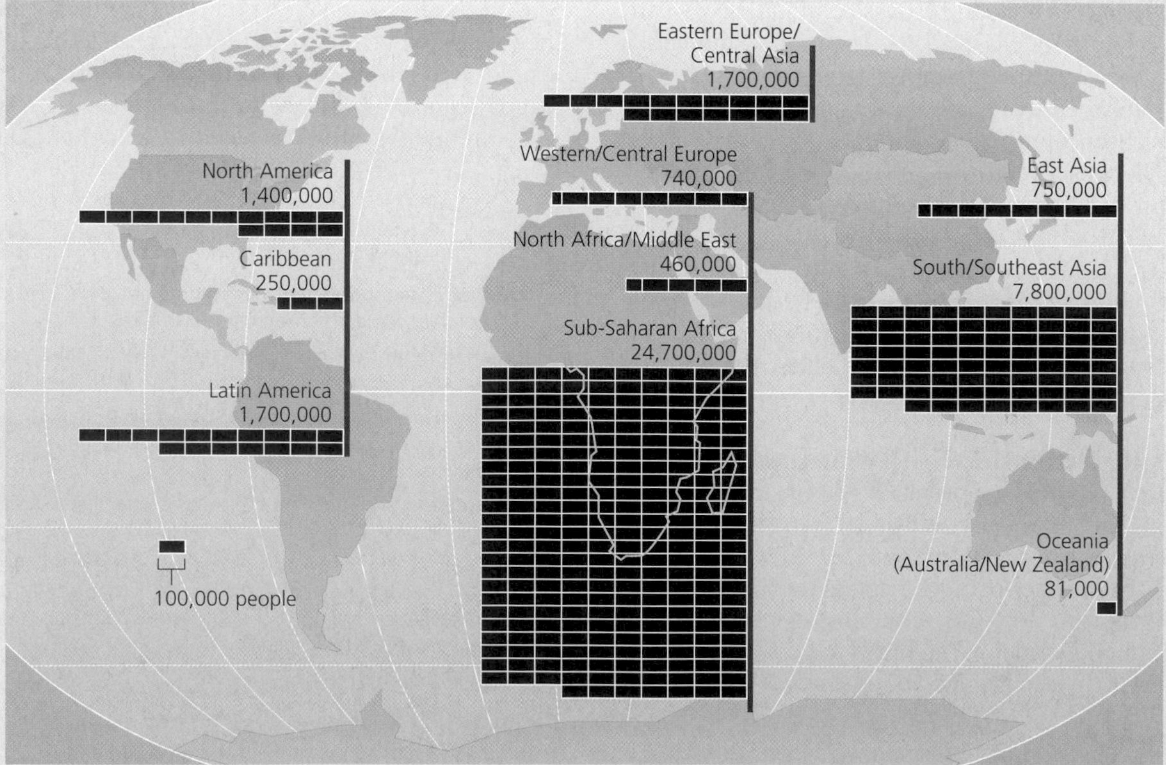

Approximate number of people living with HIV/AIDS in 2006. SOURCE: Joint United Nations Programme on HIV/AIDS (UNAIDS). *2006. AIDS Epidemic Update: December 2006*. Geneva: UNAIDS.

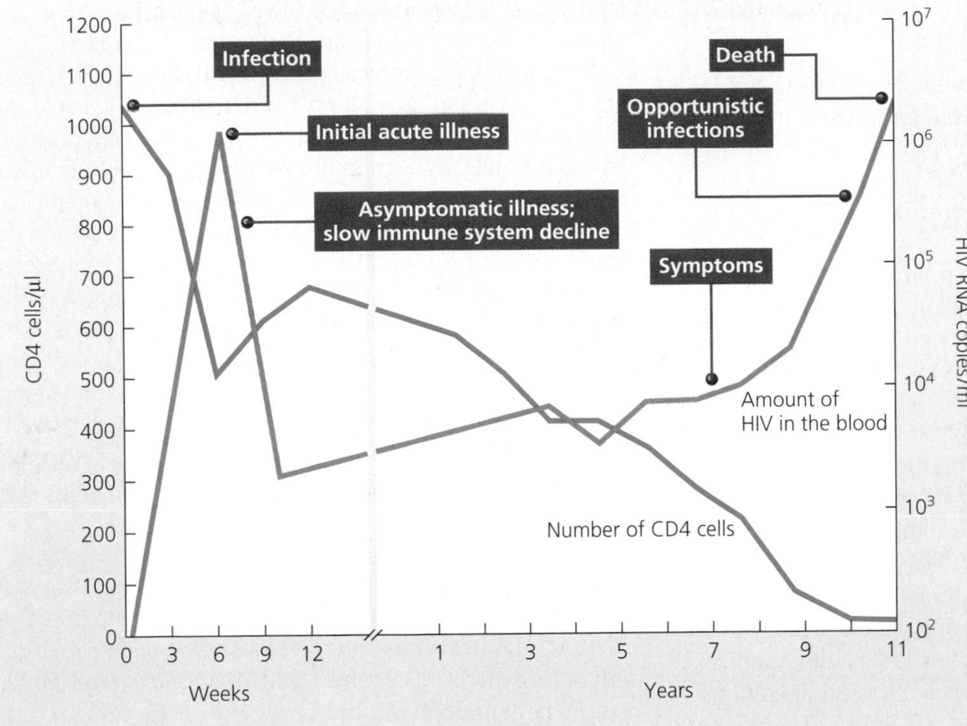
1200
1100
1000
900
800
700
600
500
400
300
200
100
0
CD4 cells/µl
Infection
Initial acute illness
Asymptomatic illness; slow immune system decline
Death
Opportunistic infections
Symptoms
Amount of HIV in the blood
Number of CD4 cells
10^7
10^6
10^5
10^4
10^3
10^2
HIV RNA copies/ml
0 3 6 9 12
Weeks
1 3 5 7 9 11
Years
During the initial acute illness, CD4 levels fall sharply and HIV RNA levels increase; more than 50% of infected people experience flulike symptoms during this period. Antibodies to HIV usually appear 2–12 weeks after the initial infection. During the asymptomatic phase that follows, CD4 levels gradually decline, and HIV RNA levels again increase. Due to declines in immunity, infected individuals eventually begin to experience symptoms; when CD4 levels drop very low, people become vulnerable to serious opportunistic infections characteristic of full-blown AIDS. Chronic or recurrent illnesses continue until the immune system fails and death results.

Figure 18-1 The general pattern of untreated HIV infection. The blue line represents the number of CD4 cells in the blood, a marker for the status of the immune system. The orange line shows the amount of HIV RNA in the blood. SOURCE: Adapted from Fauci, A. S., et al. 1996. Immunopathogenic mechanisms of HIV infection. *Annals of Internal Medicine* 124: 654–663. Reprinted with permission of the American College of Physicians.

(Figure 18-1). As the number of CD4 cells declines, an infected person may begin to experience mild to moderately severe symptoms. A person is diagnosed with full-blown AIDS when he or she develops one of the conditions defined as a marker for AIDS or when the number of CD4 cells in the blood drops below a certain level (200/µl). People with AIDS are vulnerable to a number of serious—often fatal—secondary, or **opportunistic, infections.** The infections that most often prove deadly for people with HIV are seldom serious in people with a healthy immune system. In fact, opportunistic infections are usually caused by organisms that are very common in the environment and generally do not cause illness in healthy people.

The first weeks after being infected with HIV are called the *primary infection* phase. About half of infected people develop flulike symptoms during this time. During primary HIV infection, people have large amounts of HIV in the bloodstream, making them much more infectious than they will be several months later when they enter the chronic infection stage. Experts believe that about half of all cases of HIV infection are acquired from people who are in the primary infection stage. The vast majority of people with primary infection have no idea they are infected, and even if they suspect infection and get tested, the most commonly used tests for HIV will be negative in this stage. Special tests (see below) can detect primary infection, and experts believe that increasing detection of primary infection could help reduce the spread of the virus.

The next phase of HIV infection is the chronic **asymptomatic** (symptom-free) stage. This period can last from 2 to 20 years, with an average of 11 years in untreated adults. During this time the virus progressively infects and destroys the cells of the immune system. People infected with HIV can transmit the disease to others, even if they are symptom-free. Even if they receive treatment, they remain infectious to a varying degree throughout their lives.

Transmitting the Virus HIV lives only within cells and body fluids, not outside the body. It is transmitted by blood and blood products, semen, vaginal and cervical secretions, and breast milk. It cannot live in air, in water, or on objects or surfaces such as toilet seats, eating utensils, or telephones. The three main routes of HIV transmission are (1) from specific kinds of sexual contact, (2) from direct exposure to infected blood, and (3) from

Terms

opportunistic infection An infection caused when organisms take the opportunity presented by a primary (initial) infection to multiply and cause a secondary infection.

asymptomatic Showing no signs or symptoms of a disease.

Vw

an HIV-infected woman to her fetus during pregnancy or childbirth or to her infant during breastfeeding.

SEXUAL CONTACT HIV is more likely to be transmitted by unprotected anal or vaginal intercourse than by other sexual activities. Being the receptive partner during unprotected anal intercourse is the riskiest of all sexual activities. Oral-genital contact carries some risk of transmission, although less than anal or vaginal intercourse. Still, oral sex is responsible for a small but significant number of cases of HIV transmission. HIV can be transmitted through tiny tears, traumatized points, or irritated areas in the lining of the vagina, cervix, penis, anus, and mouth and through direct infection of cells in these areas.

The presence of lesions, blisters, or inflammation from other STDs in the genital, anal, or oral areas makes it two to nine times easier for the virus to be passed. Spermicides may also cause irritation and increase the risk of HIV transmission. Recent studies of the widely used spermicide nonoxynol-9 (N-9) found that frequent use may cause vaginal and rectal irritation, increasing the risk of transmission of HIV and other STDs. The World Health Organization (WHO) recommends that spermicides containing N-9 not be used for protection against HIV and STDs. Condoms or lubricants with N-9 should never be used during anal intercourse because N-9 damages the lining of the rectum, providing an entry point for HIV and other STDs.

The risk of HIV transmission during oral sex increases if a person has poor oral hygiene, has oral sores, or has brushed or flossed just before or after oral sex. Some evidence suggests that recent consumption of alcohol may make the cells that line the mouth more susceptible to infection with HIV. During vaginal intercourse, male-to-female transmission is more likely to occur than female-to-male transmission. HIV has been found in preejaculatory fluid, so transmission can occur before ejaculation.

Studies in developing nations with high rates of HIV infection have found that circumcised males have a lower risk of HIV infection than uncircumcised males. A study in South Africa showed a 60% reduction in new infections among men who were circumcised as part of the study, and another study in Kenya and Uganda showed an approximate halving of risk among men who were circumcised. Circumcision is uncommon in most parts of the world, but these findings are heightening interest in the practice. Health officials caution that circumcision must be promoted in a culturally appropriate manner and that correct information must be given on the need for other HIV protective measures to prevent people from developing a false sense of security. In the United States, where circumcision is common and HIV infection rates are much lower, circumcision does not appear to offer any significant protection against HIV.

The odds that an infected person will transmit HIV to an uninfected person depend on a variety of factors. Let's look at an example of a heterosexual couple: Joe is HIV positive, Jane is not. Joe has a strain of HIV that is particularly infectious. He acquired the infection only 3 weeks ago and has no idea he is infected. The viral levels in Joe's blood and semen are extremely high because he is in the primary stage of infection. He also has genital herpes, which increases the likelihood that he will infect Jane with HIV. Jane is HIV-negative, but she also has genital herpes, although she doesn't know it. They have vigorous, unprotected vaginal intercourse. Will Jane acquire HIV? No one can accurately predict, but Jane's risk is substantially increased because of the strain of HIV involved, because Joe has very high viral levels, and because they both have another STD.

DIRECT CONTACT WITH INFECTED BLOOD Direct contact with the blood of an infected person is another major route of HIV transmission. Needles used to inject drugs (including heroin, cocaine, and anabolic steroids) are routinely contaminated by the blood of the user. If needles are shared, small amounts of one person's blood are directly injected into another person's bloodstream. HIV may be transmitted through subcutaneous and intramuscular injection as well, from needles or blades used in acupuncture, tattooing, ritual scarring, and piercing of the earlobes, nose, lip, nipple, navel, or other body part.

Nearly half of all new U.S. cases of HIV are caused, directly or indirectly, by sharing drug injection equipment contaminated with HIV. Drug users, their sex partners, and their children are all at extremely high risk for HIV infection. Most experts agree that syringe exchange programs combined with increased substance abuse treatment and prevention could significantly reduce the spread of HIV.

HIV has been transmitted in blood and blood products used in the medical treatment of injuries, serious illnesses, and **hemophilia**, resulting in about 14,000 cases of AIDS in the United States. Nearly all of these cases occurred in the early days of the AIDS epidemic, before effective screening tests were available. All blood in licensed U.S. blood banks and plasma centers is now thoroughly screened for HIV. The American Blood Bank Association estimates that fewer than 1 in 2 million units of blood products is capable of transmitting HIV. Unfortunately, the blood supply is much less safe in the rest of the world. In the developing world in particular, blood is often not adequately tested and blood donors are not always appropriately screened. In these countries, the risk of contracting HIV or another serious infection from a blood transfusion is very high. The WHO estimates that about 5% of all cases of HIV infection worldwide have resulted from the transfusion of infected blood and blood products.

A small number of health care workers have acquired HIV on the job; most of these cases involve needle sticks,

Term

Vw **hemophilia** A hereditary blood disease in which blood fails to clot and abnormal bleeding occurs, requiring transfusions of blood products with a specific factor to aid coagulation.

in which a health care worker is accidentally stuck with a needle used on an infected patient. The only reported cases of possible transmission *to* patients are those of 6 patients of a Florida dentist, 1 patient of a nurse in France, and 1 patient of a French orthopedic surgeon. A method of transmission was never determined with certainty in the first two cases; in the third, an injury to the hand of the surgeon during an operation may have exposed the patient to infected blood. Intensive investigations of over 22,000 patients of 63 HIV-infected health care workers showed no other cases of HIV transmission from health care workers to patients in the United States. The likelihood of a patient acquiring HIV infection from a health care worker is almost negligible; the risk to health care workers from infected patients is much greater.

What about contact with other body fluids? Trace amounts of HIV have been found in the saliva and tears of some infected people. However, researchers believe that these fluids do not carry enough of the virus to infect another person. (In the rare cases of HIV infection linked to deep kissing or biting, the virus is thought to have been transmitted in blood from oral sores rather than in saliva.) Contact with the urine or feces of an infected person may carry some risk, but contact with sweat is not believed to carry any risk. There is absolutely no evidence that the virus can be spread by insects such as mosquitoes.

MOTHER-TO-CHILD TRANSMISSION The final major route of HIV transmission is mother-to-child, also called *vertical,* or *perinatal, transmission,* which can occur during pregnancy, childbirth, or breastfeeding. About 25–30% of infants born to untreated HIV-infected mothers are also infected with the virus; treatment can dramatically lower this infection rate. Worldwide, about two-thirds of vertical transmission occurs during pregnancy and childbirth and one-third through breastfeeding.

HIV-infected children rarely appear ill at birth, but they begin to develop health problems over the first months and years of life. About 20% of infected children become very ill and progress to AIDS or death by age 4; the remaining 80% develop problems more slowly. By 2004, over 8500 cases of AIDS in American children had been reported; worldwide, about 600,000 infants are infected each year. In the United States and other developed countries, new treatments to reduce vertical transmission are in use, and the number of new cases of HIV infection has declined more than 90% since 1992. The situation worldwide, however, is bleak: In developing countries, as many as 1 in 3 children born to HIV-positive women become infected. The lack of HIV testing and treatment and common breastfeeding account for this disparity.

NOT THROUGH CASUAL CONTACT A person is not at risk of getting HIV infection by being in the same classroom, dining room, or even household with someone who is infected. Before this was generally known, many people with HIV infection, including children, were the targets of ostracism, hysteria, and outright violence. Today, it is an acknowledged responsibility of everyone to treat people with HIV infection with respect and compassion, regardless of their age or how they became infected.

Populations of Special Concern for HIV Infection Among Americans with AIDS, the most common means of exposure to HIV has been sexual activity between men; heterosexual contact and injection drug use (IDU) are the next most common (Figure 18-2, p. 554). Although the transmission of HIV occurs through specific individual behaviors, disproportionately high rates of infection in certain groups are tied to social, cultural, and economic factors. HIV in the United States is increasingly becoming a disease that affects ethnic minorities, women, and the poor. The U.S. pattern of HIV infection has changed over time: Heterosexual transmission accounts for a growing proportion of new cases, whereas the share caused by sex between men and injection drug use is falling. Women, especially African American women and Latinas, make up an increasingly large proportion of all U.S. AIDS cases. Overall, African American men and women are vastly overrepresented among people newly diagnosed with AIDS. See the box "HIV/AIDS Among African Americans and Latinos" on page 555 for more on these trends.

Another group of people at increased risk for HIV infection are young men who have sex with men. HIV infection has increased in recent years among this group, primarily because more young men are engaging in unsafe sexual practices such as unprotected anal intercourse. There are probably several factors underlying this trend. Young gay men are less likely than older men to have experienced watching friends die from AIDS and thus are more removed from the reality of the disease. They may be less afraid of acquiring HIV because of advances in treatment and a false belief that a cure is just around the corner. Drug use, especially use of crystal methamphetamine or club drugs, and the practice of meeting sex partners over the Internet are also associated with increased rates of unsafe sex and HIV infection among men who have sex with men.

There also appears to be a growing number of cases among men who acquire HIV through sex with other men but who do not identify themselves as gay. Particularly among minorities, many men who have sex with men also have sex with women, and they identify themselves as heterosexual, not gay or bisexual. Men who have sex with men and still identify themselves as heterosexual are just as likely to be infected with HIV as are gay and bisexual men who are out, but they are much less likely to know their HIV status and so may be more likely to transmit HIV to a male or female partner. Public health efforts directed toward gay men may not reach men in this group, and negative cultural attitudes toward homosexuality may make it difficult for gay and bisexual men to be

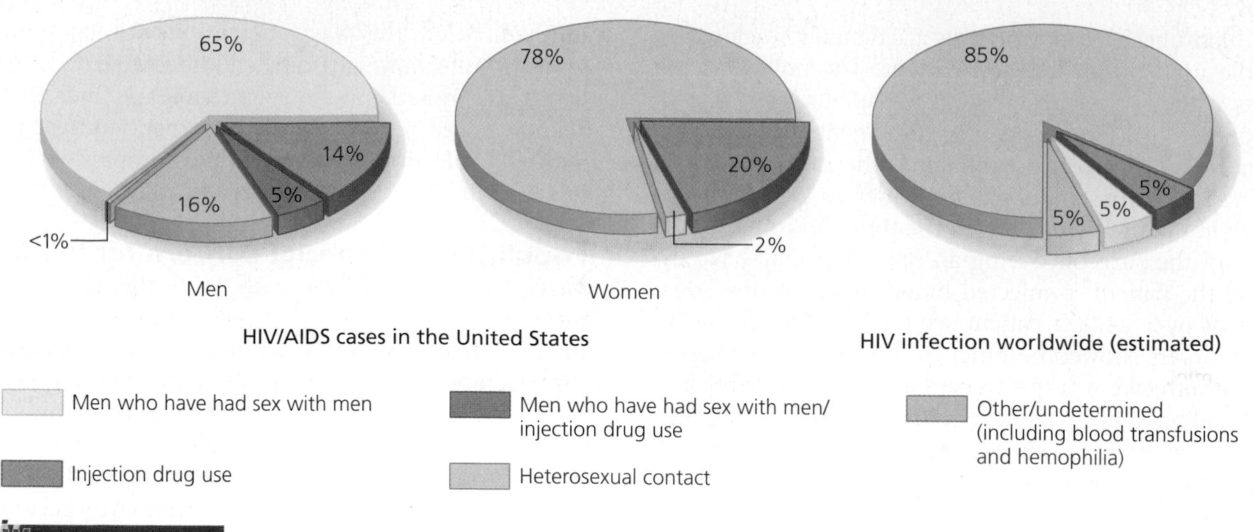

VITAL STATISTICS

Figure 18-2 Routes of HIV transmission among adults. SOURCES: Centers for Disease Control and Prevention. 2006. *HIV/AIDS Surveillance Report* 17; Joint United Nations Programme on HIV/AIDS (UNAIDS). 2006. AIDS *Epidemic Update, December 2006.* Geneva: UNAIDS; World Health Organization. 2001. Global AIDS surveillance. *Weekly Epidemiological Record* 76(50): 389–400; Centers for Disease Control and Prevention. 2006. *A Glance at the HIV AIDS Epidemic* (http://www.cdc.gov/hiv/resources/factsheets/at-a-glance.htm; retrieved September 7, 2006).

honest with their partners. This trend endangers not only the men but also their male and female partners.

These patterns of HIV infection reflect complex social, economic, and behavioral factors. Reducing the rates of HIV transmission and AIDS death in minorities, women, and other groups at risk will require dealing with the difficult problems of drug abuse, poverty, and discrimination. HIV prevention programs must be tailored to meet the special needs of minority communities.

Increased testing is one of the most important aspects of HIV prevention, but knowledge of HIV status may not be enough to change behavior. Studies show that up to one-third of people who have been diagnosed with HIV continue to have unprotected sex. Testing must be coupled with strategies not only to encourage HIV-positive people to take the steps necessary to avoid infecting others but also to encourage HIV-negative people to consistently practice safer sex.

Symptoms of HIV Infection Within a few days or weeks of infection with HIV, about half of people will develop symptoms of primary HIV infection. These can include fever, fatigue, rashes, headache, swollen lymph nodes, body aches, night sweats, sore throat, nausea, and diarrhea. Because the symptoms of primary HIV infection are similar to those of many common viral illnesses, the condition often goes undiagnosed, even if an infected individual sees a physician.

Term

HIV RNA assay A test used to determine the viral load (the amount of HIV in the blood).

Diagnosis of HIV at this very early stage of infection, although uncommon, is extremely beneficial. Immediate treatment is sometimes given to help preserve immune function, slow the progress of the disease, and reduce transmission of HIV to others. Studies are under way to evaluate the potential benefits and risks of starting treatment during primary HIV infection. It is critical for people who have engaged in behavior that places them at risk for HIV infection and who then experience symptoms of primary HIV infection to immediately inform their physician of their risk status. Standard tests for HIV will usually be negative in the very early stages of infection, so specialized tests such as the **HIV RNA assay,** which directly measures the amount of virus in the body, must be used.

Other than the initial flulike symptoms associated with primary HIV infection, most people in the first months or years of HIV infection have few if any symptoms. As the immune system weakens, however, a variety of symptoms can develop—persistent swollen lymph nodes; lumps, rashes, sores, or other growths on or under the skin or on the mucous membranes of the eyes, mouth, anus, or nasal passages; persistent yeast infections; unexplained weight loss; fever and drenching night sweats; dry cough and shortness of breath; persistent diarrhea; easy bruising and unexplained bleeding; profound fatigue; memory loss; difficulty with balance; tremors or seizures; changes in vision, hearing, taste, or smell; difficulty in swallowing; changes in mood and other psychological symptoms; and persistent or recurrent pain. Obviously, many of these symptoms can also occur with a variety of other illnesses.

Because the immune system is weakened, people with HIV infection are highly susceptible to infections, both common and uncommon. The infection most often seen

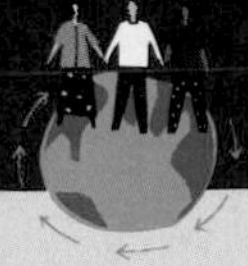

HIV/AIDS Among African Americans and Latinos

African Americans and Latinos have been disproportionately affected by HIV/AIDS since the start of the epidemic, and the disparity has grown over time.

- African Americans represent 12.6% of the U.S. population but account for more than 40% of all AIDS cases diagnosed since the start of the epidemic and 50% of new cases diagnosed in 2005 (see figure).
- Latinos represent 13.2% of the U.S. population but account for about 20% of all AIDS cases and about 19% of new cases.
- AIDS is the second leading cause of death among African Americans age 35–44; it is the sixth leading cause among Latinos and whites in the same age group. HIV/AIDS is now the leading cause of death in African American women age 25–34. AIDS deaths have declined among most groups of Americans since 1996. Among African Americans, the decline in AIDS deaths was smaller than among whites and has now leveled off. AIDS deaths among Latinos increased between 1999 and 2003; Latinos were the only group to experience an increase during this period.
- Among girls and women living with AIDS at the end of 2005, 62% were African American, compared with 19% who were white and 17% who were Latina.
- Among teens (age 13–19), African Americans represent 15% of the total population but account for about 65% of newly diagnosed AIDS cases.
- Among AIDS cases diagnosed in men, a greater proportion of cases among African Americans and Latinos are due to heterosexual sex and injection drug use compared with white men. However, the most common means of HIV transmission among men from all groups is sex with other men.

New U.S. AIDS cases, 2005
U.S. Population
100
90
80
70
60
50
40
30
20
10
0
49.8%
African Americans
12.6%
68.3%
28.7%
Whites
19.0%
Latinos
13.2%
.01%
Asian/Pacific Islanders
4.8%
.004%
American Indians/ Alaska Natives
1.2%

Distribution of U.S. AIDS cases by ethnicity compared to the ethnic distribution of the U.S. population.

What are some of the factors contributing to disparities in HIV incidence?

- *Poverty, drug use, and associated problems:* Low income is linked to lack of information about safer sex and HIV testing and treatment, higher rates of injection drug use, and lack of access to health care. Women who are poor and unemployed are more likely to be financially dependent on a male partner and less likely to use condoms; they are more likely to trade sex for money or drugs. Higher rates of incarceration among minorities also contribute to the spread of HIV. Overall, HIV prevention is likely to be a lower priority among people of low income because they are dealing with many immediate problems.
- *Distrust of physicians and public health campaigns:* Surveys suggest that a substantial proportion of blacks believe that HIV information is being withheld from the public and that a cure exists but is being withheld from the poor. These types of beliefs may deter some people from using condoms; they also highlight the need to tailor HIV prevention programs for different groups.
- *Social patterns and perception of risk:* High prevalence of infection in a group, combined with a low perception of risk, contributes to the spread of HIV as people are more likely to encounter an infected sex partner if they choose partners from a group with a high prevalence.

A recent study of young African American men who have sex with men found that despite high rates of risky behavior, most did not perceive themselves at risk for HIV infection and many thought that HIV status could be determined from someone's appearance or whether they identify themselves as straight or gay. Many of the men in this study did not identify as gay and/or were not open about their sexual identity, and nearly 20% had had recent female sex partners. It is unclear how large a role this pattern plays in the transmission of the virus, but it is a risky pattern for the men and their male and female sexual partners.

New approaches to prevention and treatment will likely be needed to combat the high incidence of HIV/AIDS among African Americans and Latinos. HIV prevention messages need to communicate effectively with the populations most at risk. Programs stressing ethnic and gender pride have been found effective for some groups. To overcome conspiracy beliefs, researchers recommend acknowledging the origin of such beliefs in the context of current and historical discrimination. For those who are already HIV-positive, resources such as peer networks, legal assistance, and on-site child care at clinics may help improve treatment access and success.

The Department of Health and Human Services' Minority HIV/AIDS Initiative Web site (www.hiv.omhrc.gov) has information about HIV/AIDS among minority populations and extensive links to relevant organizations.

SOURCES: Centers for Disease Control and Prevention. 2006. *HIV/AIDS Surveillance Report, 2005* 17. Atlanta: U.S. Department of Health and Human Services; Centers for Disease Control and Prevention. 2005. HIV transmission among black women—North Carolina, 2004. *Morbidity and Mortality Weekly Report* 54(4): 89–94; Kaiser Family Foundation. 2005. *Policy Fact Sheet: African Americans and HIV/AIDS*. Menlo Park, Calif.: Kaiser Family Foundation; Bogart, L. M., and S. Thorburn. 2005. Are HIV/AIDS conspiracy beliefs a barrier to HIV prevention among African Americans? *Journal of Acquired Immune Deficiency Syndromes* 38(2): 213–218; Centers for Disease Control and Prevention. 2004. HIV transmission among black college student and non-student men who have sex with men—North Carolina, 2003. *Morbidity and Mortality Weekly Report* 53(32): 731–734; Centers for Disease Control and Prevention. 2004. *HIV/AIDS Surveillance Report* 15.

in the United States among people with HIV is ***Pneumocystis carinii* pneumonia**, a protozoal infection. **Kaposi's sarcoma**, a previously rare form of cancer, is common in HIV-infected men. Women with HIV infection often have frequent and difficult-to-treat vaginal yeast infections. Cases of tuberculosis (TB) are increasingly being reported in people with HIV, and the CDC recommends TB testing for anyone with HIV infection.

Diagnosing HIV Infection The most common tests for HIV check for the presence of antibodies to the virus. HIV infection primarily disrupts T-cell immunity; B cells are still able to produce antibodies to HIV, which will show up in tests. Unfortunately, these antibodies do not protect against the spread of the virus. For most other diseases, the presence of an antibody to a particular pathogen may indicate protective immunity. In the case of HIV, however, the presence of the antibody indicates an active case of the disease. **HIV antibody tests** are used for screening because they are accurate and relatively inexpensive. Standard testing involves an initial test called an **ELISA;** if it is positive, a second test called a **Western blot** is done to confirm the results (see the box "Getting an HIV Test").

Not everyone with HIV infection will test positive on antibody tests, however. Antibodies may not appear in the blood for weeks or months after infection, so people who are newly infected are likely to have a negative antibody test. The infection can be detected with a more expensive test that directly measures the presence of the virus, such as an HIV RNA test. The reverse situation is seen in babies born to HIV-infected mothers: They may carry HIV antibodies, passed from their mother, without being infected with HIV. Antibodies can pass through the placenta to a fetus, but in the majority of cases, even without treatment, an infant does not acquire HIV. Thus, an infant may test positive on an HIV antibody test but actually be uninfected. Further tests such as the HIV RNA assay must be done to determine if an infant is actually infected.

If a person is diagnosed as **HIV-positive**, the next step is to determine the current severity of the disease in order to plan appropriate treatment. The status of the immune system can be gauged by taking CD4 T-cell measurements every few months. The infection itself can be monitored by tracking the viral load (the amount of virus in the body) through HIV RNA assay. Keeping track of viral load changes helps physicians evaluate the effects of treatment and can also help predict the likelihood of long-term survival in a person infected with HIV.

A 2004 survey of Americans indicates that nearly half of adults in the United States have been tested for HIV. Among those who have never been tested, nearly three-fourths say that they haven't been tested because they don't think they are at risk. Many people are not aware that rapid HIV tests, home tests, and tests that do not require a blood sample are now available. Rapid (same-day) HIV tests are effective. As of June 2006, the CDC had given out 800,000 rapid HIV tests; nearly half of those tests had been used, identifying more than 4500 cases of HIV infection.

A new diagnostic test that may help guide treatment decisions is called HIV Replication Capacity. This test shows how fast HIV from a patient's blood sample can reproduce itself. It is a measure of viral fitness and may be helpful when used in conjunction with CD4 and viral load tests in predicting how quickly a given person may progress to more serious disease.

Rather than testing only at-risk individuals, the CDC now recommends universal HIV testing as part of routine medical care for everyone aged 13–64. The CDC hopes that routine HIV testing at least once will increase the odds that people with HIV are diagnosed earlier. Early detection is important to minimizing the disease's effects and reducing the risks to others.

Diagnosing AIDS AIDS is the most severe form of HIV infection. The CDC's criteria for a diagnosis of AIDS reflect the stage of HIV infection at which a person's immune system becomes dangerously compromised. Since January 1993, a diagnosis of AIDS has been made if a person is HIV-positive and either has developed an infection defined as an AIDS indicator or has a severely damaged immune system (as measured by CD4 T-cell counts).

Reporting All diagnosed cases of AIDS must be reported to public health authorities. Before effective treatments for HIV infection were available, officials could use AIDS statistics to track the epidemic because nearly everyone with HIV developed AIDS within a fairly predictable time frame. However, the advent of more effective treatments has lengthened the time between infection and the onset of full-blown AIDS for many patients, making it more difficult to track the U.S. epidemic based on AIDS statistics alone. For this reason, the CDC recom-

Terms

VW

***Pneumocystis carinii* pneumonia** A protozoal infection that is common in people infected with HIV.

Kaposi's sarcoma A form of cancer characterized by purple or brownish lesions that are generally painless and occur anywhere on the skin; usually appears in men infected with HIV.

HIV antibody test A blood test to determine whether a person has been infected by HIV; becomes positive within weeks or months of exposure.

ELISA (enzyme-linked immunosorbent assay) A blood test that detects the presence of antibodies to HIV.

Western blot A blood test that detects the presence of HIV antibodies; a more accurate and more expensive test used to confirm positive results from an ELISA test.

HIV-positive A diagnosis resulting from the presence of HIV in the bloodstream; also referred to as *seropositive.*

seroconversion The appearance of antibodies to HIV in the blood of an infected person; usually occurs 1–6 months after infection.

Critical Consumer

Getting an HIV Test

VW

The CDC now recommends that all people aged 13–64 be tested for HIV at least once as part of routine medical care. The hope is that routine testing will increase the number of infections diagnosed early, minimizing the disease's effects and reducing the risks to others. You should strongly consider being tested if any of the following apply to you or any past or current sexual partners:

- You have had unprotected sex (vaginal, anal, or oral) with more than one partner or with a partner who was not in a mutually monogamous relationship with you.
- You have used or shared needles, syringes, or other paraphernalia for injecting drugs (including steroids).
- You received a transfusion of blood or blood products between 1978 and 1985.
- You have been diagnosed with an STD.

Testing Options

If you decide to get an HIV test, you can either visit a physician or health clinic or take a home test. A big advantage to having the test performed by a physician or clinician is that you will get one-on-one counseling about the test, your results, and ways to avoid future infection or spreading the disease. If you have good reason to think you may test positive, it is probably best to be tested by a physician or clinic, where follow-up counseling and medical care will be intensive. The home test is a good alternative for people at low risk who just want to be sure.

Physician or Clinic Testing

Your physician, student health clinic, Planned Parenthood, public health department, or local AIDS association can arrange your HIV test. It usually costs \$50–\$100, but public clinics often charge little or nothing. The standard test involves drawing a sample of blood that is sent to a laboratory for analysis for the presence of antibodies; if the first stage of testing is positive, a confirmatory test is done. This standard test takes 1–2 weeks, and you'll be asked to phone or come in personally to obtain your results, which should also include appropriate counseling.

Alternative tests are available at some clinics. The Orasure test uses oral fluid, which is collected by placing a treated cotton pad in the mouth; urine tests are also available. Oral fluid and urine tests may be helpful for people who avoid blood tests due to fear of needles; they also protect health care workers from needlestick exposure to potentially infected blood. If you suspect you have been recently exposed to HIV and might have primary infection, see your physician and ask about an HIV RNA test.

New rapid tests are now also available at some locations. These tests involve the use of blood or oral fluid and can provide results in as little as 20 minutes. If a rapid test is positive for HIV infection, a confirmatory test will be performed.

Before you get an HIV test, be sure you understand what will be done with the results. Results from confidential tests may still become part of your medical record and/or be reported (with your name or some other identifier) to state and federal public health agencies. If you decide you want to be tested anonymously—in which case the results will not be reported to anyone but yourself—check with your physician or counselor about how to obtain an anonymous test or use a home test.

Home Testing

Home test kits for HIV are now available; they cost about \$40–70. (Take care to avoid testing kits that are not FDA-approved; many such unapproved kits are being sold over the Internet.) To use a home test, you prick a finger with a supplied lancet, blot a few drops of blood onto blotting paper, and mail it to the company's laboratory. In about a week, you call a toll-free number to find out your results. Anyone testing positive is routed to a trained counselor, who can provide emotional and medical support. The results of home test kits are completely anonymous.

Understanding the Results

A negative test result means that no antibodies were found in your sample. However, it usually takes at least a month (and possibly as long as 6 months in some people) after exposure to HIV for antibodies to appear, a process called **seroconversion.** Therefore, an infected person may get a false-negative result. If you think you've been exposed to HIV, get a test immediately; if it's negative but your risk of infection is high, ask about obtaining an HIV RNA assay, which allows very early diagnosis, and about the appropriateness of retesting in a few months. If you test negative, you'll also receive information about how to avoid infection.

A positive result means that you are infected. It is important to seek medical care and counseling immediately. You need to know more about your medical options; the possible psychological, social, and financial repercussions; and how to avoid spreading the disease. Rapid progress is being made in treating HIV, and treatments are potentially much more successful when begun early.

For more information about HIV testing and a national directory of testing sites, visit the CDC National HIV Testing Resources site (www.hivtest.org).

mended in 1999 that states require reporting of both HIV infection and AIDS.

Despite efforts to safeguard confidentiality and prohibit discrimination, mandatory reporting of HIV infection remains controversial. If people believe they are risking their jobs, friends, or social acceptability, they may be less likely to be tested. At the same time, it is essential that enough information be disclosed to monitor the epidemic. The CDC recommends that states continue to provide opportunities for people to be tested anonymously; home HIV tests also allow anonymous testing.

Treatment Although there is no known cure for HIV infection, medications can significantly alter the course of

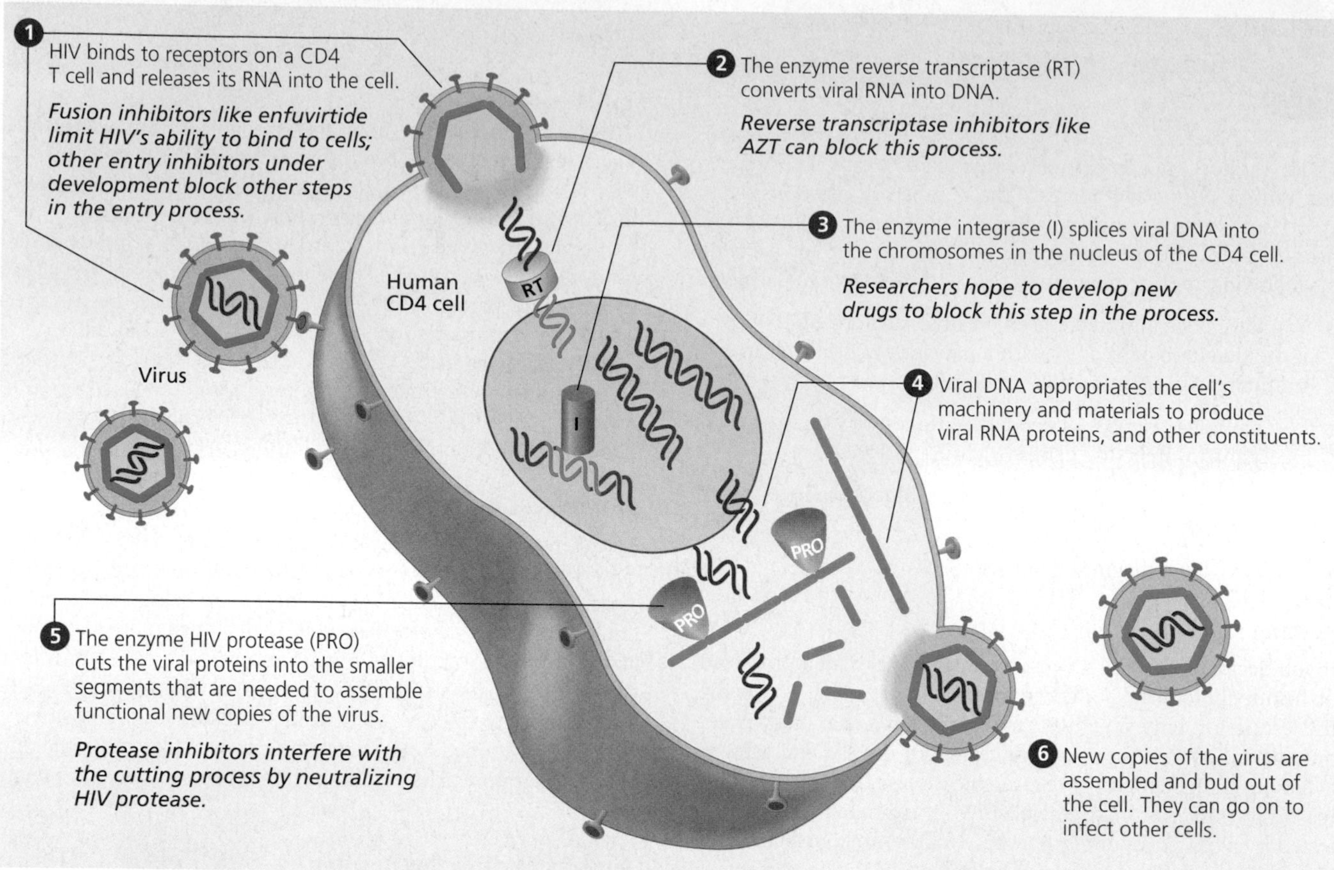

1 HIV binds to receptors on a CD4 T cell and releases its RNA into the cell.
Fusion inhibitors like enfuvirtide limit HIV's ability to bind to cells; other entry inhibitors under development block other steps in the entry process.
2 The enzyme reverse transcriptase (RT) converts viral RNA into DNA.
Reverse transcriptase inhibitors like AZT can block this process.
3 The enzyme integrase (I) splices viral DNA into the chromosomes in the nucleus of the CD4 cell.
Researchers hope to develop new drugs to block this step in the process.
Human CD4 cell
RT
I
Virus
4 Viral DNA appropriates the cell's machinery and materials to produce viral RNA proteins, and other constituents.
PRO
5 The enzyme HIV protease (PRO) cuts the viral proteins into the smaller segments that are needed to assemble functional new copies of the virus.
Protease inhibitors interfere with the cutting process by neutralizing HIV protease.
6 New copies of the virus are assembled and bud out of the cell. They can go on to infect other cells.

Figure 18-3 The life cycle of HIV: How antiviral drugs work. Different classes of drugs block the replication of HIV at different points in the virus's life cycle. SOURCES: A virus in action. 2001. *Scientific American,* November; Dickinson, G., et al. 1998. The latest recommendations for antiretroviral therapy. *Patient Care,* 15 August.

the disease and extend life. The drop in the number of U.S. AIDS deaths that has occurred since 1996 is in large part due to the increasing use of combinations of new drugs. However, this progress is irrelevant to the vast majority of AIDS sufferers, who can't afford treatment.

ANTIVIRAL DRUGS Antiviral drugs in current use to combat HIV fall into several categories based on how they block HIV replication. One category is **reverse transcriptase inhibitors,** which include the widely used drug zidovudine (AZT). These drugs work by inhibiting the enzyme reverse transcriptase, which is used by HIV to integrate its genetic material into human cells (Figure 18-3). Another category of antivirals is the **protease inhibitors;** these target the enzyme HIV protease, which is used by the virus to create a protein coat for each new copy of the virus. In 2003, the FDA approved enfuvirtide (Fuzeon), the first available medication from a category of drugs known as **fusion inhibitors;** these drugs inhibit the fusion of viral and cell membranes and can block HIV from entering and infecting cells. Treatment with combinations of drugs, referred to as highly active antiretroviral therapy, or HAART, can reduce HIV in the blood to undetectable levels in some people. However, research indicates that latent virus is still present in the body and that HIV-infected men on HAART carry potentially transmissible HIV in their semen.

Other antiviral drugs are under development, including entry inhibitors targeting the CCR-5 receptor, one of several receptors on human CD4 cells that interact with HIV and serve as doors through which the virus enters the cell. People with a specific genetic mutation have fewer than normal CCR-5 receptors. Because of this, these individuals are less likely than average to become infected with HIV, and if they do become infected, they tend to stay healthy much longer. Researchers are developing drugs that block the CCR-5 receptor as well as other cell entry components. (However, new findings show that people who lack the CCR-5 may be at higher risk of catching West Nile virus. As scientists develop new drugs, they must carefully navigate such gene-based conflicts.) Other expected treatment advances include drugs that stop HIV from integrating its genetic material into human DNA, drugs that inhibit the final step of viral processing (called maturation inhibitors), and improved versions of current drugs.

HIV/AIDS treatment is becoming increasingly complex—not only because the virus can mutate and behave unpredictably, but because so many treatment options are available. There are now nearly 30 drugs approved specifically for use against HIV/AIDS, and many others are being developed. One way to simplify treatment is by combining medicines. For example, in June 2006, the FDA approved Atripla, the first once-a-day tablet for HIV patients; Atripla combines three medicines into one and is highly effective.

New findings that may someday influence HIV prevention and treatment include the discovery that a person infected with both HIV and the virus GBV-C is more likely to do well than someone who is infected with only HIV. This may be because GBV-C somehow blocks HIV entry into CD4 cells. This information may prove useful in developing a vaccine or new treatments for HIV infection. An intriguing recent study found that Trim5-alpha, a protein produced by nonhuman primates, can block cell entry of HIV and may explain why these animals do not become infected with HIV. Future research may use this protein for drugs that prevent or treat HIV.

POSTEXPOSURE PROPHYLAXIS (PEP) Antiviral medications are being used in some cases in an attempt to prevent infection in people who have been exposed to HIV. The CDC has long recommended that health care workers who have significant exposure to HIV-infected blood or body fluids via a needle stick or other mishap consider starting antiviral medication as soon as possible (preferably within a few hours of exposure) to decrease the risk of infection. PEP is also often recommended for victims of sexual assault. In 2005, the CDC for the first time recommended PEP for people who are at risk for HIV infection from recent nonoccupational exposure to blood, genital secretions, or other potentially infectious body fluids of a person known to have HIV. Nonoccupational exposure refers to situations such as unprotected sex or contact with a contaminated needle. PEP consists of 28 days of HAART, which should begin as soon as possible after exposure, but always within 72 hours.

TREATMENTS FOR OPPORTUNISTIC INFECTIONS In addition to antiviral drugs, most patients with low CD4 T-cell counts also take a variety of antibiotics to help prevent opportunistic infections such as *Pneumocystis carinii* pneumonia and tuberculosis. A person with advanced HIV infection may need to take 20 or more pills every day. Medication side effects can become severe when so many drugs are used in combination.

HIV AND PREGNANCY Early-stage HIV infection does not appear to significantly affect a woman's chance of becoming pregnant. Without treatment, 25–30% of infants born to HIV-infected women are themselves infected with the virus. The risk of an infected mother transmitting HIV to her baby can be reduced to less than 2% by treating the mother during her pregnancy and labor, giving the baby antiretroviral drugs during the first weeks of life, avoiding breastfeeding, and delivering the baby by cesarean section if necessary. Cesarean delivery can lower the risk of infection in women who have high blood levels of HIV; women who have undergone antiviral treatment and have very low levels of HIV can usually deliver vaginally. HIV testing is strongly recommended for all pregnant women.

HIV-infected women are usually advised not to breastfeed, because this has been shown to transmit HIV. In developed countries, women infected with HIV generally have the support and resources to bottlefeed their infants. However, this is often not the case in developing countries: Infant formula is often unavailable and/or unaffordable, and many regions lack a supply of safe water with which to mix formula. In addition, bottlefeeding is socially unacceptable in some cultures and may be seen as a

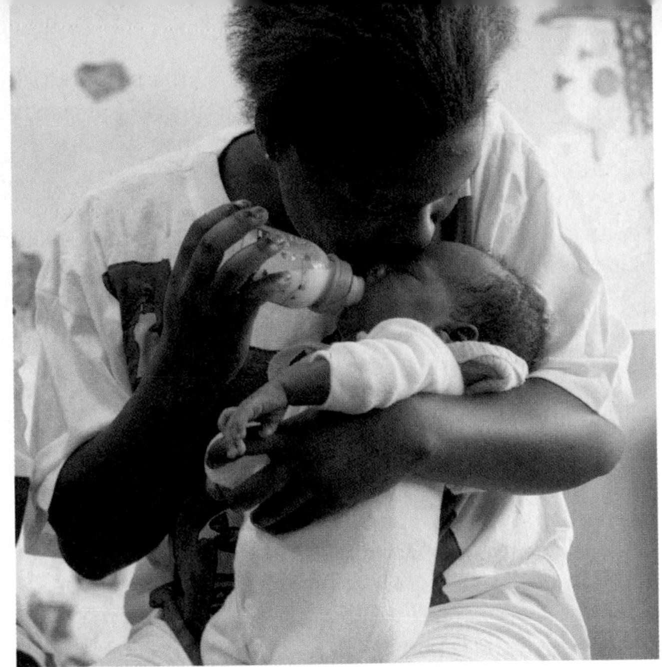

Early diagnosis and treatment of HIV infection are important for everyone, but particularly so for pregnant women. Currently available treatments can significantly increase the chance that this baby, born to an HIV-infected mother, will be free of the virus.

Terms

reverse transcriptase inhibitor An antiviral drug used to treat HIV infection that works by inhibiting reverse transcriptase, the enzyme that converts viral RNA to DNA.

protease inhibitor A drug that inhibits the action of any of the protein-splitting enzymes known as proteases. Protease inhibitors have been developed to block the action of HIV protease and thus prevent the replication of HIV.

fusion inhibitor An antiviral drug that blocks the entry of HIV into cells by inhibiting the fusion of viral and cell membranes; part of a broader class of drugs known as *entry inhibitors*.

sign that the mother has AIDS. Many infants in Africa whose mothers do receive treatment during pregnancy and delivery are born uninfected but then acquire the infection later, through breastfeeding.

Testing and the use of antiviral drugs by pregnant HIV-positive women has had a dramatic effect in the United States. Unfortunately, long-term combination antiviral therapy is very expensive and is out of reach for most of the world's HIV-positive women. As newer and less expensive drugs against HIV become available, there is hope that more pregnant women and infants will be treated, resulting in lower vertical transmission rates worldwide. Currently, some resource-poor nations are reducing the spread of HIV to infants by giving a single dose of a relatively inexpensive antiretroviral drug to mother and newborn. Although not as effective as more extensive treatment, this is a major advance in HIV prevention for many developing countries.

TREATMENT CHALLENGES The cost of treatment for HIV continues to be an area of major concern. A recent study revealed an average cost of $14,000–35,000 per year to treat an HIV-infected person in the United States. These costs are tremendous even for relatively wealthy countries. But 95% of people with HIV infection live in developing countries, where these treatments are unlikely to be available to anyone except the wealthiest few. The average per-person health expenditure in many developing countries is only about $10 per year. Pharmaceutical companies and the World Bank are working to develop combination pills and to lower drug costs in developing regions, and international aid is gradually increasing; however, it is still not nearly enough to counteract the devastating impact of AIDS on these countries.

Toxicity of antiretroviral drugs is another concern. Long-term use of HAART can cause a number of serious effects, including bone loss and dangerously high levels of cholesterol. For this reason, the National Institutes of Health issued new HIV treatment guidelines in 2001 that recommend that asymptomatic patients hold off on treatment until they are at a more advanced stage of the disease. However, immediate treatment is still recommended for anyone who is experiencing symptoms. Treatment for primary stage (very recent) infection remains controversial.

Even for those who have access to the drugs and can tolerate the side effects, treatment is difficult. The drug combinations often require people to take many pills every day at precise times. The once-a-day tablet Atripla and others like it in development will potentially improve patients' ability to adhere to treatment regimens. Some people cannot tolerate the toxic side effects of these powerful drugs, and the drugs are much more effective for some people than for others. Currently available antiviral drugs do not appear able to completely eliminate the virus from the body, even if viral levels in the blood become undetectable. The optimal duration of drug therapy is not currently known, but many scientists feel that lifelong drug therapy will be necessary. It is also unclear to what degree a damaged immune system can rebound from the effects of long-term HIV infection even if the virus is brought under control with antiviral medication.

What About a Vaccine? If an effective, safe, affordable vaccine against HIV could be developed, it might be possible to stop the worldwide HIV epidemic. Unfortunately, making a vaccine against HIV is proving to be exceedingly difficult. Methods that have been used to produce vaccines against other diseases are often ineffective or unsafe when used against HIV. Adding to the challenge is the fact that HIV comes in numerous subtypes, mutates rapidly, and destroys the very cells that normally protect the body against infectious diseases. Vaccines are currently being tested in humans, but no vaccine is likely to be ready for widespread use within the next 5 years. Vaccines are also being tested as therapy for people already infected with HIV.

Researchers are making relatively rapid progress in producing a **microbicide** that could be used to prevent HIV and other STDs. A microbicide in the form of a cream, gel, sponge, or suppository that could be inserted into the vagina or rectum could function as a kind of chemical condom. Researchers are hoping to develop a product that kills HIV and other STD organisms, is pleasant and easy to use, and can also protect against pregnancy. A microbicide could fill the urgent need for a prevention method that can be used by a woman without requiring cooperation from her partner. Several microbicides are currently undergoing human testing for safety and effectiveness.

The female condom may someday play a larger role in HIV prevention. Female condoms are more expensive than male condoms and aren't widely available in developing countries, but they offer the advantage that women can initiate their use. Scientists are developing a cheaper, easier-to-use female condom and are evaluating whether diaphragms (in combination with microbicides) protect against HIV.

Another approach is the use of preexposure treatment as prevention. HIV-negative individuals at high risk for infection would take an anti-HIV medication prior to an activity that might expose them to HIV. This approach is controversial but might be effective in stopping the spread of HIV in highly vulnerable populations such as sex workers. Unlike a vaccine, this form of prevention could be tested and put into practice in a relatively short period of time, especially if an existing HIV drug is used.

How Can You Protect Yourself? Although AIDS is currently incurable, it is preventable. You can protect yourself by avoiding behaviors that may bring you into

Term

Ww

microbicide An agent that destroys microorganisms; also known as an antiseptic.

contact with HIV. This means making careful choices about sexual activity and not sharing needles if you inject drugs.

MAKE CAREFUL CHOICES ABOUT SEXUAL ACTIVITY In a sexual relationship, the current and past behaviors of you and your partner determine the amount of risk involved. If you are uninfected and in a mutually monogamous relationship with another uninfected person, you are not at risk for HIV. Of course, it is often hard to know for sure whether your partner is completely faithful and is truly uninfected. Having a series of monogamous relationships is not a safe prevention strategy.

For anyone not involved in a long-term, mutually monogamous relationship, abstinence from any sexual activity that involves the exchange of body fluids is the only sure way to prevent HIV infection (Figure 18-4). Safer sex includes many activities that carry virtually no risk of HIV infection, such as hugging, massaging, closed-lip kissing, rubbing clothed bodies together, kissing your partner's skin, and mutual masturbation.

Anal and vaginal intercourse are the sexual activities associated with the highest risk of HIV infection. If you have intercourse, always use a condom. Use of a lubricated condom reduces the risk of transmitting HIV during all forms of intercourse. Condoms are not perfect, and they do not provide risk-free sex; however, used properly, a condom provides a high level of protection against HIV. One study of 124 couples in which one partner was infected showed that with consistent condom use, none of the uninfected partners acquired the virus during the 20-month study period. Condoms should also be worn during oral sex. Most condoms are made of latex. If you or your partner is allergic to latex, polyurethane condoms are a good substitute. Do not use natural condoms (made from lamb membranes) because pores in this material can allow STD organisms to pass through.

Remember that you should avoid using nonoxynol-9 lubricants because of the risk of tissue irritation, which can make HIV and STD transmission more likely. It is especially important to not use condoms and lubricants that contain N-9 for anal sex; rectal tissues are thin and delicate and are more prone to irritation and tearing than is vaginal tissue. Experts also suggest the use of latex squares and dental dams, rubber devices that can be used as barriers during oral-genital or oral-anal sexual contact.

Limiting the number of partners you have—particularly those who have engaged in risky sexual behaviors in the past—can also lower your risk of exposure to HIV. Take the time to talk with a potential new partner about HIV and safer sex. Talking about sex may seem embarrassing and uncomfortable, but good communication is critical for your health. Asking a partner about past sexual experiences can also be helpful, but you cannot always depend on that information. Recent surveys of HIV-positive people found that about one-third failed to reveal their HIV status to sexual partners; of these, nearly two-thirds failed to always use a condom. Take precautions with every partner. Don't agree to have intercourse or give up precautions as a way to show your love or commitment to a relationship. Your specific sexual practices can be just as important as the number of partners you have.

Removing alcohol and other drugs from sexual activity is another crucial component of safer sex. The use of alcohol and mood-altering drugs may lower inhibitions and affect judgment, making you more likely to engage in unsafe sex. The use of drugs is also associated with sexual activity with multiple partners. Some experts attribute much of the recent increase in rates of syphilis and HIV infection among U.S. gay and bisexual men to the nonmedical use of anti-impotence drugs such as Viagra in combination with crystal methamphetamine. This combination of drugs impairs judgment, increases sexual drive, and allows men to perform

High Risk

Unprotected anal sex is the riskiest sexual behavior, especially for the receptive partner.

Unprotected vaginal intercourse is the next riskiest, especially for women, who are much more likely to be infected by an infected male partner than vice versa.

Oral sex is probably considerably less risky than anal and vaginal intercourse but can still result in HIV transmission.

Sharing of sex toys can be risky because they can carry blood, semen, or vaginal fluid.

Use of a condom reduces risk considerably but not completely for any type of intercourse. Anal sex with a condom is riskier than vaginal sex with a condom; oral sex with a condom is less risky, especially if the man does not ejaculate.

Hand-genital contact and deep kissing are less risky but could still theoretically transmit HIV; the presence of cuts or sores increases risk.

Sex with only one uninfected and totally faithful partner is without risk, but effective only if both partners are uninfected and completely monogamous.

Activities that don't involve the exchange of body fluids carry no risk: hugging, massage, closed-mouth kissing, masturbation, phone sex, and fantasy.

Abstinence is completely without risk. For many people, it can be an effective and reasonable method of avoiding HIV infection and other STDs during certain periods of life.

No Risk

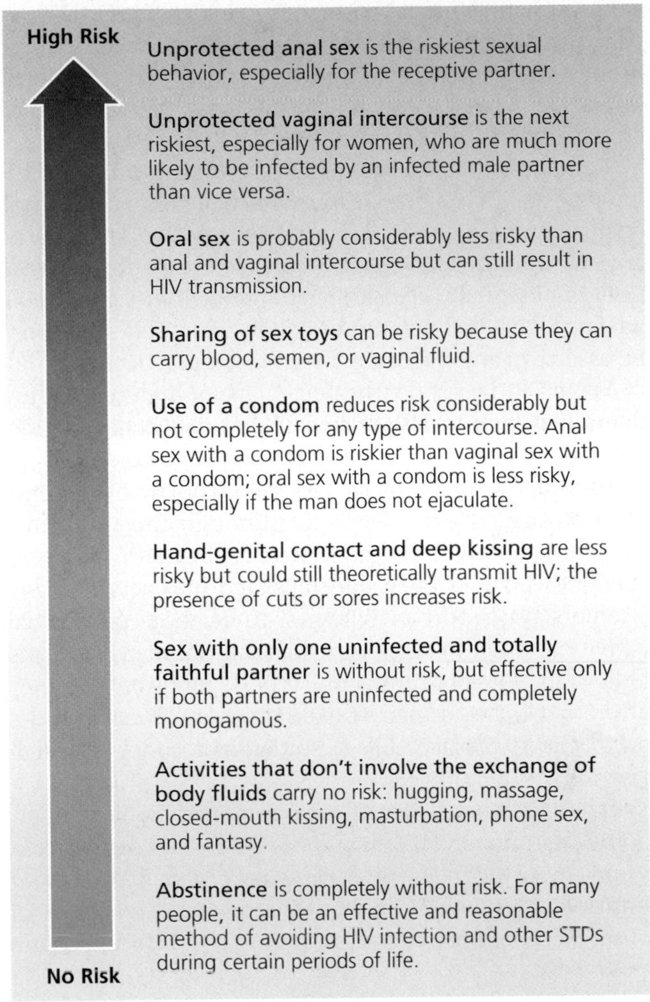

Figure 18-4 What's risky and what's not: The approximate relative risk of HIV transmission of various sexual activities. Safer sex strategies that reduce the risk of HIV infection will also help protect you against other STDs. The main point to remember is that any activity that involves contact with blood, semen, or vaginal fluid can transmit HIV.

sexually with multiple partners for many hours. Unprotected sex in association with abuse of these drugs is common, even among men who are normally more cautious. Studies show that men who use this drug combination are at very high risk for acquiring HIV and other STDs.

Remember, you can't tell if someone is infected by looking at him or her. Researchers believe that HIV has been in the United States since the mid- to late 1970s; anyone who has engaged in an unsafe behavior since that time is potentially at risk for HIV infection. Consider in advance what you will say and do in particular situations. Be assertive, and negotiate for safer sex practices.

From 1991 to 2005, the percentage of high school students engaging in HIV-related sexual risk behaviors decreased, but many still engage in such behaviors. Surveys of college students indicate that the majority of students are not engaging in safer sex. Although most students know that condom use can protect against HIV infection, this knowledge is often not translated into action. Many students also report a willingness to lie about past sexual activity in order to obtain sex. In addition, many students believe their risk of contracting HIV depends on who they are rather than on their sexual behavior. These attitudes and behaviors place college students at continued high risk for contracting HIV.

If you are sexually active, take responsibility for undergoing testing for HIV and other STDs at least once a year—more often if you have a new sexual partner or multiple partners. Prompt detection and treatment of other STDs can help decrease your risk of HIV infection.

DON'T SHARE DRUG NEEDLES People who inject drugs should avoid sharing needles, syringes, or anything that might have blood on it. Any injectable drug, legal or illegal, can be associated with HIV transmission. Needles can be decontaminated with a solution of bleach and water, but it is not a foolproof procedure, and HIV can survive in a syringe for a month or longer. (Boiling needles and syringes does not necessarily destroy HIV either.) As described in Chapter 9, obtaining sterile syringes through a syringe exchange program is much more effective than attempting to sterilize used syringes. Many prominent health organizations, including the United Nations AIDS Program and the American Medical Association, support syringe exchange programs, but these programs are unavailable and/or illegal in many parts of the world.

If you are an injection drug user, your best protection is to obtain treatment and refrain from using drugs.

PARTICIPATE IN AN HIV EDUCATION PROGRAM Many schools and colleges have peer education programs about preventing the transmission of HIV. These programs give you a chance to practice communicating with potential sex partners and negotiating safer sex, to engage in role playing to build self-confidence, and to learn how to use condoms. Studies show that educational programs in which students learn from their peers and then try out what they've learned through role playing are more likely to result in real behavior change.

Accurate information about HIV/AIDS, including where to go for testing and treatment, is available from many sources, including health professionals, community-based organizations, and national hotlines.

Many young people still believe that they are invulnerable to most kinds of harm and persist in thinking of themselves as not being at risk for HIV. The attitude of "It won't happen to me" is pervasive among high school and college students and is a major stumbling block to HIV/AIDS prevention. Until an effective vaccine and a cure are found, HIV infection will remain one of the biggest challenges of this generation. Education and individual responsibility can lead the way to controlling this devastating epidemic (see the box "Preventing HIV Infection and Other STDs").

Chlamydia

Chlamydia trachomatis causes **chlamydia,** the most prevalent bacterial STD in the United States. About 3 million new cases occur each year, down from a high of about 4 million; the drop is likely due to increased screening and treatment. An estimated 5–15% of all sexually active young American women are infected with chlamydia; rates among men are similar. The highest rates of infection occur in single people between ages 15 and 24. African American men and women have higher rates of infection than other groups for both chlamydia and gonorrhea. Up to 70% of people who are diagnosed with gonorrhea also have chlamydia. *C. trachomatis* can be transmitted by oral sex as well as by other forms of sexual intercourse.

Take Charge

Preventing HIV Infection and Other STDs

For those who don't have a long-term monogamous relationship with an uninfected partner, abstinence is the only truly safe option. Individuals should remember that it's OK to say no to sex and drugs.

Safer sexual activities that allow close person-to-person contact with almost no risk of contracting STDs or HIV include fantasy, hugging, massage, rubbing clothed bodies together, self-stimulation by both partners, and kissing with lips closed.

If you choose to be sexually active, talk with potential partners about HIV, safer sex, and the use of condoms before you begin a sexual relationship. The following behaviors will help lower your risk of exposure to HIV during sexual activities:

- Don't drink alcohol or use drugs in sexual situations. Mood-altering drugs can affect your judgment and make you more likely to engage in risky behaviors. Having sex when intoxicated significantly increases the risk of STDs.
- Limit the number of partners. Avoid sexual contact with people who have HIV or an STD or who have engaged in risky behaviors in the past, including unprotected sex and injection drug use.
- Use condoms during every act of intercourse and oral sex. Many STDs are not easy to diagnose in their asymptomatic stage, which can last for years, and asymptomatic individuals can still infect others. Even if your partner claims to have been tested for HIV and STDs, you have no guarantee that you will not contract an STD during any sexual encounter. If you choose to have intercourse, your best protection is to *always* use a condom. Condoms do not provide perfect protection, but they greatly reduce your risk of contracting an infection. Multiple studies show that regular condom use can reduce the risk of several diseases, including HIV, chlamydia, and genital herpes.
- Use condoms properly to obtain maximum protection (see Chapter 6). Use a water-based lubricant; don't use oil-based lubricants such as petroleum jelly or baby oil or any vaginal product containing mineral or vegetable oil. Avoid using lubricants or condoms containing nonoxynol-9, particularly for anal intercourse. Unroll condoms gently to avoid tearing them, and smooth out any air bubbles. If you accidentally put a condom on the wrong way, remove it and throw it away; do not flip it over and try again.
- Avoid sexual contact that could cause cuts or tears in the skin or tissue. Using extra lubricant (water-based) can help prevent damage to delicate tissues.
- Get periodic screening tests for STDs and HIV. Young women need yearly pelvic exams and Pap tests.
- Get vaccinated for hepatitis B.
- Get prompt treatment for any STDs you contract.

If you inject drugs of any kind, don't share needles, syringes, or anything that might have blood on it. If your community has a syringe exchange program, use it. Seek treatment; stop using injectable drugs.

If you are at risk for HIV infection, don't donate blood, sperm, or body organs. Don't have unprotected sex or share needles or syringes. Get tested for HIV soon, and get treated. HIV-infected people who get early treatment generally feel better and live longer than those who delay.

Both men and women are susceptible to chlamydia, but, as with most STDs, women bear the greater burden because of possible complications and consequences of the disease (see the box "Women Are Hit Hard by STDs"). In most women, chlamydia produces no early symptoms. If left untreated, it can lead to pelvic inflammatory disease (PID), a serious infection involving the oviducts (fallopian tubes) and uterus. PID, discussed later in this chapter, is a leading cause of infertility, and even an infection that produces no symptoms can cause significant scarring of the oviducts. Chlamydia also greatly increases a woman's risk for ectopic (tubal) pregnancy. Because rates of infection are high and most women with chlamydia have no symptoms, many physicians screen sexually active women at the time of their routine pelvic exam. The U.S. Preventive Services Task Force currently recommends routine screening for all sexually active women age 25 or younger and for older women who are at increased risk (such as those who have multiple sex partners).

Chlamydia can also lead to infertility in men, although not as often as in women. In men under age 35, chlamydia is the most common cause of **epididymitis**, inflammation of the sperm-carrying ducts. And up to half of all cases of **urethritis**, inflammation of the urethra, in men are caused by chlamydia. Despite these statistics, many infected men have no symptoms. Screening for chlamydia in heterosexual men currently is not routine, but some experts feel that screening young sexually active men in addition to young women would be effective in reducing chlamydia rates.

Infants of infected mothers can acquire the infection through contact with the pathogen in the birth canal

Terms

VW

chlamydia An STD transmitted by the pathogenic bacterium *Chlamydia trachomatis.*

epididymitis An inflammation of the small body of sperm-carrying ducts that rests on the testes.

urethritis Inflammation of the tube that carries urine from the bladder to the outside opening.

Gender Matters

Women Are Hit Hard by STDs

Sexually transmitted diseases cause suffering for all who are infected, but in many ways, women and girls are the hardest hit, for both biological and social reasons. Among Americans, 62% of all cases of adverse health problems from STDs occur in women. Worldwide, as many women as men now die from AIDS each year, and in the hardest-hit regions of Africa, nearly 60% of HIV-positive adults are women.

Male-to-female transmission of many infections is more likely to occur than female-to-male transmission. This is particularly true of HIV: Studies show that it is three to eight times easier for an HIV-positive man to transmit the virus to a woman than it is for an HIV-positive woman to infect a man.

Young women are even more vulnerable to STDs than older women because the less-mature cervix is more susceptible to injury and infection. As a woman ages, the type of cells at the opening of the cervix gradually changes so that the tissue becomes more resistant to infection. If an 18-year-old woman and a 30-year-old woman are exposed to the same pathogen, the younger woman is far more likely to develop a serious STD. Young women are also more vulnerable for social and emotional reasons: Lack of control in relationships, fear of discussing condom use, and having an older sex partner are all linked to increased STD risk.

Once infected, women tend to suffer more consequences of STDs than men. For example, gonorrhea and chlamydia can cause PID and permanent damage to the oviducts in women, but these infections tend to have less serious effects in men. HPV infection causes nearly all cases of cervical cancer. HPV infection is also associated with penile cancer in men, but penile cancer is much less common than cervical cancer. Women also have the added concern of the potential effects of STDs during pregnancy.

Between 1985 and 2004, the proportion of new U.S. AIDS cases in women increased from 7% to 27%. Women with HIV infection often face tremendous challenges when they are ill because they may be caring for family members who are also infected and ill. Many women are dealing with substance-abuse problems in themselves or in family members. In addition, women may become sicker at lower viral loads compared with men. Women and men with HIV do about equally well if they have similar access to treatment, but in many cases women are diagnosed later in the course of HIV infection, receive less treatment, and die sooner.

Worldwide, social and economic factors play a large role in the transmission and consequences of AIDS and other STDs for women. Violence against women is spreading AIDS, as are such practices as very early marriage for women, often to much older men who have had many sexual partners. For many women, being vulnerable to HIV can simply mean being married. Cultural gender norms that promote premarital and extramarital relationships for men, combined with women's lack of power to negotiate safer sex, make HIV a risk even for women who are married and monogamous. In addition, lack of education and limited economic opportunities can force women into commercial sex work, placing them at high risk for all STDs.

In some parts of the world, the stigma of AIDS hits women harder. Men with HIV are typically cared for by female family members, without being questioned about the source of their infection. Women, in contrast, may be accused of having had extramarital sex and receive less help and support. It is women who typically provide care to relatives with HIV as well as support the household financially when other earners are too ill to work. But if husbands die, women often do not inherit property and can be thrown deeper into poverty. Solutions to the STD crisis in women must include empowerment in the social sphere in addition to direct health care.

SOURCES: Ebrahim, S. H., M. T. McKenna, and J. S. Marks. 2005. Sexual behaviour: Related adverse health burden in the United States. *Sexually Transmitted Infection* 81(1): 38–40; Dunkle, K. M., et al. 2004. Gender-based violence, relationship power, and risk of HIV infection in women attending antenatal clinics in South Africa. *Lancet* 363(9419): 1415–1421; Joint United Nations Programme on HIV/AIDS. 2004. *AIDS Epidemic Update, December 2004*. Geneva: UNAIDS; World Health Organization. 2003. *Gender and HIV/AIDS*. Geneva: World Health Organization.

during delivery. Every year, over 150,000 newborns suffer from eye infections and pneumonia as a result of untreated maternal chlamydial infections.

Symptoms In men, chlamydia symptoms include painful urination, a slight watery discharge from the penis, and sometimes pain around the testicles. Although most women with chlamydia are asymptomatic, some notice increased vaginal discharge, burning with urination, pain or bleeding with intercourse, and lower abdominal pain. Less common symptoms in both men and women include arthritis, conjunctivitis, sore throat, and rectal inflammation and pain (in people who become infected during receptive anal intercourse). Symptoms in both men and women can begin within 5 days of infection. However, most people experience few or no symptoms, increasing the likelihood that they will inadvertently spread the infection to their partners.

Diagnosis Chlamydia is typically diagnosed through laboratory tests on a urine sample or a small amount of fluid from the urethra or cervix. The lab test may involve growing the organism in culture, using special dyes to detect bacterial proteins, or a process that quickly copies and detects genetic material from the bacteria. Testing pregnant women and treating those with chlamydia is a highly effective way to prevent infection of newborns. A home test is currently being studied.

Treatment Once chlamydia has been diagnosed, the infected person and his or her partner(s) are given antibiotics—usually doxycycline, erythromycin, or a newer drug, azithromycin, which can cure infection in one dose. Treatment of partners is important because people who have been treated for chlamydia are susceptible to getting the disease again if they have sexual contact with an infected person. The CDC now recommends that women who have been treated for chlamydia be retested 3–4 months after treatment is completed. In a 2006 study in New York City, one in eight women who had previously been diagnosed with chlamydia acquired a repeat infection within a year. A study in California yielded similar results. Both studies showed that younger women were more likely than older women to be reinfected by an untreated, infected partner.

Gonorrhea

In the United States, an estimated 700,000 new cases of **gonorrhea** are diagnosed every year. The highest incidence is among 15–24-year-olds. Like chlamydia, untreated gonorrhea can cause PID in women and urethritis and epididymitis in men. It can also cause arthritis, rashes, and eye infections, and it occasionally involves internal organs. Being infected with gonorrhea increases the likelihood that HIV will be transmitted. A woman who is infected during pregnancy is at risk for preterm delivery and for having a baby with life-threatening gonorrheal infection of the blood or joints. An infant passing through the birth canal of an infected mother may contract **gonococcal conjunctivitis**, an infection in the eyes that can cause blindness if not treated. In most states, all newborn babies are routinely treated with antimicrobial eyedrops to prevent eye infection.

Gonorrhea is caused by the bacterium *Neisseria gonorrhoeae,* which flourishes in mucous membranes. The microbe cannot thrive outside the human body and dies within moments of exposure to light and air. Consequently, gonorrhea cannot be contracted from toilet seats, towels, or other objects.

Symptoms In males, the incubation period for gonorrhea is brief, generally 2–7 days. The first symptoms are due to urethritis, which causes urinary discomfort and a thick, yellowish white or yellowish green discharge from the penis. The lips of the urethral opening may become inflamed and swollen. In some cases, the lymph glands in the groin become enlarged and swollen. Up to half of males have very minor symptoms or none at all.

Most females with gonorrhea are asymptomatic. Those who do have symptoms often experience pain with urination, increased vaginal discharge, and severe menstrual cramps. Up to 40% of women with untreated gonorrhea develop PID. Women may also develop painful abscesses in the Bartholin's glands, a pair of glands located on either side of the opening of the vagina.

Gonorrhea can also infect the throat or rectum of people who engage in oral or anal sex. Gonorrhea symptoms in the throat may be a sore throat or pus on the tonsils, and those in the rectum may be pus or blood in the feces or rectal pain and itching.

Diagnosis Several tests—gram stain, detection of bacterial genes or DNA, or culture—may be performed; depending on the test, samples of urine or cervical, urethral, throat, or rectal fluids may be collected.

Treatment A variety of new and relatively expensive antibiotics are usually effective in curing gonorrhea. Older, less expensive antibiotics such as penicillin and tetracycline are not currently recommended for treating gonorrhea because of widespread drug resistance. People with gonorrhea often also have chlamydia, so additional antibiotics are typically given to treat chlamydia. Follow-up tests are sometimes performed to make sure the infection has been eradicated. If you have had gonorrhea and have been treated, you can still get the disease again if you have sexual contact with an infected partner.

Pelvic Inflammatory Disease

A major complication in 10–40% of women who have been infected with either gonorrhea or chlamydia and have not received adequate treatment is **pelvic inflammatory disease (PID).** PID occurs when the initial infection with gonorrhea and/or chlamydia travels upward, often along with other bacteria, beyond the cervix into the uterus, oviducts, ovaries, and pelvic cavity. PID is often serious enough to require hospitalization and sometimes surgery. Even if the disease is treated successfully, about 25% of affected women will have long-term problems such as a continuing susceptibility to infection, ectopic pregnancy, infertility, and chronic pelvic pain.

PID is the leading cause of infertility in young women, often going undetected until the inability to become pregnant leads to further evaluation. Infertility occurs in 8% of women after one episode of PID, 20% after two episodes, and 40% after three episodes. The risk of ectopic pregnancy increases significantly in women who have had PID.

Women under age 25 are much more likely to develop PID than are older women. As with all STDs, the more sex

Terms

Vw

gonorrhea A sexually transmitted bacterial infection that usually affects mucous membranes.

gonococcal conjunctivitis An inflammation of the mucous membrane lining of the eyelids, caused by the gonococcus bacterium.

pelvic inflammatory disease (PID) An infection that progresses from the vagina and cervix to the uterus, oviducts, and pelvic cavity.

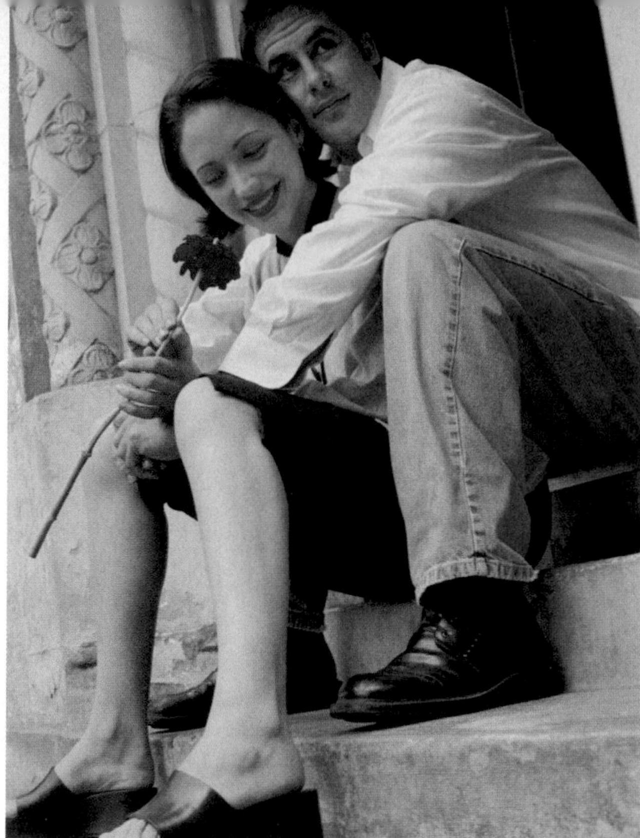

By taking a responsible attitude toward STDs, people show respect and concern for themselves and their partners. This couple's plans for the future could be seriously disrupted if one of them contracted an STD like gonorrhea or chlamydia. Either of these diseases, if untreated, could result in PID, the leading cause of infertility in young women.

partners a woman has had, the greater her risk of PID. Smokers have twice the risk of PID as nonsmokers. Using IUDs for contraception also increases the risk of PID. Research into whether the use of other contraceptives protects against PID has yielded mixed results; OC use may reduce the severity of PID symptoms.

Symptoms Symptoms of PID vary greatly. Some women, especially those with chlamydia, may be asymptomatic; others may feel very ill with abdominal pain, fever, chills, nausea, and vomiting. Early symptoms are essentially the same as those described earlier for chlamydia and gonorrhea. Symptoms often begin or worsen during or soon after a woman's menstrual period. Many women have abnormal vaginal bleeding—either bleeding between periods or heavy and painful menstrual bleeding.

Terms

human papillomavirus (HPV) The pathogen that causes human warts, including genital warts.

genital warts A sexually transmitted viral infection characterized by growths on the genitals; also called *genital HPV infection* or *condyloma.*

Diagnosis Diagnosis of PID is made on the basis of symptoms, physical examination, ultrasound, and laboratory tests. Laparoscopy may be used to confirm the diagnosis and obtain material for cultures. Cultures from the rectum or cervix may also be taken to help identify the specific organism. The symptoms of PID, ectopic pregnancy, and appendicitis can be quite similar, so careful evaluation is required to make the correct diagnosis.

Treatment Starting treatment of PID as quickly as possible is important in order to minimize damage to the reproductive organs. Antibiotics are usually started immediately; in severe cases, the woman may be hospitalized and antibiotics given intravenously. It is especially important that an infected woman's partners be treated. As many as 60% of the male contacts of women with PID are infected but asymptomatic.

Human Papillomavirus Infection

Human papillomavirus (HPV) infection is one of the most common STDs in the United States (see the box "Half of Americans Will Have an STD by Age 25"). HPV infection causes a variety of human diseases, including common warts, **genital warts,** and genital cancers. HPV is the cause of virtually all cervical cancer, the second most common type of cancer in women worldwide. (Other factors that increase a woman's chance of getting cervical cancer include smoking, sexual activity at a young age, multiple sex partners, and infection with genital herpes.) HPV also causes penile cancer and some forms of anal cancers. Genital HPV is usually spread from one person to another through sexual activity.

More than 80% of sexually active individuals will have been infected with HPV by the age of 50. Most people with HPV infection have no symptoms at all and are unaware that they are infected and contagious. The good news is that the immune system usually clears the virus, and infection disappears without any treatment. But in some cases, the infection persists and causes genital warts or genital cancers.

HPV is especially common in young people, with some of the highest rates of infection among college students. HPV infection is the most common STD for which diagnosis and treatment are sought in student health services (see the box "College Students and STDs" on p. 568). Many young women contract HPV infection within 3 months of becoming sexually active.

Human papillomaviruses cause many types of human warts. There are more than 100 different strains of HPV, and different strains infect specific locations. More than 30 types are likely to cause genital infections, and five of these are often implicated in cervical cancer; other strains are linked to anal, penile, and other genital cancers. The HPV strains that cause most visible genital warts are less

In the News

Half of Americans Will Have an STD by Age 25

The United States has the highest STD rate of any industrialized country. Estimates released in 2004 showed that half of all Americans will have at least one STD by age 25, and nearly half of all STDs that occur each year are in people age 15–24. The direct lifetime medical cost of STDs, including HIV, is estimated at $10–15 billion for the new STDs acquired each year. STDs are public health challenges for many reasons.

• *STDs are stealth diseases.* Many STDs, including chlamydia, genital herpes, trichomoniasis, and HPV infection have few, if any, recognizable symptoms. The large number of disease carriers who are unaware of their infection makes these diseases extremely difficult to control. Experts believe that in most cases, HIV is transmitted very early in the disease, before people are aware of the infection. The fact that most people are symptom-free for the first several years of HIV infection highlights the need to test people at risk often.

• *Viral STDs are persistent and incurable.* Even if detected, most viral STDs—genital herpes, HPV infection, and HIV infection—are not curable with current therapies. This means that the number of people capable of infecting others continues to grow. The best hope for controlling viral STDs is the development and widespread use of effective vaccines. The hepatitis B vaccine provides a positive example: In the years since introduction of the vaccine, the rate of new cases of hepatitis B has dropped by more than 75%, and further declines are expected.

• *Screening tests may be underutilized.* Nationwide, too many physicians and clinics fail to follow the CDC recommendations for screening, especially for chlamydia in young women. In addition, too many individuals are too unaware of or too embarrassed to request STD screening. Testing more people for STDs could potentially bring STD rates down; it would at least provide an opportunity to counsel people about risky sexual behavior. In surveys, up to 75% of people support offering STD testing in schools. Also potentially helpful would be media messages about the benefits and availability of confidential STD screening services.

• *Young people are particularly vulnerable to STDs.* Young adults are more likely to be ignorant about STDs and safer sex, embarrassed to ask for information, and unaware of how to access appropriate STD testing and treatment services. Nearly all young adults are sexually active by age 25, but young people are more likely to be unmarried, have more than one partner over time, and/or have a partner who has an STD. Young people need medically accurate information about abstinence, condoms, and other contraceptive methods—and open communication and encouragement from family, friends, and the community to behave responsibly.

Until STDs are controllable with vaccines or effective screening and treatment, the only way to reduce your risk is to limit the number of sexual partners and to use condoms consistently (see guidelines presented earlier in the chapter). For those who choose abstinence or a mutually monogamous relationship with one uninfected partner, there is no risk of STDs.

SOURCES: Cates, J. R., et al. 2004. *Our Voices, Our Lives, Our Futures: Youth and Sexually Transmitted Diseases.* Chapel Hill, N.C.: School of Journalism and Mass Communication, University of North Carolina at Chapel Hill; Weinstock, H., S. Berman, and W. Cates. 2004. Sexually transmitted diseases among American youth: Incidence and prevalence estimates, 2000. *Perspectives on Sexual and Reproductive Health* 36(1): 6–10; Chesson, H. W., et al. 2004. The estimated direct medical cost of sexually transmitted diseases among American youth, 2000. *Perspectives on Sexual and Reproductive Health* 36(1): 11–19.

likely to cause cancer than some of the other strains. A person can be infected with several different strains.

Genital HPV infection is quite contagious. Condoms and other barrier methods can help prevent the transmission of HPV, but HPV infection frequently occurs in areas where condoms are not fully protective. These areas are the labia in women, the base of the penis and the scrotum in men, and around the anus in both men and women. Still, a 3-year study showed that women who always use condoms cut their risk of HPV infection by 70%.

Many people who carry HPV have no visible warts or symptoms. And although people with visible genital warts may be more likely to transmit the disease, asymptomatic people can also infect others. Current treatments can often (but not always) eliminate visible warts, but HPV continues to infect healthy tissue nearby. So even after treatment, a person can still transmit HPV to someone else. Also, as mentioned above, condoms do not provide complete protection against the transmission of HPV.

In 2006, the FDA approved a vaccine for HPV (Gardasil), and additional vaccines are in development. Gardasil protects against four types of HPV virus that together account for 90% of genital warts and 70% of cervical cancers; the drug has also been shown to prevent cancers of the vagina and vulva. Vaccination is recommended for girls and women aged 9–26.

Symptoms HPV-infected tissue often appears normal; it may also look like anything from a small bump on the skin to a large, warty growth. Depending on location and size, genital warts are sometimes painful. Untreated warts can grow together to form a cauliflower-like mass. In males, they appear on the penis and often involve the urethra, appearing first at the opening and then spreading inside. The growths may cause irritation and bleeding, leading to painful urination and a urethral discharge. Warts may also appear around the anus or within the rectum.

In Focus

College Students and STDs

Why Do College Students Have High Rates of STDs?

- Risky sexual behavior is common. One study of college students found that fewer than half used condoms consistently and one-third had had ten or more sex partners. Another study found that 19% of male students and 33% of female students had consented to sexual intercourse simply because they felt awkward refusing.
- College students underestimate their risk of STDs and HIV. Although students may have considerable knowledge about STDs, they often feel the risks do not apply to them—a dangerous assumption. One study of students with a history of STDs showed that more than half had unprotected sex while they were infected, and 25% of them continued to have sex without ever informing their partner(s).
- Many students are infected but don't know it. A 2006 study of asymptomatic college women revealed that nearly 10% were infected with chlamydia.

What Effect Does Alcohol or Drug Use Have on My Likelihood of Getting an STD?

- Between one-third and one-half of college students report participating in sexual activity as a direct result of being intoxicated. All too often, sexual activity while intoxicated leads to unprotected intercourse.
- Students who binge-drink are more likely to have multiple partners, use condoms inconsistently, and delay seeking treatment for STDs than students who drink little or no alcohol. Sexual assaults occur more frequently when either the perpetrator or the victim has been drinking.

What Can Students Do to Protect Themselves Against STDs?

- Limit the number of sex partners. Even people who are always in a monogamous relationship can end up with extensive potential exposure to STDs if, over the years, they have numerous relationships.
- Use condoms consistently, and don't assume it's safe to stop after you've been with a partner for several months. HIV infection, HPV infection, herpes, and chlamydia can be asymptomatic for months or years and can be transmitted at any time. If you haven't been using condoms with your current partner, start now.
- Think about how you use alcohol or other drugs. If alcohol or drug use is causing problems in your life, get help.
- Enjoy sexuality on your own terms. Don't let the expectations of friends and partners cause you to ignore your own feelings. Let your own wellness be your first priority. If you choose to be sexually active, learn about safer sex practices.
- Get to know your partner, and talk to him or her before becoming intimate. Be honest about yourself, and encourage your partner to do the same. Unfortunately, studies show that many people lie about their sexual past and that, in general, people significantly underestimate their partners' sexual experience and risk for STDs. So practice safer sex no matter what.

In women, warts may appear on the labia or vulva and may spread to the perineum, the area between the vagina and the rectum. They may also appear on the cervix.

The incubation period ranges from 1 month to 2 years from the time of contact. People can be infected with the virus and be capable of transmitting it to their sex partners without having any symptoms at all. The vast majority of people with HPV infection have no visible warts or symptoms of any kind.

Genital warts sometimes grow very large during pregnancy and can occasionally be large enough to make vaginal delivery difficult. However, most pregnant women with HPV infection can deliver vaginally. HPV infection is infrequently transmitted to an infant during delivery but can occasionally cause warts to form on the infant's vocal cords.

Diagnosis Genital warts are usually diagnosed based on the appearance of the lesions. Sometimes examination with a special magnifying instrument or biopsy is done to evaluate suspicious lesions. HPV infection of the cervix is often detected on routine Pap tests. Special tests are now available to detect the presence of HPV infection and to distinguish among the more common strains of HPV, including those that cause most cases of cervical cancer. HPV subtypes 6 and 11 cause 90% of all cases of genital warts but do not normally cause genital cancers. HPV subtypes 16 and 18 cause most cervical cancers.

Treatment Treatment of genital warts focuses on reducing the number and size of warts, although most warts eventually disappear, even without treatment. The currently available treatments do not eradicate HPV infection. Warts may be removed by cryosurgery (freezing), electrocautery (burning), or laser surgery. Direct applications of podophyllin or other cytotoxic acids may be used, and there are treatments that patients can use at home. The success rates of methods vary, and warts often recur despite initial improvement. Warts are more likely to persist and become severe in people with an impaired immune system.

Even after treatment and the disappearance of visible warts, the individual may continue to carry HPV in healthy-looking tissue and can probably still infect others. Anyone who has ever had HPV infection should inform all partners. Condoms should be used, even though they do not provide total protection. Because of the relationship between HPV and cervical cancer, women who have had genital warts should have Pap tests at least every 12 months.

Genital Herpes

Genital herpes affects about 45 million people in the United States and is also very common worldwide. Genital herpes is a major factor in the transmission of HIV worldwide. Most people with HIV are also infected with HSV 2, and herpes lesions contain large amounts of HIV, making it more likely that the virus is transmitted. The presence of herpes lesions in an HIV-negative person increases the likelihood that she or he will be infected by an HIV-positive partner. Genital herpes may also interact with HPV infection to increase the risk of cervical cancer.

Two types of herpes simplex viruses, HSV 1 and HSV 2, cause genital herpes and oral-labial herpes (cold sores). Genital herpes is usually caused by HSV 2, and oral-labial herpes is usually caused by HSV 1, although both virus types can cause either genital or oral-labial lesions. Many people wrongly assume that they are unlikely to pick up an STD if they limit their sexual activity to oral sex, but this is not true, particularly in the case of genital herpes. HSV can also cause rectal lesions, usually transmitted through anal sex. Infection with HSV is generally lifelong; after infection, the virus lies dormant in nerve cells and can reactivate at any time.

HSV 1 infection is so common that 50–80% of U.S. adults have antibodies to HSV 1 (indicating previous exposure to the virus); most were exposed to HSV 1 during childhood. HSV 2 infection usually occurs during adolescence and early adulthood, often between ages 18 and 25. Approximately 22% of adults have antibodies to HSV 2; about a million are infected each year. The prevalence of both HSV 1 and HSV 2 has declined over the past decade, primarily due to changes in sexual behavior.

HSV 2 is almost always sexually transmitted. The infection is more easily transmitted when people have active sores, but HSV 2 can be transmitted to a sex partner even when no obvious lesions are present. A recent study of women with HSV-2 showed the presence of the virus in genital secretions more than one-fourth of the time when the women were symptom-free. Because HSV is asymptomatic in 80–90% of people, the infection is often acquired from a person who does not know that he or she is infected. If you have ever had an outbreak of genital herpes, you should consider yourself always contagious and inform your partners. Avoid intimate contact when any sores are present, and use condoms during all sexual contact.

Newborns can occasionally be infected with HSV, usually during passage through the birth canal of an infected mother or due to HSV infection acquired by the mother during the third trimester of pregnancy. Without treatment, 65% of newborns with HSV will die, and most who survive will have some degree of brain damage. The risk of mother-to-child HSV transmission during pregnancy and delivery is low (less than 1%) in women with long-standing herpes infection. However, a woman who acquires the infection during pregnancy, especially in the third trimester, has a much higher risk of transmitting the infection to her infant. New herpes blood tests to screen pregnant women and their sexual partners could substantially reduce neonatal herpes infections. If an uninfected pregnant woman's partner carries HSV, abstinence or the use of condoms could prevent infection during pregnancy.

Pregnant women who have been exposed to genital herpes should inform their physician so that appropriate precautions can be taken to protect the baby from infection. These precautions sometimes include a cesarean section if active lesions are present at the time of delivery. Fortunately, most babies born to mothers with a history of genital herpes do not acquire the infection, and most women are able to have normal vaginal deliveries.

Symptoms Up to 90% of people who are infected with HSV have no symptoms. Those that do develop symptoms often first notice them within 2–20 days of having sex with an infected partner. (However, it is not unusual for the first outbreak to occur months or even years after initial exposure.) The first episode of genital herpes frequently causes flulike symptoms in addition to genital lesions. The lesions usually heal within 3 weeks, but the virus remains alive in an inactive state within nerve cells. A new outbreak of herpes can occur at any time. On average, newly diagnosed people will experience five to eight outbreaks per year, with a decrease in the frequency of outbreaks over time. Recurrent episodes are usually less severe than the initial one, with fewer and less painful sores that heal more quickly. Outbreaks can be triggered by stress, illness, fatigue, sun exposure, sexual intercourse, and menstruation (see the box "Stress and Genital Herpes").

Diagnosis Genital herpes is often diagnosed on the basis of symptoms; a sample of fluid from the lesions may also be sent to a laboratory for culture. This test is helpful if the specimen is obtained within about 2 days of the lesion's development. If the lesion has been around for longer than 2 days, the culture will often be negative even if the person has genital herpes. Several blood tests can detect the presence of HSV antibodies. Older tests don't distinguish between HSV 1 and HSV 2. Because HSV 1 infection is extremely common, most people will test positive even if they have not had genital herpes. Newer tests can determine if a person is infected with HSV 1 or HSV 2 and may potentially alert many asymptomatic people to the fact that they are infected. This knowledge may help prevent transmission of HSV in couples where one partner

Term

genital herpes A sexually transmitted infection caused by the herpes simplex virus.

Mind/Body/Spirit

Stress and Genital Herpes

Patients and health care workers alike have long suspected that stress and genital herpes outbreaks are related. Research into this potential link has yielded mixed results. There is no doubt that having genital herpes is a considerable stress to many people, but does stress itself make a person with herpes infection more likely to have an outbreak? A recent study of women with genital herpes found that persistent stressors (those lasting more than a week) and persistent high levels of anxiety were associated with increased outbreaks. Short-term stress, mood changes, and brief negative life experiences did not influence the rate of herpes outbreaks.

Experts suspect that stress has a negative impact on the immune system. Studies have shown that cell-mediated immune function and antibody levels may drop in response to psychological stress. Perhaps herpesviruses that are usually dormant in nervous system tissue become activated when immune function declines due to stress.

The next logical step is to investigate whether stress-reduction techniques such as meditation or exercise result in reduced rates of herpes outbreaks. Until such research becomes available, it makes sense for people who suffer recurrent genital herpes outbreaks to do what they can to reduce stress, especially long-term stress and anxiety (see Chapter 2). If you have herpes, joining a support group may help reduce your stress and improve your ability to cope with this chronic disease. If you have several outbreaks a year, or if you have recently had your first episode of genital herpes, talk to your health care provider about suppressive antiviral medication, which can reduce outbreaks substantially. Keep in mind that regardless of stress level, genital herpes outbreaks naturally tend to become less and less frequent over time. Knowing that your outbreaks are likely to diminish can, in and of itself, help reduce your feelings of stress.

is infected and the other is not (particularly important for uninfected women who are pregnant). The more accurate tests for HSV rely on the development of antibodies to the virus, which can take several weeks or months after exposure to the virus. For this reason, doctors often recommend that people wait for 12 to 16 weeks after possible exposure before having a blood test.

Treatment There is no cure for herpes. Once infected, a person carries the virus for life. Antiviral drugs such as acyclovir can be taken at the beginning of an outbreak to shorten the severity and duration of symptoms. People who have frequent outbreaks can take acyclovir or similar drugs on a daily basis to suppress outbreaks and decrease viral shedding between outbreaks. Anyone diagnosed with a first episode of genital herpes should talk with a health care provider about suppressive treatment. A person on suppressive therapy can still transmit HSV to an uninfected partner, but the risk is probably reduced by about half. Using condoms consistently and taking suppressive medication is a reasonable way to reduce the risk of passing herpes to an uninfected sexual partner. It is always important to inform a sexual partner if you have genital herpes.

The psychological aspects of genital herpes often cause more suffering than the disease itself. Support groups are available to help people learn to cope with herpes. Despite considerable efforts, an effective vaccine has yet to be developed, but much research is ongoing.

Hepatitis B

Hepatitis (inflammation of the liver) can cause serious and sometimes permanent damage to the liver, which can result in death in severe cases. One of the many types of hepatitis is caused by hepatitis B virus (HBV). HBV is somewhat similar to HIV; it is found in most body fluids, and it can be transmitted sexually, by injection drug use, and during pregnancy and delivery. However, HBV is much more contagious than HIV, and it can also be spread through nonsexual close contact. Health care workers who are exposed to blood are frequently infected, as are people who live in close contact with each other, such as prisoners and residents of mental health care facilities. In the Far East and in developing countries, hepatitis B is extremely common, and the virus is primarily transmitted from the mother to child during pregnancy or delivery.

Hepatitis B is a potentially fatal disease with no cure, but fortunately there is an effective vaccine. The number of cases of acute hepatitis B in the United States has dropped by 75% since 1990, primarily as a result of the vaccine. In addition, mother-to-child transmission has been greatly reduced because of routine HBV screening of pregnant women. Vaccination is recommended for everyone under age 19 and for all adults at increased risk for hepatitis B, including people who have more than one sex partner in 6 months, men who have sex with other men, those who inject illegal drugs, and health care workers who are exposed to blood and body fluids.

Other forms of viral hepatitis can also be sexually transmitted. Hepatitis A is of particular concern for people who engage in anal sex; a vaccine is available and is recommended for all people at risk. Less commonly, hepatitis C can be transmitted sexually. Experts believe that traumatic sexual activity that causes tissue damage is most likely to transmit HCV. See Chapter 17 for more on these and other forms of hepatitis.

Transmission HBV is found in all body fluids, including blood and blood products, semen, saliva, urine, and vaginal secretions. It is easily transmitted through any sexual activity that involves the exchange of body fluids, the use of contaminated needles, and any blood-to-blood contact, including the use of contaminated razor blades, toothbrushes, and eating utensils. The primary risk factors for acquiring HBV are sexual exposure and injection drug use; having multiple partners greatly increases risk. As mentioned, a pregnant woman can transmit HBV to her unborn child.

Symptoms Many people infected with HBV never develop symptoms; they have what are known as silent infections. The normal incubation period is 30–180 days. Mild cases of hepatitis cause flulike symptoms such as fever, body aches, chills, and loss of appetite. As the illness progresses, there may be nausea, vomiting, dark-colored urine, abdominal pain, and jaundice. Some people with hepatitis also develop a skin rash and joint pain or arthritis. Acute hepatitis B can sometimes be severe, resulting in prolonged illness or even death.

People with hepatitis B sometimes recover completely, but they can also become chronic carriers of the virus, capable of infecting others for the rest of their life. Some chronic carriers remain asymptomatic, while others develop chronic liver disease. Chronic hepatitis can cause cirrhosis of the liver, liver failure, and a deadly form of liver cancer. Hepatitis kills some 5000 Americans each year; worldwide, the annual death toll exceeds 600,000.

Diagnosis and Treatment Blood tests can be used to diagnose hepatitis through analysis of liver function and detection of the specific organism causing the infection. There is no cure for hepatitis B and no specific treatment for acute infections; antiviral drugs may be used for cases of chronic HBV infection. For people exposed to HBV, treatment with hepatitis B immunoglobulin can provide protection against the virus.

Prevention Preventive measures for hepatitis B are similar to those for HIV infection: Avoid sexual contact that involves sharing body fluids, including saliva; use condoms during sexual intercourse; and don't share needles. If you choose to have tattooing or body piercing done, make sure all needles and equipment are sterile. The vaccine for hepatitis B is safe and highly effective.

Syphilis

Syphilis, a disease that once caused death and disability for millions, can now be effectively treated with antibiotics. Each year, there are about 7000–10,000 new cases of early syphilis in the United States, and about 70,000 people are diagnosed at all stages of the disease. The number of new cases hit an all-time low in 2000 but rose by 19% between 2000 and 2003 and continued to rise in 2004. The increase was seen mainly in homosexual and bisexual men, prompting health officials to call for increased education in safer sex practices among these groups. Studies have found an association between syphilis infection and the use of the Internet as a means to meet sex partners among men who have sex with men. Another recent trend is an increase in the proportion of cases of syphilis from oral sex; in nearly 15% of recent cases among gay men and 7% of cases among heterosexual men and women, the means of transmission was through oral sex. People with syphilis in the mouth may not have symptoms, or they may mistake the sores for another illness. The sores associated with syphilis, regardless of their location, dramatically increase the risk of acquiring HIV or transmitting it to someone else.

Syphilis is caused by a spirochete called *Treponema pallidum*, a thin, corkscrew-shaped bacterium. The disease is usually acquired through sexual contact, although infected pregnant women can transmit it to the fetus. The pathogen passes through any break or opening in the skin or mucous membranes and can be transmitted by kissing, vaginal or anal intercourse, or oral-genital contact. Although easy to treat, syphilis can be difficult to recognize, and if left untreated the disease can cause devastating damage to almost any system of the body.

Symptoms Syphilis progresses through several stages. *Primary syphilis* is characterized by an ulcer called a **chancre** that appears within 10–90 days after exposure. The chancre is usually found at the site where the organism entered the body, such as the genital area, but it may also appear in other sites such as the mouth, breasts, or fingers. Chancres contain large numbers of bacteria and make the disease highly contagious when present; they are often painless and typically heal on their own within a few weeks. If the disease is not treated during the primary stage, about a third of infected individuals progress to chronic stages of infections.

Secondary syphilis is usually marked by mild, flulike symptoms and a skin rash that appears 3–6 weeks after the chancre. The rash may cover the entire body or only a few areas, but the palms of the hands and soles of the feet are usually involved. Areas of skin affected by the rash are highly contagious but usually heal within several weeks or months.

Terms

Vw

hepatitis Inflammation of the liver, which can be caused by infection, drugs, or toxins; some forms of infectious hepatitis can be transmitted sexually.

syphilis A sexually transmitted bacterial infection caused by the spirochete *Treponema pallidum*.

chancre The sore produced by syphilis in its earliest stage.

If the disease remains untreated, the symptoms of secondary syphilis may recur over a period of several years; affected individuals may then lapse into an asymptomatic latent stage in which they experience no further consequences of infection. However, in about a third of cases of untreated secondary syphilis, the individual develops *late,* or *tertiary, syphilis.* Late syphilis can damage many organs of the body, possibly causing severe dementia, cardiovascular damage, blindness, and death.

In infected pregnant women, the syphilis bacterium can cross the placenta. If the mother is not treated, the probable result is stillbirth, prematurity, or congenital deformity. In many cases, the infant is also born infected *(congenital syphilis)* and requires treatment.

Diagnosis and Treatment Syphilis is diagnosed by examination of infected tissues and with blood tests. All stages can be treated with antibiotics, but damage from late syphilis can be permanent.

Trichomoniasis

Trichomoniasis, often called "trich," is the most common nonviral STD, with an estimated 180 million cases worldwide. It was once viewed as little more than an annoyance, but evidence shows that trich infection increases the risk of acquiring and transmitting other STDs, including HIV. Trich also increases the risk of developing cervical cancer. Trichomoniasis infection during pregnancy is associated with premature delivery and low-birth-weight infants.

The single-celled organism that causes trich, *Trichomonas vaginalis,* thrives in warm, moist conditions, making women particularly susceptible to these infections in the vagina. This protozoan can remain alive on external objects for as long as 60–90 minutes, in urine for 3 hours, and in seminal fluid for 6 hours. Thus it is possible, although rare, to contract trich by nonsexual means.

Symptoms Not everyone with trich develops symptoms. Many people carry the disease for years, even decades, without knowing they are infected. In some populations, trich is even more common in middle-aged women than in younger women.

Women who become symptomatic with trich develop a greenish, foul-smelling vaginal discharge 5–28 days after the time of contact with the organism. The discharge can cause severe itching and irritation of the vagina and vulva, causing redness and pain. Although most males do not have any symptoms, some may experience slight itching, clear discharge, and sometimes painful urination.

Diagnosis and Treatment Many doctors do not routinely test women for trichomoniasis infection, but the practice is increasing. The most common way to diagnose trichomonas in women is to examine vaginal fluid under the microscope. Unfortunately, this method fails to detect about half of all infections. Culturing the organism is more accurate but takes much longer and is more expensive. Two new rapid antigen tests have recently been approved but are not yet in widespread use.

The drug of choice for treating trichomoniasis is metronidazole (Flagyl). Partners should also be treated, to prevent the ping-pong effect that occurs when partners pass infection back and forth.

OTHER STDS

A few other diseases are transmitted sexually or linked to sexual activity. They include bacterial vaginosis, pubic lice, and scabies.

Bacterial vaginosis (BV) is the most common cause of abnormal vaginal discharge in women of reproductive age. BV involves a shift in the makeup of the bacteria that normally inhabit the vagina: Instead of *Lactobacillus* being most numerous, there is an overgrowth of anaerobic microorganisms and bacteria such as *Gardnerella vaginalis.* BV is clearly associated with sexual activity, often occurring after a change in partners. However, research on the degree to which BV is sexually transmitted is ongoing. Recent research suggests that a sexually transmitted virus that infects and kills *Lactobacillus* may be the underlying cause of BV. Douching also substantially increases the risk of BV. Topical and oral antibiotics are used to treat BV, but BV often recurs after treatment.

Symptoms of BV include a vaginal discharge with a fishlike odor and, in some cases, vaginal irritation; many women with BV have no symptoms. Studies have shown an association between BV and increased risk of PID, HIV transmission, infection following childbirth or gynecological surgery (including abortion), and, in pregnant women, premature delivery. The CDC recommends that any pregnant woman who has symptoms of BV or who is at risk for premature delivery be screened and, if necessary, treated for BV.

Pubic lice, commonly known as crabs, are highly contagious, both sexually and nonsexually. They are often difficult to see but are the color and size of small freckles; when they have fed, they become dark brown in color. Lice feed on human blood and are usually found attached to pubic hair. Separated from their human hosts, lice can survive for about 24 hours.

Easily passed from person to person, lice can also be transmitted via infested bedding, towels, clothing, sleeping bags, and even toilet seats. Intense itching is the usual symptom, and with careful examination, both the parasite and its eggs, or nits, can be seen. Treatment generally requires repeated applications of nonprescription medications. These preparations are in lotion or shampoo form and include a fine comb for removing lice or nits from body hair. Washing clothing and linen is also essential for preventing reinfestation. If the infestation persists, prescription medications are available.

Scabies is another fairly common infestation. A burrowing parasite, the scabies mite deposits eggs beneath

Assess Yourself

Do Your Attitudes and Behaviors Put You at Risk for STDs?

All sexually transmitted diseases are preventable. You have control over the behaviors and attitudes that place you at risk for contracting STDs and for increasing their negative effects on your health. To identify your risk factors, read the following list of statements and identify whether they're true or false for you.

True or False

1. I have never been sexually active. (If false, continue. If true, you are not at risk; respond to the remaining statements based on how you realistically believe you would act.)
2. I am in a mutually monogamous relationship with an uninfected partner or am not currently sexually active. (If false, continue. If true, you are at minimal risk now; respond to the remaining statements according to your attitudes and past behaviors.)
3. I have only one sex partner.
4. I always use a condom for each act of intercourse, even if I am fairly certain my partner has no infections.
5. I do not use oil-based lubricants or other products with condoms.
6. I discuss STDs and prevention with new partners before having sex.
7. I do not use alcohol or another mood-altering drug in sexual situations.
8. I would tell my partner if I thought I had been exposed to an STD.
9. I am familiar with the signs and symptoms of STDs.
10. I regularly perform genital self-examination.
11. When I notice any sign or symptom of any STD or if I engage in risky sexual behavior, I consult my physician immediately.
12. I obtain screening for HIV and STDs regularly. In addition (if female), I obtain yearly pelvic exams and Pap tests.
13. When diagnosed with an STD, I inform all recent partners.
14. When I have a sign or symptom of an STD that goes away on its own, I still consult my physician.
15. I do not use drugs prescribed for friends or partners or left over from other illnesses to treat STDs.
16. I do not share syringes or needles to inject drugs.

False answers indicate attitudes and behaviors that may put you at risk for contracting STDs or for suffering serious medical consequences from them. (For a more detailed self-assessment, take the quiz at www.thebody.com/surveys/sexsurvey.html).

the skin, especially in the creases of the body. The eggs hatch in a few days, and the new mites congregate around hair follicles. This burrowing parasite produces intense itching, especially at night. The usual sites of infestation are between the fingers, on wrists, in armpits, underneath the breasts, along the inner surfaces of the thighs, on the penis and scrotum, and occasionally on the female genitals. Scabies is easily spread from person to person, not only through sexual contact but also through any direct or close contact. Diagnosis is made by actual identification of the mite, the eggs, or the larvae in scrapings taken from the burrows in the skin of the human host. Scabies is generally treated with prescription permethrin cream. Clothing and bedding must be washed to prevent reinfestation with the scabies mite.

WHAT YOU CAN DO

You can take responsibility for your health and contribute to a general reduction in the incidence of STDs in three major areas: education, diagnosis and treatment, and prevention. To assess your current level of responsibility for STD prevention, complete the quiz in the box "Do Your Attitudes and Behaviors Put You at Risk for STDs?"

Education

Since the AIDS epidemic began, public and private agencies have grown more serious about educating the public and increasing their awareness of all STDs. This campaign may already be paying off in changing attitudes and sexual behaviors, at least among certain segments of the population. Recent surveys indicate that condom use is increasing, and the number of new cases of HIV infection in the gay population has been smaller in recent years. Most gay men with HIV practice safer sex. However, many younger gay men are participating in very high risk behaviors, and a second wave of the AIDS epidemic among homosexual

Terms

trichomoniasis A protozoal infection caused by *Trichomonas vaginalis,* transmitted sexually and externally.

bacterial vaginosis (BV) A condition linked to sexual activity; caused by an overgrowth of certain bacteria inhabiting the vagina.

pubic lice Parasites that infest the hair of the pubic region, commonly called *crabs.*

scabies A contagious skin disease caused by a type of burrowing parasitic mite.

men can be expected if younger men fail to use preventive measures. Also discouraging is the fact that the number of cases of HIV infection among harder-to-reach groups, such as injection drug users and their partners and children, is still increasing. In particular, more educational efforts are needed among U.S. ethnic minorities.

Education efforts targeted at increasing public awareness about AIDS through the media have included public service announcements, dramatic presentations, and support from well-known public figures. Colleges offer courses in human sexuality. Free pamphlets and other literature are available from public health departments, health clinics, physicians' offices, student health centers, and Planned Parenthood, and easy-to-understand books are available in libraries and bookstores. Several national hotlines have been set up to provide free, confidential information and referral services to callers anywhere in the country.

Learning about STDs is still up to every person individually. You must assume responsibility for learning about the causes and nature of STDs and their potential effects on you, those with whom you have sexual relationships, and the children you may have. Once you know about STDs—their symptoms, how they're transmitted, how they can be prevented—you are in a position to educate others. Providing information to your friends and partners, whether in casual conversation or in more serious decision-making discussions, is an important way that you can make a difference in both your own wellness and that of others.

Diagnosis and Treatment

Early diagnosis and treatment of STDs can help you and your sex partner(s) avoid unnecessary complications and help prevent the spread of STDs.

Get Vaccinated Every young, sexually active person should be vaccinated for hepatitis B; vaccines are available for all age groups. Men who have sex with men should be vaccinated for hepatitis A, and girls and women aged 9–26 should be vaccinated for HPV. In the next 5–10 years, vaccines for HSV and possibly even some strains of HIV may become available.

Be Alert for Symptoms If you are sexually active, be alert for any sign or symptom of disease, such as a rash, a discharge, sores, or unusual pain, and don't hesitate to have a professional examination if you notice such a symptom. Although only a physician can make a proper diagnosis of an STD, you can perform *genital self-examination* between checkups to look for early warning signs of infection. Women should examine the entire genital area, including the area covered by pubic hair, the outer and inner lips of the vagina, the clitoris, and the area around the urinary and vaginal openings. Men should look at the entire head, shaft, and base of the penis and the scrotum. (A mirror may be helpful for checking difficult-to-see areas.)

Throughout the exam, look for bumps, sores, blisters, or warts on the skin. Bumps or blisters may be red or light colored; they may look like pimples, or they may develop into open sores. Genital warts may appear as very small bumpy spots, or they may have a fleshy, cauliflower-like appearance. Also stay alert for other signs of STDs, including pain or burning upon urination, itchiness in the genital area, abnormal discharge from the vagina or penis, pelvic pain, and, in women, bleeding between menstrual periods. Be alert for these signs or symptoms in your partner, too.

Get Tested Remember that almost all STDs—including HIV infection—can be completely asymptomatic for long periods of time. The CDC recommends that everyone between the ages of 13 and 64 be tested for HIV at least once during routine medical care. If you are sexually active, be sure to get periodic STD checks, even if you have no symptoms. If you have a risky sexual encounter, see a physician as soon as possible (see the box "Don't Wait—Early Treatment of STDs Really Matters"). Sexually active young women should have pelvic exams and Pap tests at least once a year, with chlamydia and gonorrhea screening in most cases. Sexually active men, especially if they have had more than one partner, should have periodic STD screening.

Men who have sex with men are at especially high risk for HIV and other STDs. The CDC recommends that sexually active men who have sex with men be tested annually for HIV, chlamydia (anal and urethral), syphilis, and gonorrhea (anal, urethral, and pharyngeal). Men who have multiple anonymous partners or who are injection drug users should be screened more frequently. All sexually active gay and bisexual men should be vaccinated for hepatitis A and B.

Testing for STDs is done through private physicians, public health clinics, community health agencies, and most student health services. If you are diagnosed as having an STD, you should begin treatment as quickly as possible. Inform your partner(s), and avoid any sexual activity until your treatment is complete and testing indicates that you are cured. If your partner tells you that he or she has contracted an STD, get tested immediately, even if you don't have any symptoms. Asymptomatic partners are often treated to ensure that an infection will not spread or recur.

Inform Your Partners Telling a partner that you have exposed him or her to an STD isn't easy. You may be afraid your partner will be angry or resentful, or you may worry that your partner will think less of you or reject you. At the same time, you may be feeling afraid, ashamed, embarrassed, or angry yourself. Despite the awkwardness and difficulty, it is crucial that your sex partner or partners be informed and urged to seek testing and/or treatment as quickly as possible.

Take Charge

Don't Wait—Early Treatment of STDs Really Matters

You can't take back an unwise sexual choice, but quickly owning up to the fact that you are at risk for infection and taking action right away can make a big difference. Treating STDs like chlamydia and gonorrhea within a few days of infection is very likely to prevent complications such as PID and infertility. You will also be much less likely to pass the infection on to anyone else. If you have had a recent risky sexual encounter, visit your physician, student health center, or local STD clinic and ask for testing. Don't wait for symptoms to develop—you may never have any. Permanent damage from STDs, including infertility, can occur even if you have no symptoms.

If you feel a recent sexual encounter puts you at high risk for HIV, see a physician immediately. Unsafe sex with a person who is infected with HIV meets the criteria for PEP treatment described earlier in the chapter; if you are treated within 72 hours of possible exposure, PEP will significantly reduce your risk of HIV infection. If you develop flulike symptoms in the days or weeks following risky sexual or drug-taking behavior, see your physician and ask for an HIV RNA test in addition to standard STD tests. (HIV antibody tests may not register primary HIV infection.) If HIV treatment is begun within the first weeks of the infection, there is a good chance that damage to the immune system can be reduced or even prevented. Many physicians will not think of primary HIV infection when you describe flulike symptoms, so be sure to speak up about your recent risky activities and your concerns about HIV.

If tests come back positive for a particular STD, you need to be tested for others, including HIV infection. Infection with any STD means that you are at higher risk for all others. Women should also have a pelvic exam and a Pap test. If you are given medication to treat an STD, take all of it as directed. Incomplete treatment can result in an incomplete cure, thereby contributing to the development of drug-resistant organisms. Do not share your medication with a partner; he or she should see a physician for testing and treatment.

Do not have sexual intercourse until your treatment—and your partner's treatment—is complete. If your partner still carries the infection, you are likely to be reinfected when you resume sexual activity. If you have an incurable STD such as herpes or HPV infection, always use a condom and make sure your partner is fully informed of the potential risks of being intimate with you, even if you are using condoms.

Avoiding risky sexual encounters is by far the best course of action. But if you do make a mistake, improve your odds of staying healthy by getting tested and treated as soon as possible. And think seriously about what steps you can take to protect yourself in the future.

You can get help telling your partner if you need it. Public health departments will notify sex partners of their possible exposure while maintaining your confidentiality and anonymity. Peer counseling and student health programs often help students with practice in role playing in these circumstances, and concerned health care personnel can provide assistance.

As emphasized throughout this chapter, undetected and untreated STDs can lead to serious medical complications and even death. In asymptomatic cases, the only way infected people can find out they have a disease is by being tested. Uninformed, untested partners can go on to spread the disease, contributing to anguish for others as well as spiraling public health problems. The responsibility of informing partners is an ethical task too important to shirk.

Get Treated With the exception of AIDS treatments, treatments for STDs are safe and generally inexpensive. If you are being treated, follow instructions carefully and complete all the medication as prescribed. Don't stop taking the medication just because you feel better or your symptoms have disappeared. Above all, don't give any of your medication to your partner or to anyone else. Doing so will only make your treatment incomplete and reinfection more likely. Being cured of an STD does not mean that you will not get it again, and exposure does not confer lasting immunity, nor does it prevent you from getting any other STD—all the more reason to be informed, to inform your partners, and to practice safer sex.

Prevention

STDs *are* preventable. As discussed earlier, the only sure way to avoid exposure to STDs is to abstain from sexual activity. But if you do choose to be sexually active, the key

The use of condoms declined as more advanced methods of contraception, such as birth control pills and IUDs, became available. But condoms are once again gaining in popularity because of the protection they provide against STDs.

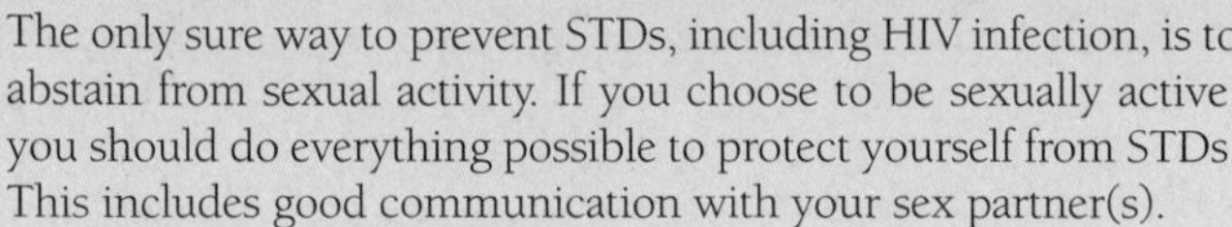

Take Charge: Talking About Condoms and Safer Sex

The only sure way to prevent STDs, including HIV infection, is to abstain from sexual activity. If you choose to be sexually active, you should do everything possible to protect yourself from STDs. This includes good communication with your sex partner(s).

The time to talk about safer sex is before you begin a sexual relationship. However, even if you've been having unprotected sex with your partner, it is still worth it to start practicing safer sex now. If you're nervous about initiating a conversation about safer sex, rehearse what you will say first. Practice in front of a mirror or with a friend.

There are many ways to bring up the subject of safer sex and condom use with your partner. Be honest about your concerns and stress that protection against STDs means that you care about yourself and your partner. Here are a few suggestions:

- "I heard on the news that more and more people are buying and using condoms. I think it shows that people are being more responsible about sex. What do you think?"
- "I'm worried about the diseases we can get from having sex because so many don't have symptoms. I want to protect both of us by using condoms whenever we have sex."
- "I've been thinking about making love with you. But first we need to talk about how to have safer sex and be protected."

You may find that your partner shares your concerns and also wants to use condoms. He or she may be happy and relieved that you have brought up the subject of safer sex. However, if he or she resists the idea of using condoms, you may need to negotiate. Stress that you both deserve to be protected and that sex will be more enjoyable when you aren't worrying about STDs (see the suggestions to the right). If you and your partner haven't used condoms before, buy some and familiarize yourselves with how to use them. Once you feel more comfortable handling condoms, you'll be able to use them correctly and incorporate them into your sexual activity in fun ways. Consider trying the female condom.

If your partner still won't agree to use condoms, think carefully about whether you want to have a sexual relationship with him or her. Safer sex is part of a responsible, caring sexual relationship, and it's smart to say no to a partner who won't use a condom. It's up to you to protect yourself.

If your partner says . . .	Try saying . . .
"They're not romantic."	"Worrying about AIDS isn't romantic, and with condoms we won't have to worry." OR "If we put one on together, a condom could be fun."
"You don't trust me."	"I do trust you, but how can I trust your former partners or mine?" OR "It's important to me that we're both protected."
"I don't have any diseases. I've been tested."	"I'm glad you've been tested, but tests aren't foolproof for all diseases. To be safe, I always use condoms."
"I forgot to bring a condom. But it's OK to skip it just this once."	"I'd really like to make love with you, but I never have sex without a condom. Let's go get some."
"I don't like the way they feel."	"They might feel different, but let's try." OR "Sex won't feel good if we're worrying about diseases." OR "How about trying the female condom?"
"I don't use condoms."	"I use condoms every time." OR "I don't have sex without condoms."
"But I love you."	"Being in love can't protect us from diseases." OR "I love you, too. We still need to use condoms."
"But we've been having sex without condoms."	"I want to start using condoms now so we won't be at any more risk." OR "We can still prevent infection or reinfection."

SOURCE: Dialogue from San Francisco AIDS Foundation. 1998. *Condoms for Couples* (IMPACT AIDS, 3692 18th Street, San Francisco, CA 94110).

is to think about prevention *before* you have a sexual encounter or find yourself in the heat of the moment. Find out what your partner thinks before you become sexually involved. Remember, you can become infected with an STD from just one unprotected encounter.

All your good intentions are likely to fly out the window if you enter into a sexual situation when you are intoxicated. If you or your partner (or both of you) is drunk, you are likely to be less cautious about sex than you would be if you were sober. Many people use alcohol and drugs as a way to deal with their anxiety in social and sexual situations. However, being intoxicated leaves you vulnerable to sexual assault and greatly increases your risk of acquiring a serious STD.

Most people don't want to think, talk, or ask questions about STDs for a variety of reasons. They may think it detracts from the appeal and excitement of the moment, that it takes away from the spontaneity of the experience, or that it will be perceived as a personal insult. For others, simply not knowing how to talk about STDs and safer sex may prevent them from bringing up the issue with a partner. (For advice on communicating with potential sex partners, see the box "Talking About Condoms and Safer Sex.")

Plan ahead for safer sex. Know what sexual behaviors are risky. Find out about your partner's sexual history and practices. Be honest, and ask your partner to do the same, but don't stake your health and life on assumptions about your partner's honesty. Even if your partner's past seems low-risk, still insist on using a condom every time you have sex. Any sexual activity exposes partners to everyone from their partner's sexual past as well everyone from those people's pasts. In one recent study, researchers mapped the sexual relationships of a group of high school students and found a chain of 288 one-to-one sexual relationships, meaning the teen at the end of the chain may have had direct sexual contact with only 1 person—but was indirectly exposed to 286 others. In addition, many honest people are simply unaware that they have an STD.

You may find that your partner is just as concerned as you are. By thinking and talking about responsible sexual behavior, you are expressing a sense of caring for yourself, your potential partner, and your future children. Taking STDs seriously is practical, courageous, and loving; it means giving yourself the respect you deserve.

Everyone can reduce the risk of infection by behaving responsibly. Aside from abstinence, the next most effective approach to preventing STDs is having sex only with one mutually monogamous, uninfected partner. If you are sexually active, use a condom during every act of intercourse to reduce your risk of contracting a disease. Although not foolproof, a properly used condom provides an effective barrier against pathogens, including HIV. A disease can be transmitted if there is contact with an infected area that isn't protected by the condom, however. The use of a barrier over the cervix (diaphragm or cervical cap) in addition to a condom may provide women with some additional protection against the organisms that cause gonorrhea, genital warts, and chlamydia (see Chapter 6).

Approaches to STD prevention that do not work include urinating or douching after intercourse, engaging in oral sex, and genital play without full penetration. Birth control pills and sterilization protect you against conception and unwanted pregnancy but not against STDs.

The decision to have a sexual relationship is accompanied by uncertainties and risks, both physical and emotional. It also carries the responsibility of safeguarding your own health and that of others. You and your partner must have mutual respect and honesty in order to make good decisions together. Caring about yourself and your partner means asking questions and being aware of signs and symptoms. It may be a bit awkward, but the temporary embarrassment of asking intimate questions is a small price to pay to avoid contracting or spreading disease. If your partner thinks less of you for being concerned, you may want to reconsider the relationship in terms of your personal values. Concern about STDs is part of a sexual relationship, not an intrusion into it, just as sexuality is part of life, not separate from it.

Tips for Today

STDs are among the most common infections you can contract—and some are among the most dangerous. Because they can have serious, long-term effects, it's important to be vigilant about exposure, treatment, and, most critically, prevention.

Right now you can

- Make an appointment with a school health clinic, Planned Parenthood, a public health department, or your personal physician if you are sexually active and have not recently been screened for STDs, including HIV.
- If you are sexually active and have not been using condoms, go to your student health clinic or a local pharmacy and buy some.
- Inform a friend or roommate that people can have an STD and not have any symptoms.
- Resolve to discuss condom use with your partner if you are sexually active and are not already using condoms.

SUMMARY

- HIV affects the immune system, making an otherwise healthy person less able to resist a variety of infections.
- HIV is carried in blood and blood products, semen, vaginal and cervical secretions, and breast milk. HIV is transmitted through the exchange of these fluids.
- There is currently no cure or vaccine for HIV infection. Drugs have been developed to slow the course of the disease and to prevent or treat certain secondary infections.
- HIV infection can be prevented by making careful choices about sexual activity, not sharing drug needles, and learning about how to protect oneself from contracting HIV.
- Chlamydia causes epididymitis and urethritis in men; in women, it can lead to PID and infertility if untreated.
- Untreated, gonorrhea can cause PID in women and epididymitis in men, leading to infertility. In infants, untreated gonorrhea can cause blindness.
- Pelvic inflammatory disease (PID), a complication of untreated gonorrhea or chlamydia, is an infection of the uterus and oviducts that may extend to the ovaries and pelvic cavity. It can lead to infertility, ectopic pregnancy, and chronic pelvic pain.
- Human papillomavirus (HPV) is the cause of both genital warts and cervical cancer. Treatment does not eradicate the virus, which can be passed on even by asymptomatic people.
- Genital herpes is a common incurable infection that can be fatal to newborns. After an initial infection, outbreaks may recur at any time.
- Hepatitis B is a viral infection of the liver transmitted through sexual and nonsexual contact. Following an

initial infection, most people recover; but some become chronic carriers of the virus who may develop serious, potentially fatal, complications.

- Syphilis is a highly contagious bacterial infection that can be treated with antibiotics. If left untreated, it can lead to deterioration of the central nervous system and death.
- Other diseases that can be transmitted sexually or are linked to sexual activity include trichomoniasis, bacterial vaginosis, pubic lice, and scabies. Any STD that causes sores or inflammation can increase the risk of HIV transmission.
- Successful diagnosis and treatment of STDs involve being alert for symptoms, getting tested, informing partners, and following treatment instructions carefully.
- All STDs are preventable; the key is practicing responsible sexual behaviors. Those who are sexually active are safest with one mutually monogamous, uninfected partner. Using a condom properly with every act of sexual intercourse helps protect against STDs.

Take Action

1. **Check out OTC contraceptives:** Go to a drugstore and examine the OTC contraceptives. Which ones provide protection against STDs? Are both male and female condoms available? Can you find, select, and purchase condoms in your local pharmacy without undue embarrassment? If not, why not? If you are sexually active, make sure you use the best protection available.

2. **Consider being a volunteer:** More and more communities have treatment and support programs for people with HIV infection. Look in the yellow pages or contact local health agencies to find out what services are available where you live. If any of these agencies use volunteers, consider donating some of your time to help.

3. **Visit a health care provider:** If you have ever engaged in unprotected sex or another behavior that puts you at risk for STDs, talk with your health care provider about being screened for common STDs. What tests are available and useful for your situation?

For More Information

Books

Alcamo, I. E. 2006. *AIDS: The Biological Basis,* 4th ed. Sudbury, Mass.: Jones & Bartlett. *A review of current information, including biological, medical, and social implications of HIV/AIDS.*

Barlow, D. 2006. *Sexually Transmitted Infections: The Facts.* New York: Oxford University Press USA. *A detailed introduction to a broad range of STDs, with discussions of testing, treatments, and prevention.*

Hayden, D. 2004. *Pox: Genius, Madness, and the Mysteries of Syphilis.* New York: Basic Books. *Presents the history, symptoms, and course of syphilis, along with accounts of key historical figures who suffered from the disease.*

Kalichman, S. C., ed. 2006. *Positive Prevention: Reducing HIV Transmission among People Living with HIV/AIDS.* New York: Springer. *An overview of "positive prevention" techniques for HIV-infected persons and their loved ones.*

King, J. L. 2004. *On the Down Low: A Journey into the Lives of "Straight" Black Men Who Sleep with Men.* New York: Broadway. *A controversial look at black men who have sex with other men but don't consider themselves to be gay; based on the author's personal experiences.*

McIlvenna, T. 2005. *The Complete Guide to Safer Sex.* Fort Lee, N.J.: Barricade Books. *Provides practical advice for STD prevention.*

Moore, E. A. 2004. *Encyclopedia of Sexually Transmitted Diseases.* Jefferson, N.C.: McFarland. *Includes a variety of information about STDs in an easy-to-use format.*

Organizations, Hotlines, and Web Sites

American College Health Association. Offers free brochures on STDs, alcohol use, acquaintance rape, and other health issues.
410-859-1500
http://www.acha.org

American Social Health Association (ASHA). Provides written information and referrals on STDs; sponsors support groups for people with herpes and HPV.
919-361-8400
919-361-8488 (herpes hotline)
http://www.ashastd.org

Black AIDS Institute. Provides public health information about a variety of topics including testing, treatment, vaccines, and health care access.
http://www.blackaids.org

The Body/A Multimedia AIDS and HIV Information Resource. Provides basic information about HIV—prevention, testing, treatment—and links to related sites.
http://www.thebody.com

CDC National Prevention Information Network. Provides extensive information and links on HIV/AIDS and other STDs.
800-458-5231
http://www.cdcnpin.org

ASHA/CDC STD and AIDS Hotlines. Callers can obtain information, counseling, and referrals for testing and treatment. The hotlines offer information on more than 20 STDs and include Spanish and TTY service.
800-227-8922

HIV InSite: Gateway to AIDS Knowledge. Provides information about prevention, education, treatment, statistics, clinical trials, and new developments.
http://hivinsite.ucsf.edu

Joint United Nations Programme on HIV/AIDS (UNAIDS). Provides statistics and information on the international HIV/AIDS situation.
http://www.unaids.org

Latex Love. Sponsored by the makers of Trojan condoms, this site includes directions for condom use and sample dialogues for overcoming excuses for not using condoms.

http://www.trojancondoms.com/quizzes/safer_sex

The NAMES Project Foundation AIDS Memorial Quilt. Includes the story behind the quilt, images of quilt panels, and information and links relating to HIV infection.

http://www.aidsquilt.org

National Institute of Allergies and Infectious Disease/STDs Information. Provides up-to-date fact sheets and brochures.

http://www.niaid.nih.gov/publications/stds.htm

Planned Parenthood Federation of America. Provides information on STDs, family planning, and contraception.

http://www.plannedparenthood.org

WHO: Sexually Transmitted Infections. Provides information on international statistics and prevention efforts.

http://www.who.int/topics/sexually_transmitted_infections/en

See also the listings for Chapters 6 and 17.

Selected Bibliography

Agot, K. E., et al. 2004. Risk of HIV-1 in rural Kenya: A comparison of circumcised and uncircumcised men. *Epidemiology* 15(2): 157–163.

American Association of Blood Banks. 2004. *Facts About Blood and Blood Banking* (http://www.aabb.org/All_About_Blood/FAQs/aabb_faqs.htm; retrieved December 2, 2004).

American Social Health Association. 2006. *Frequently Asked Questions About Cervical Cancer/HPV Vaccine Access in the U.S.* (http://www.ashastd.org/pdfs/FAQ_HPV_0606.pdf; retrieved September 7, 2006).

AVERT. 2005. *Origins of AIDS and HIV* (http://www.avert.org/origins.htm; retrieved February 7, 2005).

Baeten, J. M., et al. 2005. Female-to-male infectivity of HIV-1 among circumcised and uncircumcised Kenyan men. *Journal of Infectious Diseases* 191(4): 546–553.

Brown, D. R., et al. 2005. A longitudinal study of genital human papillomavirus infection in a cohort of closely followed adolescent women. *Journal of Infectious Diseases* 191(2): 182–192.

Centers for Disease Control and Prevention. 2004. Chlamydia screening among sexually active young female enrollees of health plans. *Morbidity and Mortality Weekly Report* 53(42): 983–985.

Centers for Disease Control and Prevention. 2004. Increases in fluoroquinolone resistant *Neisseria gonorrhoeae* among men who have sex with men, and revised recommendations for gonorrhea treatment, 2004. *Morbidity and Mortality Weekly Report* 53(16): 335–338.

Centers for Disease Control and Prevention. 2004. Transmission of primary and secondary syphilis by oral sex. *Morbidity and Mortality Weekly Report* 53(41): 966–968.

Centers for Disease Control and Prevention. 2006. *A Glance at the HIV/AIDS Epidemic* (http://www.cdc.gov/hiv/resources/factsheets/At-A-Glance.htm; retrieved September 7, 2006).

Centers for Disease Control and Prevention. 2006. Cases of HIV infection and AIDS in the United States, by race/ethnicity, 2000–2004. *HIV/AIDS Surveillance Supplemental Report* 2006 12(1): 1–36.

Centers for Disease Control and Prevention. 2006. *HIV/AIDS Surveillance Report, 2005* (http://www.cdc.gov/hiv/topics/surveillance/resources/reports; retrieved December 1, 2006).

Centers for Disease Control and Prevention. 2006. Revised recommendations for HIV testing of adults, adolescents, and pregnant women in health-care settings. *Morbidity and Mortality Weekly Report* 55(RR-14): 1–17.

Centers for Disease Control and Prevention. 2006. Trends in HIV-related risk behaviors among high school students—United States, 1991–2005. *Morbidity and Mortality Weekly Report* 55(31): 851–854.

Cohen, Myron. 2004. HIV and sexually transmitted diseases: A lethal synergy. *Topics in HIV Medicine* 12(4):104–107.

Crosby, R., and R. J. DiClemente. 2004. Use of recreational Viagra among men having sex with men. *Sexually Transmitted Infections* 80(6): 466–468.

Erbelding, E. J., and J. M. Zenilman. 2005. Toward better control of sexually transmitted diseases. *New England Journal of Medicine* 352(7): 720–721.

Food and Drug Administration. 2004. *FDA Approves First Oral Fluid Based Rapid HIV Test Kit* (http://www.fda.gov/bbs/topics/news/2004/NEW01042.html; retrieved February 7, 2005).

Gupta, R., et al. 2004. Valacyclovir and acyclovir for suppression of shedding of herpes simplex virus in the genital tract. *Journal of Infectious Diseases* 190(8): 1374–1381.

Hampton, T. 2006. High prevalence of lesser-known STDs. *Journal of the American Medical Association* 295(21): 2467.

Hightow, L. B., et al. 2005. The unexpected movement of the HIV epidemic in the southeastern United States: Transmission among college students. *Journal of Acquired Immune Deficiency Syndrome* 38(5): 531–537.

Huppert, J. S. 2006. New detection methods for trichomoniasis may help curb more serious STIs. *Patient Care for the Nurse Practitioner* 40(5).

Kimberlin, D., and D. Rouse. 2004. Genital herpes. *New England Journal of Medicine* 350(19): 1970–1977.

Mathers, C. D., and Loncar, D. 2006. Projections of global mortality and burden of disease from 2002 to 2030. Public Library of Science, *Medicine* 3(11):2011–2030.

Merson, M. 2006. The HIV-AIDS pandemic at 25—The global response. *New England Journal of Medicine* 354(23): 2414–2417.

Miller, W. C., et al. 2004. Prevalence of chlamydial and gonococcal infections among young adults in the United States. *Journal of the American Medical Association* 291(18): 2229–2236.

National Institutes of Allergy and Infectious Diseases. 2006. *HIV Infection in Women—May 2006* (http://www.niaid.nih.gov/factsheets/womenhiv.htm; retrieved September 6, 2006).

Ness, R. B., et al. 2005. Douching, pelvic inflammatory disease, and incident gonococcal and chlamydial genital infection in a cohort of high-risk women. *American Journal of Epidemiology* 61(2): 186–195.

Rodriguez, B., et al. Predictive value of plasma HIV RNA level on rate of CD4 T-cell decline in untreated HIV infection. *Journal of the American Medical Association* 296(12): 1498–1506.

Sanders, G. D., et al. 2005. Cost-effectiveness of screening for HIV in the era of highly active antiretroviral therapy. *New England Journal of Medicine* 352(6): 570–585.

Sepkowitz, K. 2006. One disease, two epidemics—AIDS at 25. *New England Journal of Medicine* 354(23): 2411–2414.

UNAIDS. 2006. *2006 Report on the Global AIDS Epidemic* (http://www.unaids.org/en/HIV_data/2006GlobalReport/default.asp; retrieved September 7, 2006).

Wang, C., et al. 2004. Mortality in HIV-seropositive versus -seronegative persons in the era of highly active antiretroviral therapy: Implications for when to initiate therapy. *Journal of Infectious Diseases* 190(6): 1046–1054.

Weinstock, H., S. Berman, and W. Cates. 2004. Sexually transmitted diseases among American youth: Incidence and prevalence estimates, 2000. *Perspectives on Sexual and Reproductive Health* 36(1): 6–10.

World Health Organization. 2004. *Antiretroviral Drugs for Treating Pregnant Women and Preventing HIV Infection in Infants* (http://www.who.int/hiv/pub/mtct/en/arvdrugswomenguidelinesfinal.pdf; retrieved December 6, 2004).

Xu, F., et al. 2006. Trends in herpes simplex virus type 1 and type 2 seroprevalence in the United States. *Journal of the American Medical Association* 296(8): 964–973.

Yeni, P. G., et al. 2004. Treatment for adult HIV infection. *Journal of the American Medical Association* 292(2): 251–265.

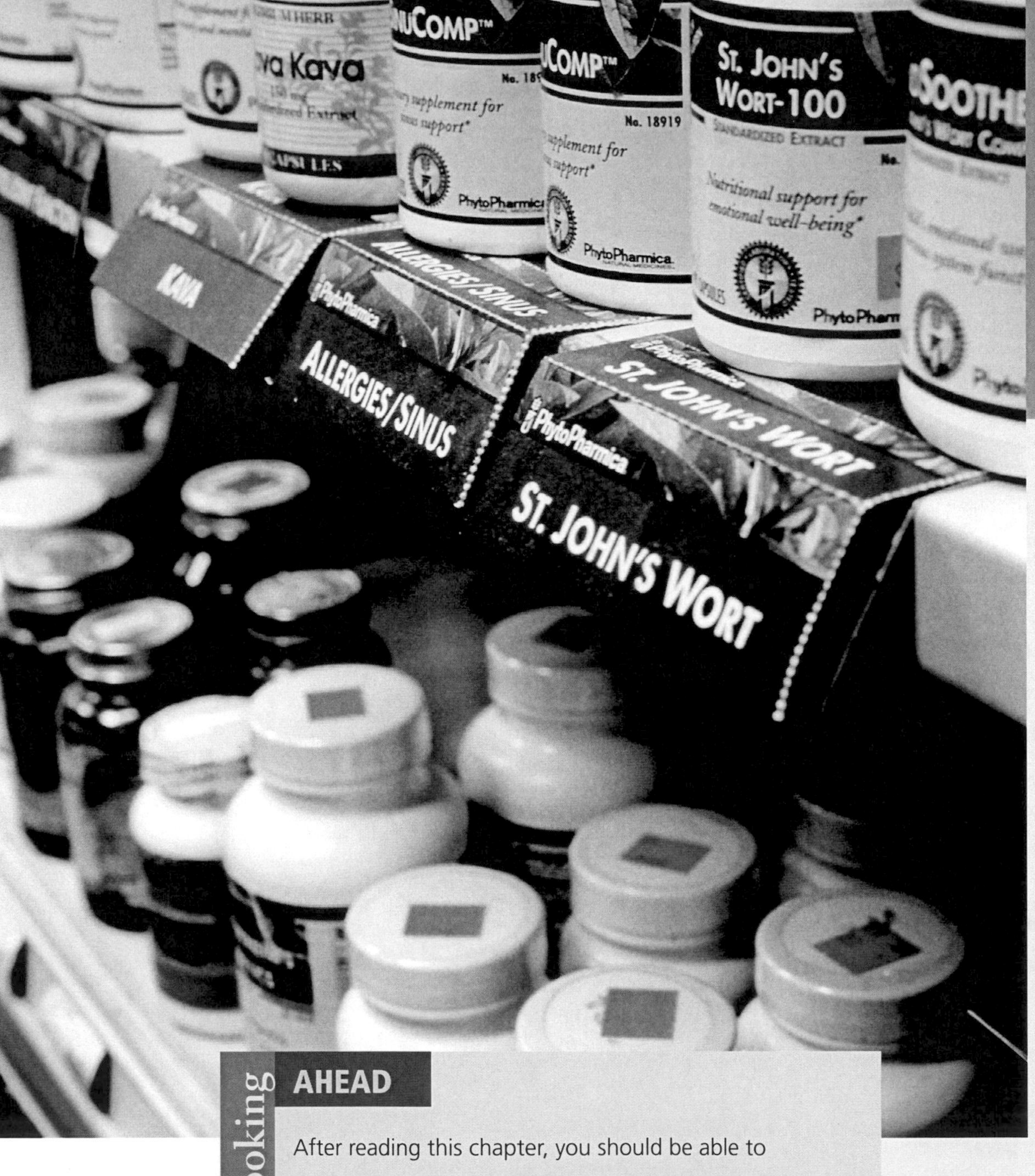

21

Looking AHEAD

After reading this chapter, you should be able to

- Explain the self-care decision-making process and discuss options for self-treatment
- Describe the basic premises, practices, and providers of conventional medicine
- Describe the basic premises, practices, and providers of complementary and alternative medicine
- Explain how to communicate effectively with a health care provider and to evaluate different forms of treatment
- Discuss different types of health insurance plans

Conventional and Complementary Medicine: Skills for the Health Care Consumer

Test Your Knowledge

1. **The people most likely to use complementary and alternative medicine are those without a regular primary care physician.**
   True or false?
2. **Which practice or interest is shared by both conventional Western medicine and complementary and alternative medicine?**
   a. careful observation of symptoms
   b. treatment with remedies derived from plants
   c. concern with the patient-physician relationship
3. **Herbal remedies and dietary supplements like ginkgo and St. John's wort must meet FDA standards for safety and effectiveness before they can be put on the market.**
   True or false?
4. **Generic drugs are generally less effective than brand-name drugs.**
   True or false?
5. **Approximately how many Americans have no health insurance?**
   a. 4 million
   b. 14 million
   c. 40 million

ANSWERS

1. FALSE. The more often a person visits a primary care physician, the more likely he or she is to use complementary and alternative medicine.
2. ALL THREE. Although there are profound philosophical differences between the approaches, they share many characteristics.
3. FALSE. Manufacturers are responsible for the safety of the dietary supplements they sell; the FDA has the power to restrict a product if it is found to pose a health risk after it is on the market. Manufacturers do not have to prove that their products are effective.
4. FALSE. Price is often the only difference. The generic version of a drug has the same active ingredient as the brand-name drug, but it may have different inactive ingredients.
5. C. According to the National Center for Health Statistics, more than 42 million Americans (including nearly 10% of all children) have no health insurance coverage. Some private estimates are as high as 50 million.

Ww Visit the *Core Concepts in Health* Online Learning Center (www.mhhe.com/insel10e) for study aids and many additional resources.

Today, people are becoming more confident of their ability to solve personal health problems on their own. People who manage their own health care gather information and learn skills from physicians and other health care providers, friends, classes, books, magazines, Web sites, or self-help groups. They solicit opinions and advice, make decisions, and take action. They know how to practice safe, effective self-care, and they know how to make decisions about professional medical care, whether conventional Western medicine or complementary and alternative medicine. This chapter will help you develop the skills both to identify and manage medical problems and to make the health care system work effectively for you.

SELF-CARE: MANAGING MEDICAL PROBLEMS

Effectively managing medical problems involves developing several skills. First, you need to learn how to be a good observer of your own body and assess your symptoms. You also must be able to decide when to seek professional advice and when you can safely deal with the problem on your own. You need to know how to safely and effectively self-treat common medical problems. Finally, you need to know how to develop a partnership with physicians and other health care providers and how to carry out treatment plans.

Self-Assessment

Symptoms are often an expression of the body's attempt to heal itself. For example, the pain and swelling that occur after an ankle injury immobilize the injured joint to allow healing to take place. A fever may be an attempt to make the body less hospitable to infectious agents. A cough can help clear the airways and protect the lungs. Understanding what a symptom means and what is going on in your body helps reduce anxiety about symptoms and enables you to practice safe self-care that supports your body's own healing mechanisms.

Carefully observing symptoms also lets you identify those signals that suggest you need professional assistance. You should begin by noting when the symptom began, how often and when it occurs, what makes it worse, what makes it better, and whether you have any associated symptoms. You can also monitor your body's vital signs, such as temperature and heart rate. Medical self-tests for such things as blood pressure, blood sugar, pregnancy detection, and urinary tract infections can also help you make a more informed decision about when to seek medical help and when to self-treat.

Decision Making: Knowing When to See a Physician

In general, you should see a physician for symptoms that you would describe as follows:

1. *Severe.* If the symptom is very severe or intense, medical assistance is advised. Examples include severe pains, major injuries, and other emergencies.
2. *Unusual.* If the symptom is peculiar and unfamiliar, it is wise to check it out with your physician. Examples include unexplained lumps, changes in a mole, problems with vision, difficulty swallowing, numbness, weakness, unexplained weight loss, and blood in sputum, urine, or stool.
3. *Persistent.* If the symptom lasts longer than expected, seek medical advice. Examples in adults include fever for more than 5 days, a cough lasting longer than 2 weeks, a sore that doesn't heal within a month, and hoarseness lasting longer than 3 weeks.
4. *Recurrent.* If a symptom tends to return again and again, medical evaluation is advised. Examples include recurrent headaches, stomach pains, and backache.

Sometimes a single symptom is not a cause for concern, but when the symptom is accompanied by other symptoms, the combination suggests a more serious problem. For example, a fever with a stiff neck suggests meningitis. If you evaluate your symptoms and think that you need professional help, you must decide how urgent the problem is. If it is a true emergency, you should go (or call someone to take you) to the nearest emergency room (ER). Emergencies include

- Major trauma or injury, such as head injury, suspected broken bone, deep wound, severe burn, eye injury, or animal bite
- Uncontrollable bleeding or internal bleeding, as indicated by blood in the sputum, vomit, or stool
- Intolerable and uncontrollable pain or severe chest pain
- Severe shortness of breath
- Persistent abdominal pain, especially if associated with nausea and vomiting
- Poisoning or drug overdose
- Loss of consciousness or seizure
- Stupor, drowsiness, or disorientation that cannot be explained
- Severe or worsening reaction to an insect bite or sting or to a medication, especially if breathing is difficult

If your problem is not an emergency but still requires medical attention, call your physician's office. Often you can be given medical advice over the phone without the

Mind/Body/Spirit

Expressive Writing and Chronic Conditions

The act of writing down feelings and thoughts about stressful life events has been shown to help people with chronic conditions improve their health. In one recent study, people with asthma or rheumatoid arthritis were asked to write down their feelings about the most stressful event in their lives; they wrote for 20 minutes a day over a 3-day period. In follow-up exams 4 months later, nearly half of the patients who engaged in expressive writing experienced positive changes in their condition, such as improved lung function or reduced joint pain. Only about a quarter of the control group, who wrote about their daily plans, experienced a positive change in health.

Investigators remain unsure why writing about one's feelings has beneficial effects. It is possible that expressing feelings about a traumatic event helps people work through the event and put it behind them. The resulting sense of release and control may reduce stress levels and have positive physical effects such as reduced heart rate and blood pressure and improved immune function. Alternatively, expressive writing may change the way people think about previous stressful events in their lives and help them cope with new stressors. Whatever the cause, it's clear that expressive writing can be a safe, inexpensive, and effective supplement to standard treatment of certain chronic illnesses.

What about the effects of expressive writing on otherwise healthy individuals? Other studies have, in fact, found a similar benefit: People who wrote about traumatic experiences reported fewer symptoms, fewer days off work, fewer visits to the doctor, improved mood, and a more positive outlook.

If you'd like to try expressive writing to help you deal with a traumatic event, set aside a special time—15 minutes a day for 4 consecutive days, for example, or 1 day a week for 4 weeks. Write in a place where you won't be interrupted or distracted. Explore your very deepest thoughts and feelings and why you feel the way you do. Don't worry about grammar or coherence or about what someone else might think about what you're writing; you are writing just for yourself. You may find the writing exercise to be distressing in the short term—sadness and depression are common when dealing with feelings about a stressful event—but most people report relief and contentment soon after writing for several days.

SOURCES: Pennebaker, J. W. 2004. *Writing to Heal: A Guided Journal for Recovering from Trauma and Emotional Upheaval.* Oakland, Calif.: New Harbinger; Smyth, J. M., et al. 1999. Effects of writing about stressful experiences on symptom reduction in patients with asthma or rheumatoid arthritis: A randomized trial. *Journal of the American Medical Association* 281(14): 1304–1309; Spiegel, D. 1999. Healing words: Emotional expression and disease outcome. *Journal of the American Medical Association* 281(14): 1328–1329.

inconvenience of a visit. To help you make wise medical decisions, a Self-Care Guide for Common Medical Problems is provided in Appendix B.

Self-Treatment: Many Options

When confronted with a new symptom, many people try to find some pill or potion that will relieve or cure it However, other self-treatment options are available.

Watchful Waiting In most cases, your body itself can relieve your symptoms and heal the disorder. The prescriptions filled by your body's internal pharmacy are frequently the safest and most effective treatment, so patience and careful self-observation are often the best choices in self-treatment.

Nondrug Options Nondrug options are often easy, inexpensive, safe, and highly effective. For example, massage, ice packs, and neck exercises may at times be more helpful than drugs in relieving headaches and other pains. Getting adequate rest, increasing exercise, drinking more water, eating more or less of certain foods, using humidifiers, changes in ergonomics when working at a desk, and so on are just some of the hundreds of nondrug options for preventing or relieving many common health problems. For a variety of disorders caused or aggravated by stress, the treatment of choice may be relaxation, visualization, humor, assertive communication, changing negative thoughts, or other stress-management strategies (see Chapter 2 and the box "Expressive Writing and Chronic Conditions").

Self-Medication Self-treatment with nonprescription medications is an important part of our health care system. Nonprescription or **over-the-counter (OTC) medications** are medicines that the Food and Drug Administration (FDA) has determined are safe for use without a physician's prescription. There are more than 100,000 OTC drugs on the market; about 60% of all medications are sold over the counter. Within every 2-week period, nearly 70% of Americans use one or more OTC drugs.

Many OTC drugs are highly effective in relieving symptoms and sometimes in curing illnesses. In fact, many OTC drugs were formerly prescription drugs. More than 600 products sold over the counter today use ingredients or dosage strengths available only by prescription

Term

over-the-counter (OTC) medication A medication or product that can be purchased by the consumer without a prescription.

Vw

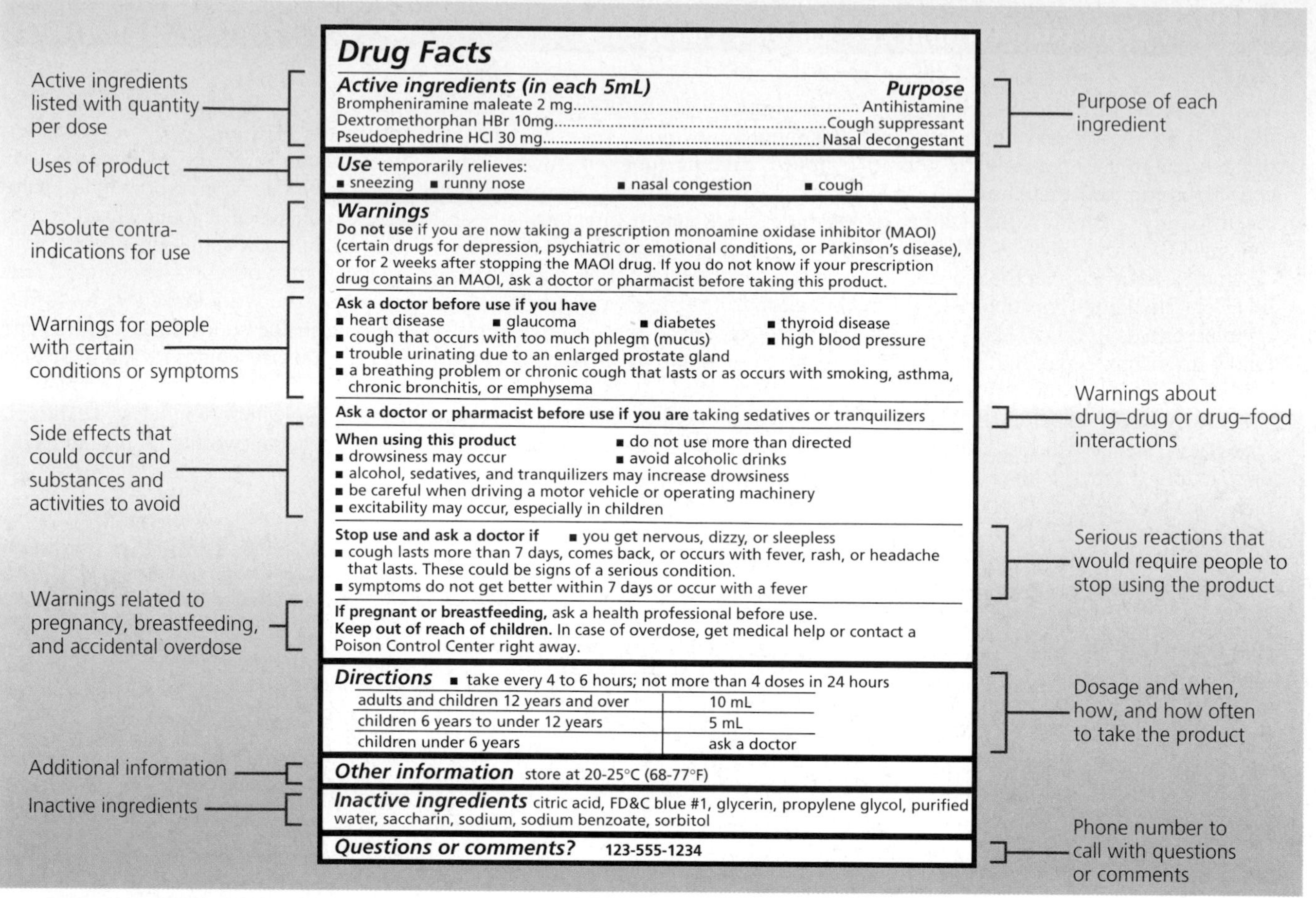

Drug Facts
Active ingredients (in each 5mL) Purpose
Brompheniramine maleate 2 mg .... Antihistamine
Dextromethorphan HBr 10mg .... Cough suppressant
Pseudoephedrine HCl 30 mg .... Nasal decongestant
Use temporarily relieves:
■ sneezing ■ runny nose ■ nasal congestion ■ cough
Warnings
Do not use if you are now taking a prescription monoamine oxidase inhibitor (MAOI) (certain drugs for depression, psychiatric or emotional conditions, or Parkinson's disease), or for 2 weeks after stopping the MAOI drug. If you do not know if your prescription drug contains an MAOI, ask a doctor or pharmacist before taking this product.
Ask a doctor before use if you have
■ heart disease ■ glaucoma ■ diabetes ■ thyroid disease
■ cough that occurs with too much phlegm (mucus) ■ high blood pressure
■ trouble urinating due to an enlarged prostate gland
■ a breathing problem or chronic cough that lasts or as occurs with smoking, asthma, chronic bronchitis, or emphysema
Ask a doctor or pharmacist before use if you are taking sedatives or tranquilizers
When using this product ■ do not use more than directed
■ drowsiness may occur ■ avoid alcoholic drinks
■ alcohol, sedatives, and tranquilizers may increase drowsiness
■ be careful when driving a motor vehicle or operating machinery
■ excitability may occur, especially in children
Stop use and ask a doctor if ■ you get nervous, dizzy, or sleepless
■ cough lasts more than 7 days, comes back, or occurs with fever, rash, or headache that lasts. These could be signs of a serious condition.
■ symptoms do not get better within 7 days or occur with a fever
If pregnant or breastfeeding, ask a health professional before use.
Keep out of reach of children. In case of overdose, get medical help or contact a Poison Control Center right away.
Directions ■ take every 4 to 6 hours; not more than 4 doses in 24 hours
adults and children 12 years and over | 10 mL
children 6 years to under 12 years | 5 mL
children under 6 years | ask a doctor
Other information store at 20-25°C (68-77°F)
Inactive ingredients citric acid, FD&C blue #1, glycerin, propylene glycol, purified water, saccharin, sodium, sodium benzoate, sorbitol
Questions or comments? 123-555-1234
Active ingredients listed with quantity per dose
Uses of product
Absolute contra-indications for use
Warnings for people with certain conditions or symptoms
Side effects that could occur and substances and activities to avoid
Warnings related to pregnancy, breastfeeding, and accidental overdose
Additional information
Inactive ingredients
Purpose of each ingredient
Warnings about drug–drug or drug–food interactions
Serious reactions that would require people to stop using the product
Dosage and when, how, and how often to take the product
Phone number to call with questions or comments

Figure 21-1 Reading and understanding OTC drug labels. SOURCE: Food and Drug Administration. 1999. Over-the-counter human drugs; labeling requirements; final rule. *Federal Register* 64, no. 51(17 March): 13254–13303.

20 years ago. With this increased consumer choice, however, comes increased consumer responsibility for using OTC drugs safely.

Consumers also need to be aware of the barrage of OTC drug advertising aimed at them. The implication of such advertising is that every symptom can and should be relieved by a drug. Although many OTC products are effective, others are unnecessary or divert attention from better ways of coping. Many ingredients in OTC drugs—perhaps 70%—have not been proven to be effective, a fact the FDA does not dispute. And any drug may have risks and side effects.

Follow these simple guidelines to self-medicate safely:

1. Always read labels, and follow directions carefully. The information on most OTC drug labels now appears in a standard format developed by the FDA (Figure 21-1). Ingredients, directions for safe use, and warnings are clearly indicated; but, if you have any questions, ask a pharmacist or physician before using a product.

2. Do not exceed the recommended dosage or length of treatment unless you discuss this change with your physician.

3. Use caution if you are taking other medications or supplements, because OTC drugs and herbal supplements can interact with some prescription drugs. If you have questions about drug interactions, ask your physician or pharmacist *before* you mix medicines.

4. Try to select medications with one active ingredient rather than combination products. A product with multiple ingredients is likely to include drugs for symptoms you don't even have. Why risk the side effects of medications you don't need? Using single-ingredient products also allows you to adjust the dosage of each medication separately for optimal symptom relief with minimal side effects.

5. When choosing medications, try to buy **generic drugs,** which contain the same active ingredient as the brand-name product but generally at a much lower cost. (Brand-name and generic drugs are discussed in more detail later in the chapter.)

6. Never take or give a drug from an unlabeled container or in the dark when you can't read what the label says.

Closet

- Analgesic (relieves pain)
- Antacid (relieves upset stomach)
- Antibiotic ointment (reduces risk of infection)
- Antihistamine (relieves allergy symptoms)
- Antiseptic (helps stop infection)
- Fever reducer (adult and child)
- Hydrocortisone (relieves itching and inflammation)
- Decongestant (relieves stuffy nose and other cold symptoms)

Medicine Cabinet

- Adhesive bandages
- Adhesive tape
- Alcohol wipes
- Calibrated measuring spoon
- Disinfectant
- Gauze pads
- Thermometer
- Tweezers

Figure 21-2 Your home medical care kit. A cool, dark, and dry place such as the top of a linen closet, preferably in a locked container and out of a child's reach, is best for storing medicines. Showers and baths create heat and humidity that can cause some drugs to deteriorate rapidly. Use your bathroom medicine cabinet for supplies that aren't affected by heat and humidity. SOURCE: Lewis, C. 2000. Your medicine cabinet needs an annual checkup, too. *FDA Consumer,* March/April.

7. If you are pregnant or nursing or have a chronic condition such as kidney disease, consult your physician before self-medicating.

8. The expiration date marked on many medications is an estimate of how long the *unopened* medication is likely to be potent. Once the package is opened, the medication will probably be potent for about a year if stored properly. Mark the date on the package when you open it, and dispose of it safely after a year by taking it to a pharmacy or hospital.

9. Store your medications in a cool, dry place that is out of the reach of children (Figure 21-2).

10. Use special caution with aspirin. Because of an association with a rare but serious problem known as Reye's syndrome, aspirin should not be used by children or adolescents who may have the flu, chicken pox, or any other viral illness.

PROFESSIONAL MEDICAL AND HEALTH CARE: CHOICES AND CHANGE

When self-treatment is not appropriate or sufficient, you need to seek professional medical care, whether by going to a hospital emergency room, by scheduling an appointment with your physician, or by accessing some other part of the American medical and health care system. This system is a broad network of individuals and organizations, including independent practitioners, allied health care providers, hospitals, clinics, and public and private insurance programs.

In recent years, many Americans have also sought health care from practitioners of **complementary and alternative medicine (CAM),** defined as those therapies and practices that do not form part of conventional, or mainstream, health care and medical practices as taught in most U.S. medical schools and offered in most U.S. hospitals. The most commonly used CAM therapies are relaxation techniques, herbal medicine, massage, and chiropractic (Table 21-1). People often use CAM therapies in addition to their conventional medical treatments, but many do not tell their physicians about it.

Consumers turn to CAM for a large variety of purposes related to health and well-being, such as boosting their immune system, lowering their cholesterol levels, losing weight, quitting smoking, or enhancing their memory. There are indications that people with chronic conditions, including cancer, asthma, autoimmune diseases, and HIV infection, are particularly likely to try CAM therapies. Despite their growing popularity, many CAM practices remain controversial, and individuals need to be critically aware of safety issues. In the next sections of this chapter, we examine the principles and providers of both **conventional medicine**—the dominant medical system in the United States and Europe, also referred to as standard Western medicine or biomedicine—and of complementary and alternative medicine, with particular attention to consumer issues.

Terms

generic drug A drug that is not registered or protected by a trademark; a drug that does not have a brand name.

complementary and alternative medicine (CAM) Therapies or practices that are not part of conventional or mainstream health care and medical practice as taught in most U.S. medical schools and available at most U.S. health care facilities; examples of CAM practices include acupuncture and herbal remedies.

conventional medicine A system of medicine based on the application of the scientific method; diseases are thought to be caused by identifiable physical factors and characterized by a representative set of symptoms; also called *biomedicine* or *standard Western medicine.*

VITAL STATISTICS

Table 21-1 Use of Complementary and Alternative Therapies in the United States

	Percent Who Ever Used Therapy
Prayer	55.3
Natural products (nonvitamin, nonmineral)	25.0
Chiropractic care	19.9
Deep breathing exercises	14.6
Meditation	10.2
Massage	9.3
Yoga	7.5
Diet-based therapies	6.8
Progressive relaxation	4.2
Acupuncture	4.0
Megavitamin therapy	3.9
Homeopathic treatment	3.6
Guided imagery	3.0
T'ai chi	2.5
Hypnosis	1.8
Energy healing therapy/Reiki	1.1
Biofeedback	1.0
Any therapy	**74.6**

SOURCE: Barnes, P. M., et al. 2004. Complementary and alternative medicine use among adults: United States, 2002. *Advance Data from Vital and Health Statistics* No. 343. Hyattsville, Md.: National Center for Health Statistics.

CONVENTIONAL MEDICINE

Referring to conventional medicine as standard Western medicine draws attention to the fact that it differs from the various medical systems that have developed in China, Japan, India, and other parts of the world. Calling it "biomedicine" reflects conventional medicine's basis in the findings of a variety of biological sciences.

Premises and Assumptions of Conventional Medicine

One of the important characteristics of Western medicine is the belief that disease is caused by identifiable physical factors. This belief can be traced back to Hippocrates, the Greek physician of the fourth century B.C. who is credited with placing the practice of medicine on a scientific footing. In Hippocrates' time, the causes of disease were thought to include the interplay of various forces and elements; today, Western medicine identifies the causes of disease as pathogens, such as bacteria and viruses, genetic factors, and unhealthy lifestyles that result in changes at the molecular and cellular levels. In most cases, however, the focus is primarily on the physical causes of the illness rather than mental or spiritual imbalance.

Another feature that distinguishes Western biomedicine from other medical systems is the concept that every disease is defined by a certain set of symptoms and that these symptoms are similar in most patients suffering from this disease. Western medicine tends to treat illness as an isolated biological disturbance that can occur in any human being, rather than as integral in some way to the individual with the illness.

Related to the idea of illness as the result of invasion by outside factors is the strong orientation toward methods of destroying pathogens or preventing them from causing serious infection. The public health measures of the nineteenth and twentieth centuries—chlorination of drinking water, sewage disposal, food safety regulations, vaccination programs, education about hygiene, and so on—are an outgrowth of this kind of orientation. (As described in Chapter 1, these public health measures are largely responsible for the 25-year increase in life expectancy that Americans experienced in the twentieth century.)

The implementation of public health measures is one way to control pathogens; another is the use of drugs. The discovery and development of sulfa drugs, antibiotics, and steroids in the twentieth century, along with advances in chemistry that made it possible to identify the active ingredients in common herbal remedies, paved the way for the current close identification of Western medicine with **pharmaceuticals** (medical drugs, both prescription and over-the-counter). Western medicine also relies heavily on surgery and on advanced medical technology to discover the physical causes of disease and to remove or destroy them.

Further, Western medicine is based on scientific ways of obtaining knowledge and explaining phenomena. Scientific explanations result from the application of the scientific method to a question or problem; they have a blend of characteristics that set them apart from other types of explanation, such as those based on common sense, faith, belief, or authority. Scientific explanations are

- *Empirical*—they are based on the evidence of the senses and on objective and systematic observation, often carried out under carefully controlled conditions; they must be capable of verification by others.
- *Rational*—they follow the rules of logic and are consistent with known facts.
- *Testable*—either they are verifiable through direct observation or they lead to predictions about what should occur under conditions not yet observed.
- *Parsimonious*—they explain phenomena with the fewest number of assumptions.
- *General*—they have broad explanatory power.
- *Rigorously evaluated*—they are constantly evaluated for consistency with the evidence and known principles, for parsimony, and for generality.

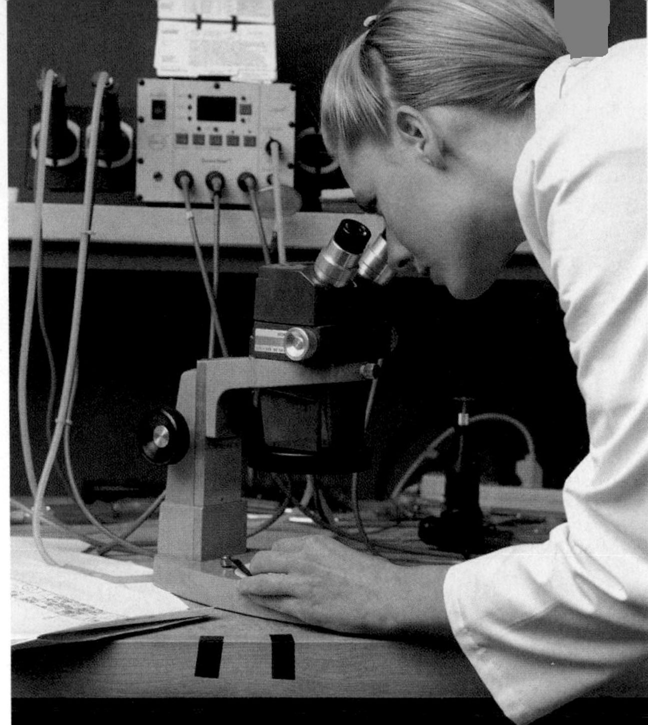

Conventional Western medicine is firmly grounded in scientific explanations resulting from the application of the scientific method to a question or problem. The identification of bacteria and other microorganisms as a key cause of disease led to many public health measures and treatments that reduced U.S. deaths from infectious diseases.

- *Tentative*—scientists are willing to entertain the possibility that their explanations are faulty.

The scientific method is both a way of acquiring knowledge and a way of thinking that involves approaching a problem by carefully defining its parameters, seeking out relevant information, and subjecting proposed solutions to rigorous testing.

Western medicine translates the scientific method into practice through the research process, a highly refined and well-established approach to exploring the causes of disease and ensuring the safety and efficacy of treatments. Research studies range from case studies—descriptions of a single patient's illness and treatment—to clinical trials conducted on large populations and carried out under carefully controlled conditions over a period of many years. The process of drug development is equally rigorous. Drugs are developed and tested through an elaborate course that begins with preliminary research in the lab and continues through trials with human participants, review and approval by the FDA, and monitoring of the drug's effects after it is on the market. The process may take 12 years or more, and only about 20% of drugs are eventually approved.

When results of research studies are published in medical journals, a community of scientists, physicians, researchers, and scholars has the opportunity to share the findings and enter a dialogue about the subject. Publication of research often prompts further research designed to replicate and confirm the findings, challenge the conclusions, or pursue a related line of thought or experiment. (For guidelines on how to interpret research when it is reported in the popular press, see the box "Evaluating Health News" on p. 636.)

The Providers of Conventional Medicine

Conventional medicine is practiced by a wide range of health care professionals in the United States. Several kinds of professionals are permitted to practice medicine independently, including medical doctors, osteopaths, podiatrists, optometrists, and dentists.

- **Medical doctors** are practitioners who hold a doctor of medicine (M.D.) degree from an accredited medical school. In the United States, an education in medicine has several stages: 4 years of premedical education in a college or university, with an emphasis on the sciences; 4 years of medical school, which teaches basic medical skills and awards the M.D. degree; graduate medical study, called a residency and lasting from 3 to 8 years, during which a specialty is chosen and studied and a medical license is obtained; and continuing medical education to keep abreast of advances in medical science. Twenty-four medical specialties are currently approved by the American Board of Medical Specialties, each with its own rule-making and certifying body. The larger specialties are further divided into subspecialties; for example, internal medicine includes subspecialties such as cardiology and gastroenterology. Visit the Web site for the American Board of Medical Specialties (www.abms.org) for a complete list. Becoming a subspecialist generally requires several more years of formal training after the completion of a residency.
- **Doctors of osteopathic medicine** (D.O.) receive a medical education similar to that of medical doctors, but their training places special emphasis on musculoskeletal problems and manipulative therapy. M.D.s and D.O.s are the two types of "complete" physicians in the United States, meaning they are trained and licensed to perform surgery and prescribe medication. D.O.s are graduates of osteopathic medical schools, which

Terms

Vw

pharmaceuticals Medical drugs, both prescription and over-the-counter.

medical doctor An independent practitioner who holds a doctor of medicine degree from an accredited medical school.

doctor of osteopathic medicine A medical practitioner who has graduated from an osteopathic medical school; osteopathy incorporates the theories and practices of scientific medicine but focuses on musculoskeletal problems and manipulative therapy.

Evaluating Health News

Health-related research is now described in popular newspapers and magazines rather than just medical journals, meaning that more and more people have access to the information. Greater access is certainly a plus, but news reports of research studies may oversimplify or exaggerate both the results and what those results mean to the average person. Researchers do not set out to mislead people, but they must often strike a balance between reporting promising preliminary findings to the public, thereby allowing people to act on them, and waiting 10–20 years until long-term studies confirm (or disprove) a particular theory.

All this can leave you in a difficult position. You cannot become an expert on all subjects, capable of effectively evaluating all the available health news. However, the following questions can help you better assess the health advice that appears in the popular media:

1. *Is the report based on research or on an anecdote?* Information or advice based on one or more carefully designed research studies has more validity than one person's experiences.

2. *What is the source of the information?* A study published in a respected peer-reviewed journal has been examined by editors and other researchers in the field, people who are in a position to evaluate the merits of a study and its results. Many journal articles also include information on the authors and funders of research, alerting readers to any possible conflicts of interest. Research presented at medical meetings should be considered very preliminary because the results have not yet undergone a thorough prepublication review; many such studies are never published. It is also wise to ask who funded a study to determine whether there is any potential for bias. Information from government agencies and national research organizations is usually considered fairly reliable.

3. *How big was the study?* A study involving many subjects is more likely to yield reliable results than a study involving only a few subjects. Another important indication that a finding is meaningful is if several studies yield the same results.

4. *Who were the participants involved in the study?* Research findings are more likely to apply to you if you share important characteristics with the participants of the study. For example, the results of a study on men over age 50 who smoke may not be particularly meaningful for a 30-year-old nonsmoking woman. Even less applicable are studies done in test tubes or on animals. Such research should be considered very preliminary in terms of its applicability to humans. Promising results from laboratory or animal research frequently cannot be replicated in human study subjects.

5. *What kind of study was it?* Epidemiological studies involve observation or interviews in order to trace the relationships among lifestyle, physical characteristics, and diseases. While epidemiological studies can suggest links, they cannot establish cause-and-effect relationships. Clinical or interventional studies or trials involve testing the effects of different treatments on groups of people who have similar lifestyles and characteristics. They are more likely to provide conclusive evidence of a cause-and-effect relationship. The best interventional studies share the following characteristics:

- *Controlled.* A group of people who receive the treatment is compared with a matched group of people who do not receive the treatment.
- *Randomized.* The treatment and control groups are selected randomly.
- *Double-blind.* Researchers and participants are unaware of who is receiving the treatment.
- *Multicenter.* The experiment is performed at more than one institution.

A third type of study, meta-analysis, involves combining the results of individual studies to get an overall view of the effectiveness of a treatment.

6. *What do the statistics really say?* First, are the results described as statistically significant? If a study is large and well designed, its results can be deemed statistically significant, meaning there is less than a 5% chance that the findings resulted from chance. Second, are the results stated in terms of relative or absolute risk? Many findings are reported in terms of relative risk—how a particular treatment or condition affects a person's disease risk. Consider the following examples of relative risk:

- According to some estimates, taking estrogen without progesterone can increase a postmenopausal woman's risk of dying from endometrial cancer by 233%.
- Giving AZT to HIV-infected pregnant women reduces prenatal transmission of HIV by about 90%.

The first of these findings seems far more dramatic than the second—until you also consider absolute risk, the actual risk of the illness in the population being considered. The absolute risk of endometrial cancer is 0.3%; a 233% increase based on the effects of estrogen raises it to 1%, a change of 0.7%. Without treatment, about 25% of infants born to HIV-infected women will be infected with HIV; with treatment, the absolute risk drops to about 2%, a change of 23%. Because the absolute risk of an HIV-infected mother passing the virus to her infant (25%) is so much greater than a woman's risk of developing endometrial cancer compared with (0.3%), a smaller change in relative risk translates into a much greater change in absolute risk.

7. *Is new health advice being offered?* If the media report new guidelines for health behavior or medical treatment, examine the source. Government agencies and national research foundations usually consider a great deal of evidence before offering health advice. Above all, use common sense, and check with your physician before making a major change in your health habits based on news reports.

SOURCES: Stevens, L. M. 2006. Medical journals. *Journal of the American Medical Association* 295(15): 1860; Nemours Foundation. 2006. Figuring Out Health News (http://www.kidshealth.org/teen/safety/safebasics/health_news.html; retrieved September 17, 2006); Tufts University. 2006. Studying Research Studies: 10 Questions You Need to Ask. *Tufts University Health and Nutrition Letter,* June, 4–5; Patient Inform. 2005. Understanding Medical Research: What to Look for When Reading Medical Research (http://www.patientinform.org/understanding-medical-research/; retrieved September 17, 2006).

emphasize training students to be primary care physicians and to practice a whole-person approach to medicine.

- **Podiatrists** are practitioners who specialize in the medical and surgical care of the feet. They hold a doctor of podiatric medicine (D.P.M.) degree; the length of training is similar to that of M.D.s. They can prescribe drugs and perform surgery on the feet.
- **Optometrists** are practitioners trained to examine the eyes, detect eye diseases, and treat vision problems. They hold a doctor of optometry (O.D.) degree. All states permit optometrists to use drugs for diagnostic purposes, and most permit them to use drugs to treat minor eye problems. (Ophthalmologists are M.D. eye specialists who care for all types of eye problems and can perform eye surgery.)
- **Dentists** specialize in the care of the teeth and mouth. They are graduates of 4-year dental schools and hold the doctor of dental surgery (D.D.S.) or doctor of medical dentistry (D.M.D.) degree; specialists receive additional education. Dentists can perform surgery and prescribe drugs within the scope of their training.

In addition to these practitioners, there are millions of other trained health care professionals, known as **allied health care providers,** working in the United States. Some of them are licensed to work independently; others are permitted to work under medical supervision or medical referral. They include registered nurses (R.N.s), licensed vocational nurses (L.V.N.s), physical therapists, social workers, registered dietitians (R.D.s), physician assistants (P.A.s), nurse practitioners, and certified nurse midwives.

Choosing a Primary Care Physician

Most experts believe it is best to have a primary care physician, someone who gets to know you, who coordinates your medical care, and who refers you to specialists when you need them. Primary care physicians include those certified in family practice, internal medicine, pediatrics, and obstetrics-gynecology. These physicians are able to diagnose and treat the vast majority of common health problems; they also provide many preventive health services. The best time to look for a physician is before you are sick (see the box "Health Care Visits and Gender" on p. 638).

To select a physician, begin by making a list of possible choices. If your insurance limits the health care providers you can see, check the plan's list first. Ask for recommendations from family, friends, coworkers, local medical societies, and the physician referral service at a local clinic or hospital. Some clinics provide brief biographies of physicians on staff who are taking new patients. If you have a particular health problem, you may want to identify physicians who are board-certified in appropriate specialties. Once you have a list of possible physicians, find out if a consumer or other independent group has rated doctors in your area; this will help you check on the quality of care they provide.

Once you have the names of a few physicians you might want to try, call their offices to find out information such as the following:

- Is the physician covered by your health plan and accepting new patients?
- What are the office hours, and when is the physician or office staff available? What do patients do if they need urgent care or have an emergency?
- Which hospitals does the physician use?
- How many other physicians are available to cover when he or she isn't available, and who are they?
- How long does it usually take to get a routine appointment?
- Does the office send reminders about preventive tests such as Pap tests?
- Does the physician (or a nurse or physician assistant) give advice over the phone for common problems?

Schedule a visit with the physician you think you would most like to use. During that first visit, you'll get a sense of how well matched you are and how well he or she might meet your medical needs. After the visit, consider the following:

- Do you feel you were listened to, and did you have a chance to ask questions?
- Do you feel you were treated with respect and made to feel comfortable?
- Do you understand what the physician told you, and did he or she spend enough time with you?
- Do you feel that the physician addressed your health problems or concerns, and do you feel comfortable with the recommended course of action?

Although you may want to give the relationship some time to develop, you should trust your own reactions when deciding whether a particular health care provider is the right one for you.

Terms

podiatrist A practitioner who holds a doctor of podiatric medicine degree and specializes in the medical and surgical care of the feet.

optometrist A practitioner who holds a doctor of optometry degree and is trained to examine the eyes, detect eye diseases, and prescribe corrective lenses.

dentist A practitioner who holds a doctor of medical dentistry or doctor of dental surgery degree and who specializes in the prevention and treatment of diseases and injuries of the teeth, mouth, and jaws.

allied health care providers Health care professionals who typically provide services under the supervision or control of independent practitioners.

Vw

Gender Matters

Health Care Visits and Gender

Americans make more than 1 billion visits per year to physicians, clinics, emergency rooms, and other treatment centers. Females are more likely than males to visit a health care provider (see figure). Women age 18–44 make nearly twice as many physician visits as do men. Women are also more likely to report use of complementary and alternative therapies.

What are some of the factors underlying this difference? Reproductive health care needs may be one key factor, with women making doctor visits related to prenatal care and childbirth. Women of reproductive age may also need to make health care visits in order to obtain prescription contraceptives and have the pelvic exams and Pap tests required to obtain certain contraceptives.

Even when physician visits related to reproductive care are discounted, however, women are more likely than men to see a health care provider, especially for preventive care. Male gender roles may be a factor in this trend, with men being socialized to be strong and tough, to ignore pain or symptoms of illness, or to feel that physician visits for preventive care (when no symptoms are present) are unnecessary. And without preventive-care visits, men may be unaware of such asymptomatic conditions as high cholesterol levels or high blood pressure, which, once diagnosed, would require regular visits for monitoring and treatment.

At all ages, it is important for both men and women to obtain recommended health care screenings and immunizations. Preventive care throughout life is important to maximize wellness. Don't wait until you are ill before you see a physician.

SOURCES: National Center for Health Statistics. 2006. *Health, United States, 2006.* Hyattsville, Md.: U.S. Public Health Service, U.S. Department of Health and Human Services; Centers for Disease Control and Prevention. 2004. Complementary and alternative medicine use among adults: United States, 2002. *Advance Data from Vital and Health Statistics* No. 343. Hyattsville, Md.: National Center for Health Statistics.

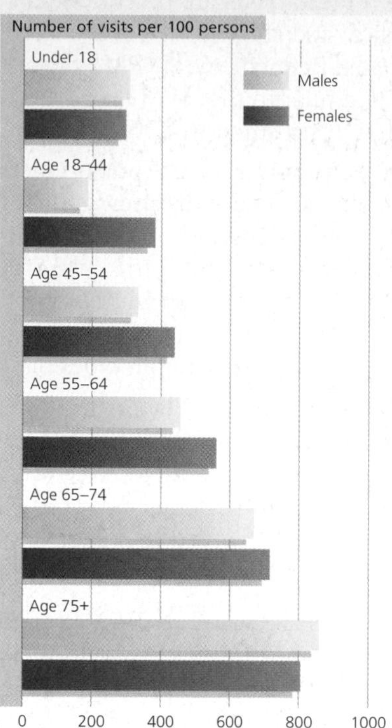

Health care visits by age and gender, 2004

Getting the Most Out of Your Medical Care

The key to making the health care system work for you lies in good communication with your physician and other members of the health care team. Studies show that patients who interact more with physicians and ask more questions enjoy better health outcomes.

The Physician-Patient Partnership The physician-patient relationship is undergoing an important transformation. The image of the all-knowing physician and the passive patient is slowly fading. What is emerging is more of a physician-patient *partnership,* in which the physician acts more like a consultant and the patient participates more actively. You should expect your physician to be attentive, caring, and able to listen and clearly explain things to you. You also must do your part. You need to be assertive in a firm but not aggressive manner. You need to express your feelings and concerns, ask questions, and, if necessary, be persistent. If your physician is unable to communicate clearly with you despite your best efforts, you probably need to change physicians.

Your Appointment with Your Physician Physicians are often pressed for time, so prepare for your visit ahead of time. Make a written list of your key concerns and questions, along with notes about your symptoms (when they started, how long they last, what makes them better or worse, what treatments you have already tried, and so on). If there are questions you're uncomfortable about asking, practice discussing them ahead of time. Bring a list of all the medications you're taking—prescription, nonprescription, and herbal. Also bring any medical records or test results your physician may not already have.

Present your concerns at the beginning of the visit, to set the agenda. Be specific and concise about your symptoms, and be open and honest about your concerns. Share your hunches with your physician—your guesses can provide vital clues. Ask questions if you don't understand something. Let your physician know if you are taking any drugs, are allergic to any medications, are breastfeeding, or may be pregnant.

At the end of the visit, briefly repeat the physician's diagnosis, prognosis, and instructions, and make sure you understand your next steps, such as making another appointment, phoning for test results, watching for new symptoms, and so on. You may also want to ask about the possibility of using e-mail for follow-up.

The Diagnostic Process The first step in the diagnostic process is the medical history, which includes

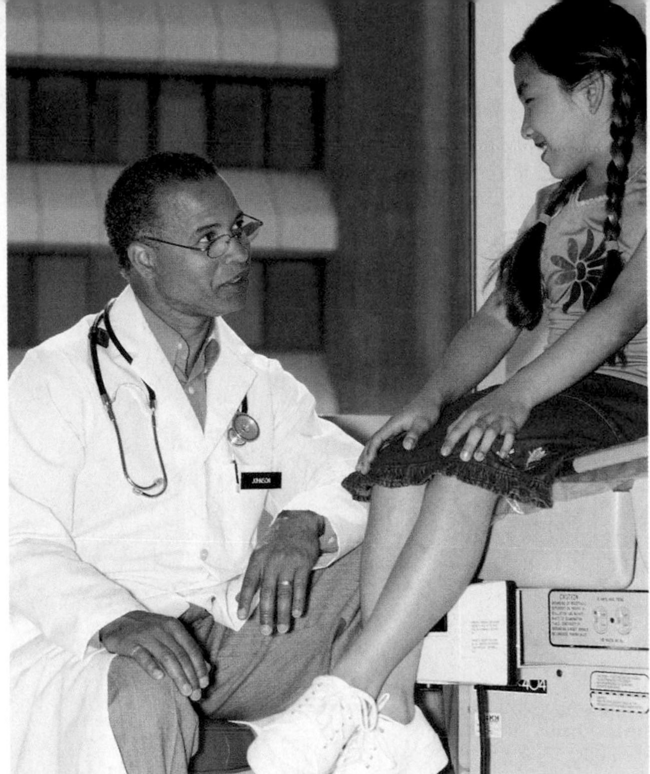

Good communication is a crucial factor in an effective physician-patient partnership.

your primary reason for the visit, your current symptoms, your past medical history, and your social history (job, family life, major stressors, living conditions, and health habits). Keeping up-to-date records of your medical history can help you provide your physician with key facts about your health (see the box "Personal Health Profile" on p. 640).

The next step is the physical exam, which usually begins with a review of vital signs: blood pressure, heart rate (pulse), breathing rate, and temperature. Depending on your primary complaint, your physician may give you a complete physical, or the exam may be directed to specific areas, such as your ears, nose, and throat.

Additionally, your physician may order medical tests to complete the diagnosis. Diagnostic testing provides a wealth of information to help solve medical problems. Physicians can order X rays, biopsies, blood and urine tests, scans, and **endoscopies** to view, probe, or analyze almost any part of the body.

If your physician orders a test for you, be sure you know why you need it, what the risks and benefits of the test are for you, how you should prepare for it (for example, by fasting or discontinuing medications or herbal remedies), and what the test will involve. Also ask what the test results mean, because no test is 100% accurate—**false positives** and **false negatives** do occur—and interpretation of some tests is subjective. Sometimes it is important to get a second opinion on a diagnosis.

Medical and Surgical Treatments

Many conditions can be treated in a variety of ways; in some cases, lifestyle changes are enough. Make sure you know the possible risks and side effects of each treatment option, as well as the likelihood that it will improve your condition.

PRESCRIPTION MEDICATIONS Each month, between 40% and 50% of Americans use at least one prescription medication; among those 65 and older, between 80% and 90% are current prescription drug users. Thousands of lives are saved each year by **antibiotics,** insulin, and other drugs, but we pay a price for having such powerful tools. A 2006 report from the Institute of Medicine (IOM) estimates that 1.5 million prescription drug-related errors—called *adverse drug events,* or ADEs—occur each year in the United States. The IOM says the average hospital patient can expect to endure at least one ADE daily. ADEs happen for several reasons:

- *Medication errors:* Physicians may overprescribe drugs, sometimes in response to pressure by patients (see the box "Prescription Drug Use and Regulation: Lessons from Vioxx" on p. 641). Adverse effects can occur if a physician prescribes the wrong drug or a dangerous combination of drugs; such problems are especially prevalent for older adults, who typically take multiple medications. The risk of ADEs increases greatly with the number of medicines you take. For example, someone who takes seven different medications is 80% more likely to suffer an ADE than someone who takes only one medication. At the pharmacy, patients may receive the wrong drug or may not be given complete information about drug risks, side effects, and interactions. Problems can occur because of a physician's poor handwriting, misinterpretation of an abbreviated drug name, or similarities between the names and packaging of different drugs. In 2004, the FDA mandated the addition of bar codes with drug names and dosages to prescription drugs to help eliminate medication errors. In 2006, the FDA required drug makers to change the format of product inserts, to make them easier to read while providing more information about medications and highlighting their potential risks. The changes are to be phased in over 5 years.

Terms

endoscopy A medical procedure in which a viewing instrument is inserted into a body cavity or opening.

false positive A test result that incorrectly detects a disease or condition in a healthy person.

false negative A test result that fails to correctly detect a disease or condition.

antibiotic A substance derived from a mold or bacterium that inhibits the growth of other microorganisms.

Assess Yourself

Personal Health Profile

General Information

Age: _____ Total cholesterol: _____ Blood pressure: ___/___ Other: _________

Height: _____ HDL: _____ Triglycerides: _____ _________

Weight: _____ LDL: _____ Glucose: _________ _________

Medical Conditions

Check any of the following that apply to you and add other conditions that might affect your health and well-being.

_____ heart disease
_____ lung disease
_____ diabetes
_____ allergies
_____ asthma
_____ back pain
_____ arthritis
_____ other injury or joint problem
_____ substance abuse problem
_____ depression, anxiety, or another psychological disorder
_____ eating disorder
_____ other: _____________
_____ other: _____________

Medications/Treatments

List any drugs you are taking or any medical treatments you are undergoing. Include the name of the substance or treatment and its purpose. Include both prescription and OTC drugs and any vitamin, mineral, or other dietary supplement you are taking.

_____________________ _____________________ _____________________

_____________________ _____________________ _____________________

Health Care Providers

Primary care physician: name _____________________ phone _____________

Specialist physician: name _____________________ phone _____________

Condition treated: _____________________

Other health care provider: name _____________________ phone _____________

Condition treated: _____________________

Health insurance provider and policy number: _____________________

To ensure that you get the most out of your medical care, you should also keep a record of your vaccinations and medical screening tests. Chapters 15–18 describe recommended vaccinations and screening tests for CVD, cancer, and STDs.

- *Off-label drug use:* Another potential problem is off-label use of drugs. Once a drug is approved by the FDA for one purpose, it can legally be prescribed (although not marketed) for purposes not listed on the label. A recent study revealed that about 20% of medications are prescribed for off-label use; three-quarters of those prescriptions are made with little or no evidence supporting such use. Many off-label uses are safe and supported by some research, but both consumers and health care providers need to take special care with off-label use of medications.
- *Online pharmacies:* A recent area of concern is the advent of online pharmacies. Although convenient, some online pharmacies may sell products or engage in practices that are illegal in the offline world, putting consumers at risk for receiving adulterated, expired, or counterfeit drugs. The FDA recommends that consumers avoid sites that prescribe drugs for the first time without a physical exam, sell prescription drugs without a prescription, or sell drugs not approved by the FDA. You should also avoid sites that do not provide access to a registered pharmacist to answer questions or that do not provide a U.S. address and phone number to contact if there's a problem. The National Association of Boards of Pharmacy sponsors a voluntary certification program for Internet pharmacies. To be certified, a pharmacy must have a state license and allow regular inspections. Many experts recommend that consumers

Prescription Drug Use and Regulation: Lessons from Vioxx

In February 2005, the FDA announced plans for changes designed to enhance its oversight of prescription drugs. Pressure on the agency had been growing following several high-profile problems with approved drugs. These cases included the risk of suicide associated with use of certain antidepressants among children and teenagers (see Chapter 3), and the risk of heart problems among people taking certain anti-inflammatory drugs for arthritis.

The Vioxx Story in Brief

Many people with arthritis take medications to reduce pain and inflammation. Traditional nonsteroidal anti-inflammatory drugs (NSAIDs) like aspirin and ibuprofen are effective, but they carry the risk of stomach irritation and even ulcers—especially if taken over long periods, as is common for a chronic condition like arthritis. Newer NSAIDs known as COX-2 inhibitors are designed to reduce pain and inflammation while causing less stomach irritation. COX-2 inhibitors include Vioxx (rofecoxib), Celebrex (celecoxib), and Bextra (valdecoxib).

Vioxx, approved in 1999, was heavily advertised and widely used. As early as 2000, studies began to find increased rates of cardiovascular problems among Vioxx users. Results of a large-scale study in 2004 found that Vioxx users were more likely to suffer a heart attack or sudden cardiac death than people using Celebrex or older NSAIDs. In response to this study, Vioxx was removed from the market. (Due to risks related to CVD and a serious skin condition, Bextra was pulled from the market in April 2005.)

The rise and fall of Vioxx has inspired debate on a number of issues relating to how drugs are marketed, prescribed, and regulated. Why weren't the risks identified before the drug was approved? Why didn't the FDA act earlier? Should such widespread drug marketing be allowed?

New Drugs and Postapproval Monitoring

Although pharmaceutical companies carry out extensive preapproval trials on new drugs, even the most extensive studies involve just a few thousand people. A large natural experiment begins when the drug is approved and physicians start prescribing it to people in the general population. Side effects and risks that did not show up in studies often become apparent when more people begin taking a drug. Problems can also develop when certain drugs are used in combination with other drugs or dietary supplements.

Preapproval studies may exclude certain groups for safety reasons. For example, initial studies of Vioxx did not include people with preexisting heart conditions, who may have been more at risk for the problems identified after the drug was approved.

Part of the FDA's 2005 proposal is for greater postapproval surveillance, including an independent review board and a Web site with emerging drug safety data accessible to both physicians and consumers. However, a 2006 report by the Department of Health and Human Services criticized the FDA for not tracking postapproval studies. The report said that 35% of annual reports from drug makers to the FDA did not mention such studies.

Direct-to-Consumer Advertising

The pharmaceutical industry spends up to 20% of its marketing budget on direct-to-consumer (DTC) advertising. Most of these ads are for a small number of the most popular drugs.

Proponents of DTC advertising claim that it enhances public health by providing educational information about underdiagnosed conditions such as diabetes, high cholesterol, and depression and by motivating people to seek care. DTC advertising may be particularly useful in getting health information to people who have no regular source of health care.

Opponents claim that DTC advertising is more promotional than educational, is misleading and omits important precautions, is designed to stimulate consumer demand by creating problems and needs, and causes patients to pressure physicians to prescribe particular drugs. One recent study found that most DTC ads fail to provide information about how a drug works, its success rate, how long it must be taken, alternative treatments, or helpful lifestyle changes. The FDA has issued guidelines regarding DTC advertising and has stepped up its enforcement efforts since 2004, issuing dozens of warnings to drug companies. In June 2006, the American Medical Association called for a moratorium on DTC ads for new products until those products had been proven safe.

There is also concern that DTC advertising leads patients to request heavily advertised drugs when older, less expensive medications may be equally effective. The COX-2 inhibitors were designed for people at risk for stomach irritation from traditional NSAIDs, but most people who used Vioxx were actually at low risk for problems from traditional NSAIDs. For most people, older NSAIDs, which have an established safety record, are just as effective as the newer drugs and much less expensive.

Selective Publication of Study Results

Many drug studies are carried out by the pharmaceutical industry, which has little incentive to publish the results of trials in which medications are found to be ineffective. In the case of antidepressants, manufacturers did not publicize studies that raised safety questions and failed to show drugs were effective for treating pediatric depression. In the case of Vioxx, the manufacturer allowed the medical community to believe that CVD complications did not arise in patients until they had taken the drug for 18 months; in reality, heart problems developed in some patients within 4 to 6 months of their first dose. Selective publication provides an inaccurate picture of the risks and benefits of a particular drug.

In response to criticism, pharmaceutical companies have set up a voluntary Web-based clearinghouse that will contain both positive and negative research findings (www.clinicalstudyresults.org). Major medical journals have pledged not to publish results of any clinical trial that is not preregistered. That is, researchers must register all trials when they begin, so unflattering or conflicting findings cannot be covered up. The U.S. Congress has also proposed legislation on this issue.

Balancing Risks and Benefits

All medications have risks and benefits. When choosing a particular medication, work with your physician to balance the risks and benefits of the drug to your own personal health.

SOURCES: Food and Drug Administration. 2005. *FDA Improvements in Drug Safety Monitoring* (http://www.fda.gov/oc/factsheets/drugsafety.html; retrieved September 18, 2006); Beardsley, S. 2005. Avoiding another Vioxx. *Scientific American,* February; Kimmel, S. E., et al. 2005. Patients exposed to rofecoxib and celecoxib have different odds of nonfatal myocardial infarction. *Annals of Internal Medicine* 142(3): 157–164; Dai, C., R. S. Stafford, and G. C. Alexander. 2005. National trends in cyclooxygenase-2 inhibitor use since market release: Nonselective diffusion of a selectively cost-effective innovation. *Archives of Internal Medicine* 165(2): 171–177.

Pharmacy information

Prescribing physician

Prescription number

Person for whom medication is prescribed

Directions for taking the drug

Generic name of drug

Brand-name equivalent

Quantity of drug in package

Number of refills remaining

MEDICAL CENTER PHARMACY

2000 Independence Way, Washington, DC 20012

555-1111 **Refill** 555-4321

Dr. KENDRA BAUER

Rx #371811 3/23/05

WATSON, TIMOTHY B.

TAKE 1 TABLET TWICE A DAY

DICLOFENAC SODIUM 75 MG TABLETS

(GENERIC FOR VOLTAREN)

QTY: 60 TABS DISCARD AFTER: 1/07

REFILLS LEFT: 2

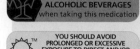

Special precautions or warnings about taking this medication

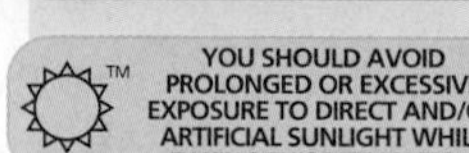
DO NOT DRINK
ALCOHOLIC BEVERAGES
when taking this medication

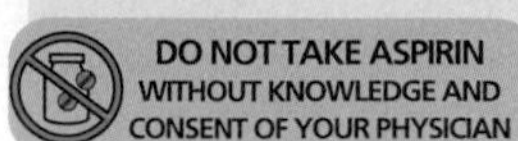
YOU SHOULD AVOID
PROLONGED OR EXCESSIVE
EXPOSURE TO DIRECT AND/OR
ARTIFICIAL SUNLIGHT WHILE
TAKING THIS MEDICATION

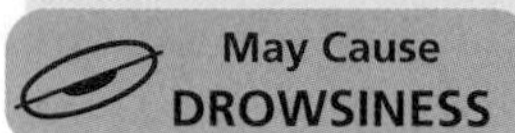
DO NOT TAKE ASPIRIN
WITHOUT KNOWLEDGE AND
CONSENT OF YOUR PHYSICIAN

May Cause DROWSINESS

Amount of medication per unit

Expiration date

Figure 21-3 Reading and understanding prescription medication labels.

use online pharmacies only to obtain medicines prescribed by their usual health care provider.

- *Costs:* Spending on prescription drugs is rising faster than the rate of inflation and is now the fastest-growing portion of U.S. health care spending. Many Americans have no or limited insurance coverage for prescription drug costs. Consumers may be able to lower their drug costs by using generic versions of medications; by joining a drug discount program sponsored by a company, organization, or local pharmacy; and by investigating mail-order or Internet pharmacies.

There is ongoing controversy about the importation of lower-cost drugs from Canada. Canada imports U.S. drugs and regulates Canadian-produced drugs, so safety should theoretically not be a concern for drugs from Canada. However, companies in Canada may make drugs for export only, thus avoiding regulation, and online pharmacies may claim they are operating in Canada but may be located in another country where there is little or no regulation. U.S. regulators have found online sites advertising Canadian drugs but shipping fake or substandard versions of medications. In addition, shipping costs can be high, and U.S. generic drugs are often less expensive than Canadian drugs.

Patients also share some responsibility for problems with prescription drugs. Many people don't take their medications properly, skipping doses, taking incorrect doses, stopping too soon, or not taking the medication at all. An estimated 30–50% of the more than 3 billion prescriptions dispensed annually in the United States are not taken correctly and thus do not produce the desired results. Consumers can increase the safety and effectiveness of their treatment by asking the following questions:

- *Are there non-drug alternatives?*
- *What is the name of the medication, and what is it supposed to do, within what period of time?*
- *How and when do I take the medication, how much do I take, and for how long? What should I do if I miss a dose?*
- *What other medications, foods, drinks, or activities should I avoid?* Other drugs, including alcohol, herbs, and OTC drugs, can interact with medications, diminishing or increasing their effect (Figure 21-3). For example, certain antibiotics, including ampicillin and tetracycline, may prevent oral contraceptives from working. Others may increase the effects of sunlight on the skin. Compounds in grapefruit juice can react with some drugs, boosting their effects to a dangerous level.
- *What are the side effects, and what do I do if they occur?* If you have a drug allergy or other medical condition, such as epilepsy or diabetes, that may require special attention in case of an emergency, wear a medical ID necklace or bracelet or carry a medical ID card. Consider joining Medic Alert (www.medicalert.org); call 1-888-633-4298 for more information.
- *Can I take a generic drug rather than a brand-name one?* Generic drugs contain the same active ingredients as the original brand-name drug, but they may contain different inactive ingredients. They are usually substantially less expensive, but sometimes physicians have reasons for preferring a particular brand.
- *Is there written information about the medication?* There are many sources of information, including the FDA-approved inserts in drug packaging and books.

Remember to store your medications in a cool, dry place, out of direct light. Never share your prescription medications with anyone else, and never use an old prescription for a new ailment.

SURGERY Surgical procedures are performed more often in the United States than anywhere else in the world. Each year, more than 70 million operations and related procedures are performed. About 20% are in response to an emergency such as a severe injury, and 80% are **elective surgeries,** meaning the patient can generally choose when and where to have the operation, if at all. Some key questions include the following:

- *Why do I need surgery at this time?* Your physician should be able to explain the reason for the surgery and what is likely to happen if you don't have it. Getting a second opinion about surgery is recommended and may be required by your health insurance plan.
- *What are the risks and complications of the surgery?* Overall risk depends on the type of operation performed, the surgeon, and your general state of health. Ask about the *mortality rate* (risk of death) and the *morbidity rate* (risk of nonlethal complications).
- *Can the operation be performed on an outpatient basis?* **Outpatient** (ambulatory) surgery has many advantages, including lower costs and fewer opportunities for hospital-associated complications.
- *What can I expect before, during, and after surgery?* Knowing what to expect can help you prepare for the surgery and speed your recovery.

COMPLEMENTARY AND ALTERNATIVE MEDICINE

Where conventional Western medicine tends to focus on the body, on the physical causes of disease, and on ways to eradicate pathogens in order to restore health, traditional medicine tends to focus on an integration of mind, body, and spirit and to seek ways to restore the whole person to harmony so that he or she can regain health. Where conventional medicine is based on science, traditional medicine tends to be based on accumulated experience.

Many alternative medical systems with long-standing traditions have concepts and theories of medicine that are very different from those of current Western medical thought. Some people consider all of CAM quackery and tell you that you can recognize a quack by his or her use of pseudoscientific language. However, the use of phrases like "bringing into harmony with nature" or "enhancing the flow of vital energy" does not necessarily mean that a practitioner is a quack; rather, it may reflect this practitioner's different concept of health and healing.

You might have heard that there are only anecdotal testimonials to support the value of many forms of CAM and that because such reports do not constitute scientific proof of effectiveness, they are therefore meaningless. Although it is correct that anecdotes and testimonials are not scientifically reliable evidence, that does not mean that they are meaningless. What is called anecdotal evidence may actually be a form of case report, a valuable and standard form of study in which a researcher describes a single patient, his or her medical history, the treatments administered, and the outcome of the case. Still, case reports alone are not sufficient to scientifically prove the effectiveness of a medical treatment. Caution is in order when choosing any mode of treatment that has not been scientifically evaluated for safety and effectiveness (see the box "Avoiding Health Fraud and Quackery").

The NIH National Center for Complementary and Alternative Medicine (NCCAM) groups CAM practices into five domains: alternative medical systems, mind-body interventions, biological-based therapies, manipulative and body-based methods, and energy therapies (Figure 21-4, p. 645). It is impossible to discuss all of these forms fully in a single chapter. Instead, what follows is a general introduction to the types of CAM available and a brief description of some of the more widely used ones. To learn more about any of these approaches, consult the For More Information section at the end of the chapter.

Alternative Medical Systems

Many cultures elaborated complete systems of medical philosophy, theory, and practice long before the current biomedical approach was developed. The complete systems that are best known in the United States are probably traditional Chinese medicine (TCM), also known as traditional Oriental medicine, and homeopathy. Traditional medical systems have also been developed in many other regions of the world, including North, Central, and South America; the Middle East; India; Tibet; and Australia. In many countries, these medical approaches continue to be used today—frequently alongside Western medicine and quite often by physicians trained in Western medicine.

Alternative medical systems tend to have concepts in common. For example, the concept of life force or energy exists in many cultures. In traditional Chinese medicine, the life force contained in all living things is called *qi* (sometimes spelled chi). Qi resembles the *vis vitalis* (Latin for "life force") of Greek, Roman, and European medical systems, and *prana* of ayurveda, the traditional medical system of India. Most traditional medical systems think of

Terms

elective surgery A nonemergency operation that the patient can choose to schedule.

outpatient A person receiving medical attention without being admitted to the hospital.

Vw

Critical Consumer

Avoiding Health Fraud and Quackery

VW

According to the Federal Trade Commission, consumers waste billions of dollars on unproven, fraudulently marketed, and sometimes useless health care products and treatments. In addition, those with serious medical problems may waste valuable time before seeking proper treatment. Worse yet, some of the products they're buying may cause serious harm. Health fraud is a business that sells false hope. It preys on people with diseases that have no medical cure and on people who want shortcuts to weight loss or improvements to personal appearance.

The first rule of thumb for evaluating any health claim is that if it sounds too good to be true, it probably is. Also be on the lookout for the typical phrases and marketing techniques fraudulent promoters use to deceive consumers:

- The product is advertised as a quick and effective cure-all or diagnostic tool for a wide range of ailments.
- The promoters use words like *scientific breakthrough, miraculous cure, exclusive product, secret ingredient,* or *ancient remedy.* Also remember that just because a product is described as natural or unprocessed does not necessarily mean it's safe.
- The text is written in medicalese—impressive-sounding terminology to disguise a lack of good science.
- The promoter claims the government, the medical profession, or researchers have conspired to suppress the product.
- The advertisement includes undocumented case histories claiming amazing results.
- The product is advertised as in limited supply or available from only one source, and payment is required in advance.
- The promoter promises a no-risk money-back guarantee. Be aware that many fly-by-night operators are not around to respond to your request for a refund.

To check out a particular product, talk to a physician or another health care professional and to family members and friends. Be wary of treatments offered by people who tell you to avoid talking to others. Check with the Better Business Bureau or local attorney general's office to see whether other consumers have lodged complaints about the product or the product's marketer. You can also check with the appropriate health professional group. For example, check with the American Diabetes Association or the National Arthritis Foundation if the products are promoted for diabetes or arthritis. Take special care with products and devices sold online; the broad reach of the Internet, combined with the ease of setting up and removing Web sites, makes online sellers particularly difficult to regulate.

If you think you have been a victim of health fraud or if you have an adverse reaction that you think is related to a particular supplement, you can report it to the appropriate agency:

- *False advertising claims:* Contact the FTC by phone (877-FTC-HELP), by mail (Consumer Response Center, Federal Trade Commission, Washington, DC 20580), or online (http://www.ftc.gov; click on File a Complaint). You can also contact your state attorney general's office, your state department of health, or the local consumer protection agency (check your local telephone directory).
- *False labeling on a product:* Contact the FDA district office consumer complaint coordinator for your geographic area. (The FDA regulates safety, manufacturing, and product labeling.)
- *Adverse reaction to a supplement:* Call a doctor or another health care provider immediately. You may also report your adverse reaction to FDA MedWatch by calling 800-FDA-1088 or by visiting the MedWatch Web site (http://www.fda.gov/medwatch).
- *Unlawful Internet sales:* If you find a Web site that you think is illegally selling drugs, medical devices, dietary supplements, or cosmetics, report it to the FDA. Problems can be reported to MedWatch or via the FDA Web site (http://www.fda.gov/oc/buyonline/buyonlineform.htm).

SOURCES: Meadows, M. 2005. Use caution buying medical products online. *FDA Consumer,* January/February; Federal Trade Commission. 2001. *"Miracle" Health Claims: Add a Dose of Skepticism* (http://www.ftc.gov/bcp/conline/pubs/health/frdheal.htm; retrieved September 18, 2006); Food and Drug Administration. 2006. *How to Report Problems with Products Regulated by FDA* (http://www.fda.gov/opacom/backgrounders/problem.html; retrieved September 18, 2006); Kurtzweil, P. 1999. How to spot health fraud. *FDA Consumer,* November/December.

disease as a disturbance or imbalance not just of physical processes but also of forces and energies within the body, the mind, and the spirit. In traditional Chinese medicine, for example, the principle of balance is expressed as yin and yang, which are opposites yet complement each other. Disease is a disturbance of qi reflecting an imbalance between yin and yang. Treatment aims at reestablishing equilibrium, balance, and harmony.

Because the whole patient, rather than an isolated set of symptoms, is treated in most comprehensive alternative medical systems, it is rare that only a single treatment approach is used. Most commonly, multiple techniques and methods are employed and are continually adjusted according to the changes in the patient's health status that occur naturally or are brought about by the treatment.

Traditional Chinese Medicine **Traditional Chinese medicine (TCM)** is based on highly abstract concepts; a sophisticated set of techniques and methods; and individualized diagnosis, treatment, and prevention. No identical diseases exist in TCM. Two patients with the same diagnosis in Western medicine will get

Domain	Characteristics	Examples
Alternative Medical Systems 	Involve complete systems of theory and practice that have evolved independently of and often long before the conventional biomedical approach	Traditional Chinese medicine; Kampo; ayurveda (India); Native American, Aboriginal, African, Middle-Eastern, Tibetan, Central and South American medical systems; homeopathy; naturopathy
Mind-Body Interventions	Employ a variety of techniques designed to make it possible for the mind to affect bodily function and symptoms	Meditation, certain uses of hypnosis, prayer, mental healing 
Biological-Based Therapies	Include natural and biologically based practices, interventions, and products, many of which overlap with conventional medicine's use of dietary supplements 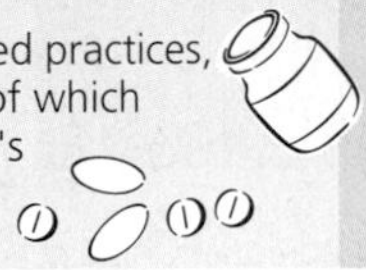	Herbal, special dietary, orthomolecular,* and individual biological therapies
Manipulative and Body-Based Methods	Include methods that are based on manipulation and/or movement of the body	 Chiropractic, osteopathy, massage therapy
Energy Therapies 	Focus on energy fields within the body (biofields) or from other sources (electromagnetic fields)	Qi gong, Reiki, therapeutic touch, bioelectromagnetic-based therapies

* Orthomolecular therapies are treatments of diseases with varying, but usually high, concentrations of chemicals, including minerals (e.g., magnesium), hormones (e.g., melatonin), or vitamins.

Figure 21-4 The five domains of CAM practices.

different diagnoses in TCM and will be given different treatments.

In TCM, the free and harmonious flow of qi produces health—a positive feeling of well-being and vitality in body, mind, and spirit. Illness occurs when the flow of qi is blocked or disturbed. TCM works to restore and balance the flow of blocked qi; the goal is not only to treat illnesses but also to increase energy, prevent disease, and support the immune system.

Two of the primary treatment methods in TCM are herbal remedies and **acupuncture.** Chinese herbal remedies number about 5800 and include plant products, animal parts, and minerals. Herbal remedies, like everything else, have yin and yang properties. When a disease is perceived to be due to a yin deficiency, remedies with more yin characteristics might be used for treatment. The use of a single medicinal botanical is rare in Chinese herbal medicine; rather, several different plants are combined in very precise proportions, often to make a tea or soup. For example, a remedy might include a primary herb that targets the main symptom, a second herb that enhances the effects of the primary herb, a third that lessens side effects, and a fourth that helps deliver ingredients to a particular body site.

Acupuncture works to correct disturbances in the flow of qi through the insertion of long, thin needles at appropriate points in the skin. Qi is believed to flow through the body along several meridians, or pathways, and there are approximately 360 acupuncture points located along these meridians. Acupuncturists use a variety of diagnostic techniques to identify the nature of the imbalance in a patient and to choose the points at which acupuncture needs to be applied. The traditional method consists of inserting the needle and then manipulating it manually, but other means of manipulation, such as heat, pressure, friction, suction, or electric stimulation, can also be used. The points chosen for acupuncture are highly individualized for each patient, and they change over the course of treatment as the patient's health status changes.

The World Health Organization has compiled a list of over 40 conditions in which acupuncture may be beneficial. At a conference called by the National Institutes of Health (NIH), a panel of experts recently analyzed the available information on the scientific evidence for the efficacy of

Terms

traditional Chinese medicine (TCM) The traditional medical system of China, which views illness as the result of a disturbance in the flow of qi, the life force; therapies include acupuncture, herbal medicine, and massage.

acupuncture Insertion of long, thin needles into the skin at points along meridians, pathways through which qi is believed to flow; needles correct imbalances in qi; a practice common in traditional Chinese medicine.

Vw

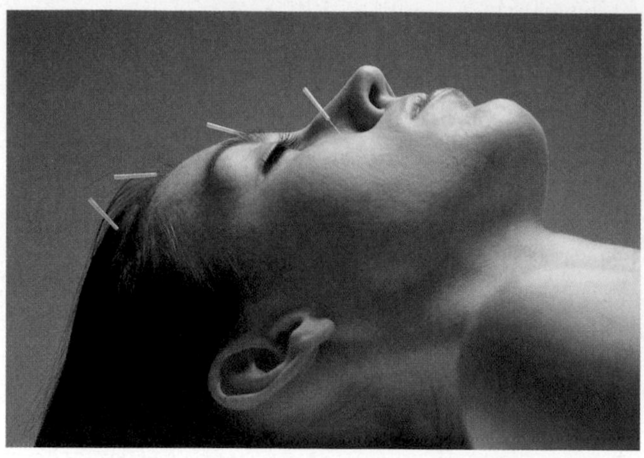

Acupuncture is one of the key treatment methods in traditional Chinese medicine. It involves the insertion of long, thin needles at appropriate points in the skin to restore balance to the flow of qi.

acupuncture in many of these conditions. These experts found evidence that acupuncture was effective in relieving nausea and vomiting after chemotherapy and pain after surgery, including dental surgery. Newer studies show that acupuncture may help relieve the painful symptoms of fibromyalgia and reduce the joint pain and stiffness of osteoarthritis. There is not yet enough evidence to show conclusively that acupuncture is effective for headaches, menstrual cramps, tennis elbow, back pain, carpal tunnel syndrome, asthma, or other conditions. Western researchers typically use a different framework for understanding the effects of acupuncture. For example, they might explain pain relief not in terms of qi but in terms of stimulation of the nervous system and release of hormones and neurotransmitters.

About 4% of Americans report having had acupuncture at least once, typically for problems such as low back pain. Very few negative side effects have been reported in conjunction with acupuncture. Nonetheless, problems can occur from the improper insertion and manipulation of needles and from the use of unsterile needles. The FDA regulates acupuncture needles like other standard medical devices and requires that they be sterile. If you consider acupuncture, you should ask your practitioner about the relative risks of the procedure and the safety practices he or she observes. Most states require licensing for acupuncture practitioners, but requirements vary widely.

Homeopathy An alternative medical system of Western origin, **homeopathy** was developed about 200 years ago by the German physician Samuel Hahnemann (1755–1843) and is based on two main principles: "Like cures like," and remedies become more effective with greater dilution. "Like cures like" summarizes the concept that a substance that produces the symptoms of an illness or disease in a healthy person can cure the illness when given in very minute quantities. Remedies containing very small quantities of a particular substance are obtained by repeatedly diluting the original solution. The extent of dilution varies, but the final extract is often so dilute that few, if any, of the original molecules are left in it. According to homeopathic thinking, such highly diluted extracts not only retain some form of biological activity but actually become more potent.

Over 1000 different substances (plant and animal parts, minerals, and chemicals) can be used to prepare homeopathic remedies, and each of these substances is thought to have different effects at different dilutions. That means a homeopath must not only choose the correct remedy for a particular patient but also decide on the specific dilution of that remedy in order to achieve the desired effect.

Like other traditional systems of medicine, homeopathy constitutes a highly individualized form of therapy; that is, the treatment of each patient is determined by the overall condition of the patient rather than by specific symptoms. In order to assess a patient's condition, homeopaths generally spend quite a bit of time talking with a patient and assessing his or her physical, psychological, and emotional health before deciding on the correct remedy at the proper dilution. This intensive interaction between the practitioner and the patient might play an important role in the success of the therapy. Indeed, critics of homeopathy often attribute its reported effectiveness to this nonspecific placebo effect (see the box "The Power of Belief: The Placebo Effect"). However, when the results of 185 homeopathic trials were analyzed recently, it was concluded that the clinical effects of homeopathy could not be completely explained by the placebo effect. At the same time, homeopathy was not found to be effective for any single clinical condition. Homeopathy remains one of the most controversial forms of CAM.

Because of the extremely dilute nature of homeopathic remedies, it is generally assumed that they are safe. To date, the FDA has not found any serious adverse events associated with the use of homeopathy, with the possible exception of situations in which a patient might have been successfully treated with standard medical approaches but chose to rely solely on homeopathy. The FDA regulates homeopathic remedies, but they are subject to many fewer restrictions than prescription or over-the-counter drugs. Remedies designed to treat conditions such as colds and headaches can be sold over the counter; products that claim to treat serious conditions such as heart disease can be sold only by prescription. A few states require practitioners to have special licenses, but most providers practice homeopathy as a specialty under another medical license, such as medical doctor or nurse practitioner.

Mind-Body Interventions

Mind-body interventions make use of the integral connection between mind and body and the effect each can have on the other. They include many of the stress-management techniques discussed in Chapter 2, including

Mind/Body/Spirit

The Power of Belief: The Placebo Effect

A placebo is a chemically inactive substance or ineffective procedure that a patient believes is an effective medical therapy for his or her condition. Researchers frequently give placebos to the control group in an experiment testing the efficacy of a particular treatment. By comparing the effects of the actual treatment with the effects of the placebo, researchers can judge whether the treatment is effective. The placebo effect occurs when a patient improves after receiving a placebo. In such cases, the effect of the placebo on the patient cannot be attributed to the specific actions or properties of the drug or procedure.

Researchers have consistently found that 30–40% of all patients given a placebo show improvement. This result has been observed for a wide variety of conditions or symptoms, including coughing, seasickness, depression, migraines, and angina. For some conditions, placebos have been effective in up to 70% of patients. In some cases, people given a placebo even report having the side effects associated with an actual drug. Placebos are particularly effective when they are administered by a physician whom the patient trusts.

A clear demonstration of the placebo effect occurred in a recent study that examined the effectiveness of a drug used to treat benign enlargement of the prostate. The men who participated in the study were randomly assigned to one of two groups: One group received the medication; the other received a placebo, a look-alike dummy pill. More than half the men who got the placebo pills reported significant relief from their symptoms, including faster urine flow—despite the fact that men on the placebo actually experienced an *increase* in the size of their prostates. How did the men in the study experience fewer symptoms despite no actual improvement in their condition? Researchers hypothesize that the patients' positive expectations of the medication's effects may have resulted in decreased nerve activity and muscle relaxation affecting the bladder, prostate, and urethra. Studies on patients with depression and people with Parkinson's disease have found that treatment with an inactive placebo results in changes in brain function. Such changes in the electrical or chemical activity of the brain may help explain the placebo effect.

The placebo effect can be exploited by unscrupulous people who sell worthless medical treatments to the scientifically unsophisticated public. But placebo power can also be harnessed for its beneficial effects. When a skilled and compassionate medical practitioner provides a patient with a sense of confidence and hope, the positive aspects of placebo power can boost the benefits of standard medical treatment. Whenever you swallow a pill, you swallow your expectations right along with the medication or herb; imagining how the pill is helping you can stimulate a positive placebo effect. Getting well, like getting sick, is a complex process. Anatomy, physiology, mind, emotions, and the environment are all inextricably intertwined. But the placebo effect does show that belief can have both psychological and physical effects.

SOURCES: Leuchter, A. F., et al. 2002. Changes in brain function of depressed subjects during treatment with placebo. *American Journal of Psychiatry* 159(1): 122–129; Nordenberg, T. 2000. The healing power of placebos. *FDA Consumer,* January/February; The powerful placebo: An effect without a cause. 2000. *Harvard Men's Health Watch,* June

meditation, yoga, visualization, taijiquan, and biofeedback. Psychotherapy, support groups, prayer, and music, art, and dance therapy can also be thought of as mind-body interventions. The placebo effect is one of the most widely known examples of mind-body interdependence.

Some forms of **hypnosis** are considered to be CAM therapies, although the use of hypnotherapy for certain conditions was accepted more than 40 years ago by the American Medical Association. Hypnosis involves the induction of a state of deep relaxation during which the patient is more suggestible (more easily influenced). While the patient is in such a hypnotic trance, the practitioner tries to help him or her change unwanted behavior or deal with pain and other symptoms. An NIH-sponsored report found strong evidence for the effectiveness of relaxation techniques and hypnosis in reducing chronic pain stemming from a variety of medical conditions, although subsequent studies have cast some doubt on this conclusion. Hypnosis is sometimes used in smoking cessation programs and as a nondrug approach to anxiety disorders such as phobias and chronic conditions such as irritable bowel syndrome. It has been shown to help some women deal with the pain of childbirth with less medication.

Hypnosis can be used by medical professionals (M.D.s, D.O.s, D.D.S.s) but is also offered by hypnotherapists. Physicians are certified by their own associations; many states require hypnotherapists to be licensed, but the requirements for licensing vary substantially. There is little regulation of practitioners of other relaxation techniques, but it is very rare that adverse events result from such techniques. Many studies have shown that support groups, friendships, strong family relationships, and prayer can all have a positive impact on health.

Terms

Vw

homeopathy An alternative medical system of Western origin in which illnesses are treated by giving very small doses of drugs that in larger doses in a healthy person would produce symptoms like those of the illness.

hypnosis The process by which a practitioner induces a state of deep relaxation in which an individual is more suggestible; commonly used in cases of pain, phobia, and addiction.

Biological-Based Therapies

Biological-based therapies consist primarily of herbal therapies or remedies, botanicals, and dietary supplements. Herbal therapies are sometimes referred to as *materia medica,* Latin for "medical matter," a term that can include a much larger variety of compounds than just herbs (which are plants that die down at the end of a growing season and do not produce woody tissue). Some herbal remedies are not technically herbs, such as the leaves of the *Ginkgo biloba* tree, and some are not even from plants, such as shark cartilage and bear gallbladder. Other items that constitute *materia medica* are algae, bacteria, fungi, and minerals. For traditional remedies that are of plant origin, many scientists prefer to use the term *botanicals.* Nonetheless, because even official government definitions use the word *herbs* to designate substances from the categories of herbs, botanicals, and other *materia medica,* the terms are used somewhat interchangeably in this chapter.

Herbal remedies are a major component of all indigenous forms of medicine; prior to the development of pharmaceuticals at the end of the nineteenth century, people everywhere in the world relied on materials from nature for pain relief, wound healing, and treatment of a variety of ailments. Herbal remedies are also a common element in most systems of traditional medicine. Much of the **pharmacopoeia** of modern scientific medicine originated in the folk medicine of native peoples, and many drugs used today are derived from plants.

A majority of botanical products are sold as dietary supplements, that is, in the form of tablets, pills, capsules, liquid extracts, or teas. Like foods, dietary supplements must carry ingredient labels (see Chapter 12). As with food products, it is the responsibility of the manufacturers to ensure that their dietary supplements are safe and properly labeled prior to marketing. The FDA is responsible for monitoring the labeling and accompanying literature of dietary supplements and for overseeing their safety once they are on the market.

Well-designed clinical studies have been conducted on only a small number of botanicals. A few other commonly used botanicals, their uses, and the evidence supporting their efficacy are presented in Table 21-2. Participants in clinical trials with St. John's wort, ginkgo, and echinacea experienced only minor adverse events. However, most clinical trials of this type last for only a few weeks, so the tests did not indicate whether it is safe to take these botanicals for longer periods of time. They also didn't examine the effects of different dosages or how the botanicals interact with other drugs.

For the vast majority of other botanicals, there are almost no reliable research findings on efficacy or safety. That is extremely worrisome because, of all the CAM approaches, the consumption of botanical supplements has the greatest potential to result in serious and even life-threatening consequences. For more information, see the box "Herbal Remedies: Are They Safe?" on page 650.

Manipulative and Body-Based Methods

Touch and body manipulation are long-standing forms of health care. Manual healing techniques are based on the idea that misalignment or dysfunction in one part of the body can cause pain or dysfunction in another part; correcting these misalignments can bring the body back to optimal health.

Manual healing methods are an integral part of osteopathic medicine, now considered a form of conventional medicine. Other physical healing methods include massage, acupressure, Feldenkrais, Rolfing, and numerous other techniques. The most commonly accepted of the CAM manual healing methods is **chiropractic,** a method that focuses on the relationship between structure, primarily of joints and muscles, and function, primarily of the nervous system, to maintain or restore health. An important therapeutic procedure is the manipulation of joints, particularly those of the spinal column. However, chiropractors also use a variety of other techniques, including physical therapy, exercise programs, patient education and lifestyle modification, nutritional supplements, and orthotics (mechanical supports and braces) to treat patients. They do not use drugs or surgery.

Chiropractors, or doctors of chiropractic, are trained for a minimum of four full-time academic years at accredited chiropractic colleges and can go on to postgraduate training in many countries. Although specifically listed by NCCAM as one of the manipulative and body-based methods of CAM, chiropractic is accepted by many health care and health insurance providers to a far greater extent than the other types of CAM therapies. Based on research showing the efficacy of chiropractic

Terms

Vw

biological-based therapies CAM therapies that include natural and biologically based practices, interventions, and products; examples include herbal remedies and dietary supplements.

pharmacopoeia A collection of drugs and medicinal preparations.

chiropractic A system of manual healing most frequently used to treat musculoskeletal problems; the primary treatment is manipulation of the spine and other joints. Practitioners hold a doctor of chiropractic degree and are licensed.

energy therapies Forms of CAM treatment that use energy fields originating either within the body or from outside sources to promote healing.

qigong A component of traditional Chinese medicine that combines movement, meditation, and regulation of breathing to enhance the flow of qi, improve blood circulation, and enhance immune function.

Table 21-2 Commonly Used Botanicals, Their Uses, Evidence for Their Effectiveness, and Contraindications

Botanical	Use	Evidence	Examples of Adverse Effects and Interactions
Cranberry (*Vaccinium macrocarpon*)	Prevention or treatment of urinary tract disorders	May prevent bacteria from infecting the urinary tract	Studies have been small and evidence mixed; taking too much can cause diarrhea
Dandelion (*Taraxacum officinale*)	As a "tonic" against liver or kidney ailments	None yet	May cause diarrhea in some users; people with gallbladder or bile duct problems should not take dandelion
Echinacea (*Echinacea purpurea, E. angustifolia, E. pallida*)	Stimulation of immune functions; to prevent colds and flulike diseases; to lessen symptoms of colds and flus	Some trials showed that it prevents colds and flus and helps patients recover from colds faster, but others found it ineffective; preparations vary widely, and so may effectiveness	Might cause liver damage if taken over long periods of time (more than 8 weeks); since it is an immune stimulant, it is not advisable to take it with immune suppressants (e.g., corticosteroids)
Evening primrose oil (*Oenothera biennis L.*)	Reduction of inflammation	Long-term supplementation effective in reducing symptoms of rheumatoid arthritis	None known
Feverfew (*Tanacetum parthenium*)	Prevention of headaches and migraines	The majority of trials indicate that it is more effective than placebo, but the evidence is not yet conclusive	Should not be used by people allergic to other members of the aster family; has the potential to increase the effects of warfarin and other anticoagulants
Garlic (*Allium sativum*)	Reduction of cholesterol	Short-term studies have found a modest effect; long-term studies are needed	May interact with some medications, including anticoagulants, cyclosporine, and oral contraceptives
Ginkgo (*Ginkgo biloba*)	Improvement of circulation and memory	Improves cerebral insufficiency and slows progression of Alzheimer's disease and other types of senile dementia in some patients; improves blood flow in legs	Could increase bleeding time; should not be taken with nonsteroidal anti-inflammatory drugs or anticoagulants; gastrointestinal disturbance
Ginseng (*Panax ginseng*)	Improvement of physical performance, memory, immune function, and glycemic control in diabetes; treatment of herpes simplex 2	No conclusive evidence exists for any of these uses	Interacts with warfarin and alcohol in mice and rats, hence should probably not be used with these drugs; may cause liver damage
St. John's wort (*Hypericum perforatum*)	Treatment of depression	There is strong evidence that it is significantly more effective than placebo, is as effective as some standard antidepressants for mild to moderate depression, and causes fewer adverse effects	Known to interact with a variety of pharmaceuticals and should not be taken together with digoxin, theophylline, cyclosporine, indinavir, and serotonin-reuptake inhibitors
Saw palmetto (*Serenoa repens*)	Improvement of prostate health	Early studies showed that saw palmetto may reduce prostate enlargement; newer studies contradict those findings	Has no known interactions with drugs, but should probably not be taken with hormonal therapies
Valerian (*Valeriana officinalis*)	Treatment of insomnia	Appears to help with sleep disorders, but further trials are needed	Interacts with thiopental and pentobarbital and should not be used with these drugs

management in acute low-back pain, spinal manipulation has been included in the federal guidelines for the treatment of this condition. In fact, electrodiagnostic tests show that chiropractic is effective in controlling back pain. Promising results have also been reported with the use of chiropractic techniques in neck pain and headaches. However, there are no well-controlled studies showing that chiropractic helps with nonmechanical problems.

A caution is in order regarding chiropractic: Spinal manipulation performed by a person without proper chiropractic training can be extremely dangerous. The American Chiropractic Association can help you find a licensed chiropractor near you.

Energy Therapies

Energy therapies are forms of treatment that use energy fields originating either within the body (biofields) or from other sources (electromagnetic fields). Biofield therapies are based on the idea that energy fields surround and penetrate the body and can be influenced by movement, touch, pressure, or the placement of hands in or through the fields. **Qigong**, a component of traditional Chinese

In Focus

Herbal Remedies: Are They Safe?

Consider the following research findings and FDA advisories:

- St. John's wort interacts with drugs used to treat HIV infection and heart disease; the herb may also reduce the effectiveness of oral contraceptives, antirejection drugs used with organ transplants, and some medications used to treat infections, depression, asthma, and seizure disorders.
- Chinese herbs contaminated through a manufacturing error with the powerful carcinogen aristolochic acid caused kidney damage and bladder cancer in patients at a weight-loss clinic in Belgium.
- Supplements containing kava have been linked to severe liver damage, and anyone who has liver problems or takes medications that can affect the liver are advised to consult a physician before using kava-containing supplements.
- In a sample of ayurvedic herbal medicine products, 20% were found to contain potentially harmful levels of lead, mercury, and/or arsenic.

These findings highlight growing safety concerns about dietary supplements, which now represent annual sales of more than $15 billion in the United States.

Drug Interactions

As in the case of St. John's wort, the chemicals in botanicals can interact dangerously with prescription and over-the-counter drugs. Botanicals may decrease the effects of drugs, making them ineffective, or increase their effects, in some cases making them toxic. Alarmingly, most patients fail to tell their physicians about their use of herbal substances. Botanicals can also interact with alcohol, usually heightening alcohol's effects. There are also complex interactions among the constituents of a single herbal preparation. And many manufacturers are offering new combinations of botanical preparations without empirical or scientific information about the interactions of the individual ingredients.

Lack of Standardization

A related problem is the lack of standardization in the manufacturing of herbal products. The Dietary Supplement Health and Education Act of 1994 requires that dietary supplement labels list the name and quantity of each ingredient. However, confusion can result because different plant species—with distinct chemical compositions and effects—may have the same common name. The content of herbal preparations is also variable. A 2003 study of echinacea supplements found that only about half contained the species and amount listed on the label; 10% of the samples contained no echinacea at all. Part of the reason for such variation is the difficulty of identifying the active ingredients in botanicals and isolating and standardizing their concentrations. The chemical composition of a supplement is also affected by the growing, harvesting, processing, and storage conditions of plants.

Contamination, Adulteration, and Toxicity

A variety of traditional Chinese and ayurvedic remedies contain heavy metals such as lead, mercury, and arsenic as part of the formula, all of which can be highly toxic and can cause irreversible damage. Some Chinese herbal remedies have been found to contain pharmaceutical drugs, including tranquilizers and steroids. Others contain herbs not listed on the label, sometimes substitute herbs that have toxic effects. Many plants are poisonous or can cause damage to the liver or kidneys if taken over long periods of time. Experts have also advised against taking supplements that contain raw animal parts, particularly central nervous system tissue, out of concern that disease may be transmissible this way. People with certain health conditions should be cautious when using herbal remedies. These conditions include Parkinson's disease, diabetes, epilepsy, hypertension, and psychiatric conditions.

The Role of Government in Safety Issues

Some European governments assume greater responsibility in regulating botanicals than the U.S. government. In Germany, manufacturing is standardized so that content, quantity, quality, and purity are guaranteed. Botanicals do not have to be proven effective to be marketed, but they do have to be proven safe.

In the United States, because herbs are considered supplements rather than food or drug products, they do not have to meet FDA food and drug standards for safety or effectiveness, nor do they currently have to meet any manufacturing standards. The manufacturer is responsible for ensuring that a supplement is safe before it is marketed; the FDA has the power to restrict a substance if it is found to pose a health risk after it is on the market. Because U.S. manufacturers can put almost anything into an herbal supplement, American consumers are at risk for buying and using products that may be not just useless but harmful as well. Part of the reasoning behind this situation is that herbal products are considered safer than conventional medicines.

medicine, combines movement, meditation, and regulation of breathing to enhance the flow of qi, improve blood circulation, and enhance immune function. **Therapeutic touch** is derived from the ancient technique of laying-on of hands; it is based on the premise that healers can identify and correct energy imbalances by passing their hands over the patient's body. **Reiki** is one form of therapeutic touch; it is intended to correct disturbances in the flow of life energy (ki is the Japanese form of the Chinese qi) and enhance the body's healing powers through the use of 13 specific hand positions on the patient.

Bioelectromagnetics is the study of the interaction between living organisms and electromagnetic fields, both those produced by the organism itself and those produced by outside sources. The recognition that the body produces electromagnetic fields has led to the development of many diagnostic procedures in Western medicine, including electroencephalography (EEG), electrocardiography (ECG), and nuclear magnetic resonance (NMR) scans. **Bioelectromagnetic-based therapies** involve the use of electromagnetic fields to manage pain and to treat conditions such as asthma. There are some indications that the use of electromagnetic fields might be useful in the areas of bone repair, wound healing, nerve stimulation, immune system stimulation, and modulation of the neuroendocrine (nerve and hormonal) system. Although promising, the available research is still very limited and does not allow firm conclusions about the efficacy of these therapies. Most scientists believe that consumer products containing small magnets have no significant effect on the human body.

Good communication between consumers and health care providers is important in both conventional and complementary medicine. It is important for consumers who choose to use CAM to discuss their choice with their physician to prevent any dangerous interactions with conventional treatments.

Evaluating Complementary and Alternative Therapies

Because there is less information available about complementary and alternative therapies, as well as less regulation of associated products and providers, it is important for consumers to take an active role when they are thinking about using them.

Working with Your Physician If you are considering a CAM therapy, your first source of information should be your physician or primary health care provider. The NCCAM advises consumers not to seek complementary therapies without first visiting a conventional health care provider for an evaluation and diagnosis of their symptoms. It's usually best to discuss and try conventional treatments that have been shown to be beneficial for your condition. If you are thinking of trying any alternative therapies, it is critically important to tell your physician in order to avoid any dangerous interactions with conventional treatments you are receiving. Areas to discuss with your physician include the following:

- *Safety:* Is there something unsafe about the treatment in general or for you specifically? Are there safety issues you should be aware of, such as the use of disposable needles in acupuncture?
- *Effectiveness:* Is there any research about the use of the therapy for your condition?
- *Timing:* Is the immediate use of a conventional treatment indicated?
- *Cost:* Is the therapy likely to be very expensive, especially in light of the potential benefit?

If you are not comfortable discussing CAM therapies with your physician, ask yourself why. Are you embarrassed about it? Do you think your doctor will think less of you? Do you think he or she doesn't know enough about the therapy you are considering? You have the right to expect your physician to take you and your concerns seriously, to respect your interest in a CAM therapy, to be informed about CAM approaches or at least make an effort to find out about them, and to be willing to discuss the evidence for and against them with you.

If appropriate, schedule a follow-up visit with your physician to assess your condition and your progress after a certain amount of time using a complementary therapy. Keep a symptom diary to more accurately track your symptoms and gauge your progress. (Symptoms such as pain and fatigue are very difficult to recall with accuracy, so an ongoing symptom diary is an important tool.) If you plan to pursue a therapy against your physician's advice, you need to tell him or her.

For supplements, particularly botanicals, pharmacists can also be an excellent source of information, especially if they are familiar with other medications you are taking.

Terms

Vw

therapeutic touch A CAM practice based on the premise that healers can identify and correct energy imbalances by passing their hands over the patient's body.

Reiki A CAM practice intended to correct disturbances in the flow of life energy and enhance the body's healing powers through the use of 13 hand positions on the patient.

bioelectromagnetic-based therapies CAM therapies based on the notion that electromagnetic fields can be used to promote healing and manage pain.

Questioning the CAM Practitioner You can also get information from individual practitioners and from schools, professional organizations, and state licensing boards. Ask about education, training, licensing, and certification. If appropriate, check with local or state regulatory agencies or the consumer affairs department to determine if any complaints have been lodged against the practitioner. Some guidelines for talking with a CAM practitioner include the following:

- Ask the practitioner why he or she thinks the therapy will be beneficial for your condition. Ask for a full description of the therapy and any potential side effects.
- Describe in detail any conventional treatments you are receiving.
- Ask how long the therapy should continue before it can be determined if it is beneficial.
- Ask about the expected cost of the treatment. Does it seem reasonable? Will your health insurance pay some or all of the costs?

If anything an alternative practitioner says or recommends directly conflicts with advice from your physician, discuss it with your physician before making any major changes in any current treatment regimen or in your lifestyle.

Doing Your Own Research You can investigate CAM therapies on your own by going to the library or doing research online, although caution is in order when using Web sites for the various forms of CAM. A good place to start is the Web sites of government agencies like the FDA or NCCAM and of universities and similar organizations that conduct government-sponsored research on CAM approaches (see For More Information).

If possible, also talk to people with the same condition you have who have received the same treatment. Remember, though, that patient testimonials shouldn't be used as the sole criterion for choosing a therapy or assessing its safety and efficacy. Controlled scientific trials usually provide the best information and should be consulted whenever possible. The absence of documented danger is not the same thing as proof of safety. Quite often, people working in health food stores are only too willing to give advice and make recommendations, particularly about botanical supplements. Many of these people are not qualified to give this kind of advice. Ask about qualifications (training or education) before accepting recommendations from anyone. Perhaps more so than for any other consumer products and services, the use of CAM calls for consumer skills, critical thinking, and caution.

Why Do Consumers Use Complementary Medicine?

Why are American consumers attracted to complementary and alternative medicine? Numerous reasons have been proposed. CAM often offers hope to people who have been disappointed by conventional medical therapies or who have chronic conditions that are incurable with conventional medical treatments. People with cancer, AIDS, and arthritis are among the heaviest users of CAM. Those most likely to use CAM are elderly people, approximately 80% of whom have at least one chronic health problem, and teenagers, who are concerned about their appearance and respond to a variety of appeals. Both these groups may be particularly susceptible to fraudulent claims for products promising new, quick, or easy ways to stay thin, strong, or attractive. A major source of CAM's appeal is that CAM practitioners often spend much more time listening and touching their patients than conventional physicians. Patients may find CAM practitioners to be warmer, more empathetic, and less rushed than their conventional counterparts.

Some experts speculate that the persuasive appeal of complementary and alternative medicine may come from the power of its underlying beliefs and cultural assumptions, which offer patients an experience they are missing in conventional medicine. People using CAM may feel they are connecting to nature or a more natural version of society; they may also feel a connection to vital energy or a life force, such as qi. They may view CAM as operating from a more holistic, person-centered body of knowledge than Western science, and they may find their quest for health imbued with an almost sacred quality. According to this view, CAM is attractive because of what it offers people when their sense of intactness and connection with the world is threatened by illness: empowerment, participation, authenticity, connection to nature and the universe, a renewed sense of purpose and meaning, and a new set of behavioral options. The assumptions of CAM can redefine the experience of illness in ways that inspire and empower the individual.

Despite many profound and irreconcilable philosophical differences between conventional medicine and CAM, there are abundant opportunities for learning, collaborating, and providing parallel care. Conventional medicine has already adopted many principles prevalent in complementary and alternative disciplines, including the ideas of health promotion, of personal responsibility for health, and of wellness as a multidimensional ideal. Western medicine is looking at the soaring use of CAM to discover what patients are missing in conventional care—perhaps more information, interest, or time from their physicians. At the same time, practitioners of CAM are looking to Western methods to modernize and optimize some of their practices, such as the preparation and standardization of herbal remedies. Within each is an enormous amount of time-tested information that has its own logic and use. In the future, greater understanding and collaboration across boundaries will certainly benefit the patient-consumer.

PAYING FOR HEALTH CARE

The American health care system is one of the most advanced and comprehensive in the world, but it is also the most expensive (Figure 21.5). In 2004, the United States spent $1.9 trillion on health care, or nearly $6300 per person. Health care costs are expected to reach $2.8 trillion, or about $9000 per person, by 2010. Numerous factors contribute to the high cost of health care in the United States, including the cost of advanced equipment and new technology; expensive treatments for some illnesses and conditions, such as cancer, heart disease, HIV infection, injuries, and low birth weight in infants; the aging of the population; and high earnings by some people in the health care industry and, in some cases, the demand for profits by investors.

The Current System

Health care is currently financed by a combination of private and public insurance plans, patient out-of-pocket payments, and government assistance. Currently, private insurance and individual patients pay about 55% of the total; the government pays the remaining 45%, mainly through Medicare and Medicaid (discussed below). Most nonelderly Americans receive their health insurance through their employers.

Not everyone is included in this financing system. More than 42 million people, the vast majority of them employed, have no health care insurance at all (see the box "Who Are the Uninsured?"). Many more are underinsured, meaning they may be uninsured for periods of time, have health insurance that does not cover all needed services, and/or have high out-of-pocket costs. People who are underinsured may skip physician visits and not take all prescribed medications. New government health insurance programs for children have reduced the number of Americans under age 18 who lack health insurance; still, almost 10% of all American children are not insured—most in working, low-income families. Among Americans age 18–44, nearly 24% are uninsured; of those age 45–64, nearly 13% have no health insurance.

People without insurance use health services less often and receive poorer care when they do use the services. Children without insurance are less likely to have screening tests and immunizations. They have fewer checkups, are less likely to be treated for injuries and for chronic conditions such as asthma, and are more likely to go without eyeglasses and prescribed drugs.

Another problem is that national health spending is growing faster than the rest of the economy, consuming an ever-increasing share of the U.S. gross domestic product (GDP). Health care spending represented 16% of the GDP in 2004 and is projected to reach 20% by 2015. Health care costs soared in the 1980s and then

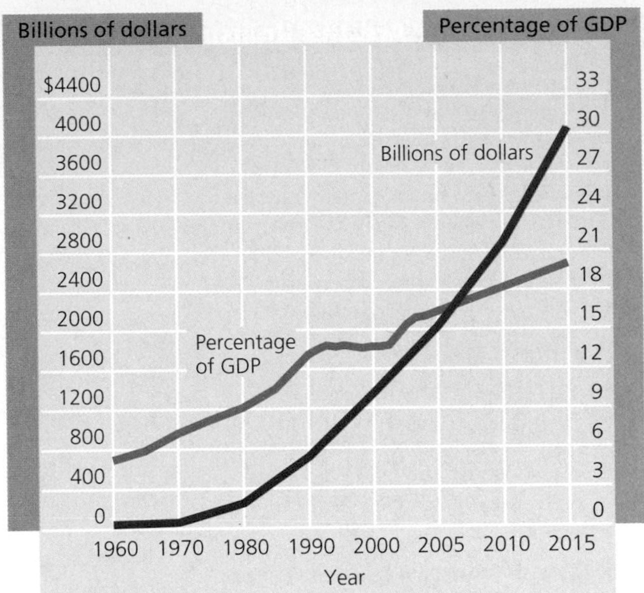

(a) National health care expenditures, beginning in 1960, when expenditures were $28 billion (actual through 2004; projected through 2015)

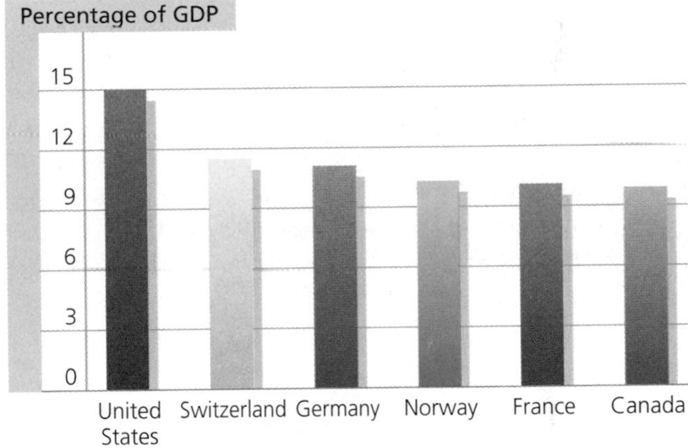

(b) Health care expenditures as a percentage of GDP, as of 2003.

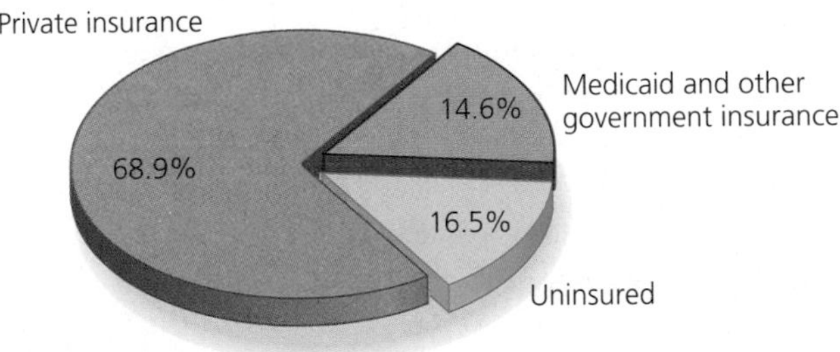

(c) Health insurance coverage of nonelderly Americans (age 0–64), as of 2003

VW VITAL STATISTICS

Figure 21-5 A statistical look at health care expenditures and health insurance. SOURCES: National Center for Health Statistics. 2006. *Health, United States, 2006.* Hyattsville, Md.: U.S. Public Health Service; U.S. Department of Health and Human Services. 2006. *National Health Expenditure Data* (http://www.cms.hhs.gov/NationalHealthExpendData/01_Overview.asp; retrieved September 17, 2006).

Dimensions of Diversity

Who Are the Uninsured?

Despite high national levels of spending on health care, many Americans under age 65—almost 17% or nearly 1 in 5—do not have health insurance. (Americans age 65 and over are often covered by government programs.) This overall statistic about the uninsured hides some important differences among groups (see table).

- *Low income:* The factor most closely associated with lack of health insurance is low income. People who are at 200% or more of the federal poverty level are significantly more likely to be insured than those in low-income brackets.
- *Age:* Young adults are less likely to be insured than older adults. Younger adults may not be regularly employed and so may not be covered by an insurance plan through work.
- *Ethnicity:* Ethnic minorities are less likely to be insured than whites. Latinos, especially persons of Mexican origin, have the lowest rates of insurance coverage. Much of the ethnic variations are explained by socioeconomic status. However, other factors may also contribute, including language barriers, differing cultural attitudes toward medical care, and living in medically underserved communities.

People without health insurance receive less health care and lower quality of care. They have fewer physician visits and less preventive care. To help overcome the health gap between ethnic minorities and the general population, the U.S. Department of Health and Human Services sponsors "Take a Loved One for a Checkup Day." Held on the third Tuesday in September, this event is designed to encourage people to obtain preventive care. People are encouraged to make an appointment for themselves or for a friend or family member who hasn't seen a health care provider recently.

People who don't have a regular health care provider or who don't have health insurance can contact a local health department or local community center to find out more about free or low-cost care. For more information, visit the Closing the Health Gap Web site (http://www.omhrc.gov/healthgap/).

	Uninsured Americans Under Age 65 (Percent)
Total	16.5
Income (percent of poverty level)	
Below 100%	31.1
100–149%	31.9
150–199%	27.6
200% or more	10.0
Age (years)	
Under 18	9.8
18–24	30.1
25–34	25.4
35–44	17.5
45–54	13.6
55–64	10.9
Ethnicity	
White	16.0
Asian American	18.2
African American	18.4
Latino	34.7
American Indian/ Alaska Native	35.0

SOURCES: National Center for Health Statistics. 2006. *Health, United States, 2006.* Hyattsville, Md.: U.S. Public Health Service; U.S. Department of Health and Human Services; U.S. Department of Health and Human Services, Office of Minority Health Resource Center. 2006. Fact Sheet: Take a Loved One for a Checkup Day (http://www.omhrc.gov/healthgap/2006drday.aspx; retrieved September 19, 2006).

were contained to some extent in the 1990s by a large-scale switch from private insurance to managed care (discussed below), which is designed to achieve cost economies. But the savings from this switch were likely a one-time phenomenon, as more than 90% of working Americans are now covered by managed-care plans. Experts predict that health costs will increase drastically in the near future, with much of the increase borne by the government and individuals.

Health Insurance

Health insurance enables people to receive health care they might not otherwise be able to afford. Hospital care costs hundreds of dollars a day, and surgical fees can cost thousands. Health insurance is important for everyone, especially as health care costs continue to rise.

Health insurance plans are either fee-for-service (indemnity) or managed care. With both types the individual or the employer pays a basic premium, usually on a monthly basis; there are often other payments as well. Insurance policies are sold to both groups and individuals; group plans tend to cover more services and cost less. Group coverage is often available through employers to workers and their families; however, millions of workers are opting out of these company-sponsored plans because of high premiums. About 3 million fewer workers signed up for such plans in 2003 than in 1998. People who are self-employed or whose employers don't offer group policies may need to buy individual plans.

Traditional Fee-for-Service (Indemnity) Plans

In a fee-for-service, or indemnity, plan, you can use any medical provider (such as a physician or a hospital) you choose. You or the provider sends the bill to your insurance company, which pays part of it. Usually you have to pay a deductible amount each year, and then the plan will pay a percentage—often 80%—of what they consider the "usual and customary" charge for covered services. You pay the remaining 20%, which is known as coinsurance. Freedom of choice is a major benefit of indemnity plans. You can see any physician you choose, including specialists. Your physician is paid based on the services he or she provides. Critics point to the fee-for-service payment system as a contributing factor in the rapid growth of U.S. health care costs because physicians have a financial incentive to order more tests and treatments for their patients. However, the vast majority of working Americans are now covered by managed-care plans.

Managed-Care Plans **Managed-care plans** have agreements with certain physicians, hospitals, and health care providers to offer a range of services to plan members at reduced cost. In general, you have lower out-of-pocket costs and less paperwork with a managed-care plan than with an indemnity plan, but you also have less freedom in choosing health care providers. Most Americans with job-based insurance are covered by managed-care plans, which may follow several different models:

- **Health maintenance organizations (HMOs)** offer members a range of services for a set monthly fee. You choose a primary care physician who manages your care and refers you to specialists if you need them. If you go outside the HMO, you have to pay for the service yourself. Physicians in the HMO agree to accept a monthly per-patient fee, or **capitation,** or to charge less than standard fees for services.
- **Preferred provider organizations (PPOs)** plans have arrangements with physicians and other providers who have agreed to accept lower fees. If you go outside the PPO, you have to pay more.
- **Point-of-service (POS) plans** are options offered by many HMOs in which you can see a physician outside the plan and still be partially covered (for example, for a specialist outside the network).

Many managed-care plans try to reduce costs over the long term by paying for routine preventive care, such as regular checkups and screening tests and prenatal care; they may also encourage prevention by offering health education and lifestyle modification programs for members. Other cost-cutting measures are less consumer-oriented. Consumers' choice of physicians is limited, and they may have to wait longer for appointments and travel farther to see participating doctors. Managed-care plans may also try to discourage overtreatment through the use of gatekeepers: In many plans, patients must get preapproval from their primary care physician or a plan representative for diagnostic tests, referrals to specialists, or hospital treatments. If a patient violates the rules for obtaining services, the plan typically will not cover the cost of the services in question. Nonemergency visits to emergency rooms are also frequently not covered.

Health Savings Accounts **Health savings accounts (HSAs)** became available in 2004. An HSA includes two parts: a health plan with a high deductible (at least $1050 per individual or $2100 per family), and a tax-exempt personal savings account that is used for qualified medical expenses. The individual makes pre-tax contributions to the savings account and later uses these funds or other cash payments to cover medical expenses until the plan's deductible is met. Once the deductible is met, the plan pays remaining medical costs according to the type of policy. The savings account can also be used for certain other types of expenses not covered by the plan. An HSA may give the consumer more control over health care spending; it can also potentially lower premiums for some people because health plans with high deductibles tend to have lower premiums. Recent research shows that HSAs are attractive to people who need tax breaks or pay high out-of-pocket health care costs. But HSAs are less likely to be used by people who don't have extra funds to set aside for future medical expenses; they are also less likely to lower health care costs for consumers who do not have high medical expenses.

Government Programs Americans who are 65 or older and younger people with certain disabilities can be covered by **Medicare,** a federal health insurance program that helps pay for hospitalization, physician services, and prescription drugs. As a result of limits placed on payments, however, some physicians and managed-care programs have stopped accepting Medicare patients. **Medicaid** is a joint federal-state health insurance program that covers some low-income people, especially children, pregnant

Terms

Vw

managed-care plan A health care program that integrates the financing and delivery of services by using designated providers, utilization review, and incentives for following the plan's policies; HMOs, PPOs, and POS plans are managed-care plans.

health maintenance organization (HMO) A prepaid health insurance plan that offers health care from designated providers

capitation A payment to health care providers according to the number of patients they agree to serve, rather than the amount of service rendered.

preferred provider organization (PPO) A prepaid health insurance plan in which providers agree to deliver services for discounted fees; patients can go to any provider, but using nonparticipating providers results in higher costs to the patient.

point-of-service (POS) plan A managed-care plan that covers treatment by an HMO physician but permits patients to seek treatment elsewhere with a higher copayment.

health savings account (HSA) Health insurance coverage that includes a health plan with a high deductible and a tax-exempt personal savings account that is used for qualified medical expenses.

Medicare A federal health insurance program for people 65 or older and for younger people with certain disabilities.

Medicaid A federally subsidized state-run plan of health care for people with low income.

Critical Consumer

Choosing a Health Care Plan

Before you choose a health plan, it's important that you understand your options and how they affect your choice of providers and services, costs, and quality of care. The following questions can help guide you in evaluating each of the health plans you are considering:

- *How is the plan rated for quality?* Find out if consumer ratings or consumer satisfaction information is available. Possible sources include the Consumer Assessment of Health Plans (CAHPS), the Health Plan Employer Data and Information Set (HEDIS), or your state health insurance commissioner (check the phone book for contact information).

- *Is the plan accredited?* Many health plans choose to be reviewed and accredited (given a "seal of approval") by the National Committee for Quality Assurance (NCQA), the Joint Commission on Accreditation of Healthcare Organizations (JCAHO), or the American Accreditation HealthCare Commission/URAC.

- *Does the plan include the doctors and hospitals you want?* If you are happy with your current physician, find out which plans he or she is in. If going to a certain hospital is important to you, investigate where a particular physician has privileges and whether a hospital is covered by the plan.

- *Does the plan provide the benefits you need?* Determine which health care services are most important to you and your family and then check to see if the plan covers them. Possible services to consider include physician office visits, preventive services, diagnostic tests and X rays, outpatient prescription medications, inpatient medical and hospital costs, physical therapy, drug and alcohol counseling, prenatal and well baby care, eye exams and glasses or contact lenses, mental health services, complementary therapies such as acupuncture, home health care, and care for preexisting or chronic conditions.

- *Do the doctors, pharmacies, and other services in the plan have convenient times and locations?* Find out about such things as after-hours care and parking as well.

- *Does the plan fit your budget?* Consider all the applicable costs of a plan: monthly premiums, annual deductibles, and copayments for doctor and hospital visits and prescription drugs. Also find out about how much more you will need to pay if you go outside the health plan's network of physicians, hospitals, and other providers to obtain services.

SOURCE: Agency for Health Care Policy and Research. 2006. *Your Guide to Choosing Quality Health Care* (http://www.ahcpr.gov/consumer/qnt; retrieved September 19, 2006).

women, and people with certain disabilities. The number of people and the number and cost of services covered by government programs has grown in recent years, challenging the ability of these programs to make all payments. The fund that pays Medicare hospital costs is currently expected to become insolvent in 2018.

Choosing a Policy

Choosing health insurance can be complicated; it's important to evaluate the coverage provided by different plans and decide which one is best for you (see the box "Choosing a Health Care Plan"). Colleges typically provide medical services through a student health center; some require students to purchase additional insurance if they are not covered by family policies. It's usually economical to remain on a family policy as long as possible.

After college, most people secure group coverage through their place of employment or through membership in an organization. If group coverage is not available, individuals should contact several different insurance companies for information about policies. Managed-care plans tend to have lower premiums and fewer out-of-pocket costs, an advantage for young adults and families with young children. Traditional fee-for-service plans tend to cost more and involve more paperwork, but they offer a wider choice of providers. If you are choosing insurance, consider a number of different plans and use your critical thinking skills to find the one that best suits your needs.

Tips for Today

Most of the time, you can take care of yourself without consulting a health care provider. You can eat sensibly, get enough exercise, manage stress, minimize your chances of getting an infection, and so on. When you do need professional care, you can continue to take responsibility for yourself by making informed, reasoned decisions about the care you obtain, whether conventional or CAM.

Right now you can

- Make sure you have enough on hand of any prescription medication that you take and that your prescription is up to date.
- Make sure you have basic first aid supplies at home and prepare or buy a small first aid kit for your car or office.
- Research any alternative or complementary practice or product you are using, either at the library or online, to find out if it is considered safe.
- Sit back in your chair and practice relaxation through breathing: Inhale slowly and deeply, imagining warm air flowing to all parts of your body; exhale from your abdomen, imagining tension flowing out of your body; continue for 5 or 10 minutes or until you feel relaxed.

Complying with Physicians' Instructions

Behavior Change Strategy

Even though we sometimes have to entrust ourselves to the care of medical professionals, that doesn't mean we give up responsibility for our own behavior. Following medical instructions and advice often requires the same kind of behavioral self-management that's involved in quitting smoking, losing weight, or changing eating patterns. For example, if you have an illness or injury, you may be told to take medication at certain times of the day, do special exercises or movements, or change your diet.

The medical profession recognizes the importance of patient adherence, or compliance, and encourages different strategies to support it, such as the following:

1. Use reminders placed at home, in the car, at work, on your computer screensaver, or elsewhere that improve follow-through in taking medication and keeping scheduled appointments. To help you remember to take medications:
   - Link taking the medication with some well-established routine, like brushing your teeth or eating breakfast.
   - Use a medication calendar, and check off each pill.
   - Use a medication organizer or pill dispenser.
   - Plan ahead; don't wait until the last pill to get a prescription refilled.
2. Use a journal and other forms of self-monitoring to keep a detailed account of health-related behaviors, such as pill taking, diet, exercise, and so on.
3. Use self-reward systems so that desired behavior changes are encouraged, with a focus on short-term rewards.
4. Develop a clear image or explanation of how the medication or behavior change will improve your health and well-being.

If these strategies don't help you stick with your treatment plan, you may need to consider other possible explanations for your lack of adherence. For example, are you confused about some aspect of the treatment? Do you find the schedule for taking your medications too complicated, or do the drugs have bothersome side effects that you'd rather avoid? Do you feel that the recommended treatment is unnecessary or unlikely to help? Are you afraid of becoming dependent on a medication or that you'll be judged negatively if people know about your condition and treatment? An examination of your attitudes and beliefs about your condition and treatment plan can also help improve your compliance.

SUMMARY

- Informed self-care requires knowing how to evaluate symptoms. It's necessary to see a physician if symptoms are severe, unusual, persistent, or recurrent.
- Self-treatment doesn't necessarily require medication, but OTC drugs can be a helpful part of self-care.
- Conventional medicine is characterized by a focus on the external, physical causes of disease; the identification of a set of symptoms for different diseases; the development of public health measures to prevent disease and of drugs and surgery to treat them; the use of rational, scientific thinking to understand phenomena; and a well-established research methodology.
- Conventional practitioners include medical doctors, doctors of osteopathic medicine, podiatrists, optometrists, and dentists, as well as allied health care providers.
- The diagnostic process involves a medical history, a physical exam, and medical tests. Patients should ask questions about medical tests and treatments recommended by their physicians.
- Safe use of prescription drugs requires knowledge of what the medication is supposed to do, how and when to take it, and what the side effects are.
- All surgical procedures carry risk; patients should ask about alternatives and get a second opinion from another physician.
- Complementary and alternative medicine (CAM) is defined as those therapies and practices that do not form part of conventional or, mainstream, health care and medical practice as taught in most U.S. medical schools and offered in most U.S. hospitals.
- CAM is characterized by a view of health as a balance and integration of body, mind, and spirit; a focus on ways to restore the individual to harmony so that he or she can fight disease and regain health; and a body of knowledge based on accumulated experience and observations of patient reactions.
- Alternative medical systems such as traditional Chinese medicine and homeopathy are complete systems of medical philosophy, theory, and practice.
- Mind-body interventions include meditation, yoga, group support, hypnosis, and prayer.
- Biological-based therapies consist of herbal remedies, botanicals, and dietary supplements.
- Manipulative and body-based methods include massage and other physical healing techniques; the most commonly accepted is chiropractic.
- Energy therapies are designed to influence the flow of energy in and around the body; they include qigong, therapeutic touch therapies, and Reiki.
- Because there is less information available about CAM and less regulation of its practices and providers, consumers must be proactive in researching and choosing treatments, using critical thinking skills and exercising caution.

- Health insurance plans are usually described as either fee-for-service (indemnity) or managed-care plans. Indemnity plans allow consumers more choice in medical providers, but managed-care plans are less expensive.
- Government programs include Medicaid, for the poor, and Medicare, for those age 65 and over or chronically disabled.

Take Action

1. **Prepare for a health care visit:** Before your next visit to your physician, prepare a written list of your concerns. Be prepared to ask questions. After the visit, review how it went. Were your concerns satisfactorily addressed? Were you able to communicate your needs? Did you feel involved and in control? What aspects would you like to handle better the next time?

2. **Compare supplements:** Visit a local drugstore and compare different brands of the same herbal remedy or dietary supplement. How similar are the supplements in terms of ingredients, recommended dosages, and price? What aspect of health do the supplements claim to benefit, and how do they make the claim? Research any unfamiliar ingredients using the resources listed in For More Information and in Chapter 12.

3. **Consider special health risks:** Ask your physician whether you have any medical condition that may require special attention in an emergency. If you do, complete a medical ID card for your wallet, or obtain a medical ID bracelet or necklace. More complete emergency service can be obtained by joining Medic Alert (888-633-4298; www.medicalert.org).

4. **Make a preventive-care appointment for yourself or someone you know:** Promote wellness in yourself and those around you by participating in "Take a Loved One to the Doctor Day." Make an appointment for preventive care for yourself and/or a friend or family member (see p. 654 for more information). If needed, help someone keep an appointment by volunteering to provide transportation or child care.

For More Information

Books

Committee on the Use of Complementary and Alternative Medicine by the American Public. 2005. *Complementary and Alternative Medicine in the United States.* Washington, D.C.: National Academy Press. *Outlines ways of integrating conventional and complementary therapies, and proposes changes to dietary supplement laws.*

Mayo Clinic. 2007. *The Mayo Clinic Book of Alternative Medicine.* New York: Time-Life. *A concise review of currently popular CAM therapies and treatments.*

Spencer, J. W., and J. Jacobs. 2003. *Complementary and Alternative Medicine: An Evidence-Based Approach.* St. Louis, Mo.: Mosby. *Provides background information and the current state of evidence for the efficacy of a wide variety of CAM therapies.*

Thompson, W. G. 2005. *The Placebo Effect and Health: Combining Science and Compassionate Care.* New York: Prometheus Books. *Describes the placebo effect and how it may be used to benefit health.*

Thomson Healthcare and PDR. 2006. *PDR for Nonprescription Drugs, Dietary Supplements, and Herbs: The Definitive Guide to OTC Medications,* 27th ed. Montvale, N.J.: Thomson PDR. *A reference covering the safety and efficacy of over-the-counter medications available today.*

Whorton, J. C. 2004. *Nature Cures: The History of Alternative Medicine in America.* New York: Oxford University Press. *Provides a history of alternative medicine in the United States, including background information on many CAM therapies.*

Organizations, Hotlines, and Web Sites

Agency for Healthcare Research and Quality (AHRQ). Provides practical, evidence-based information on health care treatments and outcomes for consumers and practitioners.
http://www.ahrq.gov

American Board of Medical Specialties. Provides information on board certification, including information on specific physicians.
866-275-2267
http://www.abms.org

American Chiropractic Association. Provides information on chiropractic care, consumer tips, and a searchable directory of certified chiropractors.
http://www.amerchiro.org

American Medical Association (AMA). Provides information about physicians, including their training, licensure, and board certification.
http://www.ama-assn.org

American Osteopathic Association. Provides information on osteopathic physicians, including board certification.
800-621-1773
http://www.osteopathic.org

ConsumerLab.com. Provides information on the results of tests of dietary supplements, including information on actual ingredients and concentrations.
http://www.consumerlab.com

Food and Drug Administration: Information for Consumers. Provides materials on dietary supplements, foods, prescription and OTC drugs, and other FDA-regulated products.
888-INFO-FDA
http://www.fda.gov/opacom/morecons.html

National Center for Complementary and Alternative Medicine (NCCAM). Provides general information packets, answers to frequently asked questions about CAM, consumer advice for safer use of CAM, research abstracts, and bibliographies.
888-644-6226
http://nccam.nih.gov

National Council Against Health Fraud. Provides news and information about health fraud and quackery and links to related sites.

http://www.ncahf.org

Quackwatch. Provides information on health fraud, quackery, and health decision making.

http://www.quackwatch.org

U.S. Treasury Department: Health Savings Accounts. Provides information about HSAs and links to relevant IRS forms.

http://www.treas.gov/offices/public-affairs/hsa/

See also the listings for Chapters 2 and 12; the box on dietary supplements in Chapter 12 (p. 361) suggests Web sites with more information on supplements.

Selected Bibliography

Allais, G., et al. 2002. Acupuncture in the prophylactic treatment of migraine without aura: A comparison with flunarizine. *Headache* 42(9): 855–861.

American Association of Retired Persons. 2006. *The Status of the Medicare HI and SMI Trust Funds: The Trustees' 2006 Annual Report* (http://www.aarp.org/research/medicare/financing/dd138_hi_smi.html; retrieved September 18, 2006).

American Medical Association. 2004. *Health Savings Accounts at a Glance.* Chicago: American Medical Association.

Bach, P. B., et al. 2004. Primary care physicians who treat blacks and whites. *New England Journal of Medicine* 351(6): 575–584.

Bordens, K. S., and B. B. Abbott. 2005. *Research Design and Methods: A Process Approach,* 6th ed. New York: McGraw-Hill.

Bren, L. 2004. Study: U.S. generic drugs cost less than Canadian drugs. *FDA Consumer,* July/August.

Brobst, D. E., et al. 2004. Guggulsterone activates multiple nuclear receptors and induces CYP3A gene expression through the pregnane X receptor. *Journal of Pharmacology and Experimental Therapeutics* 310(2): 528–535.

Budetti, P. P. 2004. 10 years beyond the health security act failure: Subsequent developments and persistent problems. *Journal of the American Medical Association* 292(16): 2000–2006.

Burke, A., et al. 2006. Acupuncture use in the United States: Findings from the national health interview survey. *Journal of Alternative and Complementary Medicine* 12(7): 639–648.

Centers for Disease Control and Prevention. 2004. Complementary and alternative medicine use among adults: United States, 2002. *Advance Data from Vital and Health Statistics* No. 343. Hyattsville, Md.: National Center for Health Statistics.

Centers for Disease Control and Prevention. 2006. *Health Insurance Coverage: Early Release of Estimates from the National Health Interview Survey, January-March 2005* (http://www.cdc.gov/nchs/nhs.htm; retrieved October 16, 2006).

Cyna, A. M., et al. 2006. Antenatal self-hypnosis for labour and childbirth: A pilot study. *Anaesthesia and Intensive Care* 34(4): 464–469.

Ernst, E. 2004. Prescribing herbal medications appropriately. *Journal of Family Practice* 53(12): 985–988.

Frazier, S. C. 2005. Health outcomes and polypharmacy in elderly individuals: An integrated literature review. *Journal of Gerontological Nursing* 31(9): 4–11.

Gan, T. J., et al. 2004. A randomized controlled comparison of electro-acupoint stimulation or ondansetron versus placebo for the prevention of postoperative nausea and vomiting. *Anesthesia and Analgesia* 99(4): 1070–1075.

Kaiser Family Foundation. 2005. *Trends and Indicators in the Changing Health Care Marketplace.* Menlo Park, Calif.: Kaiser Family Foundation.

Miller, F. G., et al. 2004. Ethical issues concerning research in complementary and alternative medicine. *Journal of the American Medical Association* 291(5): 599–604.

Morningstar, M. W. 2006. Improvement of lower extremity electro-diagnostic findings following a trail of spinal manipulation and motion-based therapy. *Chiropractic & Osteopathy* 14(1): 20.

National Academy of Sciences, Institute of Medicine. 2006. *Preventing Medication Errors.* Washington, D.C.: National Academies Press.

National Center for Health Statistics. 2006. *Health, United States, 2006.* Hyattsville, Md.: U.S. Public Health Service; U.S. Department of Health and Human Services.

National Center for Health Statistics. 2005. Trends in health insurance and access to medical care for children under age 19 years. *Advance Data from Vital Health Statistics* No. 355.

Nissen, S. E., et al. 2006. Adverse cardiovascular effects of rofecoxib. *New England Journal of Medicine* 355(2): 203–205.

Radley, D. C., et al. 2006. Off-label prescribing among office-based physicians. *Archives of Internal Medicine* 166(9): 1021–1026.

Rados, C. 2004. FDA reiterates warning against online drug buying. *FDA Consumer,* September/October.

Remler, D. K., and S. A. Glied. 2006. How much more cost sharing will health savings accounts bring? *Health Affairs* 25(4): 1070–1078.

Saper, R. B., et al. 2004. Heavy metal content of ayurvedic herbal medicine products. *Journal of the American Medical Association* 292(23): 2868–2873.

Taseng, C., et al. 2004. Cost-lowering strategies used by Medicare beneficiaries who exceed drug benefit caps and have a gap in drug coverage. *Journal of the American Medical Association* 292(8): 952–960.

The uninsured: Americans at risk. 2004. *Consumer Reports,* January.

U.S. Department of Health and Human Services. 2006. *National Health Expenditure Data* (http://www.cms.hhs.gov/NationalHealthExpendData/01_Overview.asp; retrieved September 17, 2006).

Zwillich, T. 2006. *Medicare Insolvency Creeps Closer: Hospital Fund Due Bankrupt in 2018* (http://www.webmd.com/content/article/121/114379.htm; retrieved September 18, 2006).

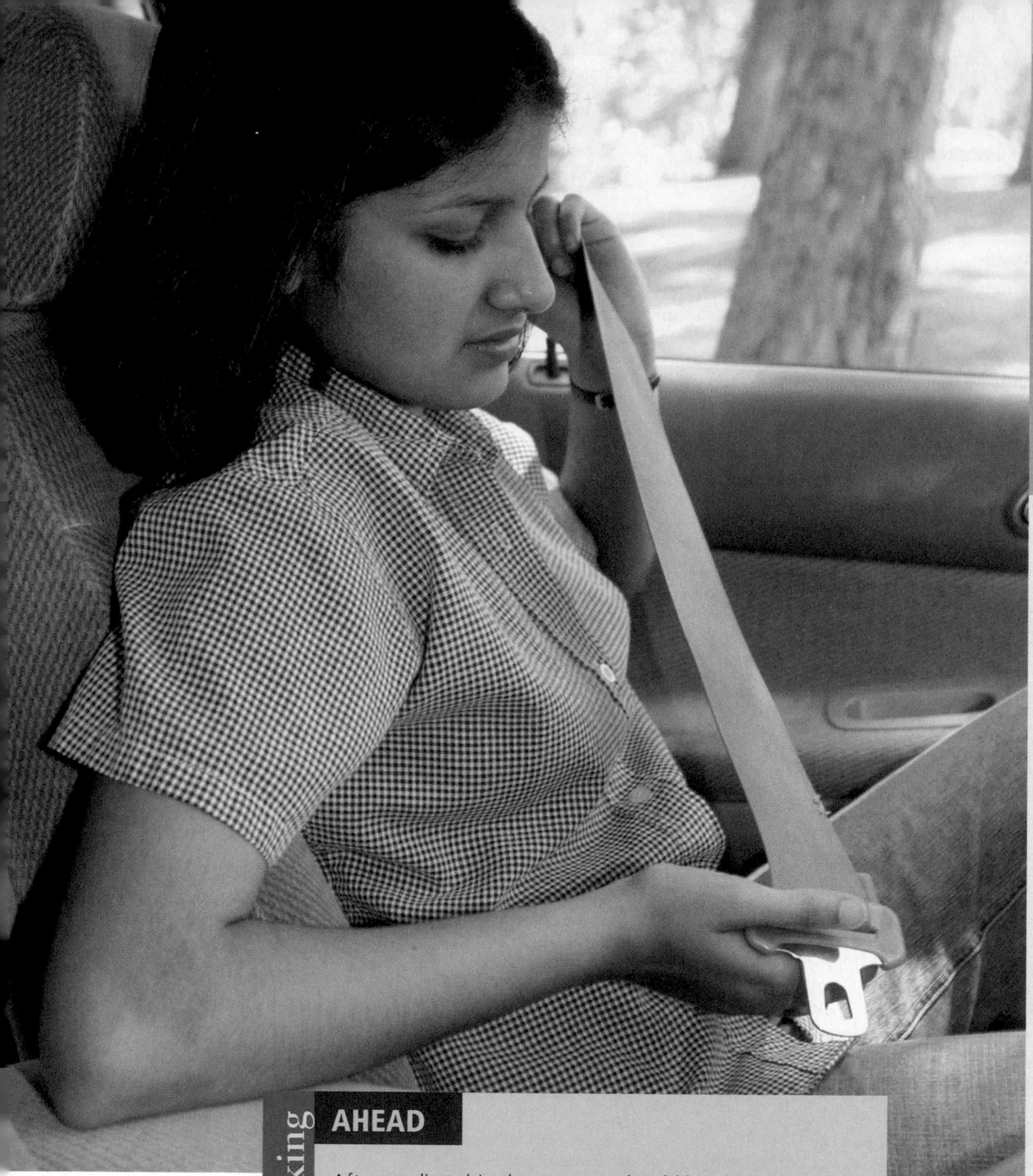

22

Looking AHEAD

After reading this chapter, you should be able to

- Discuss factors that contribute to unintentional injuries.
- List the most common types of unintentional injuries and strategies for preventing them
- Describe factors that contribute to violence and intentional injuries
- Discuss different forms of violence and how to protect yourself from intentional injuries
- List strategies for helping others in an emergency situation

Personal Safety: Protecting Yourself from Unintentional Injuries and Violence

Test Your Knowledge

1. **More people are injured each year through intentional acts of violence than through unintentional injuries (accidents).**
   True or false?
2. **It is dangerous to be wearing a safety belt if your car catches on fire or is submerged in water.**
   True or false?
3. **Your odds are greatest for being killed in**
   a. a fire
   b. a fall
   c. a plane crash
4. **Talking on a cell phone while driving increases the risk of motor vehicle crashes.**
   True or false?
5. **About what percentage of sexual assaults against women are committed by strangers?**
   a. 20%
   b. 40%
   c. 80%

ANSWERS

1. FALSE. Far more people are injured and killed each year through unintentional injuries than through violence. Your lifetime odds of dying from an unintentional injury are 1 in 35, while the odds of your being murdered are 1 in 211.
2. FALSE. Safety belts will help prevent you from being knocked unconscious, so you'll have a better chance of escaping the car. (Only 0.5–1.0% of motor vehicle crashes involve fire or submersion.)
3. B. The odds of being fatally injured in a fall are now estimated at 1 in 229. The odds of being killed by fire are 1 in 1179, and the odds of dying in a plane crash are 1 in 5704.
4. TRUE. Using a handheld or hands-free cell phone while driving decreases attentiveness and reaction time. A 20-year-old using a phone has the reaction time of a 70-year-old not using a phone.
5. A. The vast majority of sexual assaults against women are committed by friends, acquaintances, or intimate partners.

Visit the *Core Concepts in Health* Online Learning Center (www.mhhe.com/insel10e) for study aids and many additional resources.

Each year, more than 160,000 Americans die from injuries, and many more are temporarily or permanently disabled. Injuries can be intentional or unintentional. An **intentional injury** is one that is purposely inflicted, by either oneself or another person; examples are homicide, suicide, and assault. If an injury occurs when no harm is intended, it is considered an **unintentional injury.** Motor vehicle crashes, falls, and fires often result in unintentional injuries. (Public health officials prefer not to use the word *accidents* to describe unintentional injuries because it suggests events beyond human control. *Injuries* are predictable outcomes of factors that can be controlled or prevented.) Although Americans tend to express more concern about intentional injuries, unintentional injuries are actually more common. The following occur on an average day in the United States:

- 45 homicides
- 85 suicides
- 304 deaths from unintentional injuries
- 1500 suicide attempts
- 20,000 interpersonal assaults
- 63,600 disabling injuries
- 110,000 unintentional injury–related emergency room visits

Unintentional injuries are the fifth leading cause of death among all Americans and the leading cause of death and disability among children and young adults. Heart disease, cancer, stroke, and chronic lower respiratory diseases are responsible for more deaths each year than injuries, but because unintentional injuries are so common among people, they account for more **years of potential life lost** than any other cause of death. Suicide and homicide rank eleventh and sixteenth respectively on the list of leading causes of death among Americans; because they often affect young people, they also account for many years of potential life lost. Injuries affect all segments of the population, but they are particularly common among men, minorities, and people with low incomes, primarily due to social, environmental, and economic factors. Although rates of both unintentional and intentional injuries have fallen in recent years, they remain a major area of concern.

The economic cost of injuries is high, with nearly $600 billion spent each year for medical care and rehabilitation of injured people. Injuries also cause emotional suffering for injured people and their families, friends, and colleagues. Luckily, there are many steps that can be taken to reduce the risk of injuries. Engineering strategies such as safety belts can help lower injury rates, as can the passage and enforcement of safety-related laws, such as those requiring tamper-proof containers for OTC medications. Public education campaigns about risky behaviors such as driving under the influence of alcohol or smoking in bed can also help prevent injuries.

Ultimately, though, it is up to each individual to take responsibility for his or her actions and make wise choices about safety behaviors. Many of the same sensible attitudes, responsible behaviors, and informed decisions that optimize your wellness can improve your chances of avoiding injuries. This chapter explains how you can protect yourself and those around you from becoming the victims of unintentional and intentional injuries.

UNINTENTIONAL INJURIES

Unintentional injuries are the leading cause of death in the United States for people under age 35. Injury situations are generally categorized into four general classes, based on where they occur: motor vehicle injuries, home injuries, leisure injuries, and work injuries. The greatest number of deaths occur in motor vehicle crashes, but the greatest number of disabling injuries occur in the home (Table 22-1). In all of these arenas, the action you take can mean the difference between injury or death and no injury at all.

What Causes an Injury?

Most injuries are caused by a combination of human and environmental factors. Human factors are inner conditions or attitudes that lead to an unsafe state, whether physical,

Vw VITAL STATISTICS

Table 22-1 Unintentional Injuries in the United States

	Deaths	Disabling Injuries
Motor vehicle	46,200	2,400,000
Home	37,400	9,000,000
Leisure	24,700	8,200,000
Work	4,952	3,700,000
All classes*	110,000	23,200,000

*Deaths and injuries for the four separate classes total more than the "All classes" figures because of rounding and because some deaths and injuries are included in more than one class.

SOURCE: National Safety Council. 2006. *Injury Facts, 2005–2006 Edition.* Itasca, Ill.: National Safety Council.

Terms

Vw

intentional injury An injury that is purposely inflicted, by either oneself or another person.

unintentional injury An injury that occurs without harm being intended.

years of potential life lost The difference between an individual's life expectancy and his or her age at death.

Gender Matters

Injuries Among Young Men

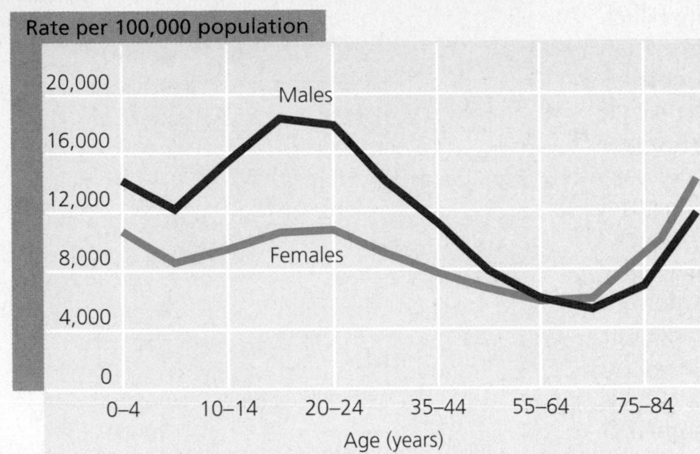

Figure 1 Nonfatal injury rate by age and sex.

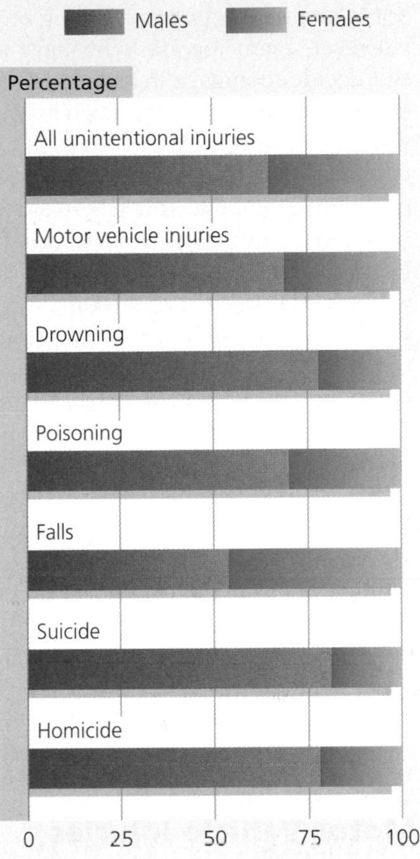

Figure 2 Injury deaths: Percentage of victims by sex.

Overall, rates of injury are highest among young adults and seniors over age 85. Except among the oldest group of adults, the nonfatal injury rate is substantially higher in males than in females—and it peaks among young adult males (Figure 1). Males also significantly outnumber females in injury deaths—whether unintentional or intentional (Figure 2).

Why do men, especially young men, have such high rates of injury? Gender roles may play a key role: Traditional gender roles for males may associate masculinity with risk-taking behavior and a disregard for pain and injury, and risk-taking behavior may be particularly common among young men. Men are more likely to drive dangerously, drink and drive, binge drink, and use aggressive behavior to control situations—all of which can lead to higher rates of fatal and nonfatal injury. Men may also have a lower perception of risk of dangerous behaviors compared with women.

Traditional gender roles may also make it more difficult for men to admit to injury or emotional vulnerability. Physical injuries may worsen or become chronic if care is not sought promptly. Untreated depression can lead to suicide.

In addition, men may have greater exposure to some injury situations. Compared with women, men may drive more miles, have greater access to firearms, and be more likely to ride motorcycles, operate machinery, and have jobs associated with high rates of workplace injuries. They may be more likely to be engage in sports and other recreational activities associated with high rates of injuries. Greater access and use of firearms plays a role in higher rates of deaths among men from assault and suicide; as described in Chapter 3, women are more likely than men to attempt suicide, but men are much more likely to succeed, primarily because they are more likely to use firearms.

Some researchers suggest that the male hormone testosterone may play a role in risky and aggressive behavior. Differences in brain structure and activity may also influence how men and women respond to stressors and how quickly and to what degree they become verbally or physically aggressive in response to anger.

Further studies are needed to identify all the factors underlying excessive risk-taking among men and how these risk behaviors can be changed to lower the rates of fatal and nonfatal injury among men.

SOURCES: Centers for Disease Control and Prevention. 2004. Surveillance for fatal and nonfatal injuries—United States, 2001. *MMWR Surveillance Summaries* 53(SS7): 1–57; World Health Organization. 2002. *Gender and Road Traffic Injuries.* Geneva: World Health Organization; Courtenay, W. 1998. College men's health: An overview and a call to action. *Journal of American College Health* 46(6): 279–290.

emotional, or psychological. Environmental factors are external conditions and circumstances, such as poor road conditions, a slippery surface, or the undertow of the ocean at the beach.

A common human factor that leads to injuries is risk-taking behavior. People vary in the amount of risk they tend to take in life; young men are especially prone to taking risks (see the box "Injuries Among Young Men"). Some people take risks to win the admiration of their peers; other people simply overestimate their physical abilities. Using alcohol or drugs is another common risk factor that leads to many injuries and deaths.

Psychological and emotional factors can also play a role in injuries. People sometimes act on the basis of inadequate or inaccurate beliefs about what is safe or unsafe. For example, a person who believes that safety belts trap people in cars when a crash occurs and who therefore decides not to wear a safety belt is acting on an inaccurate belief. However, many people who have accurate information still decide to engage in risky behavior. Young people often have unsafe attitudes, such as "I won't get hurt" or "It won't happen to me." Attitudes like this can lead to risk taking and ultimately to injuries.

Environmental factors leading to injury may be natural (weather conditions), social (a drunk driver), work-related (defective equipment), or home-related (faulty wiring). Making the environment safer is an important aspect of safety. Laws are often passed to try to make our environment safer; examples include speed limits on highways and workplace safety requirements.

When unsafe human states and unsafe environmental factors interact, an injury is often the result. A good example might be an inexperienced person borrowing a rifle to go hunting with his friends on a cold, rainy afternoon. Those in the group drink alcohol because they mistakenly believe it will keep them warmer. It is not difficult to imagine how these human and environmental factors could lead to an injury. Again, it is important to realize that injuries do not "just happen." With hindsight, we can almost always pinpoint the internal and external factors that combined to cause an injury situation.

VITAL STATISTICS

Table 22-2 Lifetime Odds of Death Due to Injury

All unintentional injuries	**1 in 35**
Motor vehicle	1 in 77
Poisoning	1 in 212
Fall	1 in 229
Drowning	1 in 1081
Fire	1 in 1179
Choking	1 in 1267
Struck by falling object	1 in 4311
Firearm discharge	1 in 4888
Air and space transport	1 in 5704
Exposure to natural cold	1 in 5766
Electric current	1 in 8205
Exposure to natural heat	1 in 10,643
Lightning	1 in 56,439
Cataclysmic storm	1 in 59,127
Earthquake or volcano	1 in 120,161
Suicide	**1 in 118**
Homicide (assault)	**1 in 211**

SOURCE: National Safety Council. 2006. *What Are the Odds of Dying?* (http://www.nsc.org/lrs/statinfo/odds.htm; retrieved September 21, 2006).

Motor Vehicle Injuries

According to the Centers for Disease Control and Prevention (CDC), more than 37,000 Americans were killed and 3 million injured in motor vehicle crashes in 2004. Worldwide, motor vehicle crashes kill 1.2 million and injure up to 50 million people each year, making motor vehicle injuries the eleventh leading cause of death overall. The groups most affected by motor vehicle crashes are people age 15–24 and over 75. It is more likely that your death will be caused by a motor vehicle crash than by any other type of unintentional or intentional injury (Table 22-2). **Motor vehicle injuries** also result in the majority of cases of paralysis due to spinal injuries, and they are the leading cause of severe brain injury in the United States.

Factors Contributing to Motor Vehicle Injuries Common causes of motor vehicle injuries are speeding, aggressive driving, fatigue, inexperience, cell phones and other distractions, the use of alcohol and other drugs, and the incorrect use of safety belts and other safety devices.

Term

motor vehicle injuries Unintentional injuries and deaths involving motor vehicles in motion, both on and off the highway or street; incidents causing motor vehicle injuries include collisions between vehicles and collisions with objects or pedestrians.

SPEEDING Nearly 60% of all motor vehicle crashes are caused by bad driving, especially speeding. As speed increases, momentum and the force of impact increase, and the time allowed for the driver to react (reaction time) decreases. Speed limits are posted to establish the safest maximum speed limit for a given area under ideal conditions; if visibility is limited or the road is wet, the safe maximum speed may be considerably lower. Many states have raised their highway speed limits since the 1995 repeal of the National Maximum Speed Limit, and overall motor vehicle fatalities have since increased. Raising speed limits on rural interstates has caused a 35% increase in crash death rates.

AGGRESSIVE DRIVING Speeding is also a hallmark of aggressive drivers—those who operate a motor vehicle in an unsafe and hostile manner. Aggressive driving, also known as road rage, has increased more than 50% since 1990, and one in four U.S. drivers admits to driving aggressively at least some of the time. Other characteristics of aggressive driving include frequent, erratic, and abrupt lane changes; tailgating; running red lights or stop signs; passing on the shoulder; and blocking other cars trying to change lanes or pass. Aggressive drivers increase the risk of crashes for themselves and others; injuries may also occur if aggressive drivers stop their vehicles and confront each other following an incident. For more on aggressive

Assess Yourself

Are You an Aggressive Driver?

To find out if you are an aggressive driver, check any of the following statements that are true for you:

_____ I consistently exceed the speed limit; I'm often unaware of both my speed and the speed limit.

_____ I frequently follow closely behind the car in front of me.

_____ If I feel the car in front of me is going too slowly, I tailgate.

_____ I change lanes frequently to pass people.

_____ I seldom use my turn signal when changing lanes or turning.

_____ I often run red lights or roll through stop signs.

_____ I react to what I feel is another driver's mistake by cursing, shouting, or making rude gestures; by blocking a car from passing or changing lanes; by using high beams; or by braking suddenly in front of a tailgater.

_____ My personality changes and I become more competitive when I get behind the wheel.

_____ I often get angry or impatient with other drivers and with pedestrians.

_____ I would consider pulling over for a personal encounter with a bad driver.

Each of these statements is characteristic of aggressive drivers; the more items you checked, the greater your road rage. If you checked even one statement, consider taking some of the following steps to reduce your hostility behind the wheel:

- Allow enough time for your trip to reach your destination without speeding.
- Avoid driving during periods of heavy traffic.
- Don't drive when you are angry, tired, or intoxicated.
- Imagine that the other drivers are all people that you know and like. Be courteous and forgiving.
- Listen to soothing music or a book on tape, or practice a relaxation technique such as deep breathing (see Chapter 2).
- Take a course in anger management.

Even if you control your own aggressive inpulses, you may still encounter an aggressive driver on the road. The AAA Foundation for Traffic Safety recommends the following strategies:

- Avoid behaviors that may enrage an aggressive driver; these include cutting off cars when merging, driving slowly in the left lane, tailgating, and making rude gestures.
- If you make a mistake while driving, apologize. In surveys, the most popular and widely understood gestures for apologies include raising or waving a hand and touching or knocking the head with the palm of your hand (to indicate "What was I thinking?").
- Refuse to join in a fight. Avoid eye contact with an angry driver, and put distance between your car and his or her vehicle. If you think another driver is following you, call the police on a cell phone or drive to a public place.

SOURCES: New York State Department of Motor Vehicles. 2006. *What Is Aggressive Driving?* (http://www.nysgtsc.state.ny.us/aggr-ndx.htm; retrieved September 21, 2006); AAA Foundation for Traffic Safety. 1997. *Road Rage: How to Avoid Aggressive Driving*. Washington, D.C.: AAA Foundation for Traffic Safety.

driving, take the quiz and review the strategies in the box "Are You an Aggressive Driver?"

FATIGUE AND SLEEPINESS Driving requires mental alertness and attentiveness. Studies have shown that sleepiness causes slower reaction time, reduced coordination and vigilance, and delayed information processing. Drowsiness can be caused by not getting enough hours of sleep, by sleep disorders that prevent sleep from being refreshing, or by disruptions caused by shift work that force people to sleep at odd hours. Research shows that even mild sleep deprivation causes a deterioration in driving ability comparable to that caused by a 0.05% blood alcohol concentration—a level considered hazardous when driving. Being awake for 18 hours can impair driving ability as much as drinking two alcoholic beverages.

CELL PHONES AND OTHER DISTRACTIONS Anything that distracts a driver can increase the risk of a motor vehicle injury. Several common causes of crashes, such as disregarding stop signs, have been linked to driver distraction. Distraction is a contributing factor in 25–50% of all crashes. Cell phones are a widely documented source of distraction for drivers. A 2006 study showed that drivers who use cell phones are nearly six times as likely to be involved in a crash as drivers who don't. The same study showed that sober drivers using cell phones can perform worse than drivers who are inebriated. Three states (New York, New Jersey, and Connecticut) and the District of Columbia have banned the use of handheld phones while driving. Other states are considering similar legislation, especially for young, inexperienced drivers (see the box "Cell Phones and Distracted Driving").

ALCOHOL AND OTHER DRUGS Alcohol is involved in about 40% of all fatal crashes. Alcohol-impaired driving is illegal in all states; the legal limit for blood alcohol concentration (BAC) is 0.08%, but people can be impaired at much lower BACs. A driver with a BAC between 0.05%

In Focus

Cell Phones and Distracted Driving

At any given moment, nearly 8% of drivers—about 1 in 12—are talking on a cell phone. In 2001, New York became the first state to ban the use of handheld cellular phones while driving; drivers there must use hand-free equipment or face fines of up to $100. In 2004, New Jersey and the District of Columbia passed similar bans, and many other states have bans under consideration. Around the world, many countries have laws against the use of handheld cell phones while driving.

Available evidence indicates that use of a cell phone while driving can increase the risk of motor vehicle crashes. In a study using a driver-training simulator, cell phone users were about 20% slower to respond to sudden hazards than were other drivers, and they were about twice as likely to rear-end a braking car in front of them. Among young adult drivers who used a cell phone, reaction time was reduced to the level of a 70-year-old driver who was not using a phone. It is unclear, however, if bans such as those in New York will help reduce the risk: Studies have not found much, if any, benefit in the use of headsets. It appears that the mental distraction of talking is a factor in crashes rather than holding the phone.

The safest strategy is not to use your phone while driving. For people who live in areas where cell phone use is legal while driving and who choose to use a phone, the following strategies may help increase safety:

- Be very familiar with your phone and its functions, especially speed dial and redial.
- Store frequently called numbers on speed dial so you can place calls without looking at the phone.
- Use a hands-free device so that you can keep both hands on the steering wheel.
- Let the person you are speaking to know you are driving and be prepared to end the call at any time.
- Don't place or answer calls in heavy traffic or hazardous weather conditions.
- Don't take notes or look up phone numbers while driving.
- Time calls so that you can place them when you are at a stop.
- Never engage in stressful or emotional conversations while on the road. If you are discussing a complicated or emotional matter, pull over to the side of the road or into a parking lot to complete your conversation.

Remember that, as a driver, your primary obligation is to pay attention to the road—for your own safety and the safety of others.

SOURCES: CTIA. 2006. *Driving Safety Tips* (http://www.ctia.org/content/index.cfm/AID/10140; retrieved September 21, 2006); National Traffic Safety Administration. 2005. *Traffic Safety Facts Research Note: Driver Cell Phone Use in 2004—Overall Results.* Washington, D.C.: National Traffic Safety Administration; Strayer, D. L., and F. A. Drews. 2004. Profiles in driver distraction: Effects of cell phone conversations on younger and older drivers. *Human Factors* 46(4): 640–649; Redelmeier, D. A., and R. J. Tibshirani. 1997. Association between cellular-telephone calls and motor vehicle collisions. *New England Journal of Medicine* 336(7): 453–458.

and 0.09% is nine times more likely to have a crash than a person who has not been drinking. The combination of fatigue and alcohol use increases the risk even further. Because alcohol affects reason and judgment as well as the ability to make fast, accurate, and coordinated movements, a person who has been drinking will be less likely to recognize that he or she is impaired.

Other substances also affect judgment and driving ability. A recent study found that hay fever sufferers who had taken diphenhydramine (an antihistamine found in over-the-counter allergy medications such as Benadryl) were as impaired as if they were legally drunk. Use of many over-the-counter and all psychoactive drugs is potentially dangerous if you plan to drive. (For a full discussion of the effects of alcohol and other drugs on users, refer to Chapters 9 and 10.)

SAFETY BELTS, AIR BAGS, AND CHILD SAFETY SEATS The improper use of safety belts, air bags, and child safety seats contributes to injuries and deaths in motor vehicle crashes. Although some type of mandatory safety belt law is in effect in 49 states (excluding New Hampshire) and the District of Columbia, only about 82% of motor vehicle occupants use safety belts even though they are the single most effective way to reduce the risk of crash-related death. Of drivers not wearing a safety belt who have been killed in automobile crashes, an estimated 60–70% would have survived if they had been wearing one. If you wear a combination lap and shoulder belt, your chance of surviving a crash is three to four times better than those of a person who doesn't wear one. Ask others in the vehicle to buckle up; in a crash, unrestrained passengers increase the risk of injury and death to others in the car. The National Highway Traffic Safety Administration (NHTSA) has mandated that, starting in 2008, all motor vehicles must have safety belts installed in the rear center seat; it is estimated that this measure will prevent about 25 deaths and 500 injuries each year.

Some people think that if they are involved in a crash they are better off being thrown free of their vehicle. In fact, the chances of being killed are 25 times greater if you are thrown from a vehicle, whether it is due to injuries caused by hitting a tree or the pavement or by being hit by another vehicle. Safety belts not only prevent you from being thrown from the car at the time of the crash but also provide protection from the second collision: If a car is traveling at 65 mph and hits another vehicle, the car stops first; then the occupants stop because they, too, are traveling at 65 mph. The second collision occurs when occupants hit something inside the car, such as the dashboard or windshield. The safety belt stops the second collision from occurring and spreads the collision's force over the body.

Since 1998, all new cars have been equipped with dual air bags—one for the driver and one for the front passenger. Many vehicles also offer optional side air bags, which further reduce the risk of injury. Advanced air bag systems include risk-reduction technologies such as sensors to detect crash severity, seat position, passenger size, and whether a passenger is wearing a safety belt. Although air bags provide supplementary protection in the event of a collision, most are useful only in head-on collisions. They also deflate immediately after inflating and therefore do not provide protection in collisions involving multiple impacts. Air bags are not a replacement for safety belts; everyone in a vehicle should buckle up.

Air bags deploy forcefully and can injure a child or short adult who is improperly restrained or sitting too close to the dashboard, although second-generation air bags are somewhat safer for children than the older devices. To ensure that air bags work safely, always follow these basic guidelines: Place infants in rear-facing infant seats in the back seat, transport children age 12 and under in the back seat, always use safety belts or appropriate safety seats, and keep 10 inches between the air bag cover and the breastbone of the driver or passenger. If necessary, adjust the steering wheel or use seat cushions to ensure that an inflating air bag will hit a person in the chest and not in the face.

Another adjustment should be made for children who have outgrown child safety seats but are still too small for adult safety belts alone (usually age 4–8). These children should be secured using booster seats that ensure that the safety belt is positioned low across the waist. The CDC estimates that 1200 children age 12 and under were killed in car crashes in 2004; another 180,000 were injured. About 45% of the injured children were not properly restrained in the vehicle. All states have child restraint laws, and more than 30 states mandate the use of booster seats for children who are too big for child safety seats. Before driving with a child, make sure that you know your state's laws; that you have an appropriate safety seat for the child; that the seat is installed correctly; and that the child is properly secured in the seat.

In the rare event that a person cannot comply with air bag guidelines, permission to install an on-off switch that temporarily disables the air bag can be applied for from the National Highway Traffic Safety Administration (NHTSA). Air bags currently prevent far more injuries than they cause and are expected to save at least 3200 lives each year once they are installed in all vehicles.

Preventing Motor Vehicle Injuries About 75% of all motor vehicle collisions occur within 25 miles of home and at speeds lower than 40 mph. Strategies for preventing motor vehicle injuries include the following:

- Obey the speed limit. If you have to speed to get somewhere on time, you're not allowing enough time.
- Always wear a safety belt. Fasten the lap belt, even if the vehicle has automatic shoulder belts. The shoulder strap should cross the collarbone, and the lap belt should fit low and snug across the hips and pelvic area. The shoulder strap should never be slipped under the arm or behind the back. Pregnant women should position the lap belt as low as possible on the pelvic area.
- Never drive under the influence of alcohol or other drugs, or ride with a driver who is.
- Keep your car in good working order.
- Always allow enough following distance. Use the 3-second rule: When the vehicle ahead passes a reference point, count out 3 seconds. If you pass the reference point before you finish counting, drop back and allow more following distance.
- Always increase your following distance and slow down if weather or road conditions are poor.
- Choose interstate highways rather than rural roads. Highways are much safer because of better visibility, wider lanes, fewer surprises, and other factors.
- Always signal when turning or changing lanes.
- Stop completely at stop signs. Follow all traffic laws.
- Take special care at intersections. Look left, right, and then left again. Make sure you have time to complete your maneuver in the intersection.
- Don't pass on two-lane roads unless you're in a designated passing area and have a clear view ahead.

Motorcycles and Mopeds About one out of every ten traffic fatalities among people age 15–34 involves someone riding a motorcycle. In more than two-thirds of crashes involving a car and a motorcycle, the driver of the car is at fault. Injuries from motorcycle collisions are generally more severe than those involving automobiles because motorcycles provide little, if any, protection. Because head injuries are the major cause of death, the use of a helmet is critical for rider safety. Still, less than 50% of motorcyclists wear helmets that meet safety standards. Riders also need to know how to operate a motorcycle safely; operator error is a factor in 75% of fatal motorcycle crashes.

Moped riders face additional challenges. Mopeds usually have a maximum speed of 30–35 mph and have less power for maneuverability, especially in an emergency. Moped riders should use caution and learn how to handle the vehicle in traffic.

Additional strategies for preventing motorcycle and moped injuries include the following:

- Maximize your visibility by wearing light-colored clothing, driving with your headlights on, and correctly positioning yourself in traffic.
- Develop the necessary skills. Lack of skill, especially when evasive action is needed to avoid a collision, is a major factor in motorcycle and moped injuries. Skidding from improper braking is the most common cause of loss of control.
- Wear a helmet. Helmets should be marked with the symbol DOT, certifying that they conform to federal safety standards established by the Department of Transportation. Helmet use is required by law in nearly half of the states.
- Protect your eyes with goggles, a face shield, or a windshield.
- Drive defensively, particularly when changing lanes and at intersections, and never assume that other drivers can see you.

Bicycles According to a 2006 estimate, bicycle crashes send more than 500,000 people to emergency rooms each year and result in about 700 fatalities. Bicycle injuries result primarily from riders not knowing or understanding the rules of the road, failing to follow traffic laws, not having sufficient skill or experience to handle traffic conditions, or being intoxicated. Bicycles are considered vehicles; bicyclists must obey all traffic laws that apply to automobile drivers, including stopping at traffic lights and stop signs.

Head injuries are involved in about two-thirds of all bicycle-related deaths. Currently, 21 states and nearly 150 cities have laws requiring cyclists to wear helmets. Wearing a helmet reduces the risk of head injury by 85%, but only 50% of cyclists wear helmets (see the box "Choosing a Bicycle Helmet"). Safe cycling strategies include the following:

- Wear safety equipment, including a helmet, eye protection, gloves, and proper footwear. Secure the bottom of your pant legs with clips, and secure your shoelaces so they don't get tangled in the chain.
- Maximize your visibility by wearing light-colored, reflective clothing. Equip your bike with reflectors, and use lights, especially at night or when riding in wooded or other dark areas.
- Ride with the flow of traffic, not against it, and follow all traffic laws. Use bike paths when they are available.
- Ride defensively; never assume that drivers have seen you. Be especially careful when turning or crossing at corners and intersections. Watch for cars turning right.
- Stop at all traffic lights and stop signs. Know and use hand signals.
- Continue pedaling at all times when moving (no coasting) to help keep the bike stable and to maintain your balance.
- Properly maintain your bicycle.

Pedestrians Pedestrians are no match for the speed, size, and weight of motor vehicles, particularly the popular sport utility vehicles. About one in eight motor vehicle deaths involves pedestrians, and more than 80,000 pedestrians are injured each year. The highest rates of death and injury occur among the very young and the elderly. About 65% of pedestrian deaths occur when people cross or enter the roadway between intersections. Alcohol intoxication plays a significant role in up to half of all adult pedestrian fatalities.

The following strategies can help prevent injuries when you're walking or jogging:

- Walk or jog in daylight.
- Maximize your visibility by wearing light-colored, reflective clothing.
- Face traffic when walking or jogging along a road, and follow traffic laws.
- Avoid busy roads or roads with poor visibility.
- Cross only at marked crosswalks and intersections.
- Don't use headphones while walking.
- Don't hitchhike; it places you in a potentially dangerous situation.

Home Injuries

A person's place of residence, whether a house, an apartment, a trailer, or a dormitory, is considered home. People spend a great deal of time at home and feel that they are safe and secure there. However, home can be a dangerous place. The most common fatal **home injuries** are the result of falls, fires, poisoning, suffocation, and unintentional shootings.

Falls About 90% of fatal falls involve people age 45 and over, but falls are a significant cause of unintentional death for people under 25. Most deaths occurring from falls involve falling on stairs or steps or from one level to another. Falls also occur on the same level, from tripping, slipping, or stumbling. Alcohol is a contributing

Term

Vw

home injuries Unintentional injuries and deaths that occur in the home and on home premises to occupants, guests, domestic servants, and trespassers; falls, burns, poisonings, suffocations, unintentional shootings, drownings, and electrical shocks are examples.

Critical Consumer

Choosing a Bicycle Helmet

VW

Wearing a bicycle helmet can help you avoid serious head injury, brain damage, or even death in the event of a collision or fall. Helmets have a layer of stiff foam, which absorbs shock and cushions a blow to your head, covered by a thin plastic shell that will skid along the ground. For maximum protection, it's important to select a correctly fitting helmet. When you go shopping, remember the four S's: size, strap, straight, and sticker.

- *Size:* Try on several different sizes before making your selection; it may take several tries before you find the most comfortable fit. The helmet should be very snug but not overly tight on your head. Pads are usually provided to help adjust the fit. A good salesperson can also help you get the right fit. When the helmet is strapped onto your head, it should not move more than an inch in any direction, and you should not be able to pull or twist it off no matter how hard you try.
- *Strap:* Be sure that the chin strap fits snugly under your chin and that the V in the strap meets under your ear. Avoid thin straps, which can be uncomfortable. Check to be sure that the buckle is strong and won't pop open and that the straps are sturdy.
- *Straight:* The helmet should sit straight on your head, not tilted back or forward (see the figure). A rule of thumb is that the rim should be about two finger widths above your eyebrows (depending on the height of your forehead).
- *Sticker:* Since March 1999, helmets sold in the United States must meet uniform safety standards established by the U.S. Consumer Product Safety Commission (CPSC). Look for a sticker or label that says the helmet meets the CPSC standard. If a helmet does not have one, it does not meet federal safety standards and should not be used.

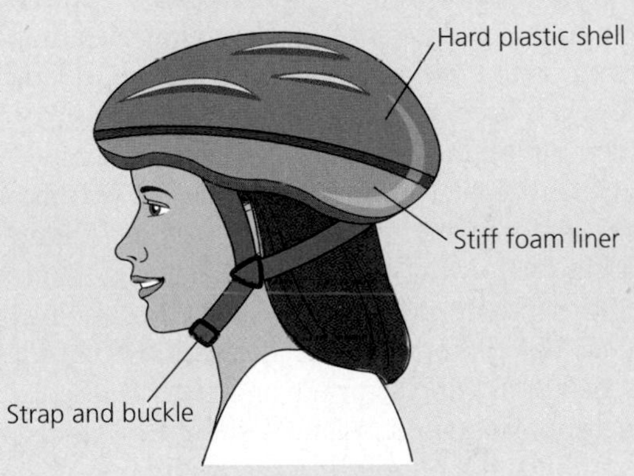

You are more likely to wear your helmet if it is comfortable, so be sure that vents on the helmet provide airflow to promote cooling and sweat control. You will be safer with a brightly colored helmet that makes you more visible to drivers, especially in rainy, foggy, or dark conditions. Reflective tape will also increase your visibility. Finally, a helmet is a good place to put emergency information (your name, address, and phone number, plus any emergency medical conditions and an emergency contact). Tape change inside the helmet for a phone call.

If you are involved in a crash, replace your helmet. Even if the helmet doesn't have any visible signs of damage, its ability to protect your head may be compromised. As the Bicycle Helmet Safety Institute says, "No one ever complains about the cost of their second bike helmet."

SOURCES: Bicycle Helmet Safety Institute. 2006. *A Consumer's Guide to Bicycle Helmets* (http://www.helmets.org/guide.htm; retrieved September 21, 2006); Bicycle Helmet Safety Institute. 2006. *How to Fit a Bicycle Helmet* (http://www.helmets.org/fit.htm; retrieved September 21, 2006); National Safety Council. 2000. *Choose the Right Helmet for Your Favorite Summer Sport* (http://www.nsc.org/pubs/fsh/archive/summr00/helmet.htm; retrieved September 21, 2006).

factor in many falls. Strategies for preventing falls include the following:

- Install handrails and nonslip surfaces in the shower and bathtub.
- Keep floors, stairs, and outside areas clear of objects or conditions that could cause slipping or tripping, such as ice, snow, electrical cords, and toys.
- Put a light switch by the door of every room so no one has to walk across a room to turn on a light. Use night lights in bedrooms, halls, stairs, and bathrooms.
- When climbing a ladder, use both hands. Never stand higher than the third step from the top. When using a stepladder, make sure the spreader brace is in the locked position. With straight ladders, set the base out 1 foot for every 4 feet of height.
- Don't use chairs to reach things; they are meant to be sat on, not stood on.
- If there are small children in the home, place gates at the top and bottom of stairs. Never leave a baby unattended on a bed or table. Install window guards to prevent children from falling out of windows.

Fires Each year in the United States, approximately 80% of fire deaths and 65% of fire injuries occur in the home; a death caused by a residential fire occurs every 2 hours. Most fires begin in the kitchen, living room, or bedroom. Cooking is now the leading cause of home fire injuries; careless smoking is the leading cause of fire deaths, followed by problems with heating equipment and arson. To prevent fires, it's important to dispose of all cigarettes in ashtrays and to never smoke in bed. Other strategies include proper maintenance of fireplaces, furnaces, heaters, chimneys, and electrical outlets, cords, and appliances. If you use a portable heater, keep it at least 3 feet away from curtains, bedding, or

The risk of dying in a fire is reduced by half if you use a smoke detector. Install detectors on every floor, check them monthly, and replace the batteries at least once a year.

anything else that might catch fire. Never leave heaters on unattended.

It's important to be adequately prepared to handle fire-related situations. Plan at least two escape routes out of each room, and designate a location outside the home as a meeting place. For practice, stage a home fire drill; do it at night, as that's when most deadly fires occur.

Install smoke detectors on every level of your home. Your risk of dying in a fire is almost twice as high if you do not use them. Clean the detectors and check the batteries once a month, and replace the batteries at least once a year. More than 90% of U.S. homes have at least one smoke alarm, but about half of the alarms are no longer functioning a year after installation, most commonly because batteries need to be replaced or dust and debris need to be cleaned out of the unit. Be sure that all residents are familiar with the sound of the smoke detector's alarm; when it goes off, take it seriously.

These strategies can help prevent injuries in a fire:

- Get out as quickly as possible, and go to the designated meeting place. Don't stop for a keepsake or a pet. Never hide in a closet or under a bed. Once outside, count heads to see if everyone is out. If you think someone is still inside the burning building, tell the firefighters. Never go back inside a burning building.
- If you're trapped in a room, feel the door. If it is hot or if smoke is coming in through the cracks, don't open it; use the alternative escape route. If you can't get out, go to the window and shout for help.
- Smoke inhalation is the largest cause of death and injury in fires. To avoid inhaling smoke, crawl along the floor away from the heat and smoke. Cover your mouth and nose, ideally with a wet cloth, and take short, shallow breaths.
- If your clothes catch fire, don't run. Drop to the ground, cover your face, and roll back and forth to smother the flames. Remember: stop-drop-roll.

Although house fires cause the most deaths, hot water causes the most nonfatal burns. Young children are particularly at risk. Place barriers around stoves and radiators, and keep young children out of the kitchen, where they might be burned by spills. Put pans on rear burners, and turn pot handles toward the back of the stove. Keep hot foods away from the edge of counters and tables, and don't put them on a tablecloth that a small child can pull. Set your water heater no higher than 120°F. Always test the contents of a baby bottle; when bottles are heated in microwave ovens, the liquid can become scalding before the outside of the bottle gets very hot.

Poisoning More than 2.4 million poisonings and over 17,000 poison-related deaths occur every year in the United States. Poisons come in many forms, some of which are not typically considered poisons. For example, even honey can be poisonous to children less than a year old. Medications are safe when used as prescribed, but overdosing or incorrectly combining medications with another substance may result in poisoning. The CDC says that each year more than 550,000 children under age 6 are treated in emergency rooms for swallowing medicines that are not meant for them. Other poisonous substances include cleaning agents, petroleum-based products, insecticides and herbicides, cosmetics, nail polish and remover, and many houseplants. All potentially poisonous substances should be used only as directed and stored out of the reach of children.

The most common type of poisoning by gases is carbon monoxide poisoning. Carbon monoxide gas is emitted by motor vehicle exhaust and some types of heating equipment. The effects of exposure to this colorless, odorless gas include headache, blurred vision, and shortness of breath, followed by dizziness, vomiting, and unconsciousness. Carbon monoxide detectors similar to smoke detectors are available for home use; they should be used according to the manufacturer's instructions. To prevent poisoning by gases, never operate a vehicle in an enclosed space, have your furnace inspected yearly, and use caution with any substance or device that produces potentially toxic fumes.

Keep the national poison control hotline number (800-222-1222) in a convenient location. A call to the national hotline will be routed to a local Poison Control Center, which provides expert emergency advice 24 hours a day. If a poisoning does occur, it's important that you act quickly. Remove the poison from contact with the victim's eyes, skin, or mouth, or move the victim away from contact with poisonous gases. Call the Poison Control Center immediately for instructions; do not follow the emergency instructions on product labels because they may be incorrect. Depending on the situation, you may be instructed to give the victim water to drink, or to flood affected parts of the skin or eyes with water. Do not induce vomiting. If you are advised to go to an emergency room, take the poisonous substance or container with you.

Suffocation and Choking Suffocation and choking account for about 4000 deaths annually. Children can suffocate if they put small items in their mouth, get tangled in their crib bedding, or get trapped in airtight appliances like old refrigerators. Keep small objects out of reach of children under age 3, and don't give them raw carrots, hot dogs, popcorn, gum, or hard candy. Examine toys carefully for small parts that could come loose; don't give plastic bags or balloons to small children.

Adults can also become choking victims, especially if they fail to chew food properly, eat hurriedly, or try to talk and eat at the same time. Many choking victims can be saved with the **Heimlich maneuver.** The American Red Cross recommends abdominal thrusts as the easiest and safest thing to do when an adult is choking (see the inside back cover). Back blows in conjunction with abdominal thrusts are an acceptable procedure for dislodging an object from the throat of an infant.

Firearms About 40% of all unintended firearm deaths occur among people age 5–29. People who use firearms should remember the following:

- Always treat a gun as though it were loaded, even if you know it isn't.
- Never point a loaded gun at something you do not intend to shoot.
- Always unload a gun before storing it. Store unloaded firearms under lock and key, in a place separate from the ammunition.
- Always inspect firearms carefully before handling.
- If you ever plan to handle a gun, take a firearms safety course first.
- If you own a gun, buy and use a gun lock designed specifically for that weapon.

Proper storage is critical. Do not assume that young children cannot fire a gun. About 25% of 3–4-year-olds and 70% of 5–6-year-olds have enough finger strength to pull a trigger. Every year, about 120 Americans are unintentionally shot to death by children under 6. About 8.3 million children live in households with unlocked guns, including 2.6 million who live in households where guns are stored loaded or with ammunition nearby.

Probably the best advice for anyone who picks up a gun is to assume it is loaded. Too many deaths and injuries occur when someone unintentionally shoots a friend while under the impression that the gun he or she is handling is not loaded. If you plan to handle a gun, avoid alcohol and drugs, which affect judgment and coordination.

Leisure Injuries

Leisure activities encompass a large part of our free time, so it is not surprising that **leisure injuries** are a significant health-related problem in the United States. Key factors in leisure injuries include misuse of equipment, lack of experience and skill, use of alcohol or other drugs, and failure to use appropriate safety equipment. Specific safety strategies for activities associated with leisure injuries include the following:

- Don't swim alone, in unsupervised places, under the influence of alcohol, or for an unusual length of time; use caution when swimming in unfamiliar surroundings or in water colder than 70°F. Check the depth of water before diving. Make sure that residential pools are fenced and that children are never allowed to swim unsupervised.
- Always use a **personal flotation device** (also known as a life jacket) when on a boat.
- For all sports and recreational activities, make sure facilities are safe, follow the rules, and practice good sportsmanship. Develop adequate skill in the activity, and use proper safety equipment, including, where appropriate, a helmet, eye protection, correct footwear, and knee, elbow, and wrist pads.
- If using equipment such as skateboards, snowboards, mountain bikes, or all-terrain vehicles, wear a helmet and other safety equipment, and avoid excessive speeds and unsafe stunts. Playground equipment should be used only for those activities for which it is designed.
- If you are active in excessively hot and humid weather, drink plenty of fluids, rest frequently in the shade, and slow down or stop if you feel uncomfortable. Danger signals of heat stress include excessive perspiration, dizziness, headache, muscle cramps, nausea, weakness, rapid pulse, and disorientation.
- Do not use alcohol or other drugs during recreational activities—such activities require coordination and sound judgment. To avoid choking, don't chew gum or eat while active.

Terms

Vw

Heimlich maneuver A maneuver developed by Henry J. Heimlich, M.D., to help force an obstruction from the airway.

leisure injuries Unintentional injuries and deaths that occur in public places or places used in a public way, not involving motor vehicles; includes most sports and recreation deaths and injuries; falls, drownings, burns, and heat and cold stress are examples.

personal flotation device A device designed to save a person from drowning by buoying up the body while in the water.

Leisure activities injure more than 6 million people each year, including 250,000 in-line skaters. The use of proper safety equipment—helmet, wrist guards, and elbow and knee pads—is critical for injury prevention.

For more on exercise safety, refer to Chapter 13. Two activities that have recently become popular and that are associated with many leisure injuries are in-line skating and the use of nonmotorized scooters.

In-Line Skating Injuries More than 26 million Americans use in-line skates, and more than 250,000 are injured badly enough each year to wind up in an emergency room. Injuries to the wrist and head are most common; many occur because users do not wear appropriate safety gear. Researchers estimate that more than one-third of all serious injuries could be prevented if all skaters wore helmets and wrist and elbow protection.

To reduce your risk of being injured while rollerblading, wear a helmet, elbow and knee pads, wrist guards, a long-sleeved shirt, and long pants. Alcohol use appears to be a significant factor in in-line skating injuries that occur on college campuses. Because in-line skating involves skill, judgment, and coordination, it makes sense not to mix skating and drinking.

Scooter Injuries Scooters are lightweight and have low-friction wheels for quickness and portability. Along with their skyrocketing popularity have come scooter-related injuries. Over 30,000 people are treated for scooter-related injuries in hospital emergency rooms each year, and several deaths related to scooter use have been reported. The most common injuries are arm or hand fractures and dislocations, cuts and bruises, and sprains; 85% of injuries involve children under the age of 15. Viewing scooters as toys more than transportation may lead riders to ignore important safety precautions:

- Wear a helmet that meets bicycle helmet standards, along with knee and elbow pads.
- Be sure that handlebars, the steering column, and all nuts and bolts are securely fastened.
- Ride on smooth, paved surfaces away from motor vehicle traffic. Avoid streets and surfaces with water, sand, gravel, or dirt.
- Don't ride after dark.
- Closely supervise young children.

Work Injuries

Since 1912, when industrial records were first kept in the United States, the work site has become a much safer place, as evidenced by a nearly 90% reduction in the unintentional death rate. That figure becomes even more impressive when you realize that the size of the labor force has more than doubled and production has increased more than tenfold. One very significant factor to account for such a marked decline in **work injuries** has been the Occupational Safety and Health Act of 1970. As a result of that act, the Occupational Safety and Health Administration (OSHA) was created within the U.S. Department of Labor to ensure a safer and healthier environment for workers.

According to the Bureau of Labor Statistics, 4 million Americans suffered injuries on the job in 2004. Certain types of injuries, including skin disorders and repetitive strain injuries, are increasing. Although laborers make up less than half of the workforce, they account for more than 75% of all work-related injuries and illnesses. Their jobs usually involve extensive manual labor and lifting, neither of which is addressed in OSHA safety standards. Skin disorders account for nearly 40% of reported occupational illnesses; the introduction of more hazardous chemicals at the work site means that these disorders are of increasing concern. Most fatal occupational injuries involve crushing injuries, severe lacerations, burns, and electrocutions; among women, the leading cause of workplace injury deaths is homicide.

Back Injuries Back problems accounted for about 280,000 work injuries in 2004; many of these could be prevented through proper lifting technique (Figure 22-1).

- Avoid bending at the waist. Remain in an upright position and crouch down if you need to lower yourself to grasp the object. Bend at the knees and hips.

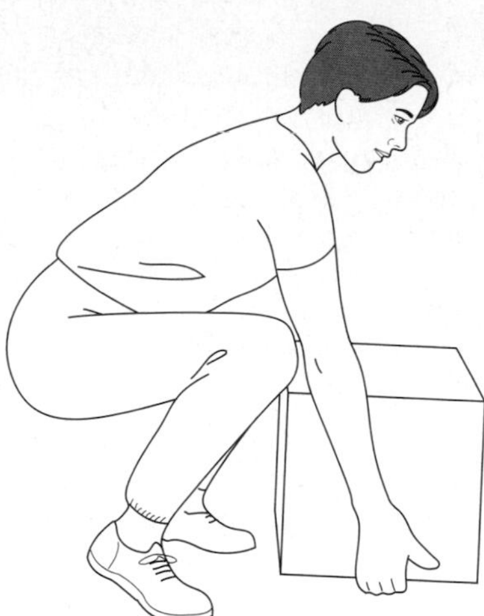

Figure 22-1 Correct lifting technique. Stay upright, bending at the knees and hips.

- Place feet securely about shoulder-width apart; grip the object firmly.
- Lift gradually, with straight arms. Avoid quick, jerky motions. Lift by standing up or pushing with your leg muscles. Keep the object close to your body.
- If you have to turn, change the position of your feet. Twisting is a common and dangerous cause of injury. Plan ahead so that your pathway is clear and turning can be minimized.
- Put the object down gently, reversing the steps for lifting.

Repetitive Strain Injuries Musculoskeletal injuries and disorders in the workplace include **repetitive strain injuries (RSIs).** RSIs are caused by repeated strain on a particular part of the body. Twisting, vibrations, awkward postures, and other stressors may contribute to RSIs. **Carpal tunnel syndrome** is one type of RSI that has increased in recent years due to increased use of computers, both at work and in the home (see the box "Carpal Tunnel Syndrome" on p. 674 for more information).

General strategies for preventing work-related injuries include following the safety instructions associated with the job, finding out where first aid equipment is located and knowing how to use it, watching for and reporting safety hazards, and using any safety equipment that is provided by the employer. Whatever the working conditions, employees should make a conscious effort to avoid hazardous situations.

VIOLENCE AND INTENTIONAL INJURIES

Violence—the use of physical force with the intent to inflict harm, injury, or death upon oneself or another—is a major public health concern in the United States. According to the Federal Bureau of Investigation (FBI), nearly 1.4 million violent crimes occurred in the United States in 2005. Worldwide, interpersonal violence is the third leading cause of death among people age 15–44. Examples of types of violence are assault, homicide, sexual assault, domestic violence, suicide, and child abuse.

It is difficult to determine the overall level of violence in our society because the major sources of data, police reports and victim surveys, are often at odds. In general, the overall violent crime rate increased between the 1950s and 1970s and then leveled off until the mid-1980s, when it again began to rise until 1992. The rate fell steadily from 1993 to 2000 and then rose slightly in 2001 and 2002, declined in 2003 and 2004, and rose in 2005 and again in 2006. Violent crime declined about 3.4% between 2000 and 2005. Possible factors cited for this general decline include the aging of the population, reduced unemployment, the decline of the crack cocaine trade, law enforcement strategies to get guns off the street, violence prevention programs for youth, and longer prison sentences. In comparison to other industrialized countries, U.S. rates of violence are unusually high in only two areas—homicide and firearm-related deaths. The U.S. homicide death rate is four to ten times that of similar countries, and the firearm death rate is eight times that of other developed countries.

Factors Contributing to Violence

Most intentional injuries and deaths are associated with an argument or the committing of another crime. However, there are a great many forms of violence, and no single factor can explain all of them.

Social Factors Rates of violence are not the same throughout society; they vary by geographic region, neighborhood, socioeconomic level, and many other factors. According to the FBI, violence was highest in the South in 2005, followed closely by the West. Neighborhoods that are disadvantaged in status,

Terms

work injuries Unintentional injuries and deaths that arise out of and in the course of gainful work, such as falls, electrical shocks, exposure to radiation and toxic chemicals, burns, cuts, back sprains, and loss of fingers or other body parts in machines.

repetitive strain injury (RSI) A musculoskeletal injury or disorder caused by repeated strain on the hand, arm, wrist, or other part of the body; also called *cumulative trauma disorder (CTD).*

carpal tunnel syndrome Compression of the median nerve in the wrist, often caused by repetitive use of the hands, such as in computer use; characterized by numbness, tingling, and pain in the hands and fingers; can cause nerve damage.

Vw

In Focus

Carpal Tunnel Syndrome

Carpal tunnel syndrome (CTS) is a repetitive strain injury characterized by pressure on the median nerve in the wrist. It is the most commonly reported work-related medical problem, accounting for about half of all work-related injuries. Women are about twice as likely as men to be affected by CTS.

The median nerve travels from the forearm to the hand through a tunnel in the wrist formed by the carpals (wrist bones) and associated tendons and covered by a ligament (see the figure). The median nerve can become compressed for a variety of reasons, including swelling of the surrounding tendons caused by pregnancy, diabetes, arthritis, or repetitive wrist motions during activities such as typing, cutting, or carpentry work. Symptoms of CTS include numbness, tingling, burning, and/or aching in the hand, particularly in the thumb and the first three fingers. The pain may worsen at night and may shoot up from the hand as far as the shoulder.

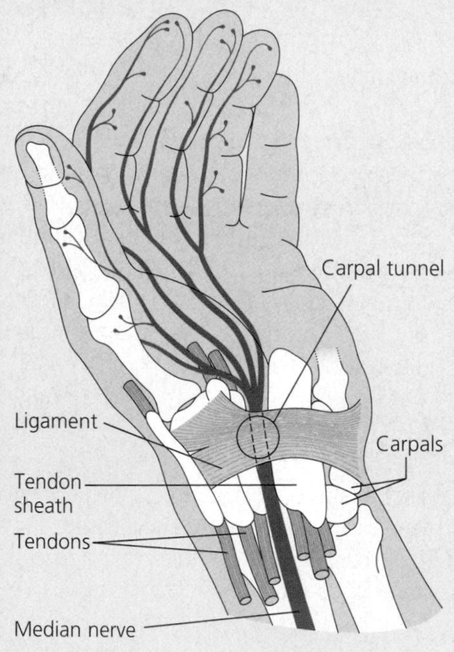

Many cases of carpal tunnel syndrome clear up on their own or with minimal treatment. Modification of the movement that is causing the problem is critically important. For example, adjusting the height of a computer keyboard so that the wrists can be held straight during typing can help relieve pressure on the wrists. CTS is often first treated by immobilizing the wrist with a splint during the night. People may also be given anti-inflammatory drugs or injections of cortisone in the wrist to reduce swelling. In a small percentage of severe cases, surgery to cut the ligament and reduce the pressure on the nerve may be recommended.

If you engage in activities like typing or cutting that involve repetitive motions, there are some strategies you can try to reduce your risk of developing carpal tunnel syndrome. Begin by modifying your work environment to reduce the stress on your wrists. Alternate activities to avoid spending long stretches of time engaged in the same motion. Warm up your wrists before you begin any repetitive motion activity, and take frequent breaks to stretch and flex your wrists and hands:

- Extend your arms out in front of you and stretch your wrists by pointing your fingers to the ceiling; hold for a count of five. Then straighten your wrists and relax your fingers for a count of five.
- With arms extended, make a tight fist with both hands and then bend your wrists so your knuckles are pointed toward the floor; hold for a count of five. Then straighten your wrists and relax your fingers for a count of five.

Repeat these stretches several times, and finish by letting your arms hang loosely at your sides and shaking them gently for several seconds.

SOURCES: Ly-Pen, D., et al. 2005. Surgical decompression versus local steroid injection in carpal tunnel syndrome: A one-year, prospective, randomized, open, controlled clinical trial. *Arthritis and Rheumatism* 52(2): 612–619; Carpal tunnel syndrome. 2002. *Journal of the American Medical Association* 288(10): 1310; American Academy of Orthopaedic Surgeons. 2000. *Exercises to Do at Work to Prevent Carpal Tunnel Syndrome* (http://orthoinfo.aaos.org/fact/thr_report.cfm?Thread_ID=5&topcategory=Hand; retrieved March 11, 2001).

power, and economic resources are typically the ones with the most violence. Rates of violence are highest among young people and minorities, groups that have relatively little power. People under age 25 account for nearly half the arrests for violent crime in the United States and about 40% of the arrests for homicide.

People who feel a part of society (have strong family and social ties), who are economically integrated (have a reasonable chance at getting a decent job), and who grow up in areas where there is a feeling of community (good schools, parks, and neighborhoods) are significantly less likely to engage in violence. American society, where more than one-third of all children live in poverty and where the gap between rich and poor keeps growing, should be expected to breed violence. Many criminologists feel we have a growing underclass of people who cannot expect to have even the worst permanent jobs. That absence of hopes and dreams, combined with family devastation and poverty, certainly contributes to violent behavior.

Studies have shown that the environment on college campuses can contribute to violence. The nature of college campuses—transitory communities rather than permanent places where people work and live together over the long term—means that there is less incentive for people to cooperate and coexist amicably. Some campus groups even promote the ideas of bigotry and bias toward others, particularly toward individuals about whom they know little or with whom they have had little contact. Ignorance and insensitivity to differences can be precursors to acts of violence. College students must become more familiar with concepts such as inclusion, tolerance, and diversity if the problem is to be addressed.

Violence in the Media The mass media play a major role in exposing audiences of all ages to violence as an acceptable and effective means of solving problems. Children may view as many as 10,000 violent acts on television and in movies each year. Computer and video games also include many violent acts, leading to concern that children's exposure to violence will make them more accepting or tolerant of it. The consequences of violence are depicted much less frequently.

A 2005 study linked TV viewing to bullying among children. Researchers found that the more hours per day that a 4-year-old spent watching TV, the more likely the child was to engage in bullying behavior in later years. Factors that reduced the rate of bullying included cognitive stimulation, such as parents reading to a child, and emotional support and attention. It is thought that emotional support from parents helps children develop empathy, social competence, and self-regulation—skills that enable them to deal with peers without resorting to aggressive or bullying behavior.

Researchers have found that exposure to media violence at least temporarily increases aggressive feelings in children, making them more likely to engage in violent or fearful behavior; the direct, short-term effects on teens and adults are less clear. It makes sense for parents to be aware of the potential influence of the media on their children. A child may not clearly understand the distinctions between the fantasy world portrayed in the media and the complexities of the real world. Parents should monitor the TV shows, movies, video games, music, and other forms of media to which children are exposed. Watching programs with children gives parents the opportunity to talk to children about violence and its consequences, to explain that violence is not the best way to resolve conflicts or solve problems, and to point out examples of positive behaviors such as kindness and cooperation.

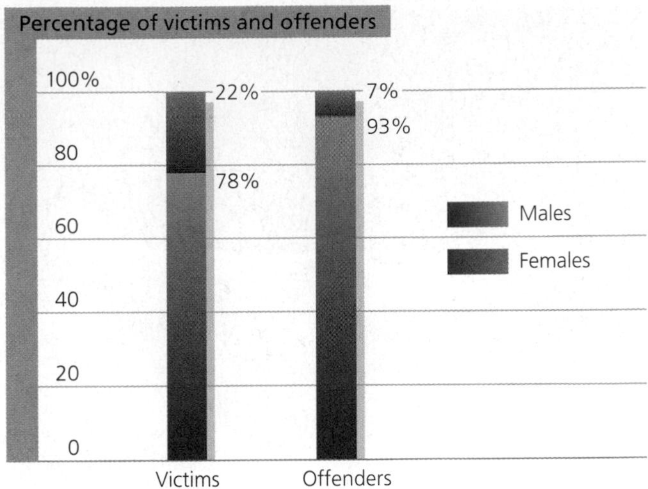

(a) Homicide victims and offenders by sex

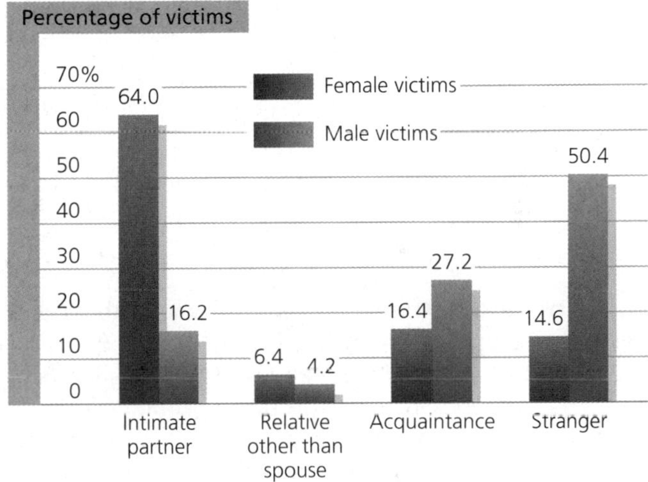

(b) Adult victims of violence by victim-offender relationship and sex of victim

VITAL STATISTICS

Figure 22-2 Facts about violence in the United States. SOURCES: Federal Bureau of Investigation. 2006. *Crime in the United States 2005.* Washington, D.C.: U.S. Department of Justice; Tjaden, P., and N. Thoennes. 2000. *Full Report of the Prevalence, Incidence, and Consequences of Violence Against Women.* Washington, D.C.: U.S. Department of Justice.

Gender In most cases, violence is committed by men (Figure 22-2). Males are more than nine times more likely than females to commit murder, and three times more likely than females to be murdered. Male college students are twice as likely to be the victim of violence as female students. Some researchers have suggested that the male hormone testosterone is in some way linked to aggressive behavior. Others point to prevailing cultural attitudes about male roles (men as dominant and controlling) as an explanation for the high rate of violence among men. However, these theories do not explain why it is that violent men are more likely to live in the West, belong to minorities, be poor, and be young.

Women do commit acts of violence, including a small but substantial proportion of murders of spouses. This fact has been used to argue that women have the same capacity to commit violence as men, but most researchers note substantial differences. Men often kill their wives as the culmination of years of violence or after stalking them; they may kill their entire family and themselves at the same time. Women virtually never kill in such circumstances; rather, they kill their husbands after repeated victimization or while being beaten.

Interpersonal Factors Although most people fear attack from strangers, the majority of victims are acquainted with their attacker (see Figure 22-2). Approximately 60% of murders of women and 80% of sexual

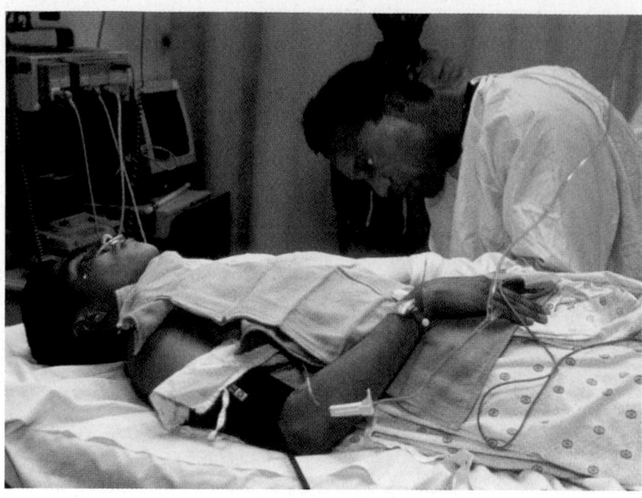

For every violent death that occurs in the United States, there are at least 100 nonfatal injuries caused by violence. The victims of most types of violence are statistically likely to be young (under age 25), poor, in a minority, urban, and—except for rape and domestic violence—male.

assaults are committed by someone the woman knows. In many cases, the people we need to fear the most live in our own household. Crime victims and violent criminals tend to share many characteristics—that is, they are likely to be young, male, in a minority, and poor.

Alcohol and Other Drugs Substance abuse and dependence are consistently associated with interpersonal violence and suicide. Intoxication affects judgment and may increase aggression in some people, causing a small argument to escalate into a serious physical confrontation. On college campuses, alcohol is involved in about 95% of all violent crimes.

Firearms Many criminologists feel that the high rate of homicide in the United States is directly related to the fact that we are the only industrialized country in which handguns are widespread and easily available. Simply put, most victims of assaults with other weapons don't die, but the death rate from assault by handgun is extremely high. The possession of a handgun can change a suicide attempt to a completed suicide and a violent assault to a murder. Every hour, guns are used to kill four people in the United States.

Over 100,000 deaths and injuries occur in the United States each year as a result of the use of firearms. Firearms are used in more than two-thirds of homicides, and studies reveal a strong correlation between the incidence of gun ownership and homicide rates for a given area of the country. Over half of all suicides involve a firearm, and people living in households in which guns are kept have a risk of suicide that is five or more times greater than that of people living in households without guns. Men between ages 15 and 34 have the highest risk of death from homicide and suicide when guns are the weapon used.

Research indicates that of all firearms, handguns are the murder weapon of choice, used in about 75% of homicides involving firearms. Teenagers and young adults are at particularly high risk for being murdered by handguns.

Assault

Assault is the use of physical force by a person or persons to inflict injury or death on another; homicide, aggravated assault, and robbery are examples of assault. Research indicates that the victims of assaultive injuries and their perpetrators tend to resemble one another in terms of ethnicity, educational background, psychological profile, and reliance on weapons. In many cases, the victim actually magnifies the confrontation through the use of a weapon.

Homicide

The FBI estimates that more than 16,500 Americans were murdered in 2005. Men, teenagers, young adults, and members of minority groups, particularly African Americans and Latinos, are most likely to be murder victims. Although homicide rates for African Americans have declined dramatically in the past 25 years, the murder rate for black males is about six times higher than the rate for the U.S. population as a whole. Poverty and unemployment have been identified as key factors in homicide, and this may account for the high rates of homicide among blacks and other minority groups.

Most homicides are committed with a firearm, occur during an argument, and occur among people who know one another. Intrafamilial homicide, where the perpetrator and victim are related, accounts for about one out of every eight homicides. About 40% of family homicides are committed by spouses, usually following a history of physical and emotional abuse directed at the woman. Wives are more likely to be murdered than husbands, and when a wife kills her husband, it is usually in self-defense.

Gang-Related Violence

Violence results from more than just the acts of individuals, as evidenced by the number of injuries and deaths resulting from gang activities. Gangs are most frequently associated with large cities, but gang activity also extends to the suburbs and even to rural areas. It is estimated that more than 800,000 Americans belong to gangs; the average age for joining a gang is 14. Most gangs control a particular territory and will oppose other gangs, as well as police and community efforts to eliminate them. Gangs may be involved in illegal drug trade, extortion, and protection schemes. Gang members are more likely than non–gang members to possess weapons, and violence may result from conflicts over territory or illegal activities.

Gangs are more common in areas that are poor and suffer from high unemployment, population density, and crime. In these areas, an individual may feel that his or her hope of legitimate success in life is out of reach and know that involvement in the drug market makes some gang members rich. Often, gangs serve as a mechanism for companionship, self-esteem, support, and security; indeed, in some areas gang membership may be viewed as the only possible means of survival.

A successful program for combating gangs that was developed in Los Angeles includes mediators to help handle disputes or negotiate truces between gangs, job skill development for ex–gang members, and programs for at-risk youths that incorporate tutoring, counseling, and recreational activities. The program helps create an anti-gang community infrastructure by promoting neighborhood watch groups, anti-gang activities, and economic development.

Hate Crimes

When bias against another person's race or ethnicity, national origin, religion, sexual orientation, or disability motivates a criminal act, the offense is classified as a hate crime. Hate crimes may be committed against people or property. Those against people may include intimidation, assault, and even rape or murder. Crimes against property most frequently involve graffiti, the desecration of churches or synagogues, cross burnings, and other acts of vandalism or property damage.

About 7500 hate crimes are reported every year; many more go unreported. Crimes against people make up about 70% of all incidents; intimidation and assault are the most common offenses. Racial or ethnic bias was cited as a motivation in 54% of the hate crimes reported in 2004. National origin or ethnicity was cited in 13% of cases, religion in 16%, and sexual orientation in 16%.

Hate crimes may be extremely brutal acts perpetrated at random on total strangers by multiple offenders. Suspects frequently are not identified, but research indicates that a substantial number of hate crimes are committed by males under age 20. Hate crimes are frequently, but not always, associated with fringe groups that have extremist ideologies, such as the Ku Klux Klan and neo-Nazi groups. The Southern Poverty Law Center tracks more than 700 hate groups and group chapters currently active in the United States; the rapid growth of hate sites on the Internet is another area of concern.

A variety of factors lead to the prejudice and intolerance that are a major force behind hate crimes. The FBI has reported a substantial increase in hate-motivated crimes in the past few years, especially since the terrorist attacks of September 11, 2001. Hate crimes against lesbian, gay, bisexual, and transgender (LGBT) people have more than tripled in recent years. A social context of unemployment and hard economic times, an influx of immigrants, and the growth of visible minority rights movements have been associated with the recent increases in hate crimes in the United States. To combat hate crimes, individuals and communities must foster tolerance, understanding, and an appreciation of differences among people.

School Violence

Tragedies like the shootings at Columbine High School in Colorado and Red Lake Senior High School in Minnesota have brought national attention to the problem of school violence. According to the National School Safety Center, more than 400 school-associated violent deaths of students, faculty, and administrators have occurred since 1992. Most of these deaths occurred in urban areas, at high schools, and involved use of a firearm; as with other types of violence, both victims and offenders were predominantly young men. Homicide and suicide are the most serious and least common types of violence in schools; an estimated 400,000 less serious incidents of violence and crime occur each year, including theft, vandalism, and fights not involving weapons.

How risky is the school environment for students? Children are actually much safer at school than away from it. Less than 1% of all homicides among youths age 5–19 occur at school, and 90% of schools report no incidents of serious violence. Children and adolescents are far more likely to be killed by an adult in their own home or away from school than they are to die as a result of school-associated violence. According to the CDC, the overall number of violent incidents has decreased steadily since 1992; however, the number of multiple-victim events may have increased. Recent school shootings received so much attention in part because they were unusual—they took place in predominantly suburban or rural schools and involved multiple victims. Despite declines in violence-related behaviors, about 17% of high school students in a national survey reported carrying a weapon (gun, knife, club) to school at least once in the month before the survey, and 9% reported being threatened with a weapon on school grounds in the past year.

Although schools are basically safe places overall, there are steps that can be taken to identify at-risk youths and improve safety for all students. Characteristics associated with youths who have caused school-associated violent deaths include a history of uncontrollable angy outbursts, violent and abusive language and behavior, isolation from peers, depression and irritability, access to and preoccupation with weapons, and lack of support and supervision from adults. Being a victim of teasing, bullying, or social exclusion (rejection) may lead to aggressive behavior and violence. Recommendations for reducing school violence include offering classroom training in anger management, social skills, and improved self-control; providing mental health and social services for students in need; developing after-school programs that help students build self-esteem and make friends; and keeping guns out of the hands of children and out of schools.

Workplace Violence

Each year U.S. workers experience an average of 1.5 million minor assaults, 400,000 serious assaults, 85,000 robberies, 50,000 sexual assaults, and 700 homicides. In about 60% of cases, workplace violence is committed by strangers; acquaintances account for nearly 40% of cases, and intimates for 1%. Police and corrections officers have the most dangerous jobs, followed by taxi drivers, security guards, bartenders, mental health professionals, and workers at gas stations and convenience and liquor stores. Most of the perpetrators of workplace violence are white males over age 21. Firearms are used in more than 80% of workplace homicides, and the majority of these homicides occur during the commission of a robbery or other crime.

General crime prevention strategies, including use of surveillance cameras and silent alarms and limiting the amount of cash on hand, can help reduce workplace violence related to robberies. A highly stressed workplace is a risk factor in cases of violence between acquaintances or coworkers; clear guidelines about acceptable behavior and prompt action after any threats or incidents of violence can help control this type of workplace violence. The OSHA Web site (www.osha.gov/SLTC/workplaceviolence.index.html) has violence prevention tips for workers.

Terrorism

In 2001, more Americans died as a result of terrorism than in any prior year; the attacks on September 11 killed more than 3000 people, including citizens of 78 countries. The FBI defines terrorism as the unlawful use of force or violence against persons or property to intimidate or coerce a government, the civilian population, or any segment thereof in furtherance of political or social objectives. Terrorism is one form of what the World Health Organization calls collective violence (see the box "Violence and Health: A Global View"). Terrorism can be either domestic, carried out by groups based in the United States, or international. It comes in many forms, including biological (see Chapter 17), chemical, nuclear, and cyber. Its intent is to promote helplessness by instilling fear of harm or destruction.

Most of the terrorism-prevention activities occur at the federal, state, and community levels. U.S. government efforts include close work with the diplomatic, law-enforcement, intelligence, economic, and military communities. The mission of the Department of Homeland Security is to help prevent, protect against, and respond to acts of terrorism on U.S. soil. It is coordinating efforts to protect electric and water supply systems, transportation, gas and oil, emergency services, the computer infrastructure, and other systems. The Patriot Act was designed to give law-enforcement agencies additional tools and improved interagency cooperation for the purpose of investigating and preventing terrorism.

One step individuals can take is to put together an emergency plan and kit for their family or household that can serve for any type of emergency or disaster (see the box "Emergency Preparedness" on p. 680). See Chapters 2, 3, and 20 for advice on coping with the stress of terrorism and mass violence and recognizing post-traumatic stress disorder.

Family and Intimate Violence

Violence in families challenges some of our most basic assumptions about the family. Family violence generally refers to any rough and illegitimate use of physical force, aggression, or verbal abuse by one family member toward another. Such abuse may be physical and/or psychological in nature. Based on reported cases, an estimated 5–7 million women and children are abused each year in the United States.

Battering Studies reveal that 95% of domestic violence victims are women; 20–35% of women who visit medical emergency rooms are there for injuries related to ongoing abuse. Violence against wives or intimate partners, or battering, occurs at every level of society but is more common at lower socioeconomic levels. It occurs more frequently in relationships with a high degree of conflict—an apparent inability to resolve arguments through negotiation and compromise. About 25% of women report having been physically assaulted or raped by an intimate partner, and more than 50% report having experienced some type of abuse—physical or psychological—in a relationship. In more than 10% of cases, the domestic violence continues for 20 years or longer. The problem of intimate violence is even apparent among young people; each year, 1.5 million high school students are victims of physical violence while on a date, according to the CDC.

At the root of much of this abusive behavior is the need to control another person. Abusive partners are controlling partners. They not only want to have power over another person, but also believe they are entitled to it, no matter what the cost to the other person. Abuse includes behavior that physically harms, arouses fear, prevents a person from doing what she wants, or compels her to behave in ways she does not freely choose. Controlling people use a variety of psychological, emotional, and physical tactics to keep their partners bound to them. Early in a relationship, a person's tendency to be controlling may not be obvious (see the box "Recognizing the Potential for Abusiveness in a Partner" on p. 681).

Dimensions of Diversity

Violence and Health: A Global View

In 2002, the World Health Organization (WHO) issued its *World Report on Violence and Health,* which examines the magnitude and impact of violence throughout the world. Each year, more than 1.6 million people die from violent acts: Suicide claims a life every 40 seconds, homicide every minute, and armed conflict every 2 minutes. Violence is among the leading causes of death for people age 15–44, accounting for 14% of deaths among males and 7% of deaths among females. Millions more victims of violence survive but are left with physical, psychological, and reproductive problems, including lost limbs, paralysis, depression, alcohol and drug abuse, sexual dysfunction, and STDs and other reproductive health problems. Beyond individual misery, violence has devastating social and economic consequences.

Interpersonal Violence

WHO defines *interpersonal violence* as the intentional use of physical force or power, threatened or actual, against another person that is likely to result in injury, death, psychological harm, or deprivation. Each year, more than 500,000 people die from interpersonal violence, and more than 60 million children and elderly adults are maltreated. It's estimated that 10–70% of women experience physical violence at the hands of an intimate partner during their lifetime; in addition, forced prostitution, child marriage, sexual trafficking, and female genital mutilation are prevalent in some areas of the world.

Worldwide, adolescents and young adults are the primary victims and perpetrators of interpersonal violence. Individual risk factors for violence highlighted in the WHO report include being young, male, and poor; being intoxicated; and having easy access to firearms. At the community and social levels, risk factors include low social capital (norms and networks that promote coordination and cooperation), high crime rates, rapid social change, poverty, poor rule of law and corruption, gender inequality, firearm availability, and armed conflict. Rates of violence are particularly high among the poorest sectors of the population in countries with high levels of economic inequality (a wide gap between rich and poor).

Collective Violence

WHO applies the term *collective violence* to violence inflicted by one group against another group to achieve political, economic, or social objectives. Collective violence includes armed conflict within or between states; genocide, repression, and other human rights abuses; terrorism; and organized violent crime. Characteristics of countries with increased risk of violent conflict include long-standing tensions between groups, a lack of democratic processes, unequal access to power, unequal distribution and control of resources, and rapid demographic changes.

In the twentieth century, an estimated 191 million people—well over half of them civilians—lost their lives directly or indirectly as a result of armed conflict, and many more were injured. In some conflicts, civilians were mutilated or raped as part of a deliberate strategy to humiliate and demoralize communities. In addition to directly causing deaths and injuries, collective violence destroys infrastructure and disrupts trade, food production, and vital services, thus setting the stage for famine, increased rates of infectious diseases, and mass movements of refugees. The resulting social turmoil also increases rates of interpersonal violence.

What Can Be Done?

The WHO report emphasizes that violence is neither an inevitable part of the human condition nor an intractable social problem. Rather, the wide variation in violence within and among nations over time suggests that violence is the product of a complex but modifiable set of social and environmental factors. Potential strategies to reduce violence include the following:

- Individual and relationship approaches to encourage healthy attitudes and behaviors, such as training in social, parenting, and relationship skills and conflict resolution; mentoring programs; and treatment for people who suffer from depression or who have inflicted abuse on partners or children
- Community-based efforts to raise public awareness and address local social and material causes of violence, such as creating safe places for children to play and adopting community policing
- Societal approaches to change underlying cultural, social, and economic factors, such as new laws and international treaties, policy changes to reduce poverty and inequality, efforts to change harmful social and cultural norms (for example, ethnic discrimination or gender inequality), and disarmament and demobilization programs in countries emerging from conflict

Tackling the problem of violence will require public investment and a collective consensus on what should be done. Only a global response can make the world a safer and healthier place for all.

SOURCES: World Health Organization. 2002. *The World Health Report 2002: Reducing Risks, Promoting Healthy Life*. Geneva: World Health Organization; World Health Organization. 2002. *World Report on Violence and Health*. Geneva: World Health Organization.

In abusive relationships, the abuser (in most cases a man) usually has a history of violent behavior, traditional beliefs about gender roles, and problems with alcohol abuse. He has low self-esteem and seeks to raise it by dominating and imposing his will on another person. Research has revealed a three-phase cycle of battering, consisting of a period of increasing tension, a violent explosion and loss of control, and a period of contriteness in which the man begs forgiveness and promises it will never happen again. The batterer is drawn back to this cycle over and over again, but he never succeeds in changing his feelings about himself.

Battered women often stay in violent relationships for years. They may be economically dependent on their

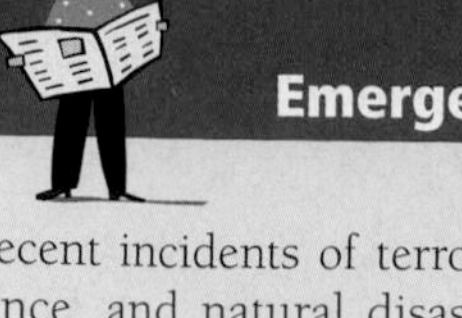

In the News

Emergency Preparedness

Recent incidents of terrorism, mass violence, and natural disasters have highlighted the need for individuals to plan ahead for emergencies. Although you usually cannot predict when a disaster situation will occur, there are things you can do to be better prepared.

Emergency Supplies

Your kit of emergency supplies should include everything you'll need to make it on your own for at least 3 days. You'll need nonperishable food, water, first aid supplies, essential medications, a battery-powered radio, toiletries, clothing, a flashlight or candles and matches, cash, keys, copies of important documents, and supplies for sleeping outdoors in any season/weather (blankets, sleeping bags, tent, and so on). Don't forget about special-needs items for infants, seniors, and pets.

In the case of certain types of terrorist attacks or industrial disasters, you may need supplies to "shelter in place"—to create a barrier between yourself and any dangerous airborne materials. These supplies might include filter masks or folded cotton towels that can be placed over the mouth and nose. Plastic sheeting and duct tape can be used to seal windows and doors.

You may want to create several kits of emergency supplies. The primary one would contain supplies for home use. Put together a smaller, lightweight version that you can take with you if you are forced to evacuate your residence and kits for your car and office.

A Family or Household Plan

You and your family or the members of your household may or may not be together when a disaster strikes. You should have a plan about where to meet and how to communicate. Choose at least two potential meeting places—one in your neighborhood and one or more in other areas. Your community may also have set locations for community shelters.

Where you go may depend on the circumstances of the emergency situation. Use your common sense, and listen to the radio or television to obtain instructions from emergency officials about whether to evacuate or stay in place. In addition, know all the transportation options in the vicinity of your home, school, and workplace; roadways and public transit may be affected, so a sturdy pair of walking shoes is a good item to keep in your emergency kit.

Everyone in the household should also have the same emergency contact person to call, preferably someone who lives outside the immediate area. Local phone service may be significantly disrupted, so long-distance calls may be more likely to go through. Everyone should carry the relevant phone numbers and addresses at all times.

Check the emergency plans at any location where you or family members spend time, including schools and workplaces. For each location, know the safest place to be for different types of emergencies—for example, near load-bearing interior walls during an earthquake, the basement during a tornado, or a safe location miles away from a hurricane (assuming there will be enough time to get there). Also know how to turn off water, gas, and electricity in case of damaged utility lines; keep the needed tools next to the shutoff valves.

Other steps you can take to help prepare for emergencies include taking a first aid class and setting up an emergency response group in your neighborhood or building. More complete information about emergency preparedness is available from the following sources:

American Academy of Pediatrics (www.aap.org)

American Red Cross (www.redcross.org)

Federal Emergency Management Agency (www.fema.gov)

U.S. Department of Homeland Security (www.ready.gov)

SOURCES: U.S. Department of Homeland Security. 2005. *Ready America* (http://www.ready.gov/index.html; retrieved September 21, 2006); Your preparedness guide for any emergency. 2004. *Consumer Reports*, September.

partners, feel trapped or fear retaliation if they leave, believe their children need a father, or have low self-esteem themselves. They may love or pity their husband, or they may believe they'll eventually be able to stop the violence. They usually leave the relationship only when they become determined that the violence must end. Battered women's shelters offer physical protection, counseling, support, and other assistance.

Many batterers are arrested, prosecuted, and imprisoned. Treatment programs are helpful in some cases but not all. Programs focus on stress management, communication and conflict-resolution skills, behavior change, and individual and group therapy. A crucial factor in changing violent behavior seems to be a partner's adamant insistence that the abuse stop.

Terms

stalking Repeatedly harassing or threatening a person through behaviors such as following a person, appearing at a person's residence or workplace, leaving written messages or objects, making harassing phone calls, or vandalizing property; frequently directed at a former intimate partner.

cyberstalking The use of e-mail, chat rooms, bulletin boards, or other electronic communications devices to stalk another person.

Stalking and Cyberstalking Battering is closely associated with **stalking**, characterized by harassing behaviors such as following or spying on a person and making verbal, written, or implied threats. In the United States, it is estimated that 1 million women and 400,000 men are stalked each year; about 87% of stalkers are men. About half of female victims are stalked by current or former intimate partners; of these, 80% had been

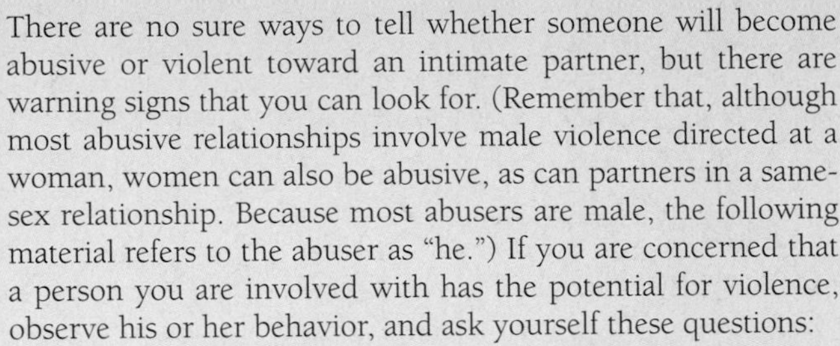

Take Charge

Recognizing the Potential for Abusiveness in a Partner

There are no sure ways to tell whether someone will become abusive or violent toward an intimate partner, but there are warning signs that you can look for. (Remember that, although most abusive relationships involve male violence directed at a woman, women can also be abusive, as can partners in a same-sex relationship. Because most abusers are male, the following material refers to the abuser as "he.") If you are concerned that a person you are involved with has the potential for violence, observe his or her behavior, and ask yourself these questions:

- What is this person's attitude toward women? How does he treat his mother and his sister? How does he work with female students, female colleagues, or a female boss? How does he treat your women friends?
- What is his attitude toward your autonomy? Does he respect the work you do and the way you do it? Or does he put it down, tell you how to do it better, or encourage you to give it up? Does he tell you he'll take care of you?
- How self-centered is he? Does he want to spend leisure time on your interests or his? Does he listen to you? Does he remember what you say?
- Is he possessive or jealous? Does he want to spend every minute with you? Does he cross-examine you about things you do when you're not with him?
- What happens when things don't go the way he wants them to? Does he blow up? Does he always have to get his way?
- Is he moody, mocking, critical, or bossy? Do you feel as if you're walking on eggshells when you're with him?
- Do you feel you have to avoid arguing with him?
- Does he drink too much or use drugs?
- Does he refuse to use condoms or take other precautions for safer sex?

Listen to your own uneasiness, and stay away from any man who disrespects women, who wants or needs you intensely and exclusively, and who has a knack for getting his own way almost all the time.

If you are in a serious relationship with a controlling person, you may already have experienced abuse. Consider the following questions:

- Does your partner constantly criticize you, blame you for things that are not your fault, or verbally degrade you?
- Does he humiliate you in front of others?
- Is he suspicious or jealous? Does he accuse you of being unfaithful or monitor your mail or phone calls?
- Does he track all your time? Does he discourage you from seeing friends and family?
- Does he prevent you from getting or keeping a job or attending school? Does he control your shared resources or restrict your access to money?
- Has he ever pushed, slapped, hit, kicked, bitten, or restrained you? Thrown an object at you? Used a weapon on you?
- Has he ever destroyed or damaged your personal property or sentimental items?
- Has he ever forced you to have sex or to do something sexually you didn't want to do?
- Does he anger easily when drinking or taking drugs?
- Has he ever threatened to harm you or your children, friends, pets, or property?
- Has he ever threatened to blackmail you if you leave?

If you answered yes to one or more of these questions, you may be experiencing domestic abuse. If you believe you or your children are in imminent danger, look in your local telephone directory for a women's shelter, or call 9-1-1. If you want information, referrals to a program in your area, or assistance, contact one of the organizations listed in For More Information at the end of the chapter.

SOURCES: Family Violence Prevention Fund. 2006. *It's Your Business.* San Francisco: Family Violence Prevention Fund; South Dakota Network Against Family Violence and Sexual Assault. 2005. *Are You in an Abusive Situation?* (http://www.sdnafvsa.com/abusive_relationship.php; retrieved September 27, 2006); National Coalition Against Domestic Violence. 2006. *2005 Domestic Violence Facts* (http://www.ncadv.org/files/DV_Facts.pdf; retrieved September 27, 2006).

physically or sexually assaulted by that partner during the relationship. Research suggests that stalking among female college students may be greater than that experienced by the general population. A stalker's goal may be to control or scare the victim or to keep her or him in a relationship. Most stalking episodes last a year or less.

The use of the Internet, e-mail, chat rooms, and other electronic communications devices to stalk another person is known as **cyberstalking.** As with offline stalking, the majority of cyberstalkers are men, and the majority of victims are women, although there have been same-sex cyberstalking incidents. Online incidents of harassment or abuse are becoming more common and more serious, and the U.S. Department of Justice estimates that over one-half million people each year experience cyberstalking. As the seriousness of the crime is being recognized, several states have passed cyberstalking or related laws, and a federal law is under consideration. The impersonal nature of electronic communication may lower the barriers to harassment and threats, because a cyberstalker does not have to physically confront the victim, and thus may make stalking more common. The popularity of online dating sites may also increase cyberstalking.

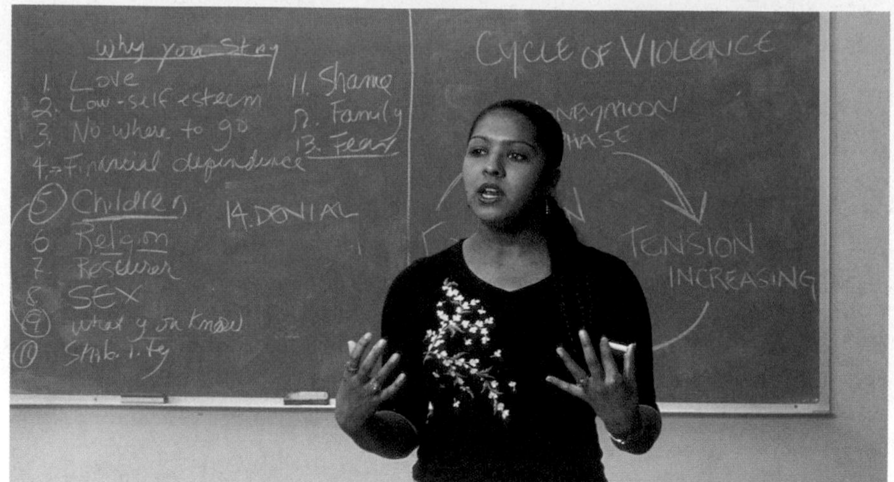

Battering and stalking are related forms of intimate violence, often involving verbal or physical abuse directed at controlling another person. Education, counseling, and support can help the victims of family violence. This college workshop helps people identify the signs of battering and the reasons why people may stay in abusive relationships.

Cyberstalkers may send harassing or threatening e-mails or chat room messages to the victim, or they may encourage others to harass the victim—for example, by impersonating the victim and posting inflammatory messages and personal information on bulletin boards or in chat rooms. Guidelines for staying safe online include the following:

- Never use your real name as an e-mail username or chat room nickname. Select an age- and gender-neutral identity.
- Avoid filling out profiles for accounts related to e-mail use or chat room activities with information that could be used to identify you.
- Do not share personal information in public spaces anywhere online or give it to strangers.
- Learn how to filter unwanted e-mail messages.
- If you do experience harassment online, do not respond to the harasser. Log off or surf elsewhere.

If you receive unwanted online contact, make it clear to that person that you want all contact to stop. If harassment continues, contact the harasser's Internet service provider (ISP) by identifying the domain of the stalker's account (after the "@" sign); most ISPs have an e-mail address for complaints. Often, an ISP can try to stop the conduct by direct contact with the harasser or by closing his or her account. Save all communications for evidence, and contact your ISP and your local police department. Many states have laws against cyberstalking. (See Chapter 4 for more on safely interacting with people online.)

Violence Against Children Violence is also directed against children. Every year, at least 1 million American children are physically abused by their parents, and another 1 to 2 million are victims of neglect. Parental violence is one of the five leading causes of death for children age 1–18. Parents who abuse children tend to have low self-esteem, to believe in physical punishment, to have a poor marital relationship, and to have been abused themselves (although many people who were abused as children do not grow up to abuse their own children). Poverty, unemployment, and social isolation are characteristics of families in which children are abused. External stressors related to socioeconomic and environmental factors are most closely associated with neglect, whereas stressors related to interpersonal issues are more closely associated with physical abuse. Single parents, both men and women, are at especially high risk for abusing their children. Very often one child, whom the parents consider different in some way, is singled out for violent treatment.

When government agencies intervene in child-abuse situations, their goals are to protect the victims and to assist and strengthen the families. Successful programs emphasize education and early intervention, such as home visits to high-risk first-time mothers. Educational efforts focus on stress management, money management, job-finding skills, and information about child behavior and development. Parents may receive counseling and be referred to substance-abuse treatment programs. Support groups like Parents Anonymous are effective for parents committed to changing their behavior.

Elder Abuse Each year, between 1 million and 2 million older adults are abused, exploited, or mistreated by someone who is supposed to be giving them care and protection; only one in six incidents is reported. Most abusers are family members who are serving as caregivers. Elder abuse can take different forms: physical, sexual, or emotional abuse; financial exploitation; neglect; or abandonment. Neglect accounts for about 55% of reported cases. Elders who have lost some mental or physical functions and must rely on others for care are most at risk and may suffer malnutrition, dehydration, mismanaged medication, or infection due to poor hygiene. Physical abuse accounts for about 15% of reported cases, and financial exploitation for about 13%.

Abuse often occurs when caring for a dependent adult becomes too stressful for the caregiver, especially if the elder is incontinent, has suffered mental deterioration, or is violent. Abuse may become an outlet for frustration. Many believe that the solution to elder abuse is support in the form of greater social and financial assistance, such as adult day-care centers and education and public care programs.

Sexual Violence

The use of force and coercion in sexual relationships is one of the most serious problems in human interactions. The most extreme manifestation of sexual coercion—forcing a person to submit to another's sexual desires—is rape, but sexual coercion occurs in many subtler forms, including sexual harassment.

Sexual Assault: Rape Sexual coercion that relies on the threat and use of physical force or takes advantage of circumstances that render a person incapable of giving consent (such as when drunk) constitutes **sexual assault** or **rape.** When the victim is younger than the legally defined age of consent, the act constitutes **statutory rape,** whether or not coercion is involved. Coerced sexual activity in which the victim knows or is dating the rapist is often referred to as **date rape,** or *acquaintance rape*. Most victims know their assailant, but less than one-third of all sexual crimes are reported.

Any woman—or man—can be a rape victim. It is estimated that nearly 700,000 women are raped each year and that 1 in 6 women and 1 in 33 men has experienced an attempted or completed rape at some point in their lives. A study of college students found that between 1 in 4 and 1 in 5 college women experience a completed or attempted rape during their college years. The majority of male victims of rape are not in prison.

WHO COMMITS RAPE? Men who commit rape may be any age and come from any socioeconomic group. Some rapists are exploiters in the sense that they rape on the spur of the moment and mainly want immediate gratification. Some attempt to compensate for feelings of sexual inadequacy and an inability to obtain satisfaction otherwise. Others are more hostile and sadistic and are primarily interested in hurting and humiliating a particular woman or women in general. Often, the rapist is more interested in dominance, control, and power than in sexual satisfaction.

Most women are in much less danger of being raped by a stranger than of being sexually assaulted by a man they know or date. Surveys suggest that as many as 25% of women have had experiences in which the men they were dating persisted in trying to force sex despite pleading, crying, screaming, or resisting. Surveys have also found that more than 60% of all rape victims were raped by a current or former spouse, boyfriend, or date.

Most cases of date rape are never reported to the police, partly because of the subtlety of the crime. Usually no weapons are involved, and direct verbal threats may not have been made. Rather than being terrorized, the victim usually is attracted to the man at first. Victims of date rape tend to shoulder much of the responsibility for the incident, questioning their own judgment and behavior rather than blaming the aggressor.

Sometimes husbands rape their wives. Strong evidence suggests that 15% of American women who have ever married have been raped by their husbands or ex-husbands; as many as 60% of battered women may have been raped by their husbands. A charge of spousal rape can now be taken to court in all states.

FACTORS CONTRIBUTING TO DATE RAPE One factor in date rape appears to be the double standard about appropriate sexual behavior for men and women. Although the general status of women in society has improved, it is still a commonly held cultural belief that nice women don't say yes to sex (even when they want to) and that real men don't take no for an answer.

Men and women also differ in their perception of romantic encounters and signals. In one study, researchers found that men interpreted women's actions on dates, such as smiling or talking in a low voice, as indicating an interest in having sex, whereas the women interpreted the same actions as just being friendly. Men's thinking about forceful sex also tends to be unclear. One psychologist reports that men find "forcing a woman to have sex against her will" more acceptable than "raping a woman," even though the former description is the definition of rape.

Men who rape their dates tend to have certain attributes, including hostility toward women, a belief that dominance alone is a valid motive for sex, and an acceptance of sexual violence. They may feel that force is justified in certain circumstances, such as if they are sexually involved with a woman and she refuses to have sex, if the woman is known to have had sex with other men, or if the woman shows up at a party where people are drinking and taking drugs. The man often primes himself to force himself sexually on his date by drinking, which lowers his ordinary social inhibitions. Many college men who have committed date rape tried to seduce their dates by plying them with alcohol first.

Terms

Vw

sexual assault or **rape** The use of force to have sex with someone against that person's will.

statutory rape Sexual interaction with someone under the legal age of consent.

date rape Sexual assault by someone the victim knows or is dating; also called *acquaintance rape*.

Take Charge

Preventing Date Rape

Guidelines for Women

- Believe in your right to control what you do. Set limits, and communicate these limits clearly, firmly, and early. Say no when you mean no.
- Be assertive with someone who is sexually pressuring you. Men often interpret passivity as permission.
- If you are unsure of a new acquaintance, go on a group date or double date. If possible, provide your own transportation.
- Remember that some men assume sexy dress and a flirtatious manner mean a desire for sex.
- Remember that alcohol and drugs interfere with clear communication about sex.
- Use the statement that has proven most effective in stopping date rape: "This is rape, and I'm calling the police."

Guidelines for Men

- Be aware of social pressure. It's OK to not score.
- Understand that no means no. Don't continue making advances when your date resists or tells you she wants to stop. Remember that she has the right to refuse sex.
- Don't assume sexy dress and a flirtatious manner are invitations to sex, that previous permission for sex applies to the current situation, or that your date's relationships with other men constitute sexual permission for you.
- Remember that alcohol and drugs interfere with clear communication about sex.

DATE-RAPE DRUGS A 2006 study showed that drugs are a factor in more than 60% of sexual assaults and about 5% of victims are given date-rape drugs. Also called predator drugs, the drugs used in date rapes include flunitrazepam (Rohypnol), gamma hydroxybutyrate (GHB), and ketamine hydrochloride ("Special K"). These drugs have a variety of effects, including sedation; if slipped surreptitiously into a drink, they can incapacitate a person within about 20 minutes and make her or him more vulnerable to assault. Rohypnol, GHB, and other drugs also often cause anterograde amnesia, meaning victims have little memory of what happened while they were under the influence of the drug. (See Chapter 9 for more on the effects of these and other psychoactive drugs.)

The Drug-Induced Rape Prevention and Punishment Act of 1996 adds up to 20 years to the prison sentence of any rapist who uses a drug to incapacitate a victim. Supporters of the law likened dropping a drug in a victim's drink to putting a knife to her throat. The makers of Rohypnol are modifying the pills so they will be a more noticeable color and will dissolve more slowly, thereby reducing the likelihood that Rohypnol can be used as a date-rape drug; however, other drugs in powdered or liquid form can be slipped into drinks unnoticed. Strategies such as the following can help ensure that your drink is not tampered with at a bar or party:

- Check with campus or local police to find out if drug-facilitated sexual assault has occurred in your area and, if so, where.
- Drink moderately and responsibly. Avoid group drinking and drinking games.
- Be wary of opened beverages—alcoholic or nonalcoholic—offered by strangers. When at an unfamiliar bar, watch the bartender pour your drink.
- Let your date be the first to drink from the punchbowl at a bar, club, or rave.
- If an opened beverage tastes, looks, or smells strange, do not drink it. If you leave your drink unattended, such as when you dance or use the restroom, obtain a fresh drink when you return to your table.
- If you go to a party, club, or bar, go with friends. Have a prearranged plan for checking on each other visually and verbally. If you feel giddy or lightheaded, get assistance.

Date rape is largely a result of sexual socialization in which the man develops an exaggerated sexual impulse and puts a premium on sexual conquests. Sex and violence are linked in our society, and coercion is accepted by some adolescents as an appropriate form of sexual expression. Both males and females can take actions that will reduce the incidence of acquaintance rape; see the box "Preventing Date Rape" for specific suggestions.

DEALING WITH A SEXUAL ASSAULT Experts disagree about whether a woman who is faced with a rapist should fight back or give in quietly to avoid being injured or to gain time in the hope of escaping. Some rapists say that if a woman had screamed or resisted loudly, they would have run; others report they would have injured or killed her. (If a rapist is carrying a weapon, most experts advise against fighting unless absolutely necessary.) A woman who is raped by a stranger is more likely to be physically injured than a woman raped by someone she knows. Each situation is unique, and a woman should respond in whatever way she thinks best. If a woman chooses not to resist, it does not mean that she has not been raped.

If you are threatened by a rapist and decide to fight back, here is what Women Organized Against Rape (WOAR) recommends:

- Trust your gut feeling. If you feel you are in danger, don't hesitate to run and scream. It is better to feel foolish than to be raped.
- Yell—and keep yelling. It will clear your head and start your adrenaline going; it may scare your attacker and also bring help. Don't forget that a rapist is also afraid of pain and afraid of getting caught.
- If an attacker grabs you from behind, use your elbows for striking his neck, his sides, or his stomach.
- Try kicking. Your legs are the strongest part of your body, and your kick is longer than his reach. Kick with your rear foot and with the toe of your shoe. Aim low to avoid losing your balance.
- His most vulnerable spot is his knee; it's low, difficult to protect, and easily knocked out of place. Don't try to kick a rapist in the crotch; he has been protecting this area all his life and will have better protective reflexes there than at his knees.
- Once you start fighting, keep it up. Your objective is to get away as soon as you can.
- Remember that ordinary rules of behavior don't apply. It's OK to vomit, act crazy, or claim to have a sexually transmitted disease.

If you are raped, tell what happened to the first friendly person you meet. Call the police, tell them you were raped, and give your location. Try to remember as many facts as you can about your attacker; write down a description as soon as possible. Don't wash or change your clothes, or you may destroy important evidence. The police will take you to a hospital for a complete exam; show the physician any injuries. Tell the police simply, but exactly, what happened. Be honest, and stick to your story.

If you decide that you don't want to report the rape to the police, be sure to see a physician as soon as possible. You need to be checked for pregnancy and STDs.

THE EFFECTS OF RAPE Rape victims suffer both physical and psychological injury. For most, physical wounds heal within a few weeks. Psychological pain may endure and be substantial. Even the most physically and mentally strong are likely to experience shock, anxiety, depression, shame, and a host of psychosomatic symptoms after being victimized. These psychological reactions following rape comprise rape trauma syndrome, which is characterized by fear, nightmares, fatigue, crying spells, and digestive upset. (Rape trauma syndrome is a form of post-traumatic stress disorder; see Chapter 3.) Self-blame is very likely; society has contributed to this tendency by perpetuating the myths that women can actually defend themselves and that no one can be raped if she doesn't want to be. Fortunately, these false beliefs are dissolving in the face of evidence to the contrary.

Many organizations offer counseling and support to rape victims. Look in the telephone directory under Rape or Rape Crisis Center for a hotline number to call. Your campus may have counseling services or a support group.

Child Sexual Abuse Child sexual abuse is any sexual contact between an adult and a child who is below the legal age of consent. Adults and older adolescents are able to coerce children into sexual activity because of their authority and power over them. Threats, force, or the promise of friendship or material rewards may be used to manipulate a child. Sexual contacts are typically brief and consist of genital manipulation; genital intercourse is much less common.

Sexual abusers are usually male, heterosexual, and known to the victim. The abuser may be a relative, a friend, a neighbor, or another trusted adult acquaintance. Child abusers are often pedophiles, people who are sexually attracted to children. They may have poor interpersonal and sexual relationships with other adults and feel socially inadequate and inferior.

One highly traumatic form of sexual abuse is **incest,** sexual activity between people too closely related to legally marry. The most common forms of incest are father-daughter (which includes stepfather-stepdaughter) abuse, brother-sister abuse (usually an adolescent boy abusing a preadolescent girl), and uncle-niece abuse; mother-son sexual activity is rare. Adults who commit incest may be pedophiles, but very often they are simply sexual opportunists or people with poor impulse control and emotional problems.

Most sexually abused children are between ages 8 and 12 when the abuse first occurs. More girls are sexually abused than boys. The degree of trauma for the child can be very serious, but it varies with the type of encounters, their frequency, the child's age and relationship to the abuser, and the parents' response. Father-daughter abuse may be the most traumatic form, in part because it is a violation of the basic parent-child relationship and because the abuse tends to be more frequent. Abused children may be depressed or moody, exhibit hyperactivity, play violently with others or with inanimate objects, talk nonsense, or unintentionally injure themselves.

Child sexual abuse is often unreported. Surveys suggest that as many as 27% of women and 16% of men were sexually abused as children. An estimated 150,000–200,000

Term

incest Sexual activity between close relatives, such as siblings or parents and their children.

Vw

new cases of child sexual abuse occur each year. It can leave lasting scars; victims are more likely to suffer as adults from low self-esteem, depression, anxiety, eating disorders, self-destructive tendencies, sexual problems, and difficulties in intimate relationships.

If you were a victim of sexual abuse as a child and feel it may be interfering with your functioning today, you may want to address the problem. A variety of approaches can help, such as joining a support group of people who have had similar experiences, confiding in a partner or friend, or seeking professional help.

Sexual Harassment Unwelcome sexual advances, requests for sexual favors, and other verbal, visual, or physical conduct of a sexual nature constitute **sexual harassment** if such conduct explicitly or implicitly does any of the following:

- Affects academic or employment decisions or evaluations
- Interferes with an individual's academic or work performance
- Creates an intimidating, hostile, or offensive academic, work, or student living environment

Extreme cases of sexual harassment occur when a manager, professor, or other person in authority uses his or her ability to control or influence jobs or grades to coerce people into having sex or to punish them if they refuse. A hostile environment can be created by conduct such as sexual gestures, displaying of sexually suggestive objects or pictures, derogatory comments and jokes, sexual remarks about clothing or appearance, obscene letters, and unnecessary touching or pinching. Sexual harassment can occur between people of the same or opposite sex. Although sexual harassment is forbidden by law, many cases go unreported. In a survey of 17,000 federal employees, 42% of women and 15% of men reported having been sexually harassed.

If you have been the victim of sexual harassment, you can take action to stop it. Be assertive with anyone who uses language or actions you find inappropriate. If possible, confront your harasser either in writing, over the telephone, or in person, informing him or her that the situation is unacceptable to you and you want the harassment to stop. Be clear. "Do not *ever* make sexual remarks to me" is an unequivocal statement. If assertive communication doesn't work, assemble a file or log documenting the harassment, noting the details of each incident and information about any witnesses who may be able to support your claims. You may discover others who have been harassed by the same person, which will strengthen your case. Then file a grievance with the harasser's supervisor or employer, such as someone in the dean's office if you are a student or someone in the human resources office if you are an employee.

If your attempts to deal with the harassment internally are not successful, you can file an official complaint with your city or state Human Rights Commission or Fair Employment Practices Agency, or with the federal Equal Employment Opportunity Commission. You may also wish to pursue legal action under the Civil Rights Act or under local laws prohibiting employment discrimination. Very often, the threat of a lawsuit or other legal action is enough to stop the harasser.

What You Can Do About Violence

It is obvious that violence in our society is not disappearing and that it is a serious threat to our collective health and well-being. This is especially true on college campuses, which in a sense are communities in themselves but sometimes lack the authority or guidance to tackle the issue of violence directly (see the box "Staying Safe on Campus"). Although government and law enforcement agencies are working to address the problem of violence, individuals must take on a greater responsibility to bring about change. New programs are being developed at the grass-roots level to deal with problems of violence directly. Schools are now providing training for conflict resolution and are educating people about the diverse nature of our society, thereby encouraging tolerance and understanding.

Looking at the problem of violence from a public health perspective points to the importance of the social environment. As with any public health problem, one potential approach is to identify and target high-risk groups for intervention. Violence prevention programs currently focus on conflict-resolution training and the development of social skills. These measures have proven effective, but for behavior change to be lasting, the focus of such programs must expand beyond individual intervention to include social and environmental factors.

Reducing gun-related injuries may require changes in the availability, possession, and lethality of the 8–12 million firearms sold in the United States each year. As part of the Brady gun control law, computerized instant background checks are performed for most gun sales to prevent purchases by convicted felons, people with a history of mental instability, and certain other

Terms

VW

sexual harassment Unwelcome sexual advances, requests for sexual favors, and other conduct of a sexual nature that affects academic or employment decisions or evaluations; interferes with an individual's academic or work performance; or creates an intimidating, hostile, or offensive academic, work, or student living environment.

first aid Emergency care given to an ill or injured person until medical care can be obtained.

Take Charge

Staying Safe on Campus

College campuses can be the site of criminal activity and violence just as any other environment or living situation can be—and so they require the same level of caution and awareness that you would use in other situations. Two key points to remember: 80% of campus crimes are committed by a student against a fellow student, and alcohol or drug use is involved in 90% of campus felonies. Drinking or drug use can affect judgment and lower inhibitions, so be aware if you or another person is under the influence. Here are some suggestions for keeping yourself safe on campus:

- Don't travel alone after dark. Many campuses have shuttle buses that run from spots on campus such as the library and the dining hall to residence halls and other locations. Escorts are often available to walk with you at night.
- Be familiar with well-lit and frequently traveled routes around campus if you do need to walk alone.
- If you have a car, follow the usual precautions about parking in well-lit areas, keeping the doors locked while you are driving, and never picking up hitchhikers.
- Always have your keys ready as you approach your residence hall, room, and car. Don't lend your keys to others.
- Let friends and family members know your schedule of classes and activities to create a sort of buddy system.
- Be sure the doors and windows of your dorm room have sturdy locks, and use them.
- Don't prop open doors or hold doors open for nonstudents or nonresidents trying to enter your dorm. Be aware of nonresidents around your dorm. If someone says that he or she is meeting a friend inside, that person should be able to call the friend from outside the building.
- Keep valuables and anything containing personal information—credit cards, wallets, jewelry, and so on—hidden. Secure expensive computer and stereo equipment with cables so that it can't be easily stolen. Use a quality U-shaped lock whenever you leave a bicycle unattended.
- Be alert when using an ATM, and don't display large amounts of cash.
- Stay alert and trust your instincts. Don't hesitate to call the police or campus security if something doesn't seem or feel right.

The Jeanne Clery Disclosure of Campus Security Policy and Campus Crime Statistics Act, named for a Lehigh University student who was murdered in her residence hall in 1986, requires colleges and universities to collect and report campus crime statistics. You can now review this information online at the Crime Statistics Web site of the U.S. Department of Education's Office of Postsecondary Education (http://ope.ed.gov/security/Search.asp).

SOURCES: Security on Campus, Inc. 2001. *Campus Safety: Tips and Evaluation Brochure* (http://www.campussafety.org/students/tips.html; retrieved September 21, 2006); U.S. Department of Education, Office of Postsecondary Education. 2000. *Campus Security* (http://www.ed.gov/admins/lead/safety/campus.html; retrieved September 21, 2006).

groups. In some states, waiting periods are required in addition to the background checks. Some groups advocate a complete and universal federal ban on the sale of all handguns.

Safety experts also advocate the adoption of consumer safety standards for guns, including features such as childproofing and indicators to show if a gun is loaded. Technologies are now available to personalize handguns to help prevent unauthorized use. Magnetic encoding, touch memory, radio frequency, and fingerprint reading are ways to identify the owner and prevent use by others. Although surveys indicate that the public may be willing to pay the increased costs for personalizing a handgun, firearms manufacturers have been hesitant to redesign their products for safety purposes. Education about proper storage is also important. Surveys indicate that more than 40% of homes with children contain guns; in about 23% of gun-owning households, the weapon is stored loaded, and in 28% the gun is kept hidden but not locked. To be effective, any approach to firearm injury prevention must have the support of law enforcement and the community as a whole.

PROVIDING EMERGENCY CARE

By following the safety guidelines described in this chapter and being aware of the potential risks associated with different activities, you can avoid many injuries on the road, at home, at work, and in public places. However, some injuries will inevitably occur. Therefore, it is also important to prepare for situations when you may need to provide emergency care for yourself or others. If you are prepared to help, you can improve someone else's chances of surviving or of avoiding permanent disability.

A course in **first aid** can help you respond appropriately when someone is injured. One important benefit of first aid training is learning what *not* to do in certain situations. For example, a person with a suspected neck or back injury should not be moved unless other life-threatening conditions exist. A trained person can assess emergency situations accurately before acting.

Emergency rescue techniques can save the lives of people who are choking, who have stopped breathing, or whose hearts have stopped beating. As described earlier, the Heimlich maneuver is used when a victim is choking (see the inside back cover). Pulmonary resuscitation (also known as rescue breathing, artificial respiration, or mouth-to-mouth resuscitation) is used when a person is not breathing. **Cardiopulmonary resuscitation (CPR)** is used when a pulse cannot be found. Training is required before a person can perform CPR, and in 2005, significant changes were made to the guidelines for lay rescuer CPR. Courses are offered by the American Red Cross and the American Heart Association. A new feature of some of these courses is training in the use of automatic external defibrillators (AEDs), which monitor the heart's rhythm and, if appropriate, deliver an electrical shock to restart the heart. Because of the importance of early use of defibrillators in saving heart attack victims, these devices are being installed in public places, including casinos, airports, and many office buildings.

As a person providing assistance, you are the first link in the **emergency medical services (EMS) system.** Your responsibility may be to render first aid, provide emotional support for the victim, or just call for help. It is important to remain calm and act sensibly. The basic pattern for providing emergency care is check-call-care:

- *Check the situation:* Make sure the scene is safe for both you and the injured person. Don't put yourself in danger; if you get hurt too, you will be of little help to the injured person.
- *Check the victim:* Conduct a quick head-to-toe examination. Assess the victim's signs and symptoms, such as level of responsiveness, pulse, and breathing rate. Look for bleeding and any indications of broken bones or paralysis.
- *Call for help:* Call 9-1-1 or a local emergency number. Identify yourself and give as much information as you can about the condition of the victim and what happened.
- *Care for the victim:* If the situation requires immediate action (no pulse, shock, etc.), provide first aid if you are trained to do so.

Like other kinds of behavior, avoiding and preventing injuries and acting safely involve choices you make every day. Ultimately, your goal is healthy, safe behavior. Take responsibility for your safety behaviors. You can motivate yourself to act in the safest way possible by increasing your knowledge and level of awareness, by examining your attitudes to see if they're realistic, by knowing your capacities and limitations, by adjusting your responses when environmental hazards exist, and, in general, by taking responsibility for your actions. You can't eliminate all risks and dangers from your life—no one can do that—but you can improve your chances of avoiding injuries and living to a healthy old age.

Terms

VW

cardiopulmonary resuscitation (CPR) An emergency first aid procedure that combines artificial respiration and artificial circulation; used in first aid emergencies where breathing and blood circulation have stopped.

emergency medical services (EMS) system A system designed to network community resources for providing emergency care.

Tips for Today

Although people worry about violence, unintentional injuries—such as those resulting from car crashes, falls, and fires—are much more common. In fact, unintentional injuries are the leading cause of death for people under the age of 35. To protect yourself from injuries, learn to incorporate sensible safety precautions into your daily life.

Right now you can

- Pick up anything on the floor of your home that could cause tripping or slipping.
- Make sure the electrical outlets in your home are not overloaded and that extension cords do not run under rugs or where people walk.
- Test the batteries in the smoke detectors in your home and replace them if they aren't working.
- Check your bike helmet to make sure it fits properly and meets the requirements described in the box "Choosing a Bicycle Helmet." Wear it the next time you go for a ride.

SUMMARY

- Injuries are caused by a dynamic interaction of human and environmental factors. Risk-taking behavior is associated with a high rate of injury.
- Key factors in motor vehicle injuries include aggressive driving, speeding, a failure to wear safety belts, alcohol and drug intoxication, fatigue, and distraction.
- Motorcycle, moped, and bicycle injuries can be prevented by developing appropriate skills, driving or riding defensively, and wearing proper safety equipment, especially a helmet.
- Most fall-related injuries are a result of falls at floor level, but stairs, chairs, and ladders are also involved in a significant number of falls.
- Careless smoking and problems with cooking or heating equipment are common causes of home fires. Being prepared for fire emergencies means planning escape routes and installing smoke detectors.
- The home can contain many poisonous substances, including medications, cleaning agents, plants, and fumes from cars and appliances.
- Performing the Heimlich maneuver can prevent someone from dying from choking.

Adopting Safer Habits

Behavior Change Strategy

Why do you get injured? What human and environmental factors contribute to injuries? Identifying those factors is one step toward making your lifestyle safer. Changing unsafe behaviors *before* they lead to injuries is an even better way of improving your chances.

For the next 7–10 days, keep track of any mishaps you are involved in or injuries you receive, recording them on a daily behavior record like the one shown in Chapter 1. Count each time you cut, burn, or injure yourself, fall down, run into someone, or have any other potentially injury-causing mishap, no matter how trivial. Also record any risk-taking behaviors, such as failing to wear your safety belt or bicycle helmet, drinking and driving, exceeding the speed limit, putting off home or bicycle repairs, and so on. For each entry (injury or incidence of unsafe behavior), record the date, the time, what you were doing, who else was there and how you were influenced by him or her, what your motivations were, and what you were thinking and feeling at the time.

At the end of the monitoring period, examine your data. For each incident, determine both the human factors and the environmental factors that contributed to the injury or unsafe behavior. Were you tired? Distracted? Did you not realize this situation was dangerous? Did you take a chance? Did you think this incident couldn't happen to you? Was visibility poor? Were you using defective equipment? Then consider each contributing factor carefully, determining why it existed and how it could have been avoided or changed. Finally, consider what preventive actions you could take to avoid such incidents or to change your behaviors in the future.

As an example, let's say that you usually don't use a safety belt when you run local errands in your car and that several factors contribute to this behavior: You don't really think you could be involved in a crash so close to home, you only go on short trips, you just never think to use it, and so on. One of the contributing factors to your unsafe behavior is inadequate knowledge. You can change this factor by obtaining accurate information about auto crashes (and their usual proximity to a victim's home) from this chapter and from library or Internet research. Just acquiring information about auto crashes and safety belt use may lead you to examine your beliefs and attitudes about safety belts and motivate you to change your behavior.

Once you're committed, you can use behavior change techniques described in Chapter 1, such as completing a contract, asking family and friends for support, and so on, to build a new habit. Put a note or picture reminding you to buckle up in your car where you can see it clearly. Recruit a friend to run errands with you and to remind you about using your safety belt. Once your habit is established, you may influence other people—especially people who ride in your car—to use safety belts all the time. By changing this behavior, you have reduced the chances that you or your passengers will suffer a serious injury or even die in a vehicle crash.

- The proper storage and handling of firearms can help prevent injuries; assume that any gun is loaded.
- Many injuries during leisure activities result from the misuse of equipment, lack of experience, use of alcohol, and a failure to wear proper safety equipment.
- Most work-related injuries involve extensive manual labor; back problems are most common. More recent common problems include repetitive strain injuries.
- Factors contributing to violence include poverty, the absence of strong social ties, the influence of the mass media, cultural attitudes about gender roles, problems in interpersonal relationships, alcohol and drug abuse, and the availability of firearms.
- Types of violence include assault, homicide, gang-related violence, hate crimes, school violence, workplace violence, and terrorism.
- Battering and child abuse occur at every socioeconomic level. The core issue is the abuser's need to control other people.
- Most rape victims are women, and most know their attackers. Factors in date rape include different standards of appropriate sexual behavior for men and women and different perceptions of actions.
- Child sexual abuse often results in serious trauma; usually the abuser is a trusted adult.
- Sexual harassment is unwelcome sexual advances or other conduct of a sexual nature that affects academic or employment performance or evaluations or that creates an intimidating, hostile, or offensive academic, work, or student living environment.
- Strategies for reducing violence include conflict-resolution training, social skills development, and education programs that foster tolerance and understanding among diverse groups.
- Steps in giving emergency care include making sure the scene is safe for you and the injured person, conducting a quick examination of the victim, calling for help, and providing emergency first aid.

Take Action

1. **Take a course:** Contact the American Red Cross or American Heart Association in your area, and ask about first aid and CPR classes. These courses are usually given frequently and at a variety of times and locations. They can be invaluable in saving lives. Consider taking one or both of the courses.

2. **Investigate local resources:** Find out what resources are available on your campus or in your community for victims of rape, hate crimes, or other types of violence. Does your campus sponsor any violence prevention programs or activities? If so, consider participating in one.

3. **Prepare for a fire:** Contact your local fire department and obtain a checklist of fire safety procedures. What would you do if a fire started in your home? What types of evacuation procedures would be necessary? Carry out a practice fire drill at home to see what problems might arise in a real emergency.

4. **Prepare for a poisoning injury:** Post the number for the national poison control hotline (800-222-1222) near your telephone. Obtain information on poisonings from a Poison Control Center, and read it carefully so you know what to do in case of poisoning.

5. **Create a public education campaign:** Choose a key behavior that prevents injuries, and develop a campaign that you think will help convince people of your age and gender to engage in that behavior—for example, use a safety belt, avoid using a cell phone while driving, wear a bicycle helmet, or change smoke alarm batteries. Consider what types of information and emotional appeals would be most effective for your campaign.

6. **Volunteer in your neighborhood or community:** Contact your local police or civic organization to find out about setting up a neighborhood watch or emergency response team. Talk with your neighbors to find out more about what you can do to help prevent crime and prepare for emergencies.

For More Information

Books

Dacey, J. S., and L. B. Fiore. 2006. *The Safe Child Handbook.* San Francisco: Jossey-Bass. *A practical handbook for keeping your family safe and coping with the stress and fear associated with many real-world dangers.*

Home Emergency Guide. 2003. New York: DK. *Provides background information on first aid and flowcharts with advice for dealing with many emergency situations.*

MacPherson, J. 2003. *AAA Auto Guide: Driving Survival. How to Stay Safe on the Road.* Heathrow, Fl: AAA Publishing. *Provides helpful strategies for choosing and maintaining a safe vehicle and for handling a variety of driving situations.*

McGrew, J. 2005. *Think Safe: Practical Measures to Increase Security at Home, at Work, and Throughout Life.* Hilton Head Island, S.C.: Cameo Publications. *A general guide to safety and crime and violence prevention.*

National Safety Council. 2007. *Standard First Aid, CPR, and AED.* Itasca, Ill.: National Safety Council. *An everyday guide to the most current first aid and emergency resuscitation techniques, with instructions for using automatic defibrillators.*

World Health Organization *World Reports. Visit the WHO Web site* (www.who.int) *to review the recent* World Reports *focusing on violence (2002) and motor vehicle injuries (2004).*

WW Organizations, Hotlines, and Web Sites

American Automobile Association Foundation for Traffic Safety. Provides consumer information about all aspects of traffic safety; Web site has online quizzes and extensive links.
800-305-SAFE
http://www.aaafts.org

American Bar Association: Domestic Violence. Provides information on statistics, research, and laws relating to domestic violence.
http://www.abanet.org/domviol/home.html

Consumer Product Safety Commission. Provides information and advice about safety issues relating to consumer products.
http://www.cpsc.gov

CyberAngels. Provides information on online safety and help and advice for victims of cyberstalking.
http://www.cyberangels.org

Insurance Institute for Highway Safety. Provides information about crashes on the nation's highways, as well as reports on topics such as speeding and crashworthiness of vehicles.
http://www.highwaysafety.org

National Center for Injury Prevention and Control. Provides consumer-oriented information about unintentional injuries and violence.
http://www.cdc.gov/ncipc

National Center for Victims of Crime. An advocacy group for crime victims; provides statistics, news, safety strategies, tips on finding local assistance, and links to related sites.
800-FYI-CALL
http://www.ncvc.org

National Highway Traffic Safety Administration. Supplies materials about reducing deaths, injuries, and economic losses from motor vehicle crashes.
888-327-4236
http://www.nhtsa.dot.gov

National Safety Council. Provides information and statistics about preventing unintentional injuries.
630-285-1121
http://www.nsc.org

National Violence Hotlines. Provide information, referral services, and crisis intervention.
800-799-SAFE (domestic violence);
800-422-4453 (child abuse);
800-656-HOPE (sexual assault)

National Youth Violence Prevention Resource Center. Provides information about violence related to college students.
http://www.safeyouth.org/scripts/topics/college.asp

Occupational Safety and Health Administration. Provides information about topics related to health and safety issues in the workplace.
http://www.osha.gov

Prevent Child Abuse America. Provides statistics, information, and publications relating to child abuse, including parenting tips.
http://www.preventchildabuse.org

Rape, Abuse, and Incest National Network (RAINN). Provides guidelines for preventing and dealing with sexual assault and abuse.
http://www.rainn.org

SafeUSA. Provides information about safety at home, in schools, at work, on the road, and in communities.
http://www.safeusa.org

Tolerance.Org: 10 Ways to Fight Hate on Campus. Offers suggestions for fighting hate and promoting tolerance; sponsored by the Southern Poverty Law Center.
http://www.tolerance.org/campus/index.jsp

World Health Organization: Violence and Injury Prevention. Provides statistics and information about the consequences of intentional and unintentional injuries worldwide.
http://www.who.int/violence_injury_prevention

The following sites provide statistics and background information on violence and crime in the United States:

Bureau of Justice Statistics: http://www.ojp.usdoj.gov/bjs
Federal Bureau of Investigation: http://www.fbi.gov
Justice Information Center: http://www.ncjrs.org

Selected Bibliography

Browne, K. D., and C. Hamilton-Giachritsis. 2005. The influence of violent media on children and adolescents: A public-health approach. *Lancet* 365(9460): 702–710.

Carr, J. L. 2005. *American College Health Association Campus Violence White Paper.* Baltimore, Md.: American College Health Association.

Centers for Disease Control and Prevention. 2004. Impact of primary laws on adult use of safety belts—United States, 2002. *Morbidity and Mortality Weekly Report* 53(12): 257–260.

Centers for Disease Control and Prevention. 2004. Surveillance for fatal and nonfatal injuries—United States, 2001. *MMWR Surveillance Summaries* 55(SS7): 1–57.

Centers for Disease Control and Prevention. 2004. Violence-related behaviors among high school students—United States, 1991–2003. *Morbidity and Mortality Weekly Report* 53(29): 651–655.

Centers for Disease Control and Prevention. 2005. Increase in poisoning deaths caused by nonillicit drugs. *Morbidity and Mortality Weekly Report* 54(2): 33–36.

Centers for Disease Control and Prevention. 2005. Unintentional non-fire-related carbon monoxide exposures—United States, 2001–2003. *Morbidity and Mortality Weekly Report* 54(2): 36–39.

Centers for Disease Control and Prevention. 2006. Nonfatal injuries and restraint use among child passengers—United States, 2004. *Morbidity and Mortality Weekly Report* 55(22): 624–627.

Centers for Disease Control and Prevention. 2006. Notice to Readers: Buckle Up America Week—May 22–29, 2006. *Morbidity and Mortality Weekly Report* 55(19): 535–536.

Centers for Disease Control and Prevention. 2006. Physical dating violence among high school students—United States, 2003. *Morbidity and Mortality Weekly Report* 55(19): 532–535.

Commission for Global Road Safety. 2006. *Global* Road Safety Fact File (http://www.fiafoundation.com/commissionforglobalroadsafety/factfile/index.html; retrieved September 21, 2006).

Cummings, P., and F. P. Rivara. 2004. Car occupant death according to the restraint use of other occupants. *Journal of the American Medical Association* 291(3): 343–349.

Cummings, P., et al. 2006. Changes in traffic crash mortality rates attributed to use of alcohol, or lack of a seat belt, air bag, motorcycle helmet, or bicycle helmet, United States, 1982–2001. *Injury Prevention* 12(3): 148–154.

Federal Bureau of Investigation. 2004. *Hate Crime Statistics, 2003.* Washington, D.C.: U.S. Department of Justice.

Federal Bureau of Investigation. 2006. *Crime in the United States. Uniform Crime Reports, 2005.* Washington, D.C.: U.S. Department of Justice.

Graffunder, C. M., et al. 2004. Through a public health lens. Preventing violence against women: An update from the U.S. Centers for Disease Control and Prevention. *Journal of Women's Health* 13(1): 5–15.

Gray-Vickrey, P. 2004. Combating elder abuse. *Nursing* 34(10): 47–51.

Grossman, D. C., et al. 2005. Gun storage practices and risk of youth suicide and unintentional firearm injuries. *Journal of the American Medical Association* 293(6): 707–714.

Iudice, A., et al. 2005. Effects of prolonged wakefulness combined with alcohol and hands-free cell phone divided attention tasks on simulated driving. *Human Psychopharmacology* 20(2): 125–132.

Kilpatrick, D. 2004. Interpersonal violence and public policy: What about the victims? *Journal of Law, Medicine, and Ethics* 32(1): 73–81.

Krug, E. G. 2004. Injury surveillance is key to preventing injuries. *Lancet* 364(9445): 1563–1566.

McGwin, G., et al. 2003. The association between occupant restraint systems and risk of injury in frontal motor vehicle collisions. *Journal of Trauma* 54: 1182–1187.

National Center for Health Statistics. 2005. Deaths: Preliminary data for 2003. *National Vital Statistics Reports* 53(15).

National Center for Injury Prevention and Control. 2005. *Sexual Violence Fact Sheet* (http://www.cdc.gov/ncipc/factsheets/svfacts.htm; retrieved April 16, 2005).

National Center for Injury Prevention and Control. 2006. *Intimate Partner Violence Fact Sheet* (http://www.cdc.gov/ncipc/factsheets/ipvfacts.htm; retrieved September 21, 2006).

National Safety Council. 2006. *Injury Facts 2005–2006.* Itasca, Ill.: National Safety Council.

National School Safety Center. 2005. *Report on School Associated Violent Deaths* (http://www.schoolsafety.us/pubfiles/savd.pdf; retrieved September 21, 2006).

National Traffic Safety Administration. 2005. *Traffic Safety Facts Research Note: Driver Cell Phone Use in 2004—Overall Results.* Washington, D.C.: National Traffic Safety Administration.

Negrusz, A., et al. 2005. Estimate of the Incidence of Drug-Facilitated Sexual Assault in the U.S. (http://www.ncjrs.gov/pdffiles1/nij/grants/212000.pdf; retrieved September 21, 2006).

Olson, C. M., et al. 2006. Association of first- and second-generation air bags with front occupant death in car crashes: A matched cohort study. *American Journal of Epidemiology* 164(2): 161–169.

Quinlan, K. P., et al. 2005. Alcohol-impaired driving among U.S. adults, 1993–2002. *American Journal of Preventive Medicine* 28(4): 346–350.

Rosenfeld, R. 2004. The case of the unsolved crime decline. *Scientific American,* February.

Silverman, J. G., A. Raj, and K. Clements. 2004. Dating violence and associated sexual risk and pregnancy among adolescent girls in the United States. *Pediatrics* 114(2): e220–225.

Strayer, D. L., et al. 2006. A comparison of the cell phone driver and the drunk driver. *Human Factors* 48(2): 381–391.

Thompson, R. S., et al. 2006. Intimate partner violence: Prevalence, types and chronicity in adult women. *American Journal of Preventive Medicine* 30(6): 447–457.

UC Berkeley School of Public Health. 2006. Cycling: Use your head. *UC Berkeley Wellness Letter* 22(9): 6.

U.S. Department of State. 2002. *Patterns of Global Terrorism* (http://www.state.gov/s/ct/rls/pgtrpt/2001/html/10220.htm; retrieved September 21, 2006).

World Health Organization. 2004. *World Report on Road Traffic Injury Prevention.* Geneva: World Health Organization.

Zimmerman, F. J., et al. 2005. Early cognitive stimulation, emotional support, and television watching as predictors of subsequent bullying among grade-school children. *Archives of Pediatrics and Adolescent Medicine* 59(4): 384–388.

23

Looking AHEAD

After reading this chapter, you should be able to

- Describe the methods used to deal with the classic environmental concerns of clean water and waste disposal
- Discuss the effects of rapid increases in human population and list factors that may limit or slow world population growth
- Describe the short- and long-term effects of air, chemical, and noise pollution and exposure to radiation
- Outline strategies that individuals, communities, and nations can take to preserve and restore the environment

Environmental Health

Test Your Knowledge

1. The world's population, currently at about 6.5 billion, is increasing by about ____ people every minute
   a. 50
   b. 100
   c. 150

2. Where ozone gas occurs naturally in the upper atmosphere, it benefits human health by protecting Earth from harmful UV radiation; when created from pollutants released at ground level, ozone gas harms human health by negatively affecting respiratory function.
   True or false?

3. Which of the following statements about sport utility vehicles is true?
   a. They currently account for about half of all new vehicles sold.
   b. They get relatively poor gas mileage.
   c. They currently have weaker pollution standards than cars and so pollute more.

4. How many species (including plants and animals) are considered to be in serious danger of extinction?
   a. 160
   b. 1600
   c. 16,000

5. Most of the energy used by a standard incandescent lightbulb is converted into light.
   True or false?

ANSWERS

1. C. Although birth rates are declining, the world's population is expected to nearly double by 2200.
2. TRUE. "Good up high, bad nearby" is how the U.S. Environmental Protection Agency characterizes ozone. The primary source of ground-level ozone precursors is motor vehicle exhaust.
3. ALL THREE. Sport utility vehicles use more nonrenewable fuels and release more pollutants than more energy-efficient vehicles.
4. C. The World Conservation Union's "red list" of animals in serious danger of extinction now includes about 16,000 species, including the polar bear and hippopotamus.
5. FALSE. About 90% of the energy used by a standard bulb is wasted because it is given off as heat, not light. If each American replaced one incandescent bulb with a compact fluorescent, the yearly energy savings would equal the total production of four nuclear power plants.

Visit the *Core Concepts in Health* Online Learning Center (www.mhhe.com/insel10e) for study aids and many additional resources.

We are constantly reminded of our intimate relationship with all that surrounds us—our environment. Although the planet provides us with food, water, air, and everything else that sustains life, it also provides us with natural occurrences—earthquakes, tsunamis, hurricanes, drought, climate changes—that destroy life and disrupt society. In the past, humans frequently had to struggle against the environment to survive. Today, in addition to dealing with natural disasters, we also have to find ways to protect the environment from the byproducts of our way of life.

Environmental health has historically focused on preventing infectious diseases spread by water, waste, food, rodents, and insects. Although these problems still exist, the focus of environmental health has expanded and become more complex, for several reasons. We now recognize that environmental pollutants contribute not only to infectious diseases but to many chronic diseases as well. In addition, technological advances have increased our ability to affect and damage the environment. Also, rapid population growth, which has resulted partly from past environmental improvements, means that far more people are consuming and competing for resources than ever before, magnifying the effect of humans on the environment.

Environmental health is therefore seen as encompassing all the interactions of humans with their environment and the health consequences of these interactions. Fundamental to this definition is a recognition that we hold the world in trust for future generations and for other forms of life. Our responsibility is to pass on to the next generation an environment no worse, and preferably better, than the one we enjoy today (see the box "Nature and the Human Spirit"). Although many environmental problems are complex and seem beyond the control of the individual, there are ways that people can make a difference to the future of the planet.

CLASSIC ENVIRONMENTAL HEALTH CONCERNS

The field of environmental health grew out of efforts to control communicable diseases. When certain insects and rodents were found to carry microorganisms that cause disease in humans, campaigns were undertaken to eradicate or control these animal vectors. It was also recognized that pathogens could be transmitted in sewage, drinking water, and food. These discoveries led to systematic garbage collection, sewage treatment, filtration and chlorination of drinking water, food inspection, and the establishment of public health enforcement agencies.

These efforts to control and prevent communicable diseases changed the health profile of the developed world. Americans rarely contract cholera, typhoid fever, plague, diphtheria, or other diseases that once killed large numbers of people, but these diseases have not been eradicated worldwide. For example, more than 130,000 cases of cholera were reported in 2005, a 30% increase from 2004, according to the World Health Organization (WHO).

In the United States, a huge, complex, public health system is constantly at work behind the scenes attending to the details of these critical health concerns. Every time the system is disrupted, danger recurs. After any disaster situation that damages a community's public health system—whether a natural disaster such as Hurricane Katrina or a humanmade disaster such as a terrorist attack—prompt restoration of basic health services becomes crucial to human survival. Every time we venture beyond the boundaries of our everyday world, whether traveling to a less-developed country or camping in a wilderness area, we are reminded of the importance of these basics: clean water, sanitary waste disposal, safe food, and insect and rodent control.

We often take for granted the well-organized system responsible for environmental health in our society, but natural disasters remind us of its fragility. Flooding such as that caused by Hurricane Katrina in New Orleans and along the Gulf Coast in 2005 can cause widespread disruption in essential services such as the delivery of electricity, gas, and clean drinking water. Sewage-contaminated water can spread cholera, typhoid, hepatitis.

Nature and the Human Spirit

In this excerpt from her book *The Sense of Wonder*, noted scientist and author Rachel Carson affirms the nurturing power of the natural world and urges us to appreciate the deep relationship between nature and the human spirit.

> What is the value of preserving and strengthening this sense of awe and wonder, this recognition of something beyond the boundaries of human existence? Is the exploration of the natural world just a pleasant way to pass the golden hours of childhood or is there something deeper?
>
> I am sure there is something much deeper, something lasting and significant. Those who dwell, as scientists or laymen, among the beauties and mysteries of the earth are never alone or weary of life. Whatever the vexations or concerns of their personal lives, their thoughts can find paths that lead to inner contentment and to renewed excitement in living. Those who contemplate the beauty of the earth find reserves of strength that will endure as long as life lasts. There is symbolic as well as actual beauty in the migration of the birds, the ebb and flow of the tides, the folded bud ready for spring. There is something infinitely healing in the repeated refrains of nature—the assurance that dawn comes after night, and spring after the winter.

SOURCE: Carson, R. 1956. *The Sense of Wonder.* New York: Harper & Row.

Clean Water

Few parts of the world have adequate quantities of safe, clean drinking water, and yet few things are as important to human health.

Water Contamination and Treatment Many cities rely at least in part on wells that tap local groundwater, but often it is necessary to tap lakes and rivers to supplement wells. Because such surface water is more likely to be contaminated with both organic matter and pathogenic microorganisms, it is purified in water-treatment plants before being piped into the community. At treatment facilities, the water is subjected to various physical and chemical processes, including screening, filtration, and disinfection (often with chlorine), before it is introduced into the water supply system. **Fluoridation,** a water-treatment process that reduces tooth decay by 15–40%, has been used successfully in the United States for more than 60 years.

In most areas of the United States, water systems have adequate, dependable supplies, are able to control waterborne disease, and provide water without unacceptable color, odor, or taste. However, problems do occur. In 1993, more than 400,000 people became ill and 100 died when Milwaukee's drinking water was contaminated with the bacterium *Cryptosporidium.* The Centers for Disease Control and Prevention (CDC) estimate that 1 million Americans become ill and 900–1000 die each year from microbial illnesses from drinking water. Pollution by hazardous chemicals from manufacturing, agriculture, and household wastes is another concern. (Chemical pollution is discussed later in the chapter.) The *Healthy People 2010* report sets the goal of increasing from 85% to 95% the proportion of Americans with drinking water that meets standards set by the U.S. Environmental Protection Agency (EPA). Worldwide, more than 2 million people, mostly children, die from water-related diseases each year.

Water Shortages Water shortages are also a growing concern. Some parts of the United States are experiencing rapid population growth that outstrips the ability of local systems to provide adequate water to all. Many proposals are being discussed to relieve these shortages, including long-distance transfers; conservation; the recycling of some water, such as the water in office-building air conditioners; and the sale of water by regions with large supplies to areas with less available water.

According to the World Health Organization (WHO), 1 billion people do not have safe drinking water and 2.6 billion do not have access to basic sanitation. Less than 1% of the world's fresh water—about 0.007% of all the water on Earth—is readily accessible for direct human use. Groundwater pumping and the diversion of water from lakes and rivers for irrigation are further reducing the amount of water available to local communities. In some areas, groundwater is being removed at twice the rate at which it is replaced. The Aral Sea, located in Kazakhstan and Uzbekistan, was once one of the world's largest inland seas. Since the 1960s, it has lost two-thirds of its volume to irrigation, and the exposed seabed is now as big as the Netherlands. People living in the area have experienced severe water and food shortages and increased rates of respiratory disease and throat cancer linked to dust storms from the dry seabed. Due to agricultural diversions, the Yellow River ran dry for the first time in China's 3000-year history in 1972, failing to reach the sea for 15 days that

Terms

VW

environmental health The collective interactions of humans with the environment and the short-term and long-term health consequences of those interactions.

fluoridation The addition of fluoride to the water supply to reduce tooth decay.

year; now, the dry period extends for more than half of each year. In the United States, the Colorado River is now diverted to the extent that it no longer flows into the ocean.

What You Can Do to Protect the Water Supply

- Take showers, not baths, to minimize your water consumption. Don't let water run when you're not actively using it while brushing your teeth, shaving, or hand-washing clothes. Don't run a dishwasher or washing machine until you have a full load.
- Install sink faucet aerators and water-efficient showerheads, which use two to five times less water with no noticeable decrease in performance.
- Purchase a water-saver toilet, or put a displacement device in your toilet tank to reduce the amount of water used with each flush.
- Fix any leaky faucets in your house. Leaks can waste thousands of gallons of water per year.
- Use organic rather than chemical fertilizers, and don't overfertilize your lawn or garden; the extra could end up in the groundwater.
- Don't pour toxic materials such as cleaning solvents, bleach, or motor oil down the drain. Store them until you can take them to a hazardous waste collection center.
- Replant your lawn and garden with plants requiring less water. Avoid watering your lawn during the hottest part of the day to minimize evaporation.

Waste Disposal

Humans generate large amounts of waste, which must be handled in an appropriate manner if the environment is to be safe and sanitary.

Sewage Prior to the mid-nineteenth century, many people contracted diseases such as typhoid, cholera, and hepatitis A by direct contact with human feces, which were disposed of at random. Once the links between sewage and disease were discovered, practices began to change. People learned how to build sanitary outhouses and how to locate them so they would not contaminate water sources. As plumbing moved indoors, sewage disposal became more complicated. In rural areas, the **septic system,** a self-contained sewage disposal system, worked quite well. Today, many rural homes still rely on septic systems; however, in many areas more than 50% of old tanks are leaking contaminants into the environment.

Different approaches became necessary as urban areas developed. Most cities have sewage-treatment systems that separate fecal matter from water in huge tanks and ponds and stabilize it so that it cannot transmit infectious diseases. Once treated and biologically safe, the water is

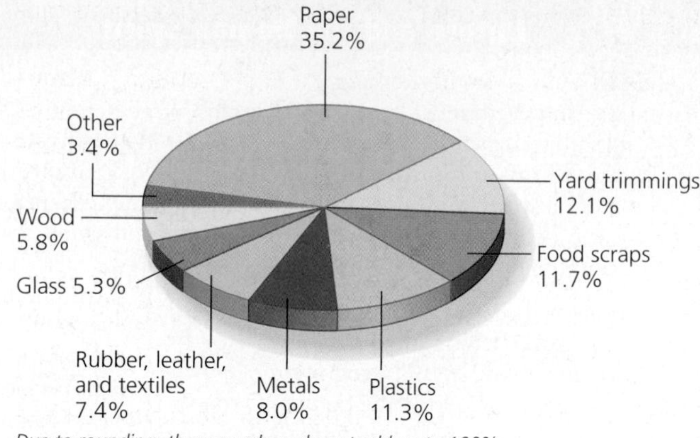

Due to rounding, these numbers do not add up to 100%.

VITAL STATISTICS

Figure 23-1 Components of municipal solid waste, by weight, before recycling. In 2003, the total amount of trash produced by U.S. residences, businesses, and institutions was the equivalent of 4.4 pounds of waste per person, per day, up from 2.7 pounds in 1960. SOURCE: Environmental Protection Agency. 2006. *Municipal Solid Waste: Basic Facts* (http://www.epa.gov/epaoswer/non-hw/muncpl/facts.htm; retrieved September 26, 2006).

released back into the environment. The sludge that remains behind is often contaminated with **heavy metals** and is handled as hazardous waste; if not contaminated, sludge may be used as fertilizer. If incorporated into the food chain, heavy metals, such as lead, cadmium, copper, and tin, can cause illness or death; therefore, these chemicals must be prevented from being released into the environment when sludge is burned or buried.

In addition to regulating industrial discharge, many cities have now begun expanded sewage-treatment measures to remove heavy metals and other hazardous chemicals. This action has resulted from many studies linking exposure to chemicals such as mercury, lead, and **polychlorinated biphenyls (PCBs)** with long-term health consequences, including cancer and damage to the central nervous system. The technology to effectively remove heavy metals and chemicals from sewage is still developing, and the costs involved are immense.

Solid Waste The bulk of the organic food garbage produced in American kitchens is now dumped in the sewage system by way of the mechanical garbage disposal. The garbage that remains is not very hazardous from the standpoint of infectious disease because there is very little food waste in it, but it does represent an enormous disposal and contamination problem.

WHAT'S IN OUR GARBAGE? The biggest single component of household trash by weight is paper products, including junk mail, glossy mail-order catalogs, and computer printouts (Figure 23-1). Yard waste, plastic, metals, and glass are other significant components. About 1% of the solid waste is toxic; a new source of toxic waste is the disposal of computer components in both household and commercial waste. Burning, as opposed to burial, reduces the bulk of solid waste, but it may release hazardous material into the air.

Solid waste is not limited to household products. Manufacturing, mining, and other industries all produce large amounts of potentially dangerous materials that cannot simply be dumped. At Love Canal (near Buffalo, New York), toxic industrial wastes had been dumped into a waterway for years until, in the 1970s, nearby residents began to suffer from associated birth defects and cancers. The government had to step in, people had to move from their homes, and huge costs were incurred.

DISPOSING OF SOLID WASTE Since the 1960s, much solid waste has been buried in **sanitary landfill** disposal sites. Careful site selection and daily management are an essential part of this approach to disposal. The site is thoroughly studied to ensure that it is not near groundwater, streams, or any other source of water that could be contaminated by leakage from the landfill. Sometimes protective liners are used around the site, and nearby monitoring wells are now required in most states. Layers of solid waste are regularly covered with thin layers of dirt until the site is filled. Some communities then plant grass and trees and convert the site into a park. Landfill is relatively stable; almost no decomposition occurs in the solidly packed waste.

Burying solid waste in sanitary landfills has several disadvantages. Much of this waste contains chemicals, ranging from leftover pesticides to nail polish remover to paints and oils, which should not be released indiscriminately into the environment. Despite precautions, buried contaminants do leak into the surrounding soil and groundwater. Burial is also expensive and requires huge amounts of space.

Industrial toxic waste poses an even greater disposal problem. In 1980, Congress enacted the Superfund program to clean up inactive hazardous waste sites that are a threat to human health and the environment. By 2005, cleanup was complete at 62% of priority sites, but further action was still needed at hundreds of priority sites; in 2005, the EPA added 18 new sites (and proposed 12 other sites) to its national priority list.

Because of the expense and potential chemical hazards of any form of solid waste disposal, many communities today encourage individuals and businesses to recycle their trash. Some cities offer curbside pickup of recyclables; others have recycling centers to which people can bring their waste. These materials are not limited to paper, glass, and cans but also include things such as discarded tires and used oils. Recycling is a good idea for two reasons. First, it puts unwanted objects back to good use. Second, it reduces the amount of solid waste sitting in landfills, some of which takes decades to biodegrade, or decay naturally. A plastic bottle, for example, may never biodegrade; a glass bottle can last a million years. Paper products usually decay in less than a year. Recycling programs have been successful in reducing the proportion of solid waste sent to landfills. In 1980, 81% went to landfills; in 2003, about 56%. (That year, about 30% of solid waste was recycled and 14% was burned.) However, the total amount of garbage Americans generate will probably continue to rise as the population increases, and researchers estimate that 80% of the nation's landfills will be closed within 20 years.

What You Can Do to Reduce Garbage

- Buy products with the least amount of packaging you can, or buy products in bulk (see the box "How to Be a Green Consumer"). For example, buy large jars of juice, not individually packaged juice drinks. Buy products packaged in glass, paper, or metal containers; avoid plastic and aluminum.
- Buy recycled or recyclable products. Avoid disposables; instead, use long-lasting or reusable products such as refillable pens and rechargeable batteries.
- Avoid using foam or paper cups and plastic stirrers by bringing your own china coffee mug and metal spoon to work or wherever you drink coffee or tea. Pack your lunch in reusable containers, and use a cloth or plastic lunch sack or a lunch box.
- To store food, use glass jars and reusable plastic containers rather than foil and plastic wrap.
- Recycle your newspapers, glass, cans, paper, and other recyclables. If you receive something packaged with foam pellets, take them to a commercial mailing center that accepts them for recycling.
- Do not throw electronic items, batteries, or fluorescent lights into the trash. Take all these to state-approved recycling centers; check with your local disposal service for more information.
- Start a compost pile for your organic garbage (nonanimal food and yard waste) if you have a yard. If you live in an apartment, you can create a small composting system using earthworms, or take your organic wastes to a community composting center.
- Stop junk mail. To cancel your junk mail, send a request to Mail Preference Service, Direct Marketing Association, P.O. Box 282, Carmel, NY 10512 (http://www.dmaconsumers.org).

Terms

VW

septic system A self-contained sewage disposal system, often used in rural areas, in which waste material is decomposed by bacteria.

heavy metal A metal with a high specific gravity, such as lead, copper, or tin.

polychlorinated biphenyl (PCB) An industrial chemical used as an insulator in electrical transformers and linked to certain human cancers.

sanitary landfill A disposal site where solid wastes are buried.

How to Be a Green Consumer

Critical Consumer

It may seem like a hassle to consider the environmental impact of the things you buy, but a few simple choices can make a big difference without compromising your lifestyle. You can quickly and easily develop habits that direct your consumer dollar toward environmentally friendly products and companies.

- Remember the four Rs of green consumerism:
  Reduce the amount of trash and pollution you generate by consuming and throwing away less.
  Reuse as many products as possible—either yourself or by selling them or donating them to charity.
  Recycle all appropriate materials and buy recycled products whenever possible.
  Respond by educating others about reducing waste and recycling, by finding creative ways to reduce waste and toxicity, and by making your preferences known.
- Choose products packaged in refillable, recycled, reusable containers or in readily recyclable materials, such as paper, cardboard, aluminum, or glass. Don't buy products that are excessively packaged or wrapped; for specific guidelines, see the section "What You Can Do to Reduce Garbage."
- Look for products made with the highest possible content of recycled paper, metal, glass, plastic, and other materials.
- Choose simple products containing the lowest amounts of bleaches, dyes, and fragrances. Look for organically grown foods and clothes made from organically grown cotton or Fox Fibre or another naturally colored type of cotton.
- Buy high-quality appliances that have an Energy Star seal from the EPA or some other type of certification indicating that they are energy- and water-efficient.
- Get a reusable cloth shopping bag. Don't bag items that don't need to be bagged. If you forget to bring your bag to the store, it doesn't matter much if you use a paper or plastic bag to carry your purchases home. What's important is that you reuse whatever bag you get.
- Don't buy what you don't need—borrow, rent, or share. Take good care of the things you own, repair items when they break, and replace them with used rather than new items whenever possible. Sell or donate used items rather than throwing them out.
- Walk or bike to the store. If you must drive, do several errands at once to save energy and cut down on pollution.
- Look beyond the products to the companies that make them. Support those with good environmental records. If some of your favorite products are overpackaged or contain harmful ingredients, write to the manufacturer.
- Keep in mind that doing something is better than doing nothing. Even if you can't be a perfectly green consumer, doing your best on any purchase *will* make a difference.

SOURCES: U.S. Environmental Protection Agency. 2006. *Consumer Handbook for Reducing Solid Waste* (http://www.epa.gov/epaoswer/non-hw/reduce/catbook/index.htm; retrieved September 26, 2006); Natural Resources Defense Council. 2006. NRDC's Guide to Greener Living (http://www.nrdc.org/cities/living/gover.asp; retrieved September 26, 2006).

Food Inspection

Diseases and death associated with foodborne illnesses and toxic food additives have decreased substantially ever since the passage of the Pure Food and Drug Act of 1906. Many agencies inspect food at various points in production. On the federal level, the U.S. Department of Agriculture (USDA) inspects grains and meats, and the U.S. Food and Drug Administration (FDA) is responsible for ensuring the wholesomeness of foods and regulating the chemicals that can be used in foods, drugs, and cosmetics. On the state level, public health departments inspect dairy herds, milking barns, storage tanks, tankers that transport milk, and processing plants. Local health departments inspect and license restaurants.

Overall, the food distribution system in the United States is safe and efficient, but cases of foodborne illness do occur. It is estimated that every American suffers an average of two or three episodes of foodborne illness every year. Recent outbreaks of serious illness have been traced to contaminated and undercooked fast-food hamburgers, unpasteurized juice, and imported produce. In 2006 raw spinach tainted with the *E. coli* bacterium sickened more than 200 people and caused more than three deaths in 26 states. The outbreak, traced to California, led to a nationwide recall of packaged raw spinach. Many cases of foodborne illness can be prevented through the proper storage and preparation of food (Chapter 12).

Insect and Rodent Control

Many illnesses can be transmitted to humans by animal and insect vectors. In recent years, we have seen outbreaks of encephalitis transmitted by mosquitoes; Lyme disease from ticks; Rocky Mountain spotted fever from another type of tick; bubonic plague from fleas on wild mammals in the West; and West Nile virus transmitted by mosquitoes. Rodents carry forms of hantavirus, tapeworms, and *Salmonella.*

Disability and death from these diseases can be prevented by spraying insecticides when necessary, wearing protective clothing, and exercising reasonable caution in infested areas. Individuals should be concerned about possible exposure to rodentborne illnesses if they see rodents or rodent droppings in the home. In public facilities, such sightings should be reported to the local or state health department. Children should be warned to never play with

VITAL STATISTICS

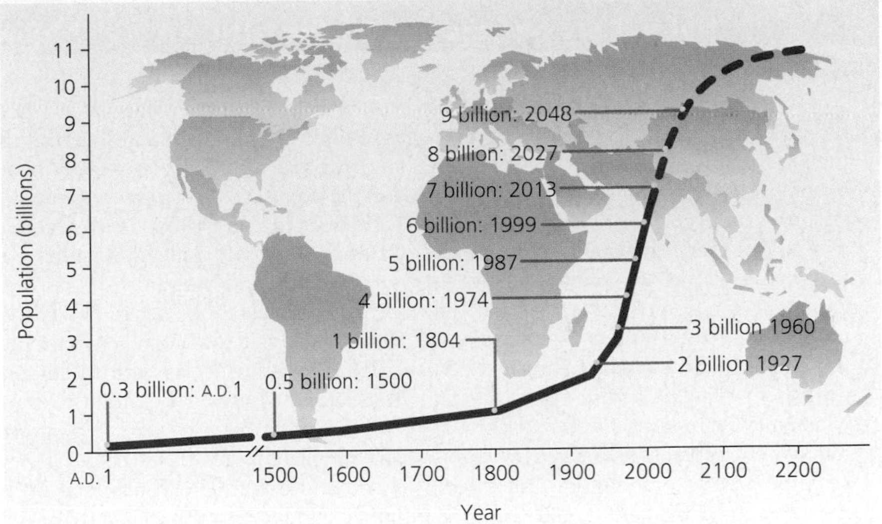

Figure 23-2 World population growth. The United Nations estimates that the world's population will continue to increase dramatically until it stabilizes above 10 billion people in 2200. SOURCES: United Nations Population Division. 2005. *World Population Prospects: The 2004 Revision.* New York: United Nations; U.S. Bureau of the Census.

sick animals. Travelers should be careful about mosquito bites, especially in developing countries and where disease warnings have been posted. For tips on avoiding tickborne and mosquitoborne illnesses, see Chapter 17.

POPULATION GROWTH

Throughout most of history, humans have been a minor pressure on the planet. About 300 million people were alive in the year A.D. 1; by the time Europeans were settling in the United States 1600 years later, the world population had increased gradually to a little over 500 million. But then it began rising exponentially—zooming to 1 billion by about 1800, more than doubling by 1950, and then doubling again in just 40 years (Figure 23-2).

The world's population, currently about 6.5 billion, is increasing at a rate of about 76 million per year—150 people every minute. The United Nations projects that world population will reach 9.1 billion by 2050 and will continue to increase until it levels off above 10 billion in 2200. Virtually all of this increase is taking place in less-developed regions. In 1950, the more-developed regions accounted for 32% of the world's population; their share dropped to 20% in 2000 and is expected to further decline to 13% in 2050. Changes are also projected for the world's age distribution: The proportion of people age 60 and over will increase from 10% in 2000 to 22% in 2050, and by 2050 there will be more older persons than children.

This rapid expansion of population, particularly in the past 50 years, is generally believed to be responsible for most of the stress humans put on the environment. A large and rapidly growing population makes it more difficult to provide the basic components of environmental health discussed earlier, including clean and disease-free food and water. It is also a driving force behind many of the relatively more recent environmental health concerns, including chemical pollution, global warming, and the thinning of the atmosphere's ozone layer.

How Many People Can the World Hold?

No one knows how many people the world can support, but most scientists agree that there is a limit. A 2006 report from the United Nation's Convention on Biological Diversity states that the population's demand for resources already exceed the earth's capacity by 20%. The primary factors that may eventually put a cap on human population are the following:

- *Food.* Enough food is currently produced to feed the world's entire population, but economic and sociopolitical factors have led to food shortages and famine. Food production can be expanded in the future, but better distribution of food will be needed to prevent even more widespread famine as the world's population continues to grow. For all people to receive adequate nutrition, the makeup of the world's diet may also need to change.
- *Available land and water.* Rural populations rely on trees, soil, and water for their direct sustenance, and a growing population puts a strain on these resources—forests are cut for wood, soil is depleted, and water is withdrawn at ever-rising rates. These trends contribute to local hardships and to many global environmental problems, including habitat destruction and species extinction (see the box "Natural Ecosystems and Biodiversity").
- *Energy.* Currently, most of the world's energy comes from nonrenewable sources: oil, coal, natural gas, and nuclear power. As nonrenewable sources are depleted, the world will have to shift to renewable energy sources, such as hydropower and solar, geothermal,

In Focus

Natural Ecosystems and Biodiversity

Our world supports an abundant variety of life. Scientists have identified some 1.75 million species, but they suspect that there are probably 10–80 million more. Different environments generate diverse life strategies, so that each **ecosystem**—from desert to tropical rainforest—contains a unique, close-knit community of organisms, linked together in a **food chain** or web. Plants use sunlight and soil for their needs. In turn, they sustain herbivores (plant eaters), which may themselves succumb to predators. When predators and surviving herbivores die, they become food for scavengers, then insect larvae, and finally bacteria, which break them down into organic substances. These substances, drawn from the soil by plants, help maintain the cycle. A similar system, based on plankton, exists in the oceans. Disruption at any point in this intricate, balanced cycle can alter or destroy an entire ecosystem.

Natural ecosystems provide humans with a wide variety of essential services. They maintain the climate and the composition of the atmosphere, cycle water and nutrients, produce food, dispose of organic wastes, generate and maintain soils, control pests, and pollinate crops; in addition, ecosystems support biological diversity, or **biodiversity,** represented by both the millions of different species on the earth and the genetic diversity within these species.

Biodiversity is critical as the basis for the future evolution of new species and as a genetic bank from which humans can draw useful genetic material and compounds. Although thus far we have examined few of these resources, the ones we have used provide many benefits, including medicines and pest and disease resistance for crops. For example, many children with leukemia can now be saved by drugs developed from the rosy periwinkle plant, and species of wild rice in India and wild tomato in Peru have provided domestic species with the disease resistance they need to be productive.

Human activity—driven by poverty and population growth in the developing world and excessive consumerism in the industrial nations—threatens biodiversity. In some cases, species and populations are being lost through direct action, such as the overharvesting of elephants, whales, and certain fish. In 2006, for example, an international team of researchers predicted the global collapse of seafood stocks in the world's oceans within 50 years if current fishing trends continue. In other cases, species and populations are lost indirectly, through habitat destruction. We are paving over, chopping down, digging up, draining, and poisoning many areas. The destruction of tropical rainforests, which are disappearing at the rate of an acre every second, is of particular concern. Rainforests cover only about 7% of the planet but are thought to harbor more than half the world's species. The World Conservation Union's "red list" of animals in serious danger of extinction now includes about 16,000 species, including the polar bear and hippopotamus.

Extinction is irreversible, and species are disappearing far faster (50–100 a day) than they can be identified and assessed for useful properties.The current extinction rate is nearly 1000 times higher than the rate over the past 65 million years. Some scientists fear that humans are precipitating a wave of mass extinction so great that the diminished stock of species will not be an adequate base on which natural selection can work to rebuild biodiversity. Even if adequate, it could take more than 10 million years for biodiversity to be restored. And because of the many ties between organisms and the physical environment, mass extinction could also threaten the functioning of the entire biological world.

What can be done to maintain biodiversity? The United States has laws that protect specific endangered species, which by indirectly preserving natural communities help maintain biodiversity. International laws and conventions also protect certain rare species, although enforcement continues to be a problem. The Convention on Biological Diversity, signed by more than 185 countries (but *not* the United States) since the 1992 Earth Summit in Rio de Janeiro, deals specifically with the issue of biodiversity. It commits countries to preserving and managing biological resources and to integrating plant and animal preservation into economic planning. It also allows countries that are rich in species but poor in cash to share in the profits from the sale of medicines or other products derived from their biological resources.

wind, biomass, and ocean power. Supporting a growing population, maintaining economic productivity, and preventing further environmental degradation will require both greater energy efficiency and an increased use of renewable energy sources.

- *Minimum acceptable standard of living.* The mass media have exposed the entire world to the American lifestyle and raised people's expectations of living at a comparable level. But such a lifestyle is supported by levels of energy consumption that the earth cannot support worldwide. The United States has about 5% of the world's population but uses 25% of the world's energy. In contrast, India has 16% of the population but uses only 3% of the energy. If *all* people are to enjoy a minimally acceptable standard of living, the population must be limited to a number that the available resources can support.

Factors That Contribute to Population Growth

Although it is apparent that population growth must be controlled, population trends are difficult to influence and manage. A variety of interconnecting factors fuel the current population explosion:

- *High fertility rates.* The combination of poverty, very high child mortality rates, and a lack of social provisions of every type is associated with high fertility rates in the developing world. Families may have to have more children to ensure that enough survive childhood to work for the household and to care for parents in old age.

- *Lack of family planning resources.* Half the world's couples don't use any form of family planning, and 300 million couples worldwide say they want family planning services but cannot get them.
- *Lower death rates.* Although death rates remain relatively high in the developing world, they have decreased in recent years because of public health measures and improved medical care.

Changes in any of these factors can affect population growth, but the issues are complex. Increasing death rates through disease, famine, or war might slow population growth, but few people would argue in favor of these as methods of population control. (The latest United Nations population estimates already project that there will be 344 million fewer people alive in 2050 than there would have been without deaths from HIV/AIDS.) Although the increased availability of family planning services is a crucial part of population management, cultural, political, and religious factors also need to be considered.

To be successful, population management must change the condition of people's lives, especially poverty, to remove the pressures for having large families. Research indicates that the combination of improved health, better education, and increased literacy and employment opportunities for women works together with family planning to decrease fertility rates. Unfortunately, in the fastest-growing countries, the needs of a rapidly increasing population use up financial resources that might otherwise be used to improve lives and ultimately slow population growth.

POLLUTION

As mentioned earlier, the classic environmental health concerns are not merely historical. They still have the potential to cause serious problems today under certain circumstances, and they take on added significance as our population grows. At the same time, new problems are arising, and some long-standing problems are gaining increased public attention. Many of these modern problems are problems of pollution. The term *pollution* refers to any unwanted contaminant in the environment that may pose a health risk.

Air Pollution

Air pollution is not a human invention or even a new problem. The air is polluted naturally with every forest fire, pollen bloom, and dust storm, as well as with countless other natural pollutants. To these natural sources, humans have always contributed the by-products of their activities. Air pollution is linked to a wide range of health problems; the very young and the elderly are among those most susceptible to air pollution's effects. For people with chronic ailments such as diabetes or heart failure, even relatively brief exposures to particulate air pollution increases the risk of death by as much as 39%. Researchers estimate that about 11,000 extra hospitalizations occur on high-pollution days, when fine particulate pollutants aggravate certain chronic conditions. Recent studies have linked exposure to air pollution to reduced birth weight in infants, reduced lung capacity in teens, and atherosclerosis (thickening of the arteries) in adults.

Air Quality and Smog The EPA uses a measure called the **Air Quality Index (AQI)** to indicate whether air pollution levels pose a health concern. The AQI is used for five major air pollutants:

- Carbon monoxide (CO): An odorless, colorless gas, CO forms when the carbon in **fossil fuels** does not completely burn. The primary sources of CO are vehicle exhaust and fuel combustion in industrial processes. CO deprives body cells of oxygen, causing headaches, fatigue, and impaired vision and judgment; it also aggravates cardiovascular diseases.
- Sulfur dioxide (SO_2): SO_2 is produced by the burning of sulfur-containing fuels such as coal and oil, during metal smelting, and by other industrial processes; power plants are a major source. SO_2 narrows the airways, which may cause wheezing, chest tightness, and shortness of breath, particularly in people with asthma; it may also aggravate symptoms of CVD.
- Nitrogen dioxide (NO_2): NO_2 is a reddish-brown, highly reactive gas formed when nitric oxide combines with oxygen in the atmosphere; major sources include motor vehicles and power plants. In people with respiratory diseases such as asthma, NO_2 affects lung function and causes symptoms such as wheezing and shortness of breath; NO_2 exposure may also increase the risk of respiratory infections.

Terms

Vw

ecosystem The community of organisms (plants and animals) in an area and the nonliving physical factors with which they interact.

food chain The transfers of food energy and other substances in which one type of organism consumes another.

biodiversity The variety of living things on the earth, including all the different species of flora and fauna and the genetic diversity among individuals of the same species.

Air Quality Index (AQI) A measure of local air quality and what it means for health. Concentrations of five major pollutants are measured and assigned index values between 0 and 500, with values above 100 considered unhealthy; the highest of the five values becomes the overall AQI for the day. Health warnings and recommendations may be issued when AQI values exceed 100.

fossil fuels Buried deposits of decayed animals and plants that are converted into carbon-rich fuels by exposure to heat and pressure over millions of years; oil, coal, and natural gas are fossil fuels.

• Particulate matter (PM): Particles of different sizes are released into the atmosphere from a variety of sources, including combustion of fossil fuels, crushing or grinding operations, industrial processes, and dust from roadways. PM can accumulate in the respiratory system and aggravate cardiovascular and lung diseases and increase the risk of respiratory infections. PM exposure is associated with increased rates of hospital admissions, physician visits, and premature death.

• Ground-level ozone: At ground level, ozone is a harmful pollutant; where it occurs naturally in the upper atmosphere, it shields the earth from the sun's harmful ultraviolet rays. (The health hazards from the thinning of this protective ozone layer are discussed later in the chapter.) Ground-level ozone is formed when pollutants emitted by cars, power plants, industrial boilers, refineries, chemical plants, and other sources react chemically in the presence of sunlight (photochemical reactions). Ozone can irritate the respiratory system, reduce lung function, aggravate asthma, increase susceptibility to respiratory infections, and damage the lining of the lungs. Short-term elevations of ozone levels have also been linked to increased death rates.

AQI values run from 0 to 500; the higher the AQI, the greater the level of pollution and associated health danger. When the AQI exceeds 100, air quality is considered unhealthy, at first for certain sensitive groups of people and then for everyone as AQI values get higher. For local areas, AQI values are calculated for each of the five pollutants listed above; the highest value becomes the AQI rating for that day. Depending on the AQI value, precautionary health advice may be provided; for example, see the AQI chart for ozone shown in Figure 23-3. Information on the AQI in your area is often available in newspapers, on television and radio, on the Internet, and from state and local telephone hotlines.

The term **smog** was first used in the early 1900s in London to describe the combination of smoke and fog. What we typically call smog today is a mixture of pollutants, with ground-level ozone being the key ingredient. Major smog occurrences are linked to the combination of several factors: Heavy motor vehicle traffic, high temperatures, and sunny weather can increase the production of ozone. Pollutants are also more likely to build up in areas with little wind and/or where a topographic feature such as a mountain range or valley prevents the wind from pushing out stagnant air.

A weather event called a **temperature inversion** also contributes to smog buildup. A temperature inversion occurs when there is little or no wind and a layer of warm air traps a layer of cold air next to the ground. Normally, the sun heats the earth, making the air closest to the ground warmer than that just above it. Warm air rises and is replaced by cooler air, which in turn is warmed and rises, thereby producing a natural circulation. This circulation, combined with horizontal wind circulation, prevents pollutants from reaching dangerous levels.

When there is a temperature inversion, this replacement and cleansing action cannot occur. The effect is like covering an area with a dome that traps all the pollutants

Index Values	Levels of Health Concern	Cautionary Statements
0–50	Good	None
51–100*	Moderate	Unusually sensitive people should consider limiting prolonged outdoor exertion.
101–150	Unhealthy for sensitive groups	Active children and adults, and people with respiratory disease, such as asthma, should limit prolonged outdoor exertion.
151–200	Unhealthy	Active children and adults, and people with respiratory disease, such as asthma, should avoid prolonged outdoor exertion; everyone else, especially children, should limit prolonged outdoor exertion.
201–300	Very unhealthy	Active children and adults, and people with respiratory disease, such as asthma, should avoid all outdoor exertion; everyone else, especially children, should limit outdoor exertion.
301–500	Hazardous	Everyone should avoid all outdoor exertion.

*Generally, an AQI of 100 for ozone corresponds to an ozone level of 0.08 parts per million (averaged over 8 hours).

Figure 23-3 Air Quality Index (AQI) for ozone. SOURCE: U.S. Environmental Protection Agency. 2000. *Air Quality Index: A Guide to Air Quality and Your Health.* Pub. no. EPA-454/R-00-005.

Terms

VW

smog Hazy atmospheric conditions resulting from increased concentrations of ground-level ozone and other pollutants. Smog most commonly occurs when oxides of nitrogen and hydrocarbons, primarily from motor vehicle exhaust, react in the presence of sunlight; also known as *photochemical smog*. (The term was first used to describe the combination of smoke and fog in early-twentieth-century London.)

temperature inversion A weather condition in which a cold layer of air is trapped by a warm layer so that pollutants cannot be dispersed.

greenhouse effect A warming of the earth due to a buildup of carbon dioxide and certain other gases.

global warming An increase in the earth's atmospheric temperature when averaged across seasons and geographical regions.

Smog tends to form over Los Angeles because of the natural geographical features of the area and because of the tremendous amount of motor vehicle exhaust in the air. The health effects of smog are most noticeable in people who already have some respiratory impairment.

and prevents vertical dispersion. If this condition persists for several days, the buildup of pollutants may reach dangerous levels and threaten people's health. Many cities have plans for shutting down certain industries and even curtailing transportation if unsafe levels are approached. State and federal governments have passed clean-air legislation that has helped improve U.S. air quality in the past 20 years. However, it is estimated that 60–130 million Americans still live in areas with unhealthy air. Many areas have elevated levels of ozone and/or particulate matter.

The Greenhouse Effect and Global Warming

The temperature of the earth's atmosphere depends on the balance between the amount of energy the planet absorbs from the sun (mainly as high-energy ultraviolet radiation) and the amount of energy radiated back into space as lower-energy infrared radiation. Key components of temperature regulation are carbon dioxide, water vapor, methane, and other greenhouse gases—so named because, like a pane of glass in a greenhouse, they let through visible light from the sun but trap some of the resulting infrared radiation and reradiate it back to the earth's surface. This reradiation causes a buildup of heat that raises the temperature of the lower atmosphere, a natural process known as the **greenhouse effect.** Without it, the atmosphere would be far cooler and much more hostile to life.

There is growing consensus that human activity is causing **global warming** (Figure 23-4). The concentration of

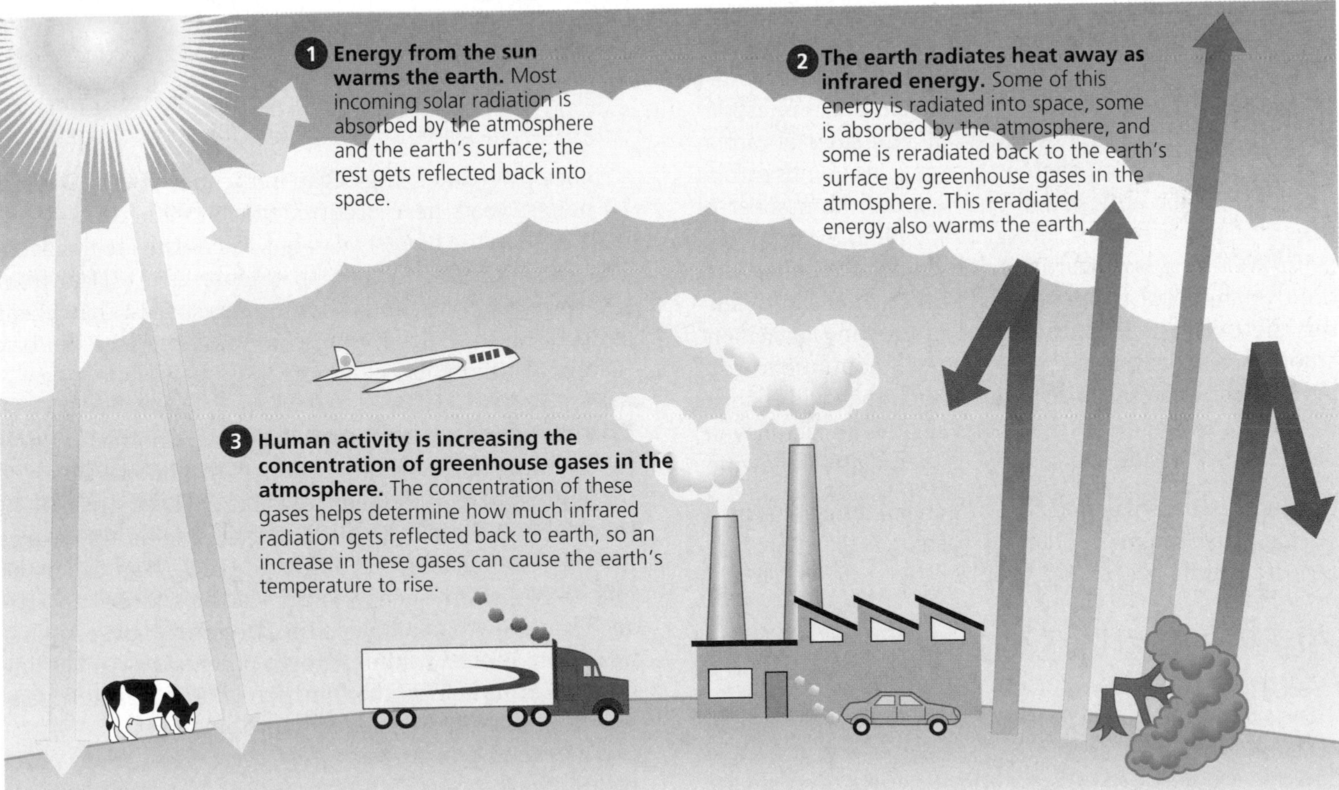

1 **Energy from the sun warms the earth.** Most incoming solar radiation is absorbed by the atmosphere and the earth's surface; the rest gets reflected back into space.
2 **The earth radiates heat away as infrared energy.** Some of this energy is radiated into space, some is absorbed by the atmosphere, and some is reradiated back to the earth's surface by greenhouse gases in the atmosphere. This reradiated energy also warms the earth.
3 **Human activity is increasing the concentration of greenhouse gases in the atmosphere.** The concentration of these gases helps determine how much infrared radiation gets reflected back to earth, so an increase in these gases can cause the earth's temperature to rise.

Figure 23-4 The greenhouse effect.

Table 23-1 Sources of Greenhouse Gases

Greenhouse Gas	Sources
Carbon dioxide	Fossil fuel and wood burning, factory emissions, car exhaust, deforestation
Chlorofluorocarbons (CFCs)	Refrigeration and air conditioning, aerosols, foam products, solvents
Methane	Cattle, wetlands, rice paddies, landfills, gas leaks, coal and gas industries
Nitrous oxide	Fertilizers, soil cultivation, deforestation, animal feedlots and wastes
Ozone and other trace gases	Photochemical reactions, car exhaust, power plant emissions, solvents

greenhouse gases is increasing because of human activity, especially the combustion of fossil fuels (Table 23-1). Carbon dioxide levels in the atmosphere have increased rapidly in recent decades. The use of fossil fuels pumps more than 20 billion tons of carbon dioxide into the atmosphere every year. In a recent report, the National Oceanic and Atmospheric Administration (NOAA) said atmospheric carbon dioxide levels have increased to a new high. Experts believe carbon dioxide may account for about 60% of the greenhouse effect. Analysis of ice core samples shows that carbon dioxide levels are now about 25% higher than at any other time in the last 650,000 years. The United States is responsible for one-third of the world's total emissions of carbon dioxide. Deforestation, often by burning, also sends carbon dioxide into the atmosphere and reduces the number of trees available to convert carbon dioxide into oxygen.

In 2006, the National Research Council reported that the overall global temperature had increased 0.6°C during the twentieth century. There is growing agreement among scientists that temperatures will continue to rise, although estimates vary as to how much they will change. If global warming persists, experts say the impact may be devastating. Possible consequences include the following:

- Increased rainfall and flooding in some regions, increased drought in others. Coastal zones, where half the world's people live, would be severely affected.

Terms

ozone layer A layer of ozone molecules (O_3) in the upper atmosphere that screens out UV rays from the sun.

chlorofluorocarbons (CFCs) Chemicals used as spray-can propellants, refrigerants, and industrial solvents, implicated in the destruction of the ozone layer.

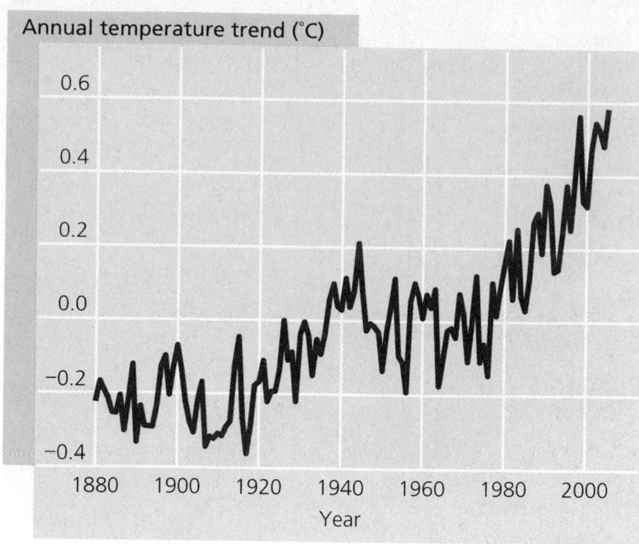

VITAL STATISTICS

Figure 23-5 Trend in annual mean temperature. This graph traces the trend in the annual mean temperature relative to the 1951–1980 mean value. There has been a strong warming trend over the past 30 years. SOURCE: Goddard Institute for Space Studies. 2006. GISS Surface Temperature Analysis, Global Temperature Trends: 2005 Summation (http://data.giss.nasa.gov/gistemp/2005; retrieved September 26, 2006).

- Increased mortality from heat stress, urban air pollution, and tropical diseases. Deaths from weather events such as hurricanes, tornadoes, droughts, and floods might also increase.
- A poleward shift of about 50–350 miles (150–550 km) in the location of vegetation zones, affecting crop yields, irrigation demands, and forest productivity.

Since record-keeping began in the mid-1800s, 9 of the 10 hottest years have occurred since 1990. 2005 is tied with 1998 as the hottest year, but when data are finalized, 2006 may surpass them both (Figure 23-5). Data from tree rings, ice cores, and other sources suggest that recent temperatures are the warmest in 400 years (see the box "Global Warming, Local Action").

Thinning of the Ozone Layer Another air pollution problem is the thinning of the **ozone layer** of the atmosphere, a fragile, invisible layer about 10–30 miles above the earth's surface that shields the planet from the sun's hazardous ultraviolet (UV) rays. Since the mid-1980s, scientists have observed the seasonal appearance and growth of a hole in the ozone layer over Antarctica. More recently, thinning over other areas—including Canada, Scandinavia, the northern United States, Russia, Australia, and New Zealand—has been noted.

The ozone layer is being destroyed primarily by **chlorofluorocarbons (CFCs)**, industrial chemicals used as coolants in refrigerators and in home and automobile air conditioners; as foaming agents in some rigid foam

Global Warming, Local Action

At current rates of consumption, we are using up the earth's resources so rapidly that they may run out sooner than anyone expects. Some experts say that humankind is already outstripping the planet's biological capacity by 20%. Indeed, a 2006 report from the Worldwatch Institute says that if fast-growing nations like China and India start using the earth's stores at the same rate as the United States, we will need the resources of *a second earth* to keep everyone satisfied.

But this problem has a second, more urgent part—that is, the way all those resources (especially minerals such as coal and oil) are being used. We use millions of tons of fossil fuel each year to power homes, cars, and factories. However unintentionally, we are also using them to destroy our planet.

Evidence of Global Warming

There is ample evidence that global warming is a reality. Here are just a few examples:

- Scientists have been measuring atmospheric carbon dioxide (CO_2) levels for years and say the amount of CO_2 is continually rising. In 2005, atmospheric CO_2 measured 380 parts per million (ppm), compared to about 290 ppm in 1850. At least one expert estimates that atmospheric CO_2 could reach 900 ppm by 2100, with a corresponding rise in global temperature of 5°–10°C.
- Glaciers and other large ice formations are melting at a quickening pace and shrinking measurably. The Greenland Ice Sheet, for example, is now melting at a rate of about 225 cubic kilometers each year. Such melting threatens to raise ocean levels around the world—possibly as much as 3 to 5 feet in the coming decades. In scenarios now envisioned, large swaths of coastline will be swamped and some small islands may disappear entirely.
- In a 2006 report, the World Health Organization said that ecological damage caused by human activities (such as burning fossil fuels and destroying forests and wetlands) is threatening our health. The report, with contributions from 1300 experts, predicted dramatic increases in disease during the next 50 years and warned that climate change could have catastrophic results in poor nations that already are unable to grow enough food or provide enough clean water for their people.

Despite the evidence, skepticism persists. Ironically, respected government agencies such as the National Oceanic and Atmospheric Administration (NOAA), NASA, and others have declared global warming to be a real phenomenon and a threat to humanity, yet many elected government officials dismiss such claims as faulty or incomplete science. In other countries, too, political and business leaders put climate change in second place after economic development. And one key component of Western-style economic development is the burning of fossil fuels to power industry and transportation.

Who Is Responsible?

To some degree, we are all responsible for climate change, just as we all stand to suffer because of it. Scientists can calculate just how much each person, house, car, appliance, and factory contributes to global warming; they call this measure an "environmental footprint." The footprint's size is determined by the amount of greenhouse gases the source generates, either directly (such as a car or factory) or indirectly (such as an electric appliance, which runs on electricity produced by a fossil-fuel-burning power plant). Here are some examples:

- For each gallon of gas your car burns, it releases about 20 pounds of CO_2 into the atmosphere. A midsize car puts out about 12,000 pounds of CO_2 per year; most SUVs put out about 22,000 pounds.
- A typical refrigerator is responsible for more than 2000 pounds of CO_2 annually. (The gas is actually released by a power plant; the amount is based on how much electricity the refrigerator uses.)
- A typical American home generates 28,000 pounds of greenhouse gases each year, both directly and indirectly.

Even though it isn't weightless, CO_2 is a gas. If you try to imagine how many CO_2 molecules it would take to make up a single pound, you can easily see why atmospheric CO_2 levels are increasing so rapidly.

What Is Being Done?

The need to slow climate change is undeniable and urgent. At the global level, many governments are taking initiatives to slow the release of greenhouse gases. One result of these efforts is the Kyoto Protocol to the United Nations Convention on Climate Change, which took effect in 2005. Under terms of this agreement, participating countries must reduce greenhouse gas emissions to an average of 5% below 1990 levels by 2012. The United States is not participating in the Kyoto Protocol, as government leaders contend the accord places too great a financial burden on industry and will stifle economic growth.

Individually, countries and states are making headway. Japan is building more nuclear power plants in an effort to reduce reliance on fossil fuel. The state of California recently added new emissions restrictions to its environmental laws, which are already the toughest in the United States—tougher, in fact, than federal pollution standards.

Industries are slowly getting on the bandwagon, too, although some must be forced to reduce their greenhouse emissions. Many companies are investing in cleaner fuel technology and "scrubbing" their emissions before they enter the environment. Du Pont, for example, has reduced its greenhouse gas emissions by 70% while decreasing energy use and increasing productivity.

Automakers are rapidly improving existing hybrid automobiles and making more models available, while focusing on the development of all-electric cars and hydrogen fuel cell technologies that virtually eliminate automotive pollution.

Individuals are making a difference, too. You can learn more about global warming and what it means to our future by checking out the organizations and Web sites listed in the For More Information section at the end of the chapter. To find out the size of your environmental footprint, visit www.myfootprint.org (what you learn may shock you). You can also follow the recommendations throughout this chapter to reduce your personal contribution to climate change.

products, including insulation; as propellants in some kinds of aerosol sprays (most such sprays were banned in 1978); and as solvents. When CFCs rise into the atmosphere, winds carry them toward the polar regions. During winter, circular winds form a vortex that keeps the air over Antarctica from mixing with air from elsewhere. CFCs react with airborne ice crystals, releasing chlorine atoms, which destroy ozone. When the polar vortex weakens in the summer, winds richer in ozone from the north replenish the lost Antarctic ozone.

Since 1979, about 15% of Antarctic ozone has been destroyed, although locally and seasonally up to 95% of the ozone disappears (forming the hole). The size and shape of the hole are affected by meteorological factors as well as by the presence of ozone-destroying chemicals. The 2000 ozone hole extended over populated areas of South America, where residents were advised to stay indoors and take other measures to avoid UV exposure. (UV radiation levels under the hole were high enough to cause sunburn within 7 minutes.) In the Northern Hemisphere, ozone levels have declined by about 10% since 1980, and certain areas may be temporarily depleted in late winter and early spring by as much as 40%. The largest and deepest ozone hole on record occurred in late September 2006, reaching 10.6 million square miles, considerably larger than the surface area of North America. The hole also had an unusual vertical extent, with nearly all the ozone between 8 and 13 miles above the Earth's surface destroyed.

Without the ozone layer to absorb the sun's UV radiation, life on Earth would be impossible. The potential effects of increased long-term exposure to UV light for humans include skin cancer, wrinkling and aging of the skin, cataracts and blindness, and reduced immune response. The United Nations Environment Programme predicts that a drop of 10% in overall ozone levels would cause a 26% rise in the incidence of nonmelanoma skin cancers. Some scientists blame ozone loss for many cases of melanoma.

UV light may interfere with photosynthesis and cause lower crop yields; it may also kill phytoplankton and krill, the basis of the ocean food chain. And because heat generated by the absorption of UV rays in the ozone layer helps create stratospheric winds, the driving force behind weather patterns, a drop in the concentration of ozone could potentially alter the earth's climate systems.

Worldwide production and use of CFCs have declined rapidly since the danger to the ozone layer was recognized. Industrialized nations agreed to eliminate CFC production and use by 2000, and limits have also been placed on other agents that destroy ozone. Metered-dose inhalers for conditions like asthma are the only significant commercial product to contain CFCs, and CFC-free inhalers are already available for some medications.

Ozone-depleting substances have very long lifetimes in the atmosphere, however, so despite these efforts, the ozone hole is expected to recover very slowly over the next 50 years. The gradual recovery is masked by annual variations caused by weather fluctuations over Antarctica. Scientists attribute the severity of the 2006 hole to record cold conditions in the Antarctic stratosphere; they expect recovery to continue.

Acid Precipitation A by-product of many industrial processes, **acid precipitation** occurs when atmospheric pollutants combine with moisture in the air and fall to earth as highly acidic rain, snow, sleet, or hail. It occurs especially when coal containing large amounts of sulfur is burned and sulfur dioxide, sulfur trioxide, nitrogen dioxide, nitric acid, and other chemicals are released into the atmosphere. These concentrations can be carried great distances by the prevailing winds and form a highly acidic mixture containing sulfuric acid and nitric acid. Most of the pollutants in acid precipitation are produced by coal-burning electric power plants. Other sources are motor vehicles and certain industrial activities, such as smelting.

Acidification of lakes and streams due to acid precipitation has completely eradicated fish and other aquatic species in some areas. Trees are also affected because acid precipitation damages leaves, strips the soil of key nutrients, and releases toxic substances such as heavy metals from the soil; in some areas of central Europe, entire forests are dying. The air pollutants that cause acid precipitation reduce visibility and cause respiratory problems in some people. Acid precipitation also corrodes metals and damages stone and paint on buildings, monuments, and cars; repairs can cost billions of dollars. Acid precipitation appears to be causing the most damage in Canada, the northeastern United States, Scandinavia, and parts of central Europe. In the United States, the areas most affected are the Adirondacks, the mid-Appalachian highlands, the upper Midwest, and high elevations in the West.

Energy Use and Air Pollution Americans are the biggest energy consumers in the world (Table 23-2). We use energy to create electricity, transport us, power our industries, and run our homes. About 85% of the energy we use comes from fossil fuels—oil, coal, and natural gas. The remainder comes from nuclear power and renewable energy sources (such as hydroelectric, wind, and solar power).

Energy consumption is at the root of many environmental problems, especially those relating to air pollution. Automobile exhaust and the burning of oil and coal by industry and by electric power plants are primary causes of smog, acid precipitation, and the greenhouse effect. The

Term

Ww

acid precipitation Rain, snow, sleet, or hail with a low pH (acid), caused by atmospheric moisture combining with products of industrial combustion to form acids such as sulfur dioxide; harmful to forests and lakes, which cannot tolerate changes in acidity/alkalinity.

VITAL STATISTICS

Table 23-2 Energy Use in Selected Countries, 2002

	Per Capita Energy Use (million Btu)
United States	342.7
Australia	264.5
Russia	208.8
France	186.1
Japan	177.7
United Kingdom	166.5
South Africa	115.2
Mexico	63.0
China	45.9
India	14.5

SOURCE: Energy Information Administration. 2006. *International Total Primary Energy Consumption and Energy Intensity: Per Capita (per Person) Total Primary Energy Consumption (Million BTU per Person): All Countries: 2004* (http://www.eia.doe.gov/emeu/international/energyconsumption.html; retrieved September 26, 2006).

mining of coal and the extraction and transportation of oil cause pollution on land and in the water; coal miners often suffer from serious health problems related to their jobs. Nuclear power generation creates hazardous wastes and carries the risk of dangerous releases of radiation.

Two key strategies for controlling energy use are conservation and the development of nonpolluting, renewable sources of energy. Although the use of renewable energy sources has increased in recent years, renewables still supply only a small proportion of our energy, in part because of their cost. Some countries have chosen to promote energy efficiency by removing subsidies or adding taxes on the use of fossil fuels. This strategy is reflected in the varying prices drivers pay for gasoline. According to the U.S. Energy Information Agency, the average U.S. per gallon price of unleaded gasoline was $2.38 in September 2006. Although U.S. gas prices are higher than in the past, they are still several dollars a gallon lower than in many European and Asian countries. It is not surprising that per-capita energy use in the United States is twice that of many European countries. The International Center for Technology Assessment estimates that the actual price of gasoline—including tax breaks, government subsidies, and environmental, health, and social costs of gas usage—is as high as $15.14 per gallon.

Despite increases in U.S. consumer gas prices, more than 70% of commuters drive alone to work, and low-fuel-economy sport utility vehicles (SUVs) remain popular. Every gallon of gas burned puts about 20 pounds of carbon dioxide into the atmosphere; some SUVs average fewer than 10 miles per gallon, and the largest SUVs increase greenhouse gas emissions by 6 or more tons per year more than an average car. A more positive U.S. trend has been the introduction of hybrid electric vehicles (HEVs), which combine a conventional internal combustion engine with an electric motor, resulting in about twice the fuel economy of conventional vehicles. Researchers hope that hybrid technology can be extended to all classes of vehicles and that Americans can be convinced to use more fuel-efficient vehicles and to travel more frequently on public transportation, in carpools, or on foot.

Indoor Air Pollution Although most people associate air pollution with the outdoors, your home may also harbor potentially dangerous pollutants. Some of these compounds trigger allergic responses, and others have been linked to cancer. Common indoor pollutants include the following:

- *Environmental tobacco smoke (ETS),* a human carcinogen that also increases the risk of asthma, bronchitis, and cardiovascular disease (see Chapter 11). Several states and cities have passed legislation known as Clean Indoor Air Acts, which state that any enclosed, indoor areas used by the public shall be smoke-free except for certain designated areas.
- *Carbon monoxide and other combustion by-products,* which can cause chronic bronchitis, headaches, dizziness, nausea, fatigue, and even death. Common sources in the home are woodstoves, fireplaces, kerosene heaters and lamps, and gas ranges. In poverty-stricken areas, especially in Asia and Africa, people commonly burn solid fuels like coal for cooking and heating their homes. The World Health Organization (WHO) says the smoke and by-products from these indoor fires kill about 1.5 million people annually—mostly children.
- *Formaldehyde gas,* which can cause eye, nose, and throat irritation; shortness of breath; headaches; nausea; lethargy; and, over the long term, cancer. This gas can seep from resins used in particle board, plywood paneling, and some carpeting and upholstery; it is also emitted by certain paints and floor finishes, permanent press clothing, and nail polish.
- *Biological pollutants,* including bacteria, dust mites, mold, and animal dander, which can cause allergic reactions and other health problems. These allergens are typically found in bathrooms, damp or flooded basements, humidifiers, air conditioners, and even some carpets and furniture.

What You Can Do to Prevent Air Pollution

- Cut back on driving. Ride your bike, walk, use public transportation, or carpool in a fuel-efficient vehicle.
- Keep your car tuned up and well maintained. Use only unleaded gas, and keep your tires inflated at recommended pressures. To save energy when driving, avoid quick starts, stay within the speed limit, limit the use of air conditioning, and don't let your car idle unless absolutely necessary. Have your car's air conditioner checked and serviced by a station

A key strategy for reducing air pollution and greenhouse gas emissions is to reduce energy consumption. Most people drive alone to commute to work or school; try to cut back on your solo driving time by riding your bike, walking, carpooling, or using public transportation.

that uses environmentally friendly refrigerants (car air conditioners made before 1994 are a major source of CFCs).

- Buy energy-efficient appliances, and use them only when necessary. Run the washing machine, dryer, and dishwasher only when you have full loads, and do laundry in warm or cold water instead of hot; don't overdry your clothes. Clean refrigerator coils and clothes dryer lint screens frequently. Towel or air-dry your hair rather than using an electric dryer.
- Replace incandescent bulbs with compact fluorescent bulbs (not fluorescent tubes). Although they cost more initially, they'll save you money over the life of the bulb. They produce a comparable light, last longer, and use only 25–35% of the energy of a regular bulb, thereby lowering carbon dioxide emissions from electric power plants.
- Make sure your home is well-insulated with ozone-safe agents; use insulating shades and curtains to keep heat in during winter and out during summer. Seal any openings that produce drafts. In cold weather, put on a sweater and turn down the thermostat. In hot weather, wear lightweight clothing and, whenever possible, use a fan instead of an air conditioner to cool yourself.
- Plant and care for trees in your own yard and neighborhood. Because they recycle carbon dioxide, trees work against global warming. They also provide shade and cool the air, so less air conditioning is needed.
- Before discarding a refrigerator, air conditioner, or humidifier, check with the waste hauler or your local government to ensure that ozone-depleting refrigerants will be removed prior to disposal.
  If you use a metered-dose inhaler, ask your physician if an ozone-safe inhaler is available for your medication.
- To prevent indoor air pollution, keep your house adequately ventilated, and buy some houseplants; they have a natural ability to rid the air of harmful pollutants.
- Keep paints, cleaning agents, and other chemical products tightly sealed in their original containers.
- Don't smoke, and don't allow others to smoke in your room, apartment, or home. If these rules are too strict for your situation, limit smoking to a single, well-ventilated room.
- Clean and inspect chimneys, furnaces, and other appliances regularly. Install carbon monoxide detectors.

Chemical Pollution

Chemical pollution is by no means a new problem. The ancient Romans were plagued by lead poisoning; industrial chemicals have claimed countless lives over the past few centuries.

Today, new chemical substances are constantly being introduced into the environment—as pesticides, herbicides, solvents, and hundreds of other products. More people and wildlife are exposed and potentially exposed to them than ever before. Many chemicals are harmless by themselves but become deadly in combination. A 2006 study of a single Nebraska cornfield revealed nine chemicals present in the soil and water; the combination was shown to cause illness, slow maturation, deformities, and higher mortality rates in nearby wildlife.

Chemical pollutants have been responsible for several environmental disasters, including thousands of deaths and injuries among people in Bhopal, India, that occurred when a powerful chemical used in manufacturing the insecticide Sevin was released from a plant. Catastrophes illustrate the short-term potential for disaster, but the long-term health consequences may be just as deadly. The following are brief descriptions of just a few current problems.

Asbestos A mineral-based compound, asbestos was widely used for fire protection and insulation in buildings until the late 1960s. Microscopic asbestos fibers can be released into the air when this material is applied or when it later deteriorates or is damaged. These fibers can lodge in the lungs, causing **asbestosis**, lung cancer, and other serious lung diseases. Similar conditions expose workers to risk in the coal mining industry, from coal and silica dust (black lung disease), and in the textile industry, from cotton fibers (brown lung disease).

Asbestos can pose a danger in homes and apartment buildings, about 25% of which are thought to contain some asbestos. Areas where it is most likely to be found are insulation around water and steam pipes, ducts, and furnaces; boiler wraps; vinyl flooring; floor, wall, and ceiling insulation; roofing and siding; and fireproof board. An experienced contractor can pinpoint asbestos-

Dimensions of Diversity

Poverty and Environmental Health

Residents of poor and minority communities are often exposed to more environmental toxins than residents of wealthier communities, and they are more likely to suffer from health problems caused or aggravated by pollutants. Poor neighborhoods are often located near highways and industrial areas that have high levels of air and noise pollution; they are also common sites for hazardous waste production and disposal. Residents of substandard housing are more likely to come into contact with lead, asbestos, carbon monoxide, pesticides, and other hazardous pollutants associated with peeling paint, old plumbing, poorly maintained insulation and heating equipment, and attempts to control high levels of pests such as cockroaches and rodents. Poor people are more likely to have jobs that expose them to asbestos, silica dust, and pesticides, and they are more likely to catch and consume fish contaminated with PCBs, mercury, and other toxins.

The most thoroughly researched and documented link among poverty, the environment, and health is lead poisoning in children. Many studies have shown that children of low-income black families are much more likely to have elevated levels of lead in their blood than white children. One survey found that two-thirds of urban African American children from families earning less than $6000 a year had elevated lead levels. The CDC and the American Academy of Pediatrics recommend annual testing of blood lead levels for all children under age 6, with more frequent testing for children at special risk.

Asthma is another health threat that appears to be linked with both environmental and socioeconomic factors. The number of Americans with asthma has grown dramatically in the past 20 years; most of the increase has occurred in children, with African Americans and the poor hardest hit. Researchers are not sure what accounts for this increase, but suspects include household pollutants, pesticides, air pollution, cigarette smoke, and allergens like cockroaches. These risk factors are likely to cluster in poor urban areas where inadequate health care may worsen asthma's effects.

A new push for research on the health effects of exposure to toxins on low-income communities is being called for by the environmental justice movement. New studies are investigating the links between environmental factors and respiratory problems, skin diseases, and cancer. While health researchers seek to quantify the health effects, neighborhood activists continue to fight against the dumping of pollution in poor communities.

containing materials in a home; they can then be analyzed by a laboratory. If any of these materials begin to release asbestos fibers, the asbestos must be sealed off, encapsulated, or removed by a professional.

Lead Lead poisoning continues to be a serious problem, particularly among children living in older buildings and adults who are exposed to lead in the workplace. The CDC estimates that about 435,000 children under age 6 may have unsafe lead levels in their blood but says the actual number could be much higher. Many of these children live in poor, inner-city areas (see the box "Poverty and Environmental Health"). When lead is ingested or inhaled, it can damage the central nervous system, cause mental impairment, hinder oxygen transport in the blood, and create digestive problems. A 2006 study linked lead exposure to some cases of ADHD in children. Severe lead poisoning may cause coma or even death. Neurological damage can be permanent. Lead damage to the brain can start even before birth if a pregnant woman has elevated levels of lead in her body.

Long-term exposure to low levels of lead may cause kidney disease; it can also cause lead to build up in bones, where it may be released into the bloodstream during pregnancy or when bone mass is lost from osteoporosis. The increased lead levels that occur as women age and lose bone mass can cause hypertension.

Young children can easily ingest lead from their environment by picking up dust and dirt on their hands and then putting their fingers in their mouth. Lead-based paints are the chief culprit in lead poisoning of children and were banned from residential use in 1978, but as many as 57 million American homes still contain lead paint. In 2006, the EPA proposed new guidelines requiring contractors to take special lead-containment measures when doing renovations, repairs, or painting in certain buildings. The use of lead in plumbing is now also banned, but some old pipes and faucets contain lead.

Lead gets into the air from industrial and vehicle emissions, from tobacco smoke and paint dust, and from the burning of solid wastes that contain lead. Levels of lead in the air have dropped sharply as leaded gas use has declined, but many vehicles still use leaded fuel. Lead occurs naturally in soil, which also collects lead from the air and other sources.

Pesticides **Pesticides** are used primarily for two purposes: to prevent the spread of insectborne diseases and to maximize food production by killing insects that eat

Terms

VW

asbestosis A lung condition caused by inhalation of microscopic asbestos fibers, which inflame the lung and can lead to lung cancer.

pesticides Chemicals used to prevent the spread of diseases transmitted by insects and to maximize food production by killing insects that eat crops.

crops. Both uses have risks as well as benefits. Take, for example, the pesticide DDT. Recognized as a powerful pesticide in 1939, DDT was extremely important in efforts to control widespread insectborne diseases in tropical countries and increase crop yields throughout the world. In 1962, biologist Rachel Carson questioned the safety of DDT in her book *Silent Spring,* pointing out that the pesticide disrupts the life cycles of birds, fish, and reptiles. DDT also builds up in the food chain, increasing in concentration as larger animals eat smaller ones, a process known as **biomagnification.** Despite its effectiveness as a pesticide, DDT was banned in the United States in 1972 because the costs associated with its use—to wildlife and potentially to humans—were too high. Most pesticide hazards to date have been a result of overuse, but there are concerns about the health effects of long-term exposure to small amounts of pesticide residues in foods, especially for children.

Mercury A naturally occurring metal, mercury is a toxin that affects the nervous system and may damage the brain, kidneys, and gastrointestinal tract; increase blood pressure, heart rate, and heart attack risk; and cause cancer. Mercury slows fetal and child development and causes irreversible deficits in brain function. As many as 600,000 babies are born each year after being exposed to levels of mercury that some studies have shown to have adverse health effects. A 2005 study estimated that the economic cost of the effects of mercury on children's brain development is $8.7 billion annually. Coal-fired power plants are the largest producers of mercury; other sources include mining and smelting operations and the disposal of consumer products containing mercury.

Mercury persists in the environment, and, like pesticides, it is bioaccumulative. In particular, large, long-lived fish may carry high levels of mercury. The FDA recommends that pregnant women, women of childbearing age who may become pregnant, women who are breastfeeding, and young children not consume shark, swordfish, king mackerel, and tilefish and limit total fish consumption to 12 ounces per week. Chapter 12 includes more information on safe fish consumption; see the box "Gender and Environmental Health" for more on issues affecting pregnant women.

Because of health concerns, some cities and stores have banned the sale of mercury fever thermometers, a small but significant source of mercury. If a thermometer breaks or is disposed of improperly, mercury can enter the environment; if it vaporizes into the atmosphere, it can be hazardous to health. To safely clean up mercury from a broken thermometer, increase ventilation in the room and pick up the mercury with an eyedropper or scoop up the beads with a piece of heavy paper. Dispose of it and any contaminated instruments by placing them in a plastic bag and taking them to an appropriate hazardous waste disposal site. Replace mercury thermometers with one of the many mercury-free alternatives.

The list of real and potential chemical pollution problems may well be as long as the list of known chemicals. To the preceding examples we can add recent concern about arsenic in drinking water, formaldehyde in synthetic building materials, prescription medications and hormones in streams, and other by-products of our industrial age. As mentioned earlier, hazardous wastes are also found in the home and should be handled and disposed of properly. They include automotive supplies (motor oil, antifreeze, transmission fluid), paint supplies (turpentine, paint thinner, mineral spirits), art and hobby supplies (oil-based paint, solvents, acids and alkalis, aerosol sprays), insecticides, batteries, computer and electronic components, and household cleaners containing sodium hydroxide (lye) or ammonia. These chemicals are dangerous when inhaled or ingested, when they contact the skin or the eyes, or when they are burned or dumped. Many cities provide guidelines about approved disposal methods and have hazardous waste collection days. Look in the government pages of your phone book under Environmental Health or Hazardous Waste.

What You Can Do to Prevent Chemical Pollution

- When buying products, read the labels, and try to buy the least toxic ones available. Choose nontoxic nonpetrochemical cleansers, disinfectants, polishes, and other personal and household products.
- Dispose of your household hazardous wastes properly. If you are not sure whether something is hazardous or don't know how to dispose of it, contact your local environmental health office or health department. Don't burn trash.
- Buy organic produce or produce that has been grown locally. Wash, scrub, and, if appropriate, peel fruits and vegetables. Consider eating less meat; animal products require more pesticides, fertilizer, water, and energy to produce.
- If you must use pesticides or toxic household products, store them in a locked place where children and pets can't get to them. Don't measure chemicals with food-preparation utensils, and wear gloves whenever handling them.

Terms

Vw

biomagnification The accumulation of a substance in a food chain.

radiation Energy transmitted in the form of rays, waves, or particles.

radiation sickness An illness caused by excess radiation exposure, marked by low white blood cell counts and nausea; possibly fatal.

nuclear power The use of controlled nuclear reactions to produce steam, which in turn drives turbines to produce electricity.

Gender Matters

Gender and Environmental Health

Although many environmental health risks are shared by all, some risks disproportionately affect women or men. Women and men often have different roles and responsibilities with respect to family, community, and the workforce. These differences can determine the types of environmental hazards that individuals are exposed to and what the potential risks of those exposures are.

In many societies, women are more often involved in day-to-day activities associated with the environment, including food preparation, agricultural work, and tasks around the home. These activities can expose women to greater levels of indoor air pollution, water pollution, foodborne pathogens, agricultural chemicals, and waste contamination. Indoor pollutants, especially soot from burning wood, charcoal, and other solid fuels used for home heating and cooking, are a particular risk for women. Exposure to this particulate pollution increases the risk of respiratory diseases, lung cancer, and reproductive problems.

All humans are exposed to chemicals in air, food, and drinking water, and we all carry a body load of chemicals. Some of these chemicals bioaccumulate in our bones, blood, or fatty tissues. Women are smaller than men, on average, and have a higher percentage of body fat; so chemicals that accumulate in fatty tissue may pose a relatively greater risk for women. On the other hand, men may be more likely to work in industries that involve significant occupational exposures to disease-related toxins; for example, coal miners have an increased risk of lung cancer (black lung disease).

Although any chemical exposure can be a concern for health, women face the added risk of passing pollutants to a developing fetus during pregnancy or to an infant through breastfeeding. Even relatively low exposure to pollutants can result in a significant chemical body load in an infant or young child because of their small body size. And because infants and children are still developing, the effects of chemical exposure can be significant and devastating. It is not unusual for dangerous environmental toxin exposures to be first recognized through noticeable effects on infants or children.

Reproductive risks are not limited to women and infants in developing parts of the world. Even in industrialized countries with strong environmental laws, infants and children are affected by such chemicals as lead and mercury. In 2005, scientists announced that they had found elevated levels of the rocket fuel chemical perchlorate in human breast milk in amounts above the safe dose set by the National Academy of Sciences. Many other chemicals, including PCBs and pesticides, have already been found in breast milk.

Studies are ongoing to identify and reduce environmental hazards in the United States and throughout the world. However, many of the people most directly affected by environmental health problems—women, children, and people living in poor communities—have limited economic, social, and political power. It is important that everyone affected by environmental problems be given a voice in determining environmental policies.

SOURCES: Kirk, A. B., et al. 2005. Perchlorate and iodide in dairy and breast milk. *Environmental Science and Technology*, Web release, February 22; McCally, M., ed. 2002. *Life Support: The Environment and Human Health.* Cambridge, Mass.: MIT Press; Population Reference Bureau. 2002. *Women, Men, and Environmental Change: The Gender Dimensions of Environmental Policies and Programs.* Washington, D.C.: Population Reference Bureau.

- If you have your house fumigated for pest control, be sure to hire a licensed exterminator. Keep everyone, including pets, out of the house while the crew works and, if possible, for a few days after.

Radiation

Many people are afraid of **radiation,** in part because they don't understand what it is. Basically, radiation is energy. It can come in different forms, such as ultraviolet rays, microwaves, or X rays, and from different sources, such as the sun, uranium, and nuclear weapons (Figure 23-6, p. 712). These forms of electromagnetic radiation differ in wavelength and energy, with shorter waves having the highest energy levels. Of most concern to health are gamma rays produced by radioactive sources such as nuclear weapons, nuclear energy plants, and radon gas; these high-energy waves are powerful enough to penetrate objects and break molecular bonds. Although gamma radiation cannot be seen or felt, its effects at high doses can include **radiation sickness** and death; at lower doses, chromosome damage, sterility, tissue damage, cataracts, and cancer can occur. Other types of radiation can also affect health; for example, exposure to UV radiation from the sun or from tanning salons can increase the risk of skin cancer. The effects of some sources of radiation, such as cell phones, remain controversial.

Nuclear Weapons and Nuclear Energy Nuclear weapons pose a health risk of the most serious kind to all species. Public health associations have stated that in the event of an intentional or unintentional discharge of these weapons, the casualties would run into the hundreds of thousands or millions. Reducing these stockpiles is a challenge and a goal for the twenty-first century.

Power-generating plants that use nuclear fuel also pose health problems. When **nuclear power** was first developed as an alternative to oil and coal, it was promoted as clean, efficient, inexpensive, and safe. In general, this has proven to be the case. Power systems in several parts of the world rely on nuclear power plants. However, despite all the built-in safeguards and regulating agencies, accidents in nuclear power plants do happen, many due to human error (as at Three Mile Island in the United States and Tokaimura in Japan), and the consequences of such accidents are far more

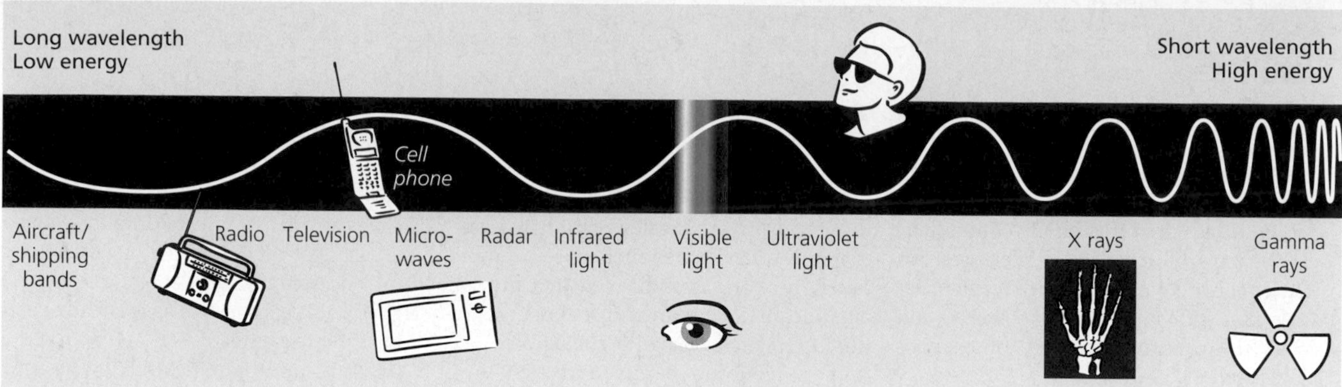

Figure 23-6 Electromagnetic radiation. Electromagnetic radiation takes the form of waves that travel through space. The length of the wave determines the type of radiation: The shortest waves are high-energy gamma rays; the longest are radio waves and extremely low frequency waves used for communication between aircraft, ships, and submarines. Different types of electromagnetic radiation have different effects on health.

serious than those of similar accidents in other types of power-generating plants. The 1986 fire and explosion at the Chernobyl nuclear power station in Ukraine caused hundreds of deaths and increased rates of genetic mutation and cancer; the long-term effects are not yet clear. The zone around Chernobyl has been sealed off to human habitation and could be unsafe for the next 24,000 years.

An additional, enormous problem is disposing of the radioactive wastes these plants generate. They cannot be dumped in a sanitary landfill because the amount and type of soil used to cap a sanitary landfill are not sufficient to prevent radiation exposure. Deposit sites have to be developed that will be secure not just for a few years but for tens of thousands of years—longer than the total recorded history of human beings on this planet. To date, no storage method has been devised that can provide infallible, infinitely durable shielding for nuclear waste.

Medical Uses of Radiation Another area of concern is the use of radiation in medicine, primarily the X ray. The development of machines that could produce images of internal bone structures was a major advance in medicine, and applications abounded. Chest X rays were routinely given to screen for tuberculosis, and children's feet were even X rayed in shoe stores to make sure their new shoes fit properly. But, as is often the case, this new technology had disadvantages. As time passed, studies revealed that X ray exposure is cumulative and that no exposure is absolutely safe.

Early X ray machines are no longer used because of the high amounts of radiation they give off. Each new generation of X ray machines has used less radiation more effectively. From a personal health point of view, individuals should never have a routine X ray examination; each such exam should have a definite purpose, and its benefits and risks should be carefully weighed.

Radiation in the Home and Workplace Recently, there has been concern about electromagnetic radiation associated with common modern devices such as microwave ovens, computer monitors, cell phones, and even high-voltage power lines. These forms of radiation do have effects on health, but research results are inconclusive.

Another area of concern is **radon,** a naturally occurring radioactive gas found in certain soils, rocks, and building materials. When the breakdown products of radon are inhaled, they cling to lungs and bombard sensitive tissue with radioactivity. Among miners, exposure to high levels of radon has been shown to cause lung cancer; overall, it is the second leading cause of lung cancer in the United States, after smoking tobacco. Radon can enter a home by rising through the soil into the basement through dirt floors, cracks, and other openings.

In 2005, the Surgeon General issued a national health advisory on radon, recommending that Americans test their homes for radon every 2 years, and retest any time they move, make structural changes to a home, or occupy a previously unused level of a residence. If elevated levels of radon are found (4 pCi/L or more), the problem should be dealt with as soon as possible through such measures as sealing cracks or installing basement ventilation systems.

Terms

VW

radon A naturally occurring radioactive gas emitted from rocks and natural building materials that can become concentrated in insulated homes, causing lung cancer.

decibel A unit for expressing the relative intensity of sounds on a scale from 0 for the average least perceptible sound to about 120 for the average pain threshold.

tinnitus Ringing in the ears, a condition that can be caused by excessive noise exposure.

More information is available at the EPA Web site or by calling 1-800-SOS-RADON.

What You Can Do to Avoid Radiation

- If your physician orders an X ray, ask why it is necessary. Only get X rays that you need, and keep a record of the date and location of every X ray exam. Don't have a full-body CT scan for routine screening; the radiation dose of one full-body CT scan is nearly 100 times that of a typical mammogram.
- Follow the Surgeon General's recommendations for radon testing.
- Find out if there are radioactive sites in your area. If you live or work near such a site, form or join a community action group to get the site cleaned up.

Noise Pollution

We are increasingly aware of the health effects of loud or persistent noise in the environment. Concerns focus on two areas: hearing loss and stress. Prolonged exposure to sounds above 80–85 **decibels** (a measure of the intensity of a sound wave) can cause permanent hearing loss (Figure 23-7). Two common sources of excessive noise are the workplace and large gatherings of people at sporting events and rock concerts. The Occupational Safety and Health Administration (OSHA) sets legal standards for noise in the workplace, but no laws exist regulating noise levels at rock concerts, which can be much louder than most workplaces.

Most hearing loss occurs in the first 2 hours of exposure, and hearing usually recovers within 2 hours after the noise stops. But if exposure continues or is repeated frequently, hearing loss may be permanent. The employees of a club where rock music is played loudly are at greater risk than the patrons of the club, who might be exposed for only 2 hours at a time. Another possible effect of exposure to excessive noise is **tinnitus**, a condition of more or less continuous ringing or buzzing in the ears.

Excessive noise is also an environmental stressor, producing the typical stress response described in Chapter 2.

What You Can Do to Avoid Noise Pollution

- Wear ear protectors when working around noisy machinery.
- When listening to music on a headset with a volume range of 1–10, keep the volume no louder than 6; your headset is too loud if you are unable to hear people around you speaking in a normal tone of voice. Earmuff-style headphones may be easier on the ears than earbuds, which are inserted into the ear canal. Experts warn that earbuds should not be used more than 30 minutes a day unless the volume is set below 60% of maximum; headphones can be used up to 1 hour.

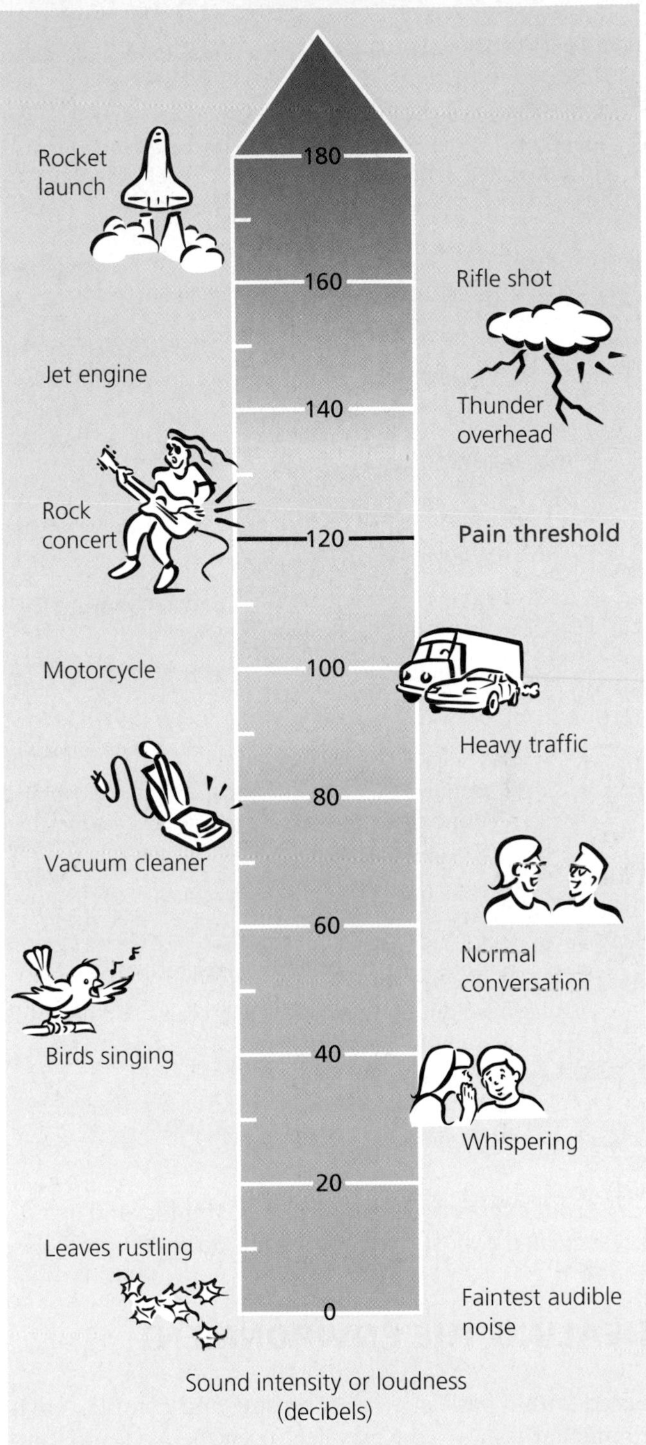

Figure 23-7 The intensity of selected sounds. Hearing damage can occur after 8 hours of exposure to sounds louder than 80 decibels; regular exposure for longer than 1 minute to more than 100 decibels can cause permanent hearing loss. Children may suffer damage to their hearing at lower levels of sound than adults.

- Avoid loud music. Don't sit or stand near speakers or amplifiers at a rock concert, and don't play a car radio or stereo so high that you can't hear the traffic.

Assess Yourself

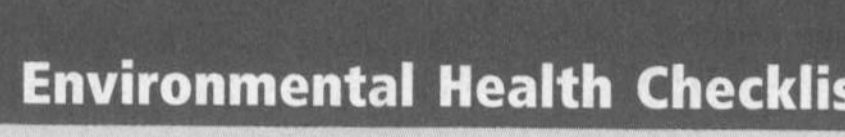

Environmental Health Checklist

The following list of statements relates to your effect on the environment. Put a checkmark next to the statements that are true for you.

_____ I ride my bike, walk, carpool, or use public transportation whenever possible.

_____ I keep my car tuned up and well maintained.

_____ My residence is well insulated.

_____ Where possible, I use compact fluorescent bulbs instead of incandescent bulbs.

_____ I turn off lights and appliances when they are not in use.

_____ I avoid turning on heat or air conditioning whenever possible.

_____ I run the washing machine, dryer, and dishwasher only when they have full loads.

_____ I run the clothes dryer only as long as it takes my clothes to dry.

_____ I dry my hair with a towel rather than a hair dryer.

_____ I keep my car's air conditioner in good working order and have it serviced by a service station that recycles CFCs.

_____ When shopping, I choose products with the least amount of packaging.

_____ I choose recycled and recyclable products.

_____ I avoid products packaged in plastic and unrecycled aluminum.

_____ I store food in glass jars and waxed paper rather than plastic wrap.

_____ I take my own bag along when I go shopping.

_____ I recycle newspapers, glass, cans, and other recyclables.

_____ When shopping, I read labels and try to buy the least toxic products available.

_____ I dispose of household hazardous wastes properly.

_____ I take showers instead of baths.

_____ I take short showers and switch off the water when I'm not actively using it.

_____ I do not run the water while brushing my teeth, shaving, or hand-washing clothes.

_____ My sinks have aerators installed in them.

_____ My shower has a low-flow showerhead.

_____ I have a water-saver toilet or a water displacement device in my toilet.

_____ I snip or rip plastic six-pack rings before I throw them out.

_____ When hiking or camping, I never leave anything behind.

Statements you have not checked can help you identify behaviors you can change to improve environmental health.

For an overall estimate of how much land and water your lifestyle requires, take the Ecological Footprint quiz (www.myfootprint.org).

- Avoid exposure to painfully loud sounds, and avoid repeated exposure to any sounds above 80 decibels.

HEALING THE ENVIRONMENT

Faced with a vast array of confusing and complex environmental issues, you may feel overwhelmed and conclude that there isn't anything you can do about global problems. But this is not true. If everyone made individual changes in his or her life, the impact would be tremendous. (To assess your current lifestyle, refer to the box "Environmental Health Checklist.")

At the same time, it is important to recognize that large corporations and manufacturers are the ones primarily responsible for environmental degradation. Many of them have jumped on the environmental bandwagon with public relations and advertising campaigns designed to make them look good, but they haven't changed their practices nearly enough to make a difference. To influence them, people have to become educated, demand changes in production methods, and elect people to office who consider environmental concerns along with sound business practices.

Large-scale changes and individual actions complement each other. What you do every day *does* count. Following the suggestions in the What You Can Do sections throughout this chapter will help you make a difference in the environment. In addition, you can become a part of larger community actions to work for a healthier world:

- Share what you learn about environmental issues with your friends and family.
- Join, support, or volunteer your time to organizations working on environmental causes that are important to you.
- Contact your elected representatives and communicate your concerns. For guidelines on how to be heard, see the box "Making Your Letters Count."

Take Charge

Making Your Letters Count

It takes only a few minutes to write to an elected official, but it can make a difference on an environmental issue you care about. When elected officials receive enough letters or e-mails on an issue, it does influence their vote—they want to be re-elected, and your vote counts! To give your letter the greatest possible influence, use these guidelines:

- Use your own words and your own stationery.
- Be clear and concise. Keep your letter to one or two paragraphs, never more than one page.
- Focus on only one subject in each letter, and identify it clearly. Refer to legislation by its name or number.
- Request a specific action—vote a particular way on a piece of legislation, request hearings, cosponsor a bill—and state your reasons for your position.
- If you live or work in the legislator's district, say so.
- Courteous letters work best. Don't be insulting or unnecessarily critical.

You can send letters via regular mail; however, increased security screenings often delay delivery. You can e-mail the president or vice president at the following addresses:

president@whitehouse.gov

vice-president@whitehouse.gov

To locate the contact information for your United States senators and representatives, visit the following Web sites:

Senate: www.senate.gov

House of Representatives: www.house.gov/writerep

Tips for Today

Environmental health involves protecting ourselves from environmental dangers and protecting the environment from the dangers we ourselves create. The two are intimately connected, and both require that we take responsibility for our actions every day.

Right now you can

- Turn off the lights in any unoccupied rooms.
- Plan to buy compact fluorescent lightbulbs to replace incandescent bulbs.
- Turn down the heat a few degrees and put on a sweater, or turn off the air conditioner and change into shorts.
- Make an appointment to have your car checked if it's not running well or needs a tune-up.
- Check your trash can for recyclable items—soda cans, plastic water bottles, white paper, magazines—and put aside any you find for recycling or put them in your recycling bins.

SUMMARY

- Environmental health encompasses all the interactions of humans with their environment and the health consequences of those interactions.
- Concerns with water quality focus on pathogenic organisms and hazardous chemicals from industry and households, as well as on water shortages.
- Sewage treatment prevents pathogens from contaminating drinking water; it often must also deal with heavy metals and hazardous chemicals.
- The amount of garbage is growing all the time; paper is the biggest component. Recycling can help solid waste disposal problems.
- The world's population is increasing rapidly, especially in the developing world. Factors that may eventually limit human population are food, availability of land and water, energy, and minimum acceptable standard of living.
- Increased amounts of air pollutants are especially dangerous for children, older adults, and people with chronic health problems.
- Factors contributing to the development of smog include heavy motor vehicle traffic, hot weather, stagnant air, and temperature inversion.
- Carbon dioxide and other natural gases act as a greenhouse around the earth, increasing the temperature of the atmosphere. Levels of these gases are rising through human activity; as a result, the world's climate could change.
- The ozone layer that shields the earth's surface from the sun's UV rays has thinned and developed holes in certain regions.
- Acid precipitation occurs when certain atmospheric pollutants combine with moisture in the air.
- Environmental damage from energy use can be limited through energy conservation and the development of nonpolluting, renewable sources of energy.
- Indoor pollutants can trigger allergies and illness in the short term and cancer in the long term.
- Potentially hazardous chemical pollutants include asbestos, lead, pesticides, mercury, and many household products. Proper handling and disposal are critical.

- Radiation can cause radiation sickness, chromosome damage, and cancer, among other health problems.
- Loud or persistent noise can lead to hearing loss and/or stress; two common sources of excessive noise are the workplace and rock concerts.
- Most health advances today must come from lifestyle changes and improvements in the global environment. The effects of personal changes made by every concerned individual could be tremendous.

Take Action

1. **Inventory household hazardous chemicals:** Find out what hazardous chemicals you have in your household. Read the labels for disposal instructions. If there aren't any instructions, call your local health department and ask how to dispose of specific chemicals. Also ask if there are hazardous waste disposal sites in your community or special pickup days. If possible, get rid of some or all of the hazardous chemicals in your home.

2. **Identify recycling resources:** Investigate the recycling facilities in your community. Find out how materials are recycled and what they are used for in their recycled state. If recycling isn't available in your community, contact your local city hall to find out how a recycling program can be started.

3. **Track your trash output:** Keep track of exactly how many bags (or gallons) of trash your household produces per week. Is it more or less than the national weekly average of 6.73 bags (87.5 gallons) per three-person household? In either case, try to reduce it by recycling, composting, and buying and using fewer disposable products.

4. **Organize a cleanup day:** With a group of fellow students or coworkers, participate in an environmental cleanup event in your community. Depending on where you live, you might clean up trash along a beach, a river, a public park, or a roadside. You can tie your event to Earth Day or International Cleanup Day, or simply choose a day that works for your group.

For More Information

Books

Ausenda, F. 2006. *Green Volunteers: The World Guide to Voluntary Work in Nature Conservation,* 6th ed. New York: Universe. *Describes a variety of opportunities to volunteer for environmental causes, in many different parts of the world.*

Brown, M. J. 2006. *Building Powerful Community Organizations: A Personal Guide to Creating Groups That Can Solve Problems and Change the World.* Chicago: Long Haul Press. *Provides advice for facing environmental (and other) challenges through local organizing and recruiting.*

Cunningham, W. P., et al. 2006. *Environmental Science: A Global Concern,* 9th ed. New York: McGraw-Hill. *A nontechnical survey of basic environmental science and key concerns.*

Maslin, M., 2005. *Global Warming: A Very Short Introduction.* New York: Oxford University Press. *A survey of the science and politics of global warming.*

Nadakavukaren, A. 2005. *Our Global Environment: A Health Perspective,* 6th ed. Prospect Heights, Ill.: Waveland Press. *A broad survey of major environmental issues and their effects on personal and community health.*

Useful annual or biennial publications include the following:

National Wildlife Federation. 2005. *2005 Conservation Directory.* Washington, D.C.: National Wildlife Federation.

World Resources Institute. 2005. *World Resources 2005.* Washington, D.C.: World Resources Institute.

Worldwatch Institute. 2006. *Vital Signs 2006–2007.* New York: Norton.

Organizations, Hotlines, and Web Sites

CDC National Center for Environmental Health. Provides brochures and fact sheets on a variety of environmental issues.
http://www.cdc.gov/nceh/default.htm

Earth Times. An international online newspaper devoted to global environmental issues.
http://www.earthtimes.org

Ecological Footprint. Calculates your personal ecological footprint based on your diet, transportation patterns, and living arrangements.
http://www.myfootprint.org

Energy Efficiency and Renewable Energy (EERE). U.S. Department of Energy. Provides information about alternative fuels and tips for saving energy at home and in your car.
http://www.eere.doe.gov

Fuel Economy. Provides information on the fuel economy of cars made since 1985 and tips on improving gas mileage.
http://www.fueleconomy.gov

Indoor Air Quality Information Hotline. Answers questions, provides publications, and makes referrals.
800-438-4318

National Lead Information Center. Provides information packets and specialist advice.
800-424-LEAD
http://www.epa.gov/lead/index.html

National Oceanic and Atmospheric Administration (NOAA): Climate. Provides information on a variety of issues related to climate, including global warming, drought, and El Niño and La Niña.
http://www.noaa.gov/climate.html

National Safety Council Environmental Health Center. Provides information on lead, radon, indoor air quality, hazardous chemicals, and other environmental issues.
http://www.nsc.org/ehc.htm

Student Environmental Action Coalition (SEAC). A coalition of student and youth environmental groups; the Web site has contact information for local groups.
215-222-4711
http://www.seac.org

United Nations. Several U.N. programs are devoted to environmental problems on a global scale; the Web sites provide information on current and projected trends and on international treaties developed to deal with environmental issues.

http://www.un.org/popin (Population Division)

http://www.unep.org (Environment Programme)

U.S. Environmental Protection Agency (EPA). Provides information about EPA activities and many consumer-oriented materials. The Web site includes special sites devoted to global warming, ozone loss, pesticides, and other areas of concern.

http://www.epa.gov

Worldwatch Institute. A public policy research organization focusing on emerging global environmental problems and the links between the world economy and the environment.

http://www.worldwatch.org

There are many national and international organizations working on environmental health problems. A few of the largest and best known are listed below:

Greenpeace: 800-326-0959; http://www.greenpeace.org
National Audubon Society: 212-979-3000; http://www.audubon.org
National Wildlife Federation: 800-822-9919; http://www.nwf.org
Nature Conservancy: 800-628-6860; http://www.tnc.org
Sierra Club: 415-977-5500; http://www.sierraclub.org
World Wildlife Fund—U.S.: 800-960-0993; http://www.worldwildlife.org

Selected Bibliography

Bell, M. L., et al. 2004. Ozone and short-term mortality in 95 U.S. urban communities, 1987–2000. *Journal of the American Medical Association* 292(19): 2372–2378.

CDC National Center for Environmental Health. 2004. *Children's Blood Lead Levels in the United States* (http://www.cdc.gov/nceh/lead/research/kidsBLL.htm; retrieved September 26, 2006).

Centers for Disease Control and Prevention. 2004. Adult blood lead epidemiology and surveillance. *Morbidity and Mortality Weekly Report* 53(26): 578.

Centers for Disease Control and Prevention. 2004. Surveillance for waterborne-disease outbreaks. *MMWR Surveillance Summaries* 53(SS-8).

Delworth-Bart, J. E., and C. F. Moore. 2006. Mercy mercy me: Social injustice and the prevention of environmental pollutant exposures among ethnic minority and poor children. *Child Development* 77(2): 247–265.

Dominici, F., et al. 2006. Fine particulate air pollution and hospital admission for cardiovascular and respiratory diseases. *Journal of the American Medical Association* 295(10): 1127–1134.

Energy Information Administration. 2005. *Impacts of Modeled Recommendations of the National Commission on Energy Policy.* Washington, D.C.: U.S. Department of Energy.

Energy Information Agency. 2006. *Gasoline and Diesel Fuel Update* (http://tonto.eia.doe.gov/oog/info/gdu/gasdiesel.asp; retrieved September 26, 2006).

Environmental Protection Agency. 2005. *Superfund National Accomplishments Summary Fiscal Year 2005* (http://www.epa.gov/superfund/action/process/numbers04.htm; retrieved September 26, 2006).

Environmental Protection Agency. 2006. *Municipal Solid Waste: Basic Facts* (http://www.epa.gov.epaoswer/non-hw/muncpl/facts.htm; retrieved September 26, 2006).

Gauderman, W. J., et al. 2004. The effect of air pollution on lung development from 10 to 18 years of age. *New England Journal of Medicine* 351(11): 1057–1067.

Kunzli, N., et al. 2005. Ambient air pollution and atherosclerosis in Los Angeles. *Environmental Health Perspectives* 113(2): 201–206.

Laden, F., et al. 2006. Reduction in fine particulate air pollution and mortality: Extended follow-up of the Harvard Six Cities study. *American Journal of Respiratory and Critical Care Medicine* 173(6): 667–672.

NASA Goddard Institute for Space Studies. 2005. *Global Temperature Trends: 2005 Summation* (http://www.giss.nasa.gov/gistemp/2005; retrieved September 26, 2006).

The National Academies. 2006. *Surface Temperature Reconstructions for the Last 2,000 Years.* Washington, D.C.: National Academies Press.

National Oceanic and Atmospheric Administration. 2006. *Billion Dollar U.S. Weather Disasters, 1980–2005* (http://www.ncdc.noaa.gov/oa/reports/billionz.html; retrieved September 26, 2006).

National Oceanic and Atmospheric Administration. 2006. *Northern Hemisphere Winter Summary 2005–2006* (http://www.cpc.ncep.noaa.gov/products/stratosphere/winter_bulletins/nh_05-06; retrieved September 26, 2006).

Parker, J. D., et al. 2005. Air pollution and birth weight among term infants in California. *Pediatrics* 115(1): 121–128.

Trasande, L., P. J. Landrigan, and C. Schechter. 2005. Public health and economic consequences of methylmercury toxicity to the developing brain. *Environmental Health Perspectives* online, February 28.

United Nations Population Division. 2005. *World Population Prospects: The 2004 Revision.* New York: United Nations.

U.S. Climate Change Science Program. 2006. Temperature Trends in the Lower Atmosphere: Steps for Understanding and Reconciling Differences (http://www.climatescience.gov/library/sap/sap1-1/finalreport/sap1-1-final-all.pdf; retrieved September 26, 2006).

U.S. Department of Health and Human Services. 2005. *Surgeon General Releases National Health Advisory on Radon* (http://www.surgeongeneral.gov/pressreleases/sg01132005.html; retrieved September 26, 2006).

U.S. Environmental Protection Agency. 2006. *Lead Safe Work Requirements to Protect Children During Renovation, Repair, and Painting Activities* (http://www.epa.gov/lead/pubs/renovation.html; retrieved September 26, 2006).

Virtanen, J. K., et al. 2005. Mercury, fish oils, and risk of acute coronary events and cardiovascular disease, coronary heart disease, and all-cause mortality in men in eastern Finland. *Arteriosclerosis, Thrombosis, and Vascular Biology* 25(1): 228–233.

World Health Organization. 2005. *International Decade for Action: Water for Life 2005–2015* (http://www.who.int/water_sanitation_health/2005advocguide/en/index1.html; retrieved September 26, 2006).

World Health Organization. 2006. Cholera, 2005. *Weekly Epidemiological Record* 81(31): 297–308.

World Health Organization. 2006. *Fuel for Life: Household Energy and Health.* Geneva: WHO Press.

Worldwatch Institute. 2006. *Vital Signs 2006–2007.* New York: Norton.

APPENDIX

Nutritional Content of Popular Items from Fast-Food Restaurants

Arby's

	Serving size (g)	Calories	Protein (g)	Total fat (g)	Saturated fat (g)	Total carbohydrate (g)	Sugars (g)	Fiber (g)	Cholesterol (mg)	Sodium (mg)	Vitamin A (% Daily Value)	Vitamin C (% Daily Value)	Calcium (% Daily Value)	Iron (% Daily Value)	% calories from fat
Regular roast beef	154	320	21	13	6	34	5	2	45	950	0	0	6	20	34
Super roast beef	241	440	22	19	7	48	11	3	45	1130	2	2	8	25	39
Junior roast beef	125	270	16	9	4	34	5	2	30	740	0	0	6	15	33
Market Fresh® Ultimate BLT	293	780	23	46	9	75	18	6	50	1570	15	30	15	25	53
Market Fresh® Roast Turkey & Swiss	357	720	45	27	6	74	16	5	90	1790	8	4	35	30	35
Market Fresh® Low Carbys™ Southwest chicken wrap	259	550	35	30	9	45	1	30	75	1690	10	10	40	10	49
Chicken Breast Fillet (grilled)	233	410	32	17	3	36	7	3	10	910	5	20	8	15	37
Martha's Vineyard™ salad (w/o dressing)	291	270	26	8	4	22	17	4	70	450	60	45	20	8	26
Raspberry vinaigrette	57	172	0	12	1.5	16	14	0	0	344	0	4	0	0	63
Santa Fe™ salad (w/o dressing)	332	490	30	23	9	40	6	6	60	1230	130	50	40	20	43
Curly fries (medium)	128	410	5	22	3	47	N/A	5	0	950	8	10	6	10	49
Jalapeno Bites®, regular (5)	110	310	5	19	7	29	3	2	30	530	15	0	4	6	55
Chocolate shake, regular	397	510	13	13	0	83	81	0	35	360	8	10	50	2	23

SOURCE: Arby's © 2006, Arby's, Inc. (http://www.arbysrestaurant.com). Used with permission of Arby's, Inc.

Burger King

	Serving size (g)	Calories	Protein (g)	Total fat (g)	Saturated fat (g)	Trans fat (g)	Total carbohydrate (g)	Sugars (g)	Fiber (g)	Cholesterol (mg)	Sodium (mg)	Vitamin A (% Daily Value)	Vitamin C (% Daily Value)	Calcium (% Daily Value)	Iron (% Daily Value)	% calories from fat
Original Whopper®	290	670	28	39	11	1.5	51	11	3	95	1020	10	15	15	30	32
Original Whopper® w/o mayonnaise	269	510	28	22	9	1	51	11	3	80	880	10	15	15	30	39
Original Double Whopper® w/cheese	398	990	52	64	24	2.5	52	11	3	195	1520	15	15	30	45	59
Original Whopper Jr.®	158	370	15	21	6	0.5	31	6	2	50	500	4	6	8	15	51
Original Chicken Sandwich	219	660	24	40	8	2.5	52	5	4	70	1440	2	0	10	20	55
Chicken Tenders® (8 pieces)	123	340	22	19	5	3.5	20	0	<1	50	840	2	0	2	4	50
French fries (medium, salted)	117	360	4	18	5	4.5	46	<1	4	0	640	0	15	2	4	45
Onion rings (medium)	91	320	4	16	4	3.5	40	5	3	0	460	0	0	10	0	45
Tendergrill™ Chicken Caesar Salad w/o dressing	299	220	31	8	3	0	7	1	2	60	710	85	40	20	10	32
Ken's® Border Ranch Dressing	57	190	2	8	1.5	0	7	2	<1	25	560	2	2	4	2	64
Croissan'wich® w/bacon, egg & cheese	115	300	12	17	6	2	26	5	<1	145	746	10	0	15	15	50
Hershey®'s sundae pie	79	300	3	18	10	1.5	31	23	1	10	190	2	0	4	6	53
Chocolate shake (medium)	447	690	11	20	12	0	114	110	2	75	560	15	6	45	10	26

SOURCE: BURGER KING® nutritional information used with permission from Burger King Brands, Inc.

A

Domino's Pizza
(1 of 8 equal slices)

	Serving size	Calories	Protein	Total fat	Saturated fat	Total carbohydrate	Sugars	Fiber	Cholesterol	Sodium	Vitamin A	Vitamin C	Calcium	Iron	% calories from fat
	g		g	g	g	g	g	g	mg	mg	% Daily Value				
14-inch lg. hand-tossed cheese	110	256	10	8	3	38	3	2	12	535.5	8	0	12	11	26
14-inch lg. thin crust cheese	68	188	7	10	3.5	19	2	1	13	408.5	8	4	12	4	40
14-inch lg. deep dish cheese	128	336	13	15	5	41	4	2	16	782	10	0	16	15	40
12-inch med. hand-tossed cheese	79	186	7	5.5	2	28	2	1	9	385	6	0	9	8	26
12-inch med. thin crust cheese	49	137	5	7	2.5	14	2	1	10	292.5	6	3	9	3	40
12-inch med. deep dish cheese	90	238	9	11	3.5	28	3	2	11	555.5	7	0	11	11	41
14-inch lg. hand-tossed pepperoni & sausage	130	350	14	16	6	39	3	2	31	863	9	0	14	13	41
14-inch lg. hand-tossed ham & pineapple	130	275	12	8.5	3.5	40	5	2	17	653	8	2	12	12	28
14-inch lg. hand-tossed ExtravaganZZa Feast®	107	200	12	16	7	7	1	1	40	780	10	10	20	8	70
14-inch lg. hand-tossed Hawaiian Feast®	82	130	8	8	4	7	3	1	25	550	10	6	15	4	62
14-inch lg. Vegi Feast®	79	120	7	8	4	6	1	1	20	480	10	10	15	4	58
14-inch lg. MeatZZa Feast®	94	210	12	17	8	6	1	1	40	810	10	4	20	4	71
Barbecue buffalo wings	43	88	9	4.5	1.5	2	2	0	50	0	20	0	25	70	45
Buffalo Chicken Kickers™ (1 piece)	24	45	4	20	0	3	0	0	10	160	0	0	0	0	44
Blue cheese sauce	43	230	2	24	5	2	2	0	30	450	0	0	0	0	91
Breadsticks (1 stick)	33	130	3	7	1.5	14	1	1	0	90	20	0	0	6	46
Cinna Stix® (1 stick)	35	140	3	7	1.5	17	4	1	0	180	0	0	0	6	43

SOURCE: Domino's Pizza, 2006 (http://www.dominos.com). © Domino's Pizza, 2004. Reproduced with permission from Domino's Pizza LLC.

Jack in the Box

	Serving size	Calories	Protein	Total fat	Saturated fat	Trans fat	Total carbohydrate	Sugars	Fiber	Cholesterol	Sodium	Vitamin A	Vitamin C	Calcium	Iron	% calories from fat
	g		g	g	g	g	g	g	g	mg	mg	% Daily Value				
Breakfast Jack®	129	305	13	14	4	0.5	34	3	0	205	715	N/A	N/A	N/A	N/A	41
Supreme croissant	155	475	16	27	8.5	3.5	41	4	1	220	815	N/A	N/A	N/A	N/A	51
Hamburger	119	310	17	14	5	0	30	6	0	45	590	N/A	N/A	N/A	N/A	41
Jumbo Jack® w/cheese	306	695	24	41.5	16	1	55	11	2	70	1305	N/A	N/A	N/A	N/A	54
Sourdough Jack®	246	715	26	51	18	2.5	36	7	2	75	1165	N/A	N/A	N/A	N/A	64
Chicken fajita pita	247	315	22	9	4	0	33	4	0	65	1080	N/A	N/A	N/A	N/A	26
Sourdough grilled chicken club	249	505	29	27	6.5	1.5	35	4	2	75	1220	N/A	N/A	N/A	N/A	48
Deli Trio Pannido™	271	645	30	34	8.5	0	53	4	2	95	2530	N/A	N/A	N/A	N/A	47
Jack's Spicy Chicken®	270	615	24	30.5	5.5	2.5	62	7	3	50	1090	N/A	N/A	N/A	N/A	45
Monster taco	110	240	8	14	5	2	20	4	3	20	390	N/A	N/A	N/A	N/A	53
Egg rolls (3)	198	445	14	19	6	3	55	10	6	15	1080	N/A	N/A	N/A	N/A	0
Chicken breast strips (5)	226	630	35	38	8	6	39	1	3	90	1470	N/A	N/A	N/A	N/A	54
Stuffed jalapeños (7)	168	530	15	30	13	4.5	51	5	4	45	1600	N/A	N/A	N/A	N/A	51
Barbeque dipping sauce	28	45	0	0	0	0	11	4	0	0	330	N/A	N/A	N/A	N/A	0
Seasoned curly fries (medium)	125	400	6	23	5	7	45	1	5	0	890	N/A	N/A	N/A	N/A	52
Onion rings	119	500	6	30	6	10	51	3	3	0	420	N/A	N/A	N/A	N/A	54
Side salad	164	155	5	7.5	2.5	0.5	16	3	0	10	290	N/A	N/A	N/A	N/A	44
Ranch dressing	71	390	1	41	6	0	4	2	0	30	590	N/A	N/A	N/A	N/A	95
Oreo® cookie ice-cream shake (small)	301	670	11	33	19	3	81	62	1	110	350	N/A	N/A	N/A	N/A	45

SOURCE: Jack in the Box, Inc. 2006 (http://www.jackinthebox.com). The following trademarks are owned by Jack in the Box, Inc.: Breakfast Jack,® Jumbo Jack,® Sourdough Jack,® Jack in the Box.® Reproduced with permission from Jack in the Box, Inc.

KFC

	Serving size	Calories	Protein	Total fat	Saturated fat	Trans fat	Total carbohydrate	Sugars	Fiber	Cholesterol	Sodium	Vitamin A	Vitamin C	Calcium	Iron	% calories from fat
	g		g	g	g	g	g	g	g	mg	mg	% Daily Value				
Original Recipe® breast	161	380	40	19	6	2.5	11	0	0	145	1150	0	0	0	6	45
Original Recipe® thigh	126	360	22	25	7	1.5	12	0	0	165	1060	0	0	0	6	64
Extra Crispy™ breast	162	460	34	28	8	4.5	19	0	0	135	1230	0	0	0	8	54
Extra Crispy™ thigh	114	370	21	26	7	3	12	0	0	120	710	0	0	0	6	62
Tender Roast® sandwich w/sauce	196	390	31	19	4	0.5	24	0	1	70	810	0	0	4	10	44
Tender Roast® sandwich w/o sauce	177	260	31	5	1.5	0.5	23	0	1	65	690	0	0	4	10	17
Tender Roast® Filet Meal	321	360	33	7	2	0.5	41	4	4	85	2010	20	6	6	15	18
Hot Wings™ (6 pieces)	134	450	24	29	6	4	23	1	1	145	1120	6	6	8	10	58
Popcorn chicken (large)	170	560	36	31	7	7	34	0	1	90	1790	4	0	4	15	50
Chicken pot pie	423	770	33	40	15	14	70	2	5	115	1680	200	0	0	20	47
Roasted Caesar Salad w/o dressing and croutons	301	220	29	9	4.5	0.5	6	4	3	75	850	45	35	25	10	36
KFC® creamy parmesan caesar dressing	57	260	2	26	5	0	5	3	0	15	530	0	0	2	0	88
Corn on the cob (5.5")	162	150	5	3	1	0	26	10	7	0	10	0	10	6	6	18
Mashed potatoes w/gravy	136	130	2	4.5	1	0.5	19	1	1	0	480	2	2	4	2	31
Baked beans	136	230	8	1	1	0.25	46	22	7	0	720	8	6	15	30	4
Cole slaw	130	190	1	11	2	0	22	13	3	5	300	25	40	4	0	52
Biscuit (1)	57	190	2	10	2	3.5	23	1	0	1.5	580	0	0	0	4	47
Potato salad	128	180	2	9	1.5	0.25	22	5	1	5	470	0	10	0	2	45

SOURCE: KFC Corporation, 2006. Nutritional information provided by KFC Corporation from its Web site (www.kfc.com) as of July 2006 and subject to the conditions listed therein. KFC and related marks are registered trademarks of KFC Corporation. Reproduced with permission from Kentucky Fried Chicken Corporation.

McDonald's

	Serving size	Calories	Protein	Total fat	Saturated fat	Trans fat	Total carbohydrate	Sugars	Fiber	Cholesterol	Sodium	Vitamin A	Vitamin C	Calcium	Iron	% calories from fat
	g		g	g	g	g	g	g	g	mg	mg	% Daily Value				
Hamburger	105	260	13	9	3.5	0.5	33	7	1	30	530	2	2	15	15	31
Quarter Pounder®	171	420	24	18	7	1	40	8	3	70	730	2	2	15	25	38
Quarter Pounder® w/cheese	199	510	29	25	12	1.5	43	9	3	95	1150	10	2	30	25	43
Big Mac®	219	560	25	30	10	1.5	47	8	3	80	1010	8	2	25	25	48
Big N' Tasty®	232	470	24	23	8	1.5	41	9	3	80	790	8	8	15	25	43
Filet-O-Fish®	141	400	14	18	4	1	42	8	1	40	640	2	0	15	10	40
McChicken®	147	370	15	16	3.5	1	41	5	1	50	810	2	2	15	15	48
Medium French Fries	114	380	4	20	4	5	47	0	5	0	220	0	10	2	6	47
Chicken McNuggets® (6 pieces)	96	250	15	15	3	1.5	15	0	0	35	670	2	2	2	4	52
Chicken Select® Premium Breast Strips (5 pieces)	221	630	39	33	6	4.5	46	0	0	90	1550	0	6	4	8	48
Tangy Honey Mustard Sauce	43	70	1	2	0	0	13	9	1	0	160	0	0	0	1	29
Bacon Ranch Salad w/Grilled Chicken (w/o dressing)	321	260	33	9	4	0	12	5	3	90	1000	130	50	15	10	31
Caesar Salad w/Crispy Chicken (w/o dressing)	313	300	25	13	4	1.5	22	4	3	55	1020	130	50	20	10	40
Newman's Own® Ranch Dressing (2 oz)	59	170	1	15	2.5	0	9	4	0	20	530	0	0	4	0	76
Egg McMuffin®	139	300	17	12	4.5	0	30	2	2	230	860	10	2	30	15	37
Sausage Biscuit w/Egg	162	500	18	31	10	5	36	2	1	250	1080	6	0	8	20	56
Hotcakes (2 pats margarine & syrup)	221	600	9	17	4	4	102	45	2	20	620	8	0	15	15	27
Fruit 'n Yogurt Parfait	149	160	4	2	1	0	31	21	1	5	85	0	15	15	4	13
Chocolate Triple Thick® Shake (16 oz)	444	580	13	14	8	1	102	84	1	50	250	20	0	45	10	21

SOURCE: McDonald's Corporation, 2006 (http://www.mcdonalds.com). Used with permission from McDonald's Corporation. For the most current information, visit the McDonald's Web site.

Subway

Based on standard formulas with 6-inch subs on Italian or wheat bread

	Serving size	Calories	Protein	Total fat	Saturated fat	Trans fat	Total carbohydrate	Sugars	Fiber	Cholesterol	Sodium	Vitamin A	Vitamin C	Calcium	Iron	% calories from fat
	g		g	g	g	g	g	g	g	mg	mg	% Daily Value				
6" Italian BMT®	243	450	23	21	8	0	47	8	4	55	1790	10	35	15	25	42
6" Meatball Marinara	377	560	24	24	11	1	63	13	7	45	1610	10	60	20	40	39
6" Steak & Cheese	250	400	29	12	6	0.5	48	9	5	60	1130	15	50	15	40	27
Subway Melt®	254	380	25	12	5	0	48	8	4	45	1620	10	30	15	25	29
Tuna	250	530	22	31	7	0.5	45	7	4	45	1030	10	35	10	30	53
Sweet Onion Chicken Teriyaki	279	370	26	5	1.5	0	59	19	4	50	1220	8	40	8	25	12
Roast Beef	223	290	19	5	2	0	45	8	4	20	920	6	30	6	35	16
Turkey Breast	224	280	18	4.5	1.5	0	46	7	4	20	1020	6	30	6	25	14
Veggie Delite®	167	230	9	3	1	0	44	7	4	0	520	6	30	6	25	13
Tuna (w/cheese) Salad (w/o dressing)	404	360	16	29	6	0.5	12	5	4	45	600	70	50	15	15	72
New England Style Clam Chowder	310	150	5	5	1.5	0	20	2	2	10	1400	2	2	10	4	33
Chili Con Carne	310	340	20	11	5	0	35	7	10	60	1100	2	0	6	15	32
Chocolate Chip Cookie	45	210	2	10	6	0	30	18	1	15	150	6	0	0	6	43

SOURCE: Subway U.S. Nutrition Info as found on http://www.subway.com, 11/17/2006. Reprinted by permission of Subway.®

Taco Bell

	Serving size	Calories	Protein	Total fat	Saturated fat	Trans fat	Total carbohydrate	Sugars	Fiber	Cholesterol	Sodium	Vitamin A	Vitamin C	Calcium	Iron	% calories from fat
	g		g	g	g	g	g	g	g	mg	mg	% Daily Value				
Taco	92	150	7	7	2.5	0.5	14	1	2	20	360	4	4	2	6	53
Taco Supreme®	113	220	9	14	7	1	14	2	1	35	360	8	6	8	6	57
Soft taco, beef	99	210	10	10	4	1	21	2	1	25	620	4	2	10	8	43
Gordita Supreme,® steak	153	290	16	13	6	0.5	28	7	2	35	520	6	6	10	15	37
Gordita Baja,® chicken	153	320	17	15	3.5	0	29	7	2	40	690	6	6	10	10	42
Gordita Baja,® chicken, "Fresco Style"	153	230	15	6	1	0	29	7	2	25	570	6	10	6	10	23
Chalupa Supreme, beef	153	400	13	24	8	2.5	31	4	2	35	620	8	6	15	15	55
Chalupa Supreme, chicken	153	370	17	21	8	3	30	4	1	45	530	6	8	15	10	49
Crunchwrap Supreme	254	560	17	24	9	3.5	70	7	4	35	1350	8	8	25	20	39
Bean burrito	198	370	14	10	3.5	2	55	4	8	10	1200	10	8	20	15	24
Burrito Supreme,® chicken	248	410	21	14	6	2	50	5	5	45	1270	15	15	20	15	31
Grilled stuffed burrito, beef	325	720	27	33	11	3	79	6	7	55	2140	10	6	35	25	41
Tostada	170	250	11	10	4	1.5	29	2	7	15	710	10	8	15	8	36
Zesty Chicken Border Bowl™ w/dressing	418	730	23	40	8	2.5	69	5	10	45	1810	15	15	15	20	52
Express Taco Salad w/chips	479	600	28	32	12	3.5	52	9	9	65	1490	25	25	25	20	48
Steak quesadilla	184	540	26	31	14	2	40	4	3	70	1370	15	2	50	15	52
Nachos Supreme	195	430	15	25	8	3.5	37	4	4	30	910	8	8	10	10	58
Nachos BellGrande®	308	730	23	41	12	7	69	7	8	35	1500	8	10	15	15	50
Pintos 'n cheese	128	180	10	7	3.5	1	20	1	6	15	700	10	6	15	6	35
Mexican rice	131	210	6	10	4	1.5	23	<1	3	15	740	20	8	10	10	43

SOURCE: Taco Bell Corporation, 2006 (http://www.tacobell.com). Reproduced courtesy of Taco Bell Corporation.

Wendy's

	Serving size	Calories	Protein	Total fat	Saturated fat	Trans fat	Total carbohydrate	Sugars	Fiber	Cholesterol	Sodium	Vitamin A	Vitamin C	Calcium	Iron	% calories from fat
	g		g	g	g	g	g	g	g	mg	mg	% Daily Value				
Classic Single® w/everything	218	430	25	20	7	1	37	8	2	65	880	8	8	4	25	42
Big Bacon Classic®	282	590	34	30	12	1.5	46	11	3	90	1510	20	15	15	25	45
Jr. Hamburger	117	280	15	9	3.5	0.5	34	7	1	30	590	0	0	2	20	29
Jr. Bacon Cheeseburger	161	370	19	17	7	0.5	34	6	2	50	790	10	6	10	20	46
Ultimate Chicken Grill Sandwich	227	370	33	8	1.5	0	44	10	2	60	1070	6	10	4	20	19
Spicy Chicken Fillet Sandwich	231	480	29	17	3	0	53	8	4	60	1400	6	8	4	15	32
Homestyle Chicken Fillet Sandwich	228	470	27	16	3	0	55	8	2	45	1210	6	8	4	15	31
Homestyle Chicken Strips	159	410	28	21	3.5	0	33	0	0	60	1470	0	0	2	6	39
Caesar Side Salad (no toppings or dressing)	99	70	5	4.5	2	0	3	1	2	15	135	100	35	10	6	57
Mandarin Chicken® Salad (no toppings or dressing)	348	170	23	2	0.5	0	18	13	3	60	480	70	50	6	10	9
Southwest Taco Salad (no toppings or dressing)	501	440	30	22	12	1	32	10	9	80	1100	80	35	45	20	45
Creamy ranch dressing	64	230	1	23	4	0	5	3	0	15	450	0	0	4	2	87
Reduced fat creamy ranch dressing	64	100	1	8	1.5	0	6	3	1	15	450	0	0	6	2	70
Large French Fries	190	590	6	24	3.5	0.5	77	0	7	0	570	4	15	2	10	44
Sour Cream & Chive Baked Potato	312	320	9	4	2.5	0	63	4	7	10	55	4	60	8	15	11
Low Fat Strawberry Flavored Yogurt w/Granola	163	163	8	6	1.5	0	42	30	1	5	90	2	2	22	6	33
Chili, small, plain	227	220	17	6	2.5	0	23	6	5	35	780	4	4	8	15	27
Crispy Chicken Nuggets™ (5)	75	230	12	15	3	0	12	1	0	35	520	0	0	0	2	59
Barbecue sauce (1 packet)	28	45	1	0	0	0	10	8	0	0	170	0	0	0	4	0
Frosty,™ medium	298	430	10	11	7	0	74	55	0	45	200	20	0	40	20	23

SOURCE: Wendy's International, Inc., 2006 (http://www.wendys.com). Reproduced with permission from Wendy's International, Inc. The information contained in Wendy's International Information is effective as of August 1, 2006. Wendy's International, Inc., its subsidiaries, affiliates, franchises, and employees do not assume responsibility for a particular sensitivity or allergy (including peanuts, nuts or other allergies) to any food product provided in our restaurants. We encourage anyone with food sensitivities, allergies, or special dietary needs to check on a regular basis with Wendy's Consumer Relations Department to obtain the most up-to-date information.

Information on additional foods and restaurants is available online; see the Web sites listed in this appendix and the following additional sites: **Hardees:** http://www.hardes.com **White Castle:** http://www.whitecastle.com

APPENDIX

B A Self-Care Guide for Common Medical Problems

This self-care guide will help you manage some of the most common symptoms and medical problems:

- Fever
- Sore throat
- Cough
- Nasal congestion
- Ear problems
- Nausea, vomiting, or diarrhea
- Heartburn and indigestion
- Headache
- Low-back pain
- Strains and sprains
- Cuts and scrapes

Each symptom is described here in terms of what is going on in your body. Most symptoms are part of the body's natural healing response. Self-care advice is also given, along with guidelines for getting professional advice. Symptoms are usually self-limiting; that is, they resolve on their own with time and simple self-care.

No medical advice is perfect. You must decide whether to self-treat or get professional help. This guide is intended to give you information so you can make better, more informed decisions. If the advice here differs from that of your physician, discuss the differences with him or her.

The guidelines given here apply to *generally healthy adults*. If you are pregnant or nursing or if you have a chronic disease, particularly one that requires medication, check with your physician for appropriate self-care advice. Additionally, if you have an allergy or suspected allergy to any recommended medication, check with your physician before using it.

If you have several symptoms, read about your primary symptom first and then proceed to secondary symptoms. If you are particularly concerned about a symptom or confused about how to manage it, call your physician to get more information.

FEVER

A fever is an abnormally high body temperature, usually over 100°F (37.7°C). It is most commonly a sign that your body is fighting an infection. Fever may also be due to an inflammation, an injury, or a drug reaction. Chemicals released into your bloodstream during an infection reset the thermostat in the hypothalamus of your brain. The message goes out to your body to turn up the heat. The blood vessels in your skin constrict, and you curl up and throw on extra blankets to reduce heat loss. Meanwhile, your muscles may begin to shiver to generate additional body heat. The resulting rise in body temperature is a fever. Later, when your brain senses that the temperature is too high, you start sweating. As the sweat evaporates, it carries heat away from the body.

A fever may not be all bad; it may even help you fight infections by making the body less hospitable to bacteria and viruses. A high body temperature appears to bolster the immune system and may inhibit the growth of infectious microorganisms.

Most generally healthy people can tolerate a fever as high as 103–104°F (39.5–40°C) without problems. Therefore, if you are essentially healthy, there is little need to reduce a fever unless you are very uncomfortable. Older adults and those with chronic health problems such as heart disease may not tolerate a high fever, so fever reduction may be advised.

Additionally, in small children (especially infants), even a low-grade fever can be a sign of a serious problem. Seek immediate medical help for any infant less than 2 months old whose temperature is 100.4°F (38°C) or higher, or for any child older than 2 months whose temperature is greater than 102°F (38.8°C). In small children, temperature should be checked with a digital rectal thermometer. Do not attempt to take a baby's temperature orally; if you have trouble taking a child's temperature for any reason, contact a medical professional right away.

Most problems with fevers are due to loss of fluids from evaporation and sweating, which may cause dehydration.

Self-Assessment

1. If you are sick, take your temperature several times throughout the day. Oral temperatures should not be measured for at least 10 minutes after smoking, eating, or drinking a hot or cold liquid. Don't use a glass thermometer that contains mercury. Digital thermometers are accurate, easy to read, and inexpensive. Follow the directions that came with your thermometer.

"Normal" temperature varies from person to person, so it is important to know what is normal for you. Your normal temperature will also vary throughout the day, being lowest in the early evening. If you exercise or if it is a hot day, your temperature may normally rise. Women's body temperature typically varies by a degree or more through the menstrual cycle, peaking around the time of ovulation. Rectal temperatures normally run about 0.5–1.0°F higher than oral temperatures. If your recorded temperature is more than 1.0–1.5°F above your normal baseline temperature, you have a fever.

2. Watch for signs of dehydration: excessive thirst; very dry mouth; infrequent urination with dark, concentrated urine; and light-headedness.

Self-Care

1. Drink plenty of fluids to prevent dehydration—at least 8 ounces of water, juice, or broth every 2 hours.

2. Take a sponge bath using lukewarm water; this will increase evaporation and help reduce body temperature naturally. Don't use alcohol rubs to reduce temperature.

3. Dress lightly. Bundling up decreases the body's ability to lose excess heat.

4. Take aspirin substitute (acetaminophen, ibuprofen, or naproxen sodium) to reduce the fever and the associated headache and achiness. Follow the product's dosage instructions carefully. Do not use aspirin in anyone younger than age 20 because some younger people with chicken pox, influenza, or other viral infections have developed a life-threatening complication, Reye's syndrome, after taking aspirin.

B

When to Call the Physician

1. Fever over 104°F (40°C), or 102°F (38.8°C) in a person over 60 years old

2. Persistent fever: 102° (38.8°C) or higher for 2 days; 101° (38.3°C) or higher for 3 days; or 100° or higher for 4 days

3. Recurrent unexplained fevers

4. Fever accompanied by a rash, stiff neck, severe headache, difficulty breathing, discolored sputum, severe pain in the side or abdomen, painful urination, convulsions, or confusion

5. Fever with signs of dehydration

6. Fever after starting a new medication

SORE THROAT

A sore throat—called pharyngitis—is caused by inflammation of the throat lining resulting from an infection, allergy, or irritation (especially from cigarette smoke). If you have an infection, you may also notice some hoarseness from swelling of the vocal cords and "swollen glands," which are enlarged lymph nodes that produce white blood cells to help fight the infection. Lymph nodes may become tender and remain swollen for weeks after the infection subsides.

Most throat infections are caused by viruses, so antibiotics are not effective against them. Most viral sore throats clear up in about a week with no treatment. But if a sore throat is accompanied by other symptoms (like a high fever, fatigue, aches, rash, or localized swelling), a more serious viral illness is possible, such as the flu, mononucleosis, or measles. These conditions should be diagnosed and treated by a physician.

About 20–30% of throat infections (called "strep throat") are due to streptococcal bacteria. This type of microbe can cause complications such as rheumatic fever and rheumatic heart disease and therefore should be diagnosed by a physician and treated with antibiotics. Strep throat is usually characterized by very sore throat, high fever, swollen lymph nodes, and a whitish discharge at the back of the throat.

Allergy-related sore throats may come with a runny nose, sneezing, and watery, itchy eyes.

Self-Assessment

1. Take your temperature.

2. Look at the back of your throat in a mirror. Is there a whitish discharge on the tonsils or in the back of the throat?

3. Feel the front and back of your neck. Do you feel enlarged, tender lymph nodes?

Self-Care

1. If you smoke, stop.

2. Drink plenty of liquids to soothe your inflamed throat.

3. Gargle with warm salt water (1/4 tsp salt in 4 oz water) every 1–2 hours to help reduce swelling and discomfort.

4. Suck on throat lozenges, cough drops, or hard candies to keep your throat moist.

5. Use throat lozenges, sprays, or gargles that contain an anesthetic to make swallowing less painful.

6. Try aspirin substitute to ease throat pain.

7. For an allergy-related sore throat, try an antihistamine such as chlorpheniramine or lorantodine.

When to Call the Physician

1. Great difficulty swallowing saliva or breathing

2. Sore throat with fever over 101°F (38.3°C), especially if you do not have other cold symptoms such as nasal congestion or a cough

3. Sore throat with a skin rash

4. Sore throat with whitish pus on the tonsils

5. Sore throat and recent contact with a person who has had a positive throat culture for strep

6. Enlarged lymph nodes lasting longer than 3 weeks

7. Hoarseness lasting longer than 3 weeks

COUGH

A cough is a protective mechanism of the body to help keep the airways clear. There are two types of cough: a dry cough (without mucus) and a productive cough (with mucus). Common causes of cough include infection (viral or bacterial), allergies, and irritation from smoking and pollutants. If you have a cold, the cough may be the last symptom to improve, because the airways may remain irritated for several weeks after the infection has resolved.

Your airways are lined with hairlike projections called cilia, which move back and forth to help clear the airways of mucus, germs, and dust. Infections and cigarette smoking paralyze and damage this vital defensive mechanism.

Self-Assessment

1. Take your temperature.

2. Observe your mucus. Thick brown or bloody mucus suggests a bacterial infection.

Self-Care

1. If you smoke, stop. Smoking irritates the airways and undermines your body's immune defenses, leading to more serious infections and longer-lasting symptoms. Most people do not feel like smoking when they have a cold with a cough. If you want to quit, a cold may provide an excellent opportunity to do so.

2. Drink plenty of liquids (at least six 8-ounce glasses a day) to help thin mucus and loosen chest congestion.

3. Use moist heat from a hot shower or vaporizer to help loosen chest congestion.

4. Suck on cough drops, throat lozenges, or hard candy to moisten your throat and relieve a dry, tickling cough.

5. If you have a dry, nonproductive cough or the cough keeps you from sleeping, you can use a cough syrup or lozenge that contains the nonprescription cough suppressant dextromethorphan. If your cough is productive, ask your physician before using a cough suppressant. Productive coughs are often protective.

When to Call the Physician

1. Cough with thick brown or bloody sputum

2. Cough with high fever—above 102°F (38.8°C)—and shaking chills

3. Severe chest pains, wheezing, or shortness of breath

4. Cough that lasts longer than 3 weeks (a chronic cough)

NASAL CONGESTION

Nasal congestion is most commonly caused by infection or allergies. With infection, the nasal passages become congested because of increased blood flow and mucus production. This congestion is actually part of the body's defense to fight infection. The increased blood flow raises the temperature of the nasal passages, making them less hospitable to germs. The nasal secretions are rich in white blood cells and antibodies to help fight and neutralize the invading organisms and flush them away. Nasal congestion associated with sore throat, cough, and fever usually indicates a viral infection. Green nasal discharge is common with viral infections; it does not mean you need an antibiotic.

Nasal congestion caused by allergies is often accompanied by a thin watery discharge, sneezing, and itchy eyes; it is sometimes associated with a seasonal pattern. In an allergic reaction, the offending allergen (such as pollen, dust, mold, or dander) triggers the release of histamine and other chemicals from the cells lining the nose, throat, and eyes. These chemicals cause swelling, discharge, and itching. Antihistamine drugs block the release of these irritating chemicals.

Self-Assessment

1. Take your temperature.

2. Observe your nasal secretions. Thick brown or bloody discharge suggests a bacterial infection.

3. Tap with your fingers over the sinus cavities above and below the eyes. If the tapping causes increased pain, you may have a bacterial sinus infection.

Self-Care

1. If you smoke, stop.

2. Use moist heat from a hot shower or vaporizer to help liquefy congested mucus.

3. Use a decongestant nasal spray or drops to temporarily relieve congestion. However, if these decongestants are used for more than 3 days, they can cause "rebound congestion" that actually creates more nasal congestion. As an alternative, use saltwater nose drops ($^1/_4$ tsp salt in $^1/_2$ cup boiled water, cooled before using) or a commercial saline spray several times a day.

4. Try an oral decongestant such as pseudoephedrine (60 mg every 6 hours) to help shrink swollen mucous membranes and open nasal passages. In some people, these medications can cause nervousness, sleeplessness, or heart palpitations. If you have uncontrolled high blood pressure, heart disease, or diabetes, check with your physician before using decongestants.

When to Call the Physician

1. Nasal congestion with severe pain and tenderness in the forehead, cheeks, or upper teeth and a high fever (above 102°F or 38.8°C)

2. Thick brown or bloody nasal discharge

3. Nasal congestion and discharge unresponsive to self-care treatment and lasting longer than 3 weeks

EAR PROBLEMS

Ear symptoms include earache, discharge, itching, stuffiness, and hearing loss. They may be caused by problems in the external ear canal, eardrum, middle ear, or eustachian tube (the passageway that connects the middle ear space to the back of the throat). The ear canal can become blocked by excess wax, producing hearing loss and a sense that the ear is plugged. An infection of the external ear canal due to excessive moisture and trauma is often referred to as "swimmer's ear." It can cause pain, a sense of fullness, discharge, and itching. Congestion and blockage of the eustachian tube by a cold or allergy can result in pain, a sense of fullness, and hearing loss. A middle ear infection often produces severe pain, hearing loss, and fever.

Self-Assessment

1. Check for fever, which may be a sign of infection.

2. Have someone look into the ear canal with a flashlight or otoscope. Look for wax blockage or a red, swollen canal indicating an external ear infection.

3. Wiggle the outer part of the ear. If this increases the pain, an infection or inflammation of the external canal is the likely cause.

Self-Care

1. If blockage of the ear canal with wax is the problem, first try a hot shower to liquefy the wax, and use a wash cloth to wipe out the ear canal. You can also use a few drops of an over-the-counter wax softener and then flush the canal gently with warm water in a bulb syringe. Do not use sharp objects or cotton swabs; they can scratch the canal or push the wax in deeper.

2. To treat mild infections of the external ear canal, you must thoroughly dry the ear canal. A few drops of a drying solution (1 part rubbing alcohol, 1 part white vinegar) on a piece of cotton gently inserted into the canal can act as a wick to dry the canal.

3. To relieve congestion and blockage of the eustachian tube, try a decongestant like pseudoephedrine or a nasal spray (but for no longer than 3 days). Hot showers or a vaporizer may help loosen secretions, and yawning or swallowing may help open the eustachian tube. For a mild plugging sensation without fever or pain, pinch your nostrils and blow gently into your nose (not through your mouth) to force air up the eustachian tube and "pop" your ears.

When to Call the Physician

1. Severe earache with fever
2. Puslike or bloody discharge from the ear
3. Sudden hearing loss, especially if accompanied by ear pain or recent trauma to the ear
4. Ringing in the ears or dizziness
5. Any ear symptom lasting longer than 2 weeks

NAUSEA, VOMITING, OR DIARRHEA

Nausea, vomiting, and diarrhea usually are defensive reactions of your body to rapidly clear your digestive tract of irritants. These symptoms may be caused by a viral infection, foodborne illness, medications, or other types of infection. Vomiting dramatically ejects irritants from your stomach, and nausea (feeling discomfort in the stomach or the sensation that you may vomit) discourages eating to allow the stomach to rest. With diarrhea, overstimulated intestines flush out the offending irritants.

The major complications of vomiting and diarrhea are dehydration from fluid losses and decreased fluid intake and a risk of bleeding from irritation of the digestive tract.

Self-Assessment

1. Take your temperature. A fever is often a clue that an infection is causing the symptoms.
2. Note the color and frequency of vomiting and diarrhea. This will help you estimate the severity of fluid losses and check for bleeding (red, black, or "coffee grounds" material in the stool or vomit; iron tablets and Pepto-Bismol can also cause black stools).
3. Watch for signs of dehydration: very dry mouth; excessive thirst; infrequent urination with dark, concentrated urine; and light-headedness.
4. Look for signs of hepatitis, an infection of the liver: a yellow color in the skin and the white parts of the eyes.

Self-Care

1. To replace fluids, take frequent, small sips of clear liquids such as water, noncitrus juice, broths, flat ginger ale, or ice chips.
2. When the vomiting and diarrhea have subsided for at least 6 hours, try nonirritating, constipating foods like the BRAT diet: bananas, rice, applesauce, and toast.
3. For several days, avoid alcohol, milk products, fatty foods, aspirin, and other medications that might irritate the stomach. Do not stop taking regularly prescribed medications without discussing this change with your physician.
4. Medications are not usually advised for vomiting. Loperamide, available without a prescription, can ease diarrhea.

When to Call the Physician

1. Inability to retain any fluids for 12 hours or signs of dehydration
2. Severe abdominal pains not relieved by the vomiting or diarrhea
3. Blood in the vomit (red or "coffee grounds" material) or in the stool (red or black tarlike material)
4. Vomiting or diarrhea with a high fever (above 102°F or 38.8°C)
5. Yellow color in skin or white parts of the eyes
6. Vomiting with severe headache and a history of a recent head injury
7. Vomiting or diarrhea that lasts 3 days without improvement
8. If you are pregnant or have diabetes
9. Recurrent vomiting and/or diarrhea

HEARTBURN AND INDIGESTION

Indigestion and heartburn are usually a result of irritation of the stomach or the esophagus, the tube that connects the mouth to the stomach. The stomach lining is usually protected from stomach acids, but the esophagus is not. Therefore, if stomach acids "reflux," or back up into the esophagus, the result is usually a burning discomfort in the chest and throat. The esophagus is normally protected by a muscular valve that allows food to enter the stomach but prevents stomach contents from flowing upward into the esophagus. Certain foods (including chocolate, garlic, and onions), medications, and smoking can loosen and open this protective sphincter valve. Overeating, lying down, or bending over can also cause the stomach acids to gain access to the sensitive lining of the esophagus.

Self-Assessment

1. Look for a pattern in the symptoms. Do they occur after eating certain foods, taking certain medications, or when you bend over or lie down? Do certain foods or an antacid relieve the symptoms?
2. Observe your bowel movements. Black tarlike stools may indicate bleeding in the stomach (iron tablets and Pepto-Bismol can also cause black stools).

Self-Care

1. Avoid irritants such as smoking, aspirin, ibuprofen, naproxen sodium, alcohol, caffeine (coffee, tea, cola), chocolate, onions, carbonated beverages, spicy or fatty foods, acidic

foods (vinegar, citrus fruits, tomatoes), or any other foods that seem to make your symptoms worse.

2. Take nonabsorbable antacids such as Maalox, Mylanta, or Gelusil every 1–2 hours and especially before bedtime, or try an acid reducer, now available without a prescription (Pepcid, Tagamet, Zantac, or Prilosec). These drugs work in different ways, so ask your physician to help you choose the right medication for you.

3. Avoid tight clothing.

4. Avoid overeating; eat smaller, more frequent meals.

5. Don't lie down for 1–2 hours after a meal. Elevate the head of your bed with 4- to 6-inch blocks of wood or bricks. Adding extra pillows usually makes things worse by creating a posture that increases pressure on the stomach. Try sleeping on your left side, which may reduce reflux compared to sleeping on your back or right side.

6. If you are overweight in the abdominal area, weight loss may help. Abdominal obesity can increase pressure on the stomach when you are lying down.

When to Call the Physician

1. Stools that are black and tarlike or vomit that is bloody or contains material that looks like coffee grounds
2. Severe abdominal or chest pain
3. Pain that goes through to the back
4. No relief from antacids
5. Difficulty swallowing solid foods
6. Symptoms lasting longer than 3 days

Recurrent or persistent abdominal pain may be a symptom of an ulcer, a raw area in the lining of the stomach or duodenum (the first part of the small intestine). About one in five men and one in ten women develop an ulcer at some time in their lives. Most ulcers are linked to infection with the bacterium *Helicobacter pylori;* people who regularly take nonsteroidal anti-inflammatory drugs like aspirin or ibuprofen are also at risk for ulcers because these drugs irritate the lining of the stomach. *H. pylori* infection is relatively easy to diagnose and treat, and other medications are available to treat ulcers linked to other causes. Many of the self-care measures described above are also frequently recommended for people with ulcers.

HEADACHE

Headache is one of the most common symptoms. There are four major types of headache: tension, migraine, cluster, and sinus. Tension headaches, migraines, and cluster headaches are described in Chapter 2 (p. 43). Sinus headaches are caused by blockage of the sinus cavities with resulting pressure and pain in the cheeks, forehead, and upper teeth. Headache caused by elevated blood pressure is very uncommon and occurs only with very high pressures.

Self-Assessment

1. Take your temperature. The presence of fever may indicate a sinus infection. Fever, severe headache, and a very stiff neck suggest meningitis, a rare but serious infection around the brain and spinal cord.

2. Tap with your fingers over the sinus cavities in your cheeks and forehead. If this causes increased pain, it may indicate a sinus infection.

3. For recurrent headaches, keep a headache journal. Record how often and when your headaches occur, associated symptoms, activities that precede the headache, and your food and beverage intake. Look for patterns that may provide clues to the cause(s) of your headaches.

B

Self-Care

1. Try applying ice packs or heat on your neck and head.

2. Gently massage the muscles of your neck and scalp.

3. Try deep relaxation or breathing exercises.

4. Take aspirin or aspirin substitute for pain relief. Over-the-counter products containing a combination of aspirin, acetaminophen, and caffeine are approved by the FDA for treating migraines.

5. If pain is associated with nasal congestion, try a decongestant medication like pseudoephedrine.

6. Try to avoid emotional and physical stressors (such as poor posture and eyestrain).

7. Try avoiding foods that may trigger headaches, such as aged cheeses, chocolate, nuts, red wine, alcohol, avocados, figs, raisins, and any fermented or pickled foods.

When to Call the Physician

1. Unusually severe headache or one that occurs suddenly
2. Headache accompanied by fever and a very stiff neck
3. Headache with sinus pain, tenderness, and fever
4. Severe headache following a recent head injury
5. Headache associated with slurred speech, visual disturbance, or numbness or weakness in the face, arms, or legs
6. Headache persisting longer than 3 days
7. Recurrent unexplained headaches
8. Increasing severity or frequency of headaches
9. Severe migraine headaches (In recent years, many new prescription medications have been approved for the prevention and treatment of migraines.)

LOW-BACK PAIN

Pain in the lower back is a very common condition; it is most often due to a strain of the muscles and ligaments along the spine, often triggered by bending, lifting, or other activity. Low-back pain can also result from bone growths (spurs) irritating the nerves along the spine or pressure from ruptured or protruding discs, the "shock absorbers" between the vertebrae. Sometimes back pain is caused by an infection or stone in the kidney. Fortunately, however, simple muscular strain is the most common cause of low-back pain and can usually be effectively self-treated.

Self-Assessment

1. Take your temperature. Back pain with high fever may indicate a kidney or other infection.

2. Check for blood in your urine or frequent, painful urination, which may also indicate a kidney problem.

3. Observe for tingling or pain traveling down one or both legs *below* the knee when you bend, cough, or sneeze. These symptoms suggest a disc problem.

B

Self-Care

1. Lie on your back or in any comfortable position on the floor or a firm mattress, with knees slightly bent and supported by a pillow. Rest for a day if the pain persists.

2. Use ice packs on the painful area for the first 3 days, and then continue with cold or change to heat, whichever gives more relief.

3. Take aspirin or aspirin substitute for pain relief.

4. After the acute pain has subsided, begin gentle back and stomach exercises. Practice good posture and lifting techniques to protect your back. Try to resume gentle, everyday activities like walking as soon as possible. Bed rest beyond 1 day is no longer advised and may even make things worse; try gentle stretching and resume activities that don't aggravate the problem. To learn more about proper back exercises and use of your back, consult a physical therapist or your physician.

When to Call the Physician

1. Back pain following a severe injury such as a car crash or fall

2. Back pain radiating down the leg *below* the knee on one or both sides

3. Persistent numbness, tingling, or weakness in the legs or feet

4. Loss of bladder or bowel control

5. Back pain associated with high fever (above 101°F or 38.3°C), frequent or painful urination, blood in the urine, or severe abdominal pain

6. Back pain that does not improve after 72 hours of self-care

STRAINS AND SPRAINS

Missteps, slips, falls, and athletic misadventures can result in a variety of strains, sprains, and fractures. A strain occurs when you overstretch a muscle or tendon (the connective tissue that attaches muscle to bone). Sprains are caused by overstretching or tearing ligaments (the tough fibrous bands that connect bone to bone). Depending on the severity and location, a sprain may actually be more serious than a fracture, because bones generally heal very strongly whereas ligaments may remain stretched and lax after healing. After a sprain, it may take 6 weeks for the ligament to heal.

After most injuries, you can expect pain and swelling. This is the body's way of immobilizing and protecting the injured part so that healing can take place. The goal of self-assessment is to determine whether you have a minor injury that you can safely self-treat or a more serious injury to an artery, nerve, or bone that should be treated by your physician.

Self-Assessment

1. Watch for coldness, blue color, or numbness in the limb beyond the injury. These may be signs of damage to an artery or a nerve.

2. Look for signs of a possible fracture, which would include a misshapen limb, reduced length of the limb on the injured side compared to the uninjured side, an inability to move or bear weight, a grating sound with movement of the injured area, extreme tenderness at one point along the injured bone as you press with your fingers, or a sensation of snapping at the time of the injury.

3. Gently move the injured area through its full range of motion. Immobility or instability suggests a more serious injury.

Self-Care

1. Immediately immobilize, protect, and rest the injured area until you can bear weight on it or move it without pain. Remember: If it hurts, don't do it.

2. To decrease pain and swelling, immediately apply ice (a cold pack or ice wrapped in a cloth) for 15 minutes every hour for the first 24–48 hours. Then apply ice or heat as needed for comfort.

3. Immediately elevate the injured limb above the level of your heart for the first 24 hours to decrease swelling.

4. Immobilize and support the injured area with an elastic wrap or splint. Be careful not to wrap so tightly as to cause blueness, coldness, or numbness.

5. Take aspirin or aspirin substitute for pain as needed.

When to Call the Physician

1. An injury that occurred with great force, such as a high fall or motor vehicle crash
2. Hearing or feeling a snap at the time of the injury
3. A limb that is blue, cold, or numb
4. A limb that is bent, twisted, or crooked
5. Tenderness at specific points along a bone
6. Inability to move the injured area
7. A wobbly, unstable joint
8. Marked swelling of the injured area
9. Inability to bear weight after 24 hours
10. Pain that increases or lasts longer than 4 days

CUTS AND SCRAPES

Cuts and scrapes are common disruptions of the body's skin. Fortunately, the vast majority of these wounds are minor and don't require stitches, antibiotics, or a physician's care. An abrasion involves a scraping away of the superficial layers of skin. Abrasions, though less serious than cuts, are often more painful because they disrupt more skin nerves. There are two types of cuts: lacerations (narrow slices of the skin) and puncture wounds (stabs into deeper tissues).

Normal healing of a cut or abrasion is a remarkable process. After the bleeding stops, small amounts of serum, a clear yellowish fluid, may leak from the wound. This fluid is rich in antibodies to help prevent an infection. Redness and swelling may normally occur as more blood is shunted to the area, bringing white blood cells and nutrients to speed healing. There may also be some swelling of nearby lymph nodes, which are another part of your body's defense against infection. Finally, a scab forms. This is "nature's bandage," which protects the area while it heals.

The main concerns about cuts are the possibility of damage to deeper tissues and the risk of infection. Damage to underlying blood vessels may lead to severe bleeding as well as blueness and coldness in areas beyond the wound. Injured nerves may produce numbness and a loss of the ability to move parts of the body beyond the injured area. Damaged muscles, tendons, and ligaments can also result in inability to move areas beyond the cut.

Wound infection usually does not take place until 24–48 hours after an injury. Signs of infection include increasing redness, swelling, pain, pus, and fever. One of the most serious, though fortunately uncommon, complications of puncture wounds is tetanus ("lockjaw"). This bacterial infection thrives in areas not exposed to oxygen, so it is more likely to develop in deep puncture wounds or dirty wounds. Tetanus is not likely to develop in minor cuts or wounds caused by clean objects like knives. You need a tetanus immunization shot following a cut under the following conditions:

- If you have never had the recommended tetanus immunization injections
- If you have a dirty or contaminated wound and it has been longer than 5 years since your last injection
- If you have a clean, minor wound and it has been longer than 10 years since your last injection

Self-Assessment

1. Look for warning signs of complications: persistent bleeding, numbness, an inability to move the injured area, or the later development of pus, increasing redness, and fever.

2. Measure the size of the cut. If your cut is shallow, less than 1/4 inch deep, less than an inch long, and not in a high-stress area (such as a joint, which bends) and you can easily hold the edges of the wound closed, it probably won't need stitches.

Self-Care

1. Apply direct pressure over the wound until the bleeding stops. The only exception is puncture wounds, which should be encouraged to bleed freely (unless spurting a large amount of blood) for a few minutes to flush out bacteria and debris.

2. When bleeding stops, wash your hands thoroughly with soap and water, then carefully cleanse the wound with clean water. Avoid getting soap in the wound, as it can irritate exposed tissues. Experts now advise against pouring hydrogen peroxide into a wound, as it may damage sensitive tissue. Do not try to remove visible dirt, debris, or objects (such as splinters or shards) from the wound; such cleaning should be done by a medical professional. If you don't see anything in the wound but suspect something may be there, see a doctor immediately.

3. Pat the area dry with a clean towel, then apply an antiseptic ointment and a clean bandage.

4. If it is an abrasion, cover the area with a sterile adhesive bandage until a scab forms. For minor lacerations, close the cut with a butterfly bandage or a sterile adhesive tape, drawing the edges close together but not overlapping. If there is an extra flap of clean skin, leave it in place for extra protection. Do not attempt to close a puncture wound. Instead, soak the wound in warm water for 15 minutes several times a day for several days. Soaking helps keep the wound open and thus prevents infection.

When to Call the Physician

1. Bleeding that can't be controlled with direct pressure

2. Numbness, weakness, or an inability to move the injured area

3. Any large, deep wound

4. A cut in an area that bends and with edges that cannot easily be held together

5. Cuts on the hands or face unless clean and shallow

6. A contaminated wound from which you cannot remove the foreign material

7. Any human or animal bite

8. If you need a tetanus immunization (see indications noted earlier)

9. Development of increasing redness, swelling, pain, pus, or fever 24 hours or more after the injury

10. If the wound is not healing well after 3 weeks

Photo Credits

Chapter 1 p. 0, PhotoDisc/Getty Images; p. 3, © Ariel Skelley/Corbis; p. 15, © Michael Newman/ PhotoEdit; p. 23, © AP/Wide World Photos; p. 25, © Jeff Greenberg/PhotoEdit; p. 26, © Steve Mason/Getty Images

Chapter 2 p. 30, © Tony Freeman/PhotoEdit; p. 38, © Richard Lord/PhotoEdit; p. 47, © AP/Wide World Photos; p. 52, © Spencer Grant/PhotoEdit; p. 56, © Joel Gordon

Chapter 3 p. 62, © Big Cheese Photo/ PictureQuest; p. 66, Ryan McVay/Getty Images; p. 70, © Michael Newman/PhotoEdit; p. 73, © Dennis MacDonald/PhotoEdit; p. 84, © Jonathan Nourok/PhotoEdit; p. 87, © Erik S. Lesser; p. 88, © Michael Newman/PhotoEdit

Chapter 4 p. 94, Suza Scalora/Getty Images; p. 97, © Michael Newman/PhotoEdit; p. 103, © Image Source/PictureQuest; p. 107, Ryan McVay/Getty Images; p. 110, © Deborah Davis/PhotoEdit; p. 115, Digital Vision/ PictureQuest

Chapter 5 p. 122, Jules Frazier/Getty Images; p. 129, © Jeff Greenberg/PhotoEdit; p. 132, © Joel Gordon; p. 138, © Spencer Grant/PhotoEdit; p. 143, © David Young-Wolff/PhotoEdit; p. 147, © Colin Young-Wolff/PhotoEdit

Chapter 6 p. 150, © Joel Gordon; p. 154, © Dana White/PhotoEdit; p. 157, 159, 161, 166, © Joel Gordon; p. 177, © Syracuse Newspapers/ Gary Walts/The Image Works

Chapter 7 p. 182, Hisham F. Ibrahim/Getty Images; p. 186, © Roberto Schmidt/Getty Images; p. 189L, © Alex Wong/Getty Images; p. 189R, © AP/Wide World Photos; p. 197, © Joel Gordon

Chapter 8 p. 202, © Spencer Grant/PhotoEdit; p. 205, © Myrleen Ferguson Cate/PhotoEdit; p. 216, © Tissuepix/Photo Researchers, Inc.; p. 218, Keith Brofsky/Getty Images; p. 224, © David Young-Wolff/ PhotoEdit; p. 230, PhotoDisc/Getty Images

Chapter 9 p. 234, © Bonnie Kamin; p. 238, © Park Street/PhotoEdit; p. 247, © Mark Antman/The Image Works; p. 255, © AP/Wide World Photos; p. 257, © Barbara Stitzer/PhotoEdit; p. 260, © Custom Medical Stock Photo

Chapter 10 p. 268, © Tom Carter/PhotoEdit; p. 271, © David Young-Wolff/PhotoEdit; p. 273, © Thinkstock/Superstock; p. 276, © James Schaffer/PhotoEdit; p. 279, © Lon C. Diehl/ PhotoEdit; p. 290, © Royalty-Free/Corbis

Chapter 11 p. 296, © Joel Gordon; p. 301, © Michael Newman/PhotoEdit; p. 306, © Dennis MacDonald/PhotoEdit; p. 312, © Mark Richards/ PhotoEdit; p. 314, © David Young-Wolff/PhotoEdit; p. 320, © Royalty-Free/Corbis

Chapter 12 p. 326, Mitch Hrdlicka/Getty Images; p. 328, © Dana White/PhotoEdit; p. 343, © Royalty-Free/Corbis; p. 347, © David Young-Wolff/PhotoEdit; p. 362, © Myrleen Ferguson Cate/PhotoEdit

Chapter 13 p. 376, © Chris Rogers/PictureQuest; p. 379, © Bob Daemmrich/PhotoEdit; p. 394, Keith Brofsky/Getty Images; p. 397, © Neil Tanner; p. 404, © David Young-Wolff/PhotoEdit

Chapter 14 p. 410, © Novastock/PhotoEdit; p. 421, © Cindy Charles/PhotoEdit; p. 425, © Mary Kate Denny/PhotoEdit; p. 430, © Tony Freeman/PhotoEdit; p. 437, © AP/Wide World Photos

Chapter 15 p. 444, © Adamsmith/Superstock; p. 452, © Michael Newman/PhotoEdit; p. 456, Doug Menuez/Getty Images; p. 466, © David Young-Wolff/PhotoEdit

Chapter 16 p. 478, © Rod Rolle/Getty Images; p. 484, © Rudi Von Briel/PhotoEdit; p. 490, © Jilly Wendell/Getty Images/Stone; p. 499, © David Young-Wolff/PhotoEdit; p. 507, © AP/Wide World Photos

Chapter 17 p. 514, © Bill Aron/PhotoEdit; p. 521, © Eye of Science/Photo Researchers, Inc.; p. 530, © John Durham/Photo Researchers, Inc.; p. 538, © David Young-Wolff/PhotoEdit

Chapter 18 p. 546, © Reuters/Corbis; p. 559, © Dave Hogan/Getty Images; p. 562, © Mary Kate Denny/PhotoEdit; p. 566, Ryan McVay/Getty Images; p. 575, © Royalty-Free/Corbis

Chapter 19 p. 580, © Royalty-Free/Corbis; p. 585, © David Young-Wolff/PhotoEdit; p. 586, © Amy C. Etra/PhotoEdit; p. 598, © Joel Gordon

Chapter 20 p. 602, © Royalty-Free/Corbis; p. 604, © John Neubauer/PhotoEdit; p. 606, 614, © AP/Wide World Photos; p. 619, © Jeff Greenberg/PhotoEdit

Chapter 21 p. 628, © Michael Newman/ PhotoEdit; p. 635, Tomi/PhotoLink/Getty Images; p. 639, Ryan McVay/Getty Images; p. 646, Anthony Saint James/Getty Images; p. 651, PhotoLink/Getty Images

Chapter 22 p. 660, © Michael Newman/ PhotoEdit; p. 670, © Tony Freeman/PhotoEdit; p. 672, © Comstock; p. 673, © Jonathan Nourok/PhotoEdit; p. 682, © Rachel Epstein/ PhotoEdit

Chapter 23 p. 692, Russell Illig/Getty Images; p. 694, Marty Bahamonde/FEMA; 703, © AP/Wide World Photos; p. 708, © Dennis MacDonald/ PhotoEdit

READINGS

What Does Science Say You Should Eat?

Most diets aren't realistic or advisable, including the U.S. agriculture department's famous food pyramid. Instead, a Harvard scientist recommends a new way of eating based on the world's largest and longest food study.

By Brad Lemley

America clearly needs dietary guidance.—More than 44 million people are clinically obese compared with 30 million a decade ago, putting them at increased risk for heart disease, stroke, type 2 diabetes, and breast, prostate, and colon cancers. In the meantime, the noun *diet* seems to attract a different adjective every week, including Atkins, Ornish, Cooper, grapefruit, rice, protein, Scarsdale, South Beach, Beverly Hills, Best Chance, Eat Smart, and Miracle, not to mention Help, I'm Southern and I Can't Stop Eating. While some of these plans overlap, others seem to specifically contradict each other, notably the meat-intensive regime of the late Robert Atkins versus the near-vegetarian program of Dean Ornish.—No wonder Americans are tempted to follow Mark Twain's admonition to "eat what you like and let the food fight it out inside." But still, we wonder: Is there really an optimum way to eat?—Although debate rages, academic nutrition researchers have begun to form a consensus around a plan with an important advantage—it is based on a preponderance of sound science. The regime does not as yet have a name, but it might well be called the Willett diet, after its leading proponent, Walter Willett, chairman of the department of nutrition at the Harvard School of Public Health.—Featuring abundant fruits, vegetables, whole grains, and vegetable oils, as well as optional portions of fish and chicken, Willett's plan resembles the much-touted Mediterranean diet shown in several studies to reduce the risk of heart disease. Nonetheless, Willett resists the comparison. "The Mediterranean diet is specific to a certain climate and culture," he says, adding that by focusing on healthy ingredients rather than specific dishes, "anyone can adapt this plan to his own tastes." The results: stable blood-sugar levels, easier weight control, clearer arteries, and overall better health.

In this case it's hard science, not just opinion. Willett's plan is based on the largest long-term dietary survey ever undertaken: the 121,700-participant Nurses' Health Study, begun in 1976 by Harvard Medical School professor Frank Speizer, with dietary assessments supervised by Willett since 1980. The study isn't just big: Willett carefully crafted it so that he and others could extract specific recommendations about food intake. Participants even surrender blood and toenail samples so that Willett can track absorption of trace elements and other nutrients. If a participant reports a major illness, such as heart attack or cancer, "we write for permission to obtain medical records for further details," says Willett. To ensure that the data include both sexes and two generations, Willett and several colleagues also launched the Health Professionals Follow-Up Study, which includes 52,000 men, and the Nurses' Health Study II, a survey of 116,000 younger women.

In the past, nutritional scientists have largely relied on studies of animals, small groups of people, and/or petri-dish biochemistry that may not reflect the vagaries of human metabolism, although Willett uses such studies when he deems it appropriate. His access to a unique quarter-million-person pool of humans who carefully track both their diets and their health lends added credibility to his research. "When you put animal, metabolic, and epidemiological studies together and they all point in the same direction, you can be pretty confident about your conclusions," Willett says.

> 'Nutrition used to be like religion. Everyone said, I have the truth, everyone else is wrong'

While soft-spoken and self-effacing in person, Willett isn't shy about using this formidable database to take on the federal establishment.

WILLETT VS. ORNISH VS. ATKINS

Walter Willett's dietary recommendations are similar in many ways to those advanced by another doctor-nutritionist, Dean Ornish, who pioneered an ultralow-fat, near-vegetarian regime that has been shown to halt or reduce coronary blockage in most heart patients. Both Willett and Ornish emphasize whole grains, fruits, and vegetables, and both minimize animal proteins. But they part ways on fats: Willett recommends replacing saturated fats in the American diet with unsaturated ones, while Ornish suggests sharply cutting fat intake altogether, especially for those at risk for heart disease. "No one has shown that the kind of diet that Walter Willett recommends can reverse heart disease," says Ornish.

For his part, Willett insists that "replacing saturated fats with unsaturated fats is a safe, proven, and delicious way to cut the rates of heart disease." He says the Lyon Diet Heart study, a French trial that tracked heart-attack survivors on an oil-rich Mediterranean diet versus those on the low-fat American Heart Association diet, showed a significant drop in second attacks for the Lyon group. Ornish responds that the drop in deaths in that study was most likely due to increasing heart-healthy omega-3 fats and decreasing intake of omega-6 fats, saturated fats, animal protein, and cholesterol, not to high overall consumption of fat. Ornish recommends that everyone consume three grams of omega-3 fats daily, either through eating fish or taking supplements.

In contrast with both Willett and Ornish, the late Robert Atkins recommended a meat-intensive, protein-rich regime. "Studies at Duke University, the University of Cincinnati, and the University of Pennsylvania all show that people can lose significant weight, lower their triglycerides, and improve their HDL [high-density lipoprotein] cholesterol levels by consuming protein and limiting carbohydrates," says Stuart Trager, an orthopedic surgeon who assumed the spokesman's mantle for the diet after Atkins's death in April 2003. Trager believes the real strength of the Atkins diet is that "it is something people are willing and able to do."

Willett concedes that Atkins "was really onto something. He believed, correctly, that most people can better control their weight by reducing the glycemic load of the diet than by other means. But there is evidence that the traditional Atkins diet, which is high in animal fat, is not optimal. There are benefits to having cereal in one's diet. There is relief from constipation, and we do see [in the Nurses' Health Study] some benefit for heart disease and diabetes. This is probably partially from the fiber in whole grains, and also partly from the other minerals and vitamins that come along with whole grains that are in short supply in many people's diets."

While at first blush the three approaches seem sharply divergent, Trager sounds a conciliatory note. "No one has ever bothered to point out that we are compatriots on many points," he says. All three nutritionists share an emphasis on reducing blood-sugar spikes by reducing the glycemic load. Moreover, all three condemn trans fats, white flour, and sugar. "There really is universal agreement that you should cut those things out of your diet," Trager says.
—*Brad Lemley*

His Healthy Eating Pyramid differs radically from the Food Guide Pyramid pushed by the U.S. Department of Agriculture. "At best, the USDA pyramid offers wishy-washy, scientifically unfounded advice," Willett argues in his book, *Eat, Drink, and Be Healthy: The Harvard Medical School Guide to Healthy Eating.* At worst, he adds, "the misinformation contributes to overweight, poor health, and unnecessary early deaths."

The numbers back him up. Men and women in Willett's studies whose diets most closely paralleled the Healthy Eating Pyramid's guidelines lowered their risk of major chronic disease by 20 percent and 11 percent respectively, according to an article published in the December 2002 issue of *The American Journal of Clinical Nutrition.* That compares with reduced risks of 11 percent and 3 percent for those whose diets most closely mirrored the USDA pyramid's guidelines.

"Nutrition used to be like religion. Everyone said, 'I have the truth, everyone else is wrong,' and there wasn't much data to refute that," says Willett. "Now we're starting to have a real scientific basis for understanding what you should eat."

JUST INSIDE THE DOOR OF WILLETT'S OFFICE AT the Harvard School of Public Health in Boston sits his bicycle, mud-spattered from his daily commute over the Charles River from his home in Cambridge. Past that, on top of a pile of medical journals, perches a plastic bag full of plump, homegrown cherry tomatoes, a late-season-harvest gift from his administrative assistant. Willett knows good tomatoes. As a member of a fifth-generation Michigan farming family, he paid his undergraduate tuition at Michigan State by raising vegetables, and today he grows "as much as possible" in his tiny urban backyard.

Behind the cluttered desk sits Willett himself, trim, toned, and turned out in a sharp gray suit. "All you have to do is take a look at Walter to see the value of his research. The proof is in the pudding," says David Jenkins, a nutrition researcher at the University of Toronto. Willett vigorously follows his own plan and at age 58 reports that his weight, cholesterol, and triglycerides are all where they should be. He is, in short, the picture of where applied nutritional science might deliver us all, if we had the proper information.

That's the problem. In recent years, Willett says, the American public has been victimized by dodgy advice. Not only has obesity skyrocketed but "the incidence of heart disease is also not going down anymore. It has really stalled."

What happened? In Willett's view, things began to go awry in the mid-1980s, when a National Institutes of Health conference decreed that to prevent heart disease, all Americans except children under 2 years old should reduce their fat intake from 40 percent to 30 percent of their total daily calories. The press touted the recommendation as revealed truth, and the USDA's Food Guide Pyramid, released in 1992, reflects this view, calling for 6 to 11 servings of bread, cereal, rice, and pasta daily, while fats and oils are to be used "sparingly."

Too bad, says Willett. "The low-fat mantra has contributed to obesity. The nutrition community told people they had to worry only about counting fat grams. That encouraged the creation of thousands of low-fat products. I call it 'the SnackWell revolution.'" Blithely consuming low-fat foods full of carbohydrates is a prescription for portliness, says Willett, adding that any farmer knows this. "If you pen up an animal and feed it grain, it will get fat. People are no different."

The problem with overeating refined carbohydrates such as white flour and sucrose (table sugar) is that amylase, an enzyme, quickly converts them into the simple sugar called glucose. That goads the pancreas to overproduce insulin, the substance that conducts glucose into the cells. But excessive sugar is toxic to cells, so after years of glucose and insulin overload, the cells can become insulin resistant and may no longer allow insulin to easily push glucose inside them. That keeps blood glucose levels high, forcing the pancreas to make even more insulin in a desperate attempt to jam the stuff through cell membranes. Willett likens the effect to an overworked, undermaintained pump that eventually wears out. Type 2 diabetes can be one result, but Willett contends that insulin-resistant people who don't develop full-blown diabetes still face significant health risks.

Other researchers agree. Stanford endocrinologist Gerald Reaven coined the term Syndrome X to describe the constellation of health problems that spring from insulin resistance. Until the late 1980s, Reaven says, "the common scientific view was that insulin resistance only mattered if it led all the way to type 2 diabetes. Looking at the data, it's clear that most people who are insulin resistant don't get diabetes but are greatly at risk for coronary heart disease, hypertension, non-alcoholic-type liver disease, polycystic ovary syndrome, and several kinds of cancer."

In the case of heart disease, Reaven says that high blood concentrations of insulin and glucose can damage the endothelium that lines coronary arteries and set the stage for the formation of plaques. "A big problem is the lack of drugs to treat this problem," he adds. "A lot of doctors' education comes from drug companies. They know about cholesterol because everyone is pushing their statin. They know about hypertension because there are multiple hypertensive drugs. But they know a lot less about insulin resistance and its consequences, and that's unfortunate."

Syndrome X, also known as metabolic syndrome or insulin-resistance syndrome, is largely unknown to the public as well. While many people avoid cholesterol and fat-laden foods, few understand the threat posed by carbohydrate excess. That needs to change, says Willett. "Cholesterol is relevant, but the danger is overblown," he says. "Syndrome X is the global public-health problem of the 21st century. Almost certainly the vast majority of Americans have a higher degree of insulin resistance than is optimal."

The Willett plan aims to even out the glucose roller coaster through an emphasis on foods with low glycemic loads—foods that convert to glucose slowly—like whole grains, plant oils, and vegetables. This keeps blood glucose levels relatively constant, sparing the pancreas overwork. Steady blood glucose also helps keep the appetite in check, which makes maintaining a healthy weight easier, says Willett. So instead of high carb, low fat, one might summarize the Willett plan's directive as good carb, good fat.

"People are being told to reduce fat and eat more carbohydrates. For many people, particularly overweight people with a high degree of insulin resistance, that produces exactly the opposite of what they need," says Willett. Randomized trials, he says, show that people on low-fat diets generally lose two to four pounds after several weeks but then gain back the weight even while continuing the diet. "Most of them would be better off reducing carbs, switching to better carbs, and increasing their intake of healthy fats."

'Instead of high carb, low fat, one might summarize the Willet plan's directive as good carb, good fat'

WILLETT, LIKE VIRTUALLY EVERY OTHER NUTRITION researcher, advises eating vegetables in abundance, consuming alcohol in moderation, and taking a daily multivitamin to cover nutritional gaps. He also touts fish as a source of protein and heart-protective n-3 fatty acids, which are also known as omega-3 acids. (Those who worry about mercury contamination in fish got some good news recently: In one study conducted in the Seychelles, a group of islands in the Indian Ocean, scientists from the University of Rochester Medical Center tracked pregnant women who ate an average of 12 fish meals a week, about 10 times the quantity of fish eaten by the average American. "We've found no evidence that the low levels of mercury in seafood are harmful," said lead author Gary Myers. Moreover, various tests indicated that the women's children suffered no adverse cognitive, behavioral, or neurological effects.)

High on the list of food ingredients Willett counsels avoiding are hydrogenated fats, often referred to

GOOD CARBS/BAD CARBS

The glycemic index (GI) is a way of measuring how quickly the carbohydrate in a given food raises the level of blood sugar. So eating a low-GI food causes a slow, mild rise, while the same quantity of carbohydrate in a high-GI food will trigger a faster, bigger rise. A GI of 55 or less is considered low, 56 to 69 is medium, and 70 or more is high.

But the GI is of limited use in the real world of pears, pork, and pudding because it ignores how much of that food a person eats. A few years ago, Walter Willett pioneered the concept of the glycemic load (GL), a measurement that factors in the quantity of carbohydrates eaten in a single serving of a particular food. The carbohydrates in parsnips, for example, are quickly converted to glucose, so parsnips have a rather high index of 97, plus or minus 19 (the numbers are sometimes imprecise because they are based on feeding foods to test subjects and monitoring their blood-sugar response, which can vary for many reasons). But parsnips have a GL of just 12, because a single 80-gram serving contains a relatively small amount of carbohydrate. A GL of 10 or less is considered low, 11 to 19 is medium, and, 20 or more is high. Consistently eating low-GL foods evens out blood-sugar peaks and valleys, which Willett says helps keep appetite and weight under control. Eating low-GL foods also reduces the risk of developing type 2 diabetes. When Willett says "good carbs," he is essentially referring to fiber-rich, low-GL foods.

Generally, whole grains have lower glycemic loads than refined grains. For example, a 150-gram serving of brown rice has a GL of 18, while the same serving of quick-cooking white rice has a GL of 29. Although the photographs in this story tally the "sugar equivalence" of the carbohydrates in various American foods, the glycemic index and glycemic load of each of these foods needs to be considered as well. The glycemic numbers accompanying the photographs in this article are from Janette Brand-Miller of the University of Sydney, based on a table published in the July 2002 issue of *The American Journal of Clinical Nutrition*. An adaptation of that table can be seen at `diabetes.about.com/library/mendosagi/ngilists.htm`.

—*B. L.*

as trans fats, which are found in shortening, margarine, deep-fried foods, and packaged baked goods. That advice was controversial when Willett published a groundbreaking paper on the subject in 1991, but it has since become close to dogma. "Both controlled-feeding studies that have examined the effects of trans fat on blood cholesterol and epidemiological studies of trans-fat intake in relation to the risk of heart disease and diabetes indicate they are considerably worse than saturated fats," he says.

Daily exercise is essential, Willett adds, and he confirms the often-cited advice that walking is the best choice for many people. The Nurses' Health Study revealed a "very strong link" between walking and protection against heart disease: Women who walked an average of three hours a week were 35 percent less likely to have a heart attack over an eight-year period than those who walked less. It may seem odd that Willett includes exercise in his Healthy Eating Pyramid, but he is adamant that exercise and diet cannot be teased apart. "It doesn't have to be extreme. I run along the Charles for 25 minutes most mornings." A half hour daily of moderate activity offers "impressive health benefits," he says, but there is "added benefit for greater intensity for longer times."

Willett's more iconoclastic conclusions include the heretical notion that soy—touted as a miracle food that fights cancer, obesity, and virtually every other human ill—may have "a dark side." He points to a British study in which 48 women with suspicious breast lumps were randomly assigned to receive either no supplement or one containing soy isoflavones (a compound in soybeans molecularly similar to estrogen) for 14 days. Those taking the supplement showed substantially more cell growth in the tissue removed than the women who were not taking the soy. Another troubling study showed memory loss and other cognitive declines in elderly Japanese men in Hawaii who stuck to their traditional soy-based diet, as opposed to those who switched to a more of a Western diet. "In moderation, soy is fine," says Willett. "Stuffed into everything, you could get into trouble." And soy isoflavone supplements, he counsels, should be regarded as "totally untested new drugs."

Willett also counsels that dairy products—which supply concentrated calories and saturated fat—are not the best way to get calcium and that the recommended daily intake of 1,200 milligrams daily for adults over 50 appears to be more than what's needed. His advice: Eat calcium-bearing vegetables, including leafy greens, take calcium supplements if you're a woman, and exercise. "The evidence for physical activity being protective against fractures is huge," he says.

> 'No research has ever shown that people who eat more eggs have more heart attacks than people who eat fewer eggs'

And he defends eggs. Although cholesterol fears have caused American per capita egg consumption to drop from 400 to 250 per year, "no research has ever shown that people who eat more eggs have more heart attacks than people who eat fewer eggs," Willett says. A 2001 Kansas State University study identified a type of lecithin called phosphatidylcholine in eggs that interferes with cholesterol absorption, which may explain why many studies have found no association between egg intake and blood cholesterol level. If the breakfast menu option is a white-flour bagel or an egg fried in vegetable oil, says Willett, "the egg is the better choice."

Perhaps the most comprehensive studies Willett has assembled compare the health consequences of eating saturated versus unsaturated fat. The term *saturated* means that every available site along each fat molecule's carbon chain is filled with a hydrogen atom; such fats—including butter and animal fat—are solids at room temperature. There are two types of unsaturated fats: monounsaturated fats such as olive oil, which are missing one pair of hydrogen atoms, and polyunsaturated fats such as soy, corn, and canola oils, which lack more than one pair. Both sorts are liquid at room temperature.

Some researchers have questioned whether saturated fat is dangerous. In his book, *The Cholesterol Myths: Exposing the Fallacy That Saturated Fat and Cholesterol Cause Heart Disease,* Swedish physician Uffe Ravnskov asserts that as of 1998, 27 studies on diet and heart disease had been published regarding 34 groups of patients; in 30 of those groups investigators found no difference in animal fat consumption between those who had heart disease and those who did not. "Anyone who reads the literature in this field with an open mind soon discovers that the emperor has no clothes," Ravnskov writes.

Willett turns to his Nurses' Health mega-study for the definitive word. "The amounts of specific fats did make a difference," he says. "Women who ate more unsaturated fat instead of saturated fat had fewer heart problems." Willett calculated that replacing 5 percent of saturated fat calories with unsaturated would cut the risk of heart attack or death from heart disease by 40 percent. Other studies—notably the French Lyon Diet Heart study, begun in 1988—show a similar correlation.

A HEALTHY DIET PLAN IS WORTHLESS IF PEOPLE won't stick to it, and Susan Roberts, director of the energy metabolism laboratory at Tufts University, contends that Willett's regimen is too severe. "Most people would say his recommendations are healthy but that other, less difficult diets are healthy too," she says.

Difficult is in the palate of the eater. The last half of Willett's book aims to dispel any taint of Calvinism with recipes that verge on the sybaritic, including pork tenderloin with pistachio-gremolata crust, chicken enchilada casserole, and grilled salmon steaks with papaya-mint salsa. On the other hand, some resolve might be required to soldier through a few of the other dishes listed there, including hearty oat-wheat berry bread or the onion-crusted tofu-steak sandwich. But most people, Willett believes, can summon the willpower to substitute whole-wheat flour for white and plant oils for shortening or lard, and eat less sugar overall. "I think what I suggest is not severely restrictive, because it can be achieved mainly by substitution," rather than slavishly following recipes, Willett says. In any case, "it does not mean you cannot eat any of those foods but rather that they should be de-emphasized."

So take heart. Even Willett has a little chocolate now and then.

BIOTECHNOLOGY: NEW FEARS FOR U.S. FOOD SAFETY

WASHINGTON, Jul 6, 2001—New concerns have arisen about the safety of the U.S. food supply and about the effectiveness of current efforts to maintain a separation between genetically engineered and conventional products.

This follows revelations this week that StarLink, a genetically modified variety of yellow corn engineered by Aventis CropScience, had been found in white corn products after consumers complained of allergic reactions.

The Food and Drug Administration (FDA) has not approved StarLink for human consumption because of its potential to trigger allergy symptoms. Although it is supposed to be fed only to animals, the modified corn was detected in yellow corn foodstuffs late last year, when people reported adverse reactions.

Some manufacturers and retailers of the foodstuffs—including tortilla chips and taco shells—switched to white corn, reasoning that this way they could be sure there was no Starlink, which is yellow, in their products. But in February, the FDA found genetic material from StarLink in Kash 'n' Karry brand white corn tortilla chips in Florida.

"The U.S. government's inability to contain StarLink shows how other undesirable biotech crops could get loose in the world food supply," says Larry Bohlen, director of Friends of the Earth's health and environment program.

Since most European countries, including Britain, France and Italy, prohibit the sale of foods containing biotech ingredients unless they are clearly labelled, the StarLink contamination has provoked concerns that bioengineered grains could get into exported food.

The controversy over biologically engineered corn and the continuing discovery of StarLink corn in products sold abroad has already prompted one country, Sri Lanka, to ban any use of the biotech corn, says Bohlen.

The World Health Organization and United Nations Food and Agriculture Organization are expected to soon approve international safety guidelines for genetically modified foods. If approved, the standards would require a tightening of U.S. safety assessment procedures if genetically modified crops from the United States are to have access to agricultural markets abroad.

The FDA does not require that all genetically modified foods be subjected to safety assessments before they are launched on the market, as they are in the European Union.

The FDA only found the genetic traces of the StarLink corn after it received a complaint by Keith Finger, a doctor living in Florida. Last year, Finger had reported suffering an allergic reaction to yellow corn products tainted with StarLink. In February, he reported a milder reaction after eating white corn chips.

The FDA's discovery of StarLink in a white corn product is significant, says Bohlen, because it comes despite manufacturers' switch to white corn, which makes up less than three percent of the U.S. corn market. It also raises serious new questions about the spread of the genetically engineered crop, adds Bohlen, because the gene could have found its way into white corn through cross-pollination.

Federal regulators are now investigating the facility that produced the white corn chips to determine how the snack food was contaminated. Both the Kash 'n' Karry and Food Lion grocery chains that sold the products voluntarily pulled the product from their shelves this week.

Finger was one of dozens of people who reported that they had suffered an allergic reaction to yellow corn products tainted with StarLink last year.

Last month, the U.S. government released a report that concluded that 17 people—including Finger—who complained of possible allergy attacks did not have any antibodies in their blood linked to StarLink's key component.

Environmentalists, however, say the report is flawed and inconclusive. They argue that the latest news proves that more comprehensive tests are needed.

StarLink is genetically altered to contain the plant pesticide Bacillus thuringienis, or Bt, which kills the dreaded European corn borer. Aventis has applied for an exemption to the government's restriction of StarLink.

While the Environmental Protection Agency (EPA) has stated that StarLink may cause allergies in humans, a special advisory panel of the administration will meet July 17–18 to discuss whether enough scientific evidence exists to safely allow small amounts of StarLink in human foods.

Bohlen, whose research last year alerted the FDA to the spread of StarLink into human food products, says the new reports of contaminated white corn should prompt the EPA to revise its estimates of people exposed to StarLink.

"Because allergies develop over time, this increase in exposure increases the likelihood that people will develop allergies to StarLink," he says.

Unable to guarantee the complete separation of StarLink from other corn varieties, U.S. corn growers also want regulators to allow a certain amount of StarLink corn in food products.

An absolute zero percent presence of StarLink corn in foods eaten by humans is not realistic, says David Uchic, a spokesperson for the National Corn Growers Association, because contamination could occur through cross-pollination and during storage.

Click With Care: New Study Spotlights Problems and Potholes in Health Information on the Internet

OAKLAND, Calif., May 23, 2001

Finding answers to important health questions using Internet search engines and simple search terms is difficult at best. And while the information consumers do find on Web sites is generally accurate, it is usually incomplete and hard for many readers to understand, according to a report featured in the May 23 issue of the *Journal of the American Medical Association (JAMA)*.

Recent surveys indicate that almost 100 million Americans go online in search of health information; 70% of them say that what they find influences treatment decisions.

The study, commissioned by the California HealthCare Foundation (CHCF) and conducted by RAND, is the most comprehensive evaluation to date of the quality, accessibility, and readability of the data in a vast, rapidly expanding e-health universe that now numbers millions of Web pages and thousands of sites. The study is also the first to analyze both English- and Spanish-language Web sites and search engines. Research focused on information about four common medical conditions—breast cancer, childhood asthma, depression, and obesity.

"We know that the Internet is revolutionizing the availability of health information for consumers. The study suggests that there are lots of good things going on, and also lots of room for improvement," said Mark D. Smith, MD, MBA, president and CEO of the California HealthCare Foundation.

"The Internet is still in its formative stages and has tremendous potential as an information resource for patients and health care providers alike. This research provides guidance both on how to use what is available on the Internet now and on the changes needed to make the information better and more reliable," said the report's lead author, RAND analyst Gretchen Berland, MD.

Key Findings

1. The study found that answers to important health questions are often incomplete. Working with nationally recognized clinical experts and patient advocates, the researchers established the basic elements of what consumers should know about each of the four conditions and compared those with the information on 18 English-language and seven Spanish-language sites.

■ On average, about 25% of those clinical elements were not covered at all by the English-language sites and 53% were not covered by the Spanish-language Web sites.

- For example, only a few sites in either language indicated that a woman with a persistent breast mass and a negative mammogram usually needs further evaluation.
- Less than half of the Spanish-language materials explained that mastectomy and lumpectomy plus radiation are equivalent treatments for early-stage breast cancer.
- One in five English-language sites provided complete and accurate information about managing the initial symptoms of a severe asthma episode.

■ Although the accuracy of information presented was fairly high, many of the sites contained contradictory information.

- A childhood asthma Web site reported in one place that using inhaled steroids does not stunt growth in children. Elsewhere it reported that using inhaled steroids does stunt growth in children.
- Conflicting information regarding depression most often concerned methods of treatment, while conflicting information pertaining to breast cancer concerned diagnosis.

2. The research showed that consumers may encounter a lot of irrelevant information when using search engines and simple search terms. The study examined 10 English-language and four Spanish-language search engines.

■ When employing English search engines, Internet users have a one in five chance of finding relevant information from the first page of results.

■ Consumers using Spanish search engines have a one in nine chance of finding relevant material.

3. The study showed that many users may not be able to read the information they find. According to a recent study of literacy in the United States, nearly half of all

adults read at an eighth-grade level or below. However, all of the English-language sites and 86% of Spanish-language sites required a high-school level of reading ability or better.

"The Internet should be a tool that anybody can use, but this shows that a good portion of its health resources may be out of reach for some," said Berland. "As the online population becomes more representative of the larger U.S. population in terms of race, age, income and education, the content available on the Internet should correspond to those changes." Berland is a Robert Wood Johnson clinical scholar at UCLA as well as a RAND researcher.

In addition to today's JAMA article, RAND and CHCF have released the full report, which elaborates on many of the article's findings and makes recommendations for consumers, consumer advocacy groups, health care providers, health Web sites, and policymakers. Among the recommendations, consumers are advised to:

1. Allow ample time to search for answers to your questions.
2. Be aware that a single site will probably not provide a comprehensive picture of what you need to know about a condition. As many as four to six sites must often be visited.
3. Discuss information you find on the Internet with your health care provider before you use it to make a treatment decision.

"This study establishes a benchmark against which to measure improvement. The findings provide a call for consumers to proceed with some caution when using the Internet, for health care providers to understand and consult with their patients about what they are reading online, and for e-health industry leaders to become more involved in monitoring content," Smith said.

The 24-page Report Summary with recommendations will be available for download at CHCF's Web site *http://ehealth.chcf.org* after 3 p.m. CDT, May 22, 2001. The 96-page Complete Study will be available at that time at *http://ehealth.chcf.org* and *http://www.rand.org/publications/documents/interneteval.* For a copy of the JAMA article, call RAND's Public Information Office (310-451-6913).

The California HealthCare Foundation (CHCF) is an independent health care philanthropy created in 1996 and committed to making the health care system work better for the people of California. This study is one in a series of activities CHCF has undertaken to enhance the role the Internet can play in improving health care. Its January 2000 Report on Privacy Policies and Practices of Health Web Sites led to improvements in privacy practices across the e-health industry.

Missed ZZZs, More Disease?

Skimping on sleep may be bad for your health

Kristin Cobb

As bleary-eyed college students in exam week will attest, lack of sleep impairs mood, performance, and judgment. They might guess, however, that the fast food and candy gobbled down during an all-nighter are far worse for bodily health than are the lost hours of slumber. After all, scientists have long been preaching that too many Big Macs and too few workouts are bad for you, but they have yet to demonstrate any definitive health costs of chronic sleep loss.

Bolstered by new evidence, however, some scientists are suggesting that poor sleep habits are as important as poor nutrition and physical inactivity in the development of chronic illness. They say that this country's sleep debt may be contributing to its current epidemics of obesity, diabetes, and cardiovascular disease.

People in the United States sleep an average of 7.0 hours on weeknights, 1.5 hours less than they did a century ago, according to the National Sleep Foundation in Washington, D.C. One-third of the population sleeps 6.5 or fewer hours, far less than the 8 hours that many sleep specialists recommend.

Several recent studies report that reducing sleep to 6.5 or fewer hours for successive nights causes potentially harmful metabolic, hormonal, and immune changes, at least in test volunteers in the sleep lab. "All of the changes are what you find in normal aging," says sleep researcher Eve Van Cauter of the University of Chicago.

It's still too early for doctors to start prescribing sleep to ward off age-related disease. Scientists agree that the findings are preliminary and that larger experiments are needed. If the story bears out, however, U.S. sleep habits may be having enormous public health consequences.

Dieter's nightmare

Early sleep-loss research focused on military personnel, rescue workers, shift workers, and others for whom on-the-job wakefulness is crucial. These studies examined the performance declines that occur with extended periods of total sleep loss.

Investigating the relationship between health and the pattern of partial sleep deprivation that the average American faces is a much newer research endeavor. Van Cauter and her colleagues helped launch the field with a surprising 1999 study that showed sleep deficits of several hours a night can impair the body's processing of the sugar glucose.

The study reported that 11 healthy, lean young men showed signs of insulin resistance after several nights of sleep restriction. Insulin resistance, a condition in which the body handles glucose poorly because cells respond inefficiently to insulin, is a precursor to type II diabetes.

Experimenters carefully controlled the men's sleep time, food intake, and exercise during their two-week stay in the sleep lab. During the sleep-restriction phase of the experiment, the men were kept awake by minimally stressful activities, such as watching television, joking with the staff, and playing games, Van Cauter says.

The restraints imposed in the study, which permitted only 4 hours of sleep a night for six nights, were more severe than most people in the United States experience. The study also excluded women. So, the scientists next compared 13 men and women who habitually slept 6.5 hours or less per night at home with 14 men and women who regularly slept about 8 hours. On the weekends, the short sleepers slept extra hours, indicating that their weekday patterns resulted from social constraints rather than biological constitution, Van Cauter notes.

Researchers verified the test volunteers' sleep patterns at home for a week and then brought them into the lab for a glucose-tolerance test. The short sleepers showed 50% more insulin resistance than the others did.

Short sleep may accelerate the onset of diabetes, Van Cauter speculates. "If you are predisposed to diabetes, and you might become diabetic at 55, are you becoming diabetic at 45?" she asks.

In further experiments, sleep-deprived test volunteers showed other hormonal changes that promote weight gain. Men who were held to 4 hours a night had markedly reduced 24-hour leptin concentrations compared with when they were fully rested, Van Cauter's research team reported at the 2001 Association of Professional Sleep Societies meeting in Chicago. Leptin is a hormone that signals satiety and regulates energy balance; mice that lack leptin overeat and become morbidly obese.

Van Cauter reported that although the men's food intake was adequate, the dip in leptin they exhibited was equivalent to that seen in people underfed by 1,600 calories a day for three days. In other words, the leptin signal was telling the men's bodies that they were short nearly a pound's worth of calories. That misleading signal might cue the body to slow metabolism, increase fat deposition, and overstimulate appetite.

A separate, ongoing study is examining sleep restriction and hunger. When held to 4 hours of sleep, volunteers reported being hungrier than when they had adequate slumber, Van Cauter says. The sleep-deprived people overwhelmingly asked for candy, starchy foods, and salty snacks such as potato chips. "There were no cravings for fruits and vegetables," she quips.

Animal studies also suggest that partial sleep deprivation leads to hormonal and metabolic changes. In one experiment, rats that normally sleep 8 to 10 hours a day were restricted to 4 hours of daily sleep for a week, mirroring Van Cauter's studies in people. During that time, the rats showed increased concentrations of stress hormones and an altered hormonal response to stressful situations, such as being confined in a small space.

Initially, such changes may help the body cope with lack of sleep, says Peter Meerlo of the University of Groningen in the Netherlands, who reported the results in the May *Journal of Neuroendocrinology*. If stress hormones are chronically altered, however, sleep deprivation may have adverse health effects, Meerlo speculates.

Inflammatory ideas

Modest sleep deprivation may also be associated with low-grade inflammation, which can lead to a host of cardiovascular problems, according to Alexandros N. Vgontzas of the Pennsylvania State University College of Medicine in Hershey.

Trying to mimic the modest chronic sleep loss that many people in the United States endure, Vgontzas and colleagues deprived 25 healthy young men and women of just 2 hours of sleep per night for a week. The scientists measured blood concentrations of immune-system molecules called cytokines, which are normally secreted during inflammation and infection.

After a week of sleeping 6 hours per night, the test volunteers had higher blood concentrations of the cytokine IL-6 than they did in their pre-deprivation state. Furthermore, the men, but not the women, had increased concentrations of the cytokine TNF-α. Increased cytokines may reflect pervasive inflammatory action, the researchers speculated last June in San Francisco at the annual meeting of the Endocrine Society.

Unremitting low-grade inflammation can damage the inner walls of the arteries, which sometimes leads to vessel narrowing, high blood pressure, stroke, and heart disease. Also, cytokines have been associated with insulin resistance, diabetes, and obesity.

Cytokines cause fatigue. By overproducing cytokines, a person's body is probably trying to say, "Go to sleep," Vgontzas says. Test participants fell asleep faster and slept more deeply when they were sleep deprived, demonstrating that their bodies were trying to compensate for the reduced sleep time, he adds. However, the more efficient sleep didn't thwart the cytokine response, which lasted the entire week. The volunteers were also sleepier and performed more poorly on an alertness test at the week's end than at the beginning of the experiment.

"There are some researchers, even in the sleep area, that say that these extra couple of hours of sleep are not important," Vgontzas concludes. "Our data say that 6 hours is not good for healthy, young people."

In a separate study, sleep of 4 hours a night for 10 nights was also associated with increased concentrations of C-reactive protein, another key inflammation mediator. Boosts in C-reactive protein might have a negative effect on health, says David F. Dinges of the University of Pennsylvania School of Medicine in Philadelphia, a researcher on the study.

Currently, the evidence linking increases in inflammatory molecules and cardiovascular disease is stronger for C-reactive protein than for the cytokines, adds Dinges' collaborator Janet Mullington of Beth Israel Deaconess Medical Center in Boston.

A recent epidemiological study also showed a direct association between short sleep and heart disease. After controlling for other factors, researchers found that men who slept 5 hours or less a night had twice as many heart attacks as men who slept 8 hours, report Japanese scientists in the July *Occupational and Environmental Medicine*.

Obstructive sleep apnea, a condition marked by temporary pauses in breathing during sleep, is a natural model of chronic sleep loss because people with the condition repeatedly wake up through the night. Several recent studies have linked sleep apnea to elevated blood concentrations of IL-6, TNF-α, and C-reactive protein, and to high blood pressure, cardiovascular problems, and stroke. However, it's hard to tease out whether these effects result from lack of oxygen due to the apnea, loss of sleep, or both, says sleep-apnea researcher Virend K. Somers of the Mayo Clinic in Rochester, Minnesota.

Virtue or indulgence?

Some scientists remain skeptical that sleeping 8 hours should be the next great health virtue. They say that getting from the current evidence to a firm link between sleep loss and disease requires a giant leap of faith.

"Some people don't have time to sleep, or they'd rather watch television. Should we condemn them before the evidence is in?" asks Daniel F. Kripke of the University of California, San Diego. Kripke argues that telling people that they'll get sick if they don't sleep enough may, ironically, worry them into insomnia.

Kripke and his colleagues published results in February that, on the surface, contradict the idea that more sleep is good for you. During a large epidemiological study lasting 6 years, people were more likely to die if they initially reported sleeping 7.5 hours or more a night than if they reported sleeping 5.5 to 7.5 hours a night. The researchers took into account such factors as age, weight, diagnosed illness, and medication use.

The amount that the average person in the United States sleeps per night, about 7 hours, is consistent with good health, Kripke concludes. "People who are saying you should sleep more don't have the evidence," he adds.

Anything more than 7 hours is optional sleep, which can be taken for relaxation and indulgence but is not necessary for good health, agrees sleep scientist Jim A. Horne of Loughborough University in England.

Pennsylvania State's Vgontzas disagrees. Underlying depression and sickness probably explain the apparent association between sleeping 8 or more hours and increased mortality in Kripke's study, he says.

However, neither Horne nor Kripke is swayed by the studies that show physiological changes in sleep-deprived subjects in the lab. The changes are probably real, they agree, but may not be meaningful—either because they're not severe enough to cause long-term health effects or because they're artifacts of the experimental situation.

The immune system probably does crank up and go on red alert when a person is awake longer, Horne explains. After all, a body is more likely to come across pathogens when it's up and about. But there's no evidence that this activity undermines health, he says.

The argument that people are evolutionarily programmed to sleep 8 or 9 hours a night doesn't hold up, at least in European history, Horne adds. Hundreds of years ago, people worked 14- or 15-hour days and were lucky to get 6 hours of sleep at night, he says. Moreover, their sleep patterns were different from those of modern slumberers. In England, people went to bed an hour after sundown, got up a few hours later for a midnight meal, and then slept a few more hours until sunup, Horne says. People are probably designed to sleep 6 or 7 hours at night and take a short afternoon nap, he suggests.

Bleary picture

Research on sleep deprivation and health is still in its infancy, Van Cauter admits. Nevertheless, she maintains that 8 or more hours of sleep a night is optimal.

"To suggest to people that you can maintain average sleep time of 6 hours and get on the road and drive your truck is criminal," she asserts. It's too early to say whether sleep loss causes disease, but it certainly hinders performance and diminishes safety, she says.

There's no reason to believe that sleeping more than 8 hours could be harmful or that insomnia could be good for you, Vgontzas adds.

"My general appraisal of the literature is, in terms of more or less normal variations in sleep amount and effects on health, we really don't know," reflects sleep specialist Alan Rechtschaffen of the University of Chicago. There's a consensus that the extreme—below 6 hours a night—isn't advisable, he says. Beyond that, distinguishing the health effects, if any, of 6 versus 7 versus 8 hours of sleep is going to take large, well-controlled studies that follow people over long periods. Optimal sleep also probably varies with age and gender, says Vgontzas.

So, as to whether millions of cases of obesity, diabetes, and cardiovascular disease could be prevented if people in the United States were simply to increase their sleep from 7 to 8 hours a night, the issue hasn't been put to bed. But the early data are at least provocative.

"We have all the dots or a lot of the dots, and it looks like there's a picture there, but the science that actually connects those dots hasn't been done yet," Dinges says.

Sleep disorders, such as sleep apnea, that were once seen as mere nuisances are now recognized by the community of sleep researchers as serious health concerns. The data suggest that even young, healthy people should give more consideration to sleep.

Of all the health prescriptions out there, it may be easier to convince people to change their sleep habits than to make other lifestyle changes.

After all, in a time when we are constantly told to eat more broccoli, eat less chocolate, and do more push-ups, wouldn't it be nice if hitting the snooze button were just what the doctor ordered?

References:

Kripke, D.F. *et al.* 2002. Mortality associated with sleep duration and insomnia. *Archives of General Psychiatry* 59 (February): 131–136. Abstract available at http://archpsyc.ama-assn.org/issues/v59n2/abs/yoa20380.html.

Liu, T., and H. Tanaka. 2002. Overtime work, insufficient sleep, and risk of non-fatal acute myocardial infarction in Japanese men. *Occupational and Environmental Medicine* 59 (July): 447–451. Abstract available at http://oem.bmjjournals.com/cgi/content/abstract/59/7/447.

Meerlo, P., *et al.* 2002. Sleep restriction alters the hypothalmic-pituitary-adrenal response to stress. *Journal of Neuroendocrinology* 14 (May): 397–402. Abstract.

Speigel, K.,…and E. Van Cauter. 1999. Impact of sleep debt on metabolic and endocrine function. *Lancet* 255 (Oct. 23): 1435–1439. Abstract.

Van Cauter, E., *et al.* 2001. Impact of sleep length on the 24-hour leptin profile. Meeting of the Association of Professional Sleep Societies. June. Chicago.

Vgontzas, A.N. 2002. Modest sleep loss increases/alters normal secretion of IL-6, TNF-α, cortisol. 84th Annual Meeting of the Endocrine Society. June. San Francisco.

Further Readings:

2002. New studies stress importance of sleep, relationship between sleep and hormones. Endocrine Society press release. June 21. Available at http://www.endo-society.org/pubrelations/pressReleases/archives/2002/sleep.cfm.

Bower, B. 1999. Slumber's unexplored landscape. *Science News* 156 (Sept. 25): 205–206. Available at http://www.sciencenews.org/sn_arc99/9_25_99/bob2.htm.

Seppa, N. 2002. Eight hours of sleep may not be so great. *Science News* 161 (March 16): 173. Available to subscribers at http://www.sciencenews.org/20020316/note10.asp.

_____. 2001. Does lack of sleep lead to diabetes? *Science News* 160 (July 14): 31. Available to subscribers at http://www.sciencenews.org/20010714/note13.asp.

In the Drink

When it Comes to Calories, Solid is Better than Liquid

"What would you like to drink with that?" asks the waitress. Think twice before you answer.

Your body may not register the calories you *drink* as well as it does the calories you *eat*. So when you down a soda or other liquid calories before or with a meal, you may not eat less food later in the day to compensate. Making matters worse: serving sizes for beverages are ballooning… as are Americans.

"Beverages are huge contributor to obesity," says Richard Mattes of Purdue University in West Lafayette, Indiana. "They're major players that often get overlooked."

Stealth Calories

In one study by Mattes, people were asked to consume 450 calories' worth of jelly beans every day for four weeks and 450 calories' worth of soda every day for another four weeks.[1] On days they ate the jelly beans, the participants compensated by eating roughly 450 fewer calories of others foods. So they ingested no more calories than usual.

But on days they drank the soda, the participants didn't compensate. They ended up eating roughly 450 *more* calories than usual.

"Liquid calories don't trip our satiety mechanisms," says Mattes. "They just don't register."

More evidence that liquid calories go unnoticed: Short-term studies show that if you drink a calorie-containing beverage with a meal, you'll wind up consuming more calories at that meal than if you drink a calorie-free beverage.[2]

But what about the long term? Researchers at the Monell Chemical Senses Center in Philadelphia gave 20 men and women about 40 ounces a day of either regular or diet cola (made with the artificial sweetener aspartame).[3] After three weeks, the women who drank the regular cola gained an average of two pounds; the men's weight didn't change. On the diet soda, the men lost one pound and the women's weight didn't change.

"It doesn't matter if you drink them with a meal or before a meal," says Barbara Rolls of the Pennsylvania State University, author of *Volumetrics: Feel Full on Fewer Calories* (HarperCollins, 2000). "The calories from most drinks add on to—rather than displace—food calories."

And that has added on to the nation's obesity epidemic, argues Mattes. "Over the last 20 years, we've gotten fatter, but what's really changed is that we're drinking a lot more calories than we ever did before."

The Bottomless Cup

In the 1950s, a "family size" bottle of Coke was 26 ounces. Now soft drink sizes at McDonald's *for one person* range from 12 ounces (for children) to 42 ounces. A "Double Gulp" at 7-Eleven convenience stores holds 64 ounces. That's eight cups—a huge serving even if you get it with ice. And the soft drinks you get at movie theaters like Loews and some AMCs (which can hit 44 ounces) often come with free refills.

"Sweetened soft drinks add more calories to our diet than any other beverage," notes Rolls.

America's appetite for soft drinks is at an all-time high, with no signs of slowing down. Soda pop dwarfs all other beverages we consume. Even if you subtract diet sodas—about a quarter of the market—it's still the number-one beverage (see "Sweetened Soda Rules").

And it's not just soft drinks. A "venti" Caffè Latte at Starbucks is 20 ounces. A large shake at McDonald's or a Dunkin' Donuts Coolata is 32 ounces. And a single-serve bottle of just about any beverage—Arizona Iced Tea, Gatorade, Fruitopia, you name it—can run as high as 20 ounces.

Look at the "Nutrition Facts" labels on those bottles and you'll see calories listed for an eight-ounce (one-cup) serving (as if people split the bottle into 2 ½ servings).

But other than children who get an eight-ounce carton of milk with their school lunch, it's hard to know who

SWEETENED SODA RULES

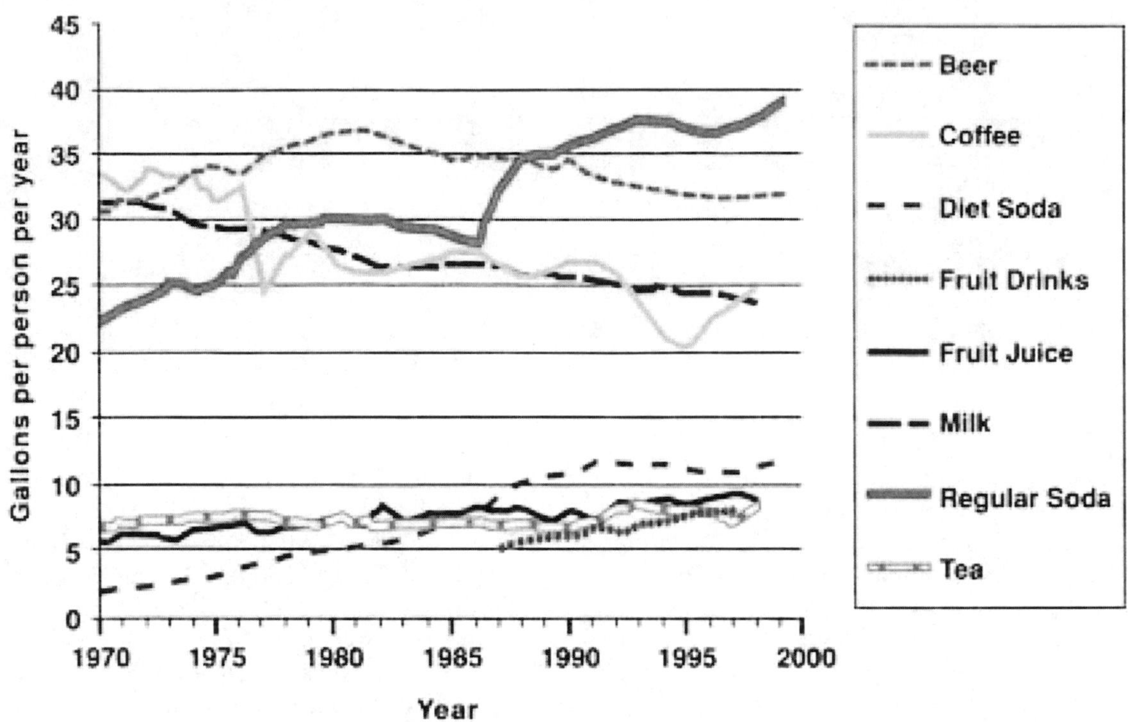

Liquid calories keep climbing. Sweetened sodas have become the most popular beverage in America. We're also drinking more fruit drinks (essentially non-carbonated soda).

Source: U.S. Department of Agriculture.

stops at one cup any more. You can't even buy an eight-ounce drink at many restaurants. A "small" drink at McDonald's is 16 ounces. And large sit-down restaurant chains like Applebee's, Chili's, Denny's, Olive Garden, Outback Steakhouse, and T.G.I. Friday's start you off with 14 to 22 ounces of soda… and offer free refills.

Even alcoholic beverages are ballooning. T.G.I. Friday's sells 18-ounce cocktails like the Ultimate Daiquiri, Hawaiian Volcano, Long Island Iced Tea, Margarita, or Mudslide.

Restaurants like Applebee's, Olive Garden, and T.G.I. Friday's offer either 16-ounce or 22-ounce draft beers. And at restaurants like Romano's Macaroni Grill and Buca di Beppo, two Italian sit-down chains, a serving of wine can be ten ounces.

(When the *Dietary Guidelines for Americans* and health authorities advise men to stop at two drinks a day and women to stop at one, they're talking about a five-ounce serving of wine, a 12-ounce serving of beer, or 1.5 ounces of liquor. Do patrons who drink alcohol at some restaurants know that each glass may contain two servings?)

And as mugs and glasses grow, so grow our bellies and bottoms. Twenty ounces of most beverages—even juice or milk—mean 200 to 450 calories. A 32-ounce large shake at McDonald's means 720 calories. A 32-ounce large Dunkin' Donuts Coolata means 820.

Good to the Last Drop

Do people drink more just because they're served more?

"Serving sizes have a tremendous effect on everyone, but a much more dramatic effect on males," says Brian Wansink, director of the Food and Brand Research Lab at the University of Illinois at Urbana-Champaign.

In a new (still unpublished) study, he gave free Coke or Sprite to 372 teens and adults who were eating at McDonald's, Burger King, or Hardee's restaurants. Roughly half were given a child-size (12-ounce) drink, while the others got a large (32-ounce) drink.

"The girls and women drank 17 ounces when they got the large size, but only 9 ounces when they got the small drink," says Wansink.

"The differences were even more extreme for the boys and men. They consume anything you give them—about 28 of the 32 ounces in the large drink and 11 of the 12 ounces in the small drink."

DRINK TO ME ONLY

All beverages are not created equal. Here's a selection of popular drinks, ranked from least number of calories to most. Some serving sizes may seem large, but we didn't make them up. All are available in bottles, in cans, or at restaurants. Restaurant drinks will have even more calories if you get no ice.

Beverage *(size)*	**Calories**	**Beverage** *(size)*	**Calories**
Water or seltzer	0	Snapple Lemonade (*16 oz.*)	240
Diet soda (*20 oz.*)	5	7-Up, Coca-Cola, or root beer (*20 oz.*)	250
Coffee, with one liquid creamer (*8 oz.*)	30	Beer, regular, draft (*22 oz.*)	280
Tea, with two packets of sugar (*8 oz.*)	50	Margarita (from mix), on the rocks (*8 oz.*)	290
V8 (*11.5 oz.*)	70	7-Eleven Big Gulp, Coca-Cola (*32 oz.*)	300
Milk, fat-free (*8 oz.*)	90	Fruitopia, The Grape Beyond (*20 oz.*)	300
Beer, light (*12 oz.*)	100	Hawaiian Punch (*20 oz.*)	300
Milk, 1% (*8 oz.*)	100	Orange soda (*20 oz.*)	300
Starbucks Cappuccino, short (*8 oz.*)1	100	Sunny Delight (*20 oz.*)	300
Apple or orange juice (*8 oz.*)	110	McDonald's Coca-Cola, large (*32 oz.*)	310
Irish coffee, w/out whipped cream (*8 oz.*)	120	Eggnog (*8 oz.*)	340
Nestea Iced Tea, sweetened (*16 oz.*)	120	Starbucks Caffé Latte, venti (*20 oz.*)[1]	350
Gatorade (*20 oz.*)	130	Tropicana Twister Fruit Punch (*20 oz.*)	350
Cranberry juice (*8 oz.*)	140	McDonald's Chocolate Shake, sm. (*16 oz.*)	360
Starbucks Caffe Latte, short (*8 oz.*)1	140	Odwalla Future Shake, Vanilla Al'mondo (*16 oz.*)	380
Beer, regular (*12 oz.*)	150	McDonald's Coca-Cola, super size (*42 oz.*)	410
Grape juice (*8 oz.*)	150	Dairy Queen Misty, large (*32 oz.*)	440
Mimosa (*8 oz.*)	150	McDonald's Hi-C Orange Drink, super size (*42 oz.*)	460
Martini (*2.5 oz.*)	160	Nestlé NesQuik Chocolate or Strawberry Milk (*16 oz.*)	460
Wine, white (*8 oz.*)	160	Jamba Juice, Strawberries Wild Smoothie, Power Size (*32 oz.*)	560
Gin & tonic, on the rocks (*7.5 oz.*)	170	7-Eleven Double Gulp, Coca-Cola (*64 oz.*)	600
Wine, red (*8 oz.*)	170	Burger King Vanilla Shake, large (*32 oz.*)	630
Milk, whole (*8 oz.*)	180	McDonald's Chocolate Shake, lg. (*32 oz.*)	720
Ginger ale (*20 oz.*)	200	Dunkin' Donuts Coolatta, large (*32 oz.*)[2]	820
Starbucks Cappuccino, venti (*20 oz.*)[1]	200	Baskin-Robbins Chocolate Milkshake, large (*24 oz.*)	1,130
Starbucks Coffee Frappuccino, tall (*12 oz.*)	200	Smoothie King, Strawberry Hulk (*40 oz.*)	1,920
Dairy Queen Misty, small (*16 oz.*)	220		
Ultra Slim-Fast, canned (*11 oz.*)	220		
V8 Splash (*16 oz.*)	220		
Arizona Iced Tea (*20 oz.*)	230		
Sobe Orange Carrot Elixir 3C (*20 oz.*)	230		

[1]Prepared using whole milk.
[2]Prepared using cream.
Source: Manufacturers and U.S. Department of Agriculture (USDA).

And what's remarkable, says Wansink, is that "people don't perceive that they're consuming any more calories with a large drink than with a small."

When asked how many calories they drank, most people had no clue, he says. "But even when we looked at people who said they could estimate calories well—usually females—they said they had consumed about 100 calories, whether they drank 9 ounces or 17 ounces."

Take Charge

Don't get us wrong. It's not just 300-calorie beverages that are making Americans pudgy. It's also 670-calorie Cinnabons, 800-calorie tuna salad sandwiches, 1,000-calorie Big Macs and Fries, 1,200-calorie orders of Stuffed Potato Skins, 1,600-calorie platters of General Tso's Chicken, and 2,400-calorie plates of Cheese Fries.

But at least some people think twice before gulping down 1,000 calories of food. They may not question the "hidden" calories in beverages.

Yet they're so easy to avoid. Dieters may have trouble eating less food over the long term. But surely they could get used to drinking noncaloric beverages with and between meals.

"People have two options," says Mattes. "Either they start consuming non-caloric beverages like water, tea, coffee, or diet soda. Or they can drink whatever they want, but compensate by eating less food."

Here are some other strategies for avoiding beverage bloat:

- Order "kiddie" or "small" sizes. At McDonald's (and many other restaurants), a child's serving is 12 ounces. And a "small" at most fast food restaurants is 16 ounces (two cups).
- Ask for ice in your drink. You'll get less beverage... and fewer calories.
- Get an empty cup or glass and split a beverage with a friend. If the waiter offers a free refill, ask for water.
- Don't have a caloric beverage as a snack to stave off hunger before a meal. It won't curb your appetite as well as solid food. Try baby carrots, slices of melon, or orange wedges instead.
- You don't have to eliminate healthy beverages like orange juice and low-fat milk. Mix OJ with seltzer for a refreshing drink with half the usual calories. And the calcium, protein, and other nutrients in that glass of milk may be worth its 100-or-so calories.
- Diet soft drinks are better than regular soda. But if you guzzle caffeinated soda, coffee, or tea all day, it may leave you jittery and unable to sleep.

Notes

1. *Internat. J. Obesity 24*: 794, 2000.
2. *Physiol. Behav. 48*: 19, 1990.
3. *Am. J. Clin. Nutr. 51:* 963, 1990

Acknowledgment

The information for this article was compiled by Jackie Adriano.

THE IMMUNE SYSTEM VS. *STRESS*

Psychological distress can suppress the body's defenses to the point of inducing physical illness.

by Paul L. DeVito

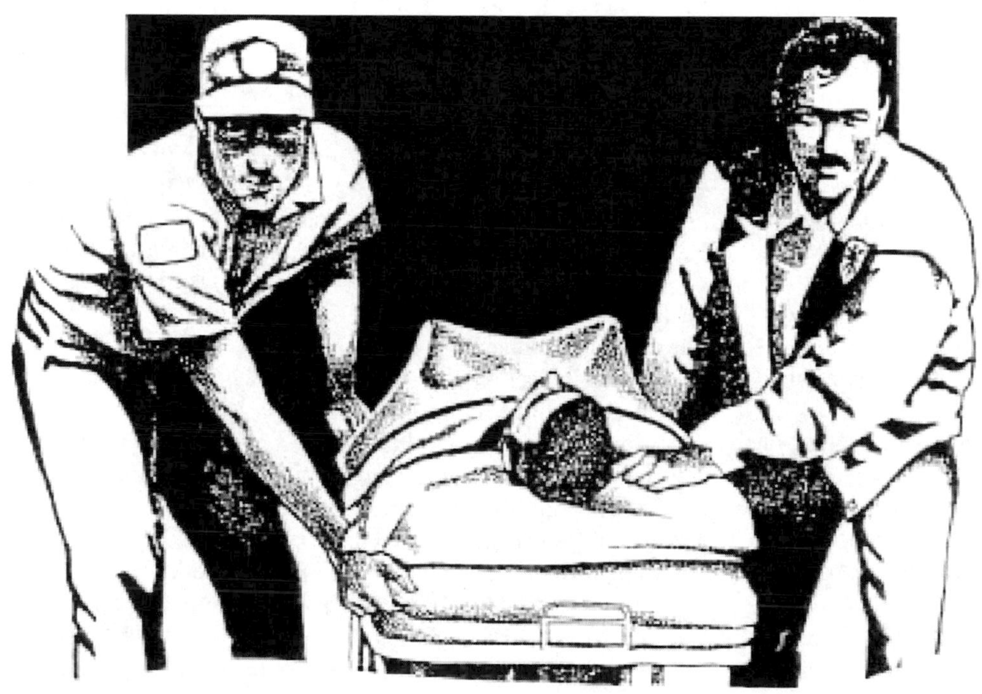

A COLLEGE student suffers from a strep throat infection while studying for final exams. A corporate executive loses her voice prior to an important presentation to stockholders. A high school senior wakes up with a horrible headache on the morning of the prom. Both parents come down with the flu after several sleepless nights with their sick child. Virtually everyone has experienced similar reactions.

Who hasn't pondered why illness strikes precisely when it can be afforded least? Often, people wonder if these maladies are real or just "psychological." Consider the following: Johnny may be faking sickness to avoid an exam. Is Melissa unconsciously postponing a date with a popular football star through her asthma attacks because she's scared to death? Is David's drinking prior to a sexual experience with his wife due to uncertainty about his performance—or guilt about an office affair? These situations are complex and require analysis in order to determine the physical and emotional sources. The diagnosis is not always simple and straightforward.

For centuries, physicians, philosophers, and psychologists have noted the apparent relationship among stress, illness, and health. Recently, medical scientists firmly have established causal relationships between them and have shown how our minds and emotions can influence the course of a disease.

Some historians have traced the word "stress" to the Latin words *strictus* (tight or narrow) and *stingere* (to tighten). Until the 19th century, stress referred more to external forces on physical objects than to internal psychological states; for instance, the stress of extreme weight on a bridge platform, rather than the stress of balancing family and professional pressures. Contemporary use of the term can be traced to 20th-century physiological psychologist Walter Cannon and Canadian physician Hans Seyle. Cannon defined the classic "fight-or-flight" reaction: When faced with stress, the body prepares for the emergency through the sympathetic portion of the autonomic nervous system. Adrenalin, a hormone, is released into the bloodstream through the adrenal glands and generates the energy to cope with the stressors, not unlike an army ready to defend its territory against an invader.

Cannon maintained that his hormonal reaction was a remnant of humans' ancient past, when most stressors could be handled only through radical and robust actions. In order to survive, our ancestors fought prey and fled from predators. Such intense reactions are not required in modern society; in fact, this kind of response potentially could be harmful to one's health and well-being. Consider how inefficient it would be to rely on "fight-or-flight" in order to pay bills, change a flat tire during rush hour, or ask a supervisor for a raise. Burnout may be the result of such overreactions to stress.

Seyle studied stress by identifying those situations in which it occurs. A stressor is an event that places inordinate demands on the body and, in turn, sets off natural adaptive bodily defenses to cope with it. The process that he labeled the General Adaptation Syndrome includes three stages: the alarm reaction, resistance, and exhaustion.

During the alarm reaction, there are increases in hormone levels, strong physical arousal, and severe emotional upheavals. When the alarm reaction is not sufficient to cope, the stressor maintains its attack. Enter resistance. During this stage, when successful, the stressor is tamed and normality returns. If coping is not successful, however, hormonal reserves become depleted, fatigue sets in, and the stage of exhaustion takes over, during which adaptation to the stressor breaks down completely. Depression and anxiety are common. Serious illness, even death, becomes likely.

Illnesses associated with stress once were known as psychosomatic disorders; today, the term psychophysiological more commonly is used. They have been referred to as diseases of adaptation since they are rooted in attempts to adapt physiologically to everyday tensions and problems. Psychophysiological disorders encompass common physical ailments such as asthma, chronic hyperventilation, peptic ulcers, colitis, hypertension, heart attacks, hives, and acne.

Research by the psychologist Marianne Frankenhauser has corroborated Seyles' landmark work. Frankenhauser found that urban commuting, job dissatisfaction, personal conflict, loss of control over individual life decisions, taking exams, noise, anticipation of aversive events, and even boredom are profound stressors.

Psychologists Richard Lazarus and J. B. Cohen have proposed three categories of stressors: cataclysmic, personal, and background. A cataclysmic stressor is one that has a sudden, powerful, and unpredictable impact on a large number of people. Earthquakes in California, hurricanes in Florida, and the ethnic-based warfare in the former state of Yugoslavia are cases in point. Personal stressors also are sudden, powerful, and unpredictable, but affect fewer people, typically limited to an individual. One's personal response to illness, the death of a close associate or relative, or the loss of a job are common examples. Background stressors are chronic, persistent, and repetitive "daily hassles." These include noise, hectic schedules, and neighborhood and family problems. Individually, these events may not pose much harm; collectively, they can be problematic.

Not all stressors are negative. Seyle, in fact, proposed two types of stress—distress and eustress. Distress refers to negative and destructive forms commonly associated with cataclysmic and personal stress—for instance, suffering the loss of a family member or losing one's job. Eustress refers to events that evoke a stress reaction even when good and happy things seem to be occurring such as celebrating a holiday, enjoying a vacation, or receiving a job promotion or personal recognition. These pleasurable occasions, oddly enough, can be stressful and have been shown to be related to illness.

Personality and health

There are both health- and illness-prone personality types: Neuroticism—a psychological term referring to emotional instability—correlates with a variety of common illnesses and cardiovascular diseases. There is clear evidence that hostility—both withholding it and chronically letting it out—contributes to hypertension and cardiovascular disorders. Introverts, who are shy, quiet, and socially withdrawn, are prone to exaggerated responses to stress. They are likely to become more ill than the average person. Extroverts, who are outgoing, sociable, and more laid back, typically are happier, more energetic, and healthier.

Coronary heart disease (CHD), the leading cause of death in the U.S., long has been associated with stress and anxiety. At the turn of the 20th century, noted physician Sir William Osler wrote that the typical coronary patient is "not the delicate, neurotic person… but the robust, the vigorous in mind and body, the keen and ambitious man, the indicator of whose engine is always at full speed ahead." Although more contemporary work has questioned his characterization, Osler's work has fueled valuable research on the relationship between personality factors and CHD. A very notable example was that performed in the 1930s by American psychiatrists Karl, Charles, and William Menninger, who validly associated the trait of aggressiveness with CHD.

During the 1960s, cardiologists Meyer Friedman and Ray Rosenman systematically explored the personality-CHD relationship. They identified with now classic Type-A person who shows hostility, excessive competitiveness, impatience, and pressured speech. An opposite behavior pattern, shown by the

Type-B personality, characterizes a more easygoing style of coping. Epidemiological studies conducted over the past two decades have been consistent in showing a strong relationship between Type-A behavior and CHD in both women and men. These psychological factors are as troublesome in this regard as smoking, hypertension, and diabetes.

Through the use of his patient's life charts, physician Adolph Meyer noted in the 1930s that illness clustered at stressful times in a person's life. Researchers Thomas Holmes and Richard Rahe extended this line of thinking in the 1960s by systematically examining the life charts of more than 5,000 patients and identifying those events that appeared at the onset of disease.

They constructed a list of 43 stressful events related to personal, family, community, social, religious, economic, occupational, residential, and vocational aspects of living. Each was given a stress score. For instance, highest on the scale and worth 100 points is the death of a spouse; lowest on the scale and valued at 11 points are minor violations of the law. Other items include divorce (second), a jail term (fourth), pregnancy (12th), outstanding personal achievement (25th), trouble with the boss (30th), and change in sleeping habits (38th). Even vacation and Christmas (41st and 42nd, respectively) made the list.

Knowledge of the immune system and its relationship to illness has grown exponentially over the past few decades. The immune system is akin to a general defense network whose primary responsibility is to protect individuals from foreign agents, known as pathogens, that do not belong in the body and can cause disease. Pathogens normally include bacteria, viruses, and allergens like pollen, but also may include transplanted tissue and abnormal cells growing within the body.

The immune system targets and destroys antigens—any substance or organism that evades the outer defenses of skin tissue and mucous membrane and enters the body. The system contains several types of white blood cells, known as leukocytes, which protect in various ways. Some destroy bacteria; others kill viruses and attack cancer cells; still others produce antibodies that selectively target and then combat particular antigens.

Leukocytes are not perfect. Their actions may backfire; they can overreact and attack a person's own body. When this occurs, the result is a disorder known as autoimmune disease, including such ailments as minor as a common allergy and as serious as arthritis and lupus.

Recent discoveries have demonstrated that the immune system is not as autonomous and independent of other body systems as previously believed. It interacts with both the nervous and endocrine systems; the latter secretes hormones, like adrenaline, directly into the blood stream. This discovery has led to an emergence of a new field of investigation known as psychoneuroimmunology. As implied by its name, psychoneuroimmunology is an interdisciplinary field that studies the relationship between the principles of psychology, neurology, and immunology, as well as the principles of endocrinology and psychiatry. Psychoneuroimmunology is the field that has identified the direct causal relationship between stress and illness, beginning with the work of Robert Ader of The University of Rochester School of Medicine and Dentistry.

Ader, a research scientist who coined the term psychoneuroimmunology, was studying a rapid and potent form of classical conditioning (associated with physiologist Ivan Pavlov and his famous dog experiments) known as taste-aversion learning in animal subjects. In it, the consumption of a distinctively flavored drink—say saccharin water—is paired with the ingestion of some nausea-inducing substance. The result of this experience is that the previously preferred and enthusiastically consumed saccharin water now is avoided permanently. Many people have suffered from the experience of associating a particular food they once enjoyed with another that is upsetting and evokes nausea. This taste-aversion procedure has been used with some success in the treatment of alcoholism. Individuals are given a drug, antabuse, that causes extreme nausea when mixed with alcohol. Subsequently, the alcoholic refrains from drinking when antabuse is ingested.

By chance, Ader used cyclophosphamide (a potent drug commonly used in the treatment of autoimmune disease and transplant surgery to slow the rejection effects of the immune system) as the nausea-inducing substance in his taste-aversion experiment. After pairing it with saccharin water, he unexpectedly found that subjects who subsequently consumed saccharin water had much higher than normal mortality rates than those who did not have saccharin water paired with cyclophosphamide. On the basis of this observation, Ader speculated that the pairing of a neutral taste with an immunosuppressive drug—one whose known result is to weaken the effectiveness of the immune system in defending against pathogens—could result in the conditioning of a weakened immune system.

Further experimentation by Ader and others confirmed this hypothesis and found that the immune system is capable of "learning" to respond to a sweet taste with a drop in immune function. This demonstration of what scientists call conditioned immunosuppression of antibody response to antigens is significant because it demonstrates a direct psychological influence on immunity. The application of this finding to the practice of medicine is equally noteworthy. Studies have shown that the rejection of transplanted tissue may be reduced through this conditioning procedure. It also may be effective in reducing the medication doses required in cancer chemotherapy and arthritis. Dramatically, Ader has shown that the presentation of saccharin water that previously was paired with cyclophosphamide effectively delayed the onset of lupus in rats. Comparable applications to the treatment of lupus in humans currently are being explored.

Psychological distress

Prior to Ader's work, most scientists believed that the brain and immune systems were separate and incapable of influencing each other. Today, scientists are finding many connections of these systems. For instance, nerve endings have been found in tissues that produce, develop, and store immune system cells. The thymus, lymph nodes, spleen, and bone marrow—each intimately involved in immune system functioning—have been shown to respond to signals from the brain. Thus, the field of psychoneuroimmunology is pursuing the relationship between stress and illness with the assumption that psychological distress can suppress the immune system to the point of inducing physical illness.

Psychologists Harry Fowler, Donald Lysle, and others have shown that physical stress and fear are capable of producing immunosuppression. In these studies, animals exposed to physical stressors like footshock (mild electric shock to the foot) were found to be in states of immunosuppression for prolonged periods of time and likely to become ill. They showed almost equivalent reactions when presented with fear-evolving stimuli previously paired with the footshock. That is, a signal—such as a light—that consistently predicted the footshock also induced immunosuppression. Thus, not only does physical stress produce a weakened immune system, but the mere anticipation of a stressful situation triggers a similar effect.

Although direct human experimentation of this nature is not ethically possible, the results of these studies seem clear and applicable to humans. When individuals are stressed, their bodies go into a state of immunosuppression; they become susceptible to those pathogens that typically are adapted to and are likely to become ill. It is not so much that the stress causes the disease as much as it sets the stage for illness. With the elimination of pathogens during stress-induced immunosuppression, it is unlikely that infection-based illness will occur.

A study by psychologist Sheldon Cohen reported comparable effects in people. He gave volunteers injected doses of a known cold virus and then waited to see who came down with a cold. There was a clear relationship between those who did catch a cold and levels of stress experienced during the past year—a striking finding. Additional human research has shown declines in immune system cells in medical students taking final exams, people caring for loved ones with Alzheimer's disease, and women who recently had experienced a nasty divorce.

It currently is believed by many health professionals that some infections, as well as the growth of tumors, may reflect a problem in immunocompetence—the degree to which an antigen is identified and successfully destroyed by leukocytes and other immune system actions. Numerous studies have found evidence for increased tumor growth as a result of stress. This offers a viable explanation for what some psychologists refer to as the Type-C personality—those individuals whose personalities seem especially prone to cancer.

As noted by psychologists Robert Gatchel, Andrew Baum, and David Krantz in their text, *Health Psychology,* the cancer-prone personality has several characteristics: "The first includes a tendency to keep in resentment and anger rather than express it and a 'marked inability to forgive.' In addition, research suggests that cancer victims are ineffective in forming and/or maintaining close, long-term relationships with other people. They are more likely to be loners without extensive social support systems. Third, they engage in more self-pity than what may be considered normal. And these people tend to have poor self-images. Thus the cancer-prone individual 'puts on a happy face' and denies any sense of loss, anger, distress, disappointments, or despair while living an inner life of self-pity, insecurity, and a certain degree of loneliness."

To underscore this notion, one is reminded of a scene from the 1986 movie, "Hannah and Her Sisters." At one point in the film, Woody Allen's character facetiously states: "In my family, we don't cope with hostility and anger... we just grow tumors!"

The record seems clear. Chronic stress without adequate coping is damaging to good health, promoting disease and illness through suppression of the immune system. The specific physiological mechanisms have yet to be identified precisely, but the successful modulation of the immune system through conditioning is an encouraging research route.

Studies currently in the pipeline are exciting and promising. For instance, there are ways stress-induced immunosuppression can be inhibited as well as enhanced. This latter effect, known as immunenhancement, ultimately may result in individuals becoming "vaccinated" for the deleterious effects of stress.

To that end, the future seems bright, possibly free of stress. Remember, though, stress does have an important function—it informs people that they are doing the wrong things or just too much. The best advice is to control one's life so as to reduce excessive stress. Heed the call, and learn to relax!

Dr. DeVito is chairman, Department of Psychology, Saint Joseph's University, Philadelphia, Pa.

Back to Health

Out with an injury?
Go from the sidelines to a starting position with these seven steps

BY MEGAN McMORRIS

IT'S WHAT EVERY athlete dreads. You're cruising along in top form when suddenly you twist an ankle during a soccer match, overextend your elbow in a basketball scrimmage or awaken with a sore knee two days before your first marathon. Even couch potatoes aren't immune. According to the American Academy of Orthopaedic Surgeons, one in seven Americans currently has a musculoskeletal condition (affecting the bones, joints, muscles, ligaments or tendons). In addition, females have a four to six times greater chance of experiencing a serious knee injury and a higher overall risk of developing shoulder pain than men do.

Sports injuries can do more than sideline you—they can drain you both mentally and physically. All-America point guard Sue Bird, now a junior at the University of Connecticut, tore her anterior cruciate ligament halfway through her first season. "Getting injured was hard, because I was a freshman and had only played eight games," she says. "Suddenly, in one day it was all over." But you don't have to be a passive patient. Here's some expert advice for getting healthy and staying that way.

Step 1: Stop playing

"The biggest mistake people make is to test their injury. That's when something minor can turn into something major," explains Dr. Lisa Callahan, medical director of the Women's Sports Medicine Center at the Hospital for Special Surgery in New York City. "They say, I twisted my knee skiing, and it hurt a little, then I tested it on another run, and that's when I blew it out."

Step 2: Ice, ice baby

As soon as possible, put the cold stuff on your sore spot. "If you can ice within the first 30 minutes, you've made a huge difference in how fast you'll heal," says Callahan. "The more swelling, the more difficult it is to recover." Ice for 30 minutes, three to four times a day, until pain and swelling diminish.

Along with icing comes the rest of RICE (rest, ice, compress, elevate). Wrap a sports bandage around the

When You Need to See the Doc

How to tell when an injury is serious? There are a few warning signs you should never ignore. If you experience any of the following, consult a doctor.

1 SNAP, CRACKLE, POP. "If you felt or heard something pop or snap, there's a good chance you've torn, broken or dislocated something," says Dr. Lisa Callahan of the Women's Sports Medicine Center at the Hospital for Special Surgery in New York City. Any impact to the head or neck should also be looked at by a physician immediately.

2 UNEXPECTED ACHES. Joint injuries often make it difficult to do things that normally would not cause a problem, such as brushing your teeth, unscrewing the lid of a jar or walking up or down stairs.

3 EXTENDED TROUBLE. Any pain, such as soreness in a muscle or joint, that lasts for more than five days or worsens during activity should be evaluated by a sports medicine expert.

injury. Keep it elevated (at or above heart level) to further reduce swelling.

Step 3: Pop a pill

Anti-inflammatory drugs such as aspirin or ibuprofen can help in the first hours after injury—but more isn't necessarily better. "Anti-inflammatories are a double-edged sword. They can reduce pain and inflammation, but they also make you think you're healthier than you are," says Callahan. Follow label guidelines, and never take any drug for more than a few days.

Step 4: Cross-train

Being injured doesn't mean it's time to hunker down. "Rarely is there an injury such that you can't do any activity," says Callahan. If you sprain your ankle, try swimming; if your shoulder aches, hop on a stationary bike. "When you're active, the brain releases certain neurotransmitters that make you feel good," says Gary Mascilak, a physical therapist at Allsport Performance Center in Sparta, N.J.

Step 5: Eat enough

Now is not the time to slash portion sizes. "Your body needs a certain number of calories every day just to keep your heart beating," says Callahan. Maintain normal caloric intake, make sure you're getting enough protein (50–65 grams for someone on a 2,000-calorie-a-day diet) and take a multivitamin.

Step 6: Ease back in

Once you start to feel improvement, test yourself—slowly. Callahan recommends starting at 50% of your normal activity level. If you have no discomfort, gradually return to your usual routine.

But the real test comes in the midnight hours, says Mascilak. "During the day your joints and tissues report to the brain, and there's a lot of stimulation," he says. "But at night your brain doesn't have as many things reporting to it, so it can respond to pain and inflammation." If you feel achy only at night, continue to RICE the injury and cut back on your workout.

Step 7: Think positive

Snowboarder Barrett Christy says that after she bruised her tailbone last year, she focused on things other than the competition. "I spent more time visualizing my technique," she says. "And I looked at it as a warning to be more careful out there."

The Female Athlete Triad: Disordered Eating, Amenorrhea, and Osteoporosis

DAWNELLA M. RUST

Although a majority of girls and women achieve positive health benefits from regular physical activity (Lopiano 2000; Tanji 2000), some develop the Female Athlete Triad, an interrelated combination of disorders that can occur in girls and women who are physically active. The three components of the triad are disordered eating, amenorrhea, and osteoporosis (see figure 1). The American College of Sports Medicine (1997) believes that internal and external pressures placed on young females to achieve or maintain unrealistically low body weight underlie the development of the triad. The disorders alone or in combination can result in declining physical performance as well as medical and psychological morbidity and mortality. School personnel who work with physically active girls should understand the components and their risk factors for the condition so that they can work to prevent it.

FIGURE 1. The Female Athlete Triad

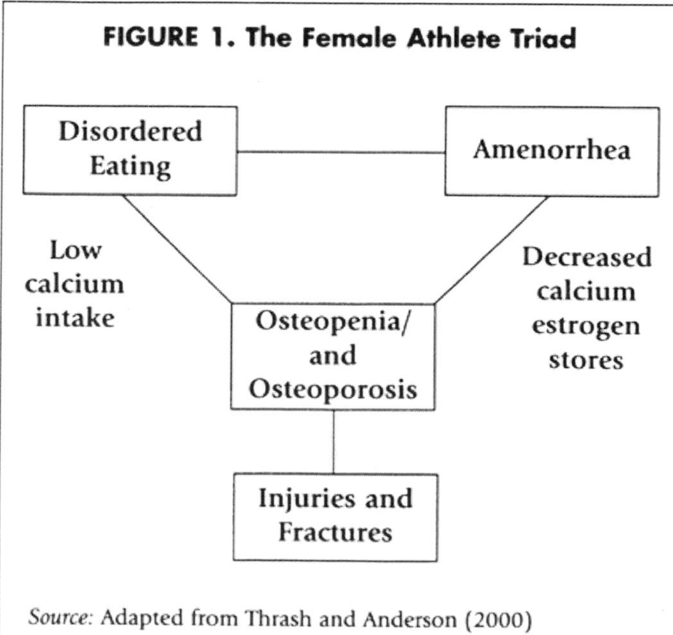

Source: Adapted from Thrash and Anderson (2000)

Disordered Eating

The association between exercise and eating disorders has received much attention (Davis 1990; Beumont et al. 1994). The advantage in athletic performance of maintaining a healthy minimal level of body fat and the strong negative connotation of overfatness in our society combine to create strong pressures for thinness. Some researchers (Nagel and Jones 1992; Yates 1991) have speculated that society's emphasis on physical fitness and leanness may promote preoccupation with low or extremely low body weight and may even result in the development of eating disorders. In addition, Yates (1992) believes that participation in strenuous physical activity is not always secondary to weight concerns but can occupy a central role in the development and etiology of clinical eating disorders. Katz (1986) has suggested that extreme exercise, such as long-distance running, can trigger anorexia nervosa in persons who are at risk psychologically and biologically for developing an eating disorder.

The American Psychiatric Association (APA) (1994) has developed descriptions of four classes of disordered eating: anorexia nervosa, bulimia nervosa, binge eating disorder, and eating disorders not otherwise classified. The fourth category was established because many females who chronically use disordered eating practices do not fit the strict APA criteria for anorexia nervosa or bulimia nervosa (see appendix A). Females diagnosed with disordered eating have more weight, eating, and body image concerns and have a higher morbidity and mortality rate (ACSM 1997).

Amenorrhea

As noted in appendix A, one of the criteria for the diagnosis of anorexia nervosa is disturbance of the menstrual cycle, more specifically known as amenorrhea, or the absence of three or more consecutive menstrual cycles. Primary amenorrhea (delayed menarche) is defined as no menses prior to the age of sixteen, and

Female Athlete Triad Resources

American Anorexia/Bulimia Association, Inc.
165 W. 46th Street, #1108, New York, NY 10036
(212) 575-6200
www.aabainc.org

American College of Sports Medicine
401 W. Michigan Street, Indianapolis, IN 46202
(317) 637-9200
www.acsm.org

Anorexia Nervosa and Related Eating Disorders
POB 5102, Eugene, OR 97405
(503) 344-1144
www.anred.com

Female Athlete Triad Video
(produced in cooperation with the AGSM)
The video describes the clinical and physiological basis of each of the components. Dr. Williams provides information regarding the warning signs and symptoms, as well as recommendation for prevention and treatment.
U.S. price: $39.95
VHS length: 33 minutes
ID: 990129-0301
www.exrx.net/Store/HL/FemaleAthleteTriad.html

National Association of Anorexia Nervosa and Associated Disorders
POB 7, Highland Park, IL 60035
(847) 831-3438
www.anad.org

National Collegiate Athletic Association
POB 6222, Indianapolis, IN 46206-6222
(317) 917-6222
www.ncaa.org

National Osteoporosis Foundation
1232 22nd Street, NW, Washington, DC 20037-1292
(202) 223-2226
www.nof.org

Saint Francis Health System
(A School's Guide to Prevention)
6655 S. Yale Ave., Tulsa, OK 74136
(918) 481-4061
www.laureate.com/services/ed/infoprof/schoolguide.asp

Sports, Cardiovascular, and Wellness Nutritionist (SCAN)
POB 4995, Buena Vista, CO 81211
(719) 395-9271
www.nutrifit.org

secondary amenorrhea is the absence of at least three to six consecutive menstrual cycles in females who have begun menstruating. Oligomenorrhea refers to menstrual periods that occur at intervals longer than thirty-five days (American Academy of Pediatrics 2000). Probable causes of amenorrhea or oligomenorrhea include hypothalamic influences; pituitary abnormalities; ovarian disorders; pregnancy; adrenal disorders; thyroid disorders; and use of medications such as anabolic steroids. Exercise-induced amenorrhea is considered to be a form of hypothalamic amenorrhea (Anderson et al. 1998). Otis (1998) describes the basis for this type of amenorrhea as follows:

> Hypothalmic amenorrhea is characterized by a reduction in the secretion of a hormone called "gonadotropin releasing hormone" (GnRH) from the brain's hypothalamus. The function of GnRh is to stimulate the pituitary gland, which in turns sends signals to the ovaries. A reduction in the secretion of GnRH and luteinizing hormone (LH) is found in amenorrhea. The lack of LH stimulation causes suppression of the ovary, which then fails to produce estrogen and progesterone. No ovulation occurs and there is no cyclic menstrual bleeding. (22-23)

Researchers speculate that this type of amenorrhea is the result not of low body weight (Frisch and Revelle 1971) or body fat (Frisch and McArthur 1974) but of energy drain (ACSM 1997; Otis 1992). Energy drain is a combination of excessive psychological and physical training and inadequate caloric intake. Professionals now agree that menstrual dysfunction is not "normal" and may lead to decreased bone density and premature osteoporosis because estrogen is needed for proper bone construction (Drinkwater, Bruemner, and Chesnut 1990; Rencken, Chesnut, and Drinkwater 1996; Shangold, Rebar, Wentz 1990s.

Osteoporosis

The third component of the triad is osteoporosis. Osteopenia is defined as low bone-mineral density (BMD), and osteoporosis is defined as a BMD greater than 2.5 standard deviations below the mean values for healthy young males (Thrash and Anderson 2000). Low concentrations of ovarian hormones—specifically estrogen—in amenorrhea and oligomenorrhea are associated with reduced bone mass, increased rates of bone loss, and increased risk of stress fractures (ACSM 1997). Sanborn et al. (2000) are alarmed by the findings of reduced bone mass in physically active females. Williamson, Netemeyer, and Jackman (1995) found that young amenorrheic female athletes in their early twenties who have consumed diets low in calcium and produced inadequate amounts of estrogen may have thin, fragile bones resembling those of women in their seventies. Even more alarming is the fact that bone loss in an amenorrheic athlete is rapid and may not be reversible (Yeager et al. 1993). In addition, female athletes, especially those with decreased BMD and menstrual dysfunction, experience stress fractures more often than men (Brukner and Bennell 1997). Thrash and Anderson (2000) report that low BMDs in athletic women should serve as an indication of risk for stress fracture.

Risk Factors

The American College of Sports Medicine (1997) considers all physically active females at risk for developing one or more components of the triad. Most vulnerable are those experiencing biological changes, peer pressure, a societal push for thinness, and the body image preoccupation that occurs during puberty. Sports or activities that emphasize low body weight also can be a risk factor. These sports or activities include

- sports in which performance is subjectively scored (dance, figure skating, diving, gymnastics, and aerobics);
- endurance sports that emphasize a low body weight (distance running, cycling and cross-country skiing);
- sports that require tightly fitting or revealing clothing for competition (volleyball, swimming, diving, cross-country running, cross-country skiing, track, and cheerleading);
- sports that use weight categories for participation (horse racing, some martial arts, wrestling, and rowing); and
- sports that emphasize a prepubertal body for performance success (figure skating, gymnastics, diving).

Prevention Strategies

The best treatment for the Female Athlete Triad is prevention. The primary prevention of the triad involves preventing occurrence; in other words, primary prevention enables healthy, non–eating disordered young females to remain healthy. Secondary prevention promotes early detection and prompt treatment of any of the triad components, increasing the chances of a quick and complete recovery. Tertiary prevention is aimed at reducing the impairment that may result from the triad. An effective prevention program should involve the athlete, the coaches, and the athlete's parents.

School personnel can promote primary prevention of the triad through dispelling body fat myths, providing sound nutrition education, addressing ways to cope with stress, and involving all school personnel. School personnel must dispel the myths that "thinner is better" and that "every sport has an ideal body weight." As Sanborn et al. (2000) point out, there is no optimal body composition for any sport. In fact, the association between body composition and performance must be individualized for each athlete. Furthermore, a specific body weight or body composition should not be recommended, but rather a range should be suggested that is realistic and appropriate for the athlete. Another myth to dispel is that the loss of the menstrual period means the young female is training well; instead, it is an indication of an unhealthy state or pregnancy.

Second, the integration of sound nutrition education and stress management techniques throughout the curriculum and school is warranted. For example, an art class can develop replicas of the food pyramid, or a math class can calculate the amount of minerals and vitamins in a daily food log. School food services can play an important role in primary prevention by providing a variety of healthy and appetizing food choices (Beals, Brey, and Gonyou 1999). Young females who are involved in strenuous physical training are prone to adopt negative coping mechanisms, such as restricted eating or purging. They need to learn about positive coping strategies such as time management skills or visualization. Last, for primary prevention to work, all school personnel, not just the coaches, physical education teachers, and health teachers, must be actively involved in dispelling the myths and providing information about sound nutrition and positive stress management and coping strategies.

To decrease the severity and duration of the triad, early identification of athletes at risk is warranted (secondary prevention). The followng questions may help identify young females at risk for the triad:

- Is the female dieting excessively to lose weight or experiencing large weight fluctuations, or does she appear to be losing too much weight?
- Are menstrual cycles irregular or absent?
- Has she had a stress fracture?
- Are her mood and self-esteem determined primarily by her weight?
- Is she a compulsive overexerciser?

If the answer to any of the above questions is "yes," express your concern and recommend that the adolescent see a health care practitioner (Otis 1998). Other resources for early detection are listed in the sidebar.

Another opportunity for early identification is the preparticipation physical exam. During the exam, clinicians should ask specific questions. For example:

- How much of an issue is weight for you?
- How much protein do you include in your diet?
- Do you currently have a regular menstrual cycle and have you always?
- How often do you take a day off from training?
- Do you consume foods that contain calcium?
- Do you have forbidden foods? (Joy et al. 1997)

Baer, Walker, and Grossman (1995) recommend a team approach to treating the triad (tertiary prevention). The team needs to include the athlete's physician, the athletic trainer, a dietitian, a psychologist, and the athlete's parents. As Beals, Brey, and Gonyou (1999) point out, tertiary prevention may not be appropriate for the school. However, school personnel should identify community and national resources that offer credible information and services relevant to the triad (see box for online resources).

Conclusion

As more and more young females become physically active, school personnel need to be aware of the importance of promoting healthy eating and training behaviors and the potential health consequences of the Female Athlete Triad (disordered eating, amenorrhea, and osteoporosis). Members of Overeaters Anonymous, a self-help group for people with eating disorders, remind us of the seriousness of these conditions. They say, "When you are addicted to alcohol you put the tiger in the cage to recover; when you are addicted to food you put the tiger in the cage, but take it out three times a day for a walk" (Yeary 1987). School personnel are in a position to foster healthy, active lifestyles and empower girls to prevent the development of the Female Athlete Triad.

APPENDIX A

Anorexia Nervosa

- Refusal to maintain minimal normal body weight
- Intense fear of gaining weight
- Disturbance in perception of body size or weight
- Absence of three or more menstrual cycles

Bulimia Nervosa

- Recurring episodes of binge eating
- Feeling of lack of control during eating episode
- Recurrent inappropriate compensatory behaviors and binge eating occurring twice a week for three months
- Persistent excessive concern with body shape or weight
- Compensatory behaviors (purging: vomiting, laxative, and/or diuretics and nonpurging: fasting and/or excessive exercise

Source: Diagnostic and statistical manual of mental disorders 1994.

Key words: Female Athlete Triad, disordered eating, physical fitness, nutrition education

REFERENCES

American Academy of Pediatrics. 2000. Medical concerns in the female athlete. *Pediatrics* 106 (3): 1+.

American College of Sports Medicine. 1997. The female athlete triad: Disordered eating, amenorrhea, and osteoporosis. *Medicine and Science in Sports and Exercise* 29: i–ix.

American Psychiatric Association. 1994. *Diagnostic and statistical manual of mental disorders*. 4th ed. Washington, DC: American Psychiatric Association.

Anderson, J. J. B., et al. 1998. Nutrition and bone in physical activity and sport. *Nutrition in Exercise and Sports*. 3d ed. Boca Raton, FL: CRC Press.

Baer, J. T., W. F. Walker, and J. M. Grossman. 1995. A disordered eating response team's effect on nutrition practices in college athletes. *Journal of Athletic Training* 30 (4): 315–17.

Beals, K. A., R A. Brey, and J. B. Gonyou. 1999. Understanding the female athlete triad: Eating disorders, amenorrhea, and osteoporosis. *Journal of School Health* 69 (8): 337–40.

Beumont, P. J. V., et al. 1994. Excessive physical activity in dieting disorder patients: Proposals for a supervised exercise program. *International Journal of Eating Disorders* 15 (1): 21–36.

Brukner, P., and K. Bennell. 1997. Stress fractures in female athletes. *Sports Medicine* 24: 419+.

Davis, C. 1990. Weight preoccupation: A comparison between exercising and non-exercising women. *Appetite* 15: 13–21.

Drinkwater, B. L., B. Bruemner, and C. H. Chesnut. 1990. Menstrual history as a determinant of current bone density in young athletes. *Journal of American Medical Association* 263 (4): 545–48.

Frisch, R. E., and R. Revelle. 1971. Height and weight at menarche and a hypotheses of menarche. *Archives of Disabled Child* 46: 695–701.

Frisch, R. E. and J. W. McArthur. 1974. Menstrual cycles: Fatness as a determinant of minimum weight for height necessary for their maintenance or onset. *Science* 185: 949–51.

Joy, E., et al. 1997. Team management of the female athlete triad. Part 1: What to look for, what to ask. *Physician and Sportsmedicine* 25 (3): 95–110.

Katz, J. L. 1986. Long-distance running, anorexia nervosa, and bulimia: A report of two cases. *Comprehensive Psychiatry* 27 (1): 74–78.

Lopiano, D. A. 2000. Modern history of women in sports: Twenty-five years of Title IX. *Clinics in Sports Medicine* 19 (2): 163–74.

Nagel, K. L., and K. H. Jones. 1992. Sociological factors in the development of eating disorders. *Adolescence* 27 (105): 107–13.

Otis, C. L. 1992. Exercise associated amenorrhea. *Clinics in Sports Medicine* 11 (2): 351–62.

___. 1998. Too slim, amenorrheic, fracture-prone: The female athlete triad—Prevention is the best therapy. *ACSM's Health and Fitness Journal* 2 (1): 20–25.

Rencken, M. L., C. H. Chesnut, and B. L. Drinkwater. 1996. Bone density at multiple skeletal sites in amenorrheic athletes. *Journal of American Medical Association* 276 (3): 238–40.

Sanborn, C. F., et al. 2000. Disordered eating and the female athlete triad. *Clinics in Sports Medicine* 19 (2): 199–213.

Shangold, M., et al. 1990. Evaluation and management of menstrual dysfunction in athletes. *Journal of American Medical Association* 263 (3): 1665–69.

Tanji, J. L. 2000. The benefits of exercise for women. *Clinics in Sports Medicine* 19 (2): 175–86.

Thrash, L. E., and J. J. B. Anderson, 2000. The female athlete triad: Nutrition, menstrual disturbances, and low bone mass. *Nutrition Today* 35 (5): 168–74.

Williamson, D. A., et al. 1995. Structural equation modeling of risk factors for the development of eating disorder symptoms in female athletes. *International Journal of eating Disorders* 17: 387.

Yates, A. 1991. *Compulsive exercise and the eating disorder.* New York: Brunner/Mazel.

___. 1992. Biological considerations in the etiology of eating disorders. *Pediatric Annals* 21 (11): 739–44.

Yeager, K. K., et al. 1993. The female athlete triad. *Medicine and Science in Sports and Exercise* 25: g775–77.

Yeary, J. 1987. The use of overeaters anonymous in the treatment of eating disorders. *Journal of Psychoactive drugs* 19 (3): 303–09.

DawnElla M. Rust is an associate professor in the Department of Kinesiology and Health Science at Stephen F. Austin State University, in Nacogdoches, Texas.

An American Epidemic
Diabetes

The silent killer: Scientific research shows a 'persistent explosion' of cases —especially among those in their prime

BY JERRY ADLER AND CLAUDIA KALB

SOMETHING TERRIBLE WAS HAPPENING to Yolanda Benitez's eyes. They were being poisoned; the fragile capillaries of the retina attacked from within and were leaking blood. The first symptoms were red lines, appearing vertically across her field of vision; the lines multiplied and merged into a haze that shut out light entirely. "Her blood vessels inside her eye were popping," says her daughter, Jannette Roman, a Chicago college student. Benitez, who was in her late 40s when the problem began four years ago, was a cleaning woman, but she's had to stop working. After five surgeries, she has regained vision in one eye, but the other is completely useless. A few weeks ago, awakening one night in a hotel bedroom, she walked into a door, setting off a paroxysm of pain and nausea that hasn't let up yet. And what caused this catastrophe was nothing as exotic as pesticides or emerging viruses. What was poisoning Benitez was sugar.

Heredity

Genes help determine whether you'll get diabetes. **In many families, multiple generations are struck.** But heredity is not destiny—especially if you **eat well and exercise.**

Benitez is a representative victim of what many public-health experts believe will be the next great lifestyle-disease epidemic to afflict the United States: diabetes. (Technically, type-2 diabetes, which accounts for 90 to 95 percent of all cases.) At five feet one and 140 pounds, Benitez is overweight; 85 percent of all diabetes sufferers are overweight or obese. She was born and reared in Mexico; Hispanics and blacks are more likely to contract diabetes than Caucasians. As the American population becomes increasingly nonwhite and obese, the disease is rapidly spreading. A study by doctors from the Centers for Disease Control and Prevention startled people last week with the finding that the prevalence of diagnosed cases of diabetes increased by a third (from 4.9 to 6.5 percent) between 1990 and 1998. But demographics explain only part of this "persistent explosion" of cases, says Dr. Frank Vinicor, director of the CDC's diabetes division; even among Caucasians—even those of normal weight—the rates are on the rise. The actual number is almost surely higher, since many cases go undiagnosed for years.

But the most alarming statistic in the CDC study was the breakdown of cases by age. For people in their 40s, the incidence of diabetes increased 40 percent over the eight years; for people in their 30s, it went up nearly 70 percent. "It's becoming a disease of the young," says Dr. Arthur Rubenstein, a leading endocrinologist and dean of the Mount Sinai School of Medicine in New York. In that light, Roman is an even more significant example. She is only 18, and she has type-2 diabetes, too.

In fact, until recently the disease Roman and her mother have was known as adult-onset diabetes, because it usually

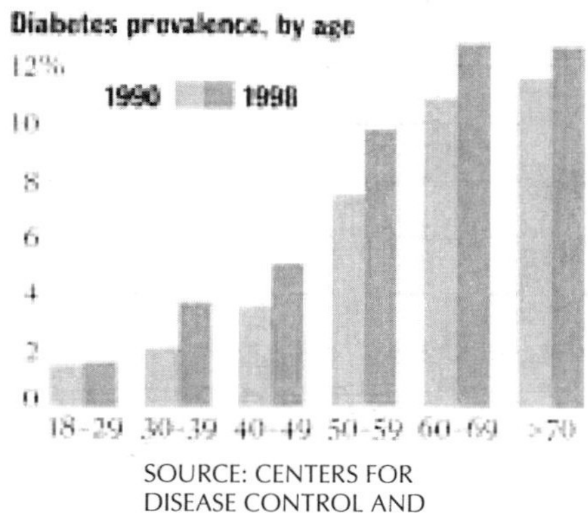

SOURCE: CENTERS FOR DISEASE CONTROL AND PREVENTION

struck people middle-aged or older. The other kind was "juvenile" diabetes, now called type 1, which is an entirely different disease altogether. But in America, getting fat is no longer a prerogative of adults, and diabetes, which is strongly linked to obesity, is spreading down the age ladder. The rise in type-2 disease among teenagers is "extraordinarily worrying," says Rubenstein, because diabetes can take decades to reveal its most appalling effects—including ulcerating sores, blindness, kidney failure, strokes and heart disease. "If people become diabetic at age 10 or 15 or 20," he says, "you can predict that when they are 30 or 40, they could have terrible complications." You can also predict that they are going to need a lot of expensive health care; on average, medical-care spending for diabetics runs \$10,000 to \$12,000 annually—three to four times higher than on healthy people, every year for life. A number of promising new drugs and therapies may make diabetes easier to live with, but it will be a medical miracle if they end up saving money.

We're Living Dangerously ...

Too many calories and too little exercise are the key risk factors for type-2 diabetes. Some 90 percent of people with type-2 diabetes are overweight.

Between a quarter and a third of U.S. adults report no physical activity. Many others get very little.

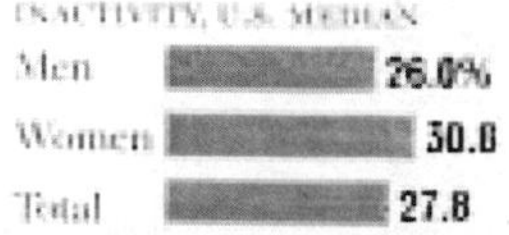

BIG COUNTRY—GETTING BIGGER

In 1991, only seven states had obesity rates over 15%. By 1998, only five states didn't.

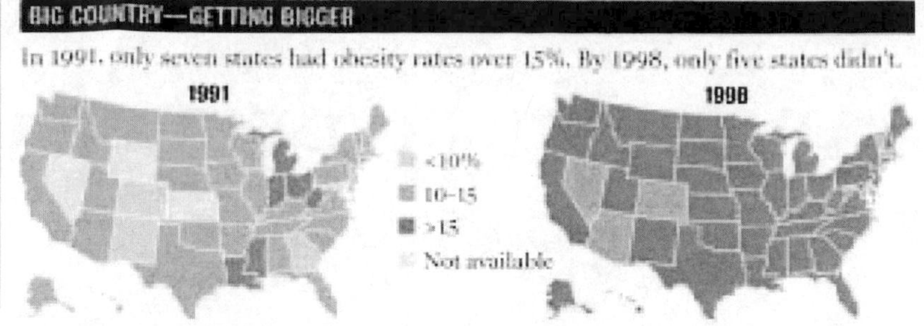

OBESITY RATE

The percentage of Americans who are considered obese, or roughly 30 pounds overweight, has soared:

PERCENT OF U.S. ADULTS WHO ARE OBESE

1991 12%

1998 18

... And Paying a High Price

During the '90s, the prevalence of type-2 diabetes increased by 33% overall, and by 70% among people in their 30s. Diabetes now affects 16 million Americans.

SHARED BURDEN

Type-2 diabetes has risen in all major ethnic groups:

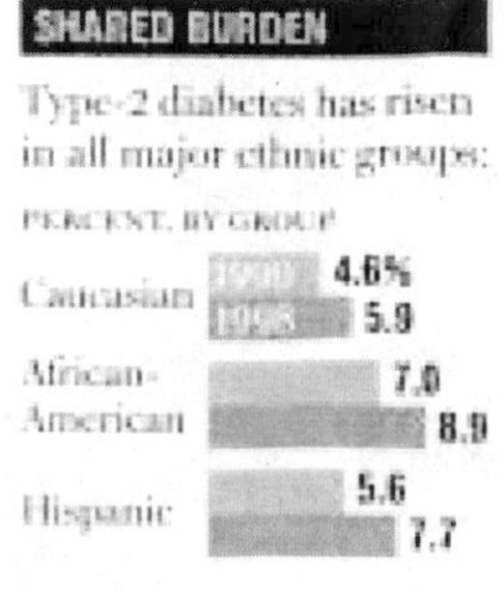

A GROWING EPIDEMIC

Nine states had diabetes rates over 6% in 1991. By 1998, 22 states crossed that line.

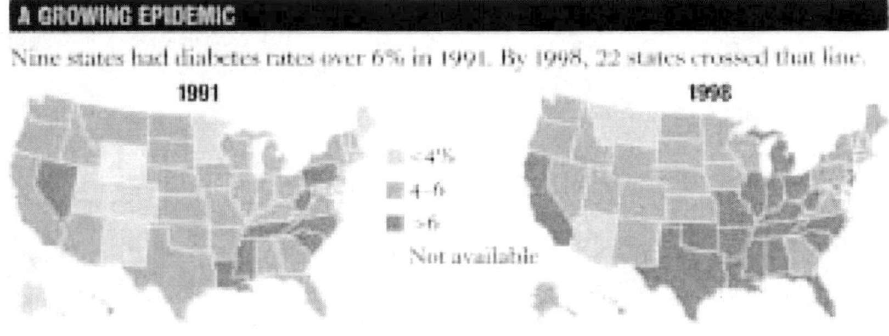

A GROWING BILL

The direct cost of treating diabetes is $44 billion per year. The total outlay, including indirect costs, is $98 billion.

RELATED COSTS, IN BILLIONS

Diabetes $98

All Cancers 107

KEN SCHILES

SOURCES: CDC, NIH, BRFSS

REX RYSTEDT, SCIENCE PHOTO LIBRARY—PHOTO RESEARCHERS (INSET)

Age

It usually strikes after 40, but new data shows **a dramatic rise among people in their 30s.** Children are now being diagnosed with type 2 as well, sounding alarms about the nation's long-term health—and **making the term 'adult-onset diabetes' obsolete.**

Diabetes is a disorder of the very engine of life, a subtle calamity at the molecular level. Its hallmark is a failure to metabolize glucose, the ubiquitous sugar molecule carried by the bloodstream to fuel every part of the body. Deprived of their prime energy supply, muscle and nerve cells slow their function, which is why early diabetes may manifest itself as lethargy and irritability. That was the experience of Maria DelMundo, 46, a Rochester, Minn., mother who weighed around 190 (she's 5 feet 2) when she stopped by her doctor's office for a checkup in 1991. "I just wasn't feeling good—tired and out of sorts," she recalls; in effect, she was undernourished even while eating her fill of the "buttery icing and whipped cream, French pastries and Häagen-Dazs" she loves.

At the same time, glucose accumulates in the patient's blood, and can reach concentrations two to three times normal and even higher. The excess is eventually excreted by the kidneys, which require copious quantities of water as a dilutant. That's how Keith Wein, 42, a mechanical engineer from Irvine, Calif., caught his diabetes—or, rather, his wife, Michelle, did. "I thought something was wrong when all of a sudden he started drinking water nonstop," says Michelle, a nutritionist. "He would come home from the grocery store with six or eight bottles of Crystal Geyser"—and spend a corresponding amount of time going back and forth to the bathroom. But these are subtle signs easy to overlook or deny. Steven Mallinson, a strapping six-foot, 190-pound hiker and cyclist, discovered he had diabetes at the age of 25 when he enrolled as a paid participant in a research study of a new drug, unrelated to insulin. The drug company took one look at his blood and urine samples and kicked him off the study, telling him to call his doctor *immediately*. "That's one of the problems," says Dr. Richard Hellman of the American Association of Clinical Endocrinologists. "A lot of people are walking around with either diabetes or a predecessor [condition] and they're not even aware of it. The symptoms are not specific, and they tend to come late."

Race

African-Americans, Hispanics and American Indians—who have the highest rates of type 2 in the world—are at greater risk than Caucasians. Still, no one is immune: **the prevalence of the disease has increased across all racial groups** over the last decade.

Researchers are still investigating all the ways in which high blood-sugar levels do damage. One obvious effect is on the arteries, especially in the eyes, kidneys and extremities; sugar seems to both weaken the capillary walls and clog the small vessels. Hemorrhages destroy the retina; im-

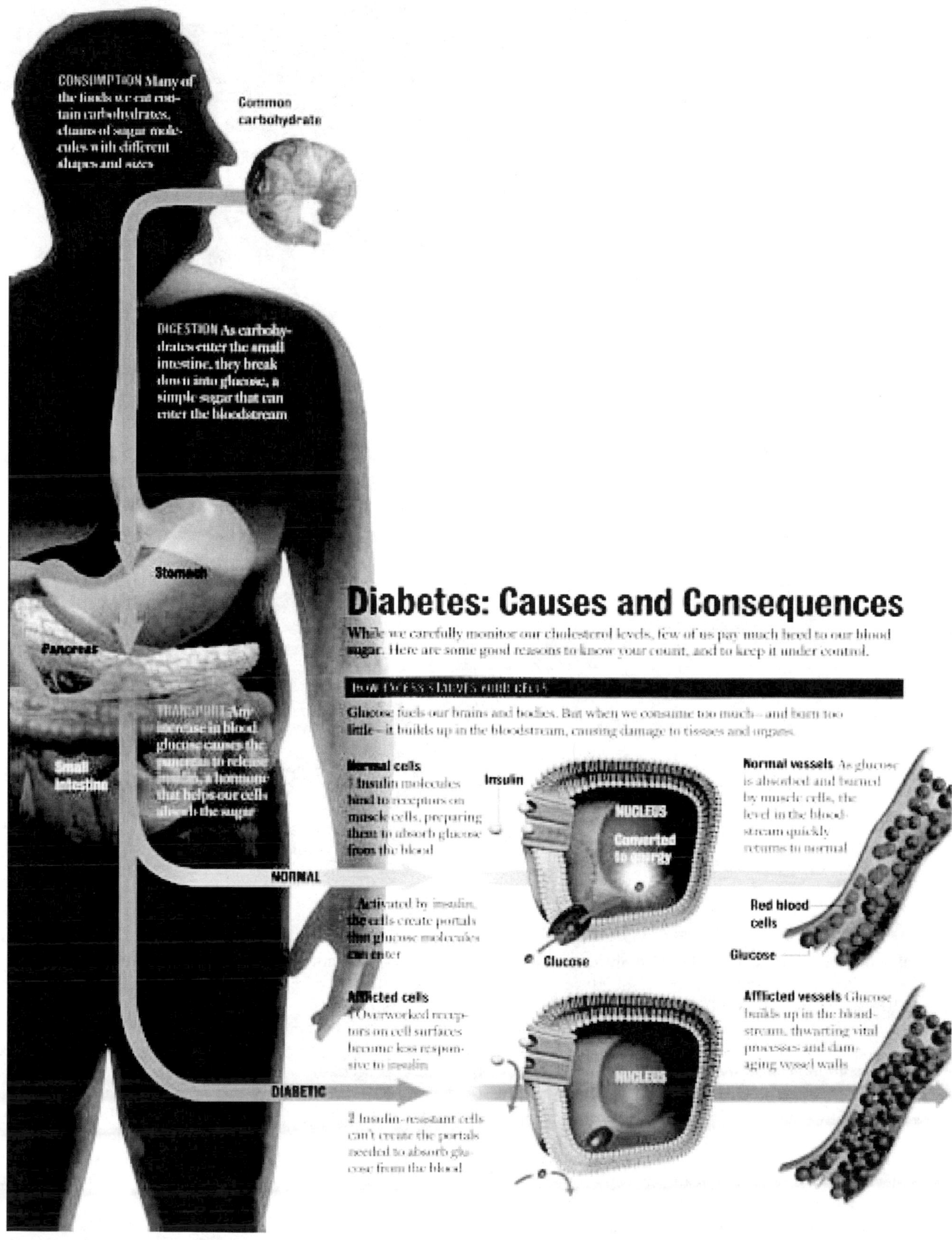

CONSUMPTION Many of the foods we eat contain carbohydrates, chains of sugar molecules with different shapes and sizes
Common carbohydrate
DIGESTION As carbohydrates enter the small intestine, they break down into glucose, a simple sugar that can enter the bloodstream
Stomach
Pancreas
Small intestine
increase in blood glucose causes the
that helps our cells
NORMAL
DIABETIC
Diabetes: Causes and Consequences
While we carefully monitor our cholesterol levels, few of us pay much heed to our blood sugar. Here are some good reasons to know your count, and to keep it under control.
Glucose fuels our brains and bodies. But when we consume too much—and burn too little—it builds up in the bloodstream, causing damage to tissues and organs.
Normal cells
1 Insulin molecules bind to receptors on muscle cells, preparing them to absorb glucose from the blood
Insulin
NUCLEUS
Converted to energy
2 Activated by insulin, the cells create portals that glucose molecules can enter
Glucose
Normal vessels As glucose is absorbed and burned by muscle cells, the level in the bloodstream quickly returns to normal
Red blood cells
Glucose
Afflicted cells
1 Overworked receptors on cell surfaces become less responsive to insulin
NUCLEUS
2 Insulin-resistant cells can't create the portals needed to absorb glucose from the blood
Afflicted vessels Glucose builds up in the bloodstream, thwarting vital processes and damaging vessel walls

SOURCES: AMERICAN DIABETES ASSOCIATION, CENTERS FOR DISEASE CONTROL AND PREVENTION, THE GLUCOSE REVOLUTION, NATIONAL INSTITUTES OF HEALTH RESEARCH BY MEREDITH SALISBURY, GEOFFREY COWLEY, AND SUSAN RAINEY. GRAPHIC BY DONGMIN SHIM AND KEVIN HAND—NEWSWEEK

TREATMENTS

When diet and exercise don't keep diabetes in check, drugs or insulin can help. There are several classes of medications:

Stimulators Drugs like Glucotrol prompt pancreatic cells to make more insulin

Sensitizers Glucophage and related treatments help make cells more responsive to whatever insulin is present in the body

Carb blockers Precose and Glyset help regulate blood-sugar levels by slowing the breakdown of carbohydrates in the digestive tract

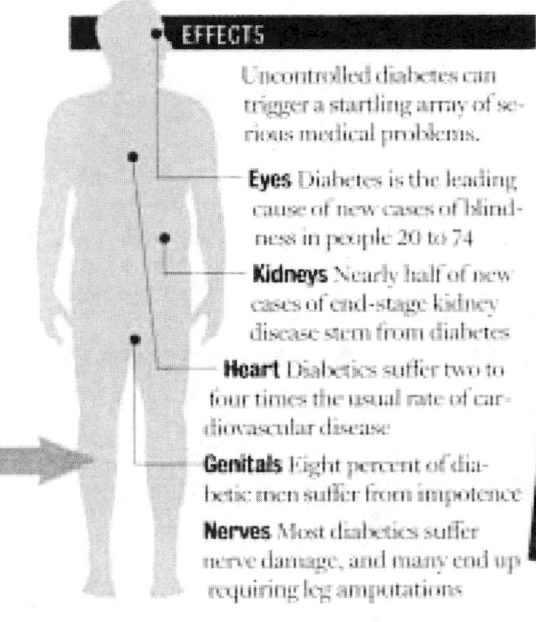
EFFECTS
Uncontrolled diabetes can trigger a startling array of serious medical problems.
Eyes Diabetes is the leading cause of new cases of blindness in people 20 to 74
Kidneys Nearly half of new cases of end-stage kidney disease stem from diabetes
Heart Diabetics suffer two to four times the usual rate of cardiovascular disease
Genitals Eight percent of diabetic men suffer from impotence
Nerves Most diabetics suffer nerve damage, and many end up requiring leg amputations

What to Eat
Foods with higher glycemic indices push glucose more rapidly into the bloodstream, taxing the insulin response.
FOOD
GLYCEMIC INDEX
Grapefruit half 25
Grapefruit juice 48
Nonfat yogurt, artificial sweetener 14
Nonfat yogurt, with sugar 33
Tomato soup 38
Green pea soup 66
Ravioli, meat-filled 39
Macaroni and cheese, packaged 64
Brown rice 55
Instant white rice 87
Pumpernickel bread 51
French baguette 95

KIM KULISH–SABA

paired circulation leads to ulcers in the legs and feet for which amputation may be the only cure. The risk of heart disease doubles for men; for women it goes up fourfold. Yet the misperception of diabetes as a relatively benign condition persists. "The word is not yet out about how serious it is," says Anne Daly of the American Diabetes Association. "There's no diabetes that's not bad. It's all serious."

Glucose metabolism is regulated by the hormone insulin, which is produced by the pancreas gland, a fist-size clump of tissue behind the stomach. In normal people, the pancreas secretes insulin in response to a rise in blood sugar, which happens after a meal. The relatively uncommon type-1 diabetes is marked by a straightforward shortage of insulin, which typically shows up around puberty. Researchers consider this an autoimmune disease, possibly brought on by a viral infection. And the treatment is straightforward in concept, if not always in practice: you supply the missing insulin, if necessary by injecting it before meals. Although the name "juvenile" diabetes has stuck, it's a disease you have for life; luckily, though, there's no evidence that its incidence is on the rise in the United States.

Type 2 is an altogether more complicated disease, a spiraling derangement in a network of positive and negative feedback loops linking the pancreas, liver (which stores and releases glucose), muscles, nerves, fat cells and brain (the only organ capable of deciding *not* to open a pint of rum-raisin ice cream). Perversely, the muscle cells refuse to absorb glucose from the blood, a phenomenon called insulin resistance. At least in the early stages of the disease, type-2 diabetics usually have normal insulin production. In fact, they may have above-normal insulin, as their pancreas produces more and more of it in a futile attempt to keep up with the rise in blood sugar. Over time, though, people may need more insulin than their pancreas can supply, and these patients, too, often become dependent on injecting themselves with insulin.

culus of food intake, energy output and dosage designed to keep blood sugar from going either too high or too low. Howard Mitchell of Bangor, Maine, 46, who weighs 280 pounds and is a type-2 diabetic, wears an insulin pump like a beeper, which he can program to deliver a measured dosage whenever he needs it. Now, he says, "my life is no different than anyone else's." An implantable version may be available soon; someday a completely self-contained unit may be able to measure blood glucose directly and deliver insulin automatically.

Are You at Risk?

Because type-2 diabetes causes no symptoms at first, it often goes unmanaged for too long. Some possible warning signs:

- **Frequent urination**
- **Constant thirst or hunger**
- **Blurred vision**
- **Numb or tingling extremities**
- **Frequent skin infections**
- **Slow healing of cuts and bruises**

Getting Tested

When people have symptoms, or clear risk factors, physicians use two basic tests to diagnose type-2 diabetes

- **Fasting test:** Blood glucose should be below 110mg/dl after an overnight fast
- **Oral tolerance test:** Blood glucose should not be higher than 140mg/dl two hours after the patient swigs a cup of glucose-laden fluid

Other drugs, such as the sulfonylureas, which have been around since the 1950s, stimulate production and release of insulin by the pancreas; many type-2 diabetics take some form of these. But newer drugs, some introduced within the last year or two, offer far more possibilities for control. Glucophage is one; it controls blood sugar directly by promoting glucose storage in the liver. A class of drugs called TZDs make muscle and fat cells more sensitive to insulin, combating type-2 disease right at the source. And there are drugs that work in the gut to inhibit starch digestion, slowing the process enough to flatten the glucose "spike." "All these are new developments since 1995," says John Buse, director of the diabetes center at the University of North Carolina at Chapel Hill. "There's 255 different combinations of drugs, insulin, exercise and diet modification; I probably use 245 of them in my practice."

But there's another surefire way to control blood sugar and lessen the complications of diabetes; it calls for eating a healthy diet in the first place. A recurring theme in the conversations of diabetics is the foods they had to give up. Maria Mendoza, a college janitor in Los Angeles, cut down from "six or seven tortillas a day" to two after she was diagnosed with type-2 diabetes in 1985, and gave up "tacos, sweets, chocolates and *pan dulce* [sweet bread]." "I can't eat what I want, and that makes me sad," she says. "At times, I feel so deprived I want to cry." But increasingly, doctors have come to believe that an absolute ban on refined sugar is too restrictive. With conscientious monitoring of their blood sugar, regular exercise and the right attitude, many diabetics can now allow themselves an occasional sweet. Provided, of course, it is part of the same low-fat, high-fiber, low-calorie diet that researchers recommend for just about every other major problem in American public health. Sophisticated patients don't just stick to a diet: they monitor what they eat obsessively, and plot it against blood-sugar levels that they measure themselves (with a blood-glucose meter and a drop of blood from a finger) as often as five times a day. "My goal is to keep my glucose level under 150," says Michael Negrin, a 41-year-old New York businessman. (The number refers to milligrams of glucose per deciliter of blood.) "Yesterday I woke up and it was 179. I took my medicine and ate breakfast, and it went down to 122. After lunch, a corned-beef sandwich, I went up to 156. I worked out in the evening, and I was down to 58."

Evidence is also accumulating that the lack of exercise contributes to diabetes. Dr. Alan Shuldiner of the University of Maryland has been studying Amish families in Pennsylvania, who have about half the rate of diabetes found in the general Caucasian population—even though their diet is no healthier and the adults are just as likely to be fat. What sets them apart is that they don't have cars; when they're not riding a buggy, they're on scooters or roller skates, and (without telephones) they spend a lot of time going back and forth just to chat. And, says Shuldiner, with the absence of television, "you never see obese Amish children. Never."

It's a tough prescription, and the doctor hasn't been born yet who could get Americans to live like the Amish—even with those great pretzels and shoofly pie. But somewhere between the contemporary lifestyle and the 18th-century one there has to be a happy medium that can let us enjoy our food and comforts—and avoid the coming scourge of poisoning by sugar.

With KAREN SPRINGEN *in Chicago*, ANA FIGUEROA *in Los Angeles*, JOHN LAUERMAN *in Boston*, JOAN FELICE RAYMOND *in Cleveland and* ERIKA CHECK, HEATHER WON TESORIERO *and* SUSAN RAINEY *in New York*

Helping to Break **Bad Habits**

Present danger: Why so many people ignore doctor's orders and put their lives at risk.

BY ROBIN S. GOLAND, M.D

IT SOUNDS SIMPLE. WITH PROPER ATTENtion to blood sugar and diet, a person with diabetes can go a long way toward staying healthy. But it's not simple. Many people with diabetes risk illness and even death by leaving their disease untreated. The vast majority of people who are referred to the diabetes center where I work have excellent access to health care and good doctors. Yet their diabetes is out of control.

A 58-year-old executive came to my office several years ago, referred for what his primary-care doctor called "noncompliance with his diabetes regimen." The patient was at least 20 pounds overweight, he did not follow his diet and he rarely checked his blood sugar, saying he didn't understand how and when to do it. His wife nagged him so often about his health that he called her the "chief of the diabetes police force." He came to my office unwillingly and feeling sheepish, the way people do when they intend to go to the gym but never get around to it.

Ignoring diabetes may seem as irresponsible as smoking cigarettes or driving drunk. But in many ways it's more understandable. For one thing, the disease moves so slowly that people with diabetes often feel perfectly fine. About one third of those with type-2 diabetes—more than 5 million people—don't even know they have it.

For those who know or suspect they have diabetes, denial can be a powerful obstacle to treatment. Because diabetes has genetic roots, many people at risk have already watched a relative go blind or lose a leg. Not knowing that treatments have improved dramatically over the past decade, these people assume, wrongly, that such complications are inevitable. Patients have asked me, "What's the point of giving up the food I love if I'm going to go blind anyway?"

Then there's the intimidating prospect of a lifetime of vigilance. To properly care for their disease, people with diabetes may have to check their glucose between sets of tennis. Or excuse themselves from a business meeting to eat a snack. Taking care of diabetes "is not for an hour, it's not for a week, it's not just for Wednesdays," a patient once told me. "Diabetes never takes a vacation." The relentlessness of the regimen creates in many a sense of isolation and fatigue. When no one else in the restaurant needs to worry about health when the food is slow to arrive, staying motivated to care for the disease gets harder and harder.

To make matters worse, people with diabetes get insufficient support from the U.S. health-care system. Diabetes centers around the country are closing because many insurers do not reimburse for preventive treatment. And many doctors, with their growing caseloads, don't have time to give people with diabetes the attention they need. Too often they tell patients to lose weight or get more exercise without ensuring that real lifestyle changes are taking place.

People with diabetes need more than preprinted menus and one-time lessons in finger pricks. They need long-term, individualized educational and nutritional counseling. Not only do people with diabetes need to learn the difference between an English muffin and a bagel; they need to learn about various glucose meters and medications—and then get comfortable using them. And then there's the matter of long-term maintenance. Some people manage diabetes well on their own. But others need ongoing attention and an understanding ear when they fall off the wagon. There's good news, though. In the three years since he visited our center, that 58-year-old executive has brought his blood-sugar level down to normal. He's stopped gaining weight and has no complications from diabetes. Now he's telling his friends and family that while treating diabetes is no fun, it's doable in an active, healthy life—and it's better than the consequences of ignoring it.

What could cause such a devastating misreading of biochemical messages? Inevitably, genetics seems to play a role. Just last week a team at the Whitehead Center for Genome Research identified a variant form of a gene on human chromosome 1 that appears to increase the risk of type-2 disease by about 25 percent—although it's carried by as much as 85 percent of the population, so having it doesn't seem to be cause for any special alarm. Certain population groups are especially prone to diabetes; among the Pima Indians of the Southwestern United States half of all adults suffer from it. Living in a harsh climate where food is naturally scarce during much of the year, they may have inherited a so-called thrifty gene that lowers metabolism in times of famine, at the price of increased susceptibility to diabetes. But it took the United States, land of the 40-ounce soda, to elevate that susceptibility to a crisis; the closely related tribe of Pimas in Mexico who farm and eat a traditional diet don't have nearly the same rate of diabetes. The correlation between type-2 diabetes and obesity is overwhelming: 13.5 percent of obese patients in the CDC survey had the disease, compared with 3.5 percent of those of normal weight. "As people get fatter, the risk of diabetes goes up dramatically," says Vinicor of the CDC. The exact nature of the relationship is extraordinarily complex and poorly understood, but the simplest way to think about it may be that for unknown reasons, the same things that make you fat also put you at risk for diabetes—lack of exercise and a high-calorie diet.

The very complexity of the glucose-insulin cycle, though, affords numerous opportunities to intervene with therapies. The obvious therapy, of course, is insulin. For years the only available form was harvested from cows or pigs, but now human insulin is being manufactured directly by recombinant DNA techniques. And not just insulin—drug companies are coming out with *new and improved insulin*, engineered with molecular changes to make it last longer in the body or be absorbed more easily into cells. Until recently, insulin had to be injected under the skin as often as five to seven times a day, in a complex cal-